Gower

HANDBOOK of MANAGEMENT

THIRD EDITION

Gower

HANDBOOK of MANAGEMENT

THIRD EDITION

edited by

Dennis Lock

BCA

LONDON · NEW YORK · SYDNEY · TORONTO

This edition published 1992
by BCA by arrangement with
Gower Publishing Company Limited

First published 1983
Second edition 1988
Third edition published 1992
Reprinted 1995, 1996

CN 3759

Printed and bound in Great Britain by
Biddles Limited, Guildford and King's Lynn

Contents

PART ONE   PRINCIPLES, POLICY AND ORGANIZATION

The beginnings of management thought – The pre-war management writers – Management theory in the post-war era – Modern management principles – Further reading

Future social attitudes – Future legal structures – Future markets – Future technologies – Future resources – Future organization and management style – Further reading

Two strategic planning philosophies – Using the planning process to create the self-reinforcing spiral of success – Further reading

The need for planned organization development – Structure, process and style – The role of the chief executive – Planning a programme or organization development – Styles of leadership – Teams and team building – Characteristics of a successful programme – Conclusions – Further reading

PART TWO   FINANCIAL MANAGEMENT

ment tasks – Case studies showing sales engineering benefits – Conclusion – Further reading

PART FIVE   PURCHASING AND INVENTORY MANAGEMENT

PART SIX MANUFACTURING MANAGEMENT

List of illustrations

Preface

In our fast-changing economic and political worlds, management philosophy and practice must adapt if companies are to survive and flourish. Technology is creating a whole series of revolutions. Priorities change. Old ideas are abandoned – even discredited. New concepts and techniques emerge, ranging from transient fashions to valuable management tools. Today's wonder company becomes tomorrow's focus for the liquidators and the Fraud Squad. All this change and challenge, coupled with managers' healthy ambition for corporate and career growth, is reflected in the proliferation of management books, with hundreds of new titles emerging every year.

It was into this dynamic environment that we launched the first edition of the *Gower Handbook of Management*. We set out to provide managers and management students with an authoritative, gimmick-free and essentially practical source of reference, covering the broadest possible range of management subjects. Our aim was to produce a book that would stand out as a unique work of reference, able to justify the claim 'If you have only one management book on your shelf, this must be the one'.

In reflective moments I like to imagine the Handbook as a kind of forum, where managers can meet expert managers from professional disciplines other than their own to gain a useful, wider appreciation of management; a place where, for example, the accountant can read about engineering management, and the production manager can gain an insight into marketing and finance.

This third edition of the Handbook follows the pattern on which the success of the earlier editions was based. It shares the same objectives and is still in ten parts, arranged in logical sequence from the corporate viewpoint in Part 1 to the needs of the individual manager in Part 10. Within that framework, however, we have made many important improvements.

The scope of the Handbook has been extended considerably. Ten additional chapters bring the total number to 73. All chapters from the second edition have been either reviewed and brought up to date by their original authors, or replaced. Every chapter now ends with a list of recommended reading, adding value by enlarging the book's reference base for those who wish to pursue any subject in greater depth.

Among the many new features of this edition are the chapters on mergers and acquisitions and on the environment. We have strengthened and updated the treatment of quality, recognizing that total quality management starts with a commitment by senior management. The new chapter on 'customer first' is one example of the greater attention given to the service industries – but we have avoided the trap of ignoring the vital role that manufacturing industry must continue to play. Those are just a few of the improvements to be found in the revised text.

In spite of its size, compiling this edition has proved to be a pleasant and trouble-free task. This has been due entirely to the enthusiasm of all the contributors. More than seventy people took part, all either expert managers or specialists in their particular subjects. Many of these people hold senior appointments and lead very busy working lives, in some cases involving extensive travel overseas. Their commitment and dedication to the book has been warmly appreciated and is gratefully acknowledged here.

I must also thank the many contributors not named in the book: people and organizations who have helped by answering all manner of inquiries, by checking or providing information and by co-operating in other ways to make this edition as accurate and informative as possible.

Dennis Lock

Notes on Contributors

Byran Atkin Bsc (Econ) *(Pricing)* has been engaged in industrial market research and business consultancy for more than 20 years. In 1984, he became a founder director of Research Solutions Limited, where he is now Managing Director of the Consultancy Division, and specializes in research and consultancy for the information technology industry. He has extensive experience of the analysis, through research, of the purchasing process and the role of price in decision taking. He has also devised and implemented specific research procedures for testing price sensitivity and/or acceptability in relation to a wide range of products and services. Bryan Atkin directed the *How British Industry Buys*, 1974 report sponsored and published by the *Financial Times* and co-authored a study into industrial pricing practices, *How British Industry Prices*, published by IMR Limited in 1975. In 1978 he spent six months on secondment to the Price Commission.

Stephen Badger *(Sources of finance)* was until recently a Director in the Corporate Finance Department of Morgan Grenfell & Co. Limited. He was educated at Sherborne School in Dorset and Pembroke College, Oxford, where he read Greats. He joined Morgan Grenfell on leaving Oxford, became a Director in 1977 and retired in 1991. He is an associate of the Chartered Institute of Bankers and of the Institute of Chartered Secretaries and Administrators.

Peter Baily *(Procurement policy; Purchasing procedures)* is a former senior lecturer in Business Studies at the Polytechnic of Wales. He started off as a telecommunications mechanic and later worked in machine tool manufacturing and textile industries as buyer, materials controller, chief buyer and assistant to company secretary. Mr Baily worked with the Business Education Council for several years as Board member, and has been chief examiner for the Institute of Purchasing and Supply. Author of several books and numerous articles, he has addressed conferences and contributed to courses in the US, Ireland, Holland, Italy, Switzerland, Singapore and the UK. He is author of *Purchasing Systems and Records* (Gower, 1991)

Brenda Barrett *(Health and safety)* studied law at Oxford and was called to the Bar at Gray's Inn. After gaining some experience in industry and at the Bar, she became a teacher. She is now Head of the Law Course at Middlesex Polytechnic. She has many years of experience of lecturing and publishing in the field of labour law. Her doctoral thesis was on employers' liability and she has also researched into management and employee attitudes in respect of safety. Dr Barrett has co-operated with Professor Howells in research into harmonization of occupational health and safety laws in the EEC and on offshore installations.

Gordon Bell *(Speaking; Reports; Meetings)* a lapsed scientist, is the Senior Partner in Gordon Bell and Partners, a firm of consultants specializing in teaching communications skills in industry and commerce. Gordon Bell and Partners have been conducting successful courses since 1956, not only in the UK but in many countries overseas. Gordon Bell is a broadcaster, and a contributor to *Handbook of Engineering Management* (Heinemann). He is the author of *Successful Speaking and Presentations*, also published by Heinemann.

Ted Bennett *(Managing the electronic office)* is an independent consultant/business analyst who entered data processing in 1967, following a degree in Chemical Engineering and a period as an engineer. He has worked in a wide variety of organizations as a systems analyst, project manager, information systems manager and consultant. He specializes in construction/project management; financial applications; office automation; and problem analysis.

William G Blyth *(Marketing research)* graduated in Economics and Social Statistics at Exeter University in 1970. He was company statistician at the British Market Research Bureau and group statistician at MIL Research, moving in 1982 to Audits of Great Britain, where he is currently director of research and development. He was recently returned for a second year as chairman of the Market Research Society, and is a fellow of both the Royal Statistical Society and the Institute of Statisticians.

Denis Boyle *(The strategic planning process)* is Managing Director of Service Management Group, a firm which specializes in the process of strategy creation and implementation for accelerated profit growth. Formerly, he was Director of the Scandinavian Institutes for Administrative Research in London and Milan, and adviser to the Institute for Industrial Reconstruction in Rome where he helped to create new approaches to state planning in such sectors as special steel, telecommunications and banking. Currently, he acts as a consultant to several leading multinationals, working particularly with developing service quality as a strategic competitive weapon. Mr. Boyle lectures widely in Europe and the United States and is a visiting professor at the University of Bocconi, Milan. His publications include numerous articles on strategic planning and implementation and he is co-author of *The Challenge of Change* (Gower, 1981). In 1990, he became a Partner in the Tom Peters Group.

Ron H Bradnam Eur. Ing. *(Corporate strategies for the future)* is a European Engineer and Chartered Engineer working as a freelance consultant in business and technology management. He has special interests in supporting the work of scientists, engineers and technologists in various management fields. After his military service he worked for EMI, Mullard and Plessey where he was responsible for the engineering design and management of research and development projects for commercial and military applications. While with EASAMS he planned and managed several important innovation projects before moving to Urwick Technology Management where his assignments were concerned with improvements to the management of technical and business functions.

Mr Bradnam has had a varied academic career, acting as a visiting lecturer at various academic institutions including the University of Southampton, Loughborough University, Cranfield School of Management, the University of Surrey, and Henley – The Management College. He also has considerable experience of designing and leading workshops and seminars in the UK and The Netherlands. As a committed Christian, he has more recently led a number of seminars on the Biblical principles of management for Christians in the work-place, and also for Christian Ministers and Leaders. He is a Fellow of the Institution of Electrical Engineers, a Fellow of the Institute of Management Consultants and a Member of the British Institute of Management.

John Bramham *(Manpower and succession planning)* after graduating in psychology, worked in various regions of British Gas including Corporate Headquarters where he was Manpower Planning Manager. He is currently Acting Industrial Relations Manager in British Gas Northern in Newcastle Upon Tyne. Mr Bramham wrote the standard text *Practical Manpower Planning* (IPM) now in its 4th reprint. He co-authored *Personnel Administration Made Simple* (IPM, 1985) and contributed to other texts including *Corporate Manpower Planning* (Gower). His current projects include a text on 'Getting a Job' and one on 'Power, Politics and Personnel'. He has lectured widely on personnel management at home and abroad. Mr Bramham is a Fellow of the IPM.

Geoff Burgess *(Overseas marketing)* is Managing Director of Wright Rain Ltd. He has been involved in technical, sales, commercial and management training for over twenty years, working both in line and staff management roles in the UK, Europe, Africa and South East Asia. He worked on distributor staff development with Massey Ferguson and subsequently as a Marketing Improvements Consultant with large national and multinational companies. He is also a Director of Birmid Qualcast (Engineering & Electronics) Ltd and Chairman of the Export Affairs Committee, Agricultural Engineers' Association.

Darek Celinski *(Training)* operates at home and overseas as a freelance training consultant, and has over thirty years' experience of training and development in industry. Previously he was with Coventry Management Training Centre, which he joined in 1972. In addition to running personnel and general management courses he specialized in the training of trainers (training managers, training officers, training advisors and similar people from commercial and industrial organizations). Before that, he was training manager at Herbert-Ingersoll. His earlier appointments in training were with the Aviation Division of Smiths Industries and with the South Wales Division of the British Steel Corporation. Mr Celinski is a Fellow of the Institute of Training and Development.

Charles Channon *(Advertising)* has been successively a researcher, an account director, a creative manager, and a director of account planning, starting at BMRB, moving to JWT on the account side, and then setting up the planning function at Ayer Barker. He was first chairman of the Account Planning Group and has written and spoken widely on advertising and planning. He became Director of Studies at the IPA in 1985.

Eric Cowell *(The environment)* is an environmental consultant whose varied career has embraced ecological aspects of agriculture, oil pollution, biological and environmental education, ecological and advisory work in many parts of the world. Before setting up his own consultancy company, he held a succession of positions over many years with a major oil company, which followed appointments with agricultural and pharmaceutical organizations. Mr Cowell has been involved, for example, in the ecological evaluation of many of the world's major oil spills. He has written over 100 papers on environmental issues, as well as editing three scientific textbooks. In addition to Brewhouse Environmental Services, he is also the director of a recording company which, among other specialized output, has produced sound tracks for environmental training videos and training cassettes for industry.

J C Craig *(Taxation)* is a taxation partner of K M G Thomson McLintock, chartered accountants, in Glasgow, where he deals with both personal and company taxation. He is a Member of the Institute of Chartered Accountants of Scotland and a former convener of its taxation committee.

Dr Barrie Dale *(Just-in-time supplies)* is Director of the UMIST Quality Management Centre. The centre is involved in four major activities: research into total quality management; the centre houses the Ford Motor Company Northern Regional Centre for training suppliers in total quality excellence and SPC; the operation of a Quality Management Multi-Company Teaching Programme involving at any one time, eight industrial collaborators; and total quality management consultancy, including the Q-share initiative. He is co-editor of the International Journal of Quality and Reliability Management and has co-written a book on managing quality.

Ken Firth *(Warehouse operation management)* has an international reputation in storage, handling and distribution in which he has been involved throughout his career. His industrial experience culminated in the position of Senior Project Manager for a large manufacturer of storage and handling equipment. He joined the National Materials Handling Centre in early 1971 and is now its Director as well as being Chairman and Managing Director of its holding body NMHC Limited. He has contributed to many publications and lectured extensively on warehouse techniques in the UK and Overseas.

Peter Foyer *(Managing sales engineering)* is a manufacturing and operations professional. He has built on operations experience as a manager in his consulting work over the last 20 years, mainly for major vehicle, engineering and food companies. Recently he has also been appointed Visiting Professor of the Principles of Engineering Design at Coventry Polytechnic.

John Gentles *(Distribution: The total cost-to-serve)* was, for a number of years, a management consultant in the London office of Booz Allen & Hamilton. In this capacity he completed a large number of manufacturing and distribution assignments for such industries as domestic consumer products, automotive supply, aerospace and medical supplies. For the last 5 years he has been with Guiness plc, latterly as Packaging Operations Director for United Distillers.

Douglas Garbutt, PhD, MEd, FMCA, ACIS *(Management accounting)* is an independent management consultant. He has taught at business schools in four continents, has published numerous articles in professional journals and has written or contributed to eleven books.

Prabhu S Guptara BA(Hons), MA, MBIM, MInstD, MITD, FRComS *(Corporate culture and competitive advantage)* is Governor of the Polytechnic of Central London. Prabhu was born, raised and educated in India, where he was a University lecturer for six years. Since coming to England in September 1979, he has worked as a management consultant and trainer, with a special interest in intercultural, interracial and international matters. He has lectured extensively at Universities and business schools.

He is founder-Chairman of Prabhu Guptara Associates (started in 1984); from January 1988 he has also been Director of Advance: Management Training Ltd.
He has presented, contributed and consulted on many radio and television programmes and in numerous newspapers and magazines.

Norman Hart *(Corporate relations)* is Managing Director of Interact International Ltd, having been Director of the CAM Foundation. His previous career with Unilever, Morgan Grampian and Roles and Parker, has been mainly in marketing, advertising and public relations. He is a regular international speaker on these subjects and has written or contributed to many books including *Marketing Handbook* (Gower, 1981). Mr Hart is a Fellow of the Institute of Public Relations and the Institute of Marketing, and holds an MSc from the University of Bradford.

Colin Hastings *(Teamworking)* is Director of Ashridge Teamworking Services, a specialist research and consulting unit. After graduating in psychology he spent eight years with the Delta Metal Group in various management posts, joining Ashridge Management College in 1980. He has been involved in consulting and training with a wide range of British and European companies, including Shell UK Oil, BP International, Renault UK, International Thomson Organisation and Marks and Spencer. He is co-author of the *Superteam Solution*, published by Gower in 1986.

Roger Henderson *(Office administration)* is Chairman of the SPS Consultancy Group plc, formerly the office planning and design consultancy, Space Planning Services plc. He took an engineering degree at Jesus College, Cambridge, and is a member of the Institution of Civil Engineers. He is past Chairman of the National Council of the Institute of Administrative Management and is a founder member of the Council of the Institute of Facilities Management. He has written many articles for professional journals on office planning, design, property markets and corporate strategy.

Richard Howells *(Health and safety)* studied law at the University of Wales and the LSE. He has experience of occupational safety in the coal industry and as a factory inspector. He has taught law for a number of years and is now Professor of Law in the Polytechnic of Central London, Faculty of Law. His research and publications have been on the interpretation and enforcement of safety law and labour legislation.

Peter T Humphrey *(Recruitment and selection)* is Group Personnel Director of Securicor Group plc. Previously he was Managing Director of Ashton Containers (Southern) and Personnel Director of The Mettoy Company Ltd. He has also spent some ten years in management consultancy with major national practices. He is a Companion of The Institute of Personnel Management, a Fellow of the British Institute of Management, and a Member of the Institute of Management Consultants. He also gained his MSc in Organization Behaviour in 1989. He is a contributor to *Administration of Personnel Policies*, edited by Torrington and Naylor (Gower, 1974) and to *Handbook of Management Skills*, edited by Stewart, D M (Gower, 1987). He is the author of *How to be Your Own Personnel Manager* (Institute of Personnel Management, 1981).

Peter Jackson *(Inventory control; Production control)* is a Principal Tutor/Consultant at CMTC Management Centre. He specializes in management techniques and computer training. He was previously with P.A. Management Consultants and started his career in GEC Telecommunications where he worked in production management and control.

C Stuart Jones PhD, MSc, FCMA, ACIS, J Dip MA *(Managing corporate mergers and acquisitions)* is a Senior Lecturer in Accountancy and Finance, School of Information Systems, University of East Anglia, Norwich. He has had wide experience in a variety of manufacturing and service industries and has held senior finance and planning positions with major international and national companies.

D Jones *(Managing sales engineering)* After serving a 5 year apprenticeship at AEI in Coventry, David moved into the Customer Service/Sales Application Engineering with various machine tool companies. During the twelve years at Ingersoll Engineers, he has worked with many clients to improve their customer focus. This has been in a variety of industries both contract and consumer driven, and has shown benefits in improving the initial response, improving the internal communications and bridging the gap between Sales Engineering and Simultaneous Engineering. The experience gained across diverse industries is a strong contribution to the chapter on Sales Engineering.

David Lascelles *(Just-in-time supplies)* is Chief Executive of Q-MAS Ltd., a total quality management consultancy operating under the auspices of the UMIST Quality Management Centre. Prior to this he was a lecturer is the Manchester School of Management at UMIST, and has held positions in sales, marketing and project management in the mechanical engineering and steel stockholding industries. His research interests include the motivational causes of quality improvement, strategic issues of TQM and supplier development. Dr. Lascelles received the 1989 European Quality Award for best European doctoral thesis on quality management.

Arthur Lawrence *(Distribution channels)* is a freelance writer and consultant. His experience includes thirty years' involvement in manufacturing, general trading and retailing in the UK and many countries overseas. For ten years he was an internal consultant with the Unilever group, specializing in organizational effectiveness, productivity and the introduction of systems to sales and marketing operations. He is author of *The Management of Trade Marketing* (Gower, 1983).

Alan Leaper *(Budgetary control)* was Financial Controller of Hoover Worldwide Eastern Region Headquarters for 10 years in which capacity he was responsible for review and control of the budgets of thirteen overseas subsidiaries. His previous experience include 3 years in Canada on cost and general accounting assignments and 11 years with the Frigidaire Division of General Motors Ltd in various factory accounting positions. Mr Leaper is now managing his own retail and wholesale business.

Dennis Lock *(Project management; International trade; Security)* qualified in applied physics and began his career with the General Electric Company, where he was an electronics engineer. His subsequent management experience has been long, successful and exceptionally wide, in industries ranging from sub-miniature electronics to mining engineering and heavy machine tool engineering. He is a Fellow of the Institute of Management Services, a Member of the British Institute of Management and of the Institution of Industrial Managers. Mr Lock has carried out lecturing and consultancy assignments in the UK and overseas, and has written or edited many management books, mostly for Gower. He is now a freelance management writer, specializing in management subjects.

Nicholas Manley *(Intellectual property rights)* is a partner in a long-established firm of patent and trade mark agents. After graduating in Physics from the University of Durham he entered the patent and trade mark profession in private practice where he qualified and became a Fellow of the Chartered Institute of Patent Agents and a European Patent Attorney.

John Mapes *(Planning for production)* is Senior Lecturer in Operations Management at Cranfield School of Management. Earlier in his career he worked for ICI in Productivity Services before taking up a lectureship in the Department of Management at Middlesex Polytechnic. Prior to his present appointment he worked as an internal consultant for Clayton Dewandre Ltd. Mr Mapes holds degrees from Cambridge and Brunel and is joint author of *Model Building Techniques for Management* (Gower, 1976).

Hamish Mathieson *(Managing employee relations)* is a Senior Lecturer in Industrial Relations in the Department of Management at Manchester Polytechnic. Following employment in the engineering industry he graduated in Administration and Industrial Relations from the University of Strathclyde and later obtained an MAS in Industrial Relations from the University of Warwick. A member of the Institute of Personnel Management, he is an active researcher in the field of public sector industrial relations.

Dr Andrew Melhuish *(Executive health)* is a general practitioner in Henley-on-

Thames. He has also been medical adviser to the staff and members at Henley, The Management College, for the last sixteen years during which time he has developed a particular interest in managerial health. With Professor Cary Cooper of UMIST, Manchester, he is involved in a large long-term prospective study of managers' health involving members of Henley and big groups from ICI Paints and Mars. He lectures widely to managers and is the author of *Executive Health* and *Work and Health*. He is at present contributing a monthly article on health to *The Director*.

Alan Mumford *(Developing effective managers)* had industrial experience with John Laing & Son, IPC Magazines and International Computers Ltd which covered management training and development. He had a period with the Department of Employment as Deputy Chief Training Adviser, where he carried out surveys on progress achieved since the passing of the Industrial Training Act. He was for six years Executive Resources Adviser to the Chloride Group, a UK multinational, responsible for senior executive selection, placement and development, and for organization work at the most senior levels. In April 1983, Alan Mumford was one of the first people appointed to IMCB, the Management Centre from Buckingham, as Professor of Management Development. In that role he is responsible for developing IMCB's approach to improving management performance through effective learning processes. He is the author of a number of articles and several books and editor of the *Handbook of Management Development* (Gower, 1986). He is a Companion of the IPM and was from 1971–1973 its Vice-President (Training and Development).

Peter Mumford *(Employee benefits)* is a management consultant specializing in Organizational and Management Development and has worked with a variety of industrial organizations, local government and the health service. He was previously a Personnel Manager in industry and a lecturer in management. His writings include: *Redundancy and Security of Employment* (Gower, 1978), a number of CBT scripts, an interactive video programme: *Styles of Leadership* and co-authorship of a computerized simulation of an insurance company's operations which is being used for training and business forecasting.

C C New *(Planning for production)* is Professor of Operations Management at Cranfield School of Management where he was also Director of the MBA Programme 1983–1986. Professor New took his first degree in Engineering at Cambridge before working with Rolls Royce Ltd in the Aero Engine Division. He joined London Business School in 1971 as a faculty member after taking his Masters Degree in Business Studies there. He completed his PhD shortly after joining Cranfield in 1978. Professor New is the author of numerous books and articles and is an acknowledged expert on manufacturing planning and control systems.

Nicholas O'Shaughnessy BA, MPhil, MBA, *(Direct mail)* is a lecturer in the Judge Institute of Management Studies at the University of Cambridge. Previous to this he worked for the American Economic Foundation and was a lecturer at the University of Wales. He is the author of numerous articles and books, including *The Phenomenon of Political Marketing* and *The Idea of a University Revisited.*

John S Oakland PhD, CChem, MRSC, FIQA, FSS, FAQMC, MASQC, MBIM *(Total quality management; Quality assurance & control)* is head of the European Centre for Total Quality Management (TQM) and holds the Exxon Chemical Chair in TQM at the Management Centre, University of Bradford, one of the largest Business Schools in Europe. Over the last ten years he has taught quality management and statistical process control (SPC) to thousands of organizations. He has directed several large research projects on quality in Europe, funded by the British Government and EEC programmes, and his work on the quality management requirements of industry and commerce has been widely acknowledged and published. He is author of several books, including *Total Quality Management* and *Statistical Process Control*, both published by Heinemann (Oxford). He started his career with the British Iron and Steel Research Association. He later worked for Sandoz, where he led a team engaged in research and development of production processes. He joined Bradford Management Centre in 1979, since when his interests have centred on quality management education, training, and research.

R Keith Oliver *(Distribution: the total cost-to-serve)* is a Senior Vice President of Booz-Allen & Hamilton, head of the firm's Worldwide Operations Management Group and leads the firm's commercial management consulting activities in Europe. He has over twenty years of consulting experience, specializing in the application of advanced management control techniques to manufacturing industries in both Europe and the United States.

He has served clients in a wide range of industries, including automotive, electronics, consumer goods, steel, paper, chemicals, food, pharmaceuticals and telecommunications.

A W Pearson *(Managing research and development)* is Senior Lecturer in Decision Analysis, Director of the R&D Research Unit and a past director of the MBA Programme at the Manchester Business School. He gained industrial experience with Pilkington Brothers Ltd and Henry Simon Ltd before becoming Lecturer in Economic and Social Studies, University of Manchester. Subsequently he was appointed Lecturer in Operational Research at MBS and has been Director of the R&D Research Unit since 1967. He is Editor of *R&D Management* and co-editor of *Transfer Processes in Technical Change* and of *Managing Interdisciplinary Research*; member of the International Advisory Board of Interstudy – International Association for the Study of Interdisciplinary Research – and a member of the Board of COLRAD – the College of R&D of the Institute of Management Science.

Christian Petersen *(Sales promotion)* was the youngest-ever member of the Institute of Practitioners in Advertising and of the Advertising Association, and is a Fellow and Life Member of the Institute of Sales Promotion. He was Chief Editor of *The Handbook of Consumer Sales Promotion* (1976–77) and is the author of *Sales Promotion in Action* (Associated Business Press, 1979). He was a founder and Managing Director of KLP Group plc, Britain's first publicly quoted sales promotion group, retiring in 1986 to read history at Oxford.

W P Ridley *(The annual accounts)* is a consultant. He worked for Merrett Cyriax Associates as a financial consultant for five years. In 1973 he joined the stockbroker firm of Wood Mackenzie and Company, which was taken over by the security companies Hill Samuel and Drunty Natwest to which was was appointed director. He read law at Oxford and became an Associate of the Institute of Chartered Accountants in 1961. He taught in Uganda and at Hendon Technical College before joining the Economic and Investment Research Department of the Bank of London and South America. Between 1965 and 1968, Mr Ridley worked for the Commonwealth Development Corporation.

F W Rose *(Company law; Contracts between companies)* is principal lecturer in the Law Department of Birmingham Polytechnic. He graduated from King's College London with a Master's Degree in Law and was called to the Bar at Gray's Inn. After working as a company secretary he began teaching full time and has acted as Course Director successively for a law degree course, the Solicitor's Final Examination Course and the Common Professional Examination Course. For several years he has also taught professional courses for a number of commercial undertakings and acted as an external examiner for various professional bodies. His publications include *Employment Law* (Ravenswood Press, 1984).

Tessa V Ryder Runton *(Capital project evaluation)* who has a Cambridge Science and Law degree, started her career as a patent examiner. She studied further at the London School of Economics and worked as a financial analyst for the Rio-Tinto Zinc Corporation. She has lectured on financial analysis at several business schools in England and Scotland. After retraining in science she has been teaching at a comprehensive school. She contributed to *Financial Management Handbook* (Gower, 3rd edition, 1988).

Philip Sadler CBE *(Principles of management)* was Principal and Chief Executive of Ashridge Management College from 1969 to 1990. He is now Chairman of the Association for Management Education and Development, and an active consultant in management and organizational development. His recent writings include *Managerial Leadership in Post Industrial Society* (Gower) and *Designing Organizations* (Mercury).

Bill Scott *(Negotiating)*, having held senior appointments in both the industrial and the academic world, is now an independent consultant specializing in communication, negotiation and management development. His clients are in industry, commerce, engineering, and international organizations. He works regularly in Europe, Asia and Australasia. Mr Scott is author of the best-selling Gower books *The Skills of Negotiating* and *The Skills of Communicating* and co-author (with Dr Sven Söderberg) of *The Art of Managing.*

Tim Seville *(Manufacturing systems)* is a freelance management training consultant and writer who specializes in the preparation of open learning material. He has more than twenty years' experience in major international manufacturing companies in engineering, chemicals and papermaking. He is a Cambridge graduate and a member of the Institute of Training and Development.

Leon Simons *(Working capital and management ratios)* is a graduate of Glasgow

University and a member of the Institute of Chartered Accountants of Scotland. He has wide experience of finance and accountancy acquired in industry, the City and the profession. He is now an independent management consultant specializing in finance and pricing, in which subjects he lectures extensively in the UK and has also lectured in Europe and America. He has contributed to and written many books and journals.

John Stapleton *(Marketing planning)* completed his full-time education at the University of Aston in Birmingham, is a recipient of the Lord Mayor of London's Marketing Award, a Queen's Award to Industry and has appeared in the British High Court as a marketing authority. Mr Stapleton has had a varied in-depth career in marketing management and practice, having been a salesman, sales manager, market research manager, marketing manager, and a senior lecturer in advertising, media and statistics. He has worked in the printing, pharmaceuticals, telecommunications, detergents, construction, publishing, and computer industries for British, American, and European companies, large and small. He has written a number of books on marketing, including *How to Prepare a Marketing Plan* (Gower, 4th edition, 1988), *Teach Yourself Marketing, Elements of Export Marketing* and *Glossary of Marketing Terms*. Since 1969 he has been an independent consultant, and provides diagnostic and monitoring services into company marketing plans, advertising campaigns, and new product promotions.

Professor Merlin Stone *(Database marketing)* is Managing Director of Tabas Midas Ltd. He has held a variety of academic and business posts, including a spell with Rank Xerox and three years as a lecturer at Henley, The Management College. He has written five books, and numerous articles, on aspects of marketing.

George F Thomason *(Pay systems and structures)* is Professor Emeritus of the University of Wales. From 1969 to 1984 he was Montague Burton Professor of Industrial Relations and Head of the Department of Industrial Relations and Management Studies in University College Cardiff. He is currently Visiting Professor in the Department of Behaviour in Organizations, University of Lancaster, and in the Departments of Town Planning and Business Studies, UWIST. He has served as a member of the ACAS Panel of Arbitrators since 1965; as a member of the Review Bodies on Doctors' and Dentists' Remuneration (1980) and on Nurses' and Midwives' Remuneration (1983). Professor Thomason is author of a number of books on personnel management and community development, including *A Textbook of Personnel Management*, now in its fourth edition; *A Textbook of Industrial Relations Management, Job Evaluation: Objectives and Methods; The Management of Research and Development: Experiments in Participation* and *The Professional Approach to Community Work*.

Denis Walker *(Customer first – a strategy for quality service)* is an independent consultant specializing in service, quality and organizational change. His previous career was with British Airways where, after holding a variety of personnel posts, he became Customer Service Manager and ultimately Deputy General Manager, Ground Operations.

Tim Warner *(Design management: a product focus)* is a product designer who has a Masters Degree in Design Research from the Royal College of Art. His research includes a study of industrial product design management.

B H Walley *(Plant layout)* is an independent training consultant. His line manage-ment experience has included directorship of Ferodo Ltd, Presswork Components & Ferodo Nigeria. He is the author of over sixty articles and eight successful books including *Management Services Handbook* and *Production Management Hand-book.*

A N Welsh *(Personal organization)* is a Senior Adviser with the Management Development Centre of Hong Kong a government funded body engaged in researching and producing new methods of managerial improvement. A graduate of Oxford University, his varied career has given him considerable industrial and commercial experience. He has been Director and Secretary of the Three Hands Evan Williams Group, manufacturers of household products and toiletries (Three Hands is now part of Cadbury Schweppes) and Director of Training for the international management consultants W. D. Scott Co. (now part of Coopers & Lybrand). He has been Managing Director of the Haverfordwest firm of agricul-ture, engineers and builders merchants S. & F. Green Ltd. and held directorships or been involved in many other enterprizes. He is the author of *The Skills of Management* (Gower, 1980), *The Hong Kong Management Development Hand-book* (1989) and many other publications and articles. He lectures and teaches widely, and is a Teaching Fellow at Hong Kong University.

Philip Westwood *(The administration of commercial property)* is a Senior Lec-turer in the Department of Building Economics at South Bank Polytechnic. A chartered surveyor and chartered builder, he holds a MPh degree in Building Legislation. Before becoming a full-time lecturer he worked for many years for Walter Llewellyn & Sons Ltd as a surveyor and estimator. He has lectured for a number of years in building economics, building technology and management to surveyors and building technologists. He is currently involved in a research programme developing an expert system for the use of physically handicapped people in the evaluation of their housing needs.

E N White *(Maintenance)* has held a number of management posts in quality control, product support, customer service and engineering maintenance, and was for ten years managing director of a technical services company. He has published many papers, is a frequent speaker in the UK and overseas, and manages a number of training programmes. His book *Maintenance Planning, Control and Documentation* (Gower, 2nd edition, 1979), has become a standard reference work for engineering training.

Dennis Whitmore *(Industrial engineering)* is Co-ordinator of Full-cost Courses at the Harrow campus of the Polytechnic of Central London. He is also a management consultant in his own right. Previously he was Senior Production Manager with Mullard and a Senior Consultant with Philips. Dr Whitmore was educated at London, Brunel and Surrey Universities and is a Fellow of the British Institute of Management. Recently he was awarded Honorary Fellowship of the Institute of

Management Services for his contribution to work measurement and control internationally. (His many books include the standard textbook *Work Measurement* (Institute of Management Services, 1976), and the standard text on work measurement for the People's Republic of China.

John Williams *(Sales promotion)* is Chairman of Innovation Limited, a Sales Promotion Consultancy. His career has involved the launch of Fosters Draught and the publication of the UK's definitive guide to sales promotion *The Manual of Sales Promotion*. He has been responsible for the introduction of various innovative sales promotion techniques into the UK market and advises companies on the strategic use of sales promotion.

Mike Williams *(Management self-development)* is an independent management consultant who operates both in the UK and Western Europe. His clients include universities, business schools, professional bodies and a wide range of companies, in both the private and public sectors. He is the author or co-author of several books in the fields of industrial psychology and management practice. His areas of specialization include senior executive development, the identification of operational and strategic managerial potential, leadership development and team building, using several unique learning methods. He has had extensive experience of the business world in personnel, marketing, sales and production. He gained his MSc from the University of Aston and he is a member of the British Psychological Society. He served full-time and as a volunteer reservist with the Royal Navy (Intelligence) and the Royal Marines (Commando and SBS) from which experience he has drawn considerably in his approach to leadership development within the business world.

M T Wilson *(Managing a sales force)* is Managing Director of Marketing Improvements Ltd, the leading international marketing consultancy and training group. Operating from offices in London and Singapore and through associates in Europe, MI covers all major markets and languages on behalf of its numerous clients in the consumer, industrial and service sectors. Marketing Improvements was formed in 1964 by Mr Wilson following experience in the Institute of Marketing and Ford Motor Company, which he joined on graduating from Manchester University. He is widely known for the seminars and courses on all aspects of marketing which he has run in all five continents, and for the highly creative consultancy advice given to companies throughout Europe, including multinationals. His *Managing a Sales Force* (Gower, 2nd edition, 1983) and *The Management of Marketing* (Gower, 1980) have both achieved worldwide success.

Frank Woodward *(Managing transport services)* is a Fellow of the Chartered Secretaries and Administrators, a Fellow of the Royal Society of Arts and a Member of the Chartered Institute of Transport with over thirty years' practical experience in all types of fleet operation. Before retiring in 1983, he was Managing Director of a large industrial fleet of over 3500 vehicles. An author, journalist and well-known speaker at conferences and seminars, he has written many books on fleet management and finance and on road transport distribution. He is co-author of *Controlling Company Car Costs* (Gower, 1985).

Prof. J G Woolhouse *(Organization development)* Director of the Centre for Education and Industry at the University of Warwick, has had 30 years experience in a career spanning industry, education and international consultancy. He spent 18 years with Roll Royce, where he started as a graduate apprentice in 1954. He became a Director of Rolls Royce and Associates in 1965 and was appointed Company Education and Training Officer for the Rolls Royce organization in 1968. In 1972 he moved to Kingston Polytechnic as an Assistant Director of the Polytechnic, and Director of the Kingston Regional Management Centre. In 1978 he joined the W. S. Atkins Group as a Director of Atkins Planning, where he was responsible for supervizing education, training and management development projects in both 'developed' and developing countries in many parts of the world.

He was seconded to the Manpower Services Commission in January 1983 as Director of the Technical and Vocational Education Initiative (TVEI) and was subsequently appointed Director of Education Programmes. He was elected to the first chair of education and industry to be created in the UK in January 1989. He has served on many public committees in education, training and management development, and was made a CBE in 1988 for services to education.

David Wragg *(Promotional public relations; Employee communications)* is the Head of Corporate Communications for the Royal Bank of Scotland. A former journalist, he entered public relations in 1974, joining the P&O Group, where he eventually became Manager, Public Relations Services, before leaving in 1979. Other organizations for whom he has worked include the Chartered Institute of Transport, Twinlock and the Bristol & West Building Society. A member of the Institute of Public Relations, Mr Wragg is the author of *Public Relations for Sales and Marketing Management* (Kogan Page, 1987), which has also been translated into Portuguese, and *Publicity and Customer Relations in Transport Management* (Gower, 1982), as well as eleven books on aeronautical history, many of which have also been published in the United States.

Foreword: The once and future manager

Nigel Farrow

Merlin, wizard and medieval management consultant, is sitting in his study. He is wrestling with one of his most difficult assignments: the tuition of the future King Arthur in the arts of management.

The course is full of practical work. Using his magical powers and the experience of already having lived in the future, Merlin often projects himself and King Arthur into the twentieth century in order to work on real business problems. Together they have designed a small car for Rover, which has taken 60 per cent of the domestic market. They have negotiated free entry into the Japanese market for British products and services and modernized French agriculture. They have found an uncontested site for the third London airport and re-financed Poland. In 1933 they bought IBM and in 1965 they sold Rolls Royce. Merlin believes in the case-study method.

But Arthur notices that whenever a particularly difficult issue arises, Merlin consults a big book which lies on his desk, along with his portable crucible, philosopher's stone, and bottled bat's blood.

Arthur	*Merlin, please tell me what's in that great volume you keep referring to? Is it a book of spells?*
Merlin	No, it's the *Gower Handbook of Management*, which I acquired on a quick trip to 1992 . . . There's no wizardry in it, just sound advice on almost every aspect of management.
Arthur	*But was it written by a wizard?*
Merlin	Not by a wizard, but by many experts. Over 70 of them.
Arthur	*(after some thought) – Merlin, there's something that's been troubling me. If there are going to be so many management experts in those days-yet-to-come and so much written and published on management and so many people tutored in the arts of management, why will they have so much trouble with their business?*
Merlin	Because they will attempt so much. It will be an heroic age. Ordinary managers, without the weapons of social privilege or personal wealth, will be required to ride out as champions of the whole kingdom to defeat poverty, ignorance and sloth.
Arthur	*You make these managers sound like a new order of chivalry. I thought that they would be arriving as bag-men and the servants of bag-men. People who will be out to line their own pockets.*
Merlin	It may well start like that, but it will have become something very different by the time *The Gower Handbook of Management* is written. I see that a little yet-to-be-history lesson is required. First, I will let you into a secret about the system of free business enterprise, which by some will be called 'capitalism'. Contrary to reports, mostly put about by its own practitioners, it will be a tremendous

success. By the twentieth century, it will provide the material means of feeding, housing and clothing huge populations. It will sustain individuals and groups of individuals regardless of their origins and promote their fortunes largely on the basis of their usefulness to society. It will transmit wealth and knowledge around the world. It will finance science and encourage the arts. In fact, it will be far too successful for its own good.

Arthur *What do you mean?*

Merlin Because of its success, governments and individuals will link their hopes and programmes for social development to its economic performance. By the middle of the twentieth century, business will be the main source of income in work and in retirement for most men and many women. Through taxation, business will contribute massively to the welfare services of the community, as well as developing many health, educational and housing schemes of its own. Through legislation, business will be obliged to advance racial and sexual equality, protect the natural world and train the young. Not content with the controls of taxation and legislation, governments will force themselves into partnership with business so as to be able to direct its resources to the achievement of their social goals.

Arthur *But will this be a bad thing? If, as you tell me, the Age of Chivalry cannot last forever, then the Age of Business Enterprise sounds as though it will provide a better life for most people than many of the ages that will come between now and then.*

Merlin Indeed it will. And that's the point. Having had their expectations raised, people and their popularly elected governments will seek to extract from business enterprise ever better conditions of living. You only have to look at the contents of this Handbook to see that by the late twentieth century the manager will have taken over many of the functions performed in previous ages by the feudal lord, the priest, the teacher, the money-lender, the physician, the lawyer, the watchman and even (*he glances with suspicion at the section on market research*) the astrologer.

Arthur *Are you saying that the decline of some businesses in the late twentieth century is therefore not the responsibility of the managers but the fault of the society?*

Merlin Of course not. Management incompetence, fraud and idleness will contribute their share of failures, as in all other occupations. But the feeling of weakness that you have observed in some areas of business and government during our visits to the mid- to late twentieth century is in large part a reflection of managers' frustration with their social roles and people's disappointment at the failure to fulfil their expectations. Indeed, some businesses will fail just because the original purposes and skills of business management – buying, making, selling – will be lost in a mass of unproductive administration. For a while, this trend will be encouraged by the very people who should stand out against it – the Business Schoolmen. They will be teaching high finance to those who need low cunning; planning to those who should be doing; organizational theory to those who need personal skills. It will take a great recession in business in the 1970s to bring some of them back to teaching the basic arts.

Arthur *Merlin, you said that the system of free business enterprise will be a success, and that to cope with this success and the expectations that it will create, the arts of business management will be developed. However, in spite of this development, the managers will not always be able to deliver all the benefits that the people expect. Does that mean that in the end management and managers will be rejected as the means of controlling business? On our study tours, we have never been beyond 1988. What happens after that?*

Merlin Ah . . . I'm not going to tell you the answers before you have done the practical research. You will have to wait and see. But you should have already observed that towards the end of the 1970s there will be significant changes in the context of management.

Small businesses, whether owned by their managers or by large corporations, will come back into favour. Governments will notice that small businesses employ the majority of people. Large corporations will realize that smaller operating units have smaller costs of administration. The costs of basic resources – manpower, energy, materials – will all rise dramatically as the owners of these resources realize that they can fix a market price for them – and that society is no longer prepared to risk wars or revolutions in order to hold down the cost of such resources. More people and nations will acquire the means of production and the skills of management, so that competition will increase faster than custom. As a function, management will be invaded by machines, which will take over the task of assembling and analysing information, and by working people, who will seek to participate in the process of decision making.

Arthur   *So, what will this mean for the manager?*

Merlin   That he needs to go back to the basics of business – and with the consent and encouragement of a society which has a better appreciation of the true role of business. Increased competition will mean getting closer to the customer and involving the whole workforce in the satisfaction of his needs. The scarcity and expense of resources will mean developing better ways of making things and generating less waste. With more machine-produced information and analysis, there will be a greater need for human judgement. Smaller business units employing better educated people will require more effective styles of leadership.

These are all reasons why the *Gower Handbook of Management* will be such a good guide for businesses in the last part of the twentieth century. It is concerned with the basic practicalities of managing a business and it also contains a section on personal skills, such as negotiation, communication, and self-development.

Arthur   *If it is so full of wisdom and management is so important to the future, I think I should have the copy of this Handbook. After all, I am the 'once and future king'.*

Merlin contemplates this suggestion. For Arthur to study the book himself would save a lot of time in tutorials. Time in which he could be earning fees from other consultancy assignments, like the plan to start a quality circle for knights called the Round Table. But Merlin considers that to let the *Gower Handbook of Management* out of his possession could be dangerous for his own business. It is the Middle Ages: wizards are two a penny, but good management consultants are few and far between. It is better not to risk spoiling the market.

Merlin   No, thank you, Arthur. I think it would be most appropriate if I kept the book – just for the next few hundred years.

With apologies to T. H. White, author of *The Sword in the Stone.*

Part One

PRINCIPLES, POLICY AND ORGANIZATION

1 Principles of management

Philip Sadler

When practising managers are faced with difficult and complex problems – for example, designing an organization structure for a new manufacturing plant, or attempting to motivate a workforce characterized by apathy and low productivity – they quite naturally feel the need for a set of principles to turn to, in order to help them reach the right decisions.

This is sensible when it involves a willingness to learn from the experience of others as opposed to a stubborn determination to learn only from one's own mistakes. There is, however, the risk that so-called 'principles' which carry all the authority of tablets of stone, but which are frequently based on limited experience, may be accepted uncritically as if they were eternal truths and used by managers as substitutes for their own thought processes.

The principles of management are, of course, quite unlike the principles of mathematics or the laws of the natural sciences. In the management field there is no universal agreement as to what the principles are, nor can it be said that the principles of management are valid for all situations. (There is little point in adding the qualification 'other things being equal' since in the human context in which management is set the 'other things' are rarely if ever 'equal'.)

It would, perhaps, be better not to use the term 'principles' at all, but to refer instead to 'guidelines'. They are, quite simply, sets of potentially useful generalizations about the factors which make for success in management. People have been making such general statements for thousands of years, usually as a result of thinking deeply about their own experiences in organizations. In modern times the wide-ranging types of experience gained by successful management consultants have been a particularly fertile source of such ideas.

In this chapter the historical development of management principles will be traced briefly in order to set the scene for a more detailed examination of some of the more recent and contemporary writings on the subject. The chapter will conclude with a statement of some management principles which have emerged from experience and research in recent years.

THE BEGINNINGS OF MANAGEMENT THOUGHT

The search for 'principles of management' – rules or 'laws' which, if observed, will result in effective managerial performance in all situations – has been going on for thousands of years (George, 1968). Early Egyptian writings show that the builders of the pyramids recognized certain basic principles such as authority, responsibility and specialization. The Babylonian Code of Hammurabi set out principles of control and responsibility and Moses developed principles of organization when leading the tribes of Israel on the flight from Egypt. Mencius, writing in China in 500 BC emphasized the importance of the systematic application of principles of management: 'Whoever pursues a business in this world must have a system. A business which has attained success without a system does not exist.' Plato, in the *Republic*, argued the merits of the principle of specialization, and Socrates stressed the universal nature of management: 'I say that over whatever a man may preside he will, if he knows what he needs, and is able to provide it, be a good president, whether he have the direction of a chorus, a family, a city or an army.'

Many instances of early management thought come from the writings of great military strategists, for example, the staff principle, probably first used during the reign of Alexander the Great (336–323 BC). Machiavelli, in the sixteenth century, developed four principles – reliance on mass consent; cohesiveness; leadership; and the will to survive. Although he was writing about government in his time, the same principles might be applied to the management of companies today.

Modern industrial management theory dates from the introduction of the factory system. Techniques for financial control, incentive payment schemes, planning systems and investment appraisal methods were rapidly developed and applied. A rational approach to management was developed in the nineteenth century, and became known as 'scientific management'. Typical of pioneering work of this kind was the development of techniques such as product forecasting, production planning and work study at the Boulton, Watt Co. Engineering Works in England in the early years of the century. At the same time, in the United States, Eli Whitney was developing cost accounting, quality control and the concept of interchangeable parts. In Scotland, Robert Owen laid the foundations of modern personnel management at the New Lanark Mill, demonstrating that concern for employee welfare and the provision of good working conditions were compatible with a profitable and thriving business.

In 1881 the first business school (the Wharton School at the University of Pennsylvania) was established – some eighty or more years before the decision to establish business schools in London and Manchester.

Thirty years later Frederick Winslow Taylor published the work which has possibly had more influence on management practice than anything published since, his famous *Principles of Scientific Management* (Taylor, 1911). He advocated that managers should gather together all the traditional knowledge possessed by workmen and then classify it and reduce it to laws, rules and formulae. They should then develop a 'science' for each element of a man's work to replace old rule-of-thumb methods and 'scientifically' select and train workmen in the new methods. Finally, managers should take over certain tasks, such as planning and scheduling of work, which were previously left to the workmen to cope with as well as they could.

THE PRE-WAR MANAGEMENT WRITERS

Taylor's work had a profound and far-reaching influence on works management and much workshop practice today still reflects this. In the field of general management, however, a number of writers, in the years up to the Second World War, exercised a similarly powerful influence – most notably Henri Fayol, a French mining engineer; Elton Mayo, a Harvard professor; Mary Parker Follett, an Ameri-

can educationalist trained in philosophy, law and political science; Chester Barnard, president of the New Jersey Bell Telephone Company; and Lyndall F. Urwick,
a British army officer who became a management consultant.

Fayol's work was first published in France in 1916 under the title *Administration
Industrielle et Générale* and failed to be noticed in Britain and North America until
translated and published by Pitman in 1949 as *General and Industrial Management*
(Fayol, 1949). He analysed management activity into five elements – planning,
organizing, commanding (or directing), co-ordinating and controlling – an analytical framework which has been borrowed and built upon by countless writers
since. He also argued that, to be effective, management should be founded upon
fourteen principles as follows:

1   Division of work and specialization
2   Authority must match responsibility
3   Discipline
4   Unity of command (one man, one boss)
5   Unity of direction
6   Subordination of individual interest to the general interest
7   Remuneration must be fair in relation to effort
8   Centralization
9   The scalar or hierarchical principle of line authority
10 The principle of order (a place for everyone and everyone in his place)
11 Equity
12 Stability of tenure of personnel
13 Importance of initiative
14 Importance of *esprit de corps.*

This represented the first attempt at a complete theory of management. The fact
that it received widespread recognition and acclaim when published in the English
language more than thirty years after it was originally written is an indication of the
extent to which Fayol was regarded as an authority on management matters.

Elton Mayo's distinction lies in the fact that his contribution was based on
research rather than on direct personal experience, and in the way he shifted
attention away from the more mechanistic issues of structure and control on to the
human factors affecting industrial performance. The now famous studies he conducted at the Hawthorne Works of the Western Electric Company (Mayo, 1933)
led to the conclusion that questions of human motivation and the emotional
response elicited by the work situation were more important than logical and
rational arrangements in determining output. Mayo also held that social relationships in workings groups were the most important factor influencing the satisfaction the workers derived from their work.

Mary Parker Follett (Follett, 1949), reached similar conclusions, but on philo-
sophical grounds rather than as a result of applied research. She emphasized the
importance of group processes in decision making and had much to say that is
relevant today on the question of resolving conflict.

Chester Barnard was a practising manager, but his analysis of the managerial
role and the nature of organizations in *The Functions of the Executive* (Barnard,
1937) constitutes an important part of our sociological literature. His analysis

linked together hitherto unrelated ideas about the factors affecting individual performance, the nature of organizations and the role of the manager.

The final figure in this group of people writing in the 1930s and 1940s is Lyndall F. Urwick, whose most influential work was *The Elements of Administration* (Urwick, 1949). He produced a new synthesis based on the work of such people as Taylor, Fayol and Follett.

The principles which Urwick gathered together in this way have come to be known as the 'classical' principles of management. They are based on a combination of experience and philosophy rather than rigorous research and have been widely criticized for this. They have attracted criticism on other grounds, also. First, the underlying assumption of their work – that there exists a common set of principles applicable to management in all types of situation – has been frequently challenged. Second, their work is criticized (perhaps unfairly) on the grounds that the world in which they had their experience no longer exists and that the principles they derived from that experience have little or no validity for the contemporary organization operating in the modern business environment. (An example of the way ideas have changed in recent years is the widespread loss of confidence in the so-called economies of scale; another is the extent to which the principle of specialization has been challenged as a result both of new ideas and much research and experimentation in the field of job design.)

Thus, changes in our ideas about management have conspired with the march of events to destroy the credibility of the classical management principles. The main changes which have affected the managerial role and altered it beyond recognition in the last quarter of a century include:

1 The impact of the computer, and more recently the microprocessor, on information processing tasks in production and administration
2 The increase in the pace of technological change generally, with consequences for the speed with which manufacturing processes and products themselves become obsolete
3 The growth of international trade and the associated intensification of competition, together with the growth of the multinational corporation and the impact on business of unstable exchange rates
4 The much greater impact of legislation on business activity – in such fields as employment protection, consumer protection, environmental care, health and safety, and so on
5 Changes in social climate leading to demands for employee participation in decision making
6 High rates of inflation.

These and other factors have brought about a geometric increase in the complexity of the management task such that decisions can not easily be taken in the light of a few clearly formulated principles or guidelines of the classical kind.

MANAGEMENT THEORY IN THE POST-WAR ERA

The post-war era has seen great expansion in the volume of literature on management. The range and variety of approaches is so great as to defy any simple grouping or system of classification into schools of thought, but some commonalities can be detected.

First, the tradition of the consultant or practitioner theorizing on the basis of his experience has continued, primarily because this approach genuinely meets the needs of many practising managers seeking to bring a greater degree of system and order into their own thinking. Often the most successful writers in this category have been those who can most clearly communicate, and elaborate into a system of thought, what practising managers already believe to be the case on the basis of their own experience. The best-known writers in this category in the English language have been such eminently successful consultants as Brech, Louis Allen and, above all, Peter Drucker.

Drucker in particular has taken account of changes in the nature of business environment and the managerial task, and has been successful precisely because he speaks to the contemporary manager and deals with the issues that currently concern him (Drucker, 1971).

Second, and closely related to the first group, is a smaller number of highly influential writers who have illuminated management thought with shafts of humour or satire. The most outstanding in this respect are C. Northcote Parkinson's *Parkinson's Law* (Parkinson, 1957); Robert Townsend's *Up the Organisation* (Townsend, 1970) and Antony Jay's *Management and Machiavelli* (Jay, 1967). The ideas of these writers are well known outside management circles and indeed Parkinson's work has a place of its own in the literature of post-war society.

Third, there are the propounders of functional principles or of principles concerned with part rather than the whole of the management task. We have already seen that the classical principles of management were developed by people such as Fayol and Urwick on the basis of earlier work in production management by Taylor and others. In the post-war period we have seen considerable elaboration of theory in such areas as principles of marketing (Levitt, 1969, and Kotler, 1976), principles of personnel management (Pigors and Myers, 1969) and corporate strategy and planning (Ansoff, 1965).

This third group differs from the previous two in that it is dominated by academics as distinct from practitioners or consultants, reflecting the growth of management studies as an academic subject in the universities and the growing influence of the business school – initially in the US but more recently in Britain and other European countries. This group, in consequence, overlaps to some extent with the fourth and perhaps most important group – the management researchers. Primarily industrial psychologists and sociologists, their work builds on the tradition pioneered by Elton Mayo of detached, empirical and comparative studies of behaviour in industrial organizations. In turn, they can be subdivided according to the main focus of their research. Looked at in this way, the field breaks down quite logically into: studies of the individual industrial worker and his motivation; studies of the behaviour of industrial work groups; studies of the factors influencing organization effectiveness; and researches into managerial and leadership behaviour.

Under the first heading three American psychologists, Herzberg, McClelland and Maslow, have had a strong and enduring influence on management theory and practice. Herzberg is best known for his distinction between 'motivators', such as the work itself, achievement, responsibility and recognition, and what he describes as 'hygiene' factors, which do not provide motivation but merely act so as to prevent workers from being dissatisfied. These factors include pay, working conditions and relations with supervisors. Herzberg's work has led to important experiments in job enrichment as well as casting doubt on the effectiveness of many financial incentive schemes (Herzberg, 1959). McClelland's researches emphasized the importance of the motivation to achieve in relation to the performance of work (McClelland, 1969), while Maslow's most important contribution was to draw attention to the way in which human needs are ordered into a hierarchical system, with basic needs such as survival and security as the foundation of motivation, but with higher-order needs such as belonging, esteem, achievement and self-actualization acting as the more important day-to-day motivators in advanced societies where survival and security can reasonably be taken for granted (Maslow, 1954).

Insight into the behaviour of industrial work groups has been provided by researchers on both sides of the Atlantic. Outstanding examples include Gouldner's study of gypsum mineworkers (Gouldner, 1954), and Walker and Guest's work on assembly-line workers in the US (Walker and Guest, 1952), while in Britain there have been equally illuminating studies, such as Lupton's participant observation of shop-floor behaviour (Lupton, 1963).

The functioning of whole organizations and relationships between different forms of organization structure and effectiveness have been the focus of a great deal of research on both sides of the Atlantic. This work in particular has had a powerful influence both in demolishing the credibility of the simple classical principles and in establishing new but more complex guidelines for management decisions.

In Britain, the work of members of the Tavistock Institute of Relations has demonstrated the importance of taking account both of the constraints imposed by technology and the needs of human beings for satisfying social relationships when designing organization structures. From their work emerged the principles of 'joint optimization of the social and technical systems', which stresses the need to search for forms of organization in which technical requirements and human aspirations are simultaneously fulfilled (Rice, 1963, and Trist et al, 1963).

Joan Woodward (in her studies of organization structures and levels of technology) conclusively showed that there is no one best way to organize a business and that the form of organization advocated in the classical principles, with its emphasis on unity of command, hierarchy and clarity of structure, was far from universally adopted by successful firms (Woodward, 1965). In a similar vein, Burns and Stalker were able to demonstrate that the classical principles worked well in firms with highly stable technologies and markets but failed to be associated with successful performance in firms faced with the need for rapid adjustment to changing conditions (Burns and Stalker, 1961).

Organization studies in the US that have contributed to the theory and practice of management include the work of Rensis Likert and, in particular, his concept of the organization as a series of interlocking groups (Likert, 1961). These US studies also include the analysis by Lawrence and Lorsch of the problems faced by firms which need, on the one hand, to differentiate their activities to be able to relate to different markets, but which must simultaneously integrate these activities into a coherent and cohesive organization for purposes of control and co-ordination (Lawrence and Lorsch, 1967).

Among the many studies of managerial behaviour, those of Mintzberg in the US (Mintzberg, 1973), and Rosemary Stewart in Britain (Stewart, 1967) have thrown much needed light on what managers actually do, and how the job content of managers with different roles in the organization varies. The relationship between leadership style and management effectiveness has also proved to be a fruitful area of research, with outstanding contributions to our knowledge of leadership processes emerging from the work of Bass (Bass, 1960), and Fiedler (Fiedler, 1971) in the US.

The fourth and final group of contributors to modern management theory can be traced in its origins to two main sources: first, the application of scientific methods and mathematical problem-solving techniques to the solution of opera-tional problems in wartime; and second, the subsequent development of computers and related mathematical approaches to solving complex problems. This fourth group is variously known as operational research or management scientists. It has included a number of eminent thinkers who have moved beyond the development and application of techniques to develop whole theories of management and organization based on concepts derived from systems theory or information theory. In the US the outstanding personalities are March and Simon of the Massachusetts Institute of Technology (March and Simon, 1958); Diebold, the 'father of automation' (Diebold, 1965) and Norbert Weiner (Weiner, 1948), the man who first developed ideas in the field of cybernetics and related them to management.

In Britain, Stafford Beer clearly falls into this category. Beer exemplifies the approach of this group of writers in several ways. He is enthusiastic about pro-spects of management becoming more 'scientific'. He regards the computer as a potential tool for revolutionary changes in the practice of management. He con-ceptualizes management as an information-processing activity and management's task as primarily one of *control*. Given that cybernetics is the science of control systems, it follows that the principles of cybernetics are also the key principles of management (Beer, 1972).

The management world described by Beer and others writing in the same vein is one with a strange language of its own – familiar perhaps to specialists in control engineering or to consultant neurologists, but foreign to generalists, and market-ing and personnel specialists, to whom terms such as 'heuristic', 'negentropy' and 'reticulum' convey little or nothing. At the same time it is a world in which problems of labour relations, emotions, attitudes, irrational conflicts and organi-zational politics have no place. The main influence of this school of writers has been in the design, development and application of mathematically based opera-tional research techniques to the solution of certain types of business problem.

MODERN MANAGEMENT PRINCIPLES

To what extent is it possible to draw from these various approaches a body of knowledge which, when summarized and distilled down to its essentials, could be said to represent the principles of modern management as distinct from the 'classical' ones? The task is a daunting one, not only because of the sheer volume of literature that now exists, but also because the principal trends have been towards divergence of theory, specialization of topic and fragmentation of knowledge, rather than reflecting convergence, integration and synthesis.

It is possible, however, to identify a number of recurring ideas or themes which, albeit given different treatment by different authorities and accorded differing degrees of importance in different conceptual schemes, would, nevertheless, command widespread acceptance. What follows is an attempt to state these main propositions, 'principles' or guidelines about management which command widespread agreement today.

The organization as a complex system

The achievement of the purposes of a human organization will involve a wide range of activities which are interconnected so as to form a system, such that changes to the pattern of activities in one part of the system will trigger related changes in other parts of it.

The technical and social sub-systems

The organization as a system is made up of two principal sub-systems – the technical and the social. The former is made up of such elements as the plant and machinery in use, the work flow between the different production stations and the system of production adopted (batch, mass production, continuous flow, etc.). The social system consists of the pattern of relations between the people who work in the organization. In designing organizations, regard must be given both to the need to adapt the structure to the technical system and to provide a structure which makes for a satisfying pattern of human relationships.

The organization as an open system

The existence of any organization depends on some process of exchange of goods or services with other organizations, social units or individuals in its environment. From this it follows that, in the long run, organizations cannot survive if they are managed exclusively in ways which meet the needs of their members. Management is, therefore, partly the process of achieving a delicate balance between the expectations and needs of such internal 'stakeholders' as shareholders, managers, employees and pensioners on the one hand, and, on the other, the demands and constraints imposed upon the organization by its markets, its customers, its suppliers, trades unions, government departments, pressure groups of various kinds and, not least, by the strategies and tactics of competitors. To create and preserve such a balance calls for the continuous monitoring of the organization's environment and the will to bring about appropriate responses on the part of the organization.

The key resource of the modern business organization in advanced industrial societies is knowledge

The key workers are the 'knowledge workers'; management, therefore, is more to do with the profitable exploitation of knowledge than with the productivity of labour or the utilization of physical capacity. 'Knowledge' in this context may mean product knowledge, process 'know-how' or knowledge of the market. It is the task of management to ensure that the organization's level of investment in the acquisition of new knowledge is sufficient to give it the competitive strength it requires to achieve profitable growth.

Management's key task is to secure the future survival of the organization by means of appropriate and timely innovation

The classical principles of management tend to conjure up a vision of some mythical factory for producing 'widgets' which has always produced widgets and always will, using the same technology for the purpose and selling them in a stable market to loyal customers and without any Japanese competition! In the modern organization, by contrast, successful innovation in both products and processes is indispensable to survival. Effective management, therefore, involves the ability to develop an innovative, creative climate, to establish an efficient system of market intelligence so as to discover needs for new products, and to generate the funds needed for R & D and investment in new plant and equipment.

Management is the process of getting things done by other people

From this proposition it follows that the achievements of an organization will reflect the degree of motivation and commitment of employees. Motivation is an extremely complex aspect of human behaviour about which we still have much to learn. We have, however, advanced beyond the naïve belief that it is a simple response to reward (in the form of financial incentives, for example) or punishment (fear of 'the sack'). Other factors such as job satisfaction, leadership and recognition clearly play an important part.

Management as an activity is universal but does not take the same form in all situations.

Managers in all organizations and at all levels have to get things done by others, have to ensure that decisions are taken, and cannot escape the need to exercise leadership. At the same time the qualities and skills required in the chief executive of a large organization are very different from those required in a first-line manager, while the qualities needed to be effective as manager of a building site differ from those required in the successful manager of an R & D group in the electronics industry.

There is no one best way to organize a business

The most successful systems of organization differ markedly from one kind of business to another. Any one business must continuously adapt its organization to meet the demands of changing circumstances.

Small is beautiful

Entrepreneurial drive, creativity, adaptability and innovation alike are stifled by the bureaucratic systems of administration and control which characterize large, monolithic organizations. Effective management structures therefore involve autonomous profit centres, served rather than directed by small head-office teams.

Management is a process involving a mix of rational, logical decision-making and problem-solving activities and intuitive, judgemental activities.

In this sense it is both science and art. An important skill is to be able to recognize which problems and decisions fall into which category and to treat them accordingly.

None of the foregoing statements, whether they are described as generalizations, precepts, principles, or guidelines, has necessarily any enduring validity. There is no point in smashing one set of tablets of stone in order to create another. Given the high level of uncertainty and, indeed, turbulence in today's business environment, coupled with the value system of our modern society, and the stage of development of our economic institutions, these statements provide some indication of the likely paths to success. Should further radical changes take place in the nature of the environment, new guiding principles will inevitably be needed.

FURTHER READING

Ansoff, H.I., *Corporate Strategy*, McGraw-Hill, New York, 1965

Barnard, C., *The Functions of the Executive*, Harvard University Press, Cambridge, Mass., 1938

Bass, B., *Leadership, Psychology and Organisational Behaviour*, Harper, New York, 1960

Beer, S., *Brain of the Firm*, Allen Lane, The Penguin Press, London, 1972

Burns, T. and Stalker, G. M, *The Management of Innovation*, Tavistock, London, 1961

Diebold, J., *Focus on Automation*, British Institute of Management, London, 1965

Drucker, P., *Drucker on Management*, Management Publications Ltd, for the British Institute of Management, London, 1971

Fayol, H., *General and Industrial Administration*, Pitman, London, 1949

Fiedler, F., *Leadership*, General Learning Press, New York, 1971

Follett, Mary P., *Freedom and Coordination*, Management Publications Trust, London, 1949

George, C.S., *The History of Management Thought*, Prentice Hall, Englewood Cliffs, NJ, 1968

Gouldner, A.W., *Patterns of Industrial Bureaucracy*, The Free Press, Glencoe, Ill., 1954

Herzberg, F.J., *The Motivation to Work*, Wiley, New York, 1959

Jay, A., *Management and Machiavelli*, Hodder & Stoughton, London, 1967

Kotler, P., *Marketing Management*, Prentice Hall, Englewood Cliffs, NJ, 1976

Lawrence, P.R. and Lorsch, J.W., *Organisation and Environment*, Harvard Business School, Cambridge, Mass., 1967

Levitt, T., *The Marketing Mode*, McGraw-Hill, New York, 1969

Likert, R., *New Patterns of Management*, McGraw-Hill, New York, 1961

Lupton, T., *On the Shop Floor*, Pergamon Press, Oxford, 1963

McClelland, D.C. and Winter, D.G., *Motivating Economic Achievement*, Free Press, New York, 1969

March J.G. and Simon, H.A., *Organisations*, Wiley, New York, 1958

Maslow, A., *Motivation and Personality*, Harper & Row, New York, 1954

Mayo, G.E., *The Human Problems of an Industrial Civilization*, Harvard Business School, Boston, Mass., 1933

Mintzberg, H., *The Nature of Managerial Work*, Harper & Row, New York, 1973

Parkinson, C. Northcote, *Parkinson's Law*, John Murray, London, 1957

Pigors, P. and Myers, C.A., *Personnel Administration*, McGraw-Hill, New York, 1969

Rice, A.K., *The Enterprise and its Environment*, Tavistock, London, 1963

Stewart, R., *Managers and their Jobs*, Macmillan, London, 1967

Stewart, R., *The Reality of Management*, Heinemann, London, 1985

Taylor, F.W., *Principles of Scientific Management*, Harper and Brothers, New York, 1911

Townsend, R., *Up The Organisation*, Michael Joseph, London, 1970

Trist, E.L., Higgin, G.W., Murray, H. and Pollock, A.B., *Organisational Choice*, Tavistock, London, 1963

Urwick, L., *The Elements of Administration*, Harper and Brothers, New York, 1944

Walker, C.R. and Guest, R.H., *The Man on The Assembly Line*, Harvard University Press, Cambridge, Mass., 1952

Weiner, N., *Cybernetics*, Wiley, New York, 1948

Woodward, J., *Industrial Organisation: Theory and Practice*, Oxford University Press, Oxford, 1965

2 Corporate strategies for the future

Ron H Bradnam

An effective corporate strategy cannot exist in isolation from the world in which its customers live, in which the business must exhibit acceptable behaviour and from which the business draws its resources. This chapter looks at possible developments for the future with the aim of helping businesses to adopt strategies that are compatible with the opportunities and threats which they may face.

Quantitative forecasts have been avoided, partly because of the inherent uncertainty of such forecasting but, more importantly, because each business must research its own data in accordance with its unique markets, technologies and resources. In so doing, it will gain its own competence in developing its strategy and contingency plans.

Strategy must take into account future:

- Social attitudes and values
- Legal structures.

It must be considered in relation to future:

- Markets
- Technologies
- Resources
- Organization and management style.

This chapter examines each of these factors in broad outline, with particular emphasis on those which are liable to affect the enterprise at a strategic level.

FUTURE SOCIAL ATTITUDES

There is more than just a feeling among the leaders of the industrialized nations that the assertion 'everyone has the right to work' (Universal Declaration of Human Rights) may need to be changed to 'everyone has the right to a personal income'. Indeed Europe and the United States have already entered an age in which:

1 If work is defined as toil in exchange for money, then providing that work for all is proving increasingly difficult
2 If work is so defined, much more creative work is now being enjoyed and undertaken for no monetary return (including 'do it yourself', home food

growing and preparation, charitable work, and arts and crafts), and is forming a significant proportion of the Gross National Product (GNP)

3   More people are finding satisfaction from working on their own, or in small groups, earning money (or engaged in barter) from efforts that may well have started as hobbies; and

4   Expectations from equal opportunities – independent of sex, race, colour, or handicap – expand each year, and are resulting in the introduction of special facilities and provisions.

Work has traditionally provided people with their means of livelihood, status in the community and an outlet for contributing. Unless an alternative means can be found of providing these three facilities, work remains the essential vehicle. It is the responsibility of management to find ways of creating suitable work opportunities for all people for reasonable periods of their lives.

In this respect, the greatest problems are still among the lower age ranges; a reducing number of school leavers who lack experience and so have less to offer employers. More co-operation between schools, colleges and universities on the one hand and industry and business on the other will provide opportunities for improvement.

However, continuing education throughout a whole career is also necessary if the work-force is to be adequately equipped for its work task. This consumes time and resources, but the consequence of ignoring the needs of both present and future employees should not be underestimated. Employees are becoming more and more aware of the way in which they are treated and the code of treatment they expect, and aware also of current ethical standards and the emerging pressures for an improved business morality. Moreover, once work has been provided, there is an increasing demand for that work to be more satisfying and 'owned' by the worker – while management, particularly with the high cost of money, is seeking primarily to improve the competitiveness of the operation.

An outcome of this situation is that employment is no longer *for life*, but may well last for less than half the span of a normal working life. New openings must therefore be sought for meaningful and continuing employment, which may well include the acceptance of other forms of work and/or career changes. The implications of this situation reach beyond the scope of most corporate plans. There is a need for the community at large to discuss the activities of businesses and perhaps also to participate (by visits, for example) in the operations being undertaken. At the same time, the resulting improvements in the relationship between business and community should be paralleled by the creation of closer and more effective links with policy makers in government and the financial institutions.

Current moves towards work sharing, and the growing call for a shorter working week, may well force medium and large companies to employ more rather than less staff – but employed for fewer hours, with shift work and part-timers becoming a very necessary feature – and despite any initial difficulties of training, change overs, continuity and planning. Also, the increasing availability of low-cost communications and other technologies may further modify this trend, bringing nearer the reality of the 'home office/business', which will eliminate (at least to a degree) the problems of commuting.

With increasing levels of resource effort being deployed in the service sector, a reassessment of national forecasts will have to take into account the changing social practices.

The 1990s have opened in a highly dramatic way. For example:

- The dismantling of the Iron Curtain, and reunification of Germany happening faster than many expected
- *Perestroika's* attempt to address the economy of Russia, and the anticipated new trade opportunities
- The inevitable reduction in the defence industries
- The decimation of huge areas of tropical forests
- The impending Channel Tunnel, and the escalating pressures of finance and competition
- Signs of growing political instability in Third World and developing countries
- The continued turmoil in the Middle East, aggravated by earthquakes and terrorism.

The development of appropriate management strategies, methodologies and auditing techniques must continue during this decade; these developments must be measured against significant performance standards in terms of their 'value for money' and their 'quality for money' – and in terms of human and other parameters.

FUTURE LEGAL STRUCTURES

In the UK people are looking forward to the opportunities of the Common Market from 1992 onwards, and all that it entails and implies. At the very least, more organizations are now taking the initiative to seek out the implications for their particular business activity; significant numbers already have working counterparts in several European countries and have initiated management plans to capitalize on the changes. This need will also apply to other countries who may well be adversely affected by the closer bonding of Europeans.

Director's responsibilities, although well spelt out in the past and in the UK Companies Act of 1980 (which requires that directors have regard to the interests of their employees), have become the focus of attention. Several substantial merger plans, or their repercussions, have become a predominant feature of public debate and concern in terms of responsibility for the total enterprise. In systems language, this encompasses an ever-widening scenario. The new legislation regarding the identification, and responsibility for the impact and reduction, of health hazards in the workplace, demands new abilities of directors. The need for them to be well informed and well advised in these matters is essential. The Financial Services Acts are also influencing the manner in which financial business is transacted, particularly with regard to insider dealing (again indicating a move toward higher ethical standards and practices).

Employees continue to seek and to achieve what they see as their legitimate rights. They have also accepted, perhaps somewhat less consciously, that they, too, have responsibilities – for product, process, and for service liability, as well as for any environmental impact.

The consequence is the need for a well-balanced and well-motivated team approach. Managers cannot contribute without the work-force, and vice versa. Both have a contribution to make of significant value, in terms of skills, knowledge and enthusiasm. Their mutual dependence will become increasingly important as the decade progresses, and the ability to co-work and problem-solve together is likely to require a high priority. There must, therefore, be a greater commitment to really understanding and appreciating each other.

FUTURE MARKETS

The 1980s saw a huge increase in the availability and impact of new computer systems, particularly in publishing, finance and manufacturing, and in personal computing. Clearly, the availability of huge amounts of routine data, and its associated processing, required better systems – but have we perhaps missed the point somewhere? The financiers with their computer systems are now responding to situations by means of algorithms (which may or may not have been always appropriate), and, as a result, their response and lead-times have been dramatically reduced. However, whether this speed of response is always desirable is quite another question (for example, Big Bang and its repercussions). There is high risk in over-reaction and in inappropriate reaction. So, management needs to decide consciously what its values are and to measure its behaviour against those values.

Advertising and the influence of the media have increased substantially, particularly in portraying environmentally responsible features. Overall, though, there is a general and growing reaction against some of the promotional techniques and, more particularly, material used and so against the product or service itself. There continues to be a genuine need for targeted and effective promotion, but the current level of promotional junk mail cannot be sensibly sustained, and the waste and cost of this medium is becoming increasingly unacceptable to the recipient. It is not unknown for two almost identical products to be marketed at widely different prices solely as a result of heavy advertising costs for one of them. Improving buyer awareness may soon render such practices untenable.

Manufacturers of custom-made products and services, particularly capital goods, will continue to find that, while marketing and selling functions must inevitably be closely linked, the manufacturing function can be hard-pressed to keep itself gainfully occupied. They may well find it is better to operate a small manufacturing facility to meet the lower levels of demand and to ensure short-term viability by using subcontractors to handle the peaks.

With both consumables and durables, skill will be required in the area of forecasting for production and procurement. Finished stock levels are of paramount importance. Organizations that succeed will be those with high flexibility and short lead-times, and an eye for the contribution and return on investment. The use of value management techniques, currently having a very high profile in the US and increasingly so in Europe, can play a particularly important role in this. The final peak of achievement can often be creamed from the effective use of stock and production capacity left 'idle' through unequal loading, and by careful use of modelling to ascertain the opportunities for improvement in any particular business situation. Access to such market and modelling information is also important for research and development departments, who will find it increasingly helpful as they strive to perform effectively and to provide value for money.

Service industries are showing significant build-up in their trading, albeit some of it overpriced, and greater care needs to be given towards ensuring that customers' needs are being properly met. The international trade in particular will continue to thrive, but is not at all easy to measure.

A further observation relates to obsolescence and the life span of products, services, machines and facilities. With the cost of money staying relatively high, the discerning purchaser will seek even better value for money, and marketing needs to take account of the longer life expectations that are being cultivated by this increased awareness. A car consumes more energy in its manufacture than in its propulsion during a ten-year life. Doubling that lifespan might well save much more energy than by making marginal improvements to fuel consumption.

Marketing competence will lead to future success, but the marketing function will be unable to work effectively in isolation from the other functions. It will be necessary for marketing to be aware of the implications of suggestions across the whole company, and to draw the other functions into their task. Obviously all orders secured must be viable, so that the product or service can be provided at a price and quality that ensures a reasonable and realistic return within a comfortable time-scale. All too often this is not known at the time of signature.

One overriding aspect, resulting from better travel, transport and communication facilities, is that the market-place is very much world-wide. It therefore provides important opportunities to meet a very wide range of needs, from the simple to the sophisticated, from the custom-made to the mass-produced. But these circumstances also provide similar opportunities for competitors; so all companies need to be far more aware and alert than in the past or their survival may be at stake.

FUTURE TECHNOLOGIES

We are becoming accustomed to technological change in our daily lives – at home, at work and at leisure – and this advance is likely to continue apace in the foreseeable future. The 1980s again showed that most things are possible in the technology field, given enough money. Particularly in the fields of microcomputer technology, medical science, robotics and automation, we can see the result of harnessing whole ranges of specializations and then integrating their contributions.

Most of the technological expectations of the mid-century have already been achieved, earlier than expected. We now need to take a fresh look at the exploratory opportunities (that is, what technology has to offer) and the normative (that is, the needs of the market place and society as a whole). All too often technology has been exploited, at great cost, for its own sake. An element of this is obviously important if technological frontiers are to be crossed, but this progress does have to be paid for by someone! As a result, better justification is being demanded, and more provision is being made for monitoring of progress and achievement, before work is authorized.

It was in the late 1960s that 'whole life' concepts first became important owing to the impact of inflation and the overall cost of maintenance and replacement –

particularly on the military scene. There is now a healthy resurgence of these concepts in the form of the total quality management (TQM) and continuous process improvement (CPI) initiatives that so many organizations are now adopting. Again, the need for multi-disciplinary inputs from all is essential for this work to be really effective and produce lasting benefits.

Unfortunately, it is not all good news. With the advent of modems and networking the availability of computing power has certainly been significantly enhanced. In the process, however, computers have become more susceptible to hackers (that is, those who gain illegal access to databases, for amusement or for industrial or other espionage purposes) and to the very insidious program viruses (whereby the virus is deposited secretly into a computer system and may lie dormant until triggered by a stimulus or time delay, at which stage it becomes active and can destroy or corrupt databases and programs). Software is becoming available which can detect and neutralize these viruses, and which can be installed to operate a policing activity. System integrity and security will warrant a high level of attention in the coming years.

Too many short cuts have been taken in the past to deliver products and services without adequate final checking and documentation – to the extent that in some cases rectification of problems and even supplying repeat orders could not be readily undertaken. An example of this was the partial failure of the $2.5 billion Hubble telescope in space owing to inadequate basic testing before final assembly. It is, of course, all too easy to be wise after the event, but some of the lessons have already been learnt too many times! The European Organization for Quality Control produced an excellent, check-list document, *General Guide to the Preparation of Specifications* (1970), which provides a very useful and comprehensive reminder of the issues to be addressed in 'communicating the needs or intentions of one party to another', whether user, designer, manufacturer or seller. It has been used to good overall effect in many organizations.

Admittedly the documentation of design and manufacturing activities is known to be costly. But it is even more costly not to have it and there are cost-effective solutions to this. The direct and the indirect cost of changes is now very significant and can cause serious problems in maintaining high inventory turns (of both materials and components). The cost of redundant stock and work-in-progress should not be ignored.

Continuing and growing public concern regarding the potential, or perceived, dangers of high technology has, yet again, demonstrated the need for extreme caution in launching many new products and processes, as well as an urgent need for monitoring and auditing those which already exist. While the public at large is now much more aware of such topics as damaging gas emissions, risk of factory explosions, fear of nuclear energy, and the opportunities for terrorism, it is not so willing to pay the premium for the demanded higher levels of safety, better quality of life, and so on. Conversely, the public is more than ready to seek handsome retribution for any mistakes that might be made.

There is also serious concern at the more obvious results of pollution by our heavy industry and the 'throw away' society. Much (but nowhere near enough) progress has already been made on the recommendations of a study report in 1979 for the UK Department of Employment, which set out six prerequisites for full employment in an environment of such technical change:

1   An adaptable and better educated work-force
2   More trained manpower in electronics and software skills
3   An expanded retraining effort
4   Less hierarchical industrial structures
5   Greater willingness by management to consult
6   Positive attitudes towards opportunities in new technology.

These criteria assume that, with the increase of technological choice, effective planning and policy making is essential. Important steps have already been taken to aid effective planning, with an accompanying change towards basic technologies and modules that require systems of management based on multidisciplinary and project, rather than functional, structures – and in this way a better environment may possibly be achieved.

The political drive, from which many of the current day-to-day benefits have been derived, is likely to be diverted by the significant economic and political changes taking place in so many countries – and this will take time to stabilize. An immediate development may well be that the considerable sums of money required for moon missions and similar projects will not be so readily available – and, indeed, the Channel Tunnel finance is an example of the questioning now needed.

FUTURE RESOURCES

As a result of the newer technologies, and shorter working hours, a far greater versatility is required in our human resources and this is spilling over into the functional areas, too. Specialization has been a virtue during the past twenty or thirty years, but it may now be a disadvantage and the trends may well become reversed. The need now is for competent professionals. The railway pioneers were examples of this type. They had to initiate and oversee the whole range of management activity, and their general manager really was a 'general' manager, in much the same way that the operations manager/director functions today.

In the area of human resources there will be more demand for (and recognition of) those with multidiscipline skills who have been appropriately trained, developed and counselled. For example, engineers, scientists and technologists with management, finance or economics enhancements who are willing to work as comfortably in their professional scene as in other working environments (the banks, government, and so on). To this end, many universities are very positively promoting 'mixed' courses, such as honours degrees in engineering with business or industrial management. Such courses are highly acclaimed by the participants and, even more importantly, by their employers. In addition, there are individuals who are returning in mid-career for MBA and similar courses in order to acquire these same attributes. The current generation of senior managers will need to adapt their style to bring the best out of this new breed of human resources.

Several large corporations have recognized the opportunities and are capitalizing on them. Within the EC, one impact of 1992 will be far greater mobility for all professionals, bringing significant cross-fertilization. The net longer-term tendency will be towards leaner organizations, with senior management involved more closely with all aspects of the day-to-day operation than for some years, and with particular specializations being bought in as and when required.

A particular problem for the strategists continues to be found in the potential problem resources, that is, those whose availability is already limited and which may become scarce by the year 2000. These include: aluminium, copper, gold, lead, mercury, natural gas, petroleum, tin, silver and tungsten. A feature of the 1980s has been the relative ease with which information on these and other resources can be obtained, processed and reviewed. All users of these materials need to model the implications of future supply, as the necessary data become increasingly available. With more reliable inputs, the decisions taken will in turn become quicker and more reliable. The need for greater flexibility is already arising within organizations if maximum advantage is to be obtained from these modelling facilities.

Implicit in the above is the continuing need for improved specification of what is to be achieved. The resource procurement function will become an even more professional activity, as the 'make or buy' and inventory management decisions are replaced by business strategy and policy decisions (with regard to procurement of subassemblies and their final assembly versus the design, development and manufacture approach). Improved decisions will be more commonplace, requiring keen awareness of:

- The practicalities of any particular situation; and
- How external changes in the environment may influence the ability to perform.

The contributor will need to leave the functional approach behind and adopt a systems-oriented approach – to map out the possibilities and make the optimum selection.

FUTURE ORGANIZATION AND MANAGEMENT STYLE

In response to the needs of more knowledge-based and innovative business, certain trends have evolved in recent years and are expected to continue to accelerate.

One of these is towards small self-sufficient units. It has been argued that:

> there is every reason why a business unit should grow to an optimum size and no good reason for going beyond it. This, of course, looks like a self-justifying statement that makes sense when 'optimum' is defined – which will never be easy. . . . A whole business might still grow on the biological principle of the divided cell. (Latham and Sanders, 1980)

Professor A. Piater (1981) argued similarly, pointing out that up to a certain size the economies of scale enhance the results but thereafter the diseconomies take over. These economic arguments have been supported by many writers from the behavioural viewpoint. Dr Sheane forecast the era of self-management within power-distributed federations. Dr Schumaker said: 'we must learn to think in terms of an articulated structure that can cope with a multiplicity of small scale units' (Schumacher, 1973).

Another trend is towards the superimposition of project teams, task forces, new venture teams – call them what you will – operating within the hierarchical structure. The leaders of more enterprising businesses have discovered that if they want entrepreneurial or innovative management, then they must delegate those responsibilities within a broadly based strategy to small multidisciplinary teams of knowledge workers. Project management has quickly become more popular in practice, in publications and in management training. Teams which can be given one single clear objective (or vision) are usually highly motivated and are an ultimate manifestation of management by objectives – and yet it is in so many of the organizations that already use such teams that change and innovations are long overdue.

As for top management and its responsibility for overall strategy, it is vital that hierarchy, small units and transient teams are not seen as alternatives or as mutually exclusive. Peter Drucker pointed out, in 1973, that:

> just as statesmen learned long ago that both laws and good rulers are needed, so organization builders will have to learn that sound organization structure requires both a hierarchical structure of authority and decision making, and the capacity to organize task forces, teams and individuals for work both on a permanent and temporary basis.

The relationship between management and unions will continue to evolve, particularly as the unions seek to find their new role in business life. Hopefully the lessons have now been learnt and a true partnership will emerge – it has been recognized by both parties that confrontation is not the way forward. Better understandings and working approaches are vital if the benefits of the 1992 process in Europe are to be attained.

The role of top management must continue to be the determination of overall strategy within which small teams can turn social and market needs into possible opportunities. Thereafter, top management must provide support and training coupled with realistic reward systems that identify contribution to overall goals rather than only functional and parochial objectives. The top manager of the future will be a spokesman and a representative of the business to the outside world in general and to the external stakeholders in particular. The top managers, and indeed all managers, will see their role as a service to the wealth generating units – a service of helping, facilitating, supporting and training. The top managers will talk and think less about 'subordinates' and more about 'colleagues' and 'teams'. They will set high standards but will never underestimate the contribution of others.

Perhaps the most important strategic role of the manager is to provide continuity in the organization. The average middle manager or project team leader (if any good) is likely to move upwards within a few years, yet the time needed to implement strategic decisions is often far longer. The activities of conglomerates and predators (those seeking short-term gains), and the influences of governments, often have far greater effect than originally envisaged.

It follows that middle managers, team leaders and executives in small units are unlikely to be motivated to give care to ten-year decisions. The top management must provide that input. To do so effectively will need a new skill and much time spent in listening, travelling, reading and debating. It will (to quote Drucker again), 'require thinking and understanding in at least three areas – the functional or operating; the moral and the political'. In the UK perhaps the initiatives on National Vocational Qualifications will be a suitable spur to managers in this respect.

A manager needs to be able to self-manage, particularly the use of his or her time. The pressures and stresses of management must be brought under control and managed; a strategy has to be developed for this, too, before the pressures and stresses have a chance to take over. To do all of this well will require a clear vision of the needs to be addressed, the values that are appropriate, and the direction which the organization should be taking to meet them.

FURTHER READING

Adair, J., *Effective Teambuilding*, Gower, Aldershot, 1986

Drucker, Peter, *The Frontiers of Management*, Heinemann, London, 1988

Goldsmith, W. and Clutterbuck, D., *The Winning Streak*, Penguin Books, 1985

Peters, T.J. and Waterman, R.H., *In Search of Excellence*, Harper & Row, New York, 1982

Richardson, Bill and Richardson, Roy, *Business Planning, an Approach to Strategic Management*, Pitman, London, 1989

Schumacher, E.F., *Small is Beautiful*, Blond & Briggs, London, 1973

Stewart, Dorothy M. (ed.), *Handbook of Management Skills*, Gower, Aldershot, 1987

Taylor, Bernard and Harrison, John, *The Manager's Casebook of Business Strategy*, Heinemann, Oxford, 1990

The following newspapers, magazines and journals provide, with regular reading, an 'automatic update' on changes in economic, technological and other areas of interest and value to the strategist:

Best of Business, Rank Xerox Corporation
Harvard Business Review
Management Today, British Institute of Management
New Scientist
Proceedings of the Royal Society of Arts and the Proceedings of chartered professional institutions and associations
Scientific American
The Economist
Financial Times
The Times
and, on BBC television:
Tomorrow's World

3 The strategic planning process

Denis Boyle

The failure of traditional corporate planning systems to resolve fundamental business problems of the 1980s has led to the development of a new approach to the strategic planning process, which is the subject of this chapter. The 'hockey stick effect' (Figure 3.1) where plans and performance are consistently not achieved, depicts graphically the reason for these new concepts. Today, in its new form, strategic planning provides corporations with a powerful tool for creating and sustaining profit growth.

TWO STRATEGIC PLANNING PHILOSOPHIES

Traditional corporate planning was to a large extent an extension of the annual budgeting process. In a highly rational process goals were set, broken down into sub-goals, and the process of implementation initiated. Diagramatically this is shown in Figure 3.2. In a stable environment where, for example, competitors are well known, industry pricing is stable, cost structures are well understood, and customers behave in a predictable fashion, such 'traditional corporate planning' worked well.

In the world of the 1980s, companies were faced by a radically different environment. Step changes and irreversible trends made detailed plans drawn up one year scarcely relevant the next. Industry invaders, new technology, deregulation and shock cost changes demanded a different kind of strategic planning process. This was concerned with formulating a view of the business and its competitive environment in the future, and also of the immediate short-run steps which must be achieved. Thus, the focus shifted from planning to implementation of action programmes which in the short run would produce visible results against which the long-run strategic vision could be further refined. This new approach is shown diagrammatically in Figure 3.3. The fundamental difference between the two philosophies is that traditional planning assumes that all relevant knowledge is available at the beginning of the process, whereas the 'new strategic planning' approach is designed to exploit information as it is acquired. The annual budgeting and financial forecasting cycle still provides a framework for systematic new strategic planning. However, the elements of strategic thinking and action are given equal weight.

New strategic planning in action

The process is cyclical, its main elements being interlinked, as shown in Figure 3.4. It begins with a review of the strategic situation of both the company and the industry in which it operates. The results of this are translated into 'high leverage'

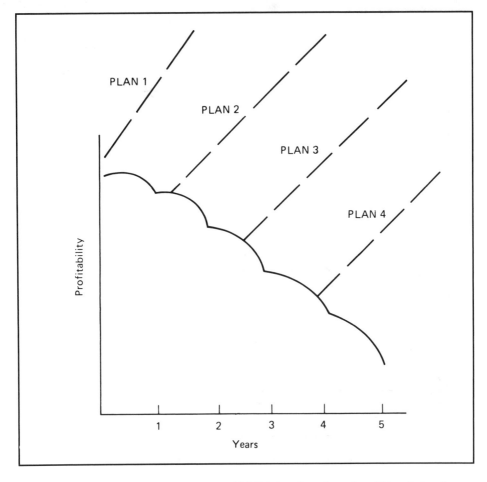

Figure 3.1   The hockey stick phenomenon, highlighting the crises of traditional planning

action plans designed to have maximum impact on the company's competitive position and profit growth.

These plans are implemented in a highly effective manner with results monitored and fed back 'real time', and with the beginning of the next planning cycle providing a systematic mechanism for an overall review before the process continues.

Organizing the strategic review

Since the process is designed to strengthen a whole business it must be organized around different business areas within the company. For example a chemical manufacturer may have four business areas such as:

- Industrial paints
- Pharmaceuticals
- Agricultural chemicals
- Special coatings.

25

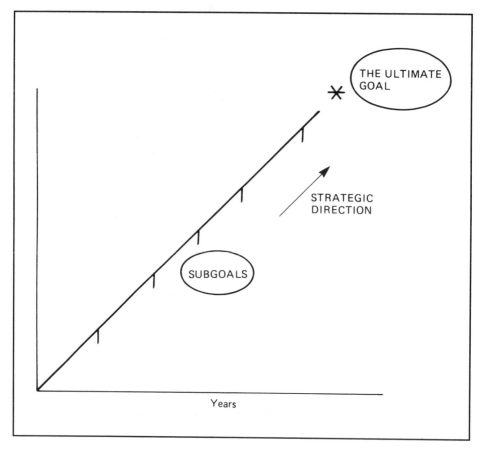

Figure 3.2   The traditional planning process with goals, subgoals and action plans

Each has its own unique success factors and needs to be treated as a distinct planning unit. To collect the necessary data for the strategic review the top management typically appoint fact finding groups of relevant managers from different functions. The strategic planning staff provide methods for analysis as well as co-ordination of the overall process. In a complex multi-business it will be essential to examine interdependencies between different business areas so that these can be optimized for the benefit of the whole company. Individual business area plans will be harmonized to maximize benefit to the total corporation while minimizing risks.

In initiating the work of the fact-finding and analysis groups the board should set challenging but realistic objectives in both financial and business performance terms. These need to be discussed and, if necessary, renegotiated.

To operationalize the conclusions of the strategic review, actions are defined as specific projects and these become the responsibility of functional departments or specially set up cross-functional teams.

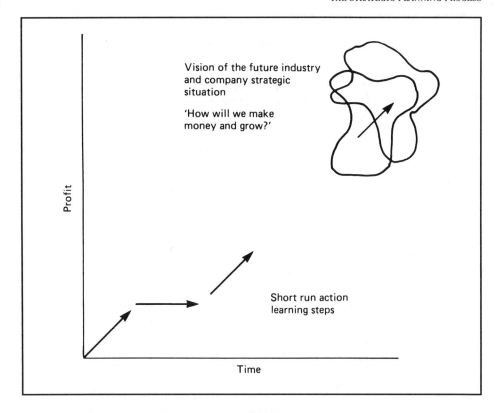

Figure 3.3   The new strategic planning approach

The importance of analysing the total business concept for each business area

Success in a particular business area does *not* come from any individual factor such as cheap raw materials, a brilliant invention, or charismatic leadership. It depends on the way a multitude of elements fit together and mutually reinforce each other. This 'total business concept' is the basis of market segment dominance and long-term profitability. During the strategic review everyone should refine their understanding of the main elements (Figure 3.5):

- The target customers: 'who are our good customers?'
- The product service price offering: 'what are they really selling?'
- The company's production and delivery systems: 'how do we produce better quality at lower cost than our competitors?'
- The company's organization structure and culture: 'how do we make our organization and systems support our way of making money and growing?'
- The corporate image: 'what image do we want and how do we project it?'

The 'fit' or harmony between these different elements is learned through success in the market place. Equally when structural changes arise they result in 'misfits', the real cause of business problems, and a weakening of competitive strength. The strategic review should identify these misfits and propose actions to resolve them.

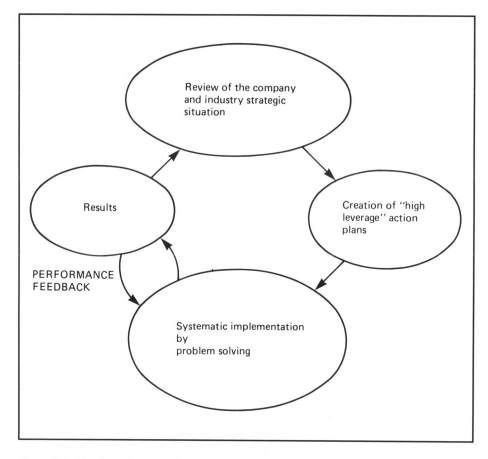

Figure 3.4   The four elements of the planning cycle

Consider an example from today's insurance industry. Most institutions are organized on product lines such as fire insurance, car insurance, house insurance and so on. This is shown diagrammatically in Figure 3.6.

Following a dramatic change in the industry environment, success now depends on customer-oriented marketing. Strategic action is therefore needed to transform organization structures and control systems to once again create fit or harmonize with the needs of the new industry.

The creation of high-leverage action plans

The objective of the strategic review is to understand the company's total business concept for each business area and how this can be effectively developed. This requires the creation of high leverage action plans. Based upon the strategic review 'diagnosis', top management focus on those actions critical to their winning strategy. For example, suppose that following its strategic review an airline decided that it must target full fare, high frequency business travellers. To get more of their business it identified several misfits which had to be tackled. Its timekeeping performance was poor, its air hostesses were not friendly and its hub

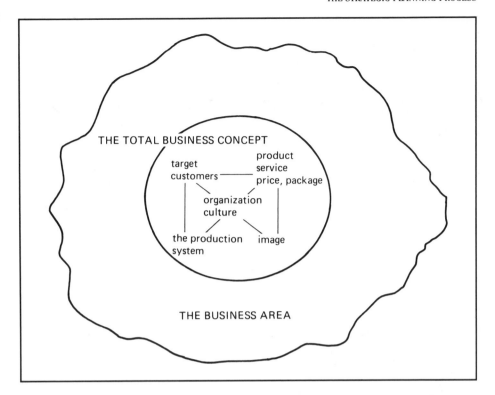

Figure 3.5   Fit and the total business concept in each business area

airport did not function very efficiently. Action programmes were focused on these in the high leverage pay-off areas.

In selecting an appropriate strategy the strategic review process will have quantified the likely outcome in approximate financial terms. As individual action programmes are developed the overall financial impact can be more closely assessed and, if necessary, appropriate adjustments made.

There are, in addition to the high leverage plans, five important preconditions for successful strategy implementation which must also be effectively planned.

Visible commitment

Top management must visibly demonstrate commitment to its strategy. Since people believe actions rather than words it is essential always to act in line with the strategy. This means, for example, that if resources are necessary for a critical programme, then they are made available.

Removing organizational blockages

The organization structure, and the people in key positions, must support the strategy. Consider, for example, a manfuacturer of jeans. Suppose that this firm's strategy is to refocus activities on its core products. To tackle this effectively, divisionalization of the single functional structure into teenage jeans wear,

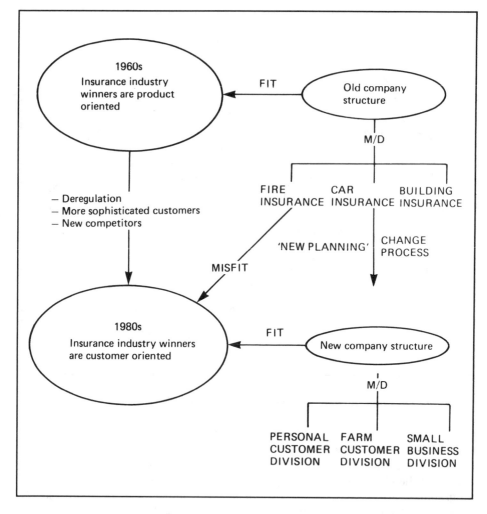

Figure 3.6   Example of an organizational problem or 'misfit' caused by a structural industry change

women's wear and men's wear becomes necessary to pin down problems and responsibilities. If, for example, the person heading up the customer service department does not like customers, then clearly he must be changed. Organizational blockages of one form or another are the most important reason for failure to implement strategies effectively.

Internal marketing

Many organizations underestimate the potential of their people for contributing to implementation if only they were to understand exactly what the strategy was. Planning internal marketing is, therefore, a crucial element of the 'new strategic planning process'. Everyone in the company should be told the conclusions of the strategic review and be given their own opportunity to contribute. Internal marketing to be effective must be carried out through the organizational lines of authority

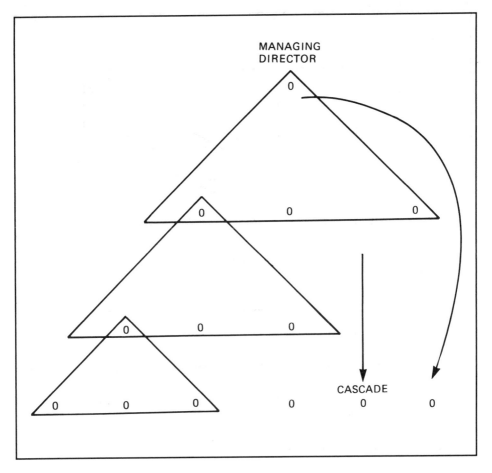

Figure 3.7   Cascade communication combined with parachuting for effective internal marketing

in a cascade fashion, but also by the top management team parachuting to the front line. This ensures not only rapid dissemination of the message but also less distortion and a high degree of involvement. This process is shown diagramatically in Figure 3.7.

Performance visibility and fast feedback

No strategy can be implemented if there are not adequate mechanisms for getting feedback on progress. Usually companies do not have a shortage of performance monitors. The secret is to select the few which are most relevant and give feedback in a highly credible way. Performance visibility systems must provide financial and qualitative data. There is a very interesting knock-on effect of using even the simplest of strategy monitors. For example, an engine manufacturer wished to develop his customer service. It was decided to measure and feed back regularly the delivery performance to its top ten customers for its top ten products. Though

31

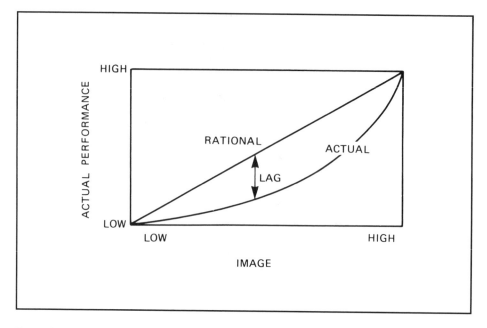

Figure 3.8   Planning to overcome image lag

this only covered a fraction of the business a dramatic improvement was made in all areas.

Performance standards should be set to be bold, challenging and capable of attainment within a relatively short time.

Systematic reinforcement of success

Motivation and the power of the problem-solving process is greatly enhanced by feeding back every possible success. People enjoy being winners and strategy implementation can be made an exhilarating 'game'.

In situations where the company has faced severe problems it may well be necessary to overcome the problem of image lag. This phenomenon is shown diagrammatically in Figure 3.8. People tend to remember performance as it was, not as it is. The classic example is that of an automobile manufacturer who once had a reputation for rusty cars. Though today they have probably one of the best records in the world, people still talk about the problem they experienced more than ten years ago. If employees see that their efforts are not being appreciated they can easily be demoralized.

USING THE PLANNING PROCESS TO CREATE THE SELF-REINFORCING SPIRAL OF SUCCESS

The new strategic planning process is a management instrument for maintaining a business in a self-reinforcing circle of success. In year one a company will focus on the 'core of the core' of its business operations. These are made up of those customers and products which generate the majority of its profits. An airline for example may choose the high frequency business travellers in Europe as its first step, or an automobile manfuacturer its top three models in its home market.

Systematic implementation by problem solving

The heart of successful implementation is decentralized problem solving. The main strategic programmes are broken down into hundreds of action programmes, each with a clearly defined responsibility and time-scale. Problems which come within one functional area are relatively easy to handle. Cross-functional problems require the establishment of special teams and careful follow-up to ensure that they do not simply fall between chairs.

As with any complex system, improving total business performance is more a question of 'one hundred changes of one per cent than one change of a hundred per cent'. This means the responsibility for problem solving implementation must be pushed all the way down the organization. Front-line supervisors are particularly important people in this process.

FURTHER READING

Carlzon, J., *Moments of Truth*, Ballinger Publishing Company, USA, 1987
Griffith, S.B., *Sun Tzu The Art of War*, Oxford University Press, New York, 1971
Kuhn, T.S., *The Structure of Scientific Revolutions*, University of Chicago, USA, 1973
LeBoeuf, M., *How to Motivate People*, Sidgwick & Jackson, UK, 1986
Normann, R., *Service Management: Strategy and Leadership in Service Businesses*, Wiley, UK, 1984
Rhenman, E., *Organisation Theory for Long-Range Planning*, Wiley, UK, 1973
Rosenbaum, B.L., *How to Motivate Today's Workers*, McGraw-Hill, USA, 1982

4 Organization development

John Woolhouse

Managing an organization in a constantly changing environment, often against formidable national or international competition, is a task that calls for exceptional skill, judgement and resourcefulness. The purpose of this chapter is to explore some aspects of this task and to describe some of the ways in which a manager can plan and implement those changes that are essential to the proper functioning of the organization for which he or she is responsible.

The term 'organization development' is used in this chapter to describe a planned programme of organizational change designed to help an organization to achieve the strategic purposes and objectives for which it was created. The concepts discussed do not apply only to the problems of changing existing organizations; they apply equally to the creation of new institutions or enterprises. In many parts of the world the creation and rapid growth of new industry, commerce, government departments and public services present serious organizational problems. There is a need, as yet too rarely understood, to apply to the design, formation and development of new organizations, the disciplines of systematic planning that are common practice in the design, construction and commissioning of buildings, plant and other physical facilities.

In discussing the relationship between strategy and organization, Professor K.R. Andrews of the Harvard Business School summed up the theme to be developed in this chapter as follows: 'It is at once apparent that the accomplishment of strategic purpose requires organization. If a consciously formulated strategy is to be effective, organizational development should be planned rather than left to evolve by itself.'

Organization development concerns not only structure, procedures or systems, but also such intangible factors as the styles of leadership, teamwork, collaboration between functions or departments, the motivation of staff, and the problems of power and influence, of co-ordination and conflict that arise in the working life of an organization.

THE NEED FOR PLANNED ORGANIZATION DEVELOPMENT

The need for a planned programme of organizational development will arise in many situations. Perhaps the most common are:

1 The creation of new institutions or enterprises in industry, commerce, government or the public services
2 Enabling existing organizations to adapt more readily to changes in their

external environment (for example in markets, in products or services, or in the range, scale or location of their operations)

3   Where the organization is failing to accomplish its objectives in terms of output, quality or profitability, and where the nature of the organization is itself limiting the performance of those who work in it

4   Where the adoption of new technology, systems or methods requires corresponding changes in the organization for their proper implementation.

Organizations vary in purpose, in constitution, in the methods and technologies which they use to achieve their purpose, and in the scope, size and location of their operations and markets. Furthermore, they exist in different economic, political and social environments, and in different cultures and subcultures.

Organizations are not merely a product of a particular technology; they are designed and directed by individuals with different values, experience and perceptions, and are to some extent a reflection of the personality of those who direct and shape them. Each organization is, in a sense, a social experiment which is constantly evolving and adapting in response to changes in the environment.

The structure and style of any particular organization, at any given time in its history, are the products of a complex mixture of technology, culture, environment and personal styles, so that there is no single solution to the problem of what constitutes the best organization in a given situation.

The management of organizational change is complex because it involves an understanding, first of organizational purpose, secondly of organizational structure, procedures and systems, and thirdly of what may be described as the 'dynamics' of organization; that is, the relationships between people and between groups, the role of leadership and teamwork, and the significance of learning and motivation in creating an understanding of the need for change, and in generating commitment to action.

The unique character of each organization indicates that the objectives and content of any programme of organizational change will vary with the situation for which it is designed, but the theme common to all programmes is that the development of an organization can be systematically planned and managed.

STRUCTURE, PROCESS AND STYLE

What exactly is an organization, and how does it work?

In the space of this chapter, it is not possible to examine this extremely complex subject in depth, but it is appropriate to identify some of the elements involved.

Industrial organizations are socio-technical systems which incorporate three main subsystems:

1   The 'executive system' by which the organization is directed and controlled
2   The 'operating system' by which it carries out work
3   A 'representative system' through which consultation and negotiation with members of the organization is conducted.

What an organization *is* can be described in terms of structure, procedures and systems. What it *does* can be defined as 'processes'. The *manner* in which it conducts those processes is usually called the 'style' of the organization.

35

The structure of any organization is a product of many interrelated factors including the culture of the society in which it was created, and the idiosyncracies of those who direct it. Among the factors on which the design of a new organization should be based, or an existing organization assessed, are:

1   The strategy or purpose which the organization is designed to achieve
2   Legal status, accountability and sources of financing
3   The methods of technology by which the strategy is to be implemented
4   The information process and procedures for making decisions, for planning and control and for operating and resourcing
5   The geographical distribution of resources and of markets or clients
6   The scale and range of the activities and resources to be controlled.

The variety of structures that have developed, particularly in large industrial, government and military organizations is so great that it has become a subject in its own right. Simple line, staff, and functional structures have been superseded by the creation of profit centres and cost centres within organizations; by project, programme and product management groups; by various forms of matrix organization for managing multi-skill or multi-discipline resources; by the extensive use of 'temporary' structures such as project teams, task forces and working parties.

What forms of both 'permanent' and 'temporary' structures are appropriate to any particular organization at any particular stage in its evolution is a question requiring detailed and thorough examination of each unique situation.

The chief executive is the architect of the organization. It is his vision of what the organization should and could become that will generate the need for change; it is his judgement as to when change is needed and what form that change should take. He must, above all, be aware that old structures are rarely an effective way of implementing new strategies.

Organizational 'processes' are the interactions, communications, and 'transactions' between people. This 'dynamic' aspect of organization is of special significance for all those involved in organizational change. Every organization is in essence an interlocking set of contracts between people. These contracts determine what people will do, and how they conduct the thousands of 'transactions' such as giving and receiving information, or authorizing the acquisition, deployment or disposal of resources. In effect all the members of an organization enter into a complex set of contracts by which they relate to other members. The majority of these contracts are not legal contracts; they are informal 'psychological contracts'. They are not written down; they are frequently changed; they are determined partly by logical factors, and partly by subjective and emotional factors.

By looking at the day-to-day activities of an organization in terms of 'contracts' regulating action and behaviour, and of 'transactions' between individuals and groups who are collaborating and communicating with each other, it is possible to gain a much clearer idea of what happens when changes are made in structure, technology, procedures or systems; the result of all such changes is that informal 'contracts' between people have to be renegotiated, not necessarily in a legal sense, but certainly in a psychological sense. Any change such as the introduction of a new piece of equipment, or of a new management information system, requires the renegotiation of the contracts which regulate what a member of the organization does and how he or she does it.

The *manner* in which relationships and transactions between people, and between groups, between managers and subordinates, between departments, divisions and functions are conducted, is usually referred to as the 'style' of the organization. A considerable amount of research has been conducted into organization and leadership 'styles', and into the psychological factors which determine or influence behaviour. Some of this research is summarized in Chapter 1 under the subheading 'Management theory in the post-war era' and the subject of leadership is discussed briefly later in this chapter.

THE ROLE OF THE CHIEF EXECUTIVE

With this perspective, it is possible to examine more closely the responsibility of the chief executive or general manager for organization development, and to do so in the knowledge that it is the will to achieve, the will to survive, the will to manage and the will to work that are the sources of the energy which drive an organization.

The chief executive and those of his colleagues who share his responsibility for the direction of an enterprise perform four basic functions. They must:

1 Define strategy
2 Specify the methods, technology and resources by which that strategy is to be achieved
3 Prepare plans and programmes
4 Create and manage an organization through which those plans and programmes will be implemented.

Andrews describes the role of the general manager in the following terms:

> The successful implementation of strategy requires that the general manager shape to the peculiar needs of his strategy the formal structure of his organization, its informal relationships, and the processes of motivation and control which provide incentives and measure results. He must bring about the commitment to organizational aims and policies of properly qualified individuals and groups to whom portions of the total task have been assigned. He must ensure not only that goals are clear and purposes are understood, but also that individuals are developing in terms of capacity and achievement and are reaping proper rewards in terms of compensation and personal satisfactions. Above all, he must do what he can to ensure that departmental interests, inter-departmental rivalries, and the machinery of measurement and evaluation do not deflect from organizational purpose into harmful and irrelevant activity.

Translating these issues into specific activities is the task of the chief executive who must ensure that:

1 Key tasks and decisions are identified and defined
2 The responsibility for carrying out tasks and making decisions is assigned to individuals or groups; the authority for acquiring and allocating resources is defined
3 Procedures are established for planning, co-ordinating and controlling the activities or work programmes to be undertaken by each work group

4 Information systems for obtaining, storing, analysing and retrieving the data needed both for management and operational purposes are designed and installed

5 Activities are arranged in a programme to be completed within defined time and resource limits

6 Individuals or groups are made accountable for the achievement of objectives and their performance is evaluated against time, quality and resource standards

7 Actual performance is monitored quantitatively against programmes, estimates or budgets, and qualitatively by the judgement of managers and supervisors, or by feedback from users, customers or clients

8 Procedures for internal consultation and communications are established so that information can be transmitted and feedback obtained on any given activity and on problems encountered in carrying it out

9 Individual staff are selected, recruited, trained and assigned to particular roles, and roles are adapted to make optimum use of the skills which are available or which can be acquired

10 A system of rewards and constraints is established, and procedures are developed for negotiating change with members of the organization or with their representatives

11 Arrangements are made to facilitate and encourage the acquisition and development of individual technical, professional and managerial skills, and for the improvement and adaptation of methods, systems and procedures.

These tasks and procedures are part of the agenda that will be considered in planning the content of any programme.

PLANNING A PROGRAMME OF ORGANIZATIONAL DEVELOPMENT

The purpose of an organization development programme may be to create a new organization, or to adapt an existing organization in ways that will enable it to achieve the purposes for which it was established. In most cases the institution will seek to achieve those purposes with the minimum consumption of time, energy and resources.

Because each institution or enterprise is unique it must define *for itself* the criteria that will guide the development of its organization. Because all institutions are subject to change these criteria will need to be redefined at intervals in response to changes in strategy, environment or technology.

Figure 4.1 illustrates some criteria that can be used in analysing the extent to which existing or proposed organizational arrangements help or hinder the achievement of purpose, and in identifying priorities for change. In practice attention and effort must be focused on a limited selection of factors which are critical to successful performance, and which the institution itself has the capacity to change. If the programme is too narrowly based it will be ineffective; if it is too ambitious it will be impossible to implement. The structure and content of each programme will vary according to the needs of the organization concerned, but most programmes will include four main stages (see Figure 4.2).

The first stage is concerned primarily with defining, diagnosing and understand-

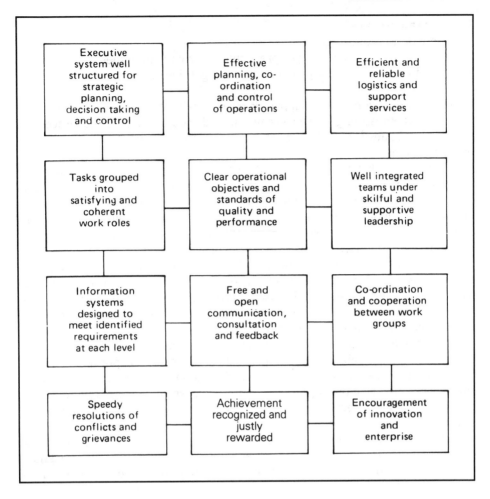

Figure 4.1   Criteria for organization development

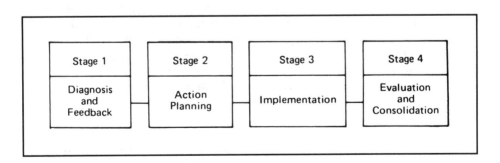

Figure 4.2   Stages in an organization development programme

ing the task to be performed or the problems to be resolved. A useful starting point for this stage is a discussion in which senior managers define the present state of the organization by seeking answers to the following questions:

1   Where are we now?
2   Where do we want to get to?
3   What are the forces helping or preventing us from getting there?
4   What do we have to change to enable us to get there?

While these questions are an apparent over-simplification, it is common experience among those engaged in organization development that the process of analysing and questioning the 'status quo' is an essential first step in the planning of a programme.

Feedback on what is happening within the organization may be obtained by informal discussion or by a systematic survey depending on the nature and complexity of the problem. What is important is that those aspects of the organization which are under review – whether they be matters of procedure, relationships, attitudes to work, or to new plans or to new technology – are tested against reactions and responses of those directly involved.

Issues arising from this examination will often become a subject for much more detailed analysis of specific problems of roles, relationships or procedures, and for action planning in the second phase. This phase is usually conducted by one or more internal management teams who will often be given training in the use of appropriate analytical and planning techniques.

In the implementation phase, which may last for many months in cases of major changes in the organization or its procedures, it is very important to obtain feedback on problems experienced in practice, and to include arrangements for making any modifications necessary to the success of the programme. Every programme is an experiment in managing change, and the implications of that statement must be understood and acted upon by everyone involved.

Evaluation should be made against realistic criteria agreed at the outset of the programme. There are several difficulties in evaluation which must be acknowledged: organizational changes may take a long time to become effective and a proper evaluation can be made only after a reasonable period of operation of new structures or procedures. Some of the most important benefits of a programme, particularly those concerned with management styles, with co-operation between teams, or with job satisfaction cannot be qualified and can only be assessed by collecting and analysing responses from managers and staff who have taken part.

At the end of the programme it is vital to consolidate and reinforce those changes that prove effective in practice. It is only too easy to lose the advantages of a programme by failing to ensure that successful procedures and processes become a permanent part of the organization's ways of working.

Diagnostic methods

Because organizations exist to accomplish strategy, any organizational design or analysis must begin with a definition of strategy, and an examination of the extent to which existing structure, systems and procedures constitute logical and effective means of implementing that strategy. It is relatively easy to conceive new ideas and new strategies. Because the time and effort needed to implement change is considerable, particularly in large organizations, there is a tendency for organization structure and systems to 'lag' so that the enterprise is trying to tackle today's or even tomorrow's problem with yesterday's organization. The time-lag problem can also be serious when major structural or procedural changes have been introduced because, in the absence of any action to accelerate the 'natural' rate of change, members of the organization can (if not helped to make the adjustment) take a long time to absorb the implications of change and to modify their actions accordingly.

In a comprehensive programme a variety of analytical or diagnostic methods will need to be employed. These methods may, for example, include:

1   Examination of work roles and co-ordination between individuals, or between departments and functions
2   Evaluation of procedures for planning, co-ordinating, allocating resources, setting performance standards, monitoring performance, output quality or cost
3   Analysis of information systems and information flows
4   Collecting and analysing feedback on operational problems, on attitudes, morale or job satisfaction
5   Assessment of leadership styles, or of the relationships within or between work groups
6   Review of rewards and incentives and of opportunities for personal development or career progression
7   Investigating internal procedures for negotiating terms and conditions of employment, or for resolving conflicts and disputes.

In programmes involving a study of work organization it may also be necessary to use such techniques as process analysis, task analysis, activity analysis, method study or operational research to analyse work flows or procedures for planning and controlling operations in the allocation of resources. Studies of this type are best carried out by small multi-discipline teams which include members with expertise in appropriate technology, in operational research and in organization development. In specialist industries and services, teams of this type can make a powerful contribution to the development of structures, systems and procedures which are properly matched to the technological requirements of the enterprise.

Underlying all structural and procedural issues there is, in every organization, a 'culture', and 'atmosphere', a set of values which is partly a reflection of the style of leadership within the institution itself, and partly of the society within which the institution operates. Technology is a major factor in determining structure and systems, but social and cultural factors are the main determinant of organizational style.

The most important and intangible of these factors are concerned with leadership, with motivation and with team work. All organization development programmes centre on the role of leadership, on the use of teams as the agents of change, and on the use of learning and feedback.

STYLES OF LEADERSHIP

There is no single 'best' style of leadership, just as there is no 'best' type of organization structure. Different situations call for different styles of leadership.

One of the problems in developing an effective organization is to develop a style that is appropriate to that organization.

The effect of leadership style on individual performance, team work and morale can be studied by analysing feedback from people in the organization. Feedback can be collected and analysed in many different ways ranging from informal interviews with individuals or groups to highly structured diagnostic procedures. Two of the best known diagnostic methods are the 'Managerial Grid' developed by Blake and Mouton and Rensis Likert's 'System 4'. In his work at the Michigan Institute for Social Research, Likert found evidence to suggest that the prevailing management style of an organization could be depicted on a continuum from 'System 1' (a very authoritarian style) to 'System 4' (a style based on teamwork, trust and confidence). In most of the companies studied, those closest to 'System 4' were more likely to have a continuous record of high productivity. The extent to which such instruments are useful in any particular situation is a matter for judgement, but the following summary by Hersey and Blanchard of Likert's four systems illustrates some of the issues which need to be explored in a study of the leadership style.

System 1

Management is seen as having no confidence or trust in subordinates, since they are seldom involved in any aspect of the decision-making process. The bulk of the decisions and the goal setting of the organization are made at the top and issued down the chain of command. Subordinates are forced to work with fear, threats, punishment and occasional rewards and need satisfaction at the physiological and safety levels. The little superior–subordinate interaction that does take place is usually with fear and mistrust. Although the control process is highly concentrated in top management, an informal organization generally develops, which opposes the goals of the formal organization.

System 2

Management is seen as having condescending confidence and trust in subordinates, such as master has toward servant. The bulk of the decisions and goal setting of the organization are made at the top, but many decisions are made within a predescribed framework at lower levels. Rewards and some actual or potential punishment are used to motivate workers. Any superior–subordinate interaction takes place with some condescension by superiors and fear and caution by subordinates. Although the control process is still concentrated in top management, some is delegated to middle and lower levels. An informal organization usually develops, but it does not always resist formal organizational goals.

System 3

Management is seen as having substantial but not complete confidence and trust in subordinates. Broad policy and general decisions are kept at the top, but subordinates are permitted to make more specific decisions at lower levels. Communications flow both up and down the hierarchy. Rewards, occasional punishment, and some involvement are used to motivate workers. There is a moderate amount of superior-subordinate interaction, often with a fair amount of confidence and trust. Significant aspects of the control process are delegated downward with a feeling of responsibility at both higher and lower levels. An informal organization may develop, but it may either support or partially resist goals of the organization.

System 4

Management is seen as having complete confidence and trust in subordinates. Decision making is widely dispersed throughout the organization, although well integrated. Communications flow not only up and down the hierarchy but among peers. Workers are motivated by participation and involvement in developing economic rewards, setting goals, improving methods, and appraising progress towards goals. There is extensive, friendly, superior–subordinate interaction with a high degree of confidence and trust. There is widespread responsibility for the control process, with the lower units fully involved. The informal and formal organizations are often one and the same. Thus, all social forces support efforts to achieve stated organizational goals.

TEAMS AND TEAM BUILDING

Teams are the building blocks from which organizations are constructed, the cells from which the various organs of the corporate body are assembled. An organiza-tion development programme is a planned programme of learning and action, carried out over a considerable period of time, in which *teams*, rather than individuals, are the agents of change. In recent years valuable research has been carried out into the dynamics of group behaviour, for example at the National Training Institute in the US and the Tavistock Institute in the UK.

Work has been carried out by these Institutes both on individual relationships within a group, described as *intra-group* relations, and on the relationships between groups, known as *inter-group* relations. The results of this research, and of experience in large industrial and military organizations, are of great practical value to managers because they provide the foundation for team-building pro-grammes which form a central part of all organization development programmes. Advice and assistance in team building is now available from many sources and the skills needed are within the capability of most competent managers.

Team-building sessions (in which diagnosis and feedback of problems at several levels in an organization are linked together as part of an integrated programme of problem identification, feedback, analysis, planning and implemen-tation) are a major component of all programmes designed to accelerate the development of new organizations, to facilitate the transfer of an introduction of new technology, and to improve the performance of existing organization. They also provide one of the main instruments for coping with conflict between levels or functions within an organization or between the organization and external groups such as suppliers and distributors.

The methods used in any particular circumstances will differ with the objectives of the programme but all processes depend on providing the group as a whole, and its individual members, with feedback or situations with which they have to cope. The intelligent and sensitive use of feedback is fundamental to any process of organization development. It is the experience of most researchers into organizational problems, first, that a significant proportion of problems whose causes are either not known, or are attributed to individual deficiences, are the result of organizational defects; and secondly that many of these defects can be identified by feedback from individuals and by methodical examination of the logic underlying the definition of responsibilities, procedures and information flows. The key to all change in behaviour is learning. Not theoretical learning, but learning about the facts, the myths and the conditions which are present in every human and social situation.

This type of learning process is one in which the 'agenda' is not a syllabus but a real problem: it draws on the combined knowledge and experience of members of a group, incorporates any 'external' advice that may be appropriate; and its purpose is to take action and not solely to acquire knowledge or skill. The result is that the approach makes a real contribution to the difficult task of changing perceptions, attitudes and behaviour in organizations. Different enterprises use different terms to define this process: action learning, group learning, achievement learning, joint development programmes, and quality circles, which have attracted so much attention in recent years, are all attempts to tap the latent energy of groups and individuals by creating opportunities for learning related to the need for action and the need for change. The management of change is a complex process; but collaborative or 'synergistic' learning is a powerful catalyst of change.

A full-scale organization development programme is appropriate only where major organizational change needs to be managed. Team-building programmes can be started, with proper preparation and instruction, by any departmental manager or project manager who wants to improve the performance of his team. A day or two spent in the early stages of team formation, given wise selection of team members, can yield rich returns in collaboration, co-operation and personal development features essential to successful project work.

There is more on the subject of team building in Chapter 69.

CHARACTERISTICS OF A SUCCESSFUL PROGRAMME

Richard Beckhard of the Massachusetts Institute of Technology in his essay on organization development lists eight characteristics of a successful programme:

1 It is a planned programme which involves the whole of an organization, or of a relatively autonomous unit within an organization
2 It is not a programme to improve managerial effectiveness in the abstract. It is designed to create organizational conditions that will directly help the institution to accomplish a specific strategy
3 The senior management of the organization are personally committed to the goals of the programme
4 It is a long-term effort, because two or three years are usually required for any significant organizational change to be planned, implemented, and its benefits realized and rewarded

5   The programme is action-oriented. In this respect an organizational development programme differs from a training programme in which the individual is
left to transfer any knowledge or skill acquired, because the programme is
designed from the outside to generate action by those involved
6   Particular emphasis is placed on changing perceptions, attitudes and behaviour, and not solely on structural or procedural change
7   It relies on some form of experience-based learning through which participants
can examine the present situation, define new goals, and explore new ways of
achieving them
8   The basis of all programmes are the groups or teams from which the organization is constructed.

CONCLUSIONS

No discussion of an organization or of organization development can be concluded
without reference to the character and quality of the people who work in it. The
selection, training and development of individual managers and staff is discussed
elsewhere in this book. It is sufficient here to observe that while the relationship
between individual competence and organizational success is widely understood,
the extent to which organization structure and style encourages or inhibits individual growth and development is not always so clearly perceived. People create
organizations; successful organizations develop capable people: capable people
to keep organizations flexible and responsive to changing needs and goals.

FURTHER READING

Beckhard, R., *Organisational Development: Strategies and Models*, Addison-Wesley, Reading, Mass, 1969

Bennis, E.G., *Organisation Development: Its Nature, Origins and Prospects*,
Addison-Wesley, Reading, Mass., 1969

Blake, R. R. and Mouton, J. S., *Building a Dynamic Corporation through Grid
Organisation Development*, Addison-Wesley, Reading, Mass, 1969

Burns, J. and Stalker, G.M., *The Management of Innovation*, Tavistock Publications, London, 1961

Campbell, A. and Tawadey, K., *Mission and Business Philosophy*, Heinemann,
Oxford, 1990

Hersey, P. and Blanchard, K.H., *Management of Organisational Behaviour*, 3rd
edn, Prentice Hall, Englewood Cliffs, NJ, 1977

Lawrence, P.R. and Lorsch, J.W., *Developing Organisations: Diagnosis and Action*,
Addison-Wesley, Reading, Mass., 1969

Schein, E.H., *Process Consultation: Its Role in Organisation Development*, Addison-
Wesley, Reading, Mass., 1969

Sutermeister, R.A., *People and Productivity*, McGraw-Hill, New York, 1969

Tannehill, R.E., *Motivation and Management Development*, Butterworth, London,
1970

Woodcock, Mike and Francis, Dave, *Organization Development Through Team-
building*, Gower, Aldershot, 1981

5   Managing corporate mergers and acquisitions

C Stuart Jones

This chapter advocates a disciplined approach to mergers and acquisitions. It starts with corporate planning and includes searching for acquisition prospects, negotiating the deal, and integrating the organizations. The chapter also outlines the legal and self-regulatory frameworks within which acquisitions of public and private companies must take place.

DEFINITION OF TERMS

Merger

A merger is a 'marriage' between two companies, usually of roughly the same size. Assets become vested in one company. It is effected by the shareholders of the one or both parties exchanging their existing shares for new shares in the other or a newly created company. 'Merger' implies the willing co-operation of each party and avoids any implication that one party is dominant.

Takeover

A takover can be defined as a series of transactions whereby control is achieved over the assets of a company. This is achieved by purchasing shares on the open stock market or exchanging shares in the offeror company for those of the offeree company, or a combination of both methods. Voting control is achieved and may occur against the wishes of the offeree company.

Reverse takeover

A reverse take-over occurs where either a listed company acquires an unlisted company whose assets or profits exceed those of the purchaser, or where control of the purchaser would change because of the large number of shares issued. Dealings in the company's shares are suspended until shareholders have approved the transaction and restored only when listing particulars have been published. These will be comprehensive because the purchaser will be treated as a new applicant for listing unless there is no material change of management or control.

Acquisition

In this chapter the terms 'merger' and 'takeover' will be used interchangeably, together with the term 'acquisition'. True mergers, in which all partners relinquish their independence in favour of a new comprehensive policy are rare. Acquisitions may be broadly classified into four types, as follows.

1 *Horizontal acquisition*   The companies are involved in the same type of business with approximately the same customers. Such acquisitions have great appeal because they occur in a business area that the acquirer understands. Because they involve market concentration they are more likely to be subject to scrutiny by the Monopolies Commission
2 *Vertical acquisition*   This concerns two companies operating at successive stages of production so that one supplies or is supplied by the other. This may improve continuity of supply and reduce stockholding and handling costs. However, the acquirer will probably lack experience in the business and it thus becomes vital to retain the goodwill and co-operation of the existing management
3 *Conglomerate acquisition*   This involves the coming together of firms in different businesses. The firms are unlikely to have any common trading interests and the only bond may be the provision of centralized financial control
4 *Concentric acquisition*   Here the firm extends its activities whilst retaining a measure of commonality with existing activities. This may be done by acquiring different technology which can be marketed to existing customer types or by acquiring new customers for the existing technology.

REASONS FOR ACQUISITIONS

Acquisitions are frequently justified on the grounds of 'rationalization' and the potential for the realization of 'economies of scale'. The underlying implication is that such activities serve the public interest. However, there is increasing evidence that casts doubt on the significance of economies of scale and demonstrates that profitability is independent of size. It seems likely that acquirers fail to think deeply enough about how they will achieve potential benefits and fail to recognize the problems that will be met. Some commentators consider that failure to meet financial and business objectives for acquisition may be as high as 70 or 80 per cent.

In addition to the many reasons embraced by economies of scale there are others which may be grouped into three categories:

1 *Growth*   This may be achieved by increasing the share of market or by entering new markets. It may be desirable for defensive reasons – to avert an unwelcome takeover bid – or to attract good quality staff and provide additional career opportunties for key managers. A less exalted reason might be fulfilling the power and reward aspirations of a chief executive. Such behavioural motives may lie behind many of the seemingly rational arguments expressed for a particular acquisition
2 *Skills*   Acquisition can capture new products, processes, patents, research and development skills as well as human abilities which it would take an unacceptably long time to generate by organic growth
3 *Financial*   Benefits can be obtained by acquiring companies with tax losses or capable of strong cash flow generation – 'cash cows'. Acquisition can also

increase the financial base of a company to facilitate a Stock Exchange listing or obtain listing by merging with a listed company.

PROCEDURE

There are undoubtedly some acquisitions still made on an opportunistic basis with little or no real planning. 'Golf-course marriages' may be less in evidence these days, but planning may not be as rigorous as merited for what is equivalent to a major capital expenditure project. If the risks of failure are to be reduced it is essential to adopt sound managerial practices in respect of acquisitions. It is also important to recognize that very few businesses possess either spare managerial resources or the neccessary in-house skills to devote to organizing all aspects of an acquisition. Thus, outside experts will be needed to supplement internal resources and they should be involved from an early stage. The programme to be followed involves planning; searching for acquisition prospects; approach and negotiation; and post-acquisition integration.

PLANNING

The desirability of having a corporate plan, whether it is rather loosely defined in the mind of the chief executive, or formally written down after extensive consultation amongst executives, applies to the development of all corporate strategies. Within such a plan, acquisition is merely one of the strategic options available to a company which must be considered along with all other options. It is particularly important to identify the impact of the post-acquisition period and what reorganization and resources may be needed to achieve successful integration. Easy assumptions regarding the release of synergy, the maintenance of high morale, and the extent of changes necessary must be avoided.

SEARCHING FOR ACQUISITION PROSPECTS

There are numerous ways of identifying acquisition prospects, and once it becomes known that a company is interested in acquiring, then unsolicited approaches are likely. 'Marriage brokers' have companies for sale but caution must be exercised when a buyer is being actively sought. During the process of corporate planning executives may identify potential targets from their own knowledge of an industry. They may have the added benefit of knowing the reputation of such a company and the personalities of its senior managers. This can help to avoid expensive personality clashes following acquisition.

There are likely to be limits to both the nature and quality of information available within the company and so the search must be widened to published sources. If consultants are used they will need careful briefing based upon the defined objectives for acquisition. There is a considerable body of published information available. Some of the publications are contained in the reference sections of good public libraries but, to gain access to a wider range of sources, it may be necessary to visit a library specializing in business matters. A short list of useful catalogues and reference works is given at the end of this chapter. Some of these are available on computer databases and this greatly facilitates searching.

An extensive search may reveal a considerable number of companies which merit further study. The selection can be refined by analysing the extent to which each company would assist the acquiring company in meeting its corporate objectives. Each objective is given a subjective weighting reflecting its importance; for example:

		Importance weight
1	A sales growth rate of at least 10 per cent annually	a
2	A pre-tax return of at least 20 per cent on investment	b
3	Continual improvement in the quality of management	c
4	Stable labour relations	d
		1.00

The performance of each prospect is then reviewed over several years in respect of each objective, and accorded a score on a scale from, say, -10 to $+10$. The sum of the individual scores multiplied by the appropriate importance weight provides an expected value for each acquisition prospect. Those above a specified cut-off value are the ones which fulfil the objectives most satisfactorily and will be selected for further in-depth study.

The ease with which in-depth evaluation can be executed depends upon the willingness of the prospect company to co-operate. If the parties believe that a merger is likely to be of mutual benefit, then co-operation may be forthcoming and extend to the disclosure of highly confidential information. In all discussions it is necessary to exercise great care to ensure confidentiality. In the absence of co-operation public sources of information must be relied upon, although it is not unknown for various subterfuges, such as the possibility of technical co-operation, to be employed to gain access to manufacturing and other facilities. By simply walking around a plant an expert can gain helpful impressions on such matters as the prevailing attitudes of the work-force, the tempo of work, and the physical conditions of equipment and production methods and stock levels.

A checklist of information that should be collected is included in Figure 5.1. Much of the information can be obtained from the annual report and accounts of registered companies. For English and Welsh registered companies, these and other company records are available for public inspection at the Companies Registration Office in Cardiff and at Companies House in London. Records of Scottish companies can be seen at the Registrar of Companies in Edinburgh.

APPROACH AND NEGOTIATION

An important part of evaluating a target company is to determine financial valuations which enable initial and maximum offer prices to be determined and the form in which they might be made. Current market prices and price–earnings ratios play an important part in both bid tactics and in the valuation of target companies. However, the valuation of a target company solely on this basis is an undesirable

General information
Company name
Location
Directors' names, ages and length of
   service
Published business objectives
General standing and reputation of
   the company
Style of management

Ownership
Capital structure and voting rights
Disposition of shares
Details of any significant share
   disposals

*Financial information (over the past
   few years)*
Turnover and profit trends
Liquidity trends
Capital expenditure
Trends in stock market price and
   price-earnings ratio

Financial information (continued)
Capital expenditure commitments
Accounting policies and any audit
   qualifications
Capital gearing
Chairman's statements

Market and product information
Main fields of activity and market
   shares
Comments on research and
   development
Overseas expansion
Product reputation
Company's reputation for fair
   dealing
Nature and extent of competition
Distribution channels

Management
Quality of senior and second-tier
   management
Ages, qualifications and contractual
   terms of key managers

Figure 5.1   Information checklist

practice and should not be permitted to displace rigorous financial analysis. This should ascertain, among other things, the short- and longer-term financial performance of the combined companies for the range of offers contemplated.

The acquiring company must also come to some broad conclusions, in advance of negotiations, as to the way which the business might be run and the role to be played by the existing senior managers. These individuals will seek their own future welfare during negotiations.

The purpose of negotiations is to explore a wide variety of business, managerial and financial issues and not merely to determine the offer price. It is desirable for the parties to draw up a letter of intent in respect of such matters, describing the scope of further investigations and a tentative timetable. However, if the board of the target company refuses to co-operate – perhaps because the offer is too low, or independence is preferred – then it may be necessary to appeal directly to the shareholders of the target company.

Professional advisers must be involved at an early stage and these may include: merchant bankers; clearing banks; stockbrokers; accountants; surveyors; actuaries; insurance brokers; pension and tax consultants. They will provide the specialized practical knowledge needed to steer the takeover procedure and complete the transaction. The frameworks of law and voluntary codes within which acquisitions take place are very important and these are now considered.

THE UK LEGISLATIVE FRAMEWORK

There are several pieces of legislation which enforce parts of the protection afforded by rules introduced by various City bodies and extend further protection to the interests of the nation, the public and employees. The legislation makes no distinction between acquisitions of public and private companies and includes the following statutes.

The Fair Trading Act 1973

The assumption behind the merger provisions of this Act is that significant mergers raise economic, social and other issues affecting the lives of many people and so merit consideration on the grounds of public interest. Thus, the Act enables the Government to exercise an effective veto over substantial UK acquisitions.

The Director General of Fair Trading is responsible for keeping merger activities under surveillance and advising the Secretary of State who, in turn, is responsible for deciding whether a particular merger warrants investigation by the Monopolies and Mergers Commission. The Secretary of State has power to make a statutory order prohibiting a merger, or requiring a divestment if the merger has taken place. There are a number of essential criteria which qualify a situation for investigation. These include: both enterprises being engaged in supplying goods or services of the same description and having, between them, at least a 25 per cent share of the UK market; and the value of assets exceeding a threshold – set at £30m in 1984. The functions and powers of the Director General were complemented by provisions to prevent anti-competitive practices, introduced by the Competition Act 1980.

Confidential advice may be obtained in advance from the Office of Fair Trading, indicating whether particular mergers are likely to be referred to the Commission.

The Financial Services Act 1986

This Act replaced the somewhat obscure Prevention of Fraud (Investments) Act 1958, under which it was an offence to make misleading, false, deceptive or reckless statements or forecasts or deceive investors. The Financial Services Act extends this provision to cover acts, practices or courses of conduct likely to defraud or deceive investors. Only authorized investment businesses have a statutory right to issue advertisements or circulars likely to lead to the sale or purchase of investments. Detailed supervision is delegated, via the Securities and Investment Board, to five self-regulatory organizations run by practitioners who specialize in particular aspects of the investment business. Non-compliance with the Act can lead to criminal and civil penalties.

The Treaty of Rome

While none of the treaty's legislation directly addresses acquisitions and mergers, it can influence such transactions. For example, Articles 85 and 86 contain far-reaching anti-trust legislation. The Commission is empowered to take action against a company which, already having a dominant position within the EC in any particular section of industry, acquires another company or companies producing similar goods. The objective is to prevent the integration of the Common Market being hindered by the conduct of cartels or monopolies.

Within the constraints of these three pieces of legislation private companies are remarkably free to strike their own acquisition bargains and to rely upon civil remedies under the law of contract. Since the vast majority of acquisitions in the UK concern relatively small private companies this is the predominant legal framework. However, the rules of the Stock Exchange and of the City Code must be observed in a private company where, for instance, the other party is a listed company or an unlisted public company.

SELF-REGULATORY CONTROLS

Although acquisitions of public companies constitute the minority of transactions, they are usually the largest in value terms and receive greatest publicity. Such companies must also observe a number of self-regulatory controls including those imposed by the Stock Exchange and The City Code. These are now outlined.

Stock Exchange controls

These are contained in a book called *Admission of Securities to Listing* (the Yellow Book). Since 1985 some of these rules have statutory backing, including the requirement of issuing listing particulars, that is, a prospectus, for all paper-for-paper acquisitions. The regulations apply to offerors, offerees and to companies listed on the Stock Exchange and traded on the Unlisted Securities Market.

The information to be disclosed and procedures to follow depend upon the category of transaction. There are four categories, the first three of which depend on relative-size criteria as between acquirer and disposer. The criteria are: value of assets; pre-tax profits; total consideration; and the ratio of additional equity capital issued as consideration. For class 1 and 2 transactions the announcement should include details of the value and profits attributable to the assets, the consideration to be paid, and expected business benefits. No such announcement is required for class 3 transactions. Class 4 transactions, which involve directors or substantial shareholders, require prior approval from the Quotations Department.

The City Code on Takeovers and Mergers

The theme of shareholder protection runs through the City Code which is issued on the authority of the Council for the Securities Industry and is administered by the Panel on Takeovers and Mergers. The Code is a voluntary code of behaviour although the panel has sanctions at its disposal. The Code comprises ten general principles of conduct and thirty-eight rules which are elaborated by practice notes.

FORM OF THE OFFER

An acquisition can be effected by various forms of cash offers or by an exchange of shares or by combination of cash, shares and loan stock. Although the value of a cash offer can be known with certainty, shareholders may become liable immediately to capital gains tax because shares have been realized. Such an offer may also place strain on the liquidity of the offeror because the exemptions from stamp duty, which can be effected using a scheme of arrangement under ss 425 to 427 of the 1985 Companies Act, do not apply.

Most bids are predominantly made on a share-for-share basis because of the potential for deferring shareholders' capital gains tax liability and preserving liquidity. However, stamp duty relief on such transactions was withdrawn in 1986. If the offerer has a high stock market price relative to the offeree it will be able to purchase on advantageous terms because fewer shares will be needed to reach the desired purchase consideration. The procedure is for shareholders in the offeree company to be offered shares in the offeror in exchange for their shares, which are then cancelled.

Another method of obtaining control of a company is to purchase shares for cash through the Stock Exchange. However, there are strict rules laid down in the 1985 Companies Act (Part VI) and City Code (rules 9 and 11) which restrict the extent to which such activity can continue undetected and the level at which an offer must be made to all shareholders. Such an offer must be made in cash at not less than the highest price paid within the preceding twelve months. Thus, the cost of control can be high because demand for the share is artificially increased.

When an acquirer buys shares they represent the company together with any underlying defects and liabilities. An alternative method of acquisition is to purchase specific assets. However, when a business is purchased as a going concern it is not possible to leave behind any unwanted employees (Transfer of Undertakings – Protection of Employment Regulations 1981). An acquiring company may prefer to buy assets because of the potential for tax relief on writing-down tax allowances.

POST-ACQUISITION INTEGRATION

When the acquisition is 'friendly' it is desirable for discussions concerning the joint future of the companies to take place before the deal is completed. Naturally, such discussions cannot be entirely uninhibited because of the conflicting interests of each company to secure the most favourable acquisition terms and because of the limitations upon disclosure implied by the City Code. It is useful to commit the programme to writing so that it forms an agreed basis, albeit in broad terms, for subsequent implementation. This helps to avoid the danger of promises being made which cannot be honoured.

In an unwelcome bid the programme cannot be agreed beforehand. Nevertheless, the bidder should prepare a tentative list of actions to be taken which can be discussed and agreed immediately after the deal is completed.

It is necessary to strike a careful balance in the post-acquisition programme between precipitous action and untoward delay. It is also important to remember that motivation and momentum must be maintained both in respect of business activities and the introduction of change. The programme should name the executives responsible and indicate an approximate timing for initiation and completion of each event. This provides checkpoints for control.

Once the legal and administrative formalities of the acquisition have been followed a possible sequence to achieve integration might be as follows:

1   Decide upon and communicate initial reporting relationships
2   Achieve control of key factors
3   Review the resources of the acquired company
4   Define corporate objectives and develop strategic plans
5   Develop a revised organizational structure.

There is little doubt that the success of an acquisition depends more upon the skilful management of post-acquisition integration than on any other phase of the acquisition procedure. For example, the effects of errors in the calculation of the purchase consideration, or in the additional pension funding needed, might be modest compared with the potential loss of motivation amongst key staff and its effect upon operations. However, remarkably few managers are experienced in post-acquisition management. Furthermore, this is an area where consultants and external experts are of limited use. Some of the main issues which can arise during the implementation of the sequence advocated above are now briefly discussed.

Perhaps the most dangerous condition created by acquisition is uncertainty. One aspect of this is frequently to be found in reporting relationships which have not been clarified. It is tempting to wait until a final form of organizational structure has been decided and hope that managers will sort out their own relationships in the meantime. This can be a recipe for falling morale and undesirable struggles for power. Generally, it is preferable to take positive action and to explain the reasons for changes, even if further revisions may be needed as integration proceeds. Great care should be taken to explain the reasons for the changes, and those affected should be encouraged to express freely any misgivings they may have.

There are several key areas where the parent company should act decisively to ensure compatibility between the activites and controls of the acquired company and those of the group. For example, borrowing limits should be set, even if the acquired company retains existing funding arrangements. Capital expenditure limits and procedures should be reviewed at an early stage. This is a sensitive area because new authorization procedures or reduced limits of delegated authority can often be perceived as reducing the status of the executive affected. Failure to institute or strengthen such controls can result in well-intentioned expansion which, without proper consideration in the context of the group, may prove to be inappropriate. Some acquisitions introduce other special factors that may require immediate co-ordination or control, including: wage bargaining; transfer pricing; competing for the same custom; recruitment and redundancy policies; advertising and public relations; and the supply of materials.

Great sensitivity is needed in introducing additional or revised controls and it may not be appropriate to introduce complete conformity in respect of accounting control procedures. If it is a successful company the existing controls are likely to have played an important part in that success and it may be a retrograde step to discard them.

Although the more obvious factors requiring co-ordination can be identified and steps taken to ensure that the staff involved in the various companies liaise with each other, such an exercise cannot be exhaustive. So it is important to foster healthy attitudes of co-operation so that individuals become aware of possible problems and are willing to seek ways of overcoming them.

The urgency to audit the physical assets acquired depends upon the information obtained prior to acquisition. This may be very scant following an opposed bid and it then becomes important to verify both the values of assets and their physical existence and to do so before the annual audit.

It is also important to form an idea of the quality of management in the acquired company. Some acquirers place top priority upon the need to acquire good management but because pre-acquisition contacts are limited to a relatively few senior executives, it is difficult to form a complete judgment regarding second-level management. Occasionally, acquirers use psychological tests to identify individuals who possess potential for further development – and those who have reached their level of incompetence. Such tests should be used only as a guide to a person's ability, potential and motivation and need to be introduced very circumspectly.

The development of strategic plans involving significant changes and a high degree of integration can be a demanding task. It can be further complicated because comparative strangers, perhaps with conflicting interests, will be working together and because business momentum must be sustained whilst the changes are introduced. Figure 5.2 illustrates the progression in complexity which occurs as more functions are changed. The least complex type of acquisition is one undertaken for purely financial reasons, with no intention to alter the pattern of manufacturing or marketing. Integrative complexity increases when overlapping product ranges or markets occur and becomes most intense when manufacturing and marketing changes have to be introduced simultaneously. For example, the logistics of running down one plant and increasing production at another, with the complications of labour problems and modified patterns of supplies to customers, make such a strategy difficult to devise and implement. This is one area where easy assumptions, at the planning stage, about the release of synergy should be carefully avoided.

Finally, it is sometimes difficult for acquiring companies to accept the need for preserving different organizational structures in acquired companies. All too often, adaptive and responsive styles of management are overwhelmed by the imposition of rather rigid and bureaucratic structures. For example, acquiring companies expect group reporting and control procedures to be uniformly followed so that information can be fed upwards through the management hierarchy; they require capital expenditure projects to be thoroughly documented and screened by committees; they expect conformity with group personnel policies, company car schemes, insurance procedures and so on. In such organizational

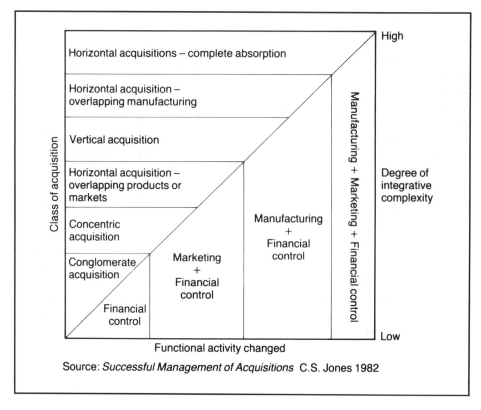

Figure 5.2   Integrative complexity during acquisition

structures the entrepreneurial flair, capable of reacting quickly to changes in the environment and to new opportunities, can be stifled.

SOURCES OF COMPANY INFORMATION

UK directories and statistical services

Who Owns Whom, United Kingdom and Republic of Ireland
Key British Enterprises
Kompass Register of British Industry and Commerce
Stock Exchange Official Year Book
Current British Directories
The Dun and Bradstreet Directory Guide
The Times 1000 Leading Companies in Britain and Overseas
Research Index – Business Surveys Ltd
Index to the Financial Times
Extel British Company Card Service
Extel Financial – Micro Exstat and UK Mergers and Acquisitions databases
Extel Unquoted Companies Service
The Small Firms Information Centres of the Department of Trade and Industry

Directories for non-UK companies

Who Owns Whom, Continental Europe/North America/Australasia and Far East
Kompass Directories
Current European Directories
Trade Directories of the World
Extel
Europe's 10,000 Largest Companies
Principal International Businesses
Million Dollar Directory Set
Dun's Market Identifiers
Standard and Poor's Corporation Records
Yearbooks of Foreign Stock Exchanges

FURTHER READING

Begg, P.F.C., *Corporate Acquisitions and Mergers: A Practical Guide to the Legal, Financial and Administrative Implications*, 2nd edn, Graham & Trotman, London, 1986

Chiplin, B. and Wright, M., *The Logic of Mergers: The Competitive Market in Corporate Control in Theory and Practice*, Institute of Economic Affairs, London, 1987

Cooke, T.E., *Mergers and Acquisitions*, Blackwell, Oxford, 1986

Cooke, T.E., *International Mergers and Acquisitions*, in association with Arthur Young International, Blackwell, Oxford, 1988

Fallon, I. and Stodes, J., *Takeovers*, Hamilton, London, 1987

Ferrara, R.C., in Gray, C.E. (ed.), *Takeovers: Attack and Survival: a Strategist's Manual*, Butterworth, London, 1987

Goldberg, W.H., *Mergers: Motives, Modes, Methods*, Gower, Aldershot, 1983

Jones, C.S., *Successful Management of Acquisitions*, Derek Beattie Publishing, 1982

Moir, C., *The Acquisitive Streak: An Analysis of the Takeover and Merger Boom*, Hutchinson, London, 1986

Monopolies and Mergers Commission Reports, HMSO, London

The City Code on Takeovers and Mergers, HMSO, London, 1988

Webb, I., *Management Buy-outs*, Gower, Aldershot, 1990

6 Corporate relations

Norman Hart

The need for a planned programme of corporate relations stems not from some new management concept but from the fact that organizations are realizing sometimes to their dismay, the need for a formalized corporate strategy. This has been dealt with earlier in the book but, simply stated, it is no longer good enough to take random actions for long-term effects: rather it is necessary to give mature consideration to future objectives and the means of achieving them. Such objectives will incorporate financial investment, labour force and staffing, marketing aspects, production, research and development and of course profit. This is no more than a move from past practices, in which future events were just allowed to take their natural course, to a position in which a company sets out deliberately to move to a predetermined position. The weakness of any attempt at corporate planning is that unforeseeable events are bound to cause the objectives to be changed, but this is no reason for not taking action to influence the course of events so as to hit the desired target as closely as possible. Corporate relations is but one of the management functions which can be used to help achieve this goal.

The need for corporate goals and for a strategy to achieve them stems from a growing number of influences, external and internal, which if ignored may well undermine the profitable development of a company and indeed threaten its very existence. The increasing tendency by governments to impose controls is a major factor as are international regulations at one extreme and a vigorous consumerist movement at the other. Thus, trade barriers and constraints, scarcity of raw materials, inflation and high taxation are factors which now play a larger part in the development of business. Equally, the growing interest by employees and trade unions with their sometimes massive influence must be taken into consideration in any future planning.

This chapter will examine corporate relations from the point of view of *what* they are, *why* they are necessary, to *whom* they should be addressed, *when*, and *how*. Finally, it will consider the all important question of the results that might reasonably be expected of such an activity.

First, *what*. Corporate relations is a term used to signify the deliberate attempt by an organization to maintain the best possible relations with each and every identifiable group of people whose interests and activities might be supposed to have an effect, for good or ill, on the prosperity and progress of the business. Such an operation is linked with communications in both directions since without communications of some kind it is difficult to see how any change or impact can be achieved. It is important at the outset to realize two things. First, that no matter how efficient any corporate communications system may be, it will be of no avail

Public	Example of communication
Consumer	media advertising
	press release
Supplier	trade exhibitions
Employees	house journal
Trade unions	statement of company policy
Competitors	public lectures
Local residents	local radio information
Trade association	journal article
Technical groups	technical journal articles
Shareholders	annual reports
Financial community	financial press release
Government	co-operation with CSO
Distributors	promotion literature
Universities	scientific information
Other pressure groups	local community action

Figure 6.1   The company public and an example of a typical outward communication for each component of that public (*Financial Times*)

unless the object of the communication is sound. In just the same way no amount of advertising will ever sell an unsatisfactory product. The second point to be made is that every single source of communications must be considered for possible use, not just the classical PR media such as press releases, factory visits, booklets and special events.

What then are corporate communications? A good example was given in a report by The *Financial Times*, as summarized in Figure 6.1. The list is not, and was not intended to be, comprehensive. It misses for instance the communications element of the product, its packaging and branding, as well as the place from which it is distributed. It does not touch on the vital role of employees, from people answering the phone and writing letters, to salesmen meeting customers. Then there is the appearance of the factory, the livery, the letterheading: the list is endless. Corporate relations then is the building-up of a good reputation with a company's many and varied publics. An old-fashioned term sums it up very well – 'goodwill'.

Clearly, the kind of activity being described is going to cost money. Hence the need to ask *why*? The fact is that all companies have an image whether they like it or not, or even if they are totally unaware of it. A company is perceived by people in a variety of ways, depending upon the messages, conscious or unconscious, they have received about it. And the perception varies from one public to another. Customers may view a supplier as a thoroughly reliable and trustworthy organization with which to do business, whereas its employees may take the very opposite view. The reason *why* corporate relations is important, then, is that it is only when relationships are positive and sound that the most effective and efficient business can be conducted. For example, is it reasonable to expect the best possible applicants for a job with a company which has a very poor reputation as an employer? It may be argued that in such a case the solution is to change the conditions of employment so that they are really attractive, but this is overlooking the essential ingredient of corporate communications for if people are unaware of a situation they cannot react to it. And if, as often happens, they are misinformed about it the opposite result to what was intended may be the outcome. The reason *why* corporate relations are important, then, is that on the one hand the company is receiving messages about itself from all the interested publics and on the other hand it is sending out messages to those same people to ensure that they are fully informed, that they understand and that they are convinced. The reason *why*, then, is in order to establish and maintain a series of relationships in which business can be conducted most efficiently.

To *whom* is corporate relations meant to apply? Once again a simplified diagram taken from the *Financial Times* shows the answer (Figure 6.2). In addition, of course, each individual company will have a number of specialist groups whose goodwill it is vital to maintain. These might be termed 'special interest groups' such as Women's Institutes, teachers, consumerists, youth movements and even, say, cycling clubs, bird-watchers and farmers.

The *when* of corporate relations can be dealt with simply. A reputation is with a company all its life. It is no use having a corporate relations function and a corporate communication programme for a couple of years and then closing it down. People's memories and attitudes are dynamic and will change over time. A company must decide whether or not it is really serious in the matter of building its reputation. If it is, and it wishes to maintain it, this can be achieved in one way only, and that is by a continuous programme of activities. It is as well also to bear in mind that achieving any major change may take years rather than months, so advance planning is required as well as continuity.

Turning now to *how* corporate relations are to be implemented. First, it is necessary to draw up plans, both strategic and tactical, to set objectives, to measure results, to co-ordinate all related and parallel activities, and to ensure that an adequate administration and professional facility exists to ensure proper execution.

STRATEGIC PLANNING

The key to successful strategic planning for good corporate relations is in the setting of comprehensive objectives. Two examples have been chosen to illustrate this point. First, a major multinational corporation which listed five aims:

1   To increase the share of people's minds available to the company
2   To engender favourable attention and acceptability from its diverse publics
3   To explain the realities of the company's social and economic contributions to the countries where it does business
4   To state the case for business in general and for multinational corporations in particular
5   To correct some of the myths and refute irresponsible allegations.

The programme which evolved consisted of a package of five interdependent activities, each mutually supporting, making its own unique contribution, but

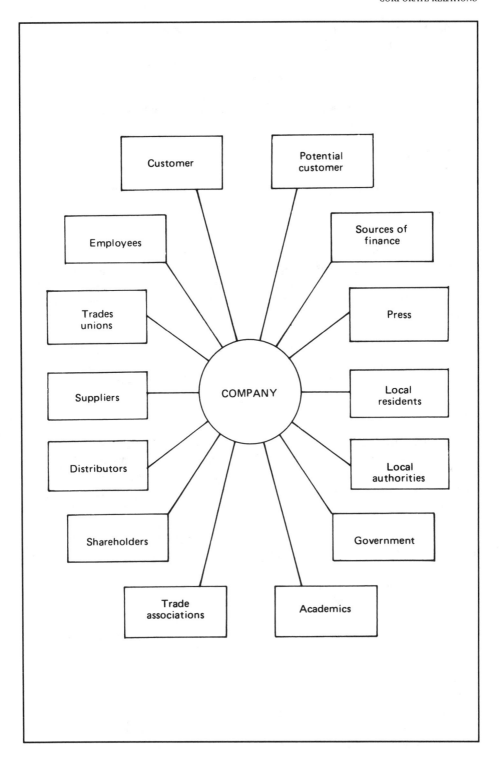

Figure 6.2   The company as a corporate citizen and its communication links
(*Financial Times*)

working to the same plan and objectives. The elements of the package were an advertising campaign, a public information brochure, an external house magazine, a press relations programme and the establishment of a speaker's panel. The complete programme was based on a publicly stated philosophy of openness, frankness and fact.

The second example is that of a well-known company in the high technology business. The programme had five objectives:

1 To extend the company's corporate identity and to improve attitudes held towards the company among the defined target audiences
2 To establish and promote the company as a leader and innovator in advanced technology
3 To promote the company's capabilities and achievements in selected areas of advanced technology
4 To create high-level awareness and knowledge among target groups in prospective market areas for the technological excellence of its products
5 To create a favourable attitude among target groups so that divisional marketing activities for particular products or systems could be carried out more effectively.

The main thrust of the campaign to achieve these aims was a very adventurous press campaign of large advertisements in the colour supplements, backed by supportive advertising in 'management newspapers' and the specialist press.

TACTICAL PLANNING

It is not sufficient to produce one big homogeneous campaign and leave it at that; it is also necessary to examine every other sector of communications with its own specialized objectives, audiences, message and media in order to ensure that these also contribute to the common objective of the company's reputation. In this way, marketing communications, employee communications, a safety campaign, city and financial news, and all the rest add together to make up a synergistic whole. It can be seen that organizationally there is a need for the provision of top management direction to ensure the proper orchestration of all the many parts which are being conducted on a day-to-day basis.

The second part of tactical operations relates to what might be termed 'reactive activities'. This is the response to events which, if not handled properly, can work against the corporate objectives, or alternatively fail to give the potential support which might otherwise be achieved. Examples might be an industrial dispute where bad handling can undo much of the goodwill which may have been built up over a period of years. Equally, but in the opposite direction, failure to exploit fully the securing of a major overseas contract is a loss in terms of the very favourable light in which such an achievement can be shown to the target groups which together make up the corporate public.

Such contingencies cannot by their very nature be incorporated in any plan, but the organization must be sufficiently flexible to be able to react quickly to each of them and to have in mind not just the event itself and how to deal with or exploit it, but also the overall objectives.

CORPORATE RESEARCH

Early in the growth of the marketing concept and of corporate planning, communications activities were characterized by 'prestige advertising' and by a narrow form of public relations which relied mainly on what was loosely termed 'press relations'. It was unusual to have specific goals, and large sums of money were spent in putting out almost self-congratulatory messages about the company without much regard to the interest of the audiences or indeed what the effect on them might be. Companies indulging in these activies became sceptical of their value and as economic conditions became tougher interest in buying prestige declined.

The growth of corporate affairs as a function, and corporate relations as an activity has been accompanied by the precise setting of objectives in quantified form, and by a programme of research to ensure that any investment was achieving results. Businessmen have begun to demand that expenditure in this area should be accountable and the effects measurable.

The starting point of any properly constructed programme of corporate communications is to make benchmark measurements against which progress can be compared as the campaign proceeds. It is no use making such measurements at the end of a campaign as by that time it is too late to take any corrective action. A company might decide that it wishes to increase the level of awareness amongst certain discrete publics and at the same time gain an improved attitude towards itself and its products. Sample groups from each segment must be chosen and an assessment made of their current level of awareness and the nature of their attitudes. Only with this information can an effective plan be drawn up. From this a budget is set with the task of moving from a perceived level A to a targeted level B in a given period of time. Using the same audience segments, methods of sampling and questioning techniques, research must be planned at intermediate stages to find out whether the results are on schedule, in advance of it or behind it. Variations can be made at this stage to bring the campaign back on course; changes may be in the direction of the campaign or it may be necessary to increase expenditure, or for that matter cut it back. So the operation breaks down into four stages – set objectives, quantify, research, verify.

ORGANIZING FOR CORPORATE RELATIONS

If corporate relations is not recognized as a top-management function it stands little chance of success. If there is not to be a corporate affairs director, at least the executive resposible must have direct access to the chief executive and the top-level strategic thinking which is going on at that level. The person concerned needs professional communications expertise across all channels of persuasion and information, but more than that he must have the perspective of an all-round businessman equally at home with financial matters as with technical, personnel and marketing.

Depending on the size of the company he may require a small staff, but increasingly there is a reluctance to add what almost amounts to a fixed overhead, and the alternative of outside services is looked upon with greater favour. It is said that outside consultants find it difficult to relate closely to the company and its inside and outside complexities. This may be so and is one of the reasons for having at least one really good staff person. On the other hand, the body of knowledge and expertise in corporate activities, particularly in effective communications, is limited and in all probability will not be found among more than a handful of consultants. The position is further complicated by the fact that many corporate campaigns have been devised and executed by advertising agencies, and so the acquired cumulative experience is shared between two professional groups of practitioners. There are signs that a new breed of total communications agencies will emerge which will set out to provide counselling at a corporate level and then follow on with a full range of services on an *à la carte* basis so that a client company can select which executive activities he will take upon himself, and which he will leave in the hands of the outside service. This combination, all under one strategic plan, facilitates the use of the respective strengths of both the consultant and the client, is highly flexible, professionally more effective, and arguably cheaper.

BENEFITS

A well-constructed and properly funded corporate relations programme can lead to many benefits of which the following are but a few of the more obvious examples.

1 Increased market reputation and market share
2 Happier and more satisfied employees
3 Rise in share price
4 Greater productivity
5 Favourable government support
6 Better quality applicants for jobs
7 Improved treatment from suppliers
8 Better understanding by, and less criticism from, outside pressure groups.

While benefits will accrue to any company as a result of a planned corporate relations effort the chances are that the larger the organization, the greater the need for a formalized corporate policy. This applies to an even greater extent where the products concerned fall into the category known as 'undifferentiated'. With little to choose between one brand and another (for example with petrol, oil, banks, cigarettes, detergents), what are the real determinants of a purchasing decision? There is a good deal of evidence to suggest that the customer will prefer the brand or name he knows best and for which he has the greatest regard. Where products are intrinsically the same, the most important factor must become that undefinable property which lies behind the product – its reputation.

THE FUTURE

There can be little doubt that corporate relations as a new management function is here to stay. Increasingly, corporations are having to accept a social responsibility and, what is more important, to be seen to accept it. Customers, employees, shareholders and all the other interested public groups wish to be better informed and to feel comfortable in the knowledge that they are not being unfairly exploited by faceless, impersonal organizations whose sole purpose is to make as much profit as they can, regardless of the feelings or sensitivities of others.

One portent of future growth is to be found by looking at the United States where there are many indicators of the firm foundation and significant benefits of corporate relations. Other industrialized countries have a long way to go in comparison, but it would be surprising if corporate relations did not become a way of business in most of them during the next decade.

FURTHER READING

Bernstein, D., *Company Image and Reality*, Holt, Rinehart & Winston, London, 1985

Hart, N.A., *Effective Corporate Relations*, McGraw-Hill, Maidenhead, 1987

Hayes, R., and Watts, R., *Corporate Revolution*, Heinemann, London, 1986

7 Corporate culture and competitive advantage

Prabhu S Guptara

Today, it is difficult to find a single large corporation whose annual report does not prominently feature the term 'culture'. By contrast, only ten years ago management people who used the word outside a theatre or art gallery were regarded as distinctly odd. This change in attitude has been caused by one book: Peters and Waterman's *In Search of Excellence*. It was the first management book to reach the top of the *New York Times*' bestseller list; it stayed there for an unusually long time; and it demonstrated that the only thing that winning companies have in common is a distinctive corporate culture.

However, Peters and Waterman were not the first people to draw attention to the importance of organizational culture. Moreover, since the publication of their book, there has been a spate of books on the subject, and their book is not superior to the others in literary skill or intellectual acumen. So why was this book particularly influential? It simply happened to touch the pulse of America at a time when it was beginning to doubt its economic pre-eminence for the first time since the Second World War: *In Search of Excellence* provided reassurance that there was much which was still excellent in America.

The jargon of America soon spreads to the rest of the business world. That is why, in spite of the growth of a considerable library on the subject of business culture, the vast majority of managers who use the word do not understand what 'culture' means – or indeed how penetrating a way culture provides into the guts of any organization.

THE NATURE OF CORPORATE CULTURE

So what is corporate culture? There are innumerable definitions. All who speak or write on the subject seem to have their own definitions of culture. Here are two:

- The way we do things round here

- The predisposition to act in certain ways.

Culture relates to every aspect of a company. For example, the ruling ideas: the values, beliefs, ways of reasoning that are accepted in defining what is desirable and undesirable. Culture relates, too, to the technology of the company: the skills, machinery and techniques that enable the company to produce the goods and services it wishes to market. And culture relates to the kind of organization that is adopted by the company, which makes it possible for members of the company to co-ordinate their behaviour effectively with the actions of others.

It is worth noting that culture is not 'natural', but is developed by each organization. Culture is not instinctive: it has to be absorbed or learned, and it is usually learned early in one's time with a particular organization, so it is emotionally charged. At an impressionable time, we become imbued with the company's ways of acting, thinking and feeling. When actual behaviour deviates from the ideal patterns of that company, sanctions are frequently applied – pressure is brought to bear on deviant individuals so that they will conform to what that company expects. The pressure can be obvious; for example: dismissal, disciplinary proceedings, or informal words from superiors or peers. But pressure can also be subtle, and, although people do not think about this very much, in this fashion it can also be a powerful moulder of behaviour. It does not take an unusual degree of observation to notice that certain forms of behaviour are rewarded or accepted, and that certain topics and ways of thinking are taboo or will simply be ignored. Whether subtle or crude, such pressure means that any departure from a company's standard begins to appear as a departure for the worse.

Once we are sufficiently imbued with a particular culture, it persists even when we are exposed to new cultures. Such persistence means that change, although not impossible, is often quite difficult. This is not to say that cultures are inflexible. In spite of our resistance to change, cultures do adapt. In fact, they change continuously, if gradually, and some organizations change faster than others.

Finally, the various aspects of a culture fit together. While a culture may have elements that appear inconsistent to outsiders, it does tend to form a consistent and integrated whole. So, two things at least must be said if we are to understand culture. First, culture relates to *what* we are growing – as in agriculture, arboriculture, viniculture and so on. In a business or organization we grow the distinctive products and services, and the ways of behaviour, which separate our group from other groups, our company from other companies. And what we produce and how we behave depends entirely, of course, on our beliefs, our values and assumptions, and our attitudes and concerns. Secondly, culture also relates to *how* we grow whatever we grow. An application of a cultural approach to our work can show us the best way of embedding in our organization whatever qualities we wish to grow – entrepreneurship, quality-consciousness, service-orientation, flexibility and so on.

The absence or presence of such qualities in our organizations is not a matter of accident. These qualities are nurtured and shaped by our culture, just as our own actions, beliefs and qualities will in turn modify that culture. So, culture is a product of actions that were taken by others before we arrived, and it will be a product of actions that are taken by us. It is rooted in the individual and collective personalities which are involved, and in the choices that have been and are being made. In other words, culture is rooted in and related to the whole of life. There have been many definitions of life, but one of the most telling was given in the 1960s by John Lennon of the Beatles. 'Life', he said, 'is what slips by while we're busy making other plans.' Culture is rather like that: it comes into being while we are doing other things.

Consider, for example, the recruitment activity of your organization. You may not consider that you are growing the culture of your organization by this activity. But what sorts of people do you look for? You may answer, 'we look for the best people, and the best people only.' That is not unreasonable, but what is 'best'?

After all, the best people are not merely those who are best technically. If that were the case, we would not need to hold interviews for graduate engineers, for example, because their exam results would tell us their level of attainment quite clearly. We are not only interested in people because they are best technically at doing their job. We are also interested in how they work, what kind of people they are, what qualities they have, and whether they can fit in with the others already in the team. Consciously or unconsciously, these latter factors are decisive in recruitment offers – and, incidentally, in offer acceptances. No wonder studies show that 87 per cent of all those who fail in a job fail because of personality, not ability.

Let us go one step further and suppose that you always recruit articulate thinkers who speak their mind and feel free to disagree with the interviewers. That does not necessarily mean that you have – or will have – a culture which fosters and rewards such behaviour. It may be that your induction process gradually dampens down such articulateness and consistently rewards conformity rather than dissent. The result could be that those recruits who cannot stomach this approach leave before or soon after the induction process is complete. You are then left with people who, for some reason, feel unable to move or are willing to conform for the sake of the job prospects involved. There are organizations well known for being like sausage machines: it does not matter what you put in at one end, what emerges at the other end is a sausage. Most armies are like that. So the induction process, too, is a powerful shaper of the organizational culture.

One can, similarly, see what values are being fostered by your reward, training and development systems, by the way in which your company's history is being interpreted and used at present, by your communication system, and so on. This is, in fact, one way in which a culture audit can be done. (For an alternative method, see Guptara, 1988.)

What is the point of auditing or mapping your corporate culture in this way? It enables you to see what you have and why you have it. You can begin to understand, for example, why your organizational strategy is formed in the way it is, and the advantages and disadvantages of this format, and the impact it has on implementability. You can begin to comprehend why performance, morale, productivity and service in your organization are at the level they are – and what you can do about it.

CULTURE MAPPING

A culture map provides you with a picture of the elements by which your present culture is being created, so that you can see which can be moved efficiently and effectively, and with minimum disruption to the other elements, in order to alter your culture. A culture map enables you to get beyond generalities, so that you can begin to understand and use your corporate culture intelligently for competitive advantage.

Cultural differences within an organization

Any culture map will reveal cultural differences within an organization. Different levels within a company have their own differences of culture, which are signalled, for example, by changes in dress code. Different departments within an organization can also have their own sub-cultures; for example, the R&D department may have a different orientation from the sales or marketing function, the accountancy division may operate by totally different criteria when compared to the manufacturing division. Different locations within a company may also have different cultures, as can different subsidiaries or acquired sections of a company. Individual managers notice cultural differences and adjust to them consciously or subconsciously – with greater or lesser success and with more or less comfort.

Nationality

There is one other dimension to which attention needs to be drawn, and to which executives and managers in multinationals tend to be blind. Because they all work in the same organization, people feel that their cultures must have the same core; but this is not so. Professor Geert Hofstede's survey of 150,000 managers in 50 countries (the largest survey ever done) revealed remarkable differences within an organization renowned for its corporate culture.

Nationality has three times more influence on shaping managerial behaviour than any other characteristic, according to Professor Andre Laurent of the Insead Business School, Paris. In surveys of his students he found, for example, that British managers did not rate communication as highly as their French or Japanese counterparts. Managers from the subsidiaries of a US multinational group differed widely in what they thought were 'the features of a well-functioning organization, the attributes of effective managers, and the most important things that effective managers should be doing'. The German managers, more than the others, believed that creativity is essential for career success. In their mind, the successful manager is the one who has the right individual characteristics. Their outlook was rational: they viewed the organization as a co-ordinated network of individuals who make appropriate decisions based on their professional competence and knowledge. The British managers, by contrast, held a more interpersonal and subjective view of the organizational world. They viewed the organization primarily as a network of relationships between individuals, who get things done by influencing each other through discussion and negotiation. According to them, the ability to create the right image and to get noticed for what they do is essential for career success. French managers, as you might expect, are different. They looked at the organization as an authority network where the power to organize and control the actors stems from their position in the hierarchy. They focused on the organization as a pyramid of differentiated levels of power to be acquired or dealt with. The French managers perceived the ability to manage power relationships effectively and to 'work the system' as particularly critical to their success.

Co-ordination

Anyone faced with such differences, and interested in using a corporate culture for competitive advantage, has to decide the extent to which it is possible or useful to unify culture. Any attempt to unify culture is doomed to failure, for the reasons given above. What can be done, and what can be useful and productive, is to harmonize the various subcultures in an organization, so that they are working in concert rather than in contrast. At least, the key values of the organization can be co-ordinated. Too many organizations, including some which pride themselves on their corporate culture, in reality do not have the co-ordination which they imagine they possess and from which they would certainly benefit.

Co-ordination can be achieved by attempting to iron out the differences between groups of employees, but a far better way is to recognize the differences and build on people's strengths. Differences can be viewed as an asset or as a handicap. Each section of your organization does things in the way it does because that way has proved the best, or least difficult, way in the past. All subcultures embody some unique insight, even if they may also have some unique weaknesses.

CULTURAL DEVELOPMENT

Cultural development, which is the next stage from culture mapping, involves the bringing together of all the subcultures in ways which can be mutually enriching and beneficial. This can be done with specific aims in view from the start, such as enhancing service-consciousness and delivery in the organization; or it can be applied to every area in a systematic way for the overall toning-up (or radical overhaul) of the organization.

RESPONSE TO CHANGE

There is one other matter worth considering. The more one operates in a genuinely global way, the more exposed one becomes to the waxing and waning of the world economy, compounded by the roller-coaster of global competition which often emerges from a direction that one least expects. For example, you are, perhaps, currently number one in the West and are desperately trying to fend off Japanese competition, when you may find that numbers four and five in the West, both well below you in size and potential, have decided to merge, with the result that you are no longer number one, even in the West.

What is the lesson? You will have to be extremely nimble if you want to cope, and you will need an organization which is capable of shifting gear and changing tack not merely from year to year, but from month to month and perhaps even from week to week. To achieve that you have to embed in your organization qualities of which you may have never even dreamed. Briefly, your organization has the unenviable job of learning to manage complete ambiguity and massive continuous change, while retaining its core work-force through the demographic collapse.

THREE MYTHS

Perhaps, by now, some light may have been thrown on three popular myths about culture and culture change.

The first is that culture is a very vague area. But the supposed vagueness of culture derives from the fact that it relates simultaneously to such a large area of business and management. Cultural differences are, instead, clearly quantifiable.

Secondly, that culture change takes a long time. Undoubtedly, culture change can take a long time. But Mrs Thatcher caused a widespread cultural revolution in

Britain and it took her only six or seven years to do it. If the culture of a country can be changed with such rapidity, you will see that it is not particularly surprising that culture change even in a fairly large company should require no more than three years.

The third myth is that culture change requires a charismatic personality. It is true that a charismatic personality may create rapid culture change; but it is also true that when that personality leaves the scene, the culture may tend to go back to what it was. To obtain an enduring culture change, what is needed is not necessarily a charismatic personality, but someone who knows how the culture of your organization is produced, and who understands that the relevant key processes and structures of the company need to be changed without affecting the bottom line adversely. If the processes and structures are changed, the resulting behaviours will inevitably change as well.

CONCLUSION

To conclude, here is a brief illustrative case study. The Japanese company Matsushita runs what it more or less a postgraduate school of business. Every year 5,000 of Japan's top graduates apply to join Matsushita's management cadre. A hundred make it. They are given four years of training. In the first year they learn nothing but Zen. Imagine what would happen if you asked your management trainees to study nothing but religion and prayer for a whole year. In the second year, at Matsushita, they learn all the quantification and methods that we teach them during an MBA at Harvard or Henley. So what do they do in their third year? They have the equivalent of a blank cheque to go anywhere in the world and do what they like. They can spend time researching a particular problem, attending courses wherever they please, doing a round of international conferences, say, on the latest advances in computers and communications, or whatever they like. And in the fourth year, all one hundred of them get together again and spend the whole year asking themselves, 'What do we do with all this material, all this information?'. It is no wonder that they produce the world-beaters. Their whole personalities are engaged in what they are doing. Their spiritual, physical, intellectual, and psychological aspects are all involved in the struggle and adventure of making that company the best there is.

Imagine what would happen if we were able to release the creativity and sense of adventure of each of our senior managers, let alone the whole of the management team, or the whole of the workforce. That is the opportunity and the challenge provided by the perspective of culture on business. It is time we stopped using the word like an incantation in annual reports and chairman's speeches. Corporate and national cultures offer a transformative and holistic perspective for individuals as well as for organizations. It is time we started using an intelligent understanding of culture to shape our organizations for competitive advantage.

FURTHER READING

Deal and Kennedy, *Corporate Cultures*, Penguin, Harmondsworth,1988
Graves, D., *Corporate Culture*, Pinter Publishers, London,1986

Guptara, Prabhu S., 'Culture Audits: Their Role in the Merger Process', *Manpower Policy and Practice*, Summer, 1988

Guptara, Prabhu S., 'Preparing for 1992; Step 1: Understand Yourself', *Training and Development.* July 1989

Hofstede, G., *Culture's Consequences*, Sage, London, 1980

Kantrow, Alan M., *The Constraints of Corporate Tradition*, Harper & Row, London, 1987

Mangham, Iain L., *Power and Performance in Organizations*, Blackwell, Oxford, 1986

Owen, Harrison, *Spirit: Transformation and Development in Organizations*, Pippa Rann Books, UK, 1988

Peters, T. J. and Waterman, R. H., *In Search of Excellence*, Harper & Row, New York, 1982

Wilkins, A. L., 'The Culture Audit: A Tool for Understanding Organizations', *Organizational Dynamics*, Autumn, 1983

Wilkins, A. L., *Developing Corporate Character*, Jossey-Bass, 1989

Wuthnow, R. et al, *Cultural Analysis*, Routledge and Kegan Paul, London, 1984

8 Customer first – a strategy for quality service

Denis Walker

Customers are the lifeblood of all organizations. Yet few organizations seem fully capable of matching their performance to the needs of their customers – in quality, efficiency or personal service. Managers must start to recognize that improving quality to their customers is not a matter of choice: the health, and ultimately the survival, of the organization depends on it.

The purpose of this chapter is to show what has to be done to create a total commitment to customers. It is aimed primarily at executives who recognize that achieving quality improvement coupled with total commitment to customer service requires a new style of management. It is a style which demands development of skilled and knowledgeable people at all levels through communication and training, and the use of their expertise to seek better ways of doing things. This style is based on agreeing clear standards and targets and the use of data and statistics to drive for continuous improvement. It combines the art of managing people with the science of reducing variability.

WHAT IS SERVICE?

Customers react differently to what appears to be the same service. The same customer can also react differently to the same service in different circumstances. The business executive flying out to make a difficult but important deal is not the same customer as the one returning home that night with a lucrative contract safely in his pocket. This represents the difficulty – and the challenge – for service providers and their organizations. Mood, culture and timing, as well as the customer's previous experience all affect the way service is perceived.

This concept is one that many business people are uncomfortable with, since it demands flexibility in the use of resources, giving discretion to staff who deal with customers and not relying on production-oriented routines. It means treating customers as individuals and setting up organizational systems which support, not hinder, this aim. Service reputation is all about what it is like doing business with you. Is it a pleasant, rewarding experience, or one your customers would rather not repeat? Is that little bit extra being done without asking, or is getting good service like going through an army assault course?

SERVICE STRATEGY

'Putting the customer first' is an admirable intention, but it will only be more than that if there is a proper service strategy for delivering it. The two main objectives of this strategy are to create a difference which is observable or measurable by the customers, and also to have real impact on the way things are done inside the company.

The service strategy must be a central part of the company's business strategy which will also cover profit objectives, markets, technology and so on. It is central because it defines the company's internal culture as well as its desired external image. It needs to be put in writing and communicated widely, so that no one is in any doubt about what it is designed to achieve. It needs to be matched by an organization structure designed for customer response. The strategy must include:

1 *Customers' needs and expectations* No company can survive if its customers' needs are either not fully defined or if they are ignored when known
2 *Competitors' activities* Without knowledge of what your main competitors are doing, it is impossible to set out to gain advantage through the quality and innovation of your services. You need to know why customers are using their products and services rather than your own
3 *Vision of the future* Listening to customers and watching the competition are obviously important processes, but they may not be sufficient to sustain differentiation and customer satisfaction over the longer term. The companies that stand apart from the rest have visionary leaders who encourage experimentation and change and enable their people to create a vision of the future. This is not a projection of the future on the basis of present position, but a picture of where you would like to be and how to get there.

Areas 1 and 2 need regular audit and assessment, which itself should be part of your service strategy.

Now consider what customers receive, or at least expect to receive for their money. It is usually a combination of material service and personal service – the tangible and the less tangible elements. If you are buying a toaster, the material aspect will be most important; if you are staying in a hotel, the personal aspects of service may be the uppermost. But in each case you hope that both material and personal service will be excellent. This is an important consideration when developing a strategy for service: it has to ensure that the customer is consistently well served both materially and personally.

Material service

Material service consists of a product plus the environment in which service takes place, and the service or delivery systems which get products to customers.

- *The product* has to be reliable and do what it is specified to do (i.e. fitness for purpose)
- *The environment* must reflect the quality of the organization – shoddy premises invariably raise questions about other aspects of a company's standards and performance. Well-organized and well-presented premises create a favourable first impression
- *The delivery systems* must work. These include distribution, scheduling, accountancy and computerized paperwork, job organization and so on. It does

not matter how good a product is if it arrives late or damaged, if it is not to the customer's specification, or if the order and account paperwork do not match.

Personal service

Personal service encompasses service style and the relationship between customers and the staff of an organization. How good a company is to deal with, usually depends on the people it employs. Their knowledge and skills are crucial to the company's ability to fulfil the expectations expressed in the service strategy. Staff who have direct contact with customers have the greatest effect on the company's reputation. But those behind the scenes must not be ignored, as they service those who are dealing with the customers, as well as creating the product and many of the delivery systems.

- *Staff attitude* towards customers can strongly support or badly undermine a company's service strategy. If they do not believe in, and demonstrate commitment to, the customer, then the service will not match the image being promoted. It is important, therefore, to know where they stand (using a carefully constructed attitude survey)
- *People systems* must be designed to motivate staff to support the service strategy. Selection criteria should reflect the need for customer focus, induction should introduce it at an early stage, 'technical' training should reinforce and not conflict, and performance appraisal should develop objectives relating to service performance. The way people are organized and the way they are managed must also be compatible with giving good service.

Service health check

Clearly, any organization determined to become more customer-oriented needs to examine its performance in each of the above areas. The activity of auditing 'organizational health' should become a natural part of the continuous improvement process. Try the following brief health check for your own organization.

- Do you know your customers and are you clear about their needs?
- Have you communicated these needs to your staff?
- Have clear service standards been set and communicated?
- Are you sure about how service can give you an edge over your competitors?
- Have you clearly defined the skills and knowledge required by your staff to deliver quality service?
- Have the skills of managing your service business been identified and programmes set up to give all managers these skills?
- Do you know how much poor quality is costing you and what the main causes of poor quality are?
- Do you have a customer complaint system?
- Do you have a corporate mission?
- Has this mission been communicated to your staff and set in the context of their work?
- Do systems exit which assure you of quality products or services?

• Do your selection procedures reflect a quality company?

Service strategy model

The elements of the service strategy just defined can be presented in the form of a model to aid auditing organizational health and devising service quality improvement programmes (see Figure 8.1).

PLANNING AND RUNNING A SERVICE PROGRAMME

The next stage is to develop a coherent framework of activities which will enable your service strategy to be implemented and create a real difference.

The coherent framework of activities is designed to produce awareness of the need to change, commitment to the process of change and an environment in which change happens. This is a complex, long-term task. Ownership and commitment at all levels of the organization, starting with management, are crucial. Commitment programmes have to be designed and run and levels of commitment monitored through regular audit and reviews of quality improvement plans and achievements. Although ownership concerns everybody, the improvement programme itself will need a 'kick-start' and continual coaxing. While the ultimate champion has to be the principal executive officer, a senior champion or co-ordinator may be required to present the total picture, co-ordinate design and implementation of activities.

The coherence of the activities is important: people must be able to understand how activities fit together and how they lead to achievement of the mission. The use of branding, traditionally an external marketing tool, helps to communicate the fact that a broad range of activities are all concerned with quality improvement.

Activities need to be designed to put the service strategy into practice – building understanding, emotional commitment and practical participation in improving service performance on a continuous basis. Improving performance requires standards of service to be defined and communicated and improvement targets set; staff need to be trained to deliver these standards and in problem solving and innovation skills and techniques, and to be involved in carefully selected improvement projects. The process of improvement is continually fuelled by new survey data, by internal audits, by customer complaints and by external audits through quality assurance (QA) programmes and supplier-partnership programmes led by your customers. In other words, there should never be a time when improvement opportunities do not arise: there will always be unexpected variations, changes to requirements to satisfy. The improvement projects need to breach traditional organizational boundaries. As the service strategy model shows, most quality problems occur in the delivery and people systems areas and these rarely have a single, clear owner. The bigger management processes cross many organizational boundaries yet still have to be improved – mechanisms for doing this have to be introduced as part of the service programme.

As the service improvement programme is to be long term, ways have to be developed for reinforcing the messages and consolidating progress. Communication systems have to be overhauled, every opportunity has to be taken to repeat

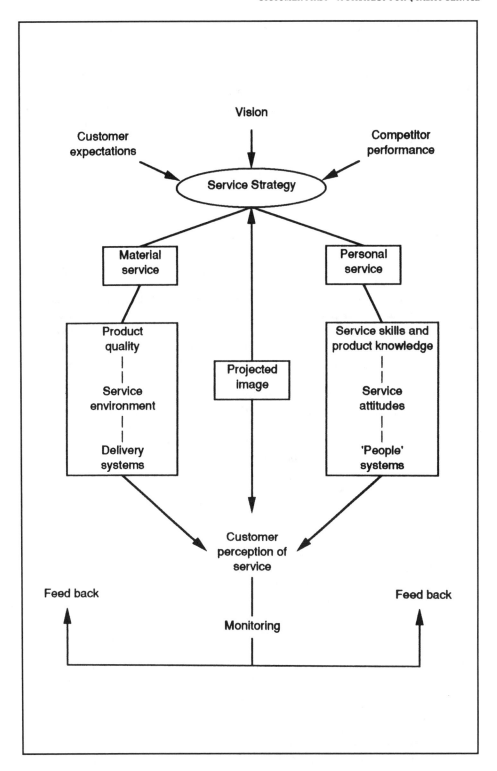

Figure 8.1   Service strategy model

key messages, and successes have to be featured to keep service quality awareness to the fore.

All training programmes provide an opportunity to reinforce the principles of 'customer first' and the need to seek continuous improvement. Technical training should no longer be perceived as separate from customer relations training, whether on the job or in a classroom. Finally, service improvements need to be recognized, rewarding individuals and teams for achievement and providing encouragement to others.

We concentrate here on the role of the manager in implementing the service strategy and bringing about performance improvement. Deming and Juran have both stated that at least 80 per cent of quality problems are to do with systems weaknesses and bureaucracy and can only be put right through management initiated activity. Very few problems can be blamed on the work-force; it is usually the systems and processes they are asked to work with. Even apparent attitude problems often have their root cause in poor training – a largely managerially-led process. Management in a quality organization involves managing change for the better rather than maintaining the status quo. Key result areas for managers should reflect this, as should management behaviour. Most employees take their behavioural cues from people only slightly higher up in the hierarchy of the company. So quality leadership has to be widely spread. Managers have to be seen to be committed to the customer, talking to them and acting on what they say, eradicating quality problems for good and encouraging subordinates to do the same.

Managers need to produce and use their own local data on customer requirements and employee attitudes. They need to devise and communicate meaningful improvement plans and use these to drive personal review systems in a non-restrictive, participative manner. They should both seek and provide training for their subordinates in change management and in customer-oriented business management. They should set up improvement projects which cross traditional barriers between departments rather than protecting parochialism. They should help their people to understand causes of variation and the control processes used to minimize them. 'Customer first' will only become a reality if managers want it and work for it.

Of course, the aim of all of these activities is to create a competitive edge which will enable the organization to prosper and grow. Image is part of the service strategy model. The way an organization promotes itself, deliberately or inadvertently, gives customers, or potential customers, certain expectations against which they will judge actual performance. Improved service can become a marketing tool, but timing is important. The organization must be sure that if it raises expectations, they will be fulfilled. Sustained improvement adds value to a basic product and has a market price. Customers will pay for reliably high quality.

The sternest test of a service strategy is its response to customer complaints, requiring clearly defined systems and procedures to handle complaints effectively.

In essence, the activites outlined above are designed to achieve:

- An awareness of customer service and quality principles
- Commitment to implementing these principles throughout the organization
- Regular review of data to show the difference achieved.

THE IMPORTANCE OF OWNERSHIP

In order that service improvement becomes a natural part of managing the business, and for its implementation and effects to be widely shared, the involvement (and therefore ownership) of managers must be deliberately cultivated by:

* Involvement in research
* Running workshops on the findings
* Testing activities with them first
* Encouraging local initiatives within the overall 'customer first' framework
* Conferences to share learning and successes and to develop next steps.

Ignoring the issue of ownership and leadership will result in piecemeal activities for which managers will not get the support of their staff, and in managers actually undermining the service strategy.

MANAGING A SERVICE BUSINESS

In any business the onus is on the managers to point the way and create the right environment for success. Employees look to their managers to set the style, to demonstrate what is important and to decide the pace of work. Nearly all changes which are needed will have to be initiated by management – revolutions rarely happen 'bottom-up'. The following are some of the principal ways for managers in service organizations to manage their own performance and that of their departments in bringing about quality improvement.

Vision

All managers need to understand the corporate vision, mission or objectives and be able to explain them in a way which makes sense to their own people. They should consider working with their team to define departmental missions which are complementary to each other. They should be able to describe the department's main purpose and motivate people towards achievement of that purpose.

Key results

The work on vision should lead to clarification of the results and targets to be achieved in the coming months. These should be expressed as between five and seven key results, at least two of which should be mainly concerned with quality and customer service. Key results should be about change – improvement, innovation, implementation – not about maintaining status quo. Targets, set in terms of quality, quantity, cost and/or timescale, should provide the milestones and review points.

It is difficult to measure some jobs in this way, but how else can their real worth to the organization be established? Objective systems designed purely to fill up the annual appraisal report, and not used to foster real performance improvement, are a waste of time. A 90-day review system is needed: two hours every three months with each direct report is managerial time well spent. A 90-day review period allows for changes in priority, correction of work which has gone off course, and reallocation of resources. The annual review and report then becomes more meaningful and less traumatic. If managers are not assessed for their contribution to customer service, then the organization is not really serious about putting the customer first.

Once a key result system is implemented, it is much easier to reward managerial performance. The reward system should reflect and support the service strategy, rather than working against it by encouraging caution and mediocrity.

Exemplifying the new values

Managers will be observed carefully by their subordinates for signals of commitment to 'customer first'. These are some of the ways in which managers can demonstrate their customer orientation:

- Referring to customers and customer data frequently
- Not accepting poor quality and 'it's near enough' attitudes
- Making direct contact with customers on a regular basis
- Breaking down barriers between departments, rather than protecting their own territory; demonstrating the importance of the internal customer concept
- Praising people for good performance, particularly where it is overtly supporting the service emphasis
- Being visible in their own department and in customer departments, and taking time to update people on performance successes
- Implementing a 90-day review system for the department
- Encouraging staff to be involved in performance improvement, problem solving and innovation, and showing an interest in team and project activity
- Keeping subjects such as quality, safety and customer high on their own and their department's agenda
- Setting high personal standards in terms of presentation, courtesy, quality and rate of work.

Managers must be careful to avoid sins of omission; not taking the trouble to acknowledge a particularly good piece of work can easily lead people to suspect lack of interest or commitment.

Performance data

Managers who are serious about performance improvement, measure it. 'What gets measured gets done' is a Tom Peters maxim which, put alongside a clear sense of priorities, is very powerful. Individuals and departments should set a handful of work standards which reflect the needs of customers (preferably developed jointly with those customers); by which performance can regularly be measured. The resulting data should be presented creatively and very visibly. Any department which cannot agree performance standards with its customers should consider whether it needs to exist at all. Some departments may even find it difficult to decide who their customers are! Using measurement in the key result areas can add meaning to the objectives and help chart progress towards them. Examples of performance standards are:

- Answering telephones in the sales department within four rings
- Accuracy of delivery to the warehouse by the production department
- Monthly accounts delivered on time by the accounts department
- Number of bug-free systems from management services department
- Pay systems with no errors
- Point of sale material available one week before product launch.

Each standard should reflect '100 per cent right first time' performance, and any which demand less must be seen as stepping stones towards that goal. This concept has to be interpreted for each department, but the sum of the parts must ultimately be perfect products and services every time. Accuracy of 98 per cent may sound great to managers who know how difficult it is to achieve, but the fact that 2 per cent of the customers get wrong or damaged orders cannot be justified.

Data can be very boring or they can provide you and your department with interest and excitement – a driving force for improvement. Displaying the data effectively is important. It should be done simply but attractively. Charts are better than columns of numbers (see Figure 71.1, for example). Use colour if possible. Provide special noticeboards and keep the data up to date. Talk about it with staff when you are on walkabout. Encourage staff to seek training in simple measurement techniques to support their problem solving. Establish statistical expertise within your department and let people know what help is available. Use the data as a regular agenda item in meetings. Have a regular performance meeting to review performance against service standards. Investigate shortfalls and praise improvements, and ensure that the right people see the data.

How to audit your department (or company, division or group)

Announce your own material and personal audit to demonstrate commitment to the organization's service programme. Involve your people in identifying all the systems, procedures and rules which are unhelpful to the customer and which impede fast response and innovation. Scrap the worst offenders and change the rest. Has the supervisor, for instance, become just the guardian of these inhibiting rules and procedures? Can the role be changed into an enabling one? How effective are your people? Do they understand what's expected of them? Are they capable of delivering it? Could they become so with the right training and other resources? If so, set this up.

Stand back from your department and make sure you know:

- Who your customers are
- What they expect of you
- How well you meet those expectations
- What needs to be done to improve
- What are the inhibitors and barriers to improvement.

Discuss these questions with your staff and check your findings with your customers.

Create action plans for improvement using task forces, champions and work teams and check these plans with your internal and external customers. With the latter group you may feel you are taking a commercial risk, but as they already know your failings, you can only enhance your reputation by showing them that you are aiming to overcome them.

Eradicate the 'manager knows best' attitude; your years of experience may have become your own worst enemy. Establish what factors influence customers' success. Talk to them regularly and use market research selectively and intelligently. Listen to your staff – the experts. Find out what they think is wrong and what needs to be done to put it right.

Training

It is the manager's job to ensure that training programmes are put into place for their staff. But managers themselves need training to manage service businesses effectively. One area in which training programmes may be needed is the management of change – understanding current and future states, managing transitions.

Managers need to become comfortable with change, accepting it as part of normal life rather than constantly striving for stability which never comes. Managers need to debate in workshops, possibly with the help of external facilitators, the need for change, the process of change and their own roles in making it happen. Techniques can include vision exercises, domainal mapping, key result generation, peer and subordinate data, action planning and critical success factor analysis. Managers need to understand why people resist change and to learn ways of overcoming the resistance of people who are territorial; who have a high need for structure; who dislike risk; who think in black and white; or who always see the negative aspects rather than the opportunities.

Other workshops may concentrate more specifically on customer service and the added value and differentiation it provides in the market-place. Discussion of customer research and critical success factors leads to an understanding of the principles behind quality and service standards and monitoring mechanisms, and an understanding of the importance of managers providing a role model for the new corporate values.

An organization introducing key result systems to support its service strategy will need a 'workshop' solely on the aspect of managing performance, to cover:

- Defining key results
- Setting targets
- Appraisal interviewing
- Giving feedback
- Counselling and coaching
- Career management.

Discussions with colleagues in the workshop will help to clarify key result areas – those parts of your job that really count. Targets for change, improvement or innovation can be given deadlines, milestones, standards, success criteria or measurement methods as appropriate.

Individual attributes

Quality organizations need quality managers. While this chapter provides a recipe of actions for managers to take, there are also some key attributes needed at a personal level:

- Total commitment to quality and customer service
- Capability of both strategic and tactical thinking
- Ability to stand back and evaluate the unit's performance
- Ability to demonstrate effective customer response by own example
- Ability to build warm, friendly relationships based on trust
- Ability to recognize good customer service and creative and innovative ideas
- Visible concern for and care about people.

PITFALLS

'Customer first' is creating change in a real and lasting way. There will, therefore, be many areas of resistance to overcome; to you these may appear to be based on illogical, irrational and emotional thinking. Just as with convincing customers to buy, people within the organization have to be motivated to 'buy-in'; so these perceptions cannot be ignored, however difficult they may be for you to accept or understand.

People facing change can undergo a whole series of negative emotions – anger, denial, frustration and, at best, resignation. All of these have to be countered if you are seeking enthusiastic, fearless commitment to change. Resistance may have to do with having change imposed, rather than the change itself. Allowing people to become involved in defining the nature of the change required and the subsequent processes for its implementation will remove much of the resistance. People must be allowed to let go of their old way of doing things in a manner which maintains their self-esteem. If you wish them to be part of the new culture, bridges with their past have to be built. Although people often resist prescribed change, there will need to be some – new structures, specific techniques, carefully chosen projects, improvement targets and so on. Therefore, time has to be taken to help people understand reasons for change in order to accept these changes. 'Customer first' or total quality cannot be achieved by system improvements alone. People make system changes work and, as such, their enthusiasm and commitment have to be won.

One obvious pitfall is not having a sufficiently coherent, essentially well-thought-out framework of activities, with the result that improvement activities are seen to be sporadic and piecemeal.

Another pitfall is not recognizing the need to have a critical mass of believers and enthusiasts with organizational influence, either in the formal structure or the informal networks which are part of any organization. Critical mass is not an absolute number but the number required to give impetus and maintain momentum, and will be different according to the stage of the change programme. These enthusiasts can be used to start convincing the persuadable neutrals who constitute the bulk of most normal populations.

The biggest hurdle is often the middle management group, waiting for repeated signals of commitment from the top or contra signals and mixed messages which allow them to stay neutral. Blaming the attitudes of their work-force for quality problems, being threatened by the changing nature of their role, feeling increasingly isolated and fearful of the future, are all characteristic behaviours, and they can be quietly and insidiously undermining progress. This particular hurdle can only be overcome by persistent leadership from the senior team providing clear championing of 'customer first' and role modelling quality behaviour, and by the training investment described earlier.

Other aspects which will soon undermine the programme if they are not anticipated are:

- Failure to start with improvement projects which are likely to be successful; teams soon get dispirited if they do not achieve success, and success in the early projects breeds confidence and hence more success
- Becoming stale after a few months as enthusiasm begins to drop. All improvement programmes will meet peaks and troughs of enthusiasm and progress. Be prepared with some new ideas, new champions and the odd surprise to keep people alert; keep the successes visible, use data constantly to renew energy levels
- Managers not listening – either to customers or employees. 'Manager knows best' behaviour is always lurking, ready to resume control at the least opportunity. Listening to customers and staff means you are constantly challenging your thinking and testing your ideas. Listening is the biggest respect you can pay to people, while it also provides you with data. Its absence will be the biggest signal to the organization of your lack of commitment to improvement.

THE POTENTIAL BENEFITS

Creating service as a key strategic value, listening to your customers and responding in a way that pleases them can have lasting benefits. The aim is to make 'customer first' behaviour a way of life by building a climate where continuous improvement in quality and innovation is natural and where the concept of the internal customer is a comfortable one for everybody in the organization.

None of this is achieved easily, it requires a long-term commitment and much effort in order for the difference to be noticed by your critical external and internal audiences. Yet your very survival may depend on making these changes. In addition to this, perhaps rather threatening, scenario there are positive benefits if you can overcome the many hurdles and pitfalls associated with bringing about change.

The vision of what can be achieved is exciting – your organization *can* be a different place in which to work and a different company to do business with. There are many opportunities for stumbling and falling, but with care these can be overcome or avoided. The question is, 'Is it all going to be worth it?' While the question can be avoided by showing that there is no choice if you want to become or remain competitive, there are also many positive, certain benefits to provide an affirmative answer to the question. Hard benefits which make a contribution to the growth and prosperity of the company are as follows:

- Guaranteed service quality becomes a marketable product in itself with a price differential acceptable to customers
- Quality improvement provides a cost-effective organization since waste, re-work and compensation become a thing of the past
- A common purpose and alignment removes ineffective training and compartmentalization and generates trust and enthusiasm
- A better educated, more numerate management and workforce are better prepared to face and handle change confidently and without fear, including market downturns; change becomes welcomed and sought after; cries for stability disappear
- Management systems and processes are uprated and the climate of continuous improvement ensures they are regularly reviewed for effectiveness, amended or removed
- Customers see the company as:
  1 responsive to their needs; good listeners
  2 adding value through innovative products and services
  3 sharing data in joint problem solving, generally seeking a partnership approach
  4 recognizing the importance of a third-party accreditation in creating customer confidence
  5 understanding the customer's business and the factors critical to their success
  6 caring about the way they deal with each customer
- Competitors see the company as formidable
- Shareholders regard the company as a safe, worthwhile investment
- The communities within which the company exists see it as a caring partner, concerned for the social and economic environment.
- Future potential employees see the company as one they would be proud to work for
- Energy and potential are released at all levels to create an altogether more powerful, innovative and more responsive organization
- Partnership programmes ensure only the best suppliers are kept and effort on new business generation is reduced as growth comes from customer loyalty and mutual development.

'Customer first' is a state of mind, producing an organization which is customer-led, quality and safety conscious, concerned for the development of its people and, as a result, highly successful. The journey is worthwhile and enjoyable. The destination is worth aspiring to. The potential payoff is immense.

FURTHER READING

Deming, W.E., *Out of the Crisis*, MIT Press, Cambridge, Mass., 1986

Normann, R., *Service Management: Strategy and Leadership in Service Businesses*, John Wiley, Chichester, W. Sussex, 1984

Oakland, John, *Total Quality Management*, Heinemann, Oxford, 1989

Peters, Tom, *Thriving on Chaos*, Macmillan, London, 1988

Walker, Denis, *Customer First: A Strategy for Quality Service*, Gower, Aldershot, 1990

9 Total quality management

John S Oakland

The reputation attached to a company for the quality of its products or services is accepted as a key to its success and the future of its employees. To prosper in today's economic climate, any organization and its suppliers must be dedicated to never-ending improvement in quality and productivity. For industrial and commercial organizations, which are viable only if they provide satisfaction to the consumer, competitiveness in quality is not only central to profitability, but crucial to business survival. If businesses in the West are to continue, they must learn how to manage quality. A comprehensive quality policy is not merely desirable: it is essential.

THE MANAGEMENT OF QUALITY

Many day-to-day issues, often taken for granted, involve quality in some form or other. For example, the safety and conformity with accepted standards of pharmaceuticals and food-processing, the continuity of performance and safe operation of nuclear plants and offshore installations, the effectiveness of weapons, the relative merits and life-cycle costs of competing products, and the efficiency of services, all attest to the need for good quality management.

The quality of products and services is important not only for users but also for suppliers. For manufacturers, quality deficiencies result in additional costs for inspection, testing, scrap, rework and the handling of complaints. Repeat sales and future market share will also be affected, with significant effects on profitability and survival. Quality must, therefore, be taken into account throughout all the areas of design, manufacture, marketing, and purchasing. It must be controlled in all these functions, and their activities co-ordinated to achieve a balanced corporate quality performance. This is just as true in the service sectors. Quality performance will not just happen; effective leadership and teamwork is the only sure recipe for success. Understanding, commitment by senior management and explicit quality policies lead to an improvement throughout the entire organization, which in turn generates a momentum for quality improvement of products, services and performance.

Management must be dedicated to the continuous improvement of quality, not simply a one-step improvement to an acceptable plateau. There must be willingness to implement changes, even in the ways in which an organization does business, in order to achieve that improvement. In addition, innovation and resources are required to satisfy the long-term requirements of the customer and the company, which must be placed before short-term profitability.

A traditional approach in many manufacturing organizations is to depend on the production department to make the product, on quality control to inspect it, and then to screen out items which do not meet specifications. This is a strategy of *detection*, which is wasteful because it allows time and materials to be invested in products or services which are not always saleable. This post-production inspection is expensive, unreliable and uneconomical. In the service sector this waste (usually in the form of time) can be massive, but less obvious to the eye. It is much more effective to avoid waste by not producing unsaleable output in the first place – to adopt a strategy of *prevention*.

The prevention strategy sounds sensible and obvious to most people. It is often captured in slogans such as 'Quality – right first time'. This type of campaigning is, however, not enough on its own. What is required is an understanding of the elements of a control system which is designed to prevent defective manufacture and unsuitable or inefficient services.

DESIGN AND CONFORMANCE

In management, one of the most commonly misunderstood words is 'quality'. What is a high-quality pair of shoes or a high-quality bank account? It is meaningless to make statements about the degree of quality of a product or service without reference to its intended use or purpose. Shoes which are to be used in the performance of a ballet would obviously have different requirements from those used in mountaineering, but both pairs of shoes may have the same level of quality, that is, they are equally suitable for the purpose for which they were manufactured.

Quality can therefore be defined as 'meeting the requirements of the customer', indicating that it is a measure of the satisfaction of customer needs. So the quality of a motor car or washing machine, a bank account or a pair of shoes, is simply the extent to which it meets the requirements of the customer. Before any discussion on quality can take place it is, therefore, necessary to be clear about the purpose of the product or service, in other words what the true customer requirements are. The customer may be inside or outside the organization and his or her satisfaction must be the first and most important ingredient in any plan for success.

A word of warning: the customer's perception of quality changes with time and the company's attitude to quality must, therefore, change with this perception. The skills and attitudes of the producer are also subject to change. Failure to monitor such changes will inevitably lead to dissatisfied customers. Quality, like all other corporate matters, must be continually reviewed in the light of current circumstances.

The quality of a product has two distinct but interrelated values:

1 Quality of design
2 Quality of conformance to design.

Quality of design

Quality of design is a measure of how well the product or service is designed to achieve its stated purpose. If it is low, the product will not work or the service will not meet the needs.

The most important feature of the design, with regard to the achievement of quality, is the *specification*. This describes and defines the product or service and should be a comprehensive statement of all the aspects which must be present to meet customer requirements.

Stipulation of the correct specification is vital in the purchase of materials and components for use in production. All too frequently the terms 'as previously supplied' or 'as agreed with your representative' are to be found on purchase orders for bought-out items. The importance of obtaining materials of the appropriate quality cannot be over-emphasized and this cannot be achieved without adequate specifications. Published standards should be incorporated into purchasing documents wherever possible.

A specification may be expressed in terms of: the maximum amount of tolerable variation on a measurement; the degree of finish on a surface; the smoothness of movement of a mechanical device; a particular chemical property, and so on. There is a variety of ways in which the specification of a service may be stated and the ingenuity of people must be constrained in order to control the number of forms of specifications present in any organization.

There must be a corporate understanding of the company's quality position in the market-place. It is not sufficient that the marketing department specifies a product or service 'because that is what the customer wants'. There must also be an agreement that the operating department can produce to that quality. Should they be incapable of achieving the desired quality, then one of two things must happen. Either the company finds a different position in the market-place or it substantially changes the production/operational facilities.

Quality of conformance to design

This is the extent to which the product or service achieves the quality of design. What the customer actually receives should conform to the design, and operating costs are tied firmly to the level of conformance achieved. Quality cannot be 'inspected-in': customer satisfaction must be designed into the producing system. The conformance check then makes sure that things go according to plan. A high level of final product or service inspection is often indicative of attempts to 'inspect-in' quality, an activity which will lead to spiralling costs and decreasing viability.

The area of conformance to design is concerned largely with the quality performance of the operations functions. The recording and analysis of data play a significant role in this aspect of quality, and it is here that the tools of statistical process control (SPC) must be applied effectively. The techniques of SPC are explained in Chapter 43.

RESPONSIBILITY FOR QUALITY

'Quality is everyone's business' is an often quoted cliché, but 'everything is everyone's business', and so quality often becomes 'nobody's business'. The responsibility for quality begins with determining the customer's requirements, and continues until the product or service is accepted by a satisfied customer. The management functions identifiable with this process, together with their duties (some of which are shared activities and appear under several functions) are as follows:

Senior management

1 Having a clear understanding of quality
2 Making a commitment to quality
3 Ensuring that the correct quality systems and attitudes pervade the organization
4 Supporting and encouraging the quality policy.

Marketing

1 Determining customer requirements
2 Knowing the competitors' quality levels
3 Setting of product/service specifications
4 Analysing customer complaints, sales staff reports, warranty claims and product or service liability cases
5 Downgrading of products for sale as seconds, and so on.

Research, development and design

1 Setting of appropriate specifications (including raw materials, processes and products/services)
2 Setting up pre-production and prototype trials
3 Designing and specifying inspection equipment
4 Analysing some rework and rectification problems
5 Downgrading of products
6 Dealing with product or service complaints and warranty claims.

Production (including production engineering) or operations

1 Agreeing specifications
2 Setting up pre-production and prototype trials
3 Training of operations personnel, including first line supervisors, foremen, and others
4 Ensuring any special handling and storage during production
5 Supervising and controlling quality at all stages
6 Arranging line or process control
7 Arranging any finished product control or service check
8 Analysing scrapped, reworked, rectified, replaced and downgraded products.

Purchasing

1 Establishing vendor rating and supplier approval
2 Procuring materials and services of the required quality.

After-sales and technical service

1 Dealing with product or service specification and performance evaulation
2 Evaluating pre-production and prototype product
3 Analysing customer complaints and material returned

Stores, transport and distribution

1 Arranging special handling and storage
2 Receiving and checking of materials and bought-out goods
3 Checking and despatching of finished products and replacement goods
4 Receiving, checking and sorting of returned products for replacement or repair.

Quality assurance

1 Dealing with quality planning
2 Providing quality advice and expertise
3 Training of personnel
4 Providing inward goods, service, process and finished products appraisal methodology
5 Analysing customers' complaints, warranty claims and product liability cases.

THE ROLE OF A QUALITY SYSTEM IN TQM

A quality assurance system (see Chapter 43) based on the fact that all functions share responsibility for quality, provides an effective method of acquiring and maintaining desired quality standards. The quality assurance department should not assume direct responsibility for quality but should support, advise and audit the work of the other functions, in much the same way as a financial auditor performs his duty without assuming responsibility for the profitability of the company.

The actual control of quality during manufacture or service delivery rests squarely on the shoulders of production or operations management, who must ensure that all the appropriate concepts and techniques are applied to this task. Organizationally, this means that staff carrying out work to control quality must be within the production/operations function.

A fully documented quality management system will ensure that two major requirements are met:

1 The customer's requirements – for confidence in the ability of the organization to deliver consistently the desired product or service
2 The organization's requirements – both internally and externally, and at an optimum cost, with efficient utilization of the resources available – material, human, and technological.

These requirements can be truly met only if objective evidence is provided in the form of information and data, which supports the system activities, from the ultimate supplier through to the ultimate customer. Chapter 43 gives further details of quality assurance systems.

THE COSTS OF QUALITY

Manufacturing a product or generating a service which has 'fitness for purpose' is not enough. The cost of achieving quality must be carefully managed so that the long-term effect of quality costs on the business is a desirable one. These costs are a true measure of the quality effort. A competitive product based on a balance between quality and cost factors is the principal goal of responsible management. This objective is best accomplished with the aid of competent analysis of the costs of quality. The balance works like this: as quality goes down, costs rise and (conversely) as quality goes up, costs fall.

The analysis of quality costs is a significant management tool. It provides:

1 A method of assessing the overall effectiveness of the management of quality
2 A means of determining problem areas and action priorities.

The costs of quality are not different from any other costs, in that, like the costs of marketing, design, sales, production/operations and other activities, they can be budgeted, measured and analysed.

Having specified the quality of design, the organization has the task of making a product or providing a service which matches this quality. This comprises activities which will incur costs that may be separated into the categories of failure costs, appraisal costs and prevention costs. Failure costs can be further split into those resulting from internal and external failure.

Internal failure costs

Internal failure costs are those which occur when products or services do not reach designed quality standards and are detected before transfer to the consumer takes place. Internal failure includes:

1 *Scrap* Defective product which cannot be repaired, used or sold
2 *Rework* or *rectification* The correction of defective material or services to meet the required specifications
3 *Re-inspection* The re-examination of products which have been rectified
4 *Downgrading* Product which is usable but does not meet specifications and may be sold as 'second quality' at a low price
5 *Failure analysis* The activity required to establish the causes of internal product or service failure.

External failure costs

External failure costs occur when products or services fail to reach design quality standards and are not detected until after transfer to the consumer. External failure includes:

1 *Repair* Either of returned products or those in the field
2 *Warranty claims* Failed products which are replaced under guarantee
3 *Complaints* All work associated with servicing of customers' complaints
4 *Returns* The handling and investigation of rejected products
5 *Liability* The result of product or service liability litigation and other claims.

External and internal failures produce the 'costs of getting it wrong'.

Appraisal costs

Appraisal costs are associated with the evaluation of purchased materials, services, processes, intermediates and products to assure conformance with the specifications. Appraisal includes:

1 *Inspection, checking* and *test* Of incoming material, process set-up, first-offs, running processes, intermediates, final products, and services, and includes service/product performance appraisal against agreed specifications
2 *Quality audits* To check that the quality system is functioning satisfactorily
3 *Inspection equipment* The calibration and maintenance of equipment used in all inspection activities
4 *Vendor rating* The assessment and approval of all suppliers.

Appraisal activities result in the 'costs of checking it is right'.

Prevention costs

Prevention costs are associated with the design, implementation and maintenance of the quality system. Such costs are planned and are incurred prior to production. Prevention includes:

1 *Product* or *service requirements* The determination of quality requirements and setting of corresponding specifications for incoming materials, processes, intermediates, finished products, and services
2 *Quality planning* The creation of quality, reliability, production, operation, supervision, inspection and other special plans (e.g. pre-production trials) required to achieve the quality objective
3 *Quality assurance* The creation and maintenance of the overall quality system
4 *Inspection* or *checking equipment* The design, development and/or purchase of equipment for use in inspection work or checking aspects of a process
5 *Training* The development preparation and maintenance of quality training programmes for staff operators, supervisors and managers
6 *Miscellaneous* Clerical, travel, supply, shipping, communications and other general management activities associated with quality.

Resources devoted to prevention give rise to the 'cost of making it right first time'.

Direct costs of quality in relation to the organization's ability

The failure, appraisal and prevention costs described above are the direct costs of quality. Their relationship with the ability of the organization to meet the customer requirements is shown in Figure 9.1. Where the ability is low, the total direct quality costs are high, with the failure costs predominating. As ability to meet the customers requirements improves, by modest investment in prevention, the failure costs drop, initially very steeply. Earlier literature on quality costs (e.g. BS6143) suggested that there is an optimum operating level at which the combined costs are at a minimum; the author has not yet found any organization in which this is true. As the customer

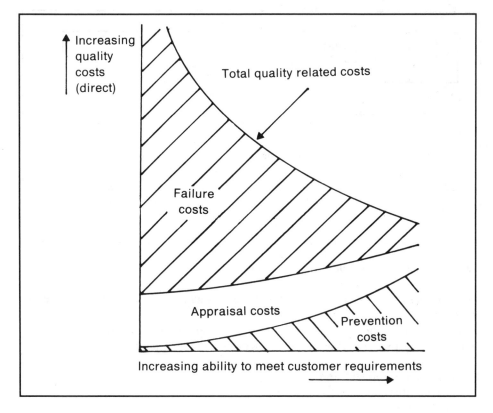

Figure 9.1   Relationship between direct costs of quality and organization capability

requirements change, the price of quality is eternal vigilance and continuous improvement.

COLLECTION AND ANALYSIS OF QUALITY COSTS

Progressive managers, always anxious to reduce costs, should be looking closely at the costs involved in achieving and maintaining conformance to a predetermined design and standard of quality. Most of those who have attempted to do so have found ample scope for economies. Work in many organizations shows that total direct quality costs can be as high as 30 percent of sales turnover or even higher. The average is around 10 per cent, and this makes them a subject worthy of attention. Indeed, it is necessary for effective management control that these expenditures be detailed and displayed. Yet efforts to discover the extent of quality costs prevailing in many companies have met with frustration for a variety of reasons. Quality costing tends to cut across normal accounting methods and cannot simply be secured by asking the accounting department for them. That will simply elicit the response 'We don't keep the books that way'.

The information must be pieced together using the 'books' where possible and resorting to estimates and finding new data when necessary. The first rule of thumb is that successful quality costing involves working closely with the accountants and with

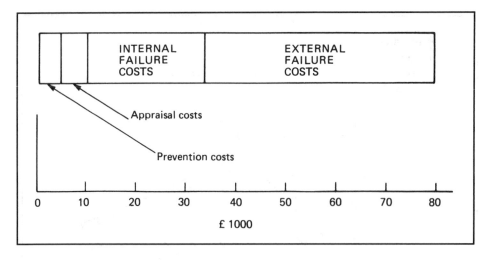

Figure 9.2   Bar chart presentation of quality costs

the managers or supervisors of the various departments to evaluate and estimate the costs associated with various activities.

Many useful reports may exist within a manufacturing company which aid the quality-costing process. These reports might include, for example:

1 Production scrap and rework
2 Machine utilization
3 Material usage
4 Salesmen's visits
5 Analysis of credit notes
6 Analysis of repairs.

A first estimate of the costs of quality in an organization can be made by combining data from such reports with estimates derived from discussions with appropriate managers and supervisors. Each assumption and estimate used in this first quality-cost computation should be published in a document which is circulated to selected managers. This will produce heated arguments about whether certain costs are part of quality costs. It is unimportant whether these 'grey' items are included or not. Provided that there is consistency in including or excluding the debatable categories, the opportunities for reducing costs are not affected.

The next rule of thumb is to consider very carefully the presentation and scope for misinterpretation of the findings. A bar-chart presentation is often the least trouble-some. A typical one is shown in Figure 9.2. To be meaningful, quality costs must be expressed as both total costs and as some financial measure. The most generally used base is sales volume or turnover. Sales have the great advantage of being understood by all as a measure of a unit's activity. A change in the quality cost:sales ratio can be immediately converted into an effect on the organization's pre-tax profitability. For a given industry, the profit to sales ratio is one of the indices of financial success, so its close relationship to the quality costs:sales ratio is another reason for favouring sales volume as the base for quality-cost reporting.

Ideally, quality costs should be recorded on a periodic basis on a running scoreboard. An annual once-off survey is a poor alternative. For regular reporting, account-ants should prepare the basic data and issue the report. This overcomes numerous problems of inconsistencies, duplication of effort, and the credibility gap created when financial data are produced from a non-financial source.

THE QUALITY–PRODUCTIVITY LINK

Total direct quality costs, and their division between the categories of prevention, appraisal, internal failure and external failure, vary considerably from industry to industry and from site to site. Work showing that total quality costs in manufacturing average 10 per cent of sales turnover means that in the average organization there exists a 'hidden plant', amounting to approximately one-tenth of productive capacity. This is devoted to producing scrap, rework, correcting errors, replacing defective goods and so on. Thus, a direct link exists between quality and productivity and there is no better way to improve productivity than to convert this hidden plant to truly productive use. A systematic approach to the control of quality is the best way to accomplish this.

QUALITY CIRCLES AND TEAMWORK FOR IMPROVEMENT

One of the most publicized aspects of the Japanese approach to quality has been quality circles. The quality circle may be defined as a group of workers doing similar work who meet:

- Voluntarily
- Regularly
- In normal working time
- Under the leadership of their supervisor
- To identify, analyse and solve work-related problems
- To recommend solutions to management.

Where possible, quality-circle members should implement the solutions themselves.

It is very easy to regard quality circles as the magic ointment to be rubbed on the affected spot and unfortunately many managers in the West have seen them as a panacea which will cure all ills. There are no panaceas and to place this concept into perspective, Juran, who has been an important influence in Japan's improvement in quality, has stated that quality circles represent only 5–10 per cent of the canvas of the Japanese success. The rest is concerned with understanding quality, its related costs, and the organization and techniques necessary for achieving customer satisfaction.

Given the right kind of commitment by top management, the right introduction, and the right environment in which to operate, quality circles can produce the shop- or office-floor motivation to achieve quality performance at that level. Circles should develop out of an understanding and knowledge of quality on the part of senior management. They must not be introduced as a desperate attempt to do something about poor quality.

A quality improvement team is a group of people with the appropriate knowledge, skills, and experience who are brought together by management specifically to tackle and solve a particular problem, usually on a project basis. They are cross-functional and often multidisciplinary. The use of the quality-improvement team approach allows the traditional definition of the 'process' to include the entire production or operating system. This includes paperwork, communication with other units, operating procedures, and the process equipment itself. Then, taking this broader view, all types of process problems can be addressed.

Structure of a teamwork organization for quality improvement

The unique feature of quality circles is that people are asked to join and not told to do so. Consequently, it is difficult to be specific about the structure of such a concept. It is, however, possible to identify four elements in a quality-improvement teamwork organization:

1 *Members* The prime element of the programme. They will have been taught certain problem-solving and quality-control techniques and, hence, possess the ability to identify and solve work-related problems
2 *Leaders* Usually the immediate supervisors or foremen of the members. They will have been trained to lead a circle and bear the responsibility for its success. A good leader, who develops the abilities of the circle members, will benefit directly by receiving valuable assistance in tackling nagging problems
3 *Facilitator* The overall manager of the quality or improvement team circle programme. This person, more than anyone else, will be responsible for the success of the concept, particularly within an organization. The facilitator must co-ordinate the meetings, the training and energies of the leaders and members and form the link between the circles and the rest of the organization. Ideally, the facilitator will be an innovative industrial teacher, capable of communicating with all levels and with all departments within the organization
4 *Management* Without the open support and commitment of management, quality circles, like any other concept, will not succeed. Management must retain its prerogatives, particularly regarding acceptance or non-acceptance of recommendations from circles, but the quickest way to kill a programme is to ignore a proposal arising from it. One of the most difficult facts for management to accept, and yet one which forms the corner-stone of the quality improvement philosophy, is that the real 'experts' on performing a task are those that do it day after day.

Training quality circles and quality teams

The training of circle leaders and quality improvement team members is the foundation of all successful programmes. The whole basis of the training operation is that the ideas must be easy to take in and be put across in a way which facilitates understanding. Simplicity must be the key word, with emphasis being given to the basic techniques. Essentially there are eight segments of training:

1 Introduction
2 Brainstorming
3 Data gathering and histograms
4 Cause and effect analysis
5 Pareto (or ABC) analysis

6   Sampling and stratification
7   Control charts
8   Presentation techniques.

Most of these are not exclusive to quality circles or quality control and find applications in most fields of management. Data gathering, stratification, graphs, histograms, cause and effect analysis, Pareto analysis, scatter diagrams, sampling and control charts form the basis of good quality control.

Management should also be exposed to some training in the part they are required to play in the quality-circle philosophy. A quality-circle programme can only be effective if management believes in it and is supportive and, since changes in management style may be necessary, their training is essential.

Operation of quality circles and quality-improvement teams

There are no formal rules governing the size of a quality circle or improvement team. Membership usually varies from three to fifteen people with an average of seven to eight. It is worth remembering that as the team becomes larger than this, it becomes increasingly difficult for all members to participate.

Meetings must be held away from the work area where members are free from interruptions and are mentally and physically at ease. The room should be arranged in a manner conducive to open discussion and any situation which physically emphasizes the leader's position should be avoided.

Meeting length and frequency is variable, but new quality circles meet for approximately one hour once a week. Thereafter, when training is complete, many circles continue to meet weekly; others extend the interval to two or three weeks. To a large extent, the nature of the problem selected will determine the interval between meetings, but this should never extend to more than one month, otherwise members will lose interest and the circle will cease to function.

A quality circle usually selects a project to work on through discussion within the circle. The leader then advises management of this choice and, assuming that no objections are raised, the circle proceeds with the work. Other suggestions for projects come from management, quality-assurance staff, the maintenance department, various staff personnel and other circles.

It is sometimes necessary for quality circles to contact experts in a particular field; for example, engineers, quality experts, safety officers, maintenance personnel. This communication should be strongly encouraged and the normal company channels should be used to invite specialists to attend meetings and offer advice. The experts may be considered to be 'consultants', the quality circle retaining responsibility for solving the particular problem.

In the formation of quality improvement teams, it is often useful to start with just one or two people concerned directly with the problem. If they try to draw flow charts of the processes involved, the requirement to include other people in order to understand the process and complete the charts will aid the team selection. This method will also ensure that all those who can make a significant contribution to the improvement process are represented.

The team leader has a primary responsibility for team management and maintenance and his/her selection and training is crucial to success. The leader need not be the highest-ranking person in the team, but must be concerned about accomplishing the team objectives (this is sometimes described as 'task concern') and the needs of the members (often termed 'people concern'). Weakness in either of these areas will lessen the effectiveness of the team in solving problems. Team leadership training should be directed at correcting deficiencies in these crucial aspects.

A MODEL FOR TOTAL QUALITY MANAGEMENT TQM

The concepts of TQM are basically very simple. Each part of an organization has customers, whether within or without, and the need to identify what the customer requirements are, and then set about meeting them, forms the core of the total-quality approach. This requires several things including understanding of the process involved, a good-quality management system, statistical process control (SPC), and teamwork. These are complimentary in many ways and they share the same requirement for an uncompromising commitment to quality. This must start with the most senior management and be communicated right through the organization. Having said that, either SPC or the quality system, or both, may be used as a spearhead to drive TQM through an organization.

The attention to many aspects of a company's operations – from purchasing through to distribution, from data recording to control chart plotting – which are required for the successful introduction of a good quality system or the implementation of SPC, will have a 'Hawthorne effect', concentrating everyone's attention on the customer/supplier interface, both inside and outside the organization. This creates the right culture of the organization, a culture in which TQM can flourish. A good quality-management system involves consideration of all the major areas: marketing, design, materials, plant, process, skills, distribution. Clearly, these each require considerable expansion and thought, but if attention is given to all areas using the concepts of TQM, then very little will be left to chance. A well-operated, documented quality-management system provides the necessary foundation for the successful application of SPC and teamwork. It is not possible simply to 'graft' these on to a poor quality system.

Much of industry and commerce would benefit from the improvements in quality brought about by the approach represented in Figure 9.3. This will ensure the implementation of the management commitment represented in the quality policy, and provide the environment and information base on which teamwork thrives, perhaps through the methods of the American gurus Juran and/or Crosby.

A systematic, structured approach to the launch of quality improvement through a balanced introduction of a quality system, SPC, and teamwork will provide a powerful spearhead with which to improve capability, and thereby market share. The importance of the use of SPC and improvement teams in quality-management systems cannot be over-emphasized. With increases in automation and the use of flexible manufacturing systems (FMS), optimized production technology (OPT) and the adoption of operations management methods such as just-in-time (JIT), the requirement for a total approach to quality is paramount. To compete locally, nationally or internationally, all organizations and their parts must adopt this professional approach to the management of quality.

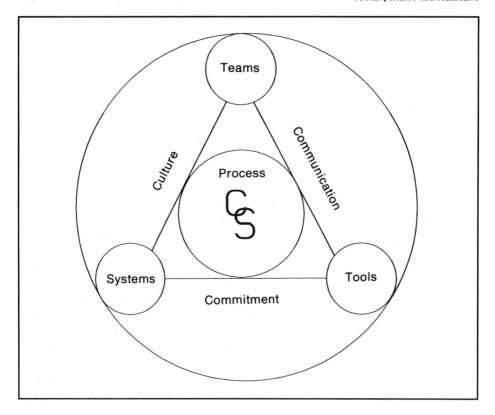

Figure 9.3   Total quality model

FURTHER READING AND REFERENCES

Crosby, P.B., *Quality is Free*, McGraw-Hill, New York, 1979

Deming, W.E., *Out of the Crisis*, MIT Centre for Advanced Engineering Study, Cambridge, Mass., 1986

Feigenbaum, A. V., *Total Quality Control*, 3rd edn, McGraw-Hill, New York, 1983

Ishikawa, K. (translated by David J. Lu), *What is Total Quality Control? – the Japanese Way*, Prentice Hall, Englewood Cliffs, NJ, 1985

Juran, J.M. and Gryna, F. M., *Quality Planning and Analysis*, 2nd edn, McGraw-Hill, New York, 1980

Lascelles, David and Dale, Barry, *Total Quality Improvement*, IFS Publications, Bedford, 1990

Murphy, J. A., *Quality in Practice*, Gill & MacMillan, Dublin, 1986

Oakland, John S., *Total Quality Management*, Heinemann, Oxford, 1989

Price, Frank, *Right Every Time*, Gower, Aldershot, 1989

Robson, M., *Quality Circles*, 2nd edn, Gower, Aldershot, 1988

10 The environment

Eric Cowell

Anyone who tries to analyse the business implications of environmental issues learns that targets are constantly moving. New topics emerge: today's standards are a foretaste of tougher standards tomorrow. Yesterday's complacency has a nasty habit of becoming tomorrow's headache.

The pursuit of environmental excellence is no longer an option for industry. It is a precondition for business success. Increasingly, the public and governmental agencies want to know what industry is doing, what the implications are, and what can be done to ensure that industry's operations are environmentally acceptable.

Environmental awareness has increased and become internationalized, scientifically based and politicized. Political parties scramble to 'outgreen' their rivals in a bid to retain or win the support of electorates. Few of the environmental issues which arouse concern are new. What is new is the public demand for action. Hardly a day now passes without media discussion and reporting of global climate warming, depletion of the ozone layer, hazardous substances, and so on. The Green Consumer movement is creating a demand for environmentally friendly products and the emergence of 'environmentally sound investment opportunities'. There is a corresponding increase in 'community right to know' legislation, legislation on transboundary waste shipment and labelling, and pressure to encourage 'environmental audit programmes' by industry.

THE NATURE OF ENVIRONMENTAL ISSUES

Environmental issues may be local, regional, national or global. They may impinge on society immediately, or be long term and difficult to assess in terms of cost and commercial effects.

Global concerns include the so-called greenhouse effect, in which climate warming from increased atmoshpheric carbon dioxide is thought to be occurring, due to the burning of fossil fuels, deforestation and other influences. The consequences include significant alterations in patterns of land use and agricultural productivity, together with resultant phenomena such as, for example, the melting of polar ice and rise in sea level. The greenhouse effect could also cause important political upheavals and affect the world's commercial climate markedly over the next twenty to fifty years.

By contrast, changes in global stratospheric ozone and the phenomenon of the hole in the ozone layer could have immediate implications owing to the increased penetration of ultraviolet light. Some skin cancer in man is attributable to ultraviolet damage. The causes of the phenomena are linked principally to releases of chlorofluorocarbons (CFCs) into the atmosphere. Global action to reduce these releases is already occurring. There are particular implications for the energy and chemical industries.

Another matter of international concern is acid rain, which results from sulphur dioxide and nitrogen oxides as products of fossil fuel burning. Legislative stringency is tightening on combustion emissions.

International argument has also been focused on toxic substances, toxic products and the disposal of toxic waste. The legislative framework is complex: compliance at all levels demands cradle-to-grave responsibility and liability for rectification of poor practice in the past (no matter how acceptable it was at the time).

Regional problems include contamination of groundwater, and the need to ensure future sources of potable and industrial supplies. The technical difficulties of cleaning up contaminated aquifers are formidable and costly, particularly where restoration to drinking quality is demanded. This problem is already occurring in a number of countries (notably the UK, US, Canada and Australia).

One matter, local or regional in nature, which is the subject of growing international study and skilled co-ordination, is that of the rights of indigenous people to preserve their own environment. In many cases, this problem is inextricably bound to their cultures (including religion), their economy and life-style.

There is global debate about some matters which are essentially regional in character. These include: loss of tropical rain forest and other widespread deforestation; regional as well as global climatic change; local erosion; loss of resources for indigenous people; and dwindling timber supplies. Concerns of this kind are founded on good science, and increasing attention is being given to industrial development as a component of the problem. Future industrial operations must be conducted to minimize harmful impact.

Local environmental issues are individual in character, relating to local geography, the perception and priorities of society and the nature of the operation. Dealing with local problems can be time-consuming and costly.

PUBLIC PERCEPTIONS

Environmental awareness in society is often well founded. Public perceptions of risk, however, are frequently out of phase with real risks. Political acitivity and legislative and regulatory regimes are often in advance of scientific understanding. Green politics, green consumers, green products, green investment are all becoming everyday catchphrases, reflecting growing public demands for good industrial practice. The concept of 'sustainable growth' put forward by the UN Special Commission on the Environment has taken root and all of the UN agencies are modifying their programmes to a co-ordinated sustainable growth approach.

Consideration for the environment has cost burdens for industry; it causes delays to projects, and affects the legislative and regulatory climate. Environmental issues must now become an integrated component of all forward planning.

INTERNATIONALIZATION

The trend for the environmental legislation of developed nations to be cascaded out into developing nations continues at an accelerated rate. It is in part driven by political moves to remove the hidden trade barriers created by the cost of regulatory compliance in the developed nations. The late 1980s saw international action on CFCs and the ozone layer, and the initiation of necessary legislative preparatory work for protecting the earth from the greenhouse effect. Moves to impose differential taxes to reduce carbon dioxide emissions to the atmosphere have been tabled in the EC and are on the OECD agenda. The environment lobby is now part of the establishment – professional, media-sustained, political and internationalized. Much of the concern expressed by society is irrational (also driven by the media and politically sustained), but the basis of concern arises from the genuine perception that *man's harmful effects on the environment are no longer acceptable.*

While most environmental topics are complex, political expediency often drives governments to legislate and regulate in advance of scientific understanding. For example, the EC nations are introducing legislation to control acid rain by reducing sulphur dioxide emissions; yet scientists still cannot give any assurance that this will reduce the problem quantitatively, or that cost effective programmes have been devised.

Such measures result in increased capital expenditure and operating costs, which reduces the competitive position of the regulated industry against its counterparts in other less stringently regulated regions. As a consequence, environmental zeal can erect invisible trade barriers and trigger political activity, regionally and internationally, to encourage the laxer nations to adopt tighter standards.

Industrialists cannot expect that their operations in underdeveloped regions can be undertaken with laxer standards than those required in the developed world. Acceptance of lower standards would expose industrialists to the risk of future penalties, heavy capital burdens, tarnished reputations and perhaps, in some cases, the need to return to the site of former activity to clean up the mess.

Clearly, industry must participate positively in the debate on a scientific and technical basis. A thorough understanding of the overall industrial problem, its perception by the public and its local, national, international and political nuances is very necessary. Without that understanding, influence on future political events will be minimal. A high profile in the organizations influencing the resolution of these matters must be initiated and maintained, either individually or collectively, through trade associations.

MAJOR ISSUES

The greenhouse effect

The question of the greenhouse effect is driven by scientific evidence and theoretical extrapolations suggesting that man's burning of fossil fuels has increased atmospheric carbon dioxide levels to a degree which (in conjunction with other trace greenhouse gases such as methane) has triggered a progressive climatic change. There are serious implications for agriculture, crop viability, disease control and for agricultural economies. The implications for developing nations may be profound. The long-term political and economic consequences may be far-reaching. For example, not only could sea levels rise as a result of melting polar ice caps, but also the grain belt could shift northwards, producing political re-grouping relating to international trade in grain supplies and national dependencies. The greenhouse effect is compounded by the release of carbon dioxide from deforestation, the production of methane in waste dumps, and methane emissions from ruminant animals (for example, cattle and sheep). The matter is complex, but scientific opinion seems to be agreed that global climate warming is happening.

Industry may have a role in slowing down, stabilizing and alleviating the problem. In the longer term (15–25 years), however, possible changes in political power balances, global ecological changes and world commercial and trading patterns need to be considered carefully. The issue is being taken seriously by governments and by the UN organizations and sections of industry.

Ozone depletion

Chlorofluorocarbon compounds are greenhouse gases in their own right, but of greater concern is the part they play in the depletion of the ozone in the stratosphere. The so-called hole in the ozone layer, recently detected over the Antarctic, has been verified and also observed over Southern Australia and over the Arctic. The issue has led to global anxiety about the increase in ultraviolet radiation reaching the earth's surface, setting off a chain of effects on living organisms including increase in skin cancer in man. Action on global reductions of CFCs is internationalized through the Montreal Protocol of 1987 (a major achievement of United Nations Economic Programme [UNEP]) but international initiatives have started to press for more stringent controls to prevent further modifications of the ozone layer.

Acid rain

Acid rain has been identified throughout Europe and North America, and now in India, Asia and elsewhere. The symptoms include damage to fish populations in lakes and rivers and alleged damage to coniferous forests in Scandinavia, Germany and the UK. The complex atmospheric processes created by emissions of sulphur dioxide, nitrogen oxides and other materials are imperfectly understood. The relationship between emissions and depositions is only now becoming clear and no consensus exists in the scientific community on the extent of actions needed to mitigate the effects. However, the costs may be signficant in terms of fuel quality and formulation. Fuels such as coal will be increasingly costly, especially if carbon taxes are imposed.

Toxic materials

There is international concern over the toxic and hazardous nature of many of the materials used in processing and manufacture, and of many of society's waste products and the methods used in their disposal. In most respects the issues are local (for example, waste disposal sites in individual locations), but the perceptions of the risks are international. Serious efforts are now being made to control transnational shipments of toxic waste materials. The issue is compounded by public misconceptions of risk and bad industrial practice reported in the media.

The public is erroneously convinced that environmental exposure to, or ingestion of, industrial products has triggered a cancer epidemic and other adverse health effects in man, and are the cause of similar effects in fish and other organisms. Problems can be attributed to a small number of man-made materials (e.g. DDT, Aldrin, Dieldrin, Lindane and intermediate compounds used in the manufacture of vynilchloride), but these are relatively rare and must be set against the benefits of these products. Political response to protect society from these perceived hazards is producing a plethora of costly and often unnecessary legislation and regulation. Many countries demand toxicity testing protocols prior to manufacture and marketing (e.g. US, UK, Europe). More than fifty countries now have toxic substances legislation and control programmes. Companies find themselves exposed to liability and litigation. There is even a growing trend for chief executives to be made liable; in the US, senior management have suffered personal fines and even prison sentences resulting from unsafe products, or the marketing of products without adequate information to ensure that their customers can take correct action to prevent environmental harm or damage to human health.

There is commercial opportunity in providing product data to the public. Conversely, the cost of testing new products to meet legislative requirements may preclude their development for a small market.

Toxic waste disposal

Anxiety about the hazards caused by disposal of toxic waste is growing. The perception of risk is, for the most part, far higher than the reality. The protection of groundwater from contamination is an important part of the concern and vigorous legislative action is being taken in an ever-increasing number of countries.

The transnational boundary movement of toxic wastes to keep the backyard clean has also become a genuine source of worry. The problem is compounded by changing disposal standards. Methods acceptable in the past are unacceptable for new waste. There is also an increasing trend to investigate and clean up long-closed waste disposal sites. Also, international moves are going ahead to assist developing nations in coping with toxic waste problems.

Industry has 'cradle-to-grave' responsibility for the consequences of its toxic waste disposal. In the US the retrospective clean-up of past practice has resulted in huge programmes, using funds raised by taxing industry. This so-called superfund now stands at over ten billion US dollars.

At the time of writing, attempts to bring the superfund concept into Europe through organizations such as OECD and the International Chamber of Commerce (ICC), and, more directly, through the European Commission, have failed. *There is no room, however, for complacency.* Every violation of legal and ethical codes which receives coverage in the media leads to a hardening of public attitudes. The developing situation opens up the prospect of legal battles of a nature not hitherto seen in Europe.

The best approach lies with active participation in trade association programmes. In immediate terms, it is essential that exposure to legal liability from toxic waste disposal is not purchased with business expansion through acquisitions. Current disposal methods merit thorough review. Particular attention must be paid to waste disposal procedures during site closures, abandonments and rehabilitation.

REGIONAL ISSUES

Many environmental concerns are primarily regional, either because of cultural divisions or, more often, because the target for the damage (for example, the rain forest) is regionally distributed.

Groundwater

In some countries groundwater is only a localized problem but others depend heavily upon subterranean sources (especially aquifers). During the last decade, contamination has been detected in widely scattered locations. Substances found vary from materials used in agriculture (for example, nitrates, pesticides and herbicides) to solvents, cleaning fluids and leachates from toxic waste disposal. Some of the contaminants are known to be toxic; others are carcinogens. Contaminated groundwater is already a serious problem in the US, Holland and Germany, and is rapidly reaching a similar status in other EC countries, including the UK, and in Canada and Australia. Clean-up costs are high, and often the water quality goals are not attainable.

Tropical rain forest

The tropical rain forests of Asia, Africa and South America are vanishing at an alarming rate, and this directly affects global environmental issues such as climatic change, extinction of species (and, therefore, loss of gene material), loss of natural medical material, erosion, desertification and consequent famine. The rain forests are valued for ecological diversity, genetic variability, water and soil conservation, control of erosion, climate regulation (both locally and globally), wildlife (often used as food by the indigenous people) and, of course, for their timber.

These forests figure prominently in the programmes of international environmental groups such as, the World Wildlife Fund, Friends of the Earth and Greenpeace. In 1988 the World Bank took the initiative to ensure that its funds for development do not damage the rain forest ecosystem. World pressure is growing to save what is left of the forests, and any industrial operation conducted in rain forest areas will be under close international surveillance by a variety of environmental organizations skilled in communicating and lobbying. Environmental protection management on a world-wide basis must be given top priority.

Wilderness

'Wilderness' has been adopted as a term to describe pristine areas on which man has had no influence. However, this notion is fundamentally flawed since man has an effect on every part of the globe. Nevertheless, the term does have strong emotional appeal. Industrial operations in wilderness areas can be very costly in terms of meeting punitive environmental protection regulations. Parts of the world now designated as wilderness include large tracts of Australia, some of the world's deserts and, of course, the whole continent of Antarctica and large areas of the Arctic.

Indigenous rights

The question of indigenous rights may be regional, national or local. The subject ranges from land and mineral rights to cultural uniqueness and religion. Recently the environment of indigenous people has itself become a point of serious debate. The destruction of habitat may effect the independence of indigenous groups through species loss, cultural deprivation or, in the worst cases, the elimination of distinct ethnic groups.

Owing to cultural diversity, the social nature of the problems embodied in indigenous rights is unique. The fight to regain these rights is political and well orchestrated. In South America national groups, themselves having failed to gain recognition by governments, are, with outside help, forming powerful lobbying groups both within individual countries and internationally. Another significant factor is that indigenous people, through self-motivation, have proved capable of co-ordinating their own efforts. International support is being made available to them through environmental groups who are also effective lobbyists and activists. Care must be taken to understand the significance of particular sites for some indigenous peoples and the implications of development of these sites in terms of cultural and spiritual values. Also, the national and state laws of some countries are in conflict with the interests of indigenous people. In such countries it is important to make every effort to minimize damage to indigenous land and life-style and to monitor any effects that are unavoidable.

Local matters

Local environmental matters are complex, highly emotional and enmeshed with vested interests and local politics. The reasons for local objection to a development will vary: health hazards from toxic or radio-active waste, the despoliation of a favourite view, smell, nuisance, and so forth. These problems are extremely difficult to deal with.

THE 'ENVIRONMENT MOVEMENT'

The influence of the environmental lobby is increasing through its mastery of communications and, in the more responsible organizations, through scientific understanding of the subjects. As this lobby has becomes more vociferous, 'green politics' has emerged. Green parties and ecology parties can have greater influence than their elected representation. In the UK the main political groups are striving to look 'greener', and green politics is on the increase in Europe. The phenomenon is a direct response to a public perception of government inertia.

The environmental movement in the UK rivals the trade unions numerically and has become the largest sectional interest. Membership of conservation bodies and pressure groups rose from 1.8 million to around five million during the 1980s. Trade union membership declined over the same period, from 12.1 million in 1980 to under nine million. In 1990 the annual income of green organizations in the UK alone was £190 million, and increasing.

The significance of these trends cannot be ignored in political, consumer and economic terms, for they indicate that the movement now has a capability to mobilize the public, raise money, protect its interests and influence perceptions. The British market has been slow to recognize the fact that the old perceived opposition between environment and the economy no longer exists. Successful firms will woo the green consumer not with green paint but with green action. *The Green Consumer Guide* sold 250 000 copies in the UK alone.

MANAGEMENT OF ENVIRONMENTAL PROTECTION

There can be no doubt that management is responsible for dealing with environmental issues. The chief executive is the person ultimately accountable.

Every company, no matter what the nature of its business must have an environmental policy that is clearly stated and understood by every employee. The environmental policy statement may in itself be a simple document but, to ensure its implementation, it requires the support of management, statements of principle, action programmes and organizational arrangements.

Every business is unique. The supporting programmes to ensure that its environmental policy is not just a paper exercise require careful preparation to suit the particular operations for which they are intended. The commitment to protect the environment must be, and must be seen to be, both sincere and factual.

Environment issues are complex. Dealing with them requires professionalism from experts either in-house or hired in an advisory capacity. In today's world nothing less than a professional approach is acceptable. It is as necessary as accountancy, production and a marketing strategy. It is an integral part of the management function.

Every business should identify the consequences of its operations, in terms of the local environment and for their possible global effect. And every company must have an environmental programme, with management and organizational arrangements that ensure compliance with its clearly stated policy.

Some form of analysis and monitoring must be instituted to back up this policy. This practice might range in scale from a simple look at resource usage in the offices (paper wastage and so on), through energy consumption in the company's premises, buildings and operations, to the monitoring of effluent, emissions to atmosphere and ecological evaluations of complex manufacturing processes or resource (e.g. mineral) extraction. Other important factors are the environmental impact of the company's products (in the hands of the user *and* after subsequent disposal) and environmental risk analysis of accident possibilities (during either operations or transportation).

Most multinational corporations have learned that strong environmental departments, supported by good environmental science, are a cost-effective necessity. Many smaller companies are beginning to recognize that environmental protection is the biggest constraint on their development.

The delegation of environmental responsibility throughout business organizations must be real and formalized, with written job descriptions incorporating the expected roles. Every employee should be aware of the person he or she answers to for environmental matters. Open lines of communication are vital, to ensure that perceived problems can be referred at once to the relevant level of management for action.

In recent years the environmental audit has become a common tool in evaluating environmental aspects of operations. The audit should use the stated policy and programmes as a yardstick for measuring future performance. Those conducting the audit should be alert for any organizational weakness, new or emerging problems and compliance with legislation and regulatory requirements. The complexity of the audit will depend on the nature of the operation. It may take only a few hours in the case of a small company, or may be a continuous process in a multinational corporation. The key is regular, routine environmental evaluation.

Lessons for industry

- Environmental issues are growing in their effects on industry and this growth can be expected to continue
- Environmental issues are probably now the biggest constraint to the development of infrastructure and industry
- The environment must be one of the most important considerations in any long-term and short-term planning
- Environmentalism is becoming increasingly institutionalized and political, and playing a significant part in government organization and planning
- Industry must be prepared to be involved at all levels, including scientific research, risk evaluation and education
- Industrial response must be based on sound science and technology
- Businesses should incorporate environmental assessment and costs into the economics of all activites from beginning to end. These considerations should take into account the short-and long-term environmental aspects, including ultimate closure and abandonment
- All acquisitions should be subjected to environmental analysis
- Some long-term issues will affect the market-place
- Public perception of environmental performance is likely to be an increasing component of customer preference
- Environmental challenges can present business opportunities, once the effort has been made to solve the main problems (for example, in renewable energy resources, forestry, alternative fuels, and so forth)
- No environmental issue can be ignored.

FURTHER READING

Commission of the European Community, *The State of the Environment in the European Community*, Commission of the European Community, Luxembourg, 1987

Elkington, John, *The Green Consumer Guide*, Gollancz, London, 1988

Holdgate, L., et al, *The World Environment*, a report by the United Nations Environment Programme (UNEP), Tycooly, Dublin 1982

IPCC, *Reports of IPCC Working Groups I and II*, IPCC, Geneva, 1989

Lean, Geoffrey, Hinrichsen, Don and Markham, Adam, *WWF Atlas of the Environment*, Arrow Books, London, 1990

Organization for Economic Cooperation and Development, *Environmental Data Compendium 1989*, OECD, Paris

Our Common Future, Report of the World Commission on Environment and Development, Oxford University Press, Oxford, 1987

United Nations Economic Programme, *Environment Auditing*, UNEP Technical Report Series No 2, UNEP, Paris, 1989

World Health Organization, *Management of Hazardous Waste*, WHO, Compenhagen, 1983

Part Two

FINANCIAL MANAGEMENT

11 Sources of finance

Stephen Badger

In theory three sources of wealth are available to a company – land, labour and capital. These are not wholly interchangeable, but to some extent the balance in any given company can be changed by the entrepreneur; land can be turned into capital by sale and leaseback (see Long-term facilities, below) or a given process can be made more capital-intensive and so generally require less labour (or vice versa). These decisions are within the scope of management, one of whose functions is to optimize the balance between the different factors of production. The first step before raising capital is, therefore, to ensure that it is really financial capital that is required.

WHY CAPITAL MAY BE REQUIRED

Capital is required to finance the conduct of the business. When a manufacturing business is first established, for instance, factory and office premises will be needed and plant and machinery and transport vehicles. These can either be bought outright or hired; in the first case the expenditure represents captial permanently invested in the business (for the second, see Medium-term facilities, below). In addition funds will be required to finance production from the initial purchase of raw materials until the sale of the finished product to an external purchaser, to pay wages and to meet overheads: these funds are known as working or revolving capital. As the business expands, fresh injections of both permanent and working capital will be required. If, on the contrary, it contracts (or is merely run more efficiently) capital will be freed for alternative uses. When the original fixed assets need replacing, more expenditure will be needed. This should have been adequately provided out of profits by depreciation provisions over the life of the assets, but in times of inflation there may well be a shortfall which will need an injection of new captial.

Capital may also be required for acquisitions.

TYPE OF CAPITAL REQUIRED

Capital is conventionally described as short-term, medium-term or long-term. The distinctions are not rigid, but short-term capital may be regarded as any liability repayable within one year; medium-term as being repayable between one and ten years in the future; and everything else as being long-term capital (this covers both the proprietor's ordinary risk capital, or equity, and long-term borrowings, or debt capital). In general, working capital requirements should be financed by short-term capital and capital permanently invested in the business should be long-term. Medium-term capital is useful to give added flexibility and balance to the overall financial structure: if a project is expected to generate sufficient cash flow to repay the initial investment within, say, seven years, medium-term financing may be appropriate.

This chapter deals primarily with sources of long-term finance (both debt and equity) but sources of short- and medium-term finance are considered in outline.

SOURCES OF LONG-TERM FINANCE FOR UNLISTED COMPANIES

The types of finance available to a company that is not listed on a stock exchange are much the same as those for one that is. The difference in the two situations is that the unlisted company is restricted to a much narrower range of sources, since many potential lenders or shareholders will be unwilling to put up funds if their investment is unlisted and so not marketable. In addition, if the company is private in the legal sense it is not permitted to make any invitation to the public to subscribe for shares or debentures.

In the first place, an unlisted company may rely on the permanent capital put up by its promoter and his friends and relations, supplemented by bank borrowings. But in due course, if the company expands faster than retained earnings by themselves allow, there will come a time when these individuals are unable to find all the funds required; or they may wish to realize part of their investment. If the company has not yet reached a stage where a public flotation is appropriate, it should be possible to find one or more institutions to put up more capital (consisting either of ordinary shares or a mixture of ordinary and loan capital) on the basis that a flotation will take place within a few years so that the institutions will then be able to realize their investment if they wish. There are a number of specialist institutions providing this kind of finance, such as 3i PLC, which is owned by the Bank of England and the UK clearing banks. The merchant banks are also active in this field, and insurance companies, pension funds and investment trusts may participate in a placing if the company is large enough.

In addition the wish of the UK government in recent years to encourage the entrepreneur has combined with an increasing appreciation of the profitability of investment made early in a company's life to produce a flourishing venture capital market. There has been a wide proliferation of institutions willing to provide both venture capital in start-up situations and what is sometimes referred to as mezzanine capital at a rather later stage. An example is Equity Capital for Industry, a body originally set up to channel institutional funds into industry, which now concentrates almost exclusively on venture capital situations. Most banks now have a venture capital subsidiary and a considerable number of other funds are active in this area, some specializing in high technology and others operating more generally. Private capital is also tapped for this purpose by Business Expansion Scheme funds, which take advantage of the legislation allowing the cost of such investments to be charged for tax purposes, and so appeal to investors with high tax rates.

Substantial funds are also available for what are referred to as management buyouts (MBOs). These are situations where, for instance, a company is willing to dispose of one or more subsidiaries and the existing subsidiary management is willing or even eager to take it over. The managers will put up a relatively small amount of capital with the bulk of it coming from institutions, usually in a mix of ordinary shares, preference shares and loan capital (see Types of security, below). But the institutions are prepared to give the management a financial incentive and thus the finance is structured so as to maximize their equity investment so long as they succeed in increasing profits. A number of MBO's have shown very good rates of return and therefore the range of institutions prepared to invest in them has increased. Syndicates have also been set up commanding large amounts of funds so that decisions can be made quickly by the syndicate leaders: there have been examples in the UK of MBOs running into many hundreds of millions of pounds, and in the USA the amounts are very much larger again. Some of the smaller privatizations carried through by the government have also involved a sort of MBO, with a high percentage of all employees being encouraged to put up at least a small amount of capital – The National Freight Corporation is one of the best examples of this.

Investments in unlisted companies (whether tiny start-ups or large MBOs) all tend to be unmarketable. There will come a time when some or all of the investors in any circumstances will need to realize their capital. At this stage the company may be taken over by another one or it may go public on the Stock Exchange.

GOING PUBLIC

Obtaining a listing on the Stock Exchange is a most important step in any company's development. But there is a total of nearly 900 000 companies registered in Great Britain, of which the vast majority are private companies (in the legal sense) with only 2 200 listed on the Stock Exchange. Many companies will therefore never reach a stage at which a listing is appropriate, or their proprietors may for various reasons not wish to seek a listing; taking in new shareholders provides an additional source of capital, but at the same time involves added responsibilities towards those shareholders typified by the Stock Exchange's requirements on disclosure. The interests of 'outside' shareholders may at times differ from those of 'family' shareholders and the future management of the company must reflect the new spread of interests represented.

The reasons for going public are usually among the following:

1   To make the shares marketable and hence more valuable
2   To diversify the family investment holdings and so to reduce the degree of risk
3   To provide funds to meet eventual tax liabilities when necessary
4   To make acquisitions of other companies for shares practicable
5   To raise new funds once the resources of the existing shareholders cease to be adequate.

This chapter is concerned with the last of these, but it is important to realize that going public does not necessarily involve raising new money for the company – the shares sold to the public are often existing shares being sold on behalf of existing shareholders.

To go public on the Stock Exchange a company must either join the Unlisted Securities Market (the USM) or else obtain a full listing. The USM caters for smaller companies – entrants do not need to wait until they can show a three-year record, advertising requirements are less and only 10 per cent of the capital need be made available to the public, often in a placing. It therefore appeals particularly to newer high technology companies which may well command a high rating. Even so, a high proportion of the money raised is often consumed by the expenses of issue. Substantial companies will tend to apply for a full listing straightaway and the mechanism used for this is usually an offer for sale. To give an idea of scale, gross issues on the USM in 1989 were £767 million and in 1990 only £364 million, whereas it can be seen from Figure 11.2 that total corporate issues of ordinary shares are typically about £3 billion.

The offer for sale will be made by a merchant bank or a firm of issuing brokers. The offer will be underwritten so that the money is available even if sufficient public subscriptions are not forthcoming. But it is most important for the company's future capital-raising ability that the issue should be successful, which means that it should be fully subscribed, that the shares should open at a premium and that a free after-market should be maintained. To achieve this it is essential that the company should have continuity of good management and attractive prospects and that large shareholders should not continue selling frequent blocks of shares once the offer for sale is complete. The amount of money that can be raised initially will depend primarily on the present and future profit levels of the company and hence on its ability to pay reasonable dividends on the increased capital: the figures can range from a million pounds to hundreds of millions depending on the size of the company.

SOURCES OF LONG-TERM FINANCE FOR LISTED COMPANIES

Once a company has taken the important step of going public it can seek to raise funds from the whole range of investors, both private and institutional, without restriction.

Historically, private investors have tended to an increasing extent to channel their equity investments through life assurance policies, pension schemes and unit trust purchases rather than making direct investments in securities them- selves. Figure 11.1 illustrates this by showing, for recent years, selected uses of funds by the personal sector and by financial institutions (other than the banking sector). This shows that there has been a steady net divestment of corporate securities by individuals, whereas financial institutions have been substantial net purchasers.

In 1986 and 1987 the growth of life assurance and pension funds slackened while there was a surge of private investment in company securities, reflecting the buoyant stock market conditions and, more importantly, the appeal of the UK government's privatization programme. In 1988, following the stock market slump, the pattern reverted to the more normal picture. All in all, any company wishing to raise funds will try to issue the sort of security that will appeal to institutional investors: that is insurance companies, pension funds and investment trusts.

Figure 11.2 shows some of the ways in which companies have in fact raised finance over the same period. Bank lending is seen to play a very important role, since banks are the first (and often the cheapest) source of finance to which all companies turn. Even more important in the overall picture are internally gener-

YEAR	PERSONAL USES OF FUNDS		USES OF FUNDS BY INSTITUTIONS		
	Investment in company securities £m	Life assurance and pension funds £m	Ordinary shares £m	Other corporate securities £m	Land, property and ground rents £m
1981	− 1 648	13 270	2 540	276	2 328
1982	− 2 525	13 996	2 707	502	2 136
1983	− 634	16 622	2 347	489	1 630
1984	− 4 506	18 523	4 479	748	1 829
1985	− 3 617	18 973	7 065	1 120	1 336
1986	− 3 336	21 029	7 784	1 770	1 132
1987	− 4 189	21 716	14 328	2 231	484
1988	− 11 048	22 344	8 454	3 486	1 779
1989	− 16 111	30 546	5 086	4 445	2 087
1990	− 8 285	31 316	11 404	1 520	1 142

Figure 11.1   Uses of funds by individuals and institutions (CSO Financial Statistics)

YEAR	BANK BORROWING £m	OTHER LOANS AND MORTGAGES £m	UK CORPORATE ISSUES £m		OTHER ISSUES £m
			Ordinary shares	Fixed interest	
1981	5 487	618	1 660	738	− 34
1982	6 563	768	1 033	245	− 43
1983	1 618	749	1 872	608	− 46
1984	7 300	596	1 127	249	298
1985	7 454	874	3 522	816	770
1986	9 095	858	5 483	2 500	1 088
1987	12 141	2 862	13 409	3 590	2 192
1988	31 124	3 691	4 352	3 586	2 482
1989	33 327	6 355	1 882	5 648	7 706
1990	18 903	5 834	2 640	3 471	5 698

Figure 11.2   Selected sources of capital funds of industrial and commercial companies
(CSO Financial Statistics)

ated funds: the amounts in Figure 11.2 must be viewed in the perspective of a total figure for undistributed income adjusted for unremitted profits of £28 222 million in 1990.

Types of security

The types of security usually issued are the following:

1 Ordinary shares
2 Preference shares
3 Debentures, secured either by a floating charge or a specific mortgage
4 Unsecured loan stocks
5 Unsecured loan stocks with conversion rights or warrants attached
6 Foreign-currency bonds.

Ordinary shares

These represent the equity or risk capital in a business. They entitle their holders to a share of the profits by way of dividend only to the extent that the directors think fit. Thus if the business prospers its ordinary shares may become very valuable, but if it declines they may become valueless. Ordinary shareholders are also usually entitled to control the company's activities by voting at general meetings.

Preference shares

Preference shares carry the right to receive a fixed dividend in every year that the company makes a sufficient profit, but to no further participation unless they are specifically participating preference shares. They may in some cases be redeemable at a fixed future time or at the company's option and they can also be issued on the basis that they are convertible in a specified ratio into ordinary shares of the company, but they will normally only carry full voting rights in special circumstances. Preference shares became relatively unpopular after the tax changes introduced by the Finance Act 1965, but more recently they have been more used as a way of increasing the capital base without diluting the interests of ordinary shareholders.

Debentures and loan stocks

The other types of capital are generically referred to as loan capital, which may be either secured or unsecured. It can be seen from Figure 11.2 that the use of these instruments has picked up in recent years but still represents a small proportion overall.

A debenture, according to s 455 of the Companies Act 1948, includes debenture stock, bonds and any other securities of a company whether constituting a charge on the assets of the company or not; but in stock exchange parlance the expression debenture normally means a secured stock, while unsecured loan stock is used to refer to a stock which is not secured. This is the terminology used here.

Unlike shareholders, holders of a debenture or unsecured loan stock are not members of a company, simply its creditors. They are therefore entitled merely to receive the agreed rate of interest (which is normally paid semi-annually) and to receive repayment of capital on final maturity. Their rights will be incorporated in the trust deed constituting the stock which will be made between the company and (usually) a trustee on behalf of the stockholders. It is a requirement of the Stock Exchange that there must be such a trustee if the stock is to be listed; the trustee will normally be one of the insurance companies or investment trusts which specialize in this type of work.

Investors in fixed-interest stocks have historically required a long life to final maturity. In fact, most stocks issued in the London market have a term of twenty to twenty-five years, although some medium-term issues have been seen. There is usually a period of five years before final maturity when the company can repay the stock without penalty and the average life of the stock may be reduced by the operation of a sinking fund. Since the creditworthiness of a company, and even the nature of its business, can change materially over an interval of this length the trust deed constituting the stock will impose certain restrictions on the company. These will vary from case to case, but they may include limitations on such things as disposing of more than a certain proportion of the business, changing the nature of the business and giving security. An unsecured loan stock deed issued domestically will also probably contain a permanent limit on the overall borrowings of the company and its subsidaries and a separate limit on secured borrowings and the borrowings of UK subsidiaries. A debenture deed will not impose a continuing limit but will require the presence of a certain level of cover in terms both of income and of assets before any further issue of another tranche of the stock can be made. In general, debenture stock holders, since their claims are supported by security, will require rather less in terms of restrictions than the holders of an unsecured loan stock who merely rank alongside trade and other unsecured creditors. But in either case the trustee will have the power to declare the stock immediately repayable if interest is not paid or if the company defaults on certain other obligations.

Convertible and warrant stocks

These stocks are a compromise between borrowing and equity. A convertible is an unsecured loan stock which initially merely carries a fixed rate of interest but which, on specified dates or within a specified period, may be converted, at the option of the holder, into ordinary shares of the company at a fixed ratio. Warrant stocks are stocks which are not convertible but which are issued together with warrants which entitle the holder to subscribe for ordinary shares of the company at specified times and at a specified price. Convertible stocks have been popular for a long time, but warrant stocks have never really become familiar in the UK domestic market.

The advantage to a company of issuing convertible stock is that for the initial period it can service the stock at a lower rate of interest than would be necessary for a stock that was not convertible, that when it is finally converted the effective price of issuing the resultant shares will be higher than it could have been initially, and that in the interval the interest payments (unlike ordinary dividends) will have been an allowable expense for tax purposes. A warrant stock gives the company a long-term borrowing (at a lower rate of interest than a simple borrowing), and when the warrants are exercised there is a further inflow of cash into the company. Both kinds of stock will impose the same sort of restrictions on the company as an ordinary unsecured loan stock with additional provisions to protect the holders' rights to convert or exercise their warrant rights.

Foreign-currency bonds

Only the largest companies will want long-term loans in foreign currencies. In the great majority of cases, the UK market will be amply sufficient as a source of capital and in general it is unwise to incur a foreign-currency liability unless one has corresponding assets in that currency. Moreover, only the largest companies would be well enough known to attract the interest of foreign lenders. However, in the 1960s a substantial international capital market developed in Eurodollars (US dollars deposited outside the USA, but not necessarily in Europe, and so not subject to any national restrictions on capital flows). A large number of US, and a smaller number of European, companies have taken advantage of this to raise quoted Eurodollar loans (both fixed interest and convertible) and there have also been issues in Deutschmarks, French and Swiss francs, Eurosterling and artificial units such as the European unit of account. Unlike domestic issues, Eurobond issues usually have a life to final maturity of not more than fifteen – and in some cases as little as five – years. With the abolition of exchange control in the UK the dividing line between domestic and Euro issues in sterling became blurred and, indeed, current trends suggest that large companies may find it most convenient to raise long-term funds on an unsecured basis in the Eurosterling market.

METHODS OF ISSUE WITH A LISTING

The four chief methods of making an issue for cash on the Stock Exchange are:

1 Offer for sale
2 Rights issue
3 Open offer
4 Placing.

Offer for sale

In this case all members of the public are invited to subscribe for the issue by advertisements inserted in the press. The offer is usually made at a fixed price. Sometimes an offer for sale by tender is used where only a minimum price is fixed and applicants decide themselves how much they are willing to pay; a striking price is then fixed at a level at which the issue will be fully subscribed and the shares issued at that price to all applicants who applied at that price or above. In either case, only a fixed number of shares are available for issue and, if a greater number of applications is received, each application is scaled down proportionately. Priority is sometimes given to existing shareholders or employees who are sent special application forms.

An offer for sale is normally used when a company goes public for the first time, as described earlier. It may also be used in an issue of loan capital where the amount of capital required is very large or where it is necessary to appeal to a particularly wide circle of investors for some other reason. In most cases, however, a placing is preferred because of its speed and simplicity (see below). By comparison, an offer for sale involves significantly larger advertising and administrative costs.

Rights issue

In a rights issue new ordinary shares or other securities are offered to existing shareholders of the company pro rata to their holdings. Shareholders can then choose between taking up their entitlement (their rights) by subscribing the set amount per share, or they can sell some or all of their rights in the market if these are quoted at a premium. If they choose to sell, they of course receive money rather than paying it out, but their percentage holding in the company is reduced so that in theory the effect is the same as if they had sold some of their existing shares. From the company's point of view the subscription money will still be received from the purchaser of the rights.

It is a requirement of a listing on the Stock Exchange that new equity shares (or other securities involving an element of equity) should only be issued for cash to existing shareholders of the company in proportion to their holdings (unless they consent otherwise in general meeting), and this has now been given wider application by the Companies Act 1980. As a result, issues of ordinary shares or convertible stocks are normally made by way of rights so that shareholders have the opportunity of maintaining their proportionate stake in the company.

Open offer

An open offer is an offer of loan capital restricted to shareholders (and possibly the holders of loan capital) of the company making the issue. However, the offer is not made pro rata to their holdings. Each shareholder can apply for as much stock as he wishes or for none; if more applications are received than stock is being issued, each application will be scaled down proportionately. This method of issue is relatively infrequent, but it may be used if it is thought that the stock being issued may attract a large premium and the benefit of this should accrue to shareholders. It is appropriate only where the company has a large number of shareholders, but in that case the effect is very similar to an offer for sale but without the attendant advertising costs.

Placing

In a placing, stock is offered direct to a relatively small number of large institutional investors who are the principal holders of fixed interest stock; it is, therefore, a quick and effective method of issue which allows the most precise pricing. Placing for an unlisted company was considered under Sources of Long-term Finance. Stock exchange permission must be obtained for a placing with a listing and it is a condition of such permission that a proportion of the stock should be available publicly in the market. As already noted, a placing of new equity issued for cash is only possible with shareholders' consent but, because of its simplicity, placing has become the most usual method of raising loan capital for UK companies.

Underwriting and expenses of an issue

Once a company has decided that it needs money, it will clearly wish to be assured of that money as soon as possible, come what may. Rather than making an issue itself it will, therefore, go to a merchant bank or issuing broker who, in addition to advising on the documentation and terms of the issue, will arrange for it to be underwritten; that is, the issuing house will undertake to subscribe or find subscribers for the issue on the terms fixed in so far as it is not fully subscribed by the public or shareholders as the case may be. In return for accepting the risk and for its overall co-ordinating work on the issue, the issuing house normally charges a total commission of 2 per cent, 1¼ per cent of which is passed on to the sub-underwriters, that is the institutions who agree to take up different amounts of the issue pro rata to the extent that it is not fully subscribed. In the case of a placing, however, the stock is placed directly with a number of the same institutions. Accordingly, no sub-underwriting commission is required and only a placing commission of perhaps ¾ per cent (varying with the size of the issue) is payable; however, the issue terms will be slightly worse so that the net proceeds receivable by the company will be much the same. The administrative costs of an issue are small by comparison, especially in a placing.

OTHER METHODS OF SUPPLEMENTING CASH FLOW

The main methods of raising long-term capital with a listing have now been outlined. It remains to consider briefly the various other possible methods of supplementing cash flow, which are of course open to quoted and unquoted companies alike. Some of these can provide relatively long-term finance, but the majority are short-term.

Long-term facilities

These include mortgages, sale and leaseback transactions, and public authority and specialist institution lending. The main sources of mortgage and sale and leaseback finance are the insurance companies and pension funds. In the case of a mortgage loan, a single lender will advance up to two-thirds of the value of a building for a specified term on the specific security of that building – the borrower retains the ownership of the building but his rights are subject to a mortgage charge for the term of the loan. In a sale and leaseback transaction he will actually sell the building (and so forfeit any appreciation in value) in return for a capital sum and at the same time lease the building back for his own use from the purchasing institution for a long period at a specified rent. Other sources of relatively long-term facilities include the Department of Industry (for specified purposes in development areas and in accordance with such schemes as may be in effect from time to time), local authorities where employment is being created in their areas, and various specialist organizations.

Medium-term facilities

These include leasing, hire-purchase, project finance and term loans.

Leasing and hire-purchase are most appropriate for items such as vehicles, plant, machinery and office equipment. In leasing, the ownership of the item remains with the lessor, but the lessee is entitled to the use of it for a specified term in return for regular payments under the lease. A tax-based lease may be particularly attractive to a company with no immediate liability to taxation. In a hire-purchase transaction the purchase price of the item and interest thereon is paid in instalments over a set period, at the end of which ownership of the item does pass to the hirer. There are a large number of finance houses which specialize in these activities.

Similarly, merchant and other banks may undertake to arrange finance for a specific project. This will involve tapping a number of different sources of finance in accordance with the cash flow requirements of the individual project and is a particularly flexible form of financing.

Finally, banks sometimes engage in term lending for periods up to five or even ten years. A term loan could come from a single bank or it might be syndicated among a number of different banks. It might be at a fixed rate of interest, but it will more usually be on a roll-over basis; that is, with interest fixed periodically at the prevailing rate. In the latter case it is also possible to arrange for drawings to be made in different currencies at different times.

Export finance

The UK Government (in common with governments of other major industrial countries) assists UK exporters to finance their contracts with overseas buyers by running an export credit programme which has two purposes: first, to provide insurance against political and commercial risks which may effect performance and payment under export contract; and second, to ensure that the terms of any credit offered to overseas buyers of UK goods and services can be made as attractive as possible. The banking system plays a crucial role as provider of funds and of specialist export finance advisory services. The official UK export credit authority providing insurance guarantees and a level of financial subsidy is the Export Credits Guarantee Department (ECGD) which operates as an autonomous government department with a direct reporting line to the Secretary of State for Trade.

Typical export funding structures

With ECGD support, finance can be made available in several different forms. For short-term transactions a supplier can insure 90 – 95 per cent of his receivables with ECGD and assign the proceeds of his insurance policy to a bank, thereby enabling him to obtain finance from his bank on attractive terms. For transactions attracting medium-term credit (usually the supply of capital goods), the structure is more complex so as to reduce the impact of deferred payments on the exporter's balance sheet. Under a medium-term supplier credit structure, the supplier would insure deferred contract receivables, evidenced by Bills or Notes accepted/issued by the buyer, with ECGD. Under a bank facility, the supplier would then be able to sell the Bills or Notes to his bank, who, in turn, is entitled to a 100 per cent unconditional guarantee from ECGD. ECGD has the right of recourse to the exporter in the event that the bank guarantee is called but the exporter may offset the recourse liability against his ability to claim up to 90 – 95 per cent under his insurance policy. Under this structure, therefore, the supplier carries a continuing residual 5 – 10 per cent financial risk on the buyer throughout the credit period. For larger sized contracts and major investment projects, the more usual structure is a 'buyer's credit', under which the supplier enters into what is essentially a cash contract. Instead of taking out insurance cover for deferred payments, the supplier is paid by means of disbursements from a loan made available by a bank to the foreign buyer. ECGD provides a 100 per cent unconditional guarantee for the principal and interest due under this loan. ECGD is entitled to take recourse on the supplier in the event of a claim by the bank under the guarantee only in circumstances where the UK supplier is in default under his contract. Although opinions differ on the real extent of this resource burden (much of the onus of proof of the contractual default lies with ECGD), suppliers would generally agree that they would have no continuing financial risk throughout the credit period as would be the case under a medium-term supplier credit.

The terms available for support of UK export finance transactions vary from straightforward commercial funding for short-term transactions to officially supported interest rates. For transactions involving a credit period of more than two years, the UK authorities acting through ECGD make it possible for exporters to offer the minimum fixed rates permitted by the international consensus on export credit terms subscribed to by OECD member countries. For particular projects in selected markets, it may be possible to obtain even finer 'soft' terms under the 'Aid and Trade' programme administered by the Overseas Development Administration and the Department for Trade and Industry. In cases where an officially supported fixed rate is to be offered to a borrower in connection with a medium-term credit, ECGD agrees with the banks providing the funds that they will receive 'interest make-up' to provide them with:

- the difference (if any) between the fixed rate and the cost of funds
- a margin over the cost of funds.

The cost of interest rate support provided by the UK authorities has continued to give rise to concern in recent years, despite a reduction in the overall cost of the scheme due to an increasing alignment between OECD minimum rates and market interest rates. Increasing attention is thus being given to funding medium-term credits from purely commercial financial sources.

If it is thought that finance will be required in connection with an export order, it is advisable to contact a merchant/clearing bank as well as ECGD sooner rather than later in view of the wide range of financing options which may need to be considered and the difficulties which can be encountered in obtaining ECGD support after a firm contract has been struck.

Short-term facilities

These include bank overdrafts and loans, bank acceptance credits, bills of exchange, trade credit, invoice discounting and factoring. Of these, bank over-drafts and loans are the most common and are used universally by companies as Figure 11.2 shows. They may be supplemented by acceptance credits, where a bank undertakes to accept approved bills of exchange up to a certain limit so that the bills can be discounted at the finest rates. Alternatively, bills of exchange can be used as a form of trade credit, whether or not discounted with a bank or discount house, or various arrangements may be made between buyers and suppliers as to the length of credit given in payment for goods. Finally, invoice discounting and factoring are undertaken by various specialist institutions. Invoice discounting means financing the collection of specific invoices (at the risk of the selling company). Factoring involves making immediate payment against invoiced debts which are then normally collected at the factor's own risk for an appropriate charge. All these methods have in common that they finance relatively small revolving trade transactions, but in aggregate they provide the finance for a vast amount of business on a continuing basis.

Current trends

The willingness of lenders to lend for long periods will depend on their being able to foresee a reasonable rate of return in real terms. In times of high inflation there is, therefore, a reluctance to tie up funds in this way except at rates so high as to be unacceptable to many borrowers. Equally, companies may prefer to borrow for relatively short periods in the hope of being able to refinance their obligations later at a lower rate. For these reasons, there has been a considerable shift over the years away from long-term issues to more flexible short-term borrowing. This has been encouraged by the greater availability of bank credit following the new monetary policy adopted by the Bank of England from 1971 onwards in its new approach to competition and credit control.

The banking market has been very competitive and in many cases lending margins have shrunk drastically. The banks have also been active in devising new products to appeal to their customers who are now offered note issuance facilities (nifs) and revolving underwriting facilities (rufs) to supplement the staid over-draft. There is also an active market in swaps both for currencies and interest rates which allow a company to optimize its own position by benefiting from the countervailing position of another party. More recently still, the UK commercial paper market has been inaugurated, thus allowing companies to obtain funds outside the banking system. It must be said, however, that many of these instruments are suitable only for the larger listed company and have little relevance for many finance directors.

LOOKING AT THE OVERALL CAPITAL STRUCTURE

We have now outlined the chief avenues open to a company wishing to raise new capital. Before raising any new capital a company should consider what the capital is needed for, whether it is permanent or likely to be repaid out of cash flow within a period and what rate of return it is likely to earn. One can then go on to decide how it can best be supplied. For instance in the case of an investment with a high degree of risk the best source of finance is likely to be equity (or risk) capital; but, if it is a relatively risk-free long-term investment, loan capital may be more appropriate. If it is a specific project of medium-term duration, project finance should be considered, while if it is a working capital requirement, bank overdraft facilities are likely to be the answer. In all cases the various methods of supplementing cash flow in other ways must be borne in mind so as to minimize the amount of new capital actually required. Finally, the rate of return must be set against the cost of the capital to ensure that an adequate margin exists to justify the investment.

One of the most important considerations is to preserve a proper balance between debt and equity in the company's financial structure. This relationship is described as the company's financial gearing; if the company's source of income is reasonably stable and assured (such as the rental income of a property investment company) it is safe for it to be highly geared, but if it is operating in a cyclical industry (such as machine tools) it is prudent to keep the gearing (that is, the element of borrowing) at a low level, for interest on borrowings has to be paid in adverse as well as favourable times and if a temporary setback combined with high interest charges results in the company making a loss, its overall status will suffer. The degree of gearing will depend both on the absolute amount of borrowing and the extent to which any of this borrowing is at fluctuating interest rates that may rise faster than the company's income. In inflationary times, borrowing at a fixed cost can be most advantageous to a company. But the closer the company gets to what is thought to be an unduly high level of borrowings, the more reluctant lenders will be to provide new funds and the more the equity interest of existing shareholders will be endangered.

The object of company financial management should be to see that the company has adequate funds at the lowest cost consonant with all these factors and so to seek to maximize its earnings for ordinary shareholders.

FURTHER READING

Admission of Securities to Listing, Stock Exchange, London, 1984 edition, with subsequent amendments

Brearley, R.A., and Pyle, C., *Bibliography of Finance and Investment*, Elek Books, London, 1973

London Business School, *Bibliography of Financial Markets*, LBS Library, London, 1987

Merrett, Howe and Newbould, *Equity Issues and the London Capital Market*, Longman, London, 1967

'New Capital Issues Statistics', *Midland Bank Review*, commentary published annually in spring edition

Ogley, Brian, *Business Finance*, Longman, London, 1981

Reid, Margaret *All-Change in the City*, Macmillan, London, 1988

Royal Commission on the Distribution of Income and Wealth (Diamond Report), Report No. 2 (Cmnd. 6172), HMSO, London, July, 1975

Rutterford and Carter (Eds), *Handbook of Corporate Finance*, Butterworth, 1988

Taylor, T., *The Financing of Industry and Commerce*, Heinemann, London, 1985
'The UK Corporate Bond Market', *Bank of England Quarterly Bulletin*, March, 1981.

The various volumes of evidence given to the Committee to Review the Functioning of Financial Institutions (the Wilson Committee) and published by HMSO may also be of interest.

12 Capital project evaluation

Tessa V Ryder Runton

Evaluating capital investment projects involves estimating their future benefits and comparing these with their costs. Such analysis is appropriate not only to the purchase of long-lived physical assets but also to any capital expenditure with impacts extending into the future (such as long-term contracts for goods and services, marketing expenditure, disinvestment by sale, mergers and plant closures).

Elements necessary to effective capital project planning are:

1 Access to the appropriate information
2 Knowledge of the company's required financial return
3 Realistic evaluation of project cash inflows and outflows
4 Analysis of these cash flows with respect to their timing
5 Evaluation by senior management of the strategic implications of large projects
6 A well-defined approval procedure
7 Consistency with strategic planning and budgeting procedures
8 A review procedure.

GOALS OF CAPITAL PROJECT EVALUATION AND PLANNING

Required rate of return: standards and the cost of capital

Cost of capital is an important standard of comparison used in financial analysis and is a vital company statistic needing careful calculation. The return on capital resources must equal or exceed the cost of that capital. Although zero or negative returns are acceptable in special cases, the necessary subsidies may lead to costs in another form.

The realities of commercial life have caused the cost of capital to be a very complex subject. Any comparisons must be made between like numbers. A percentage profit before tax made on a hotel in Bermuda bears no relationship to the same figure made after tax on a farm in Scotland. A profit expressed as a percentage of capital employed should not be compared with a discounted cash flow internal rate of return. Many measures of company performance can be devised but these are valuable only to those who are completely familiar with the definitions involved. The appraisal of projected cash flow discounted at a rate equal to a carefully estimated required rate of return leads to fewer pitfalls. In particular, the time-value of money is taken into account, all the financial effects are assessed, and tax and inflation are taken into account in the calculation of the cash flow and the estimation of the cost of capital.

Capital investment analysis aims to discover the financial truth about the plan under investigation. If it does not meet the survival standard of the organization, that fact should be stated clearly before the discussion as to its desirability begins. In practice many apparently unprofitable processes go on in any business because they enhance the profitable activities which, of course, should outnumber them. Obvious examples are the provision of catering and other services for the workforce, advertising, research and so on. It used to be thought that discounted cash flow analysis led to categorical 'yes' or 'no' judgements on any plan; in fact, all it does is marshal the financial facts for the guidance of the decision takers. In addition, it can point to the least unprofitable way of tackling a loss-making but necessary job.

The cost of capital to the firm

Most companies raise funds from many sources – retained earnings, new equity, grants and many forms of loans. The overall cost of capital to the firm is the return it must earn on its assets to meet the requirement of all those providing it with financing. Lenders require interest payments and shareholders expect dividends and capital growth. If, for example, shareholders expect dividends to be at least 8 per cent after tax and annual inflation is 10 per cent, then the minimum required return on the company's present equity and retained earnings is 18 per cent. The required rate of return will depend on the perceived risk. Shares in highly geared companies (borrowing high relative to equity funds) are more vulnerable than average and increased share risk may balance or outweigh low borrowing interest rates (see Franks and Broyles, 1979).

If a company maintains a proportion of debt capital agreed with its lenders, it can compute a *weighted average cost of capital*. For example, if the interest rate on debt is 10 per cent, and the company has 25 per cent debt and 75 per cent equity, the weighted average cost of capital in money terms including 10 per cent average inflation is $(0.25 \times 10 \text{ per cent}) + (0.75 \times 18 \text{ per cent}) = 16 \text{ per cent}$. This cost does not allow for the tax savings from interest payments. This benefit is added separately.

In deciding the appropriate standards for an organization, the marginal cost of capital is a vital guide. In a growing company, new capital will be needed and, therefore, the return on a project of normal risk should be judged against a standard of the weighted average cost of new capital. Companies making investment decisions continuously should use this marginal cost of capital as the standard for all projects with risks normal to the company's business. If a project cannot pass this test, it will diminish the company's value.

Required rates of return on projects

Obviously projects involve differing risks. Some, such as cost-saving investments and lease or buy decisions, are of low risk; others, such as research projects, involve greater than average levels of risk. A company should classify its risk categories for projects and set required returns for each. A large project of risk significantly different from normal can alter the overall character of a company, its cost of capital, its accepted gearing and the returns expected by financiers.

The required rate of return for a project can be significantly different from the weighted average cost of capital for the company. High-risk projects are characterized by high fixed operating expenditure and high revenue variability. These should be expected to earn high rates of return. The exact return required will depend upon a judgement about the level of risk in the project compared with the average risk of the company.

The use of a separate required rate of return for each individual project is most important when the projects are large relative to the company and/or when the projects being considered have long lives. A typical classification scheme, in increasing order of risk is: cost reduction, replacement, scale expansion, new products. The risks of these different types of investment differ, and so should their required returns.

TRADITIONAL TECHNIQUES FOR TESTING VIABILITY

The natural question: 'When do I get my money back?' has often been answered by the traditional technique of adding up the forecast net cash inflow (sometimes the sum of the profit before depreciation from the forecast profit and loss account) year by year until the amount of the original capital investment is reached, thereby giving the years to payback. Such a calculation is inconclusive because standards vary, definitions of the original capital vary, tax is not always deducted and most of the benefits of tax allowances are obscured. The method ignores the *time-value of money*, cannot cope with inflation and takes no account of the later profits, if any. Whether, in fact, any profit is made on the investment is not measured at all. Payback calculations give some guidance in matters of liquidity in which case the cash inflow should be carefully defined and be free of any 'accounting numbers' such as 'tax provision' instead of 'tax payable'. A better payback calculation is the discounted payback, which is computed using the present values of the future cash inflows.

Another traditional technique involves the use of balance sheet ratios for current and proposed operations. These include the ratios of profit to capital employed, of profit to sales, and many others concerning the stock, current assets and liabilities and working capital. These ratios are useful for regulating smooth operations but are unhelpful for judging profitability owing to definition problems and the choice of standards, but mostly because the time-value of money is not included.

One ratio used is the return on capital known as 'the accountant's return' or the 'book rate of return'. An average profit, before or after tax is calculated for a number of years of the proposed project and this is expressed as a percentage of the capital employed. The latter is often defined as the initial investment or the average capital employed over the years, thereby allowing for further investment and depreciation. This procedure suffers from the same snags as the techniques mentioned above and, in addition, smooths out the effect of irregular annual profits. Clearly, quick profits are preferable to a slow build-up, but advantages or disadvantages are obscured.

MODERN TECHNIQUES FOR TESTING VIABILITY

The traditional techniques take no account of the time-value of money. But money received or spent now is more valuable than the same money received or spent later. High inflation magnifies the difference. This is the principal fact used by modern techniques to improve on past methods. Analysis concentrates on the incremental cash flow of a project. The cash flow is discounted at the project's discount rate to the present time, giving a present value. The work involved has increased, but once an analysis discipline has been set up, decision takers can expect that the realities of the given data for some plan will be clearly identified. They can then concentrate on the non-financial problems involved, judge whether the data are sufficient to work with and act accordingly.

The concept of moving money in time using the relevant discount rate is not new. Today's quoted price for benefits to be received in the future can be judged by netting the price, or capital cost, from the present value of the future cash flow. A positive resultant net present value (NPV), if properly calculated, shows that the transaction is financially worthwhile. The value of the transaction can also be assessed by judging its internal rate of return (IRR).

CASH FLOW DISCIPLINE IN CAPITAL PROJECT ANALYSIS

Discounted cash flow techniques use the incremental cash flows resulting from a plan, usually scheduled monthly or annually. Provisions for depreciation are not included, but all working capital and capital expenditures are. Interest payments are part of capital cost and should therefore be included.

Projects create opportunities for cost savings and productivity improvements, not necessarily involving capital costs. What, therefore, is analysed is the total cash flow effect of an opportunity. Consequential items, such as tax savings made on other projects or any other cash effects which would not occur without the project are included. In other words the analysis should predict the net company cash flow difference between undertaking or not undertaking the project.

This analysis must either be made in real terms throughout or in money terms with respect to inflation. If necessary, alterations must be made so that cash flows in real terms are judged against a real terms standard and cash flows in money terms are judged by required return standard in money terms. Tax allowances and loan-servicing schedules are always in money terms, but sales and cost figures are usually forecast in real terms. It is usual for marketing and production departments to schedule sales or costs without allowing for external price changes, but these data must be converted to money terms to allow estimation of taxable profits and taxes. In cases of high inflation forecasts, or different effects on prices and costs, and for lengthy projects, some estimate must be made of the inflation pattern over the life of the project. This estimate could differ for use on prices, on costs and on the overall situation including the cost of capital. All figures must be converted to money terms so that expected tax payments can then be estimated.

It should go without saying that cash flows are forecast after the effects of company taxes when paid. Because tax allowances are normally in money terms, consistent cash flows almost certainly have to be forecast in money terms, unless real terms tax allowances can be calculated. Sometimes it is necessary to consider

Time in years from today	Cash flow $	Discount factor 11%	Present value $
0	(1 500)	1.00	(1 500)
1	100	0.901	90
2	1 000	0.812	812
3	1 000	0.731	731
4	100	0.659	66
		NPV	+$ 199

Figure 12.1   Calculation of net present value (NPV)

any likely future changes in tax structure. In this, as in treating inflation and in all problems of data uncertainties, it is important not to be over-meticulous, particularly at the outset. Analysis of the most roughly prepared cash flow will show whether it is worth spending any further time attending to the details.

NET PRESENT VALUE (NPV) AND INTERNAL RATE OF RETURN (IRR) IN MORE DETAIL

The use of the concept of net present value (NPV)

The net present value (NPV) of a project is the net present value of the net incremental cash flow discounted at the project's required rate of return. A zero NPV shows that the project repays the capital invested plus the minimum acceptable return on the invested capital throughout the project's life. The minimum acceptable return is equal to the opportunity cost of that capital, including a return required for the risk taken by investing in that operation for that period. NPVs show that the minimum return is achieved plus extra value.

Given a discount rate of 11 per cent for a project, the NPV is found as shown in Figure 12.1 Other things being equal, this project looks financially acceptable. One could pay up to $199 more for the opportunity and still not lose. NPV represents the analyst's estimate of the net increase in the value of the company which would accrue from the project. If the discount rate used is the capital market's capitalization rate for the risk of the project, the NPV represents an estimate of the incremental market value of the firm due to the project. The NPV technique thus gives a simple assessment tool, but is inaccurate if there is doubt or dispute as to the correct discount rate.

Tables of discount factors are published but the abbreviated table in Figure 12.2 will be found useful in many cases.

The use of the concept of internal rate of return (IRR)

The internal rate of return (IRR) is also known as the discounted cash flow yield (DCF), the DCF return or the actuarial return. IRR is defined as the breakeven financing rate for the project. This is not to say that the capital released by the project earns such a return. Reinvestments, whether wise or not, should be kept

Year	1%	2%	3%	4%	5%	6%	7%	8%	9%	10%	11%	12%	13%	14%	15%	16%	17%	18%	19%	20%
0	1.000	1.000	1.000	1.000	1.000	1.000	1.000	1.000	1.000	1.000	1.000	1.000	1.000	1.000	1.000	1.000	1.000	1.000	1.000	1.000
1	0.990	0.980	0.971	0.962	0.952	0.943	0.935	0.926	0.917	0.909	0.901	0.893	0.885	0.877	0.870	0.862	0.855	0.848	0.840	0.833
2	0.980	0.961	0.943	0.925	0.907	0.890	0.873	0.857	0.842	0.825	0.812	0.797	0.783	0.770	0.756	0.743	0.731	0.718	0.706	0.694
3	0.971	0.942	0.915	0.889	0.864	0.840	0.816	0.794	0.772	0.751	0.731	0.712	0.693	0.675	0.658	0.641	0.624	0.609	0.593	0.579
4	0.961	0.924	0.889	0.855	0.823	0.792	0.763	0.735	0.708	0.683	0.659	0.636	0.613	0.592	0.572	0.552	0.534	0.516	0.499	0.482
5	0.952	0.906	0.863	0.822	0.784	0.747	0.713	0.681	0.650	0.621	0.594	0.567	0.543	0.519	0.497	0.476	0.456	0.437	0.419	0.402
6	0.942	0.888	0.838	0.790	0.746	0.705	0.666	0.630	0.596	0.565	0.535	0.507	0.480	0.456	0.432	0.410	0.390	0.370	0.352	0.335
7	0.933	0.871	0.813	0.760	0.711	0.665	0.623	0.584	0.547	0.513	0.482	0.452	0.425	0.400	0.376	0.354	0.333	0.314	0.296	0.279
8	0.923	0.854	0.789	0.731	0.677	0.627	0.582	0.540	0.502	0.467	0.434	0.404	0.376	0.351	0.327	0.305	0.284	0.266	0.249	0.233
9	0.914	0.837	0.766	0.703	0.645	0.592	0.544	0.500	0.460	0.424	0.391	0.361	0.333	0.308	0.284	0.263	0.243	0.226	0.209	0.194
10	0.905	0.820	0.744	0.676	0.614	0.558	0.508	0.463	0.422	0.386	0.352	0.322	0.295	0.270	0.247	0.227	0.208	0.191	0.175	0.162
11	0.896	0.804	0.722	0.650	0.585	0.527	0.475	0.429	0.388	0.351	0.317	0.288	0.261	0.237	0.215	0.195	0.178	0.162	0.148	0.135
12	0.887	0.789	0.701	0.625	0.557	0.497	0.444	0.397	0.356	0.319	0.286	0.257	0.231	0.208	0.187	0.169	0.152	0.137	0.124	0.112
13	0.879	0.773	0.681	0.601	0.530	0.469	0.415	0.368	0.326	0.290	0.258	0.229	0.204	0.182	0.163	0.145	0.130	0.116	0.104	0.094
14	0.870	0.758	0.661	0.578	0.505	0.442	0.388	0.341	0.299	0.263	0.232	0.205	0.181	0.160	0.141	0.125	0.111	0.099	0.088	0.078
15	0.861	0.743	0.642	0.555	0.481	0.417	0.362	0.315	0.275	0.239	0.209	0.183	0.160	0.140	0.123	0.108	0.095	0.084	0.074	0.065
16	0.853	0.728	0.623	0.534	0.458	0.394	0.339	0.292	0.252	0.218	0.188	0.163	0.142	0.123	0.107	0.093	0.082	0.071	0.062	0.054
17	0.844	0.714	0.605	0.513	0.436	0.371	0.317	0.270	0.231	0.198	0.170	0.146	0.125	0.108	0.093	0.080	0.069	0.060	0.052	0.045
18	0.836	0.700	0.587	0.494	0.412	0.350	0.296	0.250	0.212	0.180	0.153	0.130	0.111	0.095	0.081	0.069	0.059	0.051	0.044	0.038
19	0.828	0.686	0.570	0.475	0.396	0.331	0.277	0.232	0.195	0.164	0.138	0.116	0.098	0.083	0.070	0.060	0.051	0.043	0.037	0.031
20	0.820	0.673	0.554	0.456	0.377	0.312	0.258	0.215	0.178	0.149	0.124	0.104	0.087	0.073	0.061	0.051	0.043	0.037	0.030	0.026

Figure 12.2 Table of discount factors

Time in years from today	Cash flow (£)	Cash flow discounted at:							
		11 per cent		20 per cent		17 per cent		16 per cent	
		Discount factor	value	factor	value	factor	value	factor	value
0	(1500)	1.000	(1500)	1.000	(1500)	1.000	(1500)	1.000	(1500)
1	100	0.901	90	0.833	82	0.855	86	0.862	86
2	1000	0.812	812	0.694	694	0.731	731	0.743	743
3	1000	0.731	731	0.579	579	0.624	624	0.641	641
4	100	0.659	66	0.482	48	0.534	53	0.522	55
Net present values →			199		(96)		(6)		25

Figure 12.3 Tabulation using trial rates leading to calculation of IRR (the calculation process is described in the text)

separate from the analysis of a project on its own merits. The IRR of a project is judged against the cost of capital standard or the minimum required return.

The IRR equals the discount rate which, when used to discount the net incremental cash flow, gives a net present value of zero. It can be found by carrying out a series of discounting calculations on the table of net cash flows using different discounting rates on a trial and error basis. Some rates will yield positive values and others negative, and the calculations are continued until the rate is narrowed down to that which gives zero, or almost zero NPV. The final result can be found by mathematical interpolation or extrapolation.

An example will show how this procedure applies. Suppose that the cost of capital is 11 per cent, and an investment is being considered which costs £1 500, lasts four years, and has no terminal value. All calculations are tabulated in Figure 12.3. By interpolation between the net present value calculated at 16 per cent and 17 per cent the IRR is found to be:

$$16 + \frac{25}{31} = 16.8 \text{ per cent}$$

The same result is obtained extrapolating from the 17 per cent and 20 per cent:

$$\text{IRR} = 17 - \frac{3 \times 6}{90} = 16.8 \text{ per cent}$$

Interpolation between the 11 per cent and 20 per cent figures, however, gives the answer:

$$11 + \frac{9 \times 199}{295} = 17.1 \text{ per cent}$$

which may be too inaccurate, although in this case the return would probably be quoted at 17 per cent.

The process can be simplified and speeded up using a graph. A few likely discounting rates are tested by calculating net present values from the project cash flow table. The aim is to find two or three rates which give low positive NPVs and two or three more that produce fairly small negative NPVs. These points are plotted on a graph, and when a curve is drawn through them the point at which it cuts the zero axis indicates the IRR rate.

In some cases, such as natural resource projects, which involve large negative cash flows at the end of the project, a special problem arises in using IRR. Projects of this sort can have more than one IRR, some of which may be above the required return and some below. Complex techniques have been developed to salvage the IRR method in these circumstances. These adjustments usually involve procedures similar to the present value approach, and fewer problems will be encountered by the use of the NPV rule in these circumstances.

The use of present value: mid-year discounting

Discount tables are available for all periods – weeks, quarters, years – and to various numbers of places of decimals. It is not normally helpful to calculate the cash flow in too small periods or to discount it using more than four-figure tables. It is more important to notice that the tables usually refer to points of time and the cash flows represent a total for a period. A fitting assumption is needed. It is easy if most receipts and payments occur at the beginning or at the end of the periods. For flows which are continuous and irregular over the periods, the total cash flow is often assumed to arise mid-year. The calculation should therefore be refined. If only annual discount tables are available, the half-year discount factor at r per cent can be calculated from the equation:

$$\text{Discount factor} = \frac{1}{\text{Square root of } (1 + r \text{ expressed as a decimal})}$$

Example

Suppose the investment is bought today and the operation is immediate and continuous. The NPV calculation becomes:

Time from today	Cash flow (£)	Present value at 11 per cent	
		Discount factor	Present value
0	(1 500)	1.000	(1 500)
½	100	0.949	95
1½	1 000	0.901 × 0.949	855
2½	1 000	0.812 × 0.949	770
3½	100	0.731 × 0.949	69
			NPV = 289

The IRR now needs to be recalculated to take account of the refined timing. The IRR is now 21½ per cent because of the earlier cash flow.

The use of present value – optimization of mutually exclusive alternatives

Financial analysts are constantly being asked to advise as to which of two viable alternatives is financially preferable. Such choices include large long-life machinery versus cheaper short-life machinery, labour versus automation, the choice of site, speed of construction, shaft versus open-pit mining, air versus sea transport, and so on; in each case, choice of one excludes the possibility of choosing the other alternative. Use of the net present value calculation is the easiest approach. Suppose that in a company with a cost of capital of 11 per cent the choice is between:

- Method A (which is capital-intensive) showing a NPV of + £1 500; and
- Method B (with a lower capital cost) showing a NPV of + £1 300

If the analyst calculates NPV's using the minimum acceptable return discount rate for the risk of the project, different discount rates might be appropriate to A and B. For example, one method might involve installing a possibly risky unproven technological improvement, whereas the other method would re-equip as before.

The actual question to be answered, since both methods are financially desirable, is whether the expenditure of the extra capital involved on Method A is worthwhile. The incremental investment, which is represented by the difference between the cash flows of the two alternatives (cash flow A and cash flow B, for each period), shows a NPV of + £200 (NPV A − NPV B). It is therefore worth spending the extra money. Where the patterns of the alternative cash flows are very different, the incremental approach avoids problems in comparing projects with different levels of capital expenditure. Indeed, different cash flows can arise from the same total capital invested but the incremental cash flow analysis still gives the financially preferable operational plan.

Use of the DCF/IRR approach is also straightforward but contains a snare for the unwary. The question of whether the incremental investment would be desirable is answered by finding the DCF/IRR on the incremental cash flow (cash flow A minus cash flow B, for each period). If the incremental IRR is greater than the company's minimum acceptable return, then alternative A is financially preferable. When setting out the results, however, an apparent problem frequently arises. For example:

Method		11 per cent NPV	IRR
A	Expensive	+ £1 500	14 per cent
B	Cheaper	+ £1 300	16 per cent
A–B	Incremental investment	+ £200	13 per cent

It looks as though one should choose method B because the IRR is better than that in A. This is an illusion because the capital on which the yield is earned is different in each case. The analysis of the incremental investment points to the same answer whichever method is used. It is often argued that, perhaps, the incremental capital should be spent on some other investment which might show a better return than the 13 per cent here. This could be the case in conditions of severe capital rationing when investments yielding 13 per cent cannot be financed. In other conditions there is no conflict and both investments are desirable. Of course, more than two projects might be available, in which case, several incremental investment choices would be necessary. It is easier simply to compare the NPV's – the most preferable choice has the highest NPV.

Some practitioners approve the calculation of the NPV but find the answer, which is of necessity expressed in currency, difficult to use. The *profitability index* is therefore sometimes used, particularly when projects need to be ranked because budgets are limited. The index is calculated by dividing the present value of the net cash returns by the present value of the net cash investments. In the example shown in Figure 12.3 the profitability index is $1699/1500 = 1.13$ which means that every unit of investment earns 1.13 units of present value in the project. Care must be taken not to confuse this with the IRR which is 17 per cent. In practice many analysts report the profitability of a project both in terms of NPV in currency and of IRR as a percentage to assist understanding.

When mutually exclusive opportunities are being analysed, equal project lives should be compared. This is often difficult, but a three-year life machine can be compared with a five-year machine by assuming that the longer-life machine will be sold at the end of the third year. Alternatively a fifteen-year period can be taken with five three-year machines compared with three five-year machines. The most sensible assumption will be obvious.

Present value and expected value – decision trees

Much of the capital investment planning involves arranging a continuous series of actions which may be altered in the light of future events or future actual patterns of marketing. It is possible to set out likely outcomes in a map known as a decision tree – it grows as it is extended further into the future. NPVs of each likely chain of events can be prepared and this could help the decision that must be taken later. Very often decision-tree calculations are of the expected value of the outcome. To calculate expected values the probabilities of likely intermediate events of outcomes are incorporated. Decision trees have been described extensively. A decision tree is shown in Figure 12.4.

Faced with the need to decide whether or not to install a computer, the possible courses of action or likely events might appear as shown in the figure. The decision taken would depend, financially, on the relative NPVs or expected values of the three good possibilities. Expected values are weighted by the relevant probability; for example, if there is a 60 per cent chance of an NPV of £100 and a 40 per cent chance of an NPV of zero, the expected value is £60.

COMPUTATIONAL RESOURCES

Although computers are invaluable as calculating aids for complex problems they should not be used indiscriminately. The software cost, and the time taken to learn the system and eliminate errors can become disproportionate to the problems

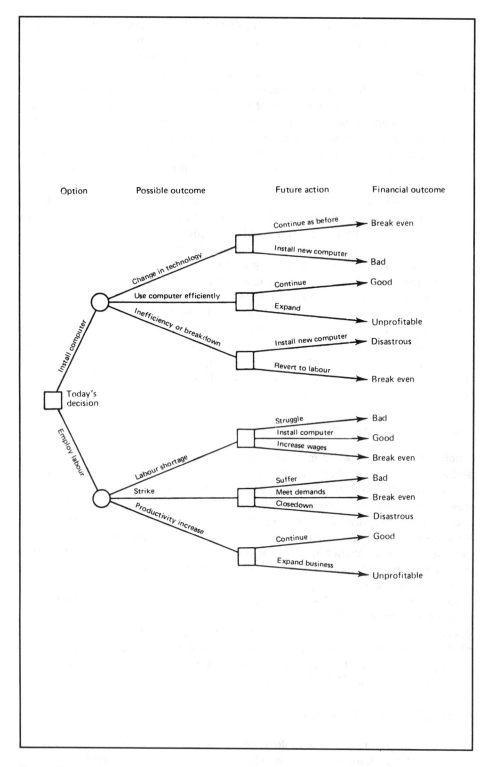

Figure 12.4   A decision tree

being analysed, especially when the user only has to make the calculations on rare occasions. There may be more justification in using a computer system when the user carries out project evaluations regularly and frequently, and is therefore able to become familiar with the software.

For practical purposes small calculators can generally be used for modern analytical methods of project evaluation. It can be useful to start by ruling up and producing photocopies of a simple proforma, the rows and columns of which help to ensure that all elements in cash flow schedules are entered in their correct periods and under their appropriate headings.

Calculation short cuts and standard procedures for all problems are often sought in this field. If, however, they are used without understanding or without necessary adaption to the different circumstances of each case, much more time can easily be wasted than if the problem were initially approached from first principles.

DATA

The collection and sifting of project data normally leads to far more problems than the analysis. This is no reason for allowing less than rigorous analytical techniques. If a quick look at the first set of data indicates a promising idea, it is sensible to re-examine the data before extending the analysis. Data are given, begged, borrowed or stolen, but in spite of (or because of) the uncertainties involved the best way to obtain good understanding leading to better decisions is to establish good communications with the project initiators as a top priority.

A special problem to be tackled is that of inflation, particularly when costs are subject to special pressures leading to price rises greater than the general rate. The analyst will have to take a view as to when it is safe to assume that, on balance, costs and revenues will be similarly inflated.

Missing data – reverse economics

Very often, data are not available for such vital factors as the achievable price for a new product, the size of the reserves in a new oilfield, the time required to obtain safety clearance or planning permission, or the market or technological life period. Reverse economics is the formal technique whereby it is possible to define the achievable or viable range for the missing data. If a graph is drawn of the profitability (NPV or IRR/DCF) of the project against invented values of the missing data, it is possible to find the value that gives the minimum acceptable result. If that value is very unrealistic, it may be possible to conclude that the new product will not be profitable, or that the oilfield cannot be economically exploited in present circumstances. A decision might then be taken to stop any further expenditure on the promotion of the idea. If a project must be killed off or frozen it is far better halted early before reputations become involved.

This technique is also useful when considering the merger, takeover or sale of a company, or its flotation on the public market. An attempt is made to forecast the foreseeable cash flow of the company – possibly including benefits caused by savings in the new managerial context. The difference between the present value of the forecast cash flow and the debt divided by the number of issued shares will give a measure of the acceptability of a quoted or offered price, or will indicate what price to set at the beginning of negotiations. In a takeover situation the buyer should use the incremental required return for the project, that is the required rate of return for the risk of the company being taken over. If the company is quoted, the value of its equity share capital is given in the market-place, unless there are undisclosed facts such as technological advance, or unless the market has anticipated a possible merger. The premium paid should be less than the NPV of the merger benefits.

Uncertain and erroneous data

A good approach to uncertain data is to attempt to identify the range in which the answer may lie. This is sometimes done by adding to the best guess two more guesses, one of which is the most pessimistic and the other the most optimistic. In this way it may be possible to exclude too much subjectivity on the part of the estimator, who might previously have thought that his future depended on the success of his estimates and who therefore, understandably, introduced too much conservatism. In large organizations a chain of conservatism may be introduced. In such cases the analyst must try to assess the realities, and it is helpful if the motivations of the personnel are adjusted so as not to interfere. Overestimating can be as wrong as underestimating and can easily lead to raising too much finance or premature expansion.

Often data are manipulated, either innocently or deliberately, to achieve the desired result – perhaps acceptance of a scheme by head office or of a contract in a tendering competition. The results can lead to public embarrassment, if not disaster. A good review discipline can help to avoid or to sort out such problems.

Once the range in which critical data lie is found, sensitivity analysis can be carried out. Alternatively, a calculation of the likely profit or loss, should everything turn out for the worst, can help in a discussion. If the organization simply cannot survive such a loss and the chances of it are significant, then the project may well have to be forgone.

Sensitivity analysis

This technique can highlight the facts and problems caused by the risks and uncertainties of the plan under discussion. It has limitations but can be carried out with a minimum of calculating aids if necessary. The aim of this analysis is to discover the value of an uncertain variable at which the project is just profitable. Two or three calculations will give the necessary sensitivity curve.

Example of sensitivity analysis

A project is showing a negative net present value at the company's cost of capital rate. What would need to be done to make it profitable? The sensitivity graph is drawn (Figure 12.5) and shows that the operating profit would need to be raised by 10 per cent to give a zero NPV of the net incremental cash flow for the project. All other things are assumed at first to remain constant (capital cost, speed of coming into operation, life of the project, tax, inflation and so on).

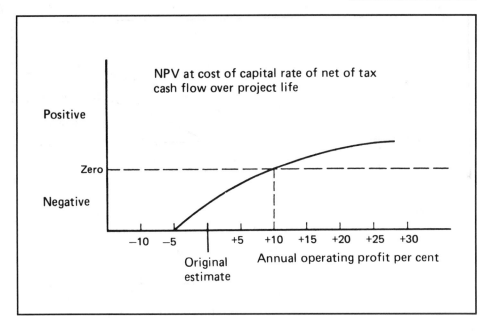

Figure 12.5 Sensitivity of project viability to profit variation

Data which give the desired result:

	Original estimate	Acceptable estimates					
Price per unit (£)	20	21	20	20	20	20	20.3
Volume/number sold	10	10	10.5	10	10	10	10.15
Labour cost (£)	40	40	40	30	40	40	38
Materials cost (£)	50	50	50	50	40	50	47.5
Overhead cost (£)	10	10	10	10	10	0	9.5
Operating profit	100	110	110	110	110	110	111.045

It is thus possible to say that the project would be acceptable if either the price could be raised by 5 per cent, or the volume sold increased by 5 per cent, or if the labour cost could be lowered by 25 per cent, or the materials cost by 20 per cent or the overhead cost by 100 per cent. Another possibility to explore would be if (as shown in the final column) both the price and volume sold could be raised by 1½ per cent at the same time as all costs are reduced by 5 per cent. However, one should try to ensure that joint changes in variables are not contradictory and fit a plausible and consistent scenario. The graph could have been plotted using IRR and the company's required rate of return as the cut-off line, but this involves more sums.

One more uncertainty can be explored to extend the analysis. Suppose, for example, that the market for the product is thought to last ten years but could be

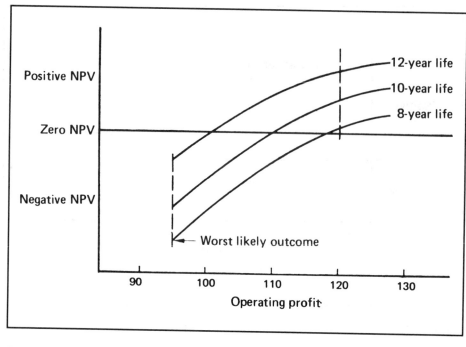

Figure 12.6   Sensitivity analysis graph with two variables

hit by competition in eight to twelve years' time; further calculations give the graph shown in Figure 12.6. Annual operating profit is thought likely to lie between 95 and 120. Assuming the variables examined to be the most critical, the profitability 'envelope' is shown by the two outer curves and the dotted connecting lines. This envelope is divided into two parts by the cut-off line of zero net present value. By inspection of the two areas it is possible to conclude that the project has roughly only a 40 per cent chance of being viable. The worst likely outcome is also shown. The decision may then be taken more easily.

Should the whole envelope be above the cut-off line it would be possible to conclude that the project is profitable in spite of the uncertainty in the variables considered, which are then defined as uncritical. Further effort could then be concentrated on other variables. This technique is limited to two dimensions. It is, however, of great value, even without calculating aids, because of its simplicity in demonstrating the effect of apparently daunting uncertainties.

PROBABILITY ANALYSIS

This is the ideal towards which sensitivity analysis is the first step, but the calculation usually requires the help of a computer. Great efforts are being made by large organizations and consultants to prepare flexible computer programs to conduct probability analyses on a wide variety of projects.

The data required are further examined to discover a range of probabilities for every variable which may lie in each part of the likely range. Subjectivity is not avoided by this, but the further discussion can sometimes help clarify the situa-

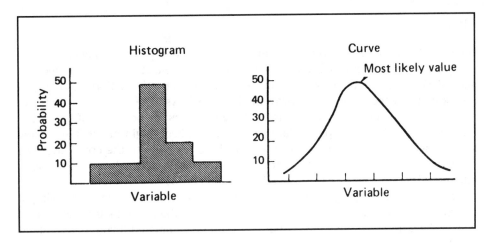

Figure 12.7   Examples of probability distributions

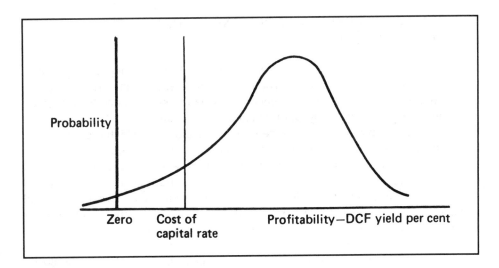

Figure 12.8   A profitability/sensitivity graph

tion. The results could be shown for each variable in a histogram, which is a practical approach to the underlying mathematical curve. An example is shown in Figure 12.7. Mathematical sampling using such data for each significant variable results in the type of profitability/probability graph shown in Figure 12.8. The peak of the curve in Figure 12.8 shows the most likely outcome, but there is a significant chance that the yield might be negative or that the original investment would not be recovered. The area under the curve being taken as unity, the area to the left of the cost of capital or required rate of return cut-off line, if measured, gives the probability of unprofitability. The use of sensitivity and probability analyses does not remove uncertainty and subjectivity of data; it helps decision takers to judge the likelihood of profit or loss in projects.

RISK

Uncertainty of data is not the only unknown bedevilling projects. There are also many possible events which could have a significant effect. Such events include acts of God (earthquake, flood), of governments (tariffs, nationalization), of competitors, of technological improvement. Some risks can be insured against. In every case it is helpful to define the risk and assess its possible effect ('what happens if . . . ?') and in particular when such an effect might occur. If the likely loss caused by risky circumstances were to be disastrous to the company, then perhaps the venture is too risky. There are several ways in which organizations of different kinds can proceed to minimize the effect of risk. Obvious examples are diversification, both geographically and in the nature of the business, the tying of customers or suppliers to long-term contracts, and the cautious introduction of new or different scale business. Other risks can be eliminated through markets in which risk is traded. A surprising variety of risks can be insured against and others, such as commodity price variation and exchange rate variations, can be hedged in future markets.

REAPPRAISAL: EX POST EVALUATION AND CAPITAL EXPENDITURE REVIEWS

It has been said that, without subsequent re-examination, formal planning appraisal techniques are largely counter-productive. *Exante* evaluation – the prior preparation of forecast results – is very necessary when raising finance for a project, either internally or externally, and obtaining the desired go-ahead. There is, however, no certainty that the combined estimates and skills which resulted in the forecasts have been optimized unless a subsequent view is taken.

There are well-established commercial routines whereby periodic (weekly, monthly, quarterly, annual) accounts are compiled of both financial and physical resources used and benefits achieved, and reports are made to relevant technical and financial monitors. Usually the results are compared with annual and three- or five-year plans for the project and for the organization as a whole. Variations are studied and adjustments are made.

Projects which were initially appraised using cash flow disciplines should be reviewed using the same disciplines. If the conclusions drawn differ, speedy action may be desirable or, if it is not, it would be nice to know that it is not.

It is unfortunately necessary to take a cynical look at projects built for less than the forecast cost, sales that noticeably exceed budget, and other such successes. If the planners' faults were not in their stars but in themselves they should remain as underlings. People have gone as far as saying that it is useless to plan at all unless one also reviews the results. But, as always, too much is as bad as too little.

It is not always clear who should conduct reappraisal reviews. Conflicts may be avoided if the project operators undertake the review in the normal course of their duties. It is highly desirable also to include some sort of outside view to ensure a balanced opinion as to why the resulting return differs from that first forecast. The review should, of course, cover all the unquantifiable as well as the measurable aspects. If the organization sets up a separate reviewing team, its members may need great powers of diplomacy as well as of detection and endurance.

FURTHER READING

Franks, J. R. and Broyles, J. E., *Modern Managerial Finance*, Wiley, Chichester, 1979

Merret, A. J. and Sykes, A., *Capital Budgeting and Company Finance*, Longman, London, 1973

Merret, A. J., and Sykes, A., *The Finance of Capital Projects*, 2nd edn, Longman, London, 1973

Mott, Graham, *Investment Appraisal for Managers*, Gower, Aldershot, 1987

13 The annual accounts

W P Ridley

Anyone interested in the management of a company, whether taking an active part or merely investing capital, needs to have financial information of two kinds concerning the company:

1 Where the capital is invested (shown in the balance sheet)
2 The return earned from the investment (shown in the profit and loss account).

Those in active management can call for financial reports and accounts to be designed according to their own requirements. But, for investors and others, forms of balance sheet and profit and loss account have been laid down by Acts of Parliament. This chapter starts by describing the formal requirements, and then proceeds to discuss other aspects of the accounts, including the interpretation of accounts in order to judge a company's financial performance.

ACCOUNTING REQUIREMENTS OF THE COMPANIES ACTS

The form of the published accounts and directors' report is largely set by the Companies Acts 1948 – 1983, although subsequent Acts have made certain amendments. The Acts set out what must be included in the profit and loss account, balance sheet and directors' report (including notes). Company accounts based on this selected information are termed the statutory accounts.

Growth of information required

The information required for the statutory accounts has grown enormously during the past sixty years, owing to pressure from investors and the general public. The pressure from investors for more information has grown with their increasing separation from management in industry and commerce. This separation has led to a need for investors to learn as much as possible of the state of the companies, in order to assess the security of their investment. The general public, which in this connection includes creditors and potential investors, are concerned to know how companies are being managed, and whether they are financially sound. (This demand for information becomes especially apparent when public confidence in company administration has been shaken by a well-publicized fraud). Successive governments have responded to these pressures in their legislation.

The government itself may wish to have more information made public if it feels that this will have a beneficial effect upon industry or commerce as a whole. Thus the publication of export figures by each company, for example, can have the effect of increasing emphasis on overseas sales and thereby stimulating trade. As a result, the successive Companies Acts tend to set increasingly stringent requirements for company disclosure while accounting standards are continually being tightened to achieve uniformity in reporting.

STANDARD PRESENTATION

While there are some variations allowed in presentation, Figure 13.1 shows the information required in a profit and loss account. Specifically, the object is to show:

1 Operating income
2 Investment income – splitting income from associated companies from other income
3 Income from ordinary activities set out separately from extraordinary income, charges or tax.

In addition, other information has to be given either in the accounts or in a statement attached to the accounts:

1 The directors' remuneration must be given, either in the accounts or in a statement attached to the accounts. All directors' remuneration and past directors' pensions, paid by the company or by any other person, either for their services as directors or for services in other capacities, must be shown. The statements or accounts must show any compensation paid by the company or any other person to past or present directors for loss of office. In addition, the statement must show the number of directors who have waived their rights to emoluments and the aggregate amount that has been waived. The chairman's emoluments must be shown separately, and also those of the highest-paid director if these are in excess of the chairman's emoluments.
    The remuneration of directors must be shown by giving the numbers of directors falling within successive bands of £5 000; that is, the number of directors whose emoluments do not exceed £5 000, the number whose emoluments exceed £5 000 but not £10 000, and so on. For each of these items the term emoluments does not include contributions paid by the company for the benefit of directors under any pension scheme
2 Auditors' remuneration
3 Amount set aside for redemption of share capital and loans
4 Turnover with analysis by geographical market
5 The average number of staff (by category) to be given with the aggregate amount of wages, social security costs and pension costs incurred.

Taxation items The more detailed requirements about disclosure of taxation items are covered by the layout shown in Figure 13.2.

1 Turnover
2 Cost of sales (*a*)
3 Gross profit or loss
4 Distribution costs (*a*)
5 Administrative expenses (*a*)
6 Other operating income
7 Income from shares in group companies
8 Income from shares in related companies
9 Income from other fixed asset investments (*b*)
10 Other interest receivable and similar income (*b*)
11 Amounts written off investments
12 Interest payable and similar charges (*c*)
13 Tax on profit or loss on ordinary activities
14 Profit or loss on ordinary activities after taxation
15 Extraordinary income
16 Extraordinary charges
17 Extraordinary profit or loss
18 Tax on extraordinary profit or loss
19 Other taxes not shown under the above items
20 Profit or loss for the financial year

Notes

(*a*) *Cost of sales: distribution costs: administrative expenses*

These items shall be stated after taking into account
any necessary provisions for depreciation or diminution
in value of assets

(*b*) *Income from other fixed asset investments: other interest
receivable and similar income*

Income and interest derived from group companies shall
be shown separately from income and interest derived
from other sources

(*c*) *Interest payable and similar charges*

The amount payable to group companies shall be shown
separately

(*d*) The amount of any provisions for depreciation and
diminution in value of tangible and intangible fixed
assets shall be disclosed in a note to the accounts

Figure 13.1   Profit and loss account format

Taxation based on profits for the year:

Corporation tax at 35%(including £   [previous
year £] transferred to deferred taxation) on
profits excluding those of associates   x   x

Less relief for overseas taxation   x   x

    x   x

Overseas taxation   x   x

Prior-year adjustments   x   x

Tax on share of profits of associates   x   x

Total tax charge   —   —

Note : No provision has been made for tax, deferment of which is
reasonably certain for the foreseeable future.

Figure 13.2   Presentation of taxation details

The balance sheet

Figure 13.3 provides a format for a company's balance sheet, together with the notes which relate to the corresponding figures shown in the table. The principles of valuation are also set out.

1 Fixed assets   The amount to be included in respect of a firm's fixed assets is normally the amount of their purchase price or production cost less provisions for depreciation. Similiar principles shall be applied where goodwill or development costs (only rarely to be treated as an asset) are given balance sheet values.

For fixed assets shown at valuations (typically property), the year in which the valuations were made must be disclosed. The names or qualifications of the valuers and the basis of valuation that they used must be given for fixed asset valuations made during the last financial year.

Freehold land must be shown separately from leasehold land, and land held on a long lease (one having not less than fifty years to run) must be distinguished from that held on a short lease (having less than fifty years to run).

There must also be shown (i) the aggregate amount of fixed assets acquired during the year: and (ii) the book value at the date of the last balance sheet of fixed assets disposed of during the year.

If the detail to be disclosed is considerable it might best be given on a statement attached to the accounts, making reference to it in the balance sheet

2 *Current assets*   Current assets shall normally be valued at production cost or purchase price (which may be calculated on last-in first-out price, first-in last-

ASSETS

A   Called up share capital not paid (*a*)

B   Fixed assets

    I   Intangible assets
         1 Development costs
         2 Concessions, patents, licences, trade marks and similar rights and assets (*b*)
         3 Goodwill (*c*)
         4 Payments on account

    II   Tangible assets
         1 Land and buildings
         2 Plant and machinery
         3 Fixtures, fittings, tools and equipment
         4 Payments on account and assets in course of construction

    III   Investments
         1 Shares in group companies
         2 Loans to group companies
         3 Shares in related companies
         4 Loans to related companies
         5 Other investments other than loans
         6 Other loans
         7 Own shares (*d*)

C   Current assets

    I   Stocks
         1 Raw materials and consumables
         2 Work in progress
         3 Finished goods and goods for resale
         4 Payments on account
    II   Debtors (*e*)
         1 Trade debtors
         2 Amounts owed by group companies
         3 Amounts owed by related companies
         4 Other debtors
         5 Called up share capital not paid (*a*)
         6 Prepayments and accrued income (*f*)

    III   Investments
         1 Shares in group companies
         2 Own shares (*d*)
         3 Other investments

    IV   Cash at bank and in hand

D   Prepayments and accrued income (*f*)

LIABILITIES

A   Capital and reserves

    1   Called up share capital (*k*)

    II   Share premium account

    III   Revaluation reserve

Figure 13.3   Balance sheet format

IV Other reserves
1 Capital redemption reserve
2 Reserve for own shares
3 Reserves provided for by the articles of association
4 Other reserves
V Profit and loss account

B Provisions for liabilities and charges
1 Pensions and similar obligations
2 Taxation including deferred taxation
3 Other provisions

C Creditors (*l*)
1 Debenture loans (*g*)
2 Bank loans and overdraft
3 Payments received on account (*h*)
4 Trade creditors
5 Bills of exchange payable
6 Amounts owed to group companies
7 Amounts owned to related companies
8 Other creditors including taxation and social security (*i*)
9 Accruals and deferred income (*j*)

D Accruals and deferred income (*j*)

Notes
(*a*) This item may either be shown as one of the two lines marked (*a*) under the heading of Assets or as Item AI under Liabilities
(*b*) Amounts in respect of assets shall only be included in a company's balance sheet under this item if either
  (i) the assets were acquired for valuable consideration and are not required to be shown under goodwill; or
  (ii) the assets in question were created by the company itself
(*c*) Amounts representing goodwill shall only be included to the extent that the goodwill was acquired for valuable consideration, or where its value has been agreed by the auditors
(*d*) The nominal value of the shares held shall be shown separately
(*e*) The amount falling due after more than one year shall be shown separately for each item included under debtors
(*f*) This item may be shown in an alternative position
(*g*) The amount of any convertible loans shall be shown separately
(*h*) Payments received on account of orders shall be shown for each of these items in so far as they are not shown as deductions from stocks
(*i*) Other creditors including taxation and social security. The amount for creditors in respect of taxation and social security shall be shown separately from the amount for other creditors
(*j*) Accruals and deferred income. The two positions given for this item are alternatives
(*k*) Called up share capital. The amount of allotted share capital and the amount of called up share capital which has been paid up shall be shown separately
(*l*) Creditors. Amounts falling due within one year and after one year shall be shown separately for each of these items and their aggregate shall be shown separately for all of these items

Figure 13.3 Balance sheet format (concluded)

out price, or average weighted price). However, the net realizable value will be substituted when this is expected to be below cost

Items requiring disclosure

Other matters to be disclosed in the published accounts (by notes if not otherwise shown) include:

1 The corresponding figures for the preceding year
2 The nature and amount or estimated amount, or any contingent liabilities not provided for; financial commitments (including pensions); charges given for other companies
3 The amount or estimated amount of any contracts for capital expenditure, so far as not provided for, and of any capital expenditure authorized by the directors but not yet contracted for
4 The bases on which foreign currencies have been converted into sterling
5 Any special circumstances affecting the company's taxation liability for the current or succeeding financial years
6 The number of employees (other than directors of the company) whose emoluments for the year (from the company, its subsidiaries or any other person in respect of services to the company or its subsidiaries): exceeded £30 000 but did not exceed £35 000; exceeded £35 000 but did not exceed £40 000; and so on in successive integral multiples of £5 000
7 Information concerning each of the company's subsidiaries
8 Similar information – normally capital reserves or profit or loss for the year:

   • where the company holds equity shares in another company (other than a subsidiary) exceeding one-tenth of the nominal value of the issued equity capital of that other company; or
   • where the company holds shares in another company (other than a subsidiary) which, in the investing company's balance sheet, are shown at an amount exceeding one-tenth of the investing company's assets (as stated in its balance sheet)

9 If a subsidiary, the name and country of incorporation of its ultimate holding company
10 Allotments of shares during the year; outstanding options; amount of redeemable shares; debentures issued, redeemed and the amount that can be re-issued. In addition, any financial assistance given by a company for purchase of the company's shares shall be noted
11 Dividends recommended; any fixed cumulative dividend in arrear
12 Reserves and provisions at the beginning and end of the year, together with any material movements. Any revaluation reserve should be shown separately
13 The amount of any provision for taxation other than deferred taxation shall be stated.

THE DIRECTORS' REPORT

The directors' report must accompany the balance sheet and profit and loss account filed with the Registrar of Companies, and must be sent to all members of the company, debenture holders and other interested parties.

The report, which is presented by the board of directors, contains much relevant information concerning a company's activities and the minimum contents, summarized below, have been considerably extended. It should be especially noted that these minimum contents are required by legislation and are not subject to directors' choice any more than the information contained in the statutory accounts.

Minimum contents of directors' report

Review

A review of the company's affairs during the period covered by the accounts: particulars of important events that have occurred since the year end; likely future developments; an indication of research and development activities.

Dividends

The amount(s) recommended to be paid by way of dividend.

Reserves

The amount(s) proposed to be transferred to reserves.

Activities

The principal activities of the company and significant changes in these activities.

Directors

The names of all directors who acted in such a capacity at any time during the period under review.

Changes in fixed assets

Significant changes in the company's fixed assets. If the market value of land is substantially different from the value shown in the balance sheet, an indication of the difference in value.

Contracts

Contracts with the company (except service contracts) in which a director of the company has an interest; the parties to the contract, the director involved, the nature of the contract, and the nature of the director's interest must be specified.

Arrangements between company and directors

Any arrangement whereby the directors are able to obtain benefits by the acquisition of shares or debentures in the company or any other body corporate.

Directors' interests

Directors' interests (at the beginning and end of each year) in shares or debentures of the company. This requirement is extended to include the directors' spouses and infant children (the directors' 'family interests')

Matters showing the state of the company's affairs

Particulars of any matter required for an appreciation by its members of the state of the company's affairs so long as, in the opinion of the directors, the publication of such information would not be harmful to the company.

Relative profitability of different activities

Turnover and profit or loss of each class of business carried on by the company, if such classes differ substantially.

Persons employed

The average number of persons employed in the UK by the company (on a weekly basis) during the year, and the aggregate remuneration paid or payable to such persons in respect of that year. This information is not required where a company has fewer than one hundred employees.

Political and charitable contributions

The amount of contributions, if exceeding £50, given for political or charitable purposes, and the identity of the political party concerned.

Exports

The turnover from exports when the value exceeds £50 000, and a note where no goods are exported.

Previous year

The corresponding amounts in each section for the immediately preceding year.

Employment policy

The arrangements for health, safety and welfare at work and for involvement in the business. Provisions for employment of disabled persons.

YEAR TO 31 MARCH 1991	
	£m
Trading surplus (before depreciation)	1.4
Less: Depreciation	0.4
Pre-interest profits	1.0
Less: Interest	0.3
Pre-tax profits	0.7
Less· Tax	0.3
Available to shareholders	0.4

Figure 13.4   Abbreviated profit and loss account of Pangloss PLC

JUDGING A COMPANY FROM ITS ACCOUNTS

Reports by a company to its shareholders are regulated in detail by law. As a result, outside assessments of the financial standing of a company are almost inevitably based on the information given in these reports (normally issued annually) rather than on other publications of the company or on its trade reputation. Increasingly, it is being realized that this outside assessment is important to the company – in raising finance, whether by loan or equity, in merger discussions with other companies, or in trading negotiations. It is, therefore, advisable for senior company executives to consider in detail the standards against which their company's financial performance – as set out in the fully audited report to shareholders – will be judged.

PROFIT AND LOSS ACCOUNT FOR PANGLOSS PLC

This chapter takes the abridged accounts of a company called Pangloss PLC to highlight information on which a financial examination is based (see Figure 13.4).

In the year to 31 March 1991 Pangloss earned £1.4m before a charge of £0.4m for depreciation; depreciation is singled out because it does not represent a direct cash outlfow but an accounting adjustment to the value of fixed assets – some of which are likely to have been bought many years before. Therefore, when considering the cash resources available to the company both the level of depreciation and retained profits will be taken into account. The trading surplus net of depreciation gives pre-interest profits – an important indicator of company trading performance – of £1.0m (see Figure 13.6).

Interest charge

The interest charge depends on the amount of loans and overdrafts outstanding, which is an integral part of the financing of the company's assets, rather than of current trading. It is therefore of prime significance to those providing finance, whether as lenders or investors. From the point of view of a potential lender, the relation of the interest charge to the level of pre-interest profits gives some

YEAR ENDED 31 MARCH 1991

Earnings for the year to 31.3.91 = £0.4m or 20p per share*
Recommended dividend = £0.2m or 10p per share*

Retained profits = £0.2m

*Issued capital 2 million ordinary shares of £1

Figure 13.5   Earnings, dividends and retentions of Pangloss PLC

indication of the security for interest payments; in this case with interest at £0.3m he is likely to be deterred by the relatively high ratio of 30 per cent of pre-interest profits (of £1m) already absorbed by interest. From the point of view of the equity investor, this ratio represents the gearing given to the amounts available to ordinary shareholders. Thus, if pre-interest profits increase by 70 per cent to £1.7m with interest remaining at £0.3m, pre-tax profits will double to £1.4m, while if they fall by 70 per cent, pre-tax profits will be reduced to nil. So the element of gearing offers both opportunity for increasing the return to shareholders where the company is successful and additional risk if trading returns fall. The degree of gearing that investors are prepared to accept varies according to the industrial risk and this must be borne in mind by the company executive when negotiating loans, overdraft facilities or equity finance.

Tax charge

The tax charge depends not only on the rates of tax ruling in the countries where profits are earned, but also on any special allowances or grants offered. Where the charge appears abnormal it will be analysed to ascertain whether this is due to temporary or permanent factors. The tax charge shown for Pangloss, however, of £0.3m on £0.7m represents a tax rate only slightly higher than normal. This leaves £0.4m available for distribution to shareholders, which will be evaluated by investors with reference to the number of shares issued.

RETURN TO SHAREHOLDERS

Earnings of £0.4m on 2 million shares (see Figure 13.5) are equivalent to 20p per share in Pangloss. The value of the share is normally directly related to this figure; thus, if the share price is £2 an investor will consider whether it is reasonable to buy or sell the share, given that £2 is equivalent to ten times the earnings attributable to that share (that is a p/e ratio of 10). The dividend must also be considered – for long-term investors, this represents the direct return. At a price of £2 the dividend of 10p per share represents a 5 per cent return on the investment, net of tax. This 5 per cent return is worth 6.67 per cent in gross terms to a taxpayer after deduction of tax at a standard rate of 25 per cent. Better returns are offered by an investment in gilts. The investor has, therefore, to judge whether

INDUSTRIAL			YEAR ENDED 31 MARCH		
AVERAGE			1989	1990	1991
	a	Pre-interest profit (£m)	0.8	0.9	1.0
	b	Turnover (£m)	8.0	8.0	9.0
11%		Margin on sales a/b	10%	11%	11%
	c	Capital employed (£m)	10.0	11.0	11.0
11%		Return on capital a/c	8%	8%	9%

Figure 13.6   Performance ratios for Pangloss PLC

or not the trading prospects of Pangloss offer scope for this dividend to be steadily increased.

TRADING PROSPECTS

The record of Pangloss will first be examined to assess the management's abilities to secure satisfactory returns. Figure 13.6 shows the ratios normally applied to the results published in the accounts to judge the management's ability in running the trading of the business.

Performance

Figure 13.6 shows Pangloss's performance measured against sales and capital employed. These criteria are used as a guide to management efficiency, as they allow comparison with other companies in the same industry, as well as to the underlying viability of the company. In this table, pre-interest profit (taken because it excludes interest which depends on the method of funding of the capital employed) has advanced by a quarter from £0.8m in 1989 to £1.10m in 1991; with turnover (up from £8m to £9m) and capital employed (up from £10m to £11m) both rising less fast, margins on sales and return on capital have increased over the period. Margins at 11 per cent in 1991 are the same as for the industry as a whole, which therefore indicates normal trading returns and one without volatile fluctations; return on capital, however, at 9 per cent is well below the industry level of 11 per cent, indicating that the amount of capital employed is high compared with other companies in the industry. Moreover, since the return of 9 per cent falls below the general level of interest rates, it is insufficient to justify the use of new capital in the business; indeed disposal of the existing assets or a change of management – whether through merger or staff recruitment – could be justified in these conditions. For the business cannot justify to its shareholders the employment of funds which could be better invested elsewhere. Thus, return on capital forms a key element in the financial assessment of a company; capital in this context, however, has to be carefully defined and this is considered in detail with reference to the Pangloss balance sheet.

BALANCE SHEET FOR PANGLOSS PLC

Pangloss's balance sheet is given in abbreviated form in Figure 13.7.

	£M
Sources of Finance	
Share capital 2 million ordinary shares of £1	2
Retained profits	4
Shareholders' funds	6
Debt finance	
4% Debenture 1992	3
Bank overdraft	2	5
Total funds	11
Assets Employed	
Fixed assets	
Property	5
Machinery	1
Vehicles	1	7
Net current assets	—	4
Total assets	11

Figure 13.7   Abbreviated 1991 balance sheet for Pangloss PLC

Value of shares

The first point of interest raised by the balance sheet is the book value of the shares. Of the £11m capital employed in Pangloss at the end of the 1990–1 year, £6m is shown to be financed by shareholders' funds giving a book value of £3 each for the 2m shares. (This allows for the assets of the company fetching the £11m shown and thus providing £6m surplus after paying off the debt finance of £5m).

Scope for raising funds

Secondly, the balance sheet gives an indication of the scope for raising further finance. In this case with borrowing at £5m against £11m capital employed, it is unlikely that lenders would be interested in advancing further funds to Pangloss. In addition to checking the company's ability to service the interest charge out of current profits, lenders are concerned with the asset backing for loans. It is rare for a company to obtain half its funds from borrowing. Within the £5m debt the £3m 4 per cent debenture explains the relatively low interest charge given in the profit and loss account. However, since it falls to be redeemed in 1992, it can be considered, with the bank overdraft, as short-term finance; the refinancing of the debenture could well be at a rate of interest of 10 per cent instead of 4 per cent, increasing the interest charge by £180 000 from £120 000 to £300 000. Thus the funding problems of the Pangloss Company are clearly likely to discourage investors; for shareholders will expect to be asked to contribute further equity finance.

Assets employed

However, close attention must also be paid to the composition of the assets shown in the balance sheet, for the value attributed to these is critical to measuring the efficiency of the company through the rate of return on capital and the potential debt finance that they can secure. In particular, the value given to the property must be considered; for if the book figure represents cost or an out-of-date valuation, the current value may be considerably higher, provided the property is freehold or on a long lease. The annual report must therefore be examined for details of the basis of valuation of the property; if the up-to-date value of the Pangloss property was for instance £8m against £5m shown, the total assets employed come to £14m; and with pre-interest profits of £1m, return on capital is little over 7 per cent, indicating that higher rewards could be gained by investing the money in gilt-edged stocks. (This assumes the machinery, vehicles and current assets, which include stocks and debtors net of creditors, raise their book value of £6m.) On the other hand, the prospect of raising debt finance is clearly less forbidding; not only does property tend to appreciate but legal rights to it can be granted to lenders. As a result, up to two-thirds of the value of the property can commonly be raised by debt finance and, provided it is invested at a rate of return that exceeds the interest charge, this offers opportunities for expansion. Property may make Pangloss attractive as a takeover prospect, whether on a break-up basis or on the possibility of improving the present returns.

Assets other than land have to be treated more cautiously; the value of the plant may be minimal on a break-up basis, while current assets, such as debtors and stock, may not fully realize their book values – particularly if the company does not impose sufficient financial control. The trend of these assets to turnover will therefore be examined closely to see whether normal business standards are being achieved. On a forced realization, these assets may recover much less than their book value if standards have not been maintained.

Other information

There is much other information that can be taken from the report, for instance on the extent of capital commitments, or the subsidiaries and associated companies of the group. These do not, however, affect the key standards applied to the balance sheet and profit and loss account that have been examined here. These standards are used for assessing the company from several standpoints. For the shareholder the attraction of the company may be measured by the trend in earnings per share. Potential lenders will look at the cover for the interest charge, the proportion of capital funded by loans and the type of security offered. Management will be assessed by the margin on sales and return on capital that it has secured. The significance of the information given in the annual report is, therefore, of fundamental importance to a company in any assessment of its financial standing and the efficiency of its management.

COMPANY LAW HARMONIZATION

Finally, it is worth considering the harmonization of company law within Europe. A number of EC directives have been agreed – for instance on consolidated accounts and the qualification of auditors. Further directives are concerned with prospectuses, takeovers and bids. More technical directives are also proposed or in preparation on insider dealing and on the publication of changes in significant shareholdings.

While these directives will not significantly affect the presentation of accounts – or indeed the assessment of a company's performance – there may be a much more fundamental impact on company law from EC legislation. The structure of boards is under discussion, with proposals for a distinction between directors who manage and those who supervise management. In addition, there are suggestions for compulsory worker participation. While there is opposition to these provisions, it is likely that non-executive directors will be given specific legal responsibilities and that staff communication will be formalized.

FURTHER READING

Firth, M., *The Valuation of Shares and the Efficient Markets Theory*, Macmillan, London, 1977

Hay D., and Morris, D., *Industrial Economics: Theory and Evidence*, Oxford University Press, 1979

How to Read a Balance Sheet, ILO, Geneva, 1975

Merrett, A.J., and Sykes, A., *The Finance and Analysis of Capital Projects*, Longman, London, 1973

Reid, W., and Myddelton, D.R., *The Meaning of Company Accounts*, 4th edn, Gower, Aldershot, 1988

Rockley, L.E., *The Meaning of Balance Sheets and Company Reports*, Business Books, London, 1975

14 Working capital and management ratios

Leon Simons

Management ratios provide valuable and quantified insight into a company's performance and financial standing, whether for potential investors or for those who manage the company and plan its strategy. This chapter uses the annual accounts of an imaginary company, Standard plc, and explains the significance of key management ratios which can be derived from them.

LIQUIDITY

The working capital of a company is its net current assets, which are its current assets less the current liabilities. In modern balance sheets current liabilities are termed 'Creditors – amounts falling due within one year'. In the balance sheet of Standard plc (Figure 14.1) the working capital is seen to be £1 406 000 (at line 11), being £5 675 000 – £4 269 000 (line 9 – line 10).

The amount of working capital indicates the liquidity of a company. Two management ratios are commonly used to express the degree of liquidity. One of these is the current ratio, which is simply the current assets divided by the current liabilities. The current ratio for Standard plc (Figure 14.1) is therefore as follows:

$$\frac{5675}{4269} = \text{approximately } 1.3$$

Some accountants consider that it is more useful to ignore the value of inventories when looking at liquidity, since these could take considerably longer to convert to cash than debtors or creditors. These accountants feel that it is more pertinent to compare the quick assets (current assets minus inventories) with the current liabilities. This is known either as the quick ratio, or the acid test ratio. Again taking the balance sheet of Standard plc as an example, the calculation of the quick ratio is as follows:

$$\frac{\text{quick assets (lines } 6 + 7 + 8)}{\text{current liabilities (line 10)}} = \frac{3389}{4269} = 0.79$$

There is no generally ideal current ratio, since companies differ so greatly from each other. A current ratio of 1.3 may be appropriate for a light manufacturing group with a short production cycle (like Standard plc). The same ratio, however, may be too low for a company with a longer cycle and a proportionately bigger stock investment. On the other hand, a supermarket with no work in progress

STANDARD plc

CONSOLIDATED BALANCE SHEET
at 31st March 1991

			1991 £'000	1990 £'000
	Fixed assets			
1	Tangible assets	10	6697	5014
2	Investments	11	1406	365
3			8103	5379
4	**Advance corporation tax**		175	151
	Current assets			
5	Stocks	12	2286	1852
6	Debtors	13	3269	2693
7	Short-term deposits		–	250
8	Cash at bank		120	206
9			5675	5001
	Creditors			
10	Amounts falling due within one year	14	4269	4616
11	**Net current assets**		1406	385
12	**Total assets less current liabilities**		9684	5915
	Creditors			
13	Amounts falling due after more than one year	15	89	1214
14	**Provisions for deferred taxation**	16	380	300
15			9215	4401
	Capital and reserves			
16	Called-up share capital	17	1944	1392
17	Share premium	18	3277	151
18	Capital reserve	18	697	697
19	Retained profit	18	3297	2161
20	**Shareholder's funds**		9215	4401

Figure 14.1   Annual accounts of Standard plc – balance sheet

(because it does not manufacture) and no debtors (because its business is purely cash) would very likely have a current ratio of less than one. In other words, it would have current liabilities which exceeded its current assets.

One should try neither to maximize nor to minimize the liquidity ratios. One should try to optimize them in relation to the objective, which in the case of a commercial public company is the maximization of profit on capital employed. The lower the liquidity ratios are, the more vulnerable the company is to pressure from creditors which it is unable to meet. The higher the liquidity ratios, the more the capital is not being fully exploited in terms of the return earned on it. One should seek, therefore, to have as little working capital as is consistent with not being unduly vulnerable to pressure from creditors. This ideal level of liquidity would vary not only from company to company, but through time within one company, as conditions changed.

STOCK

Excess stockholding has an adverse effect on liquidity. The ratio used for assessing stock level is the stock/turnover ratio. The stock/turnover ratio for Standard plc is found as follows:

$$\frac{\text{stock (line 5, Figure 14.1)}}{\text{turnover (line 1, Figure 14.2)}} = \frac{2\ 286}{15\ 220} = 0.15$$

On its own, this ratio has little significance but, as with most other management ratios, it can be used to monitor changes through time. Standard's stock/turnover ratio of 0.15 could be expressed instead as a proportion of a year which, in their case, is 8 weeks. We do not know if 8 weeks' average stock is too high or too low, or how great a deviation there is around the average. Like liquidity, stockholding has to be balanced: it should neither be maximized nor minimized, but optimized in terms of profit. Too much stock means that the money tied up in it is costing more than it is contributing. Too little stock means that the cost of lost sales (owing to stocks not being available to meet orders) exceeds the savings made by not holding the additional stock.

There are other factors to be considered in deciding the optimum stock level. For example, are there additional costs attributable to holding increased stock rather than just the interest on the capital? If the stock level were to be reduced by a given amount, would the company then be able to vacate a warehouse, with a consequent savings in rates, rent, insurance, heating, and so forth? How many storemen could be dismissed or redeployed?

Stock appreciation should also be brought into account. If the company uses volatile commodities it might save a great deal of money by holding more than its immediate requirements of a material whose market price is expected to rise during the period covered by the holding. This saving could far outweigh the extra stocking costs and throw in, as a bonus, freedom from the danger of being caught out of stock.

The stock ratio is not ideal in a number of respects. First, the turnover is at selling prices, while the stock is at cost. Second, the turnover covers a period, while the stock is quoted at a point in time which may not be typical of that period.

STANDARD plc

CONSOLIDATED PROFIT AND LOSS ACCOUNT

for the year ended 31st March 1991

Line		Notes	1991 £'000	1990 £'000
1	**Turnover**	1	15220	13124
2	Cost of sales		10083	8544
3			5137	4580
4	Distribution and administration expenses	2	2958	2799
5	**Operating profit**		2179	1781
6	Associate companies		56	–
7	Investment income	3	46	50
8	Interest payable	4	(81)	(233)
9	**Profit on ordinary activities before taxation**		2200	1598
10	Taxation	6	533	428
11	**Profit on ordinary activities after taxation**		1667	1170
12	Extraordinary income less taxation	7	70	111
13	Profit for the year		1737	1281
14	Dividends	8	583	350
15	Retained profit for the year		1154	931
	Profit for year retained by:			
	Holding company		576	411
	Subsidiaries		522	520
	Associates		56	–
			1154	931
16	Earnings per ordinary share	9	9.05p	7.52p

Figure 14.2   Annual accounts of Standard plc – profit and loss

Third, the cost of the stock is not factual but is a function of the company's costing system which includes arbitrary assumptions.

DEBTORS

Apart from inventories, a major element of working capital is in the credit taken by customers. This does not of course apply to those retailers and others who do not conduct a credit trade. The debtors/sales ratio is the measure, and this again is usually expressed in weeks. In the case of Standard plc, the debtors/sales ratio is derived from information contained in Figures 14.2 and 14.3 as follows:

$$\frac{\text{Debtors (line 1, Figure 14.3)}}{\text{Sales (line 1, Figure 14.2)}} = \frac{3\ 173}{15\ 220} = 0.208$$

(20.8 per cent, or about 11 weeks).

The debtors/sales ratio has the same disadvantage as that mentioned concerning the stock ratio, namely that the point of time at which the debtors are taken may not be typical of the period to which the turnover relates. Alternatively, there may be a strong seasonal bias within the year's total sales figure. For example, if two-thirds of the year's turnover was sold in the second six months, then the ratio is as follows:

$$\frac{3\ 173 \times 26\ (\text{weeks})}{10\ 147}$$

which is just over 8 weeks.

However, this is a problem only for external readers of the report, since managers with access to the management accounts could take the seasonal bias into consideration when calculating the ratio.

CREDITORS

Creditors are the opposite side of the coin to debtors. They are a source of funds to the company, and the more capital the company can borrow from this source, the less it requires from others (or, alternatively, the more funds it has available to deploy in various assets for building up the activity – and possibly the return – on the same net capital).

The creditors, being money owing in respect of purchases made by the company, will be compared with the purchases in the recent period and expressed in weeks. Although the cost of sales figure appears in the profit and loss account, it includes manufacturing wages as well as purchases, and purchases are not shown separately. However, the figure for purchases will be available to the managers; they should use it in the same way as the debtors ratio by allowing for any seasonal bias.

Readers of the published accounts can make the assumption that purchases are roughly thé same proportion of sales in the recent year as they were in the previous year. They can then compare the movement of creditors with that of debtors. Standard's debtors increased from £2 657 000 to £3 173 000 (line 1 in

			Group	
13	Debtors falling due within one year		1991	1990
	Line		£'000	£'000
	1	Trade debtors	3173	2657
	2	Prepayments and accrued income	96	36
	3	Amounts due from subsidiaries	–	–
	4		3269	2693

			Group	
14	Creditors falling due within one year		1991	1990
			£'000	£'000
	5	Trade creditors	1347	1477
	6	Other creditors	634	816
	7	PAYE and Social Security	172	157
	8	Accrued charges	237	182
	9	Bank overdraft	654	–
	10	Proposed dividend	408	238
	11	Corporation tax	596	641
	12	Amounts owed to subsidiaries	–	–
	13	Medium-term loan	20	20
	14	Non-convertible unsecured loan stock 1990/91	201	1085
	15		4269	4616

The bank overdraft is secured on the group's freehold land and buildings.

Interest on the loan stock is payable at the rate of 1% below the rate at which three months' deposits are offered in the London Inter-Bank Market for sterling subject to a maximum of 11% per annum. The loan stock is redeemable at par on not less than 3 months notice from stockholders and in any event no later than 31 December 1991.

Figure 14.3   Extract from notes to the annual accounts of Standard plc

Figure 14.3) or by 19.4 per cent. The creditors, however, fell from £1 477 000 to £1 347 000 (line 5 in Figure 14.3) which is 9 per cent. Since the rise in debtors is similar to the rise in sales, it is the movement of creditors which is surprising. This inference is reinforced by the increase of stock from the previous year. It would appear that either the company is voluntarily paying more quickly (which would be strange in view of the poorer cash position) or that suppliers are applying more pressure, or perhaps offering better cash discount incentives to attract prompt payment.

Whatever the reason, the decrease in trade creditors of £130 000 and the increase in trade debtors of £516 000 combine to result in a total reduction of cash flow of £646 000, which accounts for virtually the entire bank overdraft.

However, the average length of credit time taken by the company from its suppliers is still not known. Suppose, for the sake of argument, that the £1 347 000 (line 5 in Figure 14.3) represents two months' credit – meaning that average monthly purchases have been running at half that level. Then an increase by one month to three month's credit will, other things being equal, raise borrowing from this source by about £673 000, at the same time eliminating the bank overdraft. The total current liabilities will remain the same, but the company will have substituted additional borrowing from its suppliers for what it previously borrowed from the bank. The effect of this change on profit, assuming overdraft interest at the rate of (say) 14 per cent, would be a gain of about £94 000. Moreover, this is not just a once and for all gain; it will continue at that rate for as long as the additional credit is taken. This assumes that:

1 Purchases continue at the current level
2 Interest rates continue at 14 per cent
3 Relations with suppliers remain unaltered.

If there are changes in either (1) or (2), the effects can easily be ascertained, but assumption (3) requires careful consideration. If we take more credit from a supplier, will that supplier react and, if so, how will his reaction affect us?

There are a number of things the supplier can do, from writing a letter (which costs the customer nothing) to withholding supplies (which may cost the customer a great deal). Between these extremes, he may reduce quality, increase prices, cut down deliveries and so on. However, there is doubt about the validity of these intermediate reactions.

He may reduce the quality of the product or the frequency of delivery or after-sales service, but this may not be acceptable to the customer who may then withdraw his custom. Before taking any of these steps, the supplier would then have to be prepared for this eventuality, the effect of which would be the same as if he himself withheld supplies.

Similarly, if the supplier increases his prices, the higher prices may or may not be acceptable to the customer. If they are, why did the supplier not increase them previously? If they are not, he once again risks losing the business. Therefore, the question facing the supplier is whether or not he can risk losing the business.

From the customer's point of view, he must decide whether he can tolerate loss of supplies from this source because, even though it may not be in the supplier's best interest to stop supplies, he may act irrationally and the customer must be prepared for this. The summary of this discussion is that the customer's ability to take longer credit from a particular supplier depends on the balance of power between them.

Since this varies with different suppliers it follows that an individual credit policy with at least the major suppliers is necessary if optimum credit is to be taken. If a blanket credit policy is adopted to cover all suppliers, this assumes that they are all equally powerful, which is most unlikely to be the case. The consequence of this would be to take from some less credit than one could take with impunity, and to take from others more than is wise.

These arguments apply with equal force to debtor control, and since sales exceed purchases tight debtor control is even more important. It is often suggested that if a company takes longer credit from its suppliers, its own customers will in turn extend their credit and the move will be self-defeating. This is woolly thinking. Customers cannot know how a company behaves to its suppliers, save in the exceptional case where customer and supplier are the same and a two-way trade is conducted. In the normal case, the customer will take whatever credit he thinks he can get away with. This consideration is based on the same assessment of relative power as already discussed concerning creditors.

However, many companies recognize the importance of intelligent debtor control and designate it as a specific management function, whilst attention is paid to prompt invoicing and follow-up procedures. It is the treatment of credit obtainable from suppliers that is relatively neglected.

Cash discount

So far we have not considered the effect on one's credit policy if one is offered a discount for prompt payment. For example, a supplier may offer a discount of 2½ per cent on invoice for payment within 30 days.

If one pays two months from date of invoice and forgoes the discount, one has in fact borrowed for one extra month (since the first 30 days would be taken in any event) at a cost of 2½ per cent which is equivalent to a straight annual cost of 12 × 2½ per cent = 30 per cent. The discounted annual rate would be even higher than this. If one is borrowing at say 15 per cent from the bank, 30 per cent is far too dear to contemplate. Breakeven point would occur with 3 months' credit; that is, 2 extra months at a cost of 2½ per cent = 12 ÷ 2 × 2½ per cent or 15 per cent p.a. Therefore, it is only worthwhile losing the discount if one can take at least 3 months' credit. However, if bank facilities are scarce it will pay to borrow at more than 15 per cent from suppliers if the benefit derived from the utilization of the extra credit exceeds the cost.

So far in this chapter the various factors concerning liquidity have been discussed. We have seen that suboptimal utilization of working capital is expensive. At the least, it costs the interest on the unnecessary money used, but it also prevents that money from being properly employed in the company and could inhibit the company's growth through lack of cash.

Cash flow

Liquidity is the life-blood of the company and lack of cash is the only thing which could force the company out of business. Cash flows into the company by direct cash sales and the collection of debts from customers, and also, though less regularly, from the sale of assets. Cash flows out in direct purchases and payments to creditors, in payment of wages and other costs, and in the purchase of capital equipment. It also flows out in payment of taxes and interest on borrowed money and dividends to shareholders.

These flows have to be predicted and controlled. This is done by forecasting and budgeting (see Chapter 15). Cash has always to be available to meet committed expenditure. If not, the company can be forced into liquidation by its creditors even though it has an overall excess of assets over liabilities. The company can also obtain additional transfusions of cash from time to time by means of additional bank facilities, which are likely to be relatively short-term, by raising fresh loans which are likely to be long-term and by rights issues of further ordinary shares which are permanent funds.

PROFITABILITY

We shall assume, since there is not the space here to argue it, that the objective of a public commercial company is the maximization of profit on capital employed. The objective covers the total future and, of course, does not apply to any single year. Almost every company could make a bigger profit this year if in so doing it was prepared to jeopardize the future. The cessation of advertising and research, for example, would often increase this year's profit but might cripple the business in the following year.

Profit on capital employed, on its own, does not mean very much. Are we talking about profit before tax or profit after tax, shareholders' capital or total capital, for example? In fact, different definitions of profit are appropriate at different levels in a company because of varying degrees of authority to control resources and make decisions.

At parent company board level, the directors are directly accountable to ordinary shareholders, and therefore the capital for which the directors are accountable is the ordinary shareholders' funds (OSF) which consists of the ordinary share capital plus reserves. Similarly, the profit which the directors are seeking to maximize is the profit attributable to the ordinary shareholders. This profit is often referred to as the company's earnings, and the earnings divided by the number of ordinary shares in issue is the earnings per share (EPS). The earnings are the trading profit less all interest charges, taxation, minority shareholders' interest and preference dividend, since these are all the deductions which must be made before the ordinary shareholders are entitled to the remainder.

Thus the profitability ratio relevant to the assessment of directors' performance is earnings divided by OSF which, in the case of Standard plc, is:

$$\frac{£1\ 667\ 000\ \text{(Figure 14.2, line 11)}}{£9\ 215\ 000\ \text{(Figure 14.1, line 20)}}$$

which is approximately 18 per cent. Notice that the earnings figure is struck before deducting ordinary dividends. The earnings can be used by the directors, either in paying a dividend to the ordinary shareholders or by retention in the company as an addition to the OSF. How the directors dispose of the earnings is entirely within their discretion. The earnings figure is also struck before extraordinary items (line 12 in Figure 14.2) because these are of a non-trading and non-recurring nature.

Let us now look at the position of the chief executive. He is directly accountable to the board of directors and is sometimes called the managing director (if he also sits on the board) or the general manager (if he does not). The chief executive is accountable for profit since he controls both sides of the profit equation – income and expenditure. However, he does not control dividends, since he does not raise capital, and, for the same reason, he does not control loan interest. On the other hand, he does control the level of bank borrowing by, for example, his credit policies, and so he is accountable for bank interest.

Taxation is affected within the company by board decisions, particularly those regarding capital expenditure and the raising of capital. Capital expenditure gives rise to government capital allowances. New capital may be raised by a rights issue of shares (on which dividends are paid) or by the issue of loan stock (on which interest is paid). However, interest (being a cost) is allowable for corporation tax. Dividends, which are distributions of profit, are paid after corporation tax has been charged, but are paid net of income tax. With corporation tax at 35 per cent and the basic rate of income tax at 25 per cent, every £1 of gross interest actually costs the company 65p and a £1 of gross equivalent dividend costs 75p.

Minority interests are no concern of the chief executive since the decision of whether to own subsidiaries partly or wholly is a board decision. The chief executive is therefore accountable for trading profit ÷ total investment. Trading profit is defined as a profit after bank overdraft interest but before deducting loan interest, taxation, minority interests and dividends. Total investment is the total long-term capital made available by the board to the chief executive. It consists of the ordinary shareholders' funds, plus preference capital, plus loan capital, plus minority interests. In the case of Standard plc, the figures are as follows:

$$\frac{\text{trade profit}}{\text{total investment}} = \frac{£2\ 163\ 000[1]}{£9\ 255\ 000[2]} \text{ or about 23 per cent.}$$

The chief executive's ratio is different from the board's, but contributes towards it: the better the trading profit, the better the earnings (other things being equal). The chief executive's profitability is almost always higher than the board's because his is before tax and theirs is after.

These profitability ratios have little absolute significance, since both profit and capital employed are worked out in an arbitary manner, and within a given factual context there is a wide range of possibilities for both.

The elements which make annual profit arbitrary are depreciation, stock valuation and the capitalizing or writing off of expenditure. Capital employed is arbitrary because assets are often included at cost, or at cost less depreciation, or at valuation. It is not uncommon to find a balance sheet with some assets at cost less

---

[1] The £2 163 000 comprises the operating profit of £2 179 000 (see Figure 14.2, line 5) less the £16 000 bank overdraft interest. (This overdraft interest appears in notes to the accounts which are not reproduced here.)
[2] The £9 255 000 is the OSF of £9 215 000 plus a medium term loan of £40 000 (noted in a part of the accounts which is also not reproduced here).

depreciation, some assets at 1970 valuation, and other assets at 1987 valuation, all added together as if they were the same currency.

The only logical value of capital employed is the deprival value (the current market value) of the assets less the liabilities. (This argument is explained in Simons, 1986, Chapter 8, pp 103–6).

The main use of ratios is in monitoring trends. It might be thought that a given ratio at one time can be compared with the equivalent ratio at another time if, although they have certain arbitrary elements, they are calculated consistently. This would only be partly true. Suppose, for example, that assets are entered in the balance sheet at cost, or at cost less depreciation, and not at value. At a time of inflation, profit will reflect the effects as prices and costs rise, except for depreciation which is usually based on historical cost instead of replacement cost. However, capital employed, in being consistently 'valued' at cost, will depart more and more from reality and so, therefore, will the return on capital employed. The ratio will tend to rise, simply because the conventions used are holding back the denominator to a far greater extent than the numerator.

Whereas the shareholders have to accept the accounts as they are published, and make the best of what is too often a bad job, fortunately more can be done by management, in this case the board of directors. They can ensure that the accounts (at least the management accounts if not the published ones) are prepared with maximum reality in order that they can provide a basis for management decision making.

In the calculation of profit, stocks should be based on net realizable value instead of cost which is irrelevant. Depreciation should be the reduction in the market value of the assets between the beginning and end of the year plus the increase in the replacement cost of these assets during the year.

The reduction in the market value of the assets should be deducted from the asset value in the balance sheet at the end of the previous year to arrive at the balance sheet value at the end of the current year. In this way the assets will always be included at market value, which is the only treatment of relevance to the readers of the balance sheet.

The increase in the replacement cost of the asset will not be deducted from the balance sheet value as this could eventually cause a negative value of the asset, which is, of course, impossible. Instead, it is taken to an asset replacement provision on the balance sheet. Thus, when an asset is sold, a figure similar to the balance sheet value should be obtained, in addition to which depreciation has been provided between the historical cost and realizable value of the asset, and between the replacement cost and the historical cost, so that the company will have provided sufficient funds for the replacement of the asset. Conventional historical cost depreciation does not achieve this, as a result of which profit is overstated, non-existent profit may be distributed as a dividend, and the company may leave itself short of the capital necessary to continue the business at the same level as before.

Gearing

The principle of gearing is a very important one in any decision to raise new capital and it is also one of the differences between the board's profitability ratio of earnings/OSF and the chief executive's ratio of trading profit/total investment. The measure of gearing is the gearing ration, which is total investment/OSF. Most financial commentators quote a gearing percentage rather than the ratio, which is the percentage that net borrowing is of shareholder's funds.

Total investment has already been described as the total long-term capital, including OSF, preference and loan capital. OSF (ordinary shareholders' funds) is the ordinary share capital and reserves. Except for the loan of £40 000 mentioned above, Standard's long-term capital is the OSF, and it is thus virtually ungeared. The ratio of an ungeared company is 1.

Now suppose that an ungeared company has OSF (and thus total investment) of £10m, and that it makes a trading profit of £2m. The profitability ratios can be set out thus:

Trading profit	£2 000 000
Loan interest	nil
Profit before tax	2 000 000
Corporation tax (35 per cent)	700 000
Earnings	£1 300 000

The chief executive's profitability is:

$$\frac{\text{trading profit}}{\text{total investment}} = \frac{£2m}{£10m} \text{ which is 20 per cent.}$$

The board's profitability is:

$$\frac{\text{earnings}}{\text{OSF}} = \frac{£1.3m}{£10m} \text{ which is 13 per cent.}$$

The chief executive now makes an application to the board for £4m additional capital, the new funds being required for a long-term project on which the chief executive is confident of making his present 20 per cent return. The board, after examining his proposals, and comparing them with alternatives, decide to go ahead with the project and raise the necessary capital. Basically, the choice facing them is a rights issue to increase the equity (owners' capital or OSF) or an issue of 10 per cent loan stock. We shall look at both possibilities on the assumption that the chief executive (CE) meets his forecast of 20 per cent return. Here are the figures:

	Case 1 (rights issue)	Case 2 (loan stock issue)
OSF	£14m	£10m
10% loan capital	nil	4m
Total investment	14m	14m
Trading profit	2.8m (CE's ratio = 20%)	2.8m (CE's ratio = 20%)
Loan interest	nil	0.4m
Profit before tax	2.8m	2.4m
Corporation tax at 35%	0.98m	0.84m
Earnings	1.82m (board's ratio = 13%)	1.56m (board's ratio = 15.6%)

In Case 1, the board's ratio is 1.82m/14m (OSF) and in Case 2 it is 1.56m/10m (OSF).

Case 2 is preferable because money has been borrowed at 10 per cent pre-tax, and invested at 20 per cent pre-tax, the difference going to the benefit of the ordinary shareholders with no further investment on their part. The gearing ratio in Case 1 is 1 and in Case 2 is 1.4.

Gearing, however, is a two-edged weapon. It will magnify the effect of a change in trading profit on the earnings. Suppose that in the following year (year 2) trading profit doubles and in year 3 it falls to half of the year 1 level. Then, assuming the capital structure in Case 2, the positions would be as follows:

	Year 2	Year 3
Trading profit	£5.6m (CE's ratio = 40%)	£1.4m (CE's ratio = 10%)
Loan interest	0.4m	0.4m
Pre-tax profit	5.2m	1.0m
Corporation tax at 35%	1.82m	0.35m
Earnings	3.38m (board's ratio = 33.8%)	0.65m (board's ratio = 6.5%)

Notice that in the year 2 the earnings/OSF has more than doubled from 15.6 per cent to 33.8 per cent and from year 1 to year 3 it has more than halved from 15.6 per cent to 6.5 per cent.

A simple and dramatic example of the effect of gearing is to be seen in the case of the private house. A man buys a house for £50 000 and finances it by a deposit of £10 000 and a 25-year endowment-linked building society mortgage of £40 000. He sells the house for £150 000 and repays the mortgage. The gearing ratio is:

$$\frac{\text{total investment}}{\text{OSF}} = \frac{50\ 000}{10\ 000} = 5.$$

		Time of purchase	Time of sale	
Deposit	(equity)	£10 000	+1 000%	£110 000
Mortgage	(loan capital)	40 000		40 000
House	(total investment)	50 000	+200%	150 000

Although the house has appreciated by only 200 per cent, the owner's equity has increased by five times that proportion (since the gearing ratio is 5), namely, 1 000 per cent. Equally, of course, if the house had fallen in value by £10 000, which is 20 per cent, the fall in the equity would have been 5 × 20 per cent = 100 per cent. In other words, the owner would have lost his entire capital, since the remaining £40 000 in the value of the house would have been just sufficient to repay the mortgage.

There is no generally ideal gearing ratio. It can be seen that gearing adds a speculative element to a company in the method of financing it, but the degree of speculation tolerated in the financial structure of the company depends on how basically speculative the company is. A nice steady company which is relatively unaffected by seasonal and cyclical variations in profit can stand a considerable degree of gearing whereas a company whose profit fluctuates a great deal is perhaps better left ungeared or low geared.

SOLVENCY

Finally, we come to the concept of solvency. Just as liquidity is concerned with a company's ability to meet its current liabilities out of its current assets, solvency is concerned with the ability of the company to meet its total liabilities out of its total assets. The solvency ratio is:

$$\frac{OSF}{total\ assets} \times 100 \text{ per cent}$$

which in Standard's case is:

$$\frac{9215 \text{ (Figure 14.1, line 20)}}{13\ 953 \text{ (Figure 14.1, lines 3 + 4 + 9)}}$$

which is approximately 66 per cent.

This means that 66 per cent of all Standard's assets are financed by the owners and, therefore, borrowed money is the source of the remaining 34 per cent of the assets. In other words, even if 66 per cent of the assets are lost, the company is still solvent since there is enough value remaining just to repay all the borrowing and no more.

Once again, optimum solvency is a question of balance. A company financing too high a proportion of its total assets by equity is not maximizing its profitability (since the denominator of the profitability ratio is unnecessarily high) even though it is extremely safe. The art is in judging how much external financing an individual company can stand.

The true degree of solvency, like the true degree of liquidity and gearing can only be ascertained if the values of the assets in the balance sheet are realistic. Book values based on cost are of no help in making these assessments.

FURTHER READING

Simons, L., *The Basic Arts of Financial Management*, 3rd edn, Business Books, London, 1986
Westwick, C. A., *How to Use Management Ratios*, 2nd edn, Gower, Aldershot, 1987

15 Budgetary control

Alan Leaper

All businesses exercise some form of budgetary control, whether or not they call it by that name. Someone in the organization co-ordinates the business's resources in some degree to achieve some sort of plan. But whether they examine alternative plans, or consider what the ideal criteria of their objectives should be, might be another question.

There are many benefits to be derived from the introduction of a formalized budgetary control system. These include:

- Defining the organization's objectives, both in financial terms and as a whole
- Providing yardsticks against which the efficiency of designated parts of the organization can be measured
- Revealing the extent by which actual results have varied from the defined objective
- Providing a guide for corrective action
- Facilitating centralized control with delegated responsibilities.

The disadvantages of a formalized procedure are not so readily identifiable. They could include:

- Additional costs or personnel needed to perform the function
- Suspicions, aroused by its introduction, that it is merely another vehicle for implementing cost reduction programmes
- The complacency caused by paperwork becoming routine, with the eventual risk that little notice and no action will be taken.

Immediate benefits should not be expected from the introduction of a budget procedure. It may take a year or two to educate those concerned in the proper compilation of the data required and in the proper application of the data subsequently made available.

WHAT IS A BUDGET?

A budget is the expression in financial (and rather summarized) terms of a comprehensive short-term operational plan for a business entity. The financial numbers relate to specific action programmes, which give rise to asset acquisitions and disposals, the earning of revenues and the incurring of expenditure. A budget in which these financial numbers have been 'pulled out of the air' is worse than useless.

Many alternative plans may be considered before the final one showing the most practical profit is chosen. Executives and other responsible officials from all functions of the company must contribute towards the plan. Data in the unit terms of each of the functions concerned must be collected and translated into monetary terms. For example, the sales manager is primarily concerned with units of the finished article or service and he would therefore contribute the volume and models to be included in the plan. The production manager talks in standard hours and efficiencies. The personnel manager will be responsible for the levels of wage rates, absenteeism factors, welfare schemes, and so on. The chief executive must be fully convinced of the benefits to be derived from the plan and really believe in it.

Budgetary control is the process of managing these facets – planning and co-ordinating all functions so that they work in harmony and control performances and costs. It establishes the responsibility of all managers, throughout the corporate structure, for achieving the company's budgeted objectives. It entails measuring at suitable intervals how the plan is actually progressing and, if divergencies are occurring, taking the necessary corrective action to ensure that the company gets back on course again. By having a budget built up in this manner it is possible to fix responsibility at every level of the organization – and this is important.

Most managements have found that it is not sufficient to face the problems of a business on a day-to-day basis or even on a year-to-year basis; medium-term operation (or programme) planning is therefore carried out over a time-horizon of three to five years ahead. Generally, such planning involves a projection of the total market for the company's products and an assessment of what the company's share of that market should be, based on historical performance and management objectives. Obviously the degree of accuracy of the projections and plans varies with the period covered. In view of the many uncertainties involved in projecting activites over, say, a three-year period, the usual procedure is to prepare plans for the first year in considerable detail (that is, the budget) and then to resort to summary projections for the remaining two years. As each year's plan is done, refinements are made on the basis of recent experience and a new third year is added.

BUDGET CENTRES

Efficient control requires acceptance that costs are best controlled at the point where they are incurred. The transport manager should, therefore, control the transport department's cost. But the control span of any one person should not be unduly large. The area controlled by an individual is known as a 'budget centre', defined by the Chartered Institute of Mangement Accountants as 'A section of the organization of the undertaking defined for the purposes of budgetary control.'

Budgets prepared at a given level of budget centre are then consolidated at the next level up (profit centre, division or company, as the case may be). A substantial business organization will generally comprise a number of operating units, each with primary responsibility for its own profits and cash flow (profit centres) as well, perhaps, as its own capital investment (investment centres). Thus, a business may include several profit centres which, in larger organizations, may be grouped into investment centres or divisions. Every division will normally have its own financial controller, responsible for preparing the divisional master budget (see the following section of this chapter). Larger profit centres may also employ their own management accountants, who prepare draft profit and loss and cash budgets. Within each budget centre there may be other smaller areas to which costs are attributable: for example, it may be desirable to identify and control groups of trucks in a transport department. Such a smaller area of control is defined as a 'cost centre', which the Chartered Institute of Mangement Accountants describes as 'A location, person or item of equipment, or a group of these, in or connected with an undertaking in relation to which costs may be ascertained and used for purposes of cost control.'

Within each budget centre, only one person should be responsible for incurring costs. Ultimate responsibility for budgetary control lies with the chief executive.

COMPILING A BUDGET

There is really no established order in which budgets should be prepared, provided all parts are geared into a common factor. This is generally the principal limiting or bottleneck factor which varies for each individual company.

Most companies tend to establish a sales target determined on market potential and their share of the market as the basis of their budgets. Many others prefer to establish their production capacity and plan a budget to ensure the full utilization of available equipment. The ideal, of course, is to achieve a harmony of both of these important items. However, there are many other factors which may determine the level of activity to be budgeted, amongst which are insufficient cash to finance expansion, a scarce raw material, and, possibly, the non-availability of skilled labour.

Having established the basis for compiling the budget, all known external factors which could have a bearing on its fulfilment must be examined – national wage awards, sales taxes, credit squeezes, the movement of purchase prices, and so forth.

In larger organizations a budget committee is usually formed to review these items and determine, as best it can, the likely effect they will have on business during the period to be used in the budget. Having determined these external factors, the budget accountant/committee would advise functional and departmental managers of their effects and provide guidelines for the compilation of the subsidiary departmental budgets, the main examples of which are considered below.

Sales budget

The sales budget should show total sales, expressed both by value and quantity. It may be further analysed by product, by area, by customer and, of course, by seasonal pattern of expected sales. The main problems arise in determining quantities and in the calculation of standard prices. Constraints such as competitive activity have to be borne in mind (new products and aggressive pricing policies).

The budget should be compiled by the sales manager. He will seek the opinions of his salesmen and use any statistical forecasting techniques arising from market research. Other considerations include general business and economic conditions, company advertising policy, new products, supplies, product demand and plant capacity. A special pricing study is usually helpful at this stage, and this should show the complete product range, the relevant market sector, competitive models or products (taking into account both the pricing and the features available), introduction dates, discount structures and advertising strategy. In some cases, when jobbing production is involved, budgets must be made in terms of the expected sales value only.

Production budget

The production budget is a statement of the output by product, and is generally expressed in standard hours. It should take into consideration the sales budget, plant capacity, whether stocks are to be increased or decreased and outside purchases. The form the production budget would take depends on circumstances. Usually, the quantities are shown for each department (budget centre) and information is taken from machine loading charts, material specifications, time schedules and other production or time-study records.

When computing labour cost, the average labour rate used depends on the wage plan in effect. For hourly rated employees not on incentive bonuses, an overall plant rate may be sufficient. In other cases, departmental or labour grade rates may be used. When a straight piece rate plan is in force, the labour cost is the amount paid per unit produced. When other incentive plans are used, labour rates have to be computed to include estimated amounts for bonus payments. In companies using standard costs, cost accounting records can be very useful in determining budget requirements for non-productive direct labour. Many cost accounting systems are sophisticated enough to indicate the breakdown of non-productive direct labour into down time, waiting time, changeover or set-up time, and so on.

The plant manager will prepare the production budget in close collaboration with accountants, production engineers, work study engineers and other key personnel. Adequate lead times for the delivery of new equipment and the development of new processes must be considered.

At this stage, the sales and production budgets should be compared to ensure maximum utilization of capacity aligned to satisfactory sales growth. If the sales budget exceeds production capacity, then decisions on capital expenditure and new plant may be required before proceeding further. If, on the other hand, significant under-utilization of capacity is denoted, decisions on how best to use this spare capacity must be taken (to determine, for example, if sub-contract work would be profitable, if a revised pricing structure could increase the volume of sales, or if plant should be declared surplus and sold off or scrapped.).

Production costs budget

This supplementary budget should determine the 'cost of sales' allied to the required production.

Generally, by far the largest element in cost terms is direct material. This part should be compiled by the chief buyer in conjunction with the production manager. Using the sales and production budgets, it will determine the requirements of raw material and piece-parts, period by period, to meet the output, and will be evaluated in cash cost terms. Considerations should take into account bulk buying, delivery periods, stock holding, suppliers' credit terms and trade discounts, as well as recognizing any changes in material specifications, new model introductions, and so on. In timing the purchase of raw materials, piece-parts and other items, consideration must be given to the necessity to keep inventory levels to the very minimum and thereby not tie up valuable capital. Special competitive pricing exercises should be undertaken from potential suppliers to ensure that costs are strictly controlled and keen.

Direct labour is another most important element of production costs. The work study department should be called upon to establish standard times for individual units. These may then be evaluated by the required volumes and converted into direct labour requirements. The degree of labour efficiency must be determined, as must the type of employee necessary, for example skilled, semi-skilled or unskilled.

Direct expense budgets covering warehousing, transportation, warranty and special tools should be determined by the appropriate managers responsible for incurring or approving the respective expenses.

Factory overhead costs (burden) should be established by departmental foremen and consolidated by the production manager. Expenses of all types should be considered and some assistance may be necessary from the finance department in determining depreciation, insurance and other expenses possibly beyond the control of the local foremen.

Personnel budget

This is a headcount schedule of the total labour requirements necessary to carry out the sales and production budgets and, in fact, run the whole business from managing director to office boy and production worker to office cleaner. It should be prepared by the personnel department in conjunction with all other functional departmental heads.

The schedule will show the number of personnel required, the hours to be worked, wage rates, salaries and so on, and should be built up by departments. The respective costs should, of course, be incorporated in the applicable departmental budgets. The recruitment and training policies of the company will be incorporated in the budget and cognizance should be taken of all labour-related costs – for example, national insurance and pension schemes.

Operating and service department budgets

The type of department falling into this category may be administration, finance, selling, advertising and service, and might also include warehousing and shipping. The departmental head of each of these functions will be responsible for compiling his individual budget. The data included will cover personnel requirements by number and grade and be cost-determined in conjunction with the personnel manager; and departmental running costs detailed by account, for example, utilities, operating expenses, depreciation, insurance, and rates.

Special note should be taken of competitors' activity in determining the size and use of the advertising budget.

If raw material or bulk purchases are necessary, the usage and cost of these will be planned with the purchasing agent or chief buyer.

The basis of determining costs included in these budgets invariably depends on the actual trend in previous years adjusted, of course, for known changes. It should also be remembered that historical costs will include inefficiencies and these must be identified and determined if likely to continue. The considered effects of volume and activity should also be borne in mind.

Capital expenditure budget

This supplementary budget is usually compiled by senior management in conjunction with engineering and technical services.

The budget will show details of the capital expenditure proposals in the period of the master budget and will probably be prepared for a number of years because of its longer-term implications. Items included will be distinguished by the various types of asset – land, buildings, equipment, furniture, for example – and should also state the reasons for proposals – such as replacement, new methods, and capacity.

Back-up data should also accompany the proposals to justify the expenditures, and will take the usual forms of capital evaluations, such as return on investment and discounted cash flow analysis. The strain on cash resources should also be considered when compiling this budget.

Profit and loss account

The first component of the master budget is the budgeted profit and loss account. This budget will summarize the effects of all the relevant data contained in the supplementary operating and service budgets, sales, purchasing, personnel and capital expenditure (depreciation, salvage receipts) budgets. It will be prepared in months or other chosen periods and be compiled by the financial controller. A sample profit and loss statement incorporating provisions for budget and standards is shown in Figure 15.1.

Cash budget

The second component of the master budget is the cash budget, which is critical in view of the possible constraints that an unsatisfactory cash availability position may have on the required expansion of a business and hence on the acceptability of the master budget as a whole.

The financial controller, with the assistance of all other management, should determine the timing by period, usually monthly, of production, sales, fixed asset purchases and so forth, and then prepare the effects on the cash balance. The reason for this budget is to determine by period where additional cash may be required or where surplus cash may be available for short-term investments.

The income side is built up from the sales and debtors budget plus any other miscellaneous receipts, such as loans, new capital, sale of assets, grants, and

Current month	Budget	%	Standard	%	Actual	%	Variance
Gross sales							
Less: Deductions from sales							
Total net sales							
Manufacturing standard costs							
Material							
Labour							
Burden							
Direct expense							
Total manufacturing standard costs							
Standard manufacturing gross profit							
Budget and volume variances							
Actual manufacturing gross profit							
Expenses							
Selling							
Advertising							
Administrative							
Engineering							
Total expenses							
Operating profit							
Net profit before taxes							
Income tax provision							
Net profit							

Figure 15.1 Example of a profit and loss statement with provision for budgets and standards

interest. On the expenditure side will be the incurred expenses of the production and service department budgets, purchasing and capital expenditure budgets plus other payments relating to the distribution of profits, such as dividends and income taxes.

Balance sheet

The third component of the master budget is the projected balance sheet which will show the net effect of the budgets on the financial position of the company. Again, being compiled by the financial controller, it will consider information contained in the budgeted profit and loss account, capital expenditures and cash and the related movement of the working capital and financing.

Management must examine these results of the profit and loss, cash and balance sheet master budgets that result from the consolidation of the subsidiary budgets and determine if they are acceptable. Do they show the most practical overall profit to be accepted as a plan for the ensuing year or period to be budgeted? If the answer is negative then the problem areas should be determined and the departments concerned advised specifically of their short-comings. As all the budgets are mainly interrelated, such a change generally means the re-submission of all the subsidiary budgets. While this exercise may appear to be rather long-winded and even timewasting, it is one of the real values of preparing budgets in this manner in that the consideration, discussion and communication of the short-term profit objective of the company involves all levels of management in its achievement, and by this process is most likely to reveal the maximum practical profit objective for the company.

In practice, a lot of companies tend to take either sales or production in isolation and agree independently what the level of activity should be in these fields; once decided on, they proceed to build all the other budgets around them. If the resultant profit is in excess of the outlook for the current year, they are happy to leave it as such. However, assuming that the job is to be tackled properly, it is at this stage of review that any attempts at over-budgeting or, worse still, conservative budgeting, should be weeded out. The level of responsibility for performance of the plan from each manager should be agreed upon, so that he fully commits himself to its attainment.

When the master budgets have been finally agreed upon and accepted, they should be adopted formally by management as its policy and plan for the forthcoming year or period and thereby provide a budget against which performance or achievement will be measured.

CONTROLLING THE PLAN

As indicated, budgets are built up by responsibility. It follows, therefore, that operating statements will be prepared for each budget centre involved. These operating statements should form part of the management information system used to control actual performance against the budget plan.

Good budgetary control follows the theory of 'management by exception'. While management is provided with full details of expenditure, sales, production, and so on under its functional control, reports and information should be focused on matters that are adverse, or that show an unusual favourable variance, so that its energy is concentrated in the right direction and its effort is not being diluted with a lot of information which merely indicates that things are going as planned.

There are differing schools of thought on the amount of detail that should be provided to management. Some management accountants prefer to provide only data over which managers have some degree of control. For instance, if depreciation policy is decided by the board, there is no point in giving an operational manager a depreciation charge for, say, the machine shop. He has no control over what that charge will be; according to this theory, this information is unnecessary and does not help him to perform his part of the plan under normal conditions. This theory does not give management the full picture and lacks the important benefit of enabling management to see the overall effect and contribution of its department to the business as a whole. The statement may be broken down into two sections labelled 'controllable' and 'uncontrollable'. Just what is controllable or uncontrollable can be surprising. For example, a shop foreman shown a list of fixed assets in his areas on which there is a depreciation charge may well indicate items of equipment which are surplus to his requirements but for which he has not bothered to raise a disposal request. These items can then be removed from the department, sold with good salvage values being obtained, valuable floor space being released, routine maintenance checks ceasing and administration time and effort being saved in searching for and identifying equipment at physical inventory time.

Timing of feedback

Timing is of great importance. When should the measurement of control be effected, and over what period? Having decided what period the budget is to cover (usually annual) the budget itself will be divided into sub-periods: possibly months and quarters, or perhaps into thirteen four-weekly intervals, depending on the type of business. In addition to the detailed annual budget, most companies have some form of long-range planning for a number of years ahead covering, for instance, the profit and loss account, balance sheet, cash flow and capital expenditure.

This longer-term planning concerns itself primarily with determining whether or not the internal fund flow of the business will cover, for example, its commitments and capital expenditure programme, but, of course, the longer-term plans will not be prepared in anything like the same detail as the yearly short-term operating budget. It is a matter of individual company requirements to determine which data is best controlled on a quarterly, monthly, weekly or even daily basis.

An organization must generally have a fairly sophisticated accounting system to generate and disseminate information on a daily basis and this type of data is generally confined to production data. Standard hours produced, finished units, efficiencies, absenteeism, and so on all lend themselves to daily control. Billings in terms of unit sales and value would best be reviewed on a weekly basis, although for local consumption this, again, may be preferred on a rough daily basis.

All other profit and loss and cash flow data would be embodied in monthly financial statements. A balance sheet could be prepared on a quarterly basis.

Whatever is right for a business must be determined by the constraints within which it works and what is needed to control the situation. Normally, data of a daily and weekly nature are restricted to middle management to facilitate operational control and are not fed through the pyramid of top management unless a special situation demands such close control. As a general rule, the lower down the management line one goes, the sooner information should be in management's hands. The foreman should have his output in standard hours measured against budget and his material usage for his batch of machines during the following morning so that he can take the necessary action to correct any deviation from his target.

Thus it has been said that this first-line information is the life blood of the business, and the accounting results which follow at the end of the month confirm and quantify an already known situation.

FLEXIBLE BUDGETS

One criticism sometimes levelled at budgetary control is its rigidity. In practice, actual results may be the outcome of circumstances which have changed from those existing when the budget was first prepared. Budgets, when set and agreed upon, can only be based on one set of circumstances. As actual conditions seldom equate with budgeted conditions, the difference between actual costs and budgeted costs must be demonstrated. Information should therefore be available to suggest the appropriate level of expense, generally known as budget standards, which fluctuate at varying levels of production activity or sales volume.

Flexible budgetary control (as opposed to fixed budgeting) was introduced to control this situation. Flexible budgeting is applied in businesses where it is impossible to make a firm forecast of future conditions. Although fixed budgeting should be satisfactory for the more stable industries, these are very few and far between. Flexible budgeting is more widely applicable.

Flexible budgeting is designed to provide a more realistic picture of the variance between actual expenses and budgeted expenses. One expects to be able to distinguish that part of the variance which is due to volume and for which a manager will not have control, and that part of the variance over which the manager should have control. To achieve this, one must be in a position to calculate budget standards at varying levels of activity.

The application of this calculation is demonstrated below by considering first a report on the basis of fixed budgeting and then showing a similar report calculated on a flexible budgeting basis. Before looking at these reports, it must be clear that costs are classified for flexible budgeting purposes. This in itself is a most difficult task and one that may be tackled in many ways which cannot be amplified in this chapter. However, for the purpose of this exercise, the following broad categories are used:

1 *Fixed costs* Costs which do not vary in the short term with volume
2 *Variable costs* Costs which do so vary
3 *Semi-variable costs* Costs which will vary with volume but not in direct relationship.

Chapter 16 gives more details of these types of costs: of course, if standard costing is already applied in the company, the setting of a flexible budget is rendered

Expense type	Budget (£)	Actual (£)	Variance (£)
Material	10 000	12 500	+ 2500
Labour	5 000	5 900	+ 900
Rent	3 000	3 000	—
Salaries	1 000	1 100	+ 100
	19 000	22 500	+3500

Figure 15.2   Example of fixed budgeting

	Budget			Actual	Variance Analysis	
	Standard per unit	Fixed budget	Flexed budget		Control-able	Volume
Output in units		10 000	12 000	12 000	—	+ 2 000
% of original budget		100%	120%	120%	—	+ 20%
	£	£	£	£	£	£
Variable Costs						
Material	£1.00	10 000	12 000	12 500	+ 500	+ 2 000
Labour	£0.50	5 000	6 000	5 900	- 100	+ 1 000
Fixed Costs						
Rent		3 000	3 000	3 000	—	—
Salaries		1 000	1 000	1 100	+ 100	—
TOTAL		19 000	22 000	22 500	+ 500	+ 3 000

Figure 15.3   Example of flexible budgeting

considerably easier. If standard costs are not available, the technique of marginal costing will need to be applied in dealing with individual costs to determine the degree of variability. Scatter graphs or the regression theory may be used. Figure 15.2 is based on fixed budgeting and demonstrates how much the actual is off target. This type of measurement is an improvement on, say, measuring against last year's performance when circumstances may have been different. The report provides some conception of the amount by which actual experience varies from budgeted plans. However, if one is to adhere to one of the basic principles of budgetary control, that people should only be responsible for cost over which they have control, this report may not provide the solution.

Figure 15.3 applies similar information but is calculated on the basis of flexible budgeting. Thus, clearly, the advantages of flexible budgeting are demonstrated by the second report. It shows in reality that instead of the manager being responsible for an adverse variance of £3 500 as he was in the first report, he is, in fact, only responsible for the adverse variance of £500, the remaining £3 000 being due to increased volume in production which may be the result of conservative sales forecasting, or some other factor which must be taken up with some other department in the organization.

Flexible budgeting is thus extremely useful for getting behind the causes of variances, particularly if quantities, as well as costs, have been budgeted. With sales variances, for example, one can determine whether the variance is due to price, volume, outlet mixture, product mixture, or a combination of these.

USE OF COMPUTERS

Generally, manual methods of making the planning computations are time-con-suming, with the result that only a few alternative plans of operation can be fully evaluated when setting a budget and analysis of variances may be limited by time constraints. Computerized financial models have been developed to assist in simulating what the results would be under many different assumptions as to volume, products and plans of operation. Most steps in budgeting usually involve some alternative assumptions or decisions, and the final outcome of the budget process can vary greatly in terms of the profits and resources which will result from each assumption or decision. As a practical matter, the burden of making the planning and budgeting computations, under even one set of assumptions, is generally considered to be all that a company can expect its people to carry in addition to their current operating responsibilities. Very often the work is such that deadlines are missed and budgets for the new year are not available on time. The computerized financial model takes the drudgery out of the computations, once the computer programs are prepared, by applying the given relationships to different sets of assumptions and conditions. This process of stimulating different methods of operations is a big help in exploring the alternatives available in the planning process.

ZERO-BASE BUDGETING

Zero-base budgeting is a technique for short-term operational planning, whereby existing levels of expenditure on continuing activities are systematically ques-tioned. This is in contrast to the more common 'incremental' approach. In incre-mental budgeting, the benchmark tends to be the level of activity and expenditure in the immediate past, budget proposals being related to this in terms of 'more' or 'less'. In zero-base budgeting, the benchmark is the 'minimum survival' level of activity and expenditure as seen by the manager of the activity in question. If the budget proposal is only to maintain the existing level of activity, assuming this to be above the 'minimum survival' level, the proposal must explain why the addi-tional expenditure involved over and above the 'minimum survival' level is justi-fied. A manager in charge of several activities will be required to state which level of expenditure on each of these activities he would choose if he could only spend, say, 80 per cent of his budget. The point of this approach is to squeeze out 'budget slack' at the lower levels of decision making and to allow the senior levels to decide how, if at all, the balance of the budget will be spent.

INSTALLING THE SYSTEM

The organizational chart should be examined with a view to determining where the responsibility for sales, costs and profits really lies. Revisions, where appropriate, may be considered at this time. The organization structure should be so developed as to fix responsibility right down the line. There must be an organization chart which clearly defines the levels of responsibility and the chain of command, setting out who is responsible for what and to whom. It is desirable to support each functional position with a job description defining the function, duty and responsibility. Tradition must be ignored, responsibility and control being given to those who are responsible for taking the decisions, but care must be taken to preserve the 'business flair' of an organization, and those given the responsibility should be placed where their individual resources can be best used.

The key factors should then be determined before designing the system most suitable to the company's needs. The system design should cover flow diagrams of the information generated, collection data necessary for budget preparation and control reports to be subsequently prepared. During this period consideration should be given to the level of sophistication of the existing information system, whether the proposed system will provide an improvement and also the level of human resources with which one has to work the new system.

Having obtained a positive reaction to these considerations, the next step is to test the initial design with various personnel at all levels in order to determine its suitability to meet their requirements for management information.

Once initial design is finalized, it is time to prepare a series of seminars and teach-ins to explain the thinking behind the purpose and operation of the system. Questions, constructive criticisms and improvements should be invited so that all are involved and communicate at all levels.

A timetable for installation of the programme should be established. A critical path analysis is the ideal basis for identifying the order in which the budget data should be collected and which information is to be cross-referred to two or more departments.

The collection of information for the 'first budget' should now be initiated. Considerable time, assistance and guidance should be made available to staff at this stage and perseverance on behalf of those taking responsibility for the installation of the system will be required. It is vital that all levels of management go through the discipline of thinking through and preparing their portion of the budgets. Miracles should not be expected from the first results. It is not unusual for a company to take two or three years to get a control system of this nature fully operational. However, at each stage one should expect to produce some results which are usable even in the first year. What these results will be may differ from company to company but initially they usually provide a good insight to sales and cash flow data. An important by-product is management education and awareness of what the business is all about.

Budget period

There is no general rule governing the selection of a period of time for a budget. This will be decided by the particular circumstances of the business. For instance the fashion industry must, of necessity, have a very short budget period, sometimes of three or four months' duration, whereas in the shipbuilding industry a budget may range over three or four years. For most businesses, however, the calendar year is normally the accepted period: it is broken down into twelve monthly periods and the information is complementary to the published accounts.

However, if there is a strong seasonal influence affecting sales, it is sometimes prudent to have a 'model year' upon which to base the budget and this usually starts just ahead of the main selling period. Businesses which rely mainly on the summer or Christmas trade may well justify a model year. Model years, as the name implies, usually commence with the introduction of new models. A car manufacturer, for example, may run its model year from September to the following August in order to have a good start to the year following the autumn motor shows and new year car registrations. The motive behind this is that if business has not gone as well as expected there is still sufficient time before the end of the model year to curtail activity, restrict costs and reconsider expansion programmes or introduce special promotions in order to keep profits in line with, or better than, budget.

Budget manual

It is helpful to have such a document available within the company so that there is no ambiguity about what is required of each individual in relation to budgets. The type of information one might expect the budget manual to contain is a brief explanation of the purposes of budgetary control as practised within the company and organization charts and job descriptions showing quite specifically the budget responsibilities for each function; routing of budgetary control forms for collection and control documentation; timetables or programmes for completion of budgets and control data feedback; budget periods; samples of reports and statements to be employed; and accounts classification and coding data.

Budget committees

The question of who should control the preparation of budgets and who should review these controls is one that each organization arrives at during some stage of the budget preparation.

It is desirable that top and middle management contribute to and agree levels of activity to be budgeted, although it must be recognized that the human factor involved makes this difficult to achieve. A keen manager, anxious to please at a budget review meeting, will possibly incorporate a stretch element to his plan. Another manager setting his own targets against which his performance is to be measured may be inclined to be over-cautious (particularly if an achievement bonus is paid). Investigations have been made in this area and the results carry important lessons for the business man interested in making the most of his budget system.

One conclusion is that the budgets studied are used as pressure devices for constantly increasing efficiency, but because of the effects on people, the budgets tended to generate a long-run result of decreased efficiency. Naturally enough, this is attributed to the lack of participation in the budget preparation phase by those being budgeted and to the lack of sales ability on the part of the accounting personnel. Another study concludes that successful budgeting is more concerned with human relationships than with accounting techniques and that if good principles of human relationships are applied, successful budget practices become inevitable. Yet another appraisal of current business budgeting indicates that important weaknesses in practice are the result of superficial appreciation of budget concepts by management, inadequate techniques, and the absence of a disciplined environment in many organizations. Upon reflection, it becomes apparent that the requirements for a successful budget operation are not restricted to accounting or finance planning techniques but that successful managers are those who keep such considerations in mind while executing the more mechanical aspects of the budget process.

There are various views held on this point. If operating managements are made responsible for profits, then one of the objectives of budgetary control, that is, the proper co-ordination of the organization, is achieved. The same processes should be involved as with the control aspect. What an organization should attempt to achieve is the total commitment of all levels of management to the plan. Each level of management should review its plans and performances through the usual management committees, be they formal or informal groupings, right up to the chief executive, and the overall objective should be clear and unambiguous at each stage.

However, one person will be responsible for pulling together the various parts of the master budget. This job usually falls on the chief accountant or financial controller or his department. Larger companies employ a budget manager and, of course, this co-ordinating exercise naturally falls into his lap. He may be called upon to undertake a number of exercises to determine what the various results thrown up mean within the overall company objectives, but it must be emphasized that his role is one of support. The responsibility is fixed upon the persons committing and accepting stewardship over resources.

The budget organization can be regarded as analogous to a telephone company operating an important communications system; it is responsible for the speed, accuracy and clarity with which the messages flow through the system, but not for the content of the messages themselves.

Information codes

Budgetary control has extended control information beyond the more traditional accounting information to broader aspects of control, setting out data in terms of, for example, hours worked, output of production in standard hours, information on market share, and quality of product. This is all necessary for the achievement of the plan. However, looking at the pure accounting contribution to budgetary control, a suitable system of accounts coding should be designed so that the information is collected and analysed within the budget and cost centres.

The accounting code should be what is commonly called a subjective/objective system. The subjective part of the code will be used to analyse the expenditure to the cost and burden centres, that is machine X in the machine shop.

It is important to give considerable thought to the design of the coding system, as it should not only be able to cope with existing needs for information, but also have the flexibility to be expanded to meet future demands. A system of this sort should enable a company, using the subjective code, to produce information necessary for the preparation of the traditional statutory accounts. And by going through the objective section of the code, the information required for budgetary control and management accounting can be produced which should be made available to those drawing up the budgets as appropriate.

CONCLUSIONS

Budgetary control often strikes apprehension or fear into non-financial people. People tend to be sceptical or untrusting of having their performances measured against a standard. This is a human and understandable response. Most people, at some time during their careers, have had budgetary control used against them as a cost reduction tool.

It is up to finance managers to clarify and emphasize that budget flexing and control is an essential and deliberate need of modern-day management. It is a management tool designed as a *fair* basis upon which to measure performance against a predetermined plan, and conduct business in the most efficient manner possible, thereby improving profitability.

FURTHER READING

Batty, J., *Corporate Planning and Budgetary Control*, Macdonald & Evans, London, 1970

Cave, S.R., *Budgetary Control and Standard Costing*, 3rd edn, Gee, London, 1973

Garbutt, Douglas, *Get Control of Your Cash*, Wildwood House, Aldershot, 1988

Vale, Philip (ed.) *Financial Management Handbook*, 3rd edn, Gower, Aldershot, 1988

Willsmore, A.W., *Business Budgets in Practice*, 5th edn, Pitman, London, 1973

16 Management accounting

Douglas Garbutt

As its name implies, management accounting is the accounting system which provides financial information to managers to assist in formulating policies, making business plans and in controlling the organization. A few examples of specific problems tackled by management accountants are:

- Choosing the least costly methods of production
- Developing detailed plans, budgets and cost standards
- Assessing service and manufacturing performance
- Deciding on prices
- Assessing capital expenditure proposals
- Choosing between alternative methods of financing.

Some of these topics are expounded in other chapters.

A management accounting system is developed for the organization's internal needs, unlike the financial accounting system (see Chapter 13) which is set up to meet external legal requirements and accounting standards. However, the two should be combined to ensure the integrity and reliability of the information produced.

COST ACCOUNTING

Cost accounting is an important part of management accounting. Its purpose is to record and analyse the expenditures incurred on the activities and outputs of the organization. It shows how these expenditures relate to the organization's objectives and to management problems. For example:

- What does it cost to make each product or to deliver a service?
- How much profit is made each time a product is sold?

Cost classifications

Accountants classify costs in many different ways and the names used in practice are not standardized. Managers moving from one organization to another should not assume that familiar terms have the same meaning!

Elements of costs

There are three basic elements of costs:

1 *Materials* The cost of commodities introduced into, or consumed in, products or services (fixed assets are not included)
2 *Labour* The costs of remunerating employees
3 *Expenses* All other costs other than materials or labour.

Direct and indirect costs

A distinction, useful in manufacturing environments, is often made between direct and indirect costs:

1 *Direct costs* Materials, labour and expenses which become a constituent part of a specific product or service
2 *Indirect costs* Also called overhead or burden, these costs are incurred for general purposes and for more than a single product or service.

Prime cost

The combined costs of direct materials, wages and expenses are called the prime cost, which usually means direct production costs only.

Cost behaviour

Costs change over time, and management accountants examine the changes carefully for regular patterns which might be used to predict future costs. A useful distinction is made between variable and fixed costs.

Variable costs

Variable costs are those costs which vary in aggregate in direct proportion to changes in the volume of output. Variable cost should include all direct costs (prime cost) plus the variable element in overhead.

Example (dongle production)

- In April a company produces 10 000 dongles. The direct materials used cost £20 000.
- The materials cost is variable in aggregate, so the variable cost is £2 per unit produced (£20 000/10 000)
- In May 15 000 dongles are made. Because the cost is variable, the aggregate cost of materials should be £30 000
- The aggregate variable cost varies in proportion to the level of production. If production rises the aggregate variable cost will rise: if it falls the aggregate variable cost will fall. But the 'variable' cost *per unit* is constant: no matter how many dongles are made, each costs £2 in direct materials (this rule only applies within the relevant range of production levels, see below).

Fixed costs

Fixed costs are those which do not vary in aggregate in response to changes in output or activity levels. Such costs include depreciation, managerial salaries, accounting costs, research and development, permanent premises, and so on. To continue the dongles production example:

- Fixed costs are £60 000 per month. £60 000 should therefore be the fixed cost in both April and May
- The fixed cost per unit is £6 in April (£60 000/10 000)
- The fixed cost per dongle falls to £4 in May (£60 000/15 000)
- The aggregate fixed cost is not affected by the level of production. But the 'fixed' cost *per unit* varies inversely with the level of production. If production goes up, the fixed cost per unit goes down, and vice versa.

Full or total cost

Using the above distinctions there are two ways of defining full or total cost:

1 The sum of:
   - *Direct materials* (which includes supplies and components in making products)
   - *Direct labour* (the cost of employing personnel who make the products)
   - *Direct expenses* (rarely an important category, this covers payments for bought-in services for a specific product and so on. Direct expenses are often subsumed under overheads)
   - *Overheads* (which include indirect labour and materials plus various expenses such as insurances).
2 Full or total cost can also be defined as the fixed costs plus the variable costs. In the example, one dongle cost £8 (£2 + £6) to make in April but only £6 (£2 + £4) in May.

Product profit

If the fixed and variable costs (the full costs) are deducted from sales revenues, then the residue is the profit (or loss if costs exceed revenues). In the example:

- The dongles are sold for £7 each
- In April, 10 000 are sold, producing a revenue of £70 000. The corresponding aggregate cost of £80 000 (variable £20 000 + £60 000 fixed) produces a loss of £10 000
- In May, 15 000 are sold, giving a revenue of £105 000. Aggregate costs are £90 000 (variable £30 000 + £60 000 fixed) so that there is £15 000 profit.

Contribution

Contribution per unit is the difference between the selling price and the variable cost per unit. In the example, the contribution is £7 − £2 per unit, or £5 for each dongle sold. The total contribution for a stated period is the difference between sales revenues and the variable costs. In the example, the total contribution for the two months is:

- April, £50 000 (£70 000 − £20 000)
- May, £75 000 (£105 000 − £30 000)

Notice that the total contribution is proportional to the activity level. Between April and May production of dongles increases by 50 per cent, and so does the total contribution.

Relevant range

Measurement of a cost as fixed or variable is rarely accurate for the whole possible range of production from zero to maximum. If, for example, fixed costs are £60 000 per month or variable costs are £2 per unit, this will be true only within a certain range of production, say 5 000 to 20 000 units. If production exceeds 20 000 units per month, the fixed costs may rise because new fixed assets are needed. Variable costs may rise if overtime premiums become payable through extra direct labour hours. Similar processes could change fixed and variable costs if monthly production falls below 5 000 units.

COST–VOLUME–PROFIT RELATIONSHIPS

Chart method

The relationships between costs and profits can be shown by a cost–volume–profit chart. That in Figure 16.1 uses data from the dongles production example.

The total product cost line shows the result of progressively increasing production, starting at £60 000 (the fixed cost) for zero units produced. The line is straight, because £2 variable is added to the cost for each dongle.

The graph showing sales revenue starts from zero (no revenue possible at zero production). This line is also straight, showing the effect of progressive sales at £7 revenue per dongle.

The vertical gap between the two lines indicates, on the money scale, the profit or loss resulting over the range of production/sales volumes. The point at which the two lines intersect shows the volume of production and units sold at which costs just equal sales revenue. This is the breakeven point.

Solution by the C–V–Q equation

Cost–volume–profit relationships can be shown mathematically in the equation:

$$S \times Q = V \times Q + F + P$$

where S is the sales price per unit, Q is the volume of production or sales, V is the variable cost per unit, F is the aggregate fixed cost for the period and P is the profit (or loss, if negative).

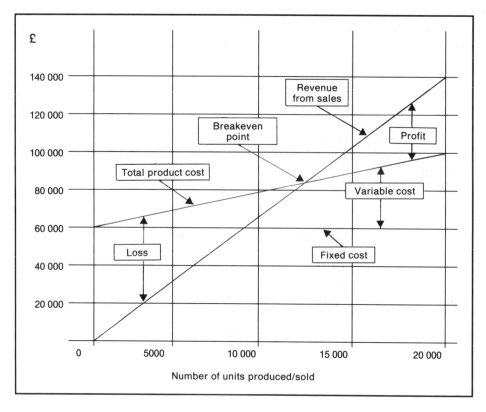

Figure 16.1   A cost–volume–profit chart

By substituting C in the equation, where C is the contribution per unit $(C = S - V)$, the equation can be rearranged as:

$$C \times Q = F + P$$

Using the equation it is possible to answer the following types of questions:

- What price will yield a target profit?
- What volume of production is needed for a stated profit?
- What must be the level of variable cost to achieve a stated profit?
- What is the maximum level of fixed costs that the firm can allow?
- What profit will result from a new production level?

Example

What price will yield a target profit of £2 000 given the following facts: $V = £5$; $F = £20\,000$; $Q = 1\,000$? The equation must be rearranged as:

$$S = (V \times Q + F + P)/Q$$

The data can now be plugged in, giving the answer: $S = £27$.

MORE COST ACCOUNTING DEFINITIONS

Cost units

A cost unit is a quantity of product, service or time in relation to which costs are recorded and analysed. Manufacturing and extractive enterprises usually have a natural measure of output to which all costs can be related: for example, a tonne of coal mined or a vehicle assembled and tested ready for despatch.

Service enterprises often have no identifiable unit of output and adopt artificial measures, such as sales of merchandise per square metre of counter or sales per customer. A bank, for example, uses a variety of measures including the costs of processing a loan, clearing a cheque, dispensing cash and so on.

Given the increasing importance of service industries, indirect costs, and new approaches to production (such as Just-in-Time), the current tendency is to identify unit costs which measure the performance of all activities undertaken by the enterprise. Realistic cost units must be developed for each component in the organization.

Cost centres

A cost centre is a process or production unit, a service centre, a particular physical location, a machine, a group of machines, in fact any grouping to which costs can sensibly be related as part of the cost control system. Eventually, cost centre costs are related to cost units.

Profit centres

A profit centre may be any unit like a cost centre to which both costs and revenues can be related, so that its performance can be judged in terms of profitability.

THE SYSTEMS APPROACH

In the systems approach, the organization is seen as a network of interdependent components. Each component performs a distinct activity which contributes to the achievement of the overall objective (which is to produce an output of service or production). The system as a whole and each component within it are regarded as 'black boxes'. Each black box accepts inputs, carries out some sort of transformation process and then yields outputs.

A 'closed system' is one which automatically controls and modifies its own operations by responding to data generated by the system itself, like a thermostatically controlled heating system.

An 'open system' does not automatically control itself. It must be supervised by people who consider data about the operations and intervene to modify inputs so that the performance becomes and remains satisfactory. Management accounting is an open system.

A good system management accounting system will produce information that will CATER to the organization's needs. The data should be:

- Consistent
- Accurate
- Timely
- Economically feasible
- Relevant.

Efficiency, economy and effectiveness

Efficiency, economy and effectiveness can be assessed in setting up a costing system and monitoring organizational performance. All three factors should be considered as follows:

1 *Efficiency* The rate at which inputs are converted into outputs:

$$\text{Efficiency} = \frac{\text{Outputs}}{\text{Inputs}}$$

2 *Economy* Paying the best price for inputs of the right quality, and getting outputs at the lowest cost
3 *Effectiveness* The extent to which the outputs from a component or subcomponent actually meet the user's needs.

COSTING SYSTEMS

Costing systems are set up to collect cost data on a continuing basis. Such systems do not meet all managerial information needs, but they are intended to meet the main regular and predetermined needs. Costing systems normally record and report material, labour and overhead costs. These are totalled to give product costs but analysed to show the costs of each department, unit or cost centre.

Each costing system must be designed for the needs of its own organization. Some of the deciding factors are:

- The number and types of product
- The organization and responsibilities
- The type of production methods used.

Cost allotment procedures

Where possible, costs are allocated directly to cost units or to cost centres.

Where allocation is not possible because the costs are indirect, the costs are apportioned on some rational or equitable basis. For example, building costs according to the space occupied, insurance according to the value of property, and so on. The overhead in cost centres is then apportioned to cost units by means of a predetermined recovery rate. Examples are:

- A percentage of direct wages
- A rate per direct labour hour
- A machine hour rate
- A rate per cost unit

- A standard cost rate.

In each case the total overhead cost is divided by the base, for example, direct wages over the budget period (normally one year).

Costing methods

Production processes differ enormously. Some firms produce only one item or job at a time, and each is different. Examples are car repairers, printers, aircraft manufacturers and bridge builders. For these, job costing is used. Service industries using job costing include professional firms (such as consultants and accountants), welfare organizations and entertainment.

At the other extreme, firms produce large quantities of a standard product, each unit of output much the same. Examples are oil refiners, chemical process plants, food processors, cement producers and mining. Service industries in this category include insurance companies, banks and fast-food outlets. All of these use process costing.

In between these two extremes are all sorts of combinations which the costing system must reflect. So the systems often combine elements of both job and process costing.

Job costing

In job costing, costs are accumulated for each job, contract or order using a job-order or job-cost sheet. As materials are issued, and as labour is used to process the materials, the cost is recorded against the job. Where machines are used, the cost of the time spent on each job is recorded. When the job is finished, all the costs are totalled and an amount is added to cover general overheads (often as a percentage of other costs). The price to the customer is often calculated by adding a further percentage to the costs to cover profit (see below for cost-plus pricing).

Process costing

In process costing, costs are accumulated by period in relation to operations, processes and departments. The period may be as short as a few hours or as long as a month of continuous operation. At the end of the period, the process costs are divided by the number of units produced to give the cost per unit for the period.

STANDARD COSTING

A standard cost is a statement of the cost which should be incurred when production or a service operation is undertaken. Standards should be based on engineering or work studies which specify the:

- Quality and quantity of materials required for manufacture (or for the provision of a service) and the price to be paid for them

- Operations to be carried out and the time required for each
- Times and rates of pay of labour involved in the operations
- Time and cost of equipment, tools, jigs, and so on.

Figures based on hunches or guesswork are *estimates* and not *standards*.

In a standard costing system, standards for each product and/or process are incorporated into the costing system. Much of the paperwork can then be simplified because standard product costs are constant. There is no need to calculate actual costs, job by job. The standard for the period is calculated by multiplying the number of products in the period by the standard cost for each product. The actual spending on materials, labour and overheads is recorded, over a period, as in process costing. This recording is separate from the standard cost calculation, but must be for the same period if variances are to be identified (see below).

Variance reporting

'Variance' is the difference between actual recorded costs and standard (or budgeted) cost. Variance reporting is based on the comparison of actual spending for a period with the standard costs over the same period. If the cost recording uses the same elements as the standards, then the actual spending for the period can be compared with the standard for the period, element by element.

An example is shown in Figure 16.2. It can be seen that the actual total costs of £47 910 are £1 910 more than they should have been. Contributing to this result, the materials cost £930 more than standard and labour £2 080 more. But machine time cost £1 100 less than standard. Thus the total excess of £1 910 is made up by an excess of £3 010 on two elements and a saving of £1 100 on the other element.

Variances are usually reported as:

- f = favourable, when the actual cost is less than standard or if a selling price or income is more than standard
- u = unfavourable, when actual costs are more than standard or selling price or income falls below standard.

'Price variance' arises whenever the price used in a cost or calculation of income differs from the standard. A 'quantity' or 'usage' variance arises whenever the actual quantity differs from standard. The elements of variance due to prices and quantities can be separated, as illustrated in Figure 16.3.

Variance analysis

Variance can be analysed in increasing detail to show how a total variance arises from different factors, such as:

- Elements of cost
- Price
- Quantity or usage.

The analysis could be extended to split the variance between:

Standard cost of one motherboard

> 3 kg of material   at £2 per kg
> 4 hrs of labour   at £5 per hr
> 1 hr of machine time at £20 per hr

June production

> 1 000 motherboards

Standard costs for June

> 3 000 kg of material   =   £6 000
> 4 000 hrs of labour   =   £20 000
> 1 000 machine hrs   =   £20 000
>
> Total standard costs   £46 000

Actual June costs recorded for making motherboards

> Materials issued   £6 930
> Wages paid   £22 080
> Cost of machine time   £18 900
>
> Total actual costs   £47 910

Comparison of actual and standard costs for June

Element of cost	Standard cost	Actual cost	Variance
Material	6 000	6 930	− 930
Labour	20 000	22 080	− 2 080
Machine time	20 000	18 900	1 100
June totals	46 000	47 910	− 1 910

Figure 16.2   Examples of variances. The figures show the standard costs for motherboard manufacture in June, compared with the actual costs recorded for this production over the same period

- departments and sections
- products
- jobs and processes
- time periods and shifts.

As the example in Figure 16.3 shows, a total variance may conceal significant variances within itself, and these may be a mixture of favourable and unfavourable results.

Value of variances to managers

The value of variances in practice depends on a number of factors:

- The managers to whom they are reported must understand them
- Managers must be prepared to accept variance reports as pointers towards problems
- Variance reports should not be seen as reports on managerial performance.

Some simple comparisons of variances which can be used are:

- The absolute value of the variance
- Variance as a percentage of the standard
- Cumulative variance
- Past period figures. Comparisons with past periods may be of value in showing business trends but they are only a guide for corrective action where it can be shown that similar factors will apply
- Similar units in the same group. Comparisons should be made with units of similar size
- Forecasts previously made.

Some variances may be hidden: not immediately apparent from direct comparison with the standard. For example, when sales have fallen, a reduction of trade debtors should occur. If relaxed terms of credit have been given, however, debtors may not fall. Investigation of the facts should lead to appropriate action.

Causes of variance

There are many potential causes for variances:

1 *External factors*, such as:

- Economic, social, legal and political changes
- Changes in competition
- Changes in supply conditions at home or abroad.

2 *Internal factors*, such as:

- Change in the operating system
- Inefficiencies

Formula for price and quantity variances

Price variance = $(SP \times AQ) - (AP \times AQ)$
= $AQ(SP - AP)$

Quantity variance = $(SP \times SQ) - (SP \times AQ)$
= $SP(SQ - AQ)$

where the letters are abbreviations for:

A = actual; S = standard; Q = quantity and P = price

Data for making motherboards in June

Standard costs per 1 000 units (see Figure 16.2)
Materials: 3 kg at £2 × 1 000   =   £6 000
Labour: 4 hrs at £5 × 1 000   =   £20 000
Machine time: 1 hr at £20 × 1 000   =   £20 000

Recorded actual costs for June

Materials: 3 300 kg at £2.1   =   £6 930
Labour: 4 600 hrs at £4.8   =   £22 080
Machine time: 900 hrs at £21   =   £18 900

Calculations

Applying these data to the formulae gives:

Materials price variance is AQ(SP − AP)
or 3 300(2 − 2.1) which is −£330

Materials usage (quantity) variance is SP(SQ − AQ)
or 2(3 000 − 3 300) which is −£600

Labour rate (rate) variance is AQ(SP − AP)
or 4 600(5 − 4.8) which is £920

Machine rate (price) variance is AQ(SP − AP)
or 900(20 − 21) or −£900

Machine usage (quantity) variance is SP(SQ − AQ)
or 20(1 000 − 900) which is £ 2 000

Labour usage (quantity) variance is SP (SQ − AQ)
or 5(4 000 − 4 600) which is −£3 000

Figure 16.3   Calculation of price and quantity variances

- Change as a result of changes in other elements. For example, stocks and debtors will change with sales, but so will production and sales expenses
- Poor standards can be responsible for variances, but accountants generally will not accept this explanation too readily.

In all cases of variances from standard, the manager responsible should be asked for explanations and recommendations for corrective action. All the explanations should be drawn together and reported to company management, who should determine the actions to be taken and issue clear directives for implementation. Implementation should be monitored and reported back. Once decisions on corrective actions have been made, operating targets should be reassessed and follow-up should be organized to check that the targets are achieved.

Standards can be used in conjunction with budgetary control (see Chapter 15) as the basis for flexible budgets, variance accounting and performance control.

PERFORMANCE CONTROL REPORTS

Reports on performance must be relevant to both the people who control and those who are controlled. Those who control can generally be provided with summary information. Those who are controlled will require detailed breakdowns of the factors contributing to their performance. The expectation is that the controller and the controlled will discuss deviations from standard and agree on action to be taken to correct unsatisfactory results.

A departmental manager may need a departmental variance report, but at board level reports will comprise a summary profit and loss account comparing budgets with actuals, and an analysis of variances by major departments. The board report would also include a summary of key inputs, such as head counts, sales by product, and market and production volumes. If the chief executive wants to investigate the cause of variances, the system allows him to 'drill down' into the supporting detail provided in reports to his subordinates.

The key factors affecting profits and costs at each level should be highlighted rather than devoting immense attention to excessive detail.

Reports should be in time for corrective action to be taken. This might mean daily or even hourly reports at low levels in the organization, while at higher levels monthly, quarterly and half-yearly reports may meet senior management needs. In order to prepare these reports in time, monitoring of actual results against budgets and at the relevant level of detail must be carried out as soon as possible after the end of each period.

In order to meet deadlines it may be necessary to estimate some items for reports requiring a lot of input (for example, profit and loss accounts). Where such estimates prove to be in serious error fresh reports must be circulated as soon as the correct figures are in.

Responsibility accounting

In responsibility accounting, reports are submitted to those people who have accepted responsibility for costs, revenues and assets, in line with their positions in the organization. In general the factors to which personnel relate tend to be non-financial at the lower levels. For instance, a foreman may need information solely on budgeted, standard and actual hours. At higher levels managers become responsible for cost and profit centres, and it is more important for the cost accounting to be more generally oriented so that comparisons can be made across the group.

FURTHER READING

Cowe, R. (ed.) *Handbook of Management Accounting*, 2nd edn, Gower (in association with CIMA), Aldershot, 1988

Hiromoto, Toshiro, 'Another hidden edge - Japanese management accounting', *Harvard Business Review*, July-August, 1988

Horngren, Charles, *Cost Accounting - A Managerial Emphasis*, 6th edn, Prentice Hall, Englewood Cliffs, N.J., 1987

Kaplan, R.S., 'Yesterday's accounting undermines production', *Harvard Business Review*, July-August, 1984.

17 Taxation

J C Craig

This chapter highlights some aspects of taxation which concern company administrators in the UK. It is based mainly on the provisions of the Income and Corporation Taxes Act 1988, the Taxes Management Act 1970, the Capital Gains Tax Act 1979, the Finance Acts 1988, 1989, 1990 and 1991, and the Value Added Taxes Act 1983.

The taxation of banks, insurance companies, building societies and other financial organizations, and of agricultural concerns, is outside the scope of this chapter.

New Finance Acts introduce changes to tax legislation at least annually, and even the existing rules are hedged round with 'ifs' and 'buts'. It is therefore important to regard this chapter as a general guide, and to check details before making major decisions.

CORPORATION TAX

Definitions

Some phrases used in the corporation tax rules are defined as follows:

- *Accounting date* The date to which a company makes up its accounts
- *Accounting period* The period for which corporation tax is charged, usually the period for which the company makes up its accounts but may be a shorter period
- *Distribution* Any dividend paid by a company, including a capital dividend. It also includes any other distribution out of the assets of the company, whether in cash or otherwise, except on the repayment of capital on liquidation or any other amount for which new consideration has previously been given. Also excluded is a company buying its own shares if certain conditions are satisfied
- *Financial year (FY)* The period for which the rates of corporation tax are fixed annually by the budget. Each FY runs from 1 April to 31 March and is identified by the year in which it begins
- *Franked investment income* Income from a source which has already suffered corporation tax and consequently is not liable to further corporation tax in the hands of the receiving company (for example dividends from UK companies)
- *Unfranked investment income* Income which has not suffered corporation tax at source and is therefore to be included in the receiving company's total income for corporation tax purposes (for example, debenture interest from other companies).

Tax returns

Every person who receives income of any kind is under statutory obligation to complete a return of income each year if required to do so; otherwise he is required to notify the Inland Revenue of any new source of untaxed income. In the case of a limited company, its officers have this responsibility and this cannot be avoided even if an agent is employed to complete the return.

Tax assessments

Local tax inspectors assess tax due based on returns, supplementary figures and the annual accounts of a business.

Appeals

Appeals must be made in writing within 30 days of the assessment and normally the appeal is settled by correspondence or a meeting. If the taxpayer and inspector cannot agree, the taxpayer may have the appeal heard by commissioners, of which there are:

1 General commissioners, who are leading local citizens without specialist tax knowledge
2 Special commissioners, comprising one or more civil servants dealing wholly with tax and who are more able to unravel complex issues. Appealing to special commissioners may involve travel and the briefing of counsel to put the case.

A commissioners' decision is binding on the taxpayer and the Revenue. Appeals on interpretation of law can be made to the courts.

Interest charged on late payment

Tax not paid on the due date, or delayed beyond a certain period pending appeal, may be liable to interest (which is itself not an allowable deduction for tax purposes). To avoid risk of interest through appeal delays the company can pay the undisputed amount and buy interest-yielding tax deposit certificates for the remainder (interest on the certificates is taxable).

Time limit

There is a time limit of six years from the end of the relevant accounting period during which assessments may be corrected on discovery of mistakes either by the taxpayer or the Revenue. The time limit does not shield the taxpayer from corrections arising from his fraud, wilful default or neglect.

Adjustment of profit and computation of amount liable to tax

The normal pattern is for a business to take account of income from all sources. For tax purposes, income is categorized according, in general, to how it was derived (for example, Schedule A is income from rents; Schedule D, Case I or II income from a trade or profession). For a company, all sources are added together to arrive at the total profits chargeable to corporation tax. As shown in Figure 17.1, starting from the ordinary profit and loss account, to calculate the Schedule D Case I or II trading profit, non-allowable expenses are added back and income which is not taxable or taxable under a different Schedule is deducted.

Apart from advance corporation tax (see later) the 'mainstream liability' amount is normally due for payment nine months after the end of the accounting period.

Pay and file

As from 1993, new arrangements (known as pay and file) require each company to file its annual accounts with the Inland Revenue, broadly speaking, not later than one year after its year end. The tax liability for that year is due for payment nine months after the year end and tax underpaid or paid late will be liable to interest from that date.

Rate of tax

The rate of corporation tax is normally announced for each financial year in the Chancellor's end-of-year budget. With a few exceptions, small companies (generally those with annual profits not exceeding £250 000) pay at a lower rate. A sliding scale applies for profits between £250 000 and £1.25m.

If a company's accounting year is different from the FY, and spans two FYs with different tax rates, the profits are apportioned on a time basis.

Allowable expenses

For any expense to be allowable, it must have been incurred 'wholly and exclusively' for the purposes of the business. Certain forms of expenditure are disallowed, either by definite statements in the Acts, or as a result of cases decided by the courts. It would be impossible to give an exhaustive list here, particularly as many of them concern only a restricted range of industries, but a selection of the more common ones is given below.

General advice is: when in doubt, check with the detailed tax textbooks. If these do not settle the doubt, claim the expense and await the inspector's reaction. There is no penalty for this approach provided the true nature of the expense is stated openly and honestly.

Salaries and wages

Salaries and wages of employees and directors are normally allowed in full. However, the deduction allowed for excessive payments to family directors is liable to be restricted if the inspector is not satisfied that the amount is reasonable considering the services rendered.

(a)

INCOME

Gross trading profit	£1 400 000
Rent from industrial premises let to tenants	20 000
Interest from bank deposit account	6 000
Dividends from shares held	10 000
Interest from debentures held (gross)	4 000
	1 440 000

EXPENDITURE

Depreciation	£26 000	
Salaries, wages, employer's contributions to national insurance and graduated pension	60 000	
Directors' salaries and fees	10 000	
Bad debts written off	300	
Specific provision for the bad debt of a named customer	100	
General provision for bad debts	800	
Legal expenses	200	
Rent, rates and insurance	3 000	
Superannuation (Company's contributions to an approved scheme)	2 000	
Heating and lighting	1 000	
Travelling expenses	2 000	
Entertainment expenses	600	
Distribution costs	20 000	
Sundry expenses	3 000	
Loss on sale of machinery	1 000	
		130 000
NET PROFIT		£1 310 000

Figure 17.1 Example of a profit and loss computation for year to 31 March 1992
    (a) Profit and loss account
    (b) Adjustment for corporation tax
    (c) Calculation of corporation tax

(b)

Net profit shown in the accounts		£1 310 000
Add back items not allowable		
Depreciation	£26 000	
General provision for bad debts	800	
Entertainment expenses	600	
Loss on sale of machinery	1 000	
		28 400
Deduct items, either not taxable or taxable under different headings		£1 338 400
Rent	£20 000	
Interest income	6 000	
Dividends	10 000	
Interest	4 000	
		40 000
		£1 298 400
Less Capital allowances		28 400
SCHEDULE D, CASE I INCOME		£1 270 000

(c)

Case I income – business profits adjusted	£1 270 000
Case III income – untaxed income from bank deposit interest	6 000
Schedule A income – rent	20 000
Income received subject to deduction of *income* tax at source debenture interest (but not dividends)	4 000
Profits chargeable to corporation tax	£1 300 000
Corporation tax at 33% on £1 300 000	£432 300

Figure 17.1 (concluded)

Entertaining

Entertainment expenses are not allowable. 'Entertainment' includes gifts of food, drink and tobacco, for example, as Christmas presents.

Bad debts

A general reserve for bad debts is not allowable, but actual bad debts and a specific provision for the bad debts of a named customer are allowable.

Depreciation

Depreciation is not allowable, but capital allowances are given in appropriate cases instead.

Capital expenditure

No kind of capital expenditure is allowable other than by way of capital allowances. Capital profit or loss on the sale of an asset is excluded from the computation of business profit, but may be subject to a separate calculation for capital gains purposes.

Legal expenses

Some legal expenses are allowable and some are not, the distinction being broadly that they are allowable if they relate to a transaction of a revenue nature, but not if they are of a capital nature. For example, legal expenses for the preparation of a service agreement for a manager, or the collection of debts, or the renewal of an existing short lease are revenue and allowable, but the legal expenses in connection with the purchase of freehold premises or a long lease are capital and not allowable.

Retirement benefits

Retirement benefits for employees are allowable whether they are direct pensions or a contribution to a superannuation scheme approved by the Inland Revenue or to the employee's personal Inland Revenue-approved scheme. A moderate lump sum to an employee on his retirement would be allowable, but an exceptional lump sum to a superannuation fund would be spread forward over future years.

Capital allowances

Capital allowances exist on seven main types of fixed assets used wholly and exclusively for purposes of the business:

1 Industrial buildings
2 Plant and machinery
3 Agricultural land and buildings
4 Mines and oil-wells

5 Capital expenditure on scientific research
6 Patents
7 Know-how.

Only the first two types will be considered in detail here.

When any asset which qualifies for allowances is purchased, the year's allowances are given in full for the company's accounting period no matter how late in the period the asset was obtained. This rule may need to be modified where the accounting period is shorter than twelve months.

It is important to consider the overall position before deciding whether or not, or to what extent capital allowances should be claimed.

Industrial buildings

The nature of the business must be industrial (as distinct from commercial, retailing or wholesaling, or professional) or storage. Even for an industrial company the allowance is not given for offices and showrooms, except where these form an integral part of the factory and account for less than 25 per cent (10 per cent prior to 16 March 1983) of its whole cost. For expenditure incurred after 31 March 1986 allowances are given to the first owner in the form of a writing down allowance of 4 per cent per year on the cost of the building.

Prior to 1 April 1986, higher initial allowances were available in the year of expenditure.

In the year of disposal, instead of the writing down allowance there is a balancing allowance or balancing charge to bring total allowances into line with net cost.

Where the building is sold for more than it cost, the balancing charge cannot exceed the total allowance already received. (There may, however, be a taxable capital gain in addition to the balancing charge.)

On the sale of a factory built before November 1962 there is no balancing adjustment if it is sold after it is fifty years old, and for factories built since November 1962 none after they are twenty-five years old.

Cost price includes: the building, plus the architect's fees, the cost of the tunnelling, levelling and preparing the land; installing main services, fences, perimeter walls and roadways on the site.

It does not include: the cost of the land, legal and estate agency fees; preparation of a lease; demolition of a former building.

When a building is demolished, the cost of demolition is added to the original cost before working out the balancing adjustment.

For the second and subsequent owners, the allowances are equal to the residue of cost spread over the remainder of the twenty-five or fifty years.

The importance of distinguishing between land and buildings is vital, with seller and buyer having opposing interests.

From 12 April 1978 industrial buildings' allowances were extended to apply also to certain qualifying hotels, the rate of annual allowance being 4 per cent.

Any industrial or commercial structure or qualifying hotel in an enterprise zone (an area designated as such by the government) qualifies for 100 per cent initial allowance; if a reduced allowance is claimed, 25 per cent writing-down allowance is available on the amount of the cost. These allowances are available only in respect of expenditure in the first ten years of classification as an enterprise zone.

Plant and machinery

Allowances may be claimed by businesses assessed on trading or professional income under Case I or Case II of Schedule D, against Schedule A assessments on income from real property, in respect of assets owned by an employee and used by the employee for his employer's business, or against profits of a trade assessed under Schedule D, Case V (foreign trades).

The definition of 'plant and machinery' spreads widely to include office and canteen equipment, furniture, dry docks and virtually every type of fixed tangible asset which is not 'building'.

The allowances for plant are based on the concept of an expenditure pool, which comprises all expenditure on qualifying plant to date less amounts claimed as capital allowances for previous years. A 25 per cent writing down allowance per annum may be claimed on the residual pool value. New acquisitions are added to the pool. When an asset is sold or scrapped its disposal figure is deducted from the pool unless sales proceeds exceed cost, in which case the reduction of the pool value is restricted to the original cost of the asset. It is possible for a company to take less than a 25 per cent writing down allowance and so defer allowances to later years.

Private cars costing over £8 000 are kept separate from other assets. Each also qualifies for a 25 per cent writing down allowance, but restricted to a maximum of £2 000 per year starting from the year of purchase. There is a balancing adjustment in the year of sale.

For assets acquired on hire purchase, allowances are given on the equivalent of the cash price, and the hire charge is treated as an allowable revenue expense in the years in which it is paid. In the case of assets on straight hire, contract hire or lease there are no capital allowances but the rental is allowed as a revenue in the year in which it is paid.

Where cars with a market value when new that exceeds £8 000 are hired, a proportion of the rental charge payable by the lessee is disallowable.

It is possible to elect for separate items of plant to be treated as short-life assets, each forming its own separate pool of expenditure. Any residual separate pools remaining after four years are transferred to the general pool.

Setting losses against profits

A trading loss (that is, Schedule D, Case I or II) arising in an accounting period may be set against:

1   Other sources of profit in the same accounting period in which the loss is suffered (for example, against Schedule A profits)
2   The trading profit of the immediately preceding accounting period, provided that the company was then carrying on the trade
3   Other sources of profit in that preceding accounting period
4   For losses in a period ending after 31 March 1991, other sources of profit in the three preceeding years.

Claims for relief under 1, 2 and 3 above are optional. If they are not made, or if they leave a balance of a loss still unrelieved, the remaining loss may be set against the first available future trading profits of that trade, but not against future profits from other sources.

The right to carry forward losses ends when the trade ceases or a majority of the shares change hands together with a major change in the nature of the conduct of the trade being carried on. The effect of this restriction has been virtually to end the sale of tax-loss companies. An example of a normal loss claim is given in Figure 17.2.

A terminal loss (suffered during the final 12 months up to the time a trade is discontinued) may be carried back and set against the trading profits of the three preceding years. To make a terminal loss claim it is sufficient that the trade has permanently discontinued. This is not necessarily the same as winding up the company, as its existence may continue through other company activities or with a fresh trade of a different nature.

Directors' remuneration as it affects loss

Skill is needed in arranging a company's affairs to take best advantage of the many variations of the loss relief rules. For example, even in a small private company it may be sound policy to pay the directors at least part of their customary remuneration, even though this makes a larger loss. Otherwise the directors might be without income from which to offset their personal tax reliefs.

ADVANCE CORPORATION TAX

When a company pays a dividend or other distribution it is required to make a payment of advance corporation tax (ACT) to the Inland Revenue. The rate is fixed annually and the formula is:

$$\text{ACT} = \frac{\text{Basic rate of income tax (for assessment year)}}{1 - \text{Basic rate of income tax}}$$

and this rate is applied to the actual dividend paid.

The year of assessment begins on 6 April in the financial year in which the dividend is paid. The rate is applied to the actual dividend paid and is treated as a tax credit at basic rate. Hence the dividend plus ACT is treated as a gross receipt by each person receiving the dividend.

Payment of ACT is due fourteen days after the end of the calendar quarter in which the dividend is paid. For these purposes the company's year-end date is treated as the end of a quarter. Failure to make payment on time can result in an interest charge.

Treatment by shareholders

Every individual in the UK who receives a dividend and tax credit can treat the tax credit as if it were a voucher for income tax paid. If he is liable to the basic rate of income tax then no further liability will arise; if he is liable to tax at the higher rate, he will be required to pay only the excess of the higher rate over the basic rate. If his income is so small that he pays no income tax, he will recover the tax credit.

Where a company receives a dividend with a tax credit the sum of the two will be treated as 'franked investment income', that is, income which has already borne corporation tax and therefore on which no further tax is payable. The company

Accounting period to 31 December annually:

Trading results — 1987 profit		£20 000
— 1988 loss		60 000
— 1989 profit		8 000
Unfranked investment income — 1987		5 000
— 1988		7 000
— 1989		6 000

Set-off of loss

1	Other income in 1988	7 000
2	Profits in 1987 (£20 000 + £5 000)	25 000
3	Trading profit in 1989	8 000
		40 000
4	Carry forward against future trading profits	20 000

Losses carried forward may only be set against future profits from the same trade and not other income, hence unfranked investment income in 1989 is taxable.
Corporation tax payable for the year to 31 December 1987 would be cancelled or, if already paid, refunded.

Note the cash flow advantage of submitting promptly the figures for 1988 and the claim for loss relief.

Note also that had the loss been incurred in the year to 31 December 1991, it could have been carried back for three years.

Figure 17.2   Example of a normal loss relief

may set the amount of the tax credit on dividends received against its obligation to pay ACT in respect of its own dividend payments, and pay only the balance to the Inland Revenue.

Treatment of ACT by a company paying dividends

In respect of dividends paid during an accounting period, ACT is treated as an advance payment on account of the corporation tax liability for that accounting period with only the balance, or mainstream liability, then being payable nine months after the accounting period. The maximum ACT which can be set off in any one year is equal to the amount of ACT which would be payable on a distribution which, together with the attributable ACT, is the size of the taxable profits for the period in question.

Any ACT not relieved in the year may be carried back for six years and a repayment of corporation tax claimed for those years. Any balance still not received may be carried forward and set against future years' corporation tax liabilities.

THE NECESSARY BOOK-KEEPING

The adjustment of profit and the computation of tax payable are made outside the double-entry book-keeping system, but settlement of tax requires three ledger accounts:

1 Corporation tax (including advance corporation tax and tax credits)
2 Income tax account for unfranked investment income
3 Income tax account for PAYE deducted from employees' income.

The reason for maintaining items under 1 and 2 is that a company suffers corporation tax but not income tax on its own account. Income tax which has been deducted at source from investment income received by the company may be offset against income tax deducted from payments made out by the company. If a net balance on the income tax account is *due by* the company it is payable to the Collector of Taxes; if a balance is *due to* the company it will be treated as a payment towards any corporation tax due for the period. It is important to keep franked items separate from unfranked, and PAYE separate from both.

The necessary entries are summarized in Figure 17.3.

GROUPS OF COMPANIES

There are special concessions in the taxation of groups of companies, their main effect being to reduce or defer the tax on certain transactions within the group. It requires skill to arrange group affairs to take the best advantage of these arrangements, and the administrator should either make a specialized study or consult the group's professional advisers before making transfer of assets or payments of dividends within the group.

The three main taxation advantages of group taxation are:

1 *Transfers of capital assets* No chargeable gain arises when capital assets are

Corporation tax account

Debit:

(a) adjustment for overprovision of last year's liability   Profit and loss (appropriation) a/c

(b) Excess tax suffered on unfranked investment income tax   Unfranked investment income a/c

Credit:

(a) Estimated tax on the profits for the current year   Profit and loss (appropriation) a/c

(b) Adjustment for under provision for last year's liability   Profit and loss (appropriation) a/c

Tax on unfranked investment income account

Debit:

Income tax suffered at source on unfranked investment income received   Unfranked investment income a/c

Credit:

Tax retained when paying out debenture interest and other annual interest payments   Accounts for debenture, etc interest paid

Where credit is greater than debit, the difference is settled by paying tax to the Collector   Bank a/c

Where debit is greater than credit, the difference is settled by transfer to corporation tax a/c   Corporation tax a/c

Advance corporation tax

Debit:

Tax credit accompanying franked investment income received   Memorandum only – not passed through books of account

Credit:

ACT paid when paying out dividends

with double entry in:

Figure 17.3   Entries to make in the tax accounts

transferred between members of a group. Care is required, however, when the company which has received an asset leaves the group within six years of the transfer.

2 *Dividends* A subsidiary may pay dividends to its parent company with or without paying ACT thereon. It may be valuable to pay the dividend without ACT when the parent is not making distributions to its own shareholders, or when it has other sources of franked investment income receivable net and no trading income of its own.

3 *Loss in one company against profits in others* When one company has suffered a trading loss (or certain other outlays such as management expenses), this may be set off against the profits of any one or more members in the group. It should be noted that this concession does not extend to capital losses and careful planning is essential prior to a disposal where there are capital losses within the group.

CAPITAL GAINS

Companies pay corporation tax on chargeable gains as well as on income. All forms of property are included as assets for capital gains purposes, but certain of them are exempt from charge. These include:

1 Wasting assets with a predictable life of less than fifty years, if they are chattels (tangible moveable objects), but excluding assets which have qualified for capital allowances
2 Gains on certain government securities and qualifying corporate bonds
3 Gains on discharge of liabilities (for example, the repayment of debentures at less than their issue price).

This list is not exhaustive and does not include assets such as dwelling houses for which the gain may be exempt if made by an individual.

If assets were acquired before 31 March 1982, an election can be made to substitute the value of the asset at that time for its original cost. In most cases this is likely to be beneficial but the administrator is advised to seek professional guidance on this matter.

When a capital gain made by a company has suffered tax and the balance is paid out to shareholders, a further round of tax is suffered. For example, if the company sells its premises and goes into liquidation the position is as shown in Figure 17.4. This example has been simplified to illustrate the principle, which in an actual company would be clouded but not overthrown by the existence of other assets.

Underlying capital gains

A company with underlying capital gains in its assets may be better sold as a going concern than put into liquidation, and to the purchaser it may be a matter of indifference whether he obtains ownership of valuable assets in the one way or the other. He is not obliged to run the company as a trading concern once he has acquired the shares. With lower rates of income tax, dividends can also be a tax efficient method of extracting cash subsequent to the sale of assets; each situation must be looked at on its own merits.

Asset whose market value is £460 000 – absorbed into the business as a fixed asset or, alternatively, the shares are purchased. (It has to be assumed that the values of the asset and the shares at 31 March 1982 are the same).

The position of the seller is as follows:

Sell the asset and then go into liquidation		*Alternatively, shareholders sell their shares*	
Selling price 1989	£460 000	Selling price 1989	£460 000
Value 31 March 1982	300 000	Value 31 March 1982	300 000
Capital gain	£160 000		£160 000
Tax at 35%	56 000		
Balance distributed to shareholders on liquidation	£104 000		£160 000
Less: Personal CGT 40%*	41 600		64 000
Net gain in the hands of the shareholders (on appreciation of the shareholding due to appreciation in the value of the asset)	£62 400		£96 000

A third option would be to pay a dividend after the asset had been sold, of such an amount that the maximum advance corporation tax (ACT) offset could be achieved. Hence a dividend of £120 000 would give rise to ACT of £40 000, which is the maximum offset (£160 000 × 25%). This ACT would be set against the corporation tax liability, leaving £16 000 payable (£56 000 – £40 000). As regards the shareholders, they would receive gross income of £160 000 (£120 000 + £40 000) with a tax credit of £40 000 (i.e. 25%) attaching thereto. Assuming the top rate of 40 per cent income tax applies, there would be an additional income tax liability of £24 000 (£160 000 × 15%). On subsequent liquidation, there is no gain as the proceeds are less than the 31 March 1982 value; consideration of a capital loss is outside the scope of this book.

If the shares are purchased, the asset will be owned by a subsidiary of the buying company. It may be sold to the parent company, which may declare a dividend to dispose of its capital gain without suffering any tax; alternatively, the proceeds may simply be lent to the parent company. If the former strategy is adopted there may be value-shifting considerations on a subsequent liquidation or sale of the newly acquired subsidiary.

Notes:

Indexation allowance has been ignored for the purpose of this example.
*The rate of capital gains tax depends on the individual's personal income tax position.

Figure 17.4   Simplified example to show that sale as a going concern is better than liquidation where assets have appreciated

The directors of a private company should give thought to the chances of 'retirement relief' before disposing of their shares in a trading company. For disposals after 5 April 1991, the first £150 000 plus one-half of the difference between £600 000 and £150 000 will be exempt if they are over fifty-five and have been full-time directors for not less than 10 years and hold either:

1 Not less than 25 per cent of the voting share capital in their own right, or
2 Not less than 5 per cent in their own right, and members of their immediate family own more than 50 per cent.

A proportionate amount of relief is available if the shares have been owned for less than ten years, but more than one year. The exemption is restricted to the underlying chargeable business assets; it is not available in respect of portfolio investments held by the company.

Replacement of assets

Deferment of tax on capital gains may be claimed where the asset has been used only for trading purposes and is replaced by fresh assets, not necessarily of a similar nature, or even serving the same function, if they are one of the following classes:

1 Land and buildings
2 Fixed plant or machinery
3 Ships, aircraft and hovercraft
4 Satellites, space stations and spacecraft
5 Goodwill
6 Milk and potato quotas.

It is important that the replacement asset is bought within twelve months before or three years after the sale of the previous asset. These time limits may be extended at the discretion of the Inland Revenue.

Deferment continues indefinitely if the replacement asset is not a depreciating asset, but if a depreciating asset is bought deferment will continue for a maximum of ten years. If the depreciating asset is sold within the ten years and is replaced by a fresh permanent asset the permanence of the deferment is established, but if it is replaced by a fresh depreciating asset the deferment ends immediately. Depreciating assets for these purposes are assets with an expected life of less than sixty years. The most common example is fixed plant.

Full deferment is given only upon making a claim and where the whole proceeds from the sale of the previous asset are used for the purchase of the replacements. Where only a portion of the sale proceeds is used, the amount on which the deferment is claimed is restricted.

THE COMPANY AS A TAX COLLECTOR

Although the company does not in itself pay any income tax, it is obliged to serve as a collector by withholding income tax when making payment of:

1 Wages and salaries, for the PAYE system
2 Annual interest such as debenture interest.

The amount of PAYE deducted in a month has to be passed to the Collector of Taxes on the nineteenth day of the month next following. For example, the month from 6 April to 5 May; tax to be paid on 19 May. Income tax on annual interest is payable fourteen days after the end of the calendar quarter in which the interest is paid. For these purposes a quarter is also deemed to end at the date on which the company prepares its annual accounts.

CONTRAST BETWEEN LIMITED COMPANY AND PARTNERSHIP

Partners pay income tax at graduated rates on the whole of their profit, which is regarded as earned income in their hands, except in the case of a sleeping partner whose share is normally treated as investment income for tax purposes. (However, the distinction between earned and unearned income has become increasingly unimportant for tax purposes and has been dealt a further blow with separate assessment of husband and wife from 6 April 1990.)

In a limited company, corporation tax is payable on the profit after deducting remuneration of its directors, who are classed as employees. Profit remains in the company after paying corporation tax is not subject to further tax, but if it is withdrawn as dividend this may be liable to income tax at the higher rate in the hands of the shareholder as personal investment income of the shareholder.

From a purely tax viewpoint, there is no longer great advantage in the tax rates applicable to a company compared with personal rates.

There are many powerful legal advantages in running a limited company and these often far outweigh the importance of any tax differences. The larger the business and the more involved its ownership, the more important it becomes to operate it as a limited company. Also, a company pension scheme for the directors can normally provide better benefits than a self-employed retirement annuity scheme or a personal pension plan. On the other hand, certain undertakings, such as some of the professions, are not allowed to operate through limited companies.

VALUE ADDED TAX

The scope of the tax

The tax is chargeable on the supply of goods and services in the UK and on the importation of goods and certain services into the UK. The tax will be charged only where the supply is a taxable supply and where the goods are supplied by a taxable person in the course of a business which he is carrying on. Tax is chargeable on the importation of goods whether for business purposes or not and the tax is payable whether or not the importer is carrying on a business. In cases where imported goods may be used for private purposes the tax cannot be the subject of a VAT input deduction but a separate claim to the Commissioners for repayment.

Where certain services including staff, consultancy work and advertising are supplied from overseas, the taxable person in the UK has to account for the tax as if he had supplied the services to himself.

The supply of services includes the letting of goods on hire and the making of certain gifts or loans.

The arithmetic of the tax

Strictly speaking, value added tax is not a tax on value added in the true economic sense. Rather it is a tax on consumption, collected at each stage in the economy, on the difference (broadly) between the purchase price of goods and services acquired to make the product and the sale price of that product. Purchases are called inputs, and the tax which a business pays on buying those inputs is called input tax; sales are called outputs, and the tax which a business charges on its customers is called output tax. The excess of output tax over input tax is payable by the business to Customs and Excise, who are responsible for administering the tax, but if the input tax exceeds the output tax the difference is repayable by Customs and Excise to the business.

Registration

Traders are required to register for VAT where their turnover exceeds certain limits (reviewed from time to time). There are penalties for failing to do so.

Small traders whose annual turnover of taxable supplies does not exceed the stated limit do not have to register but they may elect to come within the system if it is to their advantage to do so.

Rates of tax

There are three classifications of goods and services: standard rate, zero-rated and exempt.

Standard rate

At the time of writing VAT is chargeable at the standard rate of 17½ per cent on all goods and services not zero-rated or exempt.

Zero-rated items

Reference should be made to Schedule 5 of the VAT Act 1983 (and later amendments) for a list of zero-rated items. In addition, the export of all goods and the supply of certain services is zero-rated.

Exempt goods and services

Reference should be made to Schedule 6 of the VAT Act 1983 (and later amendments) for a list of exempt items of which the most important are land, insurance, postal services, certain financial services (mainly banking), education and health.

The difference between zero rating and exemption is that a business dealing in zero-rated supplies charges VAT at the rate of zero per cent but is, nevertheless, fully within the system; thus, it can recover from Customs and Excise any input tax which it has paid on its purchases. Exemption on the other hand is generally a less favourable status in that, whereas the business cannot charge VAT on its supplies, it cannot recover the VAT on its purchases; thus, the exempt business must either bear any input tax itself, or if it can, pass it on in the form of higher prices.

Many businesses are taxable on some part of their sales (whether at the standard rate or zero rate) and exempt on another part. In these cases an apportionment of the input tax is made, and only that part considered to be referable to taxable sales is deductible.

There is a possibility that certain supplies are *outside the scope of VAT*. If this is the case, there is the same restricting influence on the recovery of VAT on purchases as in cases where exempt supplies are made.

Time of supply

In order to determine which VAT accounting period a transaction falls into, the time of supply has to be ascertained. Broadly the time of supply is as follows:

Goods

1 If the goods are to be removed the basic tax point is the time when they are removed
2 If the goods are not to be removed the basic tax point is the time when they are made available to the person to whom they are being supplied
3 There are special rules for sale or return and for certain other transactions. A hire purchase transaction is deemed to be a sale. The construction industry is subject to special rules
4 Where a tax invoice is issued within fourteen days after the basic tax point, the invoice date becomes the tax point unless the taxpayer elects to use the basic tax point instead. The fourteen-day period may be extended by agreement with Customs and Excise
5 If a tax invoice is rendered before the date of the basic tax point or if payment is received in respect of a supply before the basic tax point, the earlier of the invoice date and the payment date becomes the tax point. The taxpayer in this case has no option to elect for the tax point in 1 or 2 above.

Services

1 The basic tax point in the case of the supply of services is when those services are completed
2 If a tax invoice is issued within fourteen days after the basic tax point (extendable by negotiation with Customs and Excise), the invoice date is the tax point unless the taxpayer elects to the contrary
3 In other cases, the tax point is the earlier of the tax invoice and the date on which payment is made for the services.

Businesses should ensure that where an option is open they choose the best tax point for their accounting and administrative systems.

Place of supply

Broadly, if goods are supplied within the UK for use in the UK, the supply is a taxable supply. If goods are supplied in the UK and exported, the goods are still a taxable supply but at the time of export are zero-rated. Goods supplied outside the UK but imported into the UK are liable to VAT at the time of importation. There are special accounting rules for VAT purposes which are designed to ease the cash flow problems of importers. A supply of goods made outside the UK but not imported into the UK is outside the VAT net altogether; this applies whether or not the goods are ordered from the UK.

The tax invoice

No special form of tax invoice is laid down but certain minimum requirements have to be met. In particular every tax invoice must show an identifying number, the date of supply, the name and address and VAT registration number of the supplier, the name and address of the person to whom the supply is made, the type of supply (for example, sale, lease) a description of the supply, the price for each supply before the addition of VAT, any discount offered and the rate and amount of tax chargeable. An abbreviated form of tax invoice may be used in some cases; these are generally small transactions at retail level.

It is not necessary, unless requested, for a retailer to issue a tax invoice. Tax invoices need not be rendered where the transaction is zero-rated. In the case of exempt transactions no tax invoice is to be issued.

Discounts

Where a discount is offered for prompt or immediate payment, VAT should be shown on the tax invoice as though the discount had been earned by the person to whom the goods or services are being supplied. If, in the event, the discount is not earned, no recalculation of the VAT should be made. Where a trade discount is offered, VAT should similarly be calculated on the discounted price. Where, on the other hand, a contingent discount is offered which will be available, for example, when a certain level of purchases have been achieved by the customer, the VAT should be calculated on the assumption that the volume target will not be reached.

Retrospective adjustments

Where a downwards adjustment to the price charged for a supply is made, the VAT on the original invoice will be overstated. This may be corrected by showing VAT on a credit note issued to the customer; the VAT must be at the same rate as that originally charged by the supplier. Retrospective adjustments of any kind can be made by the use of the credit note mechanism.

Bad debts

Relief for VAT on bad debts is available and was recently made less restrictive by the Finance Act 1991 for supplies made after 1 April 1989. Relief is generally available where a taxable person has written off the amount in the business accounts and a period of one year has elapsed since the supply was made.

Secondhand goods

In principle, secondhand goods are treated in the same way as new goods. There are, however, special schemes for secondhand works of art, scientific collections, cars, motor cycles, electronic organs and caravans. The effect of these schemes is to make liable to VAT only the dealer's margin rather than the full sale price.

Capital goods

In principle, capital goods are treated in the same way as any other items except in two specific instances.

From 1 April 1990 the capital goods scheme was introduced whereby, if certain assets are acquired by a partly exempt business, annual adjustments of the input tax may be required where the proportion of the use of the asset changes between taxable and exempt business. The categories of asset are:

1 Computer equipment worth £50 000 or more
2 Land and buildings worth £250 000 or more.

The adjustments are spread over five years for computer equipment and ten years for land and buildings.

In the event of any doubt, detailed professional advice should be sought.

Disallowances of VAT

Powers are given to Customs and Excise to disallow certain amounts of input tax even though the expenditure is for the purposes of a taxable business. The two main disallowances at the time of writing are for business entertaining and business cars.

Apportionments

Reference has been made above to the part-exempt business. A business whose outputs are part taxable and part exempt may have a disallowance of some part of its input tax. The formula used to calculate the apportionment must be approved by Customs and Excise. The formula used must produce the effect of allowing the recovery of VAT on expenditure to the extent to which it relates to the making of taxable supplies.

Groups

Provision is made so that groups of commonly controlled companies can be treated as one single VAT paying entity. Transactions within companies in such a group are then ignored for VAT purposes and a single return is made by the 'representative member' of the group to Customs and Excise. Not all members of a

Companies Act group need be grouped for VAT purposes, and the cash flow of a Companies Act group can be improved if the correct selection of companies is made.

Divisions

A company organized in divisions may request to have each division treated separately for VAT.

Accounting period

The basic VAT accounting period is three months but a company which is in a habitual repayment position may elect for a one-month period. This minimizes the delay between the payment of input tax by a business and its recovery from Customs and Excise.

Interest and penalties

A detailed synopsis of the scope of VAT interest and penalties is outside the scope of this chapter. Suffice to say that these can be very wide ranging and the introduction of the Serious Misdeclaration Penalty and Default interest from 1 April 1990 has added considerably to the need for businesses to give high priority to their VAT affairs and minimize the amount of any errors. There was, however, a slight relaxation in 1991 and the promise of a further review.

Accounting records

All taxable businesses are required to maintain proper accounting records. Broadly, the information required to be kept includes:

1   Taxable supplies received
2   Imports
3   Taxable supplies made by the business
4   Exports
5   Gifts and loans of goods
6   Taxable self supplies
7   Any goods used for non-business use.

From these a VAT return is completed declaring the liability for each particular VAT accounting period to Customs and Excise. The format of the records is left, by and large, to each business to decide. However, Customs and Excise can require the business to maintain certain records should they consider it appropriate.

As regards the adjustment of errors for earlier accounting periods, it is important that a system is in place to record these. If the aggregate of over and under declarations of tax discovered in an accounting period is £1 000 or less, the taxpayer is allowed to make an adjustment through the current period VAT return; if aggregate errors exceed £1 000 they must be notified separately.

Retention of records

Invoices both in and out should be retained for a minimum period of six years to enable Customs and Excise to perform their periodical audit of the business's VAT position. By agreement with Customs and Excise, invoices may be kept in micro-film or any other form. Invoices should be stored and recorded in such a way that the periodical VAT return can be completed without difficulty. The amount of record keeping which has to be done is likely to be far greater than many businesses are used to. There are penalties for failing to preserve proper records for the prescribed period.

Cash flows

The combination of the rules on the tax point and the date on which tax is payable to Customs and Excise gives rise to cash flow advantages or disadvantages. Thus a business which secures a long period of credit on its purchases will very likely not have to pay the VAT on the purchase price until after it has received credit for the tax on the purchase. On the other hand a business which allows long periods of credit on its sales may find that it has to pay the appropriate output tax to Customs before receiving payment of that tax from the customer. The rule must therefore be that the maximum credit should be obtained from one's supplies but the minimum credit should be given to one's customers. This is not at variance with normal financial strategy.

Appeal procedures

Large numbers of disputes have arisen between businesses and Customs and Excise. If agreement cannot be reached with the local VAT office, it is usually prudent to seek a ruling from Customs and Excise head office in London. If agreement is still not possible, an appeal may be lodged to a VAT tribunal. These are presided over by lawyers, and meet in various parts of the country. Their proceedings are sometimes publicized and sometimes not; in so far as they are not, Customs clearly have an advantage over the taxpayer. A determination by a tribunal on a question of fact is final but on a question of law there is a right to appeal first to the High Court (in England), then to the Court of Appeal and (with permission) to the House of Lords, or Court of Session (in Scotland).

Professional advice

It is evident, in an area of taxation which is a mixture of law and administrative practice, that the taxpayer is at a disadvantage in dealing with Customs and Excise. It is important, therefore, to take professional advice not merely in negotiations with Customs and Excise but also in the handling of appeals.

FURTHER READING

Explanatory booklets are available free from the Inland Revenue on all aspects of PAYE and corporation tax. The Inland Revenue are also responsible for collecting employers' National Insurance contributions, but the relevant booklets are provided by the Department of Social Security. VAT material can be obtained from HM Customs and Excise.

The following books may also prove useful.

Gammie, Malcolm, *Tax Strategy for Companies*, 4th edn, Longman Professional, London, 1987

Harvey, Eric, L., *Tolley's Income Tax*, Tolley Publishing Company, Croydon

Truman, M.A., (ed.), *Longman Tax Digest*, published monthly, Longman, London

Noakes, Patrick and Wareham, Robert, *Tolley's Capital Gains Tax*, Tolley Publishing Company, Croydon

Saunders, Glyn and Boulding, John, *Tolley's Corporation Tax*, Tolley Publishing Company, Croydon

Sinclair, W.I. and McMullen, J., *Allied Dunbar Business Tax and Law Guide*, Longman, London

Stein, Neil, *Business Taxation*, Heinemann, Oxford

Pritchard, Bill, *Taxation 1990-1991*, 11th edn, Pitman, London, 1990 (paperback, with new annual editions)

Whiteman and Wheatcroft on Income Tax, (with latest supplement), Sweet & Maxwell, London.

Part Three
MARKETING

18 Marketing planning

John Stapleton

Every marketing activity is an investment in time, energy and money. Few companies would spend thousands of pounds on, say, a purchase of capital equipment without a full investigation into its justification, the alternatives available, and the expected return on expenditure. Yet every year the vast majority of companies allocate a substantial part of their revenue to marketing actions without fully assessing the value or likely return on that investment. By introducing the disciplines arising from marketing planning a company should be able to ensure that the costs of marketing show an equitable return and are subject to measurement in the same way as all other business investments.

Many executives believe that the costs of marketing form an additional expense that has to be borne in order to sell their goods. While it is true that many companies use certain tools of marketing for this purpose, it is true also that the most successful companies accept marketing as an essential and integral part of the company's total commercial operation, for it is an essential cost in just the same way as production or finance.

Companies often avoid marketing planning procedures because of the effort needed to express their forward policy in a written form. Executives commonly consider that their time is too valuable to spend on anything other than pressing operational problems; those that face them from day to day. In fact, the manager who devotes his time to dealing with current administrative detail is almost certain to have ignored proper planning in the past. For if properly prepared the marketing plan will contain sufficient details of the company's policy and operational strategy for the implementation to be undertaken by an assistant. As the many alternative courses of action are programmed it is merely necessary for the assistant to activate the appropriate remedy or decision. Only unusual situations need be dealt with by the manager.

The first step in preparing a marketing plan is that of producing the information necessary for decision making. Usually, a company will have within its own administration and control system the raw material necessary for the plan's foundation. In addition, specialist data collection agencies can provide necessary information. Databases, particularly those in desktop personal computers, can be developed from these sources. The clearing banks, merchant banks, stockbrokers, specialist publishers, accountancy firms, as well as government offices and professional institutions are building international and national sources of data for business uses. Because of the scale of operations that now confronts the typical businessman it is essential that investment decisions are based on relevant information, so reducing the number of variables and, hence, business risk. Computerizing the information helps to create objective business decision making.

STANDARDS FOR MEASURING PERFORMANCE

For a marketing-oriented activity to produce lasting results the entire operation has to be systematically planned. By producing basic information in written form and establishing goals and aims for the future the company is creating standards against which actual performance can be measured. Documentation of detailed policy actions then provides the basis for monitoring and controlling the company's operation. Future trends may be predicted through the investigation of all factors that are likely to influence company results.

It is, however, unusual for future opportunities to be easily isolated or even defined. The possibilities are infinite, but it is essential that the most promising are fully investigated and the potential assessed. It is particularly important that the person responsible for planning be a senior executive, for the full appraisal of market opportunities will enable that executive to gain far more intimate knowledge of the workings and the environment of the business operation than could be achieved from a lifetime of working within the close confines of the limited philosophy and procedure of one company. The executive will be able to learn about the interactive forces that affect the company, the industry and, more important, its markets.

In studying the company's future market the businessman will try to discover basic needs for which there is no satisfaction or possibly where there is an inadequate match. It is by discovering the peculiar needs of each existing and potential customer that the enlightened company starts its marketing-orientation. It is upon such special needs that the foundations are laid. Looking at the market and listing the operational needs of each industry, then measuring the extent of each need and then the value that the market places on overcoming the problem gives an indication of the potential – in volume and in profit opportunity.

The main approach adopted by firms is to segment the market either demographically or psychographically. Having isolated part of the market, a brand differential is created sufficient to provide the company with a competitive advantage. This is the step towards a unique selling proposition.

THE NEW PRODUCT DEVELOPMENT PROGRAMME

From this stage the company will embark on a new product development programme in an effort to resolve the problems that face the market. Once a satisfactory product has been produced the basis for a promotional campaign is already apparent, as the original market assessment will have shown the prospects either by size, industry or location, and the product feasibility studies will have indicated the most appealing stimulus to demand for advertising and field selling purposes.

It must be apparent from these observations that success in marketing cannot be achieved overnight except by coincidence or good fortune. Often a minimum of three years will be required before the first hopeful signs become apparent. Successful use of certain marketing activities alone does not automatically mean a company is marketing-oriented. This situation frequently presents management with an almost insoluble problem. As the whole company has to become involved with marketing principles for success to be possible, it is unlikely that a new recruit hired for his expertise will be able to win sufficient confidence from colleagues by results in the time span that is normally allowed a new manager.

There is usually only one person in a company who can inspire the confidence and support that is necessary and who will automatically have the authority to implement the total changes that may be justified, and that is the chief executive. Introducing satisfactory marketing-orientation is more likely to be successful if the present chief executive delegates most of his daily activities to an assistant or to senior line managers and devotes his entire energies to planning, than if a manager is appointed with such responsibilities.

DETERMINING COMPANY OBJECTIVES

Few company executives have ever formally determined their company's business activity. If they have, it is often specified in terms of the means by which the business activity is achieved, for example, printing rather than communictions; or the end-product, for example, aero-engines rather than propulsion; or by convention, for example, insurance rather than security. The only sure means of defining the business activity is by thinking in terms of applications for a product, for while products, no matter how successful they are now, are heading for eventual decline, the need will usually remain – to be satisfied by the latest innovation. Companies may overcome this problem by cultivating a brand image and encouraging the development of a brand personality based on the unique selling proposition. People do not buy products; they buy brands and brands can achieve buyer loyalty. Brands can have a reputation monopoly.

Determining the appropriate business activity is the first essential step in the marketing plan. In this first step the executive will establish the parameters within which his efforts should be confined initially, but will also rely upon the know-how, expertise, market reputation, and resources the company has accumulated during its history.

At the preliminary planning stage the company will need to decide upon the course that it wishes to take and the stages that have to be reached during each step in the journey. These objectives have to be achievable and yet sufficiently challenging to enable executives and staff to take pride in their fulfilment. The aims and goals of each company have to be expressed in the marketing plan in a way that is beyond dispute while being capable of measurement and comparison. The only medium that achieves these standards is money – the means by which company prosperity is valued. The prime requirement for the survival and development of any business is profit. Too many managers still regard profit as the amount of money that is left over after all the operating expenses have been met. This view almost has connotations with a death wish, for profit is the prerequisite of all business activity and as such must be the first cost to the business.

PROFIT IS THE FIRST OPERATING EXPENSE

By writing in the profit required as its first operating expense the company recognizes its major priority and then gears all its other objectives to ensure the acquisition of that profit. The sales volume needed, the orders to be won, the tenders or quotations to be sent out, the inquiries to be solicited, and all the means by which they are obtained are secondary objectives to be achieved before the prime objective becomes possible – in practice. Properly organized, the marketing effort can be used to manage demand itself. It can be used to control the levels of demand and its timing.

Any objectives of this sort must be based upon certain assumptions. It may have to be assumed that raw materials will continue to be available or that the government will not cause a market to dry up following an Act of Parliament. Whatever the objectives they will depend for their satisfaction on certain events happening or not happening. These assumptions are incorporated in the plan with a cross-reference to the strategies that will have to be implemented or the tactics employed should the assumptions become invalid. The strategies a company adopts are the means by which the company approaches its market opportunities and by which it adjusts its resources to exploit those opportunities. Its tactics are the methods it uses to meet short-term situations or more frequently the steps it takes when in immediate contact with customers.

In documenting the preliminary marketing plan it is also necessary to list all the major problems that have faced the company during its immediate history, as well as those that are expected to confront the company in the future. At the same time it is prudent to list all opportunities that have been under consideration with the expected profit return, when they are to be achieved and under what circumstances. Both problems and opportunities are then subjected to the same appraisal as the objectives and assumptions when the company strategies are built into plan.

Every company struggles to improve its profit performance and any attempts planned for the period of the marketing plan, in detail for one year and in outline for five years, should be included. It is possible that improved productivity at the plant will make it possible for the company to improve its profitability through increased sales volume. Sales may be improved either by additional expenditure on marketing actions or by reducing price in an effort to expand the total market. It is by marketing planning that a company can be sure that whatever action it chooses will be based upon facts and information obtained from the marketplace.

Every action and every decision taken by the company executives will have an effect somewhere in the business. It may be favourable, it might be unfavourable. In formulating a marketing plan the company will be formalizing its actions, weighing its alternatives, and deciding the most appropriate route open to it. Unless each marketing decision is made with the full and detailed consideration of the known, likely and possible effects upon the business, the investment that marketing actions require will be unmonitored and the management will have lost effective control of a major asset and the benefits that should accrue from that asset.

DEVELOPING THE MARKET PLAN

Preparing a sales forecast, the basis of the total marketing plan, is not just a matter of looking at past sales and trying to establish trends, but a conscious effort to look into the future and assess potential sales opportunity.

A company has started to be objective about its future when it attempts to evaluate the future and forecast what the market will require in the way of new or improved products. Most companies, in making long-range sales forecasts, choose a period varying between five and twenty years, while more detailed sales targets are usually prepared for the financial year immediately ahead. Many products which will be available in five years' time are already on the market and firmly established in the product range. It is often possible to use such historical sales performance as the basis for projections into the future, but only as the basis, for such projections are dependent upon future events being similar to events which have happened in the past. Allowance must be made for changes due to economic circumstances and changes in competitive forces within the industry under investigation.

Demand forecasts are not based on purely functional needs. People in the affluent societies buy to satisfy psychological drives. So many successful brand personalities are based on abstract promises often appealing to the subconscious, a segmentation and brand differential all in one.

Comparison of movements, either short-term fluctuations or medium- to long-term trends, can often be achieved using the published economic data. Sometimes, acceptable degrees of correlation can be traced and these tied indicators will be useful parameters in forecasting.

The sales forecast can be as sophisticated or as simple as is justified by the business. The small- to medium-sized business is usually better placed than its larger competitors for maintaining close contact with its markets and can use elementary methods of forecasting which often produce better results than the methods employed by larger firms, where customer contact has become more remote because of larger lines of communication.

While the larger company will normally handle the research necessary to prepare a sales forecast by using its own personnel, the smaller concern cannot justify the expense of recruiting and retaining specialist staff. Where such forecasts are prepared, outside agencies are usually brought in for the task and, in recent years, multi-client projects have been evolved to cater for this demand. As the cost of research is spread over several sponsors, the research organization can afford to employ highly skilled staff and carry out projects in some depth across a wide front. In addition, the research organization is often able to prepare a report confidential to each client concerned.

BIAS TOWARDS ONE'S OWN COMPANY

Any sales forecast is subject to numerous influential factors, each of which must be isolated and measured. Some factors will have more effect than others, and the forecaster must attempt to isolate and grade those factors according to their significance in such a way that weightings can be applied and an acceptable forecast determined within tolerable limits. In forecasting, there is inevitably some bias towards the forecaster's own company and this must be avoided otherwise operating budgets, based on the forecasts, will be over-estimated, adversely affecting profitability.

It is also necessary to predict trends in related industries which provide indirect competition to the company's own products and which could have a bearing on the growth rate of the industry concerned. It is here that the forecaster can discover opportunities for product innovation or new product development. Since new products are the lifeblood of a company their discovery, development and subsequent production programming are necessary parts of the sales forecasting procedure.

To maintain a constant growth rate it is essential that every company estimates the life cycle of each of its products and introduces new products at the apex, or earlier, of an established product's life cycle in order to continue company growth. New products should not be introduced in a haphazard manner, but properly planned to fit the firm's expansion programme.

Price cutting, the most often observed tactical device in the struggles against competition, is a negative approach unless done from a position of strength with the company anticipating growth in the market and increased consumption achieved as a result of the price stimulus. Skilled marketing based on market segmentation, brand differentiation, and reputation monopoly provide a haven against price competition. People believe they are buying something unique that is superior to others. For them it seems better value even if dearer.

New markets are occasionally created following new legislation by government. Such changes can also be the cause of a substantial growth or decline in established markets and are often put forward as attempts to improve the social and/or economic life of the nation. Sudden changes in taste or fashion can cause sudden shifts in demand. Climatic changes can seriously affect sales of products which rely on extremes of temperature for their sales volume. Economic recessions, strikes or industrial disputes often bring in their train changes in purchasing habits.

CONTINGENCY PLANNING

Fortunately, many of these factors are predictable. There will certainly be any amount of published comment indicating possibilities. Research into future events is sometimes sponsored by trade and professional bodies; many thousands of words are produced by numerous authoritative writers in scores of newspapers, magazines, and trade and professional publications. These reports can be very valuable to businessmen seeking an insight into the future.

While one cannot forecast accurately what is going to happen, plans can be laid to cover any eventuality in advance of the event, at different levels of effectiveness. If the consequences of events are quantified in purely monetary terms, the businessman will be able to equate consequences with sales volume and, thus, profitability. Where necessary, contingency plans can be brought into operation.

It is true to say that many manufacturers take their products for granted and rarely investigate the uses to which they are put by customers, or how relevant they are to the customer's applications. Research can establish whether new features introduced by the manufacturer in good faith in the belief that they provide a plus for the buyer are not really required and not used, although paid for by the customer in the original selling price. It is possible, of course, that customers may not have realized the significance or relevance at the time of purchase.

In assessing product performance the businessman needs to relate application to product characteristics. Several companies have developed their share of the market as a direct result of providing superior finish or excellent design. Buyers are often impressed by tales of long life for some mechanical item and sometimes make buying decisions in favour of such devices because the cost can be amortized over several years' operational life.

Where a brand personality has been established, whether it be a consumer product or service or an industrial product or service, the need for that personality survives in the buyer's mind. The marketing-oriented company has bought that position in the consumer's mind, and has therefore bought the customers it wants. The future has been virtually secured.

In arriving at the final assessment based on established standards relating each factor to every other factor, the researcher can compare the total significance of these in terms of market share and will be able to relate the performance of individual companies according to factors on which they concentrate. Comparison of results is the only certain way of monitoring company performance in a competitive commercial environment. The standards established in the appraisal of competitor profiles provide the foundations for a full analysis of market shares. Companies desiring to break into a completely new market will need to examine the extent to which policies adopted by those already serving this market have been successful.

Having obtained full information on total market size it is necessary to assess the extent to which the market can be penetrated either by winning a share of the existing market or by concentrating on growth and winning the business which would otherwise have gone to present suppliers. Once this work has been done the company can make a full and realistic evaluation of the marketing budget necessary to achieve its objectives – objectives based on the right product (differentiated), the right target audience (segmentation) and the right message (unique selling proposition).

It may be easier in some industries to take business from established suppliers than to expand the total market. In other projects it may be more feasible to opt for developing the growth market potential than to get involved in a battle with those already active in the market. Only when the business activity of the company has been decided should any attempt be made to measure the total market and to prepare a reasoned definition of the market.

DEFINITION OF THE TOTAL MARKET

Many people are confused about the total market for a particular product. It is the total amount of money spent in satisfying a need, irrespective of the products which satisfy that need. This means that all types of food are in competition with one another, the various forms of transport are competitors, and all aids to business efficiency are locked in combat for the purchaser's money. This is direct competition, but because buyers have a wide range of choices across different product groups, the real competition is for the consumers' or buyers' money; to change their scale of preferences.

The market situation for any given company or industry is continually changing and violent fluctuations can occur in market shares from day to day. Over a period, shifts in the pattern of demand will become evident and it is imperative that a check be kept on such trends. Steadily rising sales turnover is not, in itself, a true indicator that a company is making the best use of its potential. It is quite possible for a company to achieve reasonable increases in sales year by year yet find that it has a rapidly diminishing share of the market. It will be losing sales opportunities unless sales volume is rising at least as rapidly as that of the industry as a whole.

A company also needs to keep track of its competitors' market shares and be able to explain any change that becomes apparent. There must be a reason why a competitor is expanding his market share faster than anyone else. If, on the other hand, a competitor with a strong marketing team is seen to be losing out on a market share, it could be that he has decided to diversify because of a forecast over-capacity or a decreasing growth rate. It is for these reasons that it is vital to carry out constant analyses of market share at frequent intervals, even if in a simple form, rather than rely on occasional extensive research projects, no matter how sophisticated.

Confusion sometimes arises when referring to marketing research and market research. The former is the activity which examines all the elements which make up marketing practice, including markets, products, channels of distribution, pricing behaviour and opinions. Market research is only one element of marketing research, albeit the most widely known and practised.

When it comes to getting the goods to the customer, different companies use different channels of distribution. While some use stockists or distributors, others deliver direct to the retailer or even direct to the ultimate consumer. Different channels of distribution achieve different levels of success in selling their suppliers' products, and their effectiveness can be critical to the sales volume achieved by any one company. Channels of distribution in the consumer field have undergone considerable change in recent years. The development of supermarkets and self-service stores has progressed very rapidly in some areas of retailing, more slowly in others. Some companies have achieved considerable growth through the provision of mail order facilities, while others have built their share of the market through new selling methods such as party plan or vending machines or through selling direct to the household.

In the industrial field there have not yet been such fundamental changes in the pattern of distribution, although some changes have become apparent; for example, leasing of factories and capital equipment, and the use of time sharing for data processing equipment.

CONTROL OF DISTRIBUTION

It is not generally realised that the cost to industry of distributing a product may range between 5 and 60 per cent of the final selling price, depending upon the nature of the product and the method of distribution selected. Active control of distribution can reduce these expenses and allow a substantial increase in profitability. Many related activities could be improved following an improvement in actual distribution.

The marketing executive must endeavour to reconcile the needs of the customer for a full service with his company's requirements for the provision of an economic level of service. If he decides that the most appropriate way to win sales from a competitor is by providing a superior distribution service, then that is a deliberate expense incurred in the marketing budget as an alternative to other marketing activities and expenditure.

Because of the forces of competition, demand for any one product from one source can vary considerably. It is the distributive function to provide a contingency against wide fluctuations in demand, and the businessman's responsibility to develop a distributive pattern to cater for those deviations from the norm. Some are more predictable than others and the product mix from the factory must be adjusted to cope with the demand.

Properly controlled, the distributive system can protect a company against giving customer dissatisfaction and will enable it to achieve a high level of productivity by ensuring economical production runs according to predetermined planning.

MONITORING THE MARKET PLAN

No matter how carefully a management may plan, some objectives will always be more difficult to achieve than others. Marketing planning is not a panacea for all commercial and industrial problems.

Ideally, the marketing plan will include any action which may have to be taken to avoid diminution of profits. Even if actual performance exceeds all expectations there should be built-in provisions for the favourable conditions which have become apparent. If proper care has been taken to structure the marketing plan the contingency section should be straightforward, being no more than the detailed consideration of alternative courses of action. The contingency plan should include action which may need to be taken in the short term to minimize or maximize the possible consequences of deviation from the schedule as well as the medium- to long-term action necessary to exploit a changed environment.

To ensure that the right action is taken at the right time – to ensure best results – it is essential that a barometer of company and industry performance be developed. Steps must be taken to monitor actual results against forecast company sales and forecast market shares.

There are several specialist organizations which provide, at reasonable cost, performance comparisons within an industry. If one of these organizations is used, the company needs to develop only an internal early warning system. This can be done by plotting orders received by major product groups against the purchasing industry by standard industrial classification.

In the shorter term, signals can be provided by relating actual inquiries, quotations, order received, and sales by major product groups against the forecast. Then, if the average timelag between inquiry and order is, say, six weeks, and between order and delivery is four to six weeks, the company will have, automatically, nearly three months' notice of an imminent fall-off in sales. Care must be taken to ensure that conversion ratios between each stage do not vary, or that if they do adjustment be made accordingly.

While it would not be wise to institute remedial action as a result of one deviation from plan – for occasional fluctuations *do* happen – once a trend becomes apparent, the cause should be established and appropriate action taken. In addition to showing industrial performance as a whole, some specialist comparison organizations quote the detailed performance of unspecified companies against which the performance of one's own firm can be measured.

Here, the company should be able to judge the extent to which it will be able to exert influence on the market. If the entire industry is suffering the same deteriorating position, it is probably wise to curtail any plans for expansion unless there is a clear indication that the present circumstances can be favourably exploited. The timing and extent of any cutback in this area should be provided for in the contingency plan, which should show detailed profit and loss statements for 70, 80, 90, 110 and 120 per cent actual performance against forecast. Each of the detailed accounts should include the appropriate departmental budgets and head counts. The major driving principles must be to preserve net profit and indemnify future profits. These considerations often prove incompatible in practice and a working compromise may be necessary. Sometimes, profit comes from the last 15 to 20 per cent of sales, after overheads have been covered, and when costs become marginal. Under such circumstances a reduction of 20 per cent in sales volume will warrant, perhaps, a cut of 30 per cent in expenditure in order to maintain net profit at par value.

A company can sometimes avoid the disaster of a temporarily poor market position by acquiring another company. A study of competitive profiles in the marketing plan, followed by detailed investigation of suitable partners, may disclose a competitor which could supplement, or ideally complement, the company's own operations. It is likely that acquisition will become a prominent marketing stratagem in the 1990s. While advertising is buying customers, acquisition buys branded products, market share and the all-important market connection. Acquisition is often a better and more certain investment than a lavish promotional campaign. It is becoming more than just a marketing contigency plan.

Although the possibility of making a takeover bid will almost always be considered first, realistic management must not discount the advantages of soliciting a bid for one's own company, as this may be more prudent.

Detailed consideration of both rationalization and diversification policies should form a logical part of any contingency plan. There is nearly always conflict between the sales department, anxious to meet individual customer requirements, and the production department needing long production runs and the elimination of time-consuming 'specials'.

INVESTMENT IN COMPANY RESOURCES

Although the need for improved efficiency and productivity has long been accepted by manufacturing processes in industry, and a similar need recognized for some time in the marketing function, it has never been satisfactorily resolved in the latter because of the difficulties of reconciling accounting principles with a business function which is considered part art and part science. While many marketing activites operate under disciplines not widely appreciated – let alone understood – by management, the practice of marketing is still an investment in company resources. If control is to be maintained marketing will be subject to the same accounting appraisal as any other form of investment.

The cost of handling orders of varying sizes must be ascertained if stock levels are to be controlled with great accuracy. It may be found more profitable to refuse orders selling below a price level considered to be uneconomic. Such selective selling often increases profitability. Location of warehouses, planning of sales territories and routes of salesmen can be organized, using accurate cost statistics rather than intuition. Improving direction and supervision of salesmen through the setting of performance and activity targets can result in increased selling and operating efficiency.

Management in many companies is not always able to recognize that its products or services are mediocre or even inferior to others on the market. Where such blindness exists the company is unlikely to introduce new methods or procedures to assist in rectifying or overcoming the problem. In the same way, the firm is unlikely to experiment with new ideas or make a fresh approach in an attempt to improve its future prospects. In these circumstances the only avenue left for that firm is to continue in its own fashion, no matter how much the position may deteriorate.

Because of the pace of technological change, a greater demand is manifesting itself for information to be employed in decision making. Investment decisions become more and more complex as businesses grow. The businessman must endeavour to forecast growth potential, and the factors likely to influence his company's penetration of that potential, in an attempt to reduce the risks facing every business enterprise.

Companies should be able to identify the influences on their main activities and show how they are being controlled to the benefit of the entire organization. The extent to which the information provided is relevant to the company's needs should be assessed. Executives need to eliminate unused material being prepared and to discover additional information previously unknown. Such research into the marketing effort will help to ensure that an economic level of expenditure is being maintained. Appropriate marketing policies should ensure that all products are developed according to the needs of the market and resources are not wasted on products which the market shows as unsatisfactory.

COMMUNICATING PROFIT RESPONSIBILITY

One of the important developments in marketing consumer goods is the change in emphasis to impersonal selling techniques such as advertising and point-of-sale display. Personal selling still has the most important role in industrial marketing. Improvement in the function and performance of industrial sales forces justifies more attention than is now perhaps necessary in consumer goods selling efforts. These salesmen cannot be expected to sell the ideal product mix without guidance and direction nor differentiate between the profitability of various products.

In any organization the level of profit responsibility must not only be decided but also widely communicated to ensure the satisfactory implementation of the most critical of business activities.

The marketing plan and all its ancillary documents must be used by executives as a day-to-day control and development manual. The planning process must not be treated as an annual political exercise suffered by busy executives concerned with other tasks. Planning, organization, direction and control are basic management jobs and, in a successful marketing-oriented company, will fill the management's working days. Each manager needs to understand the interactive nature of the individual tasks which have to be completed during each period of the marketing plan.

The timing of each step, at all levels, and in each function, is critical if the total plan is to be satisfactorily co-ordinated and the anticipated results achieved. A flexible attitude to planning principles needs to be adopted so that management recognizes the need for contingencies and their control within corporate stategy. Unforeseen events create a different scale of priorities, and flexibility in policy interpretation as allowed for in the plan must be recognized if the company's interests are to be best served. The results of monitoring actual performance against forecasts have a definite value in personnel development and in operating efficiency, as does the preparation of forecasts itself.

The chief executive of any marketing-oriented company retains the final responsibility for marketing policies. The marketing manager gives advice in the field of marketing and may well carry a line responsibility. If the marketing concept is to be adopted the entire company and, in particular, the management team must be oriented towards customer satisfaction. And this is the essence of planning in marketing. For the end result – the marketing plan – is not so important as the benefits gained from the input. The effort, study, appraisal, and evaluation of the business environment provides the major bonuses from the preparation of the plan and it all starts from considering customer needs.

Most companies have become heavily involved in computerization. Even if not directly concerned as users, companies have become involved by the extent to which suppliers, competitors and customers are geared to electronic data processing. Every businessman or woman must appreciate how the computer can be applied to marketing problems. He/she needs some appreciation of the effects of computers on present-day and future marketing decisions. The development of personal computers and the available software has made computerization possible and economic for many smaller firms, and will certainly assist in the scientific application of marketing. The day is not far off when a company's entire planning process will be subject to computer processing and storage.

FURTHER READING

Allen, Peter, *Marketing Techniques for Analysis and Control*, Macdonald & Evans, Plymouth, 1977

Cohen, W.A., *Developing a Winning Marketing Plan*, Wiley, Chichester, 1987

Kitler, Philip, *Marketing Management: analysis, planning, and control*, 4th edn, Prentice Hall International, London, 1981

MacDonald, Malcolm, *Marketing Plans: How to Prepare them, How to use them*, Heinemann, Oxford, 1989

Stapleton, John, *How to Prepare a Marketing Plan*, 4th edn, Gower, Aldershot, 1988

Wilson, Richard M.S., *Management Controls and Marketing Planning*, Heinemann on behalf of the Institute of Marketing and the CAM Foundation, London, 1979

19 Marketing research

Bill Blyth

Marketing research is dynamic. *Market* research is passive. Marketing research is the collection and synthesis of primary or secondary data and their transformation into *information*: information that is relevant, timely and accurate for the task. The difference between the two is principally attitudinal. Marketing research is involved in the marketing process and actively seeks to provide input that is relevant to management issues. Market research is uninvolved and takes no responsibility beyond the provision of data. Today's marketing environment needs researchers who can collect, interpret and aid the application of data in improving the profitability of their company.

DEFINING THE INFORMATION REQUIREMENTS

The principles of defining information needs are completely independent of the product being offered or conceived, be it a consumer product, a business-to-business service or heavy capital plant. Unless the user of research has a clear and concise definition of the information they require, they will carry out unsatisfactory research and, at worst, misleading research.

Once the information requirement is defined, together with a number of straightforward criteria, the most appropriate research should be apparent to a skilled market researcher. When carrying out research, use skilled professional advice and involve the researcher in defining the information need – the research brief. Research is not a science; nevertheless, it follows certain logical principles which have developed over time and which rarely fail to produce an answer, *provided that* the proper criteria are observed.

STRUCTURING THE INFORMATION NEED

In any management environment, data are continually being made available in a myriad of forms. In identifying a research need one should ask two questions:

- What do I already know?
- What else do I need to know?

To identify what one already knows, it is useful to have a simple way of structuring available and potential data. For any market there is a finite number of questions that research can answer about actual or potential purchasers:

1 Who are you?

2 What do you buy?
3 How much do you buy?
4 What do you pay?
5 Where did you buy it?
6 When did you buy it?
7 What else could you have bought?
8 Why?

From this data set one can then infer the answers to:

9 What will you buy next?
10 What if . . . (for example) price/advertising/distribution/packaging/product specification are changed?

The ultimate market research study would contain answers for questions 1 to 8, all obtained simultaneously from individual entities purchasing or potentially purchasing in a market. In practice this is never obtained, although it must be acknowledged that developments related to electronic point of sales (EPOS) technology are making this partly possible in some consumer markets in the US.

The reasons why it is not possible are the other criteria by which the information need is defined:

• Time
• Depth
• Accuracy
• Obtainability
• Cost.

Time

Research takes time. Even if the data already exist they have to be found and accessed in a relevant way. Good marketing management starts from a clear understanding of what it knows or what it can access. Then, if the information need can be quickly defined, the research has to be carried out. Typically, the more accurate the research, the longer it takes and the greater the cost. One needs to trade off these variables, particularly for tactical applications. The need for punctual and accurate information can often be met by subscribing to one of the available subscription databases, but at a cost.

Depth

Irrespective of whether the unit of information is an individual, a household, a commercial establishment or an organization, there is a limit to the amount of information that can be collected, be it by personal interview, by telephone, or by self-completion either in writing or, in some instances now, via a keyboard. Here the trade-off is between depth and breadth. The deepest information comes from 'qualitative' research, interviewing consumers either individually or in small groups. Here the questioning is unstructured, with a trained executive interviewer

Sample size	True population (within ± %)	
	19/20 of the time	9/10 of the time
250	9.0%	7.5%
500	7.0%	5.5%
1 000	4.5%	4.0%
2 000	3.0%	2.5%

Figure 19.1   Accuracy for different sample sizes

guiding the questioning. Such research can go deep into underlying attitudes and motivations. However, it is extremely expensive and rarely conducted on a scale of more than fifty individual interviews or six group discussions with six to eight individuals in each. Consequently, the findings are not quantifiable in the sense of having statistical accuracy.

In the UK, the opposite end of the spectrum is the Target Group Index, which interviews some 25 000 people about almost everything they could possibly buy, watch, read or do. In the US, similar services are operated by the MRB Group and Mediamark Research. However, the questioning is not carried out in depth in either survey and both rely for response on recall of behaviour.

This latter method will give a quick guide to the percentage of the population who ever buy a product. The former method will give an in-depth analysis of 'Why?'

Accuracy

In so far as market research has a scientific basis, it lies in statistics. The application of statistical theory provides the ability to draw a representative sample of a population, and, further, the ability to calculate the probability that the answers given by that sample lie within certain limits of the true population value.

The table in Figure 19.1 gives, in simplified format, the accuracy obtainable from various sample sizes. To halve the error, one has to quadruple the sample size. Unfortunately, costs are linear but accuracy is not. Furthermore, there are many sources of error other than that related to sample size; for example:

- The sample selection
- The wording of the questions
- The order of the questions
- The interviewers
- The analysis of the data.

All these factors potentially increase the error. Good research will reduce these errors, and will measure them. It cannot eliminate them. In a strict sense errors of this type are random.

The second factor affecting accuracy is bias. Bias is factors inherent in the research design which consistently lead to mis-estimation. Sometimes they can be built knowingly into the research, at others they occur in an uncontrolled manner. An almost universal and planned bias in much consumer research is that institu-

Type of research	Cost (£)
Depth interview	250– 500+
Group discussion	1 000– 1 500+
Hall test (200 × 20 minute interviews: housewives)	3 500– 5 500
Personal interview (1 000 × 20 minutes interviews: adults)	13 000–18 000
Telephone interview (1 000 × 10 minute interviews: adults)	9 000–11 000
Omnibus survey (1 000 × 10 questions: adults)	3 500– 4 000

Figure 19.2   Approximate *ad hoc* research costs

tional residents are excluded; for example, imprisoned criminals, members of the armed forces, students in halls of residence. An uncontrolled bias might be brought about by the difficulty of interviewing in high-deprivation areas. This probably results in underrepresenting the young, unskilled unemployed. For most purposes this does not matter in either instance, but for some it might. Accuracy requirements and key areas in which to avoid bias must be identified in advance and then traded off against other elements.

Obtainability

By this is meant:

1   Do people know the answers?
2   Are they prepared to give them to you?
3   Do they have the time?

If the answer to any of these is no, there is little point in pursuing the research without amendment. Research typically relies on the good-will of the respondents and little or no fee is generally paid. Abusing that spirit of co-operation produces bad research not only for oneself but, over time, alienates respondents.

Cost

By international standards research in the UK is still cheap. Very large amounts of data are available 'off the shelf'. Typically, subscriptions for commercial research range from £10 000 to over £100 000. Most research is still *ad hoc*, that is, tailor-made. For this type of research the market is very competitive, the price quoted varying according to quality, overhead structure and the state of the order book. The prices quoted in Figure 19.2 are provided as a rough guide. The cost will be higher for minority groups.

TYPES OF RESEARCH

The best information for any market must be:

1   What are my sales?
2   How big is the market?

The success of retail audit market research data in the 1950s was arguably founded on the fact that they told manufacturers what their own sales were and, in the 1960s, what those of their competitors were. In every gross oversimplification there is a grain of truth. Even today, in the era of expensive and complex marketing management information systems one is continually surprised by the number of companies which do not possess basic data about their own business. Examples are the inability to distinguish domestic and export sales; or in financial services, to distinguish accounts and customers; the lack of any customer classification data; the confusion of sell-in and consumer offtake. The lack of hard data about one's own business precludes most of the benefit of external data.

The size of the market can generally be simply and roughly estimated by 'desk research'. Desk research is the use of published secondary data. For almost any market, government statistics are available which enable the calculation of market size in terms of volume or value. Published data represent just the tip of the iceberg. Relevant departments are generally willing to co-operate to produce relevant data. For most consumer markets in the UK the Family Expenditure Survey (FES) gives the ability to calculate market sizes. For others, production statistics together with import and export statistics will suffice. In the UK, the Central Statistical Office (CSO) publishes a guide to what is available – *CSO Guide to Official Statistics* – and this is an invaluable tool for all marketing departments. Government data also serve to fill in the basic margins of much other data – detailed population data, employment data and many other little-known but valuable series. Great care is taken in their construction and so far as possible their accuracy should be assumed to be as good as possible. Accordingly, they also serve as an additional cross-check on other ancillary sources.

Beyond government data there are a rapidly growing number of database providers who sell data from a variety of sources. For first-time users an approach to one of them may be the most cost efficient route, rather than trying to pursue their own desk research.

With the growth in information technology this trend can only continue to grow. Much ingenuity is being addressed to repackaging existing data or cross-referencing it – for example linking census data to postcoded address lists – and the applications go beyond market research to a number of other related services, such as direct mail.

If one's sales or potential sales are low in relation to the total market, the need for formal market research will also be small, unless one is seeking difficult-to-identify sub-groups of a market. Potential customers will be contacted via point of sale or address lists; substantial sales increases will still be relatively small to the total market, and thus regular monitoring of the total market unnecessary; advertising will be low and often local or specialized, perhaps requiring testing for comprehension, but with directly identifiable effects.

Above this level there will be the need for research and, potentially, research against every aspect of the marketing business.

Over time, researchers have developed techniques suitable for providing relevant information for aiding the management of different aspects of marketing. The actual techniques will vary by type of business, depending on how the data in the overall model need to be obtained. Readers are referred to the reading list at the end of the chapter if they require further information on this subject.

For any specific information need there will be more than one way in which the information can be obtained. There are no perfect solutions. The requirement of the marketing manager is to define *all* the parameters of the information need as clearly and in as much detail as possible, and then to test the proposed research against those parameters. For those totally new to research, without an internal department to provide expertise and experience, the employment of a consultant to guide planning at the early stages would be sensible.

MARKETING RESEARCH AROUND THE WORLD

There are few countries where marketing research is not carried out. Sophisticated research agencies, offering the same range of services, exist in the US, Canada, Europe, Asia, Brazil, Mexico and elsewhere. There are a small number of US and UK owned multinational chains with local operating companies in most principal markets. In addition, there are a number of multinational associations which can provide research around the world.

Costs generally vary in line with the cost of living from country to country. Specific local conditions – for example, social security tax – may affect the costs of different types of research.

In all the main markets the same basic types of research are available. Thus, most countries have at least one supplier of retail audits for market measurement; one television audience research measure and one press/magazine readership survey to provide the basis for buying and selling advertising; a number of omnibus surveys; a number of qualitative research companies; and a number of *ad hoc* research companies.

International research practice has been dominated by American and British research agencies, and by American and British multinational manufacturers. Standards of work, both practical and ethical, are generally consistent and high in the US, Western Europe, and the Asia–Pacific region for major research companies. The competitive environment is too aggressive, and repeat business too important, for weak performers to survive.

Each country tends to have its own local practices and preferred ways of doing things. In the US, telephone interviewing predominates. In the UK there is very little use of day-after recall (DAR) measurement of advertising; in the US, the reverse is true. How qualitative research is carried out varies from country to country. What is regarded as intrusive also differs between countries.

It is not recommended that one attempts to carry out research in any country without employing those who have prior experience in the area. The Market Research Society of Great Britain publishes an international directory of market research agencies and it also provides notes compiled by local professionals on research procedures and services in every country in Western Europe, the Far East and North America.

COMPUTER APPLICATIONS

Marketing research was one of the earliest applications of computers, for the processing of survey data. Today, information technology is transforming the face of research, not only in terms of data processing, but also for the collection and distribution of data. The diversity of applications is expanding all the time. Examples include:

Data collection

- The use of hand-held terminals for face-to-face interviewing
- Hand-held terminals equipped with light pens to read bar codes for retail auditing
- Computer-assisted telephone inteviewing (CATI), where questions are displayed and routed on a display screen. The interviewer enters answers directly into the computer
- Pre-recorded telephone interviewing, with the response given by pushing keys on the telephone pad
- Remote collection of television viewing data via meters installed in private homes, with data downloaded through the telephone system
- In-home self-completion using computer terminals and pens which read bar codes
- Point-of-sale data collection, linking till-roll data with characteristics of shoppers held on electronic identity cards.
- Computerized drawing in qualitative research.

Data processing

- Survey analysis
- Data modelling and forecasting
- Database compilation
- Store location planning
- Advertising scheduling
- Fusing separate data sources into one synthesized whole
- Stock/production modelling

Data distribution

- On-line systems
- Data broadcasting
- Graphical output
- PC-based data presentation.

The growth in the power and flexibility of PC-based systems has resulted in rapid growth of analysis possibilities. That is both a benefit and a threat. In the final result, analysis is only as good as the skill of the person who designed it. Expert systems are being developed but are still in their infancy. Wherever possible, analysis should be kept as direct and simple as possible. 'Black box' techniques should be avoided. If it cannot be understood, it is probably best left alone.

COMMISSIONING MARKET RESEARCH

There are over 300 companies providing market research as their main business service in the UK alone. In addition, large numbers of other consultancies claim to provide expertise in this area. In the UK, the professional bodies of the industry – the Market Research Society and the Industrial Market Research Association – have a code of conduct covering all aspects of research which their members must observe. It is advised that research is commissioned from companies where at least the senior executives are members of one of these associations. The Market Research Society publishes an annual list of organizations carrying out research in the UK, together with details of company size and specialization. It also publishes a list of similar companies operating in other countries and a list of consultants. It is possible to commission a UK-based agency to co-ordinate research in several countries simultaneously and some companies specialize in this, either through overseas subsidiaries or associated companies.

Word-of-mouth recommendation is a good start for those new to buying research. Research companies rely on repeat business. Users need to find the right blend of technical skills, organization and people that gives them the best service.

FURTHER READING

Aaker, D.A. and Day, G.S., *Marketing Research*, 3rd edn, Wiley, New York, 1986

Bradley, U., *Applied Marketing and Social Research*, 2nd edn, Wiley, Chichester, 1987

Crouch, S., *Marketing Research for Managers*, Heinemann, London, 1984

Foxall, G.R., *Consumer Choice*, Macmillan, London, 1983

Gordon, W. and Langmaid, R., *Qualitative Market Research*, Gower, Aldershot, 1988

Kent, R.A., *Continuous Consumer Market Measurement*, Edward Arnold, London, 1989

Market Research Society, *Market Research Society Organization Book*, MRS, London, annually

Market Research Society, *International Directory of Market Research Organizations*, MRS, London, 1991

University of Warwick Business Information Service, *Sources of Unofficial UK Statistics*, 2nd edn, Gower, Aldershot, 1990

Worcester, R.M. and Downham, J., *Consumer Market Research Handbook*, 3rd edn, Elsevier North-Holland, Amsterdam, 1986

20 Database marketing

Merlin Stone

This chapter explains:

1 What database marketing is
2 Why database marketing is growing so fast
3 Who uses it and why
4 What distinguishes it from more 'traditional' approaches to marketing
5 How developments in technology have stimulated its growth
6 What competitive advantages it offers
7 The main requirements for implementing database marketing.

WHAT IS DATABASE MARKETING?

There is no universally accepted definition of database marketing. In this chapter, the following definition is used: 'Database marketing' is an interactive approach to marketing, which uses individually addressable marketing media and channels (such as mail, telephone, and the sales force):

- To extend help to a company's target audience
- To stimulate their demand
- To stay close to them by recording and keeping an electronic database memory of details of all customers, prospects and all communication and commercial contacts with them, to help improve all future contacts and to ensure more realistic planning of all marketing.

Database marketing is a new, powerful approach to marketing for large companies. Many companies are spending large budgets on it. They include telecommunications, computer and office equipment suppliers such as AT&T, IBM and Xerox, automotive suppliers such as Ford and Volvo, and financial sector companies, such as banks and insurance companies. Formerly, these companies and many like them had barely considered how database marketing could work for them. Today they use various terms to refer to their version of database marketing, such as direct response, telemarketing, direct marketing, transactional advertising, mail order and curriculum marketing. But these terms refer to one or more of the many techniques used by database marketers. 'Database marketing' at its most powerful is a new way of doing business. It is a new way of managing marketing. It leads to a new way of defining the relationship between a company and its customers.

Database marketing works by creating a bank of information about individual customers (taken, for example, from orders, enquiries, external lists). This information is then used to analyse their buying and enquiry patterns. The resulting analysis enables marketing management to target products and serivces more accurately towards specific customers. For example, it may be used to promote the benefits of brand loyalty to customers at risk from competition; it can stimulate revenue growth by identifying which customers are most likely to buy new products and services; it can increase sales effectiveness; and it can support low-cost alternatives to traditional sales methods, including telemarketing and direct mail, which can be of strategic importance in markets where margins are being eroded.

Database marketing enables marketing managers to identify precisely which marketing approaches work. This is because all forms of communication with customers are managed through the database, and all customers' responses to this communication are logged and analysed. As a result, the entire marketing function can be made more accountable for its results. If the database is used to plan all marketing actions, from new product development to sales promotion, the link between advertising and sales promotion, product management and sales channels can be much improved. If the different elements of the sales process are managed through the database, the likelihood of the customer being neglected is much reduced.

Companies come to database marketing in different ways, so not all the characteristics of database marketing are visible in all companies which use it. The characteristics of fully fledged database marketing are:

1   Each actual or potential customer is identified as a record on the marketing database. Markets and market segments are not identified primarily through aggregate data (which cannot be broken down into individual customers) but as agglomerations of individual customers

2   Each customer record contains not only identification and access information (for example, name, address, telephone number), but also a range of marketing information. This includes information about customer needs and characteristics. For consumers, this is likely to include information about the area they live in, the kinds of product they buy, and their life-style. For business customers, the information is likely to cover the type of activity carried out (industry sector), how the customer makes buying decisions, and how different products and services are used. Such information is used to identify likely purchasers of particular products and how they should be approached. Each customer record also includes information about campaign communications (whether the customer has been exposed to particular marketing communications campaigns), about customer's past responses to communications which form part of the campaigns, and about past transactions (with the company and possibly with competitors)

3   The information is available to the company during the process of each communication with the customer, to enable it to decide how to respond to the customer's needs

4   The database is used to record responses of customers to company initiatives (for example, marketing communications or sales campaigns)

5   The information is also available to marketing policy makers. This enables

them to decide such points as which target markets or segments are appropriate for each product or service and what marketing mix (price, marketing communications, distribution channel, and so on) is appropriate for each product in each target market

6 In large companies, selling many products to each customer, the database is used to ensure that the approach to the customer is co-ordinated, and a consistent approach developed

7 The database eventually replaces market research. Marketing campaigns are devised such that the response of customers to the campaign provides information which the company is looking for

8 In addition to the automation of customer information via the development of a large database and the tools to access it to handle transactions with customers, marketing management automation is also developed. This is needed to handle the vast volume of information generated by database marketing. It ensures that marketing opportunities and threats are identified more or less automatically, and that ways of capturing these opportunities and neutralizing these threats are also recommended. It makes higher quality information on marketing performance available to senior management, allowing them to allocate marketing resources more effectively.

This is fully fledged marketing automation – database marketing at its most mature. Few companies have yet succeeded in creating this, just as no company has yet completely automated the mechanism of product delivery, from design through to physical distribution. But many companies are adopting as their goal the idea that the human interface between company and customer should focus most strongly on what humans are best at – understanding and looking after each other.

For example, face-to-face sales staff may be best used in presenting difficult or radically new concepts to customers, or handling sensitive problems. Telemarketing staff may be best used in handling other sales tasks, such as managing smaller accounts, obtaining basic data needed to establish whether a prospect is a serious one, or identifying some of the facts relating to a sales problem. Both kinds of staff can concentrate more on exploiting their relative advantage if they are given the support of a powerful database marketing system. For this reason, database marketing is appearing in the strategic plans of many companies.

WHY IS DATABASE MARKETING GROWING SO FAST?

The very existence of database marketing is owed to the powerful processing capability and immense storage capacity of today's computers, and to the way telecommunications technology is being harnessed to make customer and market data available to the wide variety of staff involved in a company's marketing and sales efforts. Yet technology alone cannot explain the fast growth of database marketing. Evidence of its rapid growth comes from various sources:

1 In the US, over half of all advertising now asks for a direct response

2 In the UK, expenditure on direct mail by companies is growing much faster in real terms than expenditure on television

3   Almost every day, a new name is added to the list of large companies that have successfully added direct marketing to their communications strategy. In the US, users range from capital equipment companies to companies marketing low-budget consumer goods and services. Retailers and mail order companies have been joined by the manufacturers of fast-moving consumer goods. In the UK the rapid growth in its use by the financial sector has been greatly stimulated by continuing liberalization. Some large retailers, chary of marketing disciplines which have developed out of branded goods marketing, have appointed direct marketing agencies. They are starting to exploit one of their chief assets – the database of loyal customers who hold their credit cards

4   Telemarketing capacity in the UK is doubling annually, while in the US the telephone is now the biggest single market medium

This growth of database marketing is rooted in the philosophy of small businesses – a philosophy of getting closer to the customer. Many gurus of marketing and business thought preach the virtues of this philosophy. The idea is that every company should identify its customers, understand their needs, meet these needs, and treat customers well after the sale, in order to improve competitive position.

' All this is easily said, but less easy for large companies to put into practice. Much corporate marketing is still tied to big, general marketing campaigns that have a single message for everyone. Corporate marketing is dominated by the idea that it is the USP – the Unique Selling Proposition – that creates differentiation in the market place. In theory, the USP can be translated into one set of words and pictures which will guide all consumers to make the 'right' choice.

Developments in markets and technology are forcing large companies to question the idea of the market-wide USP. Instead, they are trying to put the small business philosophy into practice. Single USPs, spelt out to the whole market, are no longer enough. Customers can be helped to select from a wide variety of goods. But customers differ. They need different kinds of help and service. This can be provided by sending special messages tailored to specific segments of the market. Database marketing can displace the overall USP approach. It makes it a weak lowest common denominator in terms of its power to sell.

Computerizing information about customers and their relationship with the company makes it possible to address help and service more accurately. It can also be used to market a variety of additional goods and services to each customer. This combination of satisfying customer needs for more information, and marketing to the customer at the same time, is the main competitive advantage of database marketing. It provides the main motive for companies to invest in it.

THE STRENGTHS OF DATABASE MARKETING

Database marketing has special strengths; for example.

1   It is *measurable*. Responses to campaigns are measured, enabling the effectiveness of different approaches to be measured

2   It is *testable*. The effectiveness of different elements of a marketing approach – the product, the communications medium, the offer (how the product is

packaged to appeal to the customer), the target market, and so on – can be accurately tested. Tests can be carried out quickly, so a company can take quick action on the results. Test campaign results can be used to forecast sales more precisely, helping a company manage inventory more effectively

3   It is *selective*. Campaigns can be focused accurately, because communciation can be addresed to specific customers

4   Communication to each customer can be *personalized*, by including details relevant to them and not to others. This usually raises the response rate

5   It is *flexible*. Campaigns can be timed to have their effect exactly when desired.

There are other reasons why the use of database marketing is growing quickly. What were thought to be mass markets are splitting into new, distinct buying segments. In consumer markets, rising incomes are allowing people to indulge tastes for more discretionary goods. In business markets, buyers are becoming more expert. They seek information about products from a wider variety of sources. They expect to have their needs met more precisely than before. Suppliers' ability to analyse customer needs has increased with the use of new techniques and lower costs in market research. They are now better equipped for niche marketing.

The costs of mass marketing have risen. Television costs continue to rise rapidly relative to the costs of a mail shot, a sales call or a telephone call. But the costs of unstructured use of sales staff have also risen. Using advances in computing, telecommunications and print technology, more precisely targeted media – the 'narrowcast' media – are now available. They enable suppliers to address tightly defined market segments, and they enable customers to receive information more relevant to their needs.

DEVELOPMENTS IN TECHNOLOGY

In many respects, the computerization of businesses is at an early stage. Enabling technologies are developing fast. Most technologies, such as those which determine processing power and speed, memory and storage, are improving at least tenfold every ten years. Speed of access (reading, writing) to stored data is growing more slowly (about 5 per cent faster each year). Communications technology, once slow to evolve, is accelerating. Software, once a barrier, is now easier to use and more reliable. Mainframe and decision support packages are widely used for large modelling exercises and developing departmental administrative systems. Application packages (for example, database management) are also more flexible and capable of customization. Application development products have accelerated programmer productivity. Experience of using computers is widely distributed in companies.

Implications

The implications of the above developments are:

1   Computerization of more difficult areas (for example, marketing, because it

covers people not controlled by the company – the customers) is becoming easier. But no projects are easy. Large–scale projects are always difficult. Creation of a very large customer-oriented database is not to be undertaken lightly

2 Large databased systems will be used to drive customer communication and management, even in the most complex businesses

3 Companies which do not plan their marketing data and management architectures will have difficulty in exploiting developments.

IMPLEMENTING DATABASE MARKETING

The four main elements required to make database marketing happen are:

1 Corporate refocusing (creating a customer-led approach to doing business)
2 Developing the capability (data, systems, staff, suppliers and – in some cases – business partners)
3 Marketing applications development
4 Policy development.

Corporate refocusing

Database marketing demands very strong attention to customer needs. The business should develop a vision of how the business will improve its relationship with its customers and what new profit-yielding relationships can be developed with them. In a large company, creating this new emphasis may require a long campaign, including educating senior managers to the benefits of database marketing and the need to make the necessary substantial systems and human investment.

Capability development

The main elements of capability development are:

1 *Database development* Creating the database and maintaining its quality, to provide the information needed to target and attract new customers; to meet profitably more of the needs of existing customers; and to identify new, lower cost ways of reaching and selling to customers

2 *Marketing system development* Developing computer systems to hold, manage, enhance and manipulate the data. Additional systems may be needed to support specific applications, such as telemarketing, mail order, credit cards, lead generation for the sales force or dealers, exhibition invitations, and club or user-group marketing

3 *Staff development* Developing staff skills so that a company can deploy the data and system to its marketing advantage. Without these skills, even the best database marketing system will not work. Often, these skills are acquired on a temporary basis at first, from consultancies and service agencies. However, they must be brought in-house eventually

4 *Supplier development* Creating links with the many suppliers who carry out

the following functions: data provision, management and interpretation; marketing systems management; marketing application development; creative marketing services. These suppliers need to understand the company and its needs

5 *Business partner development* Initiating partnerships with other companies who benefit from one or other strand of the company's strategy. They include companies involved in joint promotions to the customers on the company's databases and in distributing the company's products.

Applications development

The development of ways in which the new capability will be applied. Applications involve fundamental commitments to a changed way of doing business with customers and business partners. Examples of specific applications include:

- Consumer and business promotion
- Targeted mailing, mail order and fulfilment facility
- Credit card management
- Financial service marketing in addition to the main product range
- Telemarketing systems
- Dealer, distributor or agent management
- Club and user group marketing
- Data marketing – the sale of data to third parties.

Policy development

Policy development is distinguished from applications development by having specific shorter-term objectives. Policies are defined in terms of one or more particular campaigns (for example, launch of a specific new life insurance policy, or a customer loyalty questionnaire campaign). Each campaign relies heavily on one or more of the capabilities and applications mentioned above.

For most users of database marketing, much of this work is delegated (at least partly) to direct marketing agencies. However, the planning of the co-ordinated series of campaigns which make up the policy must remain the responsibility of the company. If this planning and co-ordination does not take place in-house, database marketing activity may become divorced from the mainstream of company business.

CONCLUSIONS

Database marketing can affect every aspect of marketing strategy and implementation. Although it may seem quite complex, its philosophy is very simple. Every company should:

- Know who its customers are
- Keep in touch with them
- Allow them to speak to the company when they want to
- Give them good reasons (benefits) for maintaining their relationship with the company

- Do all this carefully (in a well-planned and steadily implemented manner)
- Do it cost-effectively.

FURTHER READING

Mounsey, Philip and Stone, Merlin, *Managing Direct Marketing*, Croner, Kingston, 1990

Postma, Paul and Molenaar, Cor, *Database Marketing*, Heinemann, Oxford, 1990

Shaw, Robert and Stone, Merlin, *Database Marketing*, Gower, Aldershot, 1988

Stone, Merlin, Thomson, Anna and Wheeler, Christopher, *Telemanage Your Customers*, Gower, Aldershot, 1989

21 Advertising

Charles Channon

Advertising is typically one element in the persuasive presentation of a product or service to its buying or using public. For many of those involved in it, whether as advertisers, agencies or consumers, it is *the* communication element in the marketing mix. What we really mean by this is that it is the most obvious and separately identifiable.

ADVERTISING AND THE MARKETING MIX

In fact, the whole of the marketing mix contains potential or actual communications and all of them, when they are found, are designed to be persuasive to purchase and consumption. A cleaning product may contain coloured particles to highlight certain claimed ingredients and their benefits; a small electrical product may have design elements which highlight its suitability for youth or that it is fashionable. In most instances a pack does far more than simply 'protect' what's inside – it will 'brand' the contents at the very least, and sometimes a great deal more.

Even distribution can 'say' something about a brand. So can price: whether our price is higher or lower than the competition is, potentially, a communication to our market about things other than price. As a relative price it can produce, say, lower margins and higher volume or higher margins and lower volume, and either route may mean more or less total profit. But as a communication it can say something about our quality, our market segment, our end use, and so on. In this respect it must be consistent with our strategy as expressed through the rest of the marketing mix, including, of course, promotion, of which advertising is a part.

In this sense the whole of marketing strategy, directly or indirectly, is a communication with the market-place. It must be so because in most developed market-places the buyer, the customer, the consumer is usually free to choose – to buy or not to buy, to buy our product or service or someone else's. To make that choice, consumers need *information* – information which they have in some way processed and responded to at the rational and/or emotional level, consciously or unconsciously. The response may be as vague as a heightened sense of familiarity or as definite as a feeling of total satisfaction with previous trials or the belief that the product contains added fibre or is selling with its price cut at a particular store. Of course, as we have seen, this information which is being used and responded to does not just come from advertising. In the last analysis, the response is to the whole of the marketing mix. So, advertising is not unique as a tool of marketing; rather it is like the other communication aspects of marketing, only more so. Its sole function is to evoke a response through communication in paid-for space – usually from the consumer, often (indirectly) from the trade as well, and sometimes from other audiences.

What it communicates may be a claim about value for money or a product performance benefit. It could equally be just a reminder, or it could be an association or an image in which words as such, let alone claims, have little significant role to play. Whatever it is will be (or should be) determined by the nature of the product field and the consumer needs within it, and by the part that advertising can play in the context of the rest of the marketing mix.

We should never think of advertising as isolated from the rest of marketing. It plays just one part in helping to solve a marketing problem or exploit a marketing opportunity, and, to be effective, the part it plays must be right. If the marketing problem is distribution, advertising may be able to contribute only a little to its solution; if the problem is price, advertising as such may contribute even less. And if the problem is the product itself, advertising may even be counter-productive. Advertising which generated widespread trial of an unsatisfactory product, could well render a later 'new improved' version unsaleable. On the other hand, if the problem is awareness, advertising can be very powerful, and even more powerful (because the effect lasts longer) if the problem is positioning – that is, if potential consumers have not grasped where your brand fits in to their needs or lives in a way that is different from the competition.

Where advertising fits, it will work to *simplify* consumer choice in your favour, provided that *the advertisements themselves also form a fit between the brand and the consumer in the real world*. Implicit in this statement of the obvious are some important fundamentals about the nature of advertisements and of the advertising process.

First, advertisements relate products or services to people. To do this effectively, they must be appropriate to the former and relevant to the latter *in a way that helps to express and sustain competitive advantage*. This, if you like, is the generalized or generic version of the strategy to which any advertisement is written (whether consciously or unconsciously). The specifics of the brand, the specifics of consumer needs in the product field, and the specifics of competitive advantage will determine the strategy to which a particular advertisement or campaign is written. Yet, however specific the strategy, *it will not write the advertisements* (though there are still some advertisers and some product fields where it can appear to come very close to doing so). For every given strategy there will be, in principle, an *in*definite number of possible creative solutions.

This gap, as it were, between strategy and execution is not unique to advertising. Nevertheless, it is particularly evident in advertising and helps to explain the high profile of the creative function within it. What matters is the response. Strategy will define the response we want, but it is a creative execution – an advertisement – which must elicit it. In some cases the content of the strategy and the literal content of the advertising message will be almost identical; in others this will not be so, due to the nature of the required responses and the way such responses are achieved – emotions, imagery, involvement, and values must be recreated, not just stated.

Target consumers and their needs, however, are only one side of the connection an advertisement makes. The other side is the product or service, which we often speak of as the *brand*.

ADVERTISING AND BRANDING

At the most basic level it is obvious that the one thing an advertisement must do is to identify what it is selling. However, a well-branded advertisement is no more than the final link in a whole process of *differentiation* from the competition, which good marketing will attempt to achieve in the market-place wherever it can. It is a process to which advertising is peculiarly well suited to contribute and, indeed, it is this power in advertising which has historically accounted for its prominence in the marketing of fast moving consumer goods.

We talked earlier of advertisements relating products to their target consumers in a way that helps to express and sustain competitive advantage. Looked at more closely, this statement can be seen to be almost a redefinition in communication terms of the ultimate operational objective of the whole of marketing. Although the concept of profit is not explicit in this definition, we would do well to remember that it is there by implication as the *business* objective for which all good marketing is simply the strategy: *profit defines the purpose for and constraint under which competitive advantage is created and sustained.*

Competitive advantage can take many forms but, whatever it is, the consumer needs to know about it and needs to know that it belongs to us. It could be a price advantage; it could be a performance benefit like 'washes whiter', 'gets stains out', 'kills 99 per cent of all known germs', or 'kind to hands'. Or it could be a generalized promise of reliability and value which adds up to 'the name you can trust'. It could concern *authenticity* – 'the real thing' – or be a form of social gratification like an enhancement of the role in which the product is used or of the end use (or end-user) to which (or to whom) it is addressed. It could be that our brand is easier to identify with, or has a more distinctive identity or more attractive personality – or just more fun. Being a better advertiser can sometimes constitute our competitive advantage. But whatever it is will be relevant at some level to consumer choice, and the link between it and our product will be forged by branding.

Branding links a reputation to a name and creates an *owned difference in the market-place* which is relevant to consumer needs. It provides a focus for interest, credibility and loyalty and, of course, it can be used to identify and reinforce any form of stimulus to sales. It is a powerful aid to the simplification of choice and to the creation of a *protected* franchise among your target consumers.

Branding works by counteracting the erosion of advantage which is the natural tendency of any competitive product field. It creates a sort of patent in the mind or, if you prefer, helps to build what accountants call 'goodwill', which, properly supported, has a good chance of surviving attempts by our competition to match or equal us on our own ground. Successful branding can be very valuable: it becomes our differentiated asset in the market-place and may be worth more to us than any other assets the company has.

In this sense a brand is a unique identity, a whole which is greater than the sum of its parts. You *can* build a brand *without* advertising, but many products need advertising to help them do this because the experience of the product in use will not by itself be enough to establish its unique identity without the projection, the associations and the amplification which advertising can provide.

ADVERTISING AND ADDED VALUES

Most consumers will admit that there are many products which mean something more to their users than simply what they deliver in terms of pure performance. This is most obvious in personal purchase product fields like, say, lager or fragrances, where what we buy is also a statement about ourselves. Yet most household purchases which are not retailers' 'own brands' make some statement, even if only the residual reassurance and guarantee that the product in question will deliver up to expectation. Even 'own-branding' will have a meaning in this context either because it means something anyway (Sainsbury's wines, for example) or, negatively, because we have decided that this is a product field where price alone ought to be decisive.

All these 'meanings', except the last, constitute in some sense an *added* value. For reasons that will now be obvious, added values help differentiation in the market-place, are a natural product of the creation of a brand and are usually very suited to projection and reinforcement in advertising, although, as with everything else, there are other ways of doing it.

We need to be clear that added values are not a marketing invention but are fundamental to our social nature as human beings. As anthropology has shown, we use goods to define our values, reinforce them, and express them to other people. In this perspective, if, as has been said, money is information in circulation, then *goods are information delivered and received*. Gifts, such as a box of chocolates, are obviously like this but so are houses, furnishings, cars, holidays, clothes, what we serve at a meal, and even savings and insurance. All these things serve a functional or rational purpose, but to us as human beings in society they often mean more than the purpose they serve – more to ourselves or to our families and friends or to the world at large. This does not mean that consumption behaviour is necessarily *irrational* but rather that 'rationality' must not be confined to a limited functional and economic meaning.

VALUES, ECONOMIC VALUE, AND EVALUATION

The importance and legitimacy of values and meanings in consumption behaviour have some practical implications for the relationship between marketing and advertising on the one hand and the science of economics on the other. In the end, economics can deal with *values* (that is, all the various consumer needs and satisfactions which marketing and advertising must address in the market-place) only in terms of their *economic* value, expressed in the form of such relationships as the price elasticity of demand (what percentage change in demand will result from a 1 per cent change in price) and so on. This type of analysis can be very useful *retrospectively* in evaluating what marketing has achieved but necessarily gives very little guidance on how you might set about achieving it in the real world in the first place.

The assessment of what has been achieved can still be very valuable, however, and it can be particularly valuable for an *optional and controllable* marketing cost like advertising. It is not easy to achieve because the marketing mix is not just a mix as far as sales and profit are concerned but a *blend*. It requires us to *isolate* an effect due to advertising over and above the effect of the rest of the mix (to which, of course, advertising may also have contributed – if, for example, there is an *underlying* long-term upward trend in sales). It must not only isolate an advertising effect from the rest of the mix which *we* have created but also isolate it from all those other influences on purchasing which we do not control, such as competitors' activities, and a variety of economic, social, technological and even political pressures.

It *can* be done, as the Institute of Practitioners in Advertising (IPA) Advertising Effectiveness Awards have shown, and done more rigorously than simple-minded arguments like 'advertising went up and then sales went up', which used to be the staple and inadequate basis of such demonstrations. It is easier to do if planned for in advance, and the case histories of the published books of the Awards provide extremely useful models of how to do it. The analyses they deploy, of course, are not solely those familiar from economics textbooks, indeed rather the reverse, but they do go a long way towards demonstrating how in practice advertising helps to convert values into economic value, and economic value into profit.

The bottom-line accountability of advertising will become more important as markets become more competitive and as the *business* objectives of marketing activity come into sharper and sharper focus through the stock market and its analysts. But this is only one aspect of a changing competitive environment for advertising which has tended to shift the aims of advertising activity away from the long-term brand-building effects, which can be inferred but not separately quantified (at least on a consensus basis), to strictly short-term effects where, in certain circumstances, other means of promotion may appear to be equally or more efficient.

ADVERTISING AND THE COMPETITIVE ENVIRONMENT

Two of the most important changes of this kind, apart from the ever-increasing pressure on financial performance as such, have been the growth of retailer power and the shortening life cycle of many markets.

Historically, brand advertising developed as a weapon of the manufacturer against the retailer and wholesaler. In 1964 the abolition of resale price maintenance in the UK began a process whereby retailers of packaged goods could begin to wrest some of this power back into their own hands. They could, as it were, stimulate demand (by cutting the price of brands at the expense of the manufacturer's margin rather than their own), concentrate demand (by creating larger and larger outlets whose volume would give them economies of scale), and differentiate demand (by creating 'own brands' and, latterly, by making the stores themselves into an added value 'brand' which could compete on basis other than price alone).

The effect of this in the UK over time – in the USA the relationship and its consequences have been rather different – has been a tendency to reduce the resources available for supporting manufacturer brands in ways other than cutting the price (or some equivalent incentive to stock) to the retailer. It has also created a double jeopardy for brands which are not brand leaders; the retailer can 'afford' not to stock them but they cannot afford not to be stocked. Other things being equal, it is clear that in a situation where three or four retail chains control half the sales of a brand which itself holds less than 0.1 per cent of those retailers' sales, marketing must shift its emphasis to *pushing* the product through (that is, getting product into stock) and, to that extent, less into *pulling* the product through (that is, differentiating demand among consumers.)

There are other reasons too why classic packaged goods advertising has begun to be less dominant in total advertising activity than it used to be. For one thing, there has been a growth in service markets generally and in financial services markets particularly. In many of these markets there is a tendency for the advertising task to polarize between highly generalized 'corporate' support and highly specific support and promotion for often short-lived products. Another factor is the quickening pace of the life cycle of a number of advertised products. This applies both to the financial services products which we have already mentioned and to other product fields like consumer electronics. Shorter product life cycles mean that there is less time to recover the initial investment. With manufactured goods there is also less likelihood that the economies of scale potentially open to those first into the market could offset the steep decline in the general manufacturing costs of the technology which so often characterizes technological markets. In these situations there may well be less to allocate to advertising but, equally important, what is allocated must 'move a lot of boxes' before price- and distribution-led competition absorbs most of marketing's resources.

There is also a broader thrust at work in many *high* frequency of purchase markets whose implications are harder to predict. This thrust comes from the information revolution particularly as it has affected data capture and data analysis. With (or even, on occasion, without) bar coding of goods, it is now possible to retrieve information about sales as they occur at the till and analyse these so as to control stock, facings, reordering and pricing, and, of course, to provide an up-to-the-minute information base for the buyer at head office doing a deal with the manufacturer. One effect of this is greatly to reduce the scope for traditional manufacturer influence on *in-store* marketing, but as these activities have traditionally competed with media advertising for a share of the marketing cake the result may be to increase the importance of advertising in the mix.

A stage further on (quite a bit further on) in the use of electronic point of sale (EPOS) data would be the ability *to cross-analyse sales by purchasers by media exposure* as the ultimate form of instant single-source data. Ad-lab data of this kind obviously have huge potential though it should be noted that generating them is one thing and using them effectively is quite another – most information systems in marketing and advertising have been significantly underused. Be this as it may, it seems reasonable to suppose that it would increase and sophisticate the dialogue on media policy between client and agency, provided that the client could have access to these largely retailer-generated data. This is not to say that it would always tend to increase total media spend.

With or without the ad-lab development, EPOS is part of the evolution of the retail sector towards higher margin strategies and away from price competition (in which the lever to profit is sheer volume). In principle, this should make manufacturers' added value brands (and the advertising that builds and maintains them) more attractive to the retailer. Equally, however, it highlights the fact that switched sales between brands, which change brand shares but not margin or total volume in the product field, are of no particular interest as far as the retailer is concerned. Switching sales, gaining share, are what advertising does best; it can also help to expand the market, if there is room for growth. In future manufacturers' marketing objectives may need to be at least as much margin led as they are share led. Added value competition at a price premium is more difficult than at price parity and represents a challenge both to new product development and advertising. It could also imply fewer winners unless there is a more effective segmentation of the market.

On balance, this particular development looks as if it will tend to maintain the importance of brand-building advertising, but it may also make it even more competitive for the agencies concerned as the *real* index of performance becomes sterling 'margin share'.

Increasingly, distributed computer power will also greatly expand the potential for applying statistical modelling to markets – and not only to packaged goods markets. This will, as noted earlier, sharpen the element of accountability in the client–agency relationship, but it is a long haul, requiring good data and a long time series over which the data have been collected. It also has one disadvantage, not unknown elsewhere in advertising, which is that the data are very difficult to communicate *with all their proper qualifications* to those who have to act on them. The 'boffins' should not be asked to bear the responsibility for this problem on their own – marketing and advertising management must advance half-way to meet them.

MARKETING AND THE ADVERTISING PROCESS

With one significant exception, the whole thrust of this review so far has been to emphasize the necessarily close relationship between the ways marketing and advertising work. Yet whatever the focus, short or long term, just moving unit sales or building a consumer franchise, this symmetry between the tasks and objectives of marketing and advertising is very easy to lose sight of in the real world of the client–agency relationship and the agency's way of working.

One factor here is that clients can be concerned about the confidentiality of key financial performance data, so the agency may not know, for example, the client's margin, other costs and so on. While understandable, this is also limiting, not only on the agency's ability to offer general advice but also on the extent to which the agency can really understand the total context of its work as when, for example, it recommends an advertising budget.

Two other necessary factors that arise in the translation from a marketing problem to an advertising objective, however, are just as important. One of them is the 'gap' we have already mentioned that exists between the advertising strategy and the actual advertising recommendation. Most, if not quite all, advertisements have to be based on an advertising *idea*, which is *not* the same as the advertising strategy. It will be based on the strategy of course, and designed to achieve the consumer responses which the strategy says will help the sell, but it is not created *by* the strategy: it is created *to* the strategy. The ideas that the agency's creative department devise may or may not contain words or claims that reflect the strategy in a literal and direct way.

Creative ideas and their treatment in advertisements constitute the 'language' of advertising. That language has its own conventions, resources and skills. It can draw heavily on the style and typical content of the medium in which it appears (for example, when television advertising uses a 'sit-com' idea as the basis of a campaign). It has its own conventions, too, which arise out of all those approaches, devices, and techniques which are the natural armoury of simplifying communications and persuasive communications – like product demonstration, product endorsement, analogy, imagery, humour and wit. Not every advertisement, of course, uses these resources to the same extent – an 'earpiece' advertisement (those you sometimes see either side of the name of the newspaper on its front page) may simply repeat the brand's logo – this will depend on the job the advertisement is trying to do. But every advertisement, even the simplest, will be trying to have an impact on its audience and leave an impression (consciously or unconsciously) about the product. How effective an advertisement is at doing this job will depend in part on how many target consumers it reaches (its coverage) and how often it reaches them (its 'frequency') but it will also depend on how well it uses the resources of the language of advertising which we have been discussing.

Advertising as a 'craft' – the craft of the creation and production of advertisements – is, therefore, unlike many other marketing tasks in its specific skills and in its product. Both are decisive for the character of an agency, for the work satisfaction of all those employed in it (not just the 'creatives' themselves), and for its success in winning and keeping business. So, although in the multidisciplinary world of the agency there are many relevant skills and resources which to a greater or lesser extent overlap those in the client's marketing department, there are other *defining* elements in it which make it different and mark out its operational goals as in many ways peculiarly its own.

Good advertising is one such goal, and good media planning and buying another. Indeed, media planning and buying, though it receives in its own right less attention from the general public, is the other distinguishing activity of an agency and the other service which its clients are buying, apart from advertisements themselves. They may buy these services from separate sources rather than from one full-service advertising agency but, whether they buy their media from the same source or separately from a media independent (as 'media only' agencies tend to be known), media planning and buying is a craft in its own right with its own special skills and resources. The world of media with its audience research data, its comparisons of cost-per-thousand (the cost of reaching 1 000 of a given audience or circulation), its analysis of reach and frequency, its schedules (the media chosen for a campaign together with the timing – and size or length – of the ads to appear in it), and its optimizations (maximizing what can be obtained for a given campaign cost against specified criteria of coverage and frequency) is also a very different world from that of marketing and, it should be said, from that of creating and producing the advertisements themselves.

We have spoken of these distinctive outputs of an agency as its operational goals to distinguish them as activities from the marketing ends which they both serve. It would be more accurate to speak of them as the distinctive *operational activities* of the advertising business which in their turn have their own distinctive operational goals. If this sounds like more word play on a sort of 'Russian dolls' basis (when each doll opens to reveal another doll which opens to reveal another doll ... and so on) that is because in any multidisciplinary and multistage business *one person's strategy is always likely to be another's objective.*

For example, a company's business objective may be growth in profits and its strategy to milk existing brands in saturated markets while expanding brand share for its brands in growth sectors. In the light of this, the marketing director and his or her brand people may have an objective of increasing share while maintaining margins in their growth markets and a strategy of achieving this by increasing distribution and advertising support. The agency may, therefore, have the objective of stimulating trials among non-users of the brand and a strategy of doing this by increasing awareness and emphasizing its suitability for certain end uses to which product quality is particularly relevant. The agency's creative department will have the objective of increasing awareness and improving perceptions of quality along with the salience of certain end uses, and the creative recommendation will in effect constitute its strategy for achieving this. The final strategy in this chain of objectives and strategies is the advertisement or the campaign. In the agency part of the chain, the objectives and their strategies are framed in terms of what advertising can achieve *per se* (for example, increase awareness, modify attitudes, stimulate trial – not gain share, increase volume) so that, in this respect, the disciplines of thought which guide the advertising process are distinctive of that process just as much as the craft skills and activities which constitute its end-product to the client.

This contrast between marketing's and advertising's common pursuit of differentiation in the market-place, on the one hand, and their distinctive differences in craft skills, operational goals and disciplines of thought on the other, is nothing special or unusual. Similar contrasts will be found wherever there is specialization within a common endeavour.

One other aspect worth noting, however, is how the search for differentiation in the creative product of advertising leads to a great deal of stress on the new and the original. This is *not* to say that original and creative thought are not found in the rest of the marketing mix – they are and they should be – but the importance of originality in the creative idea and the skills which make that originality work in terms of television, press, radio, posters or cinema, bring into sharp focus a necessary connection between the craft of advertisements and the arts, entertainment and editorial skills of the media in which advertisements appear.

Emphasizing this aspect of the business must be done with care. It can all too often seem like a covert plea for self-indulgence by the agency and an excuse for weakening the need for relevance. That it should neither be like this nor have this effect goes without saying. Equally, however, it is not to be despised simply because it can be abused. It can make an extremely valuable contribution to the sales effectiveness of advertising in the market-place, as is shown by the number of cases in the IPA Advertising Effectiveness Awards where the advertisements concerned win creative awards as well.

THE ADVERTISING CYCLE AND THE AGENCY ACCOUNT TEAM

Advertising is a cyclical process of which advertisements and media schedules are the recurrent product. The cycle starts with what might be called a planning baseline; this leads to the development of a strategy, which leads to the development of a creative brief and a budget, which leads to creative and media recommendations, which lead to running the advertisements, which in turn lead to monitoring our apparent progress in the market-place, which will, sooner or later, become the new planning baseline, with the cycle starting all over again.

As described, the process sounds simple enough. In practice it can be a complex process, which is feedback-intensive, prone to error, and as dependent on sound judgement as on good data. Of course, advertising accounts can differ enormously in their complexity and in the scope and nature of the feedback which is provided, while agencies themselves differ in how they are organized to apportion the various responsibilities to which the process gives rise. For this reason, it may be most useful to distinguish the responsibilities as such prior to any consideration of who fulfils them.

In fairly simplistic terms the responsibilities can be listed, as follows:

1 *Agency responsibilities to the clients:*
   - to advise them generally in their own best interest
   - to provide creative and media recommendations which are relevant and appropriate to the client's business and marketing objectives and strategy
   - to effect this at an appropriate level of quality, professionalism, timeliness, and cost-effectiveness

2 *Agency responsibilities to the brand and to the consumer:*
   - to relate the brand to the target consumer through the advertising so as to help the sell
   - in such a way as to be true to the heritage, character and performance of the brand *and* relevant to the current needs and satisfaction of the target consumers
   - to do this as far as possible so as to protect *future* sales of the brand

3 *Agency responsibilities to itself:*
   - to keep the business and handle it profitably
   - to ensure so far as possible that the client not only receives the best advice but is persuaded by it
   - not only to produce but to run work which merits the respect of its peer group agencies in the business
   - to attract and retain good talent and, as far as possible, to provide the scope and incentive for its development at every level in the agency

At first sight such a list many seem somewhat surprising in its structure and emphasis. It is not, of course, a list of legal responsibilities, so it says nothing about the fact that an agency is a principal and not an agent when it acts on behalf of its clients. It does not tell one whether the agency's remuneration will be commission-based or, as is increasingly the case, fee-based. It gives little indication of the terms of business to be agreed with the client. Furthermore, it appears to draw a surprising distinction between the interests of the client and those of the brand and an invidious distinction between both of these and the agency's own interest.

In reality, of course, all these interests overlap: they are complementary rather than contradictory, but it is important to remember that they are not identical.

They *can* clash when things get out of kilter. The advertising management task which is shared between a good agency and a good client is to ensure that all these critical responsibilities remain in their proper complementary relationship to one another.

For example, it is not in the client's long-term interest that good agency service should remain unprofitable to that agency, any more than it is in the long-term interests of consumers that a good brand should not make any money for its manufacturer. Again, clients with a portfolio of brands may well be tempted to improve the bottom line by a short-term policy of undersupporting one brand or purely price promoting it in a way that undermines its long-term franchise, securing sales today at the expense of sales tomorrow. If the agency doesn't stand up for the brand in this situation, who will?

Similarly, it is the brand's relationship to the consumer's needs and perceptions, not to those of the production manager or sales manager, that matters. Production may want to stress features or ingredients (or even, according to agency folklore, the factory) rather than consumer benefits or uses or social gratifications; sales may want to emphasize the logo, the value for money, and a slogan they think will appeal to the trade.

Again, agencies cannot best serve their clients through glorious failure. Good work which does not run is a loss to the client and a blow to the agency. True, not all 'good work' (in the agency's eyes) is necessarily sales-effective and not all 'dull work' is sales-*in*effective, but in a situation of trust such a dichotomy should be resolvable by research feedback and judgement. It can always be argued that if dull work can sell n boxes then good work *of the right kind* should be able to sell $n+$ boxes.

Not all agencies and not all clients could be induced to underwrite all the responsibilities stated here. Some on both sides set their face against creative awards, for example, as a permanent temptation to self-indulgence and irrelevance. Others, by contrast, believe the real temptation to be in the other direction: work that is nominally relevant in that you can match all the points in it against the strategy, but which never in fact comes to life and never engages the consumer such that its relevance becomes meaningful and effective. There is obviously a question here of balance and fitness for purpose, and a different balance may have to be struck in different situations.

All these responsibilities involve issues and different areas of expertise which have to be handled within the resources of the account team, drawing where necessary on internal agency resources or from outside. Leadership and the primary interface with the client will lie with the account director, media and creative responsibilities with the appropriate members of the team. In respect of those responsibilities which we have described as being to the brand and to the consumer, practice is more variable: they can be handled by the account director working with either an agency researcher or outside research suppliers when research is called for. Increasingly, and particularly in larger agencies in the UK, they will be separately identifiable as the proper sphere of the 'account planner' in the team.

The account planner in this situation will be responsible for generating the advertising strategy in the first place, and for any research-based creative development of the creative ideas produced to that strategy. The account planner will, therefore, be responsible for selecting and interpreting the research evidence both at these stages and at the final stage of evaluation in the market-place, which leads to the next planning baseline and the next round of the advertising planning cycle. In this sense, as *the representative of the consumer's needs and perceptions*, the account planner gives a separate and independent voice to the marketing principle as adapted to the agency's own specific product and way of working.

Throughout the advertising cycle, feedback in the form of research or other data has potentially a large and important role to play. The kind of research that is deployed will have much to do with the particular stage in the cycle that has been reached – at the beginning it may tend to the exploratory, the open-ended and the qualitative, at the end to the structured, focused and quantified. It will also have much to do with the respective philosophies of the agency and the client and with the way they have respectively understood the marketing and advertising task. In a nutshell, *how you think the marketing works will influence how you think the advertising works which in turn will influence how you think the research works.* This symmetry is perfectly proper and many of the arguments about research technique and methodology simply conceal a lack of congruence between the way the client and the agency understand the fundamental task. Here, as elsewhere, it would often be more fruitful to bring the assumptions out into the open and see why they differ rather than argue, often fruitlessly, about the methodological consequences that simply follow from them.

In the end there are as many models for marketing and advertising as there are types of differential advantage. Certainty is rarely attained and even more rarely held on to, because solutions wear out and problems change. In any case, the 'how' and 'why' questions, which are so important to consumer choice, do not give *actionably certain* answers whether or not we *count* the answers to them across a representative sample or simply listen to them in group discussions. So advertising decision, however well or extensively informed, is always, in the end, based on judgement, which is why respect and trust between all the parties to it, including the client, are the foundation on which everything else is based.

THE CONTROL AND REGULATION OF ADVERTISING

Advertising in the UK is carried on within a regulatory framework which acts to curb abuse and to make advertising responsive to the public consensus as well as to the letter of the law.

It has not always been so. Ninteenth-century patent medicine advertising in the UK, as elsewhere, was singularly free of any regard for the truth, however laxly defined. The gradual application of legal controls and a rising standard of education in the market-place as a whole were two important pressures in raising standards. The present regulatory system can be regarded as the product of the culmination of these two pressures in the development of consumerism in the 1960s, accelerated by a new consciousness of the potential power of advertising which followed the introduction and spread in coverage of commercial television from 1955 onwards.

As a result, the UK now has a mixed system of statutory control and self-regulation. The civil law deals also with such matters as copyright, trademark infringement, passing off and defamation. Broadcast advertising (that is, television and radio commercials) are subject to separate systems of statutory control. The Codes of Advertising Standards and Practice for these two media are the respective responsibility of the Independent Television Commission and the Radio Authority, but day-to-day implementation is the responsibility of the ITV Association and the Association of Independent Radio Contractors. The codes are specifically designed to avoid confusion between advertisements and programme material. However, there is now also a code covering sponsorship.

Print advertising is governed on a self-regulatory basis, administered by the Advertising Standards Authority (ASA) and funded by a levy on all display advertising. It is this body which deals with complaints from the public. The intra-industry complaints and issues are dealt with by the Committee of Advertising Practice, which represents all the main parties to the advertising business and is responsible for the British Code of Advertising Practice (BCAP) and the British Code of Sales Promotion Practice (BCSPP). These codes are not directly legally enforceable but bad publicity is a powerful corrective, backed up by the willingness of media to refuse space to the rule-breakers. On the whole, the system works well, not least because the spirit of the codes is regarded as being as important as the letter and because specific provision is made for difficult areas like taste and decency. It is in the interests of marketing and advertising as well as consumers that it should continue to work well. As a result of the Control of Misleading Advertising Regulations 1987 self-regulation has received some statutory back-up in the form of a reserve power by which the Director General of Fair Trading can have legal recourse in those few cases where the ASA cannot act quickly enough or cannot secure compliance.

FURTHER READING

Broadbent, S., (ed.), *Twenty Advertising Case Histories*, Holt, Rinehart & Winston, London, 1987
Broadbent, S. and Jacobs, B., *Spending Advertising Money*, 4th edn., Business Books, London, 1984
Channon, C. (ed.), *Advertising Works 3*, Holt, Reinhart & Winston, London, 1985
Channon, C. (ed.), *Advertising Works 4*, IPA/Cassell, London, 1987
Feldwick, P. (ed.), *Advertising Works 5*, IPA/Cassell, London, 1989
Feldwick, P. (ed.), *Advertising Works 6*, IPA/NTC, London, 1991
Douglas, T., *The Complete Guide to Advertising*, Macmillan, London, 1984
Jones, J. P., *What's in a Name? Advertising and the Concept of Brands*, Gower, Aldershot, 1986
King, S., *What is a Brand?*, J. Walter Thompson, London, 1970

White, R., *Advertising: What it is and how to do it*, revised edn., McGraw-Hill, London, 1988

Wilmshurst, John, *The Fundamentals of Advertising*, Heinemann, London, 1985

22 Sales promotion

Christian Petersen and John Williams

Sales promotion is an integral part of today's marketing dialogue with the consumer. Every day it reaches out to the consumer, salesman, and retailer. Promotion techniques are used to market a vast variety of goods and services. In many markets, expenditure on sales promotion equals or exceeds expenditure on advertising. In the UK, where it is of similar size to advertising expenditure, the amount spent on sales promotion is probably in excess of £6 billion.

This importance is recent. Although the techniques involved have been in use for decades, and often for centuries, the spectacular growth of promotion dates only from the mid-1960s. In many markets sales promotion expenditure (discounting inflation) has grown *five times or more* in the last twenty years.

Such dynamism reflects a change in Western economies. There has been a change from 'pull' purchasing to 'push' selling. In the 1950s and the 1960s, the growth of consumer spending power, accelerated by easily available credit, meant that people were keen to purchase whatever could be manufactured and retailed. With the slowing and then flattening of the demand trend, the primary effort has switched to 'push' selling, in order to maintain, as far as possible, the momentum of manufacturing and retailing.

The dramatic changes in how brands, products or services are retailed to the consumer have been responsible for fuelling this trend. The advent of super-markets, hypermarkets, self-service outlets (petrol stations, banks and the like) have dramatically shifted the balance of power between manufacturer and retailer. Never before have so many brands been competing for the consumer's attention.

As more inducement is now necessary to get people to purchase, sales promotion techniques have come into full play. Sales promotion is the technique which makes brands shout 'buy me' at the point of purchase.

WHAT IS SALES PROMOTION?

Sales promotion covers just about everything you can do to give people a *tangible* incentive to purchase. Everything, that is, on top of the basic sales message.

The variety of promotional techniques is as extensive as our ingenuity can devise, and as disciplined as the laws of different countries allow. New developments and refinements of technique happen every year. And because sales promotion is part of the total marketing mix, and usually co-exists with other forms of marketing, it is often difficult to decide what sales promotion is, and what it is not.

No one has yet produced a wholly satisfactory definition of sales promotion. A definition that attempts to be thorough and precise is usually too limiting for so dynamic a function. Such definitions, if accepted, cut out creative opportunism. Loose definitions hardly help either, since they give no firm idea of promotion, and often could be defining marketing as a whole. Also, the practical dimensions of sales promotion vary from country to country, so definitions adopted from other markets can be misleading and even legally dangerous.

The reader may like to experiment with his own definition of sales promotion. Any valid definition is likely to include the following elements:

1 There must be *a featured offer* (something done as a normal part of trade and not featured in any special way does not count as sales promotion)
2 The offer must be of *tangible advantage*. A message alone is intangible
3 The offer must be designed *to achieve marketing objectives* – during a defined time period – which will usually, but not necessarily, mean sales.

These are, of course, rather abstract terms. An easier, though less objective, way of recognizing sales promotion is to look for any of these four key propositions:

- SAVE!
- FREE!
- WIN!
- GIVE!

Just about every known form of sales promotion will include one or more of those propositions.

What sales promotions can do

Sales promotions can encourage the consumer or retailer to behave more in line with the economic interest of the manufacturer or supplier. Sales promotions can assist in:

1 Smoothing out costly buying troughs
2 Stimulating stock movement
3 Encouraging repeat purchase
4 Securing marginal buyers
5 Increasing penetration of new or existing products
6 Increasing volume
7 Avoiding uneconomic production runs
8 Avoiding uneconomic delivery drops
9 Bringing forward buying peaks (for example, seasonal sales)
10 Attracting customers to premises
11 Correcting poor distribution levels
12 Increasing consumer awareness
13 Increasing consumer loyalty
14 Increasing purchase frequency
15 Securing display in-store
16 Obtaining retailer support
17 Disposing of models before a new introduction

18   Drawing attention to a company's product range
19   Boosting sales in particular geographical areas
20   Stimulating a new use for the brand
21   Increasing the appeal of the brand to specific target audiences.

What sales promotions cannot do

Sales promotions cannot change long-term trends in the life of a brand or take the place of advertising or personal selling. Promotions are one element of the marketing mix and it is important to consider whether or not investment in other areas (for example, on improving the product, or changing the packaging) might meet the marketing objectives in a more cost-effective manner. In general, brand strength determines promotional effectiveness. Brands can be broadly classified into one of three types – growing, holding and declining. The effects of promotions on these are as follows:

Growing brands

Promotions enable the brands to make gains and hold them.

Holding brands

Promotions enable the brands to make short-term gains which are not held.

Declining brands

Promotions may slow down the rate of decline but cannot reverse it without a significant and lasting change in the value (product- and image-based) that the brand offers the customer.

Sales promotions act differently

Sales promotions differ widely in their effectiveness at addressing particular marketing problems. Sampling, free offers, and reduced price offers (coupons or offers) are particularly effective at increasing penetration of new or existing brands. Free draws, sweepstakes, contests and phone-ins are ideal tools to increase consumer awareness. Techniques, however, overlap considerably and consequently there will generally be more than one technique available to solve the problem. Selection of a particular technique is generally governed by four criteria:

1   The nature of the problem the promotion is to solve (penetration, repeat purchase, distribution and so forth)
2   Budget available
3   Nature of the brand (product or service)
4   Target group the promotion is seeking to influence.

THE KEY SALES PROMOTION PROPOSITIONS

Save!

People have always loved a bargain. And keen pricing is central to 'push' selling.

The promotional use of bargains, where featured offers of a price saving are made, can be classified under the following headings:

1 A retailer's price cut
2 A manufacturer's price cut
3 Coupons
4 Rebate schemes
5 Self-liquidating offers.

1 A retailer's price cut

The format is usually simple: the retailer cuts the price of a product or service and features the promotional price on store material and perhaps in his advertising.

Many retailers now consistently cut the price of the goods they stock, so that the prices they offer are no longer specially featured bargains of a promotional nature, but an integral, and often *the main*, aspect of their business.

2 A manufacturer's price cut

Again, usually a simple format. The manufacturer cuts the price of his product and features the promotional price on his pack, or on display material, or in advertising.

Most promotions of this kind are straightforward and regular aspects of a brand's existence. Sometimes, however, a price cut can be exploited in spectacular fashion.

For example, the British motorist has become aware that a car costs more to buy in the UK than the identical car bought in most parts of Europe. In March 1982 the Ford Motor Company announced substantial cuts in the UK prices of many of its more expensive models, presenting this as the company's single-handed effort to bring UK prices into line with Europe. Ford's competitors rushed into print to say that the savings were not all that exceptional, but Ford had scored a major victory in putting its proposition into the front of the customer's mind, in a believable way.

3 Coupons

A coupon is a promissory note entitling the consumer to a saving on a product or service.

Some coupons are printed on or inserted in a pack, entitling the consumer to money off his or her next purchase. Manufacturers and retailers print millions of coupons each year to stimulate consumer demand.

Coupons are a popular method of offering savings, and can be more precisely targeted than price cuts. An audience can be selected by placing a coupon in a newspaper with a particular kind of readership, or an area can be selected by delivering coupons door-to-door there. Increasingly, promoters select a retailer and make a coupon redeemable only in his stores. A development of the technique in the United States is that the manufacturer issues a coupon for, say 3 cents off his product, and an individual retailer offers to double the value of the coupon if it is redeemed in his stores.

4 Rebate schemes

The rebate scheme offers either cash or coupon by return if the consumer *mails in* a stated number of proofs of purchase.

An advantage of the rebate technique over coupons is that the promoter receives proof of purchase, whereas ordinary coupons can be wrongly used for other purchases (the two categories of wrong redemption are *malredemption*, where the wrong use is deliberate and *misredemption*, where the wrong use is accidental; because coupons are, effectively, currency, malredemption and misredemption are serious dangers).

Rebate schemes are frequently used to retain the loyalty of customers. Effectively, the loyal customer is receiving a volume discount. The proofs of purchase required can be carefully calculated against the regular user's repeat purchase pattern, and the rate can be speeded up (for example, five packs purchased over the time usually taken to purchase four packs).

A variant of the technique is the *step–sum rebate* where each proof of purchase qualifies for a rebate amount, say, 20p per proof of purchase. This variant can be used to attract the occasional purchaser or the non-purchaser sampling for the first time. And, of course, once a customer starts on the scheme, there is an incentive to go on collecting proofs of purchase in order to qualify for more and more money.

Shareouts or giveaways give a rebate scheme excitement as the rebate received depends upon the number of entries received. Here a sum of money or other divisible prize is shared equally amongst entrants according to the total number of 'shares' (proofs of purchase) received. The number of proofs or purchase that constitute a share are predetermined. So if the shareout fund consists of £10 000 and 10 000 entries are received, each entry is worth £1, with 2 000 entries the sum awarded is £5 and so forth. Usually a mimimum sum, irrespective of the number of entries received, is guaranteed.

Another variant of the technique is the accelerator rebate scheme. Here the proofs of purchase are worth different amounts, say 50p, 30p and 20p according to when they are sent in. This adaptation is designed to bring forward sales.

5 Self-liquidating offers

The first four 'save' techniques relate to savings on the price of the promoted product. The self-liquidating technique involves the offer of a bargain price on another item, which the consumer usually applies for by mail. The price the consumer pays for the offer item covers all the costs of making the offer – hence the term 'self liquidating'. Essentially, the promoter is acting as a direct marketer, buying the item in bulk and cutting out profit margins.

In a class of merchandise where regular retail prices and margins are high, significant success can be achieved with a dramatic bargain offer. But consumers can be suspicious, expecting the offer item to be of inferior quality. Therefore, it is usual to seek items which carry well-known brand names and are of that manufacturer's regular quality, or to offer the item on approval.

Of course, as mass retailing spreads to cover most classes of merchandise, and prices and margins fall, it becomes difficult to find known, branded items, which can be liquidated at a price below retail, especially when the increasing costs of postage have to be offset.

There are two ways round that problem. One is to regard the self-liquidating offer as a nil-cost opportunity to develop the character of a brand. A coffee manufacturer, for example, might offer a coffee mug imprinted with the brand name – an item unique to the product. This is a simple and frequent use of the self-liquidating technique.

A more ambitious way of communicating brand values is shown by the case of the Ovaltineys LP. Ovaltine (Ovomaltine in Europe) is a food beverage; its TV campaign recalls the brand's advertising of the 1930s, when it was known to everyone via a Radio Luxembourg show featuring the 'Ovaltineys of the Air': children who sang songs and made jokes. So, in 1980 an LP record was made of the Ovaltineys singing many of their famous songs. This was offered to Ovaltine's customers at a self-liquidating price. But the LP was also put on sale in leading record stores throughout the country (at a price £1 higher than the bargain price available to Ovaltine purchasers), and copies of the record were given to radio disc jockeys for airplay. Also a short television film of the singing Ovaltineys was made and offered to producers of suitable TV shows for inclusion in their programmes. The overall effect was to create increased awareness of the brand, not only through on-pack promotion but also via free radio and television exposure (the value of this exposure, if it had been purchased at ratecard cost, was around £750 000).

Another creative use of the self-liquidating technique was developed for Marlboro cigarettes: the mail-in element was eliminated. Marlboro retailers were offered cigarette lighters carrying the Marlboro name for resale to their customers at a price of 89p if the customer did not also purchase Marlboro cigarettes, or 69p if he or she did. This simple mechanism produced very big business – Marlboro became the biggest selling brand of cigarette lighter, and the effect on Marlboro cigarette sales was very beneficial too.

Free!

'Free' is a very powerful word. Most people are irresistibly drawn to the prospect of something for nothing.

Of course, for a free offer to be of commercial value, the something will usually be for something. And the power of the promotion will depend on whether the value offered is as good as it appears to be at first sight. It is possible to lose customers by misleading them with the word 'free', and it is also possible to attract the attention of the regulatory authorities.

There are two main types of free offer – the free product and the free item.

1 Free product

Here the promoter gives away some of his product. For example, a *free sample*, distributed door-to-door, or included in a magazine, or handed out in-store, or banded to another product. Or *extra product free*, where, for example, a product usually sold in a 100g size will be sold in, say, a 120g size at the same price. Free product promotions are often an excellent way to get occasional purchasers or trialists to buy your brand. Where the offer is being made on-pack, a devastatingly effective 'sales appearance' is achieved.

2 Free item

Here the promoter gives away an item with his product. It can be fixed on or packed inside the product; or the product can be packed in it – for example, a free storage jar containing coffee.

The free item can be handed out to the customer, and sometimes purchase is not required; the item serves as an advertising device. Such giveaways were legion in the nineteenth century. For example, that great promoter, H. J. Heinz, drew massive crowds to his stand at the World's Columbian Exposition in Chicago in 1893 by advertising a free badge to all asking for it. The badge showed a pickle with the name Heinz enamelled on it. The crowd was so dense that the floor sagged under their weight. And the pickle badge became the trademark of the company.

Or the free item can be available by mail. An attractive free item allows the promoter (where permitted by law) to 'charge' a large number of proofs of purchase.

A remarkable free offer was mounted for Chivers Jelly in the UK in the early 1970s. The marketing objective was to persuade consumers to buy the Chivers brand loyally (and to take the opportunity to try out the various flavours). In return for *eighteen* proofs of purchase mailed in, the consumer was offered a free family of goldfish! Five live goldfish were delivered to the consumer's house (in an aerated water-filled container); there was also a self-liquidating offer of a fish tank if the consumer did not already have one. Considerable planning and management went into the organization of that promotion, which was a huge success.

The free item offer gave rise to two forms which are almost techniques in their own right. The *free picture card*, inserted in or printed on a pack, was originally developed in the cigarette industry. When cigarettes were sold in paper packets, a piece of card was put in to stiffen the pack. In Canada, in 1879, someone had the idea of printing something on the card and this developed into the 'cigarette card'. Cigarette cards were issued in series, and each series had a theme – famous actors, flowers, warships – to encourage collection (and therefore loyal brand purchasing). Though cards disappeared from cigarettes a long time ago, the picture card is still a widely used free in-pack offer.

The other major development of the free item offer is the *trading stamp promotion*. A retailer issues trading stamps in proportion to the amount you spend in his store; you save the stamps and then redeem them against a wide range of gifts published in a catalogue. The same mechanism applies if you substitute a 'voucher' for a stamp: vouchers related to free gifts in a catalogue have been widely used to motivate retailers and salesmen.

Win!

Promoters did not invent the idea of winning a prize. Gambling and prize contests and games of skill have been part of life in most civilizations. In the UK in 1978, for example, gamblers laid out £7 000 000 000 on stakes (though £6 000 000 000 was returned in the form of prize money). Apart from horse-race betting, we trade fortunes in casinos and bingo halls, on dogs and in amusement machines, doing the football pools, and a host of other activities. Games of skill – crosswords, Monopoly, and now video games – provide hours, even weeks, of amusement.

All this would continue if there were no sales promotion. But sales promotion can harness the appeal of winning to marketing, and can do so very effectively.

The most important quality of a prize promotion is, or should be, *excitement*. This is often ignored. One attraction of a prize promotion is that the value of the prizes, and therefore the main cost of the promotion, is usually fixed. This appeals to promoters who want to mount activity which will not overrun budget. With such pedestrian ambition, these promoters run contests as routine and often poorly executed activities. They attract few entrants, and those few contain a proportion of *professional* contest entrants.

Lose excitement and you have lost the basic value of prize promotion. The main types of prize promotion are:

1   *A contest*, in which success depends to a substantial degree upon the exercise of mental or physical skill
2   *A free draw*, in which success depends on your name being drawn at random
3   *A sweepstake*, in which success depends on the chance receipt of a winning leaflet, or other device. Recognition or detection of success must be easy
4   *A game*, where you compete but your success does not depend primarily upon skill
5   *A lottery*, where you purchase (or make a contribution of some kind to get) a ticket which entitles you to entry into a prize draw of some kind.

It must be stressed that the laws relating to prize promotions are individual to different countries and are usually vigorously policed. Expert advice is needed when planning a prize promotion.

Some examples of prize promotions

One of the most effective prize promotions ever run in the UK is *free bingo*, tied to the sale of daily newspapers. The promotion format was pioneered by *The Daily Star*, immediately taken up by *The Sun*, and soon copied or adapted by every popular national daily and Sunday newspaper. Taking advantage of highly sophisticated random printing techniques, the promoters deliver cards with assortments of numbers to every home in the UK; you check your numbers against those published in the newspapers and, when you have matched all the numbers on your card, you can claim a large cash prize. The mechanics of the game are the same as in the traditional game of bingo played in halls and social clubs for generations: the excitement comes from the scale of the exercise and the size of the prizes. The drawback to the promoters is that since *every* popular newspaper is running its own variant of the scheme, the high expense is not being matched by additional circulation. Only a truce, or fresh creative thinking, can free the promoters from a costly battle.

A quite different kind of excitement was achieved by a British Airways contest. Everyone buying a British Airways ticket to any destination became eligible to enter; the prize was a place on a British Airways' Concorde aircraft making a special flight to the 1982 World Cup venue, Madrid. The beauty of this scheme is that it associated the excitement of the World Cup with British Airways' most exciting product – and the prize was unique. The idea justified British Airways in heavily advertising the scheme.

What is sales promotion and what is not? A remarkable kind of prize contest, demanding extraordinary skill, was the core idea of a book, *Masquerade*; the book contained a series of highly cryptic clues, woven into the storyline; if a reader correctly solved the clues he or she would find a jewel, buried somewhere in England. Finally, after phenomenal world sales of the book, someone did find the jewel. It is very rare indeed for a book to have this kind of built-in *real* dimension.

The use of prize promotions is heavily regulated in many European countries; for example, in France, entry to a contest must be open to purchaser and non-purchaser alike. This discipline should make the promoter aim for fresh ideas which create news and interest around his product. One example: a vermouth manufacturer staged an angling contest – an enjoyable day's fishing of the normal kind – but with the added bonus that some of the fish in the river had been specially marked with indelible ink. If you hooked one of the marked fish you won an angling holiday for two in Norway!

Give!

Sales promotion's 'big three' – Save! Free! Win! – have been joined by a fourth – Give!

Promotions linked to charitable causes appeared only rarely until the early 1970s. Now charity promotions form a very large and visible part of promotional activity in the United States and in the UK – less so, as yet, in the rest of Europe.

The basic charity promotion asks the consumer to collect the promoting brand's proofs of purchase, and then hand them in or mail them to the promoter, who will donate to the chosen charity a specified amount per proof of purchase. Frequently the charitable aspect is coupled with a free offer, especially where children may be involved. Badges and wallcharts relating to the charity's sphere of action can be very popular.

Charity promotions offer tremendous PR opportunities at both local and national level and they are difficult for stores to reject. Often they can provide a national link with the brand's advertising theme such as Captain Morgan Rum and the RNLI, the Andrex Guide Dogs. On the downside potential, overtones such as with the Moscow Olympics can cause problems and some charities are over-exploited.

The Olympic Games gave the first serious impetus to charitable collections – to raise funds to train a country's athletes. Rothman's cigarettes were linked to a major appeal for 1972, and many promoters have since followed the Olympic theme. Association with sporting endeavour, and the achievements of the national team, can be a very effective form of publicity.

The H.J. Heinz Co. has chosen a charitable theme for several of its annual, block-busting, multibrand promotions. Heinz twice ran an appeal to raise funds to build a new children's home. In 1980 they pursued the charitable theme into a wholly new area – the public were asked to collect labels, against which Heinz would make a donation, to provide the things needed by schools that had registered with the scheme – sports equipment, for example. Since such material had traditionally been financed out of public funds, the promotion raised some eyebrows. And you did have to collect a lot of labels to get anything worthwhile! The *Sunday Express* commented: 'Three thousand five hundred cans of baked beans for a football? Isn't it a mercy for hundreds of little tummies, not to mention the Clean Air Society, that they hadn't set their sights on a swimming pool?'

In 1980/81, Golden Wonder, makers of crisps, snacks and nuts, linked with the World Wildlife Fund to celebrate that fund's twentieth anniversary. Against the proofs of purchase received, Golden Wonder financed the cost of six specially equipped Landrovers for use by the WWF in protecting the game parks of East Africa; the scheme was coupled with the offer of a free set of badges showing the various endangered animals helped by the WWF. Thirty million proofs of purchase were sent in to Golden Wonder.

SALES PROMOTION MEDIA

Sales promotion is a combination of content – the various techniques – and 'media' – the channels via which the promoter reaches the market. All forms of advertising can be used, and frequently are used, as sales promotion media.

In addition, there are certain media specially associated with sales promotion:

1   The pack
2   Point-of-sale material
3   Field personnel
4   Direct mail
5   The telephone
6   Presentation material
7   Scratch-cards.

1   The pack

The pack in which a product travels is a fine communication medium. Admittedly, it does not have moving pictures, nor does it talk, but it is umbilically bound to the product; it is there at the point of sale at the time of sale; it goes into the home; often a pack offers space, the advantages of colour printing, and the facility of a proof of purchase. And since the pack is required in any case, the extra cost of having it carry a sales promotion message is minimal.

2   Point-of-sale material

A promotion should not exist in limbo: it should be an integral part of the marketing mix, and in many cases the most significant integration will be between the promotion and the *total effect* created at the point of sale.

The pack is an item of point-of-sale material. So too are window bills, show-cards, shelf-strips and many other vehicles for point-of-sale advertising. The trend to mass retailing through supermarkets and superstores has created many disciplines for, and often against, point-of-sale material of the conventional kind. Such material can be messy, and, in fairness, it has to be admitted that much material was produced with no idea of the real situation in-store. So many retailers have banned display material. The resulting drabness has been fashionable for some time, but is likely to give way to revived point-of-sale advertising if that material is designed with awareness and flair.

3   Field personnel

Field personnel – salespeople, demonstrators, and merchandisers – augment the regular sales teams of their clients. They can be used in many ways – to offer samples, or coupons, to show how a product works, to give information and answer questions, or just to ask people if they would like to buy the product. And specially hired personnel are often used to sell goods into the trade, reinforcing the regular sales people.

4   Direct mail

Though direct mail can succeed simply through the use of words, most direct mail solicitations include a promotional offer of some kind.

Heavy direct mail promoters, such as magazine publishers, usually offer a price cut to a new subscriber, or a free gift such as an atlas or set of cutlery.

The key to effective direct mail is the quality of the mailing list. Thorough updating of the names on a list is vital, especially if the message is to be personally addressed. Changes of status must be meticulously monitored. Don't send a message 'Dear Mr. Smith, You as a captain of industry . . .' to a man who has just been made redundant.

A great amount of thought has gone into the writing and designing of direct mail messages, and into the development and use of successful incentives. Because most direct mail asks the recipient to respond in some way, the responses can be counted and carefully analysed: every ingredient can be thoroughly tested. So direct mail can be an exceptionally accurate promotional medium.

5   The telephone

Few people today write letters as a matter of personal choice. Most people use the telephone. And since many promotional techniques require the public to respond in some way, it is natural to choose the means of response that they normally prefer.

Consumers can be asked to telephone to claim a voucher; or to enter a prize promotion; or to hear further details of an offer. Complications are that the cost of a telephone call varies by distance, and a customer may be loath to call long-distance; a list of local telephone numbers can be presented, but some administration is needed to set that up. And it is difficult to obtain proof of purchase via the telephone.

But the telephone offers considerable scope for immediacy, and creativity in promotion.

6 Presentation material

A manufacturer mounting a promotion will want to tell his salesforce and retailers about it. So printed and audio-visual media are used to communicate the message. Generally speaking, these presentations are accorded low priority by marketing departments and are often poorly executed. This is thoroughly bad business practice: improved presentation must be a chief objective for promoters in the 1990s, particularly with the advent of interactive video techniques.

7 Scratch-cards

Over the past decade, scratch-cards have evolved into an important sales promotion medium. They can be used with most sales promotion techniques from instant win and competitions through to chance/skill games and collection schemes. They can generate considerable excitement and participation. Scratch-card promotions, however, have to be carefully thought out and executed. Security is of paramount importance in the staging of scratch-card games particularly in terms of printing as well as field distribution.

SPECIAL TARGETS

Most of this chapter is about consumer promotion. But all the techniques can be used for *industrial promotion*, both to reach new customers (frequently via personal selling, exhibitions, and direct mail), and to maintain business with existing customers. There are many factors specially relevant to industrial promotion which cannot be covered in this chapter. A useful guide to these will be found in Spillard (1975).

Promoting to retailers is an important aspect of manufacturer's marketing, with techniques ranging from special discounts to free gifts to competitions. Such activity is governed by law in many countries, and there can be a fine dividing line between legitimate promotion and bribery.

And, of course, most companies will seek to motivate their own sales teams with incentives ranging from cash bonuses to holiday prizes to free items. If it is true that a salesman loves being sold to, then sales motivation must be particularly effective.

INTERNATIONAL SALES PROMOTION

The opportunity to mount international marketing campaigns will be substantially increased by the development of satellite television. It is, therefore, possible to conceive of a sales promotion campaign operating simultaneously in many countries.

But different countries have different laws. Even the individual states of the US have different laws affecting certain kinds of sales promotion. There has been much talk of a 'harmonization' of the laws of EC countries which affect sales promotion. This task, which would make Europe-wide promotion an attractive possibility, has proved to be difficult, if not impossible, to progress. Harmonization, if it comes at all, is likely to be a long way off in the future.

RESEARCHING AND EVALUATING SALES PROMOTION

Most kinds of sales promotion activity can be easily evaluated; sales performance can be measured, and redemptions and applications can be counted, and compared with track record.

Promotions are rarely researched in advance, largely because the activity is likely to be of short duration, with few strategic implications. There is an important trend, however, towards *strategic sales promotion*, where one technique, or one 'strategy platform' is intended to apply for many years. In this case, researching the technique or platform is as valuable and essential as researching a long-term advertising strategy.

SUMMING UP

A short chapter in a wide-ranging book can touch on only the most important aspects of sales promotion. More comprehensive information is available in the books listed below. And the reader must look carefully at the nature and practice of sales promotion in his or her own market, because the differences are not only interesting, but of crucial practical importance – differences of law, for example.

Moreover, sales promotion is dynamic, and what applies today can have changed dramatically in many respects within a few years. This very dynamism makes sales promotion a key marketing tool. It is especially relevant to 'push' selling market conditions, but in tough or prosperous economies modern sales promotion has a major role to play.

FURTHER READING

Petersen, C., *Sales Promotion in Action*, Associated Business Press, London, 1979

Piper, J., (ed.), *Managing Sales Promotion*, Gower, Aldershot, 1980

Spillard, P., *Sales Promotion – Its Place in Marketing Strategy*, 2nd edn, Business Books, London, 1975

Toop, A., *Choosing the Right Sales Promotion*, The Sales Machine, London, revised (paperback), 1978

Toop, A., *'Only £3.95?!' – The Creative Element in Sales Promotion*, The Sales Machine, London, 1978

Williams, J., *The Manual of Sales Promotion*, Innovation Limited, London, 1983

23 Pricing

Bryan Atkin

Setting and maintaining the right prices for its products is perhaps the most delicate and important of all the problems facing a company. It is, however, a reality of business life that there is probably no area of business activity in which practice differs so widely from theory as the area of pricing. The simple – and well attested – truth is that in a great many firms, prices are set in a way which is disorganized, inconsistent and often illogical. The reasons for this are not hard to find. Pricing decisions, even under the best of conditions, are difficult to make and frequently have to be taken against what can often seem overwhelming odds.

The purpose of this chapter is to provide a framework within which the reader can evaluate the opportunities for greater profitability available to his own firm through the development of a more rational pricing policy and implement practical procedures leading to the shaping, introduction and control of this policy.

ECONOMIC THEORY AND THE PRACTICAL BUSINESSMAN

There is a substantial body of economic theory dealing with price and pricing. The practical businessman can, however, expect little direct help from the academic in applying economic theory to the solution of everyday pricing problems. Certainly, theories of price are effective in describing *in general* the way markets behave: demand and to some extent supply volumes do respond to price approximately as predicted by theory and markets do vary in the degree of responsiveness to price changes as provided for by the concept of price elasticity. Technically, price elasticity is measured by dividing the percentage increase or decrease in the volume of demand (or sales) resulting from a change in price by the percentage change in price. 'Elastic' markets are those where the change in demand is more than a proportionate price change. Conversely, 'inelastic' markets are those in which a change in price is greater, proportionately, than the effective change in demand.

The problem is that the theory breaks down when applied in particular cases largely because the assumptions on which theoretical calculations are based turn out to be inappropriate in real life. For one thing firms rarely possess the empirical data required to construct actual demand or revenue curves for their products and are often unable to distinguish costs sufficiently clearly to construct cost curves. Second, the goals which businessmen set themselves and the constraints which surround their achievement are usually far different – and less rational – than the idealized principles and responses of the theoretical firm. Third, markets

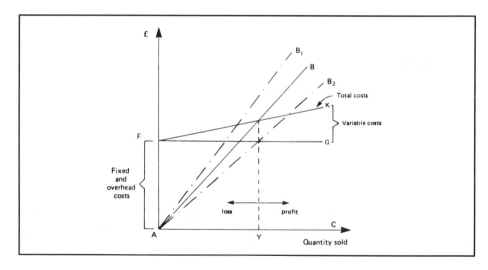

Figure 23.1   Simple breakeven chart

do not in practice display the assumed characteristics of perfect competition and rational purchasing behaviour on which theory is based.

Nevertheless, since it has long enjoyed a certain popularity, an adaptation of economic theory worth mentioning at this point is the concept of 'breakeven'. The concept, in its simplest form, purports to show the minimum quantity of its product (s) a firm has to sell simply to cover its costs. Figure 23.1 shows the classic breakeven chart in its most widely reproduced form.

In the chart, the line AB represents gross revenue from unit sales at a specified price, and the line FK denotes the total costs of making those units. These total costs are made up of fixed costs (incurred whether or not the product is made and sold at all) and variable costs (which vary according to the number of units produced). The intersection of lines AB and FK represents breakeven – the point at which gross sales income is exactly equal to the costs involved in producing those units (Y) for sales. At the price set, the firm makes increasing losses with every unit as sales fall short of Y and an increasing profit with every unit in excess of Y. The chart can be developed to show alternative breakeven points at assumed different selling prices (represented by lines AB_1 and AB_2 in Figure 23.1).

The attractiveness of the 'breakeven' idea – which in principle can be applied both to individual products and to the firm as a whole – is obvious in the context of a chart on the managing director's wall dramatizing what the firm has to do to stay in business once selling price has been determined, by indicating the volume of sales to be achieved to reach breakeven. However, the concept is of little help in actually setting prices because of the crude and unrealistic assumptions which the theory assumes about the level of, and relationship between, price, demand and costs. Thus:

1   The sales income line (AB) takes no account of the price elasticity of demand. The breakeven quantity (Y) is a 'formula' calculation – not a forecast of the actual sales, which would still need to be made to determine the profits likely to

be generated at a particular price (or indeed whether breakeven were achievable at all at that price)

2   The assumptions that variable costs increase proportionately with unit output (as represented in line FK) and that fixed costs remain the same irrespective of the level of output are poor representations of business reality.

One of the problems in applying the concept of elasticity is that the theory assumes a constant relationship between demand volume and price, when in fact research has shown that consumers (and industrial buyers) respond differently to the *size* of price changes – particularly when these are measured in a competitive (one brand versus another) rather than a global (total market change) context. Depending on the circumstances, therefore, a market can be both elastic and inelastic in terms of response to the pricing activities of the individual firm – a paradoxical situation requiring sound judgement and market knowledge.

At best the 'breakdown' concept – which is closely associated with cost-based pricing formulae described later – is mostly of value as a simple rule-of-thumb method for evaluating pricing options in the context of other market-oriented information on (potential) demand and competition.

PRICING POLICY, STRATEGY AND TACTICS

Before looking in more detail at pricing decisions and the way they are arrived at, it is useful to draw a distinction between three terms often used rather interchangeably by businessmen – in so far as they are used at all! These terms are *pricing policy, pricing strategy* and *pricing tactics*.

Pricing policy refers to the framework of rules and constraints within which pricing decisions are taken. The nature and scope of this framework can vary widely from one firm to another, even within the same industry or between firms with apparently similar pricing problems. At one extreme pricing policy can be little more than a rationalization of rule-of-thumb judgements or historical practice. At the other end of the scale can be policies devised and spelled out in considerable detail.

Simply having a pricing policy, however formal, does not imply that it is either logical or sensible in the broader arena of the market place. Nor does the existence of a policy guarantee that it will be observed in practice – policies are often more honoured in the breach than the observance. Indeed, it is entirely feasible for a firm to trade without a pricing policy at all or for decisions to be justified by reference to a policy which is to all intents and purposes a *post hoc* rationalization. This is often the case with small companies where price, like many other decisions, is in the hands of one forceful personality – a situation in which whim, prejudice and ignorance can easily play a powerful role.

Whereas *pricing policy* is the outcome of a largely internalized objective of a financial or other corporate nature, or statements of pricing principles, *pricing strategy* reflects the (longer term) market-oriented (or externalized) objectives of a firm. In effect *pricing strategy* involves the systematic manipulation or planning of pricing decisions and policies over a period of time in the context of achieving the broader objectives contained in corporate and marketing plans. It implies recognition of the role of price as an active, and important, component of the overall marketing 'mix' rather than a largely intractable obstacle which marketing has to overcome in order to compete successfully. In so far as pricing policies and strategies are the expression of needs and objectives over different time periods and on different planes it is not unusual for firms to have a pricing *policy* but no pricing *strategy*.

Whereas pricing strategy is concerned with projections over the long term, without regard to short-term fluctuations in market conditions, *pricing tactics* are concerned with the manipulation of prices themselves, and the way in which prices are presented to achieve optimum response from a targeted customer group against competition. Pricing tactics take as much from interpreting the psychology of the buyer as from more rational 'economic' judgements. Tactics are, by their nature, often short term. They may be changed several times during the life of the strategy of which they form a part. Such changes are the practical means of responding on a more day-to-day basis to changing market conditions. There are a great many variations of pricing tactics, some of which are described later in this chapter, and in practice they are often mistakenly elevated to the level of pricing strategy.

Oxenfeldt (1960) sees the pricing process involving a series of decisions taken over a period of time, rather than a single all-embracing solution. The six steps he proposes are:

1 Identification of target markets
2 Choosing an appropriate image
3 Constructing the marketing mix
4 Selecting a pricing policy
5 Determining price strategy (and tactics)
6 Definition of a specific price.

This multi-stage approach has a particular relevance to new product development but can be recycled wholly or in part as a means of reappraising existing products. The approach is particularly interesting in the emphasis it gives to broader issues of market segmentation and planning the marketing mix as the essential framework for pricing decisions.

PRICING POLICIES AND TECHNIQUES

In Wilson (1972), pricing is described as 'an exercise which must be undertaken on two dimensions. First it is necessary to think in terms of establishing the right price and second of using the correct methodology for arriving at it.' In a way this observation neatly encapsulates the practical dilemma facing most firms. At one level the pricing process takes place within a framework which is the product of many influences, inside and outside the firm. At the second level, pricing should involve a sensible and coherent procedure for determining the final selling price. That this procedure or methodology needs to be conceived and operated within a broader framework of attitudes and subjective judgements which may not always be logical (and may even be in conflict) is simply a fact of commercial life.

However, pricing policies and strategies do not necessarily define, or even imply, a particular methodology for arriving at the selling price itself. In many cases this is set as much by guesswork, trial and error, historical analogy and simple entrepreneurial judgement as it is by some more formal procedure.

There is no single 'correct' methodology or golden rule for arriving at the right price. For example, the pricing decision process and the degree of flexibility available are heavily conditioned by whether prices are *declared* or *negotiated* (the pricing system). At one extreme the executive responsible for setting catalogue or list prices is in theory at least creating a structure of 'ruling' prices for his products which will remain in force for all or a substantial proportion of sales until a change is notified; at the other extreme the executive involved in contract or tender pricing is faced with a new pricing decision with each new order or customer. The apparent coherence and stability of published prices have to be seen, however, in the context of the discounts, concessions, rebates, differentials and other devices employed by firms to manipulate the prices actually paid by customers. For many firms, list prices can be said to exist mainly as a basis for discounting with the bulk of turnover being generated from sales at discounted and negotiated prices (see Atkin, 1975). An apparently logical framework of declared prices can, therefore, be rendered meaningless and misleading by the reality of a haphazard system of informal discounts and/or individual negotiations with strong customers (see Discounts and discounting later in the chapter).

The 'right' price is not necessarily what theorists would call the 'best selling price' in the sense that it maximizes profit for a given product considered by itself. In any meaningful sense what is 'right' can only be assessed in the context of what the firm identifies as its general strategic or operational goals.

The following paragraphs look in more detail at five categories of factor which both shape pricing policy and contribute to the process of actual price setting. To the extent that one of these categories may carry the greatest weight it is possible to talk about pricing which is profit, cost, competition, demand (customer) or distribution system-oriented.

Profit targets and other corporate objectives

Perhaps the most widely quoted of all business aphorisms is that it is the objective of every firm to maximize its profits. The most cursory examination of this proposition in practice, however, shows it to be one which should not be taken too literally. Firms rarely set out even with the *theoretical* objective of maximizing profits (or return on capital employed) and often introduce criteria into pricing strategies and policies the deliberate effect of which is to contain profits at a level below that which otherwise might be achievable.

Profit is therefore a less meaningful criterion for judging performance in the longer term than other financial objectives, such as return on capital employed or return on investment. These financial objectives can consequently be expressed both as long term and immediate.

Longer-term financial objectives tend to be set in the context of achieving a targeted average level of return on investment or profit for the whole of the company which is considered to be 'reasonable' taken over a period of years (and across all products). Judgement of what is reasonable is in this context largely a pragmatic affair, owing more to general perceptions within society of what might be considered as 'fair trading profit' or to historical experience or analogy, than to the projection of a mechanistic formula. In the short term, different targets may be set either for return on capital for profit or for margins or contributions (difference between selling price and *direct* costs usually expressed as a percentage) which reflect prevailing economic and market conditions in individual years or even short planning periods.

However, financial objectives are not the only determinants of corporate policy and are, therefore, by no means the only factor underlying pricing decisions. Other goals or considerations affecting pricing include:

- (Market) growth aspirations
- Market share
- Corporate stability/expansion
- Corporate image
- Customer/public opinion
- Research and development
- Costs and efficiency
- The competitive arena
- Filling production capacity.

The role of costs in pricing

It has often been claimed that the pricing of industrial products is based on costs and very little else – a process which Wilson has derided as 'faith, hope and fifty per cent'. Research into pricing behaviour has tended to support this view of the pricing process: when asked directly about the pricing of their products firms will indeed claim that they arrive at their prices largely by the application of some formula related to costs.

How rigidly companies stand by such formulae or, indeed, whether they actually have a formula at all, is very much open to doubt. Gabor claims that 'pricing is not in fact carried out by the alleged mechanistic application of cost-based formulae' and goes on to quote Edwards: 'the manufacturer has a "hunch" as to the price at which his article can be sold and makes use of "costing" or "estimating" to justify that price.' Nevertheless, if prices are rarely based exclusively on cost, it is equally rare for costs not in some way to form the starting point either for calculating prices or for evaluating the profit consequences of various prices indicated or set by reference to other factors.

In order to use costs at all in pricing it is obviously necessary for the firm to have a clear idea of what its costs are and how these should be allocated to individual products. This is all very well for the firm producing only one product, since all costs are, by definition, attributable to that product. Where more than one product is concerned, as it is for most firms, cost allocation can be exceedingly complex and the solutions at best arbitary. The costs of producing and selling a range of products can be classified broadly into three main components:

1 *Variable (including direct) costs* Costs which vary in relation to output; for example, materials and components, labour, advertising
2 *Fixed costs* Costs which do not vary in relation to output except in the longer term, for example, buildings, machines, vehicles
3 *Overhead costs* Costs attributable to management.

The problem of allocating management overheads will be obvious, but what of fixed and variable costs? The cost accountant might be able to devise an acceptable formula for allocating costs between different products if each product was always produced in the same proportions, but the formula becomes increasingly unworkable and arbitrary where these are constantly changing. Basing a formula on historical experience is equally undesirable as it makes pricing for the future dependent on past and possibly greatly outdated sales levels. The scale of difficulty increases still further where several products are produced by the same process (as in oil refining or dairy processes), or where a marketable product is a by-product of the production process for another good.

The problems outlined above become highly relevant when costs are used as a means of calculating price. There are two main concepts or procedures for cost-based pricing – *absorption* or *full cost pricing*, and *variable or incremental cost pricing*.

Absorption cost pricing, to put it simply, involves the principle of adding a pre-determined mark-up to total unit costs. By this procedure, sometimes known as 'cost-plus', each product produced by the firm is made in theory, to cover all of its costs and make a known profit on each unit of sale or order.

Variable cost pricing is based on the principle of relating prices not to total costs but to variable costs only, with the mark-up on costs (or the price less variable costs if the price is set by a procedure independent of costs) making a *contribution* to fixed costs and to profit, the scale of which depends on sales objectives being achieved.

Absorption cost pricing is a method which has had particular appeal to the firm with a substantial proportion of its total costs in the form of fixed costs and overheads, since it places all products, in theory, on a sound profit footing and eliminates cross-subsidization and below-cost trading. It is particularly useful in tender or contract pricing as a reference basis for pricing where there are no other useful indicators and in setting some practical limits to prices of new products with no relevant competitors. However, absorption costing has a number of major drawbacks as the basis for pricing. The arguments can be summarized as follows:

1 It is not always easy to isolate the total costs attributable to a particular product where there are several product lines and ranges
2 There is, anyway, no compelling reason why any particular segment of the business, individual product, or specific order *should* be made to bear its proportionate or 'fair' share of overheads even where these can be calculated
3 Absorption costing takes no account of demand. The fact that a price can be computed by this method does not guarantee that consumers will buy the item at that price or at the predicted volumes
4 Absorption costing takes no account of competition. No firm can guarantee that its competitors will play by the same rules either by adopting the same method of costing or by allocating its overhead and fixed costs to particular products on the same basis.

The proponents of incremental cost pricing tend to use arguments which are the obverse of their criticisms of absorption cost pricing emphasizing the flexibility of the method as a means of responding to changing demand and competitive conditions. Using a direct or an incremental cost approach enables the firm to operate at different prices in different markets while maintaining overall control over the aggregated contribution derived from sales. This provides a means of assigning supply priorities in the event of demand outstripping capacity. Similarly the method enables the firm to consider and respond to individual orders in a way appropriate to specific circumstances.

Despite its apparent pragmatism, variable or incremental costing is not without its dangers. In the first place, it has been said with some truth that all costs become variable if the firm is to survive – that is, in the end, the firm depends on making sufficient revenue from its sales to cover all costs incurred whether variable, fixed or overhead. Incremental cost pricing cannot therefore be pursued unchecked. It must be conducted within some framework of required contribution based on profit targets for return on capital invested.

Second, firms using incremental cost pricing to justify accepting an order at reduced contribution may find they have made a rod for their own backs in subsequent dealings with the same customer.

Third, there is always a risk of provoking price retaliation from competitors, resulting in reduced margins all round and a steep hill to climb back to acceptable profitability in a market environment which can become accustomed with remarkable rapidity to low prices.

Finally, it must be appreciated that it is not always easy to determine clearly either the variable costs attributable to a particular product or the incremental costs associated with a particular batch or order. Some so-called variable costs are not, in fact, more than marginally variable, at least in the shorter term.

Pricing is not only difficult in practice to base entirely on costs but it renders the firm vulnerable in other respects. In a strictly competitive sense it hardly matters a jot how reasonable a profit mark-up or contribution target a firm sets in relation to its own costs if these costs are higher than those of competitors. Indeed, the costs which ultimately matter are those of the lowest-cost producer. Of course, most markets support producers who vary in efficiency, but the greater the disparity in efficiency, the greater is the pressure exerted on the least efficient.

More broadly, cost-based pricing formulae often provide little encouragement to company management to consider improving margins by reducing costs as distinct from raising prices. Firms rarely explore as rigorously as they might the various ways in which costs might be cut, from better materials purchasing to tighter control of office costs. This is not, however, the only way costs can be cut and here we return again to the need to be alive to *market* needs and conditions. Research has consistently shown over the years that products and services can quite simply be 'over-engineered' – that is contain features to which the user attaches little economic significance or which are designed to a quality standard which exceeds customer needs. By eliminating these features from the product the firm may well be able to make considerable savings in costs without reducing prices to anything like the same extent.

Competition and pricing

There are few products or services indeed for which there is no effective competition. Even when a firm has no direct competitors – as in the case of an innovative product – it usually has to take into account products capable of acting as alternatives or substitutes in some way, or the prospect of competition developing.

Long-term monopolies are therefore rare outside the realms of state enterprises but it is possible for short-term monopolies to develop on the basis of new products, particularly where high technology is involved. The short-term monopolist needs to consider pricing in the context of the breathing space he has to establish himself in the market place before competition develops, rather than in terms of the apparent freedom of action of the true monopolist.

Price acts as an element in competition, therefore, at up to three levels: it can help determine whether or not a product is bought at all (or whether the decision to purchase is taken now or at a later date); it can help determine in which of a number of alternative ways a particular need is satisfied; and it can help determine which supplier's product is selected.

It is not surprising then that in most cases prices are set and maintained with some reference to the general level and range of competitive prices. In a more specific sense, however, pricing against competition can become in itself a technique of pricing. This can work in one of two main ways:

1 By establishing the prices being charged by all (or a selected cross-section) of the competitive suppliers active in the market and positioning one's own price to occupy a certain position in the range. This may reflect either 'safety' pricing (pricing in the middle of the range) or 'aggressive' pricing (pricing at either extreme)
2 By gearing prices to those charged by a specific competitor on the basis of achieving parity with them or of achieving a designated discount or premium. This approach is often used where one company has achieved a position of such pre-eminence in the market-place that both sellers and customers accept its prices as a reference level.

In so far as competitors' prices are declared or easily established, competition-oriented pricing is relatively straightforward and has the advantage of placing prices within the known parameters of the market place. The price structure of markets is not, however, always easy to establish. Published price lists often give a highly misleading guide to actual price levels which may be arrived at largely by discounting or special negotiation.

The extent to which firms are willing and able to take a competitively independent line in setting and maintaining prices is partly a reflection of factors such as market share, established reputation, financial strength, distinctiveness of product and relative costs of production, and partly a reflection of competitive psychology. Many writers on pricing have drawn attention to the fact that price competition often tends to be of a muted and controlled nature in which a few (perhaps only one or two) dominant suppliers (price leaders) both set the price levels and pricing systems around which competition is fought, and determine the timing and scale of price changes.

In theory, price leaders 'undertake' to behave in a responsible manner with respect to price setting and act as 'policemen' for any firm threatening to take a more aggressive and independent pricing line. However, in practice the status quo is protected more by mutual compliance than any genuinely effective sanction which the price leaders can bring to bear. As Japanese companies have demonstrated repeatedly in European markets, complacent and conservative competitive environments – which in turn lead to reduced interest in increasing efficiency and cost-savings – are highly vulnerable to a bold and determined aggressor.

The attitudes and motivations of the buyer

Price is rarely, if ever, the only factor entering into the purchasing decision and is sometimes only secondary. The success of pricing decisions is therefore highly dependent on the ability of the firm to comprehend and respond to the purchasing environment into which its products are sold. Many ineffective, even disastrous, pricing policies can be traced back to misconceptions about the attitude of buyers to price and the role of price in the purchase decision.

Distinguishing fact from fiction in the market-place is therefore the first task of the would-be rational pricing executive. Consider some of the market-related factors bearing on the role of price in the purchase decision. The most important of these is the concept of 'product differentiation'. This relates to the differences in functions, performance, design and other product-related or physical attributes which a manufacturer can introduce to distinguish his products from those of his competitors. The greater the differentiation, it is argued, the more invidious direct price comparisons by the buyer become, thus giving the firm greater flexibility in turn to gear its prices to the value it believes, or can persuade buyers to believe, attaches to the features or benefits it is offering. The principle of segmentation – designing and pricing products to cater to a particular target group of customers within the market as a whole – derives from the concept of differentiation.

Economists usually assume, in theorizing on purchasing behaviour, that the buyer, being rational and efficient, will tend to purchase at the lowest price prevailing in the market-place, for the product which best fits his needs and requirements. Research into the buying decision has consistently shown this simply not to be true when considered in any detail. In the first place, economic factors are not the only criteria employed in the purchase decision. Even in the case of non-differentiated products, many other factors can intrude to justify purchases at other than the lowest price available. Second, economic considerations can go far beyond the 'price' of the product. Third, industrial buyers are perfectly capable of being irrationally influenced by factors such as a persuasive salesman; clever advertising; cosmetic product features such as colour; fashion trends within the industry and simple prejudice. And finally buyers rarely have perfect knowledge of the markets for all the products they have to buy.

It has rightly been said that the price the final buyer is prepared to pay for a product is, in the end, the best guide to optimum pricing. Because it is the best guide, however, it is inevitably the most difficult concept to employ as a practical technique in pricing. The attraction of cost-based pricing formulae and using competitors' prices as a yardstick for price setting can be attributed at least in part to the fact that they are simple to understand and employ information which, in theory at least, is readily to hand or easily generated. By contrast it is often exceedingly difficult to establish in a direct way how much customers for a product are prepared to pay for it, or put another way, how many customers would be won at different alternative prices, given the variety of factors which affect the purchase decision of individual buyers. Nevertheless, it is within the capacity and resources of most firms to develop sufficient information from their own knowledge and experience of trading in particular market-places or by talking to some potential customers, or by some experimentation or by extrapolating the results of market research surveys. Then they can make broad assumptions about the size and structure of demand for a product and responsiveness to price in a competitive context which can be used to narrow the limits within which price should be set and define the strategy and tactics which best fit market conditions.

Distribution structure

Where a product is sold direct from manufacturer to end user, as many industrial products are, the pricing executive has only to consider pricing at a single level. The situation becomes more complex when distributive intermediaries – agents, wholesalers and retailers – are involved, as he then has to consider not just the price at which the product is sold to his immediate customer, say a wholesaler, but also the price at which it ultimately sells to the final consumer after it has passed through one, two or even three sets of hands, each of which have added their own mark-up. Wholesalers and retailers tend to price by adding a designated percentage mark-up to the price they buy-in the product in order to cover overhead and sales costs and yield a profit. It is, however, relatively unusual for a single fixed percentage to be applied to all products. Rather the percentage mark-up is manipulated between products according to circumstances or design around some overall average (which may itself reflect long-standing practice or folklore in a particular industry rather than any independent judgement on the part of the distributor).

Since the ending of resale price maintenance the manufacturer is unable to dictate the ultimate selling price of his products (and therefore in effect distributors' margins). Distributors may therefore manipulate margins in a way which favours or disfavours the products of the individual manufacturer and thereby impacts on ultimate sales. Pricing to the *distributor* but with an eye to reselling prices is therefore a special component of the art of pricing.

It should also be recognized that the effect of passing on, say, a reduction (or an increase) in the cost of materials or components is heavily affected by the length of the distribution chain. Not only might the change be much smaller proportionately in respect of the final selling price than it is to the ex-factory price but distributors can choose to pass on the change across a spectrum of options ranging from no price adjustment at all to one in excess of that made by the manufacturer.

AIDS TO PRICING

Models and computer simulations

In the main, however practical or logical the basic technique adopted, pricing decisions tend to involve a great deal of individual judgement by the pricing executive. Because the individual has to apply precise weightings to the many influences bearing in practice or in theory on this decision, the final outcome is at best an approximation of the best selling price and is as good, or as bad, as the quality of judgement applied to it. Various attempts have been made to construct 'models' of a more formal nature designed to help the firm fix the optimum price of its products under actual competitive conditions. These models differ widely in their nature, purpose and origin, but most frequently relate to the pricing of goods for retail sale (particularly fast-moving goods such as baked beans and washing powder) and pricing in a competitive bid or tender situation.

All models work by simulating, in terms of mathematical relationships, the interaction of the variables – company-, competition- and demand-related – which govern the pricing decision. They share, therefore, inevitable problems in defining and assigning a value to each variable. Their success depends on the quality of research or of the market knowledge or insight the firm is able to feed into the model, and on the manipulation of the variables which normally requires access to a computer. In the past the cost and complexity of model building tended to make it the preserve of the largest firms only. However, with the development of modestly priced personal computing systems and off-the-shelf software the ability to perform at least some price modelling is now within the compass of even the smallest firm.

Market research

Whether or not a pricing model is being developed, firms still require information on customers and competitors to help them reach sensible pricing decisions. This information is rarely readily available 'off the shelf' and some level of active information gathering is therefore predicated. The most widely employed source of intelligence is the salesman. The reasons for collecting information via the salesman are, naturally, seductive; the salesman is already employed by the firm 'on the road' and he is in constant contact with customers. In theory, he ought to be particularly alive both to competitors' prices and to the price sensitivity and purchasing considerations of the buyer. In practice, however, salesmen are a highly unreliable source of pricing intelligence and tactical judgement. Research into the pricing of industrial products has suggested that it is not unusual for salesmen to convince themselves that they have lost orders on the basis of price when in fact other factors were of greater or equal importance in the purchase decision, and it seems likely that many buyers use price as an excuse for not placing an order with a particular firm rather than give the real, possibly more contentious, reason.

While it is not suggested that firms should give up monitoring price through feedback from salesmen, it would seem prudent that where key pricing decisions are concerned, such as pricing a new product or a change in pricing strategy, information should be generated where required by means of more systematic market research conducted by a reputable and competent consultancy with experience in asking and interpreting questions about price and setting these in the context of other data on market structure and the purchasing process. Market research can make a valuable contribution to the analysis of pricing situations and the selection of appropriate strategies and tactics. For example, by providing detailed feedback on actual price levels and discounting procedures operating in the market, by monitoring terms and conditions associated with pricing, and by planning price in a meaningful perspective in relation to other influences on the purchase decision. Market research by individual specialist agencies is not usually a tool for setting actual selling prices, mainly due to the difficulty of measuring likely response to hypothetical price levels. Nevertheless, research-based techniques have been developed for constructing pricing models.

DEVISING PRICING STRATEGY AND TACTICS

Entry strategies

The concept of pricing strategy as an element in the achievement of specific marketing goals was mentioned earlier. This involves the co-ordination of pricing decisions in the context of their longer-term impact and implications rather than their short-term or tactical benefits, and requires the firm to take an extended view of such factors as probable product life; volume and price sensitivity of potential demand; opportunities for segmentation of demand by price; pace of likely consumer acceptance taking into account competitive, alternative and substitute products; build-up of production capacity and the opportunity for scale economies in unit costs; and timescale for recovery of R and D costs.

It is frequently stated that at the stage of market entry the firm has a choice between two basic strategy options known as *skimming* and *penetration*.

Skimming strategies involve the deliberate setting of an initial price which is high in relation to anticipated long-term price levels towards which the price will be progressively lowered as competition and demand conditions change. The benefits of this strategy derive from the high gross margins achieved at the outset against which R and D and other 'sunk' costs, and often heavy initial promotional costs, can be set, and from the flexibility afforded for using subsequent price changes as a means of controlling market expansion (since, setting aside inflation, the direction of price changes will be downward) and meeting emerging competition by aggressive pricing. Skimming enables the firm to cream off that component of demand prepared to buy the product at its highest price before attacking the broader potential market which may exist for the product at a lower price.

Penetration strategies are intended to generate the highest possible volume of sales from the outset by keen (low margin) pricing. In practice they can be divided into two categories – demand-oriented and competition-oriented strategies. Demand-oriented penetration strategies are based in the main on a combination of an expected high level of price sensitivity among potential buyers and a need for high volume of demand to justify plant investment or achieve projected economies of scale in production (that is, some products have to be produced in volume or not at all). Competitively they have the advantage of potentially creating a strong market position or an image as market leaders before competition emerges (although this will depend on the speed and strength of the competitive response).

One specific variant of demand-oriented penetration strategies is worth mentioning – this might be called the 'razor and razor blades' strategy. Basically, it involves pricing a unit of hardware (for example, razor, labelling gun, copier, abrading machine) at a level which achieves the maximum market penetration or placement so that profits can be achieved on repeated sales of related consumables. If the consumable can be made unique in some way to the hardware, at least initially, a curious combination strategy of penetration for the hardware and what amounts to skimming on the consumable presents itself.

Demand-oriented penetration strategies usually assume a slight underlying downward tend in prices under the impetus of further economies of scale and competitive pressure. This assumption is not necessarily true of competition-oriented penetration strategies. Penetration pricing in the broadest sense can be regarded as a means of deterring potential competitors by pressuring the margins which can be achieved to offset the costs of entry implicit in product development, investment in production facilities and marketing/promotional efforts. To this extent bold penetration pricing might be employed to pre-empt the (immediate) risk of competition. Even so, the strategy may still call for prices to be kept, in relative terms, around the launch level or even drifting lower to keep up the deterrent.

Two situations exist, however, where the strategy may be one of low entry price and an underlying plan for either a sharp or gradual increase in price. First, where a new product is being launched in a market where the competition comprises substitute or alternative products, price has been used as a means of persuading potential users to try the product. The second example concerns the use of a low entry price as a means of displacing or forcing out entrenched competition from an established market-place or of gaining a substantial market share on the basis of which prices can subsequently be increased to a more profitable level.

The temptation to use price as an entry wedge becomes increasingly great the more difficult it is for the firm entering a well-established existing market to differentiate its product sufficiently clearly from those already available to ensure achievement of a satisfactory foothold on other competitive grounds. It can, however, be a high-risk strategy if competitors have the resources to fight a rear-guard battle or even to step up the price war, or if customers do not respond to the entry price as expected.

In general terms, the more innovative the product the more the firm is likely to incline towards a skimming rather than a penetration strategy, particularly if R and D costs have been high and production capacity is limited, at least in the short term.

Reviewing strategy after entry

Although pricing strategies are conceived as operating over a period of time, ignoring short-term fluctuations or pressures which may demand a tactical response, this does not mean that the strategy does not need to be kept under regular review. Nor that it is not necessary for strategies to be changed if conditions in the market place become sufficiently different from those that prompted the original plan.

The firm which has adopted a skimming strategy is faced with the need to decide when to implement the price cuts envisaged by the strategy and how large these should be on each occasion.

The firm which has implemented a penetration strategy has less room to manoeuvre in terms of price adjustments in the face of developing competition.

The major problem facing pricing executives is maintaining a long-term view of price developments when competitive pressures appear to be forcing the firm into a growing number of reactive or short-term tactical decisions most probably associated with price cuts.

It is probable that for many products, pricing decisions shade from the strategic to the tactical in the longer term whichever entry strategy is adopted as competition develops, as product differentiation becomes increasingly difficult to sustain and as sales approach saturation. Even so, it would pay the firm to be alive to the opportunities which exist for using a deliberate change in strategy to revitalize its position in the market-place or improve profits. The strategic options are legion, but they include:

1   Switching from a skimming strategy to a penetration strategy to exploit mass market potential of a product initially pioneered at a high price – perhaps by introducing a simplified and cheaper version rather than by cutting the price of the original product
2   Introduction of replacement or second generation products which can be differentiated sufficiently to command a premium price (return to skimming strategy)
3   'Re-packaging' of products in a way which takes them out of the competitive arena. A good example is the development of 'electronic office' concepts linking more conventional pieces of equipment in a unique total way (return to skimming strategy)
4   Concentration of attention on more profitable market segments even at the cost of volume – diversion of released production resources into other products
5   Improve margins by concentration on cost savings through more efficient production rather than by increasing prices (although the ability of the firm to use this strategy is limited by the long-term tendency of all production methods to ape the most efficient).

Tactical considerations

In theory, strategy precedes tactics in the pricing process, the latter providing the short-term dimension which governs the actual prices charged and the way these are expressed to the customer. In practice it is not always easy to separate the two. Tactics can be considered at two levels. First, there are tactical decisions which relate to gearing actual price levels, and the form they take, to what might be termed the 'psychology' of the customer and the nature of the purchasing process. Such tactical considerations, in so far as they hold true over a period of time, in effect form part of strategy.

The semantics of such pricing tactics tend to be those of the consumer market and retail pricing. However, many have a more universal relevance whatever the product or service being sold. Probably the most widespread tactical device is discounting and this is considered in more detail below. However, mention might also be made of such tactics (based on Wilson, 1972) as:

1   *Offset* Low basic price, 'lost' margin recouped on extras, replacement parts or consumables

2 *Diversionary* Low basic price on some products (in range or line) developing overall image of low cost
3 *Discrete* Tailoring of price to bring product within the purchasing competence of a given seniority of buyer (relevant where the location of purchase decision is determined by corporate price ceilings)
4 *Price lining* Price kept constant but quality of product or extent of service adjusted to reflect changes in costs
5 *Financing* Alternative options to purchase such as leasing and rental (can be used as a specific means of extracting greater profit by changing the bases on which 'price' is assessed by the customer); might be coupled with special credit terms, trade-in allowances and special offers.

Although the above tactics are basically concerned with price, these need to be considered alongside what might be termed non-price differentials – ways of competing which command customer loyalty outside the framework of direct price competition, such as delivery services, after-sales support, technical back-up and advice and advertising and promotion effort.

In addition to these 'tactics of strategy' there are tactical questions of a more practical day-to-day level: What is the best way to pass on a price increase forced by rises in costs? Should ways be sought of keeping prices stable by modifying the product? Is it better to make price changes at regular and infrequent intervals or often, in line with cost changes? Should prices be changed to take into account positions of short-term strengths or weaknesses in the market place? How should the firm react to changes in competitors' pricing – is it necessary to react at all? By how much?

DISCOUNTS AND DISCOUNTING

The principle of discounting, whether formal or discretionary, is entrenched in most sectors of manufacturing industry where list prices of some kind or other are employed. The variations in discounting practice in everyday use are numerous. There are four main types of discount: quantity discounts, trade discounts, cash discounts and seasonal load-shedding discounts. Other types of discount include those based on geographical factors (for example, zonal pricing based on delivery distance); delivery method (for example, discounts for customer collection); trade-in allowances on old equipment; 'free' supply of related consumables (for example, labels used in price marking equipment). There are various ways also in which discounts are actually effected: they can be based on physical volume or money sales; be a percentage discount or a cash difference from a 'list' price; be shown as a flat sum rebate or a net price; be made 'on invoice' or 'off invoice'. Finally discount structures can be formal (with details published for customer use) or discretionary (in the form of guidelines within which sales managers can negotiate) or a combination of the two.

Special contract or 'net price' arrangements with key customers are, in effect, an extension of the discounting principle but with the essential difference that the terms of the sales agreement are usually the result of direct negotiation between buyer and seller rather than a development of the existing discount formula. Prices are inevitably keen, but how much so will depend in individual cases on the bargaining strength of buyer and seller at the time and can be obscured by the introduction of product modifications, non-standard delivery arrangements and other special conditions.

Of course, in theory and in practice there are excellent reasons for operating a discount policy. Carefully operated and controlled, discounting provides firms with a flexible facility for fine-tuning response to (changing) demand and competitive conditions while retaining the overall integrity of catalogue and list price structures. The danger of discounting as general practice is that it can lead to inconsistency and lack of control. Special terms to important customers can individually be defended on the basis of pragmatism and expediency but add up in total to a jungle of prices which inevitably becomes perpetuated in successive deals with the same customers.

Discounts and special deals in effect represent the reality of pricing while formal price lists and formulae represent the theory. The greater the flexibility or informality of the discounting procedure, and the more discretion which is granted to individual sales executives in negotiating actual prices, then the more the difficulty the company faces in maintaining a firm grip over the effects of its pricing activities. Anticipating revenues and profit is a basic component of financial budgeting and control. However, the ability to make realistic forecasts and impose meaningful controls is directly related to an appreciation of the way prices are actually arrived at, the extent and 'mix' of sales at discounted prices and the relationship these prices have with formal price structures.

The firm operating discounts should keep asking itself:

1 *Do we need to discount at all?* Tradition and convention often play a major role in the operation of formal discount policies and structures. Yet firms have successfully fought the weight of conventional practice

2 *What types of discount should we offer?* The types and scales of discount appropriate in individual cases cannot be embodied within a general set of rules. What is important is that discounting procedures are subjected to rational evaluation of all the factors involved and kept consistent with changes in cost, sales structure and the market environment

3 *What proportion of sales will be made at discounted prices?* Company management must at all times be aware of the sensitivity of revenue and profit to the extent and level of discounting.

REPRESENTING PRICE TO THE CUSTOMER

Preceding paragraphs have shown how pricing can depend, legitimately, on a balance of demand and competition-related issues. It is also the case that firms can set prices in ways designed deliberately to frustrate the ability of the buyer to make direct comparisons, and even to foster price perceptions which are at variance with objective reality. Techniques which are frequently used by firms include:

1 *The 'optional extra' routine* This involves pricing a product in a basic version with a variety of enhancements priced separately as 'optional extras'.

2 *Bundling* This is, in practice, the obverse of the 'optional extra' approach,

and involves making up a package unique to a specific supplier and offered at a special price which makes invidious a comparison with a competing product without the special elements. The process can be represented as offering the buyer an attractive overall discount

3   *Artificial recommended selling prices*   Although resale price maintenance (the practice of enforcing specific resale prices) is outlawed in many countries, it is often perfectly legal for a manufacturer to declare a *recommended* selling price. A retailer can use this price if wished or, more often, as a reference to demonstrate how keen his prices actually are.

PRICING AND NEW PRODUCT PLANNING

New product development has always been a high-risk activity – various studies in the USA have shown failure rates among those actually launched running as high as 60 per cent. Many others are abandoned before they reach the production stage after large sums have been spent on R and D. The risks are, moreover, tending to become greater as the pace of technological change and competitive pressures force up development costs. The more greedy on resources new product development is, the more careful the firms needs to be that the products selected for development are those standing the best chance of achieving a good rate of return on investment when the product finally goes into production. Many writers on new product planning have emphasized the need for establishing clear frameworks of controls, systems and guidelines for appraising the relative merits of new product ideas so that management time and resources are channelled to those products offering the most attractive investment opportunity.

The process of new product appraisal is one which involves a large number of corporate and marketing considerations. However, anticipation of the price ranges at which the product is likely to sell and the market conditions or assumptions underlying those ranges is something which should normally take place at the earliest stages of product planning and be held under review throughout the development process. In effect, it is argued that firms should think far more concretely about gearing new product development to a broad target selling price derived in turn from a realistic valuation of potential demand and the nature of competition than they do at present. This would have several major benefits:

1   It would contain the tendency in R and D to 'over-engineer' products
2   It would prevent the development of products based on unrealistic assumptions about likely sales volumes
3   It would provide a framework for 'fine-tuning' the product during the later stages of development to maximize competitive success

PRICING AND PRODUCT LINES

A great many pricing decisions take place in the context of product lines or ranges rather than as entirely independent exercises. Product lines or ranges comprise individual products linked together in some identifiable way – by a common function, by a common design or structure, by a common production process, by a common user group or application area. An office equipment manufacturer may, for example, offer a range of copiers of different speeds or output capacities and with a choice of other features (such as automatic or manual operation) within each model. Other office product ranges offered by this manufacturer might include typewriters, word processors and facsimile transceivers.

The existence of product lines raises particularly complex pricing issues because of interaction in demand between individual products. Product lines as a whole may be mutually supportive but different products within a line can easily become competitive with each other, particularly with lack of care in pricing. This argues for a policy which provides for each product in a line to be individually priced according to costs and market conditions (subject to certain broad principles of consistency) to minimize the risk of anomalies that could lead to the firm competing with itself.

SUMMARY

This chapter has sought to demonstrate why pricing is perhaps the most complex and demanding – and least clearly understood – of all tasks facing company management. Some conclusions are now drawn which might help the financial executive, in particular, contribute more effectively to pricing policy formulation and price setting.

1 *Pricing is much more of an art than a science*   There is no universal formula or golden rule for arriving at the right price. Those responsible for price setting have to balance and allow for a variety of factors and influences both internal to and external to the firm itself which, far from the ordered and rational world of the theoretical economist, may not always be logical and may even be in conflict. Nevertheless, profitability can be significantly enhanced by injecting greater coherence into the rules and principles, whatever these may be, which govern the way prices are fixed and maintained. The financial executive has an important part to play in the preparation and implementation of pricing policy

2 *Successful pricing decisions cannot be based on costs alone*   Prices are far less often arrived at by the mechanistic application of cost-based formulae than is widely believed. Even so, costs and cost-related profit targets remain a major obsession of many firms in pricing, particularly in the case of industrial products. Financial executives have tended on the whole to encourage and reinforce this essentially inward-looking approach. The success of pricing decisions is, however, highly dependent on the ability of the firm to comprehend and respond to *market* needs and conditions. The contribution of the financial executive to pricing decisions would be substantially enhanced by greater recognition of the role of such factors as competition, buyer attitudes and motivations and the impact of distributive systems in optimum pricing

3 *Price is a much neglected and potentially powerful element in the marketing mix*   Price is widely treated more as a handicap which has to be borne rather than as a positive tool for achieving designated marketing goals. This chapter has looked at the ways pricing can contribute to overall marketing plans both in the longer term (pricing strategy) and in the short term (pricing tactics). The financial executive should be prepared to be 'sufficiently flexible in his own

advice and policies not to inhibit sales and marketing personnel from manipulation of price as a marketing weapon

4 *Pricing considerations are a key element in product planning* Anticipation of price ranges and market conditions are an essential precondition to effective investment and product planning. The financial executive should seek to ensure that pricing factors are introduced at the beginning and not at the end of the planning cycle for new products.

FURTHER READING

Atkin, B. and Skinner, R., *How British Industry Prices*, IMR, 1975

Gabor, A., *Pricing, Concepts and Methods for Effective Marketing*, 2nd edn, Gower, Aldershot, 1988

Oxenfeldt, A.R., 'Multi-stage Approach to Pricing', *Harvard Business Review*, July/August 1960

Wilson, A., *The Marketing of Professional Services*, McGraw-Hill, Maidenhead, 1972

Winkler, John, *Pricing for Results*, Heinemann, London, 1983

24 Distribution channels

Arthur Lawrence

'Getting distribution' for a marketed product (or even for a marketed service) is the term we give to the process of moving it through from the producer and making it conveniently available to its universe of final users. The aim is to do this through whatever channels will provide the greatest sales and the lowest costs and so generate the maximum profit.

In using distribution channels we are not concerned only with the processes of merely physical distribution; that is, the actual storage, handling, transportation and delivery of goods. It is unfortunate that only the one word 'distribution' is available to describe both the physical operations and the wider marketing concept. Perhaps a clearer distinction could be made by describing the physical operations as 'logistics', and this term is sometimes used. A whole later section of this book is devoted to physical distribution; what is being discussed here are the methods of getting a product *into* distribution, and so made available to its potential users.

MARKETS

Distribution, or trade, channels are simply the institutions which exist – or which could be created – to bring about the consummation of buying and selling between potential consumers and producers, in a given market. A market has to be defined both geographically and by the type of product in question. Geographically, the considerations are whether the product is to be marketed only in its own home town or distict; or regionally; or with full national coverage; or even further afield. Distributing beyond the national boundaries of course means 'export', which still in many minds implies a barrier beyond which everything is strange and different. Certainly, it is true that the larger the distribution area is geographically, the more possibility there is that different distribution channels will be required for different parts of it.

As to market differentiation by product, every individual product can be said to have its own market, in so far as it appeals to a unique set of users. But for purposes of considering distribution channels, there is one great divide in product classes; that is, whether the product is designed for consumption by the general public as individuals; or whether it is intended as an input product for use in other sectors of industry and business. This distinction is fundamental. The public buys its needs in the main in retail shops and stores. Equally generally, commerce and industry does not.

General public or industry?

Products aimed at the individual customer can of course be subdivided again and again from the point of view of the distribution channels they require. A main subdivision would probably be into products which are recurrent necessities for everyone (food, clothing, household supplies) and those of a rarer, more specialist appeal. The former are likely to have to jostle for a place in the main retailing market place, while for the latter more exclusive outlets may be available. Each main group can again be broken down as to the 'class' of consumer aimed at, typically as regards spending power, sophistication of interest and so on.

Supplies to industry and commerce will have their own specialized channels or routes to the user. Even when the identical product is in use by both the general public and various sectors of industry it will usually be found necessary to supply it through different channels of distribution in each case. Industry expects to deal more directly with the producer and get lower prices than are charged in the public shops; while the public does not normally have access to the channels provided for industry.

Reviewing alternative channels

The first fact of distribution is that whatever institutions and channels may exist in a particular market, their co-operation in actually providing distribution to users cannot by any means be taken for granted, either for the launch of a new product or for the continued throughput of an existing product. A new product has to be suitable for and of interest to its prospective distribution channel, just as much as it must appeal to its ultimate user. Distribution channels are constantly evolving; completely new ones become available, and old ones by degrees change their methods and their interests or even disappear altogether. New and competitive products come on the scene to oust older traditional lines, not just in their appeal to the user, but in the esteem of their distributors as well. The current arrangements for securing the distribution of a product may, therefore, not always be adequate for its development and expansion, and may at times be vulnerable to changing circumstances. The proper study and assessment of all available and alternative distribution channels is therefore a vital part of marketing planning for both new and existing items.

In considering the kind of distribution channels that could be used between the producer and the ultimate user in any marketing situation, the following main alternatives present themselves immediately. There is the choice of:

1 Using no third party intermediary or middleman between producer and end user
2 Using only one level of intermediary trader between producer and end user
3 Using more than one level of intermediary trader between producer and end user.

These alternatives apply in practically every distribution situation, whether for individual consumer goods or for supplies to industry, and in very many cases more than one of these alternatives may have to be used. Each of these categories can be considered in turn.

SELLING DIRECT TO THE USER

Where no intermediary trader is used between producer and consumer, the producer becomes a direct seller to the end user, that is, the producer himself provides or controls or buys in all the necessary services for contacting potential users in his own name, concluding sales with them, and delivering the goods to them. It is immaterial that some of the services involved may be provided by third parties. The producer may well use a transport contractor for deliveries rather than run his own delivery fleet; or use a mailing house to send out circulars; or even use commission agents to bring in orders. The essential point is that deals are concluded directly between the producer and the user, and property in the goods passes directly from the one to the other.

Direct to industry

For products intended as inputs to industry or to commerce rather than for the general public, this method of selling would probably be the first to be considered. The more specialized the product, and the fewer (and therefore the more individually important) the potential users of it, the more inclination there will be to deal with them direct. If the product is more or less tailor-made for each user, or needs complicated installation and user instruction, there may be little alternative but for the producer to see to things for himself. However widespread the market in geographical terms, the producer must contemplate undertaking all the costs of providing salesmen and other services for customer contact. On the other hand, he need not allow for any third party to make a profit out of his transactions.

Direct to the public

At the other extreme, for products aimed at the public's daily needs, it would be out of the question for the producer to contact all potential users direct – or almost so. On a purely local basis there can certainly be exceptions. The small town baker can still sell all his output through his own shop. In developing countries the peasant farmer (or his wife) takes their own produce to the market and sells it there. But where daily needs are concerned in sophisticated markets, the public tends to buy little and often and seeks as many different items as possible in the one establishment. This rules out buying from the producer direct. On the other hand, for more specialized products aimed at the general public, the possibilities for the producer to deal directly with the user begin to multiply considerably.

Mail order

To make any impact at all, products being sold by mail order must be intensively advertised, probably in the national media or by the equally expensive distribution of catalogues and mail shots. Potential sales must therefore be sufficient to carry this cost. The question is whether the allure of advertising will be enough to make up for the product not being available in the shops where the public can see it and touch it. Will the attractiveness of presentation be a substitute for active selling by the shops – if shops ever do perform active selling? As against the impulse buy, the would-be customer has the added chore of writing off for what he wants. (But perhaps local agents can be employed to do this for him).

Despite these drawbacks, mail order selling for personal possessions and household goods can be tremendously successful. Clothes, furniture, items for specialized interests, all kinds of leisure equipment, books, records – the list is so extensive that mail order cannot be ruled out as being of possible application in almost any field. Possibilities are also liable to increase if the use of 'electronic shopping' ever becomes widespread. The technology for this is already in existence – cable TV or similar arrangements can allow the customer to call up pictures and details of the items in which he is interested, and to key in his order quoting his credit card number, all in his own home.

Direct contact

For items of very high unit value, the employment of salesmen calling door to door can be cost-effective. Domestic house improvements such as double glazing and central heating are the prime examples, but personal services can be included – notably life insurance. Sixty years ago in the UK the list would have included vacuum cleaners and domestic brushware, which nicely illustrates how wage costs have increased in relation to merchandise unit value.

In a specialized field it is not wholly out of the question for a producer to operate his own retail outlets as a channel of distribution direct to the individual user. Examples exist in the clothing industry. However, with vertical integration on the one hand and the subcontracting of production on the other, it becomes quite hard to distinguish between organizations which are really producers having some interests in shops, and those which are really retailers having some control over production.

In summary, direct selling to the user can be viable both for industrial and for general public merchandise, in specific circumstances; and can be implemented either by salemen's visits, by use of the media, or even by the establishment of local sales centres.

SINGLE LEVEL DISTRIBUTORS

In the supply of consumer goods to the public, probably the most common situation is the use of a single level of distributor between the producer and the individual user. The consumer finds his or her needs in the retail shop or store, and the producer sells directly to these outlets. In the more highly developed markets, several complementary trends can be observed in this sytem of retail distribution. Producers (through mergers and growth) become larger and fewer in number, each operating as far as possible nationally; and retail establishments similarly develop into widespread chains and multiples, each covering very large areas, if not all, of the national market. Thus, a smaller number of centrally organized producers supplies an ever larger share of total needs to a smaller number of centrally organized retailers, and it is not surprising that each should deal directly with the other. At the same time, an ever wider range of merchandise is being put through the mass retailing system. The public is doing more for itself rather than employing small tradesmen for the purpose, so that materials and equipment which previously would have been distributed as trade supplies are now suitably packaged and retailed to the home user. Manufacturers have had to adapt themselves to selling a larger part of their output at retail and changing their distribution channels accordingly.

Retailing establishments can be categorized in all sorts of ways, but from the point of view of the distribution mechanism the following are the principal distinctions.

National or regional multiples

Irrespective of differences in the range of merchandise or the house style or any such qualitative aspects, retail multiples are essentially organizations which implement a uniform merchandising and selling policy throughout all their many branches. Into this category come hypermarkets, food supermarkets, clothing chains, furniture warehouses, do-it-yourself chains, multiple chemists, electrical and photographic multiples – in fact any large scale retailer exercising central control over branches. To exercise this control, multiples operate in two principal ways.

Central buying and warehousing

Very large single deals are negotiated with suppliers, for delivery in bulk to the central warehouse, which in turn supplies to branches according to their needs. Branches place no orders directly with suppliers. From the suppliers' point of view, bulk deliveries to a single point mean a great saving in transport and order processing costs, and there is no need for an expensive sales force to visit the individual stores to get orders. Since the multiple is bearing the cost of warehousing and delivery to branches, the price concession demanded from suppliers will be correspondingly steep. Suppliers may also find that in practice they still have to send salesmen to call on branches, if only to ensure that the latter remember to order stocks from their central warehouse, and to give them proper display.

Listing and local ordering

The multiple negotiates prices and terms centrally with suppliers, for estimated total requirements over a period. In return, the suppliers' products are then 'listed' to branches as items which they are authorized to order directly from the suppliers, at their own discretion. Suppliers in practice have to send salesmen to call to get these orders, and still have to bear the expense of making smaller individual deliveries to each branch. To obtain a 'listing' at all, the supplier will also have to make some price concession.

Any given multiple may operate either or both systems, and may even give a supplier the option of which system he prefers to use. It is essential in either case for suppliers to calculate all their selling and delivery costs correctly, so as to know exactly what price concessions they can afford to make.

Department stores

Originally, the classic department store was a collection under one roof of a great variety of merchandise departments, each individually managed as to its selection of merchandise and its buying policy. There would be overall guidelines and financial controls, but the department buyer had the last word on ordering. Thus, department stores were in a way the exact opposite of retail multiples; one location in place of many, but many buyers in place of one. For the specialist supplier, dealing with only one department out of a huge establishment, there would be little difference from dealing with any other single retail shop. Department stores in the classic mould, apart from one or two famous exceptions, appear to be dying out, and through mergers are evolving more into retail multiples. While outward appearances may remain the same, the indivdiual departments are becoming parts of a centrally managed chain which now makes the principal buying decisions. The supplier must therefore check carefully exactly how each establishment operates, in assessing what his costs of selling and supplying to it are going to be.

Independents

Other retail outlets fall by default into the category of independents – independent in the sense of buying decision. An independent may of course have more than one selling location, as long as there are not so many branches as to raise the status to that of a small multiple. (It is an interesting point that co-operatives can be in either category: in some areas, buying is centralized in multiple fashion; in others, quite small groups act independently.) The characteristic of dealing with the independent retailer as a channel of distribution is that each has to be sold to individually, usually through visiting by salesmen. Costs of selling are high, coupled with the higher costs of small order quantities and widespread deliveries. Against this, the supplier hopes that terms will be easier than with multiples.

Groups

Independents also are evolving, chiefly by becoming members of voluntary buying groups. In this way the group of independents begins to operate very much like a multiple, in that bulk buying decisions are now made centrally by the group headquarters, which may also operate its own warehouse. Discipline among the independent members is, of course, not nearly so tight as in a wholly owned multiple, and the supplier has less assurance that the single central negotiation will be effective in getting his merchandise into every store. To be sure of this, the supplier may have to retain as much direct contact with individual members as when they were truly independent.

Franchising

The ultimate in grouping is franchising, where the merchandising and selling policy for the particular goods or service are centrally controlled and enforced as rigidly as by any multiple. The fact that individual outlets are independently financed makes no difference to buying policy, which will usually leave the franchisee free to purchase at his own discretion only the most minor local supplies.

In all the foregoing retail categories, size of establishment and method of organization make no difference to function as a channel of distribution. Retail outlets are available to the producer as single level trading intermediaries between himself and the ultimate users, should he wish to avail himself of them. It is up to the producer to make his product of sufficient interest to those categories of retailer which offer the best channel of approach to potential users.

Industrial distributors

The producer of goods for industry and commerce will generally have more incentive to deal direct with his users than the producer of goods for the public. Nevertheless, where these users are both individually small and numerous in total, the industrial producer also has to seek intermediaries to provide an alternative channel of distribution. This will be especially the case where the product is neither so technical nor so purpose-made as to make direct contact essential between manufacturer and user. Thus, as direct counterparts to retail outlets for the general public, there exist distributors to industry and commerce in every field of product. Builders' merchants act as stockists of bricks, tiles, cement and every kind of material and accessory for construction work. Agricultural merchants stock animal feeds, seeds, fertilizer and every farm need, down to wheelbarrows and rubber boots. Steel stockholders supply engineering works. Office equipment suppliers stock everything from paper upwards. Even the hotel, restaurant and catering industry is covered by specialist wholesaling stockists, usually of the cash and carry type.

Similar categorizations exist among industrial distributors as among retail distributors. While the trend towards mergers and nationwide organizations is perhaps not so marked as in retail, it still occurs, and the equivalents of national multiples exist, in practically every field of industrial distribution. The individual producer thus has similar alternatives of central negotiation for bulk contracts with multi-branch organizations, or individual deals with a multiplicity of smaller independent traders.

A particular case of industrial distributor is the agent or stockist in a foreign market. While producers can and do still deal direct with large and important export customers, they are likely to feel more need than in the home market for an intermediary distributor to act between them and the majority of potential users abroad.

MORE THAN ONE LEVEL OF DISTRIBUTOR

When potential users of a product are too numerous for the producer to be able to contact all of them direct, he makes use of an intermediary distributor. When, in turn, the first level of intermediary distributors becomes too numerous to contact direct, the producer has to seek a higher level of distributor to deal with all the others.

This situation arises mainly in the market for the general public. Despite the trend for the displacement of small independent retailers by large centrally controlled multiples, there remain enough of the former in some sectors to constitute a problem. In the UK, for example, there are over 50 000 retail shops selling newspapers, magazines, confectionery and tobacco. There are also nearly as many grocers or general food shops. For any one producer to attempt to deal with all of these directly, obtaining their orders and making individual deliveries, is unlikely to be economic. Therefore, in each class of trade, both in the UK and in other markets, there is an important stratum of 'wholesalers' or higher level distributors between producer and retailer.

Wholesale and cash-and-carry

Many of these wholesalers operate on the basis of cash-and-carry, which is self-selection by their retail customers and payment on the spot, with the buyer providing his own transport. Others for a higher price provide delivery and credit. All of them most jealously guard against the general public being able to gain access and buy for themselves at wholesale prices, thereby short-circuiting the retailer. In dealing with wholesalers, the producer saves the cost of selling and delivering direct to thousands of retailers, but must now allow in his pricing for both wholesaler and retailer to make a profit – and probably must take steps to ensure that the position of each is protected.

Main distributors

In industrial situations the use of more than one level of distributor is perhaps rarer if only because of the smaller number of primary outlets likely to be involved. It will be unusual for there to be more first level distributors than the producer can readily deal with directly. Nevertheless, there will be instances of specialized items – agricultural machinery for example – where an advantage is found in having an upper level of main distributors who will undertake supply of occasional 'one-offs' to less specialized sub-dealers. The sub-dealer knows the customer who may prefer to deal with him rather than with a distant specialist. Again, in the export field there may be grounds for having a single main distributor in a foreign territory to handle sales to all other stockists.

CHOOSING DISTRIBUTION CHANNELS

For any producer seeking distribution for a newly launched item or reviewing the current arrangements for existing lines, the first area of decision is likely to be whether any one distribution channel will satisfy all requirements, or whether there may be grounds for using more than one channel at the same time.

Parallel channels

Many producers will find that no single channel of distribution is ideal for all the product range in all sets of circumstances. In the sector of products aimed at the general public, the manufacturer may feel that the best prospect for sales is through having the product stocked and promoted by the retail shops specializing in that class of trade. But what if retailers fail to carry stocks and large sectors of the public are left without opportunity to buy? It may be necessary to encourage direct mail ordering from the public, at the same time as stepping up pressure on retailers to stock. The advertising message will have to be: 'Available from all good retailers, or by mail direct from . . .'. Some book publishers practise this as a matter of course; as do manufacturers of specialized items where retail distribution is not widespread.

The commonest situation in the consumer goods market is where the manufacturer can and must deal directly with the largest retailers, but cannot economically sell and deliver directly to all the smaller ones. A typical case is where the larger outlets, accounting for around 20 per cent of all shops, may handle 80 per cent of all sales; while the remaining 80 per cent of smaller shops account for only 20 per cent of total sales. The manufacturer cannot afford to forego this last 20 per cent of sales altogether, but equally cannot afford to contact all of the smaller shops direct. If possible, a way must be found to interest wholesalers in handling supplies to the smaller outlets, while the main stores are dealt with direct.

In developing markets overseas, producers commonly sell their output through only a few large traders, who supply smaller outlets and market traders through possibly several levels of re-selling. But in order to stimulate sales in particular areas, the producer may have to bypass them all and from time to time sell direct to the public from mobile vans in the market place.

Goods for the industrial and commercial market face the same kind of choice. While the majority of sales can be handled through specialized merchants and stockists, very large users must be dealt with by direct negotiation, for two main reasons:

1 Large users insist on buying only from manufacturers on grounds of price
2 The size of their requirements would probably exceed the financial and physical capacity of intermediary dealers.

Very large users nowadays include governments and state organizations, for whom special terms are always necessary.

Conflicts

Where more than one distribution channel has to be used simultaneously there is thus a fundamental conflict; the producer is trying to make sales to the customers of his own customers. The reasons for trying to do so have to be compelling, and the distributors being bypassed have to be protected and their co-operation retained. Some or all of the following means can be employed:

1 Make clear in advance to intermediary distributors the circumstances in which it may be necessary to bypass them
2 Explain that the purpose is not to deprive them of business but to make the sales which they cannot get themselves and which otherwise would be missed altogether
3 Point out that gaining extra market share for the product in this way will be to their advantage in stimulating total demand for it
4 Try not to undercut distributors' prices when bypassing them to sell direct;

then there is no reason why distributors should not do this class of business themselves in future

5   If a lower price is necessary to get some special direct business, point out to distributors that they would not have been able to match this price themselves.

Whatever the arrangements for operating more than one distribution channel it is essential to make clear to all the parties involved just what these arrangements are, and also to make provision for changes should these ever become necessary. Distributors should never be allowed to think that they have a monopoly right to sales being made only through them; the manufacturer must reserve the right to intervene in special cases, giving whatever protection he can to the distributors' position.

Regulated distribution

A secondary dilemma in choosing distribution channels is whether to sell through as many distributors as are willing to handle the product, or to restrict it to selected distributors only.

Having the product available in as many outlets as possible fulfils one of the prime functions of achieving distribution. User demand is stimulated through the widespread presence of the product and no potential sale is lost through non-availability. This, however, is achieved at the risk of excessive competition between outlets, leading to price cutting and eventual loss of interest by the trade in handling the product at all.

Restricting the product to selected distributors permits a regulated market, where each distributor has a more or less exclusive position in his own area. Demand is concentrated on fewer distributors so that they can in turn concentrate on the product to the exclusion of other competitive lines. At the extreme, distribution becomes a network of exclusive dealerships.

Exclusive territories

Regulated distribution is more the norm for industrial and commercial supplies than for general public merchandise. With markets much smaller in terms of numbers of users it is the more essential not to overcrowd them. For many industrial products, technical service, support, spares and special equipment are required and distribution must be limited to those dealers who can provide them. Their investment in the product must be given some guarantee of protection thereafter. These arrangements would normally be the subject of a distribution agreement with the rights and duties of both sides clearly set out. The distributor may be given exclusivity in one particular territory, and in such cases it is essential to make provision for change if the arrangement does not work out. It may often be better to have more than one dealer in a territory so that none has a complete monopoly.

In the public sphere, regulated distribution also occurs. The sale of motor cars is an obvious example; dealers are appointed for each make on a territorial basis, again on the grounds that each has to provide specialized spares and service. Less obviously, many other lines of merchandise are restricted in their outlets. Expensive cosmetics and perfumery are on sale only in boutiques and drug stores with the requisite level of sophistication and would never be allowed to reach the shelves of a common supermarket. Technical items for specialist leisure activities will only be supplied through stores offering know-how and service.

Free consumer market

For the great majority of consumer goods, the maximum exposure in the largest number of retail outlets usually far outweighs any considerations of market regulation. Since competition is regarded as of ultimate benefit to the consumer there may be legal issues involved in trying to regulate it. In the UK – with just one or two exceptions – it is illegal to try to impose a minimum retail selling price. In practice, suppliers stipulate minimum order quantities, offer discounts for large deliveries, and require a minimum level of display. This ensures that the product is stocked only in those outlets considered suitable. The difficulty for manufacturers is usually in the other direction, in trying to keep the product on sale in all sizes of retail outlet when the larger organizations use their buying power to squeeze price concessions. With these concessions in hand, retail prices can be cut to levels with which the smaller outlets cannot compete. Given the higher costs of selling and delivering to them, manufacturers cannot reduce prices comparably to the smaller outlets.

From the manufacturers' point of view there can be considerable temptation to supply only to the large retail multiples through single negotiations, with bulk deliveries to a central warehouse, and to ignore the smaller independent retailers altogether. In this way the bulk, of the public can be reached adequately, and the costs of selling and delivery are minimal. On the other hand, terms will be onerous and, if a single sales negotiation falls through, the manufacturer may be left with no distribution at all.

THE CRITERIA FOR CHOICE

The basis for choosing a distribution channel or combination of channels is very clear in principle; it will be the one which promises to yield the highest ultimate net profit, calculated as sales volume times margin, less the associated selling and supply expenses. Estimates are therefore required of sales volume, margins attainable, and costs of selling, through different channels.

Sales volume

Sales forecasts have to be based largely on experience, but it should still be possible to estimate whether sales would be greater or less when using different distribution channels. For example, sales could be made:

1 Through mail order direct to users
2 Through retail shops
3 Through wholesalers to retail shops
4 By a combination of some or all of these methods.

Presumably sales through a channel which is shared with another would be less than if that channel were used exclusively. The question is whether total sales through shared channels would be greater than by using either one alone. Estimates should be made for all possible methods and combinations of methods.

Margins

Assessing margins entails knowing what levels of profit the different classes of distributor would require to motivate them to stock and promote the product properly. It is essential to start with the price the end user can be expected to pay, then deduct the distributors' margins. The manufacturer gets what is left, and must make his profit out of it. To start with a manufacturer's selling price, leave distributors to add what they like, and hope that end users will pay what they are asked, is not marketing – it is simply throwing a product on to the market. The complete pricing structure through all alternative levels of distribution should be worked out, allowing for distributors' costs in stocking, handling and re-selling the product, plus whatever profit will be required. The less distributors are used, the higher the remaining margin to the manufacturer; but out of this margin the manufacturer will have to provide for higher costs of his own in selling more directly.

Selling costs

The calculation of selling costs per channel must include the costs of handling orders and making deliveries as well as salesmen's wages, travel costs, telephones and so on – in fact every cost which is incurred as a direct result of using any particular distribution channel. Costs which are incurred whatever the channel can be left out of the comparison. The distributive trade is essentially passive towards suppliers, supporting its own interests rather than theirs. Customers are left to make their own choice between competitive products, rather than any one product in particular being promoted. Therefore, in addition to the cost of selling 'in' to distributors there may be further support costs in helping and persuading distributors to sell 'out'. Selling-in costs will themselves vary widely, as between making single-large-scale negotiations with central multiples and making sales calls on thousands of small shops throughout the country.

When all estimates have been made, it is a straightforward matter to work out sales times margins less costs by each alternative method and see which promises the best net result.

Intangibles

At the same time, the intangibles must not be overlooked. Alternative distribution channels may appear to produce similar financial results, but the more direct method might offer an additional advantage in closer control over the market place, and a sounder base from which to launch new products in future. Or a channel which offers a lower return in the short term might be one which provides a higher market share, greater exposure to the public, and thus better prospects for expansion. All intangibles will in the end reveal themselves in terms of financial reward, but it is as well to cross check that they have not been left out of the financial calculations.

PLANNING FOR DISTRIBUTION

Obtaining distribution channels for a product or range of products should not be looked on as a secondary matter which can be attended to once all arrangements for the presentation of the product to its users have been perfected. Except in the specific case where the manufacturer proposes to contact all users directly – as by mail order, or through own sales force – the product will only ever reach its users if the appropriate trade distributors choose to take it on. Many of the features of the product designed to appeal to users will do so only through the active participation of the trade. The appearance, performance and quality of the product will impress potential users only if the trade stocks it and allows them to see it. Its attractive price to the user depends on the trade accepting the margin proposed. Sales promotion schemes will work only if the trade co-operates. Only media advertising allows a manufacturer to appeal to his potential users directly; all other aspects of consumer marketing depend on trade participation.

Dual marketing strategies

Launching a product successfully through distribution channels therefore demands a dual marketing strategy aimed both at the intended user and at the trade sector chosen for distribution. Financial calculations will have shown which method of distribution should be the most advantageous; it remains to select the individual distributor organizations or groups or sectors most suitable for giving the product the exposure it requires. As trade outlets become concentrated into a smaller number of large organizations, it is vital to succeed in appealing to the ones whose co-operation is counted on. The absence of even one large organization from the distribution plan may mean the loss of a substantial part of the user market.

The trade's interest in a product line depends essentially on two things: the trade margin offered, and the extent to which the trade thinks the product will appeal to users. Thus, an advertising campaign addressed to potential users should not overlook the secondary aim of impressing the trade, as well as with the effect it will have on their customers.

A customer marketing plan culminates in an estimate of the volume which will be sold to users. It is essential to cross-check this with the corresponding volumes which will have to be handled through each distribution channel and to consider whether these volumes are in turn feasible. What do these volumes imply in terms of:

1 The numbers of outlets that would have to handle the product
2 The stock availability required
3 Display, storage and servicing facilities
4 The level of finance needed from the trade?

Distribution implications may therefore bring realism to consumer marketing plans, or at least provide throughput targets per channel for regular monitoring.

Working out a strategy for achieving distribution through the channels chosen should be thought of as marketing to the trade, and should be given as much priority as the strategy for consumer marketing which it is designed to complement. Only through joint marketing plans for both trade and consumer can a product attain maximum success in reaching its targets.

FURTHER READING

Foster D., *Mastering Marketing*, Macmillan, London, 1982
Lawrence, A., *The Management of Trade Marketing*, Gower, Aldershot, 1983
Stapleton, J., *Marketing*, Hodder & Stoughton, Sevenoaks, 1985
Wilmshurst, J., *The Fundamentals and Practice of Marketing*, Institute of Marketing, Heinemann, London 1978

25 Overseas marketing

Geoff Burgess

Exporting is fun – or is it? We are told by governments that we must export to survive, that exports are critical to our future and national standing in the world. Is exporting really fun? Perhaps not fun, but certainly profitable if planned and implemented properly as part of the company's overall business strategy.

In many companies the reasons for exporting are obscure: one or more of the directors perhaps likes overseas travel, or there is some excess capacity which can be usefully filled by finding an overseas order. Perhaps a little more thought has been put into the question and export is being used to overcome a seasonal capacity problem or it is seen as a way of gaining extra sales under the heading of marginal business. Some of these reasons may well be valid, but the prime reason in any company for exporting must be to make extra profit. Without real profit, exporting will not receive the commitment and support from the company staff that is needed to ensure success.

So how does a company go about setting up an effective exporting operation? Before setting off down the road of selling overseas, it is necessary to understand the wide range of methods available for entering into export markets – frequently, options that are never considered within the company's own home market.

THE OPTIONS AVAILABLE

Before launching into exporting, the company's management must consider the wide range of options open for entering into export markets, and balance the cost, risk and potential rewards that lie ahead for the business (see Figure 25.1).

Obviously, different methods will be more applicable to different parts of the world – perhaps a direct sales force seeking out large customers is suitable for Europe, whereas a licence arrangement or one single importer/distributor would be more applicable to working in Southeast Asia or African territories.

As well as understanding the wide-ranging methods of distribution open to a company planning to start an export operation, an appreciation is needed of the different opportunities that exist in export markets, and also a very honest appreciation of when opportunities will not exist. Without this very frank approach to the business of exporting it is possible for a company to waste a lot of money in market areas where no success could possibly be achieved.

MARKET NEEDS

Perhaps the most pragmatic approach to analysing the opportunities that exist in different types of export markets is to break the world down into three broad

Method of approach	Benefits	Weaknesses	Applications
1 Direct selling to end users	Total control Higher gross margins Important when selling high technology into developing countries	High cost Reduced local knowledge and contacts	To Governments To various aid organizations and consultants High-value capital plant To open-up key market
2 Through agent	Gives local knowledge and connection Can work well in conjunction with '1' above Low cost payment by results	Less control Can involve costs which are not earned Legal risks if not tied down very carefully No support back-up	As in '1' above In secondary markets When local influence needed Service industry
3 Distributor/importer/wholesaler	Local knowledge and connections Gives local support for service, spares and stock Reduces cost of establishing local dealer/distribution network	Reduced control Can be legally binding over long period despite poor performance	Capital plant and consumer durables Consumer products
4 Local/regional dealers/wholesalers within country	More direct control over distribution chain A poor performer does not impact on total sales within the country and can often be oversold by neighbouring outlet	More costly Requires more back-up May require the company to set up own central stocking in the country	As in '1' above Good way to enter very large market such as USA
5 UK export house or buying agent plus turnkey contractors	Low cost Low risk UK payment and often no shipping involvement Protection from onerous contract conditions — sometimes	Very limited control Limited direct influence with end market Watch supply conditions Lower gross margins — sometimes, but not always	Where product forms part of larger supply contract For secondary markets

Figure 25.1 Entering export markets

Method of approach	Benefits	Weaknesses	Applications
6 Aid agencies, for example Overseas Development Aid, World Bank, FAO	Lower cost / Often sizeable orders / Fairly regular business	Less control unless selling into end-user country as well (via agent often valuable) / Contracts and payment timing can be onerous / International competition	Virtually all products or services, except luxury goods
7 Supply 'own label' for local manufacture or distributor — your product and their marketing	Low selling cost / More guarantee on volume / Reasonable control	Must be legally well tied-up / No direct control over marketing	Medium-technology products into developing markets / Where company has one specialist product of interest, which cannot support independent selling
8 Joint venture and licence agreement	More control / Less direct selling cost / Often a way into a market behind protection barriers / Can result in lower cost supply point for home market / Utilizes redundant home market designs and production equipment / Less risk than '9' below	Complicated / Costly legal set-up / Examine local laws very carefully / Loss of volume for home factory / Demands high level of technical support — and always more than planned	Developing countries / Medium or older home market technology / To get round tariff barriers / Natural follow on from '7' above
9 Own company	Total control / More profits, sometimes	Very expensive / Needs a lot of management time / Highest risk	As in '8' above and can be natural. follow-on

Figure 25.1 (concluded)

Market type	Market demands/Export opportunities

1 Developed World	Higher technology
	Unique features
	Sophisticated distribution
	Superior promotional support
	Well-developed back-up and support
	For consumer products, a clear difference
	  (objective or subjective) when compared with
	  local suppliers

2 Under-developed World	Medium and lower technology especially capital
	  plant
	Good support, especially technical
	Limited luxury goods
	Specialist consultancy service
	Basic distribution (though physical
	  distribution can be a problem)
	Limited promotional support
	Longer-term finance
	Local manufacturing opportunities, especially

3 Developing World	Technology for licence agreements/local manufacture/investment Finance Luxury goods Medium- and high-technology imports Good distribution Good promotional and technical back-up

Figure 25.2   Export markets – demands and opportunities

categories:

1   The developed world: that is, Europe, North America, Australia, South Africa, Japan and some parts of the Far East
2   The under-developed world, consisting of those countries that are making little or no progress in their attempts at industrialization and economic improvement, covering many parts of Africa and some parts of Central and South America
3   The developing world, covering those countries that are at different rates of progress, moving slowly forward in their attempts to strengthen their economic position, with improving industrialization coupled with a growing consumer society; for example, several South American countries, large parts of Southeast Asia and areas where oil or mineral wealth has allowed rapid investment, such as the Middle East.

Each type of market has opportunities for a wide range of products but careful analysis needs to be made of the options open to a company for entering into that market, together with an assessment of these options against the company's own strengths and weaknesses (see Figure 25.2.).

With a clear understanding of the market types and wide range of entry options open to a company, management can then identify those markets which are most likely to yield profitable export sales in a realistic time-scale through analysing its own company's strengths and weaknesses, and matching the strengths to those countries which appear most in need of what the company has to offer.

ANALYSING THE COMPANY'S STRENGTHS AND WEAKNESSES

To enter into the business of exporting, the company will require many strengths and skills not necessarily needed for handling the home market. Before taking decisions to launch into selling overseas, it is necessary to look critically at a number of areas in the operation of the business.

The first of these must be the products. Just because a product sells well within the home market does not mean that there will be a large number of customers queuing up to buy in other countries. Attacking an overseas market with a 'me, too' product, which has no unique features, can hardly meet with success, except in the unlikely event of the export territory having a shortage of supply. To penetrate an export market, the products must have strengths in at least one of the following areas:

- technical specification
- reliability
- simplicity
- specialist application
- aesthetic features
- price.

Without at least one of these factors as a particular strength for the product range that it is intended to export, the chances of success are considerably reduced.

The one possible exception is when the company has a particular strength in offering a unique back-up service; for example, through its application design engineering, or in a specialist support area for the export customers such as arranging particularly flexible financing.

Secondly, as well as analysing the company's product strengths, there is a need to review the support services that the company can offer in relation to those required within the export markets. Developed markets will require high standards in all aspects of promotional and, where relevant, technical support, through the complete range of advertising, publicity support, shows and, if required, application engineering and service back-up.

In the less-developed markets, greater emphasis will be placed upon advisory training, technical and financial support. Without the ability to give the necessary support, any attempt to sell overseas will only meet with short-lived success.

The third area for consideration in looking at exporting is the company's strengths in product engineering and, where applicable, application engineering. This, of course, relates more to technical products, but too often companies make the mistake of assuming that a product well accepted in a home market will fit exactly into an export territory. This is rarely the case, and nearly always there is a need for some element of product engineering. This may be as simple as handling the requirements dictated by the different electrical supply systems that exist around the world, or remembering that North America still works on imperial measurements and does not like receiving metric drawings or specifications. Or the problems can be complex; for example, successfully breaking the non-tariff barriers in countries such as Germany and Japan where technical specifications and product developments are critical to meet locally imposed health and safety, performance and specification requirements. Do not be misled by the 'Common Market' concept. Each country within the EC has its own technical standards that need to be met and which are open to liberal interpretation.

The next important area for consideration is production capacity. Exporting does not exist for the purpose of filling capacity on odd occasions when the home market is not generating sufficient demand. Frequently, to maintain good export markets, there will be a conflict of demand between the home sales force and the export team. The company needs sufficient flexibility, either within its own manufacturing capacity or through subcontract capacity or a level of stocking, that will allow the demands of both markets to be met. Frequently, it is assumed that seasonality can be overcome simply by finding markets on the other side of the equator. Again an easy trap in which to fall – seasonality is often caused by different factors within different countries; for example, the demand for garden watering products in northern Europe is naturally during the European summer. What better strategy, then, than to export watering products to South Africa or Zimbabwe during the European winter? A good idea, but unfortunatley the main dry season during which garden watering is needed in southern Africa is the dry late winter and spring – July to September.

Another necessary area of support is within the administrative functions inside the company. Exporting requires far more complicated documentation, a different form of accounts control, the ability to handle a wide range of payment methods, knowledge of shipping and transport in all its forms, different packaging and labelling requirements, the skills to handle overseas visitors and, when shipping to many of the countries in the developing world, the ability to handle the buyer's inspection agency who will be required to clear all the products against the exact specification quoted before authorization for final shipment.

Even more important, it needs to be remembered that less than one-third of the world works in the English language – and even that is questionable when it comes to exporting to North America, as a wide range of terms used have a completely different meaning from European English; also South American Spanish or Canadian French differs considerably from that spoken in Europe. Selling overseas does mean selling in a foreign language.

Finally, and certainly of equal importance, is the question of the company's strength in banking support, which must be sufficiently flexible to handle the different forms of payment and financing that will be needed in the countries selected. Coupled to this will be the need for sufficient funding to cover the cash flow of exporting, which in the majority of cases will demand a higher level of working capital than most home markets.

MARKET RESEARCH

Armed with an objective analysis of the company's strengths, an understanding of the range of markets than can possibly be attacked and a clear view on the different approaches that can be used to sell into these markets, management is ready to look more closely at the specific markets where it is believed that the real demand can be identified and reasonably satisfied by the company's own product range and back-up strengths. But before sending out an unsuspecting salesman, armed with a briefcase full of samples and brochures and supported with a proper export price list, a fair degree of market research needs to be undertaken.

This does not mean vast expenditure using an outside agency. Frequently, a large amount of information can be obtained from the following sources: the various services offered by trade associations; other companies within similar industries, but not directly competitive, who are already exporting to the target markets; and the various range of services offered by the relevant government department, banks, the local chamber of commerce and, of course, the embassies of the countries that have been selected for more detailed study.

Once this information has been collected, a further refining of the list of potential countries can be undertaken, leaving six or seven potential targets for closer scrutiny. Here a research agency may be needed, depending upon the product line; if so, a company should be selected that has knowledge of the country or countries that are being investigated. A company with proven knowledge of the area, and preferably a local presence to support their claim that they can give you the detailed information that you need, is required.

Frequently, however, the most cost-effective method of undertaking detailed research is to send a member of the company's own staff on a visit to the targeted markets. With more technical products this research can include the introduction of the product for local testing with end users. (In the UK both the market research and product research may be eligible for support grants from the Department of Trade and Industry.)

This product research is most important. Mistakes are often made by companies attempting to move into new export markets who have assumed that a product, well accepted in a home or another export market, will automatically be successful in a new country.

Finally, ensure before launching into a new country that tariffs, legal barriers, product registration legislation, health and safety and other technical requirements, taxation, and personnel laws do not contain clauses that could cost the company large sums of money in the future. For example, selling to government organizations in some countries exposes the supplier to local taxation and, in the most extreme case, this taxation is levied on the company's worldwide earnings! In other areas, company personnel entering the country on business visas carry the risk of being charged income tax on the assessed level of their earnings for the period of their stay, and payment is extracted before an exit visa is issued. And do not forget product liability insurance – if you have any doubts, consult your insurance company.

EXPORT STRATEGY

If you have read this far and have not given up the whole idea of exporting, the rest of the stages are relatively easy. Do not be put off by the earlier sections: exporting, properly managed, is safe, profitable and very rewarding.

Having collected all the necessary data, the company is now in a position to plan its export marketing operation.

First, establish the objectives for the exporting operation: what level of volume, into which markets, at what prices, through which channels of distribution, to achieve what market share, and with total profitability or marginal profitability as the objective?

In establishing target markets, every company entering the export business should select a single or very few key markets, and in some cases should even narrow it down to specific regions within one country. The scatter-gun approach to exporting does not work – select specific targets and aim for those.

Setting up the organization for the export departments starts at the top – there must be a member of the board committed to managing the export operation who is clearly identified as the person with responsibility for the activity's success. In many smaller companies this will be the managing director.

Internally, there is a need for the knowledge and skills of handling the export administration function, covering everything from the enquiry and quotations to documentation, shipping, payment methods, financing and export/import legislation. In addition, in many countries, business will be carried out under contractual terms that are not in line with the company's standard terms and conditions of sale, and there will therefore be a need for knowledge of contracts, bid bonds, performance bonds, retention clauses, repayment guarantees, credit insurance, and export banking procedures. A formidable list, but knowledge and skill that can usually be found in one good export administrator or export administration manager. If possible, find a person who also has knowledge of the markets into which the company is trying to sell. Often, good export administratiors can be recruited from the band of older export salesmen who still enjoy exporting but want to stop travelling.

Next, the salesmen. The first rule: rarely do good home market salesmen turn into successful exporters. Export selling is different. In the home market the sales force is supported by a head office, a manufacturing unit, warehouse and distribution operations, sales administration back-up, sales management, and full technical support, all within the same country. The home salesmen have regular contact with managers and colleagues, plus the security of working within a country, social structure, environment and business community that is their own.

Not so the export salesmen. They are alone, working in a foreign country with alien customs, social structures, business philosophies and environment. Frequently working in a foreign language; normally operating from a hotel bedroom; always days or weeks away from contact with managers, colleagues and effective support; and without the facility of being able to switch off at home each evening or at least at the weekend.

The export salesmen need all the characteristics of the good home market salesmen, covering sales skills (but also good negotiating skills), product technical and market application knowledge, strong administration and self-discipline skills, and the ability to search out, identify and satisfy customer needs. In addition, they will need the ability to work on their own initiative without reference back to a manager, except in extreme cases, and the skill to handle a crisis – suffering a car breakdown on an autobahn, interstate or motorway when you are already thirty minutes late for an appointment is child's play when compared with running out of petrol on the Lagos to Kano road in Nigeria, or trying to deal with the problems of a stolen wallet and passport, complete with credit cards, in the middle of Lima or Teheran.

The caricature export salesman is a noisy, hard-drinking, story-telling, womanizing, devil-may-care extrovert. The *real* successful exporter is a stable, planning, hard-working, well organized, self-disciplined businessman (and, more frequently now, businesswoman) who may well drink, but only modestly, and never when flying; perhaps a good storyteller but, far more likely, just a good listener. Recruiting a good export salesman is a difficult task and if there is no one in the company with the experience to carry out the recruitment, do not hesitate to use an experienced agency.

CONTROLLING THE EXPORT FUNCTION

The decision has been taken and the company has found the right team to handle its export operation, has set the objectives, targeted the markets and is about to embark upon the first venture into overseas selling. Like all management functions, it needs controlling, but again with exporting it is a little different.

First, there must be an awareness throughout the company, at all levels of management and across all departments, that the company is embarking upon a new venture which will place strains and demands upon the business not experienced within the home market. Communications will be more difficult, orders more erratic, deadlines for delivery even more critical (ships do not wait – no, not even for twenty-four hours!).

Contact with the sales team is infrequent, and calls back to the office to ask for management approval are difficult or impossible. Controls over the level of authority, therefore, need to be far more clearly defined, with a wider band of discretion for the export sales team. Weekly, monthly or individual country or overseas trip reports need to be more detailed, and frequently circulated to a wider group of people within the company.

Monitoring of forward demand is usually more difficult, with the lead time between enquiry, quotation, order placement, confirmation of finance and dispatch often taking months, where the home market would be talking in terms of days or weeks. In addition, export orders are usually for larger quantities so, unfortunatley, usually placed less frequently, and timing – particularly with orders from the developing world – almost impossible to forecast. It is therefore essential to have a system of accurate monitoring to establish the current level of enquiry, the number and value of outstanding quotations and a system for weighting the likely delivery requirements to allow at least some forward planning by the material and production planning department.

If the exporting involves contracts, bonds, payment schedules, bank guarantees, special shipping requirements, complex documentation or any of the other special requirements associated with exporting, then a separate management control system needs to be set-up to ensure that the requirements, action dates and follow-ups are properly administered – if a letter of credit says three sets of bills of lading required within five days of the vessel sailing, no amount of arguing with the bank will get payment released to you on day 6.

The basic rules for export management control are clear guidelines, detailed operating procedures, a full set of standing instructions, very effective communication between the export staff and all other departments within the company, religious attention to detail, accurate documentation, meticulous following of timetables, and the continuous monitoring of activities, feedback and results.

Finally, in assessing and controlling the export function, organize the company's accounting function in a way that will allow the identification of all sales results, the margins achieved and a detailed breakdown of all the fixed and variable costs that are directly related to the export function. In this way, with the allowance of adequate time, a well-managed export operation will be seen to yield to the company valuable additional profits. In fact, in many companies, export operations have proved to be the most profitable section of the total business. Managed properly, then exporting *is* fun.

CHECKLIST

This checklist can be used for an existing or planned export operation.

1 Why export – what are the objectives?
2 What are the company's strengths:

- what unique points do our products have?
- how strong is our product engineering to adapt products to individual countries' requirements?
- what administrative strengths and knowledge do we have to match the demands of exporting?
- how effective is our promotional publicity, technical and service support back-up function?
- do we have banking support with detailed understanding of exporting?
- does the company have the working capital to fund the additional demands of exporting?

3 What market research information do we have on each country that may be a potential target, covering:

- the economy?
- internal politics?
- all aspects of legislation?
- tarriff and non-tariff barriers?
- market demand/need for the products/services we can offer?
- competitive activity from local manufacturers/other exporting countries/ from within our own country?
- the technical, financial and distribution stengths of the competition, particularly those involved in local manufacture?
- the distribution chains?
- the advertising, exhibition and other promotional requirements of the market?
- the likely time-scale before demand declines or barriers are imposed to stop imports?

4 What market research information is needed, and what is the most cost-effective method of entering into the market, and why?

5 What grant and aid schemes can be used to fund part or all of the market research, and, where possible, the initial market entry?

6 Which should be the key markets, and why?

7 Which distribution channel will be the most cost-effective method of entering the market, and why?

8 What detailed product modifications, plus technical support literature, will be required to enter into each market?

9 What are the objectives for each target market?

10 Who should take overall charge of the export function, and why?

11 Who should have direct day-to-day management responsibility, and why?

12 What is the ideal administration structure and profile for the staff needed?

13 What is the ideal profile for the export sales personnel?

14 What are the implications to the company's insurance policies, covering staff, travel, medical, life, pension and product liability, of entering into exporting activites?

15 How is effective communication between the export function and the other departments going to be maintained on a regular basis?

16 What management controls should be implemented?

17 How will forward likely demand be assessed and monitored?

18 What level of authority and discretion is needed by the export staff, and how will this be defined and controlled to ensure that the market place is satisfied without loss of control by the company?

19 How is the export function to be financially monitored, to be able to show its true net contribution to the business or operational profitability?

FURTHER READING

Danton de Rouffignac, Peter, *How to Sell to Europe*, Pitman, London, 1990

Hibbert, Edgar P., *Marketing Strategy in International Business*, McGraw-Hill, Maidenhead, 1988

Katz, B., *Managing Export Marketing*, Gower, Aldershot, 1987

Monk, Keith, *Go International: Your Guide to Marketing and Business Development*, McGraw-Hill, Maidenhead, 1989

Noonan, C., *Practical Export Management*, Allen & Unwin, London, 1985 Chapter 47

Paliwoda, Stan, *International Marketing*, Heinemann, London, 1986

Venedikian, H.M. and Warfield, G.A., *Export–import Financing*, 2nd edn, Wiley, New York, 1986

West, A., *Marketing Overseas*, Pitman, London, 1987

Chapter 47 complements this chapter and includes more reading references, plus a list of useful organizations.

26 Promotional public relations

David Wragg

Public relations is concerned with the relationship between an organization and those audiences regarded as being essential to the organization's success. The term 'promotional public relations', covers primarily the use of public relations techniques to help an organization market its goods or services. This fundamental element of public relations activity is often not given the weight it deserves, which could be explained by the fact that PR is a low-cost activity compared with advertising and there is the temptation in most organizations to value services by expenditure rather than by impact.

One of the most important aspects of public relations is press, or media, relations. In promotional terms, we can see the difference between media relations and advertising in that with advertising one pays for the space or the air time, and can use this in whatever way one chooses, but with media relations the space is free, but there is less control over the message. The other big difference is, of course, that generally people do not buy newspapers or tune into broadcasting stations for the advertising, and editorial coverage of an organization's products or services is more likely to be accepted because of the presumed independence of the journalist.

Obtaining the necessary media coverage requires skill and judgement, as well as the ability to target publicity material to the right type of publication and, more importantly, to the journalist who is most likely to be interested in the story. PR is often regarded as being an imprecise tool for promotional activity – it is not. The failure lies in the inability of many practitioners to target material precisely. This is difficult enough to do in countries with a substantial national press; it is still more difficult – yet, by the same standard, even more important – in those countries which lack a substantial national press (such as the United States and Spain, to give examples on both sides of the Atlantic).

PR, though, is more than simply media relations. In promotional terms, PR also extends to sponsorship, which can be one way of reaching specific audiences even more precisely. Sponsorship could be used, for example, to entertain dealers or professional connections, or to bypass a ban on television advertising of certain products, as indeed happens with the tobacco industry in the United Kingdom.

THE PUBLIC RELATIONS INDUSTRY

Most large organizations have their own public relations department – the 'in-house' PR function – while smaller businesses often find outside consultants more suitable. Consultants are also useful for work on specific projects, and a hybrid arrangement – both in-house and consultancy – can sometimes be appropriate depending on the circumstances of a particular business.

The term 'consultant' sounds imposing, but it has its origins in the difference between advertising agencies (who receive commission from the media as a contribution towards their costs) and PR consultants (who receive a retainer). Generally, there is no difference between the experience available to individual PR practitioners, whether working in a consultancy or in-house, except in the case of specialized skills. Some PR people enjoy being consultants, while others prefer to be part of a management team within an organization.

One benefit of being a consultant is that outsiders are generally viewed as being apart from the internal politics to which some organizations are prone. Also, some people, of course, would prefer advice from outsiders rather than insiders! That said, a consultancy can at times provide specialized advice to augment the skills of the in-house PR team, and can be of assistance if a new market is being developed – especially if there are likely to be language or similar problems to overcome.

When appointing a consultant, a brief should first be prepared on the organization and its products, and on exactly what is expected from the consultant. The retainer should be based on the services of a set number of the consultant's staff. Beware of any consultant who sets the retainer too low; those who do this to obtain the business in the first place are often those who will be quick to add extra items on to the bill. Many consultants follow the advertising agency practice of adding a handling fee to all work bought-in. It is advisable, therefore, to ask that all invoices from suppliers to the consultant be forwarded directly to your own accounts department for settlement, so that there is control over costs, and competitive quotes for items such as printing can be obtained and scrutinized.

MEDIA RELATIONS

Never forget that the media which will give the best publicity to your company or its products are in fact working for their own readers, listeners or viewers. Some media organizations may do favours for substantial advertisers, but the best will regard this practice as ethically wrong, except, perhaps, in a defined advertising supplement. Sometimes local newspapers or magazines will offer to carry a story if an advertisement is placed with them. The rule must be, however, that if the story is worthwhile they will want to carry it in any case as a service to their readers; or conversely, if advertising in a particular publication is such a good idea, it should not need to offer editorial space as an added inducement!

There are sometimes limitations to what can be achieved in terms of product promotion through the media. A well-established product which changes little from year to year has no news value. In this case, all that can be hoped for is that it will not be overlooked in regular surveys covering products of this nature, and that it will not be swamped by mentions of other identical offerings from your competitors. The exception, of course, is when the product gains valuable new business. There is always news space available to announce substantial new orders, especially if multimillion sums are involved. The rule is that standard products which vary little should be promoted through advertising or sponsorship.

The following points should be borne in mind when preparing media relations campaigns.

1 Targeting the right media, and the right journalists

Nothing is worse than sending material – be it press releases, features or photographs – to publications which are not interested. This undermines the credibility of your organization. For example, if your business is aircraft leasing, do not send material to publications aimed at aircraft enthusiasts! Even when the publication is right, do try to reach the right journalists; for example, avoid sending *personal* finance writers stories about *business* loans.

2 What are you offering?

Differentiate between 'news', which has to be genuinely new and significant, and 'features', which provide background information. Look at the types of stories which various publications regard as being newsworthy to judge whether your message is significant.

3 A picture is worth a thousand words

If the product is something which can be photographed, decide whether a photograph will add something to the story, but try to avoid sterile showroom photographs. Show the product in a working environment and, if practicable and realistic, with people using the product. Good pictures are so few and far between that they will be used by many publications.

4 Is a press conference really necessary?

A press conference is not a necessity. Journalists are invited to so many and too few are worthwhile. Only really big stories, and usually controversial ones, deserve this treatment.

Your media list must be up to date. There are good reference books available, some of which are updated monthly, which means that there is little excuse for not getting this aspect right. Even better, if press releases are issued frequently, subscribe to a service (for example, PNA Targeter in the UK) which is computer-based and enables word processors to link into a central computer, find the mailing lists required and print address labels. When preparing a press release, remember the following points:

1 Is the story really newsworthy? If so, to whom?
2 Which media will be most interested? National, regional, local, special interest or trade?
3 When should the news be released? Avoid weekends, but will it be worthwhile letting the periodicals with their longer lead times have the story early so that they do not lag too far behind the daily press?
4 Does it give the salient points simply, without raising fresh questions or misunderstandings? Remember:

- never say 'announces', since that is a statement of the obvious
- the essence of the news must be in the headline

- the first paragraph should include all that is necessary, so that if space or time is short it can be used on its own

5 If a photograph would help, which media would use it and will they need black and white prints or colour transparencies?
6 Should journalists be encouraged to sample the product? If so, arrangements will have to be made in advance (before the launch of a new car, for example). In some cases (although obviously not with cars) samples can be sent, but do be sure that this will add to the coverage. And be sensible about this. The purpose of samples is to help journalists to write a story, and they must not appear as a bribe
7 Provide a contact name, with a home telephone number if necessary, for follow-up enquiries by journalists. After all, journalists are often working in the evenings on morning newspapers, and also work over weekends
8 It is also worthwhile considering whether or not press releases can be localized, so that local branch or regional management have quotes attributed to them, rather than to someone at head office. This gives the story a 'local' angle, which encourages the press to consider using it and reminds prospective customers of your local presence. Using a word processor, such a system is easy to introduce. Careful planning and attention to detail will ensure that newspapers do not receive material which refers to someone outside their circulation area.

Some terrible mistakes are made – it is not unknown for radio stations to receive photographs!

Product information is sometimes carried by screen-based services. In the UK stories with an overseas angle can be distributed with the help of the Central Office of Information. Also take into account press agencies and the offices of foreign newspapers in your country. A good way of getting an urgent story (perhaps announcing a major new order, for example) to the widest possible range of publications, and to broadcast media as well, is to subscribe to Universal News Services (UNS) who operate a wire service direct into the newsroom computers of most British and some other media.

Of course, the features pages offer another possibility: covering products which might no longer be newsworthy. Regular features on personal finance, gardening, travel, and so on, should cover the main offerings by companies involved in these fields. The point is, of course, that journalists need to be aware of what is on offer, of the advantages of the product, and of its availability to their readers. Many journalists are able to sample products although much depends on the product, since one cannot really sample a mortgage, private medical care or a pension. It is usual for literary critics to receive review copies of books which are shortly to be published, and the same happens with new records or cassettes. Motoring correspondents are given the chance to test drive new cars, and new designs of pleasure craft and even new aircraft, including airliners, can be tested.

Timing is important, so that the journalist concerned can sample the product before launch, if possible. Travel companies often provide facility trips for journalists during the quieter periods when they will not be taking up accommodation which the paying customer might want. The difficulty is that the story for the

January holiday supplement may have been researched by a travel writer during the preceding autumn or even spring, and so the conscientious manager will ensure that up-dated tariffs and other details, and product changes, will be forwarded to interested journalists in good time for them to write their stories.

Travel writers are not the only journalists who often work far in advance; so do some magazines, and most especially those dealing with feminine interests. This means that information on spring fashions will have to be available before Christmas, while product information for a Christmas present idea will need to be with the magazine during August. These requirements do place strains on product launch arrangements, and force decisions on prices and distribution more quickly than might be wished.

You or your representative will meet journalists from time to time, or at least speak to them over the telephone. Do remember that everything said is on-the-record unless you preface a comment with a condition and have the agreement of the journalist. The usual conditions are:

- *Off the record*, which means that it is background briefing to stop the journalist making a false assumption and misleading his readers
- *Non-attributable*, which allows journalists to report a comment or a piece of information, without revealing their source.

Few journalists will allow their copy (that is, their story) to be vetted but, if they do, keep any changes to matters of fact, not style. If you are in any doubt on this point and do not wish to offend an important journalist by offering to vet his work, simply say that if they require clarification of any points while they are writing their story, you would be delighted to help. Quite often, especially with trade newspapers, this leads to the offer of a sight of the draft.

If you do have PR advisers, whether they are in-house or consultants, do make sure that they have someone present at meetings between you and the media, since this is a safeguard for both parties and keeps the PR person up to date on how far you and the organization are prepared to go in terms of press comment. It also acts as a briefing for the PR person, who will then have responsibility for liaising with the journalist, should the latter ask for additional material, such as further background information or photographs, which can so often be required even after the best-planned interview.

SPONSORSHIP

Sponsorship by business organizations has largely replaced private patronage. In some cases, the reasons for sponsorship have remained the same as they always were: that is, businesses have assumed the mantle of providing for activities which are worthwhile but which cannot be commercially viable. Most sponsorship by business today, however, is in pursuit of commercial objectives, using sponsorship to raise name awareness amongst a particular target audience, to entertain customers or dealers, or to establish goodwill in a particular part of the community whose support is regarded as valuable. A business which is a new arrival in a particular area will often sponsor community projects or entertainment of interest to many in the locality, in order to raise its profile and create the feeling amongst the local inhabitants that the newcomer is a valuable addition to the local business scene.

A different sponsorship angle has emerged in recent years with the ban on television advertising of tobacco products in a number of countries in the developed world. One means of bypassing this ban has been for the tobacco companies to sponsor activities, and especially sporting activites, which have been televised. Pressure to end this loophole has been growing. It will be interesting to see just how much sponsorship by the tobacco industry will survive any ban on the televising of sporting events supported by that industry.

The requirements of sponsors differ. A relatively modest sum will often suffice to provide an entertainment facility, but events worthy of televised coverage will be far more expensive. Local sponsorship is cheap for a single event or opportunity, but for a business with a nationwide coverage, a larger number of small local events will have less impact (yet cost as much) as a single major national event. Sometimes it is better to sponsor a sporting body or a series of events so that there is continuity and repetition of the sponsorship link.

It is important to be aware of the objective before considering sponsorship. If the aim is to promote a product or service, then the artistic or sporting event to be sponsored must be one which will interest the likely target market. The same can be said about image-building exercises. The interests of the target audience must be understood, and therefore the first step must be to define that audience. Sponsorship must also be appropriate to the product. For example, it makes sense for car ferry companies and motor products businesses to support motor sport, but this would be a nonsense for a pharmaceuticals manufacturer. Similarly, a life assurance business might sponsor cricket or golf because the target audience will be mainly professional and mainly male.

Certain types of sponsorship have controversy attached to them. Football is associated with violence in many countries, while horse racing has suggestions of gambling or, in some types of event, injury to animals. These circumstances might provoke an adverse reaction from some customers or potential customers. On the other hand, show jumping sponsorship seems to work for manufacturers of four-wheel drive vehicles.

Ideally, the sponsored event should allow the sponsor ample opportunities for a mention of the sponsorship, especially if it is the sole or main sponsorship. The best opportunities are those which allow the sponsor's name to be included in the title of the event or occasion, but this is not always possible. It is important at times to allow additional funds so that the sponsorship can be advertised. Sometimes the sponsor can also gain goodwill, and increase the chance of a kindly editorial mention, if assistance can be provided by the sponsor for the media at the actual events. For example, the sponsor will provide facilities and entertainment for art critics to see a preview of an art exhibition or a dress rehearsal of a play, or will ensure that there are sufficient desks, typewriters and telephones, and coffee, in the press room at a sporting event. Some journalists object to mentioning the name of a sponsor, but many will compromise. Never expect a mention in every sentence, but one mention in a report on a sporting fixture or the statutory two mentions in a broadcast are neither unreasonable nor unrealistic.

Beware of shared sponsorship, unless, of course, all that is required is an entertainment facility in return for the money! Usually, little worthwhile publicity is gained by either sponsor. Sometimes, however, shared sponsorship occurs by accident, as when two teams, sponsored by different businesses, come together for a game.

FURTHER READING

Bland, M., *Be Your Own PR Man*, Kogan Page, 1981

Gillies, Caroline, *Business Sponsorship*, Heinemann, Oxford, 1990

Jefkins, F., *Public Relations*, 3rd edn, M & E series, Pitman, London, 1988

Jefkins, F., *Public Relations Techniques*, Heinemann, Oxford, 1988

Lloyd, H., *Teach Yourself Public Relations*, Hodder & Stoughton, Sevenoaks, 1980

Turner, Stuart, *Practical Sponsorship*, Kogan Page, London, 1987

Wragg, David W., *Public Relations for Sales and Marketing*, Kogan Page, 1987

27 Direct mail

Nicholas O'Shaughnessy

Direct mail is part of the clutter of daily living. It belongs to the much larger category of direct response advertising and is, therefore, cousin to the colour supplement advertisements, televised record sales, catalogues and so forth. Yet it seldom evokes affection in the consumer. This chapter seeks to explain why and to substantiate the claim that, when properly carried out, direct mail ceases to have the character of an afterthought and can be the centre of the marketing campaign.

THE CASE FOR DIRECT MAIL

Targeting

Segmentation, the ability to target and tailor, is the critical consideration in the measurement of any marketing medium. On this, direct mail scores very highly indeed: for its distinctive merit is the potential to target market segments with greater precision than any other method, apart from the sales visit itself. Direct mailing segments can be refined to an infinite degree, as long as we can obtain further information about target prospects.

Direct mail is effective because, being personalized, it flatters people's own importance: they appear to have been chosen by invisible judges to join an elite group – perhaps they do not realize how mechanical the whole business is, and think that great effort has been invested in discovering and writing to them: 'Direct mail succeeds because unlike other media it can deliver a specialized message to distinctive groups, made personal through the agency of new technology and therefore engendering unique loyalties' (O'Shaughnessy and Peele, 1985). Because direct mail has the special ability to be made personal it can create a strong adherence, with the impression given that the needs of some particular group are being especially targeted. It can be tuned to specific elements in the market – those wanting a more lively appeal, perhaps, or those whose loyalty needs reinforcing, or people contemplating purchase for the first time.

In contrast to direct mail, television as a medium has serious deficiencies. Its costs have continued to soar above the level of inflation. There is the difficulty in targeting, since most programmes are delivered to a broad audience, so that television advertising is best suited to consumer non-durables. But the future in marketing lies in precision targeting, where direct mail excels. A general market appeal, communicated through more public media, may be bland because of the heterogeneous nature of the target audience; mail will allow us to be more lucid and vigorous with specific groups, heightening the message and tone of the original appeal. Seldom can television attain the personal, intimate voice of direct mail. But the two can work together: television makes us feel familiar with a product or personality, and direct mail is a logical extension of this association. They can create a sense of relationship in the consumer. The illusion of personality is cast over an automated process.

Other benefits

Direct mail is rich in creative possibilities. The letter can ostensibly come from a corporate potentate or a celebrity. The tone can range from bargain basement to elitist, and all kinds of imaginative ingenuity are possible – pop-ups, three dimensions, stamps, coins. All such alternatives can be pre-tested. Gifts, collectables, photos, peel-offs, numbers, seals, samples, tokens, brochures and so on – all can be experimented with. And the intangible incentives it can offer are numberless – clubs and memberships, price offers, guarantees, to name a few (Nash, 1986).

Direct mail can be speedily produced, unlike a conventional advertising campaign. Thus it can respond to fluctuations in taste, new assaults by rivals, the threat from new substitutes and the like. It is a potential public relations tool which can counter negative publicity: it does not demand the contracts, deadlines and long-range planning of other media. It is very well suited to fluid commercial operations such as share issues and financial products: anything in fact where a sudden shift is an important part of the commercial environment.

This speed and flexibility of direct mail explain its use in American political campaigning. For certain product categories and situations it could be critical – for a firm that wished to bemuse a competitor with an updated model, or introduce a new product, it would be a way of announcing the news speedily and dramatically to the target markets.

Another merit of direct mail is that its effectiveness can be accurately evaluated. The mail can be pre-tested, and we determine from a sample the impact of the final mailing. Different types of copy, package and offer are tested for their response rates. Thus, an alert direct mailer can continually improve, and learn the most persuasive types of appeal to make: the assessment and refinement of other forms of advertising and promotion are necessarily much vaguer. The consequence of this is that the labour of finding details and fashioning appeals would be handsomely repaid. Currently, the targeting potential created by the information revolution goes unexploited.

Direct mail confers many other benefits on its sponsors. For example:

1 It enables us to publish a lengthy, reasoned appeal, and in some selling contexts this could be a merit. It can lend the appearance of logical argument, of a rationally constructed case, even though the covert appeal is nearly always to emotion
2 Direct mail has curiosity appeal – our wish to unpack it and discover what is actually there. Indeed, there is a virtual guarantee that this sort of advertising is noticed, because it intrudes on our attention in a way that newspapers, magazines and even television cannot wholly match
3 Direct mail can create a latent want, with the consumer subsequently stirred

to purchase action by some other more immediate market or situation stimulus

4   While direct mail marketers incur the cost of list hire, printing and posting, they avoid many of the costs associated with wholesale/retail distribution

5   Direct mail offers great potential for comparative and even negative and alarmist advertising, although it would be tactless to advocate this. Personalized, negative mail appeals garnered high levels of support for many American politicians and pressure groups: the same tactics would probably work in some commercial situations (Crawford, 1981)

6   The use of several different media can be reinforcing and create variety, using perhaps the same motifs and personalities to lend a consistent identity

7   The mail can also compensate for weaknesses, allowing for a firmer revival than might be obtained by investing more money in more costly mediums: for example, when a few extra television advertisements may have scant effect. Again, though, it is a mistake to see these elements as conflicting: responses to a television advertisement can in themselves build a mailing list

8   It has been claimed that direct mail increases the efficiency of the sales force by 50 per cent when the two are used in conjunction (Gosden, 1985)

9   Technology in the area is constantly improving: the effects – increased speed and lower price – make direct mail more attractive and within the budget of smaller businesses. A personal computer can easily deal with 10 000 letters

10 Business-to-business direct mail is also growing in popularity, partly as a consequence of the increasing cost of the sales call (Gosden, 1985)

Historically direct mail has not been fully understood and has therefore been imperfectly exploited; often in the past it has been employed by firms which could not afford conventional distribution channels. It is bound to perform better as a habitual pattern of ordering things by mail or telephone solidifies. Indeed, younger people may adjust more easily: the more the behavioural trend moves in that direction, the better the prospects. Consumer acceptance of direct mail is growing, partly as a consequence of the increasing professionalism and sophistication of the mail itself (Gosden, 1985). It is widely believed that suspicions of a mail 'glut' are unjustified, that in fact people like it (Gosden, 1985). 'Junk' mail is only perceived as such if it looks tawdry.

SOCIAL DIRECT MAIL

Direct mail is also useful for non-commercial institutions as a highly effective technology for fund raising. Charities – as indeed commercial organizations – are finding that, having performed an initial act of commitment, people feel predisposed to do so again. This makes direct mail a powerful tool for public pressure purposes, for it is an adept lobbying instrument as a consequence of its ability to foment emotional adherence. For example, Alaskan legislators were influenced over balanced budgets by constituents encouraged by a direct mail campaign (Snyder, 1982).

It represents a device for discovering and exploiting possible supporters, and its potential in this area has yet to be fully recognized: 'it is effective because it introduces the concept of membership – people are made to feel part of a group, the essence of which is shared information' (O'Shaughnessy and Peele, 1985).

In America direct mail fund raising was the rightist response to the agitation politics of the left: conservatives were attracted by its ability to mobilize public pressure without the need for public demonstrations. It helped to defeat twelve liberal senators between 1976 and 1980. Mailers satisfied the American right's need for a ringing articulation of their values that cut through the compromise, evasion and restraint of ordinary politics, and in so doing they seemed for a time to be undermining the party system. The Republican party, however, began to draw strength itself from direct mail, expanding its donor base from 34 000 in the early 1970s to 2.7 million in 1983; contributions amounted to $8 million in 1975 and $92 million by the end of 1982, and 80 per cent of this sum was the result of direct mail solicitation (Harris, 1982).

From political mail, in particular, consumer marketing has much to learn. The mail is the demagogue's own medium, and through its agency 'new right' entrepreneurs have raised fortunes. Rightist consultant Richard Viguerie, for instance, has the names and addresses of 30 million conservative Americans on tape in a guarded vault.

America's political consultants employ the large amounts of available census data; and the so-called ethnicity tapes. They accumulate large lists of names. They are expert in the art of composing a letter, the subtle artifice in a superficially unsubtle product. The quality of political direct mail is often higher than the commercial, because the consultants have learnt to exploit the potential of precisely targeted direct mail to stir emotion. There is no endeavour to build up a reasoned, factual case. Arguments always present a picture which even true believers know to be overdrawn. By contrast, the targeting of commercial direct mail is often more vague: its sponsors make less effort to segment their audience and hence their mailings are more general, therefore less effective. Nor do they exploit emotion beyond material desire: there is no passion in what they do. And clearly, with many products, passion is irrelevant: few, for example, would feel genuinely infatuated with a food mixer. But other products do potentially involve deep emotion – the connection between insurance and fear for example.

THE CASE AGAINST DIRECT MAIL

Direct mail yields its best dividends over the long term. Testing and building lists are laborious operations: the logic of this is that mail gives its optimum performance when it becomes a permanent institution rather than an occasional experiment – to be effective it must be made an established marketing ancillary. Other limitations include the expense of prospecting (Gosden, 1985).

Direct mail suffers from many of the drawbacks conventionally associated with advertising. There is the danger of exhausting one particular kind of creative approach or thesis, and therefore a need for vigilance. Then there is the often quoted danger of over-solicitation. In America the average household now receives fifteen items of commercial direct mail every week, and there is an obvious risk when people recruit from the same list. On this subject we have argued:

Some claim that direct mail has an optimum level of impact after which its effect declines. This might be true if every direct mail shot were similar, but it is arguable that the medium can be given infinitely varied content that might push back a saturation point, if within limits it exists at all. (O'Shaughnessy and Peele, 1985)

The mail has curiosity appeal and ministers to a sense of being wanted.

Direct mail is misunderstood, especially in the UK. Mailings resemble each other too closely, they may appear cheap, they target the same lists too often and too imprecisely: it is therefore not surprising that people complain, and that the genre is discredited. Fault lies not with the concept but the tactical execution. Superior direct mailings will not arouse antagonism in people: they will be accepted and even welcomed as a mature way of seeking business among adult citizens.

THE MECHANICS OF DIRECT MAIL

Mailers must clarify their target audiences via operational criteria which state the exclusive characteristics of those in the segment. The essence of direct mail is the discovery of reliable names: the house list is the key strategic armament. This is a composite of names obtained by past prospecting and other names already in the firm's possession, and replies from lists supplied by research and commercial purchase. The quality of such lists will dictate the success or failure of direct mail operations. They must be cleared of habitual non-respondents, absentees and so on (Nash, 1986): they must be laden with detail so the list can be divided into sub-segments.

Lists are, therefore, critical. They can be derived from membership and subscription lists, banks, retailers, newspaper clipping bureaux, public records, professional registers and magazine readers. They can also be bought from professional list brokers. In America the *Standard Rate and Data Service Guide to Consumer Mailing Lists* (Skokie, Illinois) provides 1 000 pages of detail about every consumer list on offer (Nash, 1986). Lists can be bartered and exchanged between firms. There are of course business lists as well as consumer (here the rate of change is high – in America 20 per cent). Technology is supple enough to disaggregate names into every conceivable kind of list: in America there are even 'ethnicity tapes' that pinpoint the national origins of names. By way of example, Figure 27.1 shows the number of lists and list members available to certain product categories in the US.

Lists are also generated by 'geo-demographics'. The availability of local data makes it possible to label small areas according to class, social and other demographic and economic factors. We can evolve a fixed number of labels applicable throughout the country and use this as a method of targeting: the ACORN system does this in the UK. In America the richness of census detail makes it possible to use this method with some refinement – for instance, the thirty audience cell and sub-cell demographics (Gosden, 1985) which the census provides about each community include the following.

1 Percentage of households with income of $25 000 a year and over
2 Percentage of owner-occupied households
3 Percentage of households with children under three years old

List Category	No. of lists	Universe (000)
Cell 1		
Art, antiques, collectables	31	2 995
Cultural books and magazines	31	5 232
Cultural arts	7	485
Subtotal	69	8 712
Cell 2		
Upscale gifts and decorating items	24	2 088
Photography	5	969
Regional publications	20	2 732
Subtotal	49	5 789
Cell 3		
Luxury foods, home entertainment	16	3 316
Affluent, upscale life-style	8	843
Miscellaneous (credit cards)	5	1 732
Subtotal	29	5 891
Total	147	20 392*

*Reduced by 25 per cent due to duplication factor.

Figure 27.1   Art and artefacts: list markets in USA (Harper, 1986)

4   Ratio of children of five years old and under to household
5   Percentage of black households
6   Percentage of households that are one-unit structures (based on Metromail count)
7   Percentage of households that are ten or more unit structures (based on Metromail count).

Periodic mailings, rather than the isolated mail shot, may cement loyalties aroused, for the initial commitment becomes a decision precedent so that we may feel like buying again.

In direct mail, errors are often made with the letter. The evidence suggests that the more it resembles a real letter the more persuasive it is. I am not qualified to comment on the psychological intricacies of this: it simply works. Poor direct mail is a pastiche of a real letter: quality work looks exactly like a personal letter from a professional individual. The letter will be based on empirical investigation, but as in any form of copywriting its power will also be a function of intuitive insight.

The letter should motivate to action, the sole criterion of its effectiveness. Consequently, the appeal is often squarely to emotion. Details of print and layout are significant; it may even look like a handwritten letter, perhaps a rather artificial

device. It is particularly important to seek to overcome the inertia and incon-
venience of reply: the reply must be prepaid and easy to complete; telephone
payment via credit card should be available.

The envelopes should be smart; depending on the target market they may be
attractive and eye-catching. Letters are often long, though there is no set ortho-
doxy here: but usually their language is fairly simple, with reader attention
retained by subheadings, brief, snappy words and the use of colourful images.
There is ample room for vivid graphics. Business mail, of course, would be
somewhat different in tone as it performs a different function – at the very least, it
reaches the same audience in another mood and capacity.

Good copy is the way to successful direct mail. This demands skill to attain a
seemingly effortless effect: the art that conceals art. In practice much direct mail
exudes a false euphoria: it is a genre that has not really caught the popular
imagination – people perceive it as mediocre. It exhibits none of the artifice of, say,
a television advertisement: it remains marketing's poor cousin. Does the banality
really represent direct mail executives' opinion of the status of their market?

Much direct mail remains an obtuse instrument because it is imitative in vein:
success can be achieved, as in all forms of advertising, by simply going against the
convention and surprising public expectations.

CONCLUSIONS

The potential of direct mail is enhanced by several contemporary trends. The
information revolution has entailed more obtainable information about increasing
numbers of people. This means that the central conditions under which direct mail
is sustainable will be there, enabling the fine tuning of copy to segment.

Direct mail's effectiveness is magnified by the social trend to home centredness
and convenience; shopping, business, political and social activities are increasingly located in the home rather than in the external community – hence Alvin
Toffler's 'electronic cottage'. One day shopping itself will be possible on direct
response television, with electronic catalogues; printed direct mail will one day
become anachronistic. However, direct mailers now benefit from this trend to a
society of muffled introverts. Yet the medium remains only moderately exploited
because it is moderately understood – conventional wisdom in the area has not
developed the same sophistication as in other marketing media. It has the characteristic of an afterthought.

Elsewhere I have argued (in the context of politics, but the same applies to
commerce) that direct mail reflects two trends – from mass media to tailored and
targeted media, and from direct action to the armchair approach, and that having
grasped that the element of personalization is central to the success of direct mail,
technology will seek ways of taking this further. Companies will speak with an
increasingly private voice: even the television medium will become targeted as
channels and outlets expand. But at the moment 'it is infrequently trusted with a
pivotal function and this junior role may make it a relatively unfruitful use of
resources' (O'Shaughnessy and Peele, 1985). Finally, there follows a direct mail
checklist.

1 Test mail different types of copy first. Much of the profit comes on subsequent mailings, not on the first, cold mailing
2 Direct mail can be used in conjunction with other media, for example radio, telephone, personal vists
3 The identity of the person who purports to send the letter is important, and ideally has some special relevance to the person who receives it
4 The letter must be intimate and personal
5 It must completely resemble a 'real' letter
6 Direct mail is a subtle and much misunderstood medium. How the copy is written is critical to its success; copy can be much more hard-hitting than when aimed at the general, unsegmented public
7 The danger in direct mail lies in mass, undifferentiated solicitation. The key ingredients of good mail are:

- emotive copy
- smart, highly personalized letters
- ease of reply
- good lists.

FURTHER READING

Crawford, A., *Thunder on the Right*, Pantheon Books, New York, 1980

Dale, A., *Direct Mail List Building*, Post Office, London

Fairlie, R., *Direct Mail Testing and Measurement*, Post Office, London

Gosden, F.F., *Direct Marketing Success*, Wiley, New York, 1985

Harris, P.C., 'Politics by mail: a new platform', *Wharton Magazine*, pp. 16, 18, 19, Fall, 1982

Harper, R., *Mailing List Strategies*, McGraw-Hill, New York, 1986

Jefkins, Frank, *The Secrets of Successful Direct Marketing*, Heinemann, Oxford, 1989

Nash, E.L., *Direct Marketing*, McGraw-Hill, New York, 1986

O'Shaughnessy, N.J. and Peele, G., 'Money and mail markets', *Electoral Studies*, vol. 4, no. 2, August, 1985

Snyder, J.P., 'Playing politics by mail', *Sales and Marketing Management*, pp. 44–6, 5 July, 1982

Stone, Bob, *Successful Direct Marketing Methods*, 4th edn, Crain Books, Chicago, 1988

28 Managing a sales force

M T Wilson

The strategy of marketing is concerned with arranging the resources of the company so that the needs of customers can be satisfied by presenting to them a product/price offering which, when purchased, provides a profit to the firm. This strategy is implemented through a number of tactical tools, some concerned with finding out what the needs are (marketing research), some with ensuring the product/price offering is correct (product development and testing), and some with presenting the offering to the customer. The sales function is an important tactic in this last area, while having a role to play in the first two.

The importance of the sales function cannot be over-emphasized in those companies where the bulk of the presentational effort is carried by the sales force. This covers most industrial and speciality markets and many consumer goods industries. In fact, it is not exaggerating far to say that in some markets – for example, office equipment and life insurance – the main difference between competing companies lies in the quality of their sales forces.

Moreover, the sales force can make valuable contributions in the definition of market segments and customer needs, and product development and rationalization. This is particularly true in industrial markets, where formal market research is less used. Obviously, since salesmen are not usually trained researchers, the information they collect has to be treated with care.

As sales management is a function (often the most important) within the marketing strategy, it is essential for the sales manager at least to be aware of the other tactics of marketing so that he can contribute to and benefit from them. These include:

1 New product development
2 Distribution
3 Sales forecasting
4 Pricing
5 Advertising and sales promotion
6 Public relations
7 Marketing planning and control (particularly the financial aspects).

In some companies the sales manager will directly control some of these; in others, they will be looked after by marketing staff. In every firm, the sales manager must integrate his activities with the rest of the marketing effort if the maximum value is to be gained from marketing expenditure.

The sales manager is the key person in developing a successful sales operation.

He or she must do this by managing a team – not by doing their jobs for them. As a manager he or she is responsible for working through others to achieve economic objectives, but this process is hindered by the difficulties of dealing with geographically spread subordinates who spend most of their time with people other than their colleagues.

To do their job successfully, sales managers must possess knowledge and skill in four major areas: selling, management, sales management and marketing. Only then can they claim to be fully productive members of the executive team.

Sales management comprises five key elements – planning, organization, training, motivation and control. It is on these that this chapter concentrates.

HOW TO PLAN THE SALES OPERATION

The planning process is only one part of the basic and repetitive management activity necessary in any company seeking to grow. The firm must continuously answer three questions:

1 Where are we going? This is the objective-setting process
2 How shall we get there? This is the planning process
3 How shall we know if we are getting there? This is the control process.

These questions first appear at top management level and the answers constitute the corporate objectives, corporate plans and policies, and corporate control mechanisms. Typically, they will result in a statement of the profit objectives of the company (usually expressed in terms of return on capital employed), a description of the business the company is in and its desired position in that industry, its plans and policies for each function of the company, and specific goals and targets to be met within set time-periods.

The whole process will then be repeated for each function of the company. Thus, marketing, production, R and D, finance and so on, will each formulate its objectives, plans and controls. Within the marketing framework, the sales manager must specify his answers to the three questions in order to produce a format for his staff to work to. Each salesman may well be required to repeat the process with individual customers.

The sales manager's role in the continuum is obviously critical. If he fails to set clear objectives that are compatible within the hierarchy and does not initiate the appropriate action, the whole firm must suffer.

Setting sales objectives

The sales manager will commence by considering the marketing objectives, policies and strategies and control criteria. He will probably have a forecast of sales by revenue and volume, a forecast of gross profit required, perhaps an expense budget, a description of the product range available with additions and deletions, price structure, promotional support, and so on.

Forecasting sales

In many firms the sales manager will be involved as a member of the marketing team in the definition of these items. The process will normally start with forecasting sales for the next period. This is the most critical prediction in the company as it will determine the production schedule, raw materials and finished stocks, promotional expenditure, and so forth. It is best to approach the forecast in two stages. First, what will sales be, assuming all variables in the situation are the same in the future as they have been in the past? Second, which variables will change and what will the impact be? Some of the variables will be internal factors which management decides to change; others will be external factors which are uncontrollable by the company but whose effect must be predicted.

Developing the sales plan

Having set the sales forecast and targets, the manager must now consider how they can be achieved. Obviously some thought will already have been given to the plan in formulating the objectives. After the plan is written it might well be necessary to reconsider the goals that were previously identified.

The sales manager has to consider five basic questions:

1 What is to be sold?
2 To whom?
3 At what price?
4 By what methods?
5 At what costs?

In some of these areas, notably the product range and pricing structure, he may well have limited influence; they are often controlled by the marketing planning department, through a brand or product management structure. In respect of all five he will certainly have to consider the inputs of other parts of the business. What stocks will be available from production, what money is available from finance, what advertising and sales promotion support is planned, and so on?

Deciding what is to be sold

In determining what the product range should be the sales manager can at least advise his marketing planning colleagues on the saleability of the various items in the range as well as new product requirements.

From a sales management viewpoint he will have to decide whether the full range should be sold to everybody. In some capital equipment markets, for example, where the distributor has to make a heavy investment in stock, it may not be in the interests of the company to supply dealers whose resources may not be adequate to finance the more costly products. Likewise, companies who have to make after-sales service arrangements may well decide not to sell products to customers who are geographically isolated.

To whom are the products to be sold

Next, the sales manager must consider the customers and prospects for his products. First, he will study the existing markets and decide whether business with them is likely to increase, decrease or remain static. This judgement will be based on a study of previous buying records.

By analysing customers in terms of their potential and actual purchasing of the various products he has to offer, he can identify the areas to be attacked. Prospective customers can be analysed in the same way.

Choosing the methods

Having identified from the product/market analysis the segments to be attacked, the sales manager can now consider the methods most likely to achieve the objectives set.

The first question to be answered is what sort of service should the sales force provide in order to influence the buyer? For example, a crop-protection firm pondering how to increase sales to agricultural merchants will have to consider how the merchant will market the product to farmers. Perhaps the job of the sales force in this case will be to help the merchant develop his skills.

Such an analysis of the kind of sales effort needed will lead to identification of the appropriate sales methods. The complexity of seller/buyer relationships becomes rapidly obvious. It is only by such definition that the sales manager can develop the presentational approach that will enable him to succeed in the face of product/price parity.

Having identified the nature of the sales method he can then consider the scale of effort required. He must calculate how many customers and prospects should be called on and how often.

The customers are relatively easy to specify because obviously they are known by name to the company. The level of prospecting is more difficult to calculate; as in many companies potential customers cannot be identified by name. At least, however, the sales manager can indicate the characteristics of likely prospects to be called upon. Alternatively, the sales manager can plan simply to allow a certain percentage of time or calls for seeking new business, giving the salesmen the responsibility of using the time or calls wisely.

How often calls should be made is always difficult to assess. Obviously different categories of accounts will require different call frequencies. In some trades where there is an established buying pattern, usually little is gained by calling at a different frequency.

The support of the field force will also be covered by the sales manager's study of the methods required to achieve his objectives. Parts of the supplier/buyer relationship can often be more economically handled by techniques other than personal visiting by representatives. Telephone selling is one method that is successfully used to handle routine ordering, thus freeing the salemen's costly time for more creative work.

Evaluating the costs of selling

The best approach is to look at the cost-effectiveness of the methods used and particularly to try to analyse the values gained for the costs incurred. For example, if the manager were concerned with the cost of generating prospects he could compare the cost per prospect from advertising, direct mail and cold canvassing. If he were analysing sales force activity, he might question what value was gained from 'courtesy calling' (that is, routine visiting to check that the customer is satisfied with the products and service supplied). In such a case the manager might experiment by eliminating such calls in a test area and evaluating what, if anything, happened to the sales.

HOW TO ORGANIZE THE SALES FORCE

Many sales organizations have developed without objective analysis of their purpose or structure. Today they are out of date and unable to fulfil the purposes for which they were originally designed. This is because the traditional hierarchical structure is based upon conditions which no longer hold true in a great number of firms. Such organizations assume that there is a large number of relatively small, geographically separate and independent buying-points all with similar requirements, and that these can be serviced by a large number of geographically separated salesmen who can perform similar tasks and who represent the major promotional activity of the company.

Changes in buyer/seller relationships

The foregoing suppositions have been made obsolete by two fundamental changes in the buyer/seller relationship.

First, the buying power in many industries is no longer evenly distributed. In a large number of markets, a few big firms control the majority of the purchasing decisions. These oligopolies, developed largely through the processes of merger and acquisition, have resulted in a dramatic reduction in the numbers of independent outlets in the trades concerned. Thus, whilst sales organizations' structures have in many cases changed little, the number and type of customers with whom they deal have altered dramatically.

Second, the development of new marketing techniques has meant that some tasks traditionally performed by the sales force can be more economically or efficiently handled by other methods. The development of advertising and sales promotion in general, as well as the growing use of specific techniques such as telephone selling and contract ordering, have all had an impact on the nature and scale of the sales effort required. Furthermore, the reduction in sales force sizes and improvements in communications have in some cases obviated the need for regionally based management.

The prime objective of all sales staff is to gain business. From an organizational point of view, however, how they are to achieve their goals must be defined in order to identify what kind and quality of skills are required.

Matching the sales effort to customer requirements

Organizing the sales effort so that it matches the reality of the market place can alleviate such problems. First, the level and quantity of customer service must be defined and the personnel concerned identified.

Such an analysis will also begin to identify the work-loads of each level and suggest ways of grouping the various elements so that they can be better managed.

The sales force structure should also be scrutinized. A geographical split may be the most economical in that travel time is minimized. It may not, however, be the most effective. In one glass-container company it was seen that the prime service to be provided to the buyer was a technical knowledge of bottling as applied to the customer's particular industry. Thus the sales force was regrouped on an industry basis, changing the organization structure. Obviously there was some increase in travel costs because each industry group worked nationally but this was more than offset by the increase in sales.

At sales force level common groupings other than geographical are by industry, by customer size category, by buyer type (for example, purchasers and specifiers), or by service to be provided (for example, order taking and merchandising).

By conducting a customer service requirements analysis the sales manager can identify which organizational approach is appropriate.

The number of sales staff needed

The aim of building an organization is to give the appropriate level of service to each customer and the appropriate amount of work to each person. The only factor common to all sales-staff is the number of working hours and this should be the starting point for a work-load analysis, which is the only really logical way of constructing a sales force. The amount of work per salesperson can then be calculated by assessing the elements and the time taken on each. Typically, they include: prospecting, travelling, waiting, selling and report writing. If the number of actual and potential accounts to be visited and the frequency of visiting can be assessed, it is possible to calculate the number of salespersons needed as follows:

$$\frac{\text{Number of actual and potential customers} \times \text{Call frequency}}{\text{Average daily call rate} \times \text{Number of working days per year}}$$

TRAINING THE SALES TEAM

The art of selling is the presentation of product benefits in such a way that the buyer is persuaded that his or her needs will be satisfied. If the salesperson is to be successful he or she must not only be knowledgeable about product and customer but also skilful in the presentation of this knowledge.

Induction training

When a new salesperson joins a company he or she should be given some form of training. Too often, even when training is given, the whole time is devoted to company and product knowledge in the hope (usually unfulfilled) that the sales-person will somehow pick up sales techniques in the field.

This initial training can be critical to the ultimate success of the new person as it will affect both his or her ability and morale. It must therefore be very carefully planned and skilfully executed.

The programme material will obviously vary from firm to firm, particularly in terms of the company and product knowledge to be taught.

There are, however, some basic areas of the sales job that should be included in most initial training courses, although with specific biases being given by different companies. Ten principal elements should be covered.

1 *The marketing concept and the role of the sales force* The salesperson must understand fully the part he or she plays in the total effort of the company. Otherwise he or she will find it difficult to integrate his or her work with that of other departments

2 *The nature of salesmanship* It is essential that the salesperson has a clear definition of what selling is, its role in society and the basic requirements of the sales job

3 *Communications* As selling depends on persuasive communication, the salesperson must understand the inherent difficulties of interpersonal rela-tionships and be given techniques for overcoming these problems. He or she must be skilled in other forms of communication, such as reporting and talking on the telephone

4 *Preparation for selling* This is normally a very weak area of sales skill and yet if a coherent, logical approach to the customer is to be adopted, it has to be structured in advance, and the technique for doing this has to be taught

5 *Prospecting* Every business depends to some extent on gaining new cus-tomers. This is probably the most difficult part of selling and the salesperson should be taught a systematic approach to the finding of potential buyers. Having learned how to look for new business, he or she will also be better motivated and less likely to avoid prospecting, as so often happens

6 *Opening the sale* Obtaining interviews with buyers and making the right impression in the early stages of the presentation are areas where skill is required. A casual approach will lead to failure to pass the receptionist or even when that is achieved, to curtailed, unsuccessful interviews

7 *Making sales presentations* To be effective as a persuader, the salesperson must be skilled in oral presentation, visual aid handling and product demon-stration. There is a body of techniques that can be learnt which will help the salesperson to communicate convincingly

8 *Handling objections* Every sales interview is likely to produce customer objections on such topics as price, delivery, and so on. Some of these can be prevented, others overcome. Certainly most objections can be predicted and the salesperson trained in the answers to be given and the methods of expressing them

9 *Closing the sale* Again, this is normally a very weak area because the sales-person fears rejection. He or she therefore tends to avoid it by never asking for the order. If the buyer is never asked to buy, the buyer never has to refuse. Obviously the whole point of selling is to gain sales and the salesperson can

be encouraged to request orders more often and more persuasively by thorough training in proven closing techniques

10 *Work organization*   The main emphasis of initial training is on improving the quality of the salesperson's skill. Due regard should also be paid to the quantity of selling so that the salesperson knows how to utilize his or her very limited time to the maximum. He or she should be taught techniques of journey planning and day planning.

Concept of customer orientation

Throughout the initial training programme certain themes will have to be constantly emphasized as some of the basic concepts are hard to instil. One of the most fundamental of these is the philosophy of customer orientation. Without this approach, the salesperson will find it hard to succeed and yet it is difficult to ensure that it will be practised.

Every salesperson must recognize that buyers buy to satisfy needs, both rational and emotional. These needs are fulfilled by benefits of the product and these benefits are derived from product features.

Because of the difficulty of reversing the viewpoint in this way, successful training in this concept can be hard to achieve. It is helped if a product analysis is demonstrated and this technique is inculcated so that the sales staff analyse the needs, benefits and features of a situation before they commence selling.

Field training

The objective of field training is to ensure a continuous improvement in the salesperson's performance. To achieve this goal there are five tasks that must be carried out by the manager:

1 Field performance must be assessed systematically against known standards
2 Deficiencies must be identified and agreed and coaching given in the knowledge and skills necessary to correct the identified faults
3 Guidance must be given on the self-training that is expected from the salesperson
4 Information should be collected about common faults that can be more economically or effectively corrected on a collective basis
5 The effectiveness of the initial training should be assessed so that it can be improved in the future.

Sales meetings

The regular gatherings of the sales team create the other chief opportunity for developing sales force performance. In all but the smallest sales forces, these are held at local level, where the regional, area or district manager meets with his salesforce. Where there are no intermediate supervisory levels between the national sales manager and the sales force these gatherings have to be held on a national basis. The objectives of such meetings should be:

1 To administer corporate training and development

2 To inform and get feedback from the sales force
3 To stimulate and if necessary rekindle the salesforce's enthusiasm and motivation
4 To provide a meeting place and forum for all the sales staff.

HOW TO MOTIVATE THE SALES FORCE

The motivation of salespersons is probably the most common topic of conversation whenever sales managers meet. Every manager has his own pet theories on how to get the best out of his team. The reason why it is such a popular discussion point is because sales staff can be directly supervised only intermittently. It is, therefore, vital to success that they are deeply motivated to work on their own. Moreover, the sales job inevitably involves loneliness and certain customer contacts which can depress the morale of any but the most enthusiastic salesperson.

The nature of motivation

Because of the geographical separation and the wearing aspects of the job, it is vital for success that the sales manager possesses or develops the ability to motivate his sales force. In order to do so he needs a clear understanding of why people work and what they wish to gain from their work. Only then can he create an environment which will cause his staff to apply their full abilities to their jobs.

Incentives and disincentives

The basis of motivation is the provision of incentives which encourage sales staff to give of their best and the removal of discentives which prevent them from devoting their whole energies to their work. Unfortunately, far too often, motivation is equated with incentives only, although it is common to find that the elimination of discentives – for example, unfair treatment – is the more powerful influence.

It must also be recognized that virtually every incentive brings with it a disincentive, either for the same person or for colleagues. For example, a competition may be a strong motivation for the winners; but it can be demoralizing for the losers, particularly if they believe that because of the poor construction of the contest they never had a real chance of winning.

The task of the manager is, therefore, to consider the needs of his team, both individually and as a group, and to arrange a balance of motivational influences that will encourage them to achieve the company's objectives. In essence, this is best done by ensuring that the individual's own goals in life are consistent with the aims of the firm. For example, there is little point recruiting people who are highly money-motivated into a company which offers security as its major satisfaction.

Although recognizing that everyone has his own individual need pattern, there are five motivational influences that the sales manager must fully understand. These are:

1 Remuneration
2 Direct incentives
3 Job satisfaction

4 Security
5 Status.

Remuneration

First, management should define the salary grades appropriate to the job level. This grade will represent the market value of the position as well as the worth of the job to the company. The bottom of the category will represent the remuneration of a man entering the position exhibiting minimum standards of performance, the upper limit being paid to a man who can achieve completely all the criteria of the job.

Second, the position of any individuals within their grade should be determined by their performance against the job standards. An average performer would therefore be paid at the mid-point of the grade. Thus, the salary philosophy will reflect the two main elements of a logical payment structure: the degree of responsibility carried by the position, and the effectiveness with which the person discharges it.

Payment by results system

Such an approach to job grading and appraisal presupposes that the salesperson will be remunerated at least in part by salary. Many sales forces are, of course, paid in addition, to some degree or another, according to results. In a relatively small number of companies the salesforce are paid entirely on commission. The choice of remuneration system – salary only, salary plus some form of commission, or commission only – will depend upon the desired mix of security and incentive.

Direct incentives

This term is used to cover the many systems of payment in cash or in kind other than basic remuneration. It includes fringe benefits, merchandise awards, point schemes and competitions. Apart from fringe benefits, such schemes do not usually make a significant difference to total earnings and their basic intention is motivational. Merchandise awards and competitive schemes are best used to focus short-term attention on particular aspects of the business. They are a tactical rather than a strategic motivational weapon. When employed in this way, they can be very effective to concentrate sales force attention on, for example, gaining new accounts, increasing sales of lower volume products, or even submitting call reports on time!

Job satisfaction

Direct incentives in either cash or kind are important elements in any motivational scheme. The so-called 'psychic wages' of the job however must be given at least equivalent priority. Sales staff spend more than half their waking life working. It is not surprising, therefore, that they seek fulfilment in the job as well as rewards for the job. It is an essential function of any manager to ensure that such satisfaction can be gained by the sales force from their work.

Security

The need for security is a very common, although seldom admitted, motive. The nature of the remuneration system and the relative importance of salary and commission will obviously affect job security and must be considered from this aspect.

However, the less obvious facets of security should not escape the sales manager's attention. In companies where insecurity is a constant feature of the environment, morale tends to be low and, although there is often an appearance of frenetic action, achievement is usually very limited.

Status

The sales manager can help to improve the status of selling within the company and the market by ensuring that the job titles given carry as much prestige as possible. He should ensure, too, that the rest of the company realizes the importance of the function so that when a customer telephones and asks for one of the field force by name, the switchboard operator does not reply that as Mr Smith is 'only one of our salesmen (or worse still, "travellers"), he is not in the office'. Likewise when the caller is eventually put through to the sales department, he should be greeted by someone who answers as 'Mr Smith's secretary' although he or she can, of course be secretary to a number of others as well.

The salesperson should be provided with the best possible equipment for his job. Well-printed visiting cards with his name in the middle, a well-made briefcase or sample case and good literature all contribute to his status in the eyes of his customers. His car is perhaps the most significant symbol of all, not only to his buyers but also to his family and friends.

HOW TO CONTROL THE SALES OPERATION

In order to control any activity, there must first be an objective and a plan. Unless it is known what is to be achieved and how, whether it is being achieved cannot be assessed. Conversely, there is little point in setting goals and defining actions unless there is an evaluation procedure.

For example, in one business equipment firm, the sales manager developed a system whereby he could analyse the monthly performance of every salesperson under eighteen different categories of activity. Thus, he could identify how many hours each man had spent on each facet of his job. He could ascertain for instance that salesman X spent seven and half hours on prospecting, saleswoman Y eight hours on report-writing. He obviously believed that control was constituted by the collection of detailed information. Such attitudes are common among sales management and part of the impact of computerization is that data suddenly becomes available in vast quantities, thus apparently giving even more minute control.

The concept of control

It must be realized that the collection of information, however accurate, up to date and detailed, in itself in no way constitutes control. This is for the very basic reason that there is little point in knowing what *has* happened unless there is a clear conception of what *should* have happened. Control can then be exercised by comparing actual performance with planned performance and deriving variances. It is on these variances that corrective action should be based. Control can be summarized therefore as:

$$A - S = \pm V$$

where A is the actual performance, S is the pre-set standard and V is the variance between the two.

To know that salesman X spent seven and half hours prospecting is meaningless by itself. However, if the standard for this activity is ten hours then there is a minus variance of two and half hours and it is this figure which should cause the manager to take corrective action. If, however, the standard were seven and half hours, as the actual performance is equivalent to the desired standard no managerial action is required. Only by adopting such a concept can management time be economically utilized.

Setting standards of field sales performance

To identify appropriate standards for control, the manager should ask two questions:

1 What constitutes success?
2 What affects the achievement of success?

Descriptive standards

In a sales operation success can usually be defined as the achievement of the sales targets. These serve as the prime standards of control. By themselves, however, they are insufficient. The achievement or otherwise of the annual sales target constitutes a descriptive standard. It measures what has happened but it is then usually far too late to redress the balance. Moreover, it does not indicate *why* the performance has been poor.

Diagnostic standards

Diagnostic standards, which help to identify why performance is varying from target, are defined by asking the second question: 'What affects the achievement of success?'

The manager must consider in the case of a particular salesperson failing to achieve target what actions by that salesperson should lead to the goals being met. Surprisingly, there are only four and these can be identified by the following questions:

1 What kind of people does he or she call upon?
2 How many does he or she call upon?
3 How often does he or she call?
4 What does he or she do while there?

How to set standards

One of the aims of setting standards is to control the sales activity at an early stage to prevent failure to achieve orders. This aspect of control can be further refined by evaluating planned performance against standard before the activity takes place. In fact it is only by assessing the intended action of the sales force that sales managers can directly prevent failure. Obviously they must check their own plans to ensure that, if achieved, they reach the desired objectives. They can go further by assessing each salesperson's activity plans before they are put into action. This is normally done by the submission of weekly calling plans on which each person identifies whom he or she is intending to visit, for what reason and when he or she last saw this customer (if applicable).

Variance production and analysis

Variances are produced by comparing actual results against the pre-set standards. However, this simple method may need refining as high variances can result which reflect the forecast error of the standards. For example, if the average daily call rate is set at eight, there is probably no cause for alarm if this varies between six and ten. Because so many of the standards are produced by averaging past performance it may well be necessary to process the actual results before comparing them against standard.

When the actual results are compared with the standards, variances will become apparent. These discrepancies may need more careful analysis before corrective action is taken. For example, in one firm it was known from past experience that most of the selling depended upon seeing the senior management of the customers, which could only be done by appointment. The results of some sales staff, however, were disappointing despite the fact that the percentage of calls by appointment was well up to the pre-set standard. But when performance against other standards was examined it was noted that their call rate was below par. Thus, although the appointment to total call ratio was high, this was due to a smaller number of other calls rather than to an over-achievement of appointments. Furthermore, it was discovered that as they increased their number of appointments, their overall call rates decreased markedly.

What in fact was happening was that these people, in their enthusiasm to gain appointments, had not controlled the timing of such meetings. They had placed them in the middle of the mornings and afternoons, thereby limiting their ability to make other calls. The more experienced staff systematically made appointments early in the morning, immediately before lunch, immediately after lunch or late afternoon, leaving mid-morning and mid-afternoon free to make cold calls which, although not as important, resulted in enough business to make their results superior. It would have been very easy to jump to the conclusion that the disappointing results of the less experienced men were due to a lack of sales skill. It was only by careful variance analysis that the real problem of appointment timing was identified.

Taking corrective action

Having identified the true nature of the variance, the sales manager has to decide whether it results from faulty standard setting or inadequate salesperson performance. If the former, the standards will have to be modified. If the latter, the performance of the salesperson will have to be improved, usually by some form of training or instruction. If that person is to improve he or she must be given specific targets to achieve within specific time periods, otherwise little or no change will result.

FURTHER READING

Forsyth, P., *Running an Effective Sales Office*, Gower, Aldershot, 1980
Lidstone, J.B.J., *Motivating Your Sales Force*, Gower, Aldershot, 1978
Lidstone, J.B.J., *How to Recruit and Select Successful Salesmen*, 2nd edn, Gower, Aldershot, 1983
Lidstone, J.B.J., *Training Salesmen on the Job*, 2nd edn, Gower, Aldershot, 1986
Marketing Improvements Limited, *SalesPlanner*, Gower, Aldershot, 1988 (50 forms for systematic sales management, together with an explanatory book)
Melkman, A.V., *How to Handle Major Customers Profitably*, Gower, Aldershot, 1979
Strafford, John and Grant, Colin, *Effective Sales Management*, Heinemann, London, 1986
Wilson, M.T., *Managing a Sales Force*, 2nd edn, Gower, Aldershot, 1983

Part Four

RESEARCH, ENGINEERING AND DESIGN

29 Managing sales engineering

D Jones and P Foyer

Most manufacturers of goods sold to industry (equipment suppliers and subcontractors) have to customize or integrate products, or even design them from scratch, for each contract. This process starts before the order, in the preparation of proposals and quotations – sales engineering. This sequence of events is especially significant, in that it is a critical part of both obtaining (or losing) the order and the execution of the eventual contract. This chapter is concerned with the management of this process to maximize the probability of obtaining orders, and minimize the risks of losing money on the contract through error at the proposal stage. Most successful companies in this field concentrate on providing effective solutions to customers' requirements, by solving problems, and even creating opportunities for their customers. This is a long-term relationship, in which genuine mutual interest should develop.

ADMINISTRATION OF SALES ENGINEERING

The sales engineering activity's main work is to process enquiries into successful proposals. This depends upon a number of key factors:

- The quality of the enquiry and its source
- Proper allocation of resources to key enquiries
- Good quality 'base information'
- Careful customer management and liaison.

Each enquiry must have a 'champion' – the person to whom the customer can talk, and through whom he can get the information he needs. He/she will very often be a facilitator or co-ordinator of the actions of a group of people from different parts of the organization. Obviously broad experience, competence and people-handling skills are paramount in this role. Figure 29.1 shows the co-ordinator's relationships with customers and internal functions.

It is desirable to establish and manage formal procedures for handling all aspects of enquiries. These arrangements should ensure that:

- Every enquiry is acknowledged
- Each enquiry is screened before committing resources
- The actions necessary to process an enquiry are planned and managed
- Proper review procedures are built in to maximize the chance of success
- Sufficient feedback mechanisms are built in to ensure that the status of an enquiry is known, and to improve further the sales engineering activity.

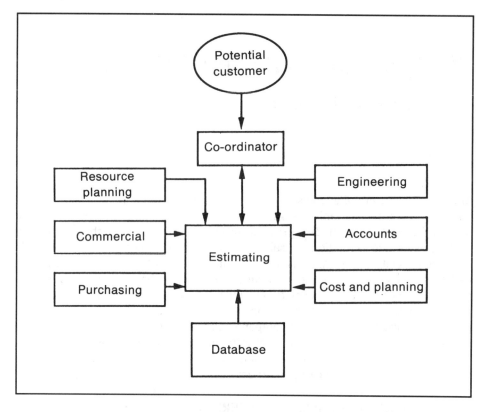

Figure 29.1   The co-ordinator function. A single point of contact both internally and externally simplifies communication

The process can be divided into:

1   Planning: screening and resource allocation
2   Proposal preparation and delivery

PLANNING AND SCREENING OF ENQUIRIES

In an ideal world, a supplier would decide which customers and types of contract he wished to work on. In practice most companies (especially those working internationally) receive requests for work from a wide variety of sources. Some of these may be very attractive, offering a strong chance of profitable work at low risk. Many will be less attractive for a number of reasons. The preparation of tenders can involve significant time and expense, especially where a considerable amount of investigation and conceptual design is needed. Before committing such expenditure, the company must evaluate the potential worth of each enquiry in a screening process. The screening process involves:

• The screening decision
• Monitoring the enquiry pattern
• Formalizing the screening process.

Undesirable enquiries must be promptly refused, and attractive enquiries pursued positively. Borderline cases can be actioned in cautious stages, with further screening stages as the risks and likely advantages become clearer. The critical decision is the initial one, because later withdrawals obviously waste resources.

The initial screening is the major part of the co-ordinator's role. In many businesses the co-ordinator's decision is sufficient, but in high-value industries like construction the decision will need authorization by the company's general management. In the latter case a summary of the enquiry and recommendations and reasons for accepting or declining should be presented to the management team. This process should be followed even where the co-ordinator has the sole responsibility, so that anyone looking at the file is aware of the reasons behind the decision.

Key criteria are normally:

- Relevance to the supplier's main products and activities
- Criteria for success and the number of bidders
- Fit to supplier's expected work-load particularly in contract, enquiry and manufacturing areas
- Value to the customer
- Likely costs of proposal and execution
- Likely margins.

It is also the co-ordinator's role to ensure that sufficient qualified enquiries are processed to allow the budgeted level and value of orders to be achieved.

The analysis of each enquiry is a useful contribution to an enquiry database, which can give useful statistics showing:

- Geographic customer and application scatter of enquiries (indicates where to concentrate or improve marketing)
- Hit rate (the ratio of orders to enquiries)
- Decline analysis (is there a potential market that is being missed, are there persistent companies which send enquiries but never give orders)
- Turnround time (useful in monitoring the performance of sales engineering).

In conjunction with a company-wide database even more useful reports can be made available and the effectiveness of the sales engineering can be improved. Possibilities are:

- Lost order report, tied into the hit rate and decline analysis
- Order analysis, geographical to see region-by-region hit rates
- Content database of previous enquiries and contracts. This can allow relationships to previous work to be recognized and hence significant economies made in tendering
- Reports on the relevance and accuracy of the company's mailing list
- Timelog: if most of enquiries come in by telephone what is the distribution of calls and is temporary manning required for parts of the day? For postal and larger contracts, when is the end of the customer's financial year? The need to spend budgets by the end of the year can increase the hit rate, therefore these may need higher priority action.

The above lists are not exhaustive but are intended to demonstrate how much useful information can be generated if properly managed, and how the screening process can be strengthened.

Another useful function of the screening process is to confirm the supplier's understanding of customer's requirements. This has the added advantage of checking the completeness of the enquiry and filling gaps or seeking confirmation at an early stage. This checklist, properly compiled, can substantially reduce the cost of the subsequent estimating and tendering stages.

From this initial screening, those enquiries which are to be pursued can be acknowledged, including confirmation of the main items off the checklist. Those which are to be declined should be politely and promptly refused.

PROPOSAL PREPARATION AND DELIVERY

Upon inclusion of an enquiry in the workplan for tendering and, where necessary, having the decision endorsed by the management team, an action plan for the subsequent tender stages must be developed. Action plans are the sales engineering equivalent of project authorizations or works orders. They authorize an expenditure budget and announce what has to be done, by whom and when. The main difference with action plans is that they authorize the expenditure of company funds which cannot be charged out directly to a customer, and which may prove to have been wasted if no order results. Action plans can provide a simple but effective system for managing expenditure and progress during the preparation of sales proposals for engineering projects. Some of the further steps involved in completing a proposal (such as cost estimating) are outlined in Chapter 42. An example of an action plan form is shown in Figure 29.2.

The main objective of the action plan is to ensure timely response, management of the contributing resources and control of the pre-order expenditure. Performance monitoring can be introduced to check the effectiveness of sales engineering and sales co-ordinator in particular. These monitors could include:

- *Hit rate*   The ratio of orders taken to the number of enquiries accepted, which provides a measure with which to monitor the effectiveness of the screening process
- *Response time*   The average time from receipt through screening to acknowledgement
- *Turnround time*   The total time from receipt of enquiry to submission of proposal
- *Enquiry expenditure*   The resources and expenditure required to process proposals.

It is essential that there is an adequate review procedure, preferably involving design, manufacture and selling people, of each major proposal before it is delivered. This increases its value to the customer and reduces risk of the contract being unachievable.

PROJEX LTD   CUSTOMER ENQUIRY

Customer Address	Enquiry number	Revision

Enquiry date:

Telephone:

Contact: Customer's reference: Telex:

ENQUIRY SUMMARY OR TITLE

SCREEN COMMITTEE

Comment:

We will not bid   Inform customer ☐

We will bid   Inform customer ☐

Clarify with customer and rescreen ☐

....
signed

ACTION PLAN

Action	For action by	Authorized costs for this action plan			Wanted by (date)
		Labour	Travel	Other expenses	
Define the task					
Review task definition with customer Develop engineering solutions					
Evaluate customer's operating costs					
Review proposed solutions with customer					
Estimate our project costs					
Write proposal and prepare artwork					
Printing and binding					
Transit time					
Deadline for proposal presentation					
Sales engineer In charge:					

Figure 29.2   Action plan for a sales enquiry. A form such as this can be used to authorize and progress the work needed to deal with a customer enquiry for an engineering project up to the preparation of a sales proposal or tender

SUMMARY OF SALES ENGINEERING MANAGEMENT TASKS

The sequence of events outlined has been successful for many companies. The process of closing an order makes change and revision to the proposal almost inevitable, and this in itself presents a significant management problem.

The sequence of events is essentially:

1 *Enquiry log* Records every enquiry and can give useful geographic information and identify new product opportunities
2 *Acknowledgement* Immediate confirmation of receipt
3 *Checklist* Summarizes the technical and commercial requirements of the enquiry and indicates at an early stage the completeness of the information available. An essential part of the screening process
4 *Screen* Decide whether or not to bid against a customer's enquiry
5 *Advice of decision to tender or decline* Confirms intention or declines to bid, and should include an understanding of the requirement based on the checklist
6 *Action plan* Allocates responsibility for tendering tasks and sets time and expenditure goals
7 *Review* Of procedure before delivery
8 *Delivery plan* Arrangements to ensure the proposal is delivered and presented to the customer in the most effective way
9 *Feedback and monitor* Improves the effectiveness of sales engineering and monitors their performance.

CASE STUDIES SHOWING SALES ENGINEERING BENEFITS

The following are examples illustrating aspects of the sales engineering management approach as applied to different industries.

Example 1

An international boiler and pressure vessel design and manufacturing company, whose product range is based on standard modules with a very high level of customization and total specials. At the top end of the product range are very large vessels which could occupy floor space for 6–12 months. The forward programme is therefore an essential part of the screening process, to assess whether capacity will be available.

The company had a functional approach to sales engineering and estimating which resulted in:

- Poor communication with other departments particularly design and manufacturing
- Duplication of paperwork and engineering effort throughout the various stages of tendering and post-order engineering
- No feedback on forward capacity available or contract performance
- No enquiry was declined
- Every enquiry was processed in the order it was received.

The net result of this situation was a long lead-time for proposals, (most of which was in the upfront sales engineering) a low hit rate and a poor sales reputation.

Having recognized the problem the company appointed a senior design engineer as a sales engineering co-ordinator. His initial prime responsibility was to screen enquiries so that time was not spent on unsuitable enquiries. His second task was to assess the potential engineering load that a possible order might require, as this function was becoming a serious bottleneck. Gradually, the role developed so that the co-ordinator would contact the customer direct if there were queries about the technical content of the enquiry or the application. This dialogue in itself helped considerably to improve relationships between the customer and contractor.

As with most jobs, aids were developed to simplify and assist the co-ordinator's role. These included:

1 A single enquiry file which would form the basis of a contract file should the order be won. This reduced some of the duplication in engineering time, and the risk of not executing the contract on time and within budgets
2 Feedback from production control about the forward capacity plan. This immediately gave an indication of whether the desired delivery date could be met, and if not was discussed with the customer before any time was expended
3 Enquiry log and analysis, to identify those customers who continually submitted enquiries but rarely or never gave orders. This enabled a simple ranking of enquiries rather than taking them sequentially
4 Development of a comparative database compiled from all contracts completed over a ten-year period, summarizing:

   • The technical aspects
   • Principal elements by time and cost
   • Notes relating to technical problems encountered
   • Contract margins.

This again proved useful in establishing the level of engineering effort required. More importantly, it acted as a pointer for the estimators to reduce the overall tendering timescale.

Similar approaches have been used by construction companies and other large 'custom built' suppliers, particularly in creating a practical database of retained engineering. One water turbine manufacturer in particular developed a simple selection programme which produced the head/power graphs for a range of turbines, superimposed the enquiry requirements and targeted to fax or post the result with an acknowledgement within 24 hours. The effect of this type of response increased their credibility considerably and, correspondingly, their hit rate.

Example 2

A European company supplying a range of standard, non-standard and special products. Enquiries were dealt with by a 'sales desk' function, with non-standard and specials passed on to designers for estimates. As some enquiries contained all three products it was estimated that some 40 per cent of enquiries needed a technical input. These naturally took a long time to process as the designers were always busy with the day-to-day problems, resulting in eight to ten weeks to respond to an enquiry. These non-standard and special items tended to carry higher margins, so that a considerable amount of profitable work was being lost.

The company brought together the internal sales function and engineering to improve communications. Analysis of enquiry receipts showed that in many cases customers requiring non-standard or specials telephoned their enquiries in. These previously had been noted down and passed on to the designers. The solution developed for the company was to have computer-aided design (CAD) terminals manned at peak periods during the day by engineers with telephone headsets. Any technical enquiry was immediately passed to the engineers who, from the information given, processed it through the CAD system, produced an A4 plot and faxed it directly to the customer to confirm the understanding of the requirement. In some cases complete estimates were also produced by the computer-aided manufacturing (CAM) capability of the processor, thus giving a near instant response to an enquiry. In many cases this resulted in an order being given the same day, thereby increasing the hit rate and the profitability of the company.

Example 3

The above cases illustrate what can be done in the 'engineered' products sector of industry. However developments in the automotive industry world-wide have changed the traditional approach to sales engineering and the management attitude.

Many of the major automotive producers have worked towards single sourcing over recent years. Most are now encouraging solution engineering by their suppliers, using specialist knowledge to design appropriate components and assemblies. This requires that the supplier has some access to the vehicle maker's CAD system, and that the major interface points are defined. The supplier then designs his product within the specified envelope. The results can be immediately vetted by the customer, modified if necessary, and confirmed so that detailed quotes can then be produced.

CONCLUSION

The above examples demonstrate that improved customer response through managing sales engineering can have a significant financial impact on any business. It will also help in developing closer relationships with the customer so that mutual benefits can be achieved.

FURTHER READING

Lock, Dennis (ed.), *Handbook of Engineering Management*, Heinemann, Oxford, 1989
Stallworthy E. A. and Kharbanda, O. P., *Total Project Management*, Gower, Aldershot, 1983
Miller and Heiman, *Strategic Selling*, Kogan Page, London, 1988

30 Managing research and development

A W Pearson

Investment in research and development must be looked at in the same way as any other investment in the business – the benefits it produces must exceed the costs. However, it is by no means easy to ensure that the practice lines up with the theory. The available evidence from a wide range of companies suggests that the costs incurred in the R and D phase of well-managed projects can be reasonably controlled, but that the time to completion is often significantly underestimated. Problems are also frequently encountered in the implementation phase and this causes further delays. Lengthening of the time-scale to completion can have adverse effects upon the benefits stream which may not only be delayed but may be significantly altered due to external influences: for example, competitive activity and changes in economic, social, political and environmental factors. It is also clear that assessing benefits is a very difficult task, which must take into account a wide range of effects and compare the anticipated futures with the likely situation if the R and D had not been undertaken.

Financial planning must recognize these uncertainties, particularly with respect to longer-term work. Appropriate monitoring or control procedures must be instituted which are capable of recognizing significant changes and indicating corrective action as early as possible.

In practice it has been found to be useful to focus attention on two critical areas of concern: first the overall allocation of funds to R and D based on identified organizational needs and, second, the planning and monitoring of individual projects. The evidence is that attention to the former has a significant influence upon the success of the latter, allowing individual initiatives to be encouraged and managed within an agreed overall framework. The two approaches are complementary and in most organizations both will be used as starting points, with links becoming apparent at a very early stage, as the next two sections aim to show.

TOP-DOWN PLANNING

In the late 1960s the word 'relevance' was frequently heard in discussions about the allocation of funds to R and D. Very simply this was meant to direct attention to the need to support R and D work which if successful would be put to effective use by the organization. In the late 1970s the phrase 'top-down planning' was used very frequently. This refers to an approach which systematically questions where the organization is going, and examines the structure of the organization in terms of its size, the nature of the component parts, their growth and profitability and their strengths and weaknesses in relation to competitive and other environmental forces. The purpose of this exercise is to identify where the organization is likely to end up if it continues in the way it has done in the past, and where it may need to change in order to improve its viability in the future. In the 1980s this led to more emphasis being placed on what has been called the strategic management of technology.

Such an analysis will usually be undertaken by individuals or groups of people who are responsible for, and knowledgeable about, a specific area of activity and will often follow organizational lines, for example, focused on products or areas of like characteristics. Within the analysis a 'technological audit' should be undertaken and this will reveal both the level and type of R and D activity which can be directly related to the support of specific areas of the organization. Such information then forms the necessary background to detailed discussion about the relationship (or 'relevance') of the R and D expenditures to the needs of the organization, with emphasis being placed on the longer- as well as the short-term needs.

The time orientation of the people involved in such discussions may be different, with R and D tending to look further ahead than, say, production or marketing people. This must be accepted. The purpose of top-down planning is to focus attention on the organization needs and each function should have an opportunity to make its view clear about these needs, bearing in mind the specialist knowledge it can contribute to the discussion. Differences of opinion are best brought out into the open at this stage, and it must be accepted that there is no certainty about the future. All opinions must be listened to. Where wide differences arise more information may need to be collected, and more views canvassed. However, it may well be that such differences still persist, and in this case it may be necessary to consider the variation of views as being a good representation of the actual situation, that is, to accept that a high level of uncertainty exists about the future. In this case a decision may have to be taken to authorize a programme of work which will cover the different views and hence allow flexibility. This will almost certainly require the allocation of more resources to the area, with a consequent reduction in the risk. If this is the accepted strategy efforts must be focused on identifying those features of the situation which can be monitored to indicate at the earliest possible time which areas should be given priority.

Top-down planning is therefore a way of focusing senior management attention on the needs of the organization. It forces people to ask questions about the relationship between the expenditures on the different functional areas and the alternative futures which the organization may encounter. In this process the R and D people should have every opportunity to put their own views forward and to make a significant contribution in respect of, for example, potential new technologies which may be seen as threats or opportunities. A thorough discussion of all these issues will reveal areas for attention and will generate commitment to a project, by the organization and by the project leader and the team. Such a commitment is a necessary condition for success.

It is not, however, also a sufficient condition, as many champions of 'non-successful' projects know to their disappointment. Many other factors need to be taken into account and as some of these change over time, for example legislation, it is important to have a planning and monitoring procedure which will provide useful information to all parties. Such a procedure can form an important part of the 'bottom-up' form of planning.

BOTTOM-UP PLANNING

This approach implies that individual activities or projects are the starting point for analysis. In many areas this is indeed the case. Ideas arise in a variety of ways: from discussions, casual meetings, problems, and so on, and they often form the basis for a request for funds to develop the idea into a proposal backing a request for a larger allocation of resources. Requests for small amounts of funds for developing ideas should always be encouraged and seriously considered. In general such ideas will lie within areas which will be of potential relevance, simply because they will utilize the skills of people who have been recruited in line with the organization's needs. The principal cost of encouraging such requests is in fact the 'opportunity' one of not applying the same resources to other continuing or preselected projects. However, the positive side of this is the increased motivation which can be generated by allowing some freedom for individuals to pursue their own ideas, and to convert them into projects which they can 'champion'.

In most organizations the decision as to how much of this type of activity to encourage, and in which direction, is left to the R and D director, whose responsibility it is to develop and maintain an exciting and creative environment which will be a positive asset to the organization. The encouragement of 'intrapreneurship' has also been found to be a key activity for section leaders and senior project managers. Many R and D directors report a lack of initiative on the part of their scientists and technologists in bringing forward new ideas, rather than any excessive demand. In some organizations this is partly due to pressure from projects of a more immediate concern to the organization's needs, which itself can be due to lack of an adequate planning and monitoring system.

The important point about the bottom-up planning approach is that it focuses attention on the level of resources which will be required to service all the projects which have been accepted into the R and D portfolio. If these projects are to be progressed well they cannot command in total more resources than are available, at any one time. This may sound an obvious statement, but the evidence is that many organizations consistently fail to complete projects on time due to the pressure on resources. If this is the case, corrective action must be taken either to reduce the number of projects which are being progressed simultaneously, or to bring in assistance from outside agencies, for example contract research organizations. Both of these are essentially short-term measures. In the long term serious consideration needs to be given either to reducing the number of projects which are accepted into the portfolio or to increasing the level of in-house resources in areas which are causing delays. If the first of these alternatives is chosen it will be necessary to examine carefully all the projects and to assess their relative importance to the organization, so that any trimming down can be done in areas which are likely to have less significant effects. This can only be done after due consideration of the plans produced by the approach discussed in the previous section, and hence the top-down and bottom-up approach will come together when questions of direction and priority are raised. An important point to note is that unless this trimming down is well managed there will be a continuing scramble for resources which will lead to the not uncommon situation in which progress meetings end up as being primarily concerned with establishing priorities. The inevitable consequence is a lowering of motivation of the people involved in low-priority projects and a reduction in financial return when compared with that planned.

Project evaluation and selection

This is an area fraught with difficulty. The literature is full of methods which have been designed to be helpful. These range from simple cash flow models, the use of net present value and internal rate of return accounting procedures, checklists, various forms of decision analysis incorporating probabilities of technical and commercial success and the more analytical approaches which are based on mathematical programming techniques. In practice the evidence suggests that the simpler approaches are the ones most commonly used, this often being justified because adequate data for the more mathematically based models are lacking. The simple cash flow models and weighted checklists are therefore much in evidence.

More recently, emphasis has been placed on the behavioural aspects of decision making, and a number of multi-criteria approaches (some using microcomputer facilities) have been described. These look very promising, and they are becoming increasingly accepted as valuable aids to decision making, helping to link project selection more closely with the strategic management process.

PLANNING AND MONITORING

The success of the approaches outlined in the previous sections will depend upon the degree to which the performance on individual projects matches up to the expectations. The purpose of a good planning and monitoring procedure is to ensure that any differences can be quickly identified and appropriate action taken. A number of methods are available for doing this, and the choice should be made in the light of the organization's needs, with one point being emphasized – the simplest and most flexible approach should be adopted. Many people still consider that the introduction of formal planning and control procedures into R and D will stifle creativity and initiative. Most attempts to impose standardized systems seem to have met with little success. It is comparatively easy for an individual or group to get around a system they do not see as useful and which takes up time they feel could be better allocated to their scientific and technical activities.

Planning and monitoring must be seen as a positive aid to the individual, the project group and the organization. Any techniques used should be seen as contributing to the team-building and leadership needs of a project. They should help focus attention on both the task and the people aspects of management. They should take into account the variables which are specific to the situation (for example, the development level of the team members) as well as the technical and organizational complexity of the project. This leads to a variety of methods being used for individual projects, the choice depending on the type of work and the project leader's management style.

There is a need for a reporting and monitoring procedure which will provide common information across the whole of an R and D establishment, and which places emphasis on obtaining and presenting information in a form which is useful for management purposes. Some approaches which have proved useful in practice are discussed in the following sections of this chapter.

Project planning

Several methods have been described in the literature, and further information can be obtained from the sources listed in the bibliography. Briefly, they fall into the following categories.

Bar charts

Bar charts are probably the oldest and yet still the most commonly used method in many R and D establishments. The chart is really a calendar planner on which activities are identified, with the time over which each is expected to be progressed indicated by a bar (see Chapter 42). The advantages of this approach are its simplicity and visual impact.

Network diagrams

Network diagrams can take a variety of forms. Until recently the most common was the activity-on-arrow diagram. Standard computer programs are available which allow easy presentation and analysis of such networks. They also include facilities for multiproject scheduling and for resource levelling, which can be very useful. Alternative forms of network diagrams are available, notably the activity-on-node method (often called precedence diagrams, among other titles). This variation is claimed to provide more flexibility at the initial project design stage and is more closely related to the engineering flow diagrams with which many scientists and technologists are already familiar. For a more detailed account of network diagrams please refer to Chapter 42.

Arguments against the use of networks have, however, been put forward by many people who believe they are too structured and inflexible and not capable of handling the uncertainties associated with R and D projects. Some of these arguments have been countered by the further development of the methods, for example, to allow alternative outcomes to be considered at any node or activity completion point. At such points allowance can also be made for recycling by incorporating feedback loops into the diagram. One such approach, known as the research planning diagram, specifically calls for the incorporation of decision nodes. This is a very valuable addition in an area like R and D and the approach has been found most useful. A point in its favour is its similarity to the logic or flow diagram which is used in other areas of business activity. A very simple example, showing the basic format, is given in Figure 30.1.

Milestone charts

The basic characteristic of the milestone chart approach is the identification of milestones or key events. These can be defined in terms of (for example) techni-

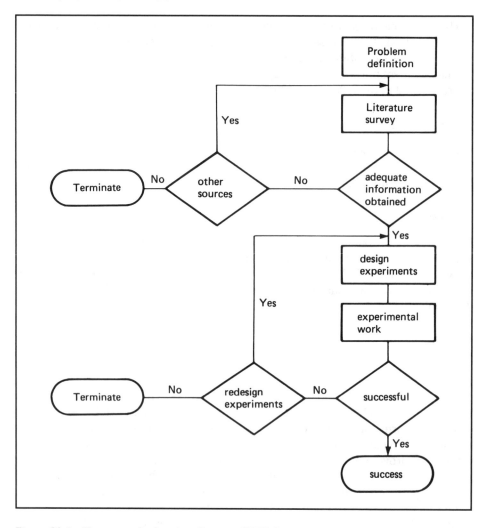

Figure 30.1 The research planning diagram (RPD) format

cal specifications which have to be met, tests which must be completed, pilot plants built, production facilities designed, or specific market research information gathered. The dates by which these activities should be completed then become the milestones.

The milestone chart is used in many organizations and expanded versions often include a breakdown of the activities by function or by individual, so that the responsibility for actions can be clearly identified. For this reason the name 'activity matrix' has been used to describe this form of presentation.

Monitoring

The purpose of outlining some of the approaches to planning individual projects was to illustrate the variety. As stated earlier, the preference for a particular method will depend upon the type of project, and the management style of the team leader. Any method must be seen as an aid to, and not as a substitute for, management. The project leader is responsible for planning, or agreeing the plans, and for progressing the project. Many aspects can change during the course of the work and corrective action may need to be taken during the life of a project. Knowing when to stop a project is important. The person to recognize this is likely to be the project leader, who is responsible for taking the necessary initiatives. The purpose of a good monitoring procedure is to record progress and to report actions which have been taken which were not originally planned and which might have consequences for the organization. In addition it should highlight, if necessary, where actions are not being taken at the correct time.

The monitoring procedure should be essentially a communication system which adds to, but does not replace, the direct contact which is always necessary between the various parties interested in a particular project. It will almost certainly provide some historical information, but its value will be significantly increased if it also focuses attention on future expectations.

Historical analysis

Most organizations require all people involved in project work to record on a standard form information about the allocation of their time on different activities. Such forms are usually completed weekly and relate to the actual expenditure of time over the immediately preceding time period. Breakdown of time may be in half-hour intervals, half or whole days. This is converted into cost information by the use of simple factors based on the salaries of different categories of individuals with overheads being added in many cases. Sometimes the accumulated costs form the basis for direct charging to customers or departments within the organization. In most cases they are presented so as to show the actual expenditure on the project alongside that originally agreed. Such information may be given in the form of a cumulative expenditure chart, but it is obvious that such information is of little value unless one can be clear about how much progress has actually been made on the scientific and technical work. That is why it is essential to have some form of plan, along the lines discussed earlier, set out in such a way that the actual work progress can be assessed at regular intervals against identifiable and agreed criteria.

Experience, however, suggests that although it is usually necessary to collect historical information on project costs it may not be of very great practical use for management purposes. Clearly it can be used as an indicator of how much effort is being applied to a project, but its value is diminished if it cannot be directly related to the expected technical progress as set out in the original plan. One way of doing this is through the milestone chart. As defined earlier, a milestone is a point at which agreed and recognizable criteria have to be met. The actual cost of reaching a given milestone can, therefore, be compared with the original estimate and a simple chart can be used to illustrate progress (see Figure 30.2). This diagram can be used to show both cost and time slippage.

The example in Figure 30.2 shows that milestone 1 was reached late, but at less than the planned cost. Milestone 2 was on time but at a higher cost. Milestone 3 was also on time, but again with the cost exceeding expectation.

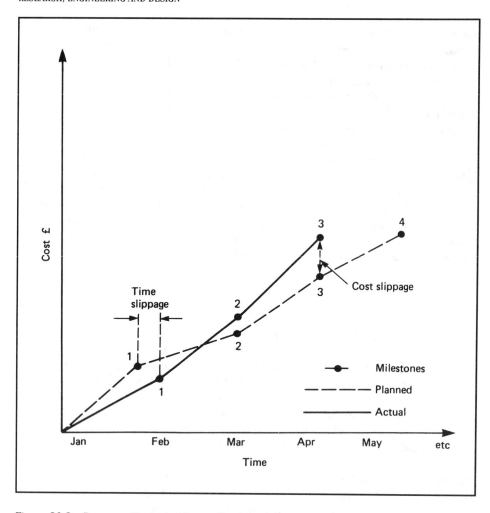

Figure 30.2   Progress illustrated by a milestone chart

Such a chart only indicates actual achievement against milestones and information about progress between these key points cannot be easily gained without a more detailed breakdown of the project into smaller activities. It is possible to do this, and at the extreme every activity can be individually monitored and progress of cost and time against expectation assessed almost continuously. This is often referred to as the work breakdown approach. In this case, computer analysis is useful, but in general the amount of information required and generated becomes too much to handle effectively, and it often leads to an anti-reaction from scientists and technologists who think too much of their time is taken up in what they see as unnecessary administration. This is particularly so in projects with a relatively high degree of uncertainty, where they feel they may require to take initiatives which were not specifically planned but which will ultimately be of advantage in steering the project to a successful conclusion. Such initiatives should be encouraged in R and D, and it has been found possible to allow a reasonable degree of flexibility by staying with the broad milestone approach but calling for information

		\multicolumn{7}{c}{Calendar time}						
		Jan	Feb	Mar	Apr	May	June	etc.
	Jan	1	2	3	4	5	6	
	Feb	1	2	3	4	5		
Review	Mar	1	2		3	4	5	
time	Apr	1	2		3	4		
	May	1	2		3		4	
	Jun							
	etc.							

Figure 30.3   Example of a slip chart

about future expectations as well as accounting for past expenditures as outlined in the following section.

Progress charts

When a project is selected, and a project leader identified, a plan is drawn up and agreed. This plan may be based on any one of the approaches outlined earlier (for example, bar chart, network, RPD) but the key point is that it should highlight important decision criteria or milestones. The number of these will depend on the type and size of project, and on the anticipated ability of the team to manage the work, including anticipated variations within the plan. The milestones need not be very close together, but they should not be so far apart that the opportunity for taking corrective action is delayed too long. They may coincide with review points, and estimates of both time and cost to reach them should be made however uncertain these may appear to be at the outset. Such estimates can be updated as more information becomes available and as such the learning of the project is more clearly indicated.

This information could be added to the simple historical analysis chart described earlier, but this would very quickly become confusing if many changes occurred in the estimates of the time and cost required to reach future milestones. An alternative is to consider the time and cost variables separately and it has proved to be most useful to emphasize the time variable in the first instance, partly because this can be more accurately monitored but also because time delays usually indicate the need for corrective action which if not taken is likely to reduce considerably the financial return on a project.

The simplest of the time-based charts in use has been referred to as a 'slip' chart, because it very clearly shows when progress is slipping (see Figure 30.3).

The numbers refer to key stages or milestones in the project, and the chart acts as an historical record of how the estimates of the time required to reach a particular stage have changed as the project is progressed. In this respect it provides future-oriented information which is extremely valuable for planning purposes. Anticipated slippage is clearly shown as a movement to the right in the

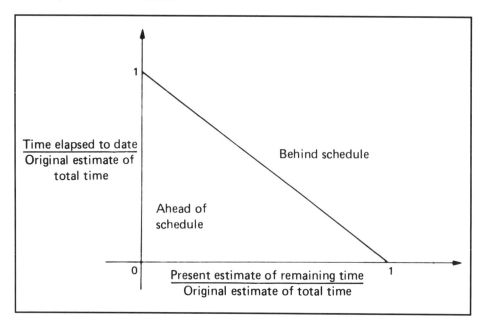

Figure 30.4 Progress against expectations for an individual project using time dimensions

number associated with the milestone, and commands the attention of all interested parties. The chart therefore acts as an extremely powerful communication
device. The information contained in the graphical presentation can quite easily be
put on to a computer. Print-outs can then be obtained as required of the progress
of any individual project or of groups of projects associated, for example, with one
area of activity or under a single management, or relevant to and perhaps supported by a particular client.

Other forms of presentation can also be of value. For example, progress against
expectations for an individual project can be portrayed graphically using ratios
(see Figure 30.4).

A plot of the progress of a project on these two dimensions will show up
deviations from plans as overruns above the line and ahead of schedule below the
line. Both these methods are simple to use and are visually very easy to understand. They clearly indicate deviations from plan, not only those that have
occurred, but also any that are expected in future periods. This is most important
if corrective action is to be taken.

The reason for choosing time as the principal variable on which to focus was
discussed earlier. Overruns on time are more frequent, often much larger, and the
effects of such overruns on the financial return can be very large.

This does not mean, however, that cost can be ignored. Historical methods of
accounting were discussed earlier, and these can be extended to include future
projections in a number of ways.

Many organizations now require a cost to completion forecast at major review
times. This information should be provided by the project leader, based on the
best possible estimates of work outstanding (including any originally unforeseen
requirements). Estimates can be derived from extrapolation from the information

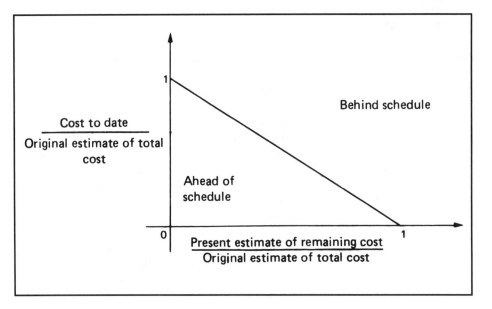

Figure 30.5   Progress against expectations for an individual project using cost dimensions

to date of actual against planned expenditures. In some cases this is not an unrealistic approach, as past problems frequently indicate future difficulties. The work breakdown method lends itself neatly to this approach through the identification of 'efficiency' factors. Care must be taken, however, to ensure that such an approach is not applied mechanistically. The aim of a good monitoring and reporting procedure should be to highlight problem areas as quickly as possible, allowing corrective action to be taken that will improve future performance.

Future cost estimates can be incorporated directly into the simple type of monitoring chart shown in Figure 30.2, or they can be presented as a cost slip chart (see Figure 30.5).

An organization may choose to emphasize time or cost reporting as its needs dictate. However, it is obvious that both can be useful and taken together will often provide additional information. For example, keeping time and cost progress charts side by side will enable slippage in either or both of these parameters to be considered at the same time. Some conclusions which might then be drawn are as follows:

1   Time overruns but not cost overruns suggest a lack of effort on the project
2   Cost overruns but not time overruns suggest problems are being encountered but extra effort is being allocated which looks like overcoming them
3   Cost overruns and time overruns suggest there are problems which are proving more difficult to handle.

Each of these will require different types of management action and the value of the reporting system is the simple indication which it provides of the possible areas for attention.

PORTFOLIO ANALYSIS

The approaches described above are essentially designed for assisting in the management of individual projects. The project leader and team are the people who supply the information and, as such, are the first people to identify deviations from the plan. They are therefore able to take corrective action if this is within their terms of reference, or to suggest alternative courses of action if they require additional resources and/or support from other key people in the organization. The value of the approaches must therefore be that they do not take away the responsibility for managing a project from those most closely concerned with its progress. Essentially what they do is recognize the uncertainty associated with research and development and encourage project leaders to provide regular position reports in the light of the progress made.

The individual planning methods focus attention on key decision points, milestones or review points. At these times the project leader will be expected to make a more detailed report on the project. Such review points will normally be agreed in advance. The progress chart, by its very nature, provides much more up-to-date information about the state of a project but without requiring this information in a detailed form. If milestones are not going to be met then the sooner this is recognized the better. In some cases this can lead to more rapid corrective action being taken; in others it may lead to an earlier decision to terminate a project which would otherwise become a cash drain with little prospect of providing an adequate financial return.

An important point about the progress chart approach is that it is first and foremost an information system, with the project leader at the centre of the information network and primarily responsible for any necessary actions. It is possible to go further than this and provide some information to management on a more general basis by presenting information in alternative forms. For example, the basic information already provided for the progress charts can be converted into ratio form, as follows:

$$\frac{\text{Cost to date}}{\text{Original estimate of total cost}}$$

$$\frac{\text{Present estimate of remaining cost}}{\text{Original estimate of total cost}}$$

which becomes:

$$\frac{\text{Original estimate of total cost} - \text{cost to date}}{\text{Present estimate of remaining cost}}$$

In this case, a ratio of one would indicate that a project was on schedule for cost (but not necessarily for time). A ratio of less than one indicates the likelihood of overspending on the project.

Ratios can be used in conjunction with other information (for example, with expenditure to date) but they must be treated with caution. They can form part of a management by exception system but here there is a danger that they will take away the main feature of the progress chart which is its value as a communication device. Management by exception systems can too easily become the tools of people who know little about either the technical side of the work or the needs of the organization in respect of the output. Some projects may need urgent attention when only very small exceptions are reported; others can tolerate much larger variations without causing undue alarm. The people who should be most concerned are those closely concerned with the project and outside interference should only be required if they are not taking the necessary actions. The use of ratios must therefore be seen essentially as a back-up mechanism, used mostly for senior management to monitor key projects. Their value will be diminished if an attempt is made to use them as the main control mechanism.

However, it is useful to consider whether additional information of a more general nature might be obtained about the overall performance of an R and D establishment which could be put to good use. There are two particular approaches which should be given serious consideration. The first focuses on the factors which cause delays to projects and the second on the outputs from projects in relation to the expectations. Obviously these two are interrelated, but can be usefully examined separately.

Constraints on individual projects

The progress chart is built up from information supplied by the project leader. Deviations from the original plan will be due to a variety of causes. A simple request for information about the nature of factors causing delays can be very illuminating. In practice, these usually fall into a few categories (for example, lack of resources, external factors, technical problems).

An analysis of all the projects in the R and D establishment usually reveals a significant number of delays due to the same factor. If so, corrective action should be taken, which will reinforce the value of the planning and monitoring system, as people will see that the information they are providing is being used to their advantage. For example, if lack of resources is a common constraint, then action to increase the level of resources or to reduce the number of projects will be much appreciated. It will also be of considerable motivational value to project leaders who will have to spend less of their time fighting for priority and working with inadequate support facilities. The advantage of the progress chart is that it concentrates attention on any likely changes in future resource requirements on individual projects due to changes in expectations about the achievement of particular milestones. Taken over the R and D establishment as a whole this information is of great value from the resource allocation point of view.

Output assessment

At the beginning of the chapter the potential value of top-down planning was discussed. The actual value of this approach will be partly determined by the ability of the R and D establishment to complete the projects which are agreed to be relevant to the different needs of the organization. A coding system can be developed which shows the relationship of an individual project to a particular need (for example, business area, short or long term, product or process development). Projects can then be identified readily and at appropriate intervals, say quarterly or annually; all projects related to a given need can be examined and their progress noted. This analysis may well reveal areas for concern; for example, that short-term projects are being progressed more effectively than long-term ones. From the financial planning point of view, it will provide a simple breakdown of the expenditures and the progress which has been made against the expectation in each area. Deviations between these two can then be examined to see whether corrective action needs to be taken.

It must also be remembered that an R and D establishment will have activities which cover a wide range of uncertainties. The proportion of low to high probability of success projects will depend upon the needs of the organization at a particular point in time as well as the attitudes to risk of the key decision makers. This balance must be reviewed at regular intervals and the monitoring procedure should highlight those projects in which the uncertainty is not decreasing over time at the expected rate. Decisions on whether to continue with such projects are not easy to make, as many major innovations have come about after sustained effort over many years with success always looking possible but always appearing to be just out of reach. In such cases the size of the potential benefits will usually be the deciding factor in obtaining further backing, but this must be balanced against the potential losses of not being successful, or of being beaten by competitive activity. There are many examples of organizations falling into difficulties through backing innovations requiring excessively large cash outflows with benefits appearing very far in the future.

CONCLUSIONS

A financial planning and control system is just as necessary in research and development as in any other area. However, it must take into account the uncertainty surrounding the activity. It must be flexible and it does not need to be complicated. It must be motivational rather than penalizing and the responsibility for management has to remain at the level at which the work is being done.

There is considerable evidence that the internal evaluation of projects is very compatible with external evaluations where the goals are agreed and accepted. The aim, therefore, is to provide the right environment in which the project leader and team are motivated to be honest with themselves and with the organization in the reporting of progress. The monitoring system can then be oriented towards signalling deviations about which other people might express different concerns than those most closely connected with the work. Such signals will encourage communication and agreement on actions which will be of benefit to all interested parties. The emphasis is on the positive aspects of monitoring which are too often hidden by disagreements about the reasons for deviations and the implied blame which often leads to the adoption of defensive positions by the different parties. The value of good feedback which can be provided through a simple planning and monitoring system cannot be over-emphasized.

Planning methods can be allowed to vary within the organization, although there may be some advantage in agreeing the type of approach which is likely to be most suitable for different types of projects. Monitoring is more useful if there is a high degree of standardization, so that comparative analysis can be done and attention paid to those factors which will improve the overall management of the R and D establishment.

In looking at possible approaches more emphasis is placed on forward than on historical analysis, with time being considered of prime importance. It must be remembered that the largest part of the cost of an R and D establishment is in the people, and unless significant amounts of outside work can be rapidly commissioned it is not easy to overspend significantly on the overall budget. The evidence is that many organizations fail to live up to their expectations in respect of completed projects in any given time period. It must therefore be more sensible to develop a monitoring system which focuses on outputs, and the approaches outlined in the previous sections are of assistance in this respect.

The basic characteristics of the suggested approaches should be carefully examined before any new system is considered, as experience suggests that the imposition of formal planning and control systems on R and D has not met with a great deal of success. Any system which is likely to be accepted and effectively used will be one which can be seen to be helpful to all parties. In this respect a monitoring of the system itself is also necessary, so that adaptations can be made in the light of experience, to ensure that the maximum use continues to be made of the information generated.

FURTHER READING

Burgelman, R. A. and Sayles, L. R., *Inside Corporate Innovation: Strategy, Structure and Managerial Skills*, Free Press, 1985

Costello, D., 'A practical approach to R and D project selection', *Technological Forecasting and Social Change*, vol. 23, 1983

Eres, B. K. and Raz, B., 'A methodology for reducing technological risk', *R & D Management*, vol. 18, no.2, April, 1988

Fahrni, P. and Spätig, M., 'An application-orientated guide to R & D project selection and evaluation methods', *R & D Management*, vol. 20, no. 2, April, 1990

Lanford, H. W. and McCann, T. M., 'Effective planning and control of large projects – using work breakdown structures', *Long Range Planning*, vol. 16, no. 2, 1983

Liberatore, M. J. and Titus, G. J., 'The practice of management science in R and D project management', *Management Science*, vol. 29, no. 8, August, 1983

Mansfield, E., 'How economists see R and D', *Harvard Business Review*, November–December, 1981

Pearson, A. W. and Davies, G. B., 'Leadership styles and planning and monitoring in R and D', *R & D Management*, vol. 11, no. 3, 1981

Souder, W. E., 'A system for using R and D project selection methods', *Research Management*, vol. 21, no. 5, 1978

Tushman, M. L. and Moore, W. L. (eds), *Readings in the Management of Innovation*, 2nd edn, Ballinger Publishing Co., Mass., 1988

31 Design management: a product focus

Tim Warner

How does managing design differ from managing any other discipline? This chapter examines that question in part by considering the subject of design management. It uses corporate design management as the model, and team-based product design as the design focus. The chapter begins with design in the context of business: this is followed by outline definitions of product design and its concerns, and product design management. General management principles are related to the management of creative individuals, after which the elements of the design process are examined. These sections collectively show what is being managed and so demonstrate the parameters of the management task involved.

CHANGE, CREATIVITY AND MANAGED CHANGE THROUGH DESIGN

The role of design in commercial and economic competitiveness is now emerging to the forefront of business concerns. Design is seen by many companies as the critical determinant of success in international markets. Consumers are increasingly discriminating, well informed, and conscious of what constitutes product quality and specification. The resulting shift has placed non-price factors alongside or ahead of price in decisions to purchase. People are well on the way to buying values, not just products. Consumers are demanding more of products as they evaluate and select those that conform to new and emerging values sets. Concern for the quality of the environment, waste, energy use, changes in lifestyles and economic constraints are now collectively pervasive influences determining and redirecting the purposes of products and manufacturing companies in the 1990s.

Creativity is the basis on which business now competes and this means change. People and businesses do not easily adapt to deal with radical change. Change must occur incrementally in order to retain some measure of company stability; it must be *managed* change. To maintain flexibility, new ways of better developing, utilizing and managing creative input to business purposes now head the agenda, with attention once again on design management. Creativity is increasingly recognized as the form of intelligence and ability best suited to dealing with the context of change both in a generative and responsive way. Design is seen as the formal focus for creativity in business and as the regulatory device by which it enters the organization. Technically oriented change enters the company through the research and development function, and socially oriented change through marketing. Design is the key linking function between these two sources, where the mix of technological values and sociological values is drawn into focus and applied to solve design and business problems.

WHAT KIND OF DESIGN IS BEING MANAGED?

The concept of 'design' is one that is generally understood but as yet remains ill-defined. As an activity design is characterized by modelling, where problems and solutions are resolved and refined together. Design problems are changeable. Progress is made by proposing and evaluating alternative solutions and by remaining solution-focused throughout. Different approaches are used side by side: the design activity can at once be analytical and synthetic, divergent and convergent, *ad hoc* and procedural, systematic and intuitive. It is an iterative process, encompassing purposes and the means to achieve goals.

Product design can be defined as: the process leading to the specification of materials, construction, mechanism, shape, colours, surface finishes and decoration for three dimensional objects produced in quantity by industrial processes.

The primary decision-making criteria used in establishing these product specifications are a concern for appearance, ease of use and maintenance, convenience, reliability, performance in operation, safety, human factors (physiological, procedural or task-related, and psychological), materials and manufacturing processes and the appropriate utilization of new technology. The designer needs to be aware of how these criteria are influenced by shifts in the more subtle, complex and changeable societal values attached to man-made products as held by individuals or collectively within society.

Product design is also strongly linked with the economic criteria and purpose of manufacturing industry and is consequently part of the wider definition of technological innovation. This has been defined as 'the bringing into a commercially viable condition some new or improved material, process, product or service' (Archer, 1974). Product design, which deals directly with new products, product improvement and stylistic change in products is the focal element in the technological innovation process. It is the point at which ideas are externalized and brought together in two-and three-dimensional forms specifying the end outcome of manufacture. It shows in what ways a product can be acceptable, operational and affordable in relation to a defined need or want.

Consequently, product design is involved not only with design problem solving, but also business problem solving. Business problems are concerned with the relative quality, specification and change in demand for products, especially with the value-in-exchange factors that alter product costing and pricing. The matching quantitative problems of design centre on an approach that allows for 'doing more with less' in the adding of perceivable value to a product, and/or reducing the material, process and manufacturing costs of the product. The true strength of product design is in its ability to balance quantitative elements with qualitative non-price factors in the resultant end product.

PRODUCT DESIGN MANAGEMENT

'Design management' is a general term that can be applied to the management of a variety of commercial design activities, including product design. In its widest sense design management can be regarded as parallel with managing the process of technological innovation (previously defined). As a specific term it needs qualifying with reference to the type of design involved and to the type of management practised.

Product design management can be defined as planning, organizing for and carrying out the motivating, co-ordinating, direction and control of the processes and creative activity of product designers. In particular cases this extends to others, from disciplines such as research and development, marketing, engineering, and manufacturing. It may also embrace consultant specialists, where these are involved with a company in the design and development of products for manufacture.

Product design management is a functional role requiring managerial and product design expertise. It is cross-disciplinary in its relations with other functions. In organizing for product design it deals with both 'permanent' traditional (hierarchical) organization and with 'temporary' non-traditional (project/matrix) organization. Ultimately, product design management is a communications and support role at, and between, each functional managerial level. This is especially true in representing the product design function at board level and in the context of multidisciplinary design teams.

Product design management is active at the following three organizational levels:

1 At the corporate level (senior management), where it assists with:
   - establishing corporate product objectives and policy
   - organizational structuring for product design
   - product and project auditing and evaluation
   - resource allocation
2 At departmental or office level (middle management), where it works to:
   - establish a creative, interactive, attitudinal climate and physical working environment within which product design can take place.
   It also deals with:
   - multiple project organization and documentation
   - technical information management
   - human resources for the product design team and its support
3 At the project level (project/matrix management) it assists in the functions of:
   - defining a design/business problem
   - selecting the designer and/or the design project team
   - establishing a mutually agreed workable method, plan, schedule and budget for the project.

With all this established, product design management can assist, direct, monitor and evaluate the product design activity and outcome to solve a design/business problem within agreed time and cost criteria. See also Figure 31.1.

MANAGING THE DESIGN PROCESS AND DESIGN ENVIRONMENT

Managing design differs from managing other functions in terms of how general management principles of planning, organizing, directing and controlling are aligned with the demands of the design process and design environment.

Corporate product design management (senior management/executive)

- Corporate product policy formulation
  — Product design component in: corporate product innovation, development and diversification process
  — Product design in: corporate strategic planning, objectives and strategies
  — Product design component in: corporate identity
  — Product design: product and project standards
- Organizational types and organization for product design
  — Organizational structures for product design: formal structures (department, division, function/matrix, committee, consultancy)
  — Role and behavioural outlines for product design and for informal structures
- Evaluation, decision-making and resource allocation
  — Final proposal evaluation (market audit, value analysis, price/profit and price, non-price factors)
  — Investment management

Product design department (middle/functional management and product design consultant and office management

- Accommodation, layout, facilities and equipment (see also communications, below)
- Organization
  — Product design support functions
- Personnel
  — Product design planning, design and design support staff
  — Design staff selection, training and education
- Project design department budgeting
- Project and product auditing
- Technical information management
  — Design project documentation
  — Design information systems
  — Communications and interdepartmental relations: establishing a creative, interactive, physical working environment and attitudinal climate in which product design can take place

Figure 31.1   A proposed grouping of the basic concerns of product design management on the basis of managerial level

Product design and project management (matrix/horizontal management)

- Nature and requirements of product design
  — Design process
  — Design methods/procedure
  — Design brief
  — Designers
  — Modelling, prototype
  — Computer aided design and modelling
  — Technical information system
  — Documentation system
  — Professional practice (product design societies, professionalism, code of ethics, designer payment, award schemes)
- Project management
  — Nature and principles
- Project definition, planning and organization (product design)
  — Brief
  — Planning methods
  — Scheduling methods (individual, scope of work, number of disciplines involved, number of staff involved, project duration, fee and leadership)
  — Budgeting methods (direct labour, other direct costs, overheads, contingency measures and profit)
  — Organization
  — Monitoring, evaluation, direction and control
- Personnel
  — Manpower planning
  — Designer selection and use of consultants (design, marketing and technical consultants)
  — Design project team selection
  — Design project manager (role, responsibilities, authority)
- Corporate client/client negotiation

Interaction with related functions

- Marketing
- Engineering
- Production and materials
- Legal
  — Contract negotiation
  — Company law
  — Product liability
  — Patents, registration and copyright
- Financial management

Figure 31.1   (concluded)

Planning is judging ahead, and involves the design manager in matters of space, equipment and staffing. This includes developing the capabilities of the existing staff and enlisting new staff with the potential to develop, or to infill where a specialized skill is required in the team.

Organizing for the design function means developing a structure that is effective in reaching objectives, yet flexible enough to accommodate individual differences in designers and in their work habits. This requires that effective channels of communication are opened and maintained for designers with the client and team members in other departments.

Directing and control are closely aligned with generating a creative and motivational environment within which design work can take place. The creative environment is established as a relationship between the designers and the design manager.

The designers employed in any one team may vary widely in skills, temperament and personality. They are, however, distinguished as creative individuals by a variety of traits, and these need to be taken into account. These traits influence how designers may relate in a team, what design methods may be adopted, through to what individual drawing equipment needs to be ordered. Creative designers tend to deal well with ambiguity and uncertainty. They are sensitive to their surroundings. They are analytical, introspective and have good conceptual ability. They gave a strong capability to visualize in the mind's eye. They can quickly perceive how things relate, by pattern, form and structure and can extract the essential from the general. This ability enables these individuals to see the same thing in different ways, to relate the previously unrelated and to generate new forms and structures. Designers tend to be non-conformist and sceptical of the status quo. They are interdisciplinary, and able to draw, integrate and organize information from a wide variety of sources in a holistic quest for solutions. They are futurists.

To a large degree the creative environment is established by the attitudes, creative philosophy and mode of leadership/direction adopted by the design manager. To bridge the gap between the stable corporate entity and its requirement for creative input, the design manager needs a participative style based upon a relationship of trust and mutual respect. Direction needs to be carefully administered, so that the business potential of the project is maximized and the designer gains sufficient freedom of movement to go beyond the strict parameters of the design brief. The design manager must be able to give support on an individual basis and motivate a team. Innovating is an emotionally and psychologically demanding process. The design manager will need to be able to:

- Listen

- Reinstate levels of confidence

- Help to reorganize the designer's thoughts

- Recognize the state of development reached in the design process

- Help the designer towards new routes of exploration or in the choice of the most appropriate solution.

Matching the designer to the design task is also critical. The tendency is to place the designer according to individual strengths at the expense of broadening the designer's abilities. Design thrives on variety, and projects need to be split carefully between designers in order to provide them with new challenges.

A designer's full commitment comes with responsibility and through being fully informed. Designers need direct contact with clients. A third party only impairs communication and eliminates the creative interaction between the main parties involved. The responsibility can then be delegated to the designer for project scheduling, quality of work and creative resolution. Shared decision making encourages trust and a positive working relationship between designer and design manager.

Control of design activities is through a shared understanding established between designer and manager at the outset of the project. This involves the laying out of a set of project performance standards against which measurement and regulation of results can take place.

In general management terms the design manager needs to relate well to the designers on his or her team, to be a part of the creative process but not interfere, to observe, comment and stimulate, and yet at other times be constructively critical. The manager needs to avoid quantifying qualitative performance, while astutely assessing the benefits of those intangibles in achieving the projected goals. Carefully balancing mutually interdependent principles is the 'art' of design management.

In specific management terms it is the design process that also forms the management structure for design. The design process can be split into two parts:

- The process (design thinking) itself, as allied to method
- The procedure (drawings and other documentation) to keep track of what is being done.

The 'procedure' also supports the design thinking process through the provision of an orderly frame of reference.

The method and thinking processes employed in designing usually result in a mix between being orderly and muddled, becoming familiar with ambiguity of context, unknown possibilities and limitations of 'the new' and coming to terms with accepting the mix that reveals that insight. Innovating requires a measure of procedural chaos, confusion and even loss of confidence. The designer must then switch to a different method that feels better, and only then restore the balancing effect of ordered procedure. Design thinking and method are still largely the domain of the individual designer and are those elements unique to each designer. These are agreed upon in principle, in an open-ended way with the design manager in relation to the nature of the project in hand.

There are also collective design methods used in larger team design situations. The design process then needs to be a specific concern of design management in how it relates as a part of the larger process of technological innovation within the company.

Procedure, on the other hand, is the middle ground where business and design meet. It is where the creative process is split into stages. This can then easily, step by step, explain the design activity to the client or senior management. It forms a

DESIGN MANAGEMENT: A PRODUCT FOCUS

framework of understanding between the two parties about what has to be done, how long it will take, how much it will cost, what results may be expected at each stage and how changes can be made. This is best achieved through a project document, which can act as a common focus throughout the life of the project, and which can act as follows:

- To enable agreement
- As a measure with which to judge progress towards goals
- To establish ways by which change can be justified within the project.

The design process commences with an initial set of goals in the form of a design brief. Measures should be included to propose alternative goals as design investigation reveals new routes or purposes. Initial expressions of objectives or goals cannot avoid the inclusion of hidden assumptions about the way those goals can be satisfied. Building in the means by which change can be made is essential to avoid a misunderstanding on the part of the client or senior management. Designing is an exploratory process and this means every part of the project is subject to change by either party, from the goals and schedules to the deliverables and the budget.

The design process in general involves; information gathering, analysis, synthesis, evaluation, selection and implementation and feedback. In the larger context of the process of technological innovation, there is a set of broad design and development stages that are now recognized as common between a wide range of industries and types of products:

- *Briefing* A general statement from management or the client about the product to be developed
- *Specification* Elaboration of the brief to include detailed market and technical requirements
- *Concept stage* Generation of alternative design solutions produced as drawings, and models to test feasibility
- *Evaluation stage* Where one or more design concepts are drawn up and/or prototyped for technical, financial and market evaluation
- *Detailing stage* Where the selected design is detailed in terms of components and materials, manufacturing process and produced as a final production prototype along with full instructions for manufacturing
- *Feedback* Added to the above process, feedback involves re-evaluation of the product in the market and takes into account changing user requirements, technical and design improvements made by competitors.

Thereafter, continuous redesign of the product or processes involved is the manner in which companies can remain successfully competitive in a dynamic market.

Design is a process that involves and depends upon the creative individual as a part in that process. The process is variable, both in terms of the design thinking involved and procedure. It is not simply a set of general principles to apply in set stages to reach a defined goal. No matter what level of procedure is employed, there is a point where intuition must be confronted.

DESIGN AND CORPORATE STRATEGIC PLANNING

In dealing with change, management's responsibility is to attempt to assess the implications of what has passed, what is now, and what may occur in the future, for the future of the enterprise. Design management's span of accountability for securing the future viability of the enterprise is in fact being enlarged.

Powerful tools which management and design have at their disposal today help to make the task more approachable. In general, a larger database of knowledge is available: this accumulated experience can be utilized to give a better understanding of the world in which we live. This can also be used to enlarge upon what we consider possible. Through the use of computers and model building, management and design are now able to simulate and manipulate possible futures in products and environments. For example, programs are now available to lighting consultants that enable the simulation of illumination within a defined environment. Computer-aided design (CAD) enables the generation of visual forms, calculation of volumes, configuration of components and simulation of product dynamics. This makes possible the configuring and 'testing' of a product before building the prototype.

One important area in which this applies is in the enlisting of design ability in the task of corporate strategic planning. The designer is a futurist, a conceptualist and an integrator of diverse information, comfortable in dealing with change, ambiguity uncertainty and hard and soft data. The designer's developed conceptual ability, allied with visualization skills, enables him or her to communicate ideas graphically to others in the planning team. Decisions on what to make, why, when and how, rely heavily on the quality of information that initially goes into planning; that results in company long-term plans, mid-term tactics and short-term goals and objectives. Design management's role is to ensure the right channels are opened for this kind of interaction to take place. This is closely allied with having a strong representation of design at board level, and in promoting and maximizing the use of design skills throughout the company.

The design manager must be on the lookout for new profitable product opportunities from inside and outside the company and bring them to the attention of senior management. In a similar sense the design manager must be willing to encourage the exploration of new concepts in areas where the potential for reward is greatest and risk highest. This builds confidence within the design team and in design management's ability to enlist the support of senior management to invest in design ability.

CONCLUSION

The strength of product design is in its ability to perceive trends, give form to concepts, and so generate a valuable qualitative definition of requirements.

Design management's strengths are in making the connections and alignments required between the company and the design function. By encouraging change through confidence in its management and understanding of the design contribution, design management will enlist greater commitment to, and investment in, creativity from senior management. The concern is no longer with design simply as a service, but for design to be incorporated as the basis and means for business to achieve a more well-designed future.

FURTHER READING

Archer, L. Bruce, *Design Awareness and Planned Creativity in Industry* Design Council, London, 1974

Burnstein, David and Stasiowsky, Frank, *Project Management for the Design Professional*, Whitney Library of Design, New York and Architectural Press, London 1982

Jones, J. Christopher, *Design Methods*, Wiley, London, 1980

Noon, Patrick and Warner, Timothy, *Product Design Management, an Annotated Bibliography*, Gower, Aldershot, 1989

Oakley, Mark, *Managing Product Design*, Weidenfeld & Nicolson, London, 1984

Oakley, Mark (ed.), *Design Management: a Handbook of Issues and Methods*, Basil Blackwell, Oxford, 1990

Part Five

PURCHASING AND INVENTORY MANAGEMENT

32 Procurement policy

Peter Baily

Key features of procurement policy in the 1990s are:

- Just-in-time production (JIT)
- Total quality management (TQM)
- Reduced supplier bases
- Continuous supplier development
- Co-makership or partnership associations with suppliers.

These developments are replacing the traditional adversarial relationships.

Single or dual sourcing based on the life of a part, instead of shopping around whenever a purchase is made, is being adopted as a policy. This has repercussions on the supply market. Large purchasers and those in a *de facto* monopoly position can exert so much leverage that they need to consider, in making a major purchasing decision, the future state of the supply market which will result from it. Such organizations as British Telecom, IBM and General Motors constantly need to bear in mind such considerations, and much research and thought may be needed to decide, for instance, whether a two-supplier market would be better than a three-supplier market.

The normal purchasing situation for the larger customer is what economists call 'bilateral oligopoly': that is, a small number of powerful suppliers dominate the supply market and a small number of powerful customers dominate the sales market. No formula will determine whether supplier or customer has the upper hand. Negotiation is used to decide the arrangements for supply: the specification, the contract quantity and the delivery quantities, the price and terms of payment, the inspection or quality assurance agreement, and so on.

PROCUREMENT STRATEGIES

Corey (1978) classified procurement strategies into three groups:

1 Cost-based negotiation
2 Market-price-based negotiation
3 Competitive bidding.

While these were distinguished from each other basically by pricing mode, they also differed according to Corey in the product scope of the procurement (which could be narrow or broad), in the number and kind of suppliers contacted (ranging from one or very few in the case of cost-based negotiation to many in the second group), in price–quantity determination (including risk-sharing arrangements and the form in which quotations were requested) and in negotiating strategy (which varies considerably between the three groups).

Supplier selection was not just a matter of selecting the type and number of source; it involved the construction of a sourcing system in which different suppliers had different roles (for instance, technical development and price leadership). Long-term supply availability, domestic versus foreign sources, distributors versus manufacturers and the strategy of numbers were some of the factors to be considered. Single sourcing and the stability of vendor relationships were topics of considerable importance, while, in certain circumstances, it could be quite difficult to persuade a supplier to accept an order. If a manufacturer needed to de-market his product, then the customer needed to market his demand – a reversal of the traditional supplier–customer relationships which may become increasingly prominent if material shortages loom larger.

Negotiation has become the subject of an enormous literature and many training courses are available for buyers, sellers, labour union representatives, management representatives, and many others with special interests. Most of this training material stresses the importance of the groundwork which precedes negotiating sessions, in which objectives are set, the relevant facts are assembled and conclusions drawn, and tentative agenda established for the negotiations.

Corey's work is based on research carried out at six very large American corporations during the 1970s. Purchasing could be carried out, and in fact in all six cases was carried out, at plant level, divisional level, and corporate level; but a strong trend was noticed to centralize procurement decision making to corporate level, mainly perhaps because of the increasing importance of the function as perceived by corporate management. Supply shortages and long-term planning of material availability, effective response to a changing business environment, profit improvement by means of purchase cost reduction, and better selection, use and development of purchasing talent were listed as reasons for this trend.

During the 1980s the main trend was towards single sourcing of major parts and materials. This resulted from the widespread adoption of just-in-time (JIT) methods in production planning and control and in stock planning and control. Goods delivered had to meet conformance standards without goods inwards inspection by the customer, so that the supplier had to comply with severe requirements for supplier quality assurance. Goods had to be delivered on time, which in terms of JIT requirements could be very specific (say at 14.20hrs on 3 March, rather than 'during the first week in March').

Suppliers had to plan ahead very thoroughly to comply with these requirements, which meant that they had to have a detailed, accurate and thorough grasp of the customer's forward planning. Inevitably, many suppliers could not or would not comply, and they had to be dropped. Other suppliers would also have to be dropped because, for one reason or another, they too failed to meet JIT requirements. More and more, suppliers of major purchases were seen as extensions to the customer's own organization. They were taken into confidence about future plans. Problems with prices, quality or deliveries were seen as common problems, to be resolved jointly for mutual benefit.

All this left less room for two or more suppliers in competition with each other, and resulted in the widespread adoption of single sourcing for major parts and materials.

INPUT MANAGEMENT

Similar trends have been reported by Farmer (1981), in his discussion of the management of input to the firm from its supply market. Input in the sense in which it is used here refers to the components and materials used in producing the firm's end products. It is argued that too many firms have confined their strategic planning to output management and the marketing of their end products, regarding the input area as operational rather than strategic. This thinking may indeed have been appropriate to the supply market conditions of the recent past, but it is doubtful if it continues to be appropriate in the present and likely that it will become quite inappropriate to future supply market conditions.

Farmer argues that while input management is one of the variables in a business system, and its importance varies from company to company and from time to time, it is, nevertheless, hardly ever to be regarded as insignificant. And while the operational aspects of input management are certainly important to the functioning of the business, it has strategic aspects which have often been overlooked in the quest for operational efficiency. The effectiveness of the whole business is not the same thing as the efficiency of the various functions which are elements within it. Co-ordination and balance should be sought between the various functions, and between input and output management, at the strategic as well as at the operational levels. To concentrate solely on cost reduction in the input and conversion stages of a manufacturing system, and to look for profit opportunities solely at the output end, may well, according to Farmer, have been a major contributing factor in the decline and even demise of many manufacturing businesses.

Purchasing policy should thus be seen as part of business policy, purchasing strategy as part of business strategy. Long-term as well as short-term aspects need to be considered, as indeed they have been by successful Japanese manufacturers of motor cars, motor bikes, and TV sets, and by successful retailers such as Marks & Spencer.

Professor Farmer in this paper was looking particularly at the long-term and strategic aspects of supply planning; but the short-term and operational aspects are also important in the determination of procurement policy. Materials requirement planning, greatly facilitated by the more powerful computers and better systems which became available in the early 1980s, brought great improvements to supply and production operations in those companies which implemented it successfully. The insistence that management should devise and authorize a rational, feasible and appropriate master schedule, coupled with the ability to explode this into detailed schedules of what parts, components and materials to make or buy, week by week, over the whole planning horizon, came like a revelation to companies which had previously operated on a chaotic mixture of stock-controlled production and customer priorities.

Materials management was a different but related approach, also intended to improve operational efficiency, but this time by a change in departmental structures.

MATERIALS MANAGEMENT

The term 'materials management' probably referred originally to the manage
ment of the activities within an organization which had to do with the planning,
purchasing, transport, storage and handling of the materials required by the
organization, using materials in the general sense to refer to the whole range of
goods and services obtained from outside the organization in order to provide
finished products for sale. However, increasingly, materials management has
come to refer to the grouping together of these materials-related activities into
one department under a materials manager. A typical theoretical approach is
shown in Figure 32.1.

In practice, surveys have shown that adoption of some kind of materials management structure has been extremely widespread in the US, and there has also
been considerable interest in the UK; but the kind of organization adopted has
often not conformed to the theoretical approach shown in the diagram. It has been
suggested that in seeking the organization structure which is right for a particular
company at a particular time, some key variables should be identified, such as:

1 Purchasing cost reduction leverage
2 Type of production: make for stock or make to customer order
3 Commonality of requirement between different divisions
4 Whether most problems occur between materials-related departments
5 Trade-offs between materials and non-materials departments.

These approaches are discussed more fully in Baily and Farmer (1982), which
also quotes evidence to suggest that the adoption of efficient computer systems
for materials management appears to have reduced the need to combine the
materials-related departments into a single materials management department.

It is obviously not easy to discuss the organizational questions in the abstract
because of the great variation in size, complexity and other dimensions which
exist between companies. Several large concerns which operate a number of
establishments favour some version of the materials management structure at
plant level, where purchasing staff are grouped departmentally with stock control,
stores, production planning and control, and transport staff while at corporate
level purchasing and contracts staff form a separate planning and negotiating
group. Similar developments can be seen in some retailing chains, where ordering
and progressing staff are grouped organizationally with stock control, warehousing and transport, while a separate headquarters purchasing unit deals with the
merchandising aspects, such as adoption of new lines and negotiation of original
prices for first-time buys.

Devising appropriate organization structures is a difficult process because so
many factors affect it. One factor is the calibre and capability of the personnel
affected. Purchasing staff who have the ability to contribute to long-term strategy
are not necessarily the same people as those who do a sound job of ordering and
progressing regular requirements from established suppliers. Another factor
arises from the fact that purchasing departments exist to arrange for the supply of
goods in accordance with the requirements of other departments, so that interdepartmental co-operation and communication is particularly important. Indeed

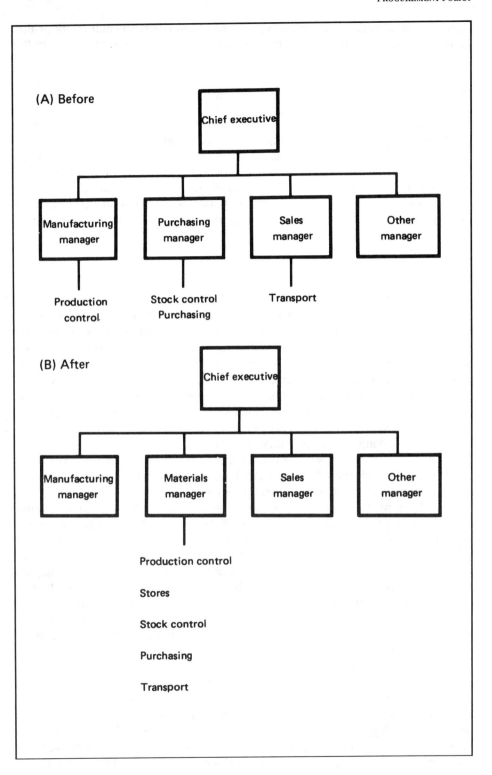

Figure 32.1   Materials management reorganization

many problems occur in practice in this area of interdepartmental relationships. An example is the matter of quality assurance, which forms the final topic in this chapter.

PURCHASING AND QUALITY ASSURANCE

Of fundamental importance in purchasing is to make sure that the right quality of goods, materials, and so on is bought. Both technical and commercial considerations are involved. The purchasing department operates jointly with other departments which also have important roles to play in this crucial aspect of arranging for the supply by outside organizations of what is required.

Although a number of different activities or stages occur in the process of purchasing quality assurance, it is convenient to group them under two headings:

1   Specification quality
2   Conformance quality.

The first part of the process is concerned with specifying the quality required. This may consist of a comparison of available merchandise and the selection of suitable brands or standards, or it may involve the preparation of engineering drawings and other forms of internally prepared specifications. Such a specification is a detailed statement of the features or characteristics required in a material, part or product. These features or characteristics may include chemical composition, such physical characteristics as ductility, viscosity, conductivity, weight, colour, surface finish, and physical size or dimensions – to name a few. The tolerance should also be stated: that is, the range of values within which a characteristic may vary without making the product unacceptable.

The second part of the process is concerned with arrangements to ensure that goods received conform with the specification, and that their important features or characteristics are within the allowed tolerances.

Normally in manufacturing industries a specialist department, such as design, engineering, or standards, is entrusted with the responsibility for specifications. Such a department needs to take account of inputs from marketing (what can be sold) and from purchasing (what can be bought), as well as the production implications. It is difficult to generalize about the role of the purchasing department in this connection beyond saying that it must play some part, and that its concern will naturally be with the commercial rather than with the technical aspects of the product. Commercial aspects include the relative cost and availability of alternative materials or products, and also the feasibility of obtaining the quantity required for bulk production at an acceptable price.

A single instance may illustrate the last point. A certain company manufactures agricultural chemical products, for use mainly by farmers but also by home gardeners. New products are continually being developed by the research and development laboratories. If approved by the new products committee, which is heavily marketing-oriented, they are put into a two-year field trial process intended to uncover any unwanted side effects as well as to provide evidence that the products will in fact produce the effect claimed. During this two-year period, a purchasing research section within the purchasing department investigates the availability on world markets of all the ingredients required by the formulation of each new product under trial. Naturally at the end of the two-year trial it is not possible to change the formulation before going into bulk production. But it would be a mistake for management to authorize bulk production if some of the ingredients could not be supplied in sufficient quantities.

The second part of the process is concerned with the selection of suppliers, the approval of their quality control systems and the inspection of goods received. Inspection is an expensive process, and should not need to be carried out at all if suppliers could be relied on to supply acceptable goods. Increasingly, purchasing organizations are taking steps to ensure that this is so.

Many organizations carry out their own investigations of suppliers, but third-party investigations are also used quite widely: the British Standards Institution and other organizations operate in this connection. Most systems for investigating the quality capability of suppliers classify the work into three levels, depending on the extent to which the customer relies on the supplier.

At the simplest level, all that the customer needs to know is whether the supplier has satisfactory instruments, test equipment and inspection procedures for final inspection of his products. Many intermediate-level products require inspection at a number of successive stages of manufacture, with a reliable system for corrective action if faults occur, so that a more comprehensive system of quality control would need to be certified.

When a supplier is responsible for design as well as for manufacture, the investigation of his quality capability needs to be still more extensive and thorough.

Industries such as aerospace, motor car manufacture, atomic energy and other parts of electrical manufacturing, are already subject to strict official regulation of certain aspects of quality (mainly those which have to do with safety) and this has been one of the factors leading to the development of British Standards such as BS 5179.

At the same time as official regulation of safety and other quality standards has increased, and official guidance as to procedures for ensuring that suppliers are capable of supplying and do in fact supply goods to the standard specified has become more widespread, a parallel development has been occurring within companies. Quality is everybody's business; job security and progression for the individual depends on the organization's ability to survive and prosper, which in turn to a large extent depends on the quality of its products.

Quality circles are a recent example of many approaches which organizations have adopted to encourage individual and small group initiative in maintaining and improving the quality of the product.

Technical inspection of incoming goods is a costly business which in principle could be dispensed with if suppliers could be relied on to supply acceptable goods. The investigation and selection process described above is intended to ensure that suppliers are in fact to be relied on, and is often used in practice to classify suppliers into three groups:

1   Accept goods on supplier's certificate
2   Accept goods after sample inspection

3   Inspect all goods received; do not order from this supplier if an alternative supplier is available.

If goods received require technical inspection before acceptance, it is often possible to obtain satisfactory results by inspecting a sample rather than every piece submitted. A large body of theory exists which can be applied in this connection to select the size of the sample and to draw conclusions from the results.

FURTHER READING

Baily, P. J. H., and Farmer, D. H., *Purchasing Principles & Management*, 6th edn, Pitman Publishing, London, 1990

Baily, P. J. H., and Farmer, D. H., *Materials Management Handbook*, Gower, Aldershot, 1982

Corey, E. Raymond, *Procurement Strategy, Organisation and Decision-Making*, CBI Publishing Company, Boston, Mass., 1978

Farmer, D. H., 'Input Management', *Purchasing & Supply Management*, Institute of Purchasing & Supply, Ascot, Berks, August, 1981

Farmer, D. H., *Purchasing Management Handbook*, Gower, Aldershot, 1985

33 Purchasing procedures

Peter Baily

Sweeping changes are occurring in purchasing procedures, due to continual improvements in computers large and small and in their software, and to comparable developments in fax and electronic data interchange (EDI). This is happening just as single market developments in the European Community and the appearance of world competitors in the Pacific Basin area could transform the trading environment in which purchasers operate and the supply chains they use.

Purchasing by organizations depends for its proper performance on good communications. The purchase department is constantly communicating with other internal departments such as users, specifiers, quality controllers, production and materials controllers, finance and budget controllers. Communications with external organizations – to obtain quotations, place orders, monitor progress, amend requirements, receive and pay for goods – are at the core of the purchasing task. Good communications are vital for good performance

Both internal and external communications often require reference to files and records. Developments in information technology (informatics as it is often called) are transforming both communications and records. This chapter outlines some of these developments, relating them to four stages in a typical purchasing transaction.

COMPUTERS AND PURCHASING

A hundred years ago many communications between trading partners were face-to-face or handwritten. Then came the era of the typewriter, the telephone and the filing cabinet.

Now small desktop computers are everywhere, linked to others in a network, or to a mainframe, or standing alone. Standard software packages readily and cheaply provide such facilities as spreadsheets, databases and word processing. Purchasing modules include as standard features, for example:

- Order/invoice checking
- Delivery date analysis
- RFQ (request for quotation) and purchase order set printing
- Outstanding order report by supplier or by product
- Supplier delivery performance analysis.

Stock records, materials requirements planning, requisitioning, price analysis and price breaks, lead-time details, ordering, open order reports, follow-up and expediting, receiving and payment are all increasingly handled by computer.

Buyers can develop supplier databases which show the names and locations of suppliers, the names of relevant executives, details of their products and prices, transaction history and performance details.

With electronic data interchange purchasers can communicate direct with suppliers, computer to computer, for ordering and other purposes. The computers can be of different types and located in different parts of the world.

Electronic data interchange (EDI)

Although face-to-face deals by word of mouth between buyer and seller have always been important in purchasing, and no doubt will continue to be so, most purchasing transactions between organizations have required a lot of paperwork. Increasingly, routine communications such as orders, delivery schedules and invoices go direct from computer to computer, rather than by typed documents sent by post which may then have to be typed in yet again. Electronic data interchange is replacing paperwork interchange. EDI transfers data from one computer to another by electronic means. Four main types of data transferred are:

- *Trade data* For example, request for quotation, purchase order, acknowledgment, delivery instructions, dispatch note, invoice, credit note and statement
- *Technical data* Product specifications, CAD/CAM data, performance data, and so on
- *Query-response* An example of this type is the airline system for querying prices and vacancies for passengers and cargo and responding by making reservations. Similar systems enable a purchaser to check the progress of an order through a supplier's manufacturing and distribution sequence
- *Monetary data* Systems for electronic funds transfer computer to computer are now widely used, instead of making payment by delivering cheques or other paper by post or by hand. Examples include bank clearing systems, electronic payment of invoices, and Electronic Funds Transfer at Point of Sale (EFTPOS). With EFTPOS a retail customer can pay for goods by means of a credit card, which is checked by the POS reader at the till. Funds are transferred from the purchaser's credit account to the retailer's account, either immediately or else overnight. Another version introduced in 1989 under the name of SWITCH uses debit cards rather than credit cards to pay for goods and services at participating stores, restaurants, garages and retail outlets. Purchases are charged to the customer's current account in about three working days, like a cheque.

Requirements for EDI

For EDI, data has to be set up in a way which can be interpreted by the receiving computers. Electronic links between sender and receiver, supplemented by short-term data storage, are required in addition to the software which structures messages.

This is emphasized in International Data Exchange Association's definition of EDI: 'The transfer of structured data, by agreed message standards, from one computer system to another, by electronic means'.

EDI services are normally provided by independent network operators, such as International Network Services (Edict), and Istel (Tradanet). These operators are usually called Value Added Networks (VAN), or Value Added Data Services (VADS).

Electronic data interchange for administration, commerce and transport (EDIFACT) is being developed as a general message standard. Well-known EDI message standards include TRADACOMS, which serves pharmacy, travel and grocery firms. More specialized standards include EDICON (Electronic Data Interchange Construction), set up by the construction industry to devise and co-ordinate electronic trading methods from design, quotation and tendering through to invoicing; CEFIC for the chemical industry, EDIFICE for electronics, ODETTE for the auto industry, DISH and SHIPNET for international shipping, ANA for retail and distribution.

A considerable saving in postage, stationery and administrative processing time is claimed for EDI. Further savings are due to shorter lead-times, which lead to lower stocks. Against this, fees have to be paid for access to networks, plus annual subscriptions and the cost of the hardware and software.

Paperless trading of this kind is increasingly used by major retailers and manufacturers, and there can be little doubt that this is how large organizations will do business in future. Already General Motors are implementing plans to trade with up to 2 000 European suppliers in seven countries through EDI; Marks and Spencer are said to be buying 95 per cent of their requirements through EDI; the National Health Service, currently spending about £6 000m a year with 10 000 suppliers, plan to order 80 per cent of the value of purchases through EDI by mid-1992.

Databases

Materials information and supplier information is increasingly available on line from databases, which buyers can search for product description and specification, supplier names, prices and availability. A huge amount of information can be stored in a very little space. The entire Encyclopedia Britannica, plus a dictionary and lots of extras, has been made available on a single compact disk in computer-readable format.

Materials databases include for instance one which gives for gas, oil, kerosene, lubricants and other materials pricing reports, pricing trend charts, and demand or usage reports, accessible by telephone or computer. Price analysis, annual time series and forecasts are available for steel, magnesium, plastic chemicals and many others.

On-line databases are also available for potential suppliers. One, for instance, lists over 110 000 actively trading UK companies with up to ten named directors. They can be listed by various criteria such as geographical location or industry sector, and listings can be supplied as print-outs or labels, or on magnetic tape or floppy disk.

Databases can be accessed via a PC or terminal with suitable software and a modem to enable telephone lines to be used for communications between computers.

Companies House in Cardiff, the agency which incorporates new companies and records statutory information, including annual returns about all existing companies, also operates a database, extracts from which can be consulted free of charge by personal callers. Additional information can be searched out quickly at reasonable charges, and many buyers use this service for information about possible suppliers.

A STANDARD PURCHASE PROCEDURE?

Forms and procedures used in purchase transactions vary considerably. On one hand, these variations reflect the differences between organizations and the operations they carry out. Purchasing managers will wish to adopt purchasing systems and records which fit the individual requirements of their organizations. Retailers, offshore contracting, and mass production of consumer durables differ so much in what they do that they could be expected to use different documentation. Variations in procedure also result, however, from individual preference and the custom and tradition of the company. By no means all such variations are valid or of equal merit. Many forms and procedures are capable of considerable improvement.

Stages in purchasing transactions

Standard procedure in most purchase transactions can be considered under the headings:

1 Originating
2 Selecting
3 Ordering
4 Completing.

A typical sequence is shown in Figure 33.1.

ORIGINATING

Purchasing for organizations involves arranging for the supply on time and at a suitable price of the goods and materials, equipment and merchandise, services and supplies which are required to meet production programmes, sales plans or operating needs. It is normally the job of the purchase department to make the purchase on behalf of production, sales or operating departments. It is not normally the job of the purchase department to determine what needs to be purchased: most purchases are initiated by *requisitions* from other departments.

A purchase requisition is a request to the purchase department from any other department for something to be purchased. It serves to initiate the purchase, and also for audit purposes to provide evidence of authorization and action taken. An example is shown in Figure 33.2.

Special purpose requisitions are also used. *Travelling requisitions,* as shown in Figure 33.3, are useful for MRO (maintenance, operating and repair) requirements and other items which are ordered several times a year. They can take the form of a card kept in the originating department. Permanent data are entered on

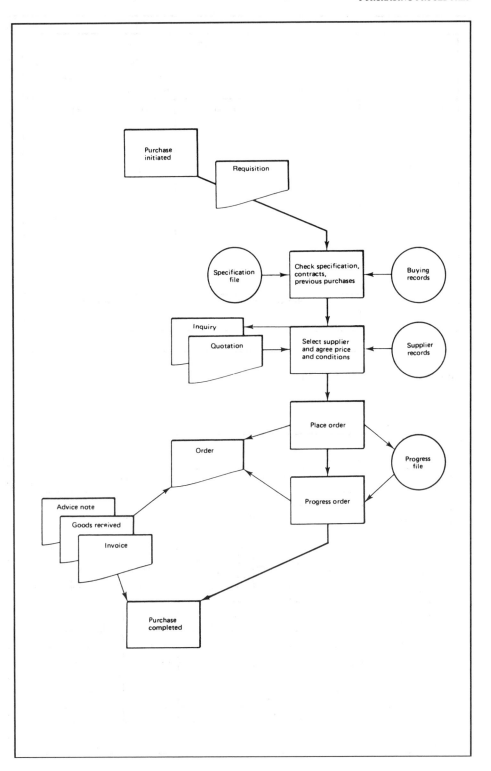

Figure 33.1   Outline of a standard purchasing procedure

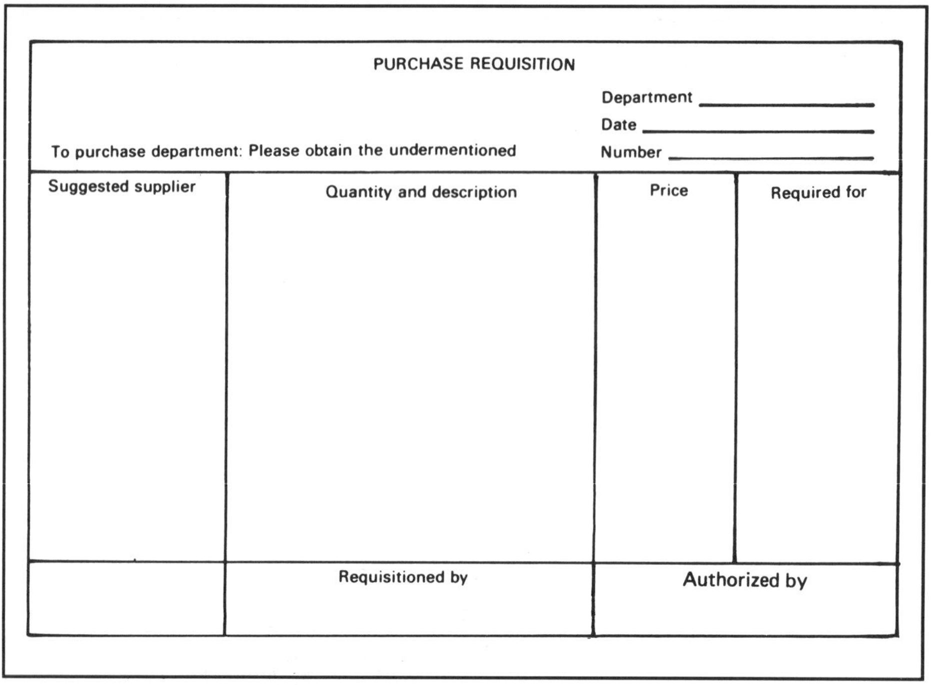

PURCHASE REQUISITION

Department _____

Date _____

To purchase department: Please obtain the undermentioned

Number _____

Suggested supplier	Quantity and description	Price	Required for
	Requisitioned by		Authorized by

Figure 33.2   Purchase requisition

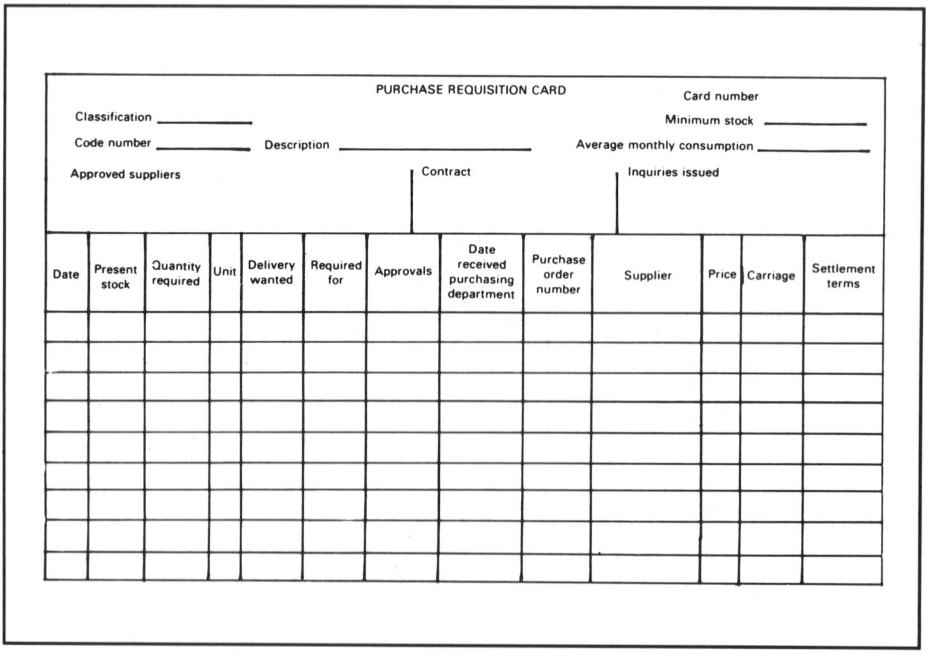

PURCHASE REQUISITION CARD

Card number

Classification _____

Minimum stock _____

Code number _____   Description _____   Average monthly consumption _____

Approved suppliers

Contract

Inquiries issued

Date	Present stock	Quantity required	Unit	Delivery wanted	Required for	Approvals	Date received purchasing department	Purchase order number	Supplier	Price	Carriage	Settlement terms

Figure 33.3   Travelling requisition

the card, such as the description. Variable data, such as the quantity required and date, are entered whenever the requisition is used. The form is sent to the purchase department to initiate each purchase, and returned to the originator (for re-use) when the purchase has been made.

Buy-lists, also known as blanket or schedule requisitions, are used when a large number of items need to be ordered to replenish stocks or to provide parts and materials for a production programme. Stock controllers issue them when using periodic review systems. Production planning systems such as material requirements planning (MRP) and period batch control also produce these buy-lists. No special form is needed: they can be retained in the computer system as planned orders to be printed out only when actioned by buyers.

SUPPLIER SELECTION

Upon receipt of a requisition, the purchasing section checks if the item in question is already covered by a contract. If it is, an order can be placed against the contract without delay. If it is not covered by a contract, the next stage is to select a supplier and agree price and terms.

There is a strong preference for continuing to deal with regular suppliers in the case of regular purchases, so long as they continue to prove satisfactory. Nevertheless, it is advisable periodically to check the market, to see what other suppliers have to offer. How often this should be done is a matter for judgement, and will vary with the type and volume of requirement and the structure of the supply market. If the market is dominated by one or two major suppliers it may be greatly to the long-term advantage of purchasers to place their business in such a way as to keep competition alive. Very large purchasers which dominate a market on the customer side often devote a good deal of time and thought to the optimum supply market structure, and sometimes take direct action to support minority suppliers or to develop new suppliers.

It is good practice for purchasing staff to know their regular supplier well, to be personally acquainted with the people who process and make decisions about their orders, to keep in touch with business plans, product developments and so forth. Suppliers are a major resource without which neither manufacturers nor traders could operate, and the management of supply markets can be a very important matter which calls for advance planning, forethought, and some difficult decisions.

When making a new purchase for which there is no regular supplier, or when checking the market for regular purchases, the usual procedure is to send a *request for quotation* to a short list of possible sources.

Who should be contacted? Names of possible suppliers can be obtained through the knowledge and experience of buyers and their colleagues, from sales representatives, trade magazines, trade associations, buyers' guides and directories. A technical library often includes catalogues and other information useful in finding sources of supply. In addition to general guides such as British Telecom's *Yellow Pages* and *Business Pages*, specialized directories are published and updated annually.

Computer databases providing similar information about product description, suppliers, and availability have the advantage that details can be updated daily –

and the disadvantage that they cost more. Buyers can obtain information from these databases by telephoning the operators or access them direct computer to computer.

Requests for information (RFIs)

General sources of information may yield a long list of possible suppliers without giving information about quality capability, financial status, performance record, and whether a firm is able to take on new work for completion within the required period. The usual procedure is to send a preliminary inquiry to the firms on the long list. These inquiries are known as requests for information (RFIs) or prequalification questionnaires. Each request outlines the requirement and asks suppliers who are able and willing to quote for the requirement to provide the information needed for the preparation of a short list (or even to provide a basis on which to decide whether or not to go ahead).

Requests for quotation (RFQs)

The request for quotation form (sometimes called an enquiry) is shown in Figure 33.4. This example is simply the company's usual letterhead, overprinted with a standard text asking the addressee to quote price, terms and delivery date for the supply of the goods listed, subject to terms and conditions which are printed on the reverse side of the sheet.

There is, however, sometimes considerable scope to structure the request for quotation in such a way as to facilitate subsequent negotiation in order to arrive at a mutually satisfactory agreement which gives better value: alternatives may be put forward as to total contract quantity, sub-quantities to be ordered against contract or delivered in particular places at particular times, terms of payment and other aspects of the deal. In some cases suppliers are asked to support their price quotation by a cost breakdown, which will be compared with a price/cost analysis prepared internally by estimating staff attached to purchasing. This latter technique is particularly favoured by mass-production manufacturers, the very scale of whose requirements limits possible suppliers to one or two in a given national economy.

Quality problems

Before making the purchase decision, purchasing staff analyse quotations. Commercial aspects such as price, discount, payment terms, legal conditions and delivery dates may not be directly comparable as submitted. The track records of existing suppliers, and the assessed capability of potential suppliers, need to be considered. Technical aspects such as differences in the specification offered or in the support provided, are also important.

For many types of purchase, the supplier's quality capability has become crucial. The international standard known as ISO 9000 in the International Organization for Standardisation (ISO) series, and BS 5750 in the British Standards Institution (BSI) series, has become the basic quality criterion for supplier selection in the single European market of the 1990s.

```
Dear Sirs,

              PURCHASE ENQUIRY

          Your quotation is invited not later than ................
    for the supply and delivery of the goods specified below, carriage
    paid, to ................

          Your tender must clearly state (a) the price which will
    remain firm, (b) the terms of payment, (c) details of appropriate
    discounts, and (d) the period required for delivery.  It must also
    incorporate all the conditions (general and special) set out overleaf.
```

```
    Dear Sirs,

              CONTRACT ENQUIRY

          Your tender is invited for the supply and delivery of the
    goods specified below to any of the Board's depots listed overleaf.

          Your tender must clearly state (a) the price which will remain
    firm throughout the period of the contract, (b) the terms of payment,
    (c) details of appropriate discounts, and (d) the period required for
    delivery.  It must also incorporate all the conditions (general and special)
    set out overleaf.

          If your tender is accepted you will then supply and deliver
    the goods in accordance with draw-off orders issued by the Board's
    supplies officers and invoices should be submitted for payment in
    respect of such draw-off orders.

          I shall be pleased, therefore, to receive your tender not
    later than .................... in a plain sealed envelope marked
    "contract enquiry number ........."

          Period of contract:
          Description of goods:

              Yours faithfully,


          (Purchasing and Stores Controller)
```

Figure 33.4   Reqest for quotation (enquiry)

The supplier's establishment may be visited by commercial and/or technical staff to assess quality capability or, when several potential suppliers are visited, to compare their facilities and to assess the likelihood of trouble-free dealings and mutually satisfactory relationships.

With the increasing importance of quality, it has been realized that it is not necessary for each purchaser to make thorough investigations of the quality capability of each possible supplier. Third party certification can be done on behalf of all purchasers by an independent body, of which the best known in the UK is the

British Standards Institution (BSI). The verdicts are published by the Department of Trade and Industry in the DTI QA Register.

Vendor rating

When considering regular purchases or established suppliers, the track record is of particular importance – although it should not be forgotten that past history is not a sure guide to future behaviour. Management does change, new developments occur, new products are launched, new customers found; nevertheless, it would not be prudent to ignore the record of how a particular supplier has behaved in the past. *Vendor rating* is an attempt to systematize this information.

Vendor rating, or supplier evaluation as it is sometimes called, is the process of systematically accumulating information about a supplier's actual performance and presenting it in numerical form. The usual aspects of performance to be measured are:

1 Quality
2 On-time delivery
3 Service (although this is usually estimated rather than measured)
4 Price.

Quality is delivered or conformance quality: essentially, the proportion of goods delivered by a supplier which are accepted. In practice several rules are used to calculate a figure appropriate to the needs of a particular purchaser. One rule, for instance, is:

$$\frac{60 \ (\text{Number of batches accepted})}{\text{number of batches delivered}} + \frac{40 \ (\text{number of parts accepted})}{\text{number of parts delivered}}$$

The delivery measure is again based on goods-received records and is essentially the proportion of goods delivered on time. Since the meaning of 'on time' may not be the same in a large-scale mass producer (within ten minutes of the due hour and date?) and a small-scale batch producer (within two weeks of the due date?), rules are specified to suit purchasing needs.

The price rating may be based on a comparison of the price quoted by the supplier in question with that quoted by competitors: the lowest price would score 100, and a price twice as high as the lowest would score 50 in one scheme. Often such a comparison is not feasible, and the price rating is based on a comparison of latest price with standard budget price, or last year's price, or latest target price.

It is not particularly difficult to calculate these ratings manually, since the system will be applied only to a minority of purchases from a relatively small number of suppliers, but computer salesmen have made much of the system as a further argument for extending the application of computers.

In most systems, after calculating individual numerical scores for the supplier characteristics being measured, a further calculation is made by weighting and combining the individual scores to arrive at an overall figure which is regarded as an index of the supplier's total performance – in fact a vendor rating or supplier evaluation figure which can be used in deciding how to allocate business between potential suppliers and also in persuading delinquent suppliers to improve their performance!

Such systems are considered in more detail in purchasing textbooks, and in books about industrial marketing, but it must be admitted that recent accounts in books which have a practical rather than a strictly academic bias are somewhat less than enthusiastic about their use in practice and tend to stress their limitations.

ORDERING

A contract is a business agreement for the supply of goods or the performance of work in return for a price, and subject usually to a number of terms and conditions. An order on the other hand is an instruction to a trader or manufacturer to supply something.

In most cases both order and contract are incorporated in a single document, the purchase order form. Normal practice is to make it a rule that all purchases, subject to certain clearly defined exceptions, must be made by means of the official purchase order form. This is for practical rather than for legal reasons. The purpose of the rule is to prevent sharp practice, whether by some unscrupulous employee or by some shady dealer outside the organization, and also to establish clearly what the organization is committed to accept and pay for. Regular suppliers are made aware of the rule by printing it on the order form, or by stipulating that the order number must be quoted on advice notes and invoices. Goods-receiving personnel can then be given instructions not to accept goods which are delivered without an official order number.

Exceptions to this procedure take several forms. The contract, or agreement with the supplier, may cover the supply of aggregated requirements over a considerable period of time, or over a large geographical area as when corporate contracts are signed by headquarters staff for common requirements at a number of divisions or branches. If such a contract is placed on the standard purchase order form it might cause some confusion if the same form is also used for instructions to supply specific quantities of goods against the contract to specific locations.

Three solutions have been observed in practice. First, a special form is used for the contract document, and normal purchase orders are used to order goods against it. Second, the normal purchase order form is used for the contract, and special forms are used for the orders; these may be known as delivery schedules, delivery instructions, contract releases, or call-offs. Third, the same form is used both for order and contract, and care is taken to state on one: 'This is an order against contract', and on the other: 'This is a contract against which goods should not be delivered until orders are placed.'

Most organizations use a preprinted multipart set of forms for purchase orders. Four or five copies are usually provided, and these are distributed to supplier, goods receiving, possibly accounts, possibly originator (department which produced the requisition), to purchase order open file, and possibly to order progress file.

Some organizations have adopted computer-output order forms and such developments as communicating word processors and computer-to-computer links.

These developments are making the traditional method of typewritten order forms sent by letter post less economic than the newer methods of electronic communication. A review of the current position, rapidly changing as it is, can be found in the third edition of Baily, P., *Purchasing Systems and Records.* Blanket orders or systems contracting methods are often used with considerable commercial advantage where it is possible to group together either numbers of different item requirements from one source, or else a sequence of requirements of one item over a substantial period of time, say, six months or a year. Instead of treating each order, or requisition, as an independent closed transaction, the idea is to look at the flow of requirements over a time and buy the flow. Instead of taking a bucket to the well every day, a waterpipe is laid on.

Take, for example, a small or intermediate value purchase such as carbon paper. Instead of placing a series of orders every month or so for the various sizes and grades required, with this technique there is an annual review of the requirements, alternative specifications and sources. Twelve months' requirements are then covered with just one or two orders which specify what and how much should be delivered each month. If stocks start to build up or fall short as the year progresses one or two adjustments may be required. Apart from that, supplies come through automatically: and the price (based on a twelve-month contract) is low.

Purchases of parts for production may not seem, at first glance, to be amenable to this approach if the production programmes are not also fixed for twelve months in advance. There will usually be a sales forecast looking forward at least a year but with the firm production programme going only one or two months ahead. The solution then may be to authorize the purchasing department to make firm commitments for 50 per cent of the sales estimate for one year, thus getting the benefit of a lower price plus the benefit of a bank stock with which to handle cyclical fluctuations. In an actual case a component X was being bought in lots of 1 000 at a price of 26p each. It was built into a product with a current sales estimate of 12 000 per year. Contracting for 50 per cent of this, that is for 6 000 pieces, with deliveries called off at 1 000 a month, enabled the buyers to bring the price down to 20p, a 23 per cent reduction in invoice cost, with further reductions in administrative costs and paperwork. Both cost and availability are improved, and if sales fall short of forecast, it may well take nine or twelve months instead of six months to clear the components but they would still be used up within the year. This is a useful technique for plastic mouldings, castings, electrical and mechanical parts.

Small order procedures

Wherever possible small orders should be put through a special procedure. If they are repeating or regular requirements they should be bought once a year in one lot, or perhaps twice a year: it is obviously uneconomic to expend £15 worth of man-hours, cheques, stamps and paperwork in procuring an item with a usage value of only £15 a year. Non-repeating small orders are often such things as maintenance requirements, design and development prototypes, laboratory requirements. The requisitioner knows exactly what he wants and where to get it and the price is often a listed price. One solution to this problem is the order/requisition/cheque form devised by Kaiser Aluminium in the USA, and adopted by other organizations, including one in the public service. Through clever forms design, the same document which the requisitioner prepares as a requisition serves as an order, and a blank cheque accompanying it (marked 'not valid above £X') cuts out the invoicing/purchase-ledger/payments procedure.

Other approaches to the small order problem include: local cash purchase (someone goes round in a van picking up requirements and paying for them along the way) and laundry list (the local stockholder calls once a week and delivers a wide range of sundry materials against a laundry list type of order, with invoices submitted monthly charging prices which are renegotiated annually).

THE COMPLETION STAGE

Contracts (or orders) are completed when goods are delivered or work is done in accordance with the agreement and payment is made as provided.

Obtaining delivery on time can be difficult: the sub-contract and component supply section of the engineering industries have got themselves a bad name for late delivery, although large numbers of purchasers throughout industry and commerce have few problems in this connection and would rightly regard late delivery as an exceptional event, to be dealt with by crisis measures when it occurs.

The fundamental step in obtaining delivery on time is to decide exactly what is wanted at what time, to communicate this decision to those concerned, and to insist that delivery is made at the time specified. All too often firms which complain of late deliveries by suppliers are themselves to blame for inaccurate delivery schedules, continually amended. When both customer and supplier are struggling to operate with production planning and control systems which are defective in practice and misconceived in principle it is astonishing that anything is ever delivered on time, yet this has been the situation in certain sections of the engineering industry. Materials-requirement planning systems, if properly designed and operated, have brought great improvements in this connection to manufacturers of complex products.

The next step is to ensure that suppliers know that on-time delivery is a very important element in their marketing mix: in the combination of characteristics which results in their customers doing business with them. If valid due dates are stipulated it becomes easy to measure supplier performance in meeting due dates, and delivery performance tends to improve significantly once it is measured and reported. Customers with accurate, stable and reliable schedules of delivery requirements, who insist on delivery at the time scheduled, and measure and report supplier delivery performance, are on the whole quite satisfied with the results they get. In many cases it has been shown that 99 per cent on-time delivery is normal when suppliers know and are fully aware that the schedule is accurate and that every time they fail to meet the schedule they are going to have to explain it to their customers. Nevertheless, progressing (chasing, expediting or follow-up) of orders remains necessary in many cases. This may be done:

1 At the date when tool or jig designs are to be ready
2 When the items from these designs should be available
3 When materials or components should be marshalled for production

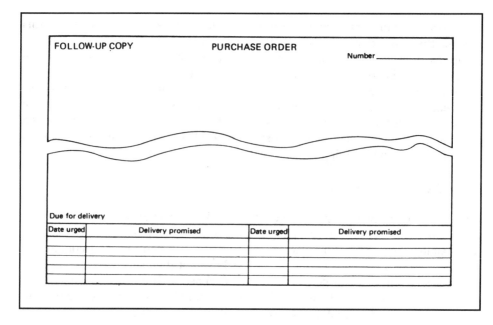

Figure 33.5   Follow-up copy of purchase order

4   When the various stages of production can be achieved
5   When final assembly and testing will be completed.

Often critical items can be identified which deserve special attention. For example, castings with long delivery times might be delivered to suppliers, only to be rejected. In consequence, some companies extend their progressing activities to include secondary suppliers (to the foundry in this example).

Methods which help to ensure that orders are chased when they ought to be include:

1   Copy orders filed in date-due order, being actioned, say, one week before that due date in general, or as necessary in the particular case
2   Five divisions made at the top of the copy order numbered one to five (representing weeks in any month). A signal of a different colour is then allocated to each month and one is attached to the relevant square in the particular case. (Thus, if January were red and the item were due in week three of that month, a red signal would be placed on square three.) The order copies are then filed in alphabetical order by supplier
3   A diary system with the serial numbers of orders which are due being entered on the appropriate page of the diary.

It is often useful to provide space on the order form to record the date of progress action, reply, and so on, as shown in Figure 33.5.

Finally, the supplier dispatches the goods to the customer, usually including a packing note and copy advice note with the goods and also forwarding an advice note by post. The postal copy is passed to the purchasing section to note that goods are in transit and, the same morning, is passed on to the goods-receiving section. Each day the goods-receiving section check through their file of advice notes and if any goods appear to have been lost or delayed in transit they initiate appropriate action. When goods are actually delivered, a goods-received note is prepared, usually on a multipart form to notify purchasing, accounting, and originating sections of the delivery.

FURTHER READING

Baily, P., *Purchasing & Supply Management*, 5th edn, Chapman & Hall, London, 1987

Baily, P. and Farmer, D. H., *Purchasing Principles & Management*, 6th edn, Pitman, London, 1990

Baily, P., *Purchasing Systems and Records*, 3rd edn, Gower, Aldershot, 1990

34 Inventory control

Peter Jackson

Investment in stocks and work-in-progress can represent a high proportion of the capital employed in any manufacturing company. The trend towards just-in-time systems has emphasized the tremendous advantages of reducing inventory, including:

- Reduced carrying costs
- Shorter lead times
- Saving in floorspace
- Improvement in quality
- Easier introduction of engineering changes.

However it is impractical to hold no stock at all and the right amount of stock at the right time in the right place can smooth out the inevitable variability of the system. This chapter covers the recording of stock, ordering methods and quantities, safety stocks and stock auditing.

STOCK CLASSIFICATION

If only a few items are stocked, control can be kept by common sense and experience. Where many thousands of items are dealt with, easy-to-use clerical or computer systems are needed. The costs of such systems can be minimized by concentrating the available effort on items which cost most to stock, and keeping their stock levels as low as possible. Conversely, larger stocks of those items which are cheap to stock can be held, reducing the need for tight control. An item is expensive to stock either because it has a high usage, or because its unit cost is high. Suppose that the annual usage value is found for each stock item (the annual usage value being the item's usage rate multiplied by its unit cost). By arranging all stock items in descending order of their annual usage value it is possible to calculate and plot a 'Pareto' curve (Figure 34.1). This shows that a small proportion of items accounts for a large proportion of the total annual usage value. From this Pareto analysis, stock can be divided conveniently into three categories:

- *A items* The 20 per cent of items which account between them for, perhaps, 80 per cent of the total usage value
- *B items* Those items which lie in the intermediate classification and require less stringent control than the A items
- *C items* Those items which form typically 70 per cent of items but which make

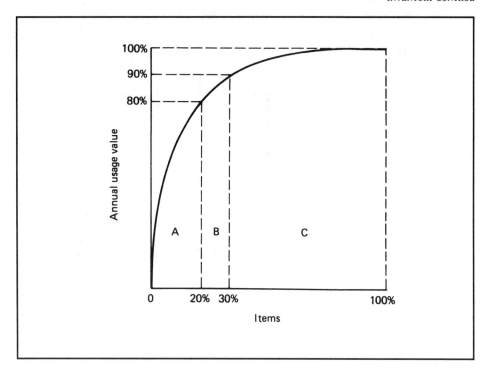

Figure 34.1   ABC classification of stocks. By concentrating stringent control on the few
most expensive A items, effective inventory reduction can be achieved for least
effort

up only a small fraction (about 10 per cent) of the annual usage value because
they are cheap or low usage or both. Holding a relatively high stock of these
will cost little and allow the adoption of simple and inexpensive control procedures.

Even with sophisticated computer systems it will be better to treat low value items
in bulk rather than control every nut, bolt and washer.

STOCK RECORDS

No control of stock can be carried out unless a firm knows, with reasonable
accuracy, the actual levels of stock held. As these levels change with time, prompt-
ness as well as accuracy is important. The more inventory levels are reduced, the
more accurate the figures need to be. Computer systems can help with speed and
accuracy of updating. Whether a computer or stock cards are used the following
data are usually required for each stock item:

- Part number
- Description
- Quantity
- Order level
- Order quantity

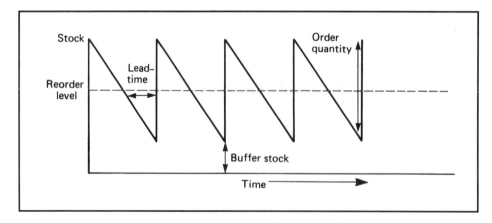

Figure 34.2   Simple stock usage pattern. Stock control tells the materials manager when to reorder, how much to order, and what level of buffer stocks should be kept

- Supplier (if bought out)
- Stores location
- Cost
- Issues
- Receipts
- Orders.

METHODS FOR CONTROLLING STOCK

There are many methods for controlling stock. Those shown here are typical and would be suitable for the stock classification indicated in each case. In general, stock will fall over a period of time and then rise suddenly as an order is received. The cycle will then repeat itself, as shown in Figure 34.2.

Ordering on past usage (max–min)

The max–min system is suitable for *B* items. When the stock level falls to a certain level a new order is raised. This reorder level is found from the following formula:

$$\text{weekly usage} \times \text{lead-time (weeks)} + \text{buffer stock}$$

For example, if 50 units of an item are used each week and it takes six weeks to get the item then fresh stock must be ordered before the stock falls to 300. Accurate lead-times and usage figures are not always available, and in any case such figures are liable to random variation and long-term change. Thus, it is necessary to carry a buffer or safety stock. The size of the buffer will vary with the availability and accuracy of the data. It can be determined statistically or, more commonly, by trial and error (for example by holding three weeks usage as a buffer and seeing what level of stockouts this gives). This system is usually controlled by stock cards. When the stock falls below the reorder level shown on top of the card, an order is placed.

Two-bin or sealed minimum method

A variation on the max–min method, suitable for C category items, dispenses with the use of stock cards and relies instead upon the physical stock levels. A quantity of stock, equal to the reorder level, is put in a sealed container at the bottom of the stores bin containing the item. A warning card telling the storekeeper to reorder is placed at the top of the sealed minimum. When the packet has to be opened the card is sent to the purchasing department. A smaller packet, containing the buffer stock, can be kept inside the sealed minimum, and this includes a progress warning to the purchasing department to chase the order. When the order is delivered the two packets are made up again and the cycle repeats.

The main advantage of this system is that stock issues do not have to be recorded. Items are given on demand. As this system of sealed minimum is commonly used for the C items, which can comprise 70 per cent of all stock items, substantial clerical savings are possible. The only record is kept by the purchasing department, who record the frequency of orders and therefore overall usage.

This system is basically the same as the Japanese 'Kanban' (or card) where a drop of physical stock triggers a signal to the previous stage of production or supply.

Ordering on predicted usage (free balance)

The assumption of max–min systems is that past usage patterns will continue. Protection against change is obtained by holding safety stock. For high-value items (such as A category stock) it may be worth the clerical effort of predicting future requirements from the forward sales plan or master schedule, and ordering to cover them. For a given period ahead the free balance is calculated as follows:

$$\text{stock in hand} + \text{existing orders due} - \text{requirements}$$

The free balance is thus the amount which would be in stock at the end of the period if all went to plan. If it is negative, or below a predetermined minimum, an order is placed. A special stock card can be used as shown in Figure 34.3.

In the simplified case illustrated, it is seen that on 4th May, 70 items will be needed in six weeks time. Posting this allocation causes the free balance to become negative. This prompts an order for the order quantity of 100 leaving the free balance at 30. When the order is delivered the stock rises by 100. When the 70 are issued the stock level falls to 30. Thus it can be seen that the left-hand side of the card anticipates the physical movements of the right-hand side. This system can only be used if usage, and therefore allocations, can be predicted further ahead than the lead-time of the item.

Material requirement planning (MRP)

Material requirement planning is a computerized version of free balance stock control. The basis of the system is a series of parts lists (bills of material) for all assemblies, showing the relationships between the items in a family tree arrangement (see Figure 34.4). The family tree stages are referred to as levels. Usually,

DESCRIPTION : Base Plate					Part No : P-123		
ORDER QUANTITY : 100							
Date	Allocations	Orders	Free balance	Receipts	Issues	Stock
4 MAY	70		-70			0
4 MAY		100	30			
3 JUNE				100		100
12 JUNE					70	30

Figure 34.3   Stock card used for reordering by predicted usage

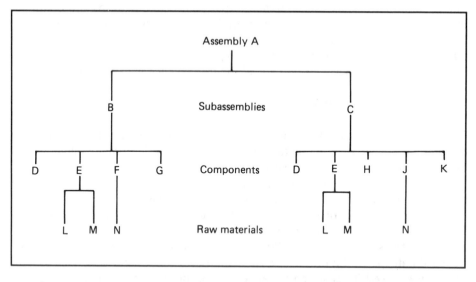

Figure 34.4   Family tree arrangement of bills of material, essential to material requirement planning

level 0 is used for assemblies, level 1 for subassemblies, and so on. The bills of material each show the quantities required to build the particular assembly or subassembly. Information held about each item will include:

- Part number
- Description

- Unit of quantity (for example, each or metres)
- Delivery or manufacturing lead-time
- Supplier code
- Order rule or batch quantity
- Stock level
- Netting.

Orders for end products are fed into the computer. These are usually for final assemblies, but could include items from lower levels ordered for spares. At each level the computer compares the requirements with actual stock, and calculates the difference.

For example; if there is an order for 10 models of type A, and there are 3 in stock, the net requirement is 7. If the order rule for the item is one-for-one, then an order for 7 will be generated. If, however, model A is made in batches, then a batch-size order will be generated. The computer will use the bills of materials to generate requirements for the components in the next level down.

Batching

As the breakdown proceeds, requirements for common parts used on different assemblies are generated. If they are required in the same week, they are simply added. If there is a series of small demands over a period of weeks, it is possible to incorporate batching rules to produce one large order rather than several small ones.

Offsetting

Given the delivery dates required for the end product orders and the lead times for each item, the computer works out when each item is required and thus when each generated order should commence. There are two snags to this:

1   Accurate lead-times are often hard to obtain and will vary. If, working from the top assembly level, a series of lead-times is added together to find out when raw material orders should be placed, the overall result might be considerably wrong owing to cumulative inaccuracies
2   The assumption is that quoted delivery dates are achievable. The MRP break-down may show that action should have started several weeks previously.

Setting up a material requirement planning (MRP) system takes time and requires a high level of data accuracy. Once the database has been set up it must be maintained and updated. There are many side benefits, such as identifying slow-moving stock and managing engineering changes.

BATCH SIZES

Whilst main items may be ordered or produced on a one-for-one basis lesser items may need to be batched. Large batches mean long lead-times, high carrying costs and inflexibility. The smaller the batches produced or purchased, the better will be the system. Two conflicting costs have to be balanced in determining batch sizes:

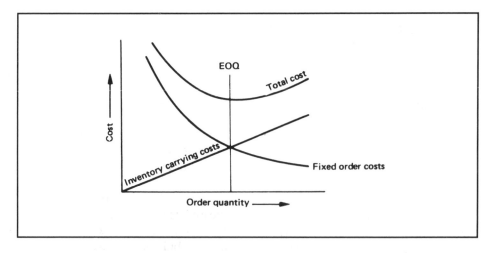

Figure 34.5   Economic order quantity. This diagram shows that the economic order quantity for each batch of purchased items will correspond to the lowest point on the curve of total costs. This curve is also of use in determining batch quantities for manufacture, in which case the set-up costs have to be considered, either instead of or in addition to the inventory-carrying costs

1   The cost of setting up a machine or the fixed cost of raising a purchase order. Clearly, in large batches this cost will be smaller in relation to each component
2   The cost of storage. A common rule of thumb is that it costs about 25 per cent of an item's value to hold it in stock for a year. For larger batches this cost will be greater per component.

These two costs together with the total cost are shown as a graph in Figure 34.5. It can be seen that the total cost falls from an initial high level and then, with increasing order quantity, starts to rise again. There is a point where the total cost is at a minimum. This is known as the economic batch quantity (EBQ) or for purchased items the economic order quantity (EOQ). It can be calculated by:

$$EBQ = \sqrt{\frac{200 \times A \times Z}{I \times U}}$$

where:

    A = annual usage
    Z = setting or order cost
    I = storage cost per cent per annum
    U = unit cost of the item

The resultant figure should only be used for guidance. Where set-up reduction programmes are carried out the setting cost can be substantially reduced, so the economic batch will be much smaller.

    One of the principles of just-in-time and optimized production technology (OPT) systems is that some machines will not be required to work all the time. When a machine is not required for production there is no time lost in doing extra set-ups, particularly if the machine has a setter operator. For such machines the batch sizes can be a lot smaller. Conversely, bottleneck machines have to be kept running as much as possible. Any interruptions (for example, for setting) lose the company sales revenue. This means that batches should be larger.

Where machines are physically close together, as in cells, components can be passed from machine to machine singly or in small numbers. What this means is that components should not necessarily remain in fixed batches throughout the production process, but that batch sizes should vary according to circumstances.

SAFETY STOCKS

Stockless production may be an ideal to aim for but reality demands a certain amount of stock to cover for the unpredictable and to allow for working batches. Just-in-time 'Kanbans' imply a certain buffer stock at each stage. MRP systems work in 'time buckets' such as weeks which implies a level of work-in-progress.

Bought out material and parts

Stock is needed at this stage to guard against poor delivery and sudden demand from the factory. While statistical controls can be applied most companies hold a certain number of days or weeks usage. This should be refined, firstly by classifying stock into easy and hard to obtain (perhaps by supplier). Less safety stock of the former and more of the latter should be kept. Secondly closer links with the suppliers should be developed in line with just-in-time philosophy to get better responsiveness and flexibility. This will mean less buffer stock needs to be carried. Above all, the number of stockouts need to be monitored and analysed. If a company never runs out of stock it is holding too much. If stockouts are frequent the reasons should be analysed to see if and where extra stock might help.

Work-in-progress

Much work-in-progress exists because of large batches and the issuing of work too early to keep operators and machines busy. There is only need for buffer stocks before bottleneck operations, to ensure they never run dry. Non-bottleneck machines by definition do not need to be kept working flat out.

Finished goods

The ability to satisfy customer demand varies with the product. No one expects to buy an oil tanker off the shelf or to wait six weeks for a packet of sweets. The service level the company sets will determine the finished stock level kept. Allowance must also be made for any seasonal demand where stocks must be built up in advance of anticipated demand. Again, by making the production system more responsive, less finished stock needs to be carried. Even with mass-produced consumer items the links between the shop's computer, the warehouse and the manufacturer are now often only a matter of days, so that production can be tied in closely to demand.

STOCKTAKING

Stocktaking is a tedious and laborious chore that has to be performed annually to the satisfaction of the company's auditors in order to evalute the quantities of stocks of materials and work-in-progress. The results are used in preparing the company's financial accounts and are also important for management control. Stocktaking verifies the accuracy of stock records and discloses possible frauds or other losses. Some large companies have full time staff to undertake continuous stocktaking. In any case, more emphasis should be placed on *A* items and less on *C* items.

Stocktaking needs careful planning to ensure that the whole exercise can be completed during the prescribed period. This is commonly arranged during a weekend or at some time when production will not be interrupted. Because of the large amount of work involved all available staff need to be deployed. Stocktaking provides an opportunity, which should not be missed, of identifying obsolete and redundant stocks, the disposal of which can release both cash and space.

FURTHER READING

Baily, P., *Successful Stock Control by Manual Systems*, Gower, Aldershot, 1971

Baily, P. and Farmer, D., *Materials Management Handbook*, Gower, Aldershot, 1982

Goldratt, E., *The Goal*, revised edn, Gower, Aldershot, 1989

Jessop, D. and Morrison, A., *Storage and Control of Stock*, 4th edn, Pitman, London, 1988

Storey, R., *Stock Control Systems and Records*, 2nd edn, Gower, Aldershot, 1984

Thomas, A. B., *Stock Control in Manufacturing Industries*, 2nd edn, Gower, Aldershot, 1979

35 Just-in-time supplies

D M Lascelles and B G Dale

Just-in-time (JIT) production has been hailed by some commentators as one of the miracles of the Japanese economic revolution. The concept of JIT is elegant in its simplicity: the production of parts in the exact quantity required just in time for use. This concept embraces not only the final user but also all preceding stages in the supply chain, both internal and external. It is an idealized philosophy of zero inventory in which the elimination of waste is the central goal. The reduction of stocks in the manufacturing system means that a company can respond more readily to the demands of the market place.

The attraction of JIT is obvious in terms of its positive effect on business, but it is a high-risk strategy because stocks are kept to a minimum and planning is short term. Key requirements, include short set-up times so that it is economical to manufacture very small batches, simple material flows, effective material handling, damage-free material, no equipment breakdowns, no product non-conformances and effective production scheduling. The ideal is make one piece just in time for the next processing operation. There is a low level of contingency in the system and failure of any part of the system can be catastrophic.

Product quality is a key issue with JIT. This has implications for the way in which the business and supplier base is managed. Suppliers need to be educated by the customer on what is required of them. The need for a continuous process of supplier development becomes critical, otherwise a company might as well forget about JIT purchasing. Supplier development revolves around the establishment of a long-term business partnership between a company and its supplier community to the competitive advantage of both parties.

This chapter opens by reviewing the concept of JIT and examines the importance of total quality management (TQM) and supplier development for the effective use of JIT. Then, drawing on the findings of a number of research projects on the subject of TQM and supplier development, the chapter examines the important issues of supplier development, outlines how such a programme might be initiated and describes its main features. Abbreviations used are:

* FMEA Failure modes and effects analysis
* JIT Just-in-time
* SPC Statistical process control
* SQA Supplier quality assurance
* TPM Total productivity maintenance
* TQM Total quality management.

THE JIT CONCEPT

JIT is concerned with the reduction and eventual elimination of waste. Hay (1984) defines waste as anything other than the minimum resources required to add value to the product. Taiichi Ohno, who is generally recognized as the 'father of JIT' due to his pioneering work at Toyota in the 1950s and 1960s, classified the waste incurred in the production process into: overproduction, waiting time at work-centres, transportation, manufacturing processes, holding unnecessary inventories, unnecessary motion and producing defective goods.

Ohno believes that overproduction leads to waste in other areas. To eliminate the problem, he devised the concept of just-in-time production; that is, bringing the exact number of required units to each successive stage of production at the required time. Putting this concept into practice necessitated a radical change in production from 'push' to 'pull'. In other words, abandoning the traditional 'push' system that is based on a forecast generated at the outset from which a production plan is developed to meet the forecast demand (the plan then drives manufacturing through the issue of work orders), and replacing it with a 'pull' system in which nothing is produced until it is needed, effectively allowing customer demand for finished goods to pull components and material through the system. The result was a significant decline in inventory levels. Even after Ohno initiated the concept on a trial basis in machining and assembly work in 1952, it took almost ten years before it was adopted in all Toyota's plants.

Once the JIT concept became established at Toyota, Ohno began extending it to subcontractors and suppliers. The Toyota JIT production system is now legendary. A critical lesson comes from the Toyota experience: a company must successfully implement JIT in-house before it attempts to extend the process to its suppliers. It is worth noting that in a number of Japanese companies products are built and shipped the same day.

By its very nature, JIT is a high risk strategy; stocks which have traditionally acted as the 'safety net' to buffer failure and hide problems are minimized and planning is short term. The prime concern of JIT is to avoid interruptions to production. A company will create for itself a number of problems by adopting JIT unless the quality of parts flowing through the system is satisfactory. In the absence of 'safety' stock, the production line will very quickly stop every time a non-conforming part is found. The effect ripples back through the previous processes and eventually the entire production system grinds to a halt. The key issue is finding the optimum level of stocks for cost effective production. Plant breakdowns will have the same effect. In addition, delays will be caused by a production scheduling system that is unresponsive to an environment with a planning horizon that is measured in hours rather than weeks. Therefore, the implementation of JIT demands a risk minimization strategy featuring Kanban, simple material flows, total productivity maintenance (TPM) and TQM.

The term 'Kanban' is often seen as being synonymous with JIT. Kanban, meaning signboard or label, is used as a communication and production control tool in the JIT system. A Kanban signifying the delivery of a given quantity is attached to each container of parts as they are fed into the production system. When the parts have been used, the same label (that is, Kanban) is returned to its origin where it becomes an order for more parts. For a detailed description of 'pure' Kanban systems the reader is referred to Schonberger (1982).

Not all Kanban systems use Kanban cards; some feature traffic-light-type signals. There are also similar pull-type production control systems in existence which use 'Kanban squares'; these are controlled inventory locations between manufacturing areas and processes. Between each process, inventory is held in a fixed-size container or fixed-area square within sight of the area producing the items held and the area consuming them. A process is not allowed to start work on an item until there is a space within the Kanban square to put the finished item after the process has been completed. In effect, the 'single bin' stock control principle has been applied to a dynamic interprocess inventory situation. This approach has been used extensively by Hewlett-Packard. However, all Kanban systems have several common characteristics: they are pull-type production control systems, they are dynamic, they are visual, the signals are easy to understand and they facilitate rapid communication.

In JIT manufacture it is essential that the layout of production processes and equipment facilitates continuous and unidirectional material flow. A parallel objective is to eliminate or at least minimize operations which do not add value to the material or cause delays (for example, inspections, transportations and storage). Therefore, material flows are a key consideration in the planning of JIT manufacture. This may require some replanning of manufacturing operations, changing the process sequence or some redesign of the product to ensure manufacturability and optimize production line efficiency. In some cases this may involve rationalizing manufacturing operations so that all products follow the same standard process sequence, in others changing the shape of flow lines. Another option may be the implementation of manufacturing cells (that is, group technology) to produce families of components (categorized by their component geometry, material, process sequence and equipment). Group technology cells reduce the need for repeatedly transporting workpieces between departments, although attention must be given to work movements and layout within the cells to ensure their efficient operation. Decisions have to be made regarding manufacturing technology and automation, whether to invest in flexible or dedicated production lines. Some flexibility is also required from the labour force in terms of job rotation and in the tasks they perform. Extra production capacity may be needed to provide cover for breakdowns and, on occasions, to smooth out loading on machine groups.

TPM is now practised by a large number of Japanese manufacturing companies. TPM is defined by the Japan Institute of Plant Maintenance as: 'aiming to maximise the effectiveness of production equipment with a total system of preventive maintenance throughout its entire life. Involving everyone in all departments and at all levels, it motivates people for plant maintenance through small group and voluntary activities.'

Preventive maintenance is usually associated with regular equipment inspection to diagnose impending failure, and servicing in order to reduce wear and so prevent or delay breakdowns. TPM goes beyond this. In Japan, TPM is seen as a company-wide activity in which everyone is imbued with a collective responsibility – just like TQM.

TQM is a way of managing the business to achieve a total quality organization.

Any organization is a network of administrative and technical processes, each of which has a supplier and a customer and where every employee is committed to continuous improvement of their part of the operation. It involves teamwork and extends to external suppliers and customers. This concept requires a fundamental change in the way in which people approach their work. It means respecting the work of all people in the company by ensuring that the output of one's work (whether it be a physical component or a piece of paper containing information) is correct before it is passed on to the next person.

TQM is an essential prerequisite for JIT. In reality, JIT has no real hope of success unless a company has embraced the TQM ethic.

THE CUSTOMER–SUPPLIER RELATIONSHIP

The simplicity of the JIT concept belies the extreme difficulty which companies experience when attempting the implementation. JIT involves cultural changes at every level within the organization and among its suppliers, and even its customers. JIT is a total concept like TQM and, therefore, organizations must adopt the complete package, not just the elements they like. The supplier must be viewed as part of the manufacturing chain, and so the JIT philosophy of producing small quantities of conforming product must be acceptable to them. They must not think that they are being forced to hold stocks for their customers.

Two surveys of JIT purchasing practices in the United States (Hutchins, 1986; Ansari and Modarress, 1986) revealed that companies were finding the implementation of JIT more difficult than they originally expected. Companies discovered that JIT is a regime which requires more than merely reducing the number of suppliers, renegotiating supplier contracts and tinkering with plant layout; changes in behaviour and attitudes are required, too. Hutchins (1986) cites several examples of unsuccessful JIT programmes. The most frequent cause of failure was the way in which companies were perceived as treating JIT as a means of getting suppliers to hold inventories on their behalf. In many cases, relationships deteriorated as suppliers complained about new inventory practices that served only to benefit the purchaser. Ansari and Modarress (1986) identified poor supplier support, followed by inadequate understanding and commitment by top management in the purchasing company as the most significant problems associated with the implementation of JIT. To minimize these problems they recommended three steps: the education and training of suppliers; the development of long-term relationships with suppliers; and encouragement of senior managers to visit companies with successful JIT programmes. Hutchins concluded that JIT suppliers need a lot of 'hand holding' from their customers, but in dealing with suppliers the old adversarial ways die hard.

The traditional relationship between the purchasing organization and its supplier community is an adversarial one, with the customer and suppliers having differing objectives. The focus tends to be on negative issues and is characterized by uncertainty. Suppliers are kept at arm's length and are provided with only the bare minimum of data on such issues as the schedule, financial information, future work programme, product changes and their own performance ratings. In general, suppliers are regarded with a certain amount of suspicion by the purchasing organization. On the other hand, the purchasing organization is seen by suppliers as not being concerned about their future business prospects and being very much price-driven in contractual negotiation; quality is a secondary consideration. If a purchasing organization starts to place some emphasis on quality, the typical reaction from suppliers is 'you can have quality but it will cost you'. Some people have likened the relationship (if one can call it that) to a game of cat and mouse.

In the traditional relationship, if the purchasing organization has not provided feedback data on performance, the suppliers tend to believe that their performance is acceptable to the purchaser. Most suppliers are not encouraged to ask the purchaser how their product is performing in practice. Lack of feedback on quality performance is a frequent complaint amongst suppliers. Suppliers, however, react to differing demands and prior experience of their customers. An example of this is the grading of their output to different levels according to individual customer requirements: 'this will not be accepted by Company X, but Company Y will take it.'

To protect themselves in this uneasy relationship with suppliers, the purchasing organization will employ a multiple-sourcing strategy, resulting in a large supplier base. Writers on the subject of single versus multiple sourcing cite a number of reasons to support the practice of multiple sourcing, the main ones being that it:

- Provides some security in the event of strikes or catastrophies
- Gives some flexibility to cater for changes in demand for the supplies
- Reduces stock
- Protects against a monopoly situation
- Facilitates competition
- Minimizes risk
- Has price-related reasons (one supplier can be 'played off' against another).

A number of the reasons given can be classified as defensive.

Another characteristic of the traditional relationship is that the customer organization does not have clearly defined responsibilities and accountability for the total quality performance of the supplier base. It is not uncommon to find that a number of people and departments are requesting and providing information to suppliers but no single area is taking overall responsibility. The points of contact are frequently ill-defined resulting in unco-ordinated data flow. In particular, the allocation of responsibilities between the purchasing department and quality department are not clear; purchasing personnel often view assistance from the quality department as interference. This results in weaknesses in the communication system and procedures used by the purchasing organization in dealing with suppliers.

Clearly, JIT requires a radically new form of customer–supplier relationship. The Philips Group (1985) coined the phrase 'co-makership' to describe it. Co-makership means working together towards a common goal. It is based on the principle that both parties can gain more benefit through co-operation than by separately pursuing their own self-interests. Co-makership means establishing a long-term business partnership with each supplier based on common aims and aspirations, mutual trust and co-operation, a desire by both parties to improve the product continuously, and to understand responsibilities clearly.

The Ford Motor Company is one major organization which has set out to build partnerships with its suppliers in which a joint approach is stressed: 'It is Ford and her suppliers who make cars.' The following points illustrate how the Ford Motor Company endeavours to co-operate with its supplier base:

- Change from supplier quality assurance to supplier quality assistance with the introduction of a new combined function of supplier quality engineering
- Participation of suppliers in process improvement teams
- Liaison with suppliers on their use of process FMEA and providing assistance
- Provision of training in SPC and other techniques to suppliers (this has been used by more than 6 000 employees from 1 200 suppliers)
- Launch of the interactive video disc programme as a continuing training aid
- Introduction to the Q1 award
- Reduction of number of suppliers from 2 100 in 1980 to 1 200 in 1988 to intensify co-operation and improve quality
- Fifty per cent of the bills of materials are now covered by long-term contracts of 3 to 5 years' duration
- Extension of early involvement and source nomination for new programmes, improved communication between prototype and production buyers and suppliers: 99 per cent of early components from final production vendors
- Introduction of just-in-time and supplier communications programme.

To develop a co-makership type of relationship, considerable changes in behaviour and attitude are required in both the customer and supplier. Customers have to be prepared to develop plans and procedures for working with suppliers, and to commit resources to this. On the other hand, suppliers have to accept full responsibility for the quality of their shipped product, and not rely on the customer's receiving inspection to verify that the product is to specification. As a prerequisite of the new relationship, both parties have to reach an agreement on how they will work together (that is, establish the ground rules).

Barriers to supplier development

As part of a research programme to investigate the effects a major customer might have on supplier awareness and attitudes towards quality management and the methods and systems employed, the authors (Lascelles and Dale, 1988) carried out a postal questionnaire survey of the supplier communities of three automotive companies (over 300 suppliers in total). In addition to the questionnaire survey, representatives from a number of the suppliers were interviewed, and time was spent in the purchasing companies observing how they operated and interacted with suppliers.

The findings of this research reveal that certain aspects of the customer–supplier relationship can act as a barrier to supplier development. They include poor communication and feedback, supplier complacency, misguided supplier improvement objectives, the credibility of the customer as viewed by their suppliers and misconceptions regarding purchasing power.

Poor communication and feedback

In general, communication and feedback in the supply chain is not good. Moreover, suppliers and customers often do not realize how poor they are at communicating with each other. It was found that while the majority of suppliers surveyed perceived as realistic the quality performance requirements of the three collaborating automotive companies, a substantial number of them felt that communications and feedback between customer and supplier could be improved. Furthermore, it was found that not all dissatisfied suppliers communicate their dissatisfaction to the customer; a typical outcome of what was seen to be an adversarial relationship.

Non-conformance of purchased items is often due to the customer's inability to communicate clearly their requirements. Ishikawa (1985) claims that at least 70 per cent of the blame for non-conforming purchased items lies with the customer. It is up to the buyer to ensure the existence of a clear specification which defines the exact requirements, but this in itself is not enough to assure conformance. The supplier must be given the opportunity to understand the function of the part and discuss design details, particularly with regard to the manufacturability of purchased or subcontracted items, before requirements are finalized.

Some purchasing managers and supplier quality assurance engineers seem to think that the quality performance of their suppliers can be achieved almost by remote control, and are disappointed and often surprised when non-conforming items are received. During the course of the study, the authors came across several people who genuinely believed they engaged in joint quality planning with suppliers, whereas, in fact, the communication process was all one-way (from customer to supplier) and feedback from suppliers was discouraged (either because it was *ad hoc* and ignored, or it was never sought in the first place). For example, in one case the supplier was asked if they remembered the non-conforming product they had shipped in some months ago. They were then told that the same problem had recurred and were instructed to visit the company with a drill to rectify the non-conformance.

Supplier complacency

Many suppliers appear complacent about customer satisfaction with the quality of their product or service and do not proactively seek out such information. Respondents to the authors' survey were asked if they had any positive way of measuring how well their product satisfied their customers' requirements. Two hundred and six respondent suppliers claimed they recorded measures of customer satisfaction: however, all but two reported only reactive measures.

Examples of reactive measures include internal failure data (for example, scrap reports, non-conformity analysis), external failure data (for example, customer rejections, warranty claims), customer assessment rating and audit reports, verbal feedback from meetings with customers, and requirements outlined in the customers' vendor improvement programme. It is clear that many suppliers see customer satisfaction in very simple terms; if the customer does not return our product then quality and reliability must be satisfactory. This is a short-term view which will ultimately result in lost business opportunities. Suppliers should, wherever possible, utilize proactive measures of customer satisfaction. These include: benchmarking, workshops, customer interviews, evaluating competitors' products, reliability analysis, value analysis and life-cycle costing and advanced quality planning carried out in conjunction with customers.

Misguided supplier improvement objectives

Companies are often not sure what they want from a process of supplier improvement. Comments made by respondents indicate that some of their customers (who may be first-or second-line suppliers to a major automotive company) do not understand the fundamentals of total quality management. Many have formal vendor audit programmes but no clear supplier development objectives. There also appears to be a dilution of the quality message as requirements are passed down the supply chain. For example, when faced with demands from customers for improved quality, suppliers are reacting by implementing specific quality techniques and, in turn, are insisting that their own suppliers use the same techniques. Very few customers are actively involved with their suppliers in helping them to solve quality problems, and there appears to be blind faith in the power of statistical process control (SPC) to do the trick. It is clear that many companies assume that introducing SPC is the same as beginning a process of total quality management. Similarly, these companies are under the equally mistaken impression that the imposition of a particular quality technique on their suppliers as a condition of purchase is the same as supplier development. But the implementation of techniques without behaviour and attitude change means that any benefits gained will only be short-lived.

Lack of customer credibility

A purchasing organization's lack of credibility in the eyes of its suppliers is another barrier to supplier development; suppliers need to be convinced that a customer is serious about quality improvement and that this is demonstrated by the customer's behaviour and attitudes. Poor purchasing and supplies management practices such as a competitive pricing policy, frequent switches from one supplier to another, unpredictable and inflated production schedules, last minute changes to schedules, poor engineering design/production/supplier liaison, overstringent specifications and inflexibility, in general all lead to a credibility gap in the customer–supplier relationship. It is not uncommon for a customer to preach the gospel of quality to its suppliers and then act quite differently by relegating quality to secondary importance behind, for example, price or meeting the production schedule. Similarly, there is little value in holding quality improvement conferences and seminars for suppliers if the purchasing organization continues to adopt an adversarial approach to its suppliers, or is seen to accord a low priority to quality unless there is a serious non-conformance. In the words of one supplier quality assurance engineer: 'No one cares about vendor performance until the production line stops.'

Failure to respond to supplier requests for information or feedback on specification requirements, component functionality, and to provide a design FMEA and so on, is a further way in which a purchaser's credibility can be seriously undermined.

Purchasing power: a misconception

Purchasing power is an important influence in the relationship between a customer and its supplier community. Lack of power is a commonly cited reason for lack of success in improving supplier quality performance. There is little doubt that a purchaser's influence on its suppliers varies with its purchasing power, and that the greater this power the more effective its supplier quality assurance activities will be.

However, companies with considerable purchasing power may well cause the supplier to improve the quality of supplied items but this may not necessarily mean that TQM becomes embedded in the supplier's organizational culture. There is a tendency for some vendors to treat powerful customers as special cases, leading to 'stratified quality assurance'. The authors' research findings indicate that a number of companies do grade the quality of their products at different levels according to past experience of individual customer expectations: 'Company A won't accept this non-conformity but Company B will.' This often stems from the traditional misconceptions that quality is an optional product attribute or extra for which the customer must pay. Such a philosophy ignores the benefits of a continuous quality improvement process (for example, positive workforce attitudes, less waste, reduced handling costs) which will accrue to the supplier.

STARTING SUPPLIER DEVELOPMENT

Before involving suppliers in an improvement process it is necessary for the purchasing organization to give attention to issues such as: the objectives of supplier development, developing a strategy to accomplish these objectives, and deciding which vendors to involve. But perhaps the first task is to carry out a critical review of the key aspects of the purchasing organization's own operation which affect supplier performance. These include purchase specifications, communications, training and organizational roles. The delivery of non-conforming product from a supplier can often be attributed to an ambiguous purchasing specification. Purchasing specifications are working documents used by both customer and supplier, and must be treated as such. A good specification will define precisely the characteristics of the material to be supplied. It is also important to recognize that the supplier is knowledgeable in his own field of operation, and should be given every opportunity to provide a design input to the preparation of the specification. This is a prerequisite in obtaining a supplier's continued commitment to his product after delivery to the customer. The authors' survey findings indicate that suppliers are more likely to accept responsibility for warranty costs if they are involved in the design of the product or formally agree the customer's specification and drawing.

At an early stage in the formulation of a supplier development strategy, the most effective mechanism for communication and feedback has to be established. Typically, purchasing, quality, design and production personnel all talk to suppliers, but with no single functional area accepting total responsibility for the price, delivery and quality of bought-out items. The need for clear accountability is an important factor in ensuring that channels of communication between customers and suppliers are effective. Both parties must nominate a representative (or 'account executive') through whom all communications are directed. Such representatives should also be given sufficient authority to ensure that all necessary actions are carried out.

Professional supplier development programmes need to be supported by well-trained personnel capable of helping suppliers achieve the objectives laid down. It is essential that purchasing staff can understand the capabilities of their suppliers' manufacturing processes and systems and have a good working knowledge of the philosophy and techniques of total quality management. The survey findings indicate that out of the sample of 300 companies, only 70 gave quality-related skills training to their purchasing staff. Embarking on a supplier development programme with insufficient regard to the needs of the purchasing organization's skills base is likely to result in frustration and possible eventual failure of the programme.

The increasing complexity of the task of obtaining conforming supplies at the right time and at the right price suggests that the conventional form and organization of the purchasing management function may no longer be adequate. Traditional staff structures based on tight functional groups (for example, purchasing, materials planning, supplier quality assurance and engineering) has resulted in compartmentalized attitudes to suppliers which hinders a co-makership approach to supplier development. Several companies have carried out some restructuring of their purchasing, quality and engineering departments to ensure that they have the right skills in dealing with suppliers, and that functional accountability and logistics are adequate for the process of supplier development.

Supplier development objectives

To assist their suppliers, some major organizations have documented the fundamental requirements for the control of quality and the achievement of quality improvement. It is a requirement of the purchase order agreement that suppliers must ensure that their product complies with these requirements. For example, Ford *Q-101, Quality System Standard* (1987) and Nissan Motor Manufacturing (UK), Quality Standard (1985).

Priorities for action

For a company with many suppliers and bought-out items, it may take several years to develop an effective supplier development programme. Before starting it is therefore essential to prioritize action in some way. One approach adopted by many companies is to concentrate on new products and new vendors. Another approach involves the use of Pareto analysis to focus priorities by ranking bought-out components and materials according to some appropriate parameter (for example, gross annual spend). It is commonly found that some 20 per cent of the bought-out items account for 80 per cent of the total purchasing spend.

Reducing the supplier base

One outcome of the trend to co-makership is that an increasing number of major purchasing organizations are awarding contracts based on the life of a part. Strategic sourcing (that is, single or dual sourcing) is considered by many writers and practitioners to be a complementary policy to co-makership. This has, in recent years, led to reductions in the size of organizations' supplier bases. In a survey of 158 suppliers in the motor industry by Dale et al. (1989) only 57 had no plans to reduce their number of suppliers; the majority of suppliers had achieved at least a 10 per cent reduction. Organizations are thinking carefully about the number of suppliers they need and how to maintain it at an optimum level. The reduction in the supplier base results in benefits such as: less variation in the characteristics of the supplied product, increases the amount of time supplier quality assurance and purchasing personnel can devote to vendors, improved and simplified communications, less paperwork, less transportation, less handling and inspection activity, less accounts to maintain and reduced costs for both parties. Nor should it be forgotten that there are competitive advantages for the supplier in being recognized as a preferred source of supply to a primary purchaser. For example, obtaining the Ford Q1 award.

It is easier to develop a long-term relationship if the suppliers are in close proximity to the customer. Consequently, a number of customers are now reversing their international sourcing strategies to develop shorter supply lines. Closeness is also a vital element in the use of just-in-time purchasing strategy.

It is worth mentioning also that it is the policy of some purchasing organizations to take up to a certain proportion only of a supplier's output – the captive supplier issue; this sometimes results in dual sourcing even though the policy is to single source. In other cases, the opposite is true.

The supplier development programme

Having selected suitable suppliers for inclusion in the development programme, the next step is to get them involved and obtain their commitment. This entails making a serious attempt to communicate to suppliers what is required and, based on a set of common objectives, to reach an understanding with them.

Initially, the most practical way of setting about this task is to hold presentations to outline to suppliers the new approach, the quality system standard to be used, how suppliers' performance will be assessed and how the assessment will be communicated to them. Presentations to suppliers can be held either on the customer's premises or at individual supplier's sites. The authors have come across several examples of how major purchasing organizations communicate their supplier development programme requirements to vendors. When the Ford Motor Company relaunched Q-101 in the UK they wrote to the chief executives of the entire supplier base to secure top management commitment. The letter was followed up by presentations made by teams from buying and quality using a specially produced video: 'Ford Cares About Quality'. At Nissan Motor Manufacturing (UK), potential new suppliers attend a meeting where the senior management outline the Nissan philosophy and quality requirements. The attendees are encouraged to discuss frankly with Nissan's management any areas of concern.

IBM, Havant, take considerable care and time in ensuring that their suppliers know how their particular material, component or subassembly fits into IBM's final product. They hold what is termed a 'road show' where IBM representatives visit suppliers with examples of their product. The supplier's personnel are encouraged to examine the product and ask questions.

From their research work, the authors have found that the best results are achieved when the chief executives of both the customer and the supplier are involved in face-to-face discussions.

Once a supplier's senior management have agreed to participate in the development programme, it is necessary for the purchasing organization to visit the supplier's factory and carry out a formal vendor approval survey. The objective of the survey is to assess the supplier's suitability as a business partner. The survey is a multidisciplinary task which in a number of cases involves the customer's purchasing, SQA (supplier quality assurance) and engineering personnel. The survey should cover areas such as control, plant, quality systems, attitude, response, tooling, planning and handling. Some form of checklist is generally used to structure the survey.

As part of its assessment a major purchasing organization should assess the supplier's commitment to advanced quality planning, this is a joint exercise involving both customer and supplier, and concentrates on the methods by which quality is designed and manufactured into the product. Advanced quality planning commences with a joint review of the specification and classification of product characteristics. Failure mode and effects analysis (FMEA) and quality function deployment would also be carried out. The supplier then prepares a control plan to summarize the quality planning for significant product characteristics. This would include a description of the manufacturing operation and process flows, equipment used, control characteristics, control plans, specification limits, the use of SPC, inspection details and corrective action methods. The supplier would provide initial samples for evaluation, this would be supported by data on machine and process capability on the key characteristics identified by both parties, plus test results. Following successful evaluation of initial samples, the supplier is now in a position to start a trial production run followed by volume routine production.

Once the customer has assessed the adequacy of the supplier's policies, systems, procedures and manufacturing methods, and the supplier is able to demonstrate the quality of his shipped product, the goods inward inspection of supplies can be reduced considerably; in some cases down to the ideal situation of direct line supply. At this point, 'preferred' or 'certified supplier' status can be conferred on the supplier in recognition of the achievement.

This assessment exercise is not necessarily confined to new suppliers; an increasing number of primary purchasing organizations will at regular intervals review the adequacy of the quality assurance systems of all their suppliers. This review is carried out to assure the purchasing organization that conformance to the assessment awarded to the supplier's quality assurance system is being maintained; most enlightened customers are looking for improvement. The frequency with which reassessments are carried out is dependent on such factors as: the supplier's current quality performance; the classification awarded to the supplier; the type of item being supplied; the volume of parts being supplied; the occurrence of a fundamental change (for example, change of management, change of facilities) at the supplier; and at the request of suppliers. A programme of continuing assessment will help suppliers and the purchaser to achieve quality improvements by providing a common database.

Supplier development does not end there; it is a continuous process aimed at building-up an effective business relationship – a relationship which demands a greater and quicker exchange of information between both parties. A number of major purchasing organizations are encouraging electronic data interchanges with their key vendors. The data exchange relates not only to quality but also covers technical requirements and specifications, schedules, manufacturing programmes, lead-times, inventory management and invoicing. Suppliers are obliged to communicate any changes to materials, processes or methods that may affect the dimensional, functional, compositional or appearance characteristics of the product. Customers are obliged to provide sufficient information and assistance to aid development of their suppliers' approach to TQM (including training where necessary). In some cases, this extends to joint problem-solving activities, with customer and supplier striving to improve the product and reduce its cost. Over the longer term it is the total cost of doing business with a supplier which is important and not the price per piece. The end results of the long-term relationship, joint problem-solving activities, and the increased level of supplier participation in the early stages of product design and development will bring about cost reductions to the mutual benefit of customer and supplier.

REFERENCES AND FURTHER READING

Ansari, A. and Modarress, B., 'JIT Purchasing: problems and solutions', *Journal of Purchasing Materials Management*, 1986, vol. 22, no. 2, pp. 11–15

Dale, B. G., Owen, M. and Shaw, P., *SPC in the Motor Industry: What is the State-of-the-Art?*, Manchester School of Management, UMIST Occasional Paper Series, Occasional Paper 8906, Manchester, 1989

Deming, W. E., *Quality, Productivity and Competitive Position*, MIT, Cambridge, Mass., 1982

Ford Motor Company, *Q-101, Quality System Standard*, Ford Motor Company, Brentwood, 1987

Hay, E. J., Will the Real Just-in-Time Purchasing Please Stand Up', in *Readings in Zero Inventories*, American Production and Inventory Control Society, 1984

Hutchins, D., 'Having a Hard Time with Just-in-Time', *Fortune*, pp. 56–8, 9 June, 1986

Hutchins, D., *Just-in-Time*, Gower, Aldershot, 1988

Imai, M. *Kaizen: The key to Japan's Competitive Success*, Random House, New York, 1986

Ishikawa, K., *What is Total Quality Control?: The Japanese Way*, Prentice Hall, Englewood Cliffs, NJ, 1985

Lascelles, D. M. and Dale B. G., *Supplier Quality Management: Attitudes, techniques and systems*, (UMIST Occasional Paper 8805), Manchester School of Management, Manchester, 1988

Mass, R. A., *World Class Quality*, ASQC Quality Press, Milwaukee, 1988

Nissan, N.M.U.K, *Nissan Quality Standard*, Nissan Motor Manufacturing (UK), Washington New Town, 1985

Schonberger, R. J., *Japanese Manufacturing Techniques*, Free Press, New York, 1982

Sloan, D. and Weiss, S., *Supplier Improvement Process Handbook*, American Society for Quality Control, Milwaukee, 1987

Voss, C. A., *Just-In-Time Manufacturing*, IFS Publications, New York, 1987.

ACKNOWLEDGEMENT

Part of this chapter is based on Lascelles, D. M. and Dale, B. G., Chapter 18, 'Product Quality Improvement Through Supplier Development', in Dale, B. G. and Plunket, J. J. (eds), *Managing Quality*, Philip Allan, Oxford, 1989.

Part Six

MANUFACTURING MANAGEMENT

36 Planning for production

J Mapes and C C New

Production management is concerned with managing the physical resources necessary to create products in sufficient quantities to meet market requirements. In manufacturing organizations the majority of the work-force and a very high proportion of the total capital investment expenditure will be devoted to the production function. Efficient production management is therefore absolutely critical to the success of such organizations.

Although production management is most closely associated with the manufacturing sector, the techniques of production management are increasingly being applied in service and non-manufacturing organizations. Because of this the modern definition of a production system has been broadened to cover systems for the creation of both manufactured items and services. The problems are very similar for both manufacturing organizations and service organizations. One of the main differences is that the 'product' of service organizations is highly perishable and must be consumed immediately.

While the primary emphasis in this chapter will be on manufacturing organizations, most of the techniques discussed are equally applicable to service organizations like banks, hospitals and public utilities.

THE PRODUCTION MANAGEMENT TASK

The production management task can be divided into two main areas. First, there is the design of the production system. This will involve decisions regarding the performance requirements and desired output levels of the production system. Then decisions will need to be made about the number of production facilities which will be required and their location, the methods of production to be used and the management control procedures to be introduced.

Second, there is the task of operating the production system in order to meet the specified performance requirements. This will include production scheduling and control, inventory management and quality control.

THE PLANNING OF PRODUCTION

The planning of production in an organization can therefore be considered at two levels, strategic and tactical. Strategic planning is concerned with the design of the production system. Tactical planning is concerned with the running of the operating system. Figure 36.1 shows the kind of planning decisions which have to be taken in production and their relative time horizons.

Strategic	Long-term	2 years +	Introduction of new products Number and location of facilities Type of technology to be used
	Medium-term	1–2 years	Relative mix of products Changes in capacity
Tactical	Medium-term	1 year	Size of workforce Subcontracting Overtime working Stockholding policy
	Short-term	3 months	Production schedule Output targets

Figure 36.1   Time-scale for planning decisions

Strategic level decisions

At the strategic level decisions will be required regarding:

The product range

While this is primarily a marketing decision the production capabilities of the organization together with any limitations on production capacity must also be taken into account.

Product design

By taking into account production implications at the design stage substantial reductions in manufacturing costs and processing time can be achieved.

Selection of processing methods, plant and equipment

Usually there are several alternative methods of manufacturing the product, each being the most appropriate for a particular output range. The choice will depend on the trade-off between capital cost, operating costs and performance requirements.

Plant location

The number of plants, the capacity of each plant and the location of each plant must be decided. This will be influenced by the transport costs for raw materials and finished goods, availability of labour, delivery performance requirements and economics of scale.

Plant layout

Within each plant the number of departments and their relative location must be decided. Within each department the location of machines, storage areas and support facilities must be decided in order to simplify movement and handling of materials between operations.

Planning and control systems

An important part of the design of a production system is the development of procedures for planning and controlling the production process.

Decisions at the tactical level

At the tactical level, decisions will need to be taken regarding:

Production control

This covers the detailed scheduling of operations, allocation of jobs to machines and monitoring of actual against planned production. The aim should be to produce a schedule which is practicable and also meets performance objectives in terms of operating costs and delivery.

Stock control

In order to ensure acceptable delivery times nearly all organizations have to carry some stocks of raw materials, subassemblies or finished products. For each item held in stock decisions must be made about when to replenish stocks and what the replenishment quantity should be.

Quality control

The quality specification will be set at the design stage. The operational task is to ensure that, as far as possible, all items which leave the factory meet this specification. Decisions must be taken on methods of inspection, on when a batch of items should be rejected or reworked and on when machines should be reset.

Maintenance

The servicing, repair and replacement of equipment is an essential part of ensuring optimum operating effectiveness. Decisions must be taken regarding the frequency of equipment overhaul, the scheduling of maintenance work and the frequency of equipment replacement.

Labour control

Labour costs are an important part of total production costs. In many industries labour costs are the main component of production costs. In order to exercise effective control the work content of each task must be determined. This enables

1   Short lead-times

2   Lead-time reliability

3   Quality

4   Ability to alter specification at short notice

5   Ability to adjust volume at short notice

6   Price

Figure 36.2   Requirements for market success

realistic work scheduling and monitoring of actual against planned performance to be carried out.

While the relative importance of these decision areas will vary for different industries and different companies every organization will need to give some attention to each of the areas mentioned.

STRATEGIC PLANNING

Clearly strategic planning of production can only take place within the context of the overall corporate planning process. Traditionally, the strategic task for the production function has been seen as the design of a production system capable of meeting the requirements of the marketing strategic plan. This is likely to lead to insufficient account being taken of the production implications of alternative strategies at the corporate planning stage. This frequently results in conflicting demands being placed on production which are impossible to resolve. Naturally, the marketing department wish to provide as good a service as possible to the customer. As a consequence, they may require production to manufacture special products to customer specifications using the same production facilities as standard products with no increase in production lead-times. Alternatively, they may ask for immediate availability of all products while insisting that the increased stockholding costs incurred cannot be passed on to the customer.

In developing a strategic plan which adequately reflects both market requirements and production capabilities, the production function must play an integral part in the process of strategy formation.

An essential first step must be to gain a clear understanding of the performance measures leading to success in the market-place. Figure 36.2 lists the most common criteria for success. While most organizations would ideally like to meet all of these criteria this is not possible as many of the criteria are in conflict. In achieving short lead-times, increased costs will be incurred leading to increased prices. If quality is an important criterion then it is unlikely that very short lead-times can be achieved.

Of course, the key criteria may be different for different product groups, provided separate production facilities are used. Problems only arise when the same production facility is required to satisfy different criteria for two product groups at the same time. Setting priorities can be almost impossible if, for example, one group of orders must be completed at minimum cost (implying high levels of machine utilization) while another group of orders must be completed as rapidly as possible (implying low levels of machine utilization).

Once the tasks which are vital to corporate success have been identified, a production capability analysis should be carried out. The main purpose of the analysis is to assess whether the organization is likely to be able to meet the performance requirements of the market with currently available resources.

If there is a mismatch between the capabilities of the existing production system and market requirements then either the production system must be modified or the strategy must be altered. Otherwise the consequences can be extremely serious. When the Babcock & Wilcox Corporation in the United States tried to enter the nuclear pressure vessel business they encountered very severe problems. They had considerable expertise in the manufacture of steam pressure vessels where the requirement was for a standard product with a short, reliable lead-time, sold at a competitive price. The nuclear power industry required absolute product reliability and reliable delivery but the length of the lead-time and the price were relatively unimportant. Also, the large size of nuclear pressure vessels, coupled with the fact that each vessel was a special item fabricated to a very precise customer specification meant that manufacturing methods suited to steam pressure vessels were quite unsuitable for nuclear pressure vessels. Consequently, during the first three years of operation only three pressure vessels were completed instead of the twenty which were scheduled. Eventually, the two main contractors transferred fourteen part-completed pressure vessels from Babcock & Wilcox to competing organizations. Between 1967 and 1969 company profits fell from $33m to $5m.

Once the production capability analysis has been completed then decisions will need to be made on the following main components of the manufacturing structure:

Plant and equipment technology

This covers the processing methods to be used, the choice of equipment and the level of automation.

Production systems

These define the procedures for detailed planning and control of production and the performance standards to be met.

Personnel policies

These specify policies on the degree of job specialization, payment systems to be employed and the type of work group organization to be adopted.

Product design

This is concerned with those aspects of product design which simplify manufacture and reduce production costs.

Organization and management

This specifies the organizational structure adopted within the production function and the allocation of responsibilities between staff.

FORECASTING DEMAND

A basic requirement for the planning of production is a forecast of demand for each product. For each forecast an indication of the likely forecasting error should be provided. For forecasts with a high expected error, contingency plans can then be made to cope with the occasions when actual demand is much higher or lower than the forecasts.

Forecasting techniques tend to be classified into short term, medium term and long term depending on the underlying assumptions which have been made. In short-term forecasting it is assumed that the underlying trend is linear and stable with changes in external factors having little effect on demand. This enables very simple extrapolative techniques to be used. However, the assumptions are only likely to be valid when forecasting just a few months ahead. The simplest method of short-term forecasting is to use moving averages to identify the underlying trend line and then to project the trend line forward. Figure 36.3 shows the results obtained using a five-period moving average.

Increasingly, however, simple moving averages of this kind are being replaced by weighted averages in which the greatest weighting is given to the most recent data. The most popular technique of this kind is called exponential smoothing. This involves updating the moving average each period, using the following calculation:

$$\text{new moving average} = a \times \text{sales for this period} + (1-a) \times \text{moving average for previous period}$$

where a is called the smoothing constant and is normally given a value between 0.1 and 0.3.

Forecasts based on exponential smoothing tend to be more accurate than forecasts based on a simple moving average, particularly when there are frequent fluctuations in the trend. Figure 36.4 shows the results of using exponential smoothing for short-term forecasting when there are marked short-term fluctuations in sales.

Medium-term forecasting techniques are based on the assumption that the underlying trend follows a regular curve. The most commonly used approach is to

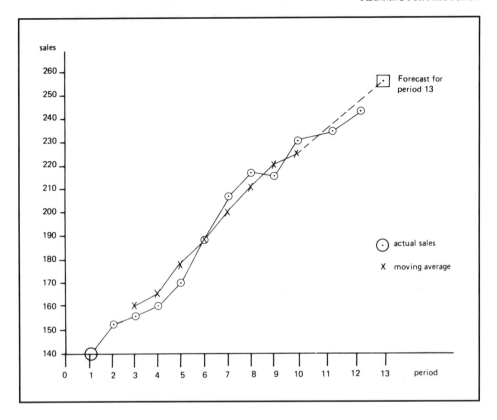

Figure 36.3   Forecast based on a 5-period moving average

fit a curve of the appropriate type to the data and then to project the curve forward to obtain the forecast.

In long-term forecasting it is recognized that external factors will have a considerable effect on the forecast. The emphasis is therefore placed on establishing the quantitative relationship between demand and those factors which influence demand, using the techniques of regression analysis. This enables an equation to be developed which can then be used to forecast demand.

THE MAKE OR BUY DECISION

One very important part of the strategic planning process is the decision regarding which items are to be manufactured and which items are to be bought in. This decision will be taken primarily on financial grounds but there are other factors which should be taken into account. Purchase of items gives greater flexibility if large fluctuations in demand occur. It also allows access to specialist skills and economies of scale which may not be available internally. On the other hand, manufacture gives greater control over quality and delivery dates.

For most items a change from manufacturing to purchase or vice versa would involve such a significant change to the nature of the company that it would not be acceptable on policy grounds. However, there will be a number of items which

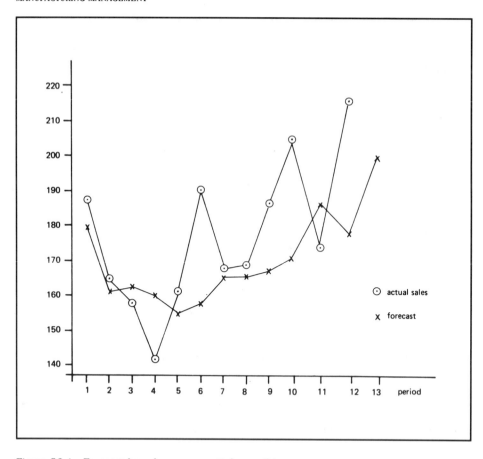

Figure 36.4   Forecast based on exponential smoothing

could either be manufactured or purchased depending on which involves the lowest cost.

When making cost comparisons it is important that only incremental costs are taken into account. Any costs which will be unaltered by a switch between manufacturing and purchasing should be ignored.

In practice the decision is very dependent on current utilization of internal resources. Manufacturing will nearly always be more attractive if labour and equipment would otherwise be under-utilized. On the other hand, buying-in is likely to be preferable if the decision to manufacture the item will involve substantial capital investment and the recruitment of labour. Purchasing will be particularly attractive if there is a possibility of a fall-off in the future level of requirements for the item in the long term.

PREPARING AN OPERATING PLAN

Once demand for each product has been forecast, and it has been decided which items will be manufactured and which will be purchased, then an operating plan

Activity	Weeks
Purchase raw materials	1
	2
Manufacture intermediates	3
	4
Manufacture base pigments	5
Standardize	6
Blend final product and test	7
Dispatch	8

Figure 36.5   Production stage chart for pigment manufacture

must be devised aimed at ensuring that the company's marketing objectives are met.

In order to predict delivery periods and decide on stockholding policy a production stage chart should be constructed. This is a diagrammatic representation of all the stages in the production process including supplier delivery periods, product design and final dispatch to the customer. Estimates of the time to complete each stage are included so that the delivery time can be assessed. An outline of a production stage chart for a pigment is shown in Figure 36.5.

If the delivery time is likely to be acceptable to customers, the organization can operate as a make-to-order company, only carrying out work on firm customer orders. Usually, however, the delivery time will be unacceptable and it will be necessary to carry out some stages in the chart in advance of customer orders. In some cases it will only be necessary to pre-order raw materials and hold stocks based on forecasts of future usage. In other cases, where customers require very short lead-times, stocks of the finished product will need to be held so that new orders can be met immediately from stock.

The next step should be to decide whether the forecast demand can be satisfied and the desired lead-time met with currently available capacity. To estimate capacity requirements, current capacity and forecast demand need to be expressed in the same units, for example, litres of paint or numbers of electric motors. However, with a varied range of products there will be no common physical unit of capacity and so forecast demand will need to be converted into standard hours of manufacturing time.

If average weekly demand exceeds average weekly capacity, a decision must be taken on whether capacity should be increased. This decision is likely to be influenced by the following factors:

1   Long-term forecasts of changes in market size and market share
2   The expected return on the capital investment required

3   Possible future innovations in the product or the production process.

If it is decided that an increase in capacity cannot be justified then one or more of the following alternatives can be considered:

1   Increase the number of purchased or subcontracted items
2   Use overtime or shift working to increase effective capacity
3   Eliminate items with low profit margins from the product range releasing capacity for more profitable product lines.

Aggregate planning

The analysis described above should ensure a reasonable match between capacity and demand on an annual basis. In addition, there will be the need to cope with variations in demand over the year. These may be due to seasonal variations, changing economic conditions or random fluctuations in orders from week to week. A company which has sufficient capacity to meet average demand will find that there are periods during the year when demand is appreciably above average. As a consequence either sales will be lost or delivery periods will become unacceptably long. On the other hand, if capacity is based on peak demand then the utilization of labour and equipment will be low during periods of below-average demand.

Aggregate planning is an attempt to schedule production over a six- to twelve-month period, taking into account forecast variations in demand. The following methods of handling fluctuations in demand can be considered:

1   Vary the number of hours worked each week by the use of overtime or additional shifts during periods of peak demand
2   Vary the size of the workforce by recruiting casual workers during peak periods
3   Use spare capacity during periods of low demand to build up stocks of finished goods for use during periods of above-average demand
4   Increase the amount of subcontracted work during periods of high demand.

Each alternative will incur substantial additional costs. The use of overtime or subcontracting involves premium charges relative to the cost of manufacturing internally during normal working hours. Changes in the size of the work-force involve recruitment and lay-off costs. Stock building involves high stockholding and obsolescence costs. The optimum solution will be the combination of these alternatives which minimizes total costs. A number of techniques for aggregate planning have been developed. The main approaches are outlined below.

The linear decision rule

This technique for obtaining a minimum-cost solution to the above problem was developed by Holt, Modigliani, Muth and Simon. The approach takes account of normal time and overtime labour rates, recruitment and lay-off costs, inventory holding, back ordering and machine set-up costs. These are used to derive two linear decision rules for computing the work-force levels and production rate for each period taking into account forecasts of sales for each period over a specified planning horizon.

This approach provides an optimum solution and is easy to apply once the two decision rules have been derived. However, the assumptions on cost structure may provide a poor approximation to reality. Also, there are no restrictions on the size of the work-force, the hours of overtime worked or the number of units held in inventory, so that the solution generated by this technique may be impractical.

Linear programming

The Simplex method of linear programming takes the same cost data as the linear decision rule approach and also generates a minimum cost solution giving work-force size and production rate period by period. An advantage over the linear decision rule method is that capacity constraints can be incorporated into the model. An important limitation of linear programming is that all constraints and cost functions must be linear. This will be unrealistic whenever economies of scale exist. A further limitation is that only a single objective can be optimized at a time, whereas aggregate planning is usually concerned with satisfying a number of conflicting objectives simultaneously.

Goal programming is an extension of linear programming which to some extent overcomes the problem of being limited to a single objective. A set of management goals is specified and a solution is generated which is as close to this set of goals as possible.

Search decision rule

An iterative procedure, the search decision rule starts with an initial solution and determines the overall cost of this solution. The procedure then searches for an alternative solution with lower costs. This continues until a solution is reached for which further alteration would not yield significant cost reductions. Unlike the first two procedures this does not yield a mathematical optimum solution. In other words, it yields a good but not necessarily minimum-cost solution. However, it has the advantages of being less complicated and requiring less computation.

Management coefficients method

By this method, developed by Bowman, management's past planning decisions are analysed statistically to determine the decision criteria which were used. A set of decision equations are then derived in which the numerical coefficients are based on this statistical analysis. These decision equations can then be used to prepare future schedules using the same criteria. This should result in an improvement in performance due to the criteria being applied more consistently.

Parametric production planning

A search procedure is used in this technique suggested by Jones to quantify four parameters associated with minimum cost in aggregate planning. The four parameters are then inserted into equations which are used to determine work-force size and production rate for each period. The method involves no constraints imposed by the mathematical structure of the model and the parameters and equations are specific to the company. While the method is non-optimizing it is claimed to produce very good results.

A performance comparison of the alternative aggregate planning procedures

Lee and Khumawala carried out a comparative study of alternative aggregate planning procedures in a company manufacturing capital goods. The aggregate planning procedures evaluated were the linear decision rule, the search decision rule, the management coefficients method and parametric production planning. The application of these procedures was simulated and the profit performance achieved compared with the actual performance of the company. All the planning methods yielded better profits than the company's own planning procedures. The greatest improvement (14 per cent) was achieved using the search decision rule.

Tactical planning

Once the aggregate plan has been prepared all the key decisions will have been made. The next step is to prepare a detailed operating plan, which will involve a series of tactical decisions regarding:

1 The operations necessary for the manufacture of each product or order and their sequence
2 Allocation of jobs to facilities
3 Scheduling the start and finish times of each operation.

These tasks are more appropriately dealt with as part of production control.

FURTHER READING

Bowman, E. H., 'Consistency and Optimality in Managerial Decision Making', *Management Science*, 9 January 1963. This article provides a detailed description of the management coefficients method of aggregate planning
Goldratt, E. M. and Cox, J., *The Goal: Excellence in Manufacturing*, North River Press, 1984. A very readable fictionalized account of a year in the life of a manufacturing plant. A thought-provoking analysis of the real objectives of manufacturing and how to achieve them
Hayes, R. H., Wheelwright, S. C. and Clark, K. B., *Dynamic Manufacturing*, The Free Press, Macmillan, 1988. A good introduction to current thinking on manufacturing strategy
Jones, C. H., 'Parametric Production Planning', *Management Science*, 13 July 1967. This article describes the parametric production planning technique for aggregate planning
Lee, W. B. and Khumawala, B. M., 'Simulation Testing of Aggregate Production Planning Models in an Implementation Methodology', *Management Science*, 20 February 1974. This article describes the comparison of alternative aggregate planning techniques referred to in the text

Makridakis, S. and Wheelwright, S. C., *The Handbook of Forecasting: a Manager's Guide*, 2nd edn, Wiley, 1987, New York. A good reference book covering the complete range of forecasting techniques currently in use

Silver, E. A. and Peterson, R., *Decision Systems for Inventory Management and Production Planning*, 2nd edn, Wiley, 1985, New York. Provides good coverage of aggregate production planning although some sections are only for the more mathematically minded

Taubert, W. H., 'Search Decision Rule for the Aggregate Scheduling Problem', *Management Science*, 14 February 1968. This article describes the search decision rule for aggregate planning

Vollman, T. E., Berry, W. L. and Whybark, D. C., *Manufacturing Planning and Control Systems*, Irwin, 1984. A comprehensive and thorough coverage of production planning and control techniques

37 Manufacturing systems

Tim Seville

Manufacturing activity is classified conventionally into jobbing or 'one-off', batch, and mass or flow production. This classification has never been very precise (some of the reasons are explored in this chapter) and recent developments in plant and in the organization of production have further blurred the boundaries. It does, however, provide a starting point for this discussion of manufacturing systems.

CONVENTIONAL MANUFACTURING ACTIVITY CLASSIFICATIONS

Jobbing or 'one-off' production

Enterprises operating in jobbing mode produce items singly or in very small numbers to meet the needs of individual customers. They range from individual creative craftsmen to large organizations building oil rigs or steel rolling mills.

In between is a vast array of businesses which operate in this way of which many are to be found in the engineering industry: trade toolrooms which produce individual die sets; sheet metal fabricators who specialize in tanks or machinery guards or ventilation trunking; forgemasters who produce heavy components for marine engines, earth moving machinery or industrial plant.

Mass or flow production

The characteristic of mass or flow production is that materials or components 'flow' through the factory in an unvarying pattern as a fixed sequence of operations is carried out. Flow production systems are appropriate where the sustained level of demand is roughly equal to or greater than the output from an economically viable unit of plant. Under such circumstances the plant can be run continuously.

Flow production systems will be found in areas of relatively low technology and low investment. But sustained high levels of demand will attract the substantial investments in plant and machinery to be found, for example, in the automobile and chemical industries. The chemical industry provides a specific instance of flow production where the output consists, not of individual items, but of bulk materials – sulphuric acid, nitrogen or cement. In such cases, raw materials and intermediates literally flow through the process.

Batch production

Probably more individual products and, where appropriate, the components from which they are made up, are manufactured in batches than by either of the other two systems.

Production in batches is appropriate where the rate of output of the smallest economic unit of plant significantly exceeds the rate of demand. Under these conditions the plant cannot be run continuously and the only alternative is to run the plant intermittently and make the product in batches. Usually with this system, at least some parts of the production plant are also used for the manufacture of other items in the product range or of complementary components.

Typical of batch production is the packaging industry, where the same basic machinery may be used to make the boxes to hold wood screws, typing paper or breakfast cereals. Similarly, in the garment industry the same items of plant – and operatives – are employed to produce a variety of styles, each in a range of sizes and perhaps of colours, too.

MANUFACTURING SYSTEMS

In practice, manufacturing systems do not fall neatly into the three categories listed above. This is not least because the activity of many production plants, taken as a whole, embraces more than one category. Major items – ships, oil rigs – built as 'one off' are constructed from components, many of which are manufactured in batches. Cardboard cases, produced in batches to customer order, are made from corrugated board manufactured in the same plant by a dedicated flow process. Automobiles are put together on mass production assembly lines from components made in batches. And in this last case, there is an added paradox: the demands of the market for a wide range of colour, trim and optional extras, to say nothing of body and engine configuration, means that each vehicle rolling off the assembly line is different from the one before it. Manufacturers can operate for weeks before building two identical vehicles. So who is operating a jobbing or 'one off' system?

System characteristics

Jobbing systems are distinguished by a high degree of flexibility in their operations. This demands plant which is itself flexible, so that general purpose machines are a commonplace. And the objective is often achieved at the cost of a relatively low level of utilization of plant: a constantly changing and unpredictable product mix can make capacity planning a nightmare.

In mass or flow production systems, all of the uncertainty for which the jobbing operation must make provision is eliminated and the designer is free to specify dedicated plant to provide the lowest processing cost. But this advantage is bought at the cost of flexibility which may be very limited indeed.

True batch production systems use the same pieces of plant to make, or carry out processing stages on a range of different parts, components or products. These are presented in batches of tens to tens of thousands of items. A demand over a period for a number of items may be satisfied by making a large number of small batches or a small number of large batches. But small batches lead to more frequent changeover of equipment with consequent loss of production. Big batches, on the other hand, lead to higher levels of inventory. Given the relevant cost data, a theoretical optimum batch size can be calculated, but the underlying problem does not go away.

WORK IN PROCESS

Where parts and components are processed in batches through a number of steps occupying different amounts of time, it is difficult to plan and route the work so as to achieve a smooth flow through the factory. A build-up of inventory between stages is therefore almost inevitable.

High levels of inventory are undesirable for several reasons. First are the handling, storage and interest costs associated with stocks of any kind. Less obvious is the inertia imposed on the system by such inventory holdings: any product or processing change must take account of the material in process. The extended overall processing time implied by the system often means that manufacturers are forced into extended periods of speculative production. Finally, the presence of inventory in the system tends to conceal other shortcomings – in meeting quality and delivery targets within the system, for example.

Reducing overall processing times

The key to reduced overall processing time is to reduce batch size. And the key to *that* is to reduce changeover time. Approaches to reductions in changeover times have followed two routes:

1 Through the way in which the work is planned. An example is planning painting or dyeing processes so that darker colours follow lighter ones in order to reduce the amount of cleaning needed between batches. A manufacturing example is sequencing batches so that machine setting changes can be made incrementally rather than by jumping between extremes
2 Through developments in manufacturing plant.

GROUP TECHNOLOGY (GT)

Carrying these ideas a stage further led to the development of the manufacturing system known as 'group technology'. Under this system, originating in the engineering industry, items are classified into 'families' according to their physical characteristics and processing requirements. This classification runs in parallel with a rearrangement of machine tools, from the conventional and functional layout of lathes, milling machines, drilling machines and so on, into groups which match the specific processing requirements of these families of parts. In this way, physical distances are reduced, lines of communication are shortened, and planning and control are facilitated through greater visibility of production problems.

Dramatic reductions in throughput times and work in process have been reported following successful applications of group technology. There are some costs – in addition to the initial classification of items and of relocation of machines – which generally show a reduction in the utilization of plant.

MULTI-FUNCTION MACHINES

So far as changes in hardware are concerned, the logic of reducing downtime between batches first led to the development of jigs and fixtures designed to assist the process, and then to the design of new machines to facilitate these changes (for example, plant with mechanical or electro-mechanical devices for resetting stops to accommodate dimensional change). This avenue of approach has been transformed by the development of the microprocessor, which has opened up a wide range of possibilities; the rapidly falling cost of such devices has also greatly increased their possible applications. These technological advances are explored further below.

A further area of hardware development is the design of machines which are capable of carrying out a number of different operations. The classic example, again from the engineering industry, is the capstan or turret lathe which allows a number of different tools to be brought to bear on the workpiece, thus permitting a sequence of turning and drilling operations to be carried which would otherwise be done on separate machines. The objective here is not a reduction in setting-up time between batches – indeed, setting-up times are likely to be extended by the additional complexity of the process – but a reduction in overall processing time. For example, it takes less time to perform three operations on each item in a batch of 500 pieces than to move the whole batch through three different processing stages.

A WIDER VIEW OF MANUFACTURING SYSTEMS

So far this account of the development of manufacturing systems has been confined to the activity on the shop floor. But there is an alternative view which embraces the characteristics of the market for the product, the design process which aims to meet the needs of that market, and the suppliers of materials and services which are inputs to the manufacturing process. This wider view recognizes that markets have become more demanding in terms of quality and variety, that product design has a profound influence on the production process and that supplier performance is critical to its success. It is against this background that the advance in microprocessor technology has brought about a revolution in modern manufacturing systems, and changes have been made both in the 'software' (the systems of control and of information handling) and in the 'hardware' (the capabilities of individual plant items).

On the hardware side new devices were produced which mechanized the loading and unloading of components to and from machines and, later, transferred them between processing stages. The target here was the replacement of manual by mechanical effort; the objective, a simple reduction in cost. This phase in the evolution of manufacturing systems led to the development of groups of 'transfer machines', where components were passed down a line of machines, each performing different operations; all the handling, loading and unloading was done without human intervention. Such systems achieved economies in direct cost but did not, in general, lead to any improvement in flexibility. On the contrary, such groups of machines were usually designed to perform a set series of operations on a particular component (for example, a cylinder block or gearbox casing).

COMPUTER CONTROL OF PLANT

In the type of arrangement described above, the sequence of operations and the precise control of each was achieved by mechanical devices, electrically or pneumatically controlled. The next step in systems development was the introduction of computerized control of individual machines. Now, instead of machines having to be set to carry out a particular sequence of operations by the careful adjustment of stops, cams and limit switches, they could be programmed with instructions coded on to magnetic or, more usually, punched paper tape. Such plant items came to be called numerically controlled (NC) machines.

From this point, two further developments have had a profound effect on manufacturing systems.

COMPUTER-AIDED MANUFACTURE (CAM)

Conventional machine tools had long been capable of manipulating either the workpiece or the tooling. A universal milling machine with dividing head is an example of the former; a conventional turret lathe an example of the latter. Within the engineering industry, control by computer has allowed both workpiece and tool system to be manipulated much more efficiently than by mechanical means. Plant is now available which has the capability not only to load and unload a single workpiece, as in the type of transfer machine referred to above, but also to handle different workpieces, and, further, to load and unload different tools as required. For example, a single 'machining centre' has been programmed to carry out a number of machining operations on no less than 32 different work pieces loaded on a specially designed pallet. Applications of this kind are referred to as computer-aided manufacture (CAM).

Clearly, this kind of development makes an impact on the old problem of reconciling the advantages of complex, multi-function plant, with the time needed to reset such machines between batches – an impact which rewrites the rules altogether. For here we have the possibility of production in a batch size of one.

FLEXIBLE MANUFACTURING SYSTEMS

Most formal definitions stress that a 'system' comprises a number of components connected together in some way. In the case of modern manufacturing systems, this definition is interpreted as comprising automated machines, of the kind just described, automated handling between plant items and, most importantly, an overall control system linking the various components together. Arrangements of plant and of linking material flows which have the degree of adaptability described are referred to as flexible manufacturing systems (FMS).

The high investment in capital and other support needed for such systems demands high levels of plant utilization. Responsibility for the kind of complex machining centre described above has confronted engineering managers with the need for extended working – on a two or, perhaps, three shift basis – as well as the kind of routine maintenance procedures which are regular practice in process industry. And because such systems are generally run with very low levels of manpower in attendance, there is a need for systems to monitor tool wear or breakage and to provide for automatic tool replacement where necessary.

The current number of FMS installations is small in relation to the number of manufacturing units worldwide, but their number is growing rapidly and their possibilities are underlined by one Japanese installation which comprises 35 NC and 10 conventional machine tools. Such installations run continuously and, perhaps with the night shift virtually unmanned, can show dramatic increases in manpower productivity as well as reductions in throughput time.

ROBOTS

So far, references have all been to systems involving advanced machines in the engineering industry. Similar developments have, however, taken place in component handling devices to serve fabrication and assembly operations. Generally recognized as 'robots', these machines have two important areas of application: in the mechanization of simple repetitive tasks; and in those situations involving stressful working environments (for example, weighing and marking hot-rolled coils of steel strip which have surface temperatures up to 800°C). In the context of manufacturing systems, the important thing to note about these applications is their *flexibility* (in the example just given, the coils vary considerably in size and weight, and the identification marks vary also).

The application of such systems of advanced technology has had an important influence on the design of the products themselves. This influence is expressed in two ways: reactive change needed in order to make such applications practicable and proactive change in order to take advantage of the opportunities which advanced technology offers. To give one illustration of the latter: the complete redesign of a system of jigs and fixtures, required for the machining of a range of components, so that they can be assembled by a robotic device which is fed with data used in the design of the jig. This application offers not only a dramatic reduction in the time and cost of assembling each fixture when compared with conventional methods but also, where such fixtures are used only infrequently, they can be dismantled and the instructions for their reassembly stored as computer input, thus making further savings in investment and holding costs.

COMPUTER-AIDED DESIGN (CAD)

Computer-controlled machines need to be provided with instructions which their processors can interpret. In early applications of numerically controlled machine tools, the designer's intentions, expressed in the form of conventional drawings, had to be translated into such instructions by a skilled programmer.

Computers have long been used as an aid to the designer: to facilitate computation (stress calculations, for example), and in the use of computer graphics in the production of conventional drawings. Details of parts and components held on computer file can now be called up at will, reducing much repetitive detailing and, perhaps even more importantly, ensuring that precise and up-to-date information is available consistently throughout the design and production process. Such applications are generally referred to as computer-aided design (CAD).

Further advances have made it possible to link design and manufacture even more closely. In the clothing industry, for example, the designer's drawings of a particular garment and of the pieces from which it is to be made are routinely converted into computer input. These data are then used to develop a family of outlines for the range of sizes in which the finished item is to be produced. This information, together with the numbers of each size specified by the customer, are used to develop a layout which minimizes waste of the material from which the pieces are to be cut. This final layout, in digital form, is used to control the machine which cuts the cloth. This type of application is referred to as 'CADCAM'.

SYSTEMS DEVELOPMENT

This brief review of manufacturing systems and their recent development might leave the impression that it is all to do with computerization in one form or another. And it is true that advances in information technology (IT) have had as profound an impact on manufacturing industry as they have had in other areas. Not least has been the ability of IT to address the problem of managing the mass of information which production activity tends to generate, particularly in the area of component assembly. For example, the availability of terminals sufficiently robust to operate under shop floor conditions, and so improve the speed of reporting, is of particular importance; while the use of bar code readers in these applications offers further improvement in quality and consistency.

At the same time, there are other important lines of thought which have influenced the design of production systems and which do not depend on computer technology. One such development has been concerned with the allocation of manual tasks in a flow production system.

The classical approach has been to divide up the total work of assembling a particular product, for example, into a large number of individual operations. This practice was based on the idea that the simple, repetitive tasks created by this approach were easy to learn by operators who could acquire very high levels of skill. Such division of labour has, however, two disadvantages. First, where tasks are subdivided in this way on a production line, there is an ever present problem of finding a practical distribution of work between all those involved so that the line is 'balanced', that is, the work is shared equally between individual operators. However, there is no natural law which says that this is possible; thus, the rate of output is inevitably determined by the operation having the longest work cycle. Secondly, the fragmentation of jobs into individually meaningless tasks can have a demotivating effect on those called upon to carry them out.

At the other extreme, instead of dividing the whole task amongst a number of operators, it is theoretically possible to allow each operator to complete the entire assembly from start to finish. To achieve this successfully requires each operator to be provided with a complete set of all the tools and equipment needed for the task, and with all the parts and components. Last but not least, each operator must be trained in the entire assembly procedure. Although there are many situations where this type of approach would be impractical there are other situations where this pattern of working has been adopted very successfully. One of the particular advantages claimed for this type of system is the improvement in quality which follows from the sense of individual responsibility for the product.

However, two alternative approaches to the general problem have been successfully applied. They have evolved between the two methods described above.

In the first of these alternative methods, the total task is assigned to each of a number of teams rather than to individuals. The small number of teams allows for a more modest investment in tools and equipment, while the problem of supplying parts and components is more manageable. Team working is also more flexible in comparison with a fixed assembly line, and this aspect can have positive motivational effects.

In a second arrangement, which relies more on the development of suitable hardware, the operator travels with the assembly on a specially designed vehicle, picking up the required parts and components from fixed stations along his route. The automatically guided vehicles (AGV) are typically controlled by a wire laid below floor level and, in the most sophisticated applications, may be routed past different supply stations to accommodate variations in product. In the assembly of automotive engines, as an example, the additional investment required in comparison with a conventional assembly track is considered to be repaid by increased flexibility.

ZERO INVENTORY AND JUST-IN-TIME (JIT)

The penalties for high levels of inventory, in terms of investment and holding costs, have already been noted. So have the less obvious costs which follow from increased inertia in the system and the tendency for inventory to obscure other operating deficiencies. Indeed, the pattern of this chapter has followed the pursuit of the economic small batch as a means of overcoming these problems. But it needed an imaginative leap to see the possibility of running a manufacturing system without any inventory at all.

Consider a business involved in the assembly of products from parts and components, some of which are manufactured in-house and some purchased from outside suppliers. The conventional way of managing the physical flows through the process has been to break down the forecast demand for finished product during the planning period into a requirement for parts and components. This requirement takes account of current stocks and work already in hand, and of manufacturing and procurement lead-times. The production plans so developed allow for any uncertainties in supply through production delays, component rejects or imperfections in the scheduling procedures. The master plan is thus used to develop detailed production plans which drive the process through to completion.

Zero inventory systems, in a sense, turn this process on its head. Planned requirement for finished product in each period is used as a precise statement of what is required and when from the preceding process stage: neither more nor less; neither later nor sooner. If components are brought in from outside suppliers, the same rules apply. The flow of material is thus *pulled* through the process rather than *pushed* in the conventional way.

Generally referred to as just-in-time (JIT) systems, arrangements of this kind make crucial demands on production management if they are to be successful. Some of the more important points are now considered.

If components are to be made available in numbers which meet the exact requirements of the next stage in the process, then production in very small batches may be necessary. Such a procedure demands an energetic attack on machine changeover times. If the demand for an exact number of components is to be met every time, then reject levels have to be reduced virtually to zero.

To operate a successful system of this kind demands a high degree of discipline in the planning and control of activities. Such systems also require a stable pattern of demand in order to function effectively.

Techniques vary. However, the overall principle is that operations are not scheduled simply to keep people and machines busy but parts are made only when they are needed for the next manufacturing stage. Although this can result in under-utilization of capacity at some work stations, this is more than offset by the dramatic reduction in inventory costs. The JIT concept is applied throughout the production cycle, right back to bought-out supplies, so that arrangements must be made with suppliers for materials to be delivered *just in time* to be used.

Several computer programs are available for controlling work in this way, but the original 'Kanban' system depends on the simplest precept that work can only be performed at a work station when that station receives a ticket requesting the work from the following work station. (*Kanban* is Japanese for a token or ticket.)

If outside suppliers are involved, they must be able to meet the same exacting standards. This thinking has had an important impact on the relationship between manufacturing companies and their suppliers. Reliability in quality and delivery needed to support a zero inventory system can only be achieved by a very close understanding between customer and supplier. This kind of intimate relationship may prove difficult to establish and sustain with more than one supplier (see Chapter 35).

Although the zero inventory or JIT system as presented might seem to be primarily an approach to inventory control, this concept would miss some important aspects of the systems. To achieve the standard of precision in every activity which is required by a true zero inventory system demands the kind of aggressive attack on every source of uncertainty and waste which can only be mounted by enlisting the energy of every employee.

CONCLUSION

This chapter has outlined some of the changes which new thinking and new technology have brought about in manufacturing systems. Those changes have been driven by two main forces: on the one hand, the demands of competitive markets for quality and variety, for an increased pace of new product development; and, on the other, the expanding capability and falling cost of computer-based systems.

These changes have conspired first to make the production-dominated, steady-rate, long-run, lowest-cost manufacturing system no longer commercially viable in many markets, and secondly, have provided production managers with tools of unprecedented power in meeting the challenge of this more turbulent environment.

FURTHER READING

Bignell, V. et al (eds), *Manufacturing Systems*, Blackwell, Oxford, 1985

Engelberger, Joseph F., *Robotics in Practice: Management and Applications of Industrial Robots*, Kogan Page, London, 1980

Hutchins, David, *Just in Time*, Gower, Aldershot, 1988

Medland, A. J. and Burnett, P., *CADCAM in Practice: A Manager's Guide to Understanding and Using CADCAM*, Wiley, New York, 1986

Scott, Peter B., *The Robotics Revolution*, Blackwell, Oxford, 1984

Vollman, T. E., Berry, W. L. and Whybark, D. C., *Manufacturing Planning and Control Systems*, 2nd edn, Irwin, Homewood, Ill., 1988

Walley, Brian *Production Management Handbook*, 2nd edn, Gower, Aldershot, 1986

38 Plant layout

B H Walley

The signs of a poor plant layout can seldom be hidden. Delays in the manufacturing process are apparent, with half-made products, components and raw materials following no direct or obvious path. Aisles are cluttered with work-in-progress. Service areas and stores are so sited that operatives are forced to leave their machines, frequently, to walk long distances to collect tools, work instructions and ancillary materials. Production plant is under-used and machines are seen to be idle, waiting for previous operations to be completed.

Putting such anomalies right demands a plant layout study, where all the factors involved in siting machinery, work stations, ancillary equipment, storage, services, manufacturing flow patterns and the functional design of the buildings are considered. The main objective is to produce a layout which will help to minimize production costs. Such a study needs the involvement of a wide range of specialists, either directly or as consultants. These can include architects, draughtsmen, ergonomists, design, mechanical, civil, electrical, process control and production engineers, work study and operations research people, production planners and controllers, safety officers, materials handling experts, shop stewards and (of course) line managers. Paradoxically, an abundance of experts with diverse aims can make the logical design of a plant layout difficult to achieve. Plant layout design is a complex task.

ENVIRONMENTAL CHANGES FOR PLANT LAYOUT

Plant layout can never be divorced from a general and well-conceived manufacturing strategy and continuing technological developments will impinge more and more on plant layout and how it is restructured.

Developments in philosophy

Factories have long been compartmentalized, with separate functions for maintenance, production and development engineering. With the advance of concepts like computer-integrated manufacturing, the departmental divisions of the past are no longer appropriate. Plant layout is now seen to be part of a computer-controlled, integrated manufacturing process. It has links with the planning process as well as with technical developments.

Optimized production technology (OPT)

OPT is one of the numerous recent developments where comparatively new thinking is being directed at the manufacturing process. Its proponents suggest that a comparatively simple appraisal is possible in plant layout, which will give considerable benefits. The central theme of OPT is to concentrate attention on production flow and elimination of bottlenecks rather than attempting to optimize capacity utilization. The production control aspects of OPT are outlined in Chapter 40.

Just in time (JIT)

JIT is a total management approach which aims to reduce inventory of all kinds and at all work stations to the minimum – even to zero stocks. The Japanese appear to have made this principle work better than Western nations. The changes in plant layout and factory utilization have been profound. Factories in Japan are, on the whole, smaller for the same level of output than those in the West. They tend to have uninterrupted material flow on the shop floor, with little work-in-progress.

JIT is outlined in Chapter 37. An essential component of a JIT system is the management of bought-out supplies, which is covered in Chapter 35.

Work organization

Group or team working, once confined to fairly esoteric examples in Sweden and West Germany, is spreading quickly in Western Europe. Teams are established which carry out many (if not all) the old compartmentalized activities, such as tool changing, maintenance and packing.

A plant layout must be established which is supportive of group working, with adjacent tool racks, maintenance equipment and packaging materials. Stores and storekeeping need to be eliminated, as far as possible. Flexibility within the team is essential. Operatives should carry out a wide range of activities, depending on their training and innate skills. Hence plant layout design should facilitate flexibility, perhaps by concentrating on ensuring maximum human resource utilization.

Robotics

Mechanization and automation have often been confused when plant layouts are being determined. Mechanization is the replacement of human muscle by mechanical means. Automation is substitution for the human brain. It is this second factor that will become more and more important in plant layout and in particular the application of industrial robots.

Industrial robots were developed when it became possible to harness digital electronic circuitry to manufacturing activities with sufficient robustness to stand up to a typical factory environment. Most robots consist of a jointed arm, a wrist, and a gripper or hand. These limbs are attached to a body and a programmable process control unit.

The very simplest programs were set up by plugging leads into a plugboard.

More modern robots can be taught to carry out all the necessary operations by driving them through the desired sequence using manual controls, committing each action and limb position to the electronic memory. The device is then programmed to do the job repetitively, accurately and reliably.

The larger robots can position workpieces weighing up to 250 kg, speedily and with accuracy repeatable to within a millimetre or so. Small robots have been developed for very fine assembly tasks.

The simplest robots are the so-called 'pick and place' devices, which can pick up an object from one given position and place it in another given attitude and position. They can be used for applications such as machine loading, and found their first major use in diecasting operations, where they excelled in handling hot workpieces straight from the moulds, in factory environments that were fatiguing to human operatives. For seam welding, paint spraying and other operations where the tool or hand has to trace a defined path, continuous path robots are necessary. Because many more positional coordinates have to be committed to memory to trace the path, these robots require considerably larger data memories.

The ambition of robot designers is to improve the 'intelligence' of their machines and to extend their abilities by giving them a sense of feel or touch to the gripper. Another development is to provide robots with some degree of visual sense. The consequences of robots for plant layout could be revolutionary.

A robot can be set among a small group of machines and sequenced to load, unload and operate them in an efficient, tireless fashion. Another application, such as the welding of car bodies on a production line, uses stationary robots with the work brought to them on a conveyor. A third arrangement has the robots mounted on tracks or conveyors, with the workpiece either stationary or carried on another conveyor.

Although each robot contains its own controls and memory, they have to be sequenced and interlocked with all the surrounding plant (and other robots). This needs the attention of control engineers during the plant layout planning stage (as with 'conventional' automation).

Robotic cell manufacture

Robotic cell manufacture combines group or team working with robotics. As the name suggests, the principle of cell manufacture is that production takes place within the confines of one dedicated manufacturing unit (the cell). This may or may not be linked with other processes or finishing operations.

The heart of the robotic cell is, of course, the robot, controlled by a local programmable processor. The manufacturing process is usually the conversion of raw materials into a finished workpiece or product. An example would be the computer weighing of raw material into a die, operation of the die, and then some further activity such as baking or enamelling. The robot acts as the handling medium from raw material to finished product.

The cell operators are a team of skilled and semiskilled operators plus first-line management. Cell manufacture of dedicated products is a major breakaway from the traditional flow line. Group technology is one aspect of this process.

Group technology

Group technology is an interesting and important development concerned with the flow of interprocess materials. As with robotic cell manufacture, it is based on the assumption that grouping manufacturing resources (such as machines) and making them interdependent in cellular fashion has many advantages over the functional layouts more usually found in batch or job shops. Each cell in group technology (but not necessarily in a robotic cell) has a mix of machines sufficient to carry out all processes on one part, or on a family of parts.

A functional layout, where (say) groups of lathes or drilling machines are brought together, produces complicated route patterns which result in high work-in-progress, bottlenecks and more orders delivered late than early.

An analysis of batch or job shop work usually reveals that products, far from being unique, can be seen to have family likenesses in their dimensions, material types, function and general appearance. This analysis is an important element in establishing group technology. So, by batching small groups of work in accordance with family features, it is possible to create large batches of basically similar work. Large batch production tends to take the place of small batch production. A precursor of group technology is therefore the design of a product classification system which can be used to batch material. A definitive coded parts numbering (drawing numbering) system is an essential adjunct to this classification system.

The design of group technology flowlines can be defined roughly as 'batch flowlines' which form an integral part of the manufacturing system. Individual operations can be formed into cells using linking roller conveyors. This ensures that batches of work do not queue jump and are processed in the same sequence as that in which they were fed into the cell.

The general applications of group technology suggest that operations can be optional, and either the machine or the labour resources may be under-utilized, with the emphasis placed on ensuring a continuous workflow. The cost of this under-utilization disadvantage is usually more than outweighed by reductions in setting-up and changeover times, work-in-progress and finished goods stock. The improvement in customer service is also important.

The size of each cell is determined by engineering considerations and span of control and, particularly, by the work relationships of the primary working group. Flexibility of labour within the cell is the norm; flexibility between cells an ideal. Incentive schemes are designed to take account of the breaks in rhythm needed when operatives move from one machine to another.

Flexible manufacturing systems

Flexible manufacturing systems (FMS), where computer control of integrated manufacture (CIM) is established, demand a radical review of plant layout. Without this a number of the benefits obtainable from FMS could be lost. This is one instance where an incremental approach to improving plant layout could be a mistake.

With the application of FMS on a production line making variations of one type of product, the plant layout might be designed around a main line incorporating the standard processing facilities. Branch lines, integrated with the main line, could then be used to carry out the non-standard operations needed to make the product variants. All activities would be programmed by a computer-coded instruction to the computer mainframe and all linked process computers. Such instructions would denote the product type, its dimensions and the variations required.

Materials handling

The truism that 'handling adds nothing to value, only to cost' suggests that materials handling should be an integral but minor part of a plant layout. Indeed, it is frequently difficult, if not impossible, to separate them.

Materials handling is a term which embraces all aspects of materials movement (other than when actual manufacturing activity is taking place). 'All aspects' are the physical transportation, equipment, methods, personnel and systems used in materials handling.

It must always be remembered that handling is not an end in itself. The objective should be to contribute to a high performance of production, stores and despatch and to help minimize the costs of production. Frequently this is synonymous with minimizing the cost of handling. Handling is a service function and should never be considered as a system independent of production or warehousing.

Many of the principles applied by materials handling specialists are similar to those which can be used in plant layout. Handling and rehandling should be avoided. Movement should be reduced in time and distance. Materials should be deposited as near as possible to the work station and be positioned ready for use. Continuous, rather than intermittent, movement should be a main aim. It is usually advantageous to establish definite routes for all material movement, vehicles and fork lift trucks.

Motion economy principles should apply wherever possible. Gravity should be used where this is feasible. Equipment and methods should be chosen to minimize the risk of in-process damage to products. Equipment should be simple and cheap, where possible. Mechanization and automation are often unnecessary.

Paradoxically, where plant layout is improved and just-in-time and computer-integrated manufacturing are introduced, materials handling could become a far less important consideration than it once was. There will be no need to store large quantities of raw material, or to have huge quantities of work in progress. A significant result of improving plant layout might, therefore, be a substantial reduction of the materials handling equipment needed.

PRINCIPLES OF PLANT LAYOUT

The skills needed to ensure success in plant layout are occasionally difficult to weld together to ensure a coherent result. While method study may be easy to apply in theory, its relationship with production engineering is not always an easy one. Potential benefits are many, but their achievement depends upon careful analysis and implementation. It is obviously far more difficult to attempt to rearrange an existing factory than to start with a 'greenfield' site. It is important, therefore, that the plant layout team should be able to refer to a set of principles which will guide its efforts and eventually provide a means of measuring whether or not the outcome is likely to be as satisfactory as first impressions might suggest. The following list of principles and expected benefits will serve this purpose:

1 The least possible space should be taken up. Any plant layout should be judged, at least in part, on the number of cubic metres and square metres needed. A useful calculation is the production added value expected per square metre. The sales value of products to be made and despatched per square metre is another test factor

2 Working conditions must produce a safe working environment, conducive to high work activity. The layout should help to promote good working practices which, in turn, help to reduce manufacturing cost, increase flexibility and maintain or improve good industrial relations

3 Interdependent operations, processes, activities and departments should be placed in proximity to each other, with as little product travel as possible

4 The layout should facilitate flow process and cellular type manufacturing operations, as these tend to utilize machines and labour

5 All product handling and re-handling should be eliminated as far as possible

6 Manual handling should be eliminated and replaced by mechanized handling wherever appropriate

7 The simplest possible materials handling equipment should be used. For example, gravity or roller conveyors are cheaper and more flexible than powered conveyor track

8 Materials and product movement should be minimized, seeking the shortest times and distances possible

9 If materials or product have to be moved any distance, they should do so as a 'unit load', as quantities rather than as unit items (perhaps on pallets)

10 Movement of product and materials should be continuous as far as possible, helping to keep manufacturing lead-times as low as possible

11 Receiving and despatch departments should be located near appropriate entrances and exits. Despatch departments should obviously be near the end of the production line

12 Machine speeds and siting should be such that few, if any bottlenecks occur. The production process should set a uniform pace which will optimize the use of machinery, handling equipment and associated personnel

13 Although machines should be utilized as fully as possible, in some instances production personnel may be the resource to utilize fully. Comparative costs, the need for flexibility, and/or imbalance in the process may determine which resource needs the most priority for efficient utilization

14 Stores and service area siting should be based on least travel between service and point of use

15 Obnoxious areas of dust, fumes or noise pollution should be isolated

16 Areas of high risk or danger need isolation (where inflammable materials are stored or used, for example)

17 Delicate or mentally arduous work should be assigned to an area which can be insulated from noise and other hazards. This does not imply banishment to an outer corner of the building: sound proofed partitions can be used provided the area is well ventilated

18   Production should be seen as a system with inputs and outputs, all of which need to be integrated within the plant layout. Management, supervision, production control, engineering and all other functions associated with the production activity should be embodied in the layout

19   Routing of services should be chosen to reduce the installation and subsequent maintenance costs of electrical, steam, gas, compressed air, ventilation and any other services

20   The most economic investment of capital in new plant, materials handling equipment, tooling, general facilities and the building itself should be sought, with each proposal for significant expenditure justified by a recognized appraisal method.

Benefits in addition to those implicit in the above principles should include at least some of the following:

1   Less need for ancillary workers, with fewer storekeepers, general labourers and internal transport drivers

2   Easier movement of staff around the factory

3   Reduced operator fatigue caused by the operation or the working environment

4   Reduced energy consumption

5   Production management made easier (production control, materials and stock control, work booking, costing, and so on)

6   More effective supervision and management

7   Better housekeeping: easier to keep everything clean and tidy

8   More easily predictable (and achievable) output and cost objectives

9   Sensitivity to changed production volume requirements, or to product mix changes and new designs

10   Improved workforce morale and promotion of good industrial relations.

CONSTRAINTS

Anyone deputed to improve an existing plant layout or to establish a new one from scratch will need to take into account a variety of constraints. It would be very unusual to start with a blank piece of paper and limitless cash. Any plant layout will be the result of numerous compromises. The following are the most important:

1   Manufacturing strategy. Many of the strategic possibilities are listed in the previous section. For example, if a JIT philosophy is being pursued vigorously and with a large degree of success, then the plant layout will certainly need to reflect the success of JIT

2   The siting, construction and layout of the building. For example, access to road and rail, structural strength, headroom, and whether it is single or multiple storey. It is still comparatively rare for a layout to be prepared and then have a factory built round it. A single-storey building will make future expansion easier and facilitate natural roof lighting but will cost more per square metre of manufacturing or storage space. The multistorey alternative will be cheaper per square metre but probably less flexible, and there may be doubts about the structural strength of upper floors

3   Environmental constraints. These could be numerous, including:

- *Oil mist pollution.* Eliminating oil mist produced by various machines could entail fully enclosing the machines, which might not be practicable. Placing them in a special location could also be prohibitive
- *Dust pollution.* There are various regulations covering such things as quarry dust and the use of asbestos. Wet manufacturing processes instead of dry ones will help to eradicate dust problems, although complete enclosure of dust producing areas is also a possibility, with the operatives within those areas wearing masks. Dust extraction equipment for reducing airborne particles to acceptable count levels may also be needed
- *Fumes and gases* are potential pollutants needing to be treated equally carefully as dust
- *Ventilation* is necessary even where dust, fumes and gases are not potential problems. Humidity also needs to be controlled
- *Lighting and heating:* in the UK must conform to the Factories Act of 1961
- *Noise* is recognized as a prime health hazard and cause of fatigue. Prolonged exposure to continuous noise can lead to permanent hearing loss. Noise suppression must be taken seriously
- *Factory amenities* such as seating, cloakrooms, restrooms, lavatories, first aid provisions and changing rooms are requirements listed in the Factories Act
- *Fire and safety precautions.* The layout must consider escape routes. The precautions will state how the building is to be used, with restrictions on its use and the number of people to be employed within it. Safety of operatives must be a prime concern in setting up machine processes

The Health and Safety at Work Act 1974 provides the framework for good housekeeping and all that this entails for plant layout (see Chapter 61)

4   Productivity requirements may sometimes impose constraints on technical excellence. For example, a case where a conscious decision is made to sacrifice some quality control or inspection space to accommodate more production machinery, in the hope that statistical process control can be substituted

5   Capital available for plant layout may be limited. The economic viability of any investment project should always be tested, using one of the recognized project appraisal techniques (see Chapter 12).

INFORMATION REQUIREMENTS

Information is a vital component in the analysis which the layout team will need to carry out. The team members themselves are unlikely to have all the information required and it will need to be obtained from market research people, the profit planning department, the accounting functions, engineering staff, who are not necessarily members of the team.

An opportunity to combine different objectives might occur as information is collected. For example, can finished goods stock be raised as a result of fast throughput time and reduced work in progress?

Information required is again set out in the form of a checklist in order to facilitate easy reference, as follows:

1 Range and volumes of production required based on marketing plans – types, quantities, raw materials, weights, volumes, product design, components, seasonality, delivery requirements

2 Budgeted revenue and costs of potential operations and, once an appropriate sequence has been determined, machines, machine speeds and potential utilization

3 Approximate costs of new plant, buildings and associated services

4 Site situations, building regulations, basic constraints of the site and any local environmental conditions which need to be taken into account – access to roads, railways or other means of transport

5 Volume of work-in-progress, raw materials and finished goods storage likely to be required

6 Labour and associated services required – canteens, rest rooms, lavatories and so forth

7 General services required – maintenance, stores, boiler-house, toolroom, fitters' shop and so forth

8 Office accommodation

9 Materials handling equipment required.

THE TECHNOLOGY OF PLANT LAYOUT

The technology of plant layout is a fundamental precept, often based on engineering principles which have become enshrined in plant layout activities. For example, the nature of the production process will normally fit a standard pattern and these patterns have become an accepted part of the technology.

1 Typical operation and process patterns are illustrated in Figure 38.1, in the following classifications:

- *Straight line* Raw materials are converted into one product by successive operations. Figure 38.1 (a)
- *Converging process* Several raw materials or components join a main line product. A motor car assembly plant is a good example. Figure 38.1 (b)
- *Diverging process* Materials converted into different products by separate processes or operations. Figure 38.1 (c)
- *Multiple process* A complex activity where cross-over between processes or operations is carried. Figure 38.1 (d).

2 Site/floor plans – the production process will tend to prescribe the site configuration, but the site itself may be a major factor in the plant layout. Several site-production processes have become fairly commonplace over the years and these are;

- *The 'I' plan* A straight-line production process established in a simple rectangular building as shown in Figure 38.2 (a)
- *The 'U' plan* The production process is often a straight line one, but because of the need to have the receipt and despatch areas adjacent to each other, a 'U' plan is adopted as shown in Figure 38.2 (b)

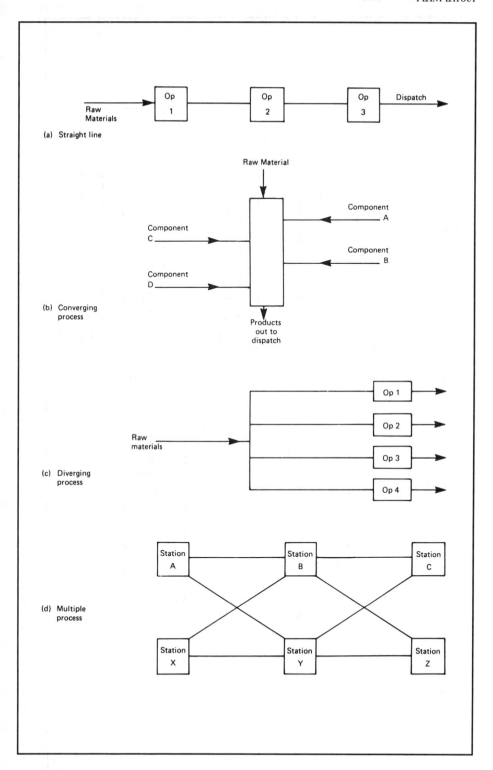

Figure 38.1   Four typical process patterns

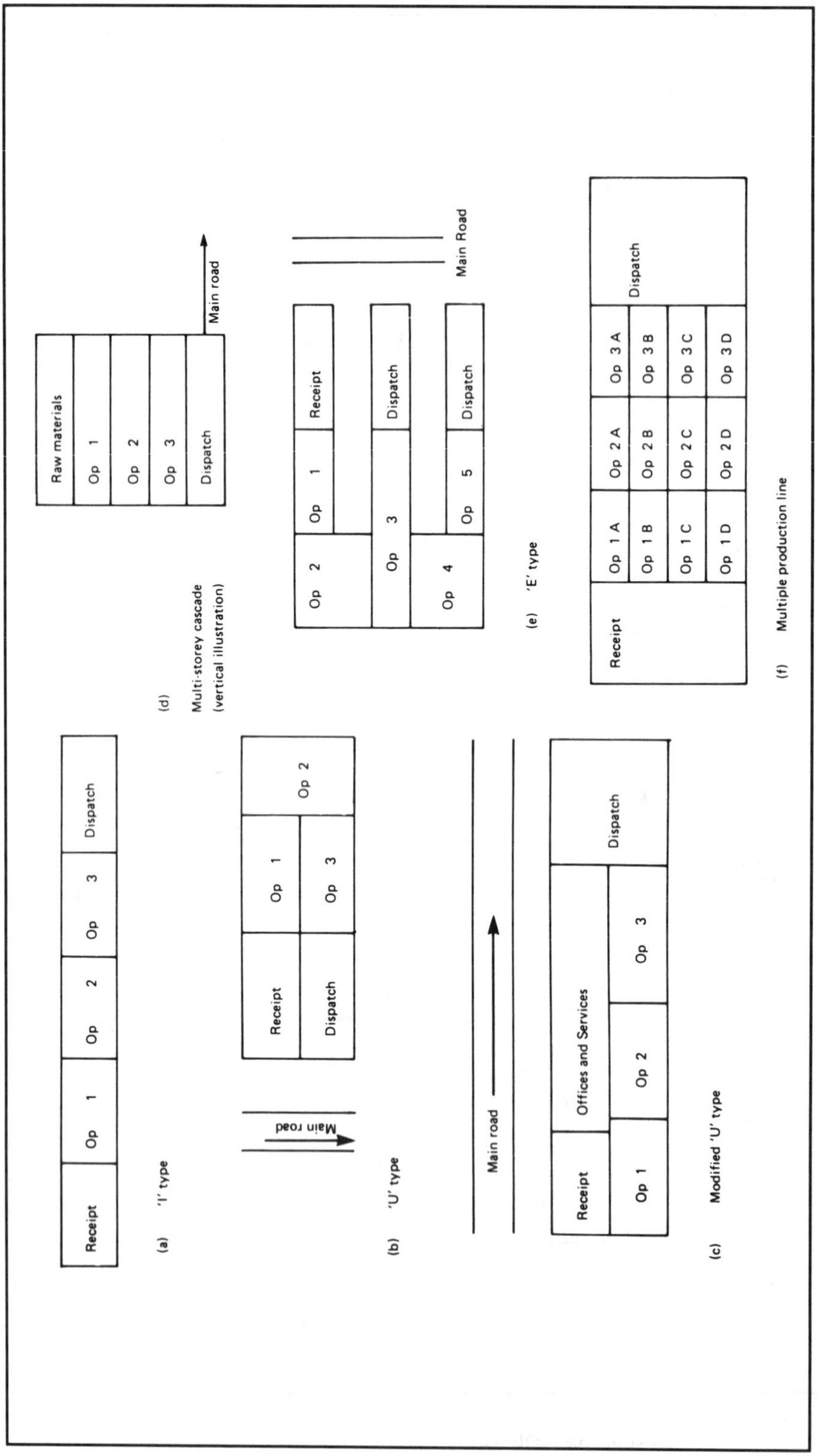

Figure 38.2   Floor plan configurations

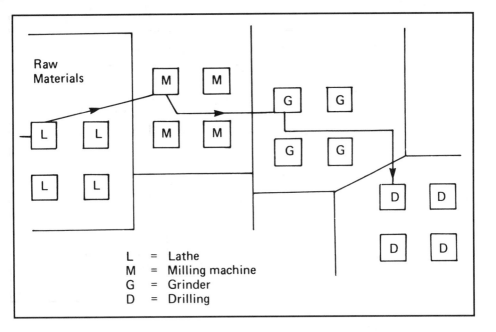

Figure 38.3 Process layout

- *Modified 'U' plan* The position of a main road and the access provided to it often promote a modified 'U' plan as in Figure 38.2 (c)
- *Multi-storey cascade* Multi-storey buildings provide the means to store raw materials on the top floor, and then allow manufacture to continue until completion on the ground floor as shown in Figure 38.2 (d)
- *'E' plan, multiple production* Multiple product lines are normally more difficult to lay out effectively than single product manufacture. The 'E' plan Figure 38.2 (e), and the multiple production line Figure 38.2 (f) are two ways of tackling the problem.

3 Process versus product layouts: process and product layouts are often in contention in optimizing plant layout. A process layout is one where flexibility can be obtained in the manufacturing activity (Figure 38.3). Like activities are put together. One machine may make several different products. The process, therefore, is specialized and can be subjected to efficient supervision and maintenance.

Product layouts (as shown in Figure 38.4) are typified in car assembly plants. Such layouts should reduce handling costs and production time. Work-in-progress should be minimized.

In many instances a combination of product and process layout is desirable

4 Functional relationships: in any factory there will be movement of products, raw materials, tools, operatives, and services personnel of all kinds between processes, machines, stores, toolroom and fitters' shop and warehouse dispatch area. Minimizing movement will be a key aspect of the plant layout.

The standard method for indicating functional relationships is a travel chart

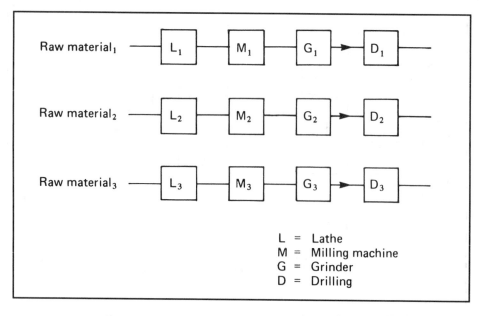

Figure 38.4   Product layout

as illustrated in Figure 38.5. Each area or unit which receives or dispatches materials, components, tools or products is listed. The number of personnel who have to travel between one location and another as part of their duties should also be recorded. The number of journeys or weight of transfers should be shown against the units or areas receiving them. A numeric system can then be used to indicate the amounts and importance of items which need to travel. The higher the number (perhaps weight or quantity x distance could be used), the nearer together the parts should be.

The principle may not apply if gravity is used in the transfer process. In that case downward rather than horizontal flow can be used to move items considerable distances, provided power is not needed to raise them later. The weighted data shown in the illustration is 568. Any layout which can reduce this total but not substantially increase cost is better than the one in existence

5   The plant layout should be designed around five major factors (illustrated in Figure 38.6):

- *The product, its design and markets*   This will help to determine unit load possibilities, economic batch sizes, the need for plant flexibility, speed of delivery, degree of 'change-over' capacity
- *The process design*   The selection of equipment, dimensions of floor area to be occupied, manufacturing operatives, operation sequences
- *The operation designs*   Methods study should help to set working patterns. Work measurement should help establish manning levels and equipment requirements
- *The design of facilities*   Materials flow, storage areas, materials handling, power, steam, heating, environmental requirements

	A	B	C	D	E	F	G	H	TOTAL
A		31	12		11	12	10	—	76
B	11			40	12	13			76
C	21	—	61					17	99
D	13					70			83
E	41		20					16	77
F	11		20			24			55
G	21								21
H			60					21	81
TOTAL	118	31	173	40	23	119	10	54	568

Figure 38.5   Functional relationships diagram

- *Site design*   Using the site and building to best advantage.

The design team should ensure that the interrelationships are well understood, with the comparative importance of each process established and suitable priorities made. The whole project should be set out as a critical path network

6   Space considerations: the allocation of space between offices and factory, productive processes and service areas, and in process and finished goods storage, needs to be done according to predetermined rules and standards. For example, aisles are often allocated far too much space. If too much is allocated an aisle will degenerate into an inter-process storage area, holding up material flow and generally hindering the reason why aisles exist – rapid transport of materials and products, and personnel of all kinds.

Storage space too is often given an over-generous allocation of floor area. Maximum height stacking should be the rule rather than the exception, and materials handling equipment should be obtained to provide this facility.

Workplace design will often determine the space required for production machinery, rather than the machinery itself. Each workplace should be designed as a microcosm of the total plant so that it has its own receiving and dispatch areas, facilities and services and production equipment, established

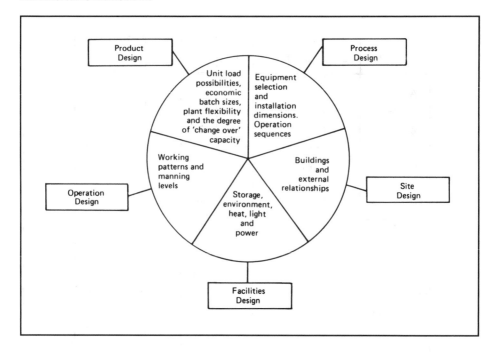

Figure 38.6   The design process

to maximize production efficiency. Workplace design should take account of potential scrap and finished production waiting to be moved, any inspection requirements, tools and tool storage, height of working surfaces, relationships between receipt and despatch of materials, hazard elimination, degree of automation and mechanization anticipated, operator comfort and conditions, floor loading constraints and general environmental considerations

7   Line balance considerations: a plant layout analysis should promote a balance between machine/labour utilization and use of in-progress storage space. This is often difficult where machines or operations have to be introduced which produce at a much higher or lower rate than perhaps the rest of the line.

The most common solution to this problem is to divide the work to be done into elements and thus combine them into activities which take up a similar amount of time. The related cost/performance calculations have been embodied into operations research techniques.

There are other ways of overcoming line balance problems, perhaps the easiest being the build-up of partly or semi-finished stocks so as to feed in production when required at the slower operations.

Another solution is to have a reasonably peripatetic work-force which has been trained to carry out work at several operations, wherever the line has become unbalanced.

Balancing the line grows increasingly difficult as the product range becomes more complex. Variety reduction will always help this problem

8   Equipment selection: equipment can be bought to satisfy one or more of the following criteria:

- to carry out a new activity
- to replace a manual activity
- to improve the environment and general working conditions
- to make use of new technology
- to improve line balance
- to replace a worn-out machine
- to reduce possibilities of accidents
- to improve quality of products

9 Method study: using the simple method study symbols to describe a material flow process is often the simplest and best way of ensuring a record is made of actual or potential plant layout designs. String diagrams too can be of help

10 The evaluation of alternative production methods and layout schemes is an essential part of any layout planning. This assumes, of course, that more than one potentially viable scheme does, in fact, exist. The merits of a proposal can be examined critically by asking how well the proposal would achieve any of the benefits listed at the beginning of this chapter, and checking that all constraint factors have been satisfied. By awarding a maximum possible number of 'score points' to each benefit factor (according to the degree of importance attached) a scale is made available against which the benefits of a scheme can be quantified. This helps to render any choice objective rather than subjective. It is obviously better still if the financial benefits of alternative schemes can be estimated and used in comparison.

FURTHER READING

Engleberger, J. F., *Robotics in Practice*, Kogan Page, London 1980

Gattorna, J., (ed.) *Handbook of Physical Distribution Management*, 3rd edn, Gower, Aldershot, 1983

Hollinggum, J., *Mass Production With Batch Work: Group Technology Explained*, Pergamon, Oxford, 1969

Walley, B., *Production Management Handbook*, 2nd edn, Gower, Aldershot, 1986

39 Productivity improvement

The British Council of Productivity Associations

Productivity improvement, in the sense of making better use of the resources employed in meeting the needs of the consumer, is a continuing preoccupation of the managers of all manufacturing or service operations. Whether by investment in more efficient plant, development of more effective systems, energy conservation, the reduction of scrap or stimulation of employee performance, the pursuit of improvements in productivity is an everyday concern. But the focus of this chapter is on improvements in these – and other – areas which are brought about in a systematic way.

A PLANNED APPROACH TO PRODUCTIVITY IMPROVEMENT

The kind of measures referred to above represent, by definition almost, a piecemeal approach to productivity improvement. Typically they are reactive, stimulated by an increase in some element of cost – labour or materials or energy or capital, or perhaps where some malfunction has focused attention on a part of the system. Even where this kind of action is co-ordinated into a more comprehensive attack on one of these elements through an organization-wide programme, the approach is still essentially a tactical one. Recent years, however, have seen a growing realization that substantial benefits can follow from a strategic approach to productivity improvement.

There are a number of reasons for this. First is the realization that there is more to the productivity equation than the measurable inputs to, and outputs from, some part of the system: man hours per unit of production or ton miles per vehicle per day. Such measures are essentially indices of the efficiency of some component of the conversion process but take no account, for example, of effectiveness (of the output's contribution to the organization's wider objectives) or of the social impact of change. Thus, investment in expensive plant in the narrow interest of reduced conversion costs can lead to a lack of flexibility in the face of rapidly changing markets. And there is nothing more demoralizing than to engage energies in bringing about operational improvements to a part of the business which subsequently falls victim to a change in business policy.

Then again, the growth of the service sector, where outputs are less tangible, has raised problems of measurement which can only be met by introducing some element of quality of service into the equation.

To recognize these additional dimensions to the output side of the productivity equation – effectiveness, quality and social impact – is to realize that to bring about an improvement is likely to involve diverse inputs also.

Conventional approaches to productivity improvement tend to be rooted in a particular discipline rather than focused on some aspect of business performance. There are many fables which describe how some problem was addressed by industrial engineering, personnel, accounting, operations research and so on, each seeing the problem and the solution in terms of their own specialization. This is not to belittle the contribution of such specialists, which is totally indispensable, but to make the point that where the effort is directed at a broader outcome, the advantages of a multidisciplinary approach become more obvious.

In discussing the subject of productivity we are, by definition, talking about manipulation of operational resources. In a commercial undertaking there are a variety of ways in which its prosperity can be enhanced by actions which, while having important impacts on the operating system, have origins which lie outside it. Thus, more astute financial management which makes more funds available for investment; mergers and acquisitions which provide the opportunity to take advantage of economies of scale; new product developments which provide wider market opportunities and so on, all originate outside the present operating system. Such actions will present those responsible for managing day-to-day operations with both problems and opportunities and their responses may well bring about beneficial change in the overall productivity of the systems in their charge. But the effect will not invariably be benign; there is a whole range of profitable change through improved service to the customer which may well have adverse effects on the utilization of resources. Where there is improvement it will be a mere by-product of the pursuit of policies which have other, wider objectives.

The argument is that the narrow pursuit of productivity of resources is not necessarily beneficial to the business as a whole. Nor, conversely, do wider policy decisions necessarily have a beneficial effect on resource productivity as such. What is required is a recognition that there is an important interaction between policy decisions and the productivity of the operating system. Initiatives taken to raise the level of utilization of input resources can have the effect of opening up opportunities for the business: business policy decisions can have important implications for the utilization of such resources.

Formal programmes of productivity improvement need to take notice of the nature of these interactions for the particular business. For example, business strategies which depend on the relationship between cumulative product experience and lowered costs will only succeed where positive steps are taken to manage the operating system down the experience curve.

A PRODUCTIVITY IMPROVEMENT PROGRAMME

To be successful, a productivity improvement programme must be based first of all on a global review of the main resources used in the business – finance, technology, plant, people. This should identify not only their potential contribution to the achievement of policy objectives but make an assessment of the organization's readiness for change. This assessment needs to consider what resources (in terms of management skills and financial strength, for example) will be required and whether they are in place or can be made available to ensure the success of the programme. If existing resources are fully stretched in coping with the day-to-day business in a tough competitive environment, then it will be unwise to proceed until some space has been created to take on the additional load.

In addition to assessing the obstacles which a shortage of resources might represent, there is a need also to consider those positive factors which contribute to organizational readiness. These would include a climate within the organization which is conducive to change, a record of innovation, of challenges successfully taken up.

If the assessment of readiness is favourable, detailed planning can begin. One of the problems with productivity improvement plans is that they have come to be associated mainly with manpower productivity and, in the prevailing economic climate, with a reduction in employment opportunity. The issue has to be faced squarely and, where the primary objective is cost reduction, it must be recognized that employees will be legitmately interested in how the savings are to be divided.

Many companies recently have found themselves in a situation where drastic action has been necessary for survival, and it has been possible to convince employees of the seriousness of the situation and secure their active co-operation in bringing about necessary change. But it has been an uncomfortable process. For others, it has seemed impossible to embark on any kind of programme which involved a collaborative approach.

In the introduction of a formal productivity improvement programme, five separate steps can be identified.

Step 1   Awareness

First is the need to establish an awareness throughout the organization of the objectives of the programme and the way in which it is to be implemented. The methods used to establish this awareness will depend on the established patterns of communications within the company. Plans have been launched which involve a considerable amount of direct training of managers, supervisors, union officers and employee representatives. Such training will often embrace some introduction to problem solving or other relevant techniques or may be confined to an understanding of the processes of change in organizations, presented in the context of the proposed plan. In other cases, information will be imparted through internal newsheets, through briefing groups, through presentations on videotape and so on.

There is much to be said for making the keynote of the campaign a very positive one: successful programmes have been run which do not look for mere improvement but challenge every item of cost to be justified in terms of contribution to profit. Other programmes have been based on the need to match the annual rate of increase in controllable costs with comparable overall savings. But it is very important to make sure these kinds of programmes are consistent with the objectives of the business. While reduction in costs is always desirable there is generally a trade-off between use of resources and service to the customer which should be recognized in the main thrust of the programme.

Step 2   Motivation

One of the objectives of measures taken to raise levels of awareness is to create a climate favourable to change. The next step is to turn that to a positive motivation. Action here will depend critically on the earlier assessments of readiness, particularly those aspects which are concerned with enthusiasm and morale. Where the management team is already innovative in style, the focus may be on convincing them that a productivity improvement programme is an appropriate weapon to use in the current situation.

Where there is a degree of inertia to be overcome, the facts revealed in the awareness campaign – of competitive pressures, for example – may of themselves create the necessary motivation. But however this phase of the exercise is directed, an essential component will be some very explicit commitment to the programme on the part of senior management. Without such a demonstration the exercise is unlikely to succeed.

The best recipe for a strongly motivated workforce is a combination of leadership and involvement. To provide leadership, senior management need to maintain a high profile where the programme is concerned, taking part in presentations where appropriate and making sure that progress reports are on the agenda at operating meetings. They can also make clear by example that attendance at team meetings enjoys a high priority. They can insist that the reward system takes account of individual contribution to the programme.

In considering the other component, there is abundant evidence that participation in teams is a powerful motivator. To spread the opportunity for participation as widely as possible consistent with sensible control is to take maximum advantage of the benefits which such involvement brings. And that participation should extend not only to the search for opportunities for improvement but to setting targets for improvement as well.

Finally under the heading of motivation is the question of reward. Programmes have been run successfully in which achievement of targets is one of the factors taken into account in assessing bonuses for managers. But it has to be stressed that other, more direct indicators of job performance dominate the system. Generally, it is held that direct financial reward is not appropriate but that some form of recognition is desirable. The method chosen should take account of any established system in the company for achievement of targets for quality, safety, lost time or other subjects of interdepartmental competition.

Step 3   Tactical planning

The next step is concerned with tactical planning – where to begin? Some form of force field analysis may be appropriate to establish a comprehensive view of the factors, both favourable and hostile, which will influence success in any proposed area of change. Early success is a great morale booster in change programmes, but avoid the fate of boxers whose reputations are built on a series of inadequate opponents only to be floored by the first serious opposition! Rather than picking the easy options there is much to be said for starting in areas where changes can be made – and be seen to be made – quickly. For it is the achievement of actual change which will build up the momentum of the programme rather than an accumulation of proposals whose implementation is necessarily delayed – by the need to purchase and install equipment, for example, or to develop computer software. Once agreement has been reached on some form of employee participation in the programme, nothing is more discouraging for its supporters than a period when nothing appears to be happening.

Step 4   Implementation

In considering the implementation of the programme there are two main areas for decision. First is the choice of an appropriate organizational framework. Most programmes involve the establishment of some structure which is divorced from the day-to-day running of the business. There are many alternatives and we explore three different examples later in this chapter. Each of these involves the establishment of one or more teams, task forces – call them what you will – which will carry out the detailed analysis of the present situation and development of alternative solutions. These teams will typically be multidisciplinary and must have access to further specialist resources, both inside and outside the organization.

In addition to such teams, there will be a need for some co-ordinating activity to ensure that individual team efforts constitute a coherent whole, and that this is consistent with the overall objectives, whose importance has been stressed at some length above. It will also be desirable to establish some means of direct communication between teams, to provide for the exchange of ideas and experiences and for mutual support.

A second important decision concerns the resources which are to be made available to the programme. Concentrating initially on the problems of raising levels of awareness and motivation, it is a common experience that managements greatly underestimate the amount of effort required to satisfy the levels of expectation that have been aroused. Of course, there are limits to the amount of change which any individual part of the organization can absorb in a given time without some aspects of performance being affected. But nevertheless, for any given amount of resource which can be made available to the programme, it will probably be wiser to concentrate it rather than spread it so thinly that early enthusiasms cannot be adequately followed up.

Step 5   Monitoring

Finally, a mechanism for monitoring the progress of the exercise will be desirable. It is not uncommon for programmes to be designed around some quantifiable target of improvement – say 5 per cent – in utilization of plant or personnel or in delivery performance or in the reduction of scrap or energy consumption, the choice being made in the light of potential contribution to the objectives of the business. Team members will want to see the cumulative effect of their efforts of progress towards such targets and management will want to monitor the outcome of the programme in relation to the resources they have made available.

Since commitment to change is the essential ingredient of success, there is much to be said for a monitoring system which requires proposals to be set out with some formality and which clearly identifies actions, responsibilities and timing.

ORGANIZATIONAL STRUCTURE

The paragraphs above have sketched in a framework for the establishment of a productivity improvement programme. Throughout there has been an implication that the programme will be based on teams. There has also been an implicit assumption that a team approach is likely to be more successful than any of the alternatives. This assumption is based on experience of the power which a small, well-managed team can bring to bear on the problems and opportunities which a productivity improvement programme can bring to light. The actual composition of such teams and the relationship between them has been only lightly touched on. Some of the alternative arrangements are illustrated in the following examples.

Company A

Company A is a subsidiary of a large engineering group and manufactures industrial products at a single site employing some 400 people. The factory has its own industrial engineering capability and is able to call on a limited range of other specialist help from the headquarters of the group. They set up their productivity improvement plan with teams consisting of departmental managers and supervisors. There are eight teams in all, one in each of the production departments, one each representing maintenance and plant services and one from production planning. The teams have four or five members and may co-opt members as they think fit. There is also a team co-ordinator and an action group. The general structure of the plan is as follows:

1 Teams meet once a week for about two hours
2 Each team has a leader whose responsibilities are:
   - To maintain records of meetings, actions agreed, responsibilities and timing
   - To maintain links with other teams and with specialist departments
   - To prepare project proposals for the team co-ordinator
3 The team co-ordinator is a senior member of the factory industrial engineering department whose responsibilities are:
   - To assist the teams to develop and progress their proposals
   - To prepare proposals for submission to the action group
4 The action group consists of the factory manager, chief engineer, chief accountant, personnel manager and the team co-ordinator. The group meets monthly, and its responsibilities are:
   - To examine project proposals
   - To decide priorities and timing for implementation
   - To progress implementation of proposals in line with agreed dates.

Before proposals are put before the action group a detailed examination of costs and benefits is carried out. Three months after changes are brought about, an investigation is carried out to establish that the benefits are being secured and that the costs are in line with estimates. The results of this investigation are reported to the action group for attention.

491

Company B

Company *B* is in the service sector and has more than twenty branches. These branches, whilst differing considerably in size, share a common technology and employ substantially similar procedures in the service of their customers.

Because of the similarity between branches, and in their way of working, it seemed that the opportunities for exchange of experiences were particularly strong. Accordingly, it was decided to set up a productivity improvement programme which would have a strong element of direction from the centre. A small team was set up at the head office under the leadership of a senior manager from one of the branches. The team was to visit each location and with the active participation of the local manager, to review each aspect of the unit's activity. The purpose of the review was to be the identification of opportunities for profitable change and to get commitment to action plans to turn such opportunities into results.

The choice of the team leader was seen as critical. He needed to be a manager whose own success had earned him the respect of his colleagues and whose personality would set a tone of encouragement and confidence. He was assisted by a member of the head office productivity services unit and an accountant with a good knowledge of branch procedures. The team leader worked to the following brief:

Work programme

The team will need to develop a programme. Its work at each site will have some aspects of an audit and must therefore be systematic and comprehensive in its review of site activities. The programme should provide for study in depth, the team spending from two to three weeks at each main site. The team's activities at each site will include:

1 Briefing sessions with the local manager to gain understanding and commitment to objectives, methods of working, confidentiality, reporting, follow-up
2 Briefing sessions with other officers, supervisors and graded staff as may be appropriate
3 Review of site activities: a useful starting point will be provided by an organization chart which accounts for every employee, and by the site budget and expenditure control reports
4 Detailed examination of selected areas with emphasis on the opportunities for profitable change
5 Establish priorities, action plans and assign responsibilites
6 Draft terms of reference for projects requiring further work. (An example of a suitable form is shown in Figure 39.1.)
7 De-briefing, agree follow-up procedure.

Control system

The essence of the programme is to gain the commitment of local management by working with them in finding opportunities for profitable change. At the same time, there will be a need to keep the programme moving forward. It is proposed that all

COMPANY B   TERMS OF REFERENCE FOR PRODUCTIVITY IMPROVEMENT PROJECT

Location ....   Project No. ....

Project title

Brief title for identification

Initiated by ....

Start date   ....   Date for completion ....

Project objective

What will the project achieve?

Present situation

What happens at present?

Reasons for project

What makes you think an improvement is possible?

Action requested and end product

What the project team is being asked to do and what the end product will be?

Constraints

What constraints are imposed on the solution in terms of costs, time, etc?

Team manager   Team members

Figure 39.1   Form used by company B to specify terms of reference for a productivity improvement team

information, notes of discussions, reports and other data generated by the team at any location should be confidential to the local manager and not disclosed to anyone else without his express permission. The local branch manager will be required to report on the projects to which he has agreed as a part of his regular reporting procedure.

General

The emphasis of the whole programme must be upon action and results. In many directions where opportunities exist, the obstacles to change are clear to see. It will be a prime task of the central team to reappraise these obstacles and seek ways in which they can be surmounted. In some areas there may be a need to re-establish the confidence of local managers. Much will depend on the ability of the central team to gain the confidence of local managers in discussing their problems; no sense of recrimination over past performance must be allowed to enter into these discussions.

Company C

Company C is a manufacturing company which has two main activities. Contracts division is concerned with meeting customer demands with products which are designed and built to individual customer specification. Products division markets a highly specialized range of industrial products which are very competitive in their field.

In considering the appropriate structure for a productivity improvement programme, the company distinguished sharply between the two divisions. It set out proposals for them in the following terms:

1 *Contracts division* This division is an important growth area for the company. The chief preoccupation of management is the planning and execution of contracts, particular emphasis being placed on the achievement of shorter delivery times through improved procurement and subcontracting procedures and on detailed planning and control of manufacturing processes.

However, if the expansion which is planned for the business is to be built on sound foundations, management information and control systems must be developed which will support such future growth. With this in mind, a team should be set up with the specific task of examining, on a regular and systematic basis, the procedures by which the operations of the business is controlled. This systems review team should comprise:

- Manufacturing manager
- Procurement manager
- Chief accountant

The team, which will report to the general manager, will draw on such outside assistance as appears helpful including, in particular, computer services

2 *Products division* This division has remained very static for some time. Control information and operating statements indicate that standards are being met and that most adverse variances arise from causes beyond the control of management.

If products division is to achieve the profitable expansion planned for it, a detailed review of the whole operation should be taken as a priority. What is needed is an approach which will challenge all the accepted constraints on the technology, and on the manufacturing and distribution operations. Resources from outside the division will be needed and structured so that creative problem analysis techniques can be brought to bear.

TEAM BUILDING

All the approaches that have been described involve the creation of teams whose composition will depend upon the circumstances and the objectives of the particular programme. Experience shows that there is benefit to be gained if a new team can take a short period of time soon after it has formed to examine how it is going to work, what its methods, procedures and work relationships will be and what the principal concerns of its members are. Training will take the form of discussions covering the following topics:

1 Statement, discussion and clarification of the team's mission – its objectives, timetable, work tasks
2 Discussion of the concerns and hopes of the team members – about their roles, relationship with the team, relationship with the departments from which they are seconded, how the group will follow or depart from tradition, what will happen when the project is complete
3 Presentation and explanation of the team leader's plan to organize the project; organization structure, relations with others, general ground rules
4 Discussion of each individual's special contribution, area of responsibility and authority
5 Development of methods of communication within the team and with people outside the team. Conduct of meetings, preparation of minutes, reports, memoranda
6 Development of the team's relationship with local managers; legitimacy, confidentiality, expectations
7 Arrangements for a follow-up meeting.

FURTHER READING

Gmelch, W. and Miskin, V., *Productivity Teams*, Wiley, New York, 1984
Gregeman, I., *Productivity Improvement*, Van Nostrand Reinhold, New York, 1984
Lawlor, A., *Productivity Improvement Manual*, Gower, Aldershot, 1985
Saunders, G., *The Committed Organisation*, Gower, Aldershot, 1984

40 Production control

Peter Jackson

Production control is concerned with producing goods in the right sequence in the least time and with the lowest inventory costs. As such it is always something of a balancing act, involving compromises and 'best fits' rather than theoretical ideals. The main aspects are:

1 Loading and scheduling work
2 Provisioning material, parts and production aids
3 Monitoring and progressing work
4 Producing management information enabling the system to be controlled.

DIFFERENCES BETWEEN SYSTEMS

Every company will have a different system depending on its products and production facilities. Some relevant factors are:

Complexity of the product

Single-operation plastic mouldings are much easier to control than components going through any combination of up to twenty operations. This is especially true if assembly of components is included.

Length of cycle time

If a job stays on a machine for a fortnight it is much easier to replan than if each operation takes only a few hours.

Repeatability of the work

Regular jobs will have predictable cycle times. The production facilities they require, such as tooling, will be known and available. One-off jobs are not so easy to control.

Forward notice available

Some companies know every job they will do for a year ahead and can plan accordingly. Others do not, or claim they do not, know a week ahead what orders will be required.

Dependence on outside suppliers and subcontractors

Where control is not completely within the company, greater allowance must be made for slippage.

Seasonal nature of the workload

Where seasonal peak loads occur capacity utilization will obviously vary.

Availability and quality of information on capacity and workload

Companies which have detailed time standards, process layouts and up-to-date capacities can load to a fuller degree and schedule to a tighter time-scale than those which have to rely on rough estimates.

Despite all these differences companies with a wide range of products and production facilities have similar problems and have developed similar solutions.

LOADING AND SCHEDULING WORK

Loading is filling available capacity with sufficient jobs in a given time period. Scheduling is determining the desired sequence of jobs. The two are interrelated and in some procedures may be indistinguishable. When work is correctly loaded and scheduled optimum use can be made of capacity, completion times can be predicted and met, and urgent jobs can be given priority without upsetting the rest of the work.

Stages

Loading and scheduling will probably be done in several stages from the overall factory planning when a new order is received to the detailed plan for each machine in the period immediately before production. The mechanics are similar at each stage. When the order is accepted little detail may be known of the work-load involved or of the machine capacity available in the proposed production period, yet some estimates must be made to enable delivery dates to be quoted. Such forward loading is done on an overall basis using broad measures.

As the time for producing the order draws near, the drawings, parts lists and process paperwork will have been extracted, enabling loads on each machine to be calculated. Also, nearer the production time available capacity can be more realistically assessed. This enables detailed short-term loading to be done.

Data required

Units

The basic need is a common unit in which both capacity and load can be expressed. The most common unit is time. Load can be measured by work study or estimation or historical information can be kept. The accuracy required of these time standards depends on the degree of repetition of the work. Often, good estimates are sufficient provided they are, on average, right. Where times for individual components are used they must be multiplied by the batch size and an allowance for setting time included.

Capacity in terms of time is easily expressed in man- or machine-hours with suitable allowances for breakdowns, rework and other contingencies.

Where times are not available a physical count may provide a suitable unit. Foundry output is often expressed in tonnes. A shoe factory may make so many pairs a day. A warehouse may process so many orders. Here the load is already defined; capacity is found from historical data.

A third measure of capacity and load is money. Orders are often considered in terms of their financial value and this may be a convenient way of loading a factory. An output of £10 000 per week may be a good measure of a factory's production. Again capacity is measured historically. Because of the nature of material and labour costs it is unusual to use money as a unit for detailed machine loading.

Load centre capacities

A load centre is the production unit to which jobs are allocated. It could be a factory, a section, a machine group or an individual machine or operator. With several stages of loading it could be all of these in turn. When it involves more than one machine either all work loaded to it should be capable of being done on any of its sub-units or the mix of work should on average match the mix of the sub-units.

Before breaking the load down to individual machines it should be considered whether the production control department are the best people to do this. The foreman or supervisor will have detailed knowledge of the capabilities of particular men and machines and be able to react to breakdowns and other immediate problems. It may, therefore, be realistic to load to machine groups, leaving the final allocation to the man on the spot.

The capacity of the load centre is calculated in the appropriate units. Some capacity may be reserved for emergency work or special customers but this must be kept to a small proportion and revised regularly.

Processes

The sequence of operations, usually called the process layout, must be known if each operation is to be loaded separately.

Parts lists

Where assemblies are manufactured the parts list of each assembly and subassembly will be needed. The requirements for common parts need to be batched up. For some components it may be more economical to make for stock than make on a one-for-one basis for final assembly.

LOADING METHODS

There are two main methods: job sequence, in which each job is loaded in strict sequence against a time-scale, and control period where a list of jobs is planned for a defined time period but can be carried out in any sequence.

Machine	Hour beginning							
	08 00	09 00	10 00	11 00	12 30	13 30	14 30	15 30
Capstan lathe	1053	1053	1053	1154	1154	1154	1154	1154
Herbert lathe	1186	1186	1186	1186	1186	1701	1701	1701
Holbrook lathe	1188	1188	1188	1188	1188	1188	1790	1790
Jig borer	REPAIR AND MAINTENANCE							
Universal miller	IDLE	IDLE	IDLE	IDLE	1185	1185	1185	1185
Horizontal miller	1081	1081	1081	1081	904	904	904	1225
Automatic – 1	1300	1300	1300	1300	1300	1300	IDLE	IDLE
Automatic – 2	IDLE	IDLE	IDLE	IDLE	IDLE	IDLE	IDLE	IDLE

Figure 40.1   A job sequence loading chart. This simple configuration is suitable for blackboard and chalk. The numbers in the squares are job numbers

Job sequence loading

To load jobs in strict sequence against a time-scale requires some visual display such as a planning board. Such boards can be purchased ready made although a home-made version can often fit particular requirements better. The load centres are usually displayed along the left-hand edge with a time-scale along the bottom. Jobs are planned to load centres either by writing on the board with an erasable medium or inserting a card in a slot (see Figure 40.1).

This method is best used close to actual production for loading individual machines. It can only be used for forward planning where contracts cannot run simultaneously. An example of this would be forward planning ships on the slipways of a shipyard.

Advantages of job sequence loading

1 Clear visual display of information
2 Full utilization of capacity possible
3 Rapid throughput of jobs loaded on more than one load centre
4 Planning boards can be used for progressing.

Disadvantages of job sequence loading

1 Updating is difficult and time consuming
2 Only suitable for limited periods ahead because of the likelihood of the situation changing
3 Relies on precise measurement of load

4   Cannot cope with overall allowances for reduction of capacity, for example, 10 per cent allowance for breakdowns.

Control period loading

A list of jobs is produced for each load centre for a fixed period of time, the control period. The total load of these jobs equals the capacity of the centre. For example, a machine group of two lathes, each worked 40 hours a week, has a capacity of 80 hours if the chosen control period is a week. A list is produced of jobs for these machines up to a total of 80 hours. Any further work is loaded into the following week.

The list becomes the programme for that load centre for that period. Jobs can be done in any sequence on any machine in the centre, provided they are finished by the end of the control period.

Multi-operational jobs are programmed at one operation per control period resulting in all jobs going through at an equal pace. The completion time of each job can be predicted.

The choice of control period depends on the length of the jobs and the sophistication of the production control system. Setting a target of one operation per week may not be very ambitious but may compare favourably with what was achieved without a loading system. It is better to start with a long control period and shorten it when experience has been gained rather than start with an unrealistically short one.

Control period loading is used in long-term planning where the overall workload can be compared with the overall capacity; for example, accepting orders up to £50 000 value a month. It is also used for short-term planning on groups of machines. This allows supervision flexibility to allocate particular jobs to individual machines or operators.

Advantages of control period loading

1   Simple to operate
2   Not dependent on completion of every job. Late jobs can be caught up without upsetting the programme
3   Allows supervision discretion in allocating jobs to particular operators or machines
4   Enables forward load picture to be produced over a reasonable period.

Disadvantages of control period loading

1   Overall throughput time is slow compared to job sequence loading, although much quicker than if no planning is used at all
2   Work progress is higher than for job sequence loading.

Forward and backward loading

Using either job sequence or control period loading it is usual to start at the present time and load jobs in the earliest available capacity, slowly building up a forward load picture. This is known as forward loading.

It is, however, possible to fix a completion date a number of weeks in advance and load backwards from this date, thus arriving at a date when the job must start. This is called backward loading.

Assuming that delivery dates have been set realistically, backward loading ensures that jobs are not started needlessly early. If all jobs are loaded in this way capacity may well be exceeded as one of the main reasons for loading is to set achievable delivery dates. It may help to backward load a certain proportion of jobs, key ones whose delivery dates are important, and then fill in the remaining capacity by forward loading the less urgent jobs.

NEW APPROACHES TO LOADING AND SCHEDULING

Several new approaches to loading and scheduling have been developed, particularly with the aim of reducing inventory. Typical of these is the just-in-time (JIT) system (see Chapters 35 and 37). Another approach is optimized production technology.

Optimized production technology (OPT)

OPT places the control system emphasis on bottlenecks. It points out that an hour saved at a bottleneck in a plant means that an extra hour's output leaves the plant. Conversely, an hour lost at a bottleneck loses an hour's production for the whole plant. Thus, the financial benefits of keeping a bottleneck working for an extra hour greatly exceed the immediate costs (such as overtime). On the other hand, an hour saved at a non-bottleneck is a mirage. By definition there should be some inactive time at non-bottlenecks. The traditional approach of keeping men and machines busy at all times to improve efficiency figures merely results in work being done that is not needed immediately, and this early production thus increases inventory.

A bottleneck is defined as any operation or activity where installed capacity is less than the current demand placed upon it. Production managers and controllers should not attempt to keep non-bottleneck operations in constant use, but should establish synchronized material flow.

Accepting that non-bottleneck work stations can be non-productive for some of the time affects batch quantities. Inactive time can be used for more set-ups, allowing smaller batches, less inventory and quicker throughput. Batch sizes at bottlenecks and at non-bottlenecks will be different.

Analysis of bottlenecks will affect investment policy in new plant. Automating a machine which is not a bottleneck may not result in any savings.

The OPT method requires that bottleneck operations are forward scheduled in detail. Buffers are provided before each bottleneck to ensure that work is always available for it. Non-bottleneck stages are scheduled more loosely, using backward loading.

PROVISIONING

Provisioning is ensuring that everything required is available when production is scheduled to start. This includes drawings, tools and gauges as well as parts and material. Such aids can hold up production just as much as material shortages and lack of them is often harder to put right.

Make or buy

Preliminary decisions must be taken on whether the part is to be made in-house or bought out or part subcontracted.

Factors affecting the decision are:

Available capacity

This may fluctuate, changing the decision.

Available skills and technology

Outside firms may specialize in certain processes.

Volume required

Normally a firm would not make its own nuts and bolts but if it used millions then it would.

Available lead-times

Much tighter control can be exercised over internal manufacture.

Where external suppliers or subcontractors are used it is vital to obtain commitment to delivery dates. Progressing is best done by personal visits. In any case, it is wise to build in latitude in the lead-times of externally sourced parts. Rating of suppliers on delivery is obviously worthwhile but cannot guard against every contingency.

Quantities

Certain items will be made on a one-for-one basis according to sales demand with perhaps a small allowance for scrap or spares. A few items may be made continuously throughout the year. The majority of items are made in batches. The size of the batch can be determined in two ways. Economic batch sizes can be calculated as shown in the chapter on stock control. Where a batch is manufactured internally the setting cost replaces the order cost in the formula.

An alternative is to make regular batches to return the stock to a desired level. These batches will vary in size but enable the factory to be programmed on a regular repetitive basis. For example, using the Pareto stock classification, *A* items might be made once a month, *B* items once a quarter and *C* items once a year.

In fact, the mathematics of both methods are not dissimilar. If batches are made regularly the average stockholding is slightly higher than if economic batches are made when a reorder level is reached.

With a set-up reduction programme, set-up times can be reduced dramatically. This allows much smaller batches to be made economically.

Kitting and pre-allocation

Before a job is issued to the shop floor it should be established that all things needed for its production are available. It should not be the job of a skilled operator to queue for drawings, tools and gauges before he starts work. Even less should he have to spend time searching on the section for missing items. All such production aids should be collected by stores staff before a job is issued. Where a job is repeated, a card can be kept recording everything required for the job.

Where assemblies are produced, kitting problems are more apparent. Often a set of parts will be collected for issue and shortages found. Either the job is issued incomplete or it is held in stores where it may tie up parts which could be used elsewhere. Such parts may be removed from the kit, further complicating the problem.

In such situations a paperwork exercise can be carried out where all the components are checked for availability though not physically collected. This dummy kitting or pre-allocation means that if it is not feasible to issue Job A because of shortages it may be possible to issue Job B using some of the components from Job A.

If parts lists and stock levels are kept on computer and are up to date such pre-allocation can be done automatically and rapidly with obvious advantages.

MONITORING AND PROGRESSING

The aims of monitoring and progressing are to:

1 Highlight jobs running late
2 Assist such jobs to catch up
3 Anticipate problems further down the production cycle that late jobs would cause
4 Enable customer enquiries to be answered.

The first principle is to progress by exception. Collecting a vast amount of information about jobs which are running to time may give people a feeling of achievement but does little real good.

The second principle is that information must be up to date. Elaborate computer runs analysing where jobs were three days ago may be ignored in favour of a physical search of the section.

Monitoring

The simplest way of monitoring the position of jobs is to utilize the work booking system. At the end of each operation the completed job card is used to update a master progress record which is held in the production control office. Problems may arise where booking is not done immediately at the completion of a job.

A similar system is to have a set of tear-off tickets attached to each job. As the job passes a control point the appropriate section of the ticket is detached and sent to update the master progress record.

Increasingly the completion of jobs is being recorded on data collection devices linked to computers. These can be on the shop floor beside the machines and can give an extremely rapid update of the production situation.

Progressing

When the current state has been monitored action has to be taken. As a job running late in its initial stages can cause problems all the way down the line progress meetings are often held for all those involved. Provided such meetings are kept short and involve more than marking up lists they can be valuable.

Progress men are often used firstly to monitor the state of jobs and secondly to urge priority jobs. Again, if this is largely marking lists it could be done better by a good clerical booking system. Progress men oil the wheels by putting urgent jobs at the front of the queue and arranging special transport between operations. However, sometimes their work can be self-cancelling. In one engineering works there were fourteen progress men to one hundred machinists. Each of the five foremen could have up to fourteen people requesting that their job be done first.

Urgent jobs

It is common for urgent jobs to be given some distinguishing mark, a red label or a star for example. The trouble is that such labels multiply until 80 per cent of the jobs have red stars. Then someone gives the really urgent jobs two red stars and so the system escalates. Fifty urgent jobs are a contradiction in terms.

A strict upper limit, ten for example, should be placed on the number of urgent jobs. If another is required an existing one should be dropped from the list. To do this the person deciding the priorities should be senior enough to resist sectional pressures and see the overall picture. A shop floor supervisor can often be approached by many different people in the management structure each asking for different jobs to be given priority.

Long-term solutions

Although it is sensible to give a few urgent jobs an extra push, if late and rush jobs are a large and constant problem then the overall situation needs to be looked at. Are delivery dates being realistically set? Is there sufficient capacity? Could the effort spent chasing rush jobs be better spent improving the throughput time?

It may be possible to chase one job through the factory with it hardly touching the ground. What is not seen is the trail of delays and increased costs on other jobs that this action causes. Many customers will ask for jobs sooner than they need them because they know only priority jobs will be chased and the rest left to drift through.

One solution to the problem of conflicting priorities is to have each progress man responsible for all the throughput of one section. When operations are completed in this section the jobs become the responsibility of the progress man in the next section and so on. This is in contrast to the usual system where a progress person is responsible for all stages of a particular range of jobs. Sometimes there is a need for both types of progress but the balance must be held.

Where two or more divisions of a company share a common resource (for example, a machine shop), conflicts over capacity and priorities will often happen. Where possible such facilities should be split. If this cannot be done the capacity may need to be expanded over what might be theoretically required to allow for interference between the user departments.

MANAGEMENT CONTROL INFORMATION

A production control department processes vast amounts of information, levels of stock, states of orders, capacities available and so on. It should, therefore, be the source of the overview of production that higher management needs. Too often, management will concentrate on solving particular problems using their authority to get things done. This may solve the particular issue but create a whole set of other problems and delays. It is management's job to look at the total picture, making decisions about capacity and load, leaving the day-to-day problems to those paid to cope with them.

The production control department can help by supplying regular information on relevant totals. The particular figures will vary but might include:

Order book

- Forecast sales
- Total orders received
- Total orders dispatched
- Total orders on hand.

Customer service

- Current average delivery times
- Delivery promise achievements
- Number of complaints.

Factory performance

- Total production
- Programme achievement
- Arrears
- Forward load versus capacity.

Stocks

- Raw material
- Work-in-progress
- Finished goods.

For most of these figures it would be difficult to set an ideal level though it is always good to aim for a target. The important thing is the direction in which the figures are going, improving, worsening or staying the same.

It may be necessary to break the total figures down into separate product lines. The temptation to produce lists of individual jobs for higher management should be avoided.

PAPERWORK

Production control departments produce a mass of paperwork, schedules, lists, tickets, progress records, computer printout. Over the years new systems may have been introduced partly duplicating existing ones. Records may be kept which are no longer required. Individuals produce and maintain their own systems.

It is possible to have a department called production control which produces a large amount of paper yet influences what happens on the shop floor hardly at all. It is said that when the weight of a ship being built exceeds the weight of paperwork required to build it then it is ready for launching.

Different production systems will require different paperwork but a typical outline is shown below.

Advanced warning

When an order is first received a document is raised to notify departments concerned. It will contain basic details of the order and the provisional delivery date quoted. An example is shown in Figure 40.2.

The receiving departments, typically industrial engineering, stock control and production, will confirm whether the provisional date can be accepted.

Job paperwork

Each job needs:

1 A loading/progress document which stays in the production control department and is used first to schedule the job and then to record its progress. It may well be a card which can be slotted into a planning board
2 An identification label which goes round with the job (job ticket)
3 Instructions for the people doing each stage of the job
4 Material or parts requisitions
5 Paperwork for booking each stage of the job. This may be in the form of cards which are returned to the production control office showing date, time, scrap and the operator's name.

Examples of production control paperwork are given in Figures 40.3 and 40.4.

Schedules

Lists of jobs will be made of work to be done on a section in a given period. These may be in sequence or highlight jobs with a higher priority. These lists will also be used to progress the work.

Methods

Various readymade paperwork systems are available, but there may be limits on their flexibility. Whatever the method used, it should be simple and functional. Paperwork systems should be reviewed periodically and improved, discarded or replaced as necessary.

WORKS ORDER

Job Number

Customer	Send to (if different)

Date issued	Customer's order No. and date	Delivery date promised	Carriage by

Items to be supplied

Quantity	Drawing number	Description	Unit price	Total price

Special instructions

£

+ VAT @   %

Total

Distribution

Catalogue items and specials			Specials only			
Stock control	Dispatch	Accounts	Chief engineer	Chief inspector	Works manager	Production control

Figure 40.2   Works order

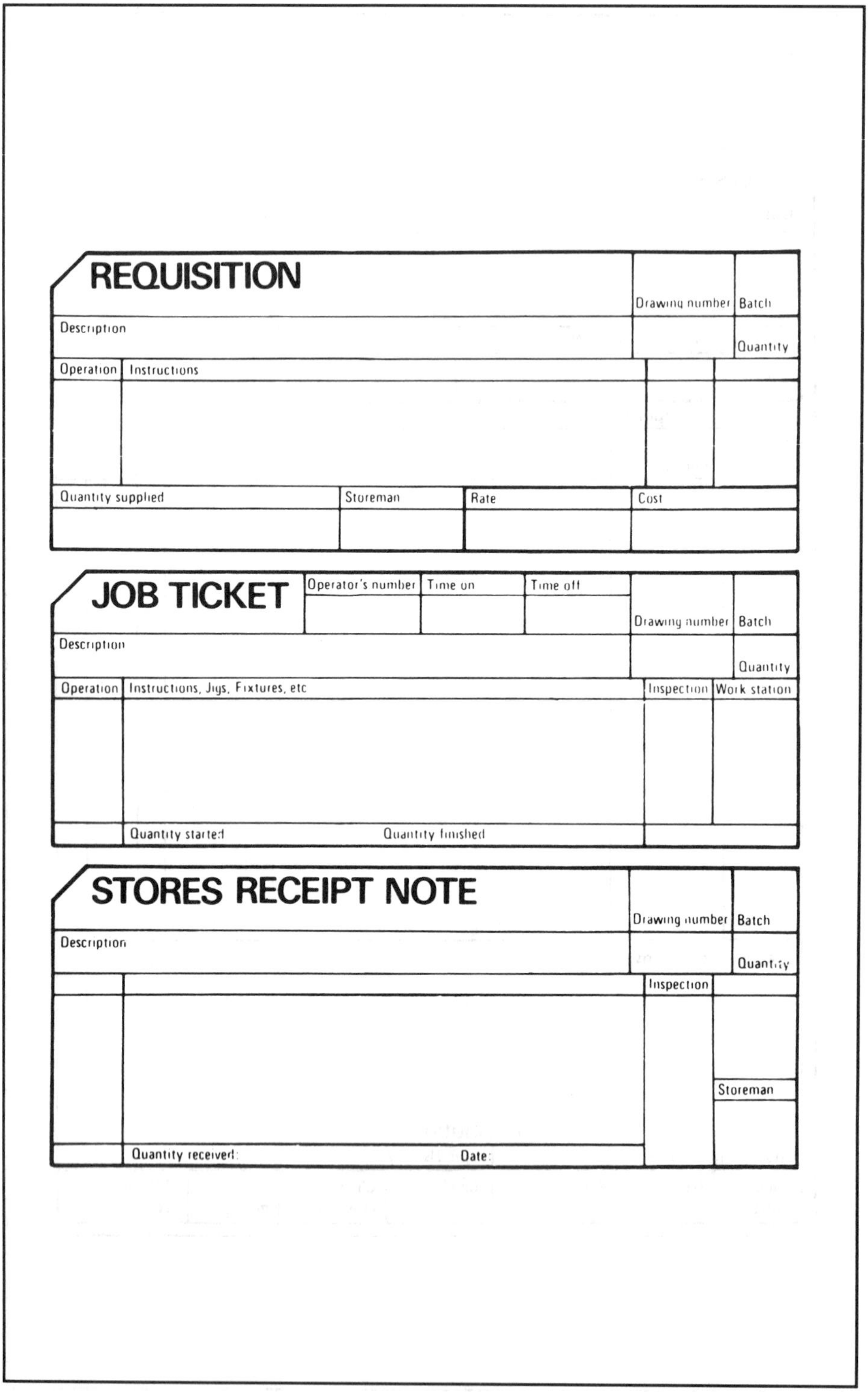

REQUISITION

Drawing number | Batch

Description

Quantity

Operation | Instructions

Quantity supplied | Storeman | Rate | Cost

JOB TICKET

Operator's number | Time on | Time off

Drawing number | Batch

Description

Quantity

Operation | Instructions, Jigs, Fixtures, etc | Inspection | Work station

Quantity started | Quantity finished

STORES RECEIPT NOTE

Drawing number | Batch

Description

Quantity

Inspection

Storeman

Quantity received: | Date:

Figure 40.3 Requisition, job ticket and stores receipt note

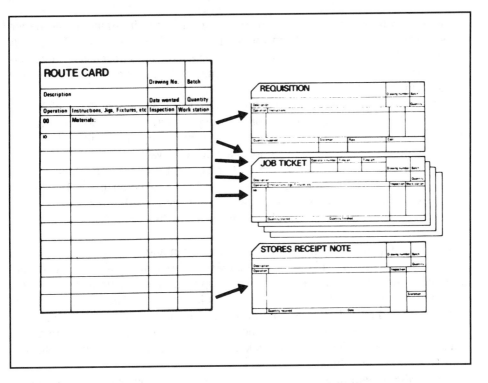

Figure 40.4   A production control document set

Stock cards

Visible edge filing can give rapid access to a large number of records.

Line selection systems

In widespread use before computer systems, these are based on special spirit duplicators. Information from a master record is selected and combined in different sequences to print sets of job cards, material requisitions, master progress cards and other required paperwork.

Computer systems

Computer systems combine large filing capacity with flexibility, plus the ability to print production documents in almost any required format. The printout can be on sprocket fed print-out paper, on cards or on A4 or other forms. A wide choice of printers is available to suit different budgets and the volume and quality of printout required.

COMPUTER SYSTEMS

Whilst computers have been used in production control for years, the advent of low-cost, high-speed rugged processors have made them much more useful.

Computers can now be dedicated to production control, information can be fed back quickly and accurately from the shop floor and schedules can be quickly recalculated. Links between computer systems enable direct access to engineering and quality departments. Some large firms send schedules to their suppliers via computer links.

The problem remains that computers require a vast amount of data which have to be maintained to a high degree of accuracy. A human being will realize that washers are not usually ordered one at a time, but a computer will merrily print out ten thousand separate requisitions, each for one washer.

Applying computers to production control is best done in stages. Most packages are sold in modules to facilitate this. The usual place to start is stock recording. Until the disciplines are established, so that the stock figures on the computer match the levels in the bins, further complications are best avoided.

The next step is usually material requirement planning (MRP). This is covered more fully in Chapter 34. Briefly, a database is built up of all parts lists and assembly and component details. The proposed build programme for final assemblies (usually called the master schedule) is fed in. The computer works down through the levels of assembly, subassembly, parts and material to work out how much of everything is required and when. In the process common items are summed together, existing stock is taken into account and each level is offset in time to allow for lead-times.

Once MRP is working successfully the system can be extended to include capacity planning. This is known as manufacturing resource planning (MRP II). This is based on the MRP database but, in addition, requires the sequence of operations for each manufactured part or assembly together with times for each operation. If desired, setting times can also be fed in. The capacity of each work centre will also be needed.

As with MRP the computer starts with the master schedule and breaks down requirements level by level. Also, it sums up the hours required on each work centre for each time period (usually a week).

The problem is that there is no guarantee that this load will be within the capacity of each centre. The master schedule may be optimistic in terms of capacity and time-scale. The result may be overloads and arrears on some or all of the work centres. However, the information is at least tabulated and the results of overenthusiastic sales promises can be seen.

Often this first MRP II run is taken as a 'rough cut' run. The problems are highlighted and the master schedule is revised in their light. The program is then run again, hopefully giving a better fit. There will still be imbalances and the option is then whether to let the computer smooth them out. To do this, rules must be fed in (for example, 'Do the most overdue job first' or 'Do jobs for customer X first'). In practice, scheduling such priorities is never a simple matter and may be best left to human intervention.

MRP and MRP II produce a series of plans. The actual stock movements, production achievements, scrap, breakdowns and so forth, must be fed in to update the computer records. Usually MRP runs are carried out weekly but some systems allow for local changes to be fed in on a daily basis.

FURTHER READING

Burbridge, J. L., *Principles of Production Control*, 4th edn, Macdonald & Evans, London, 1978. A wide-ranging and practical book

Goldratt, E., *The Goal*, rev. edn, Gower, Aldershot, 1989. A very readable and unusual introduction to production control, especially OPT

Lockyer, K. G., *Production Control in Practice*, 2nd edn, Pitman, London, 1975. A good introduction, particularly to the numerical aspects of production control

New, C. C., *Managing Manufacturing Operations*, BIM Management Survey No. 35, 1976. A survey of practice in 186 plants giving a good basis for comparisons

Shingeo, Shingo, *A Revolution in Manufacturing, the SMED System*, Productivity Press, Cambridge Mass., 1985

Walley, B. H., *Production Management Handbook*, 2nd edn, Gower, Aldershot, 1986

41 Industrial engineering

Dennis Whitmore

Industrial engineering (some prefer to call it management services) covers techniques aimed specifically at improving productivity. Its disciplines, outlined in Figure 41.1, can be separated into four main groups, concerned with improving:

1 The organization
2 Methods and equipment
3 Job conditions and the working environment
4 The product or service itself.

Techniques may overlap and be interchanged, but essentially (1) and (2) can be investigated through *work study* for most manual work, while *organization and methods* (O&M) is applicable to clerical and office work. *Operational research* (OR) is more concerned with corporate level operations, such as distribution, product mix, planned maintenance and stock control.

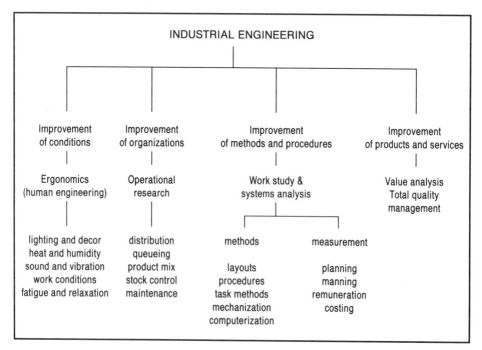

Figure 41.1 Industrial engineering applications

The safety, well-being and comfort of the operator are the concern of *ergonomics*, known as 'fitting the job to the worker'. This subject therefore uses some knowledge of anatomy and relevant medical disciplines.

Products and services may be designed to remove all unnecessary parts, or simplified to retain only those which are absolutely necessary for functional, aesthetic, or prestige purposes. When these cost-reducing devices are built in at the design stage the technique is known as *value engineering*, but its sibling, *value analysis*, may be used on existing products or services.

Over all these approaches there are the two fundamental disciplines which answer the two basic questions: how should the task be done? and how long should it take? The first of these must be tackled by a *problem-solving* technique and the second by *work measurement*.

PROBLEM SOLVING

People are always solving problems and making decisions both in their domestic and working lives. Basically, there are four types of situation:

1 An *improvement* problem, where there is a situation which needs improving in some way, such as an inefficient method
2 A *deviation* problem is one in which the situation differs from what it ought to be, or what one desires of it
3 A *creative* problem exists where one wishes to invent or design something, given the terms of reference, or objectives to be achieved
4 In *problem avoidance* one tries to anticipate troubles or problems before they actually occur, and thinks up remedies in case they do occur.

There may be an infinite variety of problems but all can be approached using a common strategy. The general procedure applies equally to method study, organization and methods, operational research or to any other technique.

1 *Problem definition* Clearly, before a problem can be tackled the true problem, as opposed to the apparent problem, must be defined
2 *Data collection* All the facts about the situation must be assembled before any solution can be attempted
3 *Examination* The facts must be critically examined in either a logical way, or in some cases, using a completely illogical approach (see the following subsection). From the results of this examination can follow:
4 *Development of a solution* Examination will show up the deficiencies and point the way to a solution. This is now developed and tested during a 'dry run' period
5 *Installation* When the proposed solution is as perfect as it can be, it is introduced to the situation
6 *Maintenance* Continual monitoring and updating is necessary as the situation develops in the future.

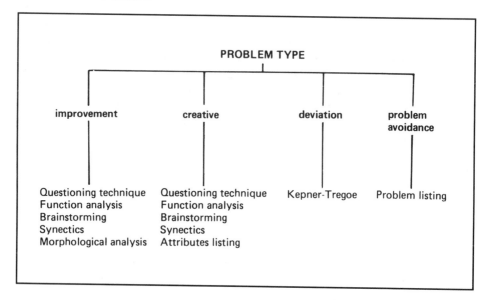

Figure 41.2   Choice of appropriate problem-solving technique

Methods of problem solving

Problem-solving methods can be separated into logical and illogical. A chart showing how a particular technique may be selected is shown in Figure 41.2.

A logical, step-by-step method is traditional *critical examination* which asks *what* is done?, *when?*, by *whom?*, *where?*, *how?* are the goals achieved? and to all of this, *why?* Often tasks need not be changed or simplified, but can in fact be abandoned altogether as unnecessary.

An illogical approach is to use analogies to describe a situation, thereby making a complex one more easily understood by equating it to similar circumstances with which the observer may be more familiar, or by acting out the role of the situation.

The Kepner-Tregoe approach is to list all things about what the situation *is* and what it *is not.* From the lists, the *causes* of deviation from the desired condition are highlighted.

Another non-logical method of collecting ideas is *brainstorming.* This requires participants to throw in ideas as they occur to them in an uninhibited way, with no criticism. This method avoids stereotyped ideas, and often generates novel and 'way-out' ideas.

Trial-and-error, or heuristic methods are often used, each trial being improved upon until the optimum solution is achieved.

IMPROVING WORKING METHODS

Problem solving may be applicable to all situations, but method study capitalizes widely on the techniques. In the clerical field, organization and methods is the principal tool for increasing effectiveness and productivity, and includes within its orbit the technique of method study.

The first stage is to define the true problem and terms of reference. For example, a goods-inwards procedure is labour-intensive and must be made more cost-effective. With such a brief must be included constraints such as costs, savings required and period of capital return.

The data collection period involves the employees through interviews about their jobs, and facts about the objectives and goals to be achieved. Information is displayed by means of flow charts, diagrams and models.

It may be necessary to investigate the document flow, goods handling and individual methods of doing the jobs (the two-handed chart). The investigator may wish to improve the layout, using a flow diagram as the basis, even using three-dimensional models, or templates which can be moved around in order to find the best configuration.

Having gathered the facts, the investigator is able to examine them and question the purpose and need for the various parts of the system. One of the problem-solving techniques outlined in the previous section of the chapter will be used. A method growing in popularity is function analysis, based on brainstorming. This technique is described later under 'value analysis', but in essence a team of specialists discusses the problem, tossing ideas for improvements into the general pool of knowledge. These suggestions are then considered and the promising ones investigated further. From the final list of recommended ideas new methods, layouts and procedures are written up as a report to management for its consideration. The parts of the report which are approved are then implemented gradually to replace the existing ones. Full consultation with staff would be maintained, of course, and their suggestions considered too. There would be many deficiencies in the new situation needing reconsideration, but eventually an integrated system would emerge.

Quite possibly the team may consider a computer configuration to be the best solution to the manual one being used at present. This is usually the province of *systems analysis*, responsible for the examination of existing or proposed computer installations and mechanization of procedures.

Situations change over a period of time, so it is important that the sixth phase of maintenance and updating is incorporated into any study of procedure, method or layout as a continuing process of monitoring.

THE MEASUREMENT OF WORK

Unless an organization knows how long a job should take it can not plan production, cost the labour or even (with incentive schemes) pay the employees. But who should say how long a job ought to take? How can this time be determined?

Regardless of what some textbooks say, work can only be measured in three basic ways: by timing it with some form of chronometer, by using manuals of predetermined times, or by estimating it. Thus all work can be measured to a greater or lesser degree of precision (see Figure 41.3).

The main objective of work measurement is to establish a time for a job which an experienced, trained person could achieve while doing the job effectively and at a workmanlike pace. This may seem rather subjective but in practice it can be done. The techniques for setting such *basic times* are many, but they all fall under the

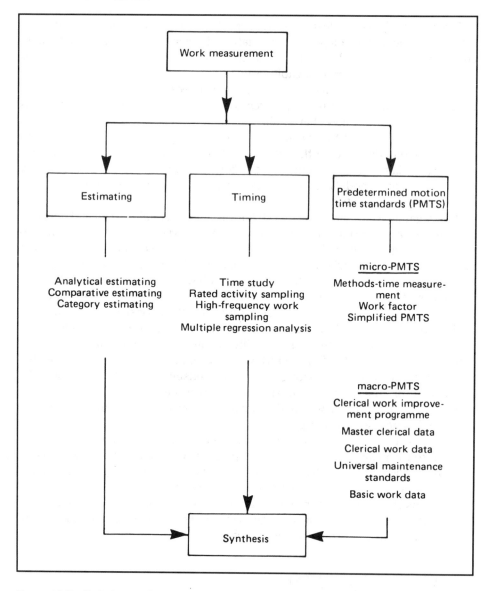

Figure 41.3 Techniques of work measurement

three basic headings as shown in Figure 41.3. The most appropriate has to be selected from the toolbag of techniques. The two main guiding factors in this selection are (a) the precision desired, and (b) the speed of application, or how long it takes the analyst to set the time standard compared with how long it takes to do the work.

The most precise standards are given by the generic group of predetermined motion time standards (PMTS). These exist in two main forms: micro-PMTS with elements measured in thousandths of a minute) and macro-PMTS (with elements of the order of seconds). Many proprietary systems exist but international ones practised in the US, Europe, the Far East and Australasia are methods-time measurement (MTM) and Work-Factor.

The principle of measuring work by PMTS is based upon the analysis of the work into suitable elements, looking up the tables of times for these, and then summing the times to obtain the overall time for the job. Typical elements of micro-PMTS are reach, grasp, release, move, walk, sit, stand, assemble, disassemble, and so on.

The micro-PMT systems are very time consuming to use, so the originating concerns have simplified them to produce higher levels of data which are far quicker and easier to apply. The two principal systems on the lowest level are Detailed Work-Factor and MTM-1. On the second level are the equivalent systems of Ready Work-Factor and MTM-2 respectively, and on the third level Abbreviated Work-Factor and MTM-3. Higher levels of data are developed in various ways including the combination of elements, the merging of moving distances, the elimination of some elements, and the simplifying of elements. For example, in MTM the first-level elements of reach, grasp, and release were combined into one new element of get, while move and position become the new element of put.

Typical elements of a mythical system are shown in Figure 41.4. The analysis of a simple operation and the derivation of the subsequent basic time for this job are illustrated in Figure 41.5. This shows how elements are identified, and times extracted for subsequent addition to obtain the time for the complete job.

In PMT systems it is appreciated that certain factors will affect the time taken to do a basic element. A reach with the hand of 45 cm will take longer to accomplish than one of only 10 cm, so distance is a factor which must be considered (see Figure 41.5). Also care must be taken if the article to be grasped is delicate or dangerous to handle; another factor. If the article is heavy, this must be taken into account. These factors and others are considered when designing a system of PMT, and due allowance of extra time must be made when any of the factors are encountered.

The basic unit of measurement in Work-Factor is called the Work-Factor Time Unit, and is equal to 0.0001 min., while the time-measurement unit (tmu) of MTM is 0.00001 hr. These tiny times originally were measured using high-speed film analyses, stroboscopic photography, stop-watches, and various electrical devices. As an example, a basic 30-cm reach with the hand with no manual control or weight would take 0.0046 min.

On the macro-PMTS level are Clerical Work Data, Clerical Work Improvement Programme, Universal Office Standards, and Office Modapts, together with Basic Work Data, MTM Maintenance Standards, Universal Maintenance Standards, and others.

A typical PMTS analysis

The exact form of the analysis of jobs for PMTS varies according to the system being employed. An illustration of how a job may be analysed and the elemental times extracted from tables using a mythical system, is given in Figure 41.5. A more complete account of PMTS is found in Whitmore (1987).

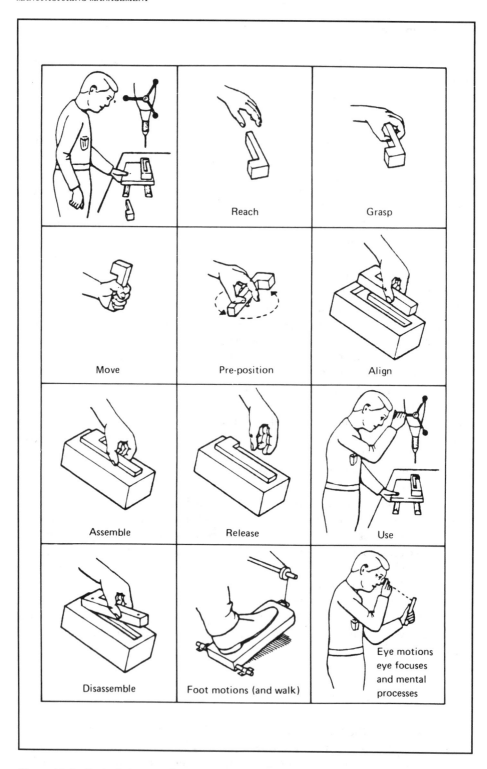

Figure 41.4 Typical elements for a system of predetermined motion times (PMTS)

ALL TIMES in millimuinutes at 100 rate

OBTAIN AND PLACE ASIDE TABLE

Times are for OBTAIN or for PLACE ASIDE (PA)

DISTANCE (CM)	SIMPLE	AVE	DIFFICULT
Up to 5cm	2	3	6
+ 5 to 10cm	3	4	7
+ 10 to 15cm	3	5	8
+ 15 to 20cm	4	6	9
+ 20 to 25cm	5	7	10
+ 25 to 30cm	6	8	11
+ 30 to 35cm	7	9	12
+ 35 to 40cm	9	11	13
+ above 40cm	10	12	15

(DEGREE OF DIFFICULTY)

MOVE TABLE (MP)

SIMPLE	AVE	DIFFICULT	WEIGHT OR RESISTANCE
2	5	(9)	
3	6	10	
4	7	11	
5	8	(12)	
6	9	13	
7	10	14	
8	11	16	
9	12	18	
10	13	20	

(DEGREE OF DIFFICULTY)

CRANK TABLE

DEGREES	WITHOUT	WITH
up to 90	4	6
+ 90 to 180	6	
+ 180 to 270	7	
+ 270 to 360	9	

TWIST OR TURN TABLE

WITHOUT	WITH
3 (7)	6 (12)

** For relocation (e.g. turn back screwdriver to slot) use M.PD.

SCREWDRIVER DATA

Element Ref	S 36
Sheet Ref	20
Study Ref	1238
Date	12 April

Screwing in medium and small screws 12 turns on average

#	Description (LH)	Diffic	Code	Time	Code	Diffic	Description (RH)
1.	Pick up screw from bin (25 cm)	Diff.	O D25	10	O A25	Ave	Pick up screwdriver from bench
2.	Move and position to pilot hole	Diff	M PD20	12	M PA20	Ave	Move and position driver to screw
3.	Hole screw upright			9	M PD5	Diff	Locate blade to screw
4.	"		H	7	T S	Simp	Turn screwdriver one turn
5.	"		H	9	M PD5	Diff.	Remove, twist back, relocate in head
6.	"		H	77	X 11		Repeat (4) 11 more times
7.	"		H	99	X 11		Repeat (5) 11 more times
8.	"		H	12	T S R	Simp	Repeat (4) for final tightening
9.	Release screw	Simp	R S	9	M PA25	Ave	Place aside driver to bench (25 cm)
			Total	244			
				0.244	basic mins		

Figure 41.5 Analysis of a job by a hypothetical system of PMT

519

Relaxation allowance

All techniques of work measurement produce basic times for each element of the job. However, it is recognized that people must have time to recover from their exertions periodically, and so a relaxation allowance (RA) is added to the basic time to allow for this. The resulting *standard time* is the one which is used by management for their various needs. The magnitude of the RA is derived from predetermined tables (see Figure 41.6) or is sometimes just estimated.

Timing techniques

The oldest method of formal work measurement is *timing* which goes back to the early part of the century to Frederick W. Taylor, Frank B. Gilbreth and Charles Bedaux. There are three basic forms of timing: time study, rated activity sampling, and timing using multiple regression analysis.

Time study is the setting of a basic time for a job (*not* for the person doing the job). This basic time is the time for one cycle to be performed with the operative working at a standardized pace, so that different jobs may be compared, and the time is absolutely unconnected with the person doing the work. Unfortunately, people do not conveniently work at this standard pace but adopt their own natural speeds. Even this may vary throughout the day as people tire.

This problem is overcome by timing (using a stop-watch) workers doing the task to be studied and then adjusting this time to what it *would* have been had the operator been working at standard pace. The process of assessing the pace is known as *rating*. Thus, if a worker took 0.6 min. to do a cycle of the job and the work study practitioner rated his pace as 50 (that is, half-standard pace) he would have done the cycle in half the time were he working at standard (100) rating. This gives a basic time of 50 per cent of 0.6 min. or 0.3 basic min. All cycles are rated in the same way, to extend observed times to basic times using the same formula, which is (observed time) × (observed rating ÷ 100).

A variation of time study, suitable for measuring long-cycle jobs, is rated activity sampling. Unlike time study, jobs are not broken down into elements, but ratings are taken at regularly defined intervals such as every minute, on the minute. A study sheet for this method is shown in Figure 41.7, together with the calculation of the basic time. To this must be added suitable RA of course.

A recent addition to the range is multiple regression analysis (MRA) which is extremely useful for measuring variable work. A description of this is beyond the scope of the present book but full accounts of this and all other techniques in this section are given in Whitmore (1987).

Estimating

The most rapidly applied set of work measurement techniques is estimating. It exists in three forms: analytical, comparative and category. The first of these requires the analysis of the job into elements to which *synthetic times* (see below) are allocated. Those for which synthetic times are not available are estimated from experience.

Comparative estimating is a method based on work content comparison. Typical

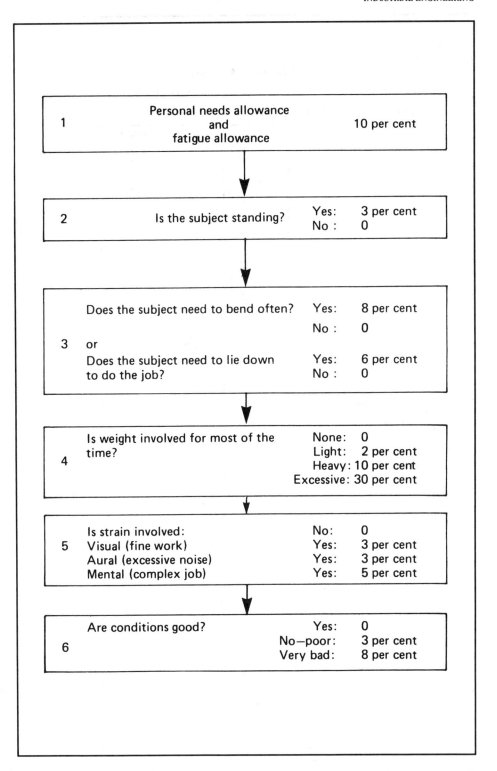

Figure 41.6   A table of relaxation allowances

RATED ACTIVITY SAMPLING

JOB: DIGGING TRENCH   ANALYST: A.J.B.

DURATION: 09.00 to 09.13   DATE: 10 JUNE

Time	DIGGING	RESTING	ABSENT
9.00.25		X	
50		X	
75		X	
1.00		X	
25		X	
50	95		
75	95		
2.00	90		
25	90		
50	90		
75	90		
3.00	100		
25	100		
50	100		
75	100		
4.00	105		
25	105		
50	95		
75	95		
5.00	95		
25	95		
50	100		
75	100		
6.00	95		
25	90		
50	90		
75	95		
7.00	85		
25	85		
50	85		
75			X
8.00			X
25			X
50			X
75			X
9.00			X
25			X
50	80		
75	80		
10.00	85		
25	85		
50	90		
75	90		
11.00	100		
25	110		
50	110		
75	110		
12.00	90		
25	110		
50	110		
75	95		
13.00			
25			
Total ratings R	**3710**		

CALCULATION

$$\text{basic time} = \frac{\Sigma R \times \text{time interval}}{100 \times \text{vol. dug}}$$

time interval = 0.25 min

Vol. = 0.4 cu. metre

$$\text{basic time} = \frac{3710 \times 0.25}{100 \times 0.4}$$

$$= 23.19 \text{ b. min per cu. metre}$$

Figure 41.7   A rated activity sampling study with calculation of the basic time

Department: Maintenance Section: Plumbing			
CATEGORY A Mean time = 9 minutes 0 to 20 minutes	CATEGORY B Mean time = 28 minutes 20 to 40 minutes	CATEGORY C Mean time = 55 minutes 40 to 80 minutes	CATEGORY D Mean time = 2 hours 80 minutes to 2¾ hours
Change tap washer Replace shower head Change short piece of burst copper pipe etc.	Change immersion heater Replace stopcock Install bath tap and shower assembly Clean and replace waste trap on bath or wash basin etc.	Install immersion heater Install stopcock in line Connect bath hot, cold and waste etc.	Change cold tank in loft Install new outside tap Connect wash basin to existing supplies etc.

Figure 41.8   A comparative estimating spread sheet

benchmark jobs are carefully measured and allocated to 'time bands' on spread sheets (Figure 41.8). Estimating is performed by the estimator comparing the job in hand with the benchmark jobs until he decides that those listed in a certain band compare in work content with the job being estimated. He then allocates the band basic time to that job. Category estimating is a variation of this but has no benchmarks, time band slotting being done purely on the experience of the estimator.

Synthetics

Much work is repetitive, so it is wasteful repeatedly to measure similar jobs over and over again. It makes more sense to create a library of study results which may be used to time future similar jobs. Such library times are *synthetic data*, which may be in the form of tables, formulae or nomographs. A typical formula may be for walking: time $= 0.006\ S + 0.01$ where S is the number of steps taken. To walk 400 steps takes 2.41 min.

Synthetic data may be compiled from time studies, PMTS, or estimating. In complex cases formulae are derived from multiple regression analysis. An example of tabulated synthetics is given in Figure 41.9.

Applications

Work measurement standards may be used for planning, assessing completion times and durations for projects, costing of jobs, calculating operator performance or utilization, and using these to assess bonuses.

As an example of the calculation of utilization, suppose an operator performed three jobs; turning twenty spindles on a lathe (12 standard minutes each), drilling forty brackets (2.5 sm each), and fettling thirty components (3.0 sm), all in 450 min. Total earned minutes are $(20 \times 12) + (40 \times 2.5) + (30 \times 3)$ which equals 430 sm. Actual time taken was 450 min., so utilization was $(430 \div 450) \times 100 =$

No. of items dusted	0	2	4	6	8	10	12
Area (sq.m)							
25	6.8	8.2	9.6	11.0	12.4	13.8	15.2
30	7.6	9.0	10.3	11.7	13.1	14.5	15.9
35	8.3	9.7	11.1	12.5	13.9	15.3	16.7
40	9.0	10.4	11.8	13.2	14.6	16.0	17.4
45	9.7	11.2	12.6	14.0	15.4	16.8	18.2
50	10.5	11.9	13.3	14.7	16.1	17.5	18.9
55	11.3	12.7	14.1	15.5	16.9	18.3	19.7
60	12.0	13.4	14.8	16.2	17.6	19.0	20.4
65	12.8	14.2	15.6	17.0	18.4	19.8	21.2
70	13.5	14.9	16.3	17.7	19.1	20.5	21.9
75	14.3	15.7	17.1	18.5	19.9	21.3	22.7
80	15.0	16.4	17.8	19.2	20.6	22.0	23.4
85	15.7	17.2	18.6	20.0	21.4	22.8	24.2
90	16.5	17.9	19.3	20.7	22.1	23.5	24.0

Data include vacuum cleaning carpets, and dusting items of furniture (times in standard minutes)

Figure 41.9 A table of synthetic data (for cleaning rooms)

95.6 (or 95.6 per cent efficiency). Furthermore, if each standard minute is costed at 20 pence, the labour cost of the spindles was 240 × 20p or £48, or £2.40 each. One thousand spindles would take 12 000 sm, or 27 days. If required within nine days, then three turners would be needed.

IMPROVING PRODUCTS AND SERVICES

The twin approaches of value analysis and value engineering are used to reduce the cost of an existing product, and a new design respectively. The philosophy of value analysis/engineering (VA) is to produce the same *function* in a cheaper way. Function, in this sense, has four facets. These are:

1 *Use function*   How the product or service performs
2 *Esteem function*   How it appears
3 *Exchange function*   How it will trade in
4 *Cost function*   Value for money.

VA procedure follows the basic problem-solving sequence:

1 Collection of data (orientation phase)
2 Examination of the situation (speculation)
3 Consideration phase
4 Recommendation phase (a report to management)
5 Implementation (when recommendations are put into operation).

VA is carried out by a team of specialists in different fields who meet at each of the phases outlined above. The orientation phase is used to collect data, costs, sales value, specifications and drawings, and specimens. The object of VA is to reduce the cost without reducing the necessary functions. This may involve removing unnecessary embellishments, combining functions, changing standards, sources of supply, designs, and simplification of the product.

Speculation uses brainstorming as its method of examination. The team suggests improvements using freethinking, with all judgements on ideas deferred until the consideration stage. Criticisms stem from prejudices against situations and methods, and generalizations which condemn certain proposals out of hand. Stereotyped thinking is another source of resistance to change. Brainstorming can sweep aside stereotype answers and come up with novel, original ideas.

After speculation, the team reconvenes to consider the ideas produced during that phase. Results of considering these ideas may be separated into 'rejected', 'recommended', or 'consider further'. Those eventually recommended are incorporated into a new design.

An example of a VA analysis sheet is given in Figure 41.10.

IMPROVEMENT OF WORKING CONDITIONS

The effectiveness of work can be improved, it can be measured and the product can be made less expensive. But the conditions under which the person is working must also be considered. The discipline which looks at this is *ergonomics*. The scope of ergonomics covers:

1 *The worker* His own physical dimensions, the stresses imposed upon him and the way in which he reacts to events and conditions
2 *The workplace* Layout of work, design of equipment, furniture and seating
3 *The environment* The effects of heat and humidity, lighting, noise, vibration and atmospheric conditions.

All of this requires some knowledge of physiology and anatomy, anthropometry and psychology.

Stresses on a worker arise from the environment, so working conditions must include suitable seating, work heights, arms rests, and footrests, correctly designed controls, good layout of controls, tools, materials, and equipment, and well-designed hours of working during shifts. Attention must also be paid to relaxation periods, both length and frequency.

The workplace must be designed so that tools and controls are within easy reach of the worker. Dials which must be read should be unambiguous, and easy to understand at a glance. Similarly controls must be simple to operate, and compatible; that is, apparatus must move in the direction which one would expect, so that a lever pushed upward should move the equipment (say fork-lift truck arms) upward. Some conventions are recognized, such as a clockwise turn of a knob for increase.

The environmental factors include noise, which may be disturbing, or can sometimes be dangerous. The most important considerations are the frequency or pitch, and the intensity of the sound. Instruments measure the intensity in

VALUE ANALYSIS

SPECULATION SHEET

SPECULATION	ANALYSIS
CONSIDER WHETHER:	

FUNCTION
the function can be eliminated,
the function can be achieved in a simpler way,
the function can be combined or integrated with any
other function.

NON-CONTRIBUTORY ITEMS
any of the items contributing nothing to the prestige
or use function can be eliminated.

TOLERANCES AND INSPECTION
the inspection can be eliminated,
quality control can replace 100% inspection,
tolerances are realistic,
gauging can replace measuring,
reduced quality of surface finish can be accepted,
alternative finish can be used,
alternative methods of applying finish can be used.

MATERIALS
standard items can be used to replace specially
made items,
cheaper items can be bought from external suppliers,
cheaper alternative material can be used,
amount of material used per part can be reduced,
dimensions can be reduced,
design changes can reduce material used.

PROCESSING
a cheaper process can be used for the raw materials,
a cheaper process can be used to produce any components,
a cheaper process can be used for the finish on the
article.

DESIGN
a new design will reduce the number of components
used
a re-design will combine two or more functions,
a re-design will eliminate any item or function,
excess material, scrap, or number of rejects will
be reduced by re-designing the item,
it would be cheaper to make the component in
more parts,
the part or component could be re-designed to
facilitate the use of power tools or plant.
the part or component could be re-designed to
facilitate the assembly by improved method.

Figure 41.10   Example of a value analysis speculation sheet

decibels (dB). Recommended maximum levels are published, and these depend on whether the noise is intermittent, or sustained. Ultrasonic sound, used for detecting cracks in metal, or for cleaning oily or dirty components, is particularly dangerous because one cannot judge the intensity as it is inaudible.

If the source is not bright enough, lighting can be a problem. The ergonomist is concerned with other factors such as the type of lighting, colour, glare and reflection, and the decor of the place of work. Minimum criteria are laid down for corridors, general work, fine work and other conditions. Factors which affect the amount of light needed are size of object, contrast between object and its surroundings and reflectivity of the surface. Shadows can also be a problem unless they are needed for a three-dimensional effect. Colours are important in designing decor because they affect the psychological well-being of the worker. For example, grey, blue and green are cold colours, while red and orange make people feel warm. Purple is a shocking colour. Colours can also give a feeling of space, or claustrophobia.

Heat and humidity affect the effectiveness and comfort of people. Ergonomists advise on heat stress, and how it can be relieved. The ambient temperature is considered, but humidity can cause more discomfort than a relatively high temperature. Protection for the worker may be afforded in several ways, such as shielding the offending heat source. Special clothing may be worn, but often this restricts the movements of the worker.

From all this, it is evident that ergonomics is an essential part of any study into the raising of productivity.

OPERATIONAL RESEARCH (OR)

Operational research, originating between the two world wars, has been developed to assist in the solving of certain problems through mathematical and statistical theory. Extensive use is made of probability theory, of queuing and replacement theories, and of logical thought. Some applications of OR are:

1 Optimization of stock levels with fluctuating demands
2 Optimum use of labour, plant and machinery
3 Determination of policy for maintenance and repair of plant and machinery, and replacement of parts and components
4 Product-mix problems and determination of the levels of output for each product consistent with demand and cost
5 Minimization of transportation costs in a distribution system such as delivery of goods to wholesalers
6 Problems where queuing or congestion occur
7 Problems of sequencing, dealt with by critical path analysis.

Applying OR

In using OR it is necessary to formulate some logical approach, so again a five-step pattern of problem solving may be used.

1 *Define the problem* It is essential to define the problem before a start is made

527

otherwise a great deal of time may be spent on unnecessary data collection and problem solving

2 *Record the facts* Once defined, the plan of action must be developed and the necessary data collected and assembled in suitable form. All variables and all constraints which may limit possible solutions must be determined and specified in order that the models, equations and inequalities may be constructed. Any information omitted may invalidate the solution. Historical data are used to assess the future. These can be gathered either by collecting data until sufficient information has been obtained, or by simulating the history with the use of 'hypothetical facts'

3 *Examine the facts* The facts are next analysed and from the data equations (or models) are formed to represent the facts in mathematical form. In certain cases actual physical models can be made as in departmental layouts. A mathematical model is an equation or inequality which may be manipulated using mathematical processes. To form the equations, statements about the job are given mathematical symbols

4 *Derive and test the solutions* The models are processed mathematically or physically and the solutions are derived. These solutions are then tested under actual operating conditions

5 *Application and maintenance* The solution is translated into practical and concrete terms and these are put into practice. Modifications may be necessary in the light of new knowledge or changing conditions.

Some techniques and situations are now described.

Linear programming

Linear programming may be used to solve such problems as product-mix or distribution (allocation). As the name linear suggests there are no powers of the variables in the equations (that is, no x^2, x^3, and so on).

Product mix

These problems are of the type where there are several factors mixed into the problem which, if taken in the correct proportions, will produce an optimum solution for cost, time or other quantity.

For example, a tyre factory may be making its tyres from several types of rubber which are mixed together. The problem is to find the most economic mix consistent with safety, wear, durability and reliability. It would be an easy matter to mix up the cheapest materials without worrying about the *constraints* given above, but these restrictions make the problem more complicated.

In solving problems of this type it is necessary to construct mathematical models relating all the factors and constraints. For example, if a dog food contained three types of meat A, B and C, where A costs x pence per pound, B costs y pence, and C costs z pence, and the total cost must not exceed 160 pence per pound, then the model would be: $Ax + By + Cz < 160$, *where* A, B and C are the weights of the meats respectively. The solution to the problem would give the amount of each meat needed to make up the dog food at an economic cost, consistent with the constraints imposed.

Distribution

The use of OR in this case is to find the most economic way for distribution of goods from dispatching points to the receiving points. For example, in distributing goods to retailers it may be possible to send one van on the round to visit all the customers over the period of one week; or alternatively to send five vans out on the same day, each serving one-fifth of the customers. In the first case it is probably cheaper but in the second case it is more convenient to the customers. These and many other facts must be considered and processed before the solution can be determined.

Queuing

A queue in the OR context is any line of items, people or products which are waiting for some sort of service or processing. Problems of queuing may include:

1 Queues at cash registers in a supermarket, ticket office or toll booth
2 Incoming calls at a telephone exchange
3 Aircraft stacking over a busy airport
4 Queues at a factory-stores hatch
5 Letters awaiting signature, or any documents or forms in an in-tray
6 Piece-parts awaiting processing in the flow line.

Characteristics of a queue are:

1 *The queue length* This may be self-regulating as when people get tired of waiting, or fruit goes bad while awaiting shipment
2 *The service time* This is the time taken by the server to deal with the situation and will vary according to circumstances, from constant to exponential time
3 *The arrivals of items joining the queue* These may be: *regular* and cyclic, and thus may be predetermined, or *random* which are unpredictable, or *random but cyclic*, being in cycles (peak and slack periods) but the numbers are unknown.

Queuing problems may be simulated in the usual way using models.

FURTHER READING

Ackoff, R. L., *The Art of Problem Solving*, Wiley, London, 1978

Grandjean, E., *Fitting the Task to the Man*, Taylor & Francis, London, 1971

Kepner, C. H., and Tregoe, B. B., *The Rational Manager*, McGraw-Hill, New York, 1964

McCormick, E. J., *Human Factors in Engineering Design*, McGraw-Hill, New York, 1976

Murrell, K. H. F., *Ergonomics*, Chapman & Hall, London, 1969

Osborne, A. F., *Applied Imagination*, Scribner's Sons, New York, 1965

Quick, J. H., Malcolm, J. A., and Duncan, J. H., *Work-Factor Time Standards*, McGraw-Hill, New York, 1962

Rivett, P., and Ackoff, R., *A Manager's Guide to Operational Research*, Wiley, London, 1963

Whitmore, D. A., *Measurement and Control of Indirect Work*, Heinemann, London, 1970

Whitmore, D. A., *Work Study and Related Management Services*, Heinemann, London, 1976

Whitmore, D. A., *Management Sciences*, Teach Yourself Books, London, 1979

Whitmore, D. A., *Work Measurement*, Heinemann, London, 1987

42 Project management

Dennis Lock

The quality which most distinguishes a project from routine commercial or industrial operations is its novelty. No two projects are ever exactly alike. Projects typically demand that scarce or expensive resources must be used for a complex pattern of tasks and neither their course not their final outcome can be guaranteed. The project manager must plan, organize and control to minimize the risks and take the project through to a successful conclusion.

PROJECT OBJECTIVES

Project objectives fall within three categories:

1 *Function or performance* The final result must satisfy the customer's specification
2 *Expenditure* With rare exceptions, costs must be kept within budgets. In large projects both client and contractor must also manage their rate of expenditure against financing plans (cash flow)
3 *Time* Delivery promises must be kept. Even projects without critical end dates risk extra costs for both contractor and customer if they run late. Effective scheduling and progress management, in addition to their obvious importance in achieving delivery dates, are also key elements of cost control.

PROJECT DEFINITION AND SPECIFICATION

Clearly the project objectives must be defined from the outset. The project specification usually starts by the customer stating his requirements. This applies equally to in-house projects, where the 'customer' is another department or company in the same group, and where proper management is just as necessary as it would be for external customers.

Experienced contractors develop checklists to avoid costly errors of omission in the specification. For example, overseas work may involve special technical standards, severe climatic conditions or other factors. If the scope of work is to include commissioning, operating and maintenance manuals and customer training, these must also be specified. Expected performance data, process charts and explanatory drawings must all be included in or attached to the specification. The specification should embody a list of all these documents, including their reference and correct revision numbers or dates. The specification has to record all aspects of what has been agreed between customer and contractor, and this includes all changes which result during discussions between contractor and customer right up to the moment when a contract is signed.

After contract award, the sales specification becomes the definitive project specification. Any subsequent change that affects the basis on which the contract was signed must be subjected to a formal contract variation procedure to ensure that its effects on performance, costs, price and delivery are all properly considered and agreed.

Changes are inevitable in most projects and the process of project definition must be continued until the final as-built drawings and other records are archived.

PROJECT ORGANIZATION

The project manager

In addition to technical proficiency a project manager needs to be:

- Perceptive (able to spot potential problems early)
- Questioning (progress claims or promises may need back-up information or proof)
- Familiar with project management techniques (which usually need a computer system)
- Active and mobile ('management by walkabout' is better than being permanently deskbound)
- A good motivator of people inside and outside the company
- A capable organizer, including the handling of meetings
- A good communicator with all levels of staff and management and with the customer.

A project may have more than one project manager. This is seen in projects with several participating contractors (such as joint ventures) where each organization appoints a manager for its own share of the work and for co-ordination with the remainder of the project organization. The customer will often have his own project manager.

Team or matrix?

Project organization is a complex subject and the organization of large projects depends on the number of contractors involved and on whether or not a managing contractor or a consultant project management company is in charge. But a question often discussed at length is whether a project should be organized as a team or as a matrix. These options are illustrated in Figure 42.1 and their relative merits are summarized in Figure 42.2.

Communications

Organizing also includes the important subject of communications, inside the company, with the customer, with other participants and (where relevant) with remote work sites. An individual should be nominated at each location as the

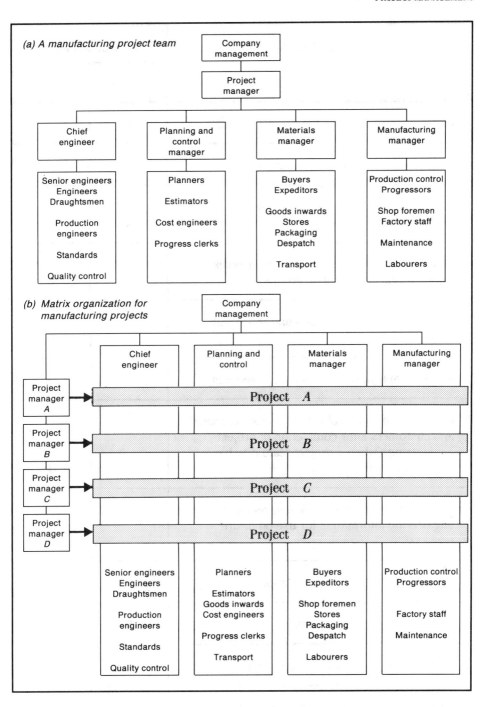

Figure 42.1 Examples of project team and matrix organizations. In (a) a project team is shown. For more than one project the company would set up more teams. In (b) the arrangement is more permanent, with a fixed organization handling several projects, and where the project managers are outside the line of command and manage through functional links with each company department

Characteristic	Organization indicated	
	Team	Matrix
Maximum authority for the project manager	●	
Clear lines of command without duplication	●	
Motivation of individuals to meet project objectives	●	
Motivation through long-term career goals, within specialist discipline groups		●
Project access to specialists and those with rare skills		●
Flexible deployment of company resources		●
Continuity of technical advice to site personnel and customers after completion of project engineering (when a project team may have been disbanded)		●
Accumulation of experience and retained engineering information for use on future projects		●
Security: self contained work area	●	
Security: restricting information spread	●	
Project employing many people for a long time	●	
Several small projects of short duration		●

Figure 42.2   Project team versus matrix organization. Some companies compromise, with project 'core' teams having access to the resources of specialist functional groups

addressee for all written communications and technical documents. Each regular channel should only carry serially numbered documents, so that any missing item can be realized from the gap in received serial numbers.

Every significant project generates large volumes of information. Computer reports especially must be sorted and edited so that each manager only receives information relevant to his/her area of responsibility on a 'need to know' basis, highlighting exceptions and items requiring action rather than routine data.

COST ESTIMATES AND BUDGETS

Cost estimates are an important (but not the only) part of of the pricing process. They also form the foundation for budgets, the benchmarks for financing and cost control.

There is no such thing as an accurate estimate for project costs. If total costs do happen to equal original estimates, that is usually by pure chance or questionable accounting. The degree of confidence in any estimate must depend on the method used, estimating skill, the degree of detail possible and the time available for preparation. Some companies find it useful to classify estimates along the following lines. The degrees of error quoted are the declared probability or intentions but, of course, far wider errors can occur in practice (usually *plus* rather than *minus*).

- *Ball-park estimates* These estimates are guesses (sometimes inspired) and the least accurate. They are useful for strategic planning and for screening customer enquiries but are otherwise very risky, with the error likely to be well over ±25 per cent.
- *Feasibility estimates* These estimates need enough conceptual engineering to have been finished for quotations for major purchases to be obtained. Such estimates are sometimes made as part of project feasibility reports for clients, where they include the end user's likely operating and maintenance costs. The accuracy aim is ±15 per cent.
- *Comparative estimates* They are made by comparing the new project with cost experience of past projects. Allowances are made for perceived differences in size and complexity and for intervening changes such as cost inflation. These estimates are commonly used as for pricing and cost control. The accuracy target is often ±10 per cent.
- *Definitive estimates* These estimates are made when design is complete, all major purchases are committed and construction or production is well advanced. They combine known costs with an estimate of costs remaining. They can be called definitive when the probable error has been reduced to ±5 per cent.

Estimating procedures and allowances

Cost estimating deserves good management because errors or omissions are so potentially damaging to profitability. Checklists to ensure a complete specification are valuable. Estimating calls for a disciplined approach, whether or not a computer is used, and standard estimating forms or tabulations are recommended.

Estimates must be supplemented by a contingency sum to offset possible errors or risks as far as price competition will allow. This forms part of the so-called below-the-line costs. An allowance for cost inflation, known as a cost escalation allowance, is usually made for projects expected to last several years.

Variations in international exchange rates are difficult to predict and may be impossible to allow for. Customary practice is to translate all costs into one common control currency, and to use this for all control and reporting purposes throughout the project.

Sometimes specific cost-risks costs can be foreseen. An example would be a customer's instruction to salvage materials during site clearance and use them in new building. The contractor may fear that the salvaged materials will not be suitable, so that new materials must be bought. In such cases provisional sums (pc sums) are listed in the estimate: these are included in the quotation as amounts that will be charged extra to price only if the additional expenses arise.

PLANNING AND SCHEDULING

Without effective planning there can be no basis for work allocation and no benchmarks for progress control. The planner may be faced with many variables and the sensible way to deal with these is to isolate them and deal with them one at a time in a logical sequence. This section of the chapter follows this sequence (although some reiteration may be needed in practice).

Work breakdown

Large projects must be split into smaller subprojects or work packages for effective management. Packages should be related and coded in a 'family tree' hierarchy. Codes should be designed so that each carries data showing the relative position of the package in the tree. If possible, the coding system should be common to costing, drawing and part numbers.

Establishing a logical work sequence

The next stage is to plan all the tasks in a practical working sequence. Bar charts (Figure 42.3) are useful and are generally preferred by artisans and site managers, and are still widely used for planning and scheduling. They are drawn to scale and easily interpreted.

Critical path networks provide a notation which can denote dependencies and work sequence between many activities. Figure 42.4 shows the project of Figure 42.3 planned as one form of critical path network (known as activity on arrow). By convention networks flow from left to right and each arrow represents the activity needed to progress from one event (circle) to the next. No activity can start until all its predecessors have been finished. Dotted arrows (called dummy activities) are used to show constraints paths between events which are not already depicted by real actual activities. Dummies usually have zero duration. See, for example,

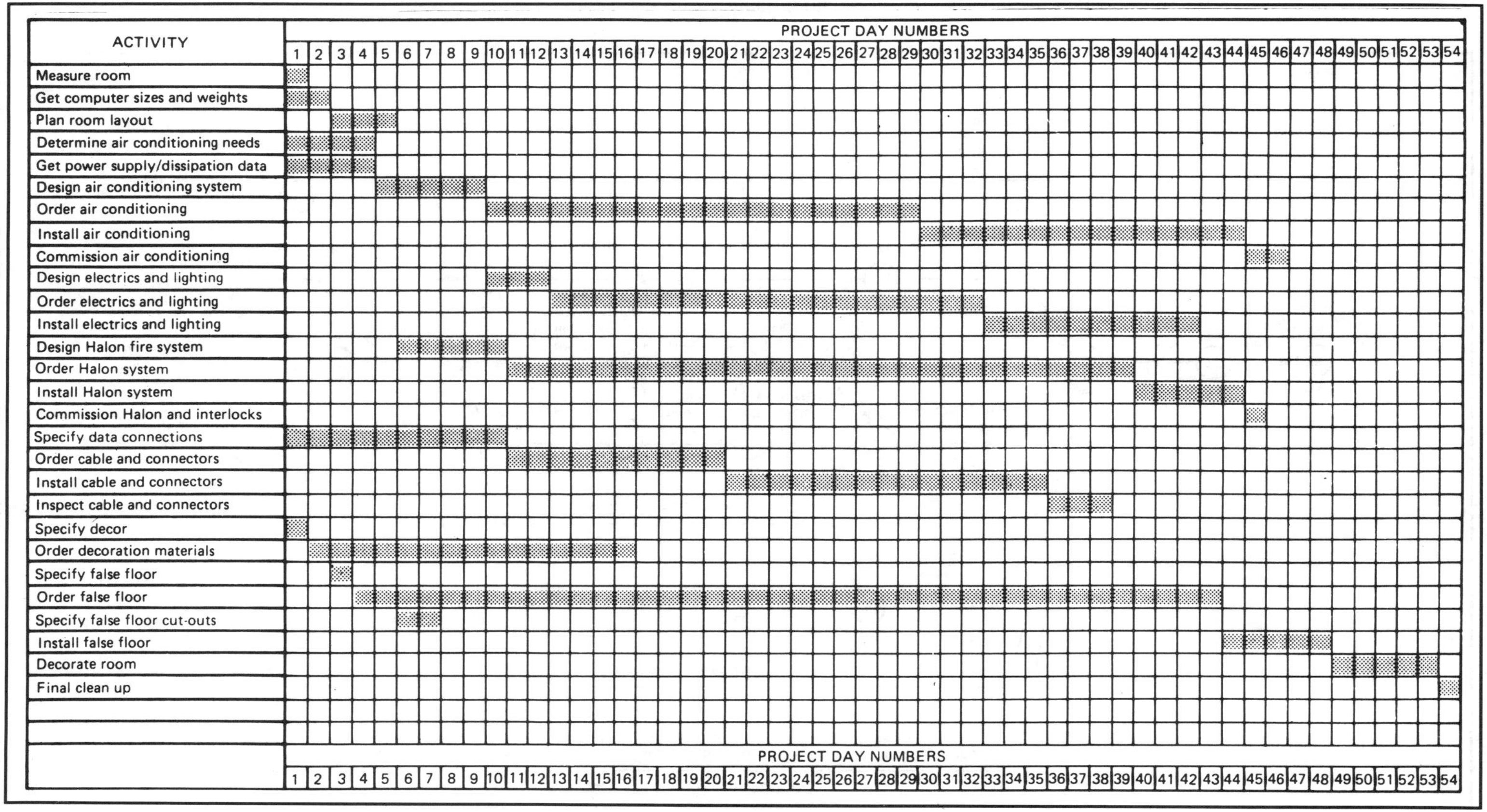

Figure 42.3   A project bar chart. This example shows the main tasks needed to convert a room into a computer suite. Compare this chart with the network diagram in Figure 42.4, which is another way of depicting the plan for this project

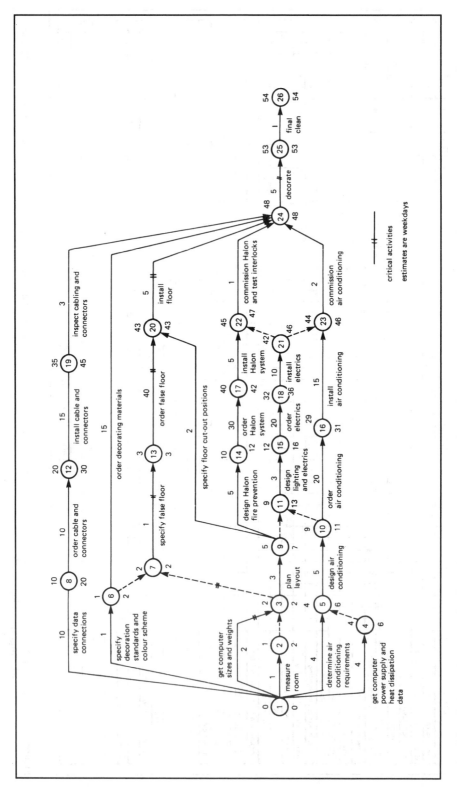

Figure 42.4   A critical path network diagram. This plan is for the same project depicted in the bar chart of Figure 42.3

Event 23 in Figure 42.4, where the air conditioning cannot be commissioned until Event 23 *and* Event 21 have been achieved.

Calculating the project duration

Bar charts are drawn to a time-scale, so that when the chart is finished the total project duration is shown by the right-hand extremity of the last task. The result is the earliest possible time at which the project could be finished, given that all goes according to plan and that there are sufficient resources.

In a critical path network the arrows are not drawn to scale, and their duration estimates are instead written alongside the arrows. Any suitable time units can be used, provided the same units are used throughout. Days or weeks are often used. The earliest possible completion time for each event is calculated arithmetically, by adding the durations of all its preceding activities. There is usually more than one possible path leading to an event, and each must be examined in turn since the highest possible path duration must give the earliest possible event time. In Figure 42.4 the earliest times are written above the events. The earliest time for the last event is obviously the earliest possible time for completing the project. As with the bar chart case, this assumes that all goes according to plan and that there are no resource limitations.

Finding the critical path

When the earliest possible time for the final event was found, the path of longest duration through the network was used. Any delay to any activity on this path must delay the whole project, and such activities are said to be critical, and lie along the critical path. All or most of the other paths will be shorter, and the activities lying on them could be delayed without affecting the earliest project completion. These uncritical activities are said to possess 'float', which is expressed as a number of network duration units.

To calculate the amount of float for each activity and event it is necessary to repeat the analysis of path durations, but this time working from right to left and subtracting durations from the time of the last event. The results give the latest permissible time for achieving each event. The latest permissible time for the end event is usually made the same as its earliest possible time, so that the latest and earliest times coincide for all critical events. The latest times are written below the events in Figure 42.4. The difference between the earliest and latest times gives the amount of float available for each event.

The concepts of the critical path and float are valuable in assigning priorities to activities which compete for attention or resources. A more detailed explanation of float and of critical path analysis is given in Lock (1988).

Scheduling resources

No project plan is complete until resource limitations have been considered. The simplest method, suitable for very small projects or for departmental scheduling, is to use bar charts set up on adjustable boards. Each bar can be coded by colour or other means to depict the type of resource needed, and the bars can be shuffled until the resources needed in each period conform to those available.

Resource scheduling with critical path networks is more difficult, at least at first sight. One method is to convert the network back into a bar chart, first ensuring that no bar is placed so that it contravenes the constraints shown in the original network. This method is impracticable for all but the very smallest project, and the preferred method is to use one of the many computer programs available.

The computer will first carry out time analysis to find the amount of float for each activity. The computer will then attempt to start all activities at their earliest times, but will delay activities with float where necessary in order to avoid using too many resources.

The planner is usually given many options when using such programs, but two of the most important are:

- A *time-limited schedule*, in which the computer will not allow the latest possible completion date to be exceeded, even if this means allocating more resources than those available
- A *resource-limited schedule*, where the computer is instructed not to exceed the stated resource limits, even if this prolongs the planned duration.

Other planning and scheduling options

The critical path method illustrated in Figure 42.4, although widely used (and preferred by this writer) is one of several network systems which have been devised or adapted during the second half of this century.

The precedence system has the activities placed in boxes and the arrows are used just to depict constraints (an activity on node system). Precedence networks allow the planner to specify more complex time relationships between different activity starts and finishes. To give just one example, it is possible to show that one activity cannot start until a specified time has elapsed after the start of another.

Other networks have been developed to deal with probabilities and with either/ or path divergencies.

A company can develop proficiency with planning to the extent that short cuts reduce the effort needed. One example of this is the use of standard library subnetworks, from which project networks can more easily be built up. These incorporate logic patterns and duration estimates based on previous experience.

When a company schedules all its projects together in one computer program it is effectively planning its total mainstream workload. Each project is treated as a subproject in a total company-wide schedule. Such multi-project scheduling is also useful for testing the workload effects on the company of proposed new projects in 'what if' modelling cases.

There is a wide range of programs available to the planner, many of which can run on microcomputers. Some of these provide integrated databases which allow data from schedules, technical data and drawing lists, progress, budgets and cost control to be combined in a total project management system.

CONTROLLING PROGRESS AND COSTS

It might seem strange to treat the control of progress and costs as one subject but, in truth, the two run hand in hand.

Using the resource schedule

Work should be initiated with the issue of an authorizing document, such as a works order, which describes the scope of work, time-scale and budget for each department. Thereafter, sensibly planned resource schedules are an invaluable tool for issuing detailed tasks (work-to lists) and for monitoring progress.

Any computer planning or reporting technique is only a forecast and guide. It cannot control progress or costs. Action can only come from management. If an activity has a float of one week but is known to be three weeks late, the project manager knows immediately that the project will end at least two weeks late if effective action is not taken at once. However, the original schedule must be updated in line with project changes and with actual achievement, so that it remains valid for work still to be issued. All computer programs have schedule updating routines which allow the input of such data.

Evaluating progress

From time to time it is necessary to gauge progress in terms of the value of work achieved. This is done for two reasons:

1 For the purposes of comparing the value of all work actually finished (as defined by the estimated costs for that same work) against the actual costs incurred. Such measurements provide a clue to the efficiency being achieved and allow predictions to be made of the probable final project costs
2 For the purposes of billing the client or customer for work done. Such work measurement usually requires certification by the customer's inspectors or by an independent professional person (such as a consulting engineer for a manufacturing project or a quantity surveyor or architect for construction work).

There are many ways in which progress can be evaluated, based either on absolute quantities (for example, tonnes of earth moved) or stated as a percentage of work completed. Percentage completion estimates made by individuals usually err on the optimistic side: one important point to remember is that a job is only 100 per cent complete when it has been passed without let or hindrance to the next scheduled activity.

Progress meetings

Most managers reading this book will be familiar with the regular meetings that take place to review progress, whether these are for sales results, for factory production management, or for a number of other specialist reasons. In project management, too, it is the accepted norm to hold regular progress meetings at intervals of a month, a fortnight, or even weekly.

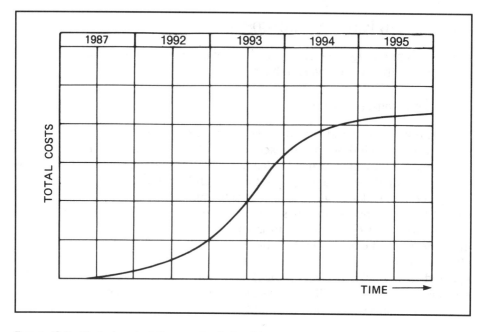

Figure 42.5   Typical project time–cost relationship

The purpose of a progress meeting is to short-circuit the usual communication routes in an organization and get key people together so that progress data can be reviewed, disputes debated, and agreements reached on the spot. The chairman must ensure that commitments made are properly defined, with specific dates (not simply 'as soon as possible') tabled and with those responsible for action clearly designated. Minutes containing this information must be brief but accurate, and they must be issued promptly while the news is still hot.

That is the conventional approach. But it is possible to control progress continuously against a detailed schedule in such a way that regular progress meetings become unnecessary. Dispensing with regular 'meetings for the sake of meetings' releases valuable senior staff time for more productive work. Meetings will still have to be called to resolve problems and in other emergencies, but these will no longer be run-of-the-mill affairs, and they will be seen as occasions demanding special attention and action.

Controlling costs

The first essential in cost control is to set up approved budgets, related item by item to each job or significant purchase, and timed according to project work schedules. The same computer program used for resource scheduling is often capable of phasing budgets in this way.

When plotted cumulatively against time, project costs typically follow an *S*-shaped curve (Figure 42.5). The initial rate is slow, as the project resources are mobilized. The final stages tend to be protracted, including late modifications and commissioning and the ironing out of snags.

The control of labour costs is largely dependent upon controlling progress, provided that staff are competent, well motivated and properly managed. The control of purchasing and subcontract costs is somewhat different and depends on an appreciation of the difference between committed expenditure and actual expenditure. Put simply, if an order is placed at a price which exceeds budget, or in such a loose contractual way that the costs can rise above budget, then overexpenditure has already been committed and any consideration of actual expenditure (when invoices are received) must be too late for remedial action. Here is another case where the use of a computer for reporting actual events is fine for historical records but valueless for control.

CONTROLLING CHANGES

One of the biggest threats to successful project completion is the introduction of unwanted changes (modifications and project variations). Sometimes modifications are unavoidable in order to secure safety or to compensate for some unforeseen design problem. When faced with any request to make a change, it is useful to consider the nature of such change, and to classify it (if possible) under one of the following headings:

1   *Customer changes*   A change requested by the customer, although possibly disruptive, must obviously be carried out under most circumstances. A customer change has the advantage of constituting a change to the original contract, and should qualify for additional costs plus consideration for an extension to the agreed time-scale. Do not under-rate the expense of such changes. Even a reduction in project scope can qualify for compensation as a result of abortive work. Under some circumstances contractors welcome customer changes, since the contractor is the sole seller, in a monopoly situation shorn of the competition that reigned when the original contract was won. If the project is running late or over budget, there might be a chance of making up some of the lost ground when the customer changes his mind over the specification

2   *Unfunded modifications*   These are modifications which cannot be charged to the customer, where any additional costs must be set against project profit, and where any extension to the time-scale has to be explained to the customer and could attract contract penalties. Unfunded modifications can be further classified as *desirable* (wouldn't it be better if . . .?) or *essential* (unavoidable if the project is to be completed to meet the customer's original specification with safety and reliability).

The accepted method for authorizing and controlling all project changes is to appoint a change committee, comprising people with the technical ability to weigh all the consequences, and with the level of authority necessary to say 'yes' or 'no' to each proposal.

FURTHER READING

Kharbanda, O. P., Stallworthy, E. A. and Williams, L. F., *Project Cost Control in Action*, 2nd edn, Gower, Aldershot, 1987

Lock, Dennis (ed.), *Project Management Handbook*, Gower, Aldershot, 1987

Lock, Dennis, *Project Management*, 4th edn, Gower, Aldershot, 1988

Lock, Dennis, *Project Planner*, Gower, Aldershot, 1990 (50 project management forms, with explanatory text)

Lockyer, Keith, *Critical Path Analysis & Other Project Network Techniques*, 4th edn, Pitman, London, 1984

Lockyer, Keith, *Critical Path Analysis & Other Project Network techniques, Solutions Manual*, Pitman, London, 1984. This manual sets out solutions to twenty questions which appear at the end of the main text (listed above)

Marsh, P. D. V., *Contracting for Engineering and Construction Projects*, 3rd edn, Gower, Aldershot, 1988

O'Neill, John J., *Management of Industrial Construction Projects*, Heinemann Newnes, Oxford, 1989

43 Quality assurance and control

John S Oakland

The foundations for good quality management through a 'total' approach, including the role of quality systems in total quality management (TQM), were set down in Chapter 9. This chapter deals in more detail with the systems and techniques necessary to assure and control quality in a manufacturing environment.

THE QUALITY SYSTEM

A 'quality system' may be defined as an assembly of components, such as the organizational structure, responsibilities, procedures, processes and resources for implementing quality management. The system should apply to and interact with all activities of the organization, involving the identification and fulfilment of all requirements at every transaction interface. The activities involved may be classified in several ways – generally as processing, communicating, and controlling, or, more usefully and specifically within a manufacturing company, as follows:

- Marketing
- Market research
- Design
- Specifying
- Development
- Procurement
- Process planning
- Process development and assessment
- Process operation and control
- Product or service testing or checking
- Packaging (if required)
- Storage (if required)
- Sales
- Distribution or installation/operation
- Technical service
- Maintenance.

A manufacturing organization should prepare a quality plan and a quality manual which is appropriate for the level of quality system required:

1 A Level 1 system related to design, production or operation and installation, which applies when the customer specifies the goods or services in terms of how they are to perform, rather than in established technical terms

Standard number	Title
ISO 9000 (BS 5750, Part 0.2)	Quality Management and Quality Assurance Standards – Guidelines for Selection and Use
	Quality System Models:
ISO 9001 (BS 5750, Part 1)	Design/development, Production, Installation and Servicing
ISO 9002 (BS 5750, Part 2)	Production and Installation
ISO 9003 (BS 5750, Part 3)	Final Inspection and Test
ISO 9004 (BS 5750, Part 0.1)	Quality Management and Quality System Elements – Guidelines

Figure 43.1   ISO 9000 (BS 5750) series of quality systems (1987)

2   A Level 2 system is relevant when an organization is producing goods or services to a customer's or published specification

3   A Level 3 system applies only to final production or service inspection, check, or test procedures.

The reader is referred to the International Standard, ISO 9000 series (UK dual numbered Standard BS 5750) which is tabulated in Figure 43.1.

A quality manual should set out the general quality policies, procedures and practices of the organization. In the quality manual for a large organization it may be convenient simply to indicate the existence and contents of other manuals which contain the details of procedures and practices in operations in specific areas of the system. (For detailed recommendations on how to develop a quality manual see Oakland, 1989.)

The format of the quality manual may reflect the standard which is chosen as the template, or it may be set out under the managerial functions and activities. For example, one company adopted the latter course for its manual, incorporating the headings tabled in Figure 43.2. These headings relate to the requirements of ISO 9001 (1987), (BS 5750, Part 1), as indicated by the clause numbers down the right-hand side of the figure. Clearly, each organization will differ in some of the details but the main criterion is to ensure that the documentation covers all the listed activities, which then provide headings for more detailed statements.

Control of quality is a managerial function through which the standards of services, materials, processes and products are verified to ensure against the release of defective goods or services. Organizations must use every device practicable to prevent, detect, and correct errors that can occur in the various operational steps. And the variables which may affect quality, and which can result from the actions of people, the nature of materials, and the performance of equipment, must be curbed in order to achieve true quality control.

Section	Functional area	ISO 9000 requirement	Clause
1	Quality management	Management responsibility	4.1
		Quality system	4.2
		Document control	4.5
		Quality records	4.16
		Internal quality system audits and reviews	4.17
		Training	4.18
		Corrective action	4.14
2	Marketing and sales	Contract review	4.3
		Servicing	4.19
3	Product research and development	Design control	4.4
4	Purchasing and subcontracting	Purchasing	4.6
		Purchaser-supplied product	4.7
		Corrective action	4.14
		Document control	4.5
		Packaging	4.15.4
		Delivery	4.15.5
5	Production	Product identification, traceability	4.8
		Process control	4.9
		In-process inspection and testing	4.10.2
		Inspection, measuring and test equipment	4.11
		Inspection and test status	4.12
		Control of non-conforming product	4.13
		Corrective action	4.14
		Statistical techniques	4.20
6	Quality control	Inspection and testing	4.10
		Inspection, measuring and test equipment	4.11
		Inspection and test status	4.12
		Control of non-conforming product	4.13
		Quality records	4.16
		Statistical techniques	4.20
		Corrective action	4.14
7	Stock control, including despatch, delivery and transport)	Product identification, traceability	4.8
		Inspection and test status	4.12
		Control of non-conforming product	4.13
		Handling, storage, packaging and delivery	4.15
		Corrective action	4.14

Figure 43.2 Arrangement of a quality manual by functional area

Technologies and market conditions vary between different industries, commercial sectors and markets, but the concepts underlying good quality systems, and the financial implications of those systems, are of general validity. The objective should be to produce, at an acceptable cost, products and services which conform to the requirements of the customer. To accomplish this, a *systematic* approach must be adopted in design, production/operations, quality assurance, purchasing, sales and all other departments – nobody should be exempt. A systematic approach to total quality is not a separate science or a unique theory of quality control. It is a set of valuable tools and systems which become an integral part of the 'total' quality approach through real commitment and teamwork.

STATISTICAL PROCESS CONTROL (SPC)

Since the responsibility for manufacture or service lies with the production or operations department, the main responsibility for achieving the appropriate quality must also lie with production/operations. Therefore production/operations staff must have the necessary tools:

1 To know whether or not the process is capable of meeting the requirements
2 To know whether the process *is* meeting the requirements at any point in time
3 To make a correct adjustment to a process which is not meeting the requirements.

Statistical process control methods, backed by management commitment and good organization, will provide objective methods of achieving process quality control.

A systematic study of any process provides knowledge of the process capability and the sources of defective output. This information can then be fed back quickly to the product design technology or service functions. Knowledge of the current state of a process enables a more balanced judgement to be made of the resources available, in terms of both the tasks within their capability and their rational utilization.

Statistical process control (SPC) procedures exist because there is variation in the characteristics of all processes. This inherent variability causes the articles produced to differ over time. If this variability is considerable it is impossible to predict the value of the characteristic of any single item or operation. Using statistical methods, however, it is possible to take meagre knowledge of data and turn it into meaningful statements which may then be used to describe the process itself. Hence, statistically based process control procedures are designed to divert attention from individual items of information and focus it on the process as a whole.

SPC techniques can be used to measure the degree of conformance of raw materials, processes, products and services to previously agreed specifications. These techniques allow a simple representative sample to be selected at random from the 'population' – which may be a batch of finished products or the output from a process – and, from an analysis of that sample, it is possible to make decisions regarding the quality of the whole batch or the current performance of the process.

TYPES OF QUALITY DATA

Numerical information on quality will arise from either *counting* or *measurement*. Data which arise from counting can only occur at definite points or in 'discrete' jumps. There can only be 0,1,2,3,... defectives in a sample of 10 items. There cannot be 2.86 defectives. The number of imperfections on a polished surface, the number of errors on an invoice, the acceptability or unacceptability of the lining of a drum, are all discrete data and are called *attributes*. As there is only a two-way classification to consider, attributes give rise to discrete data, which necessarily vary in jumps.

Data arising from measurement can occur anywhere at all on a continuous scale and are called *variable* data. The weight of a tablet, the time for a delivery, the tensile strength of a piece of rod, are all variables, the measurement of which produces continuous data.

PROCESS VARIABILITY

At the basis of the theory of process control is a differentiation of the causes of variation in quality during operation. Certain variations in the quality of products or services belong to the category of chance or random variations, about which little may be done other than to revise the process. This type of variation is the sum of the effects of a complex interaction of 'random' or 'common' causes, each of which is slight. When random variation alone exists, no main part of it may be traced to a single cause. The set of random causes which produce variation in the quality products may include: draughts, atmospheric temperature changes, passing traffic, weather, electrical fluctuations, and changes in the operators' physical and emotional conditions. This is analogous to the set of forces which causes a coin to turn up heads or tails when tossed. When only random variations are present in a process, the process is considered to be *in statistical control.* There is also variation in test equipment and check procedures, whether used to measure a physical dimension, a chemical characteristic, or any other property. The inherent variation in testing and checking also contributes to the overall process variability, and is therefore always an important factor.

Causes of variation which are large in magnitude and readily identified are classified as 'assignable' or 'special' causes. For the most part, these consist of differences among: plant, processes, operators, materials and other miscellaneous factors. When an assignable cause of variation is present, process variability will be excessive and the process is considered to be *out of control* or beyond the expected random variation.

CONTROL CHARTS

A control chart is a form of traffic signal, the operation of which is based on evidence from the small samples taken at random during a process. A green light is given when the process should be allowed to run – all too often processes are adjusted on the basis of a single measurement, a practice which can make a process much more variable than it is already. The equivalent of an amber light appears when trouble is possibly imminent. The red light shows that there is practically no doubt that the process has wandered and that it must be stopped and corrected to prevent production of defective materials or generation of poor service.

Clearly, such a scheme can be introduced only when the process is *in control*. Since the samples of data taken are usually small, typically less than ten, there are risks of errors, but these are small, calculated risks and not blind ones. The risk calculations are based on various frequency distributions.

There are different types of control charts for variable data and attributes. The most frequently used charts for variables are mean and range charts, which are used together. Number defective or errors on np charts and proportion defective or errors on p charts are the most common ones in use for attributes. Other charts found in use are moving average and range charts, number of defects or errors (c) charts, and cumulative sum (Cusum) charts. The latter offer very powerful management tools for the detection of trends or changes in attributes and variable data.

THE CONTROL OF VARIABLES AND PROCESS CAPABILITY

In the manufacture of products which have properties measured on a continuous scale, it is important to realize that no two items will ever be made exactly alike. The variation may be quite large and easily noticeable, such as in lengths of pieces of steel sawn by hand. When variations are very small the items may appear to be identical. This is, in fact, due to the limitations of measurement and instruments with greater precision would show differences.

In sampling a continuous variable (for example, the length of a piece of sheet steel), the main assumption on which the statistical analysis is based is that the variable (in this case the length) will be normally distributed – which is to say that a graph plotted of its distribution will be bell-shaped, as shown in Figure 43.3. The measure of accuracy or central tendency most frequently used in industry is the *mean* or *average* (μ) of the bell-shaped process. The measure of spread of values or precision of a process is obtained by calculating the *standard deviation* (σ).

Suppose the target length of a sheet-steel cutting process was 2 150 mm, and that the bell-shaped curve fell almost entirely within the limits 2 135 mm to 2 165 mm, then, from a knowledge of the shape of the curve and the properties of the normal distribution, the following facts would emerge:

- 68.3 per cent of the sheets are being produced within ± 5 mm of the average ($\mu \pm \sigma$)
- 95.4 per cent of the sheets are within average ± 10 mm ($\mu \pm 2\sigma$)
- 99.7 per cent are within average ± 15 mm ($\mu \pm 3\sigma$)

The usual aim in manufacturing is not to achieve every sheet with the same length, but to obtain sheets or products within specified limits of tolerances. No adjustment of the process is called for as long as there is no immediate danger of falling outside the 'tolerance zone'. Ensuring that the tolerance zone exceeds the spread of the distribution is thus necessary to avoid the production of defectives. If tolerances have been set for the sheets of metal at 2 150 ± 20 mm, then very few

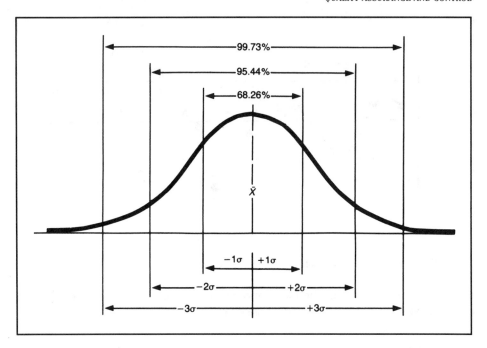

Figure 43.3   The normal distribution curve for a continuous variable

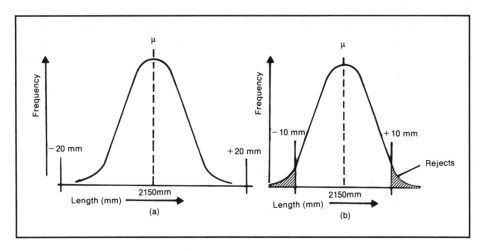

Figure 43.4   The relationship between tolerances and process variability

will fall outside the tolerances (Figure 43.4a). Conversely, if the spread of the process exceeds the tolerance zone (for example, 2 150 mm ± 10 mm, as in Figure 43.4b) then there will inevitably be reject material.

The standard deviation (σ) of a process distribution is one measure of variation. As the sample size in SPC is usually ten or fewer, a more convenient measure of spread is the sample range, which is the difference between the largest and smallest values in the sample. To control the plant or process it is necessary to

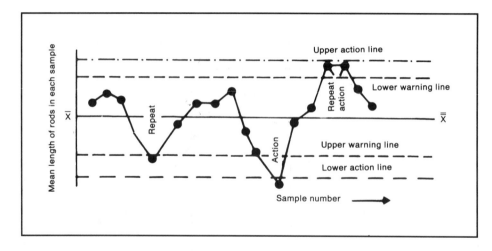

Figure 43.5   A mean chart for controlling the length of rods

check the current state of the mean and spread of the distribution. This can be achieved with the aid of mean and range charts.

Mean charts

Periodically, samples of a given sample size are taken at reasonable intervals from the process when it is under control. The variable is measured for each item of the sample and the sample mean recorded on a chart. Figure 43.5 shows values of steel rod lengths plotted on a mean chart. The sample size (n) = 5. The upper and lower action limits, and the corresponding warning limits, have been determined conventionally, as follows:

$$\text{Action limits at } \bar{\bar{x}} \pm \frac{3\sigma}{\sqrt{n}}$$

$$\text{Warning limits at } \bar{\bar{x}} \frac{2\sigma}{\sqrt{n}}$$

If the process is running satisfactorily almost all the averages of successive samples will lie between the lines marked upper action and lower action. The chance of a sample mean falling outside either of these lines is approximately 1 in 1 000, unless the process has altered in some way. If a point does fall outside, the process should be stopped immediately for investigation. This does not normally suggest a serious fault (it might for example indicate tool wear, and the need for resetting). The chances of being right in the decision to stop the process are approximately 999 in 1 000.

Figure 43.5 also shows warning limits. The chance of a sample mean plotting outside these limits is about 1 in 40, or in other words it is expected to happen once in every 40 samples. When it does happen, there are grounds for suspicion, and the usual procedure is to take another sample immediately, before making a definite decision about the state of the process.

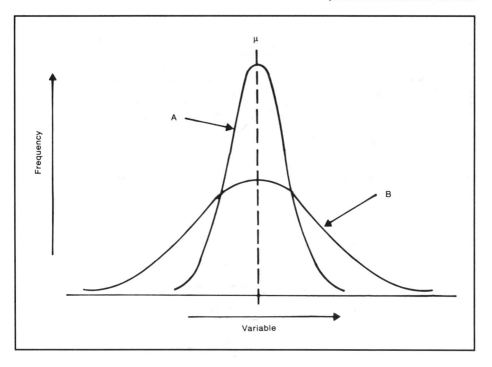

Figure 43.6   Increase of spread of a process

Range charts

A process is only in control when both the accuracy (mean) and precision (spread) of the process are in control. A separate chart for control of the sample range as a measure of process variability is required. The range chart is very similar to the mean chart, the range of the sample (the difference between the highest and lowest values in the sample) being plotted and compared to predetermined limits. The development of a more serious fault than tool wear can lead to a situation illustrated in Figure 43.6, where the process collapses from form A to form B (for example, due to failure of a tool). The ranges of the samples from B will have higher values than ranges in samples taken from A. If a range chart (Figure 43.7) is plotted in conjunction with the mean chart, similar action and warning lines can be drawn to indicate trouble.

In the case of a process which is just capable of holding the tolerances, improvements must be made to reduce the variability and control it so that:

1   The chances of producing out-of-specification material are reduced
2   The customer requirements can easily be changed without needing a completely new process.

THE CONTROL OF ATTRIBUTES

In the case of attributes (for example, colour, general appearance, errors, absenteeism, surface finish) where each classification is binary, it is clearly not possible to use the methods of measurement and control described in the previous section.

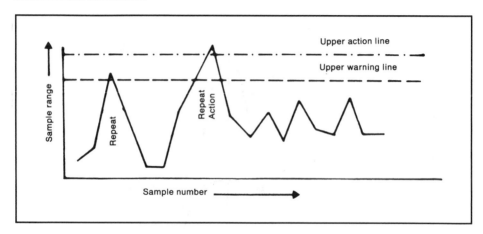

Figure 43.7 A range chart

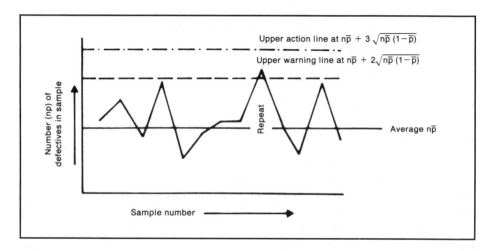

Figure 43.8 An np chart for number defective in a sample

Instead, a standard must be set with which all products or services may be compared. Control can then be exercised by means of a chart showing the number of defectives, errors, and so on, in samples of fixed size and the results plotted on a number defective or errors or np chart as shown in Figure 43.8.

It is desirable to have a constant sample size, but this is not always possible and a chart showing fraction or proportion defective or errors may be used. Before placing action and warning lines on a chart of this type, time should be allowed for the process to settle down. On many occasions the presentation of proportion defective absentees, errors, and so forth, in this form often gives staff valuable information, enabling them to make improvements. The determination of control lines is clearly justified only when this initial effect has played its part and the process has settled down to a reasonably steady level. Sometimes it is useful to insert lower warning and action limits on np and p charts. If points appear below the lower action limit, there would be only a slight chance of this happening unless

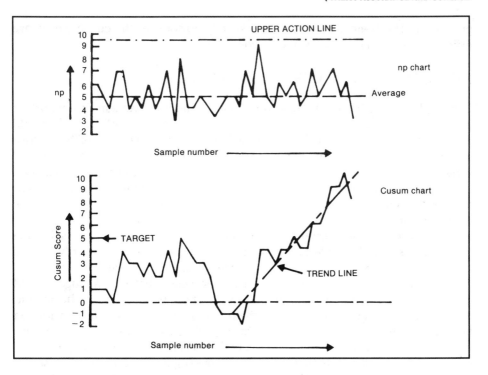

Figure 43.9   Comparison of cusum and np charts for the same data

there had been a significant change for the better in the process. In this case, it would be worthwhile investigating the cause of such a change, to discover how the improvement could be made permanent. The only other reason for a point plotting below the action limit would be inaccurate inspection (for example, defectives being passed as good, or errors missed).

CUSUM CHARTS

The cusum (cumulative sum) chart is a graph which takes a little longer to draw than the conventional control chart, but which gives much more information. It is particularly useful for plotting the evolution of processes because it presents data in a way that enables the eye to separate true trends and changes from a background of random variation. Cusum charts can detect small changes in quality very quickly and may be used for the control of variable data and attributes. In essence a reference or 'target value' is subtracted from each successive sample observation and the result accumulated. Values of this cumulative sum are plotted and 'trend lines' may be drawn on the resulting graphs. If this is approximately horizontal, the value of the variable is about the same as the target value. An overall slope downwards shows a value less than the target, and if the slope is upwards, the value is greater.

Figure 43.9 shows a comparison of an np chart and a cusum chart which were both plotted using the same data (defectives in samples of 100 polythene form products). The trends, which are immediately obvious on the cusum chart, are difficult to detect on the conventional control chart.

PROCESS CONTROL CHARTS AND IMPROVEMENT

The emphasis which must be placed on continuous improvement has important implications for the way in which process control charts are applied. They should not be used purely for control, but as an aid in the reduction of variability by those at the point of operation capable of observing and removing assignable causes of variation. They can be used effectively in the identification and gradual elimination of random causes of variation. In this way the process of continuous improvement may be charted, and adjustments made to the control charts in use to reflect the improvements. This is described in detail in Oakland and Followell (1990).

Often in process control situations, action signals are given when the assignable cause results in a desirable event, such as the reduction of an impurity level, a decrease in error rate, or an increase in order intake. Clearly, assignable or special causes which result in deterioration of the process must be investigated and eliminated, but those that result in improvements must also be sought out and managed so that they become part of the process operation. Significant variation between batches of material, operators, or differences between suppliers are frequent causes of action signals on control charts. The 'continuous improvement' philosophy demands that these are all investigated and the results used to take another step on the long ladder to perfection. Action signals, and assignable or special causes of variation, should stimulate enthusiasm for solving a problem or understanding an improvement, rather than gloom and despondency.

IMPLEMENTING PROCESS CONTROL

One of the first steps in any implementation programme must be the provision of education and training for:

- Managers
- Supervisors
- Operators and staff.

The courses, teaching methods, and materials used for this purpose must be very carefully selected, for much harm can be done by the insensitive teaching of 'statistics', which many people find indigestible. It is possible to learn and apply excellent methods of process control without undertaking complex theoretical studies.

For the successful introduction of SPC the training must have follow-up, which can take many forms. Ideally, an in-house expert can provide the lead through the design of implementation programmes. The most satisfactory strategy is to start small and then learn through a bank of knowledge and experience. Each technique should be introduced alongside existing methods of quality control (if they do exist). This allows comparisons to be made between the new and old methods. When confidence has been built upon the results of the comparisons, the statistical techniques can take over the control of the process. Improvements in one or two areas of the organization's operations, using this approach, will quickly establish SPC as a reliable tool for control of manufacturing processes.

Sometimes outside help is needed – the prophet is rarely accepted in his own land – and many organizations can offer valuable assistance. To obtain the best results, the people providing the initial training should also be involved in the follow-up activities, which should include 'workshop days' when specific process control and implementation problems are discussed.

The savings which accrue from the introduction of good methods of process control will greatly outweigh the costs. Inevitable reduction in waste, rework and rectification costs, together with the increases in resource utilization and capacity, will directly repay the investment. Increased confidence and efficiency as a result of greater process knowledge will permeate the whole organization from design, office and purchasing staff through to sales and marketing, and the introduction of good process control methods will spread the advantages of *the quality system* right through the organization.

Two of the most famous authors on the subject of quality management are Drs Walter Shewhart and W. Edwards Deming. In their book *Statistical Method from the Viewpoint of Quality Control* they state:

> The long-range contribution of statistics depends not so much upon getting a lot of highly trained statisticians into industry as it does on creating a statistically minded generation of physicists, chemists, engineers and others who will in any way have a hand in developing and directing production processes of tomorrow.

This was written in 1939. It is as true today as it was then.

FURTHER READING

Besterfield, D. H., *Quality Control*, 2nd edn, Prentice Hall, New Jersey, 1986

Caplen, R. H., *Practical Approach to Quality*, 5th edn, Business Books, London, 1988

Ishikawa, K., *Guide to Quality Control*, Asian Productivity Association, Tokyo, 1982

Juran, J. M., (ed.,), *Quality Control Handbook*, 4th edn, McGraw-Hill, New York, 1988

Lock, Dennis, (ed.), *Handbook of Quality Management*, Gower, Aldershot, 1990

Oakland, John S., *Total Quality Management*, Heinemann, Oxford, 1989

Oakland, John S. and Followell, R. F., *Statistical Process Control*, Heinemann, Oxford, 1990

Ott, E. R., *Process Quality Control – Troubleshooting and Interpretation of Data*, McGraw-Hill, Kogajusha, New York, 1975

Owen, M., *SPC and Continuous Improvement*, IFS Publications, Bedford, 1989

Price, Frank, *Right First Time*, Gower, Aldershot, 1985

44 Maintenance

E N White

The demands made on the department concerned with the maintenance of buildings, services, machinery, and equipment grow with increased dependence on these assets in today's environment. Pressures on maintenance staff increase as high cost assets call for efficient use with minimum down time, while new technology needs improved servicing and repair skills. The maintenance manager is a principal contributor to assets management and, because maintenance costs are continuous, has an important role in controlling life-cycle costs.

TEROTECHNOLOGY

The terotechnology concept grew out of a working party study on maintenance practices (see *Report by the Working Party on Maintenance Engineering*, HMSO), and it is defined as: 'A combination of management, financial, engineering and other practices applied to physical assets in pursuit of economic life cycle costs'. It covers specification and design for maintainability of all assets (plant, equipment and buildings). It extends to installation, commissioning, maintenance, modification and replacement, and includes information feedback on design, performance, costs and other management data. Typical contributions of terotechnology include:

1 Assets designed for maintainability and reliability
2 Application of 'best buy' procurement methods
3 Provision of assets with operability and maintenance features
4 Introduction of operating techniques which reduce down time and improve asset care
5 Cost monitoring and feedback for control
6 Selection and training programmes for operating and maintenance staff.

Strategies for terotechnology (new assets)

Assets management is a cradle-to-grave strategy which starts with preacquisition studies and continues throughout the life cycle. During the period of use, operation and maintenance strategies will be designed for best use at least cost. Eventually, a replacement or disposal strategy will be formulated, based on technical and economic reviews.

Asset provisioning can be considered in three stages (preparation, decision and implementation), after which come the period of use and various reviews. In more detail, these comprise:

Preparation phase

- Consideration of information fed back from operation and maintenance
- Planning (operating and maintenance policies)
- Technical forecasting
- Whole-life planning
- Life-cycle costing.

Decision phase

- Direct participation by users (past and future)
- Preparation of procurement checklists
- Reviews of supplier profiles and quality ratings
- Specification of support systems
- Review of life plans and life-cycle costs.

Implementation phase

- Design (design records, design reviews, configuration control)
- Studies (maintainability, reliability, feedback from users)
- Project planning and control
- Support planning (information, training, spare parts)
- Information systems (disclosure of design data by manufacturers and suppliers)
- Preparation of documentation (manuals, specifications, training programmes)
- Maintenance planning (management systems and resources)
- Commissioning (testing, defect action, certification)
- Handover (operation, proving, final acceptance).

Utilization phase

- Operation, maintenance, condition monitoring
- Technical and costs records
- Analysis of records
- Feedback to operations, maintenance, design, procurement
- Improvements and updating (configuration control)
- Reviews of life plans and life-cycle costing.

Reviews

- Technical and financial reviews
- Disposal or replacement decisions
- Feedback to benefit future projects.

The terotechnology system demands that a number of 'trade-off' decisions be made. For example, the comparison between increased utilization of a new asset and the attendant costs of operation and maintenance, especially if new technologies are incorporated, can be considered in a 'trade-off' against statistics for the assets to be replaced.

Strategies for terotechnology (existing assets)

Actions to implement terotechnology in the management of existing assets may be considered in two groups – actions within the maintenance function, and actions by other departments. Each of these groups further divides into actions which follow accepted practice, and actions based on analyses of feedback.

As an example, within the maintenance function, the application of planning and control to maintenance work is probably the first reaction of many managers to a terotechnology programme. The principles are well documented, case histories exist and planned maintenance is accepted practice. However, at a later date, when the feedback inherent in a planned system is analysed, the control system may well be modified and condition-based maintenance introduced. It is the action based feedback which effects the most significant improvements. But it is often necessary to improve existing systems as a first step, so that meaningful analyses can be made as justification for further progress.

MAINTENANCE PLANNING AND CONTROL

Total maintenance planning embraces all activities needed to plan, control and record work done to keep assets at the acceptable standard. This includes preventive maintenance, corrective maintenance, planned overhaul, planned replacement, spares provisioning, workshop functions, repairs and renewals, plant history records, plant modification to facilitate maintenance, spare parts manufacture, preventive maintenance on spare parts, and so on. With full control, the only unplanned time should be that spent on emergencies, which could be less than 10 per cent of the labour time available. The requirements for a planned maintenance system are:

- A maintenance programme for buildings, plant, and equipment
- Means for ensuring that the programme is fulfilled
- A method for recording and assessing the results.

In more detail, the components of a planned maintenance system are:

1 *Assets register* An essential base for the planning operation comprising an inventory of the assets to be maintained. Each asset must be identified by its name, description, reference or catalogue number and details of manufacture or supplier. The location must also be specified, in a flexible way if the asset is moved or mobile

2 *Asset coding* A numeric or alphanumeric identity code should be given to each asset (buildings, fixed and mobile plant and services installations). The code format can be devised so that it identifies the asset type, two or more levels of accounts coding, physical location, and so on. Additional numbers

can be used to link the basic codes to spare parts, special tools, work specifications, drawings and manuals filed in the maintenance library, and for corporate purposes such as investment or depreciation analyses. The codes must be attached to the assets, and used on all maintenance working documents as the key to effective communication, feedback and historical records

3   *Maintenance schedules* For inspection, lubrication, preventive maintenance and (possibly) planned overhaul of the registered assets

4   *Work specifications* Instruction cards or other stored data which identify exactly the maintenance tasks to be undertaken

5   *Maintenance control system* A trigger system which initiates all the tasks on the maintenance schedules at the specified intervals

6   *Manpower schedule* A manpower allocation system to ensure that sufficient resources are available and that they are used effectively

7   *Maintenance records* Systems for recording maintenance work and for reporting to management

8   *Maintenance support* The organization of technical data, spare parts and tools, and so on

9   *Liaison with production departments* An effective system for agreeing with the user management when maintenance work can be done

10 *Planned overhaul* Provisions for ensuring the planned overhaul of plant, either as scheduled or in response to condition monitoring

11 *Costing system* Costing procedures for adequate cost control and for the apportionment of costs in the maintenance department

12 *Training* Training operatives and supervisors to run the system.

Figure 44.1 depicts a typical maintenance control system.

Maintenance schedules

Maintenance schedules list the routine maintenance requirements of each asset. A typical schedule record includes the grade of labour required, frequency and details of the work to be done and the estimated time needed for the work. Records can be compiled in a card index or in a computer system. Where similar assets require identical maintenance, each must be given its own schedule.

Preparation of maintenance schedules is a skilled task. Not only must all necessary activities be identified, but their frequencies must be evaluated with availability for maintenance in mind, as well as other more obvious factors including suppliers' suggestions.

Grouping work by slight adjustments of the frequencies can have a most beneficial effect on the operation of a maintenance programme. Basic data can frequently be obtained from manufacturers' manuals but not all manuals have the necessary information, or have the information in the required form. The maintenance planning engineer must therefore use any available information as a basis, but must interpret it in accordance with the local requirements and with his own knowledge and experience. (Obviously care must be taken within the guarantee period of new equipment to conform with any special instructions which form part of the supplier's guarantee.)

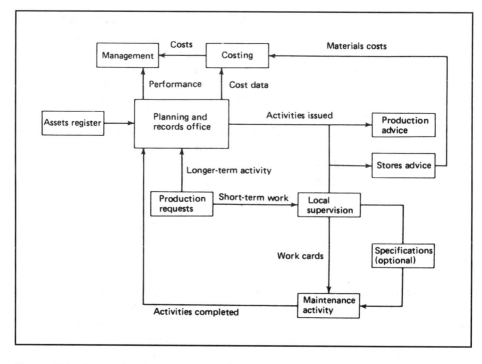

Figure 44.1   A typical maintenance control system

Maintenance controls

When the extent of the preventive maintenance activity is known, a suitable control system can be selected to trigger activities at the required frequencies. The system can be devised to print and issue the work card, materials requisition (if any) and the detailed work specification for each task at the appropriate time. When the scheduled work has been carried out the results should be fed back into the system. Obviously any additional work found to be necessary, or any amendment needed to the stored instructions should be initiated.

Manpower scheduling and allocation

When routine maintenance needs have been decided for all registered assets the estimated work hours needed for each labour grade must be estimated. Then a phased schedule can be computed by allocating the appropriate hours to suitable dates for each planned activity. Labour schedules should be compiled in detail for a medium-term control period, and in summary for longer-term planning to assist in recruitment and training plans for two or more years ahead.

Labour resourcing in the maintenance department only makes sense when full control and support for the maintenance activity is provided. Studies have shown that 15 per cent of available work time can be spent in obtaining instructions and in making journeys to the work point in an average-sized industrial installation. Planning the routing of staff is important, but unnecessary journeys to workshops or stores can be avoided if full support is given by adequate provision of test equipment, spare parts and technical manuals.

Allocation of staff with the skills appropriate for specific tasks is not always feasible in the formal schedules and may be far more a matter for the supervisor or foreman, who knows the capabilities and aptitudes of individuals. There are many local factors which may affect the decision to send either Smith or Anderson on particular routes on a particular day. The system is satisfied if two people in a given grade are matched to a two work-day load, but with the foreman left to choose which individual does which jobs.

Maintenance records

The operation of an effective maintenance records system provides the following information:

1 The percentage of planned work achieved in the period
2 The ratio of planned to unplanned work
3 Downtime for the period
4 Ratio of preventive work to corrective work
5 Maintenance requirement comparisons between individual assets, between types of asset, or between groups of assets
6 Indicators for reliability of the products of particular manufacturers
7 Trends in spare parts consumption
8 Equipment failure patterns
9 Performance detail for personnel, by individual or by trade group
10 Materials used, for guidance on restocking policies
11 Indicators on possible standardization policies.

Records are kept in many different ways, ranging from card files to computer data. The labour required for updating records or work done is a deterrent to many managers and can only be justified if use is made of the information. If a computer is used, lengthy printout sheets can be time consuming also. However, the computer is a useful tool for providing summary information on a regular basis so that trends can be observed. Whatever system of records is used, detailed investigations have to be reserved for individual situations in which the cost is justified.

Liaison with the user

Effective liaison between the operating managers or planners and the maintenance planners is essential to the operation of the maintenance programme. The extent of this liaison depends upon the method of operation, the worst situation occurring when continuous use is required. However, in continuous process plants the awareness of the requirement for liaison is generally such as to encourage efficient planning. The most difficult situations occur where the degree of use or the volume of production fluctuates and a peak period can coincide with an intended maintenance activity.

In an ideal working environment both long-term (annual) and short-term (monthly) plans are regularly reviewed. Short-term release of assets for maintenance purposes can substantially reduce the need for weekend working by maintenance staff. Among the disadvantages of weekend working are the supervision problems, non-availability of materials, spares, and other services at weekends, and possible personnel problems as the maintenance staff tend to become socially separated.

Another important aspect of liaison is the request for service originated by operatives. When standby maintenance staff are available, requests for assistance are frequently made verbally. Formal requests include details of the fault and of the particular item requiring attention together with a priority indication, advice as to whether operations have been halted and an indication of the maintenance trade needed. Cost code information is required for any work undertaken by the maintenance staff in response to requests by operatives. Depending upon the arrangements for cost codes this allows expenditure to be allocated to particular machines, to individual buildings or to operators' stations.

Analysis of down time

Maintenance records must be capable of down-time analysis, either from processing the records themselves or by summarizing the breakdown repair requests. The record cards or computer tabulation headings should at least include:

- The incident date
- The item affected (for example, compressor)
- The type of fault (for example, bearing collapsed)
- Action taken/needed (for example, spare fitted/reorder)
- The down time which resulted.

Information produced by different analyses includes:

1 An indication of down time for each building, machine and, if necessary, operator
2 The time taken for fault diagnosis and repair on various types of fault, on specific machines or by various people
3 Indications of breakdown causes.

Among the useful points made clear by analysis 1 might be:

- The true ratio of down time to use time (to answer rumours or inaccuracies being quoted against the maintenance department)
- The need for further investigation, by the operations or maintenance managements, of high down time
- The relationships between operator performance and the down time on individual assets.

Analysis 2 may help to define:

- High down time areas where permanent standby repair staff or zone workshops might be beneficial

- Suppliers to be avoided on future procurements
- A requirement for specific training (for example, electronic fault-finding) for maintenance workers
- The most efficient members of the maintenance staff for the various types of work (fault-diagnosis, repairs, renewals, for example).

Analysis 3 will define:

- The spare parts and materials requirements for the various assets
- Any requirement for increased operator training
- Problems caused by variations in the product materials used in manufacturing processes.

It will be seen that down time analysis is complementary to any cost-analysis work. However, down time recording in detail is relatively expensive and, if economies are sought, may be applied only in certain areas rather than generally. The areas chosen may be high-risk areas containing plant which is vital to a high production figure, or may be areas of rising maintenance cost as defined by the normal cost summary, or areas in which large consequential losses could occur.

Costing

The maintenance control system must provide for accurate costing of work and materials for all maintenance activities. Work cards, materials requisitions, work instructions, maintenance requests, defect reports and time sheets must all carry significant codes to indicate cost allocations. The level of accounting practice adopted will determine the structure of the code system which may define costs in terms of:

1 Individual factories
2 Process lines
3 Individual machines
4 Separate buildings
5 Office units
6 Administration departments
7 Canteens and other special areas.

There is a wide variety of functional and physical hierarchies which may be adopted. The cost codes can conveniently be incorporated in the asset codes, so that costs to a particular asset are cross-referenced at once to the correct accounts.

COMPUTER-CONTROLLED SYSTEMS

A variety of computer systems have been developed for assets registers, work control, labour resourcing, stock control, maintenance accounts and, in some cases, analyses of feedback and costs. The ideal computer system is interactive, dynamic and dedicated. Dedicated means that it is always available to the user for logging vital information or for fast retrieval of data. These requirements can be met by siting a microcomputer within the maintenance department, or providing a terminal connected to a larger computer (providing it has sufficient capacity and free time).

Computer applications in maintenance planning and control include:

1 Recording or updating asset records or asset movements
2 Managing lubrication activities and modifying the schedules if required by feedback
3 Acting upon inspection reports from lubrication operatives
4 Managing preventive and corrective maintenance activities and incorporating emergency maintenance when necessary
5 Acting upon feedback from maintenance activities
6 Resourcing for capital works programmes
7 Acting upon feedback from emergency maintenance
8 Managing spare parts stocks.

Other uses for the computer in the maintenance department can include:

1 Management of the maintenance department stores
2 Planning and control of capital works programmes
3 Management of production tools, dies, moulds, and so on.
4 Energy conservation through monitoring and control
5 Security and fire monitoring through remote sensors
6 Monitoring of automated processes or boiler plant
7 Co-ordination of condition monitoring inputs
8 Register of technical manuals and drawings
9 Register of defects and defect actions
10 Register of tests and quality documentation.

CONDITION-BASED MAINTENANCE

Condition-based maintenance is work which results from the discovery of a fault or deterioration during routine or continuous checking. Corrective work ordered after the discovery of cracks in a wall, or overheating noticed in a machine during a preventive maintenance check are examples. Condition reports arise from observations, checks and tests, or from fixed instrumentation or alarm systems grouped under the name 'condition monitoring'. Benefits expected from a condition monitoring programme include:

1 Reduced expenditure on preventive maintenance
2 No unnecessary dismantling of plant items
3 Less (or less serious) breakdowns
4 Avoidance of consequential damage.

Levels of monitoring

Condition monitoring can be considered at four levels:

1 Inspection monitoring based on the human senses, as in preventive maintenance schedules
2 Assisted monitoring, using portable equipment
3 Lubricant analysis and wear debris collection
4 Fixed monitoring systems connected to alarm systems or data logging equipment.

The inspections at level 1 of the monitoring programme form part of the normal preventive maintenance schedules and are generally included in the daily and weekly activities. The inspectors are expected to use sight, hearing, touch and smell and to obtain a sensory impression of the condition of the asset. The senses may be assisted by magnifiers, viewing devices, temperature sensing strips or paints, stroboscopes, fixed instruments or indicators.

At level 2 the inspector is assisted by a range of portable test equipment to make a variety of measurements. Examples of the tests to be made and the types of equipment used are:

Measurement	Equipment
Speed and running time	Tachometers, counters
Electrical quantities	Test meters
Fits and tolerances	Proximity testers
Temperature	Thermography
Vibration wear	Vibration analyser or shock-pulse tester
Movement	Frequency analysis
Deterioration of materials	Radiography; ultrasonics; dye penetration

This type of monitoring is applied to selected assets from the asset register for which a condition history file is built up. Quantities and characteristics are recorded and variations observed and interpreted.

Level 3 monitoring is confined to lubricated items and consists of checks on component wear together with checks on contamination of the lubricant. Wear of components is usually indicated by metal particles and debris in the lubricant. Contamination of the lubricant is detected by sampling and subsequent spectrometric analysis.

Fixed monitoring systems for level 4 monitoring range from simple remote alarm systems to comprehensive data gathering systems based on minicomputers or microprocessors. A wide range of contact points, transducers, accelerometers, counters and other sensors are employed. Data can be transmitted directly to the display or can be electronically processed on a time-shared signal transmission system.

CAPITAL PROJECT MANAGEMENT

The stages in the life cycle of a new capital project are:

1 *Conception* Formulation of project idea
2 *Approval* Preliminary discussion and agreement on study

3 *Formulation* Study of various implementation methods
4 *Procurement* Selection of suppliers
5 *Design* Development of concept
6 *Construction* Manufacture of hardware
7 *Installation* Construction and installation (often run concurrently)
8 *Commissioning* Often referred to as 'start-up'
9 *Hand-over* Buyer accepts responsibility
10 *Proving* Testing under normal conditions.

If time and money are to be spent in studying a project idea, budgetary approval must be sought. The study might involve comparison of one or more options against the alternative of keeping or reconditioning an existing asset. Among the factors are:

- Life-cycle costs and return on investment for the existing asset (if applicable)
- Predicted life-cycle costs and return on investment for each new option
- The costs of development, operating, maintenance, training and problems arising if new technologies are introduced.

The financial appraisal of capital projects was covered in Chapter 12 but aspects specific to maintenance need amplification here. Operating and maintenance must be fully taken in account and the maintenance manager should be consulted. Additional maintenance costs brought about by the new acquisition during the procurement, start-up and operation might include:

- Salaries and other payments for additional personnel
- Recruitment and training costs
- Additional accommodation
- Supplier's maintenance contract or other subcontract costs
- Spares and materials acquisition and storage costs
- Overhead charges, insurances, and so on
- Training and learning time
- Increased overtime working and premiums
- High spares consumption, excessive down time, scrap and other problems during start-up and initial operation
- Depreciation of the new assets
- Possible employment of a maintenance consultant.

The maintenance budget may be 7 to 10 per cent of the total investment required for an industrial installation (although cases vary enormously). Approximate allocations within the maintenance budget might be:

Cost item	Allowance
Materials and subcontract	25 per cent
Total personnel costs	40 per cent
Depreciation and overheads	25 per cent
Other	10 per cent

The maintenance manager might request a number of studies by the project engineers. Typical studies are:

1 Study of supplier's proposals for assistance:
   * should the proposals be accepted for training and so forth?
   * should training and product support be subcontracted to specialist firms?
   * are independent commissioning engineers to be used?
   * is a servicing contract desirable?
2 Study of operating and maintenance requirements:
   * will required utilization be achieved?
   * what numbers and grades of manpower are necessary?
   * have all services requirements been clarified?
   * are all aspects of maintenance support provided for?
3 Study of maintenance planning and control systems:
   * is planned maintenance provided for?
   * which control method will be used?
   * can this plant and others be combined to justify more sophisticated planning systems?
   * will a maintenance consultant be appointed?
4 Study of spare parts requirements:
   * are supplier's recommendations acceptable?
   * will drawings be supplied for local spares manufacturer?
   * is the spares investment at an acceptable level?
   * are original sources of spares known?
   * are spares compatible with existing stocks?
5 Study of monitoring techniques:
   * is vibration analysis or other condition monitoring included?
   * is remote control or centralized surveillance desirable?
   * are adequate alarms provided?
   * are fault diagnosis methods provided for?

These and other studies set the pattern for subsequent maintenance of the plant at an acceptable utilization factor.

The total involvement of the maintenance manager in new project work is essential if effective maintenance is to be a feature of future years. If effective maintenance planning and control methods are used in an existing maintenance department, the maintenance manager should be available for participation in new work programmes.

There are controllable risk factors that can adversely affect maintenance efficiency when a capital project is planned. These include:

* Insufficient attention to reliability and life-maintenance predictions during design and development
* Buying at the lowest quoted price without regard to the consequences
* Procurement without specifying or enforcing the product support needed at installation and start-up
* Insufficient appreciation of the maintenance role by others in the company (for example, works and production managers)

- Failure to set proper maintenance plans and budgets
- Ineffective communication in the maintenance hierarchy
- Inadequate training for maintenance staff beyond basic skills level
- Insufficient management training for engineers managing maintenance departments.

The project planner, with help from the maintenance manager or chief engineer, is responsible for setting the pattern for control in the maintenance department and for steering all concerned into a successful project. Introduction of planning methods, control systems and effective supporting organizations depends on the disciplines imposed during procurement: both by the purchaser and the supplier. Companies without the necessary experience may be advised to employ a terotechnology consultant to undertake the following duties:

1 *Formulation stage* Evaluation of maintenance aspects of various methods and development of monitoring and maintenance policies
2 *Procurement stage* Vetting of contracts for maintenance aspects
3 *Design and construction* Monitor maintainability aspects
4 *Installation and commissioning* Evaluate product support activity by vendors and enforce contract provisions. Develop planned maintenance system, plant records, and technical information system. Arrange training programmes
5 *Post-commissioning* Finalize technical information system, review planning system, update as necessary.

FURTHER READING

Report by the Working Party on Maintenance Engineering, HMSO, London
The Terotechnology Handbook, HMSO, London
White, E. N., *Maintenance Planning, Control and Documentation*, 2nd edn, Gower, Aldershot, 1979
Planning a Preventive Maintenance Programme, White, E. N., Winnersh, Wokingham, RG11 5HX

Part Seven

LOGISTICS MANAGEMENT

45 Distribution: the total cost-to-serve

John Gentles and Keith Oliver

The more management targets the company's efforts on cutting distribution costs, the less successful it is likely to be in reducing the real cost of distribution. This apparent paradox is no simple play on words. It explains why so many companies have diligently pruned distribution costs – in the warehouse, in stocks, in order processing and transport – only to find that these hard-earned savings have somehow been watered down or washed out altogether by increases in other costs scattered throughout the company.

These 'other cost' increments seem to have nothing to do with distribution. They appear, unpredicted and inexplicable, at different times, anywhere and everywhere in the business (in purchasing, in production and in administrative systems). But when traced back to their root cause they are all found to result from the way the company distributes its products.

THE TOTAL COST OF DISTRIBUTION

Some years ago the concept of a total cost of distribution (TCD) approach to evaluating distribution alternatives was introduced. The main thesis was based on two points:

1 Classical distribution costs (transport and warehousing) do not reflect the true costs of distribution. A total view of costs from supply to delivery is more realistic
2 A total cost approach is needed to ensure that the other costs are considered and presented to management as part of a fully developed business proposal.

Over the last few years this approach has evolved further. The value added in the distribution process is now seen as a source of competitive edge and there is more focus on the strategic role of distribution within the whole supply chain. The way in which cost is viewed within distribution has also changed. The cost-to-serve is now seen as less product linked, and there is a move towards looking at the cost of processing and delivering individual orders. It is now seen that the total cost-to-serve is the sum total of a large number of transaction costs which will vary by product, by market, by channel of trade, and will even vary between individual customers. It is these transaction costs – rather than those traditionally attacked in distribution cost-cutting programmes – that make up the total cost-to-serve and provide the focus for achieving competitive edge.

The important difference between distribution costs and the real impact of distribution on the total costs and total profits of the business has now been measured and dealt with by a number of hard-headed companies. Their managements have defined this cost complex and brought it under management control by applying the total cost-to-serve approach.

Benefits

The value of the total cost-to-serve approach has now become apparent to many practitioners in the field of distribution, materials and operations management. It has grown in stature with general business management as pressure on costs and efficiency have grown in step with the increasingly difficult business environment and greater competition, especially from Japan. The feasibility of the approach has also increased with the explosion of new computer tools that have allowed managers greater access to more sophisticated techniques and large volumes of data.

Some remarkable results have been achieved:

1 A food manufacturer, after applying effectively an assortment of belt-tightening techniques, found that using the total cost-to-serve approach enabled him to make additional profits of $3 800 000, enough to add 1.7 per cent to his margin of sales
2 A merchandiser, already enjoying the benefits of advanced distribution techniques, found that by using this approach he was able to cut from his corporate costs an additional 2.8 per cent of the sales value of its products – while at the same time significantly improving service to customers
3 A manufacturer of school supplies applied these techniques to his factories and warehouses and was able to cut his annual distribution costs by over $5 000 000 – a 20 per cent reduction.

These success stories from large organizations demonstrate why even companies which have tightened and tidied their distribution operations can still add substantially to their earnings by a frontal attack on the basic framework of their distribution decisions and practices. They have proved, too, that this broad and basic approach brings continuing returns. Once the total cost-to-serve has defined the most profitable pattern of distribution for the present operations of the business, management has a yardstick for measuring the impact on total profits of any proposed changes.

Case studies

The effectiveness of the total cost approach is illustrated by the two case studies which follow – each a different situation, but both using the total cost-to-serve approach. The first case shows how total cost-to-serve analysis was used to develop a fundamentally different approach to separating the market and its channels, with consequent impact on both pricing and operations strategies. The second indicates how cost-to-serve analyses provided a recommendation to restructure the supply chain fundamentally, including the later stages of manufacturing, in order to reduce costs significantly.

CASE STUDY 1: DISTRIBUTION AND MANUFACTURING IN INDUSTRIAL PRODUCTS

This case concerns the problems facing the producer and distributor of a widely used industrial product, where the upstream production could be classed as a particularly capital-intensive flow process. Downstream production concentrates on fabrication activities, labour intensive but encompassing a range of products from 'speciality', through branded, to commodity. There are three primary channels of distribution:

1 Direct to key and large customers
2 To local distributors and wholesalers, both owned and independent
3 Direct sales to professionals.

While the company is the market leader, it is facing significant competition from small, entrepreneurial companies entering its market-place. This factor has produced pressure on pricing which has significantly reduced profitability, and market share has not been maintained. The three strategic actions identified to address these challenges were to:

• Improve service (that is, reduce lead-times and increase the reliability of deliveries)
• Move towards more value-added specialities
• Reorganize manufacturing in order to decrease complexity.

In this way, it was assumed that costs could be reduced, and volume and revenues increased. The critical constraints were the wide spread of customers (both large and small, with a variety of service requirements), more than 10 000 order transactions per year, and a pricing and discount policy directed exclusively at the volume of product purchased.

Since both the reduction of complexity (*the key to cost reductions*) and the raising of service levels both implied a greater level of attention, the fundamental issue, therefore, was how to direct and segment the total supply chain to address this market-place. It was in this context that the total cost-to-serve analysis technique was of vital importance.

Traditional segmentation techniques had failed. The distinction between speciality and commodity did not show any significant variations in cost-to-serve nor did traditional channel segmentations around distributors, wholesalers, direct, and so on. The company appeared to be better positioned in the high-price, high-service end of the market rather than the low-service commodity end, but this seemed to be a natural by-product of the relative tolerances of the individual segments. Most supply chain and distribution functions appeared to be overwhelmed with complexity-related costs and poor performance typically exemplified in late deliveries, high indirect labour costs, and poor productivity to standard. Comparison between standard and real costs computed as of year end showed a total deviation

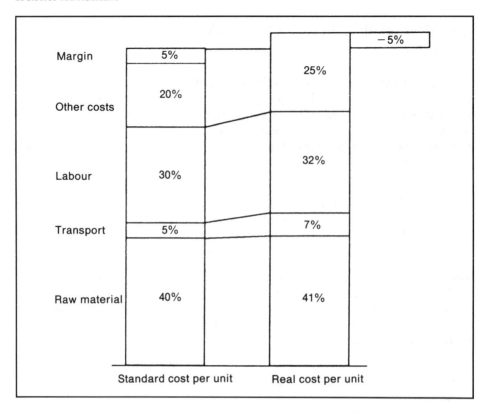

Figure 45.1 Comparison of standard cost and real cost. The standard cost system does not seem to reflect true cost and thus profitability is not controlled

of 10 per cent spread across all cost elements, as shown in Figure 45.1, but provided little insight as to what was actually going wrong or how it could be put right.

The key element of cost-to-serve is to establish what are the drivers to cost on the supply chain, and therefore what logical segmentations and techniques exist to minimize these costs. The principal element of cost-to-serve analysis therefore becomes the correct definition of the drivers to cost in each cost area:

Administration

- Size of business
- Complexity.

Marketing/selling

- Number of customers
- Number of products

- Nature of products/markets.

Distribution

- Number/location of customers
- Service requirements
- Order size.

Manufacturing

- Complexity
- Line/factory scale.

As already discussed, classic market and product segmentation had produced no clear pattern in terms of pricing flexibility, lead-time or complexity. Undertaking the full cost-to-serve analysis indicated that, with the exception of specialities, the real drivers to costs were, in fact, dependent on how easy or how difficult a total order was to process independent of either product or channel:

- Typically, a large, easy order would have a high total volume of items, few different order lines and a high number of pieces per order line
- In comparison, a small, difficult order would have a small total volume, a large number of lines per order and consequently few pieces per line.

These relationships are displayed in Figure 45.2. The differences in costs were driven by what could be identified as transaction costs, which are those costs associated with the capture, processing and execution of a given demand. They include not just the administrative and order processing costs, but also the physical handling (e.g. picking, consolidation and transportation) and, in a make-to-order environment, the scheduling and manufacturing set-up costs. These costs are, in the most part, sensitive to the number and complexity of discrete transactions to be handled, and not to volume. Hence the name 'transaction costs'.

Since it is the difficult order which typically has the high transaction costs, it became important to understand the significance of transaction costs within the total cost format. A better allocation of cost based on the complexity of handling an order was therefore undertaken. That showed a substantial difference in real cost-to-serve owing to the importance of the transactions costs (see Figure 45.3).

The insights provided by the 'cost-to-serve analyses' gave the basis for resegmenting the market and developing well-organized supply chain structures and functions to support this new objective. With the exception of speciality products, where higher manufacturing costs dominated the equation, the market could be divided quite neatly into small/difficult and large/easy orders with specific service and policy characteristics (see Figure 45.4).

The cost-to-serve analyses had shown that large/easy and small/difficult orders really do have different characteristics and ought to be treated differently. In addition, primarily because of manufacturing costs, speciality products should also be handled separately. The true cost-to-serve of a large, easy order was on

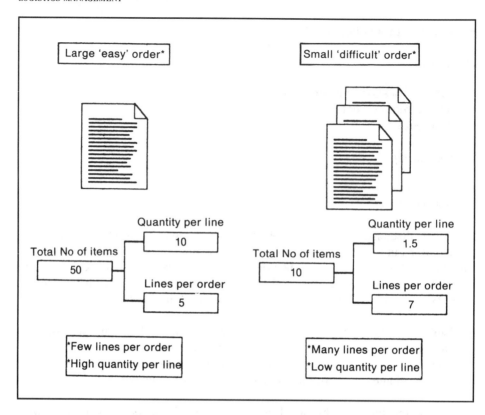

Figure 45.2   Comparison between 'easy' and 'difficult' orders

average 20 to 30 per cent less than a small, difficult order and, given this kind of range (which is by no means atypical), managing by the averages is fundamentally misleading. The implications were also not limited to distribution, since transformation plants that mixed large and small orders could also not achieve optimal performance in any segment of the business. Differentiated operating modes and operations strategies for the plants thereby started to emerge along the demand segmentation suggested by the cost-to-serve analyses (see Figure 45.5). Furthermore, the significance for pricing strategy was also rigid. Pricing by volume in a transaction-cost-dominated environment is flawed since it does not reflect true cost-to-serve and therefore the relative profitability of individual demands. In summary, the overall operations and pricing strategies of the business were becoming aligned to the implications dictated by the local cost-to-serve analyses originally conducted for the distribution functions.

The impact on total operating costs and therefore cost-to-serve was very significant. Additionally, service was considerably increased. By concentrating the small distributed plants on a service mission the adverse impact on their total operating costs was relatively insignificant. In comparison, the volume plant's costs went down by about 30 per cent. The pricing strategy for the business was also significantly changed. In summary, both the quantitative and qualitative measures indicated far better performance with the new segmentation:

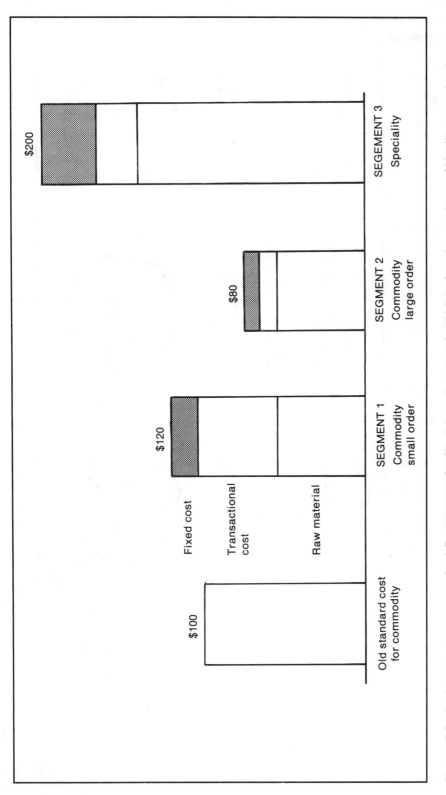

Figure 45.3   Real cost-to-serve per unit for different types of order. Better allocation of costs based on the complexity of handling an order shows substantial difference in real cost-to-serve owing to the importance of transactional costs

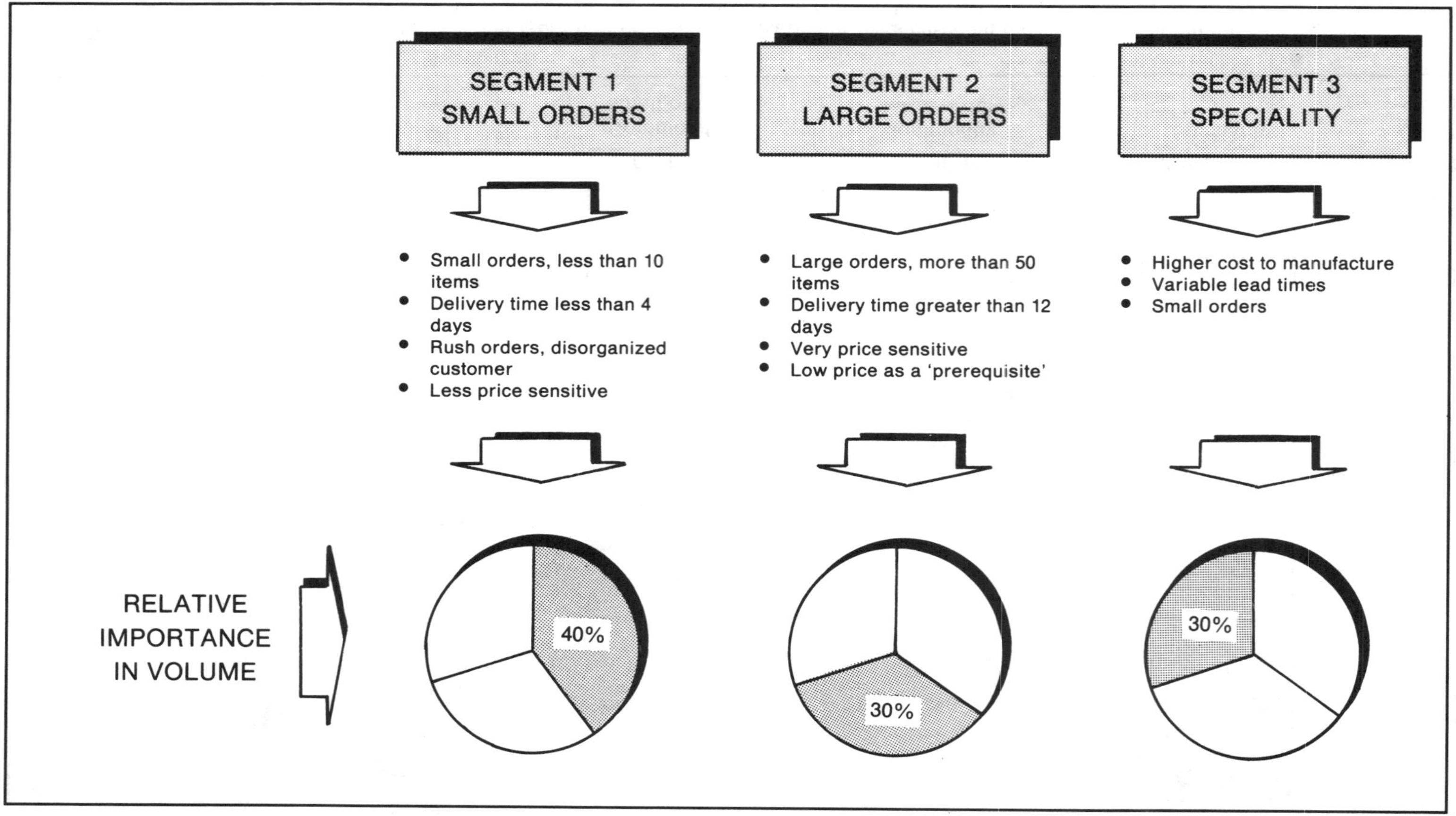

SEGMENT 1 SMALL ORDERS

- Small orders, less than 10 items
- Delivery time less than 4 days
- Rush orders, disorganized customer
- Less price sensitive

40%

SEGMENT 2 LARGE ORDERS

- Large orders, more than 50 items
- Delivery time greater than 12 days
- Very price sensitive
- Low price as a 'prerequisite'

30%

SEGMENT 3 SPECIALITY

- Higher cost to manufacture
- Variable lead times
- Small orders

30%

RELATIVE IMPORTANCE IN VOLUME

Figure 45.4 Segmentation of orders according to type of demand

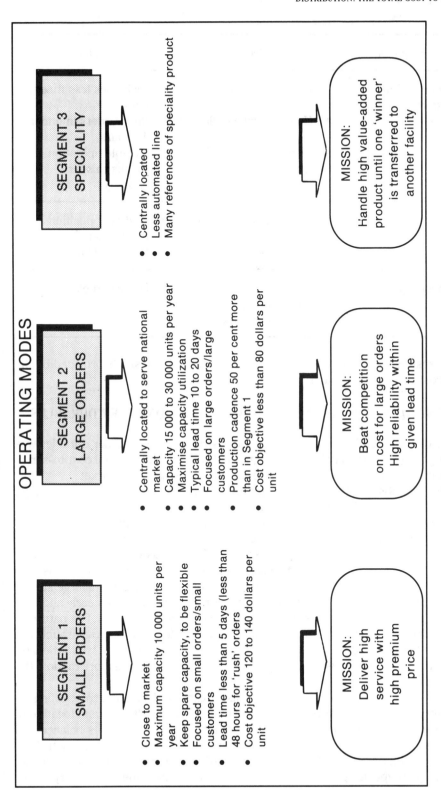

Figure 45.5 Treatment of orders according to type of demand/operating modes. Each plant shoud be focused and assigned a clear mission (for an explanation of missions and visions as used in this illustration and in Figure 45.9 please see the relevant section in Chapter 62)

Segment	Before	After
1 Small/difficult orders	• Late deliveries	• Deliveries less than five days
	• No rush orders allowed	• Rush orders in under 48 hours
	• Plants jammed with large orders	• Flexible operation thanks to spare capacity
2 Large/easy orders	• Not cost competitive	• Best cost position in the market
	• Unreliable deliveries	• Reliable deliveries
3 Speciality orders	• Mixing of speciality and commodity orders in plants	• Dedicated plants

These results would not have been possible without the insights provided by the total cost-to-serve approach.

CASE STUDY 2: SUPPLY AND DISTRIBUTION OF CONSUMER DURABLES

In this case, a pan-European supplier and distributor of consumer durables was seeking to increase profitability by a significant reduction of his total cost-to-serve, whilst improving the strategically important positioning in the market.

Initial diagnosis of the symptoms indicated poor delivery service despite high levels of inventory. The inventory was, however, radically out of balance and lead-times were both excessive and unreliable. The delivery performance to the market-place was quantified as between 55 and 85 per cent on-time delivery against promise but where the promise date often exceeded the initial customer request. In fact, when measured against request date, on-time delivery was only between 15 and 45 per cent. Perhaps more importantly, there was a large spread around the target delivery, with significant portions delivered both early and late. Typical graphs of delivery performance are shown in Figure 45.6. The nature of these graphs is that they are cumulative and therefore an S-shape around the target is the most desirable profile, indicating very little early and very little late. The corollary is that the wider the spread around the target, the more random the performance.

The total inventory for the business was in excess of $250m, representing an inventory turn of only just over twice per annum. The distribution and location of the inventory is shown in Figure 45.7, together with a sample of its balance and coverage, the latter being far more important in a cost-to-serve approach. Only inventories that are 'in balance' are capable of making a contribution to service. Too many companies pay more attention to the absolute value of inventory rather

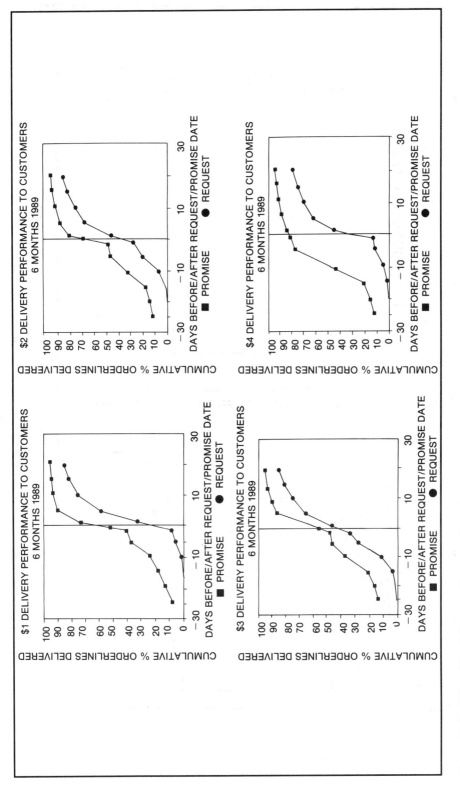

Figure 45.6 Sales office delivery performance to customer

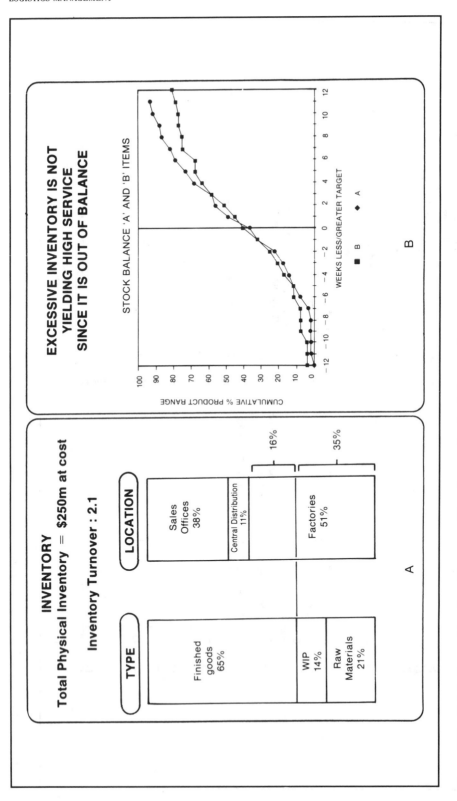

Figure 45.7 Distribution and location of inventory (A) and a sample of its balance and coverage (B) in Case 2

than to the percentages that are over- or under-target. The cumulative S-curve in the figure shows essentially random coverage against target, thereby giving the worst of all worlds – high obsolete inventories with relatively low service levels.

From the initial analyses, it became very clear that any role of central distribution inventory is relatively minimal and that the key working capital leverage was likely to be on distributed inventory in the field and on supply inventory in the factories.

Additionally, high cost-to-serve characterized the total chain. The principal cause was the excessive number of small orders, even though many of the customers were distributors or manufacturers of considerable size. Order profiles and order revenue analyses indicated both low absolute order size and (even more importantly) a very, very long tail of small orders. In fact, 80 per cent of the orders represented only 10 per cent of revenue. As in the previous case study (Case 1), the transaction costs associated with this 'tail' were substantial, and it is these transaction costs which drive the high cost-to-serve.

More fundamentally, there was also no recognition, in the way that the supply chain was structured or managed, of the different channel strategies and their requirements. Different channels had different service and response needs but there was no consideration of this in the way the distribution structures had been set up. The absence of formal supply policies exacerbated this problem by failing to manage customer expectations.

A traditional approach to fixing these issues would have concentrated on better control of inventories and an attempt (probably abortive) to raise average order sizes. The issue of how the chain should be structured, based on minimizing the cost-to-serve while maximizing the service levels, would not and could not have been dealt with in a traditional context. Two important points had to be addressed:

1   Reduction of inventory, while raising service
2   Reduction of other costs-to-serve, particularly around transactions.

The company had always had a traditional vertical, functional emphasis on the way it controlled its chain, as indicated in Figure 45.8. The current chains were therefore overendowed with assets for the relatively poor level of service.

The cost-to-serve analyses indicated that, if costs were really to be reduced without adversely impacting service, a fundamental redeployment of inventories would be required. The recommended approach was radical in that it viewed the 'distribution' function as reaching back into the assembly process of manufacturing as well as forward to the actual customer interfaces. This part of the supply chain would have a total service ethic with the emphasis on very fast response to customer demand from well-established and managed semi-finished inventory, as shown in Figure 45.9. This approach would allow the company to migrate inventory away from the market-place interface, not just to a distribution centre but back into finished inventory, where it would have both far greater flexibility as well as reduced absolute cost. Moving the inventory up the chain would have considerable leverage on asset balance. This leverage comes both from the commonality of parts and from the fact that less value added has been incurred at the semi-finished level. The relationships between these varied considerably by plant, but were in the region of 2 to 1 across the board (that is, every dollar invested at semi-finished would require $2 of finished goods inventory to deliver the same service).

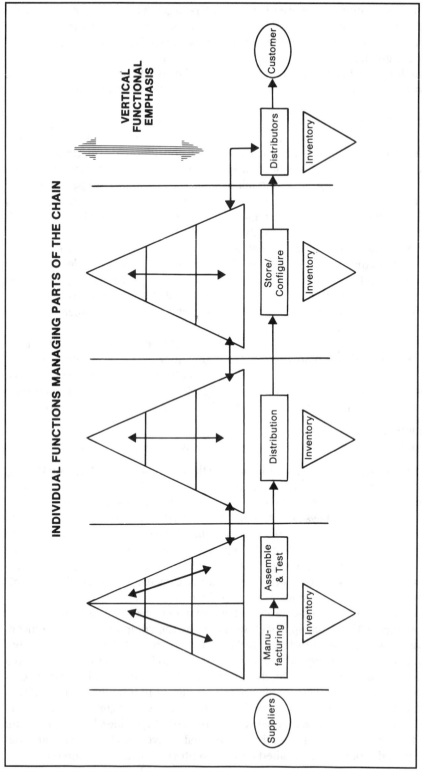

Figure 45.8   Original distribution framework of Case 2. Resulted in high inventories, major delays in processing information and excessive indirect infrastructure costs (high costs-to-serve)

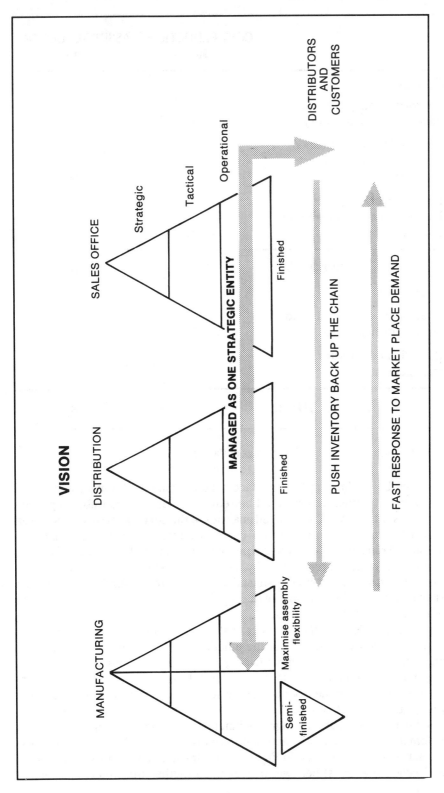

Figure 45.9 New distribution framework of (Case 2). The distribution rule is expanded to include assembly, emphasizing the 'service' mission of the front end of the chain

	COST REDUCTION $m	ASSET REDUCTION $m
INVENTORY		
• Improved management of finished goods inventory	(1.0)	33
• Trade-off between finished and non-finished product inventory	(1.0)	34
• Reduced work in process based on new manufacturing approach	(1.0)	17
SUB-TOTAL	(3.0)	84
COST TO SERVE		
• Integrated supply chain and channel management	2.5	–
• Consolidated logistics management	6.0	–
TOTAL	5.5	84

Figure 45.10   Estimated supply chain savings of Case 2

In addition, by minimizing the interface requirements at the front end of the chain the indirect infrastructure could be reduced, thereby favourably impacting the overall costs-to-serve. The detailed analyses of the cost-to-serve, as discussed above, had indicated high transaction costs, producing high levels of indirect support staff. Transactions need to be processed and in both the administrative and physical movement arenas this, by necessity, requires people. The combination of the high volume of small transactions and the highly functional approach to the management of the front end of the supply chain produces an ideal breeding ground for excessive indirect costs.

Experience has dictated that indirect costs accrue more readily at functional boundaries than in the execution of the function itself. People spend both more time and more transactions communicating with other functions than communicating within their own function. This was a typical case in point, and the simplification of the structure of the front end of the supply chain had more impact on the ability to reduce indirect cost than could have been achieved in any other way.

The ability to consolidate the logistics function from assembly right through to the customer interface offered incredible leverage on the ability to reduce the costs-to-serve. As can be seen in Figure 45.10, these amounted to an excess of $8m, and while some investment was needed to strengthen the direct management function of managing both finished and semi-finished inventories net savings were still in excess of $5m. Also while the reductions in the costs-to-serve were in themselves highly significant, the reduction in assets was even more fundamental. Conservative estimates were in the region of $80m to $90m, and the aggressive scenarios admitted to the possibility of almost halving the original $250m investment.

As in the first case, these savings, particularly given their structural nature, could not have been achieved with traditional methods. It was the cost-to-serve approach that made them possible.

WHEN THE TOTAL COST-TO-SERVE APPROACH SHOULD BE USED

1 When the company makes a significant change in its business strategy (for example, going direct versus selling to wholesalers)
2 When the size of the company changes significantly
3 When new businesses or products are added to the distribution system
4 When the mix or volume of orders and order lines changes significantly
5 When the company's geographic mix of shipments changes appreciably
6 When one or more of the main elements of cost changes significantly (for example, transportation costs or inventory holding costs)
7 When five or ten years have passed since the last evaluation
8 When any of four symptoms appear, as follows:
   • inventories high or out of balance
   • poor customer service
   • unscheduled interwarehouse shipments
   • premium freight charges.

FURTHER READING

The total cost-to-serve approach is a specialized technique: the following books offer general reading in distribution and logistics.

Christopher, Martin, *The Strategy of Distribution Management*, Gower, Aldershot, 1985
Gattorna, John L., (ed.), *The Gower Handbook of Logistics and Distribution Management*, 4th edn, Gower, Aldershot, 1990
Lewis, Robert L., *Information Technology in Physical Distribution Management*, Gower, Aldershot, 1986

ACKNOWLEDGMENT

The case study illustration material used in this chapter was provided by Booz Allen & Hamilton.

46 Warehouse operation management

Ken Firth

It cannot be said that warehousing has been a source of great inspiration to many who are in senior management positions in the UK. Too often the designing, building, running and controlling of warehousing systems have been left to individuals who have been passed over in their original speciality, or to those who are approaching retirement and have been given a supposedly less demanding job to do. Such lack of enthusiasm is unfortunate because standards of warehouse efficiency can have far-reaching effects upon customer relationships. A succession of missed delivery dates or failure to deliver a complete order influence a customer's thinking far more than the helpfulness of the salesman who originally obtained the order. Yet warehousing, as one of the least glamorous aspects of business systems, is often starved of resources in both physical and human terms.

Effective warehousing depends, like every other aspect of management, upon a clear understanding of what the system is expected to provide, a carefully outlined plan, and, above all, continuously supervised implementation with great attention to detail. The rewards can be considerable to small and large organizations alike, for although small systems cannot take advantage of economies of scale they often have a considerable edge in their ability to give personal service through effective managerial control.

MODERN WAREHOUSING

The seeds of modern warehousing operations were planted more than a hundred years ago with the arrival of crude but effective pallet handling equipment. Such equipment enabled human beings to move modular loads around manufacturing systems which would otherwise have been difficult to handle. It was not until the advent of a machine which could lift modular loads one above the other as well as undertaking horizontal movement – in the form of the early fork-lift truck – that the revolution in warehousing methods took place. This started in the 1930s and accelerated very rapidly during the Second World War when the United States Army recognized that such machinery could revolutionize their approach to logistics. The result was that warehouses ceased to be multi-storey affairs convenient to manhandling, and modern wide-span steel or concrete portal frame building predominated. Since that time there has been unremitting design effort to improve the lifting height capacity of fork-lift trucks and at the same time reduce operating aisle widths. The objective is to take maximum advantage of building cube in storage areas in the knowledge that building costs per cubic metre provided are substantially reduced between the heights of 6 to 15 metres for steel portal frame construction, thereby reducing the total systems cost. The term 'total systems cost' is important because in the context of the firm it is that cost which must be minimized – there are many circumstances where it is justifiable to increase warehousing operating costs *provided that greater savings are made elsewhere.*

The basis of modern warehousing is the principle of load unitization, combined with the remaining principles of materials handling which are:

1 Utilization of cube
2 Minimization of movement
3 Flow effectiveness
4 Safety and security
5 Communication and control,

all at lowest total systems cost.

LOAD UNITIZATION

Although load unitization is commonly associated with pallets and fork-lift trucks, there are many other forms of unit-load, large and small, which have an important place in warehousing and should not be overlooked – tote pans for small components is a typical example.

The underlying concept of load unitization is the combining of like products together on some regularly dimensioned load board or in a container, so that they may be more easily handled by man or machine. Simple though this idea is, it is only too easy to make mistakes either through not recognizing the problem involved or not being sufficiently stringent in applying the standards laid down.

Two main aspects have to be considered: on the one hand, the physical characteristics of the product including its protective packaging; and on the other, the most suitable kind of load board or container for the job in hand. When stacking products upon flat timber pallets it is preferable to have rectilinear packages or cases which are modular to the pallet dimension (to avoid loss of utilization) and at the same time ensure that the packages will 'brick' together in layers (See Figure 46.1), thereby ensuring good load stability. A package which is a perfect cube is undesirable because it cannot be bonded to its partners except by the use of strapping, stretch wrapping or other devices. Packages which overhang pallets are to be avoided because they offer scope for damage.

In building up suitable pallet patterns it is usual to construct the largest feasible load because, by so doing, movement is reduced. The achieving of this objective is conditioned by many constraints, typical of which are the overturning moment of the load, crush loading of packages, the height available within the warehouse, the lifting heights of the fork-lift trucks available, and by the type of vehicle on which the pallet might be transported.

Arriving at the best answer is often a matter of compromise but where overturning or lack of stability is the problem there are a variety of devices, such as layer interleaving, strapping, stretch or shrink wrapping which help to overcome the difficulty. In cases where pallets and loads need to be stacked simply one on top of

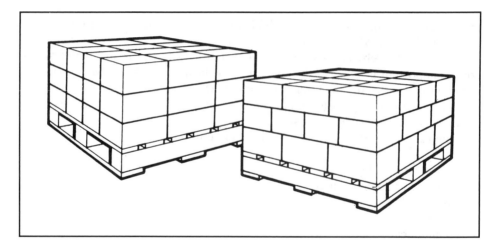

Figure 46.1   Cartons stacked on pallets. Here are two ways of stacking cartons on pallets. The wrong way (left-hand pallet) allows each pile of cartons to sway and topple. The right way prevents this, because the cartons are arranged in an interlocking pattern

another, it is essential to perform stacking tests over a period of weeks to be certain that progressive stack collapse will not take place. Such factors as poor carton design or high humidity may well cause stacking problems which cannot immediately be detected.

Once a unit load has been properly formulated and agreed it should be recorded – if necessary the pallet stacking pattern can be printed on the outer package so that anyone not familiar with the correct procedure can ensure uniformity.

In specifying a pallet board or other form of container it is fundamental to obtain a piece of equipment which will provide least cost over its *total life cycle*. The lowest available price is no criterion if the pallet has not been adequately designed and tested to carry its specified load, has poor resistance to damage and is difficult to repair. The attempts to achieve the ideal pallet have caused more contention than any other aspect of materials handling and a great lack of standardization prevails. However, the International Standards Organization (ISO) supported by the British Standards Institution (BSI) and other organizations have slowly approached the problem of standardization of through-transit pallets and dimensional and testing standards for the following sizes exist:

- 1 200 mm × 800 mm (Europal)
- 1 200 mm × 1 000 mm (Grocery pallet)
- 1 200 mm × 1 200 mm (Oil drum pallet)
- 1 200 mm × 1 800 mm (Paper and furniture pallet)

(BS 2629 Parts I, II and III.)

The 1 200 mm dimension is ideal for loading on to the side of flat vehicles in the UK, but less than convenient in box vehicles and ISO containers. A pallet size of 1 100 mm × 1 100 mm strongly advocated by the Japanese which fits perfectly into ISO containers has not been approved by ISO because it is not modular to 600 mm × 400 mm × 400 mm which is a specified ISO unit dimension.

Although there have been many attempts to depose timber as the most used material for the construction of pallets, no adequate substitute has emerged. In the manufacturing engineering industry and the motor car industry there has been widespread use of metal cage and box pallets because of their longevity under the arduous conditions in which they have to work and because of their ability to handle awkward shapes. Many experiments have been made with plastic pallets but their cost, which has escalated since the oil crisis, tends to restrict their use to applications where hygiene is a paramount consideration. The most used pallet in the UK is the 1 200 mm × 1 000 mm 4-way entry perimeter-based pallet built to BSI specification 2629. A typical life of a wooden pallet in the UK is said to be three to five years, but whether this is entirely due to fair wear and tear is a matter of some doubt. In recent years the company GKN/Chep has introduced a pallet pool exchange system which is worthy of consideration, particularly in the case of companies which have large pallet populations which have to be transported over great distances and where collection of empty pallets and their return is a costly and haphazard operation.

Loaded pallets should not normally be stacked one on top of another to a height greater than six times the minimum base dimension of the pallet and only then when the condition of the pallet and its environment have been carefully checked. For example, uneven floors can create stacking difficulties and lightly loaded pallets stacked outside can be affected by high winds. In adverse conditions the height of stack should be reduced to four times the minimum base dimension or less. There can, of course, be exceptions to such rules, but any change should be agreed with the appropriate safety representatives.

The care given to unit-load design must never be relaxed and what is certain is that as handling and storage sophistication increases, so must the attention to design. There are endless examples of mechanized equipment being damaged or rendered useless through permitting off-dimension or damaged pallets into the system.

Thus the establishment of the unit-load is the first step towards efficient warehouse operation and from this follows good use of the cube, minimization of movement, creating effective flow, all in keeping with high standards of safety and security at lowest total systems cost.

UTILIZATION OF THE WAREHOUSE CUBE

The price of new warehousing can vary quite considerably due to a variety of factors, such as location, degree of refinement of the facilities, negotiating variations and the economic circumstances prevailing. In mid-1989 a figure between £250 and £350 per square metre would not be regarded as unusual for a warehouse building complete with a limited amount of office space and services to an acceptable standard. At such prices it is commonplace to discover that the building and building services can account for as much as 40 per cent of the operating cost of the warehouse. Support for the conservation of warehouse space has long been given by UK fork-lift truck manufacturers who have always been at the forefront in the design of narrow aisle height lift trucks. Very narrow aisle equipment which will lift 1.5 tonne loads at heights of 12 metres is readily available for use in gangways only 1.5 metres wide. While reducing gangway widths is an

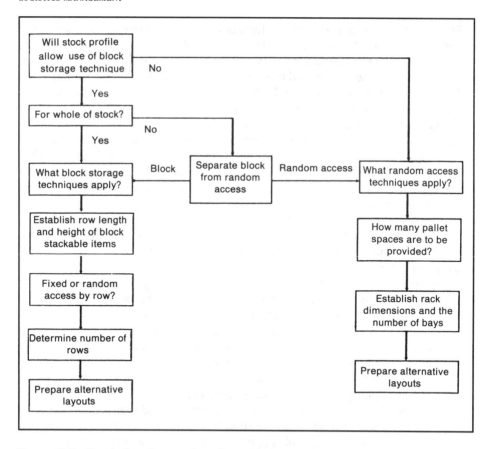

Figure 46.2   Simple flow diagram for palletized bulk storage design

obvious approach to the reduction of space costs, increased lift height is less so. Although increased lift height means more expensive equipment, which is also more expensive to maintain, the disadvantage is offset by the fact that as single-storey warehouses increase in height up to about 15 metres, their costs per cubic metre reduce because most of the cost is in the roof and floor. This fact can produce a favourable trade-off of building cost against equipment costs.

The efficient storage of palletized loads demands a careful analysis of the stockholding profile within the warehouse. That is to say, stockholding data must be collected for each product stored and the products then ranked in order of quantity of pallets held. A ranking of products in order of throughput quantities should also be prepared. Although the determination of the method of storage is primarily dependent upon the quantities by stocks held, throughput must be taken into account when considering what handling equipment is most suitable. Once the stockholding analysis has been completed it is useful to make use of the simple flow diagram (see Figure 46.2) to produce a list of alternatives which require consideration. It is important to remember when using the diagram that while all pallet profiles can be randomly stored by individual pallet, they are not all readily block stackable. The objective of using the flow chart is to eliminate looking at unnecessary alternatives.

Pallet block storage

The concept behind palletized block storage is that of stacking pallets one above the other and in rows of suitable depth. The rows of pallet stacks (identical product within each row) are assembled side by side to form a three-dimensional matrix. The operation of this simple idea can become very complicated in execution due to various constraints which can be placed upon the system, and the warehouse manager may find that because of such constraints his warehouse is badly utilized, so that only 60 per cent of the pallet spaces provided can actually be occupied by physical stock. This may be brought about by one or more of the following ways:

1 Insufficient stock per line item to form significant blocks of storage which leads to 'honeycombing' and loss of cube
2 The use of a fixed location system for products when there is a significant variation between maximum and minimum stocks. This problem may be solved by arranging rows of product randomly within the warehouse at the expense of a control system
3 Incorrect row length. At first glance, the longer the row length the better the relationship between stack and gangways. Space utilization is, however, a function of stock quantity and time occupancy which the following simple calculation illustrates:

> Twelve stacks of pallets are received into stock and the stockholding time is estimated at 24 days. The options on row length vary between 1 row of 12 stacks and 12 rows of 1 stack, but each row has the same area of gangway allocated to it.
> For example, if we say that a stack occupies 2 m² and the gangway allocation per row is 3 m² the area required for a single 12 stack row will be 27 m². Moreover, the area will be unavailable for re-use until the last pallet is withdrawn after the 24th day has elapsed (unless double handling or poor stock rotation is accepted). The 'cost' incurred amounts to 24×27 m² $= 648$ m² days. A 2-row approach will mean that half the original space occupied will be free for use after 12 days and the space cost incurred will be only 540 m² days – a significant saving. The calculation for all the variants is as follows:
>
> | | |
> |---|---|
> | 1 row | 648 m² days |
> | 2 rows | 540 m² days |
> | 3 rows | 528 m² days |
> | 4 rows | 540 m² days |
> | 6 rows | 588 m² days |
> | 12 rows | 780 m² days |
>
> In this instance a row length of 4 pallets is the most suitable choice.

It is possible to conceive that this approach to row length can be considerably refined to optimize warehouse block storage layouts
4 Limitations upon stacking height. With simple block stacking (that is, pallets simply supported one on top of each other) the problem is usually that of overturning or crush-loading. This may be prevented by the use of 'drive-in' racking which has all the attributes of block storage while separating pallets vertically (see Figure 46.3)
5 First in, first out rotation of stock can be a problem with simple and drive-in block storage systems – the best situation usually achievable is rotation by

Figure 46.3   Drive-in racking

row. When stock is fast moving this does not present a significant problem, but where it is, the options of pallet live storage, or powered mobile storage, offer a solution. Although in both cases the storage equipment cost is high, it usually represents a very small proportion of the total warehouse cost and there are many instances where the higher space utilization provided by more sophisticated systems has resulted in a favourable trade-off against building costs

6   Recent years have seen the introduction and acceptance of 'double-deep' systems. The principle is to arrange two double-sided pallet racks back to back and access two pallets deep using a telescopic forked straddle truck or a pantograph forked straddle truck. This method is ideal for stock profiles which, whilst not permitting a true block stack configuration, have sufficient pallets per line item to allow two-deep storage. The question of loss of stock rotation must be taken into account

7   The orientation of block storage in relation to building dimension and the choice of direction of entry of forks into a four-way entry pallet can materially affect the number of pallet spaces available to the system and also the distances travelled by handling equipment. Care has to be taken that the advantage of increased storage does not interfere with flow or impede managerial control.

Palletized random access storage

Virtually every form of palletized random access storage is associated with a racking system and this means, almost by definition, some form of adjustable pallet racking. A random access system, as its names implies, enables individual access to every pallet, the disadvantage being that a record of what is held in each location has to be kept, on a 'first in, first out' basis by product, and this can be prone to error. The other significant advantage of adjustable pallet racking is that it enables the utilization of headroom in a building to levels beyond what is generally acceptable for simple block storage systems (provided the building headroom is available), but when used in conjunction with counterbalance or even reach fork-lift trucks can be wasteful of space due to the relatively poor aisle space to rack occupancy relationships. This disadvantage can be largely offset by the fact that the pallet space utilization factor can be as high as 95 per cent and, when this factor is coupled with a very narrow aisle system at heights above 6 metres, can result in cube utilizations considerably superior to most block storage systems. The significant exception is powered mobile storage which combines the attributes of both block and random access and can result in total cube utilization factors in excess of 45 per cent.

The simplest way of overcoming the problem of error in placement and removal of stock is to operate a ticket system which indicates the co-ordinates of the pallet position but at the same time incorporates a random check digit which the operator has to record in placement or retrieval. If a mistake occurs this can be rapidly checked by the pallet location control clerk and the fault rectified before too much time has elapsed. Recent stock location recording systems use two-way radio between host computer and on-board truck terminals, together with bar code validation checks. The advantages of such systems are improved productivity of fork-lift truck drivers, greater accuracy and control, and faster system response to interrogation.

Damage to racking and products caused by fork-lift trucks for whatever reason is a cause of concern. The problem can be alleviated by proper training of fork-lift drivers and what is probably more important by adequate supervision once the training has been completed. It is wise to ensure that racks conform to an approved standard – that of the Storage Equipment Manufacturers Association is appropriate to the UK – and equally important that the racks are competently constructed and fixed to the floor. In the event of damage the section of the rack affected should be unloaded and remain so until the faulty component has been replaced. Efforts to straighten thin section members once distorted should be avoided.

High-bay pallet silos

The high-bay pallet silo (see Figure 46.4) serviced by automatic storage and retrieval machines (stacker cranes), although by no means a new concept, is arousing increased interest for storage and warehousing throughout the world. The reasons for this surge of interest are many but a common one is the economy of not having to move storage off an existing site as more and more companies become locked into urban sprawl with limited expansion potential. In addition, computing and control expertise has developed rapidly over the past ten years, in the area of both data and power transmission, which has greatly increased availability potential of such installations. It must be admitted that the cost justification in straightforward accounting terms can be difficult, but it is becoming increasingly apparent that this kind of equipment can offer tremendous advantage in terms of speed and accuracy of operation, which in turn makes levels of service available previously unachievable with manually operated systems.

MINIMIZING MOVEMENT

Movement, like warehouse space, is a costly resource whether it be attributable to man or machine. While there are many techniques available to reduce movement time, both in a system and an equipment sense, all can be rendered virtually uselesss if adequate standards are not imposed. A guaranteed way of ensuring continuing poor performance is to overman when setting up a new warehouse – this may be due to the absence of standards or over-anxiety by management in their desire to have a smooth start. Another failing on start-up is to do so without adequate commissioning of equipment or sufficient staff training. Warehouse planning should ensure that a start-up happens slowly and, for preference, at a quiet time of the year. Synthetic time study data for a variety of materials handling tasks is available which can be used until properly measured work standards can be applied.

Order selection tends to be the function of warehousing which is the most intensive user of labour per unit of throughput, although in some applications where load modularization and quality control is extensive goods receiving comes a close second.

An order-picking system (see Figure 46.5) should be organized in such a

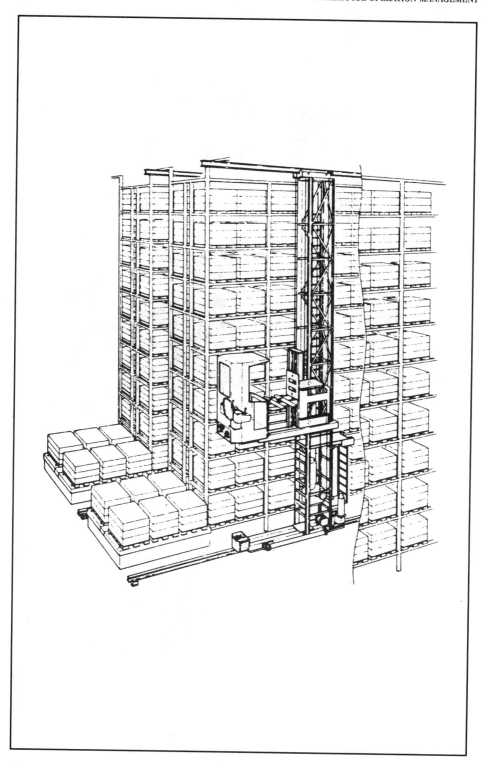

Figure 46.4   High-bay warehouse

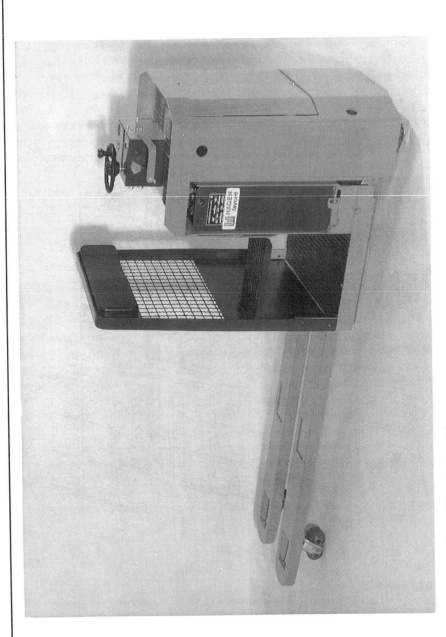

Figure 46.5 Second level order-picker

manner that a fully representative range of stock is presented in the smallest possible area conducive with safe operation, so that orders may be selected accurately at the service level demanded, avoiding unnecessary stockouts and without excessive movement from reserve to forward location. Because many of these requirements are not complementary to one another, the process is essentially one of compromise making use of the minimization techniques appropriate to the stock and throughput profiles of the picking systems under study. The techniques available are:

Functional separation

Consider whether to keep order picking and reserve storage in separate parts of the warehouse or physically integrate the two. In simple terms the answer depends on the ratio of stock held in reserve to that required in order picking. If the difference is large there is scope for holding the reserve in a specialized stockholding area making use of a space efficient storage system, such as high-rack stacking or drive-in storage. Where there is a closer relationship, say, 3 to 1 or less, it may be more sensible to hold reserve pallets in racking immediately above the order-picking pallets (see Figure 46.6). Where reserve is a very small proportion, it may be feasible to pick from multi-level locations.

Popularity

An analysis of movement within an order-picking store usually demonstrates that 80 per cent of the visits to collect product are made to only 20 per cent of locations. Knowledge relating to these products makes it theoretically possible to arrange them in a layout which minimizes the movement of the order pickers. However, there are many factors which can render the concept infeasible (for example, congestion, seasonal changes, promotions and cataloguing difficulties) which suggest that caution should be exercised in implementing the idea. Popularity is probably of greater significance when related to a fixed-location palletized bulk loading operation or when the popularity of products can be accurately monitored by computer, provided that in the latter case the stores movement involved does not result in congestion.

Batching orders

In instances where there is a large range of products covering a wide area and the average quantity picked per order is small, it is often feasible to group orders together to be picked upon a single circuit of the order-picking area. Inevitably, some sorting must be carried out either on circuit or at the end of the pick and the justification is that the cost of sorting is less than the cost of the time saved by reduction of movement around the system. The objective should be to maximize an order-picker's carrying capacity for a given picking circuit within the limits of the capability of his handling equipment. This means that if on average single orders satisfy this requirement a batching system is usually unnecessary. There are occasions where a batch pick of a day's work is brought to a forward area and sorted, the advantage being that this serves as an automatic checking device provided that balancing errors in sorting have not occurred.

Figure 46.6   Base location order-picking system

Zoning

Some large warehousing systems, notably mail order, find it advantageous to divide their systems departmentally according to merchandise or by size and throughput of product. The procedure is to route orders only to the departments concerned with the specific items required on an order and bypass the rest. Order pickers are allocated to each department or zone and only pick in that restricted area, passing the order and goods to the next department featured on the picking list, until the full order has been picked. This not only reduces pedestrian movement but permits specialization.

Randomization of order-picking locations

By far the majority of order-picking systems in the UK are based upon fixed-location systems which allow the order picker to learn, relatively quickly and easily, the location of any product. Some wide-ranging systems with constant obsolescence and introduction of lines find it impossible to cope with fixed location because when a bin has been vacated by an obsolete product, it has to be replaced by another. This automatically randomizes the locations, but does keep the picking face within reasonable dimensions. A consequence is that the location is first identified by its coordinates and secondly by its contents. Control of such systems has to be comprehensive because a product once lost is hard to find; additionally the administrative complexity is so great that computer control is almost mandatory.

Goods-to-picker techniques

It is not unknown for an order picker to have to walk more than ten miles a day to complete his or her work, which clearly may take up more than 50 per cent of the time available. Provide a system where the goods can be brought to the picker and that time is available to carry out a lot more picking (see Figure 46.7). With a few exceptions, the endeavours to achieve such savings in a case-picking environment have met with little success – the costs, under UK conditions, have been greater than using conventional techniques. On the other hand, the potential for using goods-to-picker techniques on small components applications appears considerable because these are often associated with high range and relatively small volumes and weights per line item. The control complexity required to implement an effective system should not be underestimated.

It is important to remember that while one or more of the above techniques may be used to reduce movement in an order-picking system, their applicability can only be determined through a full understanding of the system's requirements.

COMMUNICATION AND CONTROL

It has long been recognized that reductions in movement and improved productivity can be achieved by simplifying warehouse paperwork systems. In fact, the greatest improvements in recent years have been in this area, largely through the increased use of computing. There are many variations in approach but the net

Figure 46.7 Horizontal carousel order-picking machine

effect has been to provide management with immediate and accurate information and a greater ability to control their workforce.

Not only are computers used for order processing, vehicle routing and scheduling, inventory control, and so on, but we are beginning to see the emergence of near 'paperless' systems. These give instructions to order pickers through light systems and LED displays, the only paper involved being the printing of despatch notes at the packing station.

Bar coding is also being used increasingly in warehouses for a variety of purposes such as stock location, stock recording and for routing and counting in conjunction with mechanized sorting systems.

RECEIVING AND DISPATCH

A surprising number of relatively well-planned warehousing operations have been let down to some extent by the inadequacy of their load/unload facilities. One possible reason is that the work involved, particularly in the receiving area, is dependent upon external factors which can be difficult to control. Much more attention is being paid to how products are being delivered into the warehousing system, how well they are modularized, whether the quantities delivered relate accurately to the order quantity, whether the delivery is on time, early or late, and how easy is a consignment to identify. Lack of attention to these and many other factors has caused delays, congested loading docks and made unnecessary work, but above all inadequate communication has contributed to the confusion. More and more VDU terminals are being located directly at the receiving point. Their ability to identify rapidly whether a consignment is required, to state what level of quality control should be applied and to show where the product is to be located, contributes greatly to the smooth and accurate flow of product.

The other critical factors are what areas should be allocated to the function, how many loading bays are required, whether the loading bays should have raised docks or be at floor level, and whether the loading and unloading areas should share common facilities or be separated. Their determination is by analysis of the products and their load unitization, the quantities throughput per unit of time, the kinds of transport entering and leaving the systems, and other criteria such as the value of the product together with safety and environmental requirements. The increasing costs of transportation are forcing some companies to consider more carefully ways of turning around vehicles to maximize productivity – nowhere more so than in Japan, where much attention is being paid to the mass-loading of different types of road vehicle.

CONCLUSION

Much remains to be done to improve standards of warehouse operation and management but evidence exists that over the past ten years the business world has become increasingly aware of the importance of the subject and how its costs need to be controlled. This may be seen by looking at the organizational and managerial changes which have been taking place in specific companies and recognition that formalized training in the skills of distribution are a necessity. Slowly, universities and other educational establishments are beginning to introduce courses which will enable future warehouse managers to establish status which equates with that of more fashionable disciplines. Perhaps by the year 2 000 a new professional class will be fully established.

FURTHER READING

Burton, J. A., *Effective Warehousing*, 2nd edn, Macdonald & Evans, Plymouth, 1979

Gattorna, J. (ed.), *The Gower Handbook of Logistics and Distribution Management*, 4th edn, Gower, Aldershot, 1990

ACKNOWLEDGEMENT

Photographs kindly supplied by:
Apex Storage Systems Limited
Dexion Limited
Lansing Linde Limited

47 International trade

Dennis Lock

Any company wishing to exploit overseas markets may be deterred by the complexity of exporting procedures, shipping arrangements and the possibility of increased financial risk. This chapter explains some of the practices, formalities and procedures involved.

FREIGHT FORWARDING AGENTS

The use of a good freight forwarding agent will be found invaluable to any company sending goods overseas by any mode of transport. Indeed, the agent can usually advise on the most appropriate method of transport to adopt in any individual case.

In addition to wide experience of transport routes, the forwarder can help or deal with much of the documentation. Through his network of overseas offices and agents he is able to keep track of consignments world-wide and take steps to prevent or reduce delays at loading, unloading and customs points. Boakes (1989) states that a good freight forwarder should:

1 Have a good knowledge of your markets and all the transport, documentation, customs and banking requirements
2 Be well represented in the market
3 Be familiar with the requirements of your products, especially if they include dangerous goods or need specialized handling
4 Have the time and interest to help and advise you
5 Be financially sound, with good liability cover and, preferably, be a member of the British International Freight Association (which lays down strict professional standards).

One important aspect of a forwarding agent's services is found when relatively small consignments are to be made. The agent is often able to achieve economy of scale by consolidating several small loads from different clients into one bulk consignment, big enough to fill a container or truck.

TERMS OF TRADE USED IN INTERNATIONAL BUSINESS (INCOTERMS)

The manager new to exporting must become aware of the terms commonly used in quotations, purchase orders and other contract documents to define the seller's responsibilities concerning delivery of the goods to the customer. They are, of course, of equal relevance to importers and the responsibilities of buyers. These 'Incoterms' have been developed and standardized by the International Chamber of Commerce (ICC). A revised set of Incoterms was introduced in March 1990. The following account summarizes these terms, but for a fuller and more precise explanation the reader is strongly advised to obtain a copy of *INCOTERMS 1990* (see ICC, 1990).

The ICC has arranged these terms into groups *E*, *F*, *C*, and *D*, which are ranged in ascending order of the degree of responsibility undertaken by the seller. Each term is used on all documents in the form of a standardized three-letter abbreviation.

Group E Incoterm

This 'group' includes just one Incoterm, and is concerned with consignments where the seller has minimum obligation.

EXW signifies 'ex works'. This means that the seller fulfils his obligation to deliver when he has made the goods available at his premises to the buyer. He is not responsible for loading the goods on the vehicle provided by the buyer or for clearing the goods for export, unless otherwise agreed. The buyer bears all costs and risks involved in taking the goods from the seller's premises to the desired destination. This term should not be used when the buyer cannot carry out directly or indirectly the export formalities. In such circumstances, the FCA term should be used.

Group F Incoterms

In this group, the seller is called upon to deliver the goods to a carrier appointed by the buyer.

FCA is 'free carrier' (named place). The seller fulfils his obligation when he has handed over the goods, cleared for export, into the charge of the carrier named by the buyer at the named place or point. The term may be used for any mode of transport, including multimodal transport.

FAS is 'free alongside ship' (named port of shipment). The seller fulfils his obligation to deliver when the goods have been placed alongside the vessel on the quay or in lighters at the named port. The buyer has to bear all costs and risks of loss or damage to the goods from that moment. The buyer must clear the goods for export. This term can only be used for sea or inland waterway transport.

FOB is 'free on board' (named port of shipment). The seller fulfils his obligation when the goods have passed over the ship's rail at the named port. The buyer has to bear all costs and risks of loss or damage from that point. The seller has to clear the goods for export. The FOB term can only be used for sea or inland waterway transport. When the ship's rail serves no practical purpose, such as in the case of roll-on/roll-off or container traffic, the FCA term is more appropriate to use.

Group C Incoterms

This group of Incoterms includes cases where the seller has agreed to contract for carriage, but without assuming the risk of loss or damage to the goods, or additional costs due to events occurring after shipment and dispatch.

CFR is 'cost and freight' (named port of destination). The seller must pay the costs and freight necessary to bring the goods to the named port of destination but the risk of loss or damage to the goods, as well as any additional costs due to events occurring after the time the goods have been delivered on board the vessel, is transferred from the seller to the buyer when the goods pass the ship's rail in the port of shipment. The CFR term requires the seller to clear the goods for export. This term can only be used for sea and inland waterway transport. When the ship's rail serves no practical purpose, such as in the case of roll-on/roll-off or container traffic, the CPT term is more appropriate to use.

CIF means 'cost, insurance and freight' (named port of destination). The seller has the same obligations as under CFR but also has to procure marine insurance against the buyer's risk of loss or damage to the goods during the carriage. The seller contracts for insurance and pays the premium. Under this term the seller is only required to obtain insurance on minimum coverage. CIF can only be used for sea and inland waterway transport. When the ship's rail serves no practical purpose, such as in the case of roll-on/roll-off or container traffic, the CIP term is more appropriate to use.

CPT is 'carriage paid to' (named port of destination). The risk of loss or damage to the goods, as well as any additional costs due to events occurring after the time the goods have been delivered to the carrier, is transferred from the seller to the buyer when the goods have been delivered into the custody of the carrier (the first carrier if a succession of carriers is involved). The seller must clear the goods for export. CPT may be used for any mode of transport, including multimodal transport.

CIP means 'carriage and insurance paid to' (named place of destination). The seller has the same obligations as under CPT but with the addition that the seller has to procure cargo insurance against the buyer's risk of loss or damage to the goods during the carriage. The seller contracts for insurance and pays the premium, but is only required to obtain insurance on minimum coverage. The seller must clear the goods for export. The CIP term may be used for any mode of transport including multimodal transport.

Group D Incoterms

Group D Incoterms cover cases where the seller has to bear all costs and risks needed to bring the goods to the country of destination.

DAF, 'delivered at frontier' (named place) means that the seller fulfils his obligation to deliver when the goods have been made available, cleared for export, at the named point and place at the frontier, but before the customs border of the adjoining country. The term 'frontier' may be used for any frontier, including that of the country of export. Therefore, it is of vital importance that the frontier in question be defined precisely by always naming the point and place in the DAF term. The term is primarily intended for use when goods are to be carried by rail or road, but it may be used for any mode of transport.

DES is 'delivered ex ship' (named port of destination). The seller fulfils his obligation to deliver when the goods have been made available to the buyer on board the ship uncleared for import at the named port of destination. The seller has to bear all the costs and risks involved in bringing the goods to the named port of destination. This term can only be used for sea or inland waterway transport.

DEQ stands for 'delivery ex quay, duty paid' (named port of destination). The seller must make the goods available to the buyer on the quay (wharf) at the named port of destination, cleared for importation. The seller has to bear all risks and costs, including duties, taxes and other charges of delivering the goods thereto. This term should not be used if the seller is unable directly or indirectly to obtain the import licence. If the parties wish the buyer to clear the goods for importation and pay the duty the words 'duty unpaid' should be used instead of 'duty paid'. If the parties wish to exclude from the seller's obligations some of the costs payable upon importation of the goods (such as VAT), this should be made clear by adding words to this effect: 'Delivered ex quay, VAT unpaid (named port of destination)'. The term DEQ can only be used for sea or inland waterway transport.

DDU is 'delivered duty unpaid' (named place of destination). The seller's obligations are fulfilled when the goods have been made available at the named place in the country of importation. The seller has to bear the costs and risks involved in bringing the goods thereto (excluding duties, taxes and other official charges payable upon importation as well as the costs and risks of carrying out customs formalities). The buyer has to pay any additional costs and bear any risks caused by his failure to clear the goods for import in time. If the parties wish to include in the seller's obligations some of the costs payable upon importation of the goods (such as VAT), this should be made clear by adding words to this effect: 'Delivered duty unpaid, VAT paid, (named place of destination)'. The term DDU may be used irrespective of the mode of transport.

DDP is 'delivery duty paid' (named place of destination). The seller fulfils his obligation when the goods have been made available at the named place in the country of importation. The seller has to bear the risks and costs, including duties, taxes and other charges of delivering the goods thereto, cleared for importation. This term should not be used if the seller is unable directly or indirectly to obtain the import licence. If the parties wish the buyer to clear the goods for importation and to pay the duty, the term DDU should be used. If the parties wish to exclude from the seller's obligations some of the costs payable upon importation of the goods (such as VAT), this should be made clear by adding words to this effect: 'Delivered duty paid, VAT unpaid (named place of destination)'. The DDP term may be used irrespective of the mode of transport.

DUTY

Duty is the money payable by a consignee to the appropriate authorities before he can take receipt of goods imported or released from bond. Types of duty as far as the UK is concerned are:

1 Customs duty
2 Excise duty.

Customs duty

Customs duty is money payable by a consignee or his agent to the customs authorities of the importing country for according to its current tariff. *Ad valorem* duty is expressed in the customs tariff as a percentage of the CIF value of the goods (invoice value plus freight, insurance and any other dutiable charges). *Specific duty* is levied according to the quantity of goods (as opposed to their value) and will be expressed in the customs tariff at a rate per stated unit of measurement.

Payment of customs duty

Duty can be paid immediately by cash, guaranteed cheque or banker's draft.

Importers or their agents are allowed to defer payment of certain customs duty and other charges for a 30-day period subject to the lodgement of adequate security (usually a guarantee from the consignee's bank that the money will be available when called for by direct debit). Sums payable in respect of underpayment on previous imports cannot be deferred.

Duty-free goods

Customs duty is not normally payable on goods brought into the UK from other EC countries.

No duty is payable on goods imported into the UK from other countries if the goods are listed as 'free' in the customs tariff.

Duty may have to be paid on deposit to obtain the release of duty-free goods if their import is not supported by correct documentation.

Excise duty

Excise duty is a UK tax on certain imported goods, including spirits, wines, beers, tobacco, hydrocarbon oils and cigarette lighters.

Payment of excise duty

The amount of excise duty payable is shown in the customs tariff. The required amount is payable to customs by the consignee or his agent before the affected goods can be released from customs control. Payment can be made by cash, guaranteed cheque or by banker's draft.

Excise duty may be deferred, as described above for customs duty.

Importers can maintain a gross payment account with customs, with funds deposited in order to anticipate excise duty demands over a trading period. The consignee or his agent will top up the fund as necessary to replace amounts used as goods are withdrawn from stores. Each importer will maintain a separate gross payment account for each class of goods in which they deal (separate accounts for spirits, wines, beers and so on).

Goods subject to excise duty and customs duty

Goods on which excise duty is payable will generally also be subject to customs duty (duty is not normally payable on goods imported into the UK from other EC countries, when excise duty was payable).

Bonds

A bond is a cover, negotiated by a consignee or his agent with his bank or insurance company, to ensure that all sums due in respect of duty or penalties imposed will be paid by the bonder in the event of the consignee or his agent failing to meet customs demands or to comply with the regulations.

Removal bond

A bond required to cover the movement, from one place to another, of goods on which duty, customs and/or excise duty is liable and has not been paid. Such bonds can be individual for single movements or standing.

Transhipment bond

A bond required to cover the transfer of goods from an arrival port (sea or air) when such goods are subject to customs and/or excise duty. Such bonds are usually standing.

General bond

A bond which embraces both removal and transhipment, and acts as security for the payment of duty when goods subject to customs duty are moved, removed or held pending their use in manufacture.

(Penalty) bond

This is a bond in a sum laid down by customs and excise in respect of duty (customs and/or excise) payable in respect of goods stored under control, pending payment of such duty. This is the type of bond which covers the operation of a warehouse in which goods subject to excise duty are stored.

BONDED WAREHOUSES

Bonded warehouses are premises approved by the Commissioners of Customs and Excise for storage of goods without payment of duty. An authorized bonded warehouse can only be used for the storage of those goods for which it has been approved.

Types of bonded warehouse

There are four types of bonded warehouse:

1 *Customs warehouse*   For the deposit, without payment of duty, of imported goods which are liable to customs duty but which are not liable to excise duty
2 *Excise warehouse*   For the deposit, without payment of excise duty, of goods which are liable to excise duty. In this case the customs duty, if applicable, will have been paid
3 *Customs and excise warehouse*   For the deposit, without payment of customs or excise duty, of goods which are liable to both customs and excise duty
4 *Tobacco warehouse*   For the deposit, without payment of customs or excise duty, of tobacco and tobacco products liable to customs and excise duty.

Categories of bonded warehouse

There are two categories of bonded warehouse:

1 *Crown locked*   Controlled by the presence of a customs officer. The building is secured with Crown locks and the warehouse keeper's own locks, so that the warehouse keeper only has access to the goods under supervision of the customs officer
2 *Open warehouse*   In which the premises are not normally Crown locked and a customs officer is not constantly present. The warehouse keeper has unrestricted access to the goods during the hours of opening.

Classes of open warehouse

Open warehouses are described as class *A* or class *B* according to the following rules:

Class A warehouses

These warehouses are approved for beer, wines and spirits. In this class of open warehouse the goods must be kept within strictly defined and secure limits. Storage must be arranged so that consignments are easily identifiable, and to separate those goods liable only to excise duty from those which are liable to excise and customs duty. Such a warehouse will be the subject of a bond, the limits being set by HM Customs and Excise.

Class B warehouses

These warehouses are approved for goods other than beer, wines and spirits. The goods may be stored anywhere within the warehouse, subject to their being easily identifiable by a visiting customs officer. A bond is not normally required but the company is expected to maintain a duty deferment in a sum which is at least equal to the amount of duty payable on the goods stored. Class *B* open warehouses subdivide into two further kinds:

1 *General warehouse* Where the space is to be available to the general public on demand
2 *Franchise warehouse* For the storage of a manufacturer's own goods pending operation for re-export.

DOCUMENTATION

This section describes the main documents involved in international trade.

Bill of lading

A bill of lading is used when goods are transported by ship. It records the contract entered into between the shipper and exporter and, when sent to the buyer, acts as a document of title enabling him to claim the goods. An example is shown in Figure 47.1.

The principal information given on the form includes:

1 The bill of lading serial number
2 The name of the shipping company
3 The name of the ship
4 Port of loading
5 Port of unloading
6 The final destination
7 A description of the goods
8 The number of separate cases, with their weights, dimensions and markings
9 Name and address of the exporter
10 Name and address of the consignee, or the organization to be notified when the goods arrive (in the latter case the bill is made out to 'order')
11 A statement indicating whether or not freight charges have been prepaid, and where such charges are payable.

The document is usually prepared as an original plus one or more copies, the number of such copies (all called 'originals') being shown on each one. The exporter signs each original. The set customarily comprises two or three such originals, each of them signed by the ship's captain or his agent when the goods are loaded. The exporter is given all the originals, and these are known as the 'negotiable' copies, any one of which can prove title to the goods. One original, negotiable copy is sent to the buyer or his agent, by a route faster than the sea voyage, to enable him to clear the goods at the destination port. Other non-negotiable copies are prepared and kept for control and record purposes.

Air waybill

Goods sent by airfreight are consigned under cover of an air waybill (alternatively spelled airwaybill or airway bill). Air waybills do not have the same commercial significance as the bills of lading used for shipping, but they are used to control

BILL OF LADING FOR COMBINED TRANSPORT OR PORT TO PORT SHIPMENT   B/L No.

Shipper

Booking Ref.

Shipper's Ref.

LOX LINES

Lox Lines plc
100 City Street, St Albans, Herts, AL2 5ZZ
Telephone 0727 9999   Telex 8899888

Consignee

Notify Party/address It is agreed that no responsibility shall attach to the
Carrier or his Agent for failure to notify the Consig-
nee of the arrival of the goods (see Clause 20 on
the reverse)

Place of Receipt (Applicable only when this document is used as a
Combined Transport Bill of Lading)

Vessel and Voy. No.

Place of delivery (Applicable only when this document is used as a
Combined Transport Bill of Lading)

Port of loading

Port of discharge

Marks and Nos. Container Nos.	Number and kind of packages; description of goods	Gross Weight Kg	Measurement M^3

ABOVE PARTICULARS ARE AS DECLARED BY SHIPPER

†Total number of Containers/Packages

Movement

Freight and charges (please tick)	Prepayable	Collectable
Origin Inland Haulage Charge	☐	☐
Origin Terminal Handling/LCL Service Charge	☐	☐
Ocean Freight	☐	☐
Destination Terminal Handling/LCL Service Charge	☐	☐
Destination Inland Haulage Charge	☐	☐

Received by the Carrier from the Shipper in apparent good order
and condition (unless otherwise noted herein) the total number or
quantity of Containers or other packages or units indicated †,
stated by the Shipper to comprise the Goods specified above, for
Carriage subject to all terms hereof (INCLUDING THE TERMS ON
THE REVERSE HEREOF AND THE TERMS OF THE CARRIER'S
APPLICABLE TARIFF) from the Place of Receipt or the Port of
Loading, whichever is applicable. In accepting this Bill of Lading
the Merchant expressly accepts and agrees to all its terms, conditions and exceptions, whether printed, stamped or written, or
otherwise incorporated, notwithstanding the non-signing of this Bill
of Lading by the Merchant.

Number of original
Bills of Lading

Place and date of issue

IN WITNESS of the contract herein contained
the number of originals stated opposite have
been issued, one of which being accomplished, the other(s) to be void.

For the Carrier:

Copy—not negotiable

Figure 47.1   A bill of lading (reverse side not shown)

and progress the passage of goods and to identify the consignment through all its stages. In this context, the air waybill number is the vital reference. When a freight forwarding agent is used, he provides his own air waybill forms (known as house air waybills).

Commercial invoice

The commercial invoice is an invoice prepared on the exporter's usual invoice form, for despatch to the buyer as a claim for payment. However, additional copies will have to be supplied for use by the customs authorities at the exporting and importing ends of the journey. Requirements vary from one country to another, and some require additional information to be given, such as import licence number, the commission payable to local agents, details of freight and other charges, and so on.

Special requirements

Some countries add their own demands to the weight of paper needed. Such extra forms may include a *certificate of origin*, where the exporter declares the country of origin of the goods, and a *consular invoice*, which is a form of invoice dictated by (but not provided by) the government of the importing country. An example of a form which combines both of these documents is shown in Figure 47.2. The exporter usually has to obtain his own stock of such forms from a printer.

Certificate of insurance

Where the exporter arranges insurance, cover should be obtained for all stages and operations of the journey. The certificate, which must not be dated *after* the date of the bill of lading, air waybill or similar evidence of despatch, is sent to the buyer with the shipping documents.

Transport international routier

When a single consignment occupies a complete truck or container it may be possible to have the load sealed before export by customs officials. Provided that the seals are not subsequently broken, the load can then be expected to enjoy a smoother passage across frontiers where customs formalities have to be observed. The role of a freight forwarding agent is often useful in this context, since he is more likely to be able to accumulate several smaller consignments to produce a consolidated load big enough to fill the truck or container.

The document issued is known as a *transport international routier*, which abbreviates to the letters TIR. Details of the TIR system are available from any local office of HM Customs and Excise.

EC cross-border paperwork

The EC's stated aim from 1 January 1993 is to establish a frontier-free trading community. Most goods moving between member states will not be subject to

In accordance with Nigerian Government Notice 1969 of 1970.

FEDERATION of NIGERIA

Combined Certificate of Value and of Origin and Invoice of Goods for Exportation to Nigeria

C.16

CERTIFICATE OF VALUE

I, ...

of . . . .

*Manufacturers/Suppliers/Exporters of the goods enumerated in this invoice amounting to . . . .

hereby declare that I have the authority to make and sign this certificate on behalf of the aforesaid *Manufacturers/Suppliers/Exporters and that I have the means of knowing and I do hereby certify as follows :—

(1) That this invoice is in all respects correct and contains a true and full statement of the price actually paid or to be paid for the said goods, and the actual quantity thereof.

(2) That no different invoice of the goods mentioned in the said invoice has been or will be furnished to anyone.

(3) That no arrangement or understanding affecting the purchase price of the said goods has been or will be made or entered into between the said exporter and purchaser or by anyone on behalf of either of them either by way of discount, rebate, compensation or in any manner whatever other than as fully shown on this invoice.

CERTIFICATE OF ORIGIN

(1) That all the goods mentioned in this invoice have been wholly produced or manufactured in . . . .

. . . .

(2) That all the goods mentioned in this invoice have been either wholly or partially produced or manufactured in

. . . .

(3) That as regards those goods only partially produced or manufactured,

(a) the final process or processes of manufacture have been performed in . . . .

(b) the expenditure in material produced and/or labour performed in . . . . calculated subject to qualifications hereunder, in the case of all such goods is not less than 25 per cent of the factory or works costs of all such goods in their finished state   *See note below.

(4) That in the calculation of such proportion of material produced and/or labour performed none of the following items has been included or considered —

Manufacturer's profit, or remuneration of any trader, agent, broker or other person dealing in the goods in their finished condition; royalties; cost of outside packages, or any cost of packing the goods thereinto; any cost of conveying, insuring, or shipping the goods subsequent to their manufacture.

Dated at . . . . this . . . . day of . . . . 19 . . . .

(Signature). . . . . (Signature of Witness)

Note   (1) The person making the declaration should be the principal or a manager, chief clerk, secretary, or responsible employee.

(2) The place or country of origin of imports is that in which the goods were produced or manufactured and, in the case of partly manufactured goods, the place or country in which any final operation, has altered to any appreciable extent the character, composition and value of goods imported into that country.

(3) In the case of goods which have at some stage entered into the commerce of, or undergone a process of manufacture in a foreign country, only that labour and material which are expected in or added to the goods after their return to the exporting territory, shall be regarded as the produce or manufacture of the territory in calculating the proportion of labour and material in the factory or works cost of the finished article.

(4) *Delete the inapplicable.

Enumerate the following charges and state whether each amount has been included in or excluded from the above selling price to purchaser —	Amount in currency of exporting country	State if included in above selling price to purchaser
(1) Cartage to rail and/or docks ...		
(2) Inland freight (rail or canal) and other charges to the dock area, including inland insurance ...		
(3) Labour in packing the goods into outside packages ...		
(4) Value of outside packages ...		
(5) If the goods are subject to any charge by way of royalties ...		
(6) OCEAN FREIGHT ...		
(7) OCEAN INSURANCE ...		
(8) Commission, establishment and other charges of a like nature ...		
(9) Other costs, dues, charges and expenses incidental to the delivery of the articles		

State full particulars of Royalties below :—

Form No. 731 Published and Sold by FORMECON SERVICES LTD., Gateway, Crewe, CW1 1YN, England. Tel: 0270-587811 Telex: 36560 Eurofs G.

Figure 47.2   Combined certificate of value, certificate of origin and consular invoice. (In the format specified by the Nigerian Government (Formecon Services Ltd))

INVOICE No. .... 19 ....

*State here general nature or class of goods

INVOICE of*

(Place and Date).

consigned

by

of

to

of

to be shipped per

Order Number ....

....

Country from which consigned.

Country of Origin.	Marks and numbers on packages.	Quantity and description of goods.	Selling price to purchaser.	
			@	Amount

Figure 47.2 (concluded)

618

customs checks or border controls. VAT will still be payable on import, as will excise duty on certain goods. At the time of writing, definitive legislation was still under discussion by the EC. Readers should refer to their local Customs and Excise office or to their freight forwarder for up-to-date information. In the run up to 1993, community transit is covered by the use of the Single Administrative Document (SAD).

Export licences

Export licences may be needed for some goods. Details can be obtained from: The Export Licensing Branch, Department of Trade and Industry, Kingsgate House, 66–74 Victoria Street, London, SW1E 6SW. Telephone: 071-215 8070

PAYMENTS AND CREDIT

International trade involves many more formalities than those which sellers experience in sales to their home customers. Credit periods before the supplier gets paid are longer and may need bridging finance. Risk from bad debts is greater, with collection often difficult or perhaps even impossible. Sellers therefore need expert advice and services when exporting goods or services. A good place to start is the local branch of a bank. Relevant head office addresses for export departments of four major UK banks are included in the useful organizations list at the end of this chapter.

Foreign exchange

The seller may want to minimize the risk of foreign exchange dealings by pricing contracts in his own or other stable currency, but the buyer might not agree. Risks from currency exchange rate fluctuations can be reduced by including as much contingency allowance in prices as competition will allow, and by bringing payments forward by way of asking for deposits or making stage progress payments a condition of contract.

Subject to local exchange control regulations, a buyer may deal in the seller's currency if he can be persuaded to buy some or all of the necessary currency early and place it in an interest bearing deposit account. This fixes the price to buyer and seller and eliminates risk of loss (or gain) to either party should exchange rates alter before the goods are shipped and invoiced.

Another option is for the buyer to forward-purchase foreign exchange for future settlement, but this is expensive for periods longer than six months. Access to such contracts and to the foreign exchange markets generally is available through the banks.

Payments and credit methods

Advance payment

This method gives the seller maximum security, with money up front. The buyer is asked to settle in advance and the seller banks the proceeds, ensuring that any cheque is cleared before parting with the goods. But because the buyer is asked to extend credit to the seller this method is unusual. Partial protection is given by asking for a deposit in advance and for stage progress payments.

The buyer may want to protect himself by asking the seller to provide a guarantee or contract bond which can be invoked if the contract is not completed.

Documentary letters of credit

The security of payment for the seller by this method is second only to payment in advance. A letter of credit is issued by a bank for the importer, and this guarantees payment of a stated sum to the exporter within a specified time. The seller also knows that the issuing bank has confidence in the creditworthiness of the customer. Strict conditions attach to letters of credit, and they require the exporter to comply exactly with documentation demanded before payment can be made. If a letter of credit becomes time-expired because goods are shipped late, the customer must be asked to make a fresh approach to the issuing bank for the date to be extended.

The issuing bank will usually advise the exporter and arrange payments through an *advising bank* in the exporter's home country: which may or may not be the exporter's own bank. The exporter may receive the letter of credit directly, when he should ask his own bank to vet it for possible error, omission or fraud.

Letters of credit may be *revocable* (rare) or *irrevocable*. A revocable letter of credit can be cancelled or amended at any time without prior notice to the exporter. A *confirmed irrevocable* letter of credit carries an assurance from the advising bank that payment will be made. If an irrevocable letter of credit is *unconfirmed* the advising bank will merely inform the exporter of the terms and conditions, and the exporter must rely on the issuing bank's undertaking and ability to pay. An irrevocable letter of credit is illustrated in Figure 47.3.

Documents commonly required for payment by letter of credit include:

- The letter of credit itself
- A bill of exchange or draft
- A commercial invoice
- Bill of lading or air waybill
- An insurance policy or certificate such as Lloyd's MAR policy (marine all risks).

Bank charges for arranging a letter of credit may be high compared with the value of small contracts. A letter of credit may not be needed if the buyer is well known to the seller and has a good record. Some countries insist on the procedure in their exchange control regulations.

Rules for documentary credits are issued by the International Chamber of Commerce and are followed by most countries.

Bills for collection

This method can be used where the exporter is not able to get the buyer to arrange a documentary letter of credit. The shipping documents, especially the bill of lading and any other documents which give title to the goods, are sent to a bank in the destination country by the seller's bank. The documents giving title to

EXCEL BANK LTD

From:-

Excel Bank Ltd.
Registered in England
(No. 00000)

Registered Office
1074, Lombard Street,
London EC2P 2BX

Overseas Branch
P.O. Box 181760
70 St. Mary's Avenue
London EC3P 3BN
Telephone 01 000 0000 Extn:3259
Telex 000000
Telegrams Excelbank London

To:-

Camside Engineering (Cambridge) Ltd.
Chesterton,
Cambridge.

Advice of:-

Popular Bank of Africa
Mtwara
Tanzania

*Irrevocable credit which bears the confirmation
of Excel Bank Ltd.*

Dear Sirs,

We inform you that the above-named bank have opened with us their irrevocable credit in your favour on account of Haji Bwanamkubwa and Partners, of 24 Port Compound, Mtwara, Tanzania, to the extent of £8,000.00 (say Eight Thousand Pounds) valid at this office until 12 noon on 23rd September 19...., on or before which your drafts on us at sight may be paid if accompanied by the undermentioned documents evidencing current shipment from Liverpool to Mtwara, Tanzania of the goods described below. The buyer's order number and reference is U.K. 1754. Part shipments prohibited. All documents to be in English. We confirm that no import licence is required for these goods on entering Tanzania.

Set of 3 clean shipped Bills of Lading issued in favour of Popular Bank of Africa, Mtwara, Tanzania, marked "FREIGHT PAID" showing the amount of freight paid.

A clean Report of Findings must be obtained from General Superintendents, Liverpool, and must accompany the other documents; also a packing list in 3 copies.

Copy of your advice note sent to Popular Bank of Africa advising details of shipment for insurance purposes, enabling them to insure in good time.

Commercial Invoice in 9 copies, showing the F.O.B. value and freight charges shown separately, giving; in all a C & F value.

Covering 8 Water Purifying units Type SD1756 at agreed price of £640 per unit
2 aerators Type TD15 at agreed price of £540 each

We are informed that insurance will be effected by the buyers with State Insure,(Tanzania)Ltd, Mtwara, Tanzania.

Shipment must be effected in Palmate Line Vessels only. All drafts drawn under this credit to bear the clause "Drawn under Doc. Credit No 17,777,777."

We are requested to advise you of the terms of the credit, which is irrevocable on the part of our principals and also bears our confirmation. Subject to Uniform Customs and Practice for Documentary Credits (1974 Revision) International Chamber of Commerce Publication No. 290.

Figure 47.4   An irrevocable letter of credit (Formecon Services Ltd)

the purchaser will only be released by the receiving bank when the purchaser has satisfied the terms required. The actual payment arrangement can include extended credit terms provided the buyer's financial standing is satisfactory.

Bills of exchange

Bills of exchange are widely used in international trade as a means for claiming payment. A bill of exchange instructs a third party to pay a stated sum of money on a certain date or on demand. The legal definition, slightly simplified, is an unconditional order addressed by the *drawer* to the *drawee* which requires the *drawee* to pay a certain sum of money to the *payee* on demand or at a fixed determinable future time. The drawer signs the bill before issue and the drawee becomes the *acceptor* when he signs it after receipt. In our context the drawer is the customer, the drawee is the bank and the payee is the exporting seller.

Bills of exchange are often dated at 30, 60 or 90 days, and on passing them through the seller's bank they enable him to get his money early. The wording of bills must be exact, needing expert advice (that is, from the bank). The risk to the bank is covered partly by insurance on the goods, by documented evidence that the goods exist as stated (possibly with some stipulation that the goods would be readily resalable in the event of default) and by credit insurance.

Other methods for advancing payment

Other methods available to bring in payment as early as possible include bank loans or overdrafts, made against the expectation of eventual payment by the customer after all the tedious formalities have been completed. There are many other credit arrangements possible, for which advice should be sought from a bank.

Credit insurance

The UK Export Credits Guarantee Department (ECGD) is typical of many institutions, government and private, which provide credit insurance, with tailor-made policies where necessary for large capital goods. For smaller orders exporters can gain access to ECGD through their banks. ECGD guarantees can be used as security against bank loans. Normally a small proportion of the risk must be borne by the seller.

VALUE ADDED TAX

Goods on which VAT is payable at the standard rate when sold in the UK generally become zero-rated when sold as exports provided specified conditions are met. In particular the company must hold copies of the commercial documents which list the goods in specific terms and prove that they were exported. The rules allow for goods to be exported through a third party such as an export packager or a freight company that consolidates loads for containers. But goods sent to or collected by a UK customer and claimed to be for eventual export are accountable for VAT and must not be zero-rated.

Goods sent to the Isle of Man and all UK free zones are not classed as exports and normal VAT is chargeable but consignments to the Channel Islands *are* treated as exports.

UK Customs & Excise VAT publications are available from local VAT offices. Those particularly relevant to exports include:

- *Free Zones: Guidance notes for users*
- *Freight containers supplied for export*
- *Overseas traders and United Kingdom VAT*
- *Sailway boats supplied for export*
- *Tools for the manufacture of goods for export*
- 700   *The VAT Guide*
- 702   *Imports and warehoused goods*
- 704   *Retail exports* (for goods sold retail to visitors from overseas or to UK residents going abroad or crews of ships and aircraft)
- 705   *Personal exports of new motor vehicles*
- 706   *Partial exemption*
- 727   *Retail schemes*
- 741   *International services* (explains the VAT liability of exported services)

This is a brief summary of a subject which is complex and has many exceptions, special cases and grey areas. The local VAT office must be contacted in any case of doubt *before* the transaction takes place.

USEFUL ORGANIZATIONS

Barclays Bank PLC, International Trade Services Department,
PO Box 259, Fleetway House, Farringdon Street,
London EC4A 4LT
Tel: 071-489 0969

British Export Houses Association, 69 Cannon Street,
London EC4N 5AB
Tel: 071-248 4444

British Exporters Association, 16 Dartmouth Street,
London SW1H 9BL
Tel: 071-222 5419

British International Freight Association, Redfern House,
Browells Lane, Feltham, Middlesex, TW13 7EP
Tel: 081-844 2266

Dangerous Goods Advisory Service (DAGAS)
Laboratory of the Government Chemist, Cornwall House,
Stamford Street, London SE1 9NH
Tel: 071-928 7900

Department of Trade and Industry (DTI)
Export Licensing Unit
Kingsgate House, 66–74 Victoria Street, London SW1P 4QU
Tel: 071-215 8070

International Trade Policy (ITP) Department
1 Victoria Street, London SW1H 0ET
Tel: 071-215 7877

Export Credits Guarantee Department (ECGD)
Head Office, Aldermanbury House, Aldermanbury, London EC2
Tel: 071-382 7000

HM Customs and Excise, New King's Beam House,
22 Upper Ground, London SE1 9TG
Tel: 071-620 1313

Institute of Export, Export House, 64 Clifton Street,
London EC2A 4HB
Tel: 071-247 9812

International Chamber of Commerce (ICC)

Headquarters: 38 Cours Albert 1er, 75008, Paris, France
Tel: (1) 49.53.28.28

London address: ICC United Kingdom, 14–15 Belgrave Square,
London, SW1X 8PS
Tel: 071-823 2811

Lloyds Trade and Projects Limited
(*Lloyds Bank export advice and assistance*)
PO Box 19, Haye's Lane House, 1 Haye's Lane
London SE1 2HA
Tel: 071-407 1000

Midland Bank PLC (*for export advice and assistance*)
Market Department, 3rd Floor, 110 Cannon Street,
London EC4N 6AA
Tel: 071-260 6000

National Westminster Bank PLC,
International Trade Services, National Westminster Tower,
25 Old Broad Street, London EC2N 1HQ
Tel: 071-920 1588 (direct line)

Simplification of International Trade Procedures Board (SITPRO),
Almack House, 26–28 King Street,
London SW1Y 6QW
Tel: 071-930 0532

Technical Help to Exporters (THE),
British Standards Institution (BSI), Linfield Wood
Milton Keynes, Bucks, MK14 6LE
Tel: 0908 220022

FURTHER READING

Boakes, Norman, Chapter 26 'Reaching Overseas Markets', in *Marketing Handbook*, Third edn, Gower, Aldershot, 1989
Croner's Reference Book for Exporters, Croner Publications, New Malden, Surrey, UK (by subscription: updated monthly)
Croner's Reference Book for Importers, Croner Publications, New Malden, Surrey, UK
Croner's World Directory of Freight Conferences, Croner Publications, New Malden, Surrey, UK (by subscription: updated monthly)
Export Education Packages, Formecon Services Ltd, Crewe, CW1 1YN, UK
ICC, *INCOTERMS 1990*, ICC Publication 460 (Copyright © 1990) International Chamber of Commerce, Paris. This publication is available direct from ICC, whose Paris and London addresses are given above.
Katz, B., *Managing Export Marketing*, Gower, Aldershot, 1987

Note

Chapter 25 complements this chapter and includes additional further reading references.

ACKNOWLEDGEMENTS

Parts of this chapter are based on information supplied by Barclays Bank PLC, HM Customs and Excise, ICC United Kingdom and National Westminster Bank PLC.

The author is indebted to Mr Colin Beaumont of the British International Freight Association for general advice and assistance.

48 Managing transport services

Frank H Woodward

Transport services are called upon to move goods, materials or personnel for every function within industry. In all of these, the objective is to achieve a cost-effective operation that adds as little as possible to the cost burden on product prices.

ORGANIZATION STRUCTURE

Figure 48.1 illustrates organization structures for transport services in manufacturing companies of various sizes. These examples are general, for services which are not specific to a major warehousing or retailing operation. They are intended to assist readers to develop their own organization structures, after taking into consideration their own special needs.

A typical organization for the transport services function of a small company in a single factory location, with only a few cars and light vans and one heavy truck used on local deliveries, is shown in Figure 48.1(a). Dispatches are by local carrier and rail. All vehicle maintenance is carried out at local garages. A dispatch section is established which is responsible for packaging and loading goods on to vehicles.

Organization for the transport services function of a medium-sized company with two factory locations is shown in Figure 48.1(b). There are twenty cars for management and sales staff use, a number of light vans for customer after-sales service, four trucks for goods delivery to customers and a personnel carrier for personnel movement between factories. Distribution is by company transport and local carrier as well as by rail services. A company garage is available to service and repair the majority of company-owned vehicles.

Figure 48.1(c) shows the organization for the transport services function of a large group of companies with many factory locations. A mixed vehicle fleet of over 2 000 has to be controlled and administered, consisting of executive and management cars, a large sales fleet of cars and light vans, and a truck fleet exceeding 200 vehicles. A full distribution service from all factory locations to customers is carried out using company vehicles. Local carriers are used to meet peak demands. Extensive use is made of rail facilities. Company garages are established in each transport location. The whole of the transport function is based on a regional organization with line responsibility for the movement of company products. A corporate air service is the responsibility of the transport service function.

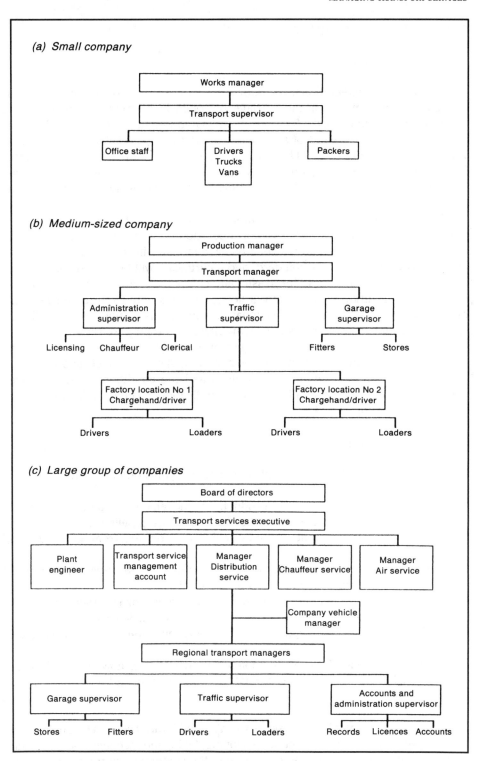

Figure 48.1 Examples of transport services organizations

TRANSPORT MANAGEMENT

Operators' licensing

Subject to certain exemptions, operators' licensing applies to all goods vehicles and combinations used for the carriage of goods in connection with trade or business and which exceed 3.5 tonnes gross plated weight or, if unplated 1 525kg unladen weight. The weight of any trailer forming part of a vehicle combination which is not in excess of 1 020 kg unladen weight is discounted in the calculation. The statutory instrument is the Goods Vehicles (Operators' Licences, Qualifications and Fees) Regulations 1984 (SI 1984 No 176) as amended by Regulation 1986 (SI 1986 No 666).

One condition for granting an operator's licence is that the 'person' named in the application to manage that transport operation is 'professionally competent'. This means that managers in the road haulage industry have to pass an examination in order to obtain this standard, and a certificate will be issued stating that the person named therein is 'professionally competent'. Although this requirement for the granting of a operator's licence applies only to 'hire and reward' operations, the Certificate of Professional Competence is a qualification available to 'own account' transport management where the transport services are not offered for hire and reward. In recruiting or promoting managers to any transport operation, this 'certificate' should be the minimum standard qualification.

Full details of how to apply for a licence, and the conditions to be met are contained in the Department of Transport Publication *A Guide to Goods Vehicle Operators' Licensing* (GV74).

Basic transport policies

Before development of any vehicle plan, a number of questions need to be asked:

1 Does the distribution of the product, or movement of personnel, need vehicles? Liquids and gases can be distributed by pipeline, personnel can communicate by telephone, closed circuit television, electronic mail, and so on.
2 If vehicles are needed, must they be road vehicles? Will railways, waterways or aircraft give a more efficient and economic service?
3 If road vehicles are needed, is the service of a haulier or contract distributor more efficient than the company operating its own vehicle fleet?
4 If road vehicles are to be operated by the company, should they be leased, on contract hire, or owned?
5 If it is finally decided to have company-owned vehicles, how should they be financed, how many are required, what types are needed, and where are they to be based?

These questions are vital. The answers will affect all future transport planning and must be based on sound commercial reasoning, taking into account not only basic costs, but also real costs, including service to the customer and the total value of the whole operation to the overall profitability of the company. The same questions can be used to test current transport policies and to change those policies should the answers differ from the time those initial decisions were taken.

VEHICLE MANAGEMENT AND VEHICLE STANDARDS

The object of setting vehicle operating standards is to obtain the most efficient utilization of a fleet of vehicles. This is the key to a minimum cost operation. Standing costs now account for more than half the total operating costs of a vehicle and it follows that the higher the utilization, the cheaper the cost per mile.

There are four main areas of vehicle operation where an attack on utilization can be made, and which can prove a basis for comparison of planned performance against actual performance.

Vehicle preparation

Preparation includes checking the vehicle before a day's work, driver administration and documentation. Work study techniques can be applied to this area of work, and standard times are easy to establish.

Vehicle loading and unloading

One way of achieving a higher productivity is to keep loading and unloading time to a minimum. The use of demountable 'swop bodies', containers and trailers are all ways of preloading vehicles while the motive unit is delivering another load. The size of pallet, side loading, double-deck loading, and lower deck height, are all areas where a work study investigation may be applied with advantage. The use of vehicle-mounted handling aids such as tail lifts, cranes and special tracking, will speed up the unloading of a vehicle at customers' premises. Standard forms of label and consignment note, colour coding identification of depots, factories, warehouses or customer delivery areas will speed up the loading procedure and assist the driver to make an efficient delivery.

Vehicle running time

The running time of a vehicle between two points is governed by the speed limit of the road over which that vehicle has to travel. Figure 48.2 shows speed limits in the UK and acceptable vehicle speeds used in transport operations as a basis for calculating time taken over road routes.

The working day of a delivery vehicle can be divided into three sections:

- Proceeding to actual delivery area
- Delivering the goods in the delivery area
- Returning to base.

The speed-limit factor will affect only the first and last sections. The main controlling factor in the delivery area is the number of delivery points and the number of units to be delivered at each point.

Type of road	Type of vehicle	Maximum legal road speed	Acceptable average speed for route calculations
Restricted to 30 mph (built-up areas)	All types of vehicle	30 mph	22 mph
Dual carriageways (other than motorways or roads restricted to a lower limit)	Car-derived van or dual-purpose vehicle	70 mph	55 mph
	Rigid goods vehicle not in excess of 7.5 tonnes gvw	60 mph	45 mph
	Articulated vehicle or rigid goods vehicle in excess of 7.5 tonnes gvw	50 mph	38 mph
	Rigid vehicle and trailer in excess of 7.5 tonnes laden weight	50 mph	38 mph
Motorways	Rigid goods vehicle not exceeding 7.5 tonnes gvw and not drawing a trailer	70 mph	55 mph
	Rigid goods vehicle exceeding 7.5 tonnes, articulated vehicles and rigid goods vehicles drawing a trailer	60 mph	48 mph
Other roads (when derestricted)	Rigid goods vehicles, articulated vehicles not exceeding 7.5 tonnes gvw and rigid vehicles drawing a trailer where the aggregate maximum laden weight of the vehicle and trailer does not exceed 7.5 tonnes	50 mph	35 mph
	Goods vehicles including articulated vehicles in excess of 7.5 tonnes gvw and rigid vehicles drawing trailers with an aggregate laden weight in excess of 7.5 tonnes	40 mph	30 mph

Figure 48.2 UK speed limits for goods-registered vehicles

Delivering the goods

Delivery is an area of uncertainty when trying to calculate standard times of performance, and the approach to the problem will differ with each company and product. Calculations can be based on:

- The number of delivery drops
- A basic time allowance for each delivery point
- Standard times for handling each parcel delivered
- An average speed for the vehicle when delivering in towns.

The setting of vehicle and operating standards in a transport operation is called 'load assessment' and there are many ways of applying this technique. The object in every case is to establish a standard against which the driver's performance can be measured.

DRIVERS' HOURS AND RECORDS OF WORK

Drivers' hours

National and international operations

EEC Directive 3820/85 sets out the drivers' hours rules for most goods vehicles with a gross plated weight in excess of 3.5 tonnes.

The rules apply to drivers of vehicles in excess of 3.5 tonnes permissible maximum weight used for the carriage of goods and passengers on public roads whether laden or unladen within the UK (regarded as a national journey) or when on a journey to or from other EC member states (regarded as an international journey). The rules are:

- *Daily driving* 9 hours maximum, extended to 10 hours maximum not more than twice a week
- *Weekly driving* Weekly driving is governed by the requirement that a driver must, after no more than six daily driving periods, take a weekly rest period. There is no maximum hours other than the limitation placed upon daily driving hours. It is possible for a driver to work up to 76 hours in one week (4 × 9 hours + 2 × 10 hours. *But,* see the restriction on fortnightly working
- *Fortnightly driving* 90 hours. Therefore if a driver drives for 76 hours in one week (see above), the following week must not exceed 14 driving hours
- *Definition of a week* A 'week' is defined as the period between 00.00 hours on a Monday and 24.00 hours the following Sunday
- *Driving hours* A driver may drive for a total of 4.5 hours, which can be continuous or accumulated, after which a break from driving must be taken
- *Breaks from driving* A break of 45 minutes minimum after an accumulated driving period of 4.5 hours or three breaks each of 15 minutes minimum spread over the driving period or immediately following it
- *Daily rest period* 11 hours minimum, with a reduction to 9 hours on three days per week subject to an equivalent rest being taken as compensation before the end of the following week

- *Weekly rest period* 45 hours minimum, with reductions to 36 hours at base or 24 hours away from base, subject to each reduction being compensated by a equivalent rest being taken *en bloc* before the end of the *third week* following the week when the reduced rest was taken.

British domestic operations

Domestic legislation as laid down in Part VI of the Transport Act 1968 (as amended) applies to drivers of vehicles which are exempt from the EC rules. These include goods vehicles not in excess of 3.5 tonnes maximum permissible weight and passenger vehicles constructed to carry not more than seventeen persons including the driver. There are many other exemptions from the EC rules, details of which are available from the Road Haulage Association or the Freight Transport Association.

There are two main limitations placed upon a driver operating under British Domestic Rules:

- *Daily driving* 10 hours maximum
- *Daily duty* 11 hours maximum.

The above rules are the only limitations placed on the driving and working hours of drivers of goods vehicles exempt from the EC rules. It is to be noted that there are no requirements to take a legal break during a driving or duty day, or any daily/weekly rest minimum.

Drivers' records of work

The law relating to the use of tachographs to record drivers' hours is covered by EC Regulation 3821/85 and the accompanying UK legislation, The Passenger and Goods Vehicles (Recording Equipment) Regulations 1979 (SI 1979 No. 1746).

All vehicles in excess of 3.5 tonnes maximum permissible weight and which are covered by EC Regulation 3820/85 (Drivers' Hours Regulations), used for the carriage of goods, and passenger vehicles constructed to carry more than nine persons including the driver (more than seventeen persons if operating in Great Britain), must be fitted with an EC approved tachograph to record the drivers' hours. A driver' is defined as: 'any person who drives the vehicle even for a short period or is carried in the vehicle in order to be available for driving if necessary'.

The tachograph record

Where a tachograph is fitted to a vehicle it must conform to the detailed specification as laid down in the EC Directive. It must be able to record:

- Distance travelled by the vehicle
- Speed of the vehicle
- Driving time
- Other periods of work of the driver(s)
- Breaks from work and daily rest periods
- Opening of the case containing the tachograph chart.

The tachograph chart must also have a facility by which the driver(s) can continue recording driving and duty time in the event of the instrument becoming unserviceable during a journey. Once a vehicle has been fitted with a tachograph, the instrument must be calibrated and sealed at an approved centre.

Employers must:

1 Issue each driver with sufficient charts for the journey
2 Organize each driver's work so that the relevant provisions of the regulations can be complied with
3 Make periodical checks to ensure that the provisions of drivers' hours and tachograph regulations have been complied with and, if infringements are found, take the appropriate steps to prevent repetition
4 Ensure that drivers return charts within twenty-one days of use
5 Retain tachograph charts for a minimum of one year after use and produce or hand over any charts on request by an authorized inspecting officer.

Drivers must:

1 Use a tachograph chart on every day in which they are driving, starting from the moment the vehicle is taken over. The same chart should continue to be used until the end of that daily driving period
2 Enter on the chart:
   • surname and first name
   • date and place where the record chart begins and ends
   • the registration number(s) of the vehicle(s) driven
   • the odometer readings:
      • at the start of the first journey
      • at the end of the last journey
      • at each change of vehicle, plus the time at which a change of vehicle takes place
3 Produce charts for inspection if requested by enforcement officers of the Department of Transport
4 Retain with them charts for the current week *and* the chart for the last day on which they drove a vehicle in the previous week
5 Return charts to their employer within twenty-one days of completion.

Written records

Drivers of vehicles which are exempt from EC drivers' hours regulations are required to maintain written records for vehicles over 3.5 tonnes gross plated vehicle weight or, if not plated, with an unladen weight in excess of 1 525 kgs. The record is required to be in a prescribed form and there is a duty on the employer to check and sign each record. There is no requirement to keep written records for those vehicles which do not exceed 3.5 tonnes gross plated weight or have an unladen weight not in excess of 1 525 kgs.

The Drivers' Hours (Goods Vehicles) (Keeping of Records) Regulations 1987 (SI 1987 No. 142), which came into force on 2 November 1987, lay down the procedure for the keeping of written records and show the layout of the *prescribed form* in which these records have to be kept.

TRUCK SELECTION

The efficiency of any distribution operation depends upon the selection of the right truck for the job to be done. For the 'own account' user it is the essential element in achieving an effective customer delivery service, and for the haulier it provides the means of maximizing profits. Selecting to meet a given set of criteria can be achieved only after full discussion with all functions within the total distribution chain – a full understanding of the size, weight and types of load to be carried is necessary as well as a knowledge of the routes over which the truck is to operate. As the product structure of a company changes, vehicles designed specifically to carry that product may become obsolete. Long-term planning is essential and a degree of flexibility needs to be built into the design features of any industrial fleet.

Specification

The body of a goods vehicle is that part on or in which the load is carried. This part of the specification must be set first, followed by a chassis specification to accommodate the body. The specification will cover:

1 Internal and external dimensions and floor height
2 Size, type and location of doors, shutters and tailboards
3 Materials to be used, including provision for insulation and temperature control equipment
4 Internal fittings and load security fitments
5 Load-handling equipment, vehicle mounted or carried
6 Requirements for carrying hazardous loads
7 Painting and company livery requirements.

The Road Vehicles (Construction and Use) Regulations 1986 (as amended) will determine the maximum dimensions and permitted gross weight of the chassis on which a truck body is to be mounted.

Environmental legislation

Within the increase in permitted vehicle operating weights up to 38 tonnes (38 000 kg), legislation has been introduced to meet higher safety and environmental standards. These include:

• Sideguards
• Antispray protection
• Rear under-run protection
• Noise levels
• Minimum ground clearance.

The choice of vehicles for the carriage of goods varies from a small van to a 38-tonne gross articulated vehicle. The design of vehicles within this range is just as varied. The use of unit load movements is an important element in achieving a high utilization of both vehicle and driver. Containers, demountable bodies, semitrailers and drawbar combinations are used in all types of distribution operations. The ultimate test of vehicle design is the efficiency of the vehicle to do the job it was intended for. In setting design specifications it is also necessary to ensure compliance with Health and Safety at Work Regulations.

ACQUIRING VEHICLES: THE FUNDING OPTIONS

The market-place is full of package schemes to tempt industrial management to acquire assets, including vehicles, by different methods of funding. Many names are used to market these options, but within all the different methods there are only two ways by which to fund a vehicle: purchase or rental.

The Finance Acts give a clear definition of determining each basic option:

If a company acquires, plant and so on, under a contract whereby that contract provides that it *may* or *will* eventually have title of such plant, then the equipment will be regarded as belonging to that company and will be a *purchase*.

If the contract does not lead to or offer an 'option' to eventual title, then the contract will be *rental*.

Purchasing

The following options fall under the 'purchase' heading:

1 Reduce current cash balances
2 Establish or increase a bank overdraft
3 Arrange a bank loan to be repaid over a predetermined period
4 Hire purchase, which is normally associated with a credit facility for a private purchaser. It has advantages for the smaller business and is usually referred to as a 'conditional sale agreement'
5 Lease with the 'option to purchase', which gives the lessee (the hirer) the option to purchase the vehicle at the end of the lease period and to acquire title by payment of a stated sum

Finance leases

A finance lease is a term generally used to mean the same as 'hire'. It excludes any option or agreement on the part of the lessee to acquire legal title. The repayment will be in the form of *equal rentals over a predetermined period*. The finance company will purchase the vehicle in its own title and the asset capitalized in the financial accounts. The lessee is responsible for all the costs of operating the vehicle, including road fund licence, insurance and maintenance. At the end of the lease period, the vehicle is sold and the lessee is usually credited with up to 95 per cent of the proceeds as a refund of rentals. In the case of trucks, a clause in the agreement may provide the lessee with the choice of continuing to lease for a secondary period at a nominal rental usually 0.5 per cent of the total rental payments per annum.

Contract hire

The use of the contract hire option by companies continues to increase year by year. It can best be described as 'paying a rental for the use of a vehicle over a stated period of time and/or miles'. A contract hire agreement will provide:

1 Supply of a vehicle ready for the road
2 Road fund licence during period of contract
3 All repair and maintenance costs of the vehicle
4 Tyres/batteries/exhaust systems, and so on
5 Replacement vehicle in the event of the contract vehicle being under repair
6 Roadside recovery and repair services.

Many contract hire companies now offer insurance as part of the agreement. The objective is to provide the user of the vehicle with no liability for costs other than the monthly rental. Most contract hire agreements have a mileage limitation. If the mileage is exceeded, an extra cost is charged based upon a 'pence per mile' calculation. Contract hire agreements for trucks, especially for periods in excess of three years, usually have the maintenance element of the rental linked to an index or a clause providing for this to be reviewed each year.

Advantages of contract hire

Fixed costs and cash flow over the period; simple and easy to forecast budgets; reduced administration; maximum availability of the vehicle; reduced downtime; no risks on residual value or maintenance costs.

Value added tax

Each funding option is affected in a different way as regards the treatment of VAT, as follows:

- *Purchase* Vehicles are subject to VAT based on the invoice price of the vehicle. This means that if higher discounts are obtained which reduce the invoice price, the VAT amount is less. VAT on goods vehicles is an input and recoverable through the VAT account on quarterly settlement dates set by HM Customs and Excise. VAT on cars, including dual purpose vehicles (estate cars) is not recoverable, so a reduction in the invoice price by negotiating discounts also reduces VAT and is a *real saving*
- *Hire purchase* VAT is payable on the invoice price of the vehicle the same as if the vehicle had been purchased outright. No VAT is payable on the repayments of capital or on the interest element of the repayments
- *Lease with option to purchase* No VAT is payable on the lease rentals when vehicles are acquired by any conditional sale agreement
- *Finance lease* VAT is payable on all rentals and this requires additional funding. For those companies registered for VAT, the charge is recoverable as an input through the quarterly VAT account
- *Contract hire* VAT is payable on all contract hire rentals.

VAT costs on finance lease and contract hire rentals is an additional cost to those organizations not registered for VAT (for example, some local government departments), and when using these two funding options to acquire cars VAT is being paid twice: on the invoice cost of the vehicle which is built into the rental, and then on the rentals paid.

Vehicle fleet management (VFM)

Fleet management is not an alternative funding option but simply the administration of the selected option by an outside agent for a fee. It is usually associated with the company car fleet. The objective is to reduce costs and administration. A vehicle fleet management package will include:

1   Operational management of the vehicles:

- acquisition
- maintenance
- fuel credit cards
- licensing
- disposal.

2   Financial analysis of costs:

- fuel
- maintenance
- depreciation.

3   Advice and consultancy:

- vehicle make and models
- replacement policies
- funding options.

What does VFM cost?

All purchases by the fleet management company on behalf of the user company are charged at cost, *plus* a set fee per vehicle per annum usually based on a percentage of the invoice cost of the vehicle.

MAINTENANCE POLICIES FOR GOODS VEHICLES

Before an operator's licence can be issued an applicant must satisfy the licensing authority that vehicles will be kept fit and serviceable at all times when used on the public roads. The licensing authority may also request a copy of any maintenance contract or letter of agreement if the servicing and repair of vehicles is carried out elsewhere than in a company garage workshop, and in all cases may request examples of the forms used for vehicle safety inspections. It is also a requirement for the issue of an 'O' licence that proper arrangements are available for drivers to report safety faults in vehicles as soon as possible. The Department of Transport publication, *A Guide to Goods Vehicle Operators Licensing* (GV74 4/84), sets the following guidelines around which vehicle operators should formulate a vehicle maintenance policy:

1 Two separate vehicle checks and inspections should be carried out: daily running checks; vehicle safety inspections and routine maintenance at set intervals on items which affect vehicle safety, followed by repair of any faults
2 The daily check is normally carried out by the driver on basic items including brakes, tyre pressures, lights, windscreen wipers and washers, and trailer couplings
3 Vehicle safety inspections and routine maintenance should be carried out at set intervals of time or mileage and should include wheels, tyres, brakes, steering, suspension, lighting and all safety components
4 Staff carrying out inspections must be able to recognize faults and be aware of the acceptable standard of performance and wear of parts
5 Records must be kept, for at least fifteen months, of all safety inspections to show the history of each vehicle. Where an outside garage carries out the safety inspections, maintenance records must still be kept
6 Adequate facilities must be available for carrying out the inspection, especially equipment for measuring braking efficiency and setting lights
7 Drivers must report vehicle faults to whoever is responsible for putting them right. The report must be in writing
8 Users are responsible for the condition of hired vehicles and trailers. The user is defined as the employer of the driver
9 Where maintenance work is contracted out to a garage or other vehicle repairer, a written agreement must be entered into setting out the conditions and periods of safety inspections.

Planned maintenance and inspection

A number of ready-made planned maintenance and inspection schemes are available to operators, all of which have been designed to ensure compliance with the legal requirements. Basically, each contains the following documents enabling a complete history of a vehicle's maintenance and inspection to be recorded and preserved:

- Driver's defect report
- Vehicle inspection check sheet
- Servicing sheet for predetermined intervals of time or mileage
- Stores requisition form
- Work order sheet or job card
- Servicing, planning and record chart
- Vehicle history folder.

No matter what method is adopted, in company premises by company employees, or by contracting out the entire task of maintenance, inspection and documentation, the onus of responsibility for the roadworthiness of the vehicle is always with the vehicle operator. He is still responsible in law even though an outside contractor providing the service and maintenance facilities has been neglectful.

The use of computers

There are many computer programs available designed to meet the requirements of all sizes of fleet. For an outlay of under £2 000 small personal computers with printer and a fleet management program are available which can handle all the records and maintenance control information for a fleet of up to 100 vehicles. It must be stressed that a computer does not replace the need for written records. The Department of Transport inspectors will require to see the original documents – invoices, service and repair sheets.

FINANCIAL CONTROL OF THE TRANSPORT FUNCTION

The only way to ensure a cost-effective operation is to establish a system of budgetary control and accounting responsibility which ensures that any overspending is immediately highlighted at the point where the cost was incurred. The best way to impose effective financial control on the transport services function is to make it an independent cost centre within the company.

The whole range of transport services is now on offer to companies which do not wish to invest in a fleet of vehicles. The acquisition of company cars through to the distribution and storage of the company product range is available on contract terms. By setting up the transport services function as an independent cost centre, a correct evaluation of both cost and service can be carried out using 'in house' services or outside contractors.

A rate schedule for the carriage of goods within the company and to customers should be produced in the same way as one would expect to see from a haulier. Similar rate schedules can also be prepared for other services such as chauffeur-driven cars, allocated company cars, and even for the repair and maintenance of vehicles in company garages. These rate schedules should be fixed for the period of a company financial year and published to all departments to be used as a basis for determining the transport and distribution costs borne by the product. By adopting such a system, the transport function receives regular revenue for its services against which it incurs costs.

To establish financial disciplines, it is necessary to keep adequate costing information for each vehicle and also to have a system of budgetary control in order that, over the whole of a financial period, regular checks can be made on areas of excessive expenditure and corrective action taken by management if necessary.

Costing the operation

There are two main components of vehicle costs:

1   Standing costs, which generally include:

- depreciation cost of the vehicle, together with a charge equivalent to the interest which the capital invested in the vehicle could earn
- licences, including road fund and operator's licences
- insurance, for both vehicle and goods in transit

- wages of the driver.

2   Running costs, which are the result of operating the vehicle on the road and include:

- fuel and oil
- repairs and maintenance
- tyres
- driver's expenses
- driver's overtime.

The most informative costs of own-account transport operation are the running costs of a vehicle.

Monthly cost record

The vehicle monthly costings record (see Figure 48.3) ignores all costs other than those directly associated with day-to-day operation.

- *Fuel*   Issues from company bulk installations are shown separately from the fuel picked up from garages by means of agency cards or cash. This helps to control the amount of fuel picked up from outside sources and to maximize the higher discounts available by having bulk stocks
- *Lubricants*   Only issues during normal running are recorded. Oil changes will be recorded on maintenance job cards
- *Tyres*   Expenditure on new tyres is recorded from invoices received. Sale of old casing will be entered as credits
- *Repairs*   A distinction is made between repairs and maintenance carried out in company garages and repairs by outside agents
- *Miles run*   This is recorded from driver tachograph charts and gives a simple but clear picture of vehicle utilization

This vehicle costing record also shows registration number or fleet number, make, vehicle group and operating base. Dividing a fleet into groups of similar vehicles (for example, vehicles under 3.5 tonnes GVW, or vehicles 3.5 to 7.5 tonnes GVW) also allows the costings to be arranged in groups and will highlight any variance within a group so that investigatory action can be taken.

Vehicle operating cost sheet

A specimen vehicle cost sheet is shown in Figure 48.4. All costs recorded refer to the direct operation of the vehicle. Overheads, rent, rates and wages are excluded as these would tend to reduce the value of the costings as a means of comparing the different types of vehicle. The following vehicle data is shown:

1   Registration or fleet number
2   Make, group, type, gross vehicle weight, unladen weight (3/3/B indicates the HGV driving licence class, the size of the vehicle in that class and 'B' denotes a box van)

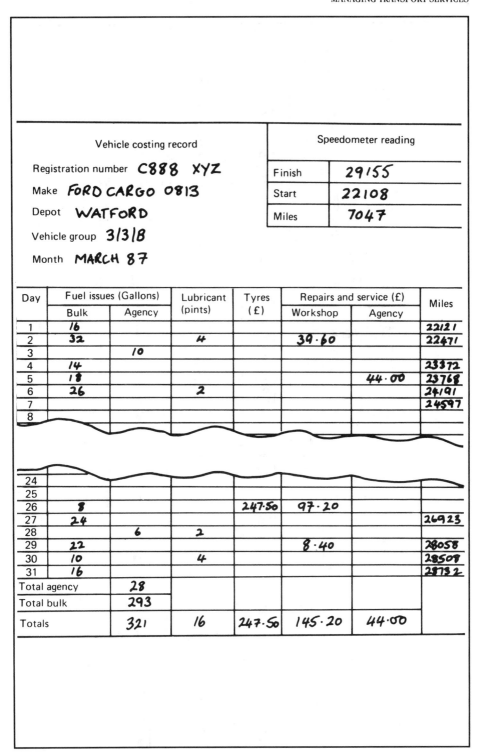

Day	Fuel issues (Gallons)		Lubricant (pints)	Tyres (£)	Repairs and service (£)		Miles
	Bulk	Agency			Workshop	Agency	
1	16						22121
2	32		4		39·60		22471
3		10					
4	14						23372
5	18					44·00	23768
6	26		2				24191
7							24597
8							
24							
25							
26	8			247·50	97·20		
27	24						26923
28		6	2				
29	22				8·40		28058
30	10		4				28508
31	16						28732
Total agency	28						
Total bulk	293						
Totals	321		16	247·50	145·20	44·00	

Figure 48.3   Layout of a simple monthly vehicle costing record

VEHICLE OPERATING COST SHEET

VEHICLE DATA

Reg. No.	C 888 X Y Z
Make	FORD CARGO 0813
Cost group	3/3/B
Date purchased	Oct. '85
Invoice cost (less tyres)	£18,473.
Estimated life	300,000 ML.
Gross vehicle weight	7490 Kgs
Unladen weight	3979 Kgs

STANDING COSTS

Interest	£1,662.
Licences	£570
Insurances	£580
Total per annum	£2,812
per month	£234.33

TYRES

Size	85 R 17.5
No. per set	6
Cost per set	£1,260.
Estimated life	40,000 MLS

ESTIMATED COST PER MILE

Tyres	£0.0315
Depreciation	£0.0616
LAST DATE COSTS UPDATE	January 1986

Month	Mileage	Fuel Gallons	Fuel Cost (1)	m.p.g.	Oil Pints	Oil Cost (2)	Tyres Est. cost (3)	Tyres Actual	Servicing/repairs Work shop	Servicing/repairs Agents	Servicing/repairs Total (4)	Depreciation (5)	Total running costs (1–5)	Running costs per mile £	Standing	Operational	Operational costs per mile £
1985																	
Oct	4284	211	321	20.3	7	2.10	135	–	84.80	3.20	88.00	264	810.10	0.19	234.33	1044.33	0.24
Nov	4291	214	325	20.0	8	2.40	135	–	16.80	55.20	72.00	264	798.40	0.19	234.33	1032.73	0.24
Dec	4838	236	354	20.5	6	1.80	152	–	93.94	2.50	96.44	298	902.44	0.19	234.33	1136.77	0.23
1986																	
Jan	6083	297	445	20.5	14	4.10	192	–	182.60	4.20	186.80	375	1202.90	0.20	234.33	1437.23	0.24
Feb	2612	124	181	21.1	7	2.00	82	–	42.90	22.70	65.60	161	491.60	0.19	234.33	725.93	0.28
Mar	7047	321	469	22.0	16	4.75	222	247.5	145.20	44.00	185.20	434	1314.95	0.19	234.33	1549.28	0.22

Figure 48.4   Example of a vehicle operating cost record sheet

3   The invoice cost of the vehicle, reduced by the value of a set of tyres and the expected life of the vehicle in miles

4   Details of tyre size and cost of complete set. The estimated tyre life is used as a basis for costing

5   Standing costs will include interest on capital invested, licences and insurance costs

6   Depreciation is calculated in terms of cost per mile, based on the actual cost and the estimated life of the vehicle in miles $(18\,473/300\,000 = £0.0616)$

7   Tyre costs per mile $(1\,260/40\,000 = £0.0315)$.

The details of running costs are taken from the monthly vehicle costing record and over the life of the vehicle a permanent record is built up. The following points are to be noted.

- *Fuel* Calculating mpg is suspect unless the tanks on the vehicle are full at the start and end of a monthly accounting period
- *Oil* Calculating mpg or miles per pint serves no useful purpose. Excessive oil use can be seen quite easily from total usage each month
- *Tyres* Calculations are based on the tyre wear. Actual purchases are shown and if the estimated mileages are correct, expenditure on tyres should balance the estimated costs over the agreed mileage
- *Depreciation* Obtained by multiplying monthly mileage by estimated cost per mile
- *Running cost* Total cost of fuel, oil, estimated tyre wear, repairs and depreciation, divided by miles run. This figure can be compared with the performance figures of other vehicles in the fleet within the same vehicle group, with its own performance figures over previous months and with cost tables published by the transport journals
- *Standing costs* These are now added to the total running costs to give the total monthly operating costs. The total operating cost per mile is of little use as this depends entirely upon the mileage recorded for the period. It will be seen from the example that total operating cost per mile varied from 22p to over 28p, whereas the per mile figure of running costs was reasonably constant

MOVEMENT OF PERSONNEL

The transport services function should be responsible for personnel movement in order to minimize the problems and increase the overall efficiency of the company by reducing the fatigue associated with people moving.

Sales and service function

The responsibility for the mobility of the sales force of a company comes within the function of transport services in that the provision of small vans, cars, and estate cars and the maintenance and servicing of such a fleet is the direct responsibility of the transport department of a company. The transport services function will need to advise on the choice of vehicle allocated to personnel of the sales and

643

service force, and will need to know the difference of law and taxation in the use of this type of vehicle.

Law on small goods vehicles

A small goods vehicle is defined in *s*60 (4) of the Transport Act 1968 as:

> One which does not form part of a vehicle combination and has a gross plated weight not exceeding 3.5 tonnes including the weight of any trailer drawn or, if not having a plated weight, has an unladen weight not exceeding 1 525 kg including the weight of any trailer drawn.

The law for the small goods vehicle and its driver can be summarized as follows.

Operator's licences

Exempt.

Vehicle testing

An annual test for roadworthiness when three years old or more.

Speed limits

1 Dual carriageways other than motorways and not drawing a trailer – 60 mph
2 Dual carriageways other than motorways when drawing a trailer – 60 mph
3 Other roads – 50 mph
  (The above subject to the road not being restricted to a lower speed limit.)
4 Motorways: not drawing a trailer – 70 mph; drawing a trailer – 60 mph.

Trailers

Subject to the weight of the vehicle not being less than the weight of the trailer being towed, the speed limit on derestricted roads and motorways is 50 mph. A 50 mph disc must be displayed on the rear of the trailer, and the kerb weight of the vehicle and the maximum permitted unladen weight of the trailer must be shown on each.

Driving licences

Ordinary driving licences group 'A' or group 'B' if restricted to automatic transmission vehicles.

Driver's hours

Goods vehicles with a gross plated weight not in excess of 3.5 tonnes including dual purpose vehicles (estate cars), are required to conform with the British Domestic Hours Rules which have been revised and simplified with effect from 29 September 1986. The rules are:

• Maximum daily driving – 10 hrs

- Maximum daily duty – 11 hrs

There are no regulations governing the hours of continuous driving, break periods, weekly duty or weekly rest periods.

Driver's records

Completely exempt (written records and tachographs).

Servicing and maintenance of sales and service vehicles

Although this class of vehicle is exempt from the requirements of operator licensing, it is important to understand that any convictions against a company or a vehicle user for contravention of the Road Vehicles (Construction and Use) Regulations 1986, or for instances of using, or causing to be used, vehicles which are found to be unroadworthy, may be taken into consideration when application is made for the renewal of, or the initial granting of, an 'O' licence. A system of reporting defects by the driver of the vehicle is recommended and a suitable form is illustrated in Figure 48.5. Drivers should also be asked to send in weekly reports showing any work done on the vehicle by outside garages.

DRIVER'S REPORT OF VEHICLE DEFECTS

Date _____

This form to be used only to report defects and must be handed to the Transport Office IMMEDIATELY on your return. No verbal reports please

Depot _____

Registration number _____   Make_____

NATURE OF DEFECT. Faults must be reported at once, even if only of a minor nature

Speedometer reading _____ If anything is wrong, don't be afraid to say so

Driver's signature _____

Date rectified _____   By _____

Figure 48.5   Form for reporting vehicle defects

The company car

Mobility of personnel costs money. Just as the cost-effectiveness of a goods distribution service is judged on its contribution to the total profitability of a company by giving an efficient customer service, the value of a fleet of company cars should also be assessed on its contribution to the efficient mobility of management and executives, as well as the part it plays in recruiting the right calibre of person to fulfil the needs of the company. There are many different approaches to determining a policy for the supply and allocation of cars to company employees. Each company will decide its own policy based on its own needs.

A company car issued to an individual is considered as a benefit in kind and as such the user is liable to be taxed on the assessed benefit. The annual Finance Bill states the taxable benefit on types of car subdivided into groups either by engine capacity or retail cost. Fuel supplied to car users for private use is also liable to tax and full details are included in the Finance Act published after each year's budget.

Replacement policies for company cars

Any replacement policy will again depend upon the cash-flow situation of a company, and should take advantage of changes in secondhand market values, or impending price increases of new cars. It is possible to negotiate guaranteed buy-back prices for cars when they are purchased, but this type of arrangement tends to become less flexible and arguments will arise over delays and damage when vehicles are returned to the dealers. A well-tested policy with in-built flexibility is as follows:

1 Outright purchase of all cars after negotiating for highest fleet discounts
2 Replacement policy:

   • cars 1600cc and under, replace after two years
   • other cars, replace after 60 000 miles or three years whichever comes first

3 Disposal policy: sell to the trade (not to the dealer who supplied the original vehicle) or through car auctions where special fleet terms are available.

With the above policy, the transport services function will be carrying out a responsible task and obtaining every possible cost benefit for the company. It is flexible in that no firm contracts are entered into and the purchase and disposal dates can be delayed or brought forward for reasons of cash flow, to avoid heavy repair bills or to take advantage of minimizing the impact of taxation balancing charges which may become due at the end of a company financial year.

Chauffeur services

One of the neglected areas in a transport function is the provision of an efficient and well-managed chauffeur operation. Even the smallest company will have a driver, whose duties will include meeting visitors at airports and stations, and driving customers between company locations. Larger companies have chauffeurs allocated to directors and executives, whose duties may include tasks other than driving a company car. A chauffeur should be trained to keep himself and his car in immaculate condition, so as to portray an image of an efficient organization. Very often a chauffeur is the first contact a visitor will have with a company and the initial impressions can be of vital importance.

Company air services

The company aircraft, owned and operated by a company for use by its personnel is now firmly established in the UK. Its justification on financial grounds is difficult to assess, but any cost exercise based solely on financial justification must fail. The task of the transport services function is to operate a service based on the highest standards of safety and also to minimize the additional costs which accompany the operating of a company aircraft. Safety, comfort, punctuality and reliability are the most important features. Safety means operating to a high standard and strict compliance with the current air navigation orders. Comfort of passengers should take into consideration cabin layout, quietness, facilities for reading and writing, temperature control and, above all, commonsense thinking of the crew to find a comfortable flying altitude for that particular journey. Punctuality and reliability are the two features which will test the efficiency of the service. Crews must ensure that the aircraft is always waiting for the passengers. Timings are important. Passengers should know the take-off and arrival times.

There are a number of ways to acquire the use of an aircraft:

1 *Charter* Specialist companies will supply the aircraft and crew, and carry out all maintenance, route-planning and management
2 *Lease* An aircraft lease is available in two forms:

- a finance lease for the aircraft only, including all the instrumentation required to meet the standards of the CAA. This will be written over a period of years at the end of which the aircraft can be made the subject of a secondary lease at a much lower rental
- an operational lease which will provide an aircraft to the required level of specification, fully maintained to CAA standards and with the provision of the crew.

The administration in both cases would be under the control of the company using the aircraft
3 *Purchase the aircraft* And contract out all maintenance and management and also the provision of crews to an operating company
4 *Purchase the aircraft* And employ your own crews as well as providing the necessary management and maintenance controls.

Operating the aircraft

Owning your aircraft does not give you the right to operate outside the public category, and if the crew is supplied by a charter company and not employed directly by your company (that is, on the payroll) the operation will be subject to all the restrictions placed by the Department of Trade and Industry on a public-category operation. By employing your own crew to fly the aircraft, it is possible to operate in the private category using aircraft with an 'all up weight' not in excess of 12 500lb. All aircraft above this weight are required to meet the full standards of operation as laid down for operating within the public category. It is, obviously, always advisable to operate at the highest standards of safety irrespective of the type of aircraft used.

Selecting the aircraft and costing the operation

A wide variety of aircraft are available which are suitable for company operation, ranging from the single-engine helicopter which flies 'point to point' at speeds of up to 150 mph to the twin fan-jet aircraft capable of speeds approaching 600 mph. The approximate costs of operating helicopters and fixed-wing aircraft are as follows:

- *Helicopters* single engine (turbine): £375–£475 per hour
  twin engine (turbine): £825–£950 per hour
- *Fixed-wing* twin engine (piston): £210–£250 per hour
  twin engine (turbine) pressurized: £500–£650 per hour
  twin engine (jet): £1250–£1600 per hour

FURTHER READING

Commercial Vehicle Buyer's Guide, Kogan Page

Cooke, P.N.C. (ed.), *Car Fleet Administration and Finance 1985*, Professional Publishing Limited (updated quarterly)

Cooke, P.N.C. and Woodward, Frank, H., *Controlling Company Car Costs*, Gower, Aldershot, 1985

Duckworth, James (ed.), *Kitchen's Road Transport Law*, 25th edn, Butterworth, 1985

Gattorna, J., (ed.), *The Gower Handbook of Logistics and Distribution Management*, 4th edn, Gower, Aldershot, 1990

Lowe, D., *A Study Manual of Professional Competence in Road Transport Management*, Kogan Page, 1978

Lowe, D., *Transport Manager's Handbook*, Kogan Page (published annually)

Tables of Operating costs (annual), *Commercial Motor*, IPC Business Publications, London

Thompson, B.A., *Croner's Road Transport Operation*, Croner Publications (by subscription, and kept up to date monthly)

Thompson, B.A., *Professional Driver's Guide*, Croner Publications, (revised every two years)

Woodward, Frank H., *Managing the Transport Services Function*, Gower, Aldershot, 1977

Part Eight
ADMINISTRATION

49 Company law

F W Rose

A company registered under the Companies Act 1985 has a legal existence and personality quite separate and distinct from that of persons holding shares in the company. Many legal formalities must be complied with before such a company comes into existence. When formed, the company has rights and liabilities in law which depends upon a careful analysis of the relevant statutory rules.

FORMATION OF A PUBLIC LIMITED COMPANY

A private company is often formed to carry on a family business. Frequently there is only a handful of shareholders, usually members of the same family. A private company cannot offer its shares for sale to the public: any disposition is through a private contractual arrangement.

A private company may trade successfully for several years, but when expansion requires additional capital that cannot be supplied by the existing shareholders, a public company may be formed to take over and carry on the business. Members of the private company will exchange their shares for shares in the new public company. The additional capital needed for such items as land, new buildings and machinery will be provided by issuing shares which the general public may purchase if they wish. About 2 per cent of all UK companies are public companies.

A public company may apply for a stock exchange quotation, so that its shares can easily be bought and sold through stockbrokers and jobbers. The company will issue a prospectus which sets out:

1 The objects it will pursue
2 Reports by experts on property owned, the company's financial position, and its future trading prospects
3 The names of directors (if the board of directors includes well-known experts this may be an inducement to buy the shares)
4 Details of the company's capital structure.

This information will enable the investor to determine whether or not to buy shares.

The company must be registered. This is effected by filing the following documents with the Registrar of Companies:

1 The memorandum of association
2 The articles of association

3 A statement of nominal capital
4 A list of persons to act as directors and secretary, together with their signatures as evidence of their consent to act as such.

These formalities are usually dealt with by a solicitor, accountant or a company formation firm specializing in this type of work. This person or body also files a declaration that the company has complied with all formalities necessary for registration. The Registrar then issues a Certificate of Incorporation which is conclusive evidence that the company has been properly incorporated.

In law the company now has an existence separate and distinct from that of the individual members who hold shares in the company. The company:

1 Can own property, and members have no rights in that property: their interest is in the shares they hold
2 Can make contracts with other individuals, companies or members
3 Will continue to exist irrespective of the death of an individual member, whose shareholding is then taken over by the person who succeeds to his property
4 Must act through the medium of human agents who will control its affairs, such as directors.

The memorandum of association

This is the charter of the company embodying its constitution and powers. It must state:

1 The name of the company indicating (where appropriate) that it is a public limited company with 'Public limited company' (PLC for short) as the last words of the name. A private company will have the word 'Limited' as the last word of its name
2 The location of the registered office of the company
3 The objects to be carried out by the company
4 A declaration that the liability of members is limited
5 The share capital and its division into shares.

The objects clause

A company's main business objectives are stated in the objects clause of its memorandum of association, the original rationale being that money subscribed to the company by its members, or loaned by creditors, should only be used for those stated purposes. Members and creditors should be aware of the risk involved in so trading.

In practice companies have relied on widely drafted objects clauses, sufficient to cover immediate and also any future objectives, however remote, that the company may wish to pursue. As a result, objects clauses are long and complex, effectively giving the company power to make a contract on a very wide range of varying issues. Since the company is a non-human legal entity, it can only exercise its contractual powers in the objects clause through the medium of agents, such as the board of directors, or the managing director or an individual director. The articles of association of the company will state how and to whom these contractual powers may be delegated.

If a company makes a contract that is outside its express or implied powers, then the basic rule is that such a contract is *ultra vires* or beyond the company's powers, and consequently void. However the Companies Act 1985, as altered by the Companies Act 1989, now provides that, in general, the *ultra vires* rule is abolished as far as an outsider making a contract with the company is concerned. To take an example, an outsider 'in good faith' agrees to provide a service for General Enterprises PLC, but the contract negotiated by the board is *ultra vires* the public company's objects clause. This contract is deemed to be free from any limitation restraining the company's contractual power in the objects clause, any resolution passed by a general meeting or class meeting of shareholders, or anything embodied in a shareholder's agreement. 'Good faith' is presumed unless the contrary is proved. An outsider does not exceed the limit of good faith if aware that the contract is beyond the director's powers. An outsider is not bound to inquire whether the contract is permitted by the objects clause or whether there is any limit placed by the members on the power of the board or its delegates to exercise the company's powers. In effect, therefore, it is possible for an outsider to contract with and legally to enforce an agreement against a company without being concerned about the validity of the contract.

The company's position in relation to the contract so made is, in the first place, that a member of the company may seek by injunction to restrain a proposed *ultra vires* act before the company enters into it. Secondly, directors, who as agents of the company contract on its behalf and make contracts, have a duty not to exceed their powers originating from the company's memorandum. If directors do contract in excess of the company's power, then the company must pass a special resolution in order to be able to enforce the contract so made. Directors remain personally liable with regard to their actions which exceed the company's powers, and could therefore be held accountable to the company if it suffers loss by the outsider enforcing the contract against it. A separate special resolution may relieve the directors of this personal liability.

In future a company, when incorporated, may have a memorandum which simply states that its objects are 'to carry on business as a general commercial company'. That company may then carry on *any* trade or *any* business whatsoever, plus all things incidental or conducive thereto. Companies not carrying out trade or business in this commercial sense will have an old-style objects clause (holding companies, for example).

A company may alter its objects clause in any manner it wishes by passing a special resolution. This means that a company with an old-style objects clause may change to the simpler formula permitted under the new legislation.

The concept of limited liability

An investor who purchases shares must pay to the company the purchase price agreed upon. Usually shares must be fully paid for at the time when they are allotted to a shareholder by the company. If they are only partly paid for, then the shareholder is contingently liable to pay the sum still outstanding, even if the company is in liquidation. Once the shares have been fully paid for, the shareholder's liability is complete. He cannot be required to make further contributions, even if the company fails and is unable to settle debts owed to creditors who have supplied goods and services to the company.

Limited liability is one of the most important attractions of shareholding in a public company. After fully paying for his shares the investor has fixed the amount of money that he is prepared to place at risk. However disastrous the company's financial collapse, he cannot be called upon to pay more.

Articles of association

These govern the internal management of the company, regulating the rights of the members among themselves on such matters as:

1 Appointment and power of directors
2 Issue, transfer and forfeiture of shares
3 Rules regulating meetings of a company
4 Payment of dividends
5 Preparation of accounts and auditing
6 Alterations to the capital structure of the company
7 Rights of different classes of shareholders.

It is usual for a company to register its own special set of articles which make specific provisions on matters of internal management, particularly suited to the needs of that individual business.

CAPITAL AND SHARES

The authorized (or nominal) capital is the amount of money that the company is authorized by the memorandum of association to raise from the public, for example, £5 000 000. In practice the company may not require this amount immediately, but it can issue shares up to the limit specified at any time when it wishes to do so.

The issued capital is that part of the nominal capital which has been actually issued to the public for cash or other consideration, such as land or buildings, in return for an allotment of shares (for example, an issued capital of £2 500 000 out of the nominal capital of £5 000 000). If a subscriber is required to pay only half the amount due on his share allotment, then the capital actually received by the company (that is, the paid-up capital) will be only £1 250 000 in the above example.

The amount not yet paid up on the shares issued is referred to as uncalled capital. This may be declared by the company to be incapable of being required from a shareholder except in a winding-up of its affairs, thus acting as a fund that is guaranteed to be available for the settlement of debts when the company is wound up.

Certificate of entitlement to commence business

A public company may not commence business after incorporation or borrow money unless it has received a certificate to this effect. This will not be granted until the issued capital is at least equal to the authorized minimum permitted (at present £50 000). In addition at least one-quarter of the nominal value of each share, plus any premium payable as part of the purchase price, must have been paid up.

Payment for shares

The person allotted shares in a company may pay for them in money or 'money's worth', that is granting some form of benefit instead of cash. Payment in a form other than cash may result in the company not receiving the full value of the shares given in return; thus, the law has been strengthened to prevent such abuses. A public company cannot accept an undertaking by an allottee of shares to do work or perform services for the company as consideration for an issue of shares. If there is a failure to observe this requirement, the allottee still remains liable to pay the required sum in cash.

A public company is permitted to allot shares in return for an 'undertaking' to transfer a non-cash asset, such as land, within five years from the date of allotment. The non-cash asset must be valued by an independent person qualified to act as a company auditor to ensure that the company is receiving proper value in return for its shares. These provisions are inapplicable where one company takes over or merges with another company and shares in the company being taken over are exchanged for shares in the company that has made the takeover.

Increasing capital and pre-emption rights

When a company has issued all of its capital and received payment in full from shareholders, it may require further cash to finance an expansion of its operations. The company will usually be authorized by its articles to alter the capital clause in its memorandum and, if the members in general meeting so decide, an ordinary resolution may be passed to increase the share capital. Shares can then be issued to raise the additional capital. Suppose that prior to the issue of the new shares for cash, an existing shareholder, Jones, holds 60 per cent of the company's total shareholding. In effect, he controls the company as a majority shareholder. The issue of new shares to other persons could take this away by reducing his percentage of the total number of shares now in issue.

A company must not allot shares for cash unless an existing shareholder has been given the opportunity to buy the new shares in proportion to his existing holding. Thus, Jones could, if he so wished, buy 60 per cent of the new shares on offer and retain the same percentage interest in the company's capital.

Power over unissued shares

A takeover bid occurs when one company (Company A,) offers to buy or has already acquired a majority of the voting shares in another company (Company B). The directors of Company B may wish to resist the takeover as undesirable, or because they fear that they will be removed from office once the takeover has been achieved. In the past, if Company B had not yet issued all of its authorized capital, the directors could have used a power, often granted to them by the articles, to issue new shares, representing hitherto unissued capital, to themselves and their supporters. This manoeuvre may have given the directors and supporters control of a majority of the voting shares and so thwart the takeover to which the other shareholders were agreeable.

Directors may not exercise any power of the company to allot shares, or other securities such as debentures which can be converted into shares at the holder's option, unless authorized to do so by an ordinary resolution of members in general meeting or by the articles. The power so granted may be a general authority to allot, or limited to a specified amount. When such authority is granted it must state the maximum amount of securities that may be allotted, the date of expiry of the authority and its duration, which must not exceed five years. The authority may be renewed for a further period (maximum again five years) by members in general meeting. None the less, members now control the directors' actions in this area, since any authority given may be varied or revoked at any time by ordinary resolution in general meeting.

MEMBERSHIP

A shareholder is a member of the company entitled to the following rights:

1 To attend meetings and vote on issues affecting company policy, including the appointment and removal of directors. He may requisition a meeting if he wishes to discuss any matter of concern provided that he alone, or in conjunction with his supporters has at least 10 per cent of the issued share capital carrying a right to vote, or some lesser proportion as prescribed by the articles
2 To receive an annual report and accounts giving details of the company's affairs
3 To share in the profits made in the form of a dividend declared by the directors
4 To share in the assets of the company if its affairs are wound up, provided any property remains when the rights of other creditors with prior claims have been met
5 To transfer his shares when he wishes by selling or giving them to another person
6 To present a petition to wind up the company or ask for an order controlling its affairs.

Different classes of shares

A company usually issues different classes of shares, each having its attractions for the investor.

Preference shareholders are entitled to the following payments in priority to ordinary shareholders:

1 A yearly dividend out of profits, at a fixed though moderate percentage of the capital invested, for example, 7 per cent. Unless the articles of association state otherwise, arrears of dividend not paid in a previous year when there were no profits are carried forward and must be paid in future years when sufficient profits are available

2   Repayments of the capital contributed to the company when it is wound up, if, as is usual, the articles so provide.

Ordinary shareholders are entitled to:

1   The remainder of profits available for distribution, which will secure a high rate of dividend if the company is successful. However, if a loss results in any trading year a dividend may not be paid at all
2   Return of capital contributed to the company when it is wound up, if sufficient assets remain to satisfy these claims.

The market value of shares will rise if the company trades successfully and the ordinary shareholder, in particular, may make a capital profit on selling his shares.

Ordinary shareholders bear the risk of substantial loss if the company fails; consequently, they have a right to vote at meetings and control the company's affairs to the exclusion of preference shareholders who are usually entitled to vote only if:

1   Their dividend is six months in arrear
2   Their rights as a class are affected by some issue under discussion at the meeting
3   On a resolution to wind up the company.

MAINTENANCE OF COMPANY CAPITAL

A company raises capital to finance its business operations by issuing shares in return for cash or property. The amount so raised may increase or decrease, depending on the relative success or failure of the company's trading activities. Suppliers of goods extending credit to the company, whether on a secured or unsecured basis, do so in the knowledge that even if the company is sustaining trading losses, there should be sufficient capital to meet their claims for payment. The capital so available must not be reduced and placed beyond the reach of creditors by returning it to the members (as where the company buys back members' shares and so refunds their capital contribution).

There are a limited number of exceptions to this rule. Preference shares may be issued on terms that permit redemption by the company, and this principle has now been extended to ordinary shares. Capital may be raised for a limited time to finance a specific programme and then returned to members, thus eliminating the need to continue paying dividends on these shares. Such shares offer temporary membership of a company, with repayment of the nominal value of these shares (in some cases plus a premium) when the period of membership expires. Membership will end after a fixed period of time or, at the company's option, in accordance with the agreed terms regarding redemption. On repaying members their share capital or redemption, the company must replace the capital by issuing other shares to raise the money so lost. Alternatively, the company may transfer a sum from its distributable profits (which would otherwise have been paid over to members as a dividend) to a capital redemption reserve, which is then treated in

exactly the same way as capital. The provisions permit listed companies to purchase issued redeemable shares at less than the redemption figure (if the company has resources available to finance a purchase at an earlier date than that
agreed) from a willing seller.

A company may redeem its own ordinary shares through a purchase from a
willing seller, even though the shares were not issued by the company on the
understanding that they were to be redeemed. Such a purchase must first be
approved by members in a general meeting. The purchase may be made through
the medium of the Stock Exchange or direct from a member who wishes to sell.

Acquisition and transfer of shares

When shares are first issued by a company an investor may make an offer to
purchase them by submitting an application form. Allotment of shares by the
company creates a binding contract with the investor. Shares may be issued at a
premium; for example, 50p may have to be paid for a share with a nominal or face
value of only 25p. This means that existing shares already issued have a market
value of 50p; thus, the real worth of a share is determined by reference to the
market value, not the face or par value.

A share certificate will be issued by the company stating the name of the
shareholder and the extent of his shareholding. The register of members, kept by
the company, will record the shareholder's name and address and the number of
shares held.

The shares of public companies are quoted on the Stock Exchange and the
shareholder can determine the present value of his shares by referring to the
Stock Exchange list which is published in leading newspapers. One of the main
advantages of shareholding is the ability to sell quickly and realize the value of the
shares.

DEBENTURES

A company needing finance for a programme of expansion may be reluctant to
raise the additional capital required by issuing more shares. The money will only
be needed until the new equipment purchased earns sufficient profits to repay the
capital borrowed, the company may not wish to raise capital on a permanent basis
for such relatively short-term needs, since regular dividends must be paid. The
company borrows money from the lender and in return issues a debenture,
redeemable at a fixed or determinable time or at the company's option. The
debenture holder is entitled to:

1 A fixed rate of interest which must be paid even if it is paid out of capital, not
profits
2 Repayment of the principal sum when due
3 A charge on the company's property. This means that if the company fails to
repay the loan and interest when due, the debenture holders may satisfy their
claims by disposing of the company's assets. These claims have priority over,
and must be satisfied before, claims by all types of shareholders.

There may be a *fixed charge* (mortgage) over a defined asset. This is often land, but can be machinery or book debts. The company cannot now dispose of the asset so charged without the mortgagee's consent.

A *floating charge* is given over an asset of a particular type, often stock in trade, which is constantly changing its precise form. The charge floats over whatever stock the company owns from time to time. The company may sell the stock (which is then freed from the charge) and buy new stock (to which the charge attaches automatically). The charge may crystallize eventually, as where the company is wound up or a receiver is appointed. The charge then fixes itself to the assets subjects to it, in the state in which these assets are to be found at the moment of crystallization.

Administrative receiver

Debenture holders are given power to appoint an administrative receiver so that company assets can be used to settle their debts, interest due and costs incurred. Power will be given to carry on the company's business, sell company property and take proceedings in the company's name. This may be a prelude to a winding up of the company, but not in every instance. After settling the debenture holders' claims the company may be financially sound enough to be managed again by its directors, and business continues without any liquidation supervening.

MEETINGS

The company is obliged to hold various types of meetings from time to time to transact business. An annual general meeting must be held every year to deal with:

1 Declaration of dividends
2 Consideration of the accounts and balance sheet and the report of directors and auditors
3 Appointment of directors
4 Appointment and fixing of the remuneration of auditors.

Members must be given twenty-one days' notice of the meeting.

An extraordinary general meeting may be called by directors if important business needs to be transacted which cannot await the next annual general meeting. Holders of one-tenth of the paid-up share capital with voting rights may requisition such a meeting, even against the directors' wishes. Members must be given fourteen days' notice of the meeting.

DIRECTORS

Every public company must have at least two directors and a secretary. A proportion of the directors, usually about one-third, retire at each annual general meeting, and the members may re-elect them or appoint others in their place. A director may be removed by an ordinary resolution passed by members, but the director may make representations on the issue showing why he should not be removed.

The directors must manage the company's affairs by taking decisions at board meetings, otherwise they may be personally liable for their actions.

A director may be required by the articles to hold a certain number of shares in the company which are called his qualification shares, otherwise he must vacate his office. This gives him a personal interest in furthering the fortunes of the company to the best of his ability.

The articles may provide for the payment of a fixed fee to a director, but his remuneration is often stated in a service contract which he makes with the company. His remuneration must be disclosed in the annual accounts. A director is not entitled to compensation for loss of office or on retirement, unless approved by the shareholders.

The powers of the company, as determined by the memorandum and articles, are usually delegated to the directors in so far as they are not exercised by the company in general meeting. Members in general meeting cannot interfere with the manner in which the directors exercise their powers, unless they alter the articles accordingly. If directors exceed their powers the members may ratify their actions, provided the act is within the powers of the company.

Publicity concerning directors

The company must make available the following information about a director:

1 A register of directors and secretaries must be kept at the registered office and open for public inspection, specifying a director's name, address, nationality, business occupation and other directorships held, except directorships in wholly-owned subsidiaries
2 Details of a director's service contract must be kept at the registered office, or place where the register of members is kept or at the company's principal place of business. It must be open for inspection by members
3 The names of directors must appear on business letters, trade catalogues, circulars and show cards
4 A register of directors' interests in the company's shares and debentures must be kept at the registered office or place where the register of members is kept. It must be open for public inspection. Such holdings by a spouse and minor children must be disclosed. This enables a check to be made upon sales and purchase of the company's shares by directors. It may be evidence of insider dealing, with the director selling shares before figures and profits are published, and buying shares ahead of an announcement of a lucrative company contract. The director is then using his position to secure an improper gain.

Managing director

Directors may appoint a managing director on terms stated, usually in a contract between the company and the appointee. The board usually has the right to delegate any of its powers to a managing director. In many instances he is given powers co-extensive with the board.

A managing director removed from this office by the board remains a director until removed by members in general meeting. However, loss of the position of director automatically terminates the office of managing director.

Chairman

Directors may appoint one of their number as chairman. Often the chairman is given a casting vote at board and/or general meetings on any issue where there is equality of voting.

Shadow directors and connected persons

The various statutory provisions that impose numerous legal obligations and duties on directors, also cover any person occupying the position of director whatever name is used to describe his office. 'Shadow' directors are also treated as if they were directors for some purposes. This concept covers persons giving directions to directors, who then are accustomed to follow them irrespective of any legal or other obligation to do so. Thus, directors may manage a company in accordance with the policy dictated by the controlling shareholder. That shareholder becomes a 'shadow' director. A person giving professional advice, such as an accountant, does not thereby become a 'shadow' director. Persons 'connected' with a director may also have the same restrictions placed upon their activities as the director himself. A 'connected person' includes:

1 Director's current spouse and his children up to the age of eighteen
2 Trustees of a trust which has as one of its beneficiaries the director, his children, his current spouse or an 'associated' company
3 Partner of the director or a partner of the director's spouse, his children or his trustee
4 A company with which the director is 'associated' where the director and his connected persons hold one-fifth of the nominal value of the 'associated' company's equity share capital, or where the director, his connected persons and any company he controls hold one-fifth of the voting rights at a general meeting.

Disclosure of interest in contracts

A director may have a personal interest in a contract made by the company with some other body, such as a partnership in which the director is himself a partner, or another company in which he holds shares. The company is entitled to the unbiased advice of a director, unfettered by conflict between personal interest and duties owed to the company. Every director having an interest, direct or indirect, in the contract which the company is about to enter, must disclose that fact to the board of directors when the matter is discussed. Such disclosure permits the director to make a personal profit from the contract which the company enters into, but failure to disclose enables the company to rescind the agreement so made. These principles also apply to 'shadow' directors.

Where directors have wide powers of management the risk arises that a director may sell his own property to the company at an inflated price with the connivance of fellow directors, or purchase the company's property at an undervaluation. An 'arrangement', which covers transactions not strictly enforceable at law as a contract of sale, cannot permit a director or his connected person to acquire a non-cash asset from the company or its holding company above the 'requisite value' of over £100 000, or one-tenth of the value of the company assets if over £1 000, whichever sum is smaller. Further, a director or his connected person cannot sell a non-cash asset over the 'requisite value' to the company or its holding company. Arrangements exceeding the requisite value are permitted, however, if approved by members in general meeting. The holding company must consent as well as the subsidiary company directly involved. Here, the shareholders have the opportunity to assess the advisability of the arrangement and will give their consent only if the company's interest have been safeguarded.

Service contract for a director

A director may be dismissed by a majority vote in favour of his removal passed by members in general meeting. To protect himself financially the director may have an express, written contract of service with the company for a fixed period of time (for example, ten years). If removed from office before expiration of the period he may claim damages for salary, less tax, that he would have earned during the unexpired portion of his service contract. The sum involved may be considerable, thus dismissal can be an expensive luxury for the company. Shareholders are given the opportunity of voting at general meetings on whether directors are to be given such long-term service contracts.

A service contract for less than five years' duration, or for over five years' duration but terminable by giving reasonable notice (which means, in practice, about six months' notice) may be approved by the board or the managing director, depending on the person or body to whom the requisite power has been delegated. The consent of the members in general meeting is required for a service contract over five years' duration if not terminable by notice, or only terminable in specified circumstances. In the absence of such consent the contract itself is valid, but the term on duration is void, and the contract may be terminated by giving reasonable notice.

These provisions are designed to prevent abuses whereby directors negotiate such contracts on terms set by themselves immediately prior to an anticipated takeover bid or removal on a vote by members, so that on loss of office they recoup substantial sums as damages for breach of contract.

Loans to directors

There are strict limitations on companies making loans to directors. Their position as managers may permit abuses at the company's, and consequently the shareholders' expense, as by making loans on terms that are commercially unsound.

A company is prohibited from making a loan exceeding £5 000 to its own or a holding company's director, or providing a guarantee, indemnity or security in connection with a loan by some other person to such a director. However, a company may provide funds for a director to meet, or avoid incurring expenditure he has or will incur for company purposes, or to enable him to perform properly his duties as a company officer. Members in general meeting must give their prior approval with knowledge of the purpose and amount of the loan, or retroactive approval before or at the next annual general meeting. In the absence of such approval the loan becomes repayable, and the resultant liability must be discharged within six months of that meeting. Not more than £10 000 must be outstanding by way of loan at any one time to a particular director or his connected person from a 'relevant' company.

Director's duty of care

Directors are trustees of company assets in the sense that, being in a fiduciary relationship with the company, they must exercise their powers bona fide for the company's benefit. If a director makes a personal profit, secret or disclosed to members, out of his position as director, then it must be paid over to the company. It is immaterial that the profit would not have been destined to swell company assets but for the director's improper behaviour.

Directors are bound by a common law duty to act honestly and without negligence. The standard imposed is that of the reasonable person when managing his own affairs. A higher standard can be imposed on an expert acting on matters within his own expertise (directors often have specialist skills in matters such as finance, accounting, legal issues, marketing and sales, for example).

If a director is sued for breach of duty, the court may wholly or partially relieve him if he acted honestly and reasonably as a normal person conducting his own affairs, and ought fairly to be excused the consequences of his acts that have caused loss to the company.

INSIDER DEALING

An insider dealer is someone connected with a company such as a director, company secretary, auditor, employee or other person in a business or professional relationship with the company, who has acquired in confidence specific information; that is, unpublished price-sensitive information, materially affecting the value of that company's shares and debentures or the securities of a company in the same group. The insider dealer then buys or sells such securities on the Stock Exchange without disclosing this information, which is not generally known to those persons who deal in, or would like to deal in, the securities affected. Persons who receive unpublished sensitive information are prevented from dealing in securities to which the information relates.

An individual who has price-sensitive information and/or is prohibited from dealing in a company's securities must not counsel or procure another person to so act, knowing or reasonably believing that such dealing would occur.

Contravention of these rules is a criminal offence under the Company Securities (Insider Dealing) Act 1985. There does not appear to be a civil remedy in this situation. In principle, if someone (such as a director) buys or sells shares in his company because he knows inside confidential information affecting their value, then the profit so made (or the loss so avoided) should in theory go to the company, since he is making an improper profit out of his official position. In such a situation it seems difficult to provide recompense to the shareholder buying from or selling to the director concerned, since the shareholder acted on his own initiative and was not induced to do so by that director. Nor is there a recognized duty to reveal the relevant information to the shareholder involved on an individual basis.

Theoretically, following a conviction for insider dealing, the court could order compensation to anyone suffering from the crime under the Powers of Criminal Courts Act 1973, though there could be problems in determining the precise amount recoverable. The register of a director's interest in shares of his company, together with the interest of his spouse and minor children, may help to establish insider dealing by illuminating his sales and purchases.

PROVISION FOR EMPLOYEES

A company may make provision for its own employees, or former employees, or those of a subsidiary company, when that company or one of its subsidiaries ceases business or transfers its business to a new owner. This provision permits a redundancy payment to an employee losing his job above the maximum sum authorized under the Employment Protection (Consolidation) Act 1978. The proposed payment must be sanctioned by members in general meeting approving an ordinary resolution. The articles or memorandum may state that a resolution by the directors suffices, or give a greater element of control to members by requiring a special or extraordinary resolution in general meeting.

DIVIDENDS

Dividends are trading profits divided among members in proportion to the number of shares held. The directors are responsible for fixing the rate of dividend, with the sanction of the general meeting. Shareholders cannot demand a dividend if the directors refuse to declare one, even though the annual profits seem to warrant some payment. Profits do not have to be distributed as dividends, as the directors may think it wiser to use them to offset past losses, or to transfer them to reserve to meet future liabilities. Once a dividend has been declared, however, a shareholder may sue to recover the sum he is entitled to receive if payment is not made.

FURTHER READING

Keenan, Denis, *Smith and Keenan's Company Law for Students*, 8th edn, Pitman, London, 1990. Some excellent background material and a useful summary of case law

Morse, Geoffrey, *Charlesworth's Company Law*, 14th edn, Stevens, London, 1991. A standard, inexpensive, straightforward text

Northey and Leigh, *Introduction to Company Law*, 4th edn, Butterworth, London, 1987. Good coverage in a style that is easy to follow

50 Contracts between companies

F W Rose

There are several elements that must be present before an agreement becomes a contract binding in law. Although the examples given concentrate on the sale of goods, the legal requirements are the same for all types of contract, whether the subject matter is a contract for the sale of goods or supply of a service by one company to another, or by a company to a private individual (or vice versa), or a contract of employment between employer and employee.

OFFER AND ACCEPTANCE

An offer is a definite indication by one party that he is willing to contract with another party on specified terms. A binding legal contract will come into existence if the terms are accepted without qualification and this fact is brought to the attention of the party making the offer. The conclusion of a contract is often preceded by lengthy discussions between the parties, but from these negotiations it must be possible to extract a firm offer followed by a firm acceptance.

Company B may ask further questions to induce better terms from Company A, but without intending to reject the original offer which will be accepted without qualification if better terms cannot be secured (for example, whether a total purchase price of £20 000 can be paid in instalments).

Any variation between the terms of the offer and the acceptance prevents the formation of a contract. For example, if Company A offers to sell Company B one hundred office desks at £500 each, the offer is not accepted if Company B agrees to buy at £400 each. Company B has rejected the original offer and made a counter-offer which is capable of acceptance by Company A. If Company A rejects the counter-offer, Company B cannot accept the original offer, unless Company A agrees. By this time Company A may have sold the goods to Company C. Company B cannot sue Company A for £10 000 damages for breach of contract if desks of the same type have to be purchased elsewhere for £600 each.

Keeping the offer open for a stipulated time

If a company offers to sell goods on stated terms, the company to whom the offer is made may be allowed a period of time to reach its decision. If an acceptance is communicated before the time allowed has elapsed, then a binding contract comes into existence. Although the company making the offer may feel morally bound to allow the company to whom the offer is made the stipulated period of time for reflection, the offer may be revoked at any time before notification of acceptance, even if the stipulated period for consideration has not ended. This right may be exercised where changed circumstances render conclusion of the contract undesirable, as, for example, where the market price of the goods has risen.

To safeguard its position the company to whom the offer is made may take an 'option' on the goods. This is a separate, binding contract whereby a period of time is given to reach a final decision on purchase. If during the period of the option the offer is revoked, the company making an offer commits a breach of contract for which damages are recoverable. Since the option itself is a contract, it must satisfy all the essential requirements of a contract. This usually means that the company making the offer must be paid for granting the option.

Lapse and revocation of an offer

An offer lapses if it is not accepted within the stipulated time. Where a given period of time for acceptance is not prescribed in the offer, there must be acceptance within the time that is 'reasonable' in the circumstances of the case.

An offer may be revoked any time before acceptance, but revocation is effective only when actually communicated to the party to whom the offer was made. It is important to choose a reliable means of communication, so that the company to whom the offer is made cannot claim that it has not heard of the revocation. If the post is used, a revocation is effective only when it is actually received. If the communication is lost in the post the revocation is ineffective. Notification of the revocation may be made through some reliable source, such as the company's sales manager.

If telex is used as a method of communication, then the contract is concluded at the time when the acceptance is actually keyed out. If the message is received in some other country, then the contract will be governed by the laws applicable in that foreign country, not by English law.

Need for a special method of acceptance

The company making the offer may request an acceptance in a particular form, such as telephone, telemessage or telex, a likely possibility where a speedy answer is required. Acceptance by another method, for instance a letter, would then be invalid. If the method of acceptance were quicker than the one prescribed by the offeror, such as a telex instead of a letter, this would probably be a valid acceptance.

Where a speedy reply is not required, but a particular method of acceptance is stipulated, use of the alternative method will not invalidate the acceptance if the circumstances suggest that there was a choice. For example, pending execution of a standard written agreement containing contractual terms, an informal letter of acceptance may suffice, especially if the party making the offer expressly or by conduct waives the condition as to the special mode of acceptance.

Sometimes when a particular method of acceptance is stipulated any alternative form of acceptance will be invalid. A company selling its goods may have drafted a written contract embodying all relevant terms to cover issues (such as problems relating to delivery) which may give rise to difficulties between the contracting parties. The seller will insist on the buyer signing the written agreement to signify assent to these standard terms. Refusal to do so will result in the seller failing to contract, or to negotiation of different terms which are mutually acceptable.

Standard contracts of this type often embody an exemption clause, a term used to describe a contractual clause which is inserted into a written contract attempting to limit or remove the legal liability of the contracting party who has insisted on its inclusion. Experience may have shown that a seller will be exposed to extensive liability in certain situations where goods supplied prove to be defective: consequently the right of action by the party suffering loss is removed at the outset, by mutual consent. The problem here is that such clauses are often imposed by the dominant party to the contract against a weaker party, who is left with little choice but to accept the exemption clause or abandon the idea of contracting. Usually most, if not all, suppliers of a particular type of goods impose similar exemption clauses.

TENDERS

A company may invite a tender from businessmen for the supply of specified goods or services. Every tender submitted is an offer and the company can accept any tender to bring a binding contract into existence.

Where tenders are invited for the supply of goods or services as and when demanded, the company submitting the successful tender is making a standing offer. There is a separate acceptance by the company requiring the goods or services each time an order is placed with the party who has submitted the tender. A fresh contract is made each time an order is placed.

Where this type of agreement includes an estimate of the quantity required, there is no obligation to order goods of any particular quantity or indeed any goods at all. On the other hand, if the buyer undertakes to purchase all his requirements in relation to specified goods from the person whose tender is accepted, there is a breach of contract if the goods are bought elsewhere.

The standing offer may be revoked at any time by the party making it, except in relation to any goods or services that have been ordered. To prevent this happening there is usually a binding undertaking between the parties to keep the standing offer open for a stipulated period. This usually means that a sum of money must be paid to the party making the standing offer.

CONSIDERATION

The majority of contracts made are simple contracts and the presence of valuable consideration is essential to their validity. This means that each party to the contract must confer a benefit on the other party in return for the benefit received. If Company A sells goods to Company B for £1 000, Company A loses the goods but receives the purchase price of £1 000. Company B has to pay the £1 000 but receives the benefit of the goods in return.

Consideration is a more complex doctrine than this simple illustration may suggest. It can take the form of an exchange of promises, with Company A promising to sell and deliver goods by 1 January and Company B agreeing to accept and pay £1 000 for them. If Company A refuses to deliver the goods on

1 January, then Company *B* may sue for breach of contract or, alternatively, if Company *B* refuses to accept delivery, Company *A* may sue for breach of contract.

Consideration must be valuable. It must have an economic character and be worth something. The court will not determine how much the goods sold are worth and then determine whether the price paid is adequate. It is for business men, not courts, to make commercially sound agreements. No attempt is made to balance the respective promises or acts of the parties to determine whether the bargain is fair, provided each party has received some benefit.

FORM OF A CONTRACT

In most cases a contract does not have to be concluded in writing, but writing is useful since the precise terms agreed upon are then easily ascertainable. The following contracts must be in a written form however:

1　Bills of exchange, promissory notes and cheques
2　Contracts of marine insurance
3　Hire-purchase contracts
4　Contracts for the transfer of shares in a public company.

The Law of Property Act (Miscellaneous Provisions) Act 1989 provides that a contract to sell or lease land must be in writing, and signed by all the parties to the agreement if it is to be legally binding. The document must cover all expressly agreed terms. Usually, each party signs a copy of the contract and then exchanges it for a copy of the contract signed by the other party. This means that the buyer has a contract with the seller's signature on it agreeing to all terms negotiated, and vice versa. The contract is then enforceable in court, if necessary, by a decree of specific performance requiring actual conveyance of the property into the name of the buyer, as against payment of the agreed price. A sale of land at a public auction is not covered by these requirements, consequently there are no requirements on writing. The contract is valid when the auctioneer, on the seller's behalf, accepts the highest bid made by a buyer.

Although writing is not essential at the time when the contract is made, writing will be needed for purposes of evidence in a contract of guarantee whereby *A* promises *B* that he will settle *C*'s debts to *B* if *C* cannot meet his own commitments. If the writing does not exist the contract cannot be enforced in a court of law. The written document may be quite informal: a letter will suffice, provided it includes:

1　The names of the parties, or a sufficient description of them
2　A description of the subject matter
3　All material terms
4　The signature of the person being sued or his agent.

A few contracts must be embodied in a deed. Such contracts are:

1　A conveyance of land or interest in land, including a lease for a term exceeding three years
2　Gifts: a promise to give embodied in a deed is binding and enforceable, although consideration is not provided in return by the recipient.

There are statutory provisions governing the execution of a valid deed. It must be in writing. The deed need not be sealed if executed by an individual, but it must be clear that it is intended to be a deed, as by describing itself as such. Sealing is still necessary if a corporation executes a deed. Anyone who is party to the deed must sign it, in the presence of a witness who attests the signature by also adding a signature to the effect that the deed has been executed by those signing as party thereto. The document is then delivered as a deed by the person who has executed it to the person who is entitled to receive it. If it is a deed of gift, the donor executing the deed will deliver it to the donee, who will receive the gratuitous benefits promised by the deed, through legal action if necessary.

Intention to create legal relations

If an agreement is supported by consideration it is assumed that the parties intended it to be legally enforceable one against the other, especially if it relates to a commercial matter. The parties are free, however, to state expressly that their agreement is not intended to be legally binding. Then it is an obligation binding in honour only and not subject to the jurisdiction of the courts.

Such an approach to commercial contract is exceptional, but there is often an arbitration agreement, which has been framed in order to prevent either party taking court proceedings under the contract until the dispute has been referred to arbitration and an award made. Arbitration may be preferred because it is cheaper, less formal, and adjudicated upon by an expert with special knowledge of the problems involved. Under the Arbitration Act 1950 if, contrary to his agreement to submit to arbitration, a party starts court proceedings, then the court (upon application by the other party) may order a stay of the court action to allow arbitration to proceed; or the court may refuse to order a stay of action (as where the only issue is a point of law), thereby breaking the arbitration agreement.

CAPACITY TO MAKE A CONTRACT

There are several types of bodies and groups of people with the power or ability to enter into contractual relations, in contradistinction to the typical contract concluded by two individual human beings each possessing full contractual capacity.

Corporations

The company may be formed in accordance with requirements set out in the Companies Act 1985 (that is, a registered company). It is a separate legal entity with its own identity, able to enter into contract with other companies and individual human beings. It may own its own property, contract and acquire rights and liabilities, and may also sue or be sued, all in its own name. It is a separate body from the members of the company and, indeed, can enter into a contract with an individual member. It may also contract with another registered company which itself is one of the members. The legal status and contractual capacity of such companies is considered in detail in Chapter 49 under the heading 'Formation of a public limited company' and also under 'The objects clause'.

The Crown may grant a Royal Charter bestowing incorporation on non-commercial bodies such as The Institute of Chartered Accountants and various universities. These institutions have the same powers in contract as an ordinary individual. The Charter may be forfeited if the body concerned pursues *ultra vires* objectives beyond those originally envisaged. As a less drastic alternative, a member can seek an injunction to restrain such activities.

An Act of Parliament may create a company with power to pursue stated objectives, usually to provide some public utility. Many of these were nationalized, such as the coal industry run by the National Coal Board.

Unincorporated associations

Some organizations do not have a legal personality separate and distinct from that of their members, although affairs are carried out in much the same fashion as for an incorporated body: for example, a society formed to provide recreational and leisure facilities for its members. The association's property is treated as the joint property of all members. A member who contracts on its behalf does so as an agent, but becomes personally liable with remaining members as co-principals if they are deemed (usually as a result of the rules of the association) to have authorized execution of the contract. Alternatively, any contract made for the members' benefit can be ratified by them.

A member lacks authority to purchase goods on credit, unless specifically authorized. In fact, it is better if purchases are made for cash, or on terms requiring immediate settlement, so that it is clear that the assets of the association are sufficient to meet the obligation.

An action against the association based on a contractual claim can be brought against all members personally if they are few in number. In other cases, a representative order is made under the Rules of the Supreme Court against only certain members who must meet any damages claim successfully established, with a right of indemnity from association funds.

Trade unions fall into this category. Often a company will need to bring legal action against a trade union. Under statute the trade union cannot be treated as if it were a body corporate. Its property is vested in trustees to hold for the benefit of the union. However, it is capable of making a contract, and suing and being sued in its own name in respect of that agreement, with execution against its property to satisfy any claim. Any collective agreement made between the trade union and employer regulating hours, wages and working conditions of a defined group of employees is presumed not to be legally enforceable in the usual way a contract may be enforced against a trade union, unless that collective agreement is in writing and contains a provision agreeing to legal enforceability. An employers' association may be either a corporate body or an unincorporated association.

Partnerships

Instead of carrying on business through the medium of a corporation, a partnership or firm may be formed by a group of individuals with the intention of pursuing some commercial, trading or professional enterprise. A partnership firm is not a separate legal entity, but merely a group of individuals pursuing a business in common with a view to profit. Rules of the Supreme Court permit a firm to sue and be sued in the firm's name.

Any property used by the partnership, such as land, is held by all partners, or by one or more of their number as trustees for the remaining partners. Each partner may act as an agent and bind the firm in contract, if expressly authorized, or if acting within the scope of actual authority as a partner, or if exercising apparent authority by virtue of his position as a partner in a firm carrying out that particular type of business, or if held out by other partners as being authorized so to act. If partnership assets are insufficient to meet contractual liability incurred, the private estate of each partner may be required to meet the deficit. If one partner pays more than his share, he may seek contribution from his co-partner's private estate if they are solvent. In contrast, a member of the limited company is only liable for the sum he agreed to subscribe in payment for shares purchased from the company. A limited partner is only liable for debts up to the limit of his agreed contribution to partnership assets.

MISTAKES IN THE CONTRACT

A contract may have been concluded under a misapprehension as to a material fact. Where both parties mistakenly believe the subject matter of the contract to be in existence when this is not so, then the contract is void.

For example, a seller may conclude a contract to sell goods which are stored in his warehouse to a willing buyer. Unknown to both parties, at the time of contracting the goods have actually been destroyed by a warehouse fire. The buyer is not obliged to pay the contract price, because the parties have contracted about a non-existent subject matter.

A mistake by both parties concerning the quality of the subject matter does not avoid the contract, where they have agreed on the same terms on the same subject matter for example, (if A and B mistakenly believe that land about to be sold has valuable mineral deposits). The buyer cannot claim his money back and return the land. In this situation the court may be willing on occasions to set the contract aside, thus relieving the party who suffers most because of the mistake. This would only apply on terms which are fair as between both parties, as for example, allowing the seller to claim any expenses incurred.

A binding contract does not exist if the parties have negotiated completely at cross-purposes and made a mistake as to the identity of the subject matter. For example, one party intends to sell a cargo leaving New York in March on board a ship named *Eastern Star*, while the buyer intends to purchase the cargo on board a similarly named vessel leaving New York in January. The ambiguity of the circumstances make it impossible for the court to determine with reasonable certainty which cargo is subject matter of the contract. Conversely, an enforceable contract will exist on the terms as understood by one of the parties, if the mistake is basically the fault of one party only. For example, if a purchaser buys land mistakenly believing that it is more extensive in area than the plot being sold, he cannot avoid the contract simply because he failed to check the specifications of the sale which were readily available to him.

A contract is void if one party is mistaken as to a fundamental fact concerning the subject matter and the other party knows of the mistake and takes advantage of it. If Company *A* offers to sell goods to Company *B* for £1 250 when Company *B*'s previous offer to buy at £2 000 had already been refused, it is obvious that Company *A* really intended the price to be £2 250. Company *B* cannot accept the offer of £1 250 and enforce the agreement against Company *A*. On the other hand, if one party's mistake is not appreciated by the other party who accepts in ignorance of that mistake, then a binding contract exists. If Company *A* offers to sell goods at £350, when, because of an arithmetical error, £400 was intended, an acceptance of the offer by Company *B* is binding, provided the circumstances do not suggest that an obvious mistake has been made in the price charged.

Mistaken signature

A party may be induced to sign a written document embodying an agreement which is fundamentally different in nature from an obligation he intended to assume and the party inducing him to sign may be aware of the mistake. The mistaken party can escape liability in pursuance of the agreement only in the most exceptional cases, such as blindness or illiteracy. Company representatives signing contractual documents should carefully scrutinize the contents of the agreement and ensure that the agreement being signed is the agreement that they intend to sign and that all the individual terms are acceptable and have not been altered contrary to any verbal understanding that preceded the execution of a formal written document.

MISREPRESENTATION

A company may be induced to contract because of misrepresentation by the other party. A misrepresentation is defined as a false statement of a fact that is material to the agreement, made by one party to the other during negotiations leading to the agreement, which was intended to operate and did operate as an inducement to enter the contract.

Fraudulent misrepresentation

A false representation is fraudulent if it is made with knowledge of the falsity, or without belief in its truth, or recklessly not caring whether it is true or false. Honest belief in the truth of a statement negates deceit, even though the representation is stupid, careless or negligent. A belief is not honest, however, if the representor deliberately shuts his eyes to the true facts or purposely abstains from investigating them. The aggrieved party may either avoid the contract with or without suing for damages for deceit, or affirm the contract and also seek damages.

Although fraud is difficult to establish, it is present in contractual situations where a seller has grossly misrepresented the profits and turnover attributable to a business that is being sold, often accompanied by the production of false accounts and returns.

A contract cannot be avoided (rescinded) where the aggrieved party elects to waive his rights by affirming the contract, for example, if he takes benefits provided by the contract with full knowledge of the misrepresentation, as by using goods purchased.

A contract further induced by fraudulent misrepresentation must be avoided within six years of either discovery of the fraud, or the time when it could have been discovered by using reasonable diligence.

If the parties cannot be restored to their original positions by taking back the purchase price and goods respectively, then the contract cannot be rescinded. A buyer may have radically altered the property he purchased before discovering the misrepresentation or electing to rescind the contract; for example, there may have been substantial extractions from a mine that has been purchased. Damages may be recovered, however, to compensate the party misled where the property is now worth much less then he anticipated because of the misrepresentation.

It is too late to rescind where property has already been sold again to a third party who now has rights to the property in question.

Negligent misrepresentation

Although a representation may be made with an honest belief in its truth, thereby negating fraud and an intention to decieve, none the less the representor may display a lack of care in either making the statement at all, or alternatively in failing to correct it before conclusion of the contract, when the true facts have been discovered, or by using reasonable diligence should have discovered, that the representative's actions were negligent.

A person possessing special skills and competence who has made a negligent misstatement may be liable in tort at common law for the financial loss suffered as a result by the person acting in reliance upon it, if he or she owed the recipient of that information a duty of care to use his or her special knowledge when making the statement. For example, a firm of accountants might over-value stock while preparing audited accounts for their client. They would be liable for a breach of duty of care to anyone foreseeably relying on those accounts as representing the true position and, in consequence, contracting to buy the business from the client.

A party induced to a contract as the result of a negligent misrepresentation may sue the representor for damages as of right in respect of losses suffered. The measure of damages is the same as for fraudulent misrepresentation. The party misled by negligent misprepresentation may also seek rescission of the contract. The representor has an effective defence to any claim against him for damages, if he can prove that he had reasonable grounds for believing that the statement was true at the time when it was made and continued to hold this belief up until the time when the contract was concluded.

Innocent misrepresentation

A false representation will be wholly innocent if reasonable care has been taken to check its accuracy before making it. The person misled may claim rescission of the contract instead. The court may award damages, if this is fairer to the party responsible and an adequate remedy for the party misled; where, for example, the falsity is of relatively minor significance in relation to the transaction as a whole. Damages cannot be claimed in the first instance as of right.

When the remedy of recission is granted, the injured party may, in some instances, also claim an indemnity for losses suffered as a result of the contractual obligations undertaken, in order to be restored effectively to the position originally occupied before contracting. The injured party cannot be placed in the same position in which he would have been if the contract had been properly performed, since the effect would be the same as the granting of an award of damages. For example, if a lessee is induced by innocent misrepresentation to take a lease of premises, an indemnity will cover losses incurred by virtue of the lease terms (such as rent, rates and repairs) but will not recover for injury to health because the premises proved to be insanitary.

TERMS OF A CONTRACT

The parties themselves may state expressly the detailed terms that are to govern the manner in which the contract will operate, such as delivery dates and time of payment. In addition to these express terms, others may be implied by custom or trade usage. For example, in a contract of employment the express terms may regulate many of the more important rights and duties of the employer and employee on such matters as salary, hours of work, holiday and duties to be discharged. However, an employee is also under an implied duty to obey lawful instructions, while the employer must indemnify his employee against any losses incurred while discharging his contractual duties.

In any type of contract the court may imply a term in order to fill in a gap left by the parties in the terms expressly agreed upon, which fail to regulate their respective rights and liabilities. The judge effects the presumed intention of the parties in order to give the contract business efficacy, by adding the kind of term that the parties themselves would have drafted if they had considered the matter.

Where the owner of a wharf contracts to permit its use by another to unload a cargo, there is an implied belief that the wharf is safe for use by that particular vessel. If the vessel is damaged because it rests on a layer of hard rock just below a muddy river bed, then the wharf owner is liable, even though responsibility for the river bed is vested in another person.

In many contracts a number of terms are automatically implied by statute, irrespective of the intentions of the parties themselves. Exclusion of the operation of these implied terms is permissible only in specified circumstances. A number of very important terms are implied by the Sale of Goods Act 1979.

The seller of goods is bound by an implied condition that he has the right to sell the goods and can therefore transfer title to the buyer as a result of the contract sale, or will have the right to so transfer title at the time when the property is to pass, where there is a mere agreement to sell at some time in the future. A consumer sale is a sale of goods by a seller acting in the course of a business where the goods are of the type ordinarily bought for private use and consumption and are sold to a person not buying them in the course of a business. Other sales are non-consumer sales, as where the seller disposes of goods to a company which buys raw material in the course of business.

In a contract for the sale of goods by description there is an implied condition that the goods shall correspond with that description; this usually covers cases where the buyer has not seen the goods and relies on the seller's description. For example, if goods are described as 'new' it is a breach of this implied term to supply secondhand goods.

Where goods are sold in the course of business there is an implied condition that they are of merchantable quality except where the defect is specifically drawn to the buyer's attention before the contract is made, or the buyer examined the goods before contracting and the defect ought to have been revealed upon examination. Merchantable is defined as fit for the purpose(s) for which goods of that kind are commonly bought as it is reasonable to expect, having regard to any description applied to them, the price (if relevant) and all other relevant circumstances. For example, a new vehicle is not merchantable if, after purchase, it has a history of continuous breakdowns due to a number of different mechanical faults.

Where goods are sold in the course of business and the buyer, expressly or by implication, makes known to the seller the particular purpose for which the goods are being bought, there is an implied condition that the goods supplied are reasonably fit for that purpose, whether or not this is the purpose for which such goods are commonly supplied. If a buyer asks the seller to recommend a vehicle that is suitable for use by a commercial salesman covering long distances, the car sold should have those qualities of reliability and comfort that the buyer is expressly seeking in his purchase.

A specially drafted clause in the contract of sale may exclude the operation of the protections given in relation to description, merchantability or fitness. Such an exclusion clause if embodied in a consumer sale is void. In non-consumer sales, exclusion or restriction of these implied terms is permitted if reasonable. Such reasonable exclusion or restriction may be imposed by express agreement, inconsistent express terms, trade usage or a course of dealings. In ascertaining reasonableness the following issues may be considered, if relevant, to the situation in question:

1 Relative bargaining strength of each party to the other, taking into account alternative means of meeting a customer's requirements
2 Whether the customer received an inducement to accept the exemption or restricting clause in relation to liability; whether when accepting it he had the chance to make a similar contract with others not imposing such a clause
3 Whether the customer knew or ought reasonably to have known of the existence and extent of the exemption or restricting clause and whether trade customs or previous dealings between the parties show that such clauses are usual
4 Where an exemption or restricting clause only operates if the customer fails to follow a prescribed procedure. For example, failing to report to the seller defects in goods purchased within a reasonable time limit, as specified. Here it is important to ascertain whether it was reasonable when contracting to expect that compliance with the procedure would be practicable
5 Whether the goods were manufactured, processed and adapted to the customer's special order.

Remedy for breach of an implied term

If goods supplied are not in accordance with the contractual description, if the seller is without title, or if the goods are not 'merchantable' or 'reasonably fit', then the seller is in breach of a contractual condition. The buyer may rescind the contract by returning the goods. He may reclaim the purchase price and additional damages, if appropriate, in respect of losses that are not too remote. Alternatively, if he wishes the buyer may claim damages only; that is monetary compensation for the difference in value between the goods delivered and the value they were supposed to have. Here the buyer retains the goods purchased. The condition is treated as a warranty, for breach of which only damages may be recovered. The buyer cannot return the goods, but may claim damages only, where 'property' in the goods has already passed to the buyer. This means that the buyer has 'accepted' the goods purchased and used them for some time before making a serious complaint. A buyer does not 'accept' goods delivered to him unless he has had a reasonable opportunity to examine them.

Unfair Contract Terms Act 1977

Liability may arise in the course of a business or from the occupation of premises used for business purposes ('business liability') for a person's death or personal injury while on the premises. If death or injury is attributable to negligence, such as failing to ensure that business premises are safe to use, then liability cannot be excluded or restricted by an exemption clause in a contract or a notice.

An occupier of premises will not be liable if a lawful visitor is injured by using a defective lift, provided that the occupier has engaged an independent contractor, who is reasonably believed to be competent, to inspect, service and repair the lift regularly. Such an occupier is not negligent. It will be otherwise if he permits an obviously dangerous situation to arise on his premises without taking adequate preventive measures, as for example where accumulations of ice and snow make it difficult to walk safely between buildings in the employment complex.

Business liability for loss or damage (other than death or personal injury) resulting from negligence, such as damage to clothing or personal belongings, can be excluded or restricted by the person responsible by a contractual clause or notice, provided it satisfies the reasonableness tests discussed above. A defaulting party may rely on a contract term or notice restricting liability to a specified sum, by proving that it is reasonable to do so by reference to his resources to meet liability and whether he could insure against it. For example, liability may be limited to a specified sum for loss or damage to goods left in a cloakroom where payment of a small fee cannot cover loss of expensive items of clothing. A non-contractual notice may exclude or restrict liability if fair and reasonable in the circumstances, with the burden of proof resting on the party relying on the notice. For example, a notice in a pub car-park may exclude liability for loss or damage to any car parked there or its contents. The injured party's awareness of the existence of a restricting or exemption clause is not, in itself, voluntary acceptance of any risk of loss or damage imposed by the clause, but if the injured party is unaware of the clause it cannot be operative.

DAMAGES FOR BREACH OF CONTRACT

If one party has broken the terms of a valid contract, the innocent party is entitled to recover damages for any loss suffered. The latter must be restored to the position he or she would have been in if the particular damage suffered had not occurred, in so far as money can be sufficient compensation.

Recovery may be confined to those losses that arise naturally in the usual course of events from the breach, and are thus assumed to be within the contemplation of the defaulting party. In a contract for the sale of goods, where there is a market for the goods, the measure of damages recoverable by the buyer is the difference between the contract price and the market price of goods at the time when the seller ought to have delivered them. The buyer can purchase goods similar to the contract goods in the market. On the other hand, if the buyer has refused to accept delivery, the seller recovers the sum by which the market price falls short of the contract price at the time when the goods ought to have been accepted. The seller can dispose of the contract goods in the market.

If there is no available market but the buyer has agreed to resell the goods, the resale price may be taken as representing their value. The buyer's damages will be the difference between the sale and the resale prices, though the seller is unaware of the sub-sale. A loss of profit is recoverable for breach of a trading contract made between experienced parties if they can be taken to understand the ordinary practices and exigencies of one another's business.

If the seller is a dealer selling goods at a standard market price, this will be the same as the contract price; for example, the contract price and the market price of machinery may be £5 000. For refusal to accept delivery the seller may recover from the buyer the profit that he would have made if the sale had been completed. Even if the item is readily sold to a new buyer, the seller has made the profit on one sale only instead of upon two sales in cases where he has plenty of stock for disposal. Conversely, if a particular item can be sold as quickly as it comes into the seller's stock, the buyer's default is a matter of indifference to the seller. In such cases, only nominal damages are recoverable; for example, where a certain type of machinery is in short supply because of strikes.

Owing to special circumstances known at the time of contracting to the party ultimately committing a breach, a loss may be suffered outside the usual course of events. The defaulting party may pay damages in respect of the exceptional loss. For example, a vendor of land may know that the purchaser intends to develop the property and make a large profit. If the seller refuses to complete the sale he is accountable for this loss of profit.

The amount of damages awarded may be reduced to reflect a claimant's liability to reduce the losses suffered, if this is possible, as by selling or buying goods elsewhere.

Distinction between liquidated and unliquidated damages

Damages are unliquidated where one party to a contract sues the other to recover whatever sum the court holds to be the proper measure of damages in the circumstances. A contract may provide that, in the event of a breach, the innocent party may recover from the defaulting party a sum stated in the contract itself: this sum is called liquidated damages. This type of arrangement has the advantage of saving the time, trouble and expense of litigation should a breach of contract occur. Only the agreed sum is recoverable, even if the actual loss suffered greatly exceeds the sum fixed by the contract. If damages are to be assessed by the contract itself, it is essential to estimate with precision the monetary effect of any possible breach.

Distinction between liquidated damages and a penalty

A sum agreed as payable in the event of a breach of the contract may be liquidated damages or a penalty. The distinction is of vital importance. If the sum is liquidated damages it can be recovered from the party in default. It is regarded as a genuine pre-estimate of the damage suffered by the innocent party.

If the sum fixed by the contract is deemed to be a penalty, then essentially it is a threat held against the party likely to violate the contractual obligations. The intention of a penalty is to attempt to compel performance of the contract by severely punishing the party who refuses to implement it. The defaulting party is made liable to pay an extravagent sum, exceeding the greatest loss that could possibly result from the breach. A penalty is irrecoverable and the injured party is limited to recovering the actual loss he has suffered. If a company wishes to guard against breach of contract, a penalty clause is not the method to use.

An example will illustrate the practical operation of these rules. Company A may agree to install machinery on the premises of Company B. A term of contract may provide that if the work is not completed by 1 January, then for every extra working day taken to complete the installation Company A must pay Company B £1 000. If a delay of twenty working days results in lost production and lost profits of £20 000, this sum is recoverable from Company A as liquidated damages if the sum is a genuine pre-estimate of the loss likely to be incurred. In the same circumstances, if the actual loss is £30 000, only £20 000 is recoverable. Here Company B is confined in its claim to the genuine, though incorrect, pre-estimate of the likely loss.

On the other hand, if Company B's maximum loss of profit for one day's lost production could not possibly exceed £200, the clause in the contract stipulating £1 000 will be recoverable is a penalty. The court will disregard the clause and only the actual loss suffered will be recovered by Company B.

Specific performance

Damages may be an inadequate remedy and the court may order the defaulting party to perform specifically the obligation undertaken in the contract. This is a discretionary remedy, usually given for breach of a contract to sell or lease land, or sell chattels with unique qualities. In these cases it may be difficult for the disappointed purchaser to acquire similar property elsewhere.

FURTHER READING

Davies, F. R., *Contract*, 6th edn, Sweet & Maxwell, London, 1991. This is a useful introductory text in straightforward language and style

Downes, T. A., *Textbook on Contract*, Blackstone Press, London, 1987. A good basic treatment of fundamental contractual concepts

51 Intellectual property rights

Nicholas Manley

Historically, patents, trade marks and designs were referred to collectively as 'industrial property'. In recent years, it has become usual to refer to 'intellectual property' so as to include more clearly copyright, know-how and trade secrets. All forms of intellectual property can be bought, sold and licensed.

PATENTS

Patents for inventions were granted by the Crown in pre-Tudor times, but the first legislation was the Statute of Monopolies 1623, which made monopolies void except those granted for 14 years (now 20) in respect of 'any manner of new manufacture'.

The latest of many enactments is the Patents Act 1977 (referred to in this chapter as 'the 1977 Act') which came into force on 1 June 1978. There are still in force some patents ('existing patents') granted under the Patents Act 1949 (referred to here as 'the old Act'). Another major change was the coming into force (also on 1 June 1978) of the European Patent Convention (EPC), with the opening of the European Patent Office (EPO) in Munich. A further development is the Community Patent Convention (CPC), which has been signed by the EC members, but will not come into force for a considerable time because ratification of the EPC and the CPC by Denmark and the Irish Republic will entail amendments to the constitutions of these two countries.

The EPC provides a system whereby a single application at the EPO designating a number of member countries (which will include all the Western European countries when all the signatories have ratified the convention) selected by the applicant will be examined by the EPO and, if accepted, will result in the grant of a bundle of identical patents in the designated countries. The CPC will go further, in that an application at the EPO designating the EEC will, if successful, result in the granting of a single 'Community patent'. Thus, there will be three kinds of patent in the UK:

1 National Patents, granted by the UK Patent Office (UKPO) and effective only in the UK

2 European Patents (UK), granted by the EPO and effective only in the UK (although identical patents in the bundle will be effective in the other designated countries)

3 Community Patents, granted by the EPO and effective as a single entity throughout the EC (not yet applicable).

All three kinds of patents are, or will be, enforceable by the UK courts, but validity of Community Patents will be under the jurisdiction of the EPO with an appeal to a Community Patent Court (COPAC) yet to be established.

Invention

An adequate guide to the meaning of 'invention' for present purposes is that an invention is a new article or substance, or a new machine, or a new method or process of carrying out an industrial operation – the word 'industrial' including agriculture and horticulture. Computer programming is not included, but new computer programs now enjoy copyright protection (see 'Copyright', below).

Further types of activity may, with the advance of technology, become suitable for patenting in the future, and the 1977 Act provides that such new developments can be included within its scope by Statutory Instrument without the need for legislation.

Not all inventions can be *validly* patented; certain attributes are necessary to make an invention patentable. Before considering these, we need to know more about the nature of patents.

Patent specification

The grant of a patent can be regarded as a contract under which the State grants the patentee a twenty-year monopoly in making or using the invention in return for a disclosure to the public of the invention and how to put it into practice. The vehicle for this disclosure is the patent specification – a document printed and published by the Patent Office as a prerequisite to every granted patent.

The claim

Besides disclosing the invention, the specification has another essential function: the definition of the area of monopoly to which the patentee claims to be entitled, this being contained in the claims of the specification.

It has long been recognized that to confine the patentee's monopoly exactly to his invention would stultify the whole system, since a competitor could evade the monopoly simply by making an inconsequential variation. The patentee is therefore allowed to include in his monopoly a range of constructions or processes centred on the original invention, but in return he must by means of the claims define precisely the scope of the monopoly for which he wishes to have protection and to which he believes himself to be entitled.

A simple example will help to clarify this rather difficult concept. Suppose the invention is a ballcock for a cistern. It is a piece of mechanism which includes a float in the form of a hollow sphere. If the patent monopoly were confined to the exact mechanism as conceived by the inventor, a competitor might be able to evade it quite easily by replacing the sphere by an egg-shaped float or even perhaps a rectangular one. So the patentee does not refer in his claim to a 'hollow spherical float' but to a 'hollow body serving as a float' or perhaps just to a 'float'.

The extent to which the inventor can extrapolate from his original invention is dealt with in the 1977 Act by the provision that the claims must be supported by the matter disclosed in the specification $(s14(5)(c))$, but this can in the last analysis only be a subjective judgment by the tribunal considering the matter.

Explaining the nature and function of patent claims is not made easier by the fact that the word 'invention' is used not only as above to mean the concrete article or process devised by the inventor, but also in the quite different sense of 'the invention claimed' – that is the area of the monopoly. Although these two meanings are hallowed in the legal phraseology of patents and by time-honoured usage generally, the word will in this chapter be used only in the first of the above senses, thus removing at least one semantic obstacle from the reader's path.

What is a patent?

A patent can be likened to a fence erected round an area of technology and bearing the sign 'trespassers will be prosecuted'. The area of technology will be recognizable as the claims discussed above, while somewhere near the middle of the area is the 'invention'.

By way of illustration, consider a process for making sulphuric acid by passing sulphur dioxide over a catalyst at a temperature of $x°$C. The patentee will probably have been allowed to include in his claims a range of catalysts and a range of temperatures on either side of x. The fence delimits these ranges.

It will be observed that the fence in itself does not prevent anyone from trespassing on the forbidden area, or *infringing* the patent as it is called. But once the fence is crossed the patentee has a cause of action in the High Court or the new Patents County Court, claiming damages and, usually much more significant, an injunction to stop the infringer from doing it again.

Validity of patents

The validity of a granted patent can be the subject of Proceedings in the Patent Office acting in a judicial capacity, or the Patents Court, which is a branch of the High Court. A new Patents County Court is now also available for patent actions. If the patent is held to be invalid, it is revoked.

The grounds of revocation under the new Act are of three types:

1   That the invention is not patentable
2   That the patent was granted to somebody who was not the inventor (s) or a person deriving title from him or them
3   That the specification does not adequately tell the expert (in the 1977 Act, 'person skilled in the art') how to put the invention into effect.

The state of the art

The fundamental requirements of patentability are concerned with the relationship of the invention to the 'state of the art'. This phrase means the sum total of the knowledge available to the public in the relevant 'art' (that is, technology) at the 'priority date' of the patent. The knowledge can be documentary, as, for example, in the technical journals or, above all, in prior patent specifications (usually referred to for short, but inaccurately, as 'prior patents'), or it can be by virtue of what has been done before (so-called 'prior use'), provided the nature of the use was known to the public (for example, as a product available on the market).

Under the old Act the knowledge had to exist in the UK to be effective, but under the 1977 Act it can be anywhere in the world. This will not make as much difference as might be thought, because most technical publications, including patent specifications, become available in the UK shortly after publication.

Novelty

The first requirement for patentability is that the invention shall be new. This means that if a comparison is made between the alleged invention and the state of the art, there must be some genuine difference between them. In making the comparison, account must be taken not only of the express wording of the relevant documents, but also any clear implications. The approach is to ask the person skilled in the art what, on a fair reading, the document actually means to him.

Obviousness

The commonest ground of invalidity is probably that the invention is 'obvious and does not involve any inventive step' having regard to the state of the art. This means that while there is some difference between the invention and the prior art, so that it can properly be described as new, the difference would have been obvious to the person skilled in the art, such as, for instance, a 'mere workshop variant'. To justify a monopoly, the inventor must have taken an 'inventive step'. This need not be of breakthrough proportions; quite the contrary. In one case it was held that a 'mere scintilla of invention' will suffice. What is certain is that there is no definition of what it consists of. It is a matter for the subjective judgement of the tribunal considering the case.

One criterion enters into most arguments on obviousness. What this amounts to is that if there had been an incentive for some time for a new development but no one had thought of it before the inventor, it is not possible to regard it as having been an obvious thing to do.

Secret prior use

It is fundamental that a patent should not be granted which could stop a person continuing to do what he was doing before, even if he were doing it 'secretly'. The 1977 Act (recognizing that secret use is not part of the state of the art) provides that, if a person other than the inventor was using the technology 'secretly' before the priority date of the patent, he shall be free to continue to doing so. The patent remains valid and enforceable except against the individual or company which operated the invention before the priority date.

Is the technology an invention?

This question must be asked before patentability is considered. The 1977 Act, in s1, defines the requirements of a patentable invention.

Grounds of invalidity concerned with the specification

The specification must disclose the invention in a fair and intelligible manner and must reflect the breadth of the scope of the claims; it must not withhold significant information on its optimization, because this information is the consideration for the grant of the patent. Failure to comply with this requirement is a ground of revocation.

Employees' inventions

In the absence of any rule or law to the contrary, an invention and its patent rights belongs to the inventor or joint inventors. But an invention made by an employee is the employer's property if:

1 The employee's normal or specially assigned duties might reasonably be expected to lead to the making of an invention; and
2 The invention was made in the course of those duties.

The first is a legal question for the Patent Office or courts in a particular case. They could be assisted if a job description agreed between employer and employee stated specifically that the job was expected to result in inventions. But a blanket statement in a service contract that all inventions made during the employment will automatically belong to the employer will not be enforceable unless conditions 1 and 2 above are met.

Compensation to employee inventors

The 1977 Act (s40) introduced the concept of awarding compensation to employee inventors in appropriate circumstances. Entitlement can arise in either of two cases:

1 An invention made after 1 June 1978 belongs to the employer and a resulting patent is of outstanding benefit to the employer
2 An invention belongs to the employee and a resulting patent has been assigned or exclusively licensed to the employer after 1 June 1978, and the benefit derived by the employee from the assignment or licence is inadequate in relation to the benefit derived by the employer.

An application for an award can be made by the employee (even if his employment has ceased) to the UKPO or to the Patents Court or Patents County Court, at any time up to one year after the patent has ceased to have effect and any number of applications may be made. The 1977 Act (s41) sets out the considerations which the tribunal must have in mind.

An employee is debarred from making a claim to the UKPO or the court for an award of compensation if he is a member of a trade union which has entered into a 'collective agreement' with his employer relating to payment of compensation.

Contracts on employee inventions

The 1977 Act overrides the ordinary law of contract in certain cases. Thus, s42 renders unenforceable any contract between an employer and employee inventor which reduces the statutory rights of the employee, if the contract was made *before* the invention. A contract relating to an invention belonging to an employee which was entered into after the invention was made is clearly enforceable, and presumably the same applies to inventions belonging to the employer.

A collective agreement with a trade union relating to employee inventions is enforceable in respect of members of the union only. It appears that non-members retain their full statutory rights under the Act, even if they benefit from the collective agreement, but the tribunal could probably take this into account in awarding compensation.

Infringement of patents

A patent is infringed by anyone who makes, imports, keeps, uses or sells an article or machine protected by the patent, or uses a process protected by the patent, or sells the direct product of such a process, whether the process is conducted in the UK or abroad. To decide whether a given article is protected by the patent it is necessary to construe the definition constituted by the patent claim and determine whether the article falls within or without the definition.

British patent law is strict in holding the patentee to the words of his claim, but there are two qualifications. The first is that the *de minimis* rule (that the law takes no account of trifles) applies as always. The second is the doctrine of *equivalents* or 'pith and marrow', according to which a man infringes a claim if he substitutes an element of it by an equivalent (as, for instance, a non-spherical float in a ballcock claim confined to a spherical float) so as to take the pith and marrow of the claim even if it is not within its exact wording.

This doctrine has been modified by recent case law in that the 'purposive construction' of a claim rather than just its literal wording must be considered in matters of patent infringement, so that an article or process which might avoid infringement of the strict wording of a claim might nevertheless still infringe that claim. Expert advice is therefore desirable in patent infringement matters.

Contributory infringement

Contributory infringement applies to patents where the invention essentially involves the use of some unpatented material, substance or article. Section 60(2) of the 1977 Act provides that anyone selling such unpatented material, substance or article, knowing that the customer intends to use it for infringing the patent, is guilty of infringement. Section 60(3) makes the additional qualification that if the material and so forth is a 'staple article of commerce', the supplier must actually induce the customer to infringe before he (the supplier) can be held to infringe. A typical example would be the issue of a data sheet to customers recommending the infringing use.

Pharmaceutical use

A method or process of treating the human body is not a patentable invention (*s2*(6)). However, the 1977 Act provides that a patent can be obtained for a new pharmaceutical use of a substance and such patent will be infringed by a person supplying the substance for the patented use, even though the use itself, being a treatment of the human body, is not deemed to be an infringement. In other words, the pharmaceutical manufacturer can be sued, but not the doctor.

Court action

If the patentee wishes to go to the limit in enforcing his patent against a supposed infringer, he must issue a writ for infringement in the Patents Court or the Patents County Court.

If the patentee cannot tell from any product sold by the alleged infringer whether what the latter is doing infringes the patent (as in the case of a chemical process, for example) he can ask the court for an order for discovery and inspection on the basis of a reasonable suspicion.

It is routine in an infringement action for the defendant to counter-claim for revocation of the patent on the basis that it is invalid on one or more specified grounds. The question at issue at the trial is, therefore, whether any valid claim of the patent has been infringed.

Threats

Under *s*70 of the 1977 Act anyone who makes unjustified threats to bring proceedings for infringement against somebody who is reselling an article or product (such as a retailer) is liable to an action to restrain these threats. But the patentee is free to threaten the manufacturer or importer.

European patent law

The function of the EPO was mentioned at the start of this chapter and the procedural aspects will be dealt with later. The substantive law embodied in the EPC is mainly confined to the criteria for granting and validity of patents; in other words, what is a patentable invention? It is the intention of the 1977 Act to bring UK law into line with the EPC as far as is practicable. It follows that EPC law on patentability is essentially as set out in relation to UK law.

The 1977 Act had to make provision for eventual ratification of the CPC. Community patents, granted by the EPO under the EPC, will be effective in the UK. It is therefore important that British law should be assimilated to the law of the EPC.

Patenting procedure in the UK

Each country has its own system of patent law and administrative procedure. In broad outline the principles set out in the preceding sections, although directed primarily to the UK and EPC law, are valid for overseas countries, with a few important exceptions which will be referred to later. Administrative procedures, however, differ substantially from country to country. Those obtaining in the United Kingdom will be considered first.

Priority dates

The first step in obtaining a patent is to file an application at the UKPO. It has always been a special feature of the British system that the application need be accompanied only by a 'provisional' specification, which does not require the inclusion of the monopoly-defining 'claims' and that the application need not be completed until twelve months after the filing date.

For the sake of harmony with the EPC, the 1977 Act has formally abolished provisional specifications, but the substance of the system has been retained by an ingenious device.

Under the 1977 Act, the applicant need only file a description which can be informal; in particular, he does not need to include claims. In fact, the description can be just the same as a provisional specification under the old Act. Such a document serves to establish the applicant's priority date for his invention. But in order to proceed to the granting of a patent, the claims must be filed within twelve months. Alternatively, a new application containing a specification with claims may be filed and this is particularly useful if the applicant wishes to add new matter to his description. If such new application is filed within twelve months of the first application, the priority date established by the latter remains effective. The system is thus essentially the same as the old provisional and complete specifications.

Publication

The specification with claims is published, usually just as it is filed, at 18 months from the priority date. The specification is printed and indexed in a comprehensive classification system, and copies can be bought at the Sales Branch of the UKPO. It should be noted that this document only fulfils one part of the function of a patent specification – the provision of technical information about the invention. The other function – defining the scope of the claimed monopoly – cannot be fulfilled until the patent has been granted.

On publication of the specification, the Patent Office file of the case becomes open to public inspection, and remains so thereafter.

Search and examination

When the claims have been filed and the prescribed search fee has been paid, the application is remitted to an examiner who makes a search among prior documents (in practice, existing patent specifications) and reports those which are relevant to the invention as claimed in the claims. The applicant then has the opportunity of deciding whether, in the light of the search report, it is worth proceeding to the next step. The sort of considerations which usually arise can be illustrated with reference to the ballcock invention.

Suppose that the applicant thinks he is entitled to claim a ballcock with any kind of float but that an elliptical float is especially advantageous. The examiner cites a specification describing a ballcock with a spherical float. This destroys the patentability of the broad claim to any kind of float, but not of a claim limited to the elliptical float. To cater for this common type of situation the law provides that the applicant can make a series of claims directed to successively smaller 'fenced-off' areas, each within the confines of the previous one, and that in litigation the validity and infringement of each claim is to be considered separately. In the ballcock example the applicant would simply strike out claim 1 and accept the grant of a patent based on claim 2.

The applicant must decide whether there is enough chance of securing allowance of a claim of worthwhile scope to justify spending the further fee for *examination* of the application. If so, the case is sent back to the examiner. He/she determines whether the prior documents destroy the patentability of the invention, in which case the examiner will refuse the application. If (more likely) there is something left which could be patented, the applicant can amend the claims accordingly. When the examiner is satisfied a patent is granted.

Acceptance by the examiner does not guarantee validity of claims. In our illustration the examiner could have missed the ballcock specification in his search, so that a patent was granted containing claim 1 as well as claim 2, and this could be challenged in litigation by a defendant who managed to discover the prior specification the examiner had missed. The court would then hold claim 1 invalid but might hold claim 2 valid. If the defendant had made a ballcock with an elliptical float, the court would order an injunction and, subject to a defined discretion, damages for infringement of claim 2, at the same time ordering the cancellation of claim 1.

The patent in its granted form is reprinted, using the same number as the previously published specification but with the letter B added. The letter A is used for the first published version.

Conflict between pending patent applications

Suppose that Jones files an application during the 18 months between the priority date and publication of Smith's application for a closely similar subject (particularly possible in intensively research-based industries). The paradox is then created that Jones's specification was still secret at Smith's priority date and therefore ought not to count against Smith, yet patents ought not to be granted to both for the same invention.

To overcome this difficulty, both in the EPC and the 1977 Act, Smith's earlier specification, during the period before publication, is deemed to be part of the state of the art. However, the prior unpublished specification is only halfway to being in the state of the art: it counts against the *novelty* of Jones's later application but cannot be used as a basis for proving *obviousness*.

Adjudication of patents

Under the 1977 Act, the UKPO has jurisdiction over the validity of patents granted both by the UKPO and by the EPO, although in the latter case the jurisdiction is confined to the UK part of the bundle. Opposition before grant of a UK patent has been abolished. Anyone interested in securing the revocation of a patent at any time in its life can apply to the UKPO for revocation under s72 of the 1977 Act. There is a right of appeal to a new branch of the High Court called the Patents Court, but appeal from this to the Court of Appeal lies only in respect of particular grounds listed in the 1977 Act (s97(3)).

The Patents Court can also adjudicate on validity at first instance; for example, if a defendant in a patent infringement action puts in, as he invariably does, a counter-claim for revocation of the patent. (See also 'Patents County Courts' below.)

Patenting procedure in Europe

Since procedure under the 1977 Act has been devised to correspond closely with that under the EPC, only a few further points need be added under this heading.

Language

The EPO is an autonomous international organization set up by a treaty (the EPC). It has no connection with the EC. It is staffed by officials from all member countries.

Patent applications must be filed in one of the official languages: English, French or German. Since the system is accessible to nationals of any country, a large number of applications originate in USA and Japan. More applications are therefore filed in the English language than in either of the other two languages. When a patent is granted, the claims will have to be translated into the other two official languages. Most countries, including the UK, require that the specification be translated into their national language when this differs from the language of publication of the grant. The UK has introduced this requirement only recently, so there will still be many European patents effective in the UK whose specifications are in French or German.

Application for a European patent

There are two main differences between procedures in the EPO and the UKPO. The first is that there is no counterpart in the EPO of the British specification without claims. Priority can be claimed in the EPO from a British preliminary specification, but this is part of the International Convention system (see below) rather than a specifically EPC procedure.

Secondly, as mentioned above, the applicant has to 'designate' the countries in which he wishes the European patent, if granted, to be effective (a designation fee being payable for each country, including of course the UK).

Opposition

Although the EPO is basically concerned only with the *granting* of patents, which then revert to the national jurisdictions of the respective designated countries, there is one exception. Within nine months after grant, a European patent can be 'opposed' at the EPO. This is similar to British revocation proceedings at the UKPO. If an opposition is successful, the European patent as a whole (that is, in respect of each designated country) is revoked.

Which route: European or national?

If a prospective applicant wants to cover his invention in more than one member country of the EPC, he has the option of applying at the EPO (the 'European route') or of filing separate national applications in each of the countries concerned (the 'national route'). The following considerations arise:

1 Obviously the greater the number of countries involved, the greater the financial advantage of the European route. The calculation is complicated because it involves professional as well as official Patent Office fees, and both of these vary from country to country in the case of national applications. It also involves the cost of translation of the granted European patent for those countries where such translation is required. As a rough guide it can be said that there is a breakeven point of three or four countries at which the European route becomes less expensive than the national route
2 National patents can be obtained very easily in a number of member countries; for example, France, Belgium, Italy, Spain. If the European route is chosen, fairly strict criteria for allowing an application will be applied by the EPO, and also the applicant will be restricting his or her opportunity to one source
3 In the case of a European patent, a single opposition can destroy the patent in all the designated countries
4 The amount of time and effort which has to be spent by the applicant and his or her patent agent in securing protection in more than one country should be less by the European than the national route
5 British patent agents who are also European patent attorneys can act directly at the EPO, whereas if the national route is used local agents have to be employed for each country.

Community patent convention

The nature of the CPC has already been indicated briefly. It will eventually provide for the granting of a single patent for the whole Common Market. This will raise interesting questions of jurisprudence. Procedure under the CPC should fit comfortably into that of the EPO and UKPO, but annual renewal fees to keep patents in force will be very high. At the time of writing the CPC has not been ratified by all member countries and further discussion is inappropriate here.

Foreign patents

Nearly all the countries of the world have their own patent offices and fully autonomous patent systems. This includes the members of the EPC, whose national systems will continue to operate in parallel with the EPO. There are two treaties which operate worldwide:

1 The International Convention for the Protection of Industrial Property
2 The Patent Co-operation Treaty (PCT).

The PCT is concerned with providing a single filing and searching facility for all the countries which a patent applicant may wish to cover. This sounds like a simple matter, but in fact the technical and procedural complications are immense and so the PCT is not popular amongst patent agents.

The International Convention

This dates from 1883 and now includes all the industrial countries and many more. The EPC counts as a 'Convention country' on the same footing as each individual European or other member country. The main provisions of the Convention are:

1   That the laws of a Convention country will be applied equally to citizens of all Convention countries
2   That if a patent application for an invention is filed in one Convention country and within twelve months an application for the same invention is filed in one or more other Convention countries, then such other applications will have the priority date of the first one. Hence, it is very desirable for a UK applicant to file foreign applications within twelve months of his British application. Thus, if the latter was filed within a preliminary specification, the filing of the claims in the UK normally coincides with the filing of foreign 'Convention applications'
3   If a ship or aircraft, which has on board equipment used for the operation of that craft, temporarily enters a country where such equipment has been patented by a third party, no proceedings for infringement may be taken.

If an applicant, usually from abroad, files a Convention application in the UK, he files a certified copy of the original foreign application plus a certified translation thereof if not in English, and this serves to establish his priority in much the same way as a British preliminary specification does for a British applicant in the UK.

Diversity of laws

It is not possible here to touch on the different procedures in different countries and only salient differences in substantive laws can be mentioned.

In the US and, until recently, Canada, the inventor's priority does not stem from the date of filing a patent application, but from the date he 'conceived' the invention.

No country except the UK and some of the old Commonwealth countries has the preliminary specification system.

The examination to which a patent application is submitted before grant varies as follows:

1   Full examination of all possible grounds of invalidity – for example, the US, Japan, Germany and other northern European countries including the UK
2   Little or no examination at all – for example, Italy, Belgium, Spain and Latin countries generally. France has provision for an official search, although it is left to the applicant whether or not to take action on the search report
3   Germany, Holland, Australia and Japan have adopted the system of 'deferred examination' whereby the application is not examined unless the patentee or an interested party requests it and pays the appropriate fee within the specified period, typically several years, failing which the application lapses.

There used to be a fundamental difference in the way the UK, on the one hand, and the civil law countries and most of the rest of the world on the other, approached the questions of definition of the monopoly area and validity (with the US somewhat nearer the UK). In those countries (including the UK) which participated in the Strasbourg Convention on the Unification of Certain Points of Substantive Law on Patents for Inventions, Steps are being taken to bring laws on validity and infringement into line.

Renewal fees

Renewal fees have to be paid in virtually all countries to keep a patent in force. The sums vary greatly but are generally payable annually and usually increase with the life of the patent. Fees are particularly onerous in the West, and particularly in Germany.

Licensing

Instead of using his 'fence' to keep out the competition, the patentee may decide to exploit it by allowing one or more parties in for a consideration. A licence in its simplest form is a promise not to sue the licensee for infringement if he enters the forbidden territory. If at the same time the patentee agrees not to let anyone else in, and to stay out himself, the licence is 'exclusive' within the meaning of the 1977 Act. Such an exclusive licensee has most of the rights and privileges of the patentee, including the rights to sue for infringement.

If the patentee undertakes to grant no further licences, but does not exclude himself from working the invention, the licence is known as a 'sole' licence. This carries none of the statutory rights of the exclusive licence. Licences which permit any number of licensees are termed 'non-exclusive'.

Territory

A licensing agreement may include licences in other countries where there are corresponding patents. The licensee does not need a licence to sell in countries where there are no patents but, subject to possible national legal restrictions, may agree collaterally *not* to sell in specified countries.

Financial arrangements

The consideration for the grant of a licence is normally monetary, and may take the form of a royalty based on use of the invention, an annual minimum payment and/or a down payment. The royalty can conveniently be expressed as a percentage of the sales value of an article, or the product of a process, covered by the patent.

If the licence is exclusive, the patentee has a prime interest in ensuring adequate performance by the licensee. This is usually provided for by requiring the licensee to make up the royalty payment to a stated annual minimum payment. The licensee for his part is willing to do this since he is effectively buying a monopoly as well as a right of entry. The licensee may either covenant outright to pay the annual minimum or he may reserve the right not to pay it in which case he submits to a penalty such as termination of the licence or conversion to a non-exclusive one.

A down payment is appropriate if the deal includes the initial transmission of technical information ('know-how') such as drawings, to enable the licensee to commence manufacture.

Miscellaneous terms

If the parties so agree, the licence may permit the licensee to grant sub-licences to third parties.

The duration of a licence is normally for the life of the relevant patent and it is provided in the 1977 Act (s45) that it shall be terminable by either party when the patent expires.

Know-how and improvements

It often happens, especially if an exclusive licence is contemplated, that the parties agree to transmit know-how and improvements to each other. The point to note here is that an essential part of such an agreement is an exact definition of the technological field. If this is to be coterminous with the fenced-off area of the patent, the agreement should say so; it is not, as is often believed, an accepted meaning of the word 'improvement'. The agreement should also be clear about what rights will accrue in respect of *patentable* improvements. Possibly each party will be able to exploit these in his own territory.

Another important point is the right to use the know-how after termination of the agreement. In the absence of an explicit provision there is no such right, and this can have very serious consequences for the recipient of the know-how.

Know-how licence

Of course, technology does not need to be patented to enable it to be licensed. It is not unreasonable for secret unpatented know-how to be licensed in return for a royalty payment so long as the know-how remains secret. In the case of know-how which is not secret, a single payment or stage payments are more appropriate as all the licensee is doing is saving himself the trouble of seeking out know-how for himself.

Forbidden terms

In English law the parties can negotiate a patent licence, or for that matter any other intellectual property licence, on any terms they please provided it is not in restraint of trade – a common-law doctrine of fairly narrow compass – and, when a patent is included in the licence, does not contravene s44 of the 1977 Act. This provides that the patentee shall not exceed his monopoly right by making it a condition of a licence that the licensee shall buy from the patentee unpatented raw material, such as unpatented phosphoric acid for use in a patented metal-finishing process. This is, in fact, frequently done, especially by implication, but the patentee is risking the enforceability of his patent if the practice ever comes to light.

In the US and the EC the antitrust or competition laws restrict what a licensor and licensee can lawfully agree. It is important not to fall foul of these laws. The practice of applying restrictions to licence agreements has spread, especially in developing countries, where the main motives are to foster local development and reduce royalty payments to other countries.

Existing patents

Existing patents are patents granted under the old Act, that is, on applications filed before 1 June 1978. Existing patents can be recognized by numbers in the 1 000 000 range, whereas patents granted under the 1977 Act are numbered from 2 000 000 onwards. The law on validity of existing patents differs from that applicable to patents granted under the 1977 Act but it is rare for these differences to be of great significance.

The law on infringement of existing patents, on the other hand, is that prescribed under the 1977 Act as described above, unless the infringement commenced before 1 June 1978. Since, at the time of application for an existing patent, the term of the patent was sixteen years, an existing patent is deemed endorsed 'licences of right' for the seventeenth to twentieth years of its life. This means that anyone wishing to take a licence under the patent must be given one. If the prospective licensee cannot agree terms with the patentee, these will be settled by the UKPO.

TRADE MARKS AND SERVICE MARKS

It has long been part of the common law that if A has a reputation in a trade name or trade mark and B sells his goods in association with the trade mark in such a way as to lead the public to believe that his goods emanate from A, then A has a cause of action against B for 'passing off' his goods as A's. In such an action, A has the onus of proving both the reputation of his mark and the confusion caused by B's use of it.

By the Trade Marks Act 1875 the owner of a trade mark was given a new right: to enter his mark on a Register of Trade Marks, thereby gaining an entitlement to stop anyone else from using the mark, always assuming that the registration was valid. The current registration is provided by the Trade Marks Act 1938.

Under pressure from trade mark agents and persons providing services rather than selling goods and in anticipation of a future Community Trade Mark Regulation, the Trade Marks (Amendment) Act 1984 was passed to provide for registration of service marks. Applications to register service marks have been possible since 1 October 1986.

An essential part of the system is that the registration must be in respect of a specified range of goods on which the owner uses or intends to use the mark or services which he offers or intends to offer, and that the registration is infringed only by use of the mark in connection with goods or services within this 'specification of goods' or 'specification of services'.

An important amendment introduced by the Copyright, Designs and Patents Act 1988 makes it an offence, punishable by imprisonment, to apply a registered trade mark, or a confusingly similar mark, to goods without permission, when it is intended that the goods should be accepted as those of the person entitled to use the registered trade mark, and when the fraudulent mark is applied with a view to gain. This is intended to help in the fight against counterfeiting.

The Register of Trade Marks

The Registrar of Trade Marks is in fact the same person as the Comptroller of Patents. An application to register a mark is examined to see if it complies with the Trade Marks Act. The examination extends to almost all the grounds on which a registration could be held invalid. The mark must be distinctive, distinguishing the owner's goods or services from those originating or provided elsewhere, either inherently or because past use has made it distinctive.

All goods are divided into thirty-four classes and separate applications must be made for goods in different classes. Services are divided into eight further classes.

A further requirement of registration is that the mark must not resemble too closely a mark already on the register for the same or similar goods or services, unless the applicant for registration can prove 'honest concurrent use' of the two marks for a period of some years.

There is provision for opposition to the registration and for an action to 'rectify the Register' by removing an existing registration. One ground of removal which will not have been considered at the registration stage is that the owner had no bona fide intention to use the mark and has not in fact used it; or that he has not used the mark for a continuous period of five years.

Trade mark and service mark use

It is most important that a mark, whether registered or not, should be used correctly if the proprietor is to retain his exclusive rights in the mark.

Specifically, the proprietor should aim to prevent his mark (in the case of a word mark) from becoming a generic name for the goods or services in question. To this end, it is recommended always to use the mark in conjunction with the conventional noun for the goods or services and to write the mark in some special way, such as between quotation marks, in capital letters or in bold letters. The proprietor should monitor the trade press to ensure that any reference to his trade mark which may appear includes a reference to the ownership of the mark.

Licensing

The right to use a trade mark or service mark, whether registered or not, can be licensed by the owner, but he must be careful to require the licensee to adopt his standards of quality for the goods in question, since otherwise the public may be deceived, with the result that the owner will lose his rights in the mark. It is advisable in the case of a registered mark to get the official seal of approval on the terms of the licence by making the licensee a 'registered user' under $s28$ of the Trade Marks Act. This has the further advantage that use of the mark by the registered user counts as use for the purpose of $s26$.

International

Trade marks, but not service marks, are included in the International Convention for the Protection of Industrial Property, but the priority period is six months as distinct from twelve months in the case of patents. The trade mark laws and practice of other countries differ from each other about as much as they do for patents, the main point being that in some countries, notably France, there is no concept of ownership of a trade mark until and unless the mark is registered, prior use being of no consequence. Hence, a company that has failed to register a valuable mark in France can see it lost to a third party simply by registration.

Discussions have been in progress for some years under the aegis of the EC for the setting up of a Community trade mark system. It will be at least a couple of years, probably more, before this is finalized and put into operation. As in the case of the EPC, national systems will continue to exist in parallel with that of the EC.

DESIGNS AND COPYRIGHT

The protection of the appearance of articles arises by virtue of two main pieces of legislation, the Copyright, Designs and Patents Act 1988 and the Registered Designs Act 1949. The Copyright Act 1956 and the Design Copyright Act 1968 have now been repealed. Three forms of protection for designs, not all or any of which may be relevant to any particular article are available:

1 Registered design
2 Design right
3 Copyright.

Registered designs

A design registered under the Registered Designs Act 1949 must be in respect of a named article, and gives the proprietor the exclusive right to make, import, use for business, sell or hire such articles to which that design is applied. The design may be in respect of the 'shape or configuration' of the article, which is usual in the case of three-dimensional articles, such as furniture, or in respect of the 'pattern or ornament', which is more usual in the case of two-dimensional articles, such as wallpaper and textiles.

However, the registered design cannot protect a method or principle of construction, or features of shape or configuration which are dictated solely by the function of the article (for example, a screw thread) or which are dependent upon the appearance of another article of which the article is intended to form an integral part (for example, a car body panel). A design will also be unregistrable if the appearance of the article is not material, that is, if aesthetic considerations are not normally taken into account by a purchaser or user. An example of this might be a vehicle oil filter.

A design registration is infringed by anyone who, without permission, makes, imports, uses for business, sells or hires articles to which the same or a similar design has been applied. There need not be any actual copying for infringement to be found. The reliefs available are an injunction to restrain further infringement and damages. Care is needed when threatening to bring a design registration infringement action since the person threatened has the possibility of bringing an action for restraint of threats which are unjustified. As with threats of patent infringement proceedings, the proprietor of a registered design is free to threaten a manufacturer or importer.

Filing registered design applications

Unlike design right and copyright, it is necessary to apply to register a design before any rights under registered designs exist. The Designs Register is kept by the Registrar, who is again the same person as the Comptroller of Patents. An application to register a design is filed at the Designs Registry and must be accompanied by 'representations' illustrating the article to which the design is applied. The representations can be drawings or mounted photographs but, in either case, there should be sufficient views to illustrate the whole of the exterior of the article. Only features which are judged by the eye are protectable so views of the interior of the articles need not be included.

The author of the design is taken to have the right to apply for registration, unless the design was made by an employee in the course of employment, in which case the employer has the right, or if the design was made in pursuance of a commission for money or money's worth, in which case the person commissioning the design has the right.

The design must be new at the date of filing of the application. Novelty is judged in relation to what was available to the public in the UK before the filing date. Thus, the proprietor of a design must file his application *before* making his design available in the UK by publication or by sale of articles to which the design is applied. The application is examined by the Registry and a search confined to previous design registrations is carried out. An opportunity is given to correct formal defects and to reply to any objections.

The registration is dated as of the filing date and lasts for five years, renewable for four further periods of five years each on payment of the prescribed fees, making a total of twenty-five years. However, by virtue of the Copyright, Designs and Patents Act 1988, registered designs having an application date before 1 August 1989 will be limited to two further five-year periods, making a total of fifteen years.

The Copyright, Designs and Patents Act 1988 has also amended the Registered Designs Act 1949 by increasing the restrictions on the registrability of designs. In this regard, as a transitional measure, the registration of any designs registered in respect of an application made after 12 January 1988, which would not be registrable under the Registered Designs Act as amended, will expire on 1 August 1999, if they do not expire sooner. Moreover, any person is entitled to a licence as of right in respect of such designs, and in the absence of agreement between the proprietor of the registered design and the licensee, the Registrar will settle the licence terms.

Design right

Design right is a new form of protection, introduced under the 1988 Copyright, Designs and Patents Act upon the repeal of the Copyright Act 1956. It is intended to give relatively short-term protection to all functional industrial designs created on or after 1 August 1989. (For designs created before that date, see 'Enforcement of copyright in designs made before 1 August 1989' below.) The 'design' means the design of any aspect of the shape or configuration, whether internal or external, of the whole or part of an article. However, design right does *not* extend to:

1 A method or principle of construction
2 Aspects of the shape or configuration of an article which enable the article to be connected to, or placed in, around or against another article so that either article may perform its function (the so-called 'must-fit' exception, as, for example, the connecting portions of an exhaust pipe)
3 Features of shape or configuration which are dependent upon the appearance of another article of which the article is intended by the designer to form an integral part (the so-called 'must-match' exclusion, as, for example, the door of a car)
4 Surface decoration.

Design right subsists only when the design has been recorded in a 'design document' (for example a drawing) or an article has been made to the design. There is no provision for registration of design right – the right comes into existence as soon as the design is recorded in a design document or an article has been made to the design. It is thus important to be able to show when a design was made. In respect of drawings, it is good practice to get into the habit of dating every drawing made.

The owner of a design right has the exclusive right to reproduce the design exactly or substantially (that is, copy the design) for commercial purposes by making articles to that design or by making a design document recording the design for the purpose of enabling such articles to be made.

Design right is infringed by anyone who, without licence of the design right owner, imports into the UK for commercial purposes, possesses for commercial purposes, or sells, lets for hire or offers or exposes for sale or hire in the course of a business, an article which is and which he knows or has reason to believe is a copy of the design in which design right exists. Design right (unlike a registered design) is *not* infringed if no *copying*, either direct or indirect, has taken place.

Design right lasts for a maximum of fifteen years from the end of the calendar year in which it originated. However, if articles made to the design are made available for sale or hire within five years from the end of that calendar year, the design right then only lasts for ten years from the end of the calendar year in which such articles made to the design were made available for sale or hire. The articles can be made available for sale or hire anywhere in the world, by or with the licence of the design right owner, and not just in the UK.

Any person is entitled to a licence in the last five years of a design right. The Comptroller of the Patent Office will settle terms if parties cannot agree.

The period of overall exclusivity to the design right owner can therefore be as little as five years, and the overall term might only be ten years. This contrasts sharply with the provisions of registered designs, where no such automatic licences of right exist, and where the maximum period of protection is twenty-five years. The obvious conclusion to be drawn is that wherever it is possible for a design having design right to be registered as a registered design, then such registration is most desirable.

The remedies available for infringement of design right are an injunction to restrain further infringement, and damages or an account of profits.

It is most advisable to mark on articles protected by design right, and on packaging for such articles, that design right exists in respect of the article. This is important in an infringement action, since an infringer who can show that he was not aware, of the existence of the design right in a particular article and that he had no reason to suppose that the right existed may be able to avoid payment of damages.

As with patents and registered designs, care is needed when threatening to bring a design right infringement action, since the person threatened has the possibility of bringing an action for restraint of threats which are unjustified. As with threats of patent and registered design infringement proceedings, the proprietor of a design right is free to threaten a manufacturer or importer.

Copyright

Copyright protects original literary, musical and artistic works and performing and broadcasting rights. In the light of changes brought about by the Copyright, Designs and Patents Act 1988, copyright is now of much less significance in the protection of industrial designs. Many new designs which would previously have been protected by copyright will now be protectable only by the new design right. In respect of three-dimensional articles, it is intended that copyright should protect only true artistic works and artistic aspects of otherwise functional, non-artistic works. For copyright works made before 1 August 1989, in respect of non-artistic articles, see the following section. It is important to note, however, that computer programs are considered to be 'literary works', and thus qualify for copyright protection.

Referring specifically to artistic works, this term clearly covers paintings, sculptures, photographs and works of architecture. Strictly speaking, copyright also exists in any drawing, irrespective of its artistic quality, which includes, for example, engineering drawings. However s 51 of the Copyright, Designs and Patents Act 1988 removes the enforceability of such copyright, other than for aspects of the surface decoration, when it relates to a *non-artistic* article where a design right also exists, and the design right prevails in such circumstances. Conversely, where copyright and design right both exist for an *artistic* article, the combined effect of s 51 and s 236 is to remove the enforceability of design right, and copyright prevails in such circumstances. Thus, a sculpture would be considered as an *artistic* work and would benefit from copyright protection, and be effectively excluded from design right protection, whereas a drawing of a machine part, which clearly is a *non-artistic* article would benefit from design right protection and be effectively excluded from copyright protection.

There is no procedure for registration of copyright. Copyright is an inherent right which arises when the original work is made. Thus, as with design right, it is important to be able to prove when a particular copyright work was made. The copyright term in respect of most artistic and literary works is for the life of the author and for fifty years after his death. One notable exception to this term is where an artistic work has been 'industrially applied' – where more than fifty articles are made – in which the copyright effectively endures for twenty-five years from the end of the calendar year in which such articles are first marketed. The author of a copyright work is the owner of the copyright, unless the work was made by an employee in the course of his employment, in which case the employer is the owner of the copyright.

Artistic and literary copyright is infringed by anyone who, without permission *copies* the author's work or a material part of it and sells the copies. It is not an infringement if no *copying* has occurred. In the case of artistic copyright, it is also an infringement to copy a three-dimensional reproduction of a two-dimensional drawing of an artistic article. This means that an artistic product which has been made or reproduced from original drawings or sketches effectively enjoys copyright under the Copyright, Designs and Patents Act. Functional, non-artistic articles do not attract enforceable copyright protection and must rely on design right for protection of their appearance, other than their surface decoration, which can attract copyright protection, even if the rest of the article is protected only by design right. 'Original' means that the drawing is not merely a copy of an earlier drawing or of a model.

Copyright is also infringed by anyone who imports, possesses in the course of business, sells or hires or exhibits or distributes in the course of business an article which is, and which he knows or has reason to believe is, an infringing article.

The remedies available for infringement of copyright are an injunction to restrain further infringement, and damages or an account of profits.

Enforcement of copyright in designs made before 1 August 1989

The Copyright, Designs and Patents Act 1988 incorporates transitional provisions with respect to copyright for functional, industrial articles. Since design right can exist only for designs created on or after 1 August 1989, the design of any functional, non-artistic article created before that date which was protected by copyright (for example, in an engineering drawing) under the former law will still be protected by copyright until 1 August 1999 (unless the copyright would have expired sooner) under the new law.

However, the transitional provisions alter the transitional copyright protection so that any aspects of the existing copyright for non-artistic works which would have qualified for the new design right protection if the design had been made on or after 1 August 1989, will expire on 1 August 1999, unless the copyright would have expired sooner anyway. Copyright in any other aspects (for example, in surface decoration) can exist after that date.

Moreover, the transitional provisions also provide that any 'transitional copyright' as described above will be subject to licences of right during its final five years, in the same way as design right.

Copyright in existing *artistic* works is unaffected by the transitional measures described above.

Licensing

Registered designs, copyright and design right can be licensed in much the same way as patents. An exclusive licence of copyright or design right carries with it a right of the licensee to sue infringers. While an exclusive licensee under a registered design does not have any statutory right to institute infringement proceedings, a true exclusive licence will probably include the right of the licensee to sue. A restrictive condition concerning articles not the subject of a design registration, copyright or design right should be avoided, for fears of running foul of EC anti-trust laws.

International

Registered designs are covered by the International Convention but, as with trade marks, the priority period is six months. A design filed under convention is dated as of the priority date, not the filing date.

There are two copyright conventions, the Universal Copyright Convention and the Berne Copyright Union. Each of these conventions in principle extends the copyright under domestic legislation of each member country to nationals of all other member countries. The Berne Union imposes more conditions on member countries as to the content of their copyright laws. The UK is a member of the Universal Copyright Convention but not of the Berne Union. The UK recognizes countries party to either or both of these conventions for the purpose of providing copyright protection under the Act.

Only those countries whose copyright or design laws follow closely those of the UK provide for 'industrial copyright' or design right protection of the kind described above. On the other hand, many countries have an unfair competition law which can provide remedies similar to those under the UK passing-off law and UK industrial copyright and design right law.

Marking

Since patents, registered designs, trade marks, copyright and design right are exclusive to the proprietor, it is to his benefit that he should advertise those rights. Therefore, the proprietor is well advised to advertise that he has such rights by marking the patented product, or article protected by a registered design with the patent or design number or by indicating the number of any trade mark which is registered. Indeed, such marking is compulsory, failure to mark may result in failure to obtain damages for infringement.

A false claim to protection is, in general, an offence punishable by a fine or imprisonment or both. Accordingly, when an application for a patent, a design registration or a trade mark registration has not been granted, it is necessary to use wording such as 'Patent applied for, No. 86 54321'.

In the case of unregistered trade marks, it is useful to include the marking such as 'ACME is a Trade Mark of PQR Ltd'. This makes it clear that PQR Ltd has staked its claim to the trade mark.

Copyright and design right are somewhat different in that they do not have an identification number and that they can automatically extend to many different countries. The marking in accordance with the copyright conventions consists of the letter C in a circle followed by the year of publication followed by the name of the copyright owner, thus '© 1986 XYZ Ltd'. Failure to use this prescribed marking may mean that, in some countries, no damages can be recovered for infringement. There is no agreed marking for design right, but wording along the lines of 'Protected by Design Right' followed by the year when the design was made, or the year of first offer for sales of articles to the design, if this is within five years of making the design, and the owner of the design right, would seem appropriate.

PATENTS COUNTY COURTS

With a view to making litigation in patents and designs more accessible to those of relatively limited means (such as small companies) the Copyright, Designs and Patents Act 1988 has introduced the concept of Patents County Courts to hear proceedings relating to patents and designs and associated matters.

The idea is that a party need not necessarily be represented by a barrister in High Court proceedings but can instead be represented by a registered patent agent, solicitor or barrister in a county court. This provision is intended to reduce considerably the cost of litigation in respect of intellectual property rights.

Although the Act makes possible the provision of Patents County Courts, at present only a single Patents County Court has been established. However, the success and popularity of that court make it likely that further Patents County Courts will be established in due course.

FUNCTIONS OF PATENT AND TRADE MARK AGENTS

Patent agents have a function in relation to patent law and practice which is analogous to that of solicitors in relation to other branches of law. Until recently, practice in the field of patents was restricted by law to those who held a high level of technical expertise, usually to degree standard, and who had passed qualifying examinations which the Chartered Institute of Patent Agents administers on behalf of the Department of Trade and Industry. In accordance with recent attitudes to the encouragement of competition, any person may now act in the field of patents, but it should be noted that the titles 'patent agent' and 'patent attorney' are reserved for those on the Register of Patent Agents, for which entry requirements and examinations will be broadly the same as those which previously existed for the profession as a whole. Also, it should be noted that registered patent agents will have right of audience in the proposed Patents County Courts.

There are very few matters connected with patent law or practice in which it is safe to proceed without consulting a patent agent.

Like the profession of patent agency, that of trade marks is not closed, but there is an Institute of Trade Mark Agents which administers a rigorous examination as a condition of membership. It is usual for patent agents to include trade marks in their practice and many are members of both institutes. There is now also a Register of Trade Mark Agents, for which entry requirements exist.

The day-to-day work of the patent agent consists of: the preparation of patent applications, the main part of which is the patent specification, for filing in the UK and abroad in accordance with the local procedures; dealing with objections raised by the various examiners and with any oppositions; securing the grant of a patent; and ensuring the renewal fees are paid on it as long as the patentee requires.

Representation before the UKPO in connection with design registration application is also an open profession. Nevertheless, it is usually conducted by patent agents and sometimes by trade mark agents.

The role of the patent agent in design right and copyright questions is purely advisory. Many patent agents develop a substantial expertise in industrial copyright and design right because of the overlap of interests with other intellectual property matters.

European patent attorneys

Professional representatives (practitioners) of any EPC country can act directly at the EPO in contradistinction to the national patent offices which require the representation to be held by a local patent practitioner. Qualification to act before the EPO is by an examination of similar scope to that in the UK, run by the EPO. Qualification leads to membership of the European Patent Institute (EPI).

Most foreign practitioners, when speaking English, call themselves 'patent attorneys'. Recognizing that this could put British agents at a disadvantage when competing for EPO business (for example, in USA and Japan) Parliament approved the name 'European Patent Attorney' for use by British practitioners qualified to act before the EPO, in s 85(1) of the 1977 Act. The same expression was subsequently approved by the EPI for use by all professional representatives, irrespective of nationality and equivalent expressions in French and German have also been approved.

COSTS

The costs of obtaining and maintaining patents contain two components: government fees and professional charges. The Patent Office in each country has to carry out a number of clerical and technical operations on each patent application, the latter requiring skilled manpower, and the objective is to charge applicants and patentees enough to make the Patent Office self-supporting. The fee in the UK for an application is a nominal £15, the search fee is £120 and the examination fee is £130. The patent agent's charges depend on the nature of the job but they are not likely to be less than £500 for a preliminary specification and £750 for an application with claims. Much higher charges may be made for lengthy or complex work.

The costs for foreign applications vary a good deal from country to country. A large fraction of the costs in foreign-language countries goes for translation. An idea of the order of magnitude of the costs and of their range can be given by quoting estimates of £700 for an average case in India, and of £1 500 in Germany.

It is impossible to estimate the cost of prosecuting an application since it depends on the nature of the subject-matter, the procedure of the country concerned and the objections the examiners happen to turn up. The cost can vary from a few pounds in some countries to hundreds of pounds for a difficult US case.

The annual renewal fees necessary to maintain a patent in force also vary enormously from country to country and over the life of the patent, generally increasing with its age. The UK is in a range of about £102 to £406 exclusive of agent's charges.

Charges for trade mark work follow a similar pattern but on a lower scale, perhaps a quarter to a half of the charge for analogous patent work. Renewal fees are required only at relatively long periods; for example, in the UK every fourteen years after an initial period of seven years. Charges for design registration applications are generally of the same order as those for trade marks.

FURTHER READING

Blanco White, T. A. and Jacob, Robin, *Patents, Trade Marks, Copyright and Industrial Designs*, 3rd edn, Sweet & Maxwell, London, 1986

Baillie, Iain C., *Business Licensing Law & Practice*, Longman, London, 1990

Chartered Institute of Patent Agents, *European Patents Handbook*, Longman, London (expensive but comprehensive in four looseleaf volumes with updating service)

Flint, Michael F., *A User's Guide to Copyright*, Butterworth, London, 1985

Hearn, Patrick, *The Business of Industrial Licensing*, 2nd edn, Gower, Aldershot, 1986

Meinhardt, Peter and Havelock, Keith R., *Concise Trade Mark Law and Practice*, Gower, Aldershot, 1983

Phillips, Jeremy and Hoolahan, Michael J., *Employees' Inventions in the United Kingdom Law and Practice*, ESC Publishing Ltd, 1982

Phillips, Jeremy, *Introduction to Intellectual Property Law*, Butterworth, London, 1986

52 Insurance of company operations

Commercial Union plc

More than ever before it is important for business owners and executives to protect their companies. Competition, health and safety legislation, the complexity of products, environmental considerations, a whole host of natural disasters from fire to flood, and man-made catastrophes from burglary to fraud, can spell disaster for any size of company.

Insurance is one form of protection against many of the accidental or natural disasters. For over 300 years there have been 'risk takers' who, for a fee called a 'premium', are willing to assume financial responsibility for losses incurred following a variety of events. The premiums of the 'many' pay for the claims of the 'unfortunate few'.

Not all business risks are insurable; some are pure business risks which involve the successful businessmen and women in making good business decisions. 'Risk management' involves the appraisal of the risk which might affect the performance of the company. Once the risks have been established a business plan is designed to cope with them.

A number of risks are unavoidable and have to be catered for in business plans – obsolescence or overestimation of the market, for example – their remedy lies in research, development and marketing. Other corporate problems can be answered by advice from accountants, bankers and solicitors.

What about the unpredictable? This is where the insurance company or broker play a significant part in your company's prosperity. The purpose of insurance is to provide a financial indemnity against loss from accidental and unpredictable risks. Its aim is to put your company in the same position as it was before the advent of the fire, storm damage, burglary or other disaster. What follows explores some of the factors involved in business insurances.

There are over 300 insurance companies and Lloyds who make up the UK insurance market today. Some of those companies handle only life or pensions business; those who handle general insurance and life or pensions business are known as composite insurers. They are predominantly the large companies, the nationally known names. All non-life and composite companies are limited liability companies. Lloyds, however, is different. Insurance is placed only by Lloyds insurance brokers with syndicates of individual underwriters who act for the syndicate members. The members have to satisfy Lloyds of their financial standing and integrity and are liable without limit to the full extent of their individual wealth. Most Lloyds syndicates specialize in specific classes or risk; for example, marine, aviation, motor, property, and so on.

INSURANCE LANGUAGE

Before looking at the insurance cover itself, it might be useful to look at some common expressions used in the insurance industry. While many present-day insurers attempt to produce contracts in a 'plain English' format, there are still some fundamental principles on which most insurance contracts are based. In addition, some words have developed a common usage within the insurance industry. The following glossary gives a basic description of some of these principles and terms.

- *Adjuster* A specialist appointed by the insurer to investigate the circumstances and negotiate settlement of a loss. Usually an independent specialist whose fee is paid for by the insurer
- *Assessor* A person who acts on behalf of the insured at the insured's expense to negotiate claims with the insurer and, where necessary, the insurer's adjuster. An assessor can also negotiate on behalf of third-party claimants
- *Average (non-marine)* A principle of insurance (mainly insurance of property) where the insurer will only pay for the same proportion of a loss as the sum insured bears to the actual value of the property at the time of the loss. For example, if an item covered by the policy is 'subject to average' but is only insured for half its value at the time it is damaged, the insurer will only pay half of the claim for repair
- *Betterment* See *Indemnity*
- *Broker, insurance* A professional insurance adviser who, following discussions of the cover required with his client, will negotiate and place the business with insurers. The broker must meet the standards required by the Insurance Brokers (Registration) Act 1977, which includes a statutory code of conduct. Brokers may be members of BIIBA (British Insurance and Investment Brokers Association). The description 'insurance broker' may only be used by individuals who have registered (enrolled, if a firm) under the Act. Sometimes the term 'broker' is used colloquially to mean any professional insurance adviser, whether registered or not
- *Code of conduct/codes of practice* Brokers are required to follow a statutory code of conduct under the Insurance Brokers (Registration) Act. Other general (non-life) insurance intermediaries are required to follow the Code of Practice issued by the ABI (Association of British Insurers) with the support of the DTI (Department of Trade and Industry). These other intermediaries are either 'independent' or 'company agents'
- *Days of grace* When a non-life policy falls due for renewal, the insurer is usually willing to hold cover under the terms for renewal, pending payment of the premium, provided that the policyholder intends to renew.
  Under motor policies there are no days of grace. However, as it is necessary for a certificate of motor insurance to be delivered to a policyholder for it to be effective, insurers usually provide 15 days' temporary cover beyond the renewal date to enable the insurer to date the new certificate from the renewal date and deliver it within the period of temporary cover.
  Should a life assured die within the days of grace specified under a life policy

before the renewal premium is paid, the position must be ascertained from the policy or the insurer

- *Debris removal* Under a policy covering buildings and/or machinery against damage, the cost of removing debris can be included provided that the costs have been allowed for when deciding on the sums to be insured. If the costs are insured as a separate item under a policy covering commercial property, they are not subject to average. Similarly, debris removal of stock can also be insured as a separate item under a policy covering commercial property

- *Disclosure* The rule of law whereby a prospective policyholder must tell ('disclose' to) the insurer any facts known to the prospective policyholder which are likely to affect acceptance by the underwriter or his assessment of the risks proposed. If the prospective policyholder fails to do this, the policy may not provide the cover required, or the policy may be invalidated

- *Ex gratia* Voluntary payment made by an insurer as a gesture of goodwill, without admission of liability under the policy

- *Excess* If expressed in money terms (which is usual) excess is the uninsured amount for which the insured is responsible in the event of a claim. See also *Franchise*

- *Fees, professional* Under a policy covering buildings and/or machinery against damage, it is possible to insure the professional fees (for example, architects) incurred in rebuilding or repairs in a variety of ways. These are normally calculated as a proportion of the value of buildings or machinery, and are limited to the scales of professional bodies. If insured separately under a policy covering commercial property, such fees are not subject to average

- *Fidelity guarantee* This insurance protects employers against 'direct pecuniary loss' which they suffer by all acts of fraud or dishonesty committed by any of their employees. The term 'direct pecuniary loss' refers to the loss of monies, stock and other items of value belonging to the employer, where the loss can be proved and the employee or employees responsible can be identified (although insurers do not insist on prosecution). Unaccountable deficiencies of losses are not covered

- *Franchise (money)* There is no payment by the insurer if a total claim is below the stated figure. Above that amount, however, the agreed claim is payable in full. Some policies – for example, certain personal accident or engineering contracts – may have time franchises

- *Franchise (time)* May apply in certain personal accident or engineering contracts. The claim will only be payable if the time franchise is exceeded, but then the agreed amount will be paid in full

- *Indemnity* This is a common law principle by which the policyholder after a loss shall be put in the same financial position as he was immediately before the happening of the event insured against. In practice this often means that, payment of a claim is based first on what it would cost to replace new a lost or damaged item, but then an amount is deducted to take account of wear and tear. Such a deduction is sometimes called 'betterment'.

  This principle naturally does not apply to life assurance, permanent health or pensions contracts. Nor does it apply to personal accident and sickness cover, although medical expenses insurance does provide indemnity for costs incurred

- *Insurable interest*   A policyholder has an insurable interest if the insured event would involve him in financial loss or diminution of any right recognized by law or any legal liability, or for the consequences of his own bodily injury or illness. As regards life and personal accident policies, a person is deemed to have an unlimited interest in his or her own life, or in the life of his or her spouse. Insurable interest may also exist between employer and employee, debtor and creditor and other cases
- *Insurance agents*   An insurance agent is primarily the agent of the policy-holder, not least when passing information to the insurer with a view to obtaining insurance cover. He can also be the agent of the insurer, in particular when collecting premiums due to the insurer
- *Insurance broker*   see *Broker*
- *Insurance consultant*   Is a professional insurance adviser whose business is similar to that of an insurance broker, but who has not registered/enrolled under the Insurance Brokers (Registration) Act. While unlikely, therefore, to meet the standards required under the Act, they are required to follow a code of practice agreed between insurers and the Department of Trade and Industry
- *Introducer*   An insurance intermediary who merely introduces a prospective policyholder to an insurer, but who takes no part in the subsequent selling process
- *Local authorities clause*   In the event of damage, current building regulations may well be applied to the structure, thereby involving additional expense when rebuilding. If the insurance is on a reinstatement basis, this clause can be added to extend the policy to meet the additional expenses on rebuilding for the damaged portion, although the sum insured must have been increased to allow for such expenses
- *Proposal form*   The form completed by a proposer. A completed life proposal forms the basis of the contract between the insured and the insurer
- *Reinstatement*:
  1 Where property is destroyed, it means the rebuilding of the property if a building, or, in the case of other property, its replacement by similar property. In each case the replacement is to be a condition equal to (but no better or more extensive than) the condition of the property when new
  2 Where property is damaged, it means repair of the property to a condition substantially the same as (but not better or more extensive than) its condition when new

  The sum insured needs to represent what it would cost fully to rebuild/replace, at the time the property is actually rebuilt/replaced, and any under-insurance will result in a proportionate reduction of the amount paid in accordance with the average principle (see *Average*)
- *Renewal notice*   Form sent to the insured advising the approaching renewal date and inviting renewal on payment of a stated premium. The insurer is not bound to issue a notice but it is the normal practice.

  The renewal invitation is provided on the basis of information already given to the insurer. Other than for individual life, pension or permanent health insurance, if that information is affected by any change of circumstances or additional fact known to the policyholder, the insurer (or the authorized agent) should be told. It could be that, as a result of the additional information, the insurer will wish to revise the terms on which renewal is being invited.

- *Subrogation* The substitution of one person or thing for another so that the same rights and remedies which attached to the original person/thing attach to the substituted one
- *Surveyor* Person who inspects property to advise the underwriter about the risk. He/she may also require or recommend improvements to the risk to lessen the likelihood of fire, burglary or other incidents occurring, or to minimize their effects
- *Time-on-risk-charge* This is a premium charged for a period (often limited to a number of days) during which an insurer is holding a risk covered, for example, by means of a cover note
- *Underwriting* The process whereby a risk is assessed for insurance purposes, on the basis of information supplied to the underwriter (often by means of a proposal form). The underwriter must decide whether the risk is acceptable to the insurer, the terms on which it may be acceptable, and the premium to be charged before issue of the policy
- *Utmost good faith* A legal duty imposed on both parties to an insurance contract to disclose all facts material to the contract (see also *Disclosure*)
- *Warranty* A policy condition or requirement which, if not complied with, may have the effect of invalidating the policy. It may relate to woodworking in a motor garage or to the absence of certain property (for example, no oil to be stored in the hardware shop or only certain types of oil kept).

Insurance cover

There are four basic categories of insurance which can be arranged for companies. These are outlined in the remainder of this chapter and are:

1 Property protection
2 Loss of income
3 Legal liabilities
4 Personnel.

PROPERTY PROTECTION

The insurance arrangement is essentially a complete form of protection where, if a loss occurs, within certain criteria, the insurer will resolve the problem by way of financial compensation. Such an insurance will include wide cover for your stock, machinery, fixtures and fittings and furniture, employees' belongings, and other items for which you may be responsible. The structure, if you own it, would come within this category or, if you are a tenant, you can arrange for the insurance to cover that portion of the structure and interior decorations for which you are responsible. Specific requirements within a lease would obviously have to be complied with.

Fire insurance

There was a tendency in the past for companies to be selective in terms of which contingencies to insure against. It has now become almost standard practice for insurers to offer a package which includes the basic traditional calamities such as fire, lightning, explosion and so on. There are many special features and extensions on the market which are worthy of consideration.

Many insurers now refer to 'all risks' cover which could be more accurately described as accidental damage cover. 'New for old' cover is also offered which requires the sums insured to be at full reinstatement value.

Additional standard extensions include property which has been temporarily removed, architects', surveyors' and other specialist fees, removal of debris costs, special provision for local authority legislation, and even damage to the underground service pipes and cables on which the business might rely.

Theft

Theft and loss of money are now two of the prime security considerations in many businesses and cover will almost inevitably carry a proviso from the insurer that a certain degree of minimum security is observed. Certain manufactured goods, and even raw materials, have become prime targets to the criminal world, and insurers require their policyholders to improve the safes, locks and alarm protections at their premises rather than rely solely on charging a higher premium for a risk as it stands.

Cash

Money cover carries a variety of limitations and requirements and particular attention should be paid to the observance of such conditions in the day-to-day business of the company. For example, certain safes will have insurance limits as to the amount of cash which can be kept in them overnight and there may be conditions relating to the sum which can be taken in transit on any one trip. Where large-volume cash transits are involved the use of security companies has become more prevalent. On a lower degree, the insurer may require more than one of your employees to be present during a delivery of cash either to the bank or to a point of wages payment.

Loss of money as a result of theft should not be confused with fidelity guarantee insurance, which would be dealt with separately.

Glass insurance

Apart from the traditional concept of insuring against breakage of glass in doors, windows, and so forth, extensions apply which include breakage of sanitary ware, damage to neon signs and burglar alarms, foil lettering, painting, and so on.

Again, insurers expect policyholders to take positive steps to reduce risk in certain areas, for example by the use of grills or roller shutters. Large excesses could apply in areas where the insurers' experience has been particularly poor.

LOSS OF INCOME

Insurance against loss of income is a feature of the insurance portfolio which protects the business when it is interrupted as a result of loss or damage under the above sections.

It covers loss of gross profit due to a reduction in the business income. It also covers increased costs of working incurred to reduce the loss of profit, so long as these do not exceed the loss of profit which would otherwise have been paid.

Once more, a variety of extensions are available to protect the business against financial loss and these include damage to property in the vicinity, causing denial or access to your own premises, or damage at the premises of any supplier (which would normally carry a limit in respect of any one supplier).

This particular style of insurance has its own special definitions, the principal one being 'indemnity period', which relates to the maximum period of time during which the business might suffer loss as a result of the interruption. Traditionally, the indemnity period has run for a period of twelve months following the incident, although longer periods are now commonplace.

Such insurance normally requires the service of a professional accountant should a claim arise and the insurer will usually include the professional accountant's charges as part of the sum paid.

Careful consideration should be given to the calculation of the sum insured in this context and future company projections should be taken into account. It is not appropriate to rely on your previous year's gross profit as a basis for fixing sums insured. For example, if a two-year indemnity period were to be selected and the loss were to take place at the end of a particular insurance year, then at the expiry of the indemnity period it is possible that the original sum insured could be almost three years out of date.

To compensate for future projections the insurer will accept audited declarations in retrospect and adjust premiums to reflect the actual risk as compared with the projected one, paying appropriate rebates to the policyholder.

Following the rise in inflation insurers have developed more sophisticated means by which to adjust this cover. Consultation with a professional intermediary or insurance advisor is highly recommended in this context.

LEGAL LIABILITIES

If any one thing could bankrupt a company at a stroke it would be a heavy court award. No matter how far a company may consider that it can set aside the need for insurance this particular form is imperative.

The cover relates to legal liabilities to pay compensation:

1 *To employees* For bodily injury, illness or death arising out of and in the course of their employment in the company for an unlimited amount. Any person working for the company for the purpose of gaining work experience is automatically included. This cover is a statutory requirement of the Employers' Liability (Compulsory Insurance) Act 1969
2 *To members of the public* For bodily injury, illness or disease or loss of or damage to material property, which arises in connection with the business,

including liability arising from the sale of goods (product liability) for an amount of, say, up to £1m for any one event. In the case of liability arising from the sale of goods, this amount would be the limit applying to all claims happening in any one year of insurance. Increases on cover are available on the payment of an additional premium.

In addition, all litigation costs and expenses are paid when incurred with the insurers' agreement

Certain extensions and special features include:

3 *Defective premises* Cover for liability incurred by the company under s3 of the Defective Premises Act 1972
4 *Damage to rented premises* Cover for damage to premises rented or hired by the company (other than if liability is assumed by the company under an agreement which would not have attached in the absence of such agreement). The insured may be asked to pay the first £100 or thereabouts of each loss unless the damage was caused by fire or explosion
5 *Health and Safety at Work Act* Cover for legal costs arising out of any prosecution under Part 1 of the Health and Safety at Work Act 1974, but excluding any fines or penalties imposed and any costs incurred as a result of a deliberate act of omission
6 *Contingent liability* Cover for liability incurred by the company as a result of the use by an employee of his own vehicle on the company's business.

As a result of the tendency in the US towards very large court awards, the UK insurance market is now particularly sensitive to this area. Therefore, if a UK company is involved in the supply of materials or products to that part of the world your insurer should be informed.

In 1988 the Consumer Protection Act created a strict liability for claims arising from many types of goods. This liability should automatically be embraced by any policy covering product liability.

It is common for insurers to exclude public liability claims which arise from motor vehicles licensed for road use, professional negligence, or for property which is held in the company's custody or control. Special arrangements should be made to cover these areas.

PERSONAL

Personal accident insurance

This is the least expensive of the covers and takes one of two forms:

1 *Occupational accident cover* This type of cover applies to all accidents at work including those not directly the fault of the employer. It is one of the cheapest forms of protection and can be extended to include accidents on the way to and from work
2 *24-hour accident cover* This cover applies 24 hours a day, every day of the year at home and at leisure anywhere in the world. Clearly, as the cover is

extended, the costs increase and will vary depending upon the occupation of the staff involved. These covers can be arranged either for specific members of staff by name, specific groups of staff or for all employees.

Personal accident policies usually include capital sums and weekly benefits. They can be arranged either by a fixed benefit or a figure related to the employee's earnings. Capital sums are paid following accidental death or serious injury and can be used as compensation to the injured employee or made payable to the firm to offset the very high costs often involved in replacing a key individual (see key employee assurance). Weekly sums, usually for short-term absence by reason of accidents, are normally payable for 104 weeks only.

Personal accident and sickness insurance

The personal accident only cover can be supplemented in respect of sickness. This extension of the policy would normally provide a weekly benefit in the event of illness on the same lines as for personal accident only. There is usually a two-year limit (104 weeks) on the benefit payable.

Rates of premium are often based on a percentage of the wage roll and the rates vary according to occupation. In general, the employer would collect premiums and pay them in bulk to the insurance company. From the insurance company's point of view the group schemes covering most or all employees would be at a cheaper rate as there is a wide spread of risk among administrative as well as manual staff.

Personal accident insurance, including or excluding sickness, is renewable every year. This means that if there is a run of bad accidents or illness, the insurer may wish to revise the terms of the cover. For key employees permanent health insurance may be the answer.

Permanent health insurance

Permanent health insurance has two advantages over personal accident and sickness insurance. Firstly, it provides regular monthly income for as long as the employee is ill, without limitation. Payments can continue, if necessary, right up to retirement age. Because the possible amount payable by an insurer is far greater, premiums are higher. To keep premiums at a reasonable level, it is usual for the first thirteen or twenty-six weeks of disability, known as the waiting period, to be excluded from the cover. An employer will often pay full salary for the first six months of illness and there would be a duplication of payment if this was included in the permanent health cover.

The second advantage is that, once effected, the insurer cannot subsequently withdraw cover or change the terms of that cover, however disabled the member of staff becomes through recurrent health problems. Furthermore, if the employee becomes totally disabled and takes an early retirement pension through illness, or has to take some lower-paid professional occupation, a reduction benefit will still be paid under the permanent health policy.

Key employee assurance

There are some men and women who are so valuable to a company that their loss, either permanently or temporarily, could affect its financial stability. Statistically, it is more likely that a 45-year-old senior or chief executive will die before 65 than that the business premises will suffer a serious fire in the same period. But while management would not dream of failing to insure premises and contents against fire, very few take steps to combat the equally serious loss following death or prolonged illness of a key person.

Key employee assurance can be made-to-measure to cover exactly what is needed and nothing more. It is specific to the individual and refers to that person's contribution to the company. Also, because no employer knows precisely what the future holds, benefits can be changed to suit changing circumstances.

Here are the basic kinds of assurance for a key person:

To protect profits against a key person's death

The cheapest way to offset the effects on profits of a key person's death is by means of term assurance or convertible term assurance. In either case, the policy is arranged to pay a lump sum in equal instalments spread over, say, ten years to minimize corporation tax. The sum to be assured will depend on the value of the employee.

With term assurance, cover ceases after a set number of years. With convertible term assurance there is the option of converting at any time into a permanent whole-of-life or endowment policy, or a further term or convertible term policy, without the employee having to undergo a further medical examination.

Premiums may be reduced if the key person is a non-smoker. Insurers have found that non-smokers are much better insurance risks than smokers and this is reflected in the levels of life cover provided.

The premiums for life assurance are remarkably good value, £100 000 cover on a ten-year term assurance, assuming a non-smoker, would cost £21.30 per month for a man aged 35. Corporation tax would often be deductible from these payments.

Key employee permanent health insurance

The long absence of key people through illness or injury can be as disruptive as their deaths. A regular income for the company while the employee is unable to work is best provided by permanent health cover. Statistically, there is a one in six chance of a forty-five-year-old key employee suffering long-term disablement through illness or accident during the next twenty years.

The policy is usually for a period of ten years, but a slightly higher premium will secure an option to extend for a further ten years without further medical evidence. Monthly benefits are usually limited to two years including the 'waiting period' of thirteen or twenty-six weeks. The loss of a key person may not be a problem in the very short term and, similarly, the firm might reasonably be expected to replace or retain by the end of two years.

The key employee permanent health policy is designed to tide the company over the short-term financial difficulties arising from the serious incapacity of a key employee. If the key person is incapacitated more than once, benefits start again on the same terms as on the first occasion provided a different illness or injury is responsible. If there are separate periods of incapacity due to the same illness or injury, these are aggregated and benefits are paid for only two years in total, less the original waiting period. The waiting period is not repeated for related illnesses.

If, while in receipt of payments under the policy, the employee takes early retirement and a pension, or takes up some lower-paid occupation, a reduced benefit is payable during the remainder of the period.

Again, premiums are relatively inexpensive. For example, an employer would pay a monthly premium of £5.20 for a male aged 35. This would provide a benefit of £10 000 per annum payable for 104 weeks, less a waiting period of twenty-six weeks, assuming the employee was in an administrative or clerical occupation.

Medical expenses

Substantial discounts are available for groups of employees from firms specializing in medical expenses insurance schemes, such as BUPA and Private Patients' Plan. A common practice is for the employer to arrange such schemes on behalf of their employees, as an employee benefit, with premiums paid by the employee by deduction from salary.

The advantage to employees is that they obtain the benefit of private medical insurance at comparatively low cost because of the group discounts, while the employer has the advantage of faster medical attention available to his employees who can then resume work much more quickly.

The employee has the choice as to which plan he wishes to opt for, but it is recommended that as hospital accommodation charges form a large part of the claim it is better to assume hospital treatment at London rates rather than take up cover on the basis of provincial hospital charges.

'Death in service' benefits

Benefits following death from any cause are usually part of a company pension scheme. None the less, provided it is arranged by the employer, cover can be paid for by deduction from salary or subsidized by the employer. There are two basic forms of 'death in service' schemes:

1 *Capital sums* In this type of arrangement a lump sum is payable which is either a sum directly related to salary (for example, one, twice, three or a maximum of four times the employee's salary at death) or a sum which bears no direct relationship to salary
2 *Widow's 'death in service' benefits* This scheme can be in addition to the lump sum benefits. It provides an income to the widow or dependants of the deceased employee from the date of death until he or she would have reached retirement age.

Under both these schemes there are certain limitations laid down by the Inland Revenue. In respect of lump sum benefits the maximum is usually four times current salary. The maximum death in service benefits for widows is normally 44 per cent of current salary.

CONCLUSION

The previous sections have covered the principles of insurance in relation to business practice. There are, however, many specialist forms of insurance designed to cater for the huge variety of activities in which the business community is involved.

Insurance is now a highly competitive market which is no longer inhibited by tariffs or market agreements. As a result the need for specialist advice is paramount, particularly if your business has any degree of specialism in itself. The events against which a company insures itself were traditionally described as 'perils'. Perhaps the greatest peril of all would be to ignore the existence of insurance altogether.

FURTHER READING

Association of Insurance and Risk Managers in Industry and Commerce (AIRMIC) (eds), *Company Insurance Handbook*, 2nd edn, Gower, Aldershot, 1984

53 The administration of commercial property

Philip Westwood

The nature of a company's property will obviously depend on its activities. It may consist of retail outlets, administrative offices, warehouses, garages for the repair and maintenance of the company's transport, factories, research and development facilities, leisure and training facilities, and company houses for the accommodation of its staff.

All proprietary interests in land are at law 'real' property, as distinct from other property including chattels, animals, stocks and shares, and so on, which are 'personal' property. Thus, 'real estate' includes freeholds and easements, which are rights by virtue of land ownership over the land of others (for example, a right of way).

As with all other aspects of a company's activities, the continuing suitability of its premises should be reviewed regularly. This chapter is intended to aid that process and assist in the correct decisions being taken as the company expands or contracts to meet changing circumstances.

If a great deal of property is involved, the company would be best advised to employ its own staff with professional expertise in the selection and maintenance of its buildings. A small company might feel unable to afford such help and will look to the office manager or company secretary to fulfil these duties, while taking professional advice when the need arises.

FACTORS AFFECTING THE SELECTION OF A BUILDING

Selecting a building to suit the needs of a company will involve the review of a number of factors, including the location of the building, choice of site, type of building proposed, and the extent of refurbishment, repair, or new building work needed to meet the company's requirements. The choice of freehold or leasehold purchase is dictated by the availability of suitable buildings and will generally have little effect on the decisions taken.

Location

A modern business should be sited where it can achieve the most efficient use of its resources. Traditionally, businesses are located near their markets, their raw material, or the labour and power necessary for the conversion of that material into goods for sale. In the nineteenth century the development of the railways allowed the increased separation of these elements and introduced the additional need for proximity to railway depots and marshalling yards. Many heavy industries had their own railway sidings. The decline of the railways coupled with improvements in the road network and suitable vehicles has resulted in a major transfer of distribution of raw materials and goods to the roads. As trade becomes ever more international, the use of alternative means of fast distribution remains an important consideration in the location of a company's premises.

The location of industry and commerce is, therefore, dependent upon easy access to raw materials, easy delivery of products to markets, docks or airports, and the availability of a suitable labour force.

Commercial undertakings generally begin in locations which favour the small scale of the enterprise. As the company grows the commercial environment may alter to an extent where the factors which worked in its favour in its early development are either neutralized or may begin to work against its interests. Relocation could be a solution to inefficiencies resulting from the unavailability of space for expansion, the need for reorganization of production lines without interruption of output, or shortages of suitably trained labour.

Selecting a site

A company wishing to establish itself on a new site, either by conversion of an existing building or by building afresh, will find its choice of site limited by planning legislation, which controls the location of commercial and industrial development. This control, as well as preventing certain types of development in particular areas, also encourages the establishment of special commercial and industrial zones or estates. Sites within such zones are available for light industrial use, allowing the letting of existing purpose-made factory or office units, or the erection of buildings to the company's own design.

The choice of site may be influenced by incentives provided by the national government. In the UK, for example, the government, in partnership with local authorities, attempts to direct the location of new business to areas of high unemployment. The incentives include taxation and local rates allowances. If the business is large or politically important enough, local authorities will generally be prepared to consider proposals for new development and negotiate special terms, consisting of low interest loans, rate reductions, and so on, in order to attract the business to its area. A company considering relocation would be well advised to explore all the options open to it before settling on a suitable site.

New towns, established to take the overspill population from major cities, were designed as self-contained economic units. Each has its own commercial and industrial centres. The sites for these new towns were generally chosen to take advantage of good communications and other facilities, and offer many amenities to attract business and labour.

The long-term benefits to companies of relocation include continuing rate and insurance bills lower than in the centre of the major cities, and a more contented work-force, not hidebound by traditional working practices.

The following is a checklist of factors to be considered when choosing a building location:

1 Communications:

- standard of trunk roads available
- proximity of railhead
- access to international airport
- access to seaport
- average distance from suppliers and consumers (as small as possible).

2 Services:

- electric power available without restriction
- mains gas supplies available
- adequate water supplies.

3 Climate and topography:

- temperate climate throughout the year
- area/site well drained and free from flood danger
- site sheltered from high winds and extreme weather
- surrounding area pleasant; good outlook from site.

4 Government and local authority:

- area scheduled as development area, or enterprise zone, and eligible for investment grants
- planning restrictions in the area minimal
- friendly and co-operative local authority.

5 Labour and labour relations:

- local branches of trade unions moderate and co-operative
- key staff willing to move into area
- good supply of skilled or suitable work people already living in the area.

6 Amenities:

- housing prices low, good supply of houses of all types (private and local authority)
- good schools, with possibilities in the area for higher education
- good local transport facilities for commuters
- good local health services and hospitals
- adequate recreational facilities in the area
- theatres, cinemas and other entertainments
- police and fire services efficient
- churches of all denominations accessible.

7 Specific site factors:

- means for disposal of waste/effluent
- access on good local roads
- as required by the particular industry.

Choosing a building

The choice of building will depend on a number of factors which must be considered carefully together.

The activities and processes which are to be undertaken within the building must be analysed so that their requirements can be satisfied in its design. A report of the requirements of manufacturing processes, the storage of raw materials and finished products and the methods of packing and distribution should be requested from the managers responsible. All the data must be considered and a brief prepared to enable the appropriate building to be sought.

Unless the requirements of the firm are extremely specialized, it is likely a choice will be made from among a number of buildings with varying degrees of suitability. The first consideration is whether the firm wishes to rent or purchase the property and, if the latter, whether an existing building is being sought or specially built premises are required. The time factor is very important – a new building may take one or two years to complete, depending on its complexity, after all necessary consents are to hand. The design stage may add a further six to twelve months to the process. If the company can afford to purchase the freehold the building will represent a valuable asset and surety against the rent reviews inevitable in leases.

Any building taken over either by lease or purchase may require capital expenditure in adapting it to the needs of the company. A complete refurbishment, with the installation of air conditioning, improved insulation, and modern welfare facilities may be necessary, or just minor redecoration work and carpeting. If the use of the building is to be changed, then work may be needed to meet the requirements of special legislation or a licensing authority and planning permission may have to be obtained.

Professional advice

At this stage it is wise to consider appointing a professional who will be able to advise on the selection, conversion or construction of suitable premises. This appointment should be made at an early stage in order to avoid the problems which may arise from the selection of a building which is ill-fitted to the company's requirements for technical reasons. There are many considerations which require professional expertise in their assessment: for example, the suitability of the structure to carry the loads required: the capacity of the existing drains to cope with the possible increased use: and the requirements of the fire authorities.

The range of suitable qualified professional help has never been wider. In the past the architect has dominated this area, and may well be the only professional who springs to mind when considering building work. Of recent years the emergence of the surveyor, particularly of the building surveyor, as an expert in conversion and refurbishment work, has allowed the client greater choice and a range of skills which go beyond that offered by the architect.

Building surveyors and quantity surveyors are able to offer a full range of services which include structural surveys, cost feasibility studies, advice on the appointment of contractors and the design and supervision of the conversion work. Other professionals may be required to provide specialist advice (for example, civil engineers, landscape architects, general practice surveyors and town planners). All the leading professions publish registers of practitioners which are available in most public libraries.

The correct choice of someone who is going to be closely linked with major expenditure on your company's behalf is of vital importance. Prospective candidates should be interviewed, references from recent clients should be sought, and work in progress or recently completed should be inspected.

The architect/surveyor may be appointed to carry out the complete task, from advising at the inception of the scheme to the final handover of the completed work, or he may be appointed to deal with specific stages of the work, perhaps for the feasibility study only, or up to the selection of the contractor to carry out the work. The scale of fees would be varied accordingly. However, fragmentation of the work into small parcels frequently leads to difficulties arising from the lack of continuity and separation of responsibilities which is a consequence of that approach, and should be avoided by the appointment of a professional to supervise the project as a whole.

He or she will require a brief of the company's requirements, with particular emphasis on any special areas of concern. For example, special provision will have to be made for areas of high fire risk, heavy loads such as safes or heavy equipment, ventilation and air conditioning. He must be aware of any constraints upon the layout of offices and workshops arising from working practices, manufacturing production lines, policy on open plan or individual offices, vehicular access and parking for staff and deliveries, catering facilities, and special service needs requiring high voltage electrical substations or generators (for computers or large machinery).

Selecting a contractor

One of the architect's/surveyor's duties will be to advise on the selection of a contractor to carry out the building work. Since it is particularly difficult to control building costs associated with conversion work, that selection process must produce a contractor and price for the works which can be relied upon. The traditional method of choosing a contractor is by a process of competitive tendering, whereby a number of contractors are selected to bid for the work. The contractor offering the cheapest price is generally awarded the contract. The architect/surveyor will normally invite contractors, capable of undertaking work of the type and value required, selected prior to the tender itself. The preparation of a list of suitable contractors circumvents any difficulties which may arise if an unknown contractor submits the lowest price in an open tender. Doubts may exist as to such a contractor's ability to carry out the work satisfactorily, on time, at the quality and price tendered. The additional confidence in a contractor chosen by the selective tender process, and the time saved in his selection may well be worth the possibility of a higher contract price.

A number of other systems of selection and contracting are available which may be used where suitable. These will now be discussed briefly in turn.

Management fee contracts

The contractor undertakes to manage the contract for a fee established in advance. This allows him to be appointed at an early stage in the design process as an important member of the professional team. The intention is that he cannot be said to gain from increases in the value of the work, a useful factor if major refurbishment is contemplated.

Package deal and turnkey systems

The whole of the design and construction work is undertaken for a total cost, the client being handed the key to the building on completion (hence 'turnkey'). Contracts of this type are offered by companies with an interest in providing a standardized form of construction, and are often used for standard factory or warehouse units on industrial estates. They are therefore more suitable for new-build work rather than for refurbishment, for extensions to existing buildings, or for a new building within a factory site.

Design and build contracts

These contracts are similar to package deal contracts, but with a greater emphasis on the client's special design requirements.

Separate contracts

Also known as the Alternative Methods of Management System (AMM), these contracts involve the use of the architect/surveyor as usual, but lets the various aspects of the work to various contractors as appropriate, thus avoiding the appointment of an individual main contractor. The architect/surveyor manages the contract. This approach involves the client in the selection of a number of contractors, each carrying out their own part of the works. Much refurbishment work could be successfully carried out using this system.

Project management contracts

These contracts place the responsibility for all the various aspects of the work, design, supervision and performance, on one organization. No single profession has emerged as the legitimate holder of this title. Architects, surveyors, and main contractors are all conducting contracts under this title at present. The functions of each are being carried out by a team consisting of architects, surveyors and contracting staff, but all under the one contract. It generally depends on the historical background of the team leader as to which profession can claim to be the project manager. Advantages of the system are the removal of the litigious barriers between the members of the team, who can all be seen to be working together for the good of the project.

It is as well to remember with all the available contracts and tendering procedures, that the cheapest initial price may not prove to be the cheapest final contract figure. Costs arising from delays, claims or the bankruptcy of contractors caused by the enforcement of onerous contract conditions may not be assessable or recoverable. It is worthwhile spending some little time ensuring that the right designer, supervisor, and contractor are chosen, and that the building requirements are fully worked out and understood before work is started on site.

BUILDING LEGISLATION (UK)

There are approximately 200 Acts and nearly 300 regulations affecting building operations.

Of course, not all the legislation applies to any particular building. Many types of buildings or uses to which a building may be put have their own specific regulations, but some of the general legislation, such as the building regulations, applies in most cases, and should always be considered.

Many of the regulations apply only to particular classes of building, or to buildings used for special purposes; for example, the Asbestos Regulations, which apply only to premises where asbestos processes are carried out or asbestos products are handled.

Legislation affecting particular commercial and industrial applications would normally be well known to a company working in that field. It is therefore proposed to discuss only the more important items of legislation of general concern to building owners.

Planning control

The use to which a building may be put is controlled by planning legislation exercised by the local authority under the Town and Country Planning Act 1971. The Use Classes Orders 1972 and 1987 categorize a number of uses for land. Although land, and the buildings on the land, may continue to be used for purposes within the same use class – for example, a greengrocer's may become a newsagent's, or a factory producing clothing may switch to the assembly of electronic components – any change in use class constitutes development and requires planning permission.

Planning permission can be sought in two stages. Initial application can be made for outline planning approval. A prospective user can explore the likelihood of permission to use land for his purpose without the need to develop the scheme fully, even before he has obtained any legal interest in the site. Care needs to be taken here, since the value of the land may increase considerably if planning consent is given. For this reason, consent is generally given to a particular individual or company, and may lapse if that company sells its interest to another party. Before development can take place, detailed proposals must be put forward and full planning consent obtained.

As well as the nature of the use of the development, the local authority will be concerned with the appearance and height of the building, means of access, car parking provision and, increasingly, the employment opportunities offered by the development.

If it is felt that planning approval may be required, then the advice of the planning authority should be sought. The local authority is able to order the removal of any building for which planning permission was not obtained, and the restoration of the land to its former use.

Building control

In addition to the need to satisfy the planning authorities, any development which involves the construction of new work or alterations or extensions to existing buildings may have to satisfy the requirements of the building regulations. Building control is also exercised by the local authority, and it is common practice to submit plans for building regulation approval at the same time as an application is made for planning approval. The practice of submitting plans for scrutiny and approval prior to the commencement of building work has been criticized in the past as causing unnecessary delay, particularly in circumstances where the work required is straightforward and simple, like the installation of a washbasin or the erection of a small shed.

Since November 1985 alternative methods have been available whereby the local authority is notified that the work will be carried out, and inspection takes place on site, without the prior approval of plans. The building owner loses certain protection afforded under the older system, but gains time in circumstances where the risk of failure to comply with the regulations is less likely.

A third method, using inspectors approved under the Approved Inspectors Regulations instead of the local authority has also been introduced, but at present the only approved inspectors are the National House Builders Registration Council, who deal with private housing developments.

The building regulations lay down standards of design and construction essentially in the interests of public health and safety, and to conserve power and the water supply. Sections of the regulations deal with structural strength, means of escape in case of fire, drainage and sanitation, ventilation, thermal insulation and water supply.

Whichever of the alternative inspection systems is followed, the building owner is held responsible for compliance with the building regulations. Failure to do so can lead to a fine, and an order to put right or remove offending work.

Fire precautions

Fire precautions are an important consideration in the safety of premises, and are dealt with in two ways. New building work is dealt with primarily under the building regulations, but existing buildings are covered by the Fire Precautions Act 1971 and related legislation.

The Act deals with the adequate provision of means of escape in case of fire. It includes the provision of fire fighting equipment, alarm systems, and so forth. It is primarily concerned with the protection of life, but the measures necessary to meet the requirements will provide some protection to property in the event of fire. There is also a requirement to instruct staff on necessary action in case of fire, and records must be kept of fire drills, alarm tests, maintenance checks and incidents involving fire. Registers are provided for the purpose. The provision of special equipment, sprinkler systems and the like, may be used in order to prolong the time available for escape and to protect property where there is special risk. Sprinklers and smoke detection devices may be required in special circumstances, such as basements and storage areas for inflammable materials.

In order to invoke its powers, the Minister must place before Parliament a designating order, which brings the types of buildings specified by the order under the Act. The Act was intended eventually to cover all buildings which fall into one of the following categories of use:

1   Recreation, entertainment or instruction or for any club, society or association
2   Teaching, training or research
3   Institutions providing treatment or care
4   Any purpose involving the provision of sleeping accommodation
5   Any use involving access to the building by members of the public, whether on payment or otherwise
6   Since the enactment of the Health and Safety at Work Act 1974, premises used as a place of work.

At the time of writing there have been only two such designating orders. The first dealt with hotels and boarding houses. The second includes premises previously covered by the Factories Acts and the Offices Shops and Railway Premises Act. In both cases there is a minimum size (stated as employees or customers) below which certification is not required, but there is still an obligation to provide a means of escape.

Under the Act, the owner of premises which come in a category designated by a designating order must make application to the fire authority for a fire certificate.

The fire authority is required to inspect the premises and advise on necessary standards. If necessary, they may provide written notice of the steps required to achieve a certificate, and stipulate a date by which the work must be carried out. After the period of time specified, a final inspection takes place. On being satisfied the appropriate precautions have been taken, a fire certificate is issued. If the work is not carried out to the satisfaction of the fire officer, then the business must cease trading until such time as he is satisfied. If the owner feels that the schedule of requirements, or any decision of the fire officer, is unreasonable, he has 21 days to appeal.

Other categories of building are presently covered by further regulations with respect to fire control. For example, nursing homes and residential care homes are among the categories which may come under the Act with the introduction of a future designation order. At present, the fire officer's requirements in this area are covered by the Residential Homes Act 1984 and the Residential Care Homes Regulations 1984. In this case the registration by the area health authority under the Act includes the requirement to satisfy the fire officer in the same areas of concern covered by the Fire Precautions Act.

The provision of fire protection systems may be prudent in situations not at present covered by the Fire Precautions Act. Suitable detection and fire control systems can prevent serious damage from fire by early detection and local control, and may allow normal business to recommence more quickly after an incident involving fire. Constant vigilance and inspection is necessary to maintain standards and ensure that the measures taken are not undermined by careless action. A fire in a basement at a major oil company's head office caused £100 000 damage despite almost instant detection and the attendance of the fire services after less than two minutes. The subsequent disruption caused by repair work added a further £200 000 to the bill. Fire doors had been wedged open, and communication ducting and the air-conditioning system conducted the smoke as far upwards as the tenth floor.

Insurance companies will look favourably on a company with a sound fire prevention policy. While it is unlikely that there will be a reduction in premiums, the additional premiums required to cover high-risk areas or materials may be avoided.

FUTURE ALTERATIONS AND EXTENSIONS

When reviewing the suitability of a company's property, due allowance for future expansion should be made. If considering the purchase of existing property, the possibility of taking over adjacent property in the future or buying a building with a greater floor area than present requirements demand should be explored. The extra space may be let on a short-term lease until required. If a new building is contemplated then the architect or surveyor responsible for the design should be informed of future plans so that he may make allowance within his design. The additional cost of strengthening the foundations and structure to take an extra storey in the future will be minimal compared with the cost involved later. Such considerations may influence the location of the building if site investigations show that the proposed additional loads take the design beyond the bearing capacity of the ground. The incorporation of larger capacity service mains or space for additional plant to accommodate the expanded needs may also be considered.

Provided that there is space within existing boundaries, a company is entitled to extend its property within normal planning constraints up to 10 per cent of the original development without further planning approval being required. If an extension of less than the full 10 per cent is made, then further expansion up to the total of 10 per cent of the original development is possible. If expansion beyond the gross 10 per cent is contemplated, then new planning approval must be sought.

If the property is leasehold the lessor's consent will be required, and at this stage it should be considered whether notice should be served under the Landlord and Tenant Act 1927, to protect the tenant's position at the end of the lease.

DISPOSAL

In addition to the initial design, alteration or extension to any building it is well to have in mind the possibility of eventual disposal. The more specialized a building in design the more difficult it is to sell, as it cannot easily be adapted for use other than that for which it was purpose-built, although there are a few well-known examples where imaginative developments have given buildings such as power stations, warehouses, mills and railway stations new leases of life in greatly changed roles.

In office buildings, partitioning arrangements may be unsuitable to a subsequent occupier. Flexibility can be provided by subdividing open office areas with demountable partitions which can easily be removed or adapted.

MAINTENANCE AND REPAIR

An important aspect of the management of property is that of maintenance and repair. Buildings consist of materials of varying durability, with 'lives' ranging from a few years to centuries. Some, such as timber joinery, can be protected by impregnation at the manufacturing stage or by the application of surface treatments (paints, stains, or varnishes) throughout their life. Others, such as heating appliances, wear out after a number of years' use and need overhaul or replacement well before the rest of the building deteriorates.

Failure to carry out repair and maintenance at the appropriate time can lead to a considerably more expensive replacement becoming necessary or even danger to the building occupants, if, for example, a faulty gas appliance continues to be used.

While not all equipment and materials need to last the whole life of the building, those used in parts of the building which are difficult to reach without severe disruption should be designed to do so. Mechanical systems should have a reasonable service life before wearing out. However, the replacement of a boiler may provide an opportunity for a review of the heating and ventilating requirements of the property, resulting in the introduction of more efficient systems.

There is little advantage in designing all systems to last the life of the building. Technological advances, improvement in materials and equipment and changes in working practices lead to obsolescence in design which may result in the replacement of equipment before it wears out, just because something better becomes available. There can be very few buildings over twenty-five years old which still boast the original heating system, or even retain the same internal layout as envisaged in their original designs.

When evaluating the suitability of an existing building, or approving the design of a specially commissioned one, the importance of ease of maintenance should not be underestimated. There are a number of hidden costs associated with maintenance which may be overlooked when comparing alternative materials. In addition to the cost of carrying out the work itself, there is the cost of disruption to the normal routine while the work is carried out. The cost to the company of documents or files misplaced because they were moved to allow the painters in, or of a vehicle access blocked by scaffolding, may be extremely high. Also, the additional security risk of unauthorized access via scaffolding cannot be overlooked. Some of these maintenance costs cannot be avoided, but choices taken during the design or refurbishment of premises at the time of purchase can reduce their effect or frequency.

In some cases, the initial cost of incorporating materials or design solutions requiring low maintenance will be greater than would otherwise be required. The loss of earnings or interest on the extra capital should be balanced against the expected savings in the future. Maintenance is an area which is particularly vulnerable to the company's financial circumstances. It is all too easy to delay maintenance to save costs and balance the budget. For this reason the temptation of agreeing to a cheap specification and relying on future maintenance being carried out on a regular basis should be avoided.

The idea of spending money today in anticipation of problems which may not arise for twenty or thirty years is a difficult one, particularly if a board of directors or shareholders has to be persuaded. Companies are often more concerned with current expenditure than future expense. The value of designed maintenance is, however, becoming better appreciated, and may be reflected in the value of the property if it comes to the market before the maintenance is required. A compromise between designing a cheap specification with high maintenance costs or an expensive specification with little or no maintenance must be reached, and the architect or surveyor should be able to advise here. The terms 'costs in use' or 'life cycle costing' describe procedures where, on paper, future expenditure is discounted to present values for comparison purposes.

Programmes of planned maintenance

These programmes should be prepared by the prudent building owner. In order to identify the maintenance requirements of the building a survey should be carried out and a programme of maintenance appropriate to the materials and design incorporated within its construction should be prepared. This programme can form the basis of a maintenance budget which should be approved at the highest level, particularly in view of the vulnerability described above.

The varying needs for maintenance in different parts of the building must be established. Little-used or carefully used rooms and corridors will require less frequent redecoration with consequent savings in the maintenance budget. Reception areas and other prestigious parts of the building require redecoration more frequently than is strictly necessary in order to maintain or promote the corporate image of the company. Where the fabric of the building is exposed to corrosion or where hygiene requirements must be considered (for example, in food preparation areas) more frequent redecoration will be required.

Provided the building is brought up to a good standard of repair when purchased, expenditure on maintenance should not be great in the first few years of occupation. If low maintenance materials are incorporated, maintenance will be limited to the repainting of external painted surfaces every three to five years and redecoration internally as required. The replacement of boilers or electrical rewiring can be planned in advance and included within an annual maintenance budget.

Labour for maintenance

This labour may be provided by a contractor selected by the procedures described earlier in this chapter. The contractor may carry out specific tasks in accordance with the previously agreed maintenance programme, or be retained to cope with emergencies. Minor repairs and the replacement of consumable equipment like fluorescent light tubes is usually carried out by staff directly employed by the company. In some areas of high office concentrations, it is now possible to obtain all such services from specialist maintenance contractors who will undertake a twenty-four hour comprehensive service.

All those responsible for managing property will be aware that many contractors are competing to provide regular services which range from simple cleaning to highly specialized professional care of architectural finishes or mechanical services. There is always a risk that such companies will either skimp work or fail to carry it out altogether. A simple example is the window cleaning company whose computer generates invoices monthly whether or not the work is actually done. Another is the office cleaning company which charges for 15 early morning cleaners but actually provides 8, some of whom sign the register twice using different names. Yet another instance is where a main ventilator fan fails during a heatwave and, upon inspection, it is found that the bearings have not been greased for years by the contractor responsible. These examples are from the experience of this author.

In all cases where reliance is placed on outside contractors for regular services and maintenance, it is essential to nominate a reliable member of staff to act as a supervisor or monitor, whose job must include ensuring that the scheduled work is done before any invoice is paid.

LEASEHOLD PROPERTY

A high proportion of commercial property is leasehold, and most leases contain a clause which allows the rent to be reviewed at fixed intervals during its term. At each review date the current market rent is assessed and substituted for the rent previously payable. The dates or interval between reviews should be expressly stated in the lease, together with the procedure which must be followed. Recent court decisions have been concerned with the rights of the parties if the procedure is not followed. For example, if the landlord does not give notice of the review at the time stipulated by the lease, the view is that the landlord will forfeit the right to a review until the next review date if time is of the essence of the agreement. Time will be of the essence only if it is expressly so provided in the terms of the lease, or if there is some indication in the lease or in the surrounding circumstances that time is to be of the essence. Generally, surveyors or valuers acting for each party meet and negotiate the new rent. Provision is usually made within the lease for the appointment of a third independent surveyor to settle the matter by arbitration if agreement is not reached.

Full repair convenants

Leases for commercial property may contain a full repair covenant, which will require a tenant to leave the property newly decorated and in a condition of good repair at the end of the tenancy. Even if in disrepair at the commencement of a lease having a full repairing covenant, a tenant must put the premises into good repair and so hand them back at the end of the term.

The law of dilapidations is complex and a subject for experts; but the principle should be borne in mind that the measure of dilapidations when they have to be valued is the amount of injury to the landlord's revisionary interest. If it is the landlord's intention to demolish the building for redevelopment, he will fail in a claim against the tenant if the building is in disrepair as he has suffered no loss.

A tenant of business premises may be entitled to a new lease on the expiration of an existing lease should he desire to continue in occupation under the terms of the Landlord and Tenant Act 1954. The rent of the premises is subject to review under the new terms, and the landlord can regain possession, thus avoiding granting of a new lease if he proves intention to redevelop the premises or requirement for his own occupation. Provision is made in the Landlord and Tenant Act 1927 for compensation for tenants making improvements, or establishing goodwill in business premises at the end of the term of the lease. Alternatively, a new lease may be granted.

VALUATION

The valuation of freehold or leasehold property should be carried out by an expert valuer familiar with the value of similar properties in the same market. The value depends on the purpose of the valuation. Valuation for insurance purposes will be the full cost of rebuilding on the existing land, and consequently should not include the value of the land. The cost of rebuilding should include the cost of site clearance, professional fees and legal expenses. Insurance should also be taken out to cover the cost of disruption to production, or of temporary accommodation required while the work is carried out. The value of a property for the purpose of sale or the setting of rents will depend on its location, and the demand for property of its type and condition in the area. It has very little direct relationship to the cost of building, particularly where the advantages of the location may be overwhelming, and there is a scarcity of building land in the area. A revaluation of a company's real estate should be undertaken at regular intervals, as it represents an asset which is often undervalued in the accounts with a consequential effect on the company's value in the market-place.

RATING

All premises used for business purposes have a rateable value, which is used to assess the contribution to the local authority made by that business for the provision of local services.

The responsibility for valuing property for rating purposes rests with valuation officers of the Inland Revenue, who establish a gross value for the property or hereditament concerned. Valuation lists for England and Wales contain all rateable hereditaments for each rating area together with their assessments. Rates are levied on the occupier of a property, although the owner may be liable for rates on unoccupied premises.

The basis of the valuation is an estimate of the rent at which the particular property might be let according to the statutory definition. Until 1 April 1990, the current valuation lists were those which came into force on 1 April 1973, and any subsequent alterations to those assessments, or properties being assessed for the first time, were valued as if the hereditament had existed in the year prior to 1 April 1973. It was becoming increasingly difficult to assess new buildings satisfactorily the further removed the 1 April 1973 became. Accordingly, the method of rating was subjected to review in parallel with the domestic rating system, and a new system came into effect on 1 April 1990.

Under the reform, the rate in the pound, or poundage, is set nationally, rather than individually by each local authority as in the past. An exception to the rule is a small area served by the City of London Corporation, which continues to set a local poundage. Business rates are not now retained by the local authority, but are paid into a national pool and redistributed to each area as an equal amount per community charge payer.

All non-domestic properties are to be, or have been, revalued to provide a fair and up-to-date basis for the new system. The Government claims that the rateable values will rise by about eight times, but the new business rate set at a uniform poundage will ensure that in real terms the amount taken from the business sector in 1990/91 broadly matches the figure for 1989/90. After revaluation subsequent annual increases in the business rate will be linked to the retail price index, although the treasury has the power to specify a lower rate if it wishes. It is claimed that business rates have risen faster than inflation over the last fifteen years, so the change will provide firms with greater stability in future.

There will be some adjustment to the rates bill of individual properties as a result of the introduction of the new system. Some firms are benefiting from lower rates, while others are paying more. How a firm fares depends on the combined effect of the revaluation and the switch to the national poundage. Types of property whose rents have increased by less than the average since 1973, the previous base date, benefitted, since they were previously too heavily rated. Types of property which were undervalued because their rents rose by more than the average suffered above average increases. At the same time, if the poundage set by the local authority was higher or lower than the national poundage, the overall effect of combining the two may be exaggerated or minimized.

Transitional arrangements

Firms facing substantial rises will not have to pay the full amount of the increase immediately, as a ceiling will be set on rate bill rises in any one year. The largest increases will be phased in over at least five years. Phasing arrangements will generally only apply to properties which were occupied on 31 March 1990, or those which had only been vacated temporarily by the occupier. The transitional arrangements will cease to apply if the property changes hands, and the new ratepayer will pay the new rate. There will be a similar scheme for businesses who will benefit by substantial reductions in their rates bills. The reduction will be limited in a similar manner.

Empty properties will normally be eligible for a 50 per cent rate bill, subject to being empty for three months. Some premises, such as factories or warehouses, will not be subject to rates while empty.

Businesses will be able to propose a change in their new rateable value within six months of the publication of the revised lists. If the valuation officer does not accept the proposal and cannot agree some other figure, the business can appeal to the local Valuation and Community Charge Tribunal. After the initial six months, proposals and appeals will only be possible in limited circumstances. The Local Government Finance Act 1988 provides that there must be a revaluation of non-domestic property at five-year intervals after 1990.

ADJOINING OWNERS

The owner and occupier of a property has a responsibility to his neighbours and the community at large in respect of his use of the site. Nuisance and negligence are legal torts which may arise between adjoining owners as the result of the use of the property. Nuisance can arise in the generation of smoke, fumes, noise, and so on, causing grievance. If a substance is dangerous, such as toxic chemicals, or is stored in a dangerous manner on a neighbour's land, (for example, a reservoir of water) he will be liable should it escape and cause damage. There is also a legal responsibility embodied in legislation such as the Health and Safety at Work Act 1974 and in planning legislation. Failure to comply can result in prosecution.

The boundary to a property is usually defined on the site by a boundary wall or fence. Disputes can often develop concerning boundaries, particularly about their ownership, maintenance and repair. The title to the property may define the ownership of the enclosure, but in the absence of such evidence, the convention is that the fence stands on the property of the owner, for example the posts are on the owner's side, and the face of the fence usually represents the boundary. Boundary walls may be built on the owner's land, or they may be party walls, built with their centre lines on the boundary. Walls separating buildings are usually party walls. In London the law relating to party walls is well defined in the London Building Acts, which require notice to be served by the party initiating the works on the neighbours, and if the works are not agreed surveyors have to be appointed by both parties, to negotiate agreement. A third surveyor may be required to arbitrate if agreement cannot be reached.

There may be right of way across an owner's land in favour of an adjoining property. Such easements may be limited to a particular purpose or use, and generally are limited to a predetermined path or route. If access is taken and used openly and as of right by a neighbour across an owner's land a prima facie right will be established if continued for twenty years, and this could become a burden and frustrate development. In the same manner, rights of light can be acquired by the windows of a neighbour's building enjoying light and air across an owner's property for a similar period. Such rights cannot be obstructed, and can restrict the future development of an owner's property.

FURTHER READING

The Building Act 1984, HMSO, London

Cross, C.A., *Principles of Local Government Law*, 6th edn, Sweet & Maxwell, London, 1981

Department of the Environment, *The New Business Rate: A Brief Guide*, HMSO, 1990

The Fire Precautions Act in Practice, Architectural Press, 1977.

Fire Precautions Register, FPR Distribution, 37 Dumbarton Road, Glasgow.

Franks, J., *Building Procurement Systems*, The Chartered Institute of Building, London, 1984

Hirst, R., *Underdown's Practical Fire Precautions*, 3rd edn, Gower, Aldershot, 1989

Housing and Building Control Act 1984, HMSO, London

Mole, J.M., *Landlord and Tenant*, 2nd edn, M&E Handbooks, 1984

Taylor, N., *Property Managers' Guide to Fire Legislation in Commercial and Industrial Premises*, FPR Distribution, 37 Dumbarton Road, Glasgow

Town and Country Planning (Use Classes) Order 1972, HMSO, London

West, W.A., *Law of Dilapidations*, Estates Gazette Limited

Woodfall's Law of Landlord and Tenant, Sweet & Maxwell, London, 1978, with updating service

54 Security

Dennis Lock

The security risks facing any company depend greatly on the location and nature of the business. A company dealing with highly sensitive information is concerned that access to its premises shall be restricted to authorized people. At the other extreme, a retail store may try to attract large numbers from the general public during business hours. Every organization has its own combination of security problems and each decides its own policy and strategy for reducing the risks.

Some risks can be covered by insurance (Chapter 52) but every responsible manager (and the insurer) will want to see steps taken to reduce the likelihood of unwanted incidents. This is, of course, especially important where the safety of people is in question.

Most companies are concerned to protect:

- Premises
- Property (including cash and valuables)
- People
- Proprietary information.

This chapter outlines a few of the security considerations common to companies in general. For more detailed study of this complex subject there is a list of relevant books at the end of the chapter.

SECURITY MANAGEMENT

Security policy is a matter which should concern management at the most senior level but the company must nominate an individual who can be held responsible for co-ordinating security policy, implementing security measures and acting in case of any incidents. In a large organization this might be a specialist security manager, possibly with senior management status and commanding a sizeable department. Such managers are often retired senior police officers or others having relevant experience and suitable credentials. In a smaller company the security management role is often combined with that of office services or some other job, in which case the person responsible might have no previous security experience at all.

For simplicity, the person responsible for security will be referred to in the remainder of this chapter as the 'security manager'.

PROFESSIONAL ADVICE

Whether the risks are from criminal intent or from accident or fire, any company wishing to install or review security measures must have access to professional advice from the legal, criminal and practicable viewpoints. Free and expert advice is available from three main external sources:

1   The crime prevention officer from the local police station
2   The local fire prevention officer
3   A surveyor from the company's insurers.

Each of these experts should be given an outline of the company's business activities and interests and be conducted over the company's premises to survey potential risks.

If possible, the security manager should arrange a subsequent joint meeting with these experts on site. Specific and general risks can then be assessed. The combined experience of this 'expert committee' will be found invaluable in formulating detailed measures that:

- Are based on practical experience of past incidents
- Are recommended by those who know the relevant statutory obligations that must be fulfilled by the company
- Recognize special risks (for example, to a cashier, or of stored combustible materials)
- Do not include unnecessary or wasteful measures (for example, too many detectors in an automatic alarm system, or the employment of guards where there is insufficient risk)
- Will be accepted by the insurers (since their surveyor will have been party to the recommendations).

Other specialists or professional organizations may need to be consulted in cases where specialist knowledge is required, such as goods loading and transport operations, commercial fraud prevention or where computers and their data are at risk (subjects not covered in this chapter).

POLICY AND STRATEGY

Most security measures cost money and some are very expensive. The company must decide what it is prepared to pay to protect its security. The extremes range from spending and doing nothing to committing huge and regular sums (which could even exceed the value of the risks to be protected). It is also very easy to waste money on ineffective measures or with incompetent security firms.

One essential step before committing expenditure is to try and evaluate the size of the risks. If possible, the extent of likely losses or incidents must be visualized and used to gauge what might be a sensible level of expenditure – a provisional budget, in fact.

The company has to decide how much it expects to rely on external security companies and organizations and whether or not it will employ its own security staff. Company size will obviously be a principal deciding factor. Larger companies may be in a position to employ their own security staff but this always means recruiting and keeping sufficient numbers to cover periods of sickness and holidays, especially important where a 24-hour guard service is required. Those considering the direct employment of security staff are referred to the security manuals listed in the further reading section.

The security industry has grown enormously in recent years and there is no shortage of companies willing to offer protection against all manner of risks. The services offered range from mobile patrols or on-site guards to the provision of highly sophisticated equipment and anti-terrorist measures. Some companies are very good, capable of offering excellent advice and services. Others are so bad that their use actually introduces risks. It is often difficult to tell good from bad and it is easy to be beguiled by glossy brochures, impressive claims and professional sales presentations. The field is big enough to confuse all but the experts.

When choosing an outside security organization, either to install equipment or to provide other services, the advice of the experts will prove invaluable. Although they may not be prepared or allowed to recommend a particular company, they should be able to give a list of companies that have earned reasonable reputations for providing the types of services envisaged and which, backed by their professional memberships, can offer some guarantee of performance.

This preplanning approach places the company in an advantageous purchasing position. It can seek competitive quotations from several security companies against specifications based on independent expert advice. The initiative is with the buyer, who need not be influenced by the sellers' own proposed schemes. The aim is to achieve measures that are adequate and effective without being excessive and wasteful.

PREMISES

Locks and keys

A lock is as good as its price. Its key is as good as the precautions taken to restrict the number of holders and the opportunities for it to be copied. For security purposes a five lever deadlock is the minimum insurance requirement, but cheaper locks are often adequate for simple privacy. The strength of the door and its frame is also important.

Where padlocks are used, these should be close-shackled with the vulnerable parts made of hardened steel. The hasps must be of equal quality and must be correctly fitted.

There are often external doors which, because they are unattended by guards or receptionists, must be kept securely locked against intruders even when the premises are occupied. Where these are intended to provide a means of escape during fire the locking device must be of a type approved by the local fire authority. The usual design criterion is that the device shall be simple to operate from inside even in cases of panic or dense smoke. Security of such doors can be put at risk if staff use them when there is no emergency (for example, to take short cuts). Labelling such doors 'fire exit only' does not usually have the desired effect and the fitting of individual simple door alarm bells can provide the necessary deterrent.

A system for the safekeeping of keys should be instituted, which would usually include such measures as keeping keys for the premises and its installations in a locked cabinet, from which keys can only be issued in exchange for signed receipts from authorized persons.

Identification and passes

Many thefts are the work of opportunists who gain entry using a plausible excuse. Such people may be dressed in smart clothes, authentic-looking uniforms, or even in overalls bearing the name of a well-known and perfectly legitimate contractor (for example, a window cleaning company). Beware of technicians, complete with tool kits, looking for office equipment to service. In addition to the risks to company property or information, a walk-in thief can cause loss and much discontent among employees, especially at lunch times, when staff (in spite of advice and warnings) leave wallets, cheque books and other valuables in their brief cases, jacket pockets, handbags and unlocked desk drawers.

The company should operate a rule that all visitors must be conducted about the premises by a member of staff, and all staff should be encouraged to challenge any person unfamiliar to them who is seen to be unaccompanied. *A work-force which is security and safety conscious is a company's strongest security safeguard.*

Identity cards bearing photographs can be issued to all permanent staff, with suitable temporary passes for casual or agency workers. Such passes authorize the relevant people to be on the premises and can be produced if they are challenged. Their more usual purpose is to authorize entry to the premises, but this presupposes that every entry point will be manned at all open times by guards or receptionists, and that the passes will in fact be properly scrutinized, without fear or favour, before their holders are admitted.

The issue of passes must be strictly controlled and registered, preferably under the control of the security manager or the personnel department. Passes must be withdrawn (reclaimed from the holders and destroyed) when people leave employment, are suspended, or otherwise lose the right to enter the premises.

Identification pass systems lead to a considerable amount of administrative work if they are to satisfy all the above conditions, but they are necessary in very high-risk areas. Automatic access systems may be preferable in many situations for easier administration and because they cause less disruption to staff movement.

Automatic access control systems

The simplest form of automatic access control system consists of a remote-controlled solenoid door lock. The person inside can interrogate the visitor using an intercom device before pushing a button to energize and release the lock. Where it is not possible to see the person outside the door, a closed-circuit television monitor may also be provided.

Solenoid locks can also be released by keying a four-digit number into a keypad mounted outside the door. It is possible in some devices to have a reserve number, to be used by any member of staff who is forced to admit an intruder under duress or threat: use of the reserve number allows entry, but alerts security staff or activates a remote alarm without warning the intruder. No keys or identity cards are needed but all of these entry systems rely on restricting the code number to staff. It will not remain so restricted for very long, and must be changed at suitable intervals.

More sophisticated systems release solenoid locks when coded identification passes are inserted into a detector box. Better still are the devices which work when a coded pass card merely comes within range of a remote detector – the so-called 'hands free' systems.

When automatic access systems are linked to a central computer, the administrative problem of pass cards is greatly simplified, it being easy to cancel a pass simply by removing its number from the data or (better) by transferring it to a list of cancelled numbers. With such systems zoning is possible, so that staff can be allowed access only to those areas of the building which are relevant to their jobs and status. In some modern systems the computer might also be used for controlling other more general building services (such as lighting, heating and ventilation) and alarm systems.

No system is foolproof and all depend on the integrity of staff. A common problem is that people find it difficult to disobey the normal rules of politeness: they will hold a door open for any person rather than allow it to close as intended for its security purpose.

Lighting

Lighting can play a big part in reducing risks from accidents or crime.

It is always essential to maintain adequate lighting where there are stairs or steps, or where other hazards to people exist. If possible, switching should be controlled centrally so that staff or energy-conscious managers cannot switch the lighting off.

Care must be taken to avoid sudden changes of illumination at boundaries between different areas; for example, staff leaving a brightly lit office should not encounter a dimly lit corridor or staircase, but the lighting should be designed so that there is a graded reduction in intensity over sufficient distance for eyes to adjust.

Where emergency lighting is provided, particularly along routes designated as means of escape in case of fire, it is important to arrange for regular testing and maintenance. Such lighting depends on rechargeable batteries which deteriorate with time and need occasional replacement.

Bright lighting of stockyards and external areas in general is a powerful deter-rent to intruders. Where security guards are employed, the lighting should be arranged so that they can patrol or be housed behind the main security lights, so that potential intruders outside a fence or gatehouse see the lights but no detail beyond them.

If closed-circuit television is used for remote surveillance it is obviously necessary to provide adequate lighting if the equipment is to provide good definition at night.

It is one thing to design a good lighting system, but quite another to keep it working at its planned level. Regular testing and planned maintenance is essential. Some high-intensity lamps (such as tungsten–halogen) have a relatively short life and, if they are operated by time switches or other automatic devices, their failure can easily go undiscovered when they are protecting premises outside normal hours of occupation. Where the colour quality is unimportant, energy-efficient, long-life, low-maintenance luminaires (such as sodium or mercury vapour) are suitable, especially for external floodlighting.

Guarding

If it is decided to employ security guards to protect premises outside working hours there is a choice between using mobile patrols, which visit at intervals to make checks, and 'static' guards stationed on the premises.

Whatever arrangement is adopted, the company should work with the security organization responsible to produce a security specification that gives precise details of the service to be provided. Such specifications include instructions for the guards themselves, with a list of duties, clocking points, 'do's' and 'don'ts', items of high risk, routine communications, and what to do in the case of specified emergencies.

Mobile patrols

Mobile patrols are the cheaper option but are of limited use without additional facilities. Their visits can be witnessed by lurking villains, who then know that they have ample time to break in once the patrol has been seen to depart. But mobile patrols can be effective in conjunction with automatic alarm systems (see the section on automatic alarms below).

Static guards

Static guards have a useful role in detecting and reporting incidents, provided that they are backed by an efficient security company with whom they are in constant communication. The usual arrangement is to arrange for the guard to patrol the premises, with clock-punch points at strategic places to allow subsequent audit of the guard's movements. The guard would also be expected to communicate with base at regular intervals (typically every hour), failure to do so resulting in some form of emergency investigation.

Among the risks from using static guards are neglect of duty (falling asleep, reading, private study, or even temporary absences from the premises), theft of property or information by the guards themselves, admittance of unauthorized persons (for example, for amorous purposes), abuse of telephones or other office facilities and equipment, and fouling of premises (outside or indoors) where a dog is used. These risks should not deter any company wishing to use static guards, but they must be countered by ensuring adequate supervision including occasional spot checks. Where the guards are provided by an external company, this means establishing good and regular contacts with that company's operations management.

Apart from obvious special cases (such as museums and art galleries) it may be advantageous for some companies to consider employing static guards from the same security company on a 24-hour basis. They can often provide internal messengers and personnel for reception and access control duties at rates which compare favourably with the total employment costs of their permanent staff counterparts. Such arrangements can engender a closer and more effective relationship with the security company, which in turn can enhance the service provided out of hours.

Automatic alarm systems

It is possible to festoon a building with detectors capable of detecting fire, flood or unwanted intruders and have the results transmitted by telephone line or other means to a 24-hour manned station that can inform the police. This is fine in theory, but may be less so in practice owing to the high incidence of false alarms. Police will ignore alarms known to generate false calls. Criminals know this, and have been known to activate alarms deliberately several times before finally committing their planned burglary in earnest. It is well known that a thunderstorm can produce a crop of false alarm activations. A purely local bell or sounder is no answer because it is likely to be ignored until someone eventually complains about the noise.

Alarm detectors should therefore be chosen and sited to avoid false activation as far as possible and the system has to be well maintained and tested at regular intervals. Those responsible for securing the premises when employees leave must follow a checklist for closing all windows and access points, and for setting the intruder alarms.

Typical alarms might comprise a system of automatic heat and smoke detectors for fire, plus another with detectors that can sense the presence of intruders. The types of detectors and their siting should be as recommended by the expert committee mentioned at the start of this chapter. The systems can be fitted with automatic dialling equipment which sends a recorded message to the emergency telephone service, but a better arrangement is a direct link to a reliable security company's control room by secure, monitored land lines.

Additionally, a concealed personal attack button which alerts some responsible and remote security control post should be provided for each employee considered to be at high personal risk (such as a cashier).

Local bells for personal attack or intruder alarms should be on a time delay, so that they do not panic the criminals into precipitate action.

Upon alarm activation the central station will call the appropriate emergency service immediately and alert the company's nominated keyholder. It is usual to provide more then one keyholder, listed in the order in which they should be called by the local police station. The central station can be asked to act as first-call keyholder. Those who would take longer than 20 minutes to reach the premises should not be nominated as keyholders, for all the obvious reasons and to avoid wasting police time.

Where the risks are not unduly high, but are of a normal commercial nature (for example, office premises) there is an arrangement that virtually eliminates the wasting of police time through false calls. This only works where the security company has local radio patrols operating in the area and only applies to intruder alarms (never to fire or personal attack alarms). Upon receipt of an intruder alert the control room directs a mobile patrol to the premises by radio. The police are only called if the patrol discovers signs of a break-in or otherwise suspects that intruders are on the premises.

CASH

Money in any form is just about the most attractive target for thieves because it is easily disposable and usually impossible to trace back to its rightful owner. The best security measure against the loss of cash is not to handle it at all, and to let it be widely known that no cash is kept on the premises. Failing this ideal, the amounts of cash handled and the numbers of people with access to it should be kept to a minimum.

If it is intended that wages or any other large sums are to be carried and handled the insurer must be informed. They will usually insist on special precautions, such as the use of a reputable security company for transporting the cash, with appropriate guards (such companies can also be employed to make up wage packets). Strict procedures must be followed for authorizing collection from banks against cheques, including adequate means of identification and signature arrangements.

Where cash has to be carried by members of staff, police crime prevention advice should be sought and their recommendations followed. Special waistcoats, alarmed bags, and bags which can deface the contents or eject dye or smoke are commercially available.

Cash, other negotiable items and cheque books should all be kept in safes. Each safe will be 'rated' by the insurers according to its age, type and location as being suitable for holding a certain maximum value, which should not be exceeded.

Careful attention (with expert advice) must be paid to the construction and siting of cashiers' offices. Serious consideration must be given to the strength of the doors, walls, and all windows and hatches, from possible attack. Robbers often use shotguns, sledgehammers and pickaxe handles, and, while maximum physical protection for the staff should be provided, they must be instructed never to attempt heroics in the face of weapons. A concealed button, remote-indicating, personal attack alarm should be installed.

The accounts department should be responsible for supervising and auditing disbursements and holdings of petty cash by any department.

INFORMATION

Safekeeping of documents

The modern company has to maintain many books, documents, records and other sundry items, either because of statutory requirements or in its own interests. Some of these must be retained permanently (minute books, registers of members and directors, certificates of incorporation and of business name registrations, and the common seal). Others have to be kept for the full term of their viability (title deeds and leases) or for their term plus 12 years (correspondence and papers relating to property transactions, particular types of contract, and so on). In certain other cases six years' cover has to be maintained (including sales and purchase ledgers with their associated records, wages and salaries registers, and so on).

Other documents have to be protected to prevent loss of the information contained in them, either because this would be helpful to a competitor or because the company's operations depend on being able to retrieve the information whenever it is needed.

The loss of any of these documents would at least be inconvenient and could be very serious. They have to be protected against fire, theft, vandalism, rodents, damp, and water from any source. Specially constructed fire safes or cabinets are expensive but necessary items for important documents. Their purchase should be undertaken only after taking specialist advice. The company's insurers will be able to help. Obsolete safes can be considered, but these may not offer adequate protection against fire. Worse, small safes are at risk of being taken away by thieves for breaking open elsewhere, and they should be bolted down to a concrete base.

Where records are held as computer media it is even more important to use the correct type of protective cabinets, since cabinets which are suitable for papers may allow damage to data through condensation of steam in the event of fire.

An important factor in preventing the unauthorized removal of documents is to ensure that only appropriate personnel have access to the premises where they are kept. There is more on this subject under the 'premises' heading.

Where the problem is simply prevention of loss through accident or fire, information can be duplicated and stored on two separate sites. The use of microfilm or a more modern digital storage medium greatly reduces the amount of space needed. There are companies which offer storage of bulk documents in secure premises or vaults, usually allowing retrieval of documents within one day on request.

Theft of information

If a document is actually stolen, the law of theft can be applied. If information is simply taken by memorizing or copying, the law is vague. If an employee sells information it may be possible to prove corruption and take criminal proceedings, but cases (under the Prevention of Corruption Act 1906) have been rare. Civil actions are more likely to benefit the lawyers than the participants.

Cases have failed on the grounds that the firm took no steps to ensure privacy of what it subsequently claimed to be important and did not emphasize to employees that the operations were regarded as being in any way secret. The Data Protection Act 1984 (see Chapter 56) has introduced the term 'reasonable security' into law and imposes statutory obligations, but only for data covered by the Act.

Electronic surveillance (bugging)

Although suspicions of bugging are likely to be unfounded, many devices are sold; they can be very small and are easy to conceal. Detection of electronic bugs may be difficult, and very expensive multi-band sweep-frequency receivers are required. If strong suspicion exists, it is possible to hire the services of a professional company who will undertake to scan the premises – at a price. Even then it is possible that a bug can remain undetected. Where leaks are suspected there is merit in holding vital meetings at off-site venues arranged at short notice.

Document classification

It is important to establish a policy and procedure for classifying information according to its value to the company and its customers. Where a company is working on a government contract or for a customer with sensitive commercial interests a classification system may be obligatory. Adoption of a simple system, used and understood by everyone, will prevent the proliferation of ambiguous terms and the tendency to classify everything, whether it really matters or not.

Fixing the degree of restriction is the responsibility of the originator, after which all recipients must be bound by the classification. In a typical system, 'confidential' implies that the information is not for general dissemination but allows discretion in divulging it to those who need to act upon it or must know of it for their work. 'Secret' is much more emphatic, and is completely restricted to those on the distribution list (which must be attached to or marked on the document). Other classifications sometimes used include 'proprietary confidential', 'restricted' and 'staff confidential' (the last of these referring to personnel or medical records).

Document preparation and handling

Highly sensitive papers should be typed only by trusted personnel who are informed of the importance of secrecy. Ideally, only these people should be allowed to make photocopies. This is no job for temporary employees from an agency, who might work for a competitor or otherwise be able to make unauthorized and damaging use of the material in their hands. A danger lies in recipients making further copies for their own use or for secondary distribution to others: where this must be prevented the documents should be overstamped 'not to be copied' and retribution handed out to anyone found violating the rule.

Any spare copies, notes, carbons, and used 'one strike' typewriter ribbons associated with secret documents should be destroyed (by shredding in the case of paper, and by burning or a mechanical destructor for other items). There are contractors who can dispose of information safely, including bulk quantities, but the client should insist on being allowed to accompany the items and witnessing the process.

The wider the distribution of any classified information, the greater the risk and the more difficult it is to investigate the source of a leak. Originators must therefore compile distribution lists with great care, strictly on a 'need to know' basis. Secret documents should be sealed in two envelopes, with the inner marked 'secret' and the outer marked with something less obvious, such as 'personal'. If the information is particularly sensitive it may be necessary to have the documents delivered in person, and to ask for a signed receipt. One risk to avoid is having sensitive documents delivered to general office mail in-trays, where they are at the disposal of any potential miscreant who can recognize the significance of a particular envelope.

Longstanding and trusted employees should be used for the sorting and internal distribution of mail. Secretaries who open mail must be given instructions concerning the opening of classified mail. Where the originator is in any doubt, the inner envelope can be marked 'secret, to be opened only by . . .'

A checklist of precautions

- Define key jobs and apply stringent selection and vetting procedures to applicants
- Identify sensitive areas and restrict access to them
- Establish procedures for classifying, handling, copying and keeping documents and data
- Provide means for destroying sensitive documents and items associated with them from which information can be deduced
- Ensure that wall charts or other visual aids are not left where they can be freely seen
- Instigate occasional out-of-hours checks for documents carelessly left out, and to check on the conduct of security staff, cleaners, and so forth
- Educate staff to be security conscious
- Set up a procedure for dealing with any person with access to sensitive information who is due to leave the company's employment for any reason.

FIRE

Full use should be made of the services of the local fire prevention officer. In the UK the Fire Services Act 1947 requires the local fire authority to respond to requests for advice on fire prevention, means of escape and the restriction of the spread of fires.

The terms of a company's fire certificate will detail the numbers and types of extinguishers to be kept on the premises. Staff should be given basic instruction in the different types and their applications and operation. The company providing the extinguishers will probably be able to offer training to selected staff, or to arrange an on-site demonstration.

Although sprinkler systems are widely used as a means of automatic fire extinguishing, they are obviously not allowed in areas such as computer suites. Effective fire prevention can be achieved by having a gas system (CO_2 or Halon) which is activated by automatic detectors. The system should be linked so that it shuts down the mains power supply to the area affected and activates the main fire alarms and central station or fire brigade alarm.

All extinguishers, alarm systems, hosereels, sprinklers and roller fire shutters must be maintained and tested on a regular basis, with the results recorded in a fire log book.

The fire authority will advise on the wording of notices that must be displayed at key points in the building, which advise staff on what to do in the event of a fire. Fire drills should be held occasionally in order to ensure that staff are familiar with evacuation procedures and assembly points. If the building is not cleared in a short-time during a fire drill, the causes must be investigated, rectified, and the drill repeated.

Some members of staff should be designated as fire marshalls, responsible for given areas of the building. Their routine duties should include checking that fire extinguishers are in place, that fire and smoke-screen doors are not wedged open, that designated means of escape are not obstructed, and that specified areas are not used for storing any combustible materials. Fire marshalls should keep a list of personnel normally working in their areas, for use in the event of roll-calls at the fire assembly point.

DISCIPLINARY POLICY

A high proportion of disciplinary actions arise from incidents which have a security connotation. It is therefore advisable to have clearly defined policies for dealing with incidents. These could include:

1   Action to be taken in respect of a criminal offence against the company:

- by employees – suspension, dismissal, prosecution
- by contractors – expulsion from site, summary termination of contract, financial redress, prosecution
- by others – prosecution or other alternatives

2   Which matters should be referred to the police and at whose discretion
3   Dealing with lost and found property
4   Working of notice by a person resigning from a position of special risk
5   Sales of products and other items to employees
6   Use of the company's purchasing facilities for private purchases
7   Loan of equipment to employees for use off site
8   Work permitted for company staff, using the company's facilities and labour on repayment
9   Policies in respect of giving references
10   Communications sources for public media in the event of newsworthy items (accidents, losses, industrial action, and so on)
11   Policy towards losses by employees of personal belongings, cash, and so on. Includes disclaimers, extent of insurance cover (if any), possible provision of safekeeping facilities
12   Policy concerning collections of cash by staff, and (if allowed) provision of facilities for safekeeping cash
13   Policy for dealing with drug abusers.

These are really only a selection of matters and policy statements could include the use of insurance to offset risks (including the fidelity bonding of employees), bomb threats, major incidents, cash handling procedures, plus those already mentioned in connection with document security.

Theft

Theft is generally accepted by industrial tribunals as a valid reason for dismissal. It is therefore important to have a firm policy and no grounds should be allowed where an appeal could arise through some legal nicety.

Discretionary offences

It does not follow that all criminal activities should necessarily be grounds for dismissal.

Whether or not to prosecute for any offence is left to the ultimate discretion of the company, which can take into account any mitigating circumstances. The prime objective is to have a consistent policy on what constitutes grounds for dismissal rather than whether or not to prosecute.

It is stressed that for theft by non-employees the police must always be informed and prosecution pursued where possible.

Right of search

Even where a company includes a search clause in its conditions of employment there is no legal right of personal search without consent. In these circumstances, refusal to submit to a search may constitute grounds for dismissal, but not where there is no such clause in the employment conditions. It is probable that a search which reveals stolen property would be considered justified, dismissal resulting from the discovered theft and not from the refusal.

PRECAUTIONS AGAINST TERRORIST ACTION

Terrorism can unfortunately take many forms; for example, kidnapping, bomb threats, incendiary devices, and letter bombs. The attentions of a number of extremist groups may be directed against companies which they perceive as legitimate targets.

As with all security, staff should be warned always to be on the lookout for anything suspicious. Simple precautions against explosions outside the premises can include protection of windows using a suitable film. Good housekeeping generally, avoidance of accumulated rubbish, and a clear site will reduce the opportunities for concealing bombs and make searching easier. Mail room staff should be trained to recognize packages or letters which may contain explosive or incendiary devices and report them to the police.

Probably the most common occurrence is the call warning of a bomb on or near the premises. The call may be a hoax, but must always be taken seriously and reported immediately to senior management who will decide what should be done. There are three basic courses of action:

1 Ignore the warning and assume it is a hoax
2 Make a search
3 Evacuate the premises and organize a search before re-entry.

Amongst the points to be considered are:

1 Nature of the call – apparent age of the caller, speech, attitude, general approach, and so on
2 Recent history of such threats, genuine or otherwise, locally and nationally
3 Prevailing conditions of industrial tension, strikes and political unrest in the neighbourhood and at the recipient's premises particularly

Signal your supervisor and conform to prearranged drill for nuisance calls: tick through applicable word below, insert where necessary.

TIME . . . . DATE . . . .

Origin	STD		Coin box		Internal
Caller	Male	Female		Adult	Juvenile

Voice	Speech	Language	Accent	Manner	Background
Loud	Fast	Obscene	Local	Calm	Noises
Soft	Slow	Coarse	Regional	Rational	Factory
Rough	Distinct	Normal	Foreign	Irrational	Road traffic
Educated	Blurred	Educated		Coherent	Music
High pitch	Stutter			Incoherent	Office
Deep				Deliberate	Party
Disguised				Hysterical	atmosphere
				Aggrieved	Quiet
				Humorous	Voices
				Drunken	Other

Text of conversation

Figure 54.1   Bomb-threat checklist (Oliver and Wilson)

4   Any connection likely to arouse the antipathy of Animal Liberation Front activists
5   Any trading relationships between the company and countries whose opponents have used bombs
6   The implications and dangers of an evacuation.

In all instances, police and fire authorities should be informed immediately, whether an evacuation is to be ordered or not. As a neighbourly gesture, adjoining firms should be told what is happening.

It is important that telephone operators have clear instructions what to do if they receive a message, so that there is minimum confusion and as much derived information as possible. In addition to the instructions suggested below, a form similar to that in Figure 54.1 can be placed on hand for use by the operators, its mere availability possibly also useful in relieving natural tension.

Guidelines to telephonists

1   Let the caller finish his message without interruption
2   Get the message exactly – bearing in mind the points shown
3   If it is possible to tie the supervisor or another operator into the conversation, do so
4   Ensure that senior management or a predesignated person are told exactly the contents of the call as soon as possible
5   If the caller is apparently prepared to carry on a conversation, encourage him to do so and try to get answers to the following:

   • *where* has the bomb been put?

- *what time* will it go off?
- *why* has it been done?
- *when* and *how* was it done?

In general, if the caller is prepared to continue, try to get him to talk about possible grievances as they affect the firm, and anything which bears upon the truthfulness of the message and the identity of the caller.

Letter bombs

Letters or parcel bombs mainly take the form of substantial envelopes (not less than 5 mm thick) or of parcels containing paperback books delivered through normal postal channels. The weight in letter form is unlikely to exceed 120 g. Points which may make unfamiliar material suspect are:

1 The postmark, if foreign and unfamiliar
2 The writing, which may have an 'un-English' appearance, lack literacy, or be crudely printed
3 Name and address of sender (if shown), if address differs from area of postmark
4 'Personal'/'Only to be opened by' or 'Private' letters addressed to senior management under the job title (for example, Managing Director)
5 Weight, if excessive for size and apparent contents. Thickness: 5 mm or more
6 Weight distribution, if uneven may indicate batteries inside
7 Grease marks showing on the exterior of the wrapping and emanating from inside may indicate 'sweating' explosive
8 Smell – some explosives smell of marzipan or almonds
9 Abnormal fastening – sealing excessive for the type of package. If such an outer contains a similar inner wrapping, this may be a form of booby trap
10 Damaged envelopes which give sight of wire, batteries or fluid-filled plastic sachets should be left strictly alone; those that rattle or feel springy should be teated with caution; and, naturally, any ticking noise should be treated as a 'red' alert. Pinholes in the outer wrapping may indicate where devices for the safety of the bomb-maker have been removed. Where conventional paperback books have been used, the resultant bomb may be discernibly softer in the centre than at the edges.

If suspicions cannot be alleviated

1 Do not try to open the letter/parcel or tamper with it
2 Do not put it in water or put anything on top of it
3 Isolate it where it can do no harm but needs minimum handling (that is, enclose it in a nest of sandbags but ensure that it is in a position for easy visual inspection)
4 Open any windows and doors in the vicinity. Keep people away from it
5 Inform the police and seek their guidance; give them full details of the letter/parcel, its markings and peculiarities which have led to suspicion.

FURTHER READING

Bologna, Jack, *Corporate Fraud*, Butterworth, London, 1985

Bottom, Norman R. and Kostanoski, J., *Security and Loss Control*, Macmillan, London, 1983

Comer, M., Ardis, P. and Price, D., *Bad Lies in Business*, McGraw-Hill, Maidenhead, 1988

Evans, A. and Korn, A. in association with Percom Limited, *How to Comply with the Data Protection Act*, Gower, Aldershot, 1986

Hughes, D. and Bowler, P., *The Security Survey*, Gower, Aldershot, 1982

Jones, P., *Modern Loss Control Concepts, A Manager's Guide*, Longman, London, 1987

Lyons, S., *Security of Premises, A Manual for Managers*, Butterworth Scientific Ltd, 1988

Oliver, E., and Wilson, J., *Practical Security in Commerce and Industry*, 5th edn, Gower, Aldershot, 1988

Purpura, P.P., *Modern Security and Loss Prevention Management*, Butterworth, London, 1984

Saddington, T., *Security for Small Computer Systems*, Elsevier Advanced Technology Publications (UK), 1989

Walsh and Healey, *Protection of Assets Manual*, Merritt Co, Columbus, OH

Walsh and Healey, *Industrial Security Management: A Cost Effective Approach*, Merritt Co, Columbus, OH

55 Office administration

Roger Henderson

Recent years have seen a massive increase in office-based employment while, particularly in the West, manufacturing industries have been in relative decline. The deregulation of the financial sector, coupled with rapid developments in communications technology, has had far-reaching effects on the so-called service industries which, in turn, have increased the importance of the office as a place of work. Indeed, these highly successful and profitable businesses play a substantial part in the national economy. At their hub is not a factory but an office, an office as a productive unit. But even where this is not so, in manufacturing and processing industry, a large part of the organization will depend on the office for its smooth running. In all cases the effectiveness of the office administration will have a considerable impact on the degree of success the business enjoys.

SCOPE AND ORGANIZATION

The scope of work covered by the heading 'office administration' will vary widely with the type and size of the organization. For a small business many of the activities will be inappropriate or absorbed within other routines. For others there will be a single point of responsibility covering all tasks, the ubiquitous office manager, and for medium- to large-sized companies special departments will be needed to provide administrative support.

Whatever the actual arrangement, the potential scope of work can be considered under a number of headings, as shown in Figure 55.1.

As many and varied as the types of administrative services are the job titles of the individuals responsible for their management: administration manager, office manager, office services supervisor, house or premises manager, and the latest to gain acceptance – the facilities manager. The implications of this most recent development will be discussed later in the chapter. These variations often have little to do with actual job content and more with custom and practice.

Figure 55.2 shows a typical organization chart for a medium-sized business employing some 300 people in one building. Common variations on this include dealing with property matters through another specialist department (surveyors, architects, for example) and having purchasing handled by the accounts department. Such fragmentation of responsibility is not to be encouraged. The provision of a high-quality service to the user departments is dependent upon the effective co-ordination of diverse activities. If one of the key activities, such as premises management, is dealt with by a separate in-house specialist whose prime function is to respond to external business demands, it will receive only part-time atten-

Reprographics	Post	Reception
Printing, publishing	Postal services	Main reception
Photocopying	Messengers	Commissionaires
Stationery supplies	Document movement	Booking of meeting rooms
Microfilming		Travel arrangements

Security and safety	Central services	Purchasing
Security services	Filing, archives	Stationery supplies
Fire precautions	Word processing	Furniture and equipment
Emergency procedures	Library and information services	Leasing agreements
Commercial espionage protection	Conference management	Contract arrangements
Statutory requirements	Bulk storage	
Health and safety precautions		

Staff welfare	Telecommunications	Transport
Social/recreation	Telephone systems	Company cars/vans
First aid/medical centre	Paging, public address	Chauffeurs/drivers
Rest room	Telex, facsimile	Transport records, licensing
Staff shop/banking facilities	Data links, networks	and tax
Creche	Dealing systems	
	Satellite communications	Catering
	Teleconferencing	Staff restaurant and dining rooms
		Refreshments, vending machines
		Entertainment facilities

Buildings
Cleaning, upkeep, repairs, decoration, rubbish and waste disposal, goods, delivery, external upkeep.
Leases, landlord liaison
Local authority liaison
Improvements, acquisitions and disposals

Plant and equipment
Maintenance contracts for heating/ventilation/airconditioning, lifts, window cleaning gear

Day-to-day maintenance of plant, plumbing and electrical services, data distribution networks

Space allocation, planning and office layouts
Planning layout revisions
Alterations to partitions
Lighting
Building Services
Furniture moves

Office furniture and equipment
Maintenance and replacement of all items of office furniture and equipment

Figure 55.1   Potential scope of office administration

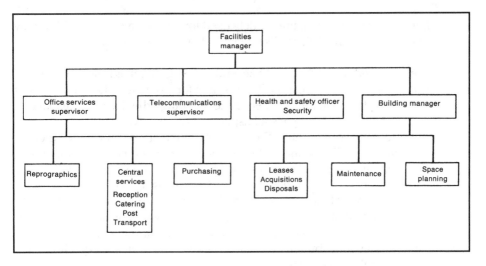

Figure 55.2 Typical organization chart for facilities management department in a medium-sized organization

tion. This particularly applies to estates departments in, for example, retail businesses which have a large portfolio of property to look after. Inevitably, the office building which houses company administration is low down on the list of priorities.

In setting up an office administration unit, senior management should consider the following:

1 The person they charge with running the building and its supporting services and facilities will probably have one of the largest budgets and work-forces in their organization. The department is not a profit centre, but it has tremendous significance in terms of total operating cost

2 The quality of the service provided by this department impinges on all aspects of the business, including the profit centres. If that service is efficient, reliable and flexible it will contribute towards profitability

3 To maintain a high level of service the office manager must be able to anticipate future demands to be made upon the department, particularly in respect of the provision of office space. This will only be possible if the manager is kept fully informed of company strategy, changes in policy and all matters affecting company administration.

These three points lead to the clear conclusion that the management of office administration should not be regarded as an inferior occupation. It should have a clearly defined place in the organizational structure with direct links to top management. Only in this way can channels of communication be maintained and control exercised to ensure that administrative support meets the demands of the business at all times.

FACILITIES MANAGEMENT

During recent years with the growing recognition of the importance and size of the investment being made in the office workplace a new profession has emerged, that of 'facilities management'. The title, widely used for a long time in the US but only recently emerging in the UK, is, like many labels, imprecise and varied in its interpretation.

In a large organization, perhaps with several buildings in mixed use, the facilities manager and his team have responsibility solely for premises, their upkeep and use. In others, with a single, smaller office building, the facilities manager's responsibilities will also encompass all aspects of office services.

It might be said "twas ever thus'. With a larger range of responsibilities there is a need to create specialist posts, and facilities management is perhaps merely a manifestation of this. Whereas there is some truth in this, it does not do full justice to the success this new profession has achieved in making itself heard. Its message is simple. Business profitability depends heavily on the performance of its work-force and a key contributor to that performance is the way in which it is housed. Facilities managers ensure that the business premises, in this context the office building, makes that contribution in an effective way. The principle equally applies to the factory, warehouse or processing plant.

To provide an effective facilities management service in an office-based organi-zation above a size of, say, 100 staff is a complex matter and can only be touched on here.

The key is to establish and work within an accommodation strategy developed to reflect the needs of the business. The business plan, if one exists, should be the starting point, interpreting projections for growth and change in premises terms. Anticipating the unexpected requires flexibility, not only in the way accommo-dation is planned but also in the thinking behind the process. The accommodation strategy should become the reference point for all premises related decisions – acquistion and disposal, maintenance and refurbishment, the way they are used and the facilities provided.

Even the day-to-day reorganization of space, an important issue in dynamic businesses, should be planned within the longer-term framework of the strategy.

Application of CAD and CAFM systems

Computer-aided drafting (CAD) systems, which have been expressly designed as a space planning tool, are now widely available for use on personal computers (PCs). They give the facilities manager a quick and accurate way of creating, storing and reproducing layout drawings in as much or as little detail as is required.

Block plans can be produced which allocate space in buildings to departments, automatically recording the areas occupied for charge out purposes. Detailed layouts created on CAD not only position each item of furniture and equipment, but also record it in inventory form for use as an assets register.

More complex and powerful systems have also been developed specifically for use in facilities management. Known as CAFM (computer-aided facilities manage-ment) the systems use a database interactively so that a vast fund of information about the building, its contents and use may be stored and made available for use by management at any time.

Typical CAFM reports include:

1 Analyses of space usage, alternative projections of demand and consequential effects on the property portfolio
2 Assets register listing all items of furniture and equipment in as much detail as is required and giving source, specification, original cost and current book value
3 Location of each item, again in as much detail as required, by building, floor, department, section or individual's name or payroll reference
4 Space allocations to departmental cost centres automatically updated to match layout changes and including a proportional allowance for non-allocated circulation space. This report will provide monthly premises costs for each department for inclusion in management accounts
5 Maintenance programmes and work schedules
6 Cable management reports.

CABLE MANAGEMENT

Cable management is an important element in managing the modern electronic office. The aim should be to provide a flexible arrangement which allows for change or expansion, to adhere to equipment suppliers' technical recommendations concerning maximum permitted cable lengths and avoidance of cross-talk or interference, and the personal safety of the building's occupants (particularly avoiding cables trailing over floors). In some cases where high confidentiality of information is involved it may be necessary, also, to consider the security of the cabling system.

All office buildings have a cable distribution system of some kind, both vertically through the building and horizontally at each floor level. Horizontal systems range from ductwork at the perimeter to fully accessible raised floors beneath which cables are routed along trays to relocatable outlet points in the floor panels.

The proliferation of information technology (IT) systems in the office brings increasing demand for new networking arrangements, data links, special power requirements and, inevitably, modification and replacement of cable installations. Keeping pace with these demands is part of the facilities manager's role and the maintenance of accurate records of the costly cabling arrangements is essential.

REPROGRAPHICS

Reprographics is the business of reproducing the written word, picture or graphic image. It covers all aspects from the now commonplace photocopying machine through to sophisticated in-house printing facilities. It also includes the printing of plans and technical drawings, microphotography (or microfilming) and more recently desktop publishing. An ambitious reprographics department can compete in quality terms with bought-in work from a commercial printer. There is a danger, however, of underestimating the additional overhead cost of providing and maintaining the equipment and the space it occupies when analysing comparative prices. Effective supervision of the reprographics function in all its manifestations is essential in order to control operating costs.

Photocopying

It is necessary to be aware of the abuse to which the simple photocopier can be subjected, from the illicit production of private copies to the bigger problem of wastage by taking more copies than are really needed. In the same way as the original Mr. Colman is said to have made his fortune from the mustard left on the side of the plate, so must the paper and copier manufacturers be doing from the high volume of unnecessary copies.

The most effective way to control copy quantity – and quality – is to place every photocopier within a central reprographics department, staffed by one or more trained operators, and with copies only given against duly authorized requisitions. Under such supervision, the machines will prove more reliable, and print quality can be maintained at a good level.

In a large organization, a centralized photocopying facility may not be convenient to all staff, where the ability to obtain a few copies quickly saves the time of senior people and helps to promote efficiency. The wastage inherent in allowing staff free access to unsupervised copiers can be more than offset by the time saved. One solution to cut down wastage at local copier stations is to lock the machines, and provide suitable staff with keys. Another, less cumbersome approach is to provide machines for local use capable of giving the cheapest possible copies consistent with readable quality and reliable performance. Copies for internal use do not have to be up to exhibition standard. Where high quality or large numbers are justified, then the central facility has to be used.

Photocopying technology continues to develop rapidly. Plain paper copying using an electrostatic process known as xerography is now the industry norm but it will no doubt be superseded by laser printing before too long. As far as the end users are concerned quality of output, speed and ease of use, cost and reliability will remain key factors in their choice of equipment, rather than the basis of the technology.

Many factors need to be taken into account when choosing a copier for the first time. The market is such a competitive one that there is a danger of being swamped by eager salespeople in response to the first set of enquiries. It is advisable to set out a simple statement of requirements, covering such things as size of paper to be used, reducing and enlarging facilities, automatic feed and collating and so on. Beware over specifying in terms of added features and underestimating copy quantities.

As with the purchase of all office equipment, it is prudent to seek out other users of similar equipment and find out whether they would recommend it. The supplier will usually be willing to give introductions to such referees, although he is unlikely to be very open about sites where significant problems have occurred.

The total cost approach is necessary when choosing copiers. The starting point is to determine the number of copies to be made each month at each copying station. This is bound to be a variable figure, depending on seasonal factors and the level of activity in the business generally. In addition to an estimated average usage per month (for annual budgeting) it is also necessary to estimate the maximum and minimum numbers. Knowledge of the maximum number of copies will eliminate some copiers at the outset because they would simply be too slow or too unreliable to cope with the work-load predicted. Manufacturers often specify the maximum capability of their machines, although they sometimes tend to be optimistic.

Printing and duplicating

Although some large plain paper photocopiers are able to produce fairly cheap long runs, spirit duplicators or stencil machines can still be considered where low cost is the only consideration, to the exclusion of high-quality prints. If it is essential to maintain decent print quality, then offset litho printing commends itself.

In the offset process, an image is prepared on a printing plate by direct typing or by photography. The image is transferred to an intermediate surface in the machine (and reversed) and thence to the paper (reversed back again). Thus, it is not necessary to work with a reverse print master. Copy quality is excellent, long runs are possible, and the process is cheap. A skilled operator is required for best results.

An alternative to the off-set litho machine is the photo-printer which is effectively a high volume photocopier. Although the quality falls short of the best an offset litho can produce, particularly on illustrations, the machine is simple and clean to operate and the initial cost is lower.

Plan printing

Printing of engineering and architectural drawings and plans has for many years been carried out using the diazo process. Masters are drawn on translucent or transparent material, and in the printing process a coated material is exposed to ultraviolet light, passed through with the original in close contact with the print, and the positive image is developed by ammonia. Such machines consume a considerable amount of electrical power – often in excess of 10 kW – and the heat and ammonia fumes produced have to be extracted into a flue. The process is ideal for producing large-sized prints on paper, or on any other film or sensitized medium.

Dry copying

Plain-paper printers, using the xerographic process, are now available which will take A0 size originals.

These offer many advantages over diazo equipment. They are quiet, emit no fumes and use less power. Other advantages are that they will print on to a wide variety of materials and input drawings no longer have to be made on translucent material. Indeed, the latest developments in laser printing have led to direct reproduction on A0 plain paper from digital input from a CAD system. This dispenses with the intermediate pen plotter process.

Desk-top publishing

Desktop publishing now competes strongly with the traditional in-house printing facility. There are many systems based on PCs with a wide range of cost, operating speed and quality of end result.

At the lower end of the scale, though cheap to install using existing hardware, the systems can be disappointingly slow and cumbersome to use and the output variable in quality. With the right choice of software and a good laser printer it becomes possible to produce reports and other documentation to the highest standards. Word-processed texts and diagrams can be 'imported' from other PCs, and illustrations included via a simple scanning device.

Document style and quality

The computerization of office equipment has brought about a convergence of applications so that it is no longer appropriate to think of reprographics as a separate function. The high-speed laser printer is far removed from the early duplicating machines, yet effectively performs the same task, that of reproducing images for communication. The most significant difference, apart from speed and quality lies in the ability to bypass a number of intermediate processes. It is now possible to link the input device, the word processor, for example, directly to the printer to produce the finished document in multiple sets ready for binding.

This technology means that any secretary or other member of staff with access to an appropriate keyboard, and with the necessary operator training, is able to produce reports, brochures and company stationery. The best equipment gives the user choice from a wide range of typestyle and typesizes. The results may, however, be far from desirable because technical competence in operating the equipment is not enough. Production of high-quality documents needs a good eye for design and page layout. Some very unfortunate results have been produced by amateurs, with inappropriate and mixed typestyles and horrible layouts. It is recommended that some form of control is introduced to ensure that all documents conform in style to an approved company standard. This need not stifle innovation, but it should aim at documents that reflect the desired corporate image.

Standardization of forms and stationery

Much time and money can be wasted by the proliferation of forms and other stationery. Some large organizations, for example, have achieved useful cost and time savings by having an audit of the stationery and forms used in the business, often reducing dramatically the numbers of different form designs in use. This is a role which can be undertaken, for instance, by an organization and methods practitioner.

The reprographics department can sometimes be used as a filter to prevent the reintroduction of unnecessary forms and stationery by the simple expedient of ensuring that no new form or new item of stationery shall be printed without suitable authorization.

The aim should be to use (and therefore stock) a preferred range of paper sizes

ISO A series		ISO B series (less common)	
Sheet code	Dimensions (millimetres)	Sheet code	Dimensions (millimetres)
A0	1 189 × 841	B0	1 414 × 1 000
A1	841 × 594	B1	1 000 × 707
A2	594 × 420	B2	707 × 500
A3	420 × 297	B3	500 × 353
A4	297 × 210	B4	353 × 250
A5	210 × 148	B5	250 × 177
A6	148 × 105	B6	177 × 125

Figure 55.3   ISO standard document sheet sizes (International Standards Organization)

(see Figure 55.3), and operate with the minimum number of designs for forms, letterheads, and other items of stationery. This will save storage space, result in more efficient procedures, allow more competitive purchasing of supplies and result in less scrap when organizational or other changes render existing designs obsolete.

MICROFILMING

Any office manager responsible for providing office space is aware that document filing is usually very space consuming, and staff continually request more and more filing equipment. Indeed, it could be said that any company will eventually choke to death on its own paper files if the growth of such files is allowed to continue unchecked. Clever filing equipment, some of it mechanized, is available to minimize the space needed; this is achieved by transporting the documents within the system in such a way that waste space (for example, roof voids) can be used. Other measures include the provision of storage space off site, in a warehouse or similar building, where files can be boxed and held available for occasional reference at, say, a day's notice.

A more drastic and usually sensible way to reduce filing bulk is to question the need to keep documents at all. Certainly, when a member of staff asks for an additional filing cabinet, he or she should be asked first to clear out unnecessary paper from the other cabinets and drawers in the office. Nevertheless, a considerable amount of information has to be stored within easy reach in most companies, and a cost-effective and convenient approach to the problem is to hold the documents on microfilm, which dramatically reduces the space needed for storage. Properly managed, access time to any required document can also be reduced, simply because the files are concentrated in a small area, and no walking is needed to retrieve items. Accurate and sensible indexing is the essential requirement for microfilm retrieval.

Microforms

There are several variations on the microfilming theme, each suitable for a particular office application.

16 mm film is used widely for the storage of complete files. The original documents can be any size up to A3. Longer documents can sometimes be filmed so that the image lies along the major axis of the film. By mounting the film in a cassette, and using viewing equipment with a suitable indexing device, rapid retrieval of the document required is possible. Approximately 1 500 A4 original documents can be held on a 100 ft (30 m) roll of film. The roll-film method is only really suitable for files which will not be updated because the replacement of a document would entail cutting and splicing the film.

16 mm jacket fiche is a system based on the use of 16 mm roll film, but which allows editing, additions and revisions. Documents are filmed on to the roll, which is then processed and cut up into individual documents or groups of documents according to the file index. For example, one subject could be the name of an individual in a personnel records system. Using a special jig, the strips of film are inserted into transparent plastic sheets, which allow a grid of frames to be assembled. The sheets contain a series of horizontal channels to accommodate the film. Outdated information can be removed from the jacket fiche using tweezers. Additional or revised information is filmed and inserted in the appropriate place in the jacket.

Retrieval is achieved with a special fiche viewer, using an index system that first identifies the particular jacket fiche, and then locates the frame on the sheet by a grid reference system.

Microfiche is similar in some respect to jacket fiche, but the degree of reduction is greater. Many more documents can be held on one fiche, which is a single piece of photographic film of a size suitable for filing in a card index tray. Every frame is photographed on to the fiche sequentially to form a pattern of images in regular columns and rows. As with jacket fiche, any single frame can be identified by a grid system of co-ordinates but, since microfiche is a direct photographic image on film, it can only be updated by changing a whole fiche. Microfiche is applicable to whole books (since books do not get updated in general, and a whole book can be contained on only a very few microfiche sheets). The method is also used for catalogues and spare parts lists, the whole set of fiche being replaced when a new issue is required.

35 mm film allows larger documents, such as engineering drawings, to be microfilmed without the loss of definition which would result from any attempt to use 16 mm. Drawings up to A0 size can be filmed successfully on 35 mm. *70 mm film* is used in limited applications where even greater definition is needed.

35 mm aperture cards are similar in appearance to data processing punched cards, but a rectangular aperture in the card carries a single 35 mm image frame. Usually, drawings are filmed on to a 35 mm roll, which is then cut up into individual frames for mounting into jackets cemented on the face of the aperture cards. Aperture cards can also be obtained in magazines, with the film already in place on each card. Exposure takes place in a special camera, which also develops and processes the image automatically. The advantage of aperture cards over unmounted roll film is in the ease of handling and retrieval made possible. In fact, provided care is taken not to damage the film, aperture cards can be punched and printed with the relevant drawing number and title, and mechanical sorting and automatic feeding to a printer becomes possible. A more recent development is to use bar codes or optical recognition (OCR) for sorting.

Quality control and techniques

With all microfilms, quality control is essential at every step in the process. The exposure must be right, the original document must be well and evenly illuminated (sometimes from underneath using a glass table), the degree of reduction should be accurate in order to maintain the correct scale on reproduction, and, of course, the image must be in focus over the entire area. Developing, fixing and washing also require careful control to ensure that the film will keep without deterioration – especially important for archive microfilming. Good conditions can be obtained using automatic equipment which is computer controlled. Otherwise, a reliable bureau should be employed. An incidental, but extremely important, extension of quality control and supervision is the care given to the original documents during the process to prevent damage or loss. Obviously, such originals must be protected until the microfilm has been processed and the image quality checked.

Storage and copying

Ordinary photographic film, using a silver halide emulsion, is referred to as 'silver' microfilm for short, and this is the material with the longest storage life for archival purposes – say, up to fifty years or more. The diazo process can be used to make cheap contact copies from roll film or from aperture cards or fiche. Such cheap copies are usually of very high quality, with adequate storage properties for normal use. For widespread publication of books, catalogues and the like in microfilm, diazo copies are ideal. In engineering offices, 'satellite' reference files of drawing aperture cards can be arranged in a number of locations to give local access to drawing information while the silver masters are locked away for security.

Viewing and printing

A wide range of commercial viewers, viewer-printers and printers is available. There are also projectors. Many of these viewers are fitted with a retrieval device, allowing a particular frame to be found easily on a roll-film cassette or fiche. Printing methods include xerography on to plain paper, an electrolytic process, and heat-developed image using photographically sensitized paper.

Computer output on microfilm (COM)

COM is a system in which the need for a paper document is discarded. Instead, the data output from the computer is photographed directly on microfilm from a viewing screen. More modern techniques use lasers and video discs will replace some microfilm techniques altogether, with information stored in digital form from which an image can be printed out or projected on a viewing screen. At this point the discussion leaves the realm of office services and becomes more a question of data processing.

TELECOMMUNICATIONS

The subject of telecommunications continues to be a complex and rapidly developing one. With the latest systems and distribution networks capable of transmitting voice, data and video messages, conventional telephone system requirements should no longer be considered in isolation from other communications needs.

As far as the provider of office services is concerned, the simple telephone call into the office remains potentially the single most important piece of communication the business receives. The way it is received, routed and responded to influences the judgement of potential new customers and reinforces satisfaction with existing ones. In selecting a new telephone system this basic requirement should not be overlooked. Before final commitment it is advisable to have the switchboard operator 'test drive' the new model, preferably in a live situation.

The range of facilities offered to telephone users by modern digital exchanges is impressive. Indeed, it is possible to install so many facilities that every member of staff will need a training session or, at least, an instruction manual in order to exploit all the capabilities of the system. These include *inter alia* such things as:

- Short dialling codes for frequently called numbers, stored in the private exchange
- Short dialling codes for frequently called numbers, stored in individual extensions and programmed by the users
- Access barring, which disallows calls from certain extensions to: all outside lines; to outside lines except local calls; and to international numbers, as required
- Automatic dial back, so that an engaged internal extension will automatically be called when it becomes free
- Conference facilities, allowing more than two extensions to engage in conversation
- Hold for enquiry, so that the user can hold an incoming call while talking to another extension
- Automatic call transfer, allowing users to transfer incoming calls to other extensions without recourse to the operator
- Distinguishing ringing tones, different for incoming calls from the public exchange and from other internal extensions
- Call queueing
- Direct dialling-in to extensions from the public network
- Audible signals to the user signifying that the operator is listening-in or that an incoming call is queuing
- Paging facilities
- Music, which plays to incoming callers kept on hold by the operator

- Night arrangements, allowing certain extensions to become direct lines to incoming calls when the operators shut down.

One valuable facility which should always be considered seriously is call-logging. The equipment is able to monitor many aspects of operator performance, and much data on incoming and outgoing calls. It is particularly useful in saving costs, by monitoring and deterring unauthorized use, or in recovering call costs from clients (where professional service contracts allow). Provided the system is properly and continuously managed, savings can be very considerable (30 per cent savings in total company call charges are not unknown).

SECURITY AND SAFETY

Not so long ago security measures were aimed at preventing pilfering and, occasionally, thought was given to safeguarding confidential information. Now vandalism and even bombings can necessitate converting buildings into fortresses and, once again, it is the office manager who is responsible for seeing that the drawbridge is raised. It is a manifestation of our rapidly changing society that buildings planned and designed only a few years ago for ease of access for goods and staff and the general public are now considered vulnerable, and therefore ill-conceived.

As usual, technology leaps to the rescue and sophisticated services abound to cope with each new problem as it arises: protective film for windows, electronic locks, closed circuit TV systems to monitor the thieves' progress; anti-bugging devices to confound the electronic eavesdroppers – all these and many more are readily available to cope with specific security problems. The drawback is, however, that apart from the cost, they nearly all impose constraints and discipline on the law-abiding users of the building. It is important, therefore, to strike a balance between security risk and acceptable constraints. The office manager should assess the risks and make recommendations so that management can decide the appropriate level of security precautions necessary.

No avoidable risks should be countenanced, however, when it comes to fire precautions. These really fall under two headings – minimizing the risk of fire breaking out and spreading, and the provision of safe means of escape from the building in the event of fire. For further discussion of this subject, and of security, please turn to Chapter 54.

While under the provisions of Health and Safety at Work Act the employer has a legal obligation to ensure as far as is reasonably practical the health, safety and welfare of all his employees, the office manager must relate the spirit of the law to the services for which he is responsible. For example, there are a number of very real hazards which can be created by the misuse or irregular maintenance of electrical services. Frayed or trailing cables, the use of multi-socket adaptors, damage to electric cabling caused by inadequate protection at outlets, and changes to electrical heating systems without consideration of current loading all are common examples of dangerous practices. Similarly, with the increasing use of furniture systems it is essential that the components are put together strictly in accordance with the manufacturer's instructions to avoid, for example, accidental tipping of screens carrying storage units.

The subject of health and safety is discussed more fully in Chapter 61.

SICK BUILDING SYNDROME

The term 'sick building syndrome' (SBS) refers to a group of ailments affecting people working in office buildings. Building-related or work-related illnesses would be more accurate, if less picturesque, descriptions of these complaints which manifest themselves in headaches, sore throats and other 'flu-like symptoms.

An enormous amount of research has produced inconclusive and inconsistent results. There is little doubt that poorly maintained air-conditioning systems can result in an unhealthy and even dangerous environment. Legionnaires Disease is one manifestation of this. SBS symptoms do not only occur in air-conditioned buildings and investigations can result in other factors being found to blame. Badly designed lighting or glare from windows are often contributory causes and posture at VDU work stations should not be overlooked as the possible source of the problem.

The office manager should treat any such complaints seriously. The mere process of consultation and being seen to be taking some action often goes a long way to solving the problem.

BUILDING MAINTENANCE

Chapter 53 deals with the administration of commercial property, but some aspects of building maintenance are worth touching on here in so far as they fall within the ambit of the office services manager.

There are, of course, the routine daily processes of cleaning the building and disposing of rubbish and waste, and there is the contract maintenance of a wide range of items from computer equipment to lifts. These, though, can be dealt with satisfactorily, once the contracts have been set up, with only routine supervision and an occasional detailed check on performance. All too often overlooked, however, are the opportunities for preventive maintenance and planned replacement procedures.

For example, most office building leases require tenants to redecorate externally and, sometimes, internally on a regular basis. Apart from financial planning, or budgeting for what could be a substantial item of expenditure, it makes sense to plan ahead for the disruption that internal redecoration can cause. With forethought it can be done progressively, taking advantage of the inevitable changes of layout as they occur and which take place regularly in any dynamic organization. This is far better than expensive out-of-hours working with attendant security problems, or having to shuffle people around to create working space for decorators.

FURTHER READING

Beattie, Derek (ed.), *Company Administration Handbook*, 7th edn, Gower, Aldershot, 1991

Mills, Geoffrey and Standingford, Oliver, *Modern Office Management*, 7th edn, Pitman, London, 1986

Titman, Lionel G., *The Effective Office: A Handbook of Modern Office Management*, Cassell, London, 1990
Walley, B. H., *Handbook of Office Management*, Business Books, London, 1982

56 Managing the electronic office

Ted Bennett

Development in the office environment is rapid and wide-ranging. Not long ago most office workers thought than an electronic typewriter represented advanced technology. Now equipment based on microcomputers is the norm, with widespread use of communications technology linking the different elements together. Because of these changes, the problem of managing the electronic office has changed. It is no longer a search for the facilities which workers need; now we must control the acquisition, development and use of the wide range of hardware and software which is available. Standards for the procurement and use of resources must also be set and enforced.

Much of this chapter is devoted to problems of defining a suitable strategy for office systems, implementing that strategy, and then keeping up to date with changes in technology. Other sections deal briefly with the storage and retrieval of information, and with the Data Protection Act.

THE STRATEGIC FRAMEWORK

A 'strategy' can be defined as 'a plan which determines how to use available resources to achieve planned objectives'. The strategy will depend upon the funds available plus:

1 Current availability of physical resources (hardware, software, communications, training)
2 Scope of development
3 Existing resources in place
4 Objectives for the development.

Current availability of physical resources

The range of hardware and software available for office systems seems limitless, and includes:

- Word processing
- Business graphics
- Optical disk storage, read only, write once and read, and reusable
- Impact, ink jet and laser printers
- Graph plotters
- Desktop publishing

- Diary management
- Accounting/book-keeping
- Electronic mail
- Telex/facsimile transmission
- Networking and communications
- Project management software
- Programming languages
- Financial services – for example, TOPIC
- Money transmission – SWIFT and/or BACS.

Any or all of these, and others, may be required by staff within one organization.

Within any particular function, products appear with monotonous regularity, so that the choices presented, and the temptations to procure the latest product, are great enough to present a problem in themselves. One way to reduce the number of options is to produce a specification of the functionality required, projected cost, and so on, for the type of product required. The available products should then be compared rigorously with the specification and with each other to eliminate those which are not entirely suitable.

Scope of the development

The areas of the organization to be included in the exercise must be stated explicitly. Both the types and levels of staff involved as well as the physical areas of the business must be specified. This is especially important where the business is physically dispersed.

The physical aspects of office systems are often ignored, mainly because most people are now familiar with personal computers; indeed, many have one at home. In the office, however, it is most likely that there will be a large number of these devices. This may lead to problems, the most serious of which are:

- *Lack of space* No matter how small the personal computer, it will still occupy about one sixth of the area of an average desk. There will also be printers, control boxes, and so on, to be accommodated, as well as diskette storage boxes, manuals, paper and so forth
- *Heat and noise* Each piece of equipment generates heat, and most are cooled by fans, which make noise. Any printer will make some noise – an impact printer when it is working, and a laser printer when it is both idling and printing. The effects of both the heat and 'white noise' can lead to complaints of the so-called sick-office syndrome
- *Trailing cables* Unless great care is taken to use specially designed furniture which allows for cables, and unless the office itself is modified to run cables within walls or ceilings, power and data cables will trail across the office. This is at best unsightly, and at worst hazardous: on either count, it should be avoided.

The technical scope of the project will depend to a large extent upon the objectives set, in terms of the levels of function to be made available, and the budget limits set. (See under the heading 'Budgets'.)

Existing resources

A good starting point for a development strategy is a survey of the existing resources in terms of hardware, software, communications and staff skills. Some, if not all, of these resources may be incorporated into the new environment, depending upon the deliberations of those producing the strategy, and upon the costs of such integration.

Objectives

For any exercise, the objectives must be framed in such a way that it may be determined whether or not they have been met satisfactorily. The objectives set must therefore be in terms of business requirements, rather than vague statements. 'Everyone should have access to a personal computer' is an admirable objective, but is not very useful. Conversely, that all staff of a certain job description should have access to spreadsheet software is a *business* objective. Whether or not these facilities are supplied via PCs is part of the strategy.

Some likely objectives are:

- *Improved secretarial services* Faster document production, improved final document quality, more effective use of secretarial time
- *Improved communications* Better voice, telex, facsimile and data communications
- *Reduction of paper volumes* Reduced consumption, reduced storage requirements, faster information dissemination, better security via passwords and encryption
- *Operational improvements* Increased flexibility, wider availability of facilities, lower unit costs, more robust systems.

Project objectives should be related to:

1 *Time* It is essential to specify when particular facilities should be made available
2 *Performance* Some measurable criterion must be specified so that the utility of the individual facility can be assessed
3 *Cost* The importance of conformance to budgets cannot be overstated.

Adherence to these three criteria concentrates the mind when planning and carrying out a strategy project.

PRODUCING THE STRATEGY

Important elements of a strategy include: a knowledge of the users' needs; and an idea of the timescales and budgets to be applied. Using these factors, a selection of the elements from which the system will be built may be made. This is discussed below.

Marshalling data

Producing a strategy is like planning a motoring holiday. You begin with a start point and a destination; the route is determined by a variety of parameters – technical, financial, the best scenery, good restaurants and so on.

The starting point for an office systems strategy is decided by the scope of the project and the existing resources. The destination is set by the needs of the workers for the functions which are, or may be, available. Naturally enough, a survey of requirements is necessary, although the difference between what people feel is desirable and what they actually need to do their jobs should be recognized.

Once you have discovered what the functional requirements are, and the approximate budget available, then a plan to meet the expressed needs within a sensible timescale can be produced.

Information

Before deciding upon the facilities and products required for the general office system it is worth considering the organization's basic information needs. Information is the life-blood of any organization. It can range from an on-line list of stock prices to a library of company annual reports on a shelf somewhere in the basement.

The systems will themselves generate operating data, and reference data will come from many sources, both internal and external. Information will be both volatile and static, and the technology to be applied will depend, among other things, on the following criteria:

- The usefulness of the information to the organization
- Frequency of updating
- Frequency of access or use
- Volumes to be stored
- Security requirements
- Processing requirements, both for storage and after retrieval
- Costs associated with storage, processing and retrieval.

All of these should be considered in order to produce an idea of the costs and benefits of storing and using information.

An example of this is the several on-line feeds of stock prices and other data which are available, and which many mergers and acquisitions departments have as a matter of course. Whether or not the speed at which they work requires an up-to-the-second price display is debatable, but its availability is at least reassuring. Here is a case where the cost of the information is small compared to the fees generated by the groups.

Consider the availability of relatively static data on magnetic media or laser disk (CD–ROM). The prices of these services compare favourably with the on-line search and retrieval process from a database which may be on the other side of the world. Even information formerly considered as primarily paper-based, such as company reports or Acts of Parliament, can now be passed through scanning devices and stored on magnetic or optical disks, and made available via work stations or personal computers.

By the use of a wide range of storage media and techniques, the most suitable and cost-effective retention of a wide range of information is made possible. Such information can be retrieved via the individual's work station. Once retrieved, information can be marshalled into a format suitable for manipulation through desktop publishing software and can be reproduced as a coherent document. Recipients of such a document need never know of its diverse sources.

Choosing facilities and products

The choice of facilities will be helped by the survey of the organization, its workloads and so on. Choice of products which could provide those facilities is more problematical, as there is a wide range of individual products which appear to do the same job.

There are, for instance, many word processing systems and several spreadsheet packages. Additionally, there are integrated products which offer word processing, spreadsheets and other facilities combined in one piece of software. Whether you choose individual or integrated packages will depend on circumstances and policies. An example of policy would be the use of a single software supplier as much as possible in order to reduce the number of supply and support sources.

Hardware

As office automation systems are essentially software based, they can be developed using any type of computer platform – micro, mini or mainframe. Some of the deciding factors are:

- *The availability of existing equipment* If, for instance, a large mainframe computer system with attached terminals is already installed, it may make economic sense to use it as a development base
- *Resilience* A communications system which is built up from linked local area networks (LANs) is more resilient when technical failures occur than a single large network. In this system local facilities will be preserved, allowing some work to continue while repairs are undertaken
- *Flexibility* It is important that any installation be easy to change or reconfigure in response to changing circumstances. This would include changes in organizational structure and workloads as well as improvements in technology
- *Ease of installation* The prime example of this is use of previously installed cable ducts in buildings, or using a digital telephone system as the basis of an organization-wide data network. Bear in mind that this type of short cut should be used with care, as it may reduce other options for resilience and flexibility
- *Choice of processor architecture* In the past, the choice of processor, or manufacturer, tended to lock out many software suppliers. The advent of 'open systems' (at present this means using the Unix operating system or one of its variants) has meant that the choices available are more varied. It is still the case that the majority of micro systems installed are based on the Intel chip series and are thus 'IBM compatible'. Beware, however, that there are still some software products which are only available for a particular chip set, even with the Unix system

- *Choice of network architecture* This may be based on a single type of network, or a mixture, and will be discussed in more detail below. It is, however, a very important decision, which may influence the office environment well into the future.

All these factors will determine the direction of your systems for some years to come. They will provide the infrastructure for office and, probably, data processing systems for your organization. Such decisions are strategic for any organization and must be treated as such.

Software

In some ways it is more difficult to choose software than it is to choose hardware, because the range of choices is so much wider. Almost any application requirement can be satisfied by a range of software packages. The final decision on the most suitable mixture of software to provide all of the required functionality can be time-consuming, difficult and expensive in the making.

Bear in mind that now and in the future users of any office system will demand that their applications work together – in terms both of transferring data between software on a single PC, and of transmitting data between PCs across a network. These functions can be aided by: using integrated software packages, especially those designed for networked use; common file formats; standard data transmission protocols; a single network management package, and so on. If the facilities provided cannot be operated as a single resource, workers will only use separate parts of the systems, and there will therefore be little overall gain from their installation.

Some suggested selection criteria for software are:

- Ease of use, ease of learning, availability of training
- Support offered by suppliers
- Financial stability and viability of suppliers
- Availability of multi-user versions for networked use
- Supplier policy on the release of new software versions and upgrade paths
- Interfaces and/or working with other software packages, especially from other suppliers
- Functionality available, both in relation to the user's requirements and in respect of extra features contained in the package.

Communications

Communications – both inside and outside the office environment – form the backbone of any office system.

External communications are generally well catered for, and some of the facilities available are:

- Telex
- Facsimile
- Packet-switching circuits
- Dial-up telephone circuits

- The Integrated Services Data Network (ISDN)
- Digital satellite services for data, voice and pictures.

Access to these systems can be obtained through a variety of devices. Using any or all of the services, communication is possible between remote offices of the same organization, between different organizations and between organizations and external sources of reference or operational information.

Internal communications – local area networks (LANs) – will be needed to provide shared facilities to system users within an area that can vary in size from a radius of a few metres to kilometres. When discussing LANs, people will talk of 'token rings', 'ethernets', and a variety of standards. Concentrate, however, on the following points:

- The facilities and functions to be supported
- The locations in which those facilities and functions are to be supplied
- The resilience to failure which is required of the network (s)
- Maximum allowable delays before failures are repaired
- Whether or not large quantities of data are to be transferred across the network
- Use of existing cabling or networks
- Costs of the various solutions, especially remembering the continuing costs of maintenance.

You may not feel able to design a network system yourself; if so obtain professional help, from either inside or outside your own organization. Approach at least three network suppliers for proposals. Make certain that any alternative proposals with which you are presented comprehensively cover all the points listed above, and that comparisons can sensibly be made between the proposed systems. Most importantly, do not be afraid to seek advice and help until you are sure that all your questions have been answered satisfactorily.

Budgets

Discussion of budgets – arguably the most important topic – is left until last. While this comment may not be too helpful, it is tacitly understood in the trade that no development involving computers was ever *overfunded*. The project which came in under budget is a myth!

Therefore, the first decisions in deciding how the money is to be spent – assigning priorities to the facilities that are required – must be taken at high level. Then the provision of each of those facilities must be costed individually. At this stage, bear in mind that, in addition to the procurement and installation of a system, the investment in training, the building works to accommodate the system, and the operating costs of consumables and maintenance must also be costed.

At some stage, when it is realized how much each element will cost, high-level decisions will again be required. This time, either the functionality will be reduced or the budgets will be extended, or possibly both.

In the computer business, the old adage 'you get what you pay for' is not necessarily true. Some cheap products are surprisingly good, and some expensive products are not as good as their price would suggest. Others are hard to learn but excellent when you have invested in the training required to use them.

The right strategy?

In the course of an office automation development it is easy to spend large amounts of money to procure a system which does some things well but most things indifferently. It is also possible – although not simple – to produce an environment which will almost satisfy almost everyone. This result is probably the best that can be hoped for, but there is no straightforward way to achieve it. A great deal of clear, careful thought is required before any purchases are made – plus, above all, the ability to remain calm and not panic. Persevere with care and you *will* succeed, *and* survive.

THE DATA PROTECTION ACT (1984)

The scope of the Act

The Data Protection Act, although it strenuously avoids the use of the word computer, refers to data which are or have been, processed on a computer. The Act is also restricted to personal data, which refers to an identifiable, living, human being.

The requirements of the Act are, broadly:

1   That all personal data and the uses of it shall be registered
2   That personal data shall not be used, disclosed, or sent abroad except as defined in the registration document
3   That every computer bureau handling personal data must be registered
4   That the person about whom the data are held (referred to as the data subject) is entitled to know (on request) what those data are
5   That a data user shall abide by the principles of the Act.

The principles of the Act

There are eight principles, based on articles of the Council of Europe Convention, and similar to the ten principles set out in the Younger Report. The principles are:

1   That the information to be contained in personal data shall be obtained fairly and lawfully, and shall be so processed
2   That personal data shall be held for only specified and lawful purposes
3   That personal data held for any specified purpose or purposes shall not be disclosed in any matter which is incompatible with that purpose or those purposes
4   That personal data held for any purpose shall be adequate, relevant and not excessive in relation to those purposes
5   That personal data shall be accurate and up to date
6   That personal data shall not be kept for longer than is necessary for the stated purpose

7   That an individual shall have the right, at reasonable intervals, and without due delay or expense:

- to be informed by any data user whether he holds data of which that individual is the subject;
- to have access to any such data held by a data user; and
- to have such data corrected or erased, where appropriate

8   That appropriate security measures shall be taken against unauthorized access to, or alteration, disclosure or destruction of, personal data, and against accidental loss or destruction of personal data.

These principles should be followed by all data users, these being persons who control the contents and use of data. Computer bureaux are expected to abide only by the final principle, the others being the responsibility of the users of the data processed at the bureaux.

The operation of the Act

The data user shall apply to the Registrar for details of his data to be entered in the Data Protection Register. He will receive from the Registrar notice of acceptance or refusal, and may also receive:

1   An enforcement notice, telling him to change his practices to comply with the Act
2   A transfer prohibition, preventing data being sent abroad
3   A deregistration notice, removing his details from the Register and so preventing any further legal processing.

The data subject will apply to the data user for copies of records concerning himself, and may also request any errors to be corrected. He may inspect the Data Protection Register and, for a fee, obtain a copy of part of it. He may also make complaint to the Registrar if he cannot obtain satisfaction.

The Registrar deals both with the data users and data subjects and keeps the Register up to date. The Registrar must promote the observance of the eight principles, and give advice on data protection matters. He may investigate complaints, encourage the adoption of codes of practice and issue appropriate guidelines.

The data user must register his data and also comply with the principles.

Some definitions related to the Act

Data are defined as 'Information recorded in a form in which it can be processed by equipment operating automatically in response to instructions given for that purpose'. In today's world, this is a parliamentary draughtsman's way of saying 'data held on a computer'.

Data are personal if they consist of 'Information which relates to a living individual who can be identified from the information'. The information need not include the name of the individual; anything which uniquely identifies the person will suffice, (for example, the Prime Minister in 1963). The identifying information need not be held on the computer; it might just be in the possession of the data user.

Personal data include 'any expression of an opinion about the individual, but not any indication of the intentions of the user in respect of the individual'. The interpretation of this phrase is unresolved; nobody is really certain what it means except that intentions passed on to the data user from a third party are not excluded.

A data user is one who controls the contents and the use of data. The data must be part of a collection of data which are, or are to be, processed. Processing is defined as amending, augmenting, deleting or rearranging the information or extracting the information and, in the case of personal data, means performing any of these operations by reference to the data subject. This seems to exclude any chance reference to any individual within any otherwise non-personal file.

Exemptions

Exemption may be gained for a variety of reasons, apart from those of national security, government use and medical/caring services ethics, and data which are by law available to the public.

Exemptions for the normal business user are only concerned with:

1   Exemption from the Act as a whole:

- payroll, pensions and accounts data
- names, addresses and so forth, held solely for distribution purposes

2   Exemption from subject access:

- statistical and research data
- data held under the Consumer Credit Act
- all back-up data

3   Exemption from the non-disclosure principles:

- disclosed to the data subject or his agent
- disclosed to persons working for the data user
- disclosed in response to urgent need to prevent injury or damage to health.

In many of these cases, the definition is not explicit, and will have to be tested in the courts before all becomes clear. In conjunction with this, if exemption is to be claimed, it is essential that the user is certain that any future use of the data will not cause loss of the exemption. The most straightforward advice is that, if there is any doubt at all, the data user should register the data.

Registration under the Act

Each entry in the Register must include the following:

1 The name and address of the data user, and the registered company number if the user is a limited company
2 A description of the data and the purposes for which it is used
3 A description of the sources of the data
4 A description of the data recipients
5 A statement of any other countries to which data may be sent
6 The address to which data subjects must apply for access to their records. It is not a good idea to name a responsible person, as the Register would require amendment every time the name changed.

A decision must be made regarding single or multiple registrations. Multiple entries are simpler to make and maintain, and restrict the volume of data to which access is available via a single enquiry. As each such registration uses up about two working days, multiple registrations may be expensive.

If there is any doubt regarding the particulars of registration, or usage of the data, then the opinion of the Registrar should be sought. It is better to find out that usage is prohibited *before* an application is developed, rather than be forced to scrap it afterwards.

The rights of data subjects

A data subject has the right to be told if a data user holds personal data about him. If the data user does hold such data, then the subject has the right to see the record. If there are errors in the record, the subject may also demand that it is corrected or erased. These rights may be enforced by the Registrar, or by the courts.

A request for a copy of the data should be accompanied by sufficient information to identify the enquirer and to locate the required record. A fee may be demanded by the data user, and each request for data will cover only one entry in the Register. If records from more than one entry are requested, multiple requests (and multiple fees) are required.

It is stipulated that a response should normally be made within forty days, except for examination results which may be delayed for up to five months or until the results are published (presumably, whichever is the longer).

It is not necessary to provide computer-produced output; hand-written or typed information will suffice. The data must however be comprehensible, so that anything which is coded or encrypted must be translated or accompanied by a translation table. Note that computer installations in Wales should be prepared to provide information in English or Welsh, but not both, to an enquirer.

Disclosure of data

Disclosure, in the sense of misuse of data, has two meanings under the Act:

1 The deliberate passing of data to a third party not declared in the registration. This also includes passing exempt data in a way which invalidates the exemption
2 Unauthorized disclosure, where data are passed through carelessness or

whatever, without the consent of the user. This contravenes the eighth principle, and such disclosure could bring a claim for compensation.

The Act obviously requires that any form of data misuse be avoided by all means.

FURTHER READING

Blaazer, Caroline, and Molyneux, Eric, *Supervising the Electronic Office*, Gower, Aldershot, 1984

Harvey, David, *The Electronic Office in the Smaller Business*, Gower, Aldershot, 1986

Judkins, Phillip, West, David and Drew, John, *Networking in Organisations, the Rank Xerox Experiment*, Gower, Aldershot, 1986

Lucas, Henry C., *Information Systems Concepts for Management*, 4th edn, McGraw-Hill, New York, 1990

Welsby, R.S., *How to Buy a Business Computer*, Gower, Aldershot, 1985

Zorkoczy, Peter, The Open University, *Information Technology*, Pitman, London, 1990

Journals

PC User, EMAP Business and Computer Publications
Personal Computer Magazine, VNU Publications
Which Computer?, EMAP Business and Computer Publications

For information on the Data Protection Act 1984 contact:

Office of the Data Protection Registrar, Springfield House, Water Lane, Wilmslow, Cheshire, SK9 5AX, tel. 0625-535777

Part Nine

HUMAN RESOURCE
MANAGEMENT

57 Manpower and succession planning

John Bramham

Manpower planning can be defined as 'a strategy to acquire, utilize, retain and develop people by formulating sound manpower policies agreed with employees and their unions'. Though any definition must have limitations, this one at least contains most of the key points of manpower planning.

PLANNING FOR PEOPLE

Personnel managers and line managers engaged in manpower planning must not be overly concerned with operations. 'Planning for people' attempts to convey the idea that we must of course, recruit the people we need today (operations) but we must also have an eye on the future (planning). We should have policies about what sort of work-force and culture we are trying to develop: the extent of skilled, semiskilled or unskilled manpower; more or fewer graduates, more or fewer managers; more labour saving devices; a desire to give our customers a better service; more work done by outside support companies. Policies should be designed to achieve the objectives which the organization sets itself. At the same time, operations and policies are not separate items; they are complementary sides of the same task.

Why manpower planning?

Why should resources be devoted to manpower planning? Management has at its disposal three basic resources: physical, economic and human (materials, money and people). It is now accepted that, along with the management of money and the management of materials, it makes sense to work at the management of people. This approach, which we are calling 'manpower planning', takes place at the organizational level (where policies are considered and decided) and then at the tactical level, when it is necessary to match the requirement for people (demand) with the availability of people (supply).

THE PROCESS OF MANPOWER PLANNING

Investigating

Information should be gathered which will provide the basis for forecasts, as well as regular monitoring. Although a perfect definition of manpower planning may elude us, it is nevertheless possible to point to the essential matter with which it is

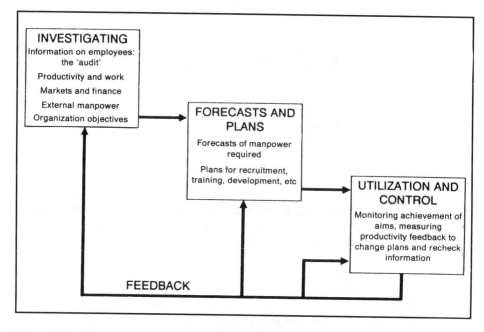

Figure 57.1   The process of manpower planning

concerned, namely matching manpower requirements and resources. Figure 57.1 indicates the comprehensive nature of information required. For example, marketing and financial information will take the form of cost, sales and profit targets. The manpower implications of such objectives will need to be carefully considered. Information on manpower productivity and working practices will take the form of an analysis of project work study schemes, method studies and working practices.

Crucial to the task of identifying the organization's current position is the 'manpower audit'. One aspect of this is passive: the identification of employees (how many, what grades, what their designations are, age distributions and so on). The purpose is to count the various employee 'stocks' and 'flows' (recruits and leavers) of the manpower system that was referred to earlier and highlight the dominant features relating to them.

Information needs

A number of guidelines apply when considering information needs, as follows:

- Lack of information hinders planning
- Information is for making decisions (that is, which decisions are to be made and therefore what information is needed)
- There is a need for different levels of detail of information
- Use available data (for example, from an existing payroll).

It has already been noted that without information it is difficult to think of planning taking place at all. However, if planning is for decisions, the manager must know what has to be decided before being able to specify and gather all the relevant

Information required	Possible reason
Age	as an estimate of experience and likely retirement
Length of service	to assess level of experience and likelihood of leaving
Occupation now	to know the current stock of skills
Occupation previously	to assess the stock of skills not currently used directly
Education/training	to classify the skills available
Number by department	need over a period of time to help assess future needs in light of business plans
Wage and salary	to assist in identifying costs
Employees leaving	to forecast labour turnover and assess problem areas
Overtime, contractors, temporaries, part timers	to assess degree of flexibility available to the organization
Recruitment/promotion patterns	to establish promotion and recruitment problems, promotion blockages/expectations
Absence framework	to ensure that absence levels are allowed for when calculating requirements. To draw attention to any problems and possible increases/ reductions

Figure 57.2   Information needs

information. Information which the manager requires about the people employed is summarized in Figure 57.2.

External manpower review

External manpower review is concerned with the potential external supply of labour. Again, this is largely a matter of information flow to ensure that knowledge about the availability of labour is to hand. In addition, government policy is included under the review. Another consideration is the continuing growth of higher education and demographic changes which will affect the availability of suitable 16- to 18-year-old school leavers.

FORECASTS AND PLANS

The provision of information is, of course, not an end in itself. It is necessary to formulate coherent forecasts and plans to determine personnel strategy.

The reason for planning

Recruitment levels

By knowing more about manpower requirement over a period of time, future recruitment can be planned carefully and ill-prepared recruitment drives can be avoided, to ensure that the correct type and number of employees are available as management require them.

Training and retraining requirements

Again, by having forecasts of skill requirements the manager can ensure that correct levels of trained employees are available and that employee development programmes are planned.

Manpower costing

Detailed information should be retained relating to manpower costs, so that costs can be controlled and perhaps reduced. Cost data will also be required on manpower for new projects or alternative strategies.

Redundancy

By identifying problem areas in advance alternative employment may be highlighted or, if redundancy is unavoidable, at least employees can be made fully aware of the implications for them personally and assisted by all possible means to ease their transition to a new job or early retirement.

Timescale of forecasts and plans

It is important to recognize the limitations imposed by any time-scale (the 'planning horizon'). First, the manager should be aware of the organization's priorities. There is no point in concentrating on the next century if there are doubts as to whether the company will survive the next year. Having ascertained the priorities, it is essential to realize how they affect the type of decision that may be taken.

This point is illustrated in Figure 57.3, the purpose of which is to show that timescales for manpower planning and forecasting vary. The manager can deal in the short-term, over, say, 0–6 months, but flexibility is limited by the current manpower employed and by the degree of ability to control resources (that is, overtime, recruitment or redundancy policies). If the manager is concerned with longer-term strategic planning, then the time-scale will be in terms of some years, possibly five years or more. Over this period the manager may look at wholesale reorganizational changes, such as fundamental modifications to job structuring, management development programmes and organizational development.

Forecasts and plans of jobs

In preparing plans and forecasts of jobs there are three aspects that can be considered:

1 *Identification of key jobs* This is probably the main area to consider. The manager should concentrate on those jobs that are central to the organization
2 *Time needed for training new employees* Where an apprenticeship or management trainee scheme is involved, anything up to four years has to be allowed. It is therefore necessary to identify the need in good time

	Basis of requirement	*Basis of availability*	*Possible actions*
0–6 months	Current budget	Current manpower	Contractors Overtime Recruitment Redundancy
6–18 months	Forward budget	Current manpower less projected leavers	Promotion Transfer Recruitment
18 mths– 5 years	Forward budgets and plans	Projected current manpower plus those completing training	Recruitment plan rundown Training programmes
More than 5 years	Predicted market and technological changes	Expected labour market and education system supplies	Organization development and job restructuring Management development programmes

Figure 57.3   The time-scale of manpower planning (C. J. Purkiss)

3   *Shortage or surplus in the labour market*   Particular emphasis should obviously be given to areas of likely shortage.

The importance of setting out assumptions

When forecasting and planning, the manager will have to make certain assumptions. The particular importance about setting out these assumptions is that in the future it will be possible to go back and check what has occurred against what was originally expected or intended. For example, if the assumed labour turnover rate proved to be underestimated, it might be necessary to go back and change some fundamental parts of the plan.

A number of factors affect these assumptions, such as:

1   Investment decisions (for example, capital investment)
2   Productivity and motivation (for example, incentive bonus schemes)
3   Marketing changes (for example, sales and product changes)
4   Technological changes (for example, the use of robots)
5   Social and political factors (for example, government or legislative changes).

1	Classify work		
	Meters	hours per job	0.5
	Installation		2.2
	Maintenance		1.6
	Emergency		1.1

2	Forecast work in jobs '000			
		1995	1996	1997
	Meters	12	13	10
	Installation	95	104	123
	Maintenance	29	34	38
	Emergency	8	6	5

3	Convert into employee hours '000			
		1995	1996	1997
	Meters	6	7	5
	Installation	209	229	271
	Maintenance	46	54	61
	Emergency	9	7	6
	Total	270	297	343

4	Convert into employees required assuming 1 800 hours/employee			
		1995	1996	1997
	Employees	150	165	191

Figure 57.4   Using the workload method

Approaches to forecasting

Having considered the general background to forecasting and planning it is necessary to review the techniques available to assist in preparing forecasts. Personnel specialists have a real contribution to make here. The three broad approaches now to be described have been found useful.

The workload method

An attractive method which is being used with some effect to separate the work to be done into its discrete parts. Each part is then forecast using a mixture of judgement and statistics or financial necessity. Figure 57.4 shows how such data can be converted into manpower requirements.

Productivity ratios

In concept, this is a straightforward method. The idea is to relate units of work, financial activity and so on, to levels of employment required. A direct application is given in Figure 57.5.

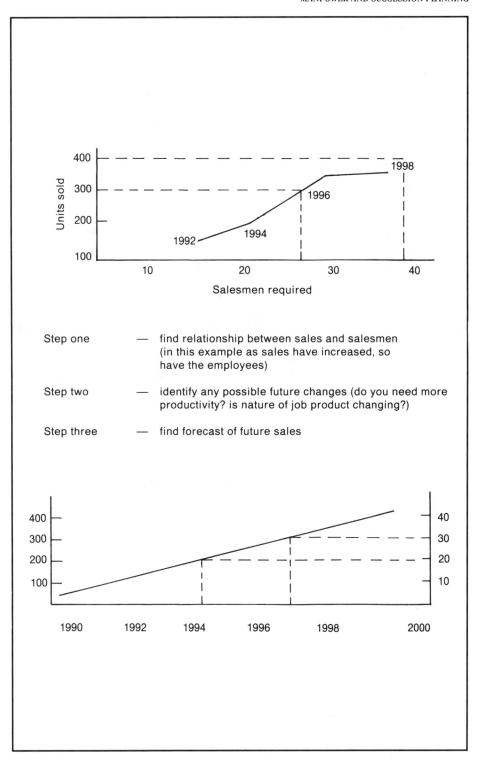

Step one — find relationship between sales and salesmen (in this example as sales have increased, so have the employees)

Step two — identify any possible future changes (do you need more productivity? is nature of job product changing?)

Step three — find forecast of future sales

Figure 57.5   Using the ratio method

The use of trends

The first two methods imply some knowledge of the work to be done, which may not always be available or possible. They will also require the use of some statistical methods. In addition, however, the statistical approaches can themselves be used for forecasting manpower levels.

The levels of employment or output, when recorded over a period of time, will reveal five distinct elements, known as 'time series':

1 A trend, as shown in Figure 57.6(a)
2 Cyclical effect, as shown in Figure 57.6(b)
3 Seasonality, as shown in Figure 57.6(c)
4 A step, as shown in Figure 57.6(d). This is a sudden change in the level of employment which will probably accompany some identifiable change (for example the EC 1992 changes)
5 Random fluctuations, as shown in Figure 57.6(e).

The forecasts can be derived by projecting the trends.

Care must be taken when interpreting the information. For example, a distinction should be made as to whether a sharp change in employment is a once-and-for-all step or a random fluctuation, or whether underlying circumstances have changed.

It is also possible to forecast manpower using business and financial information (for example, what can we afford?). If all else fails, the judgement of managers (within a systematic framework) is better then nothing.

Forecasting manpower availability

Labour turnover

There are several strongly marked characteristics of wastage. The three most important are:

1 Wastage decreases as length of service increases
2 Wastage decreases as the amount of skill exercised increases
3 Wastage decreases as age increases.

Of these, the first is particularly important and, indeed, so well validated that it approaches the status of a natural law. The object is to measure these flows. How can the manager measure and interpret wastage information?

Labour turnover can be expressed as a percentage using the following equation:

$$\text{Labour turnover} = \frac{\text{Wastage} \times 100}{\text{Average number employed}}$$

Usually, but not necessarily, the average number employed and the wastage (leavers) refer to a particular year.

At first sight this seems a sensible measure of wastage, and is easy to compute. But there is still widespread ignorance as to how misleading this statistic can be. The following is an example taken from a much-quoted paper:

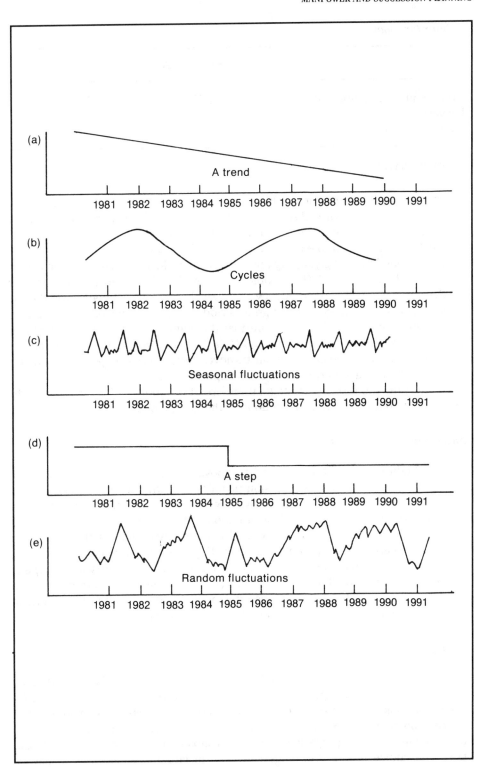

Figure 57.6   The components of time series

Labour turnover

	Departent A1	Department A2
Average number employed	1,117	382
Leavers	98	65
Index of turnover	8.8%	17.3%
Average service	5 years	7 years

Using the standard index it would seem that Department A1 was considerably more stable then Department A2. However, on closer analysis it transpired that an individual's expectation of service in A1 was five years and in A2 was seven years. A1 was therefore less stable than A2. Why this discrepancy?

As mentioned previously, a very important factor affecting wastage is the length of service of an individual (the probability of leaving decreases as the length of service increases). The discrepancy between the two departments was due to Department A2 having gone through a period of rapid expansion, bringing in a large number of new staff. This meant that the length of service distribution has been pulled sharply to the lower end, and it is the people at that lower end who are most likely to leave. The crude labour turnover index therefore gave a misleading picture of the wastage pattern of the two departments.

To interpret and forecast wastage, therefore, it is important for the manager to look at the length of service distribution in the groups being considered.

Succession and career planning

The methods of forecasting referred to above cannot be used in planning for managers. The concern in 'succession planning' is with such questions as 'who will be the next chief accountant?' or 'what will happen when the chairman retires at the end of the next summer?' The attention is directed towards *which* person.

In 'career planning', however, the organization is concerned with more strategic questions of career development, which is distinguished from succession planning because the concern is less with the individual employee and more with the *type* of employee required to fill a particular post (that is, whether the company should employ more graduates, more engineers, more scientists; whether the chairman of the board should be an accountant or a marketing expert, and so on).

Managing careers

In career management it is possible to use statistical methods supported by information technology approaches (and even personal computers). Figure 57.7 shows the possible use of succession and career progression techniques. The information required to draw these diagrams is simple. It is necessary to know only the number of employees in each age group and their grade in the organization. The choice of age groupings can vary. In larger organizations it may be possible to use every incremental age step between 20 and 65. However, in smaller

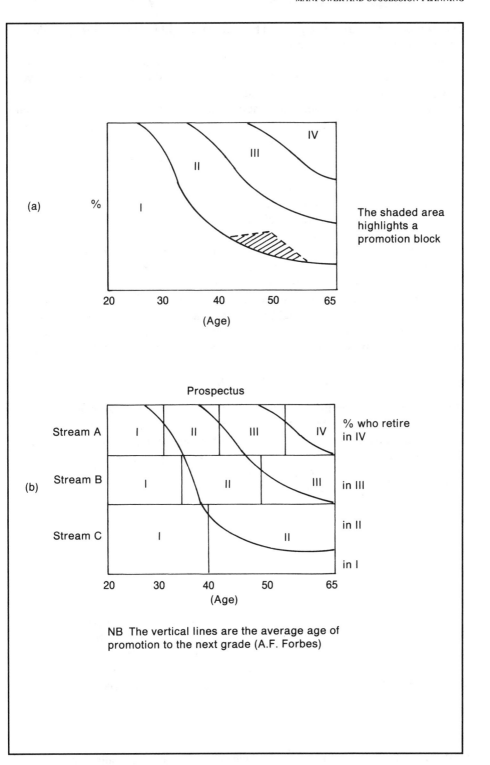

Figure 57.7   Succession and career progression

organizations or where more general trends are sought it may be more practicable to use groupings of people's ages.

The grade is simply some classification of hierarchy in the organization. It could be a salary band or managerial level. The purpose of these diagrams is to give a clear picture of promotional routes and achievement, and from that picture to make some estimation about future succession and career plans for individuals and groups. The advantage of diagrams such as these is that they give a definition of the present situation (that is, how many employees move from one grade to another at a certain age), from which it is possible to get some idea of promotion paths and prospects.

Also, using a technique such as this, an indication is given of the problems and advantages of various existing situations and future policies. For instance, the upwards deviation in the line in Figure 57.7 (a) would indicate a promotional blockage. Conversely, had this deviation been downwards it would indicate that, for some reason, employees at that particular age were breaking through quickly into the next grade, which might point in turn to inexperienced managers and a requirement for special emphasis on training.

Comparisons can be drawn between departments, especially in larger organizations. These can be most enlightening and can highlight different promotion patterns between graduates and non-graduates, between engineers and marketing experts, or between different sites or divisions within the corporate group.

MANPOWER UTILIZATION AND CONTROL

If there is a forecast and information, then there is a basis for the plans. However, we have to be sure either that these plans will materialize, or if they are not materializing, we have to be able to so something about it. A system of manpower control is therefore neeeded: a system for measuring achievements in terms of utilization compared to the original forecast.

There are three methods for controlling manpower:

- Head counts
- Costs
- Productivity ratios.

Head counts

For many organizations, control consists of head counting. Certainly, there are advantages in this method, since it measures manpower in terms that the manager understands (that is, people). It does not mean very much initially if a manager is told that too much money has been spent or that productivity levels are below expectation. However, if the manager is told to get rid of 10 people out of a budget of 35, that has an immediate impact!

Costs

Cost control has an element of ruthless efficiency. The manager allocates a certain amount of money to a department and says, 'That is all you have got: do not spend any more.' The main problem with this method in respect of manpower control is that, in many circumstances, it is difficult to allocate costs accurately. It is more than likely that the costs centres are so vague, especially in larger organizations, that it is difficult to make local managers define their costs clearly.

Production ratios

Ratios of productivity are less useful as a mechanism for controlling managers, but more useful as centralized measures of how productivity is progressing in the organization. Here we are concerned with expressing manpower in relation to output in some way. It is only necessary to record whether productivity is improving and whether the plan for improvements has been achieved.

Any document called 'a plan' would not remain relevant for long. A plan is dynamic, made up of goals which are themselves changing. Constant monitoring of information will warn the organization when forecasts or targets or utilization are going awry, so that corrective action may be taken.

The overall purpose of manpower planning, then, is the achievement of better utilization of human resources from a strategic, not tactical, perspective.

Mapping the manpower environment

Given the uncertainty that surrounds the future, the manager should not divert resources that could be put to better use elsewhere to forecasting. In manpower planning the suggestion is that those resources should be directed towards analysis of objectives and alternatives backed up by a thorough understanding of the organization and its environment – that is, the 'manpower map'. A recognition has emerged that managers' sense of security about the future will come not from knowing what the future holds in store (because that is impossible) but from the confidence of knowing that the organization can adapt to any eventuality. It follows from this that the personnel function will seek to improve flexibility and adaptability – to create a 'flexible firm' – by the careful use of contractors, flexible trade union agreements, and so on. In this way, the manager's job will become easier and new developments will be dealt with efficiently.

CONCLUSIONS

Manpower planning, therefore, is a process rather than a set plan or well-defined technique. It goes on within a framework of continuous debate about goals which are themselves dynamic. No final blueprint is either possible – or, perhaps, desirable. Nevertheless, although manpower plans and planning cannot be exact they are still valuable since, providing they are adequate, they will help to decide how best to deal with new and unforeseen circumstances.

FURTHER READING

Bramham, John, *Human Resource Planning*, Institute of Personnel Management, 1989
Bramham, John, *Practical Manpower Planning*, 5th edn, Institute of Personnel

Management, 1990 (from which much of the material and thinking set out in this chapter has been derived)

Pettman, Barrie O., *Manpower Planning Workbook*, 2nd edn, Gower, Aldershot, 1984

58 Recruitment and selection

Peter Humphrey

Whatever has been written or said about recruitment and selection, everyone believes that they are experts in this field. But while the ultimate decision is the seemingly simple 'to employ or not to employ', recruitment and selection is quite a complicated process. In addition to the legal and quasi-legal frameworks, there is the 'answer back' facility in the form of candidates, some of whom will readily make known their views of the selection process and its end results. Thus, the principle of normal courtesy underpins the recruitment and selection procedure, particularly in the face-to-face situation and also at all other points of contact during the decision-making process. Attention must therefore be paid to the underlying social processes, especially since the decision-making process is not one-sided.

The process does not end with a job offer, but only when the applicant says 'Thanks, I accept your offer'. The whole procedure is aimed at reaching such a conclusion. Four important phases can be identified in this process, and these are described in the following sections.

PHASE ONE: PRE-RECRUITMENT

Both actual and hidden costs of recruitment and selection are significant. The total outlay for one employee can involve anything from 6 to 40 per cent of the annual basic salary. Costs of advertising, agency/search/selection consultancy fees, royalties, fees for occupational testing – all these soon mount up, without taking into account administrative costs and the recruiter's own time. If no appointment is made these costs escalate, and there are the unquantifiable but significant costs of the time delay involved in repeating the recruitment exercise. Thus, it is important to establish an effective recruitment system, if only because such significant sums of money can be put at risk.

The system should ensure the availability of statistical information for manpower planning, job information, and administrative support to deal with responses from candidates. A realistic understanding of the different time-scales needed for filling vacancies is vital. This is not a call for sophisticated back-up services, merely a pragmatic statement of the main foundation on which successful recruitment procedures rest.

PHASE TWO: RECRUITMENT

Requisitions

Many organizations are quite indifferent to the way in which requests for replacement or additional staff are made. Yet in many respects the underlying attitudes which allowed this have been changed by economic circumstances. There is now closer scrutiny of labour costs, and the requisition for staff at all levels has acquired almost the same cachet as capital applications. Information on a staff requisition should include:

1 Name and location of originating department
2 Job title
3 Main job function
4 Salary or grade
5 Reason for requisition, for example:

   • replacement
   • new appointment
   • additional appointment

6 Required by: (date)
7 Signature . . . . (department head)

Completing a requisition takes up a little management time but its value to the recruiter is incalculable. It leaves no room for doubt. No one has to rely on remembering what was said about the job during informal conversations, when valuable managerial time can be wasted in referring back by telephone or personal visit to verify the position. The recruiter's time can be better spent in the next step of the process.

Job information

A great deal of confusion exists over terms used in this area. In the UK, the Department of Employment's *Glossary of Management Terms* defines 'job description' as a broad statement of the purpose, scope, duties and responsibilities of a particular job, whereas a 'job specification' is a detailed statement of the physical and mental activities in a job.

Job description

Jobs must be viewed as part of a dynamic organization, thus the job description is, at best, only a point-in-time interpretation. Consequently, hard-pressed managers may question the need for preparing a job description. But there are sound reasons for countering such resistance, as follows:

1 The job description acts as a basic means of communication between the manager and the recruiter as far as the position to be filled is concerned

2 It is an invaluable mechanism for discussing and finalizing the tactical approach to the selection process

3 It can yield vital information for the candidates who have come to have a high level of expectation in terms of job information. This certainly has a useful 'plus effect' in promoting confidence about the organization amongst the candidates

4 It ensures that there is an accepted factual basis from which information can be selected for advertising purposes

5 Finally, it provides the reference point against which all decisions taken and judgements made can be evaluated.

Time spent on this preparatory work can yield dividends in preventing over-interviewing and in ensuring that advertising and other expense is used to maximum effect. What information, therefore, should be included? The following items are essential, whatever the vacancy level:

1 *Job title* This must be self-explanatory wherever possible, and certainly where either unusual technical terms or terms specific to the organization are used, adequate explanation must be given

2 *Name of department* Also in understandable terms

3 *Accountability* The job title of the person to whom the job holder is responsible

4 *Main job function* A brief but lucid statement of the purpose of the job

5 *Responsibilities for people and/or equipment* No need to detail every nut and bolt, but include categories and numbers of people to be supervised together with main items of equipment

For managerial, supervisory or technical positions, additional items are required as follows:

6 *Limits of authority* Particularly in relation to spending money

7 *Levels of contact* This is of special importance in a multi-divisional organization and with working relationships outside the organization.

During this information gathering process it is useful to question the completeness, fairness and accuracy of the information, and whether it is presented clearly. It may be desirable to seek a second opinion in some cases.

The job specification

It might appear that there is considerable difference in requirements at the various levels of appointment but five basic categories can be identified, as outlined in the following paragraphs. These categories can be qualified as appropriate for each selection by a scale of relevance (vital/desirable/useful).

1 *Qualifications* This category is the bane of every recruiter's life. The standpoint to take must be 'is it relevant?' Is a PhD really vital? A sense of reality must be maintained, for it is as easy to be swayed by academic and professional qualifications as it is by medals and decorations. Instead of qualifications it is sometimes better to list required areas of knowledge (for example, export procedures for a shipping clerk)

2 *Specific skills, abilities and aptitudes* This category should not be just a jumble of popular management phrases which divert attention from the main purpose. The intention is to define accurately (and quantify if possible) factors seen as necessary for success in the job. For instance, skills in negotiating with trade union officials or the different skill required in negotiating commercial contracts; the ability to sell an idea or a product. Aptitudes might be verbal, numerical or mechanical. All must be related to reality, Simplicity is the keynote here

3 *Experience* It is most important to build an accurate picture of the previous experience needed. This can lead to better advertisements, easier preselection and more searching interviews. It should include the early, formative years and, depending on the post specified, positions of responsibility held. A relationship must be established between these details and the environments in which they occurred (for example, for the post of foundry manager, experience of specific materials or castings sizes). The general standing of the organizations where the experience was gained is also very relevant. The other most important aspect of experience, at all levels, is its relevance to the major tasks of the job

4 *Personal attributes* More attention is being paid now to this category. The impact of the new individual on an existing work group (and vice versa) can be vital, particularly where incentives are based on group performance. Some attempt must be made to analyse the 'chemistry' of the situation – 'acceptability' is probably the key word. However, on occasions it may be necessary to specify apparently unwelcome attributes (for example, abrasiveness for stimulating a complacent team)

5 *Physical attributes* A great deal of emphasis has been placed, through legislation, on employing the disabled. This is more obvious in relation to physical disabilities but it is often found that only lip service is paid to the mental health aspects of the working situation. The question of the individual's capacity to absorb stress is very important, especially at certain decision-making levels, or where long hours or a harsh environment can have a serious effect on an individual's domestic or social relationships. These attributes must be specified accordingly. (The amateur doctor or psychologist can do untold harm here, and professional advice should be obtained whenever possible.)

Internal sources for candidates

Many companies overlook the talent in their existing work forces. It is very important to look internally to identify potential candidates from all parts of the enterprise. In doing this, the political pressures of the organization will come into play and it is important to maintain an independent stance throughout. This independence is sustained by the factual nature of the job description and subsequent job specification. None the less, it is vital that internal candidates are subjected to the full selection process. This must not be regarded as unnecessary bureaucracy: its purpose is to safeguard the integrity of the process for the organization and for all those involved in it, especially the candidates.

Advertising

The main purpose in advertising a job is to attract sufficient candidates of the right calibre, thereby securing a reasonable field from which to choose the most appropriate person. How does one tackle this attraction process?

1 Define the audience (that is, the type of people to be reached)
2 Decide on the means and establish the cost of making the contact
3 Write the message
4 Monitor the results.

The audience

The nature of the vacant position will largely define the size and geographical spread of the audience. At the operational level there is usually a local audience which can be tapped. When the necessary skills are not available locally an initial investigation is needed to establish the location of the required audience and the potential available. This also applies at the clerical and technical level, though there is a tendency for technical people to restrict their own availability by becoming identified with particular processes, even within one organization. This does not seem to be the case with computer staff, whose skills and knowledge have almost universal application and whose mobility transcends national boundaries. It is at managerial level that the audience becomes national and international and it is pertinent to define this audience in broad functional terms (for example, accountants, engineers, buyers). Consideration must also be given to defining current salary levels from which candidates can be drawn.

The means

Detailed information abounds on the circulation and readership of newspapers and professional journals and advertising costs. Decisions have to be made on the worth of national coverage against local coverage, the space needed and whether to cover any wider public relations aspects. It seems natural to turn to press advertising but other methods should also be considered, as follows:

• Television or cinema advertisements
• Posters in appropriate public places
• Leaflet distribution, especially on housing estates
• Word of mouth (with the inevitable discount for misstatements)
• Notice boards either in or outside the place of work
• Job centres
• 'Recruitment circus' using a travelling roadshow or hotels
• Pre-recorded tape for distribution or access by telephone
• Commercial radio.

Most of the above methods are more appropriate when considerable numbers of people are required at the same time, especially during expansion or when staffing a new site. Organizations typically use a mix of methods according to their needs and funds.

The message

There is an art in constructing a message with the necessary basic emotional appeal to the audience. Simplicity is the keynote, together with the need to use technical terms on a restricted, meaningful basis. But one must present sufficient hard information. The message includes everything within the physical boundaries of the medium: words, black or white space, line drawings, company symbols. Sometimes it may be important for the text to be in a foreign language. A great deal of help on these details is available from advertising agencies and public relations consultants. The aim is to make candidates reach for their writing pads, telephone or even visit.

The results

Keeping a record of the response to advertisements enables the user to evaluate in financial terms the relevance of certain media in reaching the required audience. The main statistic is 'cost per reply' which can be refined in relation to numbers interviewed, shortlisted or appointed from that particular source. A simple form can be used by a clerk or secretary to record information such as the appointment title, medium used, size of advertisement, cost, number of replies, cost per reply, number interviewed, number shortlisted and the number appointed. Such information is invaluable for advertising budgets, and also in settling arguments and destroying preconceived ideas.

Equally at this stage, use can be made of the advertising agency in obtaining comparative statistics on a confidential basis from other agency clients.

Processing of applications

The greatest sin in recruitment is not to acknowledge an application. Most applicants are prepared for occasional lost letters but none will tolerate being ignored. This, again, is related to natural courtesy. Keeping track of applications over a prolonged selection period demands a good office system, preferably dovetailed with the sorting process. A suggested outline appears in Figure 58.1. The application form itself can be designed to signal and record actions required at appropriate points.

With the advent of word processing there is an even stronger argument for having individually addressed standard letters. The timesaving is considerable, apart from the important question of maintaining cordial relations with candidates. Typical standard letters cover acknowledgment of application, invitation to interview, request for further information and rejection.

A well-thought-out and proven system will keep candidates and recruiter happy and help to avoid the embarrassing letter to the chairman from an aggrieved candidate.

PHASE THREE: SELECTION

Previous work has been directed inwardly to the job to be filled and outwards only in terms of a remote audience. At the selection stage this changes and many managers feel quite exposed. Although confrontation with individuals is a large

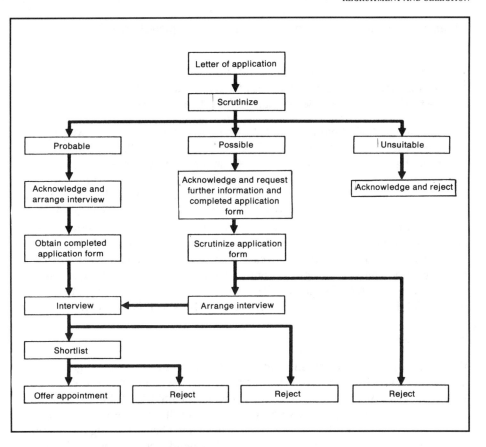

Figure 58.1   Processing of applications

part of a manager's job, this tends to be in a specific commercial or operational context where individuals are aware of the institutional constraints surrounding meetings. The selection situation cannot be classified in the same way, and therefore a specific framework and ground rules must be established.

Planning and setting up the interview

For any situation to be described as an interview it must meet the following criteria:
1   It is a tool of the communication process
2   It is a vehicle for the transmission of information from one person to another
3   It focuses upon specific subject matter that is relevant to its situation, occasion and purpose
4   It requires the participation of at least two people who interact freely with each other
5   It is initiated to achieve one or several objectives
6   It takes place in a particular physical and social setting
7   It occurs as part of a procedural sequence of events.

It is also of value to understand the various levels or planes on which the interview takes place:

1 The primary level deals mainly with facts
2 The secondary level deals with both facts and judgements
3 The tertiary (or depth) level deals with motivation and attitudes.

This background will help to establish a framework for the interviewer and help him/her to develop a pattern and style appropriate for handling the interview.

Sufficient attention must be paid to preliminary administrative arrangements. All relevant papers must be to hand: correspondence, application form, job description and specification plus other documents which may be needed such as company reports, product/service brochures and conditions of contract booklets.

It is vital to brief all who will meet the candidates, including receptionists and others responsible for greeting them properly. Domestic arrangements should not be neglected: awkward situations can arise through inadequate provision for travel arrangements, overnight accommodation (where necessary) and prompt reimbursement of travel expenses. These considerations help to set the interview tone, which is just as important for junior applicants as it is for the most senior.

The interview setting

Privacy is a prime requirement, for nothing can be more disturbing than being knowingly overheard. Although the interview has a social element it is, nevertheless, a business meeting and the room furnishing has to be functional, especially if the room is kept specifically as an interview room. If an office is used it may be necessary to consider tidiness, positions of desk and chairs, barring the telephone and turning off loudspeakers (privacy includes avoidance of interruptions).

The social setting and tone of the interview is important to the interviewer and the candidate. Every effort must be made to establish rapport with the candidate. If this consideration is missing, chances are that the objectives will not be achieved, unless a deliberate stress situation has been created for a purpose. Try to establish cordial relationships by setting the necessary tone during the exchange letters. It is also important to ensure that necessary courtesies are extended to candidates during any waiting period: feelings of being isolated or ignored can easily be aroused by lack of attention and it takes much time and effort to overcome these effects. Never cause interviewees to lose their dignity.

Conducting the interview

Although this chapter has so far discussed the one-to-one employment interview, there are other types of interview, as follows:

1 Preliminary interviews, often for simply meeting a person to exchange information and form initial judgements
2 Background information interviews, for example, when helping a candidate to complete an application form
3 Discussion interviews, where the objective is to elaborate on information already available and to talk over problems

4   Group interviews, where a candidate faces a number of interviewers together. Control is easily lost in these circumstances, and then only the candidate benefits – for he acts on his own behalf and therefore becomes the only consistent factor in the proceedings.

When the interviewer has defined the context, he has to decide on which level to operate and on the style to adopt. Levels were listed earlier. Style can be directed, non-directed or probing.

- *Directed interviews*   Use direct questions needing definite answers. Such questions are often needed but there are occasions when the style is necessary for the whole interview. It is especially appropriate for school leavers, for applicants with complicated job histories and when there is a suggestion that 'facts' are in dispute
- *Non-directed interviews*   Rely on open questions that allow the respondent to choose an answer. This is the best way of searching out or developing a person's views on any matter. Prompting is a useful technique. The question 'and then what happened?' places the onus on the respondent to continue the story or reveal something unintentionally. Another ploy is for the interviewer to keep silent, building pressure on the interviewee (who usually cannot resist the need to fill the vacuum by continuing to talk)
- *Probing interviews*   Cover and recover the same ground by a series of questions. The interviewer may need to check on claimed experience, on perceived inconsistencies in the job history or even on attitudes displayed which may not seem to be in character.

The interview sequence

Every interview has its own sequence: opening, exchanging information, recording, guiding and closing.
- *Opening*   The interviewer must attempt to put the interviewee at ease and win his confidence. A useful opening gambit is to outline the time limits for the interview, or to clear up any problems over travelling, or, best of all, to try to establish a common link which assists in forming a bond between the two people. This latter gambit must be free from any social, racial or sexual overtones. In addition, the interviewer must be able to conceal any prejudice, particularly in relation to ethnic origin, forms of dress, regional speech, sex or physical appearance. Conversely, he or she must not appear to be attracted by affinities such as experience of the same school or interest in a certain sport
- *Exchanging information*   The why, what, where, whom and how – this is the kernel of the interview. It is now that the quality of preparatory work is tested. Properly prepared, the interviewer should be able to answer most questions, but it is a rule of the professional recruiter not to overstretch the truth and to admit openly when it is not possible to answer a question. An honest response to difficult or unanswerable questions will usually be accepted by the interviewee. Candidates must be given every chance to ask pertinent questions and have them fully answered, but the interviewer must be certain to leave enough time for getting and checking all relevant details of the candidate's background

Date:	Time:	Ref. Number:
Name:	Age:	Job:

Education, training and qualifications	*Impact*
	Appearance
Relevant experience	
	Personal

Figure 58.2   Interview notes

and work history. If an answer is missed or not properly heard the interviewer must be strong enough to ask the candidate to repeat the answer

- *Recording* Interviewers cannot hope to remember all answers received during an interview and it is necessary to have some policy and method for taking notes. Most candidates will expect this, but it must be done in the least obtrusive way possible. A standard form is useful, particularly if it allows the interviewer to record a preliminary assessment as soon as the candidate has left. An example is shown in Figure 58.2

- *Guiding* A part of the control process. In most cases the interviewer has control at the start, but this control must be maintained throughout. It is important to keep discussion within the bounds of subject and time. The hallmark of a good interviewer is the ability to listen, not to intrude while the candidate is speaking and not to hog the conversation with rhetorical questions or personal anecdotes. But it is surprising how often candidates are

Name:	Age:	Job:
Impact and appearance	very good/good/acceptable/poor	
Training and qualifications	very good/good/acceptable/poor	
Other abilities	very good/good/acceptable/poor	
Motivation	very good/good/acceptable/poor	
Adjustment	very good/good/acceptable/poor	
Experience	very good/good/acceptable/poor	
Assessment (all factors)	very suitable/suitable/reserve/unsuitable	

Figure 58.3   Initial assessment and interview summary. This list should be attached to the interview notes

allowed to dwell on unimportant points, wasting time and therefore degrading the interview.

Interviewees occasionally try to assume control. Such attempts can be thwarted by rapidly changing the subject or by asking innocuous questions. The ploy is to buy time in which to regroup one's thoughts and then resume questioning along the desired lines

- *Closing*   The interviewer must know how to end the interview. A lot obviously depends on the place of the interview in the selection procedure but it is very easy to mishandle the situation and promote unnecessary uncertainty and suffering in the candidate. Above all, a positive approach must be taken, telling the candidate what to expect next (for example, a letter giving the outcome within ten days; you are sorry that you will not be able to take this application any further, or that the candidate will be placed on the short list).

Assessment

An initial assessment of each candidate should be made immediately after the interview. Always valuable, this practice is especially important when there is a long delay between interviews and the final decision. A simple form based on J. Munro Fraser's five point plan (see Figure 58.3) can be used, and this should be attached to the interview notes. The scale assigned to each of the factors is rather crude but simple methods such as this provide a useful framework which allows the interviewer to summarize his/her thoughts and make an initial judgement.

Administering appropriate tests

Although not usually included under this heading, the test most commonly applied is the medical one (whether this is a screening by a trained nurse or a rigorous medical examination). Most companies have their established policy and practice, usually dependent upon the nature of the work, its environment and the seniority of the appointment. Guidance is therefore probably already available to the recruiter.

Apart from medical examinations, questions inevitably arise about the value of using tests in the selection process. A case can often be made for using appropriate tests, especially where available information points to their validity in the particular context. But caution is needed. In Britain (for example) safeguards for the administration of tests have been introduced by the National Foundation for Education Research in England and Wales in conjunction with the British Psychological Society. Where there are any possible problems over the use of tests in selection or management development, reference to a suitably qualified independent person or organization is essential.

Tests can yield important information on manual dexterity, intelligence, aptitudes, abilities, interests, colour blindness and various personality aspects. The results of relevant tests can help the recruiter to make a full and final assessment about the suitability of candidates for the job in question.

Most test packages include detailed instructions on procedure. Test administration is important and the recruiter should ensure that conditions for all test sessions are the best possible. The correct physical conditions and the right psychological tone are essential to good test performances by the candidates. If these conditions are not available test sessions can become a futile exercise in apparent sophistication.

A guarantee of confidentiality is highly important to candidates. The approach to be encouraged with respect to test results is that of the medical profession when dealing with personal information of this nature.

Making the appointment

The decision to offer the position to one of the candidates is one-sided and the recruitment task is not completed until the offer has been accepted.

At this stage the 'evidence' on all the candidates should be available for review and final assessment. In all probability, at least two people will be concerned in the final decision, and in most cases they should meet to discuss the matter as fully as necessary. Sometimes one candidate stands out among all others, and consequently the decision comes easily. But on many occasions a debate occurs with an informal cataloguing of the pros and cons, and inevitably some sort of compromise has to be made in relation to the 'ideal' job description and candidate specification prepared at the beginning. Indeed, increasingly the selection decision is made, not by comparing candidate against candidate, but by assessing the candidate in relation to the specification.

The important point here is to approach the decision-making session in a systematic way, so that the reasons for the choice of one candidate and the rejection of the other become quite clear. No one should be afraid of stating and, if necessary, restating that a liking for a candidate has tipped the scales in his favour. As Robert Townsend says in *Up the Organization*, 'The important thing about hiring is the chemistry of the vibrations between boss and candidate; good, bad, or not there at all'. Any manager who denies this truism has already reached his level of incompetence.

Once made, the decision must be conveyed in writing to the successful candidate. The formal offer of employment should be qualified with the phrase 'subject to satisfactory references' (unless, of course, these have already been obtained). No self-respecting potential employee will accept and act upon a verbal offer, and the employer cannot regard the appointment as made until an acceptance letter has been received. It is important at this stage to identify and clear any remaining questions concerning the conditions under which the appointee is to be employed.

PHASE FOUR: POST-RECRUITMENT

With the offer and acceptance of employment, the main subject of this chapter – recruitment and selection – ends. But there are important post-recruitment activities which must be mentioned.

Introducing the new employee to the organization

Any new employee will need a period of familiarization before the job can be performed properly. An established induction programme for new recruits is useful, especially when this includes a formal introductory course through which new employees learn about the policies, practices and nature of the organization. Sometimes these can be group courses, but for some cases the introduction may have to be tailor-made. Perhaps the best basis from which to start is to ask, and answer, the question 'What does the newcomer need to know?' The main aim of induction, however conducted, is to integrate the newcomer as soon as possible.

Follow-up

Contact needs to be maintained with new employees until it becomes apparent that they have settled down and become part of the team. Following up the progress of the new employee is particularly important where the appointment is subject to a probationary period of employment of not more than 13 weeks. In these cases administrative procedures must ensure regular reviews (typically weekly or monthly) and adequate records.

The employee must be kept informed of the progress which he or she is seen to be making. This need not be on a formal basis, for, given good supervisors and managers, the result of an informal chat can be a mending of ways or a spur to even better performance.

Reviewing and evaluating the recruitment and selection process

Most organizations check their recruitment and selection methods on the exception principle – the new recruit who does not fit in becomes the stick with which the recruiter is beaten about the head, no matter how many previous successes can be listed! However, it is possible to examine the actual methods by which the final decision is reached in a more objective way. Such questions must be asked: are we advertising a vacancy properly? Are we attracting the right sort of candidates? Are we treating the candidates in the right way? Have we got the right system for obtaining the preliminary information about the job? Generally are the candidate specifications lucid enough? Are we getting the right sort of information about candidates from the tests we use? How long do new employees of various categories stay with us? Is this a result of over- or under-recruitment?

It is people who, collectively or individually, make or break the company. The cost-effectiveness of the recruitment and selection process must be of prime concern for top management, especially as the annual company report now discloses the average numbers of people employed over the year and the amount of wages and salaries paid to them. In the last analysis, the criterion for the selection decision must be value for money.

FURTHER READING

Higham, M., *The ABC of Interviewing*, Institute of Personnel Management, London, 1979

Institute of Personnel Management, *Code on Occupational Testing*, IPM, London, 1989

Institute of Personnel Management, *Code on Recruitment and Selection*, IPM, London, 1990

Plumbley, P., *Recruitment and Selection*, 2nd edn, Institute of Personnel Management, London, 1976

Sidney, Elizabeth (ed.), *Managing Recruitment*, 4th edn, Gower, Aldershot, 1988

59 Pay structures and systems

George F Thomason

A pay *system* aims to control the relationship between the workers' efforts or contributions to production and the financial returns (remuneration) obtained for them. It must do this within the different patterns of objectives and constraints imposed by the organization's product and labour markets; it also has to take account of differences in workers' goals and preferences. All these factors create variations in both pay levels and pay structures, even between units in the same industry or locality.

Whatever the immediate context, the pay system must serve two organizational purposes:

1 Controlling worker mobility, by attracting and retaining enough workers of adequate capability to meet its labour requirements as these are established by product or service demand
2 Maintaining motivation, by inducing sufficiently high levels of performance from employees to enable the employer to meet competition in the product/ service markets (see Figure 59.1).

The system must secure these ends as cheaply as possible and with sufficient flexibility to permit the organization to respond to changes in its operating circumstances. Market position and the nature and strength of the competition it faces are likely to determine the pressures upon the organization to achieve these objectives. The relative scarcity and solidarity of the workers will, in turn, affect the organization's ability to respond to those pressures effectively.

An organization's pay *structure* refers to the relationship between the pay rates of different jobs. The structure is established partly as a result of the way the organization develops its pay system to achieve these objectives, but is more the consequence of the way in which work tasks are defined and organized by the organization as skilled, semiskilled, and so on. Traditional definitions of work have different implications for pay differentials from innovative definitions.

If only to reduce the number of pay rates to a manageable size, the organization is very likely to follow certain social conventions concerning the way in which jobs are linked with one another for pay purposes. Trade unions and professional associations, which have often organized themselves around traditionally defined occupations and jobs, tend to support these same conventions in seeking to influence pay levels and differentials. Consequently, jobs are grouped into categories such as unskilled, semiskilled and skilled, with flat-rated blue-collar jobs differentiated from incrementally-rated white-collar jobs. The effect is a discrete

Mobility-related, time-based elements include:

1   The basic rate of wage or salary expressed in terms of an hourly, weekly, monthly, quarterly or annual rate

2   The premium rate to be paid for time availability beyond the standard weekly, monthly or yearly hours

3   The premium or allowance to be paid for availability during (what have come to be referred to as) unsocial hours and during holiday and vacation periods

4   A potentially infinite range of so-called fringe benefits (particularly sickness payments, hospitalization cover, educational provision, pension payments, car provision and cheap loan facilities) where the purpose is essentially that of securing commitment to the enterprise (or 'retention'), even though they will often also form incentives to increased effort.

Effort-related or contribution-related elements (associated with performance-related pay (PRP)) include:

1   Payments based on measurable results of the employee's contribution (piece-work payments, payment-by-results (PBR), profit-sharing schemes for senior management, and stock option schemes)

2   Payments based on measurable results of the contribution of a group of employees (including any of the above where they are related to the group rather than the individual, but bringing in also across-the-board gain-sharing schemes such as the Scanlon, Rucker, Priestman plans)

3   Payments based on the individual's assessed input of skill, effort or contribution deemed relevant to achievement, even though the results are not readily measurable – as occurs particularly in non-profit-making organizations and with application of many management-by-objectives (MBO), behaviourally-anchored-rating-scales (BARS), and performance-related pay (PRP) plans.

Figure 59.1   Elements of payment systems. Descriptions of the various types of payment plan are to be found in Armstrong and Murlis (1988), Fowler (1988) and Smith (1984)

number of pay rates, pay grades or 'families' of pay rates forming the organization's pay structure. Non-traditional jobs are then 'fitted into' this structure by one means or another.

BASIC PAY STRUCTURES

An organization's pay system is intended to create financial mechanisms for controlling three labour processes:

1 The basic pay rates which have to be offered to influence mobility, and which establish the organization's terms for interacting with the external labour market
2 Any additional payments (usually linked to age, seniority or length of service) considered necessary to retain employees in the employment
3 Other additional payments (such as bonuses) necessary to raise and maintain (above the minimum necessary to sustain the employment relationship) the workers' contributions to achieving the undertaking's market or service objectives.

These have to be assembled in a package in a way which consistently links the different elements of pay to the kind of contribution the employer wants to achieve: skilled, diligent, compliant, enduring, creative, loyal, and so on. They require careful selection and alignment if overall consistency is to be achieved, because different elements in the package produce different effects. Service-based increments, for example, serve a quite different end from performance-related bonuses; and payment-by-results schemes usually relax pressures on quality whereas measured daywork can be structured to increase them.

They must also be related closely to the class or category of contribution expected, if only to prevent the intended effects on one category of labour from contaminating another category. This was the benefit accruing from the traditional divisions into skilled, semiskilled, white collar, and so on. Separate pay systems could be applied to each in a highly concentrated way. It was possible to ensure, for example, that the pay structure applied to wage-earners differed from that applied to salaried workers, and that each self-contained structure met both employer requirements and employee expectations.

Recent market and technological changes have, however, made the continuation of these traditional divisions much less relevant and much more difficult to maintain. The need for teams to work across the boundaries between blue- and white-collar jobs and across skill boundaries, has produced the response of 'harmonization', in which pay structures and systems become realigned to cope with the new working relationships. Also, the appearance of new aspirations amongst workers often combines with these same changes to challenge the other convention that work (and therefore its remuneration) must be full-time and related to a standard working day, week or year. Atypical contracts, designed for 'less than full-time' workers and involving only parts of the traditional working year are, in consequence, much more prevalent.

Determining structures

Both the pay conventions and the structures they supported, provided a degree of security to workers and employers alike. Consequently, it usually proves difficult to create new and more operationally-relevant pay structures, even on 'greenfield' sites, when changing market conditions and changing methods of work organization threaten the continued relevance of the old systems. Trade unions do not *always* seek to maintain the traditional patterns but, where no alternative structure or system of protecting the worker's pay status is provided in the new scheme of things, resistance from them or their members is most likely.

Part of the problem is caused by the operation of another convention governing the methods of pay determination. This rests on the assumption that the employer is in the labour market to buy what the worker warrants he has to offer by way of skill and commitment, and that individual or collective bargaining processes are concerned (almost) exclusively with fixing the rate at which it is to be purchased. Any day-to-day variation in the effort or contribution required is something for the employer and the worker to determine by another process in another context (even if the union will still stand ready to defend the worker's interest in the matter). Effectively, this system ensures that the determination of remuneration on the one hand, and effort or contribution levels on the other, occurs in separate (and often unlinked) processes.

The recent resurgence of interest (after an interregnum of about twenty years) in schemes which relate pay to performance threatens this dichotomy. As negotiated (or market) rates come to form a smaller share of total remuneration, and performance-related-pay (PRP) a larger one, the more individualized approach to determining pay assumes ascendancy over the traditional collective-bargaining approach. As it does so, it gives greater weight to the exercise of the employer's discretion, and allows less weight to be given to comparisons with what others are paid for the 'class' of work involved.

The employer's freedom to establish more open structures of remuneration is, however, constrained by new conventions, stemming mainly from protective legislation. These conventions are designed to eliminate discrimination in pay (or any other employment terms) on the basis of gender, marital status, ethnic origin or (in some circumstances) religion. Clearly, such considerations ought to be outlawed as irrelevant to employment or to job performance or pay. Many existing systems and structures have therefore to be reviewed, in the light of the new values and norms, in order to eliminate unacceptable biases.

Nevertheless, the employer retains considerable discretion to decide, even within this structure of constraint, what basic pay structure he needs to aim at. He must exercise that discretion in a way which meets the exigencies of both trading and of working.

Pay grades and spines

Discretion will be directed primarily to decide: which jobs need to be related together and which separated in the new structure; how many pay grades or pay progressions are desirable; and how the whole should hang together in a coherent way. These questions may be decided separately for manual and white-collar workers, but increasingly often the two are now put together.

Manual grades

A pay structure for a manual worker traditionally contained three distinct base rates, one for each of the unskilled, the semiskilled and the skilled grades of worker. Developments in production technologies and upward pressure on wages often led to the extension of this convention by interposing two intermediate grades and adding an extra one to the top. Individual rates for workers with special skills and abilities sometimes existed alongside these grades, but trade unions usually tried to eliminate them.

Organizations employing comparatively large numbers of such workers in conditions of relative market stability met the need for administrative convenience and accommodated worker pressure for pay equity by using job evaluation methods to decide basic rates. The common aim is to create a defensible basis for any variations in basic remuneration. All varieties of the method attempt to establish differentials in pay on the basis of the different demands made upon the worker by the jobs themselves. Job demands in turn are usually assessed in terms of the qualifications, experience, effort and responsibility needed to do the job. These are factors which workers themselves generally consider appropriate to relative worth (Thomason, 1980, pp 5–6).

Technological innovation, such as that associated with information technology, threatens to overwhelm these simple banded pay structures. Employers have found it necessary not only to reduce the numbers engaged in manual activities, but also to increase their investment in manual worker training. This encourages a demand for more 'qualification' or 'skill' pay. To accede to it results in more individual rates appearing in the banded structure, so that it begins to resemble the more ramified white-collar pay structure in which different patterns of job demand are usually identified. It raises the question whether the two might not be harmonized and evaluated by similar procedures.

This tendency is reinforced by the workers' and employers' separate demands for more varied working schedules (see Connock, 1985) to meet personal or operating circumstances. This reduces the relevance of the simple standard working day or week to pay determination. Remuneration could now be fixed on some basis other than the full-time worker's standard day or week, plus overtime, plus compensation for unsocial hours. If so, the range of choice for both employer and employee will increase, and will result in more diversified pay structures.

White collar grades

White-collar work has always been somewhat less structured and less standardized than manual work. This has been part of the difference identified by the concepts of 'wage-earning' and 'salary-earning'. The greater variability has been reflected in the white-collar pay structure, which normally contains more bands or grades and more individual rates (even if these are organized into a hierarchy or a progression for career reasons). Salaried workers also tend to receive pay which acknowledges their qualifications, and a wider range of fringe benefits aimed at maintaining their loyalty and their commitment to work tasks.

The progressive development of office technology, which has routinized and standardized a good deal of office work, plus the changing ratio of blue-collar to white-collar labour costs (as manual work is more quickly replaced by machines), has led to the application of more standardized pay grading, previously more associated with manual work. Job evaluation methods are more often used to establish greater rationality and equity in the face of similar pressures. Attempts to preserve a salary and career progression, in which movement is determined by traditional factors such as age, seniority or qualification, have often failed, although they have been more successful in the public sector than in the private.

However, in both sectors there is now considerably more pressure to base progression, in pay or career terms, on the employee's merit or assessed contribution. This pressure appears in the guise of performance-related pay (PRP), which replaces the simple grade or band progressions with a variety of individual rates set by reference to assessed performance. A first consequence of worker pressures for equitable treatment, allied with desire for administrative convenience in these circumstances, is the creation of a larger number of separated pay bands or pay grades, which offer some pay progression but effectively limit the amount of upward movement possible.

Attempts have also been made to marry greater individual pay flexibility with overall cost control by introducing a common 'pay spine'. This usually has a constant interval between the separate pay points but, unlike the former pay grades, runs from top to bottom of the job and pay hierarchy. Where separate pay grades, bands or ranges are retained for distinct job families, these are clipped on to the spine at appropriate points. When conditions (such as labour shortage or appraisal results) warrant, individual rates and ranges can be switched to different positions on the spine without distorting the structure.

Many organizations are already finding it convenient to treat manual and white collar workers in the same manner within a single spinal framework, as the wage-earner/salary-earner distinction disappears and both categories are required to give a similar kind of performance.

PAY LEVEL

The level of pay to be offered is clearly crucial to the realization of the business and staffing objectives. Some employers may be in the position of 'price-takers' in the labour market – facing the necessity of paying a wage rate over which they have little influence – but certainly not all of them are. Furthermore, some employers obviously influence the pay levels for their area. There is always some discretion to determine either the pay level or the level of minimum contribution required for it. But the employer's efforts to secure workers' commitment of time and energies are always restricted by what the employer has available to offer as inducement, and are influenced (at least in part) by the demands that workers bring to bear on the employer's decisions (in either individual or collective bargaining).

The employer's capacity

The employer's ability to use pay to influence mobility and motivation is variable, being influenced by his market position and his level of funding or profitability on the one hand, and by the conditions found in the external labour market on the other. Product and labour market positions with high and low capacities may correlate with the undertaking's size, although this may be no more than a proxy for the kind of work and technology involved.

The categorization by market position (market share related to market growth) and stage reached in the product life cycle, developed by the Boston Consulting Group (1970), suggests that the availability of cash for improving staffing or productivity (and not required more urgently for other purposes) will be greater in organizations with high shares of growing or stable product markets. They are likely to use some of their cash for mobilization and incentive purposes in order to protect their market positions, whereas those with less cash available (because of their low shares in growing or declining markets) will have other urgent uses for it.

This categorization does not apply readily to the public service sector, where few 'stars' or 'cash-cows' are likely to be found. Their measure of success in controlling pay costs in the past has usually flowed from their position as single buyer (or nearly so) of a category of labour and from their ability to rely on status rather than pay to provide satisfactions to their workers.

The demand upon the employer to meet the costs of labour also varies with the condition in the external labour market. If the quantity of the kind of labour needed is readily available to the employer from the labour market, the pressure applied is confined to meeting the current rate for hiring. If this condition is not met, the employer may be pressured into creating his own supply by internal action and into incurring higher labour costs in so doing. Both responses are visible and have been classified by the labour market relationship involved as follows:

1   Some organizations, usually those reliant on standardized work tasks, are able to hire the labour of the kind they need, to run any type of job, directly from the external labour market and to discharge it to that market when the need diminishes

2   Other organizations cannot secure labour with the abilities they seek and therefore hire untrained labour into the bottom positions of their various job hierarchies and invest resources in training and developing it to the standards of competence required, creating what is, in effect, an internal labour market on which they can draw to staff their work tasks.

Both must match market rates in hiring workers, but the level of the pay bill and the structure of the reward package tends to differ significantly between them, reflecting their different approaches to the labour market. The first type of organization will tend to pay market rates to mobilize and use standard payment-by-results schemes to motivate. The second is likely to pay above the market rates to secure the quality of trainable labour that it seeks, and thereafter develop complex pay structures both to secure the needed functional flexibility and to protect its investment in employee training.

In either case, however, management must consider which 'pay division' it wants to play in, given that there is very rarely a single market rate for any major category of labour. Management must decide whether it wants to pay wages and salaries in the upper quartile or the lower quartile of the range of rates (or, of course, elsewhere). While much will be dependent on the profitability of the enterprise, this decision is forced upon the management by the demands of the tasks that have to be performed.

The quality of staff obtained is likely to vary according to the level adopted as policy. Some high-technology enterprises find it necessary to adopt a policy of paying in the upper decile, or at least the upper quartile, in order to get the calibre of personnel necessary to push their products forward. The British Civil Service has in the past sought to pay somewhere in the middle (within the inter-quartile range) and some public sector organizations have been forced by their funding or efficiency levels or both to remain in the lower quartile.

Worker's demands

Pay levels are also affected by the factors which influence the workers' decisions on whether to join and stay in an organization, and whether to expend energy on achieving the organization's task objectives. This influence is opposite in direction to that which stems from the needs of the organization itself. The workers' decisions to take employment are likely to be based upon their perceptions of what constitutes:

- An *appropriate* amount of return in money value for their qualifications and experience, skill and responsibility, effort and diligence; and
- A *fair* return in comparison with what others (those whom they regard as their comparators) receive and what the employer retains by way of profit or (in public services) secures by way of increased value for money.

This amount will vary with the individual's circumstances (the stage reached in the life–cost cycle or the 'status' of his or her occupation) and the general economic conditions (cost of living, taxation, or earnings levels).

Workers' decisions to contribute extra effort (that beyond the minimum necessary to retain employment) rest upon a calculation of whether the extra reward available (whatever form it takes) is seen as an adequate return for the extra effort. The fundamental calculation is whether the amount of effort demanded is rewarded adequately (where adequacy is determined by comparison with what others are required to give for their rewards) and in line with conventional effort–reward ratios in the trade or occupation. This kind of calculation affects the response to incentive schemes designed to elicit additional contributions. These schemes vary in form according to the type of work being performed, the kind of contribution (for example, quality or quantity) to be stimulated, the worker's job status, and the employer's capacity to meet the installation and maintenance costs.

The workers' calculations are necessarily affected by the power that they have to insist upon their own terms. This may be increased where the workers possess the skills in demand in a condition of shortage, or where they can draw upon the strength of union solidarity. Higher qualifications being generally in shorter supply than lower ones, or none at all, those possessed of them are usually able to command higher levels of remuneration than the others. Solidarist groups are similarly better able to secure, at least marginally, higher rewards than those who negotiate on their own.

However, the pay or general reward level is rarely something determined by one side or one set of considerations alone. It is the product of the interaction of two sets of decisions.

PAY SYSTEMS

Influencing workers' decisions to take or stay in a job is chiefly attempted by offering a basic rate of payment for it, although they may also be affected by the other elements in the total package. Basic rates tend to vary according to the factors already mentioned. Since jobs differ in their demands for these qualities and qualifications, base rates have to be established by a method which will meet the criteria of fairness and equity.

Retention of employees is likely to be only partially dependent on this basic rate, although it is usually the biggest element in any pay package. There should also be a significant positive response to any additional pay or benefits which accrue by virtue of length of service or bonuses. Some of these financial benefits are fixed by reference to the basic pay rate, but others are fixed independently. Some so-called fringe benefits are determined almost at the whim of the employer; sometimes they are not as costly as they might seem and the employer secures a 'bonus' by using them. For example, benefits (such as company cars, pensions or health care schemes) which are dependent on the tax arrangements may be valued more highly by those who receive them than they actually cost the employer to provide.

The fixing of basic rates depends on the assessment of market or negotiated rates of pay for the kinds of job on offer, or possibly for broader categories of them (such as skilled, semiskilled and unskilled). Where the employer aims to base rates on the factors on which workers are thought to place most weight, his assessment of the strength of those factors may be linked to observation of worker behaviour or published information about it. Published statistics and labour market surveys of rates indicate what workers have accepted in the past. Negotiations with individual workers or their representatives reveal something of what workers might be prepared to accept in future.

In the organization which neither engages directly in negotiation of pay with trade union representatives nor follows negotiated rates, the necessary assessment may be based on some more or less formal survey of the rates offered in the external labour market. Where rates are fixed directly or indirectly by negotiation, this process substitutes for this assessment, the negotiated rates becoming the best estimates of what is required to hire in labour. In either case, the comparison of existing rates with assessed or negotiated rates indicates the extent and direction of any adjustments needed. However, the employer must still decide what he is able and willing to afford by way of general pay level in order to attract and retain the amount and quality of labour he thinks he needs.

The test of whether the correct hiring-in rate has been established, by whichever method, is whether the organization can attract sufficient labour to fill its vacancies. Failure of this market test might then lead to further adjustment of rates – as recently happened in areas like the South-East of Britain in the face of increasing labour shortage. But the rate found in the external labour market is not always to be relied upon, because organizations determine their pay rates for a range of purposes, not all of which (particularly in organizations with internal labour markets) are related to recruitment or mobilization. The challenge is to ensure that comparisons are made only with like situations and conditions.

The test of whether the total package is adequate to retain such employees as the employer wishes to hold on to is made by examining the rate of voluntary labour turnover. All organizations experience a level of labour turnover, and what is significant in relation to decisions about the form and level of the reward package as a whole is whether the rate of turnover is changing from its normal level. Where it increases suddenly or over a short period of time, this might be taken as prima-facie evidence that some other organization's package is becoming relatively more attractive; attention to it is therefore indicated.

Incentive payments

The basic rate or basic package is generally assumed to cover a minimum worker contribution to achieving the organization's goals. To induce higher levels of performance is considered to require the offer of some additional incentive pay (where 'incentive' is defined as any available benefit which is sufficiently attractive to a person to lead him or her to decide to expend effort in obtaining it). The incentive system links whatever 'extra' the employer wishes to elicit to an offer of extra reward.

The underlying theory is that the higher the reward offered above some notional standard level, the more likely people will be to do more or to contribute more. In practice, the amount of extra incentive pay offered falls somewhere within the range of an additional 20 to 40 per cent above basic pay (the evidence of the *New Earnings Survey* suggests that incentive payments account for something like 25 per cent of manual workers' remuneration, and much less for white-collar workers). This additional pay may well secure increased performances within the same range, although rarely on a simple point-for-point basis. The extra payments may be related to measurements or assessments of individual performance or of the performance of a cohesive working group or team, but the incentive effect is usually greater in the first case.

This theory forms the basis of both payment-by-results (PBR) and performance-related pay (PRP), and, indeed, many other schemes. In their nature, these systems require that either outputs (effects or results) or inputs (skill or contribution) must be capable of either measurement or assessment. In PBR, output is usually countable or measurable, and in PRP more weight is usually placed on the supervisor's assessment of performance defined by reference to input – and partly for this reason some prefer to refer to this as appraisal related pay (ARP) (see ACAS, 1990).

Output is usually more easily measured in the cases of routine, short-cycle tasks performed in factory or office and of organization-wide tasks of top executives. It can be done by counting pieces or volumes produced or by calculating profit performance, respectively, where responsibility for each can be identified fairly readily. The determination of how much any extra output is worth for pay purposes is usually based on some conception of added value (expressed, that is, in terms relevant to the product's market price).

The added value may be divided in different proportions between the enterprise and the individual(s) responsible for it. Extra money can be made available on the basis that the performer receives either the full value or a part of the value of the production or profit results achieved (as in payment-by-results (PBR) and some profit sharing schemes). There is no absolutely right answer to the question about how the division ought to be made. There has to be some return on capital employed, and the producer needs to receive enough to maintain the incentive effect but this may be significantly below the full market value of the output).

If output is not easily identifiable or measurable, or where more intangible quality considerations are important, output-related schemes are less feasible, but a need or desire to provide some incentive may remain.

One response to the problem is to pay an organization-wide bonus based on the organization's profit or overall gain (as in the Rucker, Priestman or Scanlon plans). These wide-group gain-sharing plans usually have more effect on loyalty and commitment than upon individual or small-team productivity. This is true of conventional profit-sharing or employee share-ownership schemes, and of the newer versions developed in response to the tax concessions made in UK national budgets in the 1980s. They are often introduced for just this reason, or because of their 'educational' value (in helping employees to understand the 'realities of business') (Mason and Terry, 1990). However, they have more positive effects than 'lieu-bonus' schemes, in which the bonus of one group such as service workers (whose performance is thought not to be measurable) is linked to that of another such as production workers (where it is).

Another idea (more generally associated with white-collar work) is to link extra payments to the individual's inputs (qualities or qualifications), on the ground that they contribute to the achievement of desired (but unmeasurable or unattributable) outputs. It is then often necessary to rate personal qualities, such as 'application to work' or 'cooperativeness' as well as skills to give a foundation for making extra payments. In the typical merit-rating scheme, however, there is usually some attempt to mix the criteria, some being related to definable outputs and others to personal qualities or characteristics of work performance.

Performance-related pay

Management by objectives (MBO), behaviourally-anchored rating scales (BARS), and performance-related-pay (PRP) schemes are examples of such responses (although they create their own problems of assessment).

Such schemes commonly identify the actions ('key tasks') that the individual is to take within the job, attempt to give these some quantifiable form, and use them as targets against which, at some later date, actual performance can be assessed. Typical schemes may identify key tasks in terms of improving output, reducing error rates, cutting expenditures, completing named projects, or reducing accidents or similar incidents. It is common to tie inputs (such as application) to behaviours which can be measured (such as time-keeping or attendance) where this is possible, but others have to be left for more subjective assessment (for example, improving relationships with others, increasing job knowledge, developing awareness of safety considerations).

Because these schemes rely upon subjective judgement, some attempt has to be made to control the exercise of such judgement in order to produce realistic and equitable effects. The ways in which this is done, and the ways in which the recruitment assessments are aligned with pay, are both numerous and diverse in the principles applied (ACAS, 1990).

Control of assessments is usually attempted by requiring the use of a five-point scale (exceptional or excellent, good or highly effective, satisfactory or effective, fair or less than effective, and poor or unacceptable) for the purpose. These may be assigned a (purely notional) numerical value to facilitate other operations (such as linking the ratings to pay). In order to thwart human (rater) tendencies to be lenient and to bunch assessments in the central category, some schemes also force the assessors to distribute their ratings to personnel according to a predetermined pattern (for example, no more than 5 per cent in the highest category and no more than 15 per cent in the second highest, and about 60 per cent in the middle one). This helps to keep costs in check, but it is likely to raise doubts about the equity of the assessment scheme.

In spite of the many and varied attempts to control the assessment process (for example, by the use of judgemental scales, assignment quotas and close supervision) problems persist. Most frequently encountered are those problems which can be linked to concerns about equity – perceptions of unfairness in the assessments and the rewards, leading to reluctance to carry out ratings or to express judgements, or creating predispositions to use middle categories in scales, and the like.

The linking of assessments to pay usually increases management's control over the awarding of any pay increases. It is becoming increasingly common, for example, for the annual pay bill 'cost-of-living' increase to be negotiated with worker representatives, but for its *distribution* to individuals to be determined on the basis of assessments. It is also becoming more common in white-collar occupations to make entitlement to increments (within a grade or along a spine) dependent on assessments. In some schemes, a defined proportion of the basic rate (say 10 per cent), or a defined potential addition to the basic rate, may be varied annually on this same basis.

The actual relationship between the assessment and the amount of money received by way of increase also varies. In principle, the higher the assessment, the higher will be the amount added to pay. The maximum amount which might be added annually in this fashion may be limited to about 10 per cent, but provision might be made for adding more than this for consistent high performance over a period. In all cases some ceiling is necessary to prevent simple pay 'drift'. The level of the assessment score at which some additional pay becomes due also varies; commonly, no increase is given for the lowest assessment, and only a small increase for the second level assessment (perhaps only the cost of living increase or half an increment on an incremental scale).

Such schemes are clearly designed to concentrate more employee attention on the need for improved performance, and to provide a basis on which to reward the kinds and levels of performance which the employer considers he needs. They do not always succeed in their aims, and often create a degree of resentment unless the controls are well constructed and adequately supervised from the top of the organization. So far, they have been applied more often to top management groups or white-collar personnel: their real test will occur when, in adjusting pay systems to new patterns of teamworking, they are applied to those whose previous experience of them has been nil.

CONCLUSION

Pay is a powerful tool in the hands of management, facilitating achievement of appropriate staffing and performance. It is, however, subject to a wide variety of conventions which help to ensure that both employers' and workers' expectations of the relationship between work and pay will, generally, be met.

Currently all private or public sector organizations face new market challenges and new forms of competition, which at least question the continued relevance of the conventions and the pay structures to which their application gives rise. Workers, for their part, are making new demands on their employers.

To meet the new circumstances, some pay conventions are being abandoned and pay structures made more flexible and more in accord with the realities of work and the emergent aspirations of workers. Opportunities for change are, however, still constrained by the organization's cash position and the capacity of workers to accommodate the greater element of uncertainty which these changes usually introduce. But the future will most probably see the growth of less structured and more personalized pay arrangements intended to meet the new conditions.

The main development occurs in the incentive system, where changes aim to focus more attention on the need for performance. The spread of newer electronic technologies generally reduces the extent to which variation in output is controlled by the workers, and older methods of computing their contribution are no longer valid or feasible. The development is, therefore, dependent on creating better and more acceptable assessment methods than those which have been applied in the past.

FURTHER READING

Advisory Conciliation and Arbitration Services (ACAS), *Appraisal Related Pay*, ACAS, London, 1990

Armstrong, Michael and Murlis, Helen, *Reward Management: A Handbook of Salary Administration*, Kogan Page, London, 1988

Boston Consulting Group, *Perspectives of Experience*, BCG, 1970

Bowey, Angela (ed.), *Managing Salary and Wages Systems*, 3rd edn, Gower, Aldershot, 1989

Connock, S., 'Workforce flexibility: juggling time and task', *Personnel Management*, October 1985

Cummings, L.L. and Schwab, D.P., Systems for Appraisal and Development, *Performance in Organisations: Determinants and Appraisal* (pp. 118–30), Scott Foresman, 1973

Fowler, Alan, *Performance Related Pay*, Southern Provincial Employers' Organisation, Winchester, 1988

Incomes Data Services, *Paying for Performance in the Public Sector – A Progress Report*, IDS/Coopers and Lybrand Public Sector Unit, London, 1989

Local Authorities Conditions of Service Advisory Board, *Handbook on Performance Related Pay*, LACSAB, London, 1990

Mason, Bob and Terry, Michael, *Trends in Incentive Payment Systems: Into the 1990s*, University of Strathclyde, June, 1990

Smith, I, *The Management of Remuneration*, Gower, Aldershot, 1984

Thomason, G.F., *Job Evaluation: Objectives and Methods*, IPM, 1980

60 Employee benefits

Peter Mumford

Some indication of the importance of benefits used to supplement the attraction of basic salary can be found by studying the job advertisements in any leading national daily newspaper: 'the remuneration package includes negotiable basic salary, commission, bonus, car and pension scheme'; 'this position offers an attractive benefits package . . . as well as an excellent salary we will offer a full range of large company benefits'; 'the exceptional benefits package includes an above average salary, bonus, pension, executive car, medical insurance, relocation expenses . . .'; 'subsidized travel'.

The practice of adding a range of benefits was developed during the period when salaries and wages were strictly controlled by government legislation. These benefits were seen as the only means of rewarding achievement and keeping or attracting good quality staff. Once given, such benefits are difficult to reduce or eliminate, so they continued even in times of high unemployment. When a period of high employment occurs, together with a shortage of many types of staff, there is a tendency for the practice to develop further.

If such things as interest-free loans and mortgages are included, share options and performance bonuses for senior executives, plus say £25 000 for an executive car every two years, the cost of these benefits can easily exceed the cost of salaries.

The elements of the benefit or, as it is sometimes called, compensation package, arise from a variety of causes. The work of dispensing them would be simplified if wages or salary were the only element, but this is hardly likely to be attained. Therefore, it is worth examining these packages to try and establish some comparison between their actual and assumed benefits.

SALARY AND BENEFITS

Basic salary

The main factor in most packages is basic salary, and it is frequently the key to other benefits (for example, the type of car is often related to the salary band).

Although a different approach – guaranteed incomes and so forth – is increasingly being used for production workers, it is still common for the basic salary to be considerably less than bonuses or allowances. This creates many anomalies. For example, a foreman, whose performance in arranging work and maintaining good relationships can have a material effect on the output of many workers, may be paid a fixed salary, while the workers can earn a bonus. The foreman has to go sick to obtain tangible benefit from the fixed salary.

Benefits

Good benefits can sometimes make up for a poorly-planned salary structure, but unless they are used flexibly to suit a variety of needs they may exacerbate problems. The offer of further benefits to overcome these problems or to placate groups will result only in added costs. It is much sounder policy to get the basic salary anomalies ironed out and then build a series of benefit packages which meet the real needs of the employees and the organization and give a positive return on top of this.

Many unions have recognized that so-called fringe benefits can be just as attractive to their members as straight wages increases, especially when they create the risk of advancing into a higher tax bracket. Recent examples which have caused consternation among other unions have included private health scheme membership and share schemes.

The boundaries between blue- and white-collar workers are becoming even more blurred under pressures of social change, the desire for increased status, and the well-publicized approaches of Japanese and other companies setting up local manufacturing plants, who bring with them their own concepts of equality in dress, canteens and so on.

All these pressures make it even more imperative that the basic salary and wage structures are soundly based, felt to be fair and administered openly. Openness is a fairly new concept to many organizations, but where the benefits of more open styles of management are being sought, it is anomalous to preserve secrecy over the rewards for greater involvement and commitment. Resentment and jealousy are far more a product of assumption made about another person's earnings for a perceived level of work than awareness of what different scales and pay brackets mean.

It is worth noting that in local government, where salary scales are well publicized, there is little cause for comparing one individual's earnings with another. There might, of course, be discussion about how an employee was promoted to a particular salary bracket, but this is on a far smaller scale than might be the case in private industry, where such matters are frequently surrounded in secrecy and hence are prime grounds for speculation.

COMPANY CAR

Chief of the benefits currently being offered is the company car. Starting from the basis of an essential tool for representatives and others who genuinely have to travel to do their jobs, the company car has developed into an essential perk for all jobs above quite a modest level and an important status symbol for middle- and senior-level managers. As such, it can become a cause of friction among those employees who seek to get into a better car bracket, or who have more extras than the next person, or merely spend hours of work time discussing the merits of one type or another. In addition, if a car is provided it must be seen as essential, so it has to be used – with the result that many executives spend much time as drivers when they could be more productive.

Taking into account the capital, running and repair costs, as well as the savings on travel to work, a company car is probably worth an average of £6000 p.a. to the recipient, a significant factor in any benefits package. As well as the financial benefits, there is the status effect of the company car, and the subsequent two-car family which it makes possible. Since some 50 per cent of cars on the road are company owned, it is very unlikely that this item could be replaced by other forms of benefit. Certainly, the level of salary increase required to provide the equivalent value would be very high and, because of this, it would undoubtedly set off a chain reaction of pay claims to restore previous differentials.

So powerful is the company car market that it has had a significant influence on the design of most mass production models, in spite of increased taxation on the benefit of the car.

PENSIONS

Pensions represent another area where the distinction between blue- and white-collar is being eroded and most organizations now offer them right across the whole spectrum of employees.

Pension schemes usually impose restrictions on age and service to avoid the starting up of a multitude of small agreements with little hope of survival. This is particularly important in the light of current regulations for portability which could present major administrative problems where there is high labour turnover. The intention is that everyone in full-time employment shall be entitled to a pension to which they and their employers may contribute and which may be taken with them, without loss of benefit, each time they change jobs.

From 2000 onwards the value of these pensions will, to some extent, be offset against reductions in the present supplementary earnings-related pension (SERP) scheme which, because of the ageing of the population, will become an increasing burden on those who are working.

The basis of most company pension schemes is a contribution of 5 to 6 per cent of salary by the employee, backed by contributions of around 6 to 8 per cent by the employer. The pension due at retirement age is calculated at 1/60 of the final or average of three final years' salary for every year of service, with a maximum of 60 per cent. Schemes vary enormously from those to which the employee does not contribute, to 'top-hat' policies for senior executives and directors, giving particularly generous terms. In education and other parts of the public service, 1/80 of final salary is more common, but the apparent meanness is offset by better index-linking arrangements. In times of high inflation these are most valuable.

The cost of pension provision is bound to increase as living standards improve, expectations are higher, retirement age falls and life expectancy increases.

LOANS AND MORTGAGES

Access to loans and mortgages at cheap or nil interest rates are a special incentive to younger staff who may be setting up home or buying the first car, and hence have good attraction power. Loans and mortgages are more generally the province of organizations in the finance business (banks, building societies, finance houses, and so on) but in times of high inflation they are often used by other companies to attract staff. Local authorities may also offer these facilities. They can, of course, have a prison effect, whereby employees will be reluctant to leave because of the high cost of obtaining a new loan.

It should be noted that low-interest mortgages from the organization cannot be used to exceed the £30 000 limit on tax-free interest payments on, for example, building society loans.

DISCOUNTS ON GOODS AND SERVICES

Discounts can be particularly valuable and attractive where the services or goods are desirable consumer products. Of particular interest are low-cost travel for airline, rail and shipping staff, and semi-luxury goods. Control must be exercised on these to prevent abuse by friends and relations of employees.

In times of full employment it is not unknown for staff to plan a progression of jobs through various organizations in order to set themselves up with possessions at substantial savings.

MEALS AND ENTERTAINMENT

It is doubtful if anyone has ever worked harder because of a good canteen or the provision of subsidized meals. However, these facilities – often provided at great cost in terms of staff and space as well as running expenses – are undoubtedly a great incentive to people to join the organization, especially where outside catering facilities may be remote or expensive.

It is at least arguable that where signs of malnutrition are reappearing in the population because of overindulgence in junk foods, absentee and sickness costs could be reduced by the provision of attractive real food at unrefusable prices. Communal dining facilities also provide opportunities for discussion of work problems, often between staff who would not normally meet. In the case of senior managers, substantial saving of time can be achieved by use of dining rooms where visitors can be entertained rather than by taking them to expensive restaurants outside.

However, staff and works canteens, like railway sandwiches, have a reputation for poor quality, which is frequently undeserved and is often caused by the behaviour of the staff rather than the quality of meals. A 'Tom's cafe' arrangement in a works, serving little more imaginative food than egg and chips, can enjoy a very high rating because of Tom and his staff.

It is possible for a canteen to become a negative benefit, the subject of endless niggles and involvement by the personnel department who would be more profitably employed on other activities. To overcome this problem one organization successfully reduced overheads by turning over the management of the canteen to the staff association. The subsidy was maintained at the prevailing level, but in all other respects the staff had total control. The benefit rapidly became tangible and, as a side issue, the staff association become more willing to appreciate the management's point of view on other issues. One leading retail organization is so convinced of the value of adequate canteen and refreshment facilities as an aid to productivity and quality that it advises and assists its suppliers to improve theirs.

Rather than run the restaurants themselves many organizations subcontract to specialists, agreeing the level of subsidy and the prices to be charged.

As a move towards single status some companies have only one canteen which is open to all. While this creates problems – oily overalls may create difficulties for other staff who have to work in smart clothes – in general, it does help to improve relations and reduce the 'them and us' or works *v* staff divide. On the other hand head offices of large companies retain strict segregation arrangements, with several tiers of canteens, restaurants and dining rooms used according to status and reflecting the culture of the organization.

The alternative, where in-house facilities cannot be provided or the attractions outside are too great, is to provide luncheon vouchers. While the amount is limited by tax rules, they do provide a small incentive when recruiting and help to encourage staff to eat at lunch time, with consequent health benefits.

Entertainment as a specific benefit is usually confined to executives, but attractions such as subsidized social clubs could also be considered under this heading. With increased varieties of entertainment available elsewhere, however, the attractions of sports and social clubs have diminished. It is likely that a comparatively small number of staff will use the facilities, and therefore the cost will be high in terms of the returns.

As a by-product of publicity and advertising activities, many executives, and even in some cases the whole of the staff, are able to benefit from sponsorship of sporting or cultural activities. The provision of hospitality at major sporting and social events, membership fees for golf and other clubs, are all seen as legitimate business activitites and an attraction and incentive to the users.

GIFTS AND SPECIAL BONUSES

These often represent a carry-over from the days of paternalism, but many organizations still use gifts or bonuses in cash or kind, as a means of maintaining good relations, rewarding special efforts or expressing general goodwill (for example, the case of wine at Christmas). In sales and marketing departments it is quite common to find events such as 'salesman of the year' which are rewarded by gifts, a special bonus or holidays. An underlying, but frequently very powerful, motivator is the fact that by involving wives and families in the largesse and rewards they will exert pressure for, or accept the penalties of, additional efforts.

Cash bonuses, paid at regular intervals, should ideally relate to the profitability of an organization, otherwise they are taken for granted and may cause ill will if for any reason they have to be omitted or reduced on occasion. It is important, too, that people receiving them are able to relate their own efforts to the value of the reward, otherwise the incentive value is lost.

HEALTH INSURANCE

Private medical care has become increasingly appreciated by the employee, who can obtain speedy treatment by the desired specialist. The organization benefits in terms of recruitment and, perhaps more importantly, through the earlier return to fitness of key staff.

If the organization does not want, or is unable, to carry the cost itself, the formation of a group scheme provides substantial savings to staff who participate.

The provision of private health facilities offends the political and social convictions of many unions and individuals. Nissan UK faced this dilemma when drawing up terms of employment for their plant at Sunderland. Their solution, which seems to work well, is to offer the facility to all staff, but to allow each individual freedom to join or not. In terms of the growth of a more prosperous, less socially divisive work-force, it is undoubtedly a move to be encouraged by management.

A corollary to medical insurance, although the service is frequently a part of the policy, is the preventive aspect. This may range from health checks of various sorts, provided free or at discounted prices, to membership of sports clubs in an endeavour to encourage exercise and an increased level of fitness by staff.

SABBATICALS

Although the concept of sabbaticals has been part of the academic scene for a very long time, they are an innovation for industry and commerce and may take many forms. The traditional one is a period of leave in which to study something related to the individual's job or development and/or the needs of the organization.

It may also be used as a reward or period of recovery from an exceptionally demanding or valuable piece of work, or even as a privilege to recognize rank. In some cases the sabbatical has already progressed through these stages to become an extra period of leave after a given length of service which can be aggregated over several years and used for almost any purpose, such as an extended trip abroad.

One leading organization has used the concept, if not the title, to combine a number of benefits: to extend the interests of an individual, perhaps in preparation for retirement; to meet the organization's social or community objectives; and to reduce an excess of staff at particular levels caused by changes in the structure. While retaining full salary, the individual works for the charity, community project or other activity seen to be socially desirable by them and their organization.

A few companies are recognizing the benefits of staff exchanges with, for instance, the services, police, education or government departments. An extension of the idea which could be particularly valuable would be an exchange between supplier and retailer or customer.

TRAINING AND DEVELOPMENT

The benefits to be gained by both trainees and the organization from a properly designed training and development programme are difficult to overestimate. While there is always the risk that a person who has received expensive training may seek the opportunity to exploit these abilities elsewhere, there is a great benefit to the organization not only to have the skills available, but no less important, to ensure that it makes effective use of the staff it has trained and so retains their services.

Some companies have set up open learning centres where staff may study, especially through C.A.L. or distance learning courses that have nothing to do with and may far exceed the companies' expected needs. They believe that this provision acts as a powerful motivation, a generator of goodwill and togetherness in the organization.

SHARE OWNERSHIP

Share ownership has been hailed by many as the cream of benefits. It gives all employees a stake in their organization and its success. It is assumed that commitment and dedication will increase as a result. In the UK, government backing has been given for these schemes through tax relief and there are now some 3 000 in British industry, with approximately 1 000 profit-sharing or savings-related share schemes. They will be given a great boost when a porportion of earnings related to company profitability are allowed to be tax free.

The ultimate in owner schemes is seen where employees are owners of the whole company, either as a result of a buyout or by gift.

But what will happen when profit share forms a major component of earnings and the organization has a bad year? This may well be in spite of the best efforts of the staff and could result in frustration and large pay claims to restore the level of earnings at a time when the organization is least able to support increased costs.

The following conditions must prevail in order for these schemes to be successful:

1 The organization must be well managed and forward thinking
2 There must be good relationships
3 Staff must be able to have a material influence on results
4 Results should not fluctuate too widely from year to year
5 Staff should be trained to interpret results
6 Staff should be committed and informed.

As a subdivision of employee shareholding schemes there are executive share options. This is perhaps the fastest growing area and is now seen as an essential element in attracting high-calibre senior executives.

Against the enthusiasm for share participation it must also be admitted that a recent survey by the Wider Share Ownership Council is at least open to the interpretation of a less than fully enthusiastic response to the value of such schemes.

CRECHES AND DAY NURSERIES

The make-up of the working population is changing, with more women returning to work and fewer school leavers available. It is estimated that women returning to work will make up 40 per cent of the workforce by the year 2000.

The provision of child-care arrangements while parents work will become an increasingly important attraction. Some surveys by companies finding difficulty in attracting staff have shown the availability of this facility as an important factor in influencing the choice of workplace.

Changes in the 1990 UK Budget allowed employers to charge creche facilities against tax and removed the liability to tax from those using them. But this can only benefit employees living near enough to their work to bring their children with them. Few parents would be willing to expose children to the perils of regular rush-hour commuter travel. To assist those parents who travel some distance to work and to make the provision of child care a real benefit, efforts are being made to set up a system of vouchers similar to luncheon vouchers which could be exchanged at any convenient centre.

This still leaves the problem of adjusting work hours to suit school hours. Systems of job share could, with flexible crèche arrangements, make it possible for two or more people to share both the job and the child care to the benefit of all.

KEEPING UP TO DATE

As needs and fashions change, it is essential to review the benefits package so that its cost brings the best return in terms of increased performance, attraction of staff, length of service, commitment to organizational aims, reduction in disputes or whatever the objectives of the policy are.

When reviewing its benefits policy, an organization should take the preferences of staff into account through individual consultation, through negotiation with employee representatives or by opinion surveys. While there is no point in increasing costs unnecessarily, a company which is aware of the needs and aspirations of its employees will be able to be proactive and gain much goodwill, rather than have to react under pressure and be perceived as old-fashioned or mean – a reputation which can be gained at very great expense.

Some preferences expressed by groups of employees might appear to be predictable – young employees would be less concerned with pension benefits than older ones who are nearer to retirement age. A recent survey in a large retail organization showed very definite preferences by staff for various types of benefits. The order of preferences was:

1   Pension scheme
2   Profit share scheme, + Christmas bonus
3   Staff discount
4   Private health scheme
5   Commission
6   Staff canteen
7   Extra holiday entitlement
8   Clothing allowance
9   Mortgage assistance
10   Free hairdressing
11   Interest-free credit, + free uniform
12   Luncheon vouchers
13   Long-service award
14   Extra sickness leave
15   Company car
16   Time off for study
17   Businesswear discount scheme
18   Personal loans
19   Holiday discount scheme

20 Relocation assistance
21 Subsidized chiropody service
22 Sports facilities
23 Social club
24 Season ticket loan.

It is interesting that in the case of the first choice, the percentage of staff opting for this varied according to age. Also worthy of note is the high preference expressed for commission as opposed to higher salaries:

Age group	Percentage
16–30	67
30–45	100
45–55	100
55+	71

This survey was, of course, valid only for the circumstances of the company in which it was conducted. It is likely, for example, that, for a firm based in a large conurbation with many commuting staff, the 24th choice (season ticket loan) would have been much higher up the scale. Dearer house prices and higher mortgage interest rates (both of which occurred since the survey was carried out) would undoubtedly have increased the attractiveness of the 9th item, especially among staff in the 19 to 30 years age group. These factors confirm the need to investigate which items will be voted most valuable by recipients, and hence more likely to represent value for money for the organization.

It is of course, relatively easy to carry out such surveys amongst the existing work-force. It is much more difficult to obtain relevant information from potential employees whom the organization may be having difficulties in recruiting. As an example, the provision of child-minding facilities may not be rated too highly by existing staff because they are already managing the situation, or may not have any children of that age. To potential employees, however, it may be the main reason why they are unable to join the organization.

Surveys and opinion polls are expensive to carry out amongst the general public but their results can be invaluable in helping to shape employment policies. The Department of Employment may be able to help by carrying out surveys. Job centres are also a useful source of assistance, as could be the local further education colleges or polytechnics which are invariably on the lookout for suitable projects for groups of students to tackle.

In structuring the benefits package it is also important to ensure that there is no discrimination on account of race, sex, and so on. Following a recent European Court ruling, differences in retirement ages and pension benefits between men and women will probably be eroded, allowing either sex greater freedom of choice in the matter.

A number of organizations have already lowered the normal retirement age to sixty-three. Such moves will have important implications for the cost of funding pensions which will be likely to start earlier and go on longer. Contrary to this thinking, pensionable age limits may rise rather than fall because of changes in the make-up of the population and the number of people available for work.

The subject of benefits has become such a complicated and important area of personnel management that many companies have set up separate employee compensation or benefits package departments. This brief insight should indicate that opportunities exist for both the organization and its employees to gain significant benefit from the costs which can be involved. Conversely, unless those benefits are applied with discretion and are well though out and planned, they can become just a drain on profits for very small return.

THE TAX POSITIONS

The Inland Revenue regards nearly all benefits in kind as well as cash as additional income and therefore taxable, unless they are expenses directly incurred for the purpose of the business.

However, within this broad definition there are many exceptions and anomalies. For instance, if a subsidized canteen or restaurant is provided for a small section of the work-force only (for example, a managers' dining room), this would be considered a taxable benefit for those entitled to use it. On the other hand, if subsidized meals are available to all staff, then there is no liability to tax.

The tax position on company cars is particularly complicated. It is affected by the age and value of the car, its engine cubic capacity and the earnings of the person concerned (that is, the charges generally apply only to people earning more than £8 500 per annum and most directors.

THE EUROPEAN COMMUNITY

The type of benefit available in different countries varies greatly. The high level of company cars is a uniquely British institution, so that, in the nature of things, these will be a natural target for harmonization if the increased tax levels have not overtaken events by that time. With high provision of maternity leave, for both parents in many countries, it is probable that crèche facilities will be encouraged together with such things as subsidized canteens.

Fortunately, the bureaucracy of the Community is usually slow-acting, so there should be ample warning of important changes. It may, however, be necessary to buy out – at considerable expense – some benefits which are not agreed to by the commissioners.

FURTHER READING

Bowey, Angela M. (ed.), *Managing Salary and Wage Systems*, 3rd edn, Gower, Aldershot, 1989

Copeman, G., Moore, P. and Arrowsmith, A., *Shared Ownership*, Gower, Aldershot, 1984

Green, F., *Unequal Fringes: Fringe Benefits in the UK*, Bedford Square Press, 1984

Lupton, T. and Bowey, A., *Pay and Benefits*, CCH edns, 1985

Smith, Ian, *The Management of Remuneration*, Gower, Aldershot, 1984

Toulson, Norman, *Managing Pension Schemes*, Gower, Aldershot, 1986

61 Health and safety

Brenda Barrett and Richard Howells

In the Health and Safety at Work Act 1974 (the 'Act') the UK Parliament addressed the problems of health and safety from a commonsense viewpoint. This approach sought a positive response from management, not in terms of minimal compliance but with wholehearted commitment to the ideal of making its enterprises safer and healthier for all concerned.

The Act remains the principal UK legislation governing safety at work, although it has been implemented by a number of regulatory codes relating to particular hazards, imposing duties of varying degrees of strictness. Increasingly such regulations are the national response to EC directives and the impact of the EC is likely to increase. However, the Act is expected to remain in force for the foreseeable future, although it may need some amendment to accommodate the EC's Framework Directive (the 'Directive').

FRAMEWORK OF GENERAL DUTIES

The Act was intended to have the effect of securing the health, safety and welfare of persons at work and protecting persons other than persons at work against risks to health or safety arising out of or in connection with the activities of persons of work. The legislature appreciated that these ambitious objectives could only be achieved within a framework of broad general duties. Thus, ss2–8 of the Act identify those persons, such as employers, contractors, controllers of premises and suppliers of articles and substances, whose conduct might create hazards at the workplace, and impose upon them general duties to have regard for the safety of others, enforced by criminal sanctions. In particular s2(1) imposes the duty on every employer to ensure, so far as is reasonably practicable, the health, safety and welfare at work of all his employees.

The Act differs from previous safety legislation in that it protects almost the whole of the work-force. It does not distinguish for this purpose between employees and self-employed persons, nor between management and shop floor, or blue-collar and white-collar status.

The Act demands well-organized and safe systems of work. The philosophy of the Act is, therefore, that all persons within an organization should be involved in the effort to achieve safer and healthier working conditions, and it is of paramount importance to managers devising strategies for the use of human resources. All managers need to examine their safety responsibilities in the light of their other functions, but the personnel manager has special safety responsibilities, such as the drafting and implementation of contracts of employment, the selection and training of personnel at all levels, and the formulation and administration of disciplinary and dismissal procedures. If managers fail to pay proper attention to these matters they cannot hope to achieve and maintain within the workforce the high level of safety competence which is necessary in order to comply with the spirit of the Act and the express provisions of regulations made under it.

THE CONTRACT OF EMPLOYMENT

The relationship between employer and employees and their mutual rights and duties is, in matters concerned with safety (as in all others), dependent first upon the express and implied terms of the contract of employment. In the absence of contractual duties, the employer and employee, whatever their respective obligations under labour legislation, would have no private rights, either of enforcement or other redress against each other. A satisfactory contract of employment should be couched in terms which provide adequately for the introduction, maintenance and enforcement of the safe systems of work which the Act requires employers to organize in discharge of their statutory duties.

A firm that has not formulated clear terms and conditions of employment, so that each employee knows the scope of his/her responsibility and authority, is unlikely to be either efficient or safe. The organization which attempts to treat safety in isolation is likely to run up against resistance as individuals suspect that they are being required to undertake new responsibilities and to sacrifice existing rights. Except where individuals have special safety functions (such as a safety officer) it should not be necessary to negotiate special contractual terms in order to comply with the Act.

The requirements of s2(2)(c) that an employer supply 'such information, instruction, training and supervision as is necessary to ensure the health and safety at work of his employees' may be facilitated by the general contract of employment. An employer could, for example, go some way towards discharging his obligations to inform the employee by incorporating into the contract an indication of the particular hazards to which the employee is likely to be exposed and the appropriate safeguards to minimize the risks. The contract might describe the job in terms which imply that it is a condition that the employee holds himself out as having certain skills to deal with specific hazards (for example, a person employed as an electrician would be expected to assimilate and observe the obligations imposed on the worker by the Electricity at Work Regulations 1989).

The contract of employment is also the source of the duties that may be required of an employee. These contractual duties may include detailed requirements for the employee's own protection, and for the protection of others. The general duty of an employee under s7 of the Act is 'to take reasonable care for the health and safety of himself and other persons and to cooperate with his/her employer, or any other persons', so far as is necessary to enable the others to perform the duties imposed on them by safety legislation. It is likely that the terms of a contract of employment will throw considerable light upon what the individual employee can be expected to do to display reasonable care for the safety of others.

The statutory requirement that the employee co-operate with the employer to enable that employer to perform the duties imposed upon him by safety legislation means that the employee is required, in order to discharge his/her contractual obligations fully, to obey reasonable orders in the context of safety, and also to exercise personal competence in safety as well as in vocational skills. Regard should therefore be paid not only to the provisions of clear job specifications which may involve an express delegation of safety duties to the employee, but also to the utilization of disciplinary procedures for those who do not comply with the standards expected of them by the terms of their contracts.

COMPANY SAFETY POLICY

Many firms may well already have, or may wish to introduce, safety rules within their organization. These may be published in the arrangements for the implementation of a safety policy required under s2(3), or within a firm's handbook, or quite separately as codes of practice related to special tasks. However, where such rules are actually spelt out in detail it is advisable to refer to them and the place in the safety policy at which they may be found. There can be few firms who do not have some sort of safety rules, if it is only 'no smoking' signs. It is unlikely that these rules form contractual terms for individual workers, but they are likely to be deemed reasonable orders for the employer to give the employee, so that it would be a breach of the employee's contract to disobey them, and there is judicial support for this view in *Secretary of State* v *ASLEF* (1972). In this case the Court of Appeal was asked to decide whether railway workers engaged in an industrial dispute were in breach of their contracts of employment when they had 'worked to rule' by carrying out unnecessary safety checks and thus delaying trains. Their Lordships were of the opinion that the employee's interpretation of the rule book was unreasonable. They also held that, although the rule book was not itself part of the contract of employment of each individual employee, failure to obey it was a breach of contract. The words of Roskill L J summarize the position well:

> It was not suggested that strictly speaking this formed part of the contract of employment as such. But every employer is entitled within the terms and the scope of the relevant contract of employment, to give instructions to his employees and every employer is correspondingly bound to accept instructions properly and lawfully so given. The rule book seems to me to constitute instructions given by the employer to the employee in accordance with that general legal right.

A firm wishing to raise its standards of health and safety will be well advised to review its rules on safety, to amend and supplement them when necessary, to make sure that they are known and understood by employees and, finally, to take care that they are actually observed in practice.

Relationship between safety rules, disciplinary rules and grievance procedures

The Employment Protection (Consolidation) Act 1978 s1(4)(a) requires that the written particulars of terms of employment, which all full-time employees are entitled to receive by the thirteenth week of employment, shall include a note specifying any disciplinary rules applicable to the employee, or referring to a document which is reasonably accessible to the employee and which specifies such rules. Similarly, the employee is entitled to be informed as to the grievance procedure which he may invoke. However, s1 (5) of that Act expressly states that these requirements shall not apply to rules, disciplinary decisions, grievances or procedures relating to health and safety at work.

It is suggested that s1 (5) is intended for the protection of the rights of the employee. Disciplinary and grievance procedures often contain agreements for the maintenance of the status quo pending the resolution of the dispute. Thus, without this subjection the situation might arise where an employee who reported an allegedly unsafe situation might be required to go on working with it until an enquiry discovered whether the allegation was correct.

The safety policy

Section 2 (3) of the Act requires every employer of five or more persons to set out in a written statement the firm's general policy on health and safety at work, together with the organization and arrangements for carrying out that policy.

In large organizations, or in companies which operate from a number of sites, it is not uncommon to find that the policy statement relates to the whole organization and delegates responsibility for provision for safety organization and hazard arrangements to local level. Sometimes the responsibility may be imposed upon a site manager. Quite apart from any legal requirements, no company can be said to have achieved a safe system until this local task has been properly executed. This is a task which appears to fall within the province of the site office, to be carried out within the requirements of existing managerial structures at local level and with regard to the existing job specifications of individual employees.

Steps should be taken to ensure that a copy of the policy is received – and understood – by each new employee and the organization should monitor its performance to ensure that the systems set out in the policy are maintained. The safety policy, like the corporate plan (to which it ought logically to be related) should be kept under review and updated as circumstances demand, in consultation with employees.

CONSULTATION AND DISCLOSURE

Section 2 of the Act places emphasis upon disclosure of information and consultation with employees. The Safety Representatives and Safety Committees Regulations 1977 give recognized trade unions the right to appoint safety representatives and provide them with a statutory floor of rights. The functions of safety representatives are based on consulting with the employer with a view to the making and maintenance of arrangements which will enable both the employer and the employees to co-operate effectively in promoting and developing measures to ensure the health and safety at work of the employees. The safety representative has the following specific functions:

1 To investigate potential hazards and dangerous occurrences at the workplace and to examine the causes of accidents at the workplace
2 To investigate complaints by any employee they represent relating to that employee's health, safety or welfare at work

3   To make representations to the employer on matters arising out of (1) and (2)
4   To make representations to the employer on general matters affecting the health, safety or welfare at work of the employees at the workplace
5   To carry out safety inspections
6   To represent the employees they were appointed to represent in consultations at the workplace with inspectors of the Health and Safety Executive and of any other enforcing authority
7   To receive information from inspectors in accordance with s28 (8) of the 1974 Act (that is factual information about the workplace which the inspector has obtained in the course of his duties)
8   To attend meetings of safety committees in their capacity as safety representatives in connection with any of the above functions
9   To undergo such training in aspects of those functions as are reasonable having regard to the Code of Practice on Time Off for Training of Safety Representatives.

In workplaces where there are one or more recognized trade unions it is likely that the work-force will have opted to exercise the rights granted under the regulations. However, the regulatory provisions leave room for negotiation between employer and union on many aspects of the system, such as how many representatives may be appointed, the inspection procedures and the paid time off needed for safety representatives' functions. The better the climate of industrial relations at the workplace the more effective the system is likely to be.

Regulation 7 entitles safety representatives (or the employees whom they represent), if they have given the employer reasonable notice, to inspect and take copies of any document relevant to safety at the workplace which the employer is required to keep, except a document consisting of or relating to any health record of an identifiable individual. The employer is also required to make available to safety representatives, subject to certain exceptions, the information within the employer's knowledge necessary to enable them to fulfil their functions.

The Directive recognizes the importance of employee involvement. While it purports to authorize the use of existing national systems for worker involvement, it is difficult to reconcile this with its requirement for consultation with, and provision of, information to the whole work-force without reference to their being unionized. It seems likely, therefore, that UK law and practice will have to be changed at least to the extent necessary to ensure that all employers consult with and inform all their work-force.

Whatever the system of employee participation, its long-term effectiveness can only be assured if the employer keeps under review both the arrangement for its operation and the provision of trained persons to represent management in the consultation process.

TRAINING

The Act expressly requires employers, as one of the matters to which they must attend in order to discharge their general duty, to provide instruction and training to ensure the safety of their employees. This requirement makes it desirable to keep under review all aspects of the enterprise's existing training schemes and also to consider whether new training programmes should be introduced to deal with other areas which have hitherto been neglected. In particular, attention should be given to the following.

Induction courses

New employees, or employees starting work in a new capacity, need to be trained in the systems and practices of their firm. At the induction stage they should be made conversant with any safety rules which are of general application, in particular with emergency procedures for contingencies such as fire or other dangerous occurrences. Emphasis should be placed on the necessity for following such rules and the consequences of not doing so. Rules are more likely to be obeyed if the reason for them is understood, especially when training young employees.

Training for the job

Training in the operation of machinery and equipment should be given not only when employees start work, but whenever new methods are introduced. Such training should include safety, by making the operatives familiar with both the hazards and the means to protect themselves against accidents and ill health when carrying out routine operations. Workers should also be trained to respond to emergencies: for example they should know the procedure for obtaining the assistance of a trained first aider.

Special competence

The Directive imposes a general requirement on employers to designate competent employees. More detailed regulations already identify situations in which this duty may arise (for example, the Electricity at Work Regulations 1989 and the Control of Substances Hazardous to Health Regulations 1988). Compliance with such obligations calls for the special training of relevant employees.

It may be that such persons will be needed more generally, some for monitoring and maintaining systems for the control of hazards and others to bear special responsibilities in the event of catastrophe (for example, persons trained in first aid in accordance with The Health and Safety [First Aid] Regulations 1981). Indeed the Directive's reference to the allocation of responsibiliites to competent persons may well be related to the general obligation it places on employers to take such measures as are necessary to avoid risks and to evaluate those risks which cannot be avoided. Employers will be well advised to anticipate the implementation of the Directive and allocate special roles to named key employees who have been trained to the appropriate level of competence, to ensure a safe system of operation given the particular hazards inherent in the organization.

Specialist management training for safety

The firm may well decide that it should appoint managers (such as safety officers) with special responsibilities for safety, if it has not already done so, and to keep the status of the appointment under review. Special regard should be paid to the relationship of the safety officer to the general management structure. The question will probably be asked whether it is likely to be more effective to have one professionally trained safety manager at a fairly senior level or a number of safety officers, who have had some safety experience, at foreman level, or a combination of the two. It may be necessary to ask whether these could be full-time appointments, or whether these tasks should be carried out in conjunction with other duties. If other new appointments of this nature are being made, or if there are existing staff in posts who have had some safety training, the question should be asked whether the people concerned have been properly trained for the task.

Training in the requirements of legislation

The requirement of s2 (2) (c), that the employer provide information and training, has been interpreted as requiring the employer to train the employees to understand and observe the statutory duties imposed upon them.

Before the Act, the law required an employer to accept responsibility where an employee had suffered injury because he/she had not understood or complied with the full extent of his/her duties under specific regulations (for example, The Construction Regulations; see *Boyle* v *Kodak* (1969)). The basis of liability was the employer had failed to instruct the employee in the meaning of the regulations and his/her obligations under them. It seems unlikely that the Act requires a lower standard than this: indeed, this requirement is spelt out in recent regulations such as the Control of Substances Hazardous to Health Regulations 1988 and the Noise at Work Regulations 1989.

Management training

The Act does not confine training requirements to the provision of training for operatives to enable them to look after their own safety; it also requires training of managers in order to ensure safety. Thus, it takes into account the need to install and operate safe systems of work. Compliance with the Act therefore requires training of managers to enable them to introduce, operate and enforce safe systems of work.

Refresher courses

Initial training may not be adequate if nothing is done thereafter to ensure that the matters dealt with during training are observed in practice, and also that techniques are brought up to date in the light of changes in technology or the systems used in the organization. Therefore, any effective training scheme must include refresher courses.

Subcontractors and other persons

Section 3 of the Act requires every employer to conduct his undertaking in such a way as to ensure, so far as is reasonably practicable, that persons not in his employment who may be affected by it are not thereby exposed to risks to their health or safety. It is, therefore, the more important that work systems should have regard to the safety both of the general public and of visitors or subcontractors operating in circumstances where they might be endangered by the activities of the company's employees. It has been decided that an employer should make available to subcontractors' employees the same information as he/she gives to his/her own employees where that information is necessary to the safety either of the employer's own employees or employees of the subcontractor. (*R* v. *Swan Hunter Shipbuilders Ltd* [1981]). There may be circumstances where UK law makes it desirable to offer other workers the training intended for employees, although the Directive goes no further than to require communication of information.

Safety representatives

The Code of Practice for Time Off for Training of Safety Representatives provides that as soon as possible after their appointment safety representatives should be permitted time off with pay to attend basic training facilities approved by the TUC or by the independent trade union or unions which appoint the safety representative. Further training, similarly approved, should be undertaken where the safety representative has special responsibilities or where such training is necessary to meet changes in circumstances or relevant legislation.

The Code did not attempt to lay down standards for the length of training but said that basic training should take into account the functions of the safety representative. It should provide an understanding of the role of safety representatives, safety committees, and of trade union policies and practices in relation to:

1 The legal requirements relating to health and safety of persons at work, particularly the group and class of persons they directly represent
2 The nature and extent of workplace hazards and the measures necessary to eliminate or minimize them
3 The health and safety policy of the employer and organization and arrangements for fulfilling this policy.

Additionally, the Code suggests that safety representatives need to acquire particular skills in order to carry out their functions (including safety inspections) and to use basic sources of legal and official information provided by, or through, the employer on health and safety matters.

The Code states that when a trade union wants a safety representative to attend a course it should inform management of the course it has approved and supply a copy of the syllabus, indicating the particular relevance of its contents, if the employer asks for it. It should normally give at least a few weeks' notice of the safety representatives it has nominated for attendance. The number of safety representatives attending training courses at any one time should be that which is reasonable, bearing in mind the availability of the relevant courses and the operational requirements of the employer.

Unions and management are advised to reach an agreement on appropriate numbers and arrangements, and refer any problems which may arise to the relevant agreed procedures. Sometimes the employer himself may wish to provide the appropriate training (*White* v *Pressed Steel* (1980)).

It will be noted that the Code places the primary responsibility for defining the type of training needed for safety representatives upon trade unions. Nevertheless it is suggested that the personnel manager should consider what, if any, further training, possibly related to the special hazards and systems of the organization, should be provided for safety representatives beyond the basic statutory training. It must remain for the time being a matter of speculation what provisions, if any, will be necessary in the light of the Directive to ensure training of representatives drawn from non-unionized sectors of the workforce.

DISCIPLINE AND DISMISSAL

Operating a safety policy requires not only the introduction of a safe system of work but also its observance. There can be little doubt that the best mechanism for encouraging the adoption of safe systems of work by employees is by training and by example. Individual workers will usually follow the pattern of behaviour set by their colleagues and superiors, but even in the best run organizations there tend to be the occasional situations where people prefer to persist in their own unsafe practices rather than follow the good example of others. In these, presumably rare, cases the employer should be able to take disciplinary action to bring this behaviour to an end.

If the employer has laid down, and consistently sought to enforce, a system of work, together with rules of conduct for the promotion of safety, it should not be difficult to establish that a recalcitrant employee was aware of his responsibilities. There may be occasions when instant dismissal is warranted but, except in the most flagrant and serious cases of disregard for safety, the employer should follow his normal warning procedures for dealing with cases of misconduct.

It is possible that the provisions for worker involvement in safety matters already discussed will help to inculcate in employees generally the need to observe safety requirements and that the group may in turn exercise influence over the recalcitrant few.

Dismissal as a result of a prohibition notice

An employer may feel obliged to dismiss employees because a prohibition notice has been served which prevents the use, until further notice, of the plant or premises at which the employees are engaged. Under the Employment Protection (Consolidation) Act s57 (2) (d) the employer may dismiss an employee where, by continuing to work, the employer would be in breach of a duty or restriction imposed by or under an enactment. It must, however, be reasonable in all the circumstances to dismiss and, in particular, the employer should offer alternative employment when it exists.

Alternatively, it would seem that the situation might amount to a redundancy under s81 of the Employment Protection (Consolidation) Act.

The employer might wish to suspend his employees during the time the notice is in force, but he cannot thus avoid payment of wages unless there is an express term in the contract permitting suspension. An employer faced with a prohibition notice requiring cessation of work would be likely, at least, to have to make guarantee payments, in accordance with s12 of the Employment Protection (Consolidation) Act, even if he were contractually entitled to lay off his employees.

COMPANY HEALTH POLICY

Protection of health

The need to protect workers from health risks has received increased emphasis in the years since the Act came into force. Regulations, such as the Control of Lead at Work Regulations 1982, imposed duties on employers for the protection of their employees against specific hazards. The Control of Substances Hazardous to Health Regulations now require assessment of the health hazards at the work-place, the setting up of systems for their control and, if necessary, the provision of protective equipment to workers. In some situations it is necessary to monitor the health of individual employees and to keep medical records over along periods of time.

Incidentally, the fear of suspension and dismissal may well have deterred employees in the past from participating in employers' schemes for medical inspection and testing. But now the employer may, in many cases, have statutory authority to carry out medical tests. It might, however, be advisable for employers to consider whether it would be beneficial to negotiate contractual terms under which an employee agrees to have regular medical inspections, whether or not these are legally required. Under such a scheme the employee might be required to accept the decision of the company's doctor on his fitness for work in exchange for insurance rights to cover sickness or possibly early retirement. Such a scheme might be particularly attractive to employers in future since the new regulations (such as the Noise at Work Regulations) might well encourage litigation for compensation for ill health which has been caused by working conditions. The operation of the system might provide the evidence of the ill health and its cause and the regulations are likely to enable the victim to found his civil claim on the employer's breach of statutory duty.

Dismissal on grounds of ill health

There may be occasions when a dismissal is fair because the employee's health is such that the employer cannot provide work without exposing that employee, and/or other workers' or the public, to unwarranted risk of personal injury. For example, a road transport firm might well be able to justify the dismissal of a driver found to be liable to diabetic coma while driving. The view emerging from unfair dismissal case law is that before dismissing for reasons of ill health the employer should endeavour to obtain a medical opinion and to discuss with the employee the needs of both parties. The dismissal will be fair if the ill health of the employee is causing the employer to break his duty to provide reasonably safe working conditions for other employees. Employees who are dismissed in contravention of the Employment Protection (Consolidation) Act's provisions relating to medical suspension will, of course, be deemed to have been unfairly dismissed.

HOW THE SYSTEM WORKS

External authorities

Managers may be better placed to comply with the law and to work towards achieving a safe workplace if they have some knowledge of the legislative and administrative framework within which safety laws are made and enforced.

Primary responsibility for implementation of the Health and Safety at Work Act rests with the Health and Safety Commission. This is a corporation consisting of not more than nine and not less than six persons. Its duties include assisting and encouraging people to carry out the general purposes of the Act and making arrangements for carrying out, and publishing, the results of research. The Commission is also required to make such arrangements as it considers appropriate to ensure that government departments, employers, employees, employers' organizations and unions are provided with an information and advisory service on the implications of the Act.

There is also a corporate body, consisting of three people, known as the Health and Safety Executive: this body employs most of the inspectors who visit workplaces to advise on and enforce the law. Some enforcement, particularly in relation to shops, offices and services, is undertaken by local authority inspectors on behalf of the Health and Safety Executive.

As well as, or instead of, instituting criminal proceedings for breach of regulatory duties, the inspectorate is empowered to issue improvement and prohibition notices. Under s21 of the Act an inspector may serve an improvement notice on a person (in practice this is frequently an employer) when the inspector is of the opinion that the person is contravening one or more statutory provisions. It will require that person to remedy the situation within a specified period. An inspector may serve a prohibition notice, under s22, upon a person who is in control of activities, which, in the inspector's opinion, involve a risk of serious personal injury. Where an immediate prohibition notice is served the activities to which the notice relates must stop immediately.

It is not the practice of the inspectorate to institute proceedings or even serve notices where they have confidence in the standards achieved by, and the attitude of management to, safety issues. An important part of the function of the inspectorate is to advise management how to achieve safe workplaces and the managers should not hesitate to take advantage of this facility. Similarly the publications of the Commission are frequently of great value since they indicate both the expectations of the Commission and the way in which safety can be achieved. Copies of the Act and regulations and codes of practice made under the Act, are obtainable from HMSO. EC directives are not generally applicable in member states until they have been implemented through the national legislative process.

Corporate, management and employee responsibilities

The main emphasis of the Act is upon duties of the employer to ensure health and safety at his workplace. The law does not allow employers to avoid their legal responsibilities merely by delegating to others (even employees of management status) the task of achieving safety at the workplace. However, the corporate employer will not in all situations have to accept the sole, or indeed any legal, responsibilities for unsafe practices at work. Section 36 of the Act provides that where the commission of an offence is due to the act or default of some other person than the one upon whom the law has imposed the duty, that other person shall be guilty of the offence, whether or not proceedings are taken against the person primarily responsible. Thus, prosecution of an employee under this section may or may not relieve the employer of his/her primary responsibility. This is a matter for the discretion of the Health and Safety Executive.

The 'other person' might well be a line manager, who could commit an offence under the Act in a number of ways. For example, where the obligation laid upon the employer is necessarily delegated to the manager for discharge, the latter may be guilty of an offence under s36. The point may be illustrated by the instance of an unfenced machine in a factory. The basic obligation to fence under s14 of the Factories Act or s2 of the Act will fall upon the occupier or the employer respectively. This may well mean in practice that the duty is imposed upon a corporate body. However, responsibility for safeguarding the machine within the organization under the corporate safety policy will actually be assigned to a named manager. If the latter neglects this obligation, that manager may be prosecuted under s36.

Again, in the same circumstances, the line manager may be guilty of an offence as an employee who, under s7 (above) has failed to 'co-operate' with his employer to enable the latter to discharge his duty to safeguard the machine. Another possibility is that there may be Regulations which impose an obligation upon a line manager personally; in such a case the primary responsibility for performance of this duty will rest upon the manager and not the employer.

Finally, s37 of the Act contains a standard director's liability clause imposing criminal liability upon any director, manager, secretary, or other officer of the firm whose consent, connivance or neglect has caused or contributed to an offence which the firm has committed. In one case a director was convicted under this section even though no charges were laid against the company itself (*J. Armour* v *J. Skeen* (1977)).

Whether a manager is deemed to be subject to liability at board room level or line manager level must clearly depend upon the status of the appointment and the nature of his/her responsibilities. In each case, however, the probability of personal liability being incurred under the provisions listed in this chapter will be minimized if the manager has done all that is possible, for a person in his/her position, to ensure health and safety at the workplace within the resources available.

Where there is special regulatory legislation, such as the Act, the UK tradition until recently has been to prosecute for safety offences under that legislation rather than under the general criminal law. However, there is now some evidence that this practice is changing. In some cases where there has been loss of life, the corporate employer, managers and other employees may be charged additionally or alternatively with a general criminal offence such as manslaughter.

FURTHER READING

Of the many codes and regulations on health and safety at work Croner's *Health and Safety at Work*, Croner Looseleaf Service, provides the best quick source of reference.

Howells, R. and Barrett, B., *The Health and Safety at Work Act*, Institute of Personnel Management, 1982

Redgrave's *Health and Safety in Factories*, Butterworth, 1976.

62 Training

Darek Celinski

This chapter is about training people who work in organizations. Adapting the usual dictionary definition, 'training' can be described as 'bringing people who work in organizations to desired standards of job performance through instruction and practice'. The role of training never varies, and the methods and procedures required to design, organize and conduct training are the same for every organization.

INTRODUCTION

Training within organizations can be divided into two main areas:

1 Training young people for their first adult jobs
2 Training newly appointed and established adults, including managers and supervisors.

Young people in their first jobs

The usual reason why organizations recruit and train young people for their first adult jobs in life is to secure a continuous supply of appropriately qualified men and women needed to fill future vacancies for key personnel. Organizations achieve this by operating special training schemes for young people which, depending on the qualifications they are designed to provide, take two, three or four years to complete. The training itself is mainly in the form of attachments to a series of departments within the organizations, usually integrated with periods of related studies at further or higher education establishments. Participants usually receive a formal, recognized qualification on successful completion of the training.

Each organization decides what training schemes are appropriate to its needs. These may be for craftspeople, technicians, technologists, administrators and other specialist and professional personnel.

The organizations which operate any of these schemes normally decide each year on how many young people to recruit and for which jobs they should be trained. When making these plans, future needs for key personnel are estimated by reference to the corporate or equivalent long-range plans.

The skills used when operating these schemes are mainly organizational and administrative; they are not relevant to the chief purpose of this chapter. Thus, the remainder of this chapter deals with the training of adults who work in the organizations.

Adults

Training adults within organizations is a specialist service function. In each case it starts with the managers and supervisors identifying training needs and defining job performance targets for their subordinates. Training then provides the specialist service of bringing these people to those desired standards.

Training produces the greatest benefits when it is structured so that all the separately identified training needs equate as a whole with the organization's corporate or long-range plan. Thus, it is for the organization's top management to decide the results they want to achieve, and it is the role of training to help top management in achieving them.

MISSIONS AND VISIONS

Probably the best approach to explaining the training of adults within an organization is to provide an example of the organization's mission and vision statements and describe the strategy for achieving them.

Stating missions and visions is a modern management practice that can be used by organizations when developing their corporate, or equivalent long-range plans. This process starts with the organization defining its 'mission' by providing a concise, single-sentence answer to the question 'What business are we in?' The next step is to state its 'vision', which means defining the results that the organization has decided it needs to achieve in order to be successful and to grow and prosper. The final step is to develop strategies which provide answers to the question 'What must we do to achieve each vision statement?' The answers are then presented in the form of the organization's corporate or equivalent plan.

For example, an international airline might make the following mission and vision statements:

- *Mission* To provide a world-wide air travel and transport service
- *Vision* To be voted the world's best airline by *Executive Travel Magazine* (which conducts such voting each year and publishes its findings).

After defining the mission and vision of the whole organization, the best results are obtained when the mission and vision of each principal function and of each department are also defined. For training, these might be stated as follows:

1 *Mission* To help the organization fulfil its corporate plans by raising job performance standards so that the people who work there, their sections and their departments become as efficient as desired by management
2 *Vision* That *every* training need which arises anywhere in the organization is promptly and fully satisfied so that:

- there are no complaints of any kind received from clients or customers about any product or service supplied by the organization
- all work is 'right first time', with no scrap or rework produced anywhere in the organization
- all work is produced on time, with no delays or wasted time anywhere within the organization

- all materials, machines and equipment are correctly used, so that there is no misuse or damage to any of these anywhere in the organization
- everyone complies with the relevant safety rules and regulations and uses safe working practices, so that no notifiable injuries take place in the organization
- the efficiency and productivity of all sections and departments, and of the whole organization, is increased each year by the amounts specified in the corporate plan.

If the results that management expect from training can be set out as precisely as those in the above examples, their satisfaction is almost guaranteed. With such precise definition of training needs it becomes a relatively simple matter to design and conduct training that satisfies each vision statement. Should subsequent performance fall short of any of these vision statements, this would immediately be recognized and, again, precise training or retraining can be planned and carried out. Post-training satisfaction of vision statements is the best possible indicator that training has been effective.

Stating training missions and visions is a highly flexible process that can be used by all kinds and sizes of organizations and in all areas of training (including management and supervisory). The greatest benefits accrue when these statements reflect the organization's long-term plans and objectives. Top management sets these plans and objectives, they should therefore be involved in formulating the training mission and vision statements because only they have the necessary information.

The return on investment in training should be far greater than the cost. Satisfaction of properly formulated training vision statements produce significant financial benefits. Popular estimates suggest that as much as 25 per cent of the operating costs of organizations which fail to provide adequate training is spent on correcting mistakes, wasted time and materials, and other inefficiencies.

STRATEGY FOR SATISFYING TRAINING VISION

There are two prerequisites that must be fulfilled before a strategy can be developed. These are:

1 That the organization employs at least one specialist who has been trained to design, organize and conduct training (in the manner described in this chapter)
2 That the managers and supervisors are willing to give their full support to the training specialist, and to comply with the necessary disciplined methods and procedures (again, as described in this chapter).

The strategy should be aimed at fulfilling the vision statement that 'every training need which arises anywhere within the organization is satisfied in full'. The strategy in this case will amount to setting up and maintaining strict controls so that systematically conducted training is provided whenever anyone who works in the organization is:

1 *Newly appointed* After being newly recruited into the organization; after

being newly transferred within the organization to do a different job; or after being newly promoted into a higher level job within the organization

2 *To be affected by changes* When his or her job is to be affected by changes to products or services, methods of working, procedures, technology, machines, materials, equipment, and any other changes that require him or her to do some aspects of their job differently from existing practice

3 *Required to improve his or her job performance* In this case the immediate manager or supervisor requires an individual to do specific aspects of the job better than he or she is doing it at present. This includes the situation where any one of the training vision statements is not being satisfied in full, so that an improvement in its level of fulfilment is required.

The above defines the only circumstances in which organizations need to provide training. This means that when every one of the above statements has been satisfied, training within the organization is producing the greatest benefits of which it is capable.

To emphasize that these are the only situations where training is essential, it is in these cases that people will learn for themselves even if no formal training is provided. For example, if a newly recruited person is not given any training immediately after joining, he or she will not just sit and wait but will do his or her best to find out what is required and will attempt to learn the new job by trial and error. Unavoidably, such learning is slow, inefficient, uncertain, and likely to result in low standards of performance. By providing expertly conducted training whenever any need arises, organizations eliminate all need for learning by trial and error thus their efficiency and productivity are measurably increased.

Conversely, there is never any need for training other than because of a new appointment, a change, or to produce a precisely defined improvement in job performance. As there is no need, any learning acquired cannot be applied on the job. Hence, the training makes no contribution towards improving efficiency and productivity of organizations. Therefore, it should never be provided.

TRAINING TO SATISFY THE ORGANIZATION'S NEEDS

Systematic on-the-job training is the main training method of satisfying learning needs that arise within organizations. 'Systematic' means that it is conducted by part-time *departmental trainers*. They are people who have been trained in using, and actually use, an *instructional technique* when they are instructing. 'On the job' means that the training is conducted at the place of work where the job that is being learned is normally performed.

People who work in organizations learn their jobs by actually doing them. This means that even when a job has been learnt on a training course, the learning is not completed until it has been applied on the job so that, through practice, the desired standard of its performance is achieved. Thus, on the job is by far the best place for training people who work in organizations.

In addition to its high effectiveness, systematic on-the-job training is the only form of training that can be provided at a very short notice at almost any time, at practically every workplace, within every section and department. Thus, it is in practice the only form of training that can satisfy the very high volumes of learning needs that arise within organizations. This means that systematic on-the-job training is the only form of training that can produce measurable improvements in the efficiency and productivity of organizations, and that without it, none of these improvements can be achieved.

There are organizations where attendance at courses is the only form of training provided. Even when as much of this kind of training as possible is provided, it caters for only a small fraction of the organization's learning needs. This is why reliance on external courses alone will not improve efficiency and productivity. But, although systematic on-the-job training can satisfy most learning needs, it cannot satisfy them all. Most organizations must therefore supplement their on-the-job training with some form of off-the-job training and attendances at training courses'.

Later sections of this chapter outline the procedures for on-the-job and off-the-job training.

TRAINING PROCEDURE

For training to fulfil its objectives, strict controls have to be established and maintained. The most fundamental control is the following of a four-step procedure. The steps are:

1 Identify training needs

No training need can be satisfied unless its existence has been identified. Also, it is not possible to bring anyone to the desired standard of performance without first defining precisely what is actually desired. This first step should be carried out by the relevant managers and supervisors because they are responsible for the results of their departments and the people who work in them. More particularly, needs should be identified for:

- *New appointments* Define, in job performance terms, precisely what the new recruit should be able to do after training that he/she is unable to do now
- *Changes* Define precisely what the affected person should be able to do that, owing to the impending change, is different from his/her present job
- *Need for improvement* Define precisely what he/she should be able to do better, and to what standard, compared with current performance.

2 Preparation – getting ready to satisfy the need

This is the step that is carried out by the organization's training specialist. His/her first decision is to choose the most effective form of training for the particular need. Depending on this, one of the following will be carried out:

- Preparation for systematic on-the-job training
- Organizing and designing systematic off-the-job training
- Organizing and designing a training course.

Where the decision means arranging for training outside the resources of the organization, preparation means selecting the necessary off-the-job training or training course and making the appropriate bookings and arrangements.

3   The training itself

This step, carried out by training specialists, can be:

- Systematic on-the-job training by instruction and practice, using an instructional technique
- For off-the-job training an instructional technique is used for operating tools, equipment and machines
- A training course should also be conducted by instruction and practice, structured so that the previously defined standard of performance is achieved during the course.

4   Post-training, on-the-job application of learning

Here is the acid test. Is the required standard actually being applied at the workplace? The desired standard of job performance is, in practice, achieved when the learning produced by the training is actually applied on the job. In order that this application is as complete as possible, it is necessary that the managers and supervisors responsible help those who have just finished the training. The need for such post-training help is, however, minimal for training carried out systematically on the job, because this most effective form of training promotes easy learning, and all the knowledge gained is applied to the job.

In practice it is often difficult to comply strictly with every requirement of the above four-step procedure. However, there is no alternative. Taking short-cuts or attempting simplifications will result in ineffective training.

Managers and supervisors have to play their key role in this process and must be willing to act precisely according to the procedure. It is unlikely that many managers and supervisors would be able to identify every training need that exists or to define with adequate precision the desired performance standards. Thus, it is important for managers and supervisors to discuss their departments' training needs with the organization's training specialist. Assistance to managers in such identification and definitions is part of the service to be expected of the training specialist.

SYSTEMATIC ON-THE-JOB TRAINING

First a recapitulation: 'systematic' means that the on-the-job training is conducted by a departmental trainer using an instructional technique.

A departmental trainer is an experienced, non-managerial and non-supervisory job holder who has volunteered and has been formally appointed by his or her immediate manager or supervisor to work as a part-time trainer within the section or the department. After being trained in using the instructional technique, the departmental part-time trainer does his/her usual job but conducts on-the-job instruction whenever the need arises.

The instructional technique requires the departmental trainer to prepare in advance by learning:

1 How to get ready to instruct
2 How to instruct.

One of the best ways to approach the first of these stages is to find out from the relevant manager or supervisor who, in the department, is currently best at doing the job in question. After making the necessary arrangements, the trainer observes the job being done and notes the methods and procedures used on a formal 'job instruction breakdown sheet'. Using this method, the aim is to train everyone in the department to produce the same quality and quantity of work as the person previously recognized as the best. Thus, very high levels of efficiency and productivity are attainable.

To accomplish the second stage, 'How to instruct', the departmental trainer must work through four steps:

1 *Preparation* Prepare the trainee for the instruction
2 *Presentation* Present the instructions to the trainee. This should be done clearly, completely and patiently, one stage at a time, following the instructional job breakdown sheets
3 *Try out* The learner practises the job in front of the trainer. This process is continued until the trainer is satisfied that the learner has completely mastered the job
4 *Put to work* Provide information that will help the learner to apply the newly acquired knowledge on the job.

In organizations without systematic on-the-job training it is usual for the managers and supervisors to provide the training themselves, as and when the need arises. Such training is apt to be by trial and error, because it is unstructured. Further, managers and supervisors often have urgent calls upon their time, with higher immediate priorities than training, so that frequent interruptions to any programme of instruction can be expected. These busy people will also have less time available in which to prepare themselves or the instructions for the training. Reliance on managers or supervisors to carry out on-the-job training is generally far less efficient than using specially assigned part-time departmental trainers.

The benefits of systematic on-the-job training are likely to include:

- At least 50 per cent reduction in time and costs of satisfying the relevant learning needs
- At least 10 per cent improvement in quality and quantity of the work produced
- Elimination of mistakes, scrap and rework
- No misuse of machines, materials and equipment
- Managers and supervisors do not need to be involved personally in conducting the training and correcting mistakes, thus releasing their time for their more pressing tasks and more senior work
- Improved safety at work and reduction in accidents (properly trained employees use safe methods and procedures)
- Morale is generally higher, there is better co-operation between departments and increased motivation. All these are characteristics noticeable in organizations that are efficient and staffed by well-trained people.

There are other benefits, not listed above. All are attainable without incurring additional costs. Indeed, the use of part-time departmental trainers is likely to cost less than training by managers and supervisors. Reduced learning times and increases in the quality and quantity of work means that the total costs of providing systematic on-the-job training will be recovered many times over.

OFF-THE-JOB TRAINING

The main reasons for providing off-the-job training are:

1 The particular need cannot be satisfied through on-the-job training. For example, training in basic managerial and supervisory skills or in the skills needed for dealing with the organization's customers and clients
2 Training in basic skills of newly recruited people or those subjected to a change of job, where such training is more efficient before they join their departments. For example, training garment-sewing operators to operate sewing machines or the basic training of electronic-wiring operators in wiring skills
3 Training in the operation of machines or equipment which is not available or cannot be spared for on-the-job training. For example, training in machine operation provided by the machine manufacturers before similar machines are installed in the organization's own premises, or learning to operate computers in specially equipped classrooms
4 Training groups of people, where the numbers affected by a change warrant setting up special courses. For example, the introduction of a total quality control system, or training the company's fire marshals in their duties.

Off-the-job training can be conducted either in-house or externally. In-house training can often be arranged in 'training bays', which adjoin the departments for which the particular training is being provided. External facilities include specially equipped training centres. These attempt to simulate the working environment, examples of which are a 'working' branch of a bank with all the live facilities needed for its operation, or a retail shop which is set out to imitate any one of the company's portfolio of high-street branches. A classic example would be the training of airline pilots in flight simulators.

Training in all these cases is conducted by full-time trainers employed by the organizations responsible for conducting the training. All should be trained to use an instructional technique, in exactly the same way as for systematic on-the-job training.

A distinctly different form of off-the-job training takes place in lecture rooms, which may be in-house or external (often the conference suite of a hotel). Unlike on-the-job training, these courses do not by themselves bring the participants to the desired standards of job performance. Full proficiency is only achieved later, when the newly acquired learning has been repeatedly applied back at the workplace, on the job and with encouragement and further help from managers and supervisors.

TRAINING COURSES

A training course is a course which has been designed to bring each learner to the desired standard of job performance by instruction and practice.

In reality, this is possible to achieve only after the learner's immediate superior has defined the 'desired' standard. This process was described as step 1 earlier in this chapter, under the heading 'Training procedure'. If a manager or supervisor is unable to identify and define these requirements precisely, there is probably no training need at all, and certainly no one should be attending a course. When, however, training needs have been identified positively, with targets set for post-training performance, a course can be planned and designed or (alternatively) a 'bought-out' course can be selected from an external source.

Although it is not possible to use the on-the-job instructional technique during training courses, these should be based on instruction and practice (using one or more of the various methods and techniques available). If a course has been properly conducted the participants should be able to achieve the desired standards of performance before the course ends.

On return to work, the most effective way to carry over the benefits of the course into practical application on the job is for the immediate supervisor or manager to draw up an 'action plan' with the trainee (or group of trainees). The plan should set out the expected results against a timetable. Performance can then be monitored against the plan to ensure that the learning received on the course is properly developed and consolidated. Monitoring must continue until the final performance standards have been achieved.

Any course that is properly designed and conducted exactly as described above can be guaranteed to bring people who work in organizations to the desired standards of job performance. Courses that are not so conducted are of little practical value. This applies to all kinds of training courses, including those for the training of managers and supervisors.

CONCLUSION

It is surprising how often managers can be heard to express the view that: 'In this organization we believe that training is very important. We know that we ourselves do not provide much training, but this is only because we are very busy and simply have no time or money to spare.' When such views are questioned it becomes clear that these managers' perception of training is confined to sending people on external courses. But training courses can have only marginal effects on the results that organizations can achieve because, at best, only a very small proportion of the work-force can be trained in that way.

Systematic on-the-job training, however, can be applied right across the organization, to all who work there. It replaces the usual hit and miss, trial and error form of learning with much faster and more reliable planned instruction. In practice, it is the only form of training that can be guaranteed to raise the performance of individuals, departments and the whole organization to the standards desired by management.

Thus, it is usually little loss when organizations declare that they have no time or money to spare for people to attend courses. But it is a considerable loss when organizations fail to take advantage of systematic, on-the-job training.

FURTHER READING

Bennett, R. (ed.), *Improving Trainer Effectiveness*, Gower, Aldershot, 1988

Buckley, R. and Caple, J., *The Theory and Practice of Training*, Kogan Page, London, 1989

Jackson, T., *Evaluation: Relating Training to Business Performance*, Kogan Page, London, 1989

Mager, R.F., *Preparing Instructional Objectives*, Pitman, London, 1984

Mager, R.F., *Making Instruction Work*, Pitman, London, 1988

Mager, R.F., *Measuring Instructional Results*, 2nd edn, Pitman, London, 1984

Mager, R.F. and Pipe, P., *Analysing Performance Problems*, 2nd edn, Pitman, London, 1984

Pepper, A.D., *Managing the Training and Development Function*, Gower, Aldershot, 1984

Rae, L., *How to Measure Training Effectiveness*, Gower, Aldershot, 1986

Smith, B.J. and Delahaye, B.L., *How to Be an Effective Trainer: Skills for Managers and New Trainers*, Wiley, Chichester, 1987

63 Developing effective managers

Alan Mumford

Managers should be effective in meeting the particular purpose of the organizations in which they work. However, while the development of effective managers is necessary and appropriate from an organizational point of view, managers are by no means a subservient tool of the organization's purpose; it is also in the interests of the individual manager to develop his or her effectiveness in order to meet personal goals.

WHAT IS MEANT BY 'EFFECTIVE'?

The apparently obvious sentence with which this chapter starts in fact brings out one of the most significant points about management development. First, as Drucker told us, 'Efficiency is doing things right. Effectiveness is doing the right things' (1974). This is significant, not only because it is important about the management development process itself that it should be effective and not just efficient, but more crucially that development activities should be concentrated on effectiveness and not just on efficiency. In their different ways Rosemary Stewart (1982), Henry Mintzberg (1973) and John Kotter (1982) have built on the essential Drucker propositions and exploded the classical authors on management – perhaps not so surprisingly, because the work of all three is based on detailed observation, questioning and analysis rather than on theoretical propositions about what 'all' managers do. An important theme for all of them has been that, although there are some important similarities in what managers do, the requirements to meet the different needs of different organizations are at least as significant. What the effective manager has to do, and therefore what he or she has to be developed to do, ought to be determined by careful analysis of the specific and contingent nature of the manager's job in specific organizations.

In the United Kingdom there has recently been increased attention to what the particular competences of managers need to be. Based on the detailed work done by the Stewarts (1978) and Boyatzis (1982), and popularized through the Management Charter Initiative, the interest in *competence* potentially provides a very powerful route for management development. Again, however, the seductiveness of generalizations in which the Management Charter Initiative has been involved, particularly in association with the possibility of educational qualifications, has

---

This chapter is a slightly abbreviated and updated version of a chapter which first appeared in *Personnel Management Handbook*, Gower, 1986

been given undue prominence as compared with specific competences for particular organizations.

Finally, but still in the context of what it is that managers have to do, we should note the impact of company culture, and also the impact of national culture. On the first issue, the most popular book is that, of course, of Peters and Waterman (1983). Probably a more useful understanding of the impact of organizational culture and management development is that offered by Handy (1985) who shows that the type of management development process most likely to be effective is related to the four cultures he identifies: Power, Role, Task, and Person. The national differences, of course, are particularly important in any multinational organization, and the most extensive description of differences in the ways in which managers relate to each other is still that given by Hofstede (1980).

All these points relate to the central proposition that, all too often, management development schemes, or parts of them, are introduced because other organizations work that way, or someone else's statement of what managers do looks attractive, or someone else's appraisal scheme seems to be particularly up to date. Generalizations and short cuts do not provide a successful route towards effective management development.

WHAT IS MEANT BY 'DEVELOPMENT'?

We shall concentrate here on the development of managers in their roles at work, rather than describing the process by which the whole person may be developed, although concentration on the manager at work does not exclude reference to the larger issues of the manager as a person. It is certainly necessary to be aware of some of the fascinating material on stages of development and life cycles discussed by Kolb (1983). The idea that people are more or less responsive to particular kinds of development at particular stages of their life is important. These factors can, however, be expressed at a more immediate and, indeed, more practical level, in terms of identifying specific factors which will encourage or discourage managers to undertake development processes.

There is one theory of motivation which is particularly significant for management development and which is relatively easy to understand and implement. It is neatly described in Handy (1985) as the motivation calculus:

1   The strength or salience of the need
2   The expectancy that energy or effort will lead to a particular result
3   The instrumentality of that result in reducing the need shown at one.

In management development terms this is illustrated as follows:

1   Managers feel a need to improve their relationship with their colleagues
2   They believe it is possible to produce improvement by working at the problem
3   They believe that discussions with their bosses and colleagues would be a useful way of bringing about the desired result.

The essence of this theory is that a suggested management development process can go wrong in motivational terms because the prospective recipient lacks belief at any of the three stages. The manager may not feel a strong need; may have a strong need but not feel that it is possible to do anything about it; or may have a strong need and feel that something could be done, but that bosses and colleagues would not be of any assistance. In any of these instances management development is unlikely to be successful.

Is there any difference between learning and development?

Most authors and certainly most practising managers do not distinguish between learning and development. The word development is often used because learning is seen as a relatively unattractive term to many practising managers. If you take the view that development is essentially concerned with personal growth, then it could be argued that learning is a process through which personal growth is achieved. Learning as a word is often, mistakenly, equated with formal training processes, whereas development carries wider implications of the large variety of activities of an unstructured and certainly non-training variety through which managers may learn. It is very often appropriate to use the word 'development' because it does seem to cover a wide area and because it is more acceptable. Equally, because of the grotesquely inadequate attention paid to the actual process of learning, a useful definition is given:

1 A manager knows something not known to him or her earlier and can show it
2 A manager is able to do something he or she was not able to do before.

One other issue of definition arises about the word 'development'. For some people development has been seen as an exclusively future-oriented process; developing managers has meant helping them to be effective in a future job, usually after promotion. The decline of both the actuality and the prospect of organizational growth, and, therefore, promotion opportunities, in many organizations has substantially reduced what is often an error. Managers very often need to be developed in order to meet the demands of their current jobs more effectively.

Learning on the job

Processes of learning and development for managers arise far more from the variety of opportunities to learn on the job than they do from off-the-job activities. Sadly, the opportunities are often ignored or misunderstood. Managers fail to make use of some opportunities usually because they see themselves only as managing and not as managing and learning at the same time. It has, however, become clearer over the last ten years or so that effective management development revolves more practically around the learning opportunities on the job than neatly contrived experiences off the job.

EFFECTIVE DEVELOPMENT PROCESSES

Effective management development depends on a clear understanding of the specific features determining effectiveness in any particular management job as already explained. Without such a recognition of the facts of managerial life, management development schemes and activities may concentrate on systems, skills, activities and processes which are not actually of prime significance.

A second, but closely associated, reason for emphasizing the need to work on effectiveness issues is that such an approach is both stimulating and more acceptable to the managers involved. It is more stimulating because it makes them think harder about the results which can be sought from development processes. It is more acceptable because it produces more realistic statements of what managers in an organization actually set out to achieve. In particular, for off-the-job experiences, it provides a very sharp answer to any managers inclined to say that the content of a programme is irrelevant. Sadly, off-the-job programmes are often irrelevant precisely because they have not been based on a proper analysis of what managers do.

Thirdly, the requirement to concentrate on how to help managers improve what they were actually doing, rather than designing programmes to show them how to do the things the textbook says they should be doing, can have substantial rewards for increasing the efficiency with which the organization's goals are achieved.

Having focused on effective managerial behaviour as one important requirement for developing effective managers, we can now move to another effectiveness requirement, namely, the need to ensure that any development process is itself effective. It is unfortunate that, just as too much management development in past years has depended upon generalizations about management jobs and managerial behaviour, unrelated to specific circumstances and specific individuals, so the process of learning itself has been subject to large-scale generalization about the way in which managers learn. It is no excuse to say that managers have themselves assisted in this unhelpful process of generalization by offering simplistic statements about managers learning through experience. Unfortunately, many of those who have the duty to provide a more appropriate answer have failed to meet their responsibilities. Managers with the same development needs will respond differently to any particular process offered to satisfy those needs. Hence, case study methods, T groups, interactive exercises or action learning often fail to achieve the results expected. There are two substantial reasons for this, an understanding of which will avoid a great deal of wasted effort, frustration and negative feelings about management development.

The first reason is partially expressed through some of the comments made earlier about the differences of organizational culture and the effect of this on what is objectively needed and subjectively acceptable in any particular organization. Undoubtedly, some organizations provide a more appropriate developmental climate than others. There are organizations where a positive and open acceptance of the need to develop and learn is regarded as normal and helpful. On the other hand, there are organizations where all risk-taking is discouraged.

One can, however, go further in identifying blockages to development within any particular cultural environment. The job itself may suffer from a number of disadvantages from the point of view of giving scope and practice for improving management abilities. It may be too restricted in authority or content; it may be entirely responsive to rules and procedures, offering little opportunity to think. It may alternatively be so vaguely described and so lacking clear priorities and objectives that the manager swims in a turbulent sea, uncertain of direction and purpose.

Perhaps even more powerful is the role of the boss in providing opportunities, encouragement and reward for the development of subordinates.

Roles of the boss

Far too little has been written about the role of the boss in the development of subordinates. It is insufficient and unhelpful to say that the manager is responsible for the development of subordinates and to imply that this will be achieved by a combination of fruitful appraisal, participation in coaching and giving high priority to the attendance of subordinates at off-the-job training courses. Much the most substantial responsibility for the boss is the identification and use of opportunities for learning on the job (see also Mumford, 1989). The boss can certainly provide some of the opportunities: by acting as a direct coach in some situations, if the boss's style in coaching is suitable both to the need and to the recipient; and by providing an example both in directing the priorities of others toward learning and in showing a personal commitment to learning.

The individual learner

The other main element helping or hindering development is the combination of personal characteristics and behaviour of the individual manager. Again, it is important to look at the individual. The single most useful step towards improving management development over the last ten years has been the recognition of the different characteristics and learning preferences of the individual. One approach to this is to review those obstacles to learning, as set out by Boydell and Temporal (1981). This is a useful approach and successful with some individuals. Not all managers, however, will want to go into some of the deeper causes of blockages which can be reviewed through that process.

Rather more managers are responsive to the idea of different preferences within the learning process. The idea that some individuals learn well from a case study and others do not, that some seem to learn only by 'hands on' implementation and others learn something useful by relatively abstract study of books or lectures, has so far been too devastating for most institutions of learning to take on. David Kolb's (1983) elegant experiential learning theory and its accompanying memorable figure of the learning cycle has as yet been taken up in the UK by remarkably few people and only one institution. The elegance of his theory arises not only from the persuasiveness of the view that the learning process involves having an experience, thinking about it, generating a model for subsequent behaviour and then taking action in the light of this new view. It is also clearly a process which is relatively easy to explain and relatively easy to get managers to connect to.

Developing on the job

If there were no management training centres, no management development advisers and no management educators, managers would still learn. They can be helped to learn either by expanding the number of on-the-job opportunities or by helping them to recognize that normal managerial activities contain learning opportunities within them. An extensive list of opportunities for learning in working time from the manager's existing job is given in Honey and Mumford (1989). Managers can and do learn from discussing problems in advance and reviewing the results of solutions adopted. They can learn from watching others at work and modelling what they see as appropriate behaviour. They can set objectives for the results of an interview or a negotiation and then review afterwards what actually happened and why. They can seek explanations from others of what has happened and why during some managerial activity. They can look for new opportunities to stretch themselves, to try out new ideas and new techniques. All these processes are available, though many of them are unrecognized and managers need to be helped to recognize them.

It is, of course, also possible to learn from a job by taking on different kinds of activity by assignments to special tasks, to committees or working parties, or by partial or full-time secondment. All these are examples of opportunities to learn through relatively normal on-the-job activities where the prime purpose of the activity is to manage to get things done and where the subsidiary purpose of learning may be identified. This aspect is covered by McCall et al (1988).

Contrived learning on the job

There is another range of opportunities on the job where the situation may have been created, initiated or stimulated by the need to give someone a learning opportunity, but in which the content of the managerial activity remains real and responsible. The UK has been the centre of the development of this sort of approach in the last fifteen years, represented in slightly different forms by action learning (Revans 1980) and joint development activity (Morris 1981). The crucial idea behind these activities is that managers learn most effectively when they are exposed to a real rather than a simulated experience, and where they have to take responsibility for the results of the activity as they would for any other managerial activity. The other outstanding advantages of the process are that in most but not all cases the work undertaken can be centred on the organization's own problems and opportunities, and ease of 'transfer'. The problem created for themselves by management trainers and educators largely disappears. Secondly, the unreality of some management development processes in which the absence of responsibility means that managers learn to analyse but not to implement again largely disappears. For example, a manager who has to determine a totally new rewards policy for a previously unsuccessful sales force, and a manager who has to work on a total review of the location of a large number of retail stores, in neither case operate as quasi-consultants; both are faced with the fact that they will have to implement whatever is decided.

Self-development

The other substantial UK contribution to improved management development has been the self-development movement. In the discussion of the role of the boss above it was stressed that the boss is not wholly responsible for the development of subordinates. An important feature of the self-development process is exactly the understanding that development is not something which can be injected from outside or slapped on like a suit of clothes, but is rather a process which happens within an individual. Nobody can be totally responsible for the development of another person. At best, the boss can help to provide the conditions in which development will happen more effectively.

The crucial themes of self-development spring, therefore, from this prime understanding that it is the person who is being developed who has the greater function, and not the boss or the provider of education and training. Self-development does not mean that the individual is the only person involved, but means the individual takes responsibility for using any offers of help on development which come along (or indeed rejecting such offers). It is a dramatic and fundamental shift from a 'done to' process to a 'done with' process. Learning is the responsibility of the learner and not of the provider. The learner is involved not only in the analysis of needs but also in discussing potential solutions, rather than being the recipient of professional advice from others on what the solutions might be. Involvement and responsibility for solutions mean that there are fewer excuses to be offered about either relevance or applicability of solutions. There is a much heightened sense of taking personal responsibility for one's own actions rather than following someone else's prescription about what useful actions might be. It is interesting and relevant to note that the origins of this movement rest partly on a value judgement about the right of individuals to choose their own development process, and partly on the pragmatic position that involvement, participation and discussion actually lead to better and more acceptable solutions at the level of practical implementation. Pedler et al. (1986) have deservedly had a considerable success in providing a workbook to help managers to develop themselves.

Colleagues and mentors

There are many opportunities to learn from colleagues at work. Colleagues may be more expert in a particular subject; more experienced with a particular activity; they may know a particular person better; or know sources of information which other managers do not know. They can certainly therefore help managers learn by discussing in advance issues and problems. They can also help in the process of review and reflection after a managerial experience by offering feedback, guidance and suggestion.

The mentor is in many respects a half-way house between a boss and a colleague. It is confusing to talk, as some writers have, about bosses being mentors as well, because all the activities in which the boss engages as a mentor are really no more than their role should be as a boss. A mentor is normally a person who takes particular care and responsibility for bringing on someone junior in either age or status. The fact that a mentor may have a protégé at the same organizational level is rather underemphasized in the literature. The mentor may take action in regard to a more junior manager in a variety of forms. It may be a case of opening doors and providing pathways for a more junior manager to have the opportunity to succeed. It may be looking out for particularly attractive assignments or advocating promotion to a particular job. It may mean a frequent and direct personal association in which the mentor offers counsel or guidance to a more junior manager on how to behave. A convenient summary of the mentoring process is provided in Clutterbuck (1991).

This is another area in which formal management development follows the realities of how managers always have been developed, because, just as with the recognition that managers learn best by responsible experience, so the practice of mentoring has existed for centuries. While this is a powerful and important process, it is not easy to introduce it as part of a formalized management development scheme, certainly to the extent of some United States companies who offer rewards for mentor of the month. It is far preferable that it is taken up as something of mutual interest to a mentor and a protégé, with some advice and guidance being offered to both parties on the likely difficulties involved in the relationship.

Off-the-job training

So far, this chapter has concentrated on developing managers on the job. There is, however, an important industry offering processes for helping to develop managers off the job, including a range of things such as courses, seminars, programmes or workshops. There is a considerable irony in the distribution of attention in this chapter to on-the-job development activities as compared with off-the-job because in general the literature emphasizes the reverse. This is probably because the people who run off-the-job activities are relatively literate, have discrete processes to describe which have a beginning and an end, and in many cases come from a context in which it is either institutionally or individually desirable to publicize the activities being described in the articles or books.

If an analysis can be made of what off-the-job training can do better than on-the-job processes, managers will be more effectively developed. One of the pleasing changes over recent years has been the evolution at business schools of a large number of programmes in which at least some attempt has been made to turn general programmes open to a wide variety of managers into programmes of more specific utility to the needs of a particular organization. However, many in-company programmes are only cosmetically shifted from the general programmes of the organizations offering them. The problem stems partly from intention and partly from economics. Not all sponsoring organizations and not all academic institutions want to go to the trouble of designing a specific programme. There are problems about the rewards involved, whether academic or financial, for the academic staff involved. The more likely process is for a course to be run largely as an in-company activity with perhaps sometimes (on the more senior programmes) an external input or, alternatively, as a purely external programme. The reasons for choice between one or the other will again often be made in terms of what the company is prepared to invest in terms of money, time and personal credibility in the construction of an in-company programme. (There is another small variant in that there are a few examples of programmes drawn up and run for a group of companies to meet the apparently similar needs of senior managers in say half a dozen organizations.)

In-company programmes offer the prospect of a greater attention to specific issues within the organization. They do not always take advantage of the opportunity for specific concentration on the particular characteristics of effectiveness amongst those managers attending, but this position is gradually improving. However, while some courses do focus, for example, on a retail sales manager's job, rather than sales management in general, this is insufficient. The challenge is for the designers of the programme to deal with the issues of effectiveness specific to their organization rather than to provide company interpretation of generalized management skills.

There are two reasons for choosing to send managers on a general external course rather than a specific internal programme (if the organization can afford the choice). One is to send individual managers on programmes of the short variety because they have hit the public eye. All too often in these cases, nominations for the programme are based not on a logical development process but on current excitement about a subject. A variation is to send complete groups of managers, as has been done, for example, with programmes in team building or managerial grid. Decisions in favour of this kind of approach are likely to be better founded simply because the decision to spend large sums of money in this way improves reflection and analysis.

However, the vast majority of users of external programmes are not persuaded by a flavour-of-the-month excitement, nor by a desire to make a significant shift in total management behaviour through a course providing a particular approach. Most managers are probably still sent as individuals to individual programmes to meet individual needs. Surveys continue to show that the greatest problem for external courses, even more than for internal, is in fact the correct definition of needs and the involvement of the potential participants in that definition. If we presume the need has properly been defined, then the manager is sent on a course in order to acquire certain skills or knowledge. Decisions about the type of programme and choice between programmes are usually the main concern for specialists in management development in large organizations and it is clearly more difficult for those organizations not able to devote resources to investigating which programmes provide which kind of result. There is, however, no need to act in an isolated fashion on this since managers and advisers can use personal networks, can read the brochures with care and, for example, can use the Management Training Index. A useful account of how to choose an external programme is given by Abrahams (1991).

There are good resources available to run effective in-company programmes and to run effective external programmes. At their best, in-company programmes will: offer greater specificity; address real problems and, indeed, even work on significant real issues of direct and present concern; and generate more involvement and subsequent action from both participants and bosses. External programmes for all but the very largest and diverse organizations offer the alternative merits of: opening managers to ideas from outside their organization; greater freedom to experiment with different behaviours because of the increased security felt by managers outside the company; and an opportunity to stand back and look at one's organization from outside. Internal programmes can be particularly effective in fitting managers to the particular culture and way of doing things of the organization. Indeed, some programmes are in a sense too effective – they produce clones. External programmes may produce challenges and stimuli which may be found by some managers to be a good thing and by others to be too risky or uncomfortable.

The main justification for courses of any variety are that they provide something which is not available through on-the-job processes. Although effective management development may revolve around normal work opportunities, clearly not all needs will or can be satisfactorily met in this way. Courses are particularly useful when:

- There is a need to learn something quickly
- There is no opportunity to learn that through normal work experience, or the skill or knowledge is simply not available within the organization
- The balance is in favour of designing situations specifically for learning rather than taking advantage of task processes with subsidiary learning benefits
- The managers need to be placed in a situation away from their environment in order to learn effectively
- The opportunities for learning from others represent a significant characteristic and opportunity within the course being offered.

THE EFFECTIVE LEARNER

The capacity of individual managers to learn is affected by the working environment, particularly by the boss, by the motivations and prospects of rewards felt by the individual manager, and by the relative strength of any preferred learning styles held by the individual. The effective development process for any individual takes account of all these factors, of which the most identifiable is now the learning style preference. This can be discovered by using the work of Kolb (1983) or Honey and Mumford (1986).

MANAGEMENT DEVELOPMENT SYSTEMS

Do we need a system?

The first principle for any system is that it should meet the needs of individual managers effectively. Many management development systems meet the needs of personnel managers or management development advisers rather than managers. A system should give answers and show how actions should be implemented. It should also be designed with the full involvement of at least a representative group of managers rather than being designed by a management development adviser and then sold to a management committee. A management development system which has worked very well elsewhere in an apparently similar company will not necessarily work in what may well be a different culture. A system designed by an eager and well-educated management development adviser who has toured the country looking at the best systems may in practice turn out to be unworkable because it does not meet felt needs within the organization. Those wishing to design or redesign a management development system should return to the issues of what is meant by effective management and what the nature of the organizational culture is.

The main features of a management development system are:

- A process for identifying individual development needs

- A process for reviewing the results across a unit, division or company of individual development analysis
- A clear process for taking action on the results of analysis (preferably placing the main responsibility on the manager and the manager's boss)
- An overall review of resources dealing not only with succession and development but with performance issues
- A process for meeting all the action requirements emerging from these reviews.

The emphasis is on the need for a management resource plan rather than simply a succession plan. This derives from the proposition that development needs for managers may have nothing to do with future prospects. Moreover, discussion on potential and succession is too often an easy once-a-year discussion for managers enabling them to avoid discussing some of the more immediate issues about developing managers.

There is no hard-and-fast rule on whether it is desirable for an organization to have a stated management development policy. There are organizations where the process of working out what should go into such a policy is itself productive in the sense of highlighting issues and generating action. In other organizations, however, the production of words may have taken months with no useful end product.

Relating to the needs of the business

One of the observable improvements in management development processes in organizations over the last ten years has been the attempt, and sometimes the achievement, of a close association with the organization's business plan. The emphasis so far on identifying the specific characteristics of existing jobs has to be complemented by an awareness of the future direction of the organization. Even if there is no formal business plan it is possible to discuss with the senior executives what the likely changes in the business may be. Is it to grow, to contract, to change its core nature? What resources will be needed to meet the organization's requirements over the next three or five years? One advantage of looking ahead in this fashion is that it may help to develop requirements for particular kinds of job or for numbers of jobs which cannot be identified by looking at the present situation. Another advantage is that looking ahead encourages the identification of useful actions over a long period of time. It becomes easier to recognize that an action is necessary now in order to meet a long-term need and, in consequence, it is sometimes easier to get people to recognize that long-term action is necessary for more familiar development objectives.

Women and management development

Women as a group tend to have particular problems and needs in terms of management development. Until relatively recently this was an area in which male unconcern or ignorance meant that these needs were not properly identified. There is now much more guidance on what can and should be done specifically for women. A good review of this is available in Hammond (1984). Sadly, nothing of substance has yet emerged in the literature on what will clearly be an important issue on the specific needs of other minority groups.

CONCLUSION

Ten years ago a quite different chapter would probably have been written for this handbook, with a much greater concentration on systems and procedures, a much more substantial coverage of courses, much less about on-the-job development and practically nothing on the processes of learning and the desirability of stressing effectiveness. More is now known about the reasons why management development has succeeded and failed in the past. Margerison (1982) gives an excellent summary of many of the requirements for ensuring success. It is important to reaffirm as he does the view that the responsibility for developing effective managers rests first with the manager and secondly with his or her boss. The role of the management developer, educator or trainer is to provide support for the manager to fulfil this responsibility, not to take it over. Mumford (1989) provides a series of exercises through which specialist advisers can assess their current management development systems.

FURTHER READING

Abrahams, M., 'Choosing resources', in Mumford, A., *The Gower Handbook of Management Development*, 3rd edn, Gower, Aldershot, 1991

Boyatzis, R.E., *The Competent Manager*, Wiley, 1982

Boydell, T. and Temporal, P., *Helping Managers to Learn*, Sheffield Polytechnic, 1981

Clutterbuck, D., *Everyone Needs a Mentor*, 2nd edn, Institute of Personnel Management, 1991

Drucker, P., *Management: Tasks, Responsibilities, Practices*, Harper & Row, 1974

Hammond, V., 'Practical Approaches to Women's Management Development', *Industrial & Commercial Training*, July, 1984

Handy, C., *Understanding Organizations*, Penguin, 1985 (particularly useful further reading)

Hofstede, G., *Culture's Consequences*, Sage, 1980

Honey, P. and Mumford, A., *Manual of Learning Styles*, Honey, 1986

Honey, P. and Mumford, A., *Manual of Learning Opportunities*, Honey, 1989

Kolb, D., *Experiential Learning*, Prentice Hall, 1983

Kotter, J.P., *The General Managers*, Macmillan, 1982

Lawrence, P.R. and Lorsch, J.W., *Organization and Environment*, Harvard, 1967

McCall, M., Lombardo, M. and Morrison, A., *The Lessons of Experience*, Lexington, 1988 (particularly useful further reading)

Margerison, C., 'Delivering success in management development', *Journal of Management Development*, vol. 3, 1982 (particularly useful further reading)

Mintzberg, H., *The Nature of Managerial Work*, Prentice Hall, 1973

Morris, J.F., 'Joint development activities', in Cox, C.L. and Beck, J. (eds), *Advances in Management Education*, Wiley, 1981

Mumford, A. (ed.), *The Gower Handbook of Management Development*, 3rd edn,

Gower, Aldershot, 1991 (provides a wide range of material and gives details of some processes not highlighted in this chapter)

Mumford, A., *Management Development Strategies for Action*, Institute of Personnel Management, 1989 (unusual because it covers both formal and informal development processes)

Pedler, M., Burgoyne, J. and Boydell, T., *A Manager's Guide to Self Development*, 2nd edn, McGraw-Hill, 1986

Peters, T.J. and Waterman, R.J., *In Search of Excellence*, Harper & Row, 1983

Reddin, W.J., *Managerial Effectiveness*, McGraw-Hill, 1970

Revans, R.W., *Action Learning*, Blond & Briggs, 1980

Stewart, A. and Stewart, V., *Managing the Manager's Growth*, Gower, 1978

Stewart, R., *Choices for the Manager*, McGraw-Hill, 1982

Taylor, B. and Lippitt, G. (eds.), *Management Training and Development Handbook*, McGraw-Hill, 1984 (provides a variety of comments on many aspects)

64 Employee communications

David Wragg

Most managers, and indeed most employees, will be familiar with employee communications. Few of us have not known an employee magazine or newspaper, and many will have come across or even have been involved with video. Those who have experienced these more sophisticated and expensive media will have seen how they have been complemented by the simpler forms – posters and circulars – which still offer certain advantages, including speed in preparation and low cost.

One still finds those who question the need for employee communications, or perhaps misunderstand the importance of employee communications and prefer to leave this function to the staff social club, for example. Employee communications is not a luxury, but a necessity of modern business life. It informs employees of what is happening, and why, by giving them news and information about the business, and it also helps to create a team spirit, providing a form of 'social cement' through sports and social coverage.

This in itself is only a part of the story. Most senior managers or directors would like to be able to talk directly to their employees, especially during difficult periods, and there is no doubt that employees like this approach. All research shows that employees prefer to receive information from their superiors at a meeting, so that the message is adjusted to their own involvement, with the opportunity to ask questions. Unfortunately, in large organizations with employee numbers running into thousands, this approach is difficult.

Another reason for having effective, managed, employee communications is consistency. Pass a message down the line, and it is likely to be misinterpreted as it passes from one part of the network to another. Establish a form of managed employee communication, and the message will be controlled and consistent. This is not to say that local initiatives should be discouraged, or that local managers should not enhance the message, especially if they have been briefed on what to say and how to respond to questions. But such communication cannot be left to chance.

Given the brief to implement, augment or simply improve employee communications, most managers can be expected to have some idea of what to do. In the larger organizations they will often have professional advice on hand, or a budget sufficient for them to be able to seek such advice and assistance from outside the organization. Actually getting employee communications started is only part of the problem, since it is also necessary to ensure that the communications work, that they are effective, and that the overall communications strategy reflects the nature and the aims of the organization.

Employee communications is usually regarded as being part of the public relations function, although it is not unknown for it to belong to the personnel function or, occasionally, to stand alone. In common with other aspects of public relations, employee communications benefits from consistency, by which is meant that one is looking for a sustained and planned programme of communications, eschewing too many *ad hoc* exercises. One does not suddenly develop employee communications to counter a threat of industrial action or to enlist employee support at a time of crisis, although one might well augment the existing programme at such times.

EMPLOYEE EXPECTATIONS

While managers are usually familiar with employee communications, so too are modern employees, who have a good idea of what they expect from employee communications. Just as a good journalist appreciates that a story has to be relevant to a substantial number of his readers to be worth publishing, employees do expect employee communications to be relevant to them. As mentioned already, for the most part the preferred means of communication is by word of mouth direct to the employee from his or her boss, since this allows clarification and ensures that the message is tailored directly to the audience. But this is not practical in large organizations. While passing messages down through the management chain has much to commend it, it is slow and can mean a loss of consistency in the message.

The content of an employee communications programme, the media used, and the way in which the programme is split to target specific audiences, can be aided by an employee attitude survey. This can reveal employee perceptions of the organization and their expectations or misgivings, and also identify differences which could mean that employees in one company or division prefer a lighter tone to communications than others who prefer greater depth and more background. Produce something which is too heavyweight, and most of the audience will quickly lose interest: produce something which is seen as being too lightweight, and there are those who will treat it with contempt. Of course, managers and other senior personnel should be left in no doubt that the programme is aimed at the mass of the workforce, but if a significant proportion of the total are specialists, for example, a separate communication could be necessary.

As a general rule, employees expect communications to provide them with information on:

- What is going to happen, rather than items which have happened already, especially if one bears in mind that the low frequency of many communications means that the 'news' is often stale
- Events, with information on what is happening, and the background to it
- The impact which changes or developments will have upon them personally
- Decisions, but with the background coming from those responsible rather than through the grapevine – it does help if the decision makers in the organization can be identified and given the opportunity to explain why they have taken a particular decision.

It can be seen that much of the emphasis is on what is likely to happen rather than on what has happened, and that employees takes these matters very personally. Research generally shows that an overwhelming majority of employees are interested in their own operating unit, and that loyalty is more often to the team than to a larger organization which may, in some cases, seem fairly remote and even irrelevant. Indeed, the message is that employees will be more responsive if they feel that they are treated as adults rather than as children, and the attitude of employees to communications does seem to bear this out.

It is imperative that news is fresh, and this is one reason why circulars still have value. They are easy to organize and can be more immediate than a magazine or newspaper which will take some time to produce. Organizations with a good centralized computer network, such as banks and building societies, often find that the computer system is suitable for transmission of messages (being quicker and cheaper than a telephone call, especially for short concise messages), with more complete information following later.

SELECTING THE MEDIA

In recent years, the media available for employee communications have extended beyond workplace meetings, posters and circulars, through publications, to video and computer-based systems. The advent of new media has sometimes been a triumph of salesmanship over need, but in many cases, new forms have contributed to presentation (as in the case of video) or the speed of dissemination (as with the computer-based systems).

It is important to be clear about the advantages and drawbacks of the different media, which, broadly, are as follows.

Circulars

Ideal for urgent messages, although efforts must be made to ensure that these are passed on quickly, and not delayed, lost or misdirected. Simply marking 'urgent' or 'pass on quickly' will not do. Mandatory instructions also lend themselves to circulars.

Notices

Also ideal for urgent messages, or for instructions with a definite life, such as the suspension of a staff facility for a period.

Electronic mail

Obviously only relevant to organizations based on a major mainframe computer or with good data links. Immediate notification is possible to everyone whose terminal is on line, with the possibility of checking whether or not the message has been seen, and of targeting a confidential message to certain recipients only. Another benefit arises if the system offers access to printers, in which case it can assist with the rapid distribution of circulars and notices to remote locations.

Electronic notice boards

Expensive, and only worthwhile if these can be viewed by a substantial work-force. Nevertheless, these offer immediacy, providing remote programming is possible, and impact, although of an impersonal nature.

Facsimile

Not so much a medium on its own as a superb means of ensuring rapid and accurate transmission of a circular or notice to locations for photocopying and distribution.

Loudspeaker announcements

Also somewhat impersonal, these should be used only for messages which are very short and absolutely vital to the personal interests of the staff (for example, as a warning of blocked roads on the way home).

Meetings

Important urgent information concerning, for example, mergers or acquisitions or critical problems which could affect the organization, are best raised at meetings, which can be arranged quickly. The crucial requirement is to ensure that those conducting the meeting are well briefed and able to handle any questions.

Video

Superb for subjects of visual interest and detail, making the most of the old adage that 'a picture is worth a thousand words', but time consuming to make, often costly, requiring equipment on which to watch the video to be available for employees, and, of course, time in which to watch. Video may also need written material to support the medium, especially if used for training or for such matters as the annual results, so that employees can refer to this afterwards.

Video conferencing

Ideal for two-way or even three-way meetings. Nevertheless, there are limits on the numbers who can be involved in any one location. But this is one way of improving communication at managerial level or of conducting negotiations with union leaders, for example. The system is available internationally, and, indeed, one British company has a system with links across the North Atlantic and into Europe as well as within the UK. Drawbacks are cost, and the need to have private studios on your own premises if security is to be guaranteed.

Satellite links

Still in their infancy and used to date primarily for briefings of large audiences gathered together in television studios, companies can use specialized satellite links aimed at the business market or even use surplus satellite television channels. While the initial equipment is expensive, the system is claimed to be cheaper than using telecommunications networks, which are the basis of many computer systems and even some video conferencing facilities. One good application for such a system is claimed to be for staff training in branches, but obviously important announcements could also be made using a company newscaster.

Periodicals

Excellent for background, but their value for news coverage will depend on the frequency of publication. They can cover some of the material suitable for video, or can complement video by enlarging upon the message and providing more detail, as well as giving employees something to refer to after they have seen the video. As with video, periodicals can suffer in taking time for publication. One will have to decide on whether to opt for a simple, low cost, newsletter, or for a more sophisticated and expensive newspaper or magazine layout. Magazines are best for articles and are often appreciated by office workers, while newspapers are better for news, and have an appeal for manual workers. Much really depends on the type of story available. If the organization has good solid news stories about substantial new orders, then a newspaper, regardless of the nature of the reader-ship, offers more scope. But if such momentous events are lacking, then a magazine is best. There is nothing worse than not having a strong front page story for a newspaper, except, perhaps, not having something good enough for an attractive and readable centre page spread.

Audio tapes

Short, personal or semi-personal messages can be transmitted using this medium, which is also quicker in production than video or even periodicals. Usually audio tape can be discounted for urgent material, but can be used as an introduction to written matter.

Annual reviews for employees

Such reviews are effectively employee versions of the annual report, but the term 'review' recognizes that employees will often need the figures to be simplified, and to have more emphasis on developments during the year under review, and in the year ahead. Some organizations have discovered shareholder interest in such material, and, indeed, this is reflected by recent changes, in the UK, to allow companies to produce a simplified form of annual report for shareholders (with the traditional, more comprehensive document still available on request). Employees who are able to handle complex financial reporting will be happy to take the official annual report.

Regardless of the medium or combination of media chosen, the desired aim is that employees should want to read, or watch or listen. Success is close when employees pester the post room or the messengers for their copy of the news-paper or magazine – and when they contribute a substantial amount of material, (although, depending on the nature of the business, 'substantial' could mean anything between 20 and 50 per cent, and seldom more). The encouraging news is that employees can, and do, find employee communications readable and likeable, and will support communications programmes which are relevant to them.

This growing variety of media makes it even more important to make the right choice, and often to be able to do this in advance so that preparatory work can be started even before the announcement is ready. In working on a programme of regular communications, which may well be augmented by a number of special items, you will have to decide:

- Which combination of media to use
- The type of message each medium will be used for
- The audience to be targeted with each medium
- The frequency of each medium.

In reaching a decision, you will have to bear in mind the:

- Nature and structure of the organization
- Audience
- Resources available to you, both in financial and skill terms
- Time-scale within which the message will need to be communicated.

There is much which can be handled within the organization but it is important to be realistic about the skills available. Desktop publishing can enhance the quality of circulars and make simple newsletters or magazines easier, quicker and cheaper to produce, just so long as someone can handle the equipment and appreciate the niceties of layout. Production of a full-colour newspaper or magazine is a highly skilled business, and if a full-time editor (or, even better, editorial team) cannot be justified, outside help will be essential. Bringing typesetting and layout in-house is one thing, especially with word processing and desktop publishing, but beware the temptation to become involved in printing which can involve a massive outlay in equipment.

While video and some publications can be used for special items, video is sometimes also used in a magazine format, augmenting the magazine or newspaper. This is much as television news programmes add to, rather than replace, quality newspapers. Even video programmes dealing with an ad hoc item should be accompanied by briefing notes, since ideally video programmes should be shown to staff in the presence of a manager or supervisor who can provide additional information, and report back on whether the programme met its objectives.

In preparing a video magazine programme or periodical publication, the value of the news or feature value must be the criterion for use and for the position occupied by a particular story. The audience is interested in people like themselves, so the success of a senior manager in a gardening competition is only of marginal importance compared to the success of a shopfloor worker in gaining a first-aid prize, or the works cricket team's victory against a competitor's team. One can use the publication so that senior managers become better known, and the personal side is relevant too, but not in every story.

A major announcement can be handled by:

- Providing brief details in a meeting

- Confirming the story with a circular or by placing a notice on the notice board
- Producing a video documentary on the new development.

The extent to which a periodical or a video programme can be used will depend on the frequency of these media: the less frequent they might be, the more likely it is that news will be stale and hardly worth mentioning. This problem has led to many organizations moving away from newspapers and magazines towards simpler and cheaper newsletters, which can be produced more easily and frequently. This is not to say that the more sophisticated media should be abandoned, but they can then be used more successfully for background information, profiles of individuals, departments, or branches, or for articles on policy and future developments, rather than attempting to keep pace with the news. In some cases, bimonthly magazines can be cut back to quarterly. But less frequent publication than this can result in a loss of interest and, from the point of view of the reader, it might seem to be a less regular publication, and so become one which is not looked out for.

On a more positive note, a simpler and more frequent newsletter can sometimes assist in stemming the flow of paper into departments and branches, with many items carried in the newsletter rather than in separate circulars. Few organizations use such newsletters for announcing internal vacancies, but many could find that successful management of a good newsletter would cut out circulars announcing staff appointments, and, indeed many other routine matters of no immediate urgency.

The key to good linking between media lies in leaving one department to handle all internal communications. Many, including the author, would suggest that external media should also come under the same department, since consistency between the internal and external message is necessary for credibility. It also saves time if one individual is briefed rather than two or more. External relations do not usually include advertising, which is sales-, marketing- and product-related, although it is a good idea for the public relations department to know what advertising is planned (in case there should be any media or other external affairs implications), while employees also are often interested in what is being done to promote the company. Another reason for adopting this approach is that the external media are also read by employees and can often reach them more quickly than the house publication ever could.

Ideally, the PR function should also be the repository of the skills necessary for employee communications. Even so, only the largest organizations can keep all of these skills in-house. Even quite large companies will usually resort to video production companies for their video programmes, although there will be an in-house adviser to co-ordinate, select video producers or production companies, and ensure that quality is controlled. Again, it is usual to use specialized magazine or newspaper printers, even though the editor should be an employee, ideally with sound journalistic experience.

One should never feel that because video programmes or the employee periodical are of little interest to management that they are unappreciated by the main target audience. Conversely, if managerial and professional staff love it, unless it is aimed at them and is in fact a management communication, treat this as a warning sign that the target audience on the shopfloor or in the branches is being neglected. A good mainstream communication will aim at the broad mass of the audience. Then smaller, less expensive, communications can be added for any minority audiences with different interests. Nor should one be tempted into filling a periodical with those items which employees can get elsewhere. They do not need motoring, travel, gardening, angling, cookery or other such columns, all of which they can find in daily newspapers and weekly magazines. What they do want is to know more about people like them, within the same organization, and what the future holds in store. Not a lot to ask!

FURTHER READING

Barnard, M., *Magazine and Journal Production*, Blueprint Publishing, London, 1986

British Association of Industrial Editors, the Association's Handbook

Seekings, D., *How to Organize Effective Conferences and Meetings*, Kogan Page, London, 1987

Watford College, *Desktop Publishing: Design Basics*, Blueprint Publishing, London, 1989

See also Chapters 70, 71 and 72

65 Managing employee relations

Hamish Mathieson

In their response to changes in the wider environment large employers in particular have been recognizing the importance of developing new 'social strategies' in the management of employment to complement material changes in production organization and methods. Organizational renewal and revitalization are increasingly perceived to depend not only on management skills in 'traditional' areas such as finance, production and marketing, but also critically in the intertwined fields of 'people-management' and 'organizational culture'. The values, beliefs, attitudes and behaviour of the enterprise's employees are held to occupy a strategic role in corporate success. Of particular significance in this regard is the emergence of 'human resources management'.

HUMAN RESOURCES MANAGEMENT (HRM)

HRM, American in origin, has aroused a wave of interest and, indeed, controversy in recent years on this side of the Atlantic. As Thomas (1988) has commented:

> For some it is an emergent philosophy, arguably a new discipline that cross-cuts the business school boundaries of organizational behaviour and organizational psychology, personnel and industrial relations. For others it is industrial relations without unions – an enigmatic discipline which may or may not supplant industrial relations depending on the shape of the post-industrial economy. Then, for a hardy few, it is the past revisited, a recycling of an old managerial ideology which promised industrial peace but delivered fear when all else failed.

The growing appeal of an HRM approach to employee relations is partly rooted in perceived deficiencies in the record of 'traditional' personnel management practice, particularly in relation to its contribution to productivity. The 1960s and 1970s saw a period of unprecedented growth in the numbers and influence of personnel specialists in both the private and public sectors, reflecting a response to increasing organizational size and complexity, tight labour market conditions, substantial trade union growth, the proliferation of labour legislation, and the influential analysis and recommendations of the Royal Commission (Donovan) Report of 1968. In proposing that a much greater level of professionalism be introduced into the management of employee relations Donovan sought to shift control in labour management from discredited line managers and instead deal with key employment issues through formal company policies administered by a cadre of personnel professionals. Consequently, a much expanded role for personnel specialists became crystallized around the tasks of regularizing and standardizing employment relations, applying expertise in interpreting and administering legal regulations and in building stable, accommodative relations with representatives of organized labour.

The 'proceduralization' of industrial relations has been a marked feature of the past twenty years. So much so that the *Workplace Industrial Relations Survey* (1984) shows that 94 per cent of establishments surveyed reported operating some kind of IR procedure (the comparative figure for 1980 being 85 per cent). Procedures represent a type of 'constitutional' framework for IR within which management and unions voluntarily agree limits on the use of power in various aspects of their relationship. Such procedural rules, if they are to be effective and have 'moral' legitimacy, should be the product of joint determination: rules which one party perceives to have been imposed on it are unlikely to be observed and may generate rather than prevent conflict.

The main areas regulated by procedures are:

1 *Negotiation* The procedure typically will lay down the occupational groupings over which particular union representatives have bargaining jurisdiction; lay down substantive *collective* issues for negotiation; and how and when changes to terms and conditions may be made
2 *Disputes* The procedure will typically specify at what point the use of sanctions may be undertaken and lay down a stage-by-stage process by which the resolution of *collective* disputes over substantive terms and conditions may be sought
3 *Grievances* The principal concern of procedure is to provide channels through which *individual* employees can express grievances against management and seek their resolution
4 *Discipline* The procedure will normally specify the 'disciplinary steps' which can be taken against *individual* employees and provide for the representation of the employee in disciplinary hearings.

Other commonly found procedures cover redundancy and health and safety at work.

The advantages of concluding joint procedures have been concisely summarized thus: they 'lay down accepted standards of conduct and behaviour in the workplace; help management and employees to avoid conflict; provide early warning of potential problems; place emphasis upon fairness and rationality; and reduce the possibility of inconsistent and uncontrolled action' (White, 1987).However, while formalized procedures may bring the virtues of clarity and consistency to industrial relations they may also act as an obstacle to flexibility of manoeuvre and also inhibit adaptation to external change.

Viewed from the era of 1980s 'cost-effective' management, post-Donovan personnel practice has attracted criticism for its 'passive', bureaucratized approach to managing employee relations through procedures and union structures. Its apparently central concern with maintaining a 'temporary truce' between management and work-forces through institutionalized compromise had caused it to be accused of administering a status quo which rests on a now inappropriate adversarial view of employee relations. In other terms, the traditional personnel perspective is seen to be insufficiently active in breaking down the long-standing legacy of 'low trust' relations in industry characterized by 'us and them' attitudes, a minimum sense of mutual dependence and a 'zero sum' win/lose approach to management-union relations. In sum, the policy objective of building employee relations policy around *simply* maintaining industrial law and order is criticized for its lack of ambition and relevance in contemporary conditions.

Proponents of HRM seek a reconstruction of the 'people management' role to focus upon the 'virtuous circle' of 'high trust' relations, characterized by mutual self-preservation, openness, co-operative problem solving and disclosure of information. In this formulation, management's role is 'pro-active', flowing from a consciously held philosophy of aligning the values and behaviour of employees with those of the enterprise by means of a package of policies (to be considered in detail below) designed to elicit 'moral' commitment as opposed to minimum 'instrumental' compliance.

A second impetus to the growth of interest in HRM is the emergence of employee relations as an area of 'strategic contingency'. As Strauss (1984) explains: 'Strategic contingency theory argues that power goes to the organisational function which deals with critical uncertainties.' In the turbulent climate created by recession, intensified global competition, technological change and shifting public policy, employee relations considerations such as labour costs and productivity are increasingly moving 'centre stage' in company policy making. The emphasis is upon the integration of human resources policies into corporate plans, based on the idea that gaining the competitive edge is dependent on building a strategic linkage between employee relations and production, marketing and finance strategies. A total approach to employment management thus replaces traditional reliance on short-term, 'fire-fighting' and compartmentalized personnel policies. The shift to an HRM approach symbolizes a move from dealing with employee relations questions in exclusively functional terms – 'employee relations is too important to be left to personnel managers' – to an approach based on a vision of organizational transformation hinged on the development of 'human capital', which is the responsibility of all managers.

An example of just such an approach is contained in the following extract from the corporate 'mission statement' of espoused employee relations policy formulated by the Eaton Corporation, a US multinational corporation with several plants in the UK.

Eaton understands that the success of the company depends ultimately on performance of its employees.

Sustained, high level performance is most likely when there is a high level of individual commitment to the goals of the organisation. This Easton philosophy strives for such commitment by recognising the potential for positive contributions from all employees, and by committing the organisation to work toward the development of an atmosphere in which these contributions can, and will, be made.

The following principles are intended as target conditions to be pursued at every Eaton facility. They form the foundation for a work environment that is characterised by mutual trust, mutual respect, and the individual freedom necessary for exceptionally high employee performance.

- Focus on the positive behaviour of employees
- Encourage employee-involvement in decisions
- Communicate with employees in a timely and candid way with emphasis on face-to-face communications
- Compensate employees competitively, under systems which reward excellence

- Provide training for organisation/individual success
- Maintain effective performance appraisal systems
- Emphasise promotion-from-within throughout the company
- Select managers and supervisors who demonstrate an appropriate blend of human relations skills and technical competence.

(reproduced by permission of Eaton Corporation)

A third factor underpinning the rise in interest in HRM has been the publication of an influential literature purportedly revealing the distinctive characteristics shown by the most successful or 'excellent' American companies. According to such writers 'excellent' companies are those whose employee relations policies are anchored to the 'marketplace' goals of good customer relations and service. The role of employee relations policy, in reinforcing the 'company culture' of shared values, is seen primarily as a *means* to the achievement of business goals.

Before we move on to review the implementation of HRM in practice it may be useful to summarize the principal features of an HRM approach in contrast to 'traditional' personnel management (Guest, 1987):

	Personnel Management	HRM
Time and planning perspective	Short term	Long term
	Reactive	Pro active
	Ad hoc	Strategic
	Marginal	Integrated
Psychological contract	Compliance	Commitment
Control systems	External controls	Self control
Employee relations perspective	Pluralist	Unitarist
	Collective	Individual
	Low trust	High trust
Preferred structures	Bureaucratic	Organic
	Centralized	Devolved
	Formal defined roles	Flexible roles
Specialist roles	Professional control (personnel)	Integrated line control
Evalation criteria	Cost minimization	Maximum utilization (human asset accounting)

HRM IN PRACTICE

The implementation of HRM centres attention on three employee relations policy areas: employee involvement and communication; labour flexibility; and line management responsibility for employee relations.

Employee involvement and communication

Companies are attaching increasing importance to the encouragement of greater employee identification with company objectives such as productivity and flexibility by extending the range and quality of methods of employee involvement and communications.

The underlying rationale is simple: that employee performance is more likely to be enhanced, employee relations improved and resistance to change overcome where employees feel that they are being properly informed and where they are perceived as responsible, trusted members of the organization. Of particular significance in an HRM context are forms of 'direct involvement' where the emphasis is on the greater participation of the individual employee in the management of his immediate work task, and also upon face-to-face communications between (predominantly line) managers and employees.

The past decade has seen steady growth in employer initiatives in this area. Of particular interest are employee communications techniques and quality circles.

Employee communications techniques

The Confederation of British Industry (CBI) has outlined the principal reasons for attributing importance to good employee communications (CBI, 1980), as follows:

1 *Organizational size* As firms get bigger and more complex there is a great danger that managers can become remote from the shop floor or the office, without realising it
2 *Attitudes to work* Rising employee expectations and aspirations among employees mean that motivation is not just a matter of financial incentives
3 *Economic education* In a highly competitive economic context there is a growing need for companies to explain the economic 'facts of life'
4 *Co-operation* People give of their best if they know what is expected of them, how well they are doing and how they can contribute to decision making at their own level – to facilitate this information is essential.

Chapter 64 deals with the subject of employee communications in greater detail.

Quality circles

The aims of quality circle programmes (see Chapter 43) are not confined to technical aspects of improving efficiency and cutting costs. Their objectives are also behavioural in character — to build commitment to the organization through teamwork and regular management/workforce interaction; to improve morale and job satisfaction; and, above all, to provide an opportunity for genuine, if restricted, employee involvement in traditionally managerial activities.

The significance of quality circles as an element in HRM strategy lies in their role of promoting organizational changes from the 'bottom up'. The implications for employees and management are potentially far reaching. For employees they offer the prospect of a more open and contributory organization and the opportunity to extend control over work. As Shea (1986) puts it: 'once people start having a say they want more. Consequently quality circles are not experienced by their members as simply problem solving groups. QC members set about their work with items on their agenda other than solving problems.'

Financial participation

Recent years have witnessed the spread of schemes designed to increase the involvement of both managers and work-forces in the financial fortunes of their companies. Profit-sharing and share-ownership schemes have a longish pedigree in Britain, but a combination of changing tax laws, the privatization of nationalized concerns and a rising stock market have given it a substantial boost. Advocates of financial participation claim that it increases employee identification and commitment as well as concentrating employee attention on the long-term prosperity of the company and not just upon its short-term profitability. Employee motivation will thus be more directed towards improving the quality and output and not just be aimed at 'quantitative productivity'. Others see in employee ownership the prospect for more radical change in the relationship between labour and capital. For example Leadbeater (1988) argues that employee share ownership poses a challenge to the traditional definition of a job:

> Even limited forms of employee ownership such as profit sharing, share savings schemes and personal equity plans, challenge the idea that a wage is a defining characteristic of a job. Employee share ownership is based on a more open recognition that people do not appear in the economy merely as 'workers' but as savers, investors and consumers as well. The trend towards employee share ownership is part of a broader approach to how people can lead their economic lives.

Yet it would be wrong to exaggerate the importance of financial participation as a principal lever of corporate culture-change unless it is accompanied by real opportunities for employees to become involved in managerial decision making. The British experience to date would appear to be more often than not that 'employee-owned' companies tend to retain many of the managerial prerogative features of non-employee-owned enterprises. Nevertheless, employee share-ownership's more ambitious objectives are clearly consistent with an HRM approach which seeks to replace the traditional 'minimum' relationship between the organization and its employees resting unstably on a narrow, contractual basis with a view of the employment relationship as more than merely a wage-effort trade off, and of the employing organization as a 'collective' not identified with any particular sectional interest.

Labour flexibility

A second disinctive feature of HRM practice is emphasis on labour flexibility. While by no means a novel managerial concern a considerable impetus to the development of a more adaptable labour force has been given in recent times by the combination of recession-driven organizational restructuring, the urgency of implementing new technology to gain competitiveness and the prevailing uncertainty and volatility of markets.

Labour flexibility may take a number of forms: the Institute of Manpower Studies (IMS) has suggested a model of the 'flexible firm' based on an employer strategy of segmenting the labour force into 'core'/primary and 'periphery'/secondary sectors (Atkinson, 1984). 'Numerical flexibility', or flexibility in numbers, is permitted via the introduction of forms of contract which allow rapid change in staffing levels in response to 'external' market fluctuations. A variably sized peripheral fringe labour force composed of temporary workers, part-timers, subcontractors and homeworkers can be created whose terms and conditions of employment will typically be inferior to those regular employees who comprise the 'core'.

It is to the principal form of flexibility applied to the core work-force – 'functional flexibility' or 'flexibility of task'– to which we turn. The implementation of an HRM approach implies a radical review of practices in the use and control of labour. In terms of production organization and job design the trend over the past century had been towards the increasing subdivision of fragmentation of work, involving much 'de-skilling' and resulting in a structure of highly 'task-specific', repetitive, short-cycle jobs each sharply demarcated from the other. Control over the work process is exercised directly and hierarchically through tiers of management and supervision whose role is to ensure compliance to managerially prescribed working methods and performance standards. Worker motivation is held to depend predominantly upon individual financial incentives.

While this 'Fordist' approach (so called since it originated in Henry Ford's Model T assembly plant) may have been appropriate to mass consumption patterns requiring high volumes of standardized products, it is recognized that it embodies limitations given a shift in emphasis to a more differentiated pattern of consumer demand and the growth in worker expectations of job satisfaction. Concerns about the implications for productivity and competitiveness of rigid, bureaucratized authority structures and highly individualized forms of job design and employee motivation which require from employees mere obedience, have stimulated rising management interest in alternatives.

Drawing to some extent on the experience of Japanese industry, HRM strategy places greatest emphasis on the division of work on a team basis with correspondingly 'looser' definitions of the individual employee's share of work, fluid job boundaries and a high degree of interdependence among team members. Workers freed from the constraints imposed by direct supervision have greater discretion and autonomy in arranging their own work. For example, teams of workers involved in the differing stages of a production process are constituted as self-contained units in which all of the workers are trained to do any of the separate tasks, thus expanding the scope of each individual's job function. In addition, workers may also have the authority to stop the production process – previously a managerial prerogative – in order to correct defects, allowing greater responsibility and accountability for quality control plus the exercise of supervisory functions. A parallel objective is to rationalize and streamline grades to produce, for example, one or two multi-skilled categories of versatile worker.

Attainment of labour flexibility and integration is dependent upon several facilitating factors. Prominent among these are policies which sweep away traditional status differentials between employees relating to terms and conditions of employment. Clearly, greater interchangeability in the use and deployment of human resources is assisted where 'harmonized' (that is, the extension of 'staff' status to manual employees) terms and conditions prevail. At the same time, the equalization of status is aimed at breeding among manual employees the sort of co-operative attitudes to the enterprise historically associated with non-manual employees.

Secondly, innovation in payment structures and systems is an important element in the promotion of labour flexibility. As Rothwell (1987) remarks:

> Whether in manufacturing organisations struggling to improve on their recently restored profitability and productivity, service companies seeking to take even better advantage of new market opportunities ... or in branches of the public sector seeking to stimulate and reward merit, new or additional methods of relating individual pay to the performance of either the individual, the group or the organisation are

being introduced ... the emphasis is very much on rewarding achievement and encouraging involvement.

For manual workers the emphasis is shifting away from the idea of the 'rate for the job' and, particularly for salaried workers in 'integrated' pay structures, towards merit-related increases linked to performance appraisal. For other groups bonuses may be introduced where reward is tied to the efficiency of team performance – for example, in diagnosing and ironing out faults in the production process – rather than merely for quantity of output.

Thirdly, labour flexibility places considerable importance upon the quality of training and employee development in the organization. Given the significance attached by an HRM approach to seeking employee loyalty to the organization and to developing interdependence and collective responsibility, a consequent premium is placed on skill development within the organization's internal labour market. The emphasis is upon 'growing your own' skills rather than relying overly on the uncertainties of the external labour market. Training is seen as vital not only in 'technical' terms – preparing employees for detailed changes in working practices – but also for its role in 'attitudinal structuring'. Employee commitment and preparedness to embrace change is felt to be more likely to be generated in circumstances in which there is a perception of a strong corporate commitment to continuous training and development opportunities. In sum: greater employee integration into the organization is an important product of training-based career development systems which offer the prospect of personal advancement and mobility to production workers while simultaneously upgrading work-force competencies in making use of new technologies.

Finally, the overall organizational context affects the capacity of the enterprise to respond flexibly to environmental change. Following Burns and Stalker (1961), organizations faced with uncertainty and pressures for innovation must reject hierarchical, bureaucratic structures which harbour entrenched interests in favour of 'flatter' more organic forms which emphasize decentralization and delegation and permit employee autonomy and discretion. A further organizational factor which appears to sponsor labour flexibility to some extent is geographical location. Perhaps the most ambitious programmes of labour flexibility in Britain have been those introduced in 'greenfield' sites without a legacy of low-trust adversarial relations.

Organizing for employees relations

The introduction of a human resource management approach has potentially far-reaching consequences for the division of labour within management in handling employee relations. In particular, attention is focused on the respective roles of line and personnel managers. For personnel specialists, especially in manufacturing industry, HRM may be perceived to represent a challenge, if not a threat, to traditional practice built around the monopolization of 'people' expertise in formalizing employment rules and relations through joint regulation with union representatives.

The radicalism of HRM lies in shifting the centre of gravity in 'people management' from personnel to line management. At corporate policy-making levels this entails the meshing of personnel considerations with strategic business planning processes as an integral part of general management. At operational level the emphasis is on line managers as change-agents through their role in 'driving' employee relations initiatives. The nature of this trend is indicated by Storey (1987):

> A key change to the role of the line manager appears to be one of expansion. In part this is thrust upon them, that is top management no longer judge it sufficient for their line managers simply to meet schedules. They are additionally expected to improve quality, to become adept at budgeting, to be innovative and to plan: in sum to treat their units as mini-businesses.

The implication is that all managers are expected to be 'people managers' critically involved in a range of employee relations questions. Accountability for employee relations is shifting or being devolved to managers on the front line, advised by personnel specialists.

A particular case in point is that of the reformulation of the role of the first line supervisor, the most 'up-front' of all line managers. Traditionally the supervisory role was centred on task management – controlling the pace of output on behalf of higher management. The role often involved a measure of direct control over the work-force, expressed sometimes in autocratically imposed sanctions. Within an HRM context emphasizing participation and worker commitment a new responsibility is being placed on supervisors – responsibility for the way in which others complete their jobs. The requirement is for the exercise of proactive leadership skills of motivation and communication in the management of changes in working methods, and involvement in goal setting with individual workers where appraisal schemes exist (Leicester, 1989).

Overall an HRM approach would appear to imply a significant shift in the distribution of authority within management in the conduct of employee relations and a qualitative enlargement in the role of line managers from traditional task management to include people management.

HRM and the trade unions

The spread of HRM methods, stressing the primacy of employee loyalty and accountability to the enterprise, direct management–employee communications, and the downgrading of collectivized industrial relations channels, potentially represents a not inconsiderable cause for trade union concern. American experience suggests that such fears are justified, given evidence that companies anxious to avoid unionization have been enthusiastic adopters of HRM. As one American commentator remarks:

> The idea is to provide an employment package that so effectively addresses employee needs and desires that union dues will appear a needless cost ... (our) results support the hypothesis that human resources policies which are often part of employers' union substitution efforts do inhibit unionization. (Fiorito et al., 1987)

To what extent is this true of the UK? Evidence suggests that while formal union derecognition policies 'continue to be rare' (ACAS, 1988), employers are, nevertheless, actively reviewing existing recognition and bargaining arrangements. Unions seeking recognition are finding that the least liberal of employer policies prevail in the fastest growing sector of the economy (private services), while on 'greenfield' manufacturing sites 'employers are clearly exercising a range of options from single union recognition through partial recognition for representational rights, to no unions at all' (Towers, 1988).

Trade union recognition

A key area of 'strategic choice' in the management of employee relations surrounds the question of union recognition for the collective determination of terms and conditions of employment. The profound implications of recognition are perhaps summed up by Torrington and Chapman (1983) who suggest that it signals 'an irrevocable movement away from unilateral decision-making by the management'. Given its significance and widespread ramifications for the future conduct of employee relations in an enterprise, it would appear prudent for management to devise clear and consistent policy towards claims for union recognition, By so doing, management will be in a better position to ensure that the terms on which dealing with unions will be conducted are compatible with wider business objectives, but also take into account employee aspirations. Formulation of recognition policy thus provides an opportunity actively to shape employee relations and avoid problems associated with *ad hoc* reactive responses to claims.

Assuming that an organization has, in principle, accepted the value of a policy of union recognition (as opposed to the lesser stance of accepting the right of individual employees to join a union, or a contrary policy of non-recognition), what initial considerations will be relevant? Hawkins (1979) has suggested a number of 'strategic' objectives to which recognition policy may be tied:

1   To negotiate recognition arrangements and bargaining structures which will be effective and viable in the long term
2   To ensure that bargaining structures are consistent with the structure of decision making in the organization
3   To negotiate arrangements which are conducive to the orderly, peaceful settlement of disputes. For example, some of the current crop of 'single union' deals have been prompted in part by a concern to avoid demarcation disputes developing in the future. In circumstances in which the majority of employees recruited to a new 'greenfield' site are already union members, management policy might be to award sole bargaining rights to a single union at the outset, rather than be faced with competing claims from a number of unions for recognition at a later date with potentially destabilizing consequences for industrial relations
4   To ensure that the conduct of collective bargaining is consistent with the ability of management to manage the business by ensuring that conflict is contained by effective joint procedures.

In responding to a claim for union recognition management will typically first require to determine the level of support in the work-force for union representation and the appropriateness of the union seeking to be the 'bargaining agent'. The work of ACAS in this field might be of assistance: the criteria used by ACAS under the procedures activated by $ss11$–16 (now repealed) of the Employment Protection Act 1975 were those of 'actual union membership' and 'potential union membership'. Although neither ACAS nor the law specified any minimum level of support it became clear that ACAS did not expect a union claiming recognition necessarily to have recruited an actual majority of the employees affected for the claim to succeed. However, the key factor in circumstances in which 30–40 per cent of the employees were in membership was the level of potential membership as measured by tests of worker opinion, prevailing trends in union membership and the distribution of union membership by occupation or department. A ballot of workers affected by the recognition claim might be employed to test support: if it is, the arrangements need to be carefully and jointly agreed in order for it to possess legitimacy and for its results to have credibility.

A decision to recognize will also depend on an assessment of the 'appropriate-ness' of the union making the claim. Relevant considerations will centre on whether the organizational and staff resources of the union are sufficient to service its membership; the union's record and experience of negotiation for similar employees elsewhere; and the union's ability to represent all the sectional or occupational interests covered in its claim.

A second important concern in the mechanics of the union recognition process relates to the composition and boundaries of 'bargaining units', that is, the groupings of employees to be covered by the collective agreements. In determin-ing which employes should be grouped together in a bargaining unit the (now defunct) Commission on Industrial Relations, whose experience was considerable in this field, identified a range of factors which might be utilized to establish homogeneity of interest among employees. These are as follows:

1 *Characteristics of the work group* Job skills and content; payment systems; similarities in hours, holidays, sick pay, physical working conditions; qualifica-tions of work group members
2 *Trade union membership and collective bargaining arrangements* Employee preferences regarding work group association; employee wishes towards rep-resentation through collective bargaining; the existence and operation of existing collective bargaining arrangements; existing membership or non-membership of unions or staff associations
3 *Management organization and decision making* Extent of unilaterally oper-ated management procedures in areas such as discipline and grievance settle-ment; management structure (for example, the division of the organization into separate units); recruitment and promotion patterns and practices; and geographical factors such as the dispersion of employees.

Contemporary developments in the management of employee relations have had direct consequences for the structure and composition of bargaining units. The trend towards the decentralization of bargaining in multiplant companies has in some cases led to the redefinition of bargaining units. A more publicized develop-ment has been the growth in the incidence of 'single union' packages not only as a feature of 'greenfield' site operations, but also as a substitute for formerly multi-union arrangements.

Recognition arrangements featuring the assignment by management of sole bargaining rights to a union (often following intense competition between unions) typically involves a 'package deal' including 'single status' (all employees enjoy common conditions such as hours, holidays and sick pay), enhanced job flexibility and 'pendulum' arbitration. While managements in such companies have extolled the benefits of simplified bargaining arrangements, particularly in achieving greater flexibility in the ultilization of labour, opinion in the trade union movement has been sharply divided on the issue of whether a single-union organization chosen by management can properly reflect the representational interests of entire work-forces.

A third consideration in recognition policy is to decide the appropriate degree of recognition to be accorded. In essence there are two options open to management:

1 A restricted or partial form – 'procedural recognition' – in which recognition rights are limited to the representation of union members in, for example, grievance and disciplinary questions. While this may be an appropriate course of action in the short term – perhaps justified by a relatively low level of union membership – it may not be seen as an acceptable substitute for progressing towards:

2 Full negotiating recognition. Under such arrangements unions participate as equal negotiating partners with management in determining a range of substantive terms and conditions of employment including pay and working practices. Over time the range of issues subject to negotiation, and the scope of recognition, may widen as the bargaining relationship matures.

At the same time, care must be taken not to exaggerate the role of HRM thinking in stimulating employer initiatives in the field of union recognition. Wider political and economic considerations must also be taken into account. The 1980s, for instance, saw a lessening of public policy support for union recognition. The statutory provisions embodied in the Employment Protection Act 1975, under which a union might enlist the assistance of ACAS in pursuing recognition, were repealed by the 1980 Employment Act. Moreover, public sector employers have, through their actions at GCHQ and in unilaterally withdrawing support from closed shop agreements (UMAs) elsewhere, signalled similar messages. Another factor is the impact of high levels of unemployment on the ability of unions to advance claims for recognition (or resist its erosion or abolition).

At this point in time it is not possible to be conclusive about the implications of HRM for trade unions. Much depends upon the conviction with which British employers pursue HRM and also upon unions taking a less equivocal attitude towards it than they are are present. In its 'purest' form (for example, as practised in the US) HRM exists as a clear expression of assertive anti-union unitary ideology. Research in the UK, on the other hand, suggests that HRM policies typically tend to exist in parallel with, rather than as a substitute for, existing bargaining relationships. A dual system of employee relations combining, for example, a stress on communications, consultation and involvement, with a 'pluralist' joint regulatory framework appears to reflect current mainstream practice. The force of tradition is strong in British employee relations as is reflected in the mounting empirical evidence indicating remarkable stability in workplace employee relations procedures and institutions in the 1980s. As ACAS (1988) observes: 'Despite continuing shifts in patterns of employment and a decline in trade union membership in recent years, collective bargaining remains the dominant determinant, either directly or indirectly, of the terms and conditions of the majority of employees.' It is possible, however, that we may be in a transitional phase and that unions require to adopt a more proactive position in regard to HRM. For example, some long-standing union goals – such as a more open and less authoritarian workplace, increased worker control and flexibility in work, and greater job satisfaction – are consistent with espoused HRM policies. The unions' task would appear to be to ensure that the terms on which employers expect greater moral commitment from their employees are not largely set by the employers.

FURTHER READING

ACAS, *Annual Report*, 1988

Atkinson, J., 'Manpower Strategies for Flexible Organisations', *Personnel Management*, August, 1984

Burns, T. and Stalker, D. M., *The Management of Innovation*, Tavistock Publications, London, 1961

Confederation of British Industry, *Employee Communications*, 1980

Collard, R. and Dale, B. G., 'Quality Circles', in Sisson, K. (ed.), *Personnel Management in Great Britain*, Blackwell, Oxford, 1989

Eaton Corporation, *The Eaton Philosophy: Excellence Through People*

Fiorito et al., 'The Impact of Human Resource Policies on Union Organising', *Industrial Relations*, vol. 23, Spring, 1987

Guest, D., 'Human Resources Management and Industrial Relations', *Journal of Management Studies*, September, 1987

Hawkins, K., *A Handbook of Industrial Relations Practice*, Kogan Page, London, 1979

Leadbeater, C., Employee Ownership, *Financial Times Supplement*, 9 March 1988

Leicester, C., 'The Key Role of the Line Manager in Employee Development', *Personnel Management*, March, 1989

Mathieson, Hamish, 'Employee Relations', in *Company Adminstration Handbook*, 7th edn, Gower, Aldershot, 1991 (extracts from which were used to compile this chapter)

McIlroy, *Trade Unions in Britain Today*, Manchester University Press, Manchester, 1988

Piore, M. and Sabel, C., *The Second Industrial Divide*, Basic Books, New York, 1984

Rothwell, S., 'Human Resources Update', *Journal of General Management*, Summer, 1987

Shea, G., 'Quality Circles, the Dangers of Bottled Change', *Sloan Management Review*, Spring, 1986

Storey, J., 'HRM – the Line Management Dimension', *IRRU Paper*, University of Warwick, 1987

Strauss, G., 'Industrial Relations: Time of Change', *Industrial Relations*, 23 (1), Winter, 1984

Thomas, R. J., 'What is Human Resource Management?' *Work, Employment and Society*, 2 (3), September, 1988

Torrington, D. and Chapman, J., *Personnel Management*, 2nd edn, Prentice Hall, 1983

Towers, B., 'Derecognising Trade Unions', *Industrial Relations Journal*, 19 (3), Spring, 1988

White, P. 'Industrial Relations Procedures', in Towers, B. (ed.), *Handbook of Industrial Relations Practice*, Kogan Page, London, 1987

Part Ten

THE SKILLS OF MANAGEMENT

66 Management self-development

Michael Williams

It is widely believed that management development = management training = 'send him/her on a course'. This view assumes that management development is 'done' by someone to someone else – applied like an external treatment. Management development planned in this spirit rarely involves the subject in either the diagnosis of the problem or in formulation of the prescription and follow-up. Thus, the person tends to play a largely passive role in important activities concerned (as the case may be) with his/her:

- Growth as a person
- Development for promotion or transfer
- Current performance improvement
- Increased contribution as a manager
- Ability to make the transition from specialist to managerial role
- Development of skills in specific areas.

Traditional forms of management training, moreover, are more likely to be ready-made than tailor-made, and may not always be suitable for an individual.

Perhaps most serious of all is the constant failure to recognize that ultimately the company, a boss, or the management development manager is *not* responsible for the development of the organization's managers. The managers themselves are. The boss's responsibility is to encourage, support and facilitate the process of subordinates' self-development – principally to help them to develop themselves and become more effective.

At its most fundamental, management development means self-development – a conscious response on the part of individuals to deal with what *they* recognize as their development needs. Real development takes place when individuals see, for themselves, the need to modify their behaviour, change attitudes, develop new skills, or improve their performance or themselves for different roles. The idea that 'only the learner will learn' is accepted in some organizations and by a growing number of management development specialists, tutors and trainers.

Because many of the barriers to self-development that exist in companies and within boss–subordinate relationships are self-imposed and psychological, the process needs stimulation, guidance and sensitive managing. The next level up in the management hierarchy often serves as the best excuse for not getting things done and provides a frequent let-out for the individual who chooses to deny his responsibility for his own development: 'I'm employed by the company: it's up to my boss to decide what my development needs are. I don't know which way my career is going to go.' Such self-imposed constraints are not strategies for success. They need to be recognized by managers as recipes for mediocrity. The evidence that such self-protective behaviour is prevalent at managerial and supervisory levels usually takes the form of:

- Scepticism and a general 'don't want to know' attitude
- Unwillingness to take ownership of problems
- Reluctance to exercise initiative and authority
- Opting out and buck-passing
- Failure to take necessary risks, leading to a record of lost opportunities
- Forfeiture of influence as a 'power source' within the organization.

The true basis of self-development – namely, that the individual takes responsibility for his own learning – may be quite alien to some managers. Traditionally, much education (schools, further education and training) has put the emphasis on teaching rather than on learning. That approach tends to create inappropriately high levels of student passivity towards developing new attitudes and behaviours ('It's up to *them* to teach *me*').

To some people the idea of taking responsibility for their own learning is even seen as threatening, because it involves a personal shift from a largely uncommitted or passively receptive state to one which demands the individual's commitment and action. Others may be so disillusioned with their particular lot or with the company in general that they are demotivated and demoralized to the extent that they cease to care about self-development altogether. To people in such negative states of mind the process is likely to be seen at best as 'pie in the sky'.

More probably it will be viewed with suspicion as a management confidence trick, personnel department propaganda or (by the real cynics) as a 'do-it-yourself hangman's kit'. Some managers may take a tougher, more calculative view and expect to see direct links between any effort on their part in self-development and the company's reward system.

Finally, there will always be managers (usually senior executives) who assume inviolability. They claim, with or without coyness, that they have already 'arrived' and that 'this sort of thing is all right for other people'.

SELF-DEVELOPMENT IN THEORY AND PRACTICE

There are two aspects of the human personality which are relevant to the understanding of self-development. These are:

1 The 'self image' (the 'me as I see myself') by which each individual identifies himself, his personal values, beliefs, knowledge, wants, needs and fears as well as his physical presence
2 The 'ego ideal' (which amounts to the individual's 'me as I would really like to be'). In essence this consists of the attainable 'plus me' which exists in every individual in addition to the hopes, dreams and wishes which may make up the idealized or fantasy self.

Personal growth (which by definition is largely determined by self-development)

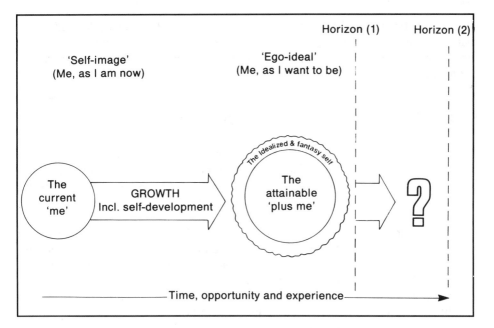

Figure 66.1   Personal growth

is the linking route from the self-image to the ego ideal. This is illustrated in Figure 66.1.

Practical self-development in management is concerned, necessarily, with attainable realities – what have been termed the 'plus me', rather than simply with the individual's fantasy world. The 'plus me' represents the difference between what the individual currently does, how effectively he operates, what contributions he makes in his present role and what that person is realistically capable of doing and being, within *self-selected periods of time*. The concept of the 'plus me', therefore, is related to a series of progressively emerging horizons – rather than to some ultimate limit which he or others have put on his potential. The horizons become more readily discernible as the individual consciously links his current behaviour and performance to what he feels are, for him, *requisite* standards, levels or modes of behaviour and which he judges are within his identifiable capacity. In practical terms the 'plus me' can be related to and reinforced by what Hodgson and Myers refer to as the 'plus job'. This is an attainable, realistic and viable role in which there are opportunities for increased satisfaction for the individual, coupled with increased contribution to the organization in which he operates.

Identifying the 'plus me' and the 'plus job' involves the individual manager working through a series of key questions, preferably with his boss and (where available) a management development specialist. From the responses are built up pictures of how the individual wants to grow as a person and how his job, or role, might be realistically developed to cater for and capitalize on that person's growth. The next stage is to evolve appropriate action plans, principally within the scope of the manager's work environment. Exercises are given later in this chapter which illustrate the processes and show how more diagnostic information can be obtained in order for the prescriptive action plans to be evolved for individual managers and for managerial teams. The crucial following activities are monitoring, review and follow-through, without which there would only be action plans – not action.

SELF-DEVELOPMENT: DISCLOSURE AND FEEDBACK

The self-diagnosis described above represents a systematic analysis of a manager's performance, especially his behaviour in role and, therefore, his *management style*. The evidence of his immediate boss, his boss's superior, his peers and his subordinates represents crucial feedback to help him identify his real training and development needs for himself.

Informal performance reviews by his boss, periodic discussions with colleagues whose opinions and judgement he values, together with the data available to him from formal appraisal interviews all help to place himself in relation to the demands of his job. Similarly, discussions with effective and experienced management development or training managers should provide valuable feedback and insights into how others see him and his contribution.

The process of feedback, however, is often best enhanced by *disclosure*, that is by disclosing expectations, needs or concerns which invite response and discussion. By specifically asking for information about personal effectiveness, management style, role as a colleague or boss, or contributions as a subordinate, a manager can build up a picture of both confirmatory and contradictory evidence about his perceived competence in his job. For example, he can turn what is so often the rather sterile ritual of the annual appraisal into a fruitful discussion by taking the initiative himself and encouraging his boss to ask the right questions. By using a simple self-appraisal instrument which more or less parallels the questions and areas of analysis of the company appraisal form he can prepare himself (and his reviewer) for a worthwhile and relevant diagnosis of his real performance improvement or development needs. One of the hallmarks of the really effective manager or specialist is his capacity to 'manage upwards'.

Influencing superiors is not the same as falling into the trap of self-weakening by *delegating* authority and responsibility upwards. Rather, it means letting a boss know exactly what you need from him, in order to do your own job more effectively. Equally, it means finding out from him where he needs you to change your behaviour in some way. The process is about helping a superior to act as a necessary and appropriately supportive source of organizational authority in order to open doors or give sanction to requisite innovation. Some managers may well feel vulnerable when the significance of their epaulets is drawn to their attention by a subordinate who is saying, in effect – 'Come on, you're the boss, so act like one and give me the authority to go and do what we need to get done'.

Generally most far-reaching changes require management at at least three levels within the organization, as Figure 66.2 illustrates. First, there is the level at which the innovation or change is to be implemented. Immediately above that is the superior who may have to go out on a limb in order to give the necessary 'go-ahead'– hence the sense of vulnerability at this level. Then, above him is the 'umbrella' often necessary to provide senior managerial or organizational cover

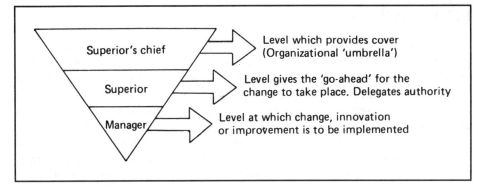

Figure 66.2 Hierarchical support needed for change to be implemented. This diagram shows the levels of support required to implement and sustain far-reaching change and improvement

for the venture, even though all the evidence suggests that the change will result in necessary performance improvement.

Much of the art of the process lies in the extent to which both joint and mutually exclusive areas of accountability are identified and spelled out. In this way, mutual perceptions and expectations about obstacles to effective results and about opportunities that should or should not be exploited can be clarified. Such disclosure and feedback need to be 'core' features of any boss – subordinate relationship in management, as a matter of course not just during periods of innovation and change. As an essential part of the personal (and hopefully mutual) stocktaking which is what the annual performance appraisal should be, then at least the following questions need to be raised and worked through from the subordinate's point of view:

1 'These are what I see as my current priorities'
2 'This is what I believe (d) you (my boss) expect (ed) from me' or 'This is what I believe is/was expected of me in my job'
3 'These are the results I believe I have achieved'
4 'This is what I feel I have done well'
5 'This is where I see I need to improve'
6 'This is where/how I need you (my boss) to act on my behalf (or to give me support) in order for me to do my job more effectively'
7 'These are areas where I see our relationship as:

• good'
• less than satisfactory'

8 'What do you need to do differently in order for you to:

• act more effectively as my boss?
• do your own job more effectively?'

9 'I see these as my main training development needs'
10 'What training or development do you feel I need?'

THE 'FLY ON THE WALL'

A process which provides detailed minute-by-minute data about a manager's role and performance over several short periods of time is that of direct observation, accompanied by feedback and discussion. The purpose of the observation is to identify, record and review what a manager actually *does* in the course of several working days. Observation takes the form of a 'fly-on-the-wall' technique, which involves the observer sitting in with the manager so that the latter's every work activity can be recorded under appropriate headings and subsequently fed back to him for review and analysis. As a tool for learning, self-development and performance improvement it is invaluable, given an observer who is a credible, competent and sensitive individual in whom the manager being observed has confidence. The observer, therefore, may be a management development or training manager, external consultant, colleague, superior, or in some cases a subordinate.

The process can be structured to suit the situation, status and role of the manager being observed and the relationship between the observer and the observed. A case study later in this chapter illustrates a structured observation over a period of several hours. The subject in this case was a typical middle manager at work. His activities have been recorded in detail, in this format, in order to provide him with accurate data about:

1   How he spends his time in a variety of management situations, covering a range of managerial activities. In particular, where he needs to create periods of uninterrupted time for himself
2   Where he could or should delegate and make greater use of other people – especially his secretary
3   In which situations and with which people he needs to control his 'boundaries' more effectively by developing more assertive approaches
4   How he could acquire vital information from other functions in a more timely way, with less effort
5   Where he needs to develop a more effective 'eyes and ears', or 'field intelligence' service through other people to reduce the amount of time he personally spends seeking information.

The amount of time required and frequency of observation for a 'fly-on-the-wall' exercise will vary, dependent upon:

1   The purpose and intended outcomes of the observations
2   The role and nature of the activities of the manager under observation
3   Whether or not remedial work is to begin after the first session or once all observation is at an end and diagnostic feedback has been completed.

Generally the process takes place in four or five phases, which are described below.

1   Initial discussion and decision to mount the exercise

This includes:

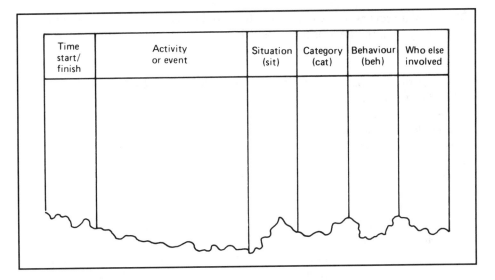

Time start/ finish	Activity or event	Situation (sit)	Category (cat)	Behaviour (beh)	Who else involved

Figure 66.3   Format for activity log

- Agreement of the 'contract' between the observer and his client about mutual expectations and intended outcomes (Note: the client may well not be the person to be observed; it could be his immediate superior, or other more senior executive)
- Ice-breaking and establishment of relationship between observer and observed
- Agreement on whether to hold observation sessions on set dates, or turn up on a random basis
- Confirmation of what are and are not legitimate activities for observation.

2   Observation

This phase may consist of any number of sessions but, typically, four or five half-days over a period of two weeks represents the minimum necessary. During those sessions the observer is virtually 'glued' to the manager so that he may record the latter's activities and *reactions* in adequate detail. Normally, the observer will use a log with appropriate headings under which he can detail what he sees happening (or not happening, since part of the observer's role during later stages will be to talk through significant omissions in the observed manager's behaviour). A typical log is illustrated in the case study later in this chapter (see Figure 66.3). Codes used are also explained in the case study. Others may be added as necessary. This is largely a matter of matching the tool to the task and evolving a relevant shorthand vocabulary which is convenient and quick to use.

3   The feedback stage

At this stage copies of the log are given to the manager. This may be done either at the end of each observation session, when his memory is fresh, or as a complete 'package' at the end of the exercise.

To stimulate review and analysis and to help the manager draw out the necessary learning points the observer usually works through a series of relevant questions, typified by the following:

- How far do the observations match your understanding of what happened?
- Are there any surprises in the data contained in the log?
- Does time actually spent on some activities fit your recollections of the time you believed you spent?
- What can you learn about the way you analyse situations, make decisions and take action?
- When are you most effective? Which situations do you handle well?
- When are you least effective? Which situations could you handle better?
- What could and should you be delegating?
- How well do you plan against contingencies and cope with events that you could not plan for?
- How effective are you in obtaining the information you need to do your job?
- How well do you warn others of impending difficulties, or actions likely to affect them?
- What exactly do you need to do differently in order to be more effective at your job?
- From all the above data what skills do you need to improve in order to be more effective and how best can you develop them?

4 The action plan stage

Both the data presented and the manager's response to that feedback provide the basis for his personal development action plans. Where appropriate the action plans may well be discussed with the manager's superior and a specialist from the personnel department or an external consultant. The plans need to be implemented and followed through to ensure that the requisite changes in operation, management style and personal development *are* taking place.

5 The development stage

As a variation on a theme, a team workshop consisting of all the managers who have been through a 'fly-on-the-wall' exercise may be run to confirm development needs and action plans to meet the needs. Each manager (who is well known to the others) presents the essence of his feedback and the lessons drawn from it, together with his action plans for treatment. These are added to, modified and ratified by his colleagues or team-mates on the basis of their knowledge of him. They are then implemented by the team on a mutually supportive basis which ensures a high level of monitoring, review and follow-through.

CASE STUDY IN ACTIVITY ANALYSIS

John Walton is a transport manager. In this exercise the procedure is described by which over three hours of his working day his actions were recorded on an activity log in order to obtain an impression of his typical work pattern. The activity key looks fairly complicated, but it becomes relatively simple when considered under the four right-hand columns, as described below.

Format of the activity log

A proforma is used to record the activities, with the layout shown in Figure 66.3. A shorthand key is used to speed up the entry process and condense data into the limited space available on the form. In this example, the shorthand codes used were as follows:

Under 'sit' (the situation in which the individual was observed):

AW	working alone
TI	taking an incoming telephone call
TO	making an outgoing telephone call
D	discussion with one other person
MI	meeting – informal
MF	meeting – formal
O	outside own office

The above can be used in combination, and might have been supplemented by:

WSP	with superior
WSB	with subordinate
WSBS	with more than one subordinate
AD	dictating to secretary
AT	working alone – thinking

Under 'cat' (the category of managerial activity observed) the codes used were:

PA	establishing causes of problems
SA	clarifying situations or problems
GD	giving data/information
BV	briefing verbally
XCA	checking data for relevance and accuracy
SDI	seeking data/information
E	evaluating or reviewing progress
O	organizing
OGI	organizing and giving instructions
RH	requesting and requiring help

Other possibilities which might have been used under this heading are:

DA	making decisions (choosing between alternatives)
P	planning
PP	protecting the plan (contingency planning)
CO	controlling
S	social chat

A   arbitrating

The following codes were applied under the 'beh' column, where the behaviour of the observed individual was recorded:

PA	positive/assertive
LA	listening attentively
Q	questioning
D	disagreeing
X	confused
U	constructive
C	composed (when under stress)

To these codes might have been added:

UN	uncertain/indecisive
CR	critical
DI	dominant
DG	domineering
E	emotional
DF	defensive
SWO	switched off
DY	switched on (dynamo)
GA	playing psychological games
AG	aggression
H	humour
NU	nurturing/building

Codes under 'who else' are simply the initials of others involved in the observed situation.

Activity log for Mr John Walton

The activity log compiled for John Walton is shown complete in Figure 66.4. The impression gained is that the period of observation involved activities and work patterns which were typical of John Walton's normal work-load and working style. Assuming this to be so, then what emerges as a representative picture is the following:

1   About 5 per cent of his time is free to work alone (thinking and planning time)
2   95 per cent of his time is spent face-to-face with someone, or on the telephone
3   50 per cent of his time is spent seeking information and clarifying situations
4   30 per cent of his time is spent giving instructions or briefing
5   The remainder is spent in arranging/organizing transport, solving problems, and so on.

Some questions raised by the analysis

Given that the above *is* typical of John's working day then some questions that need to be asked are:

Manager observed: John Walton
Position   :   Transport manager
Date(s) observed   :   3 August 19XX
Times observed   :   11.09am-12.30pm and 1.45pm-3.45pm

Time on/off	Subject/activity/event	sit	cat	beh	who else?
11.09		AW	PA	PA	
11.10	Arthur collects notes on transport routes	D	SA	LS	ART
11.11	Graphic statistics – analysing what, where and when	D	SA	Q	BRI
11.12	Checking|details/facts/figures with supervisor	D	SA	Q	
			PA	PA	BRI
11.13	J. goes out to collect outwork book, disagrees on section III; agrees on sections I and II	D	SA	D	BRI
			GDI	PA	BRI
			BV	Q	BRI
	J. seeking reliable accurate information		BV	X	BRI
	(given contradictory 'facts')			Q	
11.18			SA	U	
11.19	Telephone call to Transport Haulage Company	TO	SDI	PA	
	– seeking information on lorries and drivers		SDI	Q	
11.26	– ? work completion notes to clerk	D	E	PA	CLE
11.27	Recommences work with BRI	D	BV	PA	BRI
11.28	Query work in progress	AW	O	PA	NEV
11.28	Telephone call	TI	SDI	PA	
11.28	Second telephone rings (J. also takes this one over from secretary)	TI	SA	PA	
11.29	First call finished and first 'phone rings again	TI	SDI	PA	Visitor
11.31	Organizing people to do things, including	D	SA	PA/Q	Secret
11.35	gathering information	D	OGI	PA	MIK
		D	OGI	PA	DON
11.38	Given more wrong data (goes out to TER next door)	MO	SA	X	TER
	Checks paperwork with loader (loader unhelpful)	MO	SDI	PA	LOA
11.39	Wrong feedback – visitor gets data/information	D	SA	XQ	DON
	mixed up	D	SDI	Q	
11.40	Talks to driver	D	GI	PA	Driver
		D	SA	PA	
11.40	Clarifying delivery situation on goods	D	SA	PA/Q	MIK
11.42	Discussion with driver – gives more information	D	GI	PA	Driver
11.46	Reaffirms delivery date on goods	D	SA	PA	MIK
11.47	MIK returns regarding possible shortages	D	E	Q/PA	MIK
11.47	Checks numbers of 'look in'	MO	GI	Q	TER
11.52	Checks/queries tonight's deliveries	D	GI	LS	PAC
11.55	Gives routes/delivery runs and quantities	D	SA	PA	BRI
12.00	Request for transport	TO	RH	PA	
			XCA	Q	
12.05	Availability of drivers' mates for twilight shift	TO	SI	Q	RON
			DA	PA	
12.07	Call for information (no-one there)	TO	RH	Q	
12.09	Request to J. for transport and driver	TI	GDI	PA	ANON
	J. goes out to talk to driver	MO	SDI	Q	Driver
12.13	Request for situation report	TI	GDI	PA	RAY
			DA	PA	

Figure 66.4   Activity log example. In practice entries would be hand-written

Time on/off	Subject/activity/event	sit	cat	beh	who else?
12.14	Checks up on transport availability	TO	SDI	Q	VIC
		D	SA	PA	TER
	Do we have a car? Do we have a driver?		SA	Q	
12.19	Spare driver?	D	SA	Q	MIK
12.19		TO	SA	Q	CLI
12.20	Situation report	D	E	PA	MIK
12.21	No driver	TO	GDI	PA	
12.22	Briefing caller	TI	BV	PA	RAY
			GDI	PA	WIL
12.23	Situation report	D	BV	PA	MIK
		TI	DA	PA	PAU
		D	SA	PA	WIL
		TO	GDI	PA	CLE
12.25					
12.28					
LUNCH					
1.49	Planning procedures	D	GDI	PA	CLE
1.51	Making up loads for tomorrow	AW	DA	PA	CLE
2.06	Phone call	TI		PA	?
2.11	Clarifying schedule	D	PA	PA	MIK
2.12	Taking message	TI	A	PA	DIC
2.14	Phone (wrong number)	TI	A	PA	?
2.15	Call TER	TO		PA	out
2.17	TER calls back	TI	XCA	Q	TER
2.22	Goods (southern deliveries)	TI	SDI	Q	PAT
2.24	Meeting	MI	SDI	Q	NOR
			GI	PA	
2.28	Goods (Midlands deliveries)	TO	SA	Q	PAT
2.30	Parcel arrives – goods components				PET
2.31	Makes out rail notes	MIO	DSI	PAQ	
2.32	Clarifying/explaining procedures	TI	E/BV	PA	CLI
	+ action: sorts out detail		O/DA	QPA	JON
2.42	Parking ticket from driver	M	XCA	QPA	Driver
2.42	Clock card	D	GI	PA	PAC
2.44		D	GI	PA	Driver
2.50	Calls for notes	D	SA	X	Driver
2.57	Writing	D	SA	PA	CLE
2.57	Sorts out Midlands/North deliveries	D	E/	C	ART
			GDI		
3.09	Delivery of two reels of cable	D	SDI	Q	Driver
3.10	Electricians call	TI	BV	QPA	RAY
3.15	Ring for transport	TO	SA	PA	PAU
3.22	Needs information for PAT for goods (southern)	D	DA	PA	Visitor
3.24	Despatch priorities: goods (southern)	D	SA	PA	DER
3.28	Phone call	TI	SA	PA	DON
	Another call holding		SA	Q	ADR
	OBSERVER REJOINS PERSONNEL DEPARTMENT				

Figure 66.4   (concluded)

1 How could JW create more thinking and planning time for himself?
2 How much of the time he personally spends chasing up data and information could be reduced by:

- using other information sources (production planning and control)
- delegating to his subordinates the task of securing much of the information
- the introduction of an up-to-the-hour information service to JW from production (or production planning and control)?

3 How much more, generally, could and should he use his subordinates and push responsibility for solving problems back down to them?
4 The very nature of a transport manager's role especially when combined with that of chief despatcher, is fraught with fire-fighting problems. Being at the 'end of the line' inevitably means collecting everyone else's rubbish, to some extent. BUT, there is much that JW's immediate superior could do to reduce the pressure on John by:

- sitting down with him and analysing the what, how, when and who of JW's work
- assuming a higher profile and more assertive stance in managing the boundaries between finishing and transport/despatch.

Ultimately, of course, many of the decisions to delegate or not delegate rest with John himself.
5 Finally, there is the question of organization. Is the structure of work done and current reporting relationships appropriate, or is there a need to rethink and reorganize the whole question of ordering and using transport both at incoming and outgoing stages? This is obviously a far wider issue, but inevitably the organization structure is a major determinant of work loads, work patterns and comparative efficiency/inefficiency of managerial time.

ACHIEVEMENT OBJECTIVES

Used either as a natural consequence of discussions at the end of a 'fly-on-the-wall' exercise or as an alternative approach, specific achievement objectives can lend structure, direction and impetus to a manager's self-development. Based on a diagnosis of needs, set within the context of a manager's role and agreed with his boss, achievement objectives represent yardsticks of attainment against which the manager can measure his performance and development.

Obviously, the practice of setting objectives takes various forms in business. These range from formalized management by objectives (MBO) schemes to informal (but specific) targets set between bosses and their subordinates or within a work group set up to resolve a particular problem. The very process of management is about moving from a current situation (X) to a requisite state of affairs (Y) – usually within a set time limit. Typically managers work to the basic criteria as part of their day-to-day role, namely: quantity (how many and how much); quality (how well done or in what manner); cost (how much in financial terms); deadline (by when started/completed).

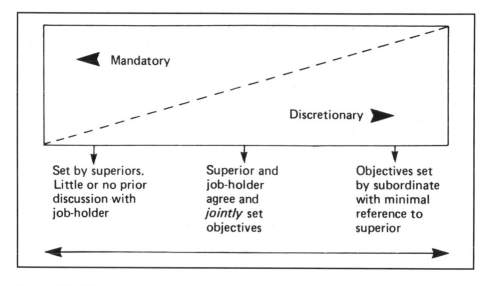

Figure 66.5   The extent to which objective setting between superiors and subordinates may be mandatory or discretionary. Some objectives will be mandatory themselves by their very nature (budget targets for instance) but *how* they are to be achieved may be largely discretionary within the boss–subordinate relationship

At the most senior levels, philosophy, policies and strategies are normally based upon certain corporate goals – even though they may be sometimes more implicit then explicit. Normally corporate objectives are then translated appropriately at different levels down the line so that, necessarily, there will be a mandatory aspect to manager's objectives as well as a discretionary one.

In setting and agreeing personal achievement objectives as a means of stimulating self-development and improving manager's effectiveness, the diagram in Figure 66.5 illustrates the basic scope open to bosses and their subordinates. That scope can be refined by a structure which enables managers to select, define and sharpen objectives in a disciplined way that more closely relates the performance of individuals to the goals of others.

First, it is helpful to determine what objectives are and what they are not. Management objectives:

are:	*are not:*
required results	activities
achievements	effort
accountabilities	duties
what is required	how it must be done
'musts'	'shoulds'

Second, there are different types of management objective. The principal categories are those which reflect the results to be achieved, under the following headings:

1   *Targets*   To meet a deadline, programme of activities or product launch

2 *Improvements*   For example, to increase profitability levels, productivity rates or quality standards
3 *Resolution of specific problems*   Examples are the removal of obstacles or constraints in order to correct deviations and restore previous conditions
4 *Innovation and change*   This would include introducing and implementing something new which represented a departure from previous practice
5 *Control*   Aimed at ensuring or maintaining a given set of conditions
6 *Personal or team development*   Principally aimed at acquiring the behavioural knowledge and levels of skill needed to operate more completely.

Undoubtedly some areas of activity are easier to measure than others in terms of results. It is usually possible to apply at least one specific, quantified objective. This is particularly the case where the type of objective has been determined ('target', 'improvement', 'problem solving', 'innovation', and so on). Even in areas of activity such as research and development or operational research, where the final outcomes might be very difficult to predict realistically, it is still possible to set quantified objectives. This can be done by making the objectives of the form 'submit and present an interim report at the progress review meeting on 13 May and show all findings to date' (for example).

Objectives need to be realistic, attainable, accurate and expressed in clear language if they are to appear credible and relevant as a self-development exercise. They must not be couched in vague terms. For example:

1 'Reduce the use of consumable materials on numbers 1 and 2 lines to budget level by the end of December, and by a further 10 per cent by the end of March' NOT 'Cut down drastically on consumables'
2 'Submit proposals by the end of the month for reducing steel procurement costs by at least 12 per cent. Method: by the use of alternative transport arrangements from the mills' NOT 'Investigate methods for reducing steel procurement costs'
3 'Revise your own and your subordinates' job descriptions by mid-January, clarifying the principal accountabilities for each person. Progressively ensure that only agreed principal accountabilities are retained and that all other work is delegated and reallocated to section heads by 31 January' NOT 'Delegate as much as possible to subordinates'.

In some organizations people of high potential may be deliberately moved into the 'fast line' in terms of career progression by being appointed to specially designed 'development posts'. Although they usually carry out necessary functions the real purpose of their move is to groom them for a more senior, longer-term position. In most organizations this probably does not happen and only selected tasks and objectives may be available for the job-holder's development. Where this is the case the opportunities for self-development could well lie outside the mainstream of the role, in the areas of:

- Short-term tasks and objectives
- Priority objectives
- Innovation and change programmes

- Trouble shooting and problem solving.

SOME VEHICLES FOR SELF-DEVELOPMENT

Once the task and personal objectives have been agreed, there is the question of work opportunities through which to achieve those objectives and ensure the process of development. A crucial factor in the process is the extent to which the manager's boss facilitates his subordinate's self-development by:

- Providing the necessary 'trigger' and encouragement
- Sustaining and restimulating it
- Capitalizing on it to the advantage of both the individual and the organization
- Pressing on the appropriate 'nerves' when unnecessary obstacles get in the way.

Learning is fundamental to self-development and most people in managerial roles tend to learn as the result of *experience*. However, that experience needs to be analysed, discussed and worked through in order to draw the appropriate lessons from it.

Learning by experience, within a management job, is likely to involve the 'learner' in at least:

- *Doing* – followed by analysis and review
- Experimenting with new or different experiences and activities
- Questioning and testing out existing knowledge, custom and practice, prejudices, values and beliefs
- Experiencing (and reviewing) both success and failure
- Examples and models (other managers) against which the learner can compare, assess and, if necessary, modify his own management style
- Study and reflection, in order to put experience into perspective and context.

Well-tried learning vehicles which provide opportunity for experiential learning and self-development including the following:

1   Keeping a work diary which is reviewed daily or, at least weekly, by the learner with his boss and/or a management development specialist
2   Setting up projects which are *relevant* and *realistic* and which have *real payoff* for the company, the department and/or the individual. Such projects often carry far more weight when there is major representation to be made by the trainee to the chief executive or a senior panel, so that a sense of occasion is attached to the experience and it is seen to be important
3   Cross-functional assignments involving multidisciplinary teams of subordinates working together (for example marketing, product planning and engineering or production, industrial engineering and finance) where end results rely on co-operative, co-ordinated effort
4   Presentations on key issues – or contributions to key issues – to top management

5   Team development workshops in which members review:

- 'our key objectives and priorities'
- 'obstacles to achieving them'
- 'my personal contribution to the team's goals'
- 'our strengths and weaknesses as a team and as team members'
- 'our action plan for the next 12 months'

6   'Bespoke' tutorials for individuals or groups using external professionals who test thinking and action plans by inputs of expertise, rigorous questioning and a wider perception

7   'Action learning', involving co-operation with managers from other companies and organizations, in the identification and resolution of each other's operational problems

8   Participation in junior 'boards', working parties, 'think tanks' or research teams, with or without senior executives involved, but where the outcomes are deemed to be important and relevant

9   Deputizing for the boss:

- by representing him at meetings, or on committees
- visiting important external contracts, on his behalf
- acting in his capacity for days/weeks/months at a time as appropriate

10   Setting up and running an entirely new product, department, function or small subsidiary company

11   Lecturing on personal accountability or a field of expertise to:

- internal courses and seminars
- professional courses run by universities, polytechnics or local colleges
- educational programmes run by national, local or professional bodies

12   Planned reading, regularly reviewed and discussed with the trainee by one or more of the following acting in a mentor role:

- his immediate superior
- his superior's chief
- appropriate in-company specialists, managers or supervisors
- external professionals

Planned reading also involves keeping up-to-date by regularly choosing different areas of developing technology, important disciplines or relevant current events and systematically scanning the appropriate professional journals.

These, then, represent some of the learning opportunities that are available to enable a manager's self-development to take place at little or no cost to the company and with minimal interference with the day-to-day job that he is there to do.

The term 'self-development' means exactly what it says. The real drive to make it happen must come from within the individual himself, but his superiors can do much to ensure an encouraging supportive climate in which self-development can thrive and become regenerative.

FURTHER READING

Austin, B., *Time and the Essence – A Manager's Workbook for Using Time Effectively*, British Institute of Management, London, 1979

Burgoyne, J., Pedler, M. and Boydell, T., *A Manager's Guide to Self-Development*, 2nd edn, McGraw-Hill, Maidenhead, 1986

Carnall, Colin, *Managing Change*, Routledge, London, 1990

Cranwell-Ward, Jane, *Thriving on Stress*, Routledge, London, 1990

Humble, J. W., *Management by Objectives*, Gower, Aldershot, 1975

Mumford, A., *Making Experience Pay*, McGraw-Hill, Maidenhead, 1980

Mumford, A., *Developing Top Managers*, Gower, Aldershot, 1988

Pedlar, M. and Boydell, T., *Managing Yourself*, Gower, Aldershot, 1990

Revans, R. W., *Action Learning*, Blond & Briggs, London, 1981

67 Personal organization

A N Welsh

It has been suggested that the better manager is the better organized manager, who makes the best use of his time and best use of the time of his staff. However, just as there is no such thing as a born manager, so the effectiveness of a good manager cannot really be taught. *Effectiveness has to be learned* and the suggestions in this chapter are only some pointers as to how you can look at your work, develop a personal approach, and make the best use of your time.

THE NEED FOR PERSONAL ORGANIZATION

When I had my first managerial job, I naturally found it very exciting and very demanding. I would come in on or before time, and to digress, a good manager should sometimes come in before time and perhaps stay after time. All sorts of things happen outside normal working hours: some people who get their work wrong or do not complete it within the day will stay behind or come back later to finish off, others will use company facilities for private purposes. However, I would come in on or before time and work furiously throughout the day, and by the end I had never completed all that had to be done and my head was full of all that was happening. In particular, I was concerned by matters affecting the well-being of others, and also attacks on my department's activities or my own standards of performance.

When I arrived home my head was buzzing and I would wake up in the middle of the night remembering things I had forgotten to do or thinking of new ideas. I had the choice then of lying awake during the rest of the night remembering whatever it was, or going to sleep again and forgetting the matter. At least I did not decide to hold a meeting about the situation!

CREATING A LIST

I listed all the jobs which I had to do, all the work in my in-tray and the functions which I had to supervise. I kept a diary, and a brought-forward file. The latter in my case was a concertina file with slots for the days 1–31 and for the remaining months of the year. I would pop into the brought-forward file any correspondence, assessments, buying orders and the like which I wanted to review at a future date; these items were brought into the list as they 'came up'. Having made the first rough list, I then sorted it into order of importance and urgency. At the end of each day I used to go through the list and cross off what I had done and also any items which had ceased to be relevant. I would add to the list new jobs or problems which had arisen and then I would note which jobs I planned to do the following day.

In the morning there was my list telling me what I had to do that day. Obviously unexpected matters arose – in an operational situation one can almost budget for the unexpected – but by and large I worked through the list each day.

I use ordinary stationery and a large desk diary, but there are several proprietary 'time management' systems available. These of course cost more and can be less flexible, but they are elegant and compact – particularly if you travel a lot – and have special sections for telephone and fax numbers, addresses, personal details, and so on, and pockets for cards.

Communications

One of the standing items on the list, apart from going through the diary and brought forward file, was to see *all my subordinates*. I kept at hand a list of all subordinates and made a point of seeing each one even if only to say 'hello', every day. It could be, of course, that you are often away, or that you have too many staff to see. Perhaps, in the first case you should consider whether you are away too much to do your job properly; in the second case either you may have too many people directly under you or should delegate some of the communication process to subordinates. Communications is the name of this game: people require *regular contact* and in particular from their boss, and they will often say things, or you will be able to sense a problem which they would be diffident about bringing to your office.

Incidentally, what does your office look like to a subordinate? Can he come and talk to you, or are you involved most of the time in meetings, discussions or telephone calls? Communications can only exist on face-to-face basis, and they are of prime importance at every level. Many managers with considerable responsibilities in large organizations do not know the names or faces of their top management and directors. An even greater proportion never see, or are seen by, their top management in any operational situation from year to year end. *No amount of personnel work can make people think you care about them if they never see you.*

Personal planning

The first list of work is much more difficult to produce than the subsequent amendments, and to help you produce it there is a checklist of questions in Figure 67.1. These are general and analytical questions to be used in any review of your responsibilities, but they would assist in preparing the first list. When, you may ask, would there ever be time to do this, and is it possible with everyone rampaging around and the telephone constantly ringing?

Well, do you intend to spend the rest of your life in a managerial pigsty, and are you seriously going to say you are too busy to do your job? Half an hour's planning can save hours – even days – of misdirected effort; the crisis anticipated proves to be no panic, and you should find in the normal situation that if you pursue this type of personal planning for a few months, you will get right 'ahead of the game' and that you can start looking for additional responsibilities.

Decide now on a specific half hour in the coming week to go through the list. Ask

1 What are the objectives of my department or function?
2 Am I satisfied that I feel these can be achieved – that I have a plan(s) for this?
3 In what ways can my department or area be improved?
4 Is the work in my area altering in nature, quantity or quality?
5 Can the work be done in a better way?
6 Have I the right equipment and facilities?
7 Have I the right number of staff?
8 Am I happy that all my subordinates are correctly placed and loaded?
9 Are my staff doing what I want them to do?
10 Do any of my staff need further training or experience? Have I a training plan?
11 What are the staffing trends?
12 Are my staff happy? Do I spend enought time with them?
13 Have I a trained deputy?
14 Am I satisfied personally? Have I defined my personal objectives?
15 Is my authority defined and adequate?
16 Is may relationship with my senior management satisfactory?
17 Where is my next promotion coming from?
18 Am I doing too much routine or administrative clerical work?
19 Have I enough time for thinking?

Figure 67.1   Checklist for reviewing your function

someone else to take the telephone calls and say you do not want to be disturbed (unless it is the Chairman!). Some of the questions will require further investigation, but whenever you reach an unsatisfactory answer, answer the question: 'What am I going to do about it?'

THE CONSTRAINT OF TIME

Managing is conducted within a large number of constraints. What is your biggest constraint? Is it capital, working finance, material resources, machinery, property or is it people? People can be a big limiting factor, but you can always train them. Are you limited by the presence of other aspects? Many factors can constrain you, but *the biggest restriction of all is your own time.* You never have enough of it. There are only twenty-four hours in a day, seven days in a week, 52 weeks in the year and so many years in your career. You cannot produce more time; it keeps slipping away. Yesterday can never come back.

We would say, therefore, that we do not have as much time as we need, but would this be equally true for everybody, or would it apply in particular to you? Time can be replaced. Certain tasks can be performed by machinery and certain office work can be done by computers. Some tasks can be delegated to other people, although this is really a transfer of time. However, *the manager cannot delegate his management work* to a machine and seldom can he share it with anyone else. There is no substitute for time as far as he is concerned. Everything he does takes time. All business, all activity, all work uses time and takes place in time.

However, we do not manage our time naturally – as a whole we take it for granted. Now we could talk for a long time about this problem, and we could say that the unhurried, unheroic manager with a clear desk, and a reliable organized office is the efficient or effective manager, but what do you do about it?

Step 1

First of all, accept that, other things being equal, *the best and happiest manager* is the one who *makes the best use of his time*. If you do not accept this, then this chapter was not written for you. But if you feel that you can make better use of time, and that if you do so you will be a better manager, then please read on.

Step 2

The second step comprises finding out what you are doing now. A simple method of doing this is to list the various activities which you perform, and record for a week or a fortnight (or on random days over a longer period) how much time you spend on them. This can be done by using a simple daily diary sheet. At the end of the period the daily diary sheets are analysed into what is called a work distribution chart. This work distribution chart will show quite clearly what you are doing and what proportion of your time is spent on your various activities.

A specimen manager's activity list (with the activities given for example only) is as follows:

1   Visiting customers
2   Visiting suppliers
3   Queries from staff over technical matters
4   Customer complaints
5   Planning and control work
6   Training
7   Supervision
8   Reading mail
9   Chasing overdue accounts
10 Checking stocks and reordering
11 Management meetings
12 Recruiting
13 Staff problems
14 Personal.

Simple forms for the daily diary sheet and for the work distribution chart are shown in Figures 67.2 and 67.3.

The work of a manager is variable, particularly as regards the subject involved. Completing a work distribution chart will not give a 100 per cent accurate picture of what the manager does or should do, but it will give a representative view of the proportions of his time spent on various activities; for example, queries: accounts queries may relate to different transactions, but they will still be accounts queries.

Date:				1. Ines- sential	2. Some- body else could do	3. Wasting others' time	
Time	Activity	Inter- ruptions	Phone calls				Notes
8.30 8.45 9.00 9.15 9.30 9.45 10.00 ,, ,, ,, ,, 5.30 5.45 6.00 Evening	Enter number against time whenever activity changes	Enter a '1' for each, e.g., 1, 11	As for interruptions. Note incidence and quantity. Analyse if too many.	Record impressions, if any, at the time.	Record impressions, if any, at the time.	Record impressions, if any, at the time.	Note anything unusual or 'special'.

Figure 67.2 Specimen manager's diary sheet

Once the work distribution chart has been completed, one can then move on to the next step.

Step 3

The third step is the analysis of the work distribution chart. A number of questions need to be asked at this stage.

WASTED TIME

1 What would happen if I did not do this kind of activity?
2 Am I spending too long on it?
3 Am I doing it ineffectively – for example, am I getting it properly set up and spending enough time on it? Short periods of supervision are of limited value with persons engaged on complex work
4 Am I failing to do any task which would contribute to the business because of the lack of time?

Activity no.	Activity title	Daily times										Total time	% of total	Comments and action
		1	2	3	4	5	1	2	3	4	5			(You can also do this kind of analysis with your staff.)
														These are taken to the nearest quarter hour.
											(No) (No)			If phone calls and interruptions occur which are separate from the activity being recorded – multiply by 3 minutes; if the totals exceed 15% of the day, then analyse them. Possibly something is wrong.

Figure 67.3 Manager's work distribution chart

Supervision

A manager should be able to spend time with his staff – encouraging, training, supervising, and just getting to know them and keeping in touch. The time required for this varies with the staff and the complexity of the work, but a rough quick figure is an average of forty minutes per person per day. This includes normal management duties, reports and 'personnel' work. It does not include 'checking' as distinct from normal supervision and training.

Checking

Checking should be considered carefully. Twenty or thirty years ago commercial convention looked for a high degree of literal accuracy, and salary costs were lower in proportion to other expenses than they are now. There is a satisfaction in getting everything 'right', but we should first consider what the customer really needs. Checking is expensive and frustrating: it is no longer a motivating factor (if it ever was) for staff to have all their work checked.

Your work distribution chart will show how much of your time is spent checking, but you should consider whether the cost of checking is justified by the errors discovered and how much these matter. If the errors do matter you may have to continue to check, but you can consider whether random checks, occasional and unexpected, will serve as well where generally quality standards and methods are the main concern.

List of jobs

In the end you will finish with a list of jobs which you want to do and which you have to do, and a subsidiary list of jobs which you feel you should not be doing but perhaps you still have to do for one reason or another. (We are, of course, well aware that you cannot get rid of all inessential tasks, but you can reduce them.) You will *rank the list of jobs in order of their importance* to the business, and estimate what general proportion of your time and energy should be spent on each.

You will have considered where time is being wasted on unnecessary work, and where time could be saved by better personal organization and work methods. You should move to the next heading in your analysis of the work distribution chart.

DELEGATION

Ask yourself which of your activities could be done by somebody else to an adequate standard, or as well as you, or even better. The manager is paid to do his work, but if there are others at lower salaries who can do part of it and have the time, then is it better for the manager to be fully occupied or for the junior staff?

Another factor which comes out of this analysis is that the more senior people become, the larger becomes the proportion of their time spent on moving about and travelling, and you should think about this.

There will be certain customers who are very important, and who are accustomed to dealing with you personally; it may well be that you can introduce them to someone else who can deal with the routine parts of the account but, of course, you will remember to watch what is happening to the account from time to time subsequent to this arrangement. This would apply also to 'important jobs' and to important senior managers!

The present managing directors of several companies in the UK were in very humble positions only a few years ago; in fact, consider where you yourself were five years ago, and now you are performing much more important work. Quite possibly within your area you have the managers or senior managers of the future, and you should keep a look out for them and give them a 'chance' as soon as you can. Not only will this be good for them, but it will also free you. Think about how to develop the business and to perform your other managerial tasks.

One thing which is very irksome to staff is to see people senior to them performing activities at greater salaries which they could perfectly well do themselves. In one major British company staff are asked the question 'What does your supervisor do that you could do yourself?' Could you ask this question of your staff, and would they know how to answer it? It is worth considering that they may have views on this subject themselves.

SUBORDINATES' TIME

A manager becomes a manager by promotion or appointment. He learns to be a manager by observing other managers, who themselves have been taught by observation, and by being shown, and from what is called the 'hard way'. There are certain training courses, but they are normally very short, and as a result most managers devise their style and system of management from their own experience. Often this is very good, but once personal inclinations creep in, funny things start to happen.

You should ask yourself the following question: 'Is there anything I do which wastes subordinates' time without contributing to their effectiveness?' You can begin to answer this question from your analysis of the work distribution chart, and you may even be able to ask it of the subordinates themselves.

Waiting around

For instance, how much time do your staff spend waiting for answers from you, items to be checked or approved, action to be taken, or for you to be available? Consider whether in your area you ever have two or more people involved in work which should be done by one person only. Normally, it is more satisfying and efficient for a job which can be done by one person to be done by one person and not split between two or three. Staff learn from observing you (or colleagues), but sometimes you may be playing to an audience unnecessarily (and distracting the others).

Remember when you were a member of staff or a worker. Did your manager or foreman ever waste any of your time while you waited for him when he was late, when he had to check your work, while he had to get around to this or that but was (or allowed himself to be) interrupted by a variety of other matters? Did this frustrate you as well as waste your time? Staff are paid less than managers, but with overheads, the difference is not as great as it once was. Are you working too hard; are you paying the proverbial dog then doing the barking yourself?

Crises

One thing which wastes time, particularly of subordinates, is a crisis. In many organizations crises occur regularly, and there are so many things which are unforeseen that one could almost describe crises as routine. However, a recurrent crisis is a symptom of slovenliness. Certain crises such as making up the returns, the budget figures, sales figures, payroll, the peak season, are all known in advance. If the manager uses sensible planning and scheduling techniques he may well be able to provide for these, in which case they will become routine occurrences and not crises.

Panic action is expensive. People rushing off to make special deliveries, special visits to the post office, special trips out to acquire stationery, other things that are needed, people dropping things in the middle of picking up others and so on, all lead to ineffective use of time and also mistakes.

IMPROVEMENTS

The question here is, how can you use your time more effectively? The first thing to consider is your attention span. Are you a person who works best by sitting down quietly and for extended periods looking at a particular problem, or do you keep things running around in your mind? What are your best methods of working, and with whom and when?

Discretionary time

You need to have a certain amount of 'discretionary time', that is, time at your free disposal, time available for important matters, perhaps the things you are paid for, and this must be kept in usable chunks. Not many managers feel they have much discretionary time, even after cutting out wasted time, but they can generally set aside an hour or so each week. The question arises as to how much discretionary time is desirable. This is rather like maintenance on a car; you do not buy a car in order to service it, but if you do not carry out a certain amount of maintenance on the car it will not perform satisfactorily.

Your function

The same applies to your function. You need from time to time to review the total operation of your area and to go through the checklist given previously; you need to make sure you see the staff regularly and review their situation. On a daily basis you may want to keep a list of the tasks which you have to do, and the problems with deadlines and priorities, and perhaps revise these either last thing at night or first thing in the morning. Also, you may well want to use a brought-forward file or diary system so that you are automatically reminded of things that need to be done in the future. How long this should take is like the service on the car, except that it is you rather than the garage that must make the diagnosis and the decisions.

Suggestions

Simple suggestions for using your time more effectively are to concentrate on one thing at a time; deal with first things first, and one at a time. Allow enough time for what you are doing – nothing ever goes completely right and one thing you can always expect is the unexpected. Do not hurry, do not try and do several things at once. Do not assume that everything that was important yesterday is important today. Ask yourself the question 'If we had not already started on this activity would we start it now?' It is just as difficult and just as risky to do something small as something which is big, so allocate your time to the most important parts of the business.

When you have analysed your work distribution chart comparing the proportions of time spent on the various activities with their importance in terms of obtaining income, business and profit or other advantage for the company, you will most certainly find that you are spending a lot of your time on small irritating matters. Consider whether some of these can be allowed to slide without damage to the business, and whether things would be improved by concentrating on the main managerial requirements of the organization.

FURTHER READING

Douglass, Merrill E. and Douglass, Donna N., *Manage Your Time, Manage Your Work, Manage Yourself*, AMACOM, New York, 1980

Drucker, Peter F., *The Effective Executive*, Heinemann, London, 1967

Goodworth, Clive T., *How You Can Do More in Less Time*, Business books, London, 1984

Lakein, Alan, *How to Get Control of your Time and your Life*, Gower, Aldershot, 1985

Reynolds, Helen and Tramel, Mary E., *Executive Time Management: Getting 12 Hours' Work out of an 8 Hour Day*, Gower, Aldershot, 1981

Welsh, A.N., *The Skills of Management*, Gower, Aldershot, 1980

68 Negotiating

Bill Scott

This chapter is in three parts. The first describes a style of negotiating designed to produce the greatest area of agreement in the joint interest of both parties. This is a pattern of negotiating in which the parties work together, creatively, *towards agreement*. The second pattern is one in which each party is concerned more with its own advantage than with the joint advantage. Goodwill and agreement are still important, but the overriding consideration is that which is *to independent advantage*. Third, when goodwill is not important, negotiations can sometimes deteriorate into a pattern of *fighting*.

NEGOTIATING TOWARDS AGREEMENT

When the parties are concerned to work together creatively towards agreement the key activities are exploration of one another's position, and creative recognition of what is in their joint interests.

Those phases of exploration and creativity, however, hinge on having first created a suitable climate and on having some procedure which helps the parties to work together. There is no cause for heavy use of negotiating tactics but there is a need for effective preparation. The sequence in this section will therefore be: creating the climate – opening procedure – sequence in negotiations – exploration – creativity – subsequent phases – preparation.

Creating the climate

Negotiators usually operate best when the climate is brisk and businesslike. When negotiating towards agreement, they need a climate which is also cordial and co-operative.

The pace of a negotiation, be it brisk or lethargic, is set very early. Within seconds of the parties coming together, during the rituals of meeting and greeting, a pace is established which is durable. It should be a brisk pace – briskness established by the pace at which the parties are moving about and by the speed at which they are communicating.

The cordial character is established in an ice-breaking phase. As the parties first meet and interact with one another, they need to adjust and to build their regard before getting into possibly controversial areas. The ice-breaking, therefore, needs to be a period in which they discuss neutral topics – the football, the weather, the journey and so on.

The ice-breaking is an indispensable preliminary, so important that it deserves possibly 5 per cent of the prospective negotiating time: a couple of minutes even at the outset of short negotiations; a preliminary dinner and evening out before protracted negotiations.

The brisk and cordial character is thus very soon established. The development of the businesslike and co-operative characteristics comes as the parties sit down and move towards business. Timing and the form of first remarks at the negotiation table should provide the 'business-like': timing, by an immediate statement so that there is no long gap as members get seated; and the form of the opening remarks concentrates on business, towards agreement.

The co-operative character can be set, too, at this early stage. This depends on effectiveness in handling the opening procedure.

Opening procedure

There is nothing more likely to produce a co-operative atmosphere than the immediate question, on sitting down: 'Well, ladies and gentlemen, can we first agree on procedure?' Note that the word 'agree' is used at the outset. Note that the question is one which will almost certainly produce the answer 'Yes'. Note that both parties establish the 'agree' mood from the outset.

There are four procedural terms which should be explored and agreed in this opening stage – the four Ps:

Pace – Purpose – Plan – Personalities

The *pace* is the speed at which the parties need to move together. There needs to be harmony on this pace if parties are to work together effectively. There will not be such harmony if one believes that there is a whole afternoon available whereas the other has another engagement in half an hour.

The *purpose* is the reason why the parties are meeting. If one party thinks that the meeting is purely exploratory, while the other believes the purpose is to achieve a final settlement, then the parties are going to be working at cross-purposes. Even when the purpose has been established in preliminary communication, it is still important at the outset to refresh the consciousness of that purpose, and to take the chance to emphasize that both parties *agree* on that purpose.

The *plan* should be in the form of a short agenda – some four main stages through which the meeting should move.

These first three Ps – Pace, Purpose and Plan – should be agreed at the outset of every negotiation.

The fourth P in the opening procedural stage is Personalities: the introduction of members who do not know one another, their backgrounds, what they can contribute to the meeting. Skilfully used, this opening procedure has great advantages:

1   The meeting can proceed with both parties recognizing joint objectives and a joint means of moving forward
2   The plan gives a framework for control of the remainder of the meeting
3   The mood of agreement can be quickly stated and established

4 The groundwork is set for a smooth and co-operative entry into the later stages of the negotiation.

There is a consistent sequence in these later negotiation stages, which is: exploration – creativity – shaping the deal – bidding – bargaining – settling – ratifying. These phases are – or should be – found in any negotiation, even though they may sometimes become mixed and muddled. The importance of each phase varies a great deal, however. In negotiating towards agreement, the key phases are those of *exploration* and *creativity*.

Exploration

When two parties come together, each has its own distinctive view of the aims and possibilities for the negotiation. If the parties want to work together to bake the biggest possible cake, it is imperative that each should:

* Recognize what both see in the same way
* Recognize and respect what others see in a different way; and
* Be clear about the way in which their own interests are distinctive.

From such recognition can spring the creative spark of what is then most in their joint interests. To achieve that recognition each party should independently make a broad statement of its own position, and give opportunity for the others to seek clarification. Then get a comparable 'broad picture' of the other party's position, and clarify that.

Each opening statement needs to cover:

* *Our understanding* The broad area within which we believe the negotiation will take place
* *Our interests* What we would like to achieve through the negotiation
* *Our priorities* What are the most important aspects for us
* *Our contribution* The way in which we can help to our joint advantage
* *Our attitudes* The consequence of our previous dealing with the other party; their reputation as it has come to us; any special hopes or fears which we may have for collaboration.

Characteristic of the opening statement are the following points:

1 The opening statements of each party should be independent. Each should state its own position, and not attempt at this stage to state the joint interests of the two parties
2 They should not attempt to put assumptions about the position or interests of the other party. (The giving of this assumption serves only to irritate, to confuse and to introduce disharmony.)
3 The statements should be general, not detailed, not yet quantitative
4 The statements should be brief. Each should give the other party an opportunity to come into the discussion quickly, both so that the parties can quickly interact and so that others do not get a sense of being overwhelmed by either the duration or the complexity of an opening statement. Keep it short.

As one party makes its opening statement, the other party needs to listen, clarify and summarize.

- *Listen*   Do not waste energy by thinking up counter-arguments
- *Clarify*   If in doubt, question to get clear what he/she is trying to say. But note: question for clarification. Do not question for justification – that forces the other negotiator on to the defensive and runs counter to the creative climate being sought
- *Summarize*   Feed back the key points of what you understand has been said, so that he/she can check.

Having got clear the view of one party then comes the time for the other party to offer its own opening statement, and for first party's corresponding response – listen, clarify, summarize.

For really creative negotiations, there is a need for these opening exchanges to be carried through frankly in an environment of mutual trust and respect. For these reasons great attention has been paid to creating a positive climate and to underlining agreement and preparing minds in the opening process.

Skilled negotiators are skilled at giving and getting information. They are also conscious that some other parties will seek to exploit them. They therefore look out for danger signals which would suggest a need to change strategy.

If, during the ice-breaking, the other party insists on probing about business matters ('How's trade? cash-flow? quality?'), beware. Probably he is simply an unskilled negotiator, but possibly he is aggressive, seeking information that he can later use aggressively. If he is highly assertive in the phase of proposing and agreeing procedure – then again we must beware. An amber light is flashing.

If he is excessively anxious, that we should be the first to make an opening statement or in challenging that opening statement: then a further amber light is shown – indeed, this is virtually a red light.

Given a succession of amber lights, or just one red light, then the skilled negotiator will be prepared to change his strategy. He should seek a recess, even though it is still an early stage of the negotiation, reconsider the other party's behaviour and decide whether he needs to change to either of the strategies in later sections of this chapter.

But skilled negotiators practising this characteristic style of negotiating towards agreement can normally produce a positive response.

There is thus a great need for negotiators to develop the skills of creating a co-operative climate, of agreeing procedure, and of openness in the exploratory phase.

Creativity

Agreement-oriented negotiators now have a unique opportunity to achieve something to joint advantage, something bigger than either party could get when negotiating to independent advantage. This is the moment to be seeking together to bake the biggest possible cake.

To achieve that creativity, they need first to be imaginative. Later they must impose the forces of reality, but the most productive of ideas may not be seen unless the parties are prepared to range as far as the borderline between reality and fantasy. Be imaginative.

Scandinavian negotiators have a special phrase to launch into this phase. Having summarized the respective positions of the parties as discussed in their opening statements, they say 'All right then – what are the creative possibilities?' In looking for those creative possibilities there are a few guidelines:

1 The pattern of generating the ideas must be broad in its sweep, and interdependent
2 It must be broad because immediately the parties concentrate on one suggestion (either criticizing or exploring in depth), their minds cannot revert to broad and imaginative thinking
3 It must be interdependent, not only to sustain the co-operation between them, but also because each fresh suggestion can kindle a new spark in the imagination of the other. The parties have great potential to be creative together.

This process of recognizing creative possibilities should generate a number of different ideas. There then comes the need to form a bridge between the world in which the parties have been thinking imaginatively, and the world of reality in which their performance must be measured by business criteria. They must decide which of their imaginative ideas offer realistic possibilities. They must then assess and agree on the action needed to turn possibility to mutual advantage.

Subsequent stages

The critical periods of negotiations towards agreement are the exploratory and creative phases. From them springs the recognition of mutual interest. There is, of course, need for the later realities to be foreseen, for agreement on the commercial conditions, and for the establishment of realistic plans to implement decisions. Given, however, the creative atmosphere, then views and possibilities for these commercial and planning discussions can be developed in a similarly open atmosphere,

The approach – 'Let us now explore together' – can be sustained through these later stages without the need to get into the tough bidding and bargaining encountered (and to be further discussed) in the context of other strategies.

However, before starting any negotiation, each party must arrive at the negotiating table well prepared.

Preparation

For any form of negotiation, the negotiator must have done his homework beforehand. He must know the facts, the figures, the arguments.

He needs also to have prepared in two other respects. First, preparing for the procedure. He should think through the Pace, Purpose and Plan which he will suggest for the meeting. And having thought them through, it is advisable to jot down the headlines of pace, purpose and plan on a postcard, to serve as a reminder during the meeting.

Second, he needs to have prepared his opening statement: his understanding of the matter for discussion, his interests, priorities, contribution, attitudes; and again, to jot the headlines on a postcard.

It is important, when negotiating towards agreement, not to over-prepare. The negotiator who has built a detailed framework of prices, deliveries and so on in his preparations is so mentally committed to those preparations that he obscures the possibilities for being creative in any wider sense.

To summarize, when their strategy is negotiating towards agreement, the parties must first create a climate which is brisk, businesslike, cordial and co-operative. They must then establish and agree on a procedure helping them to work together effectively. From the opening procedural discussion they move into important exploratory and creative phases, and thereafter should be able to sustain the high co-operation already established. This must be founded on effective preparation by each party before the event.

NEGOTIATING TO INDEPENDENT ADVANTAGE

Different skills are needed when the negotiator is concerned with gaining special advantage for his party. In some ways these skills mirror those needed when negotiating towards agreement; in other ways, new and different skills are needed.

In particular, bidding and bargaining become the crux of the negotiation. Early moves set the framework; and a different form of preparation is needed. The sequence of this section will therefore be: opening moves – bidding – bargaining – preparation.

Opening moves

The negotiator working to independent advantage must approach the negotiation with a difference of attitude. No longer is his concern to work creatively together with the other party. Rather it is to establish the best deal in the interests of his own side.

Assuming, however, that the deal will need the other party's co-operation to be implemented, or that there will in due course be a need to negotiate some other deal with the same party, it is important that goodwill should be sustained. Aggressive tactics and power struggles should be avoided.

The negotiator's attitude should not be that he will work towards the other party's disadvantage. His attitude must be to find the best way to divide the cake to give satisfaction to both parties. If he likes icing more than fruit, and the other party likes fruit more than icing – there is no problem. Both sides can 'win'. The skilled negotiator thus works towards influencing the other party to value the fruit more than the icing.

The opening moves will again establish the climate for the meeting. Because of the concern for sustaining goodwill it is again important that the climate should be brisk, businesslike, cordial and co-operative; and it is again important that pro-cedure should be agreed at the outset.

Exploration now takes a different form. It becomes necessary to identify the shape of the deal quickly, rather than to look creatively for some new shape. In this process, both parties become more concerned with 'what our party wants'.

The response to the other party needs to be one of probing, to find out which issues or which ingredients are important to the others. Are they, for example, more concerned about price than delivery, quality, terms of settlement?

It is important in these exploratory stages to keep the dialogue on a broad front. If the move to discussion of a particular item (such as price) is taken too soon or too deeply, it is likely to lead to a premature conflict and also to erode some of the most effective possibilities for later bargaining.

Bidding

In negotiating to independent advantage, the guideline to bidding is to start with that which is the highest defensible. (For buyers, the corresponding phrase is of course 'lowest defensible offer.')

The opening bid needs to be 'the highest' because:

1   The opening bid sets a limit beyond which the party cannot aspire. Having once made it, no higher bid can reasonably be put at a later stage
2   The first bid influences others in their valuation of our offer
3   A high bid gives scope for manoeuvre during the later bargaining phases. It gives something in reserve with which to trade
4   The opening bid has a real influence on the final settlement level. The higher the level of aspiration, the greater the prospective achievement.

The opening bid needs to be high. At the same time it must be defensible. Putting forward a bid which cannot be defended does positive damage to the negotiating process. It is found to be offensive by the other party; and if it cannot be defended when challenged in subsequent bargaining; there is soon a loss of face, a loss of credibility, a forced retreat.

The content of the bid of course usually needs to cover a range of issues. The components of the opening bid in a commercial negotiation will not simply be price, but a combination of price, delivery, payment terms, quality specification and a dozen other items.

The 'highest defensible bid' is not an absolute figure; it is a figure which is relevant to the particular circumstances. It is specifically a figure which relates to the way in which others are operating. If they are pressing to their independent advantage, then we must open with a high bid; but if faced with a lot of competition, the bid must be tailored to the level at which it will at least enable us to be invited to continue the negotiations. If we have established cordial relationships with others, possibly over a long period of time, then we shall know the style in which they will operate and the degree of co-operation we can expect – we know the level at which it is prudent for us to make our bid.

On each individual item the opening bid needs to be the highest defensible. We are certain, when negotiating to independent advantage, to be pushed by others to compromise on one or two issues. We cannot be sure which until the bargaining process is under way; we must aspire high on all issues and keep room to manoeuvre.

The manner in which the bid is stated is important. It should be put firmly – without reservations, without hesitations – so that it may carry the conviction of a conscientious negotiating party.

It should be put clearly so that the other party recognizes precisely what is being asked. The creation of a visual aid, that is, taking a sheet of paper and writing figures on it within the sight of the other party, while stating the bid, is powerful reinforcement.

It should be put without apology or comment. There is no need to apologize for anything that can be defended. There is no need to comment since the other party can be expected to raise questions on matters which concern it. And voluntary comment (before others ask for it) simply makes them aware of concern about issues which they might never have considered.

Those then are three guidelines to the way in which a bid should be presented: firmly, clearly, without comment.

In responding to bids by the other party there is a need to distinguish between clarification and justification.

The competent negotiator first ensures that he knows what the other party is bidding. Precisely. He asks any questions which are needed to ensure that he gets the picture clear. He makes sure, in the process, that the other party recognizes that these are questions for clarification and not demands to justify. And once satisfied, he summarizes his understanding of the other party's bid, as a check on the effectiveness of communication between them.

First party should at this stage deflect questions which demand that he justifies his position. He has put a bid, and he has a perfect right to know what the other is prepared to offer in return.

Bargaining

The first two steps in the bargaining process should be:

1 Get it clear
2 Assess the situation.

It is vital to establish a clear picture of the other party's requirements at the outset. We should have got a clear picture of *what* he is bidding already. Now we need to know *why*.

The need is increasingly to build an understanding of what will give him satisfaction and of how to trade to advantage while giving him that satisfaction. We must discover what for him are essentials and what else is desirable but not essential, and what aspects of his bid are really of fringe interest only – where he could readily give.

To achieve this clarity, the guidelines are:

1 Check every item of his bid. Enquire why. Ask how important the item is and how much flexibility he could introduce
2 Never speculate on his opinions or on his motives. A speculation only irritates. Moreover, it is often misconceived – it is out of our frame of reference, not his, and confuses the negotiations between the pair of us. Never put words into his mouth
3 Note his answers without comment. Reserve our position. Avoid deep diving or premature diving into any issue. Keep it on a broad front.

Assuming significant difference between the parties there are now three options for the negotiator:

1 He can accept
2 He can reject
3 He can carry on negotiating.

If he decides to carry on negotiating then he must be prepared for the next round. His options at this stage are:

1 To make a new offer
2 To seek a new offer from the other party
3 To change the shape of the deal (vary the quantity or the quality or the use of third parties), or
4 Embark on give-and-take bargaining.

The steps for preparing for that give-and-take are:

1 Issue identification – list the issues in the package
2 Prepare the bargaining position:

- An essential conditions list – those issues on which it is impossible to concede anything
- A concessions list – those issues on which concession is conceivable. For each such issue, a progression stepped from the minimum which could be offered (against counter-concessions from the other party) in the next round of bargaining, to that ultimate limit which might be forced in successive rounds.

During the bargaining stages, each successive negotiation meeting should be opened with a new round of climate formation and with agreement on procedure. Each round should be concluded with the establishment of some means of resolving outstanding difficulties.

In between, the negotiations should be conducted laterally rather than vertically. That is to say, the aim should be to reach agreement in principle on a broad front, then to tackle more detailed negotiations, still on a broad front. A sequence of several successive moves across the broad front; not a succession of narrow penetrations.

When the time comes for compromise, neither party will readily 'lose face'. Neither party will readily concede on one issue without having some corresponding concession on another. It is thus important to solve difficulties on a broad front or, at the least, two at a time; not simply one at a time.

For example, when the parties have been exploring a difference between them in price and when they are reaching the stage of preparedness to make concessions, it is helpful to both parties if one of them interjects a comment such as 'Well, just before we finish that discussion on price, could we at the same time tie in this question about (for example, the shipping risk) and who is to be responsible for that?'

927

And so sustaining goodwill and sustaining efforts to keep a co-operative climate even through tough bargaining – the negotiation should move towards settlement to independent advantage.

Preparation

As ever, preparation is of critical importance, and the general pattern of preparation should repeat that previously described – with one important difference: the need to be more specific during preparation processes. Whereas in creative negotiations it is important to keep one's preparations general and to preserve flexibility, in more divisive negotiations the negotiator needs to be protected from exploitation. He needs to have considered his bids at an early stage. There is this constant dichotomy between the need for flexibility and the need for precise preparations. The one is the enemy of the other. The choice should reflect the strategic situation which will be referred to at the end of this chapter.

To summarize: bidding and bargaining are the key phrases in negotiating to independent advantage. It is a type of negotiation needing distinctive attitudes and skills. Bidding and bargaining become more important than exploration. Climate formation and procedural development remain important. So does preparation though it takes a slightly different form.

FIGHTING

Warfare is not a commendable form of negotiation. Nevertheless, negotiators do become involved in confrontations in which the aim has to be 'win' – or, at any rate, to ensure that they do not 'lose' at the hands of an aggressive party.

The use of fighting methods

The fighter's aim is to win and to make the other party the loser.

This is a dangerous attitude to negotiations. It puts goodwill at risk; it obscures the possibility of creative co-operation; it naturally provokes the other party to fight back, causing delay and putting at risk the fighter's chances of success. Even when the fighter batters an 'opponent' into submission, he is not likely to find the deal implemented energetically.

The means which the fighter uses are powerful. Both by his personal behaviour and by the negotiating tactics which he uses, he seeks to reinforce the power of his position. His methods include:

- A constant search for gain at every opportunity
- At each successive stage in the process of negotiating, he wants fresh advantage
- Any withdrawals must be deliberate, tactical withdrawals, designed only to promote greater advance
- Power-methods; high in terms of the pace, size and forcefulness of demands, low in readiness to listen or to yield
- Task-centred. Concern for his special advantage. Not concerned with other party's pride or dignity nor with their feelings. Forcing them to 'accept or else'.

The pattern of a fighting negotiation

The central concern of the fighting negotiator is to win. This winning takes place in the fighting phase of the negotiation – a special version of the bargaining phase, at which he is expert and best able to use his personal characteristics. Quickly he leads the negotiation to the point at which his form of bargaining becomes the dominant activity.

This leaves little time or interest for the early stages of negotiating, little time to get on the same wavelength as other party, or to agree on a plan; little time to explore mutual interests. Even issue identification is hastened and the negotiation quickly becomes centred on the first chosen issue.

The pattern of the negotiation is then 'vertical', deep diving on the first selected issue. He aspires high and pushes until he 'wins' on that and each successive issue.

Fighting tactics

He knows a lot of tactics and manoeuvres, and regularly uses a number. He has his own repertoire, and admires (and tries to emulate) tactics which have been used 'against' him by other negotiators. Here are some of them:

- *Probing from the start* The fighter enters the negotiating room, shakes hands and wishes us 'Good morning' and immediately starts probing – about our business situation, about the product or service, even about one's personal situation. The advantages sought are in getting information, in building a picture about the other party and especially in recognizing weaknesses and vulnerabilities. The fighter also establishes a power position, a pattern of aggressive leadership
- *Get/give* The fighter is concerned to get something before giving anything – to get a small concession before giving a small concession and to get a big concession before giving a big concession; to get information before giving information; to get the other party's bid before making a bid; to get the power of being the first to make an opening statement. Get/give tactics used by skilled negotiators can have positive commercial advantages in the short term. They may well gain ground during early negotiating stages but in the long run lead to delay and deadlock (neither party being willing always to give before it gets)
- *Showing emotion* For example anger. Making loud and emotional statements, possibly banging the table; the form of eye contact, posture, gesture and voice, all displaying emotions
- *Good guy/bad guy* This is the tactic for use by a team of two negotiators. One takes the role of the 'bad guy', being aggressive, making excessive demands, dominating and uncooperative. When these tactics have softened up the 'opposition' the 'good guy' takes over the lead role, constructively offering solutions, quietly trying to reach a mutual understanding. The tactic parallels the archetypal method for prisoners of war; ruthless interrogation by a tough investigator followed by sympathy from one with a different personality to whom, with luck, the prisoner would open up

- *Poker-faced* Giving nothing away by expression, tone, posture or gesture; an important part of the fighting negotiator's armoury
- *Managing the minutes* Taking responsibility at the end of each session for producing the record, slanting interpretations of what has been agreed (always to self-advantage). Readiness to include the odd item which 'ought to have been agreed' even though there was no time to discuss it – provided, of course, that the odd item is favourable
- *Getting upstairs* When unable to come to an agreement, taking steps to contact the other negotiator's boss, or boss's boss's boss!
- *PR* Many fights are conducted by negotiators acting on behalf of other group-ings. For examples, the union negotiator who represents the work-force and the government negotiator representing a country. Here it is important for the group represented to be kept informed and influenced so that it continues to give its backing to the negotiator. Ability at public functions is thus another important part of the fighter's armoury
- *Forcing moves* There are, of course, yet other moves which some negotiators use: bribery, sex, blackmail, bugging. Most negotiators would see such devices as rankly unethical, but people negotiating very important deals are at risk and need to be on their guard.

Counter measures

Counters to those who fight are in two forms: long-term and short-term measures.

In the long term, where there is expectation of repeated rounds of negotiations (for example, in labour negotiations) there is a need for the development of attitudes, skills and relationships.

This development takes place best when the parties can come together at a place remote from their normal battlefield, and at a time during the off-season for fighting. Especially fruitful is the practice, which has been well developed in Scandinavia, of holding joint working seminars for two or three days. The product of such seminars is not only the development of relationships but the planning of subsequent joint activities.

That is a long-term approach. In the short term, measures to counter the fighter fall into three categories:

1 Head him off
2 Control the battlefield
3 Cope with his tactics.

The most satisfying way of coping with him is of course to head off the fight before it develops. If this is to be achieved it must be done in the critical opening seconds and minutes:

- Deflect his opening questions
- Preserve a neutral ice-breaking period
- Do not be drawn by his probing questions
- Do not let him assert leadership
- Do not let him dominate the early moments – what is being talked about, when to stand and when to sit, the seating arrangements.

We are able to control the skirmishing if we can somehow control the battlefield. In negotiating terms, this 'control of the battlefield' is control of the procedures of negotiating. Guidelines are:

1 Seek for form and plan for the proceedings
2 Seek for opening discussion of purpose, plan and pace
3 Keep bringing him back to the agreed plan
4 Keep things fluid. Use the 'broad front' approach
5 Seek compromise. He will be impervious either to searches for creative resolution of differences, or to sensitive attempts to influence him. His *métier* is that of compromise. If his position is that he is asking £120 and ours is that it is only worth £100, then settlement is likely to be at the compromise amount of £110. Bargain slowly until you get him down to at most £110.

Above all, keep control of the process – keep control of what is being negotiated and in which sequence – keep to the plan. It will irritate him. He much prefers to be able to run free, but do not worry. A caged fighter cannot do as much damage as one on the loose.

To cope with some of the fighter's tactics: when he is using the 'get/give' tactic, we must not give too easily, for if we give before we get, he will regard this as a sign of weakness. He will want to get yet more and will change the tactic into 'get/get/give' and soon will be aspiring even higher to 'get/get/get'.

We must not give in. We must trade scrap of information for scrap of information, scrap of readiness for scrap of readiness, scrap of concession for scrap of concession.

The only counter to displays of anger is to suspend negotiations, either temporarily or permanently. The human brain is such that emotions (such as anger) are handled in one part of it, rational thinking in another part. Once the brain becomes focused on emotive thinking, then the rational part is cut off. The angry party cannot receive rational messages and it is no use the other party trying to instil them. So the counter is to suspend operations.

It does not matter if first party's anger is simply a display rather than real anger. Second party has no way of being sure about the matter. First party has behaved in ways which are not acceptable and second party should immediately suspend.

The 'good guy/bad guy' tactic is difficult to recognize and difficult to counter. But, of course, if it has been recognized in one round of negotiating then the negotiator will be alert for it during later rounds and must hope either to be able to ignore the bad guy or to separate the two 'opponents'.

The counter to 'getting upstairs' is to state strong objection to the tactic and then to arrange for our own boss to come in and make it clear that theirs was a losing tactic.

Formality is, inevitably a device used to try to bring order to such negotiations. However, the fighting negotiator becomes expert in framing and fighting by a rule book which is to his advantage. He is expert not only in drafting and amending rules but in interpreting and manipulating them. The effective negotiator from the other side therefore is forced to build his own corresponding expertise.

Preparation is, as ever, of critical importance for effectiveness in negotiating. When faced with a fight it is imperative to be well prepared procedurally and to have precise objectives, targets and prepared concession lists. There is special need to prepare options ('scenarios' in the current jargon), alternative approaches which could enable both parties to move forward while minimizing loss of face.

The counter to his competence at public relations is to develop equal competence and to ensure that the relevant public is suitably influenced.

In meeting with a fighting 'opponent', then, the negotiator is operating in a world of power. He needs skill to control the battlefield and to prevent his being exploited. But that is a short-term approach. The longer-term interest demands that he should work for some joint development of attitudes, skills and relationships with the other party.

SUMMARY

This chapter has been concerned with three distinct forms of negotiation. First, with negotiations in which two parties seek to move forward co-operatively to create the best possible deal in their joint interests. Second, with patterns of negotiation in which both parties aim to preserve goodwill while at the same time trying to maximize their independent advantage. Third and finally, with fights in which continuing goodwill is not treated as being important.

The choice among these approaches to negotiating will depend on a number of strategic issues:

1 The extent to which the parties will need to come together again from time to time
2 The respective strength of the parties in the market-place
3 The character and quality of their negotiators
4 The time-scale and the importance of the prospective deal.

These strategic issues are considered at greater length in Marsh (1984) and Scott (1981).

FURTHER READING

Karrass, C.L., *Give and Take*, World Publishing Co., 1974. A good treatment of the tactics used by American negotiators.
Marsh, P.D.V., *Contract Negotiation Handbook*, Gower, Aldershot, 2nd edn, 1984. Excellent treatment of negotiating strategy of general interest. Preceded by a mathematical/economic analysis of bidding – also excellent, but demanding a reader with mathematical talents.
Scott, Bill, *The Skills of Negotiating*, Gower Aldershot, 1981. A highly readable expansion of his ideas by the author of this chapter of the handbook.
Winkler, John, *Bargaining for Results*, Heinemann, Oxford, 1981.

69 Teamworking

Colin Hastings

A consistent theme running through most recent studies of effective organizations is the importance of teamworking. The word has historically been used to describe permanent functional teams such as production and sales. However, in its recent resurgence it is cross-functional and multidisciplinary teamworking that is seen as an important ingredient of success. This form of collaboration is vital to solving complex problems fast, gaining commitment to change, and tapping the full reservoir of latent energy and ideas possessed by most organizations.

As a result, much of the work in organizations is now carried out by temporary project groups or task forces. Their briefs are often complex and frequently difficult to define. They range from organizing an office move to launching a new product, from testing a new drug to making a bid for a new advertising account, and from implementing a new process to managing a merger. Whatever the objective, and even where multiple project teams are used, a wide range of skills and experience now exists to make teamworking successful. It does not always come naturally, especially in organizations that think mainly in terms of hierarchy and functions. Learning how to assemble and develop teams to full advantage and how to create the organizational culture in which they survive is a challenge to which senior management, line management, team leaders, human relations specialists and external consultants can all contribute. This chapter summarizes the key conclusions from the author's research and consultancy on how to make teamworking work in your organization.

THE ROLE OF SENIOR MANAGEMENT

Senior management must create the conditions within the organization that help both functional and cross-functional teams to perform. Teams without senior management sponsorship are like plants without water. Some of the most important 'do's' and 'don'ts' for this sponsorship role are:

1 *Divest responsibility and authority to teams* If senior management provide an exciting vision, ask much of the teams, train them and then trust them, they will achieve significant results
2 *Ensure that you are open to the teams' ideas* The teams will become very authoritative. If management respect them and learn from them, they and the organization will benefit hugely
3 *Do not delegate responsibility for the project elsewhere* A common pattern is that senior management are much in evidence only at the interesting time

when a team project is launched. Managers should ensure their continuing commitment and visibility

4 *Demonstrate commitment by removing obstacles* Find out about and act against organization blockages facing teams. This is another test of commitment

5 *Ensure that the budget is there to develop teams and their leaders* Just as in capital investment, underinvestment in human resources is often wasted investment. Outstanding teams do not just happen

6 *Ensure that teams are clear about what is expected of them* This often takes time and a lot of discussion. Do not assume that the objectives are clearly understood.

CREATING HIGH PERFORMANCE TEAMS

Planning the 'how'

Many teams seriously underperform. Even those whose performance is acceptable often look poor when compared with outstanding teams. Successful teams do spend planning time developing ground rules about how they need to operate in order to be successful. Some of the general ground rules or values that characterize high-performing teams include:

1 A shared belief in, and excitement about, what they are trying to achieve
2 A persistent and obsessive pursuit of their goals while maintaining flexibility in their strategies for reaching them
3 A realization that no team is self-sufficient: it needs resources from the organization and elsewhere
4 An attitude which is always looking to find a better way to do things
5 An action orientation; they do not wait for things to happen, they go out and make things happen
6 A realization that the team exists to produce something for someone, a client or user, allied to a deep-seated commitment to understand and deliver what they want.

In practical terms, however, there are a number of things that outstanding teams get right. There are seven key aspects to a team's functioning; these are covered in the following sections.

Negotiating success criteria

Teams seldom specify their own success criteria. These usually come from a number of external sources, both inside and outside the organization. They need to map out who expects things from them and what it is that they would want.

Who is the client?

A systems development team in a life assurance company had a number of customers to satisfy. The board as overall sponsors of the project had crucial expectations about overall cost and timing. The sales forces wanted the system to be able to provide specific information within certain time frames to their customers. The head of systems wanted compatibility and uniformity with other systems. What they all forgot was the users, that is, those clerks who were going to make the system work for the company! It is very important to get a team to consider all the different people they need to satisfy and their differing requirements and expectations.

What are they looking for?

Many people find it difficult to express what they need and many teams find it equally difficult to be precise about what they are trying to achieve. However, the greater the clarity and understanding the greater the chances of success.

Some of the ways in which this clarity of purpose can be achieved are as follows:

1 Help the team to use good open questions to draw information out of clients. Some useful ones include:

   - What *must* we do?
   - What must we *not* do?
   - If we were to satisfy your most outrageous hopes, what would we be doing?

2 Get the team to suggest a range of alternative approaches from the conservative to the way out. Then make them get clients to list systematically what they like and dislike about these. This helps both client and team to be much more specific.

3 Distinguish hard (tangible, quantitative) criteria and soft (intangible, qualitative) criteria. Most teams concentrate on the former because they are easier to specify, but clients and sponsors make their judgements on both.

Keeping success criteria in sight

Once teams are involved in their tasks it is very easy for them to lose sight of what they are really trying to achieve. Make sure in the first place that all the team fully understand all the subtleties of what is expected of the team. Secondly, make sure that they constantly come back to the key question: what are we trying to achieve and for whom?

Managing the outside

A design team in an engineering consultancy was bemoaning the fact that it could never get prints of drawings done when they were needed and that the woman in charge of the print room was always uncooperative. Eventually they realized that they always made demands on her at the last moment, and had never thought about the conflicting priorities that she faced.

They cannot go it alone

Teams never have all the resources that they need. They are frequently dependent on other departments, external specialists, subcontractors, consultants and even their clients for help and information. Some teams may need help to locate and make contact with external resources (known as the invisible team).

Tangible and intangible resources

Most teams will seek the tangible resources such as money, people, materials and information that they require. What they may ignore is the intangible resources of support, commitment, protection and clout that they need, as well as resistance or ignorance in others.

In particular, a team should be coached to anticipate the opportunities and problems presented by the invisible team. These key outsiders should be involved at an early stage. The team should prepare the ground, cultivating positive relationships and above all motivating them to want to help the team achieve its purpose.

Planning the 'what'

It is surprising how many teams launch themselves into a task without defining the problems adequately, evaluating alternatives or developing a coherent plan to guide their efforts.

Make sure they do some planning together

We have found that it is not so much a team's plan that is fundamental to success, but rather how they go about the process of planning. Above all, it is vital that all team members develop a clear and shared understanding of the 'big picture', that is, the broad plan to be taken by the team with key time, role and cost milestones. These factors provide important and frequent targets for achievement. If it is a small team, the best way to do this is to have all involved in developing the plan, which ensures that it is both realistic and believed in. In a larger team, beware of the leader or planner who wants to prepare a plan for the team in isolation. Each level should plan their own work in detail within the big picture.

In predictable situations, where the team has considerable experience, the plan can be prepared at the beginning and the team can reasonably expect to keep to it. However, in more ambiguous situations where there are many unknowns, you should encourage a different approach. Do not let the team spend too much time trying to plan detail. Encourage them instead to go and find out by doing and also to bring the information back quickly to use in more informed planning. In short, do not let a team waste time on trying to plan the unplannable. Equally do not allow a plan to become a straightjacket where the situation has clearly changed. The outstanding team is one that does plan but can also adapt and improve a plan as it learns and discovers better ways to do things.

Leading a team

A big food firm promoted one of their best scientists to lead an important new research team. He rapidly discovered that he was out of his depth, as the work and the team disintegrated about him. An alert personnel manager spotted his predicament and realized where the company, not the scientist, had gone wrong.

Choosing team leaders

Effective team leaders will have a record of success in their own specialism combined with a broader technical view of how different specialisms integrate. Equally, they should be known and respected within the organization. Leaders like this have a head start when it comes to negotiating success criteria and resources with the team's sponsor, resource providers or users. However, specialist achievement and credibility is insufficient in the leader role; for this role contenders should also have demonstrated ability to inspire and motivate others towards a goal. They must be able to plan and prioritize their own and other people's work, being able to stand back from detail, monitor progress and anticipate problems before they become serious.

The role of the personnel function is to help identify and then train suitable candidates for these roles and to influence those who make the selection to apply not just technical, but managerial criteria to the process. See Briner, Geddes and Hastings (1990) for a comprehensive guide to selecting and developing such team leaders.

Preparing leaders

The ideal leader is seldom available and any appointment is a compromise. Additionally, more and more organizations are using their more talented specialists to lead teams as an important personal and career development opportunity. Senior management should ensure that team leaders are fully prepared for, and supported in, their new and demanding roles. There is a range of options available:

1 Ensure each team leader has a sponsor at senior level who is prepared to spend time coaching that leader
2 Ensure that leaders get regular feedback from senior management, users, service departments and even the outside client about their own and their team's performance
3 Provide training and development opportunities in skills and knowledge areas that are lacking (having previously helped leaders assess their strengths and weaknesses). Programmes are particularly relevant that look at the human aspects of managing teams and projects, for these are the skills most specialists lack
4 If feasible, bring a number of team leaders together as a regular support Group. Get each to bring a success and a problem to each meeting. Share and analyse the successes, and motivate them to help sort out each other's problems
5 Suggest to leaders that they run team development workshops with their teams, using either internal or external consultants to help them improve performance.

Team members

A team's members are its life-blood. Senior managers and personnel specialists should be giving thought to how the organization plans its resources to ensure that the team gets the right people for its job.

Getting the right mix

The range of specialist technical knowledge required by team members is dictated by the task. Care should be taken not to define this too narrowly. One new product development team consisted purely of marketing and technical specialists. Their progress was slow and they met tacit resistance from other departments when they made demands of them. Their solution was to diversify the team so that it had representatives of all those parties who had a key role to play at any stage in the process. So they acquired an accountant and a production engineer. They also asked the account executive from their advertising agency to join them regularly. The result was a relatively conventional new product but one that was manufactured and packaged in a revolutionary new way, and to which the whole company became involved and committed.

Membership qualities

In addition to their technical skills, however, members should be good team-workers. Ideally, they are people who can accept leadership and direction – which does not mean that they should be passive and compliant individuals. On the contrary, personnel specialists should be looking out for individuals who have the confidence to contribute actively and take a share of the responsibility within a team. They need to be active followers. They should also be people who are not so blinkered in their own specialism that they cannot appreciate the contributions of other specialists. But, perhaps most important of all, team members should have a fundamental commitment to quality of performance not only in technical terms but also in terms of being sensitive to the needs of clients, the leader, fellow members and the rest of the organization. They should also be reliable in meeting targets and deadlines and be honest when facing problems.

The team together

Everyone has their ultimate story about boredom, wasted time and lack of results from badly planned and badly run meetings. For those experienced in meetings it is easy to forget that it is a skill that requires learning and one that many specialists have little experience of until they suddenly find themselves in a team. Nor should it be just the leader who develops the skills; no team can function fully unless all members share the basic discipline needed to work effectively together.

The organization should ensure that teams receive this basic training, and that they actually do use the knowledge. A few informal questions to team members after a meeting will soon establish whether they practise what they preach.

Another simple technique is to get a team to end each meeting with a simple review of how effectively they have worked. Team leaders or personnel specialists can give them the following checklist for discussion:

- Are agenda, discussion notes, and information circulated in advance for people to digest?
- What are we trying to achieve as a result of this meeting?
- Given what we have on the agenda, how much time do we need for each item and which is the most important?

- Do people listen, summarize, clarify and demonstrate interest and attentiveness to others?
- Do people ramble off the particular agenda item without realizing?
- Do they use the full skills and diversity present, or do just a few people dominate?
- Do they search for better alternatives or just grab the first idea at face value?
- Is conflict ignored, smoothed over or used positively as a source of ideas and energy? Do they have ways of resolving conflicts? Can they compromise?
- Do members ever make observations about how the meeting is going or ask to stop the discussion momentarily to discover how best to proceed on a problem?
- At the end of the meeting, do they tie each other down to producing specific actions by particular times?

The team apart

A group of companies formed a purchasing team from buyers in its five divisions spread round the country. The team met for a day every three months. Little seemed to happen in between meetings and each meeting appeared to go over the same ground as before. In the end the team was disbanded on the grounds that no area for significant cost saving had been identified.

This is an extreme example. But it is true for all teams that they spend relatively little time actually working *together*. It is also true that most of the problems occur when the team disperses between meetings. The problems are exacerbated when team members work on different floors, in different buildings, on different sites or even in different countries.

Keeping it together

The paradox of the team apart is that it merely highlights the importance of the team coming together. If you survey teams in your organization that seldom get together, you may find that they lack identity, the 'we-feeling' that is so important to a good team. The organization should be encouraging these dispersed teams to meet regularly, not just to work but to spend social and leisure time together to build the bonds. One highly dispersed team we know found they have had to come together at least every six weeks just to keep all their efforts on track. They used to rotate their meetings round the different sites and always met the evening prior to their meeting with a social event organized by the local host. The personnel or human relations department can influence members to come together through its ability to organize company conferences, briefing sessions and training courses.

Out of sight – but not out of mind

It is a frequent complaint of people in distant sites that they get ignored and forgotten by the centre. This is a direct challenge to the leader. The leader often has great difficulty in visiting and staying in touch regularly. Human relations or personnel department members can help by visiting, staying in regular contact and ensuring that all housekeeping issues (which often assume greater importance at a distance) get speedily sorted. Personnel can, in fact, become an extra pair of eyes and ears for the team apart, being aware of what is happening and in particular looking out for any early warning signals that things might be going wrong in the human system.

Communication, communication and more communication

Outstanding teams think hard about how they are going to preserve their sense of urgency and identity when they are working apart. They will develop formal methods such as regular reports, meetings and circulation lists. Subgroups within the team that are perhaps not too far from each other will agree to meet in between formal meetings. Members will talk frequently on the telephone and the leader in particular will act as a central communications for disseminating up-to-date information to those who need it.

The growing power of information technology to link distant sites has important implications for a company's communications policies. It can make a dramatic difference to helping the 'team apart' to stay in touch.

DEALING WITH CONSULTANTS

In many cases the organization will lack the experience of high-performing teams, their development and the multiple ways in which teams can be used to help transform the organization. In these circumstances an internal or external consultant, with the necessary experience and skills, has an important role to play. Consultants will work directly with senior management, personnel department, service departments and teams.

The consultants' first role is to take the broader view, reviewing teamworking within the organization and agreeing action as necessary to improve it. Their second role is to work on the ground in a training, development or consultancy role with senior management sponsors, leaders and members of their teams to help them improve their performance.

Senior management and personnel departments have a leading role in assessing and selecting consultants for projects of this nature. Here are some of the considerations to test out:

1 *Check they are results-oriented* Sometimes consultants in this area are only interested in group process and relationships as an end in themselves and are not sufficiently performance-oriented, nor interested in the real work issues facing teams and organizations
2 *Test them out on senior management to assess their credibility* Senior management must feel comfortable with them because much of the consultant's role is to influence them in their role as sponsors
3 *Check that they can work on the team's external relationships and not only on its internal workings* If they only work on the team's internal functioning they are missing important factors that affect a team's performance
4 *Assess their flexibility and realism* Do they just offer a standard package, questionnaire or workshop? This is unlikely to have a real impact in helping teams with real performance issues or create the conditions for teamworking success within your organization

5 *Can they also work with leaders and members on an individual basis* Do they have good counselling skills and sensitivity to help individuals improve their personal contribution?

6 *Would they be prepared to call a halt?* Consultants are employed to use their professional experience and judgement in order to help their clients' teamworking projects to succeed. If the consultants find that some of the ground has not been properly prepared, or if insufficient support or investment is forthcoming to make it work, then they must confront those issues with their client and sponsors. The motivation is twofold. First, they do not want their client and all the others in the organizations to waste time, energy and money only to fail or at best achieve mediocre results. Secondly, they themselves like to be associated with success not failure.

CONCLUSION

Creating the teamworking organization that is able to mobilize the talents of all its people in order to adapt fast and solve complex problems is one of the basic management challenges. When successful, the results are spectacular but no organization should be under any illusion about the investment of time and money needed to make it work.

FURTHER READING

Belbin, R.M., *Management Teams – Why they succeed or fail*, Heinemann, London, 1981. A very useful look at the different roles that an effective team needs

Briner, W., Geddes, M., and Hastings, C., *Project Leadership*, Gower, Aldershot, 1990. A practical book on the neglected role of project leaders in organizations. It also gives more insight into the nature of the teamworking organization

Francis, D. and Young, D., *Improving Work Groups: A practical manual for team building*, University Associates Inc., 1979. Just what it says – a practical manual of 'do it yourself' team building exercises

Hastings, C., Bixby, P. and Chaudhry-Lawton, R., *The Superteam Solution: Successful teamworking in organisations*, Gower, Aldershot, 1986. A more extended treatment of the ideas described in this chapter, with many examples and suggestions for performance improvement. Also has case studies of the different ways that improved teamworking can contribute to organizational performance. Readable

Moss Kanter, R., *The Change Masters*, George Allen & Unwin, London, 1984. A heavyweight study of corporate entrepreneurs at work. Especially good on how to 'manage the outside'. Good insights, but needs patience

Peters, T.J. and Waterman, R.H., *In Search of Excellence*, Harper & Row, New York, 1982. A modern management classic that is very readable. In particular, demonstrates the crucial contribution of multi-disciplinary teams in successful USA companies

70 Speaking

Gordon Bell

From the chairman of the largest group to supervisors and staff, everybody uses words. Every businessman and woman writes letters, reports, memoranda, orders. Reasonable people will agree that words are a vital tool in industry and commerce. The higher we go up the ladder of management, the more important words become. Communications are the nub of effective management. Time and effort invested in developing your own skills as a communicator must produce dividends.

In this part of the book we shall discuss three aspects of communications:

1 Speaking (this chapter)
2 Reports (Chapter 71)
3 Meetings (Chapter 72).

EFFECTIVE SPEAKING

Speaking is for other people. This fact about effective speaking is so obvious and so simple that many overlook it. An audience always evaluates a speaker subjectively. What did they get from the talk? The answer to this question measures the speaker.

A manager needs to command attention at conferences and other meetings: he must be able to make oral presentations to his board and to professional organizations; to brief his staff, to persuade, to convince. Particularly if he is a specialist, he must be able to clarify specialized concepts so that others, not necessarily qualified, can share his thoughts. Even the most brilliant person is useless until his ideas can be shared by others who can use them.

A successful speaker is one who gives the audience a success. Many managers suffer from the delusion that speaking in public is the same as a theatrical performance, or something suitable only for extroverts. This delusion often serves as a defence. The plain truth is that they fear exposure of their limitations as speakers. This state of affairs is deplorable. If a person has something worth saying, he should not only say it but also learn how to say it with full effect. 'Why should the devil have all the best tunes?' asked General Booth. It is also pertinent to ask, 'Why should the image-makers and the tricksters have a monopoly of effective speech?'

Let us examine the fear, sometimes amounting to terror, that afflicts otherwise intelligent people when they are asked to speak. What causes this fear? The unpopular but accurate answer is vanity – too great a concern with 'How am I going to do?' and not enough concern with 'How are they – the audience – going to do?' This truth is a hard one to face yet it applies at both ends of the scale. Vanity causes the glib, arrogant, loud-mouthed, no-nerves-at-all-I-can-talk-at-the-drop-of-a-hat person to subject his audience to a flood of waffle; it also causes the timid to worry about themselves at the expense of their hearers. If you face this fact now you can save yourself a lot of trouble.

A successful speaker is one who gives the audience a success. The speaker's success stems from the audience reaction. If the audience reacts in the desired manner, the speaker has been effective. There is no other criterion.

Newton's third law of motion says, roughly, 'To every action there is an equal and opposite reaction.' A given stimulus creates the same response if conditions remain constant. Herein lies one of the most important points that a speaker must consider. An audience is never a constant factor. There is no such thing as a production-line human being. Everyone is unique. People in an audience vary in social levels, technical knowledge, prejudices, age, sex. Even the same pepole gathered together at different times or under different conditions can change as an audience.

Effective speaking is a human relationship. It is not something that one person does in isolation. Any speaker wishing to get a desired reaction must begin by studying the audience, the source of the reaction. Unfortunately, many speakers begin with themselves and end in disaster.

So, the first point for a would-be speaker to think about is his attitude to the audience. This thinking must be positive and outward – not so much 'what subject am I going to talk about?' as 'How can I create a powerful relationship with my audience using the subject as both the generator and the cement which binds that relationship?'

Can you imagine anyone erecting a building or constructing a locomotive who would begin by laying the first brick or polishing the whistle? A rational person starts with a purpose and a plan. So does a professional speaker – and you, whether you realize it or not, are a professional speaker, a professional report-and-letter-writer and a professional meeting person. If you analyse your job as a manager you will find that you do little else but talk, write and discuss. Given equal knowledge of the business, a person who knows how to speak, how to write and when to listen always has the advantage over one who does not.

PREPARING AN EFFECTIVE TALK

Many speakers complain that they have no time to prepare properly. If you know your subject you can prepare a talk in one hour. The method we shall discuss now is the one-hour method. There are three stages, roughly twenty minutes each. (When you have ample time, say, three weeks or six, simply extend each stage accordingly.)

1   Gathering subject matter

Arm yourself with plenty of large sheets of paper and write down at great speed *every* idea on your subject that enters your mind. Make no attempt to think these ideas through. Get them down in rapid notes, symbols or any other shorthand form that will enable you to recognize them when you arrive at stage 2 – the plotting stage. Work at speed. Your aim during stage 1 is quantity; to amass hundreds of facts about your subject, various opinions, prejudices, misunderstandings, possible visual aids, thoughts about the audience, the occasion – anything which in any way may bear on your proposed talk. Note direct facts, oblique, tangential and even remotely relevant facts. Set down page after page of rough notes.

During stage 1 it is most important that you concentrate and work non-stop at great speed. If time allows, do this several times until you have at least ten times more material than your final talk demands. Fix nothing, solidify nothing. Bear in mind that what might be old stuff, obvious to you, might well be new or in need of explanation to your hearers. So get it all down. Note everything. A thought unnoted often disappears for ever.

Give yourself all the options. Review the whole subject. This review jogs your memory, gives you flexibility, acts as a solid background for your talk and can prove particularly helpful if you are required to answer questions. Instead of having to excavate facts from the deep recesses of your mind, you have them near the surface, fresh and ready for use.

Quantity. Now you have raw stuff to work on, stacks of it.

2   Purpose and people

Establish your precise purpose. What reaction do you wish to induce in your hearers? What job has the talk to perform? Write down your purpose; rewrite it several times until you express, exactly, in a few cogent words, the effect you wish to achieve. Know what you are doing, explicitly. Be thorough about this. Do nothing else until you have got your objective clear.

Now that you have ample subject matter and a vividly clear purpose, you must ponder on the real material for your talk – the people who will listen to you. Examine every link they have or might have with your subject because they will be completely uninterested until what you say has something to do with them. Obvious isn't it? What is their technical level, their social, financial level; what are their needs in connection with you and your subject? Study the people until you can see their view of your subject. You can only put your view across in relation to theirs. If you do not know anything about your audience, you would be well advised to find out at once. A discussion with the organizers, even a telephone call, can prove useful. Get to know your audience and integrate them into your presentation *now*; it will be too late when you are on your feet talking.

So, *purpose* and *people*. These two essential elements for an effective talk rarely receive enough thought or attention.

Stop here, please.

You must go no farther until you have checked that you have the driving force of a clear purpose working for you. You must go no farther until you have developed a real interest in your audience and their needs. These two factors should already be allies helping you to establish a partnership with your audience.

After your talk, what message will your hearers carry away with them? What big points supported your thesis? No audience will remember everything that you said. Decide at this stage in your preparation what basic theme you wish them to remember. As with your purpose, write down your *theme* and work on it until it becomes simple, straightforward and crystal clear.

Next, separate the one, two or three really important points from the lesser points. Which are the *main points* that you want them to have working in their minds? If you do not establish them clearly now, they will not stand out prominently enough in your delivered talk. Your job as a speaker is to clarify the subject for your audience. You cannot do this unless you first clarify it for yourself.

Now build your talk on your foundation of:

Purpose – People – Theme – Main points.

A few reminders

- A successful speaker knows his subject and is enthusiastic about it
- He makes certain that he is well prepared
- He has considered the audience and believes that the subject is important to them
- Bad speakers are usually people who think about themselves too much.

Pertinent questions to be answered at the end of stage 2

1 What exactly is my subject?
2 Why am I speaking about it to this audience and what do I know about them?
3 What are the most important things I must tell them?
4 Have I picked out the main points which must be highlighted?
5 Have I arranged these points so that this particular audience will fully understand them and be involved in them?
6 Have I ruthlessly eliminated matter not pertinent to my purpose? (No self-indulgence)
7 Have I made sure that there is a glowing, dominant theme?
8 What will the audience gain from this talk?

3 Delivering the goods

The audience must at once be made confident that the speaker knows what he is doing. They must find his first thoughts intensely interesting. This, of course, rules out the usual dreary opening, for instance, where the speaker talks about himself and his worries as a speaker.

The three-sentence technique can secure a telling impact on opening:

- *Sentence 1* You make any vivid, unexpected, off-beat, truly interesting remark you like (always, of course, bearing in mind your audience)
- *Sentence 2* You link, skilfully, sentence 1 to your subject and make clear exactly what your subject is
- *Sentence 3* You *involve* the audience in both your opening remarks and your subject.

It is essential that you economize and discipline yourself to use only three sentences for this effect. There must be no woolly edges around these three sentences, no 'hums' and 'hahs', no interpolated oddments, no clutter. You are

945

seeking a clean, crisp, immediate communication, a direct response. Experiment until you have got a really good beginning. Excite, Link, Involve. Do not be satisfied with the first openings you think of: try at least six ways before you decide.

Avoid the word 'I' for at least one minute. Substitute 'you,' 'your', or group words describing the audience, such as engineers, Scotsmen, managers. Be as specific as you can. Talk about them and their links with the subject. Get the attention firmly on to them and away from yourself.

As soon as your impact has been achieved and the audience knows what your broad subject is, define your limits so that they will not waste their attention on parts of the subject outside the scope of your talk. Tell them where you intend to take them within your subject, sometimes even which aspects you intend to leave out. From the start, concentrate their mental energy on the relevant aspects. Give them clear signposts, briefly.

Now, you have a dynamic purpose in your mind; you and your audience know where you are going. They have been intrigued by your opening remarks and are ready for the statement of your basic theme, ready for the development of your first main point supporting that theme – and they are eager to find out how and where they fit in and what you have to say.

The elements are prepared for you – the catalyst – to do your work.

There are no dull subjects. Everything under the sun teems with interest. From even such beginnings as a dirty ashtray or the Industrial Training Act a lively mind could create a fascinating talk. How are you going to tell your story, how give your facts their full value as facts plus that life which also gives them interest? The key to power in story-telling is to bind everything you say to people and things – the concrete rather than the abstract. You might well be talking about some entirely abstract technical concept. Human beings and physical, tangible things judiciously woven into your presentation will vitalize even the unlikeliest subject for a potent talk, Also, wherever you can, link your examples directly to your listeners. A distant earthquake killing thousands could leave your audience unmoved: but a gas explosion in nearby Main Street will engender great interest – especially to those of your audience who live in Main Street.

Facts are sacred and must not be tampered with. Concrete examples emphasize facts and make facts stick in the mind. The closer the examples are to the experience and the environment of the audience the more surely your points will find their target.

Contrary to a common opinion, facts do not always speak for themselves. They need good people to speak for them. No fact of life need be colourless or less interesting than fiction. You must adroitly develop the story of each fact, giving it a good beginning, a lively motif, substance, excitement, strong, close-to-home examples and a language suitable for your hearers.

Words worry people. They say 'I have plenty of ideas but I haven't the vocabulary to express them'. This assertion is based on a fallacy. Words (or some other set of symbols such as mathematical formulae) are essential to clear thought. If you are fumbling for words, you have not clarified the thought.

Technical language and jargon incur much scorn and contempt; but they have their uses as a shorthand for the initiated. On the other hand, to use such esoteric stuff to show how clever you are or because you lack consideration for your hearers is unpardonable. Use your audience's language or explain your own. Otherwise you will waste your breath and, what is worse, waste their time.

SPEAKING STYLE

A hypnotist wishing to put someone to sleep employs a subdued, monotonous voice and a single soporific thought repeated and repeated and repeated until the patient gives up and slumbers. To arouse the patient he makes some sharp noise and brings his own voice to life by using a complete change of tone. the patient wakes up.

Human voices possess an immense range of volume, tone, pace, attack. Why be monotonous? Why be dull? Why mutter or bawl like a bull? Why not work out beforehand how you can give variety and the appropriate vocal clues to each part of your talk? Think in terms of main headlines and paragraphs and make sure that each new idea comes to the audience with a change in vocal approach. Particularly when introducing a fresh point, give your voice a lift. Watch sentence length; see to it that a few crisp short ones intervene between a series of protracted sentences. Watch the ends of sentences: a rising pitch holds more interest than a dying fall.

It is an odd fact of speaking technique that absolute silence for a few seconds – under control – can be the most effective part of a speech. Try to find, perhaps, two such moments when you can hold your audience to your thoughts during your calculated pauses.

The human voice is only one of the channels through which ideas can flow. Sound, sight, touch, smell, taste all provide means of conveying to other people. A good speaker gives his audience a chance to use as many of their senses as the occasion permits. With a little ingenuity you can give their ears a rest and switch channels. One obvious way of doing this is to show them the point, to demonstrate it. The term 'visual aids' does not mean only blackboard – chalk-and-talk stuff – or flipcharts or films or overhead projectors; solid physical, three-dimensional objects have much more effect. If it is practicable, show them the actual thing you are talking about. Let them handle it, smell it, taste it. Use your zest, imagination and enthusiasm to create a worthwhile experience for your audience. You can develop a reputation as a first-class speaker if you work at it and stop worrying about yourself. They will say you simply have a flair for this sort of thing, a gift. You must not mind that. A judicious use of the five senses will help you. However prosaic your subject, give it vigour, colour – life.

Please arm yourself with a pencil and a sheet of paper because we are going to create a graph. I would appreciate your comments in it and your physical co-operation. Please read the notes in Figure 70.1A and draw the axes exactly. Then proceed to Figure 70.1B.

Commentary

The shading at the foot of Figure 70.1B represents the grey sludge area at the beginning of so many talks, during what the speaker calls 'warming up'. The monologue here tells how unaccustomed the speaker is and what a trying ordeal he is experiencing in facing such a difficult, awesome set of people. In general, the self-centred blockhead isolates himself and destroys the goodwill of the

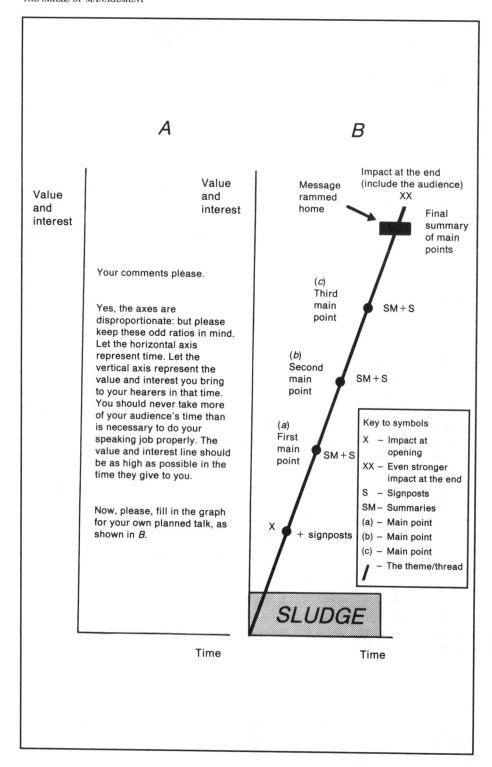

Figure 70.1   Graph of value and interest against time

audience by turning attention in the wrong direction. No wonder he is nervous. No wonder the audience already begin to doubt whether they should have come.

Eliminate the sludge area altogether. Instead, get some vigour, elevation and impact into your beginning. Hoist, the value-and-interest line clean through the sludge up to X, which marks your impact at opening.

Signposts help your hearers to concentrate on the special aspects of the subject that you intend to cover. Define your limits, briefly.

Now drive towards your first main point (a). You have it clear. You have already worked out how to make your facts come to life, how to link your vivid example both to the facts and to your audience. Follow your line, the theme, and support that theme with facts. Develop your message.

Summaries are a matter for your judgement. At least you must make certain that each main point holds fast in the minds of your audience before you tackle the next point.

Signposting internal to the talk, again, is a matter for you to decide. Will summaries and signposting help the audience? If so, use them.

When you reach the climax of your talk, when you ram home your message you must remind your audience of the main facts which support your theme. Summarize crisply: remind them how the matter of your talk affects them and do have a powerful line at the end. (Make a really sharp, hard, strong point and sit down on it!)

SOCIAL SPEAKING

Social speaking has one simple purpose: to give pleasure. What will make your audience purr? What will cause them to cry 'Hear! Hear!'? What will make them laugh? What will make them proud that they belong to this club, this company, this band of people brought together with a common cause? What sentiment will bring a lump into their throats? What will make them say afterwards 'Oh, I did enjoy that'?

Deliver the answers to these questions and they will be glad that you spoke, especially as you delivered with obvious affection for them and warm appreciation of their values, and you did so without going on and on and on. Work out a good line to end your speech and do not separate it by too long a time from your first-class opening line. Give them pleasure and enjoy the pleasure of their company.

CONCLUDING THOUGHTS

Make contact with people. Use your eyes. Look at them. Include them in what you say. This is simply good manners. Take the trouble to prepare properly to ensure that you give them value in exchange for the time they are giving you. Develop a respect, even an affection for your audience. Remember that, however expert you may be, every man and woman there is superior to you in some way and could teach you something.

Speaking is probably the oldest form of human communication. It is certainly the most natural to modern man but, unless other minds can process and use what is said, speaking is just a useless shifting of wind.

There are few things more exhilarating than an audience reacting with interest, excitement and the sheer pleasure of enjoying a first-class speaker. Deserve such a reaction and your world will be that much better for having you around.

FURTHER READING

Bell, Gordon, *The Secrets of Successful Speaking and Business Presentations*, Heinemann, London, 1987

Stuart, Cristina, *Effective Speaking*, Gower, Aldershot, 1989

See also the further reading list at the end of Chapter 72

71 Reports

Gordon Bell

John Logie Baird's discovery of the principles of television was useless; Einstein helped nobody with his thinking on relativity nor did Fleming with penicillin until they made their facts and theories known to other people. Knowledge locked away in the recesses of a single mind has little value until other minds receive the key and gain access to it. Many specialists believe that their work stops when they have uncovered the facts. A question was asked of them. They worked on it, investigated it thoroughly and found the answer. And that, they say, is the end of their job. But is it?

Why do industrial concerns employ scientists, accountants and other specialists? The answer to that question is simple. Industrial concerns employ specialists in order to get from them information, and expert guidance towards profitable action. Yet although specialists study and sweat for 5, 10, 15, 20 years, a lifetime, to equip themselves as experts they rarely study the techniques of passing their hard-gained information to other people. And their readers do the sweating.

A report is a working document that helps the other man to do his job. A record may well form the basis for a report but it is not a report. Samuel Pepys's diary recorded his times, brilliantly, but scholars had to delve to extract the meat. Nobody expects to have to delve into a modern business report; readers expect you to present the meat ready for digestion. A long report is not necessarily better than a short one, if only because fewer people will bother to read it. On the other hand, if you are writing for qualified people who want to know not only the conclusions and recommendations but also the detailed results and the methods used to obtain them, your report must contain such facts in full.

A report is not a detective story. Agatha Christie could take a set of facts and cloak them so skilfully that few readers can get the crucial point until the final page. The facts are all there if only one has the common sense to spot them. There should be no mystery about a report. The facts should be clear and the development logical so that the conclusions and recommendations follow them naturally.

There are five main considerations in thinking about reports:

1 Circulation and distribution
2 Physical layout
3 Numerical information
4 Visual aids
5 Language.

CIRCULATION AND DISTRIBUTION

All communications are a struggle for other people's interest and attention. The furniture in any busy person's office always includes a yawning wastepaper basket. If you have put this busy person on your circulation list for reasons of self-advertisement or because his name happened to be on a routine list, unedited for years, beware! Before you begin to shape your report, please take the trouble to sort out the people whom it will help in their jobs. Nobody else should have it.

Many a report suffers from a false start. The managers who asked for it did not bother to discuss with the writer either the purpose of the report or the intended readership. Or the writer just said 'Yes' and ploughed on blindly into a document which did not meet the real requirements. Such a report will fail or at least have to be rewritten. Both the senior person and the writer contributed to the failure and caused the extra labour, the frustration, perhaps the anger ensuing from a job badly done. So, before you write a syllable, establish who is going to use your report and what they have a right to expect from you. What is the purpose of the report from their point of view?

In many companies, the circulation is tacked on to the completed report as an afterthought. This deplorable custom should be opposed vigorously. Additions to the circulation list should be exceptional; better still, they should have been considered and meshed into the writer's reckoning from the start.

All this does not mean, however, that the facts should be coloured or slanted to affect the truth; no specialist worth his salt would wish to gain a point by distortion or trickery. His credibility would quickly disappear if he did, and rightly so.

Above all, your reader must find your report useful and the facts presented in such a way that he can absorb them easily and accurately. You cannot use suitable language, suitable layout or even select the material properly unless you know whom you are talking to and what he wants from the report. Consider your reader from the beginning. You cannot expect to do this unless you fix the circulation list at the outset. A report looks so forlorn in the wastepaper basket or even put aside – to be read 'later'. Do not plague people with reports they do not require for their own work. People have enough to do. All they want from you is help. Your useful reports will receive a welcome at the right time, at the right place and from the right man.

PHYSICAL LAYOUT

Your company has probably issued instructions on how its reports should be laid out. Such instructions were not written to while away an idle hour and it is the duty of every report writer to study them. The research department requires for its reports a different approach from the sales or public relations departments. Monsieur Ritz, the hotelier, made a fortune by following the precept 'the customer is always right'. The layout of a report depends almost entirely on how the readers like it. There are no rules, just a few principles. Your reader must be able to find his way about the report. If he is accustomed to a summary on the first page, that is where you put it. If he prefers all the graphs, tables, charts and detailed figures in appendices, put them there.

Reports should look as if they expect a welcome and want to be read. The ninety-third copy from a worn-out duplicator lacks inspiration and deserves neglect. The general appearance of a report must be appropriate to the contents and its purpose.

First appearance

The cover should immediately indicate the type of report that is inside: glossy for the chairman's annual report and other such public relations stuff; perhaps blue for research, green for personnel, or whatever the company's standard practice demands. The title and security classification must, obviously, be prominent before a page is turned.

The busy person's page

The first page must include the date of the report, the title, the author's name and that of the issuing authority and a reference/file number. Some readers also like a short circulation list on the title page – it is often useful to know who else has the report – and a very brief synopsis. This 'busy person's page' should tell the busy man or woman the object of the report and the reason why the work was done. It should provide a well-pruned summary of the investigation, the *main* results and the *main* recommendations for action. If possible, the busy person should get the guts of the report on one page in fewer than 200 words.

Any report longer than six pages should have a table of contents, clearly indicating where readers can find the special bits of the report that are all they intend to read. (Do not flatter yourself that everyone will read the whole of your tome.) Even avid readers will want to know where things are. A table of contents, reflecting a logical layout with clear, expressive headings, immediately creates an impression of order, thought and consideration.

So, you have already given your reader:

- *A cover* that immediately tells him the style, title and security classification of the report
- *A title page* that tells who wrote it, when it was written, who authorized it and, sometimes, who else has the information
- *A synopsis* – the main elements of the report in a nutshell
- *A table of contents* that tells him where he can find all the details he wants.

Many of your readers, especially top management and laypeople, will go no further into a report. They have all they need – a general appreciation of your work and enough information for discussion or appropriate action at their level. It is advisable to avoid technical language at this stage.

Your fellow specialists will now wish to dig into the report. They will expect an introduction which informs, or reminds, them of the circumstances which prompted your work. They will want to know how you set about your investigation, what methods, what tests, what equipment you used. They will expect a complete validation of your results and figures and to know what standards of accuracy you worked to. They will expect you to separate facts from opinions. The headlines for the main body of the work could read:

1 Introduction
2 Experimental details
3 Results
4 Discussion
5 Full summary
6 Recommendations
7 Appendices.

This format cannot fit all circumstances and must be adjusted to suit the needs of your readers and the purpose of the report.

Please acknowledge the work of other people who have helped you, if only in a bibliography.

NUMERICAL INFORMATION

Numbers form the backbone of most reports. Measurements of time, frequencies, distances, and so on, are fundamental in presenting facts. Few readers need all the numbers; all readers need the significant numbers and wish them to be displayed significantly. Do not bury them or wall them up behind the background data. When you are planning your report, establish the vital numbers early on so that you can give them due prominence when writing.

Your reader will want to know your tolerances and to what degree of accuracy your figures are presented. Do not bother him with five decimal places if the approximate whole number will suffice. The main body of the report will flow more easily if the script is uncluttered by a mass of figures. Many thoughtful writers quote only those figures that make the point and then guide those people who may be interested in greater detail to an appendix which contains more complicated items such as mathematical formulae.

With numbers, significance is all – or nearly all.

VISUAL AIDS

The opportunity for using well-drawn and effective visual aids in reports has been much widened in recent years with the spread of computers and their powerful software. It is no longer necessary to suffer the expense and delays of outside studios. High-quality graphics can be produced in-house by suitably trained secretaries as a matter of routine.

If you were a sales director, how would you prefer to have the sales figures from May to October presented – as in (a), (b), (c) or (d) of Figure 71.1?

Sometimes readers would rather be able to see the point than have it related to them. Please consider this.

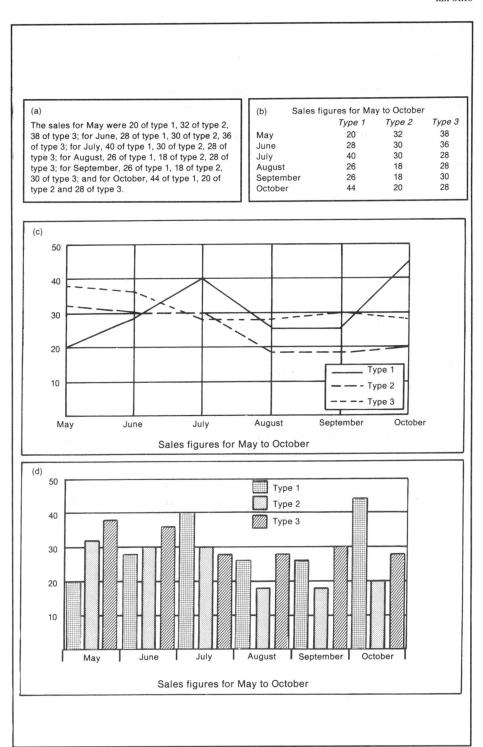

Figure 71.1   Four ways of displaying a set of numerical results. This shows how careful
thought can result in a more effective display

LANGUAGE

'Tests showed that the handle gets too hot'

or:

'The results of a period of *ad hoc* experimentation supplemented by both statistical analysis and consideration of empirical factors thought to be universally viable in the context of the areas in which utilization could be expected to approach a maximum indicated that the thermal conductivity of that portion of the equipment designed for prehensile digital contact was such as to present a surface whose temperatures would markedly exceed the generally accepted threshold of sensory discomfort?

Why do so many technicians, trained in logic and precision, write such twaddle? Is it because they are suspicious of the arts, afraid that what they do might lose 'mystique' or is it that they cannot bother to bring logic and precision into their use of language? Many a brilliant young person, on reaching middle age, wonders what went wrong with his career. Let him reread some of his reports. The answers could be found in them.

We have no space here to discuss grammar and the techniques of clear English, but you should learn a few basic points of control in your writing. You can then leave the rest to your genuine wish to help people to understand you. For instance, most readers will want to recognize, without much effort, two things about each of your sentences:

1 The grammatical subject – whom or what you are talking of
2 What happens – the action.

Let us look at 1 first. Concrete words such as 'polecat', 'sewing-machine', 'policeman' give your reader an exact image of what is in your mind. Abstract words and phrases leave room for doubt. So prefer concrete words as subjects of your sentences.

Now 2. Your reader will readily understand the 'what happens' part of your sentence if you convey the action as simply as you can with power verbs, preferably active. Let us clarify this. Please examine these four sentences:

1 *Oil lubricates bearings.*
  The subject of the sentence, 'oil', is concrete, tangible, clear.
  The subject does the deed of the verb so the sentence is active.
2 *Bearings are lubricated by oil.*
  The subject, 'bearings', is concrete.
  The subject does not do the deed of the verb: it gets done to, so the sentence is passive.
3 *The lubrication of bearings is carried out by the use of oil.*
  The subject, 'lubrication of bearings', is an abstract phrase.
  The subject does not do the deed of the verb: it gets done to, so the sentence is both abstract and passive.

Structure 3 often leads to:

4 *In so far as the process of lubrication with respect to bearings is concerned, this is carried out by the use of an application of oil.*

Exaggerated as it is, sentence 4 shows the beginnings of the decay that attacks so many specialists from about the age of twenty-eight. In any large organization roughly one-third of the people over the age of twenty-eight are dead. They have accumulated sufficient cliché phrases and routine attitudes to lean on until their pensions turn up. There seems to be no reason for them to think any more. It is enough just to react according to the rule book and the jargon – 'We are in receipt of your favour of the 19th instant to hand, and it must be pointed out that in view of the fact that . . .' 'The conceptual philosophy of commonality and standardization at this point in time could be said to have, perhaps, groundings in feasibility which, with the basic assumption that . . .' '. . . the viability of these parameters, shiftwise. . . .'. All non-think stuff, torture for the reader and highly dangerous for the writer.

Danger? What danger? We live in a sea of words. What is wrong with drifting along in the fashionable waters, swallowing the stuff and regurgitating it into the faces of our fellows? Why not? It's easier than thinking.

What happens to a muscle that gets no exercise? It becomes flabby. What happens to a machine that lies idle for years? It becomes rusty and useless. What happens to a brain that does nothing but gather verbal cobwebs? Adult thinking is impossible without a language or some other set of symbols that label the elements we develop into thoughts. If words, for instance, are the bricks and mortar with which we build the wall of thought does it not follow that the sort of words we habitually use is the sort of thinker we are? Near-enough words, that'll-do words, other people's tired old clichés provide neither keep-fit exercise nor nourishment for an active mind.

Technical language has the advantage of being clearly defined. Used properly, it assists constructive thought and communication among those who understand it. Abused, or flaunted because you want to imply that you are superior to people outside 'the club', it can cause trouble – for you as much as for your victims. The English language provides one of the most precise, subtle, flexible and vigorous aids to clear thought and effective reports. No manager can claim to be more than half-baked if he does not learn how to control it.

REPORT WRITING CHECKLIST

Before drafting a report ask yourself:

1 Have I insisted on a thorough briefing from whoever requested the report and discussed with him/her in detail:

- that there is a need for the report?
- the exact purpose of the report?
- who is going to read the report?
- the exact scope of the report?

2 Have I collected all the information I may need?
3 Have I selected from this the information the readers need?

When drafting a report, ask yourself:

1 Does the layout comply with any company standard and does it make things easy for the reader?

2　Is there a 'busy person's page' and does it contain the right information for him/her?

3　Does the report look good and can it be reproduced using the equipment available?

4　Is everybody who 'needs to know' on the circulation list?

5　Have I arranged for library copies and spare copies?

6　Is the circulation too wide?

7　Does the report need a security classification?

8　Have I used powerful verbs and concrete nouns?

9　Have I used short sentences and simple construction?

10　Are any technical or scientific words likely to be unknown to the readers?

11　Have I avoided padding and waffle-words?

12　Will the reader easily understand what I have written?

13　Have I avoided slant and bias?

14　Have I clearly stated conclusions and recommendations?

15　Have I used sufficient visual aids?

16　Are the visual aids in the right place, clearly labelled and cross-referenced?

17　Have I shown scales, dimensions and magnifications on my visual aids?

18　Are the tables and charts displayed in the best way?

19　Have I shown the units? Are units consistent and do they comply with British or other accepted standards?

20　Will the visual aids still be clear and easy to follow when reproduced by the available process?

21　Should I invite someone else to read the draft and discuss it with me?

A report is a working document that helps the other person to do his or her job. Managers who learn to write effective reports add value to themselves and to their work.

FURTHER READING

Bosticco, Mary, *Personal Letters for Business People*, 3rd edn, Gower, Aldershot, 1986

Janner, Greville, *The Art of Letter Writing*, (audio cassette and manual), Gower, Aldershot, 1989

Jay, Antony, *Effective Presentation: the Communication of Ideas by Words and Visual Aids*, Management Publications Ltd, London, 1970

Mort, Simon, *Report Writing for Managers*, Gower, Aldershot, 1991

There is a more comprehensive reading list on personal communications at the end of Chapter 72.

72 Meetings

Gordon Bell

Believe it or not, some companies use up more cash at meetings than they spend on the raw materials with which they make their products. Much of this cash goes straight down the drain. Before you dismiss this thought as whimsical, consider the cost of meetings – air and rail fares, cars, hotel bills, salaries and expenses, conference and boardroom rents, rates, cleaning, postage of reports and other documents, typing and more money for many more items. Any large organization spends millions of pounds each year so that people can discuss, decide and, one hopes, energize some profitable action. The waste is colossal.

Money is important – only a fool would deny that – but much more important is human life. Ineffective meetings not only waste money but they also devalue people's time and shrink the people concerned with them. Human relationships can be soured by bad meetings. A wise person takes the trouble to find out how meetings work and how to make them work for him and his associates.

WHY, WHO, HOW, WHEN AND WHERE?

A definition of 'business meetings' might be: two or more people getting together for a specific business purpose.

The meeting itself forms only one link in a chain of events. If the other links lack strength the meeting can become merely the place where the chain breaks. Ninety per cent of an effective meeting happens before the meeting starts. Forging the before-the-meeting link requires thought, horse-sense and skill. If you intend to call a meeting, be completely clear about its intended purpose. What specific business should the meeting achieve? Is it to decide on action, to brief people, to inform, to persuade? What in specific terms – no vague abstractions – is the business purpose of the meeting? You must then face what might be a deflating question: is a meeting necessary at all? Must you deprive people of their time and put the company to expense? Can the business be done – the decision made, for instance – in some other way (for example, by a few telephone calls or half a dozen letters)? Why are you proposing to call the meeting?

So you decide that your meeting is a necessity; the business cannot be accomplished without a combination of other minds, interest and experience. Which people can provide you with such a combination? Nobody else should be invited. You want to get some business done. Avoid the hangers-on and the strange creatures who go to meetings just to get out of their own offices for a while. If your business is to get a decision and action, beware of the second-string person who cannot give a firm 'yes' or 'no'. He has to report back to his boss. Then there will have to be another meeting for his boss or even his boss's boss. Invite and accept only the people who can do the job properly. Do not forget, as so often happens, to invite the person who will have to take any action you decide upon. If your meeting decides to change the production line you cannot expect joyous co-operation from the production manager who was elsewhere when you decided how to run his department.

When and where the meeting takes place depends on the urgency of the business and the convenience of the people concerned. Be considerate about this. Merely the fact that you operate from Plymouth does not necessarily mean that your Glasgow and Ipswich colleagues will agree that your office is the perfect location. Must you start your meeting at 0900, which means an overnight trip for everyone except you? Timing, the date and the hour, can show you to be a thoughtful organizer.

If your colleagues have to examine reports, plans, figures or must equip them-selves in other ways in preparation for the meeting, give them a fair chance to do so. Also make it clear to them precisely what the business of the meeting will be and that you expect them to come prepared. A meeting which has to be recalled because the relevant facts are missing reflects no credit on the convenor or the members. More meetings fail because the preparation has been neglected or skimped than for any other reason. No one should go to a meeting ill-prepared. Even if the meeting happens to be a quick get-together, and at short notice, a few minutes' thought beforehand will increase your value to the meeting. At least one person – you – will be able to talk sense.

The businesslike chairman will see to it that he or his secretary arranges a suitable conference room. He will indicate when the meeting is likely to finish; he will arrange breaks for the creature comforts of the conferers, and for telephone messages to be collected, outside the conference room – no interruptions will be allowed except for desperately urgent calls. He will plan an approximate timetable for the agenda so that timeworthy items get their due. Documents and, if required, suitable equipment for presentations must be available. Name cards help people to know who's who; make them bold and do have them spelled correctly. There are of course a hundred and one other details, any of which might be important. A meeting succeeds in direct ratio to its intelligent preparation.

The formal rules for running meetings become more important when the gath-ering is a large one. For most business meetings, formal rules matter little. It is the spirit in which people attend the meetings that produces a good or bad meeting.

No real progress can be made without agreement. The object of meetings is to produce agreement. Even if, after disagreement, action results because of fear or force of personality, the action will only be half-hearted and possibly poorly performed. The chairman of a meeting must always be striving for agreement, not surrender.

PREPARING FOR THE MEETING

The chairman

The chairman must decide whether the meeting is really necessary (especially important with routine meetings which often occur even when there is nothing to be discussed or decided). He must also:

- Decide on the purpose of the meeting
- Decide on the subject or subjects
- Decide on the place and time
- Decide who is going to attend the meeting. Only those with something to contribute or who need to know exactly what was said and by whom should be present. Other people can get any necessary information from the minutes. The chairman should ensure that those attending are of sufficient standing, that they really represent their departments, and have the authority to commit them to action
- Decide on the agenda and roughly how much time to allow for each item. It is imperative that items are stated in concrete terms. Abstractions will inevitably result in rambling discussion that leads nowhere. One or two simple items first will get the meeting off to a good start. Even if the meeting is summoned hurriedly by telephone, members should be told what they are going to discuss. This is the agenda
- Study the subjects. The chairman must be sufficiently familiar with the subjects being discussed to be able to keep the discussion on the right lines
- Study the people attending. He/she must know the personal alignments that will help or hinder the meeting, those who will not talk when they have valuable contributions to make and those who will talk even when they have not.

The secretary

The secretary is responsible for all the mechanics of the meeting; he/she must obtain for the chairman any points for the agenda and names of those attending; suitable accommodation; arrange for paper, and so on, arrange for refreshments to be available when the chairman wants them, and arrange to disconnect the telephone.

He/she must circulate the agenda in good time and must prepare all the papers the chairman may require.

The members

The members must:

- Study the subjects to be discussed and, if necessary, departmental opinions and agreements
- Study the chairman and his idiosyncrasies
- Study the other members
- Work out how they are going to sell their ideas. (Please see the section on presenting a proposal to a board or committee, which appears later in this chapter)

CONDUCT OF THE MEETING

The chairman

The meeting must start on time, even if there are absentees. If the chairman is absent, the next most suitable person should start instead. If the speaker on the first point is absent, switch the agenda items.

Start briskly, laying down the purpose, the time available, and any other conditions that will help to control the meeting. A chairman cannot demand respect: it can only be earned – usually by giving it to others.

The chairman must watch the time. If the meeting is getting behind time the chairman must decide whether to accelerate the proceedings or allow an extension into extra time. In any case, the chairman must warn the members early, so that they can either get a move on or make any necessary arrangements for a late departure.

The chairman must keep feeding back to the members the state of the discussion, to ensure that everyone understands the situation. This is particularly important at the end of each item. This will also enable the secretary to set down an immediate, accurate record of the decisions reached, who is to take action and by what date, without any risk of error.

The chairman must try to be impartial and only produce his own opinions late in the discussion, if at all. Otherwise he will inhibit proper discussion.

The chairman may have to keep reminding members of the subject and aim in order to keep them to the point.

The chairman must ensure that everyone has the opportunity to express his opinion, at the same time preventing any individual from taking up an excessive amount of time. A member with very strong views that he is determined to express should be given his head, unopposed, the chairman, at least, giving all his attention to what is being said. The chairman should try to extract the relevant points from what may be a confused discourse and ensure that they are properly considered by the meeting.

The chairman must summarize, clarify and emphasize the action arising from the meeting, name specifically who is to be responsible for taking action and record who should do what in precise terms.

The meeting should finish at the stated times unless the members have agreed to go on late.

The chairman and the secretary should leave the room immediately after the meeting is over; otherwise another meeting might ensue.

Reminders for the chairman

Before the meeting

- Ensure that there is a clear, worthwhile purpose
- Check who will be attending
- Check on the points to be discussed
- Ensure, with the secretary, that everything has been organized

During the meeting

- Introduce the meeting and its purpose
- Define the limits of the subject and the time available
- Keep the meeting to the point. Be quick to spot when people are wandering off the subject
- Be impartial
- Show and earn respect
- Feed back. Ensure that everyone is keeping up with discussions and understands the points which are emerging
- Sum up at the end. Make sure that all know the conclusions reached and especially who is to take action.

The chairman must always remember, and occasionally remind members, that the object of the meeting is to benefit the whole organization and not any section or individual. He/she should strive to ensure that the meeting results in profitable action.

The secretary

During the meeting

During the meeting the secretary must take copious notes unless he/she can be sure that the chairman will provide minutes as the meeting goes along. It is therefore usually impracticable for a person to act as a member and secretary and do both jobs adequately.

After the meeting

As quickly as possible after the meeting the secretary should write up the minutes, either for rapid circulation or to go on the files. The minutes should be kept as short as is practicable.

The essential parts of the minutes are the decisions, agreed action and who is to take it and when. These must stand out.

At an appropriate time after the meeting someone, probably the secretary, should check that members are getting on with action they undertook or were instructed to take.

Members

Members who disagree must do so without being disagreeable.

A member must be clear about the points to be made and proceed with the aim of convincing the other members that he/she is right. At the same time, the members must have a sufficiently open mind to be able to change it if someone else produces better arguments or ideas.

The members must:

- Study the subjects to be discussed and, if necessary, departmental opinions and agreements

- Study the chairman and his idiosyncrasies
- Study the other members
- Work out how they are going to 'sell' their ideas
- Avoid distracting personalities.

PRESENTING A PROPOSAL TO A BOARD OR COMMITTEE

Please engrave this sentence into your mind: Nothing induces agreement faster than self-interest – the other fellow's self-interest.

Many business people have to recommend changes that will cost money. In most companies there is a procedure for this. The proposer has first to prepare a document setting out his/her proposal in detail. This goes through normal channels and may sometimes be agreed to or rejected as it stands. More frequently the proposer will be asked to appear before some board or committee to explain his/her proposal and to answer questions about it.

The written part of a proposal is a persuasive report and should be written with that in mind. The oral presentation is part speech, part meeting and part interview.

In preparing such a presentation, the proposer should ask him/herself these questions:

1 Do you know exactly what you want?
2 Do you really believe in your case?
3 Have you got all the facts that support your case and have you checked them?
4 What are the strongest arguments for your case?
5 What are the benefits for your listeners?
6 Why must the present situation be changed?
7 What is their problem?
8 Who else is affected? (Unions, other divisions, and so on)
9 What are the arguments against your plan?
10 What are the alternatives to your plan?
11 Do your benefits clearly outweigh these arguments and alternatives?
12 To whom are you presenting your plan? Have you done any lobbying? Do you need to?
13 Do you know who your probable allies and opponents are?
14 Have you discussed the finances with the experts?
15 Have you prepared hand-outs of any complicated figures?
16 It was a good idea when you first thought of it. Is it still – from their point of view.
17 Have you prepared a really effective presentation? (Time plus the value and interest ratio are particularly important in case presentation.)
18 How will you sum up and end?
19 Are you ready for questions?
20 Have you emphasized the benefits they (your listeners) will gain? Remember: nothing induces agreement faster than self-interest – the other fellow's self-interest.

The board is probably only interested in this question: 'Have they a problem and does your proposal solve it for them?' Ask yourself: 'Will your proposal satisfy their need, their greed, their self-esteem – or all three?'

ONE-TO-ONE MEETINGS

An encounter across a desk can often make or break a manager. Failure follows almost inevitably if you present your ideas at the wrong time or if you insist on pushing a proposal from your own point of view.

By all means be relaxed but before you go in to win your point, or before the other fellow calls on you, do your homework. Get your purpose clear, have your facts ready. Know the other person's problems in relation to your suggestion and start the discussion on the basis of them. Until you have established those problems and have shown that you understand them and are in sympathy with them, you must not try to sell anything. You want the other person to react, to say 'yes'. You will not get this favourable reaction if you spend your time putting yourself across. Try it the other way round. Put the other person and his/her problems in the forefront. If what you have to sell solves those problems, you will get the agreement that you seek.

IN THE FUTURE

In the year of our dreams our transport systems will have been perfected; perfect roads, perfect railways, perfect passenger aircraft all toing and froing to perfection; punctual and clean with no squashed commuters breathing each other's used air. Comfort and space will be guaranteed, because nobody will be using the roads, the railways or the airlines – not for business anyway. We shall all be working from home.

Going to meetings will be a thing of the past. Business men and women will no longer need to travel to their meetings. Our meetings will become telephonic and televisual affairs. Today's normal conference room meetings will be regarded as anachronisms, fit only for backwoodsmen and fuddy-duddies who still prefer personal contact with their colleagues and customers. At least, that's what the purveyors of telecommunications systems are saying. No sensible manager should scoff at their claims. They could be right.

Teleconferencing is already becoming commonplace at top level in the more progressive organizations. It will become general but, like the telephone, it will take time.

Alexander Graham Bell patented the telephone in 1876. Most people regarded the instrument with awe and trepidation. Few ordinary folk knew how to use one. The telephone had obvious uses for emergency services. Rich people could add it to their advantages over the commonalty. But even in 1952 the number of telephones per hundred inhabitants was still only:

- United States – 31
- United Kingdom – 12
- France and Germany – 6
- USSR – 1

Now almost everybody has easy access to a telephone and practically anywhere in the world can be reached in seconds.

Telemeetings will probably make more rapid progress into our lives than the telephone. Does that mean the end of person-to-person meetings as we know them? Of course not. In the 1920s the cinema threatened to kill the living theatre stone dead but was itself badly bruised by television. Flesh and blood theatres continue to flourish in the larger cities; human beings prefer each other to shadows. So will it be with meetings. But business men and women will ignore televisual conferencing at their peril. It is incumbent upon every manager, every salesperson, every designer, every director, every production boss to develop personal expertise and awareness in telecommunications.

The successful businessman or woman needs the meetings skills outlined in this chapter but will need more in the future. Distance, it is said, lends enchantment to the view. But it also creates new problems. Anybody lacking meetings skills by satellite will be left among the also-rans.

A good communicator uses all the assets at his/her command.

CONCLUSION

Anybody can hold a meeting but only the person able to obtain the desired responses ranks as a good communicator. A computer memory and its processing unit can store great quantities of data; but the machine is simply a speedy automaton, entirely dependent upon its program. The human memory and its processing unit contain facts, experiences, feelings, prejudices, social attitudes, business needs, expediency, cussedness, warmth, love, hatred and much more.

Programming the computer to obtain useful output – the response – demands skill and knowledge. How much more demanding is the need for a manager to acquire the knowledge and skills for better human relationships? At least you can start by making your meetings successful.

FURTHER READING

In addition to books on meetings, the following list includes books which combine the personal communications subjects covered in this chapter and in Chapters 70 and 71.

Bell, Gordon, *The Secrets of Successful Speaking and Business Presentations*, Heinemann, London, 1987

Bell, Gordon, *The Secrets of Successful Business Meetings*, Heinemann, Oxford, 1990

Honey, Peter, *Face to Face: A Practical Guide to Interactive Skills*, Gower, Aldershot, 1989

Janner, Greville, *Janner on Meetings*, Gower, Aldershot, 1986

Janner, Greville, *Janner on Chairing*, Gower, Aldershot, 1989

Jay, Antony, *Effective Presentation: the Communication of Ideas by Words and Visual Aids*, Management Publications Ltd, London, 1970

McCann, Dick, *How to Influence Others at Work*, Heinemann, London, 1988

Scott, Bill, *The Skills of Communicating*, Gower, Aldershot, 1986
Wells, Gordon, *How to Communicate*, McGraw-Hill, Maidenhead, 1978

73 Executive health

Dr Andrew Melhuish

There are two things to aim at in life; first to get what you want and after that to enjoy it. Only the wisest of mankind achieve the second.

Logan Pearson Smith

The objective of this chapter is to encourage executives to look at their lifestyles: to discover if there are ways in which they can enjoy life more and remain well longer.

THE BENEFITS AND HAZARDS OF EXECUTIVE LIFE

First let us look at executives in general. Is there scope for improvement? The answer, coming from modern research, is a firm 'yes'. Executives enjoy good health compared with the population in general but are equally prone to heart disease. They certainly could improve their health and happiness. Second, and most important, can you yourself improve? Consider your present life-style. Do you whole-heartedly enjoy work; or are there times when it is too demanding, too time-consuming – or boring? Do you have time to enjoy the expensive home and holidays you earn by your hard responsible work? Do you have enough time with your wife and children? Even more important, would they agree? If you have the balance right, well done! I fear you are in a minority. Unfortunately, most executives can manage with expertise their complex jobs, but fail to manage effectively the apparently more simple balance of work and home life and the maintenance of their own bodies.

The reasons for this are many. There will always be a high demand on the successful executive's time at work, creating pressures on his time at home. His success is usually due to his commitment, independence and drive at work; and these qualities can lead him to neglect or underrate his own health and happiness. Many managers would die rather than admit they are exhausted, unable to cope, unfit. Some do! Executives are usually well trained to do their job; it is rare for them to be trained to manage their own lives.

In order to manage his body and his life successfully the executive needs to know the particular challenges he faces from his executive life-style. Then, with sufficient motivation, he can use this knowledge to devise strategies to modify his life-style and improve his health. Before proceeding further, it may well be helpful for the reader to list his own satisfactions at work and the pressures which go with them. Each executive has his own unique life-style with its own rewards and problems. Awareness of these will help him to review the balance of his life.

Some benefits of executive life

1 *Job satisfaction*   Most executives are involved in challenging and, usually, interesting jobs
2 *High financial rewards*   These benefit the manager and his family
3 *Autonomy*   Most executives exercise some degree of control over their working hours, work content and working conditions.

Risk factors to be weighed against benefits

The demands of the job

Much is known about the problems faced by executives at work. Cary Cooper's book *Coping with Stress* summarizes these well. My own experience is that most executives can produce high quality work; their main problem is that they do not have enough time to achieve this quality. The more senior they become, the greater the responsibility they have, the more they must come to terms with deadlines and priorities. There is very real conflict between high standards and expediency.

Interpersonal relationships also create much pressure; dealing with people is so much more difficult than dealing with things, and the more senior the executive becomes the less the support he can expect from his colleagues at work. It is lonely at or near the top. The relationship which has a great effect on most executives however is with his 'boss', but colleagues and staff can be equally demanding.

Work-load can also be a problem. To complete his work satisfactorily the manager may spend long hours at work, returning home late. Worse, however, is the automatic assumption in most firms that the executive's work does not stop when he leaves the office. The bulging briefcase is the obvious sign of the pressure he faces: work to be completed during the evening, during the weekend and even during his holidays, that is, if he feels able to take his full allocation of holiday entitlement.

Finally, concerns about his career structure together with the politics and infighting associated with high position and authority can create great pressures.

Sedentary nature of the job

Most executives work behind a desk and move around very little during the working day. The more senior they become, the less they move; staff and colleagues come to them, they park close to the office and they may not even have to walk to lunch. Executives tend to be concentrated in big cities so, if they choose to set up home outside the city limits, they must travel to and from the office by car or train. This is sedentary, unhealthy and takes valuable time. When the executive reaches home his ability to take exercise as relaxation or enjoyment will be reduced by his long hours at work and the extra work he may take home. Executives spend many hours flying. Air travel is a particularly striking example of remaining sedentary for long periods. Few British companies provide good exercise facilities at the office or encourage organized activity breaks during the day –

unlike their Japanese, Russian or North American counterparts. It is difficult for most British executives to get enough physical exercise.

Entertainment as part of the job

The entertainment of customers is a necessary part of many executives' jobs. Important customers expect to be well entertained, and it is difficult to entertain well without drinking or smoking too much. Entertainment at lunchtime will affect work performance later in the day while entertainment in the evening can lead to neglect of home life. Expectations about entertaining are changing: successful firms, such as IBM, ban alcohol during the working day, and most German executives bargain over a frugal healthy lunch.

Insecurity of executive employment

Estimates of redundancy in executives vary, but all figures are unacceptably high for, if an executive should lose his job, he and his family are at high risk as they have high expectations from life. High mortgages are encouraged by the British tax system and private schooling is expensive. Loss of his job can be a total disaster for the executive – both to his morale and to his ability to support his family in the way to which they are accustomed.

Relocation as a way of life

In many companies executives move regularly; it is a necessary part of a success-ful career structure. Relocation is a great pressure on the executive and, increas-ingly, on his family. More than 60 per cent of wives in Britain now work regularly. For them, finding new employment in a new locality may be difficult. Children need stability to benefit from their education. Job uncertainty can only make relocation even more frequent and stressful, for the executive must prove himself in a new company in addition to moving location. Change is a major cause of executive stress. There is no greater change for an executive than relocation.

THE HEALTH OF EXECUTIVES IN GENERAL

This long list of pressures and short list of benefits might suggest that many executives are unhappy or unwell. But the most recent health census in Britain showed that, as members of social class 1, they are about 40 per cent less likely to die between 35 and 65 than the lowest social class. Sickness absenteeism shows an even more dramatic difference in favour of social class 1. The death rate in the group of managers being researched by Professor Cary Cooper and myself is at present about 10 per cent of that predicted for the population in general.

The two most important factors contributing to this good health are:

1 *Job satisfaction* In a 1977 survey by *Which* magazine executives were high among those satisfied with their jobs, with a high level of control over how the job was done
2 *Habits* In general, executives share with other members of social class 1

greatly reduced smoking, and better eating and exercise habits compared with the other social classes. But the risk of alcohol problems is highest in class 1.

Current health patterns

Although at less risk than most other workers, the executive's health will still be influenced by the prevailing pattern of illness. Today the most important causes of death in the age group 35 to 65 are coronary heart disease and lung cancer.

The emergence of these 'modern killers' reflects the variety of the spirits released from the Pandora's box of modern Western civilization. Good living conditions and advances in medical care have wiped out malnutrition and greatly reduced infection. At the same time the abundance of pleasures – smoking, eating and drinking – and the freedom to indulge them, often to excess, have led to the dramatic rise in heart disease and lung cancer. Too many cigarettes contribute to lung cancer; excess food, cigarettes and alcohol are important risk factors for heart disease.

Once established, coronary heart disease and cancer are dangerous and destructive. But much can be done to prevent them. The occurrence of coronary heart disease in young people can be dramatically reduced by simple changes in diet and cigarette smoking. Lung cancer would be a fairly uncommon illness if no one smoked. Finland has long been known to have the highest rates of heart disease in Europe. In the late 1970s The Karelia programme offered to a selected group of Finns regular health screening along with practical advice on diet and stopping smoking. It nearly halved the occurrence of heart attacks in this group. In America, the increased awareness of the importance of weight reduction, diet and cigarette smoking has resulted in a significant fall in heart disease.

Executives share equally with the general population the increased risk of coronary heart disease. Sensible modification of their life-style will reduce this risk. Indeed, they stand to benefit even more than other workers for there is convincing evidence to implicate their particular life-style as contributing to coronary heart disease.

Figure 73.1 summarizes the factors known to influence the onset of coronary heart disease. Coronary heart disease is the result of clogging up of the arteries supplying the heart itself – the coronary arteries – by atheroma. Blood flow to parts of the heart can be reduced (causing angina) or fully blocked (a heart attack or coronary thrombosis).

Atheroma is a fatty deposit containing cholesterol and other fatty materials. The formation of atheroma is clearly associated with cigarette smoking, so the executive who uses cigarettes to help him to cope with his working pressures is at risk in this way. Raised blood pressure is also an important factor in increasing the risk of heart disease. Success in executive life is often related to the ability of the manager to control and to hide his emotions. He learns to carry on calmly; but at what cost to his system? It is probably no coincidence that the Italians, who enjoy expressing their emotions, are relatively free from heart disease. But probably the greatest risk to the executive lies in the combination of his hard-working responsible job and the lack of exercise that goes with it. To understand this better we need to

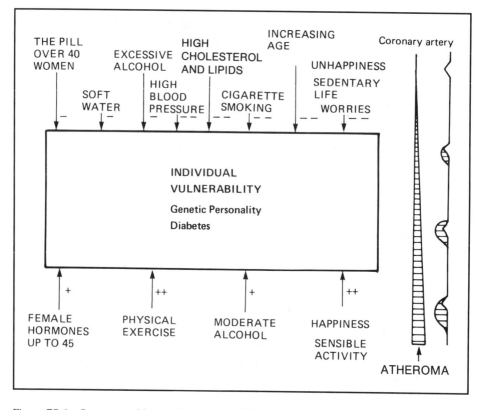

Figure 73.1   Summary of factors known to influence the onset of coronary heart disease

look briefly at the natural response to stress or challenge. This will show that it can now be inappropriate, and so a danger, to the modern executive's life-style.

The stress response

Inert matter and living organisms respond to increased challenge or stress by improved performance. But the pattern of this response is different. Figure 73.2 shows how the physical response of inert matter is entirely predictable, performance increasing steadily to a maximum beyond which the system is destroyed. Physiological response, from living organisms, be they animal or man, is quite different. At low to moderate levels of pressure the response is dramatic, with small increases in pressure resulting in much improved performance. Then, as the levels of pressure become higher, the response falls steadily away. Finally, the organism will fall apart, like the machine. The time of such collapse is not predictable, however, because the organism is complex, with a mind and body of its own.

The practical applications for man are obvious. Very little challenge or stress (boredom) produces poor performance. Too much stress (overload, burn-out) destroys. In between, there is the area where stress enhances performance, improves life. Stress cannot be avoided; it must be kept at a manageable level. Executives, through their natures and their jobs, will be at risk from too much stress. So it is important to know how excessive stress can harm – and what clues

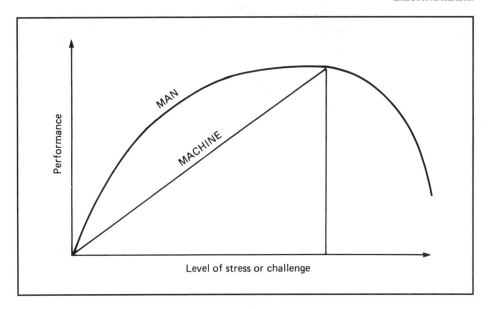

Figure 73.2 The stress reponse. For a machine or an inert material, the response to
increasing stress is gradually improved performance, up to a point where
breakdown suddenly occurs. The human response to stress is more rapid
initially, with the eventual collapse less easy to predict owing to the
complexity of mind and body

can be detected to warn that it is becoming excessive. The answer lies in the
physical and emotional response to stress.

Physical response to stress

Faced by challenge, animals and man respond in the same well-known, scientifically proven, way – the 'fight or flight response'. Figure 73.3 shows how the
organism is helped to survive. The message comes from the brain and is mediated
through the adrenal glands which produce adrenalin and the steroid hormones.
The result is increased blood supply to the brain and muscles. The heart and
lungs work harder to provide this extra blood. Other systems lose blood. At the
same time, glucose and small fat molecules flood into the bloodstream to provide
the fuel. The result is a body primed for action, the choke is pulled out, the
booster let in.

Unfortunately, a new type of animal has evolved over the last forty years, 'homo
executus'. He faces just as many challenges and pressures as did his predecessors
– perhaps more; but his response to these challenges is not physical; it is
emotional. His habitat is sedentary and his response to stress is controlled. He
cannot hit his difficult boss or unhelpful colleague; nor can he run away. He must
smile and cope. But he cannot stop his body priming itself for the physical activity
it feels appropriate and it is the unused products of that priming – the raised blood
pressure and pulse, the surge of fats into the bloodstream which can harm. If the
stress is acute and quickly resolved the benefits far outweigh the potential
problems. But if the stress is chronic – if work is frustrating, unhappy and the

	 Normal (relaxed)	 Under pressure	 Acute pressure	 Chronic pressure (stress)
Brain	Blood supply normal	Blood supply up	Thinks more clearly	Headaches and migraines, tremors and nervous tics
Mood	Happy	Serious	Increased concentration	Anxiety, loss of sense of humour
Saliva	Normal	Reduced	Reduced	Dry mouth, lump in throat
Muscles	Blood supply normal	Blood supply up	Improved performance	Muscular tension and pain
Heart	Normal rate and Blood Pressure	Increased rate and Blood P	Improved performance	Hypertension and chest pain
Lungs	Normal respiration	Increased respiration rate	Improved performance	Coughs and asthma
Stomach	Normal blood supply and acid secretion	Reduced blood supply Increased acid secretion	Reduced blood supply reduces digestion	Ulcers due to heartburn and indigestion
Bowels	Normal blood supply and bowel activity	Reduced blood supply Increased bowel activity	Reduced blood supply reduces digestion	Abdominal pain and diarrhoea
Bladder	Normal	Frequent urination	Frequent urination due to in-creased nervous stimulation	Frequent urination, prostatic symptoms
Sexual organs	(M) Normal (F) Normal periods, etc.	(M) Impotence (decreased blood supply) (F) Irregular periods	Decreased blood supply	(M) Impotence (F) Menstrual disorders
Skin	Healthy	Decreased blood supply, dry skin	Decreased blood supply	Dryness and rashes
Biochemistry	Normal: oxygen consumed, glucose and fats liberated	Oxygen consumption is up. Glu-cose and fat consumption is up	More energy immediately available	Rapid tiredness

Figure 73.3   Effects of stress on bodily functions

future uncertain – then Figure 73.3 shows how the inappropriate stress response can damage nearly every organ in the body, and in particular the heart.

Emotional response to stress

The natural emotional response of the body to stress or challenge is a powerful adrenalin-induced stimulation. Concentration is high, reflexes are quick. The mood is serious. Sleep or relaxation are impossible. Faced by a crisis this stimulation is beneficial; a difficult job can be completed more quickly and efficiently. The loss of relaxation and sleep does not matter. As with the physical response, problems will only arise if the stress response continues for too long. Unfortunately, for many executives it does; adrenalin-induced stimulation seems to become an addiction in just the same way as can alcohol or heroin. As so many addicts cannot stop gambling, so the executive cannot stop working under intense pressure. If he finishes the job in hand he will find another to maintain the pressure.

Many executives can cope with this lifestyle and do so happily. But there are several disadvantages to it. One is that the ability to work long hours and the inability to relax at the end of that work easily create pressures at home. A second is that such a dependence on work for satisfaction leaves the executive desperately at risk when he cannot work. Twenty years ago this problem was postponed until retirement. In 1968 superannuation figures from a large British firm showed that 65 per cent of their senior executives, who retired at 65, died during the next year. Early retirement has taken away this particular risk: usually the executive can decide when to retire and most of those taking early retirement remain reasonably well. Early retirement seems the silver lining to the cloud of redundancy, evidence that there is worthwhile life after work. Unwanted redundancy has replaced retirement as the medical hazard.

In general, the executive fares well in terms of mental health compared with other workers. But mental illness, particularly anxiety and depression, is common; and executives are not exempt. Such executives, such as those involved in research, may be vulnerable by virtue of their brilliance. There is a real association between genius and mental instability. Others may be put at risk by the increasing pressure of competition at work or the dual career family at home. Few women now see their role in life as the passive supporter of a successful husband. So the support of a solid stable home base for a successful career is fast becoming an illusion. Our research at Henley has already identified lack of social support as an indication of risk for mental illness and breakdown.

HELPING OURSELVES TO BETTER HEALTH

Happiness and good health are the two objectives that executives should be seeking to achieve. Happiness for ourselves and for our families is the most important. Health is part of this happiness – but only a part.

Figure 73.4 shows diagrammatically the complex factors which determine our health and happiness. Each of us floats in a sea of life. Whether we float or sink in the sea depends on our response to the many factors affecting us. How we respond is governed physically by our bodies and emotionally by our minds or personalities. Each of us is unique, with different bodies and different personalities, the

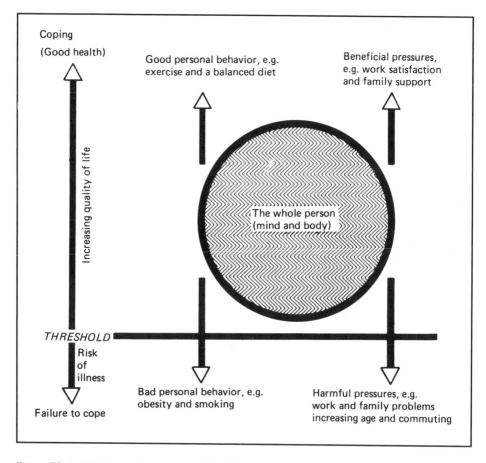

Figure 73.4   Habits, environment and health

products of nature and nurture, heredity and environment. Therefore our responses cannot be predicted. There can be no precise rule as to what makes us buoyant, giving good health and happiness, in just the same way as there is no precise rule as to what makes a good executive. But there are many guidelines, which will help most executives to live well, just as there are management procedures which will help most executives to manage well.

The factors affecting us divide easily into two areas: what we do to our bodies and what our environment – work and home – does to us. What we do to our bodies, body maintenance, is mainly determined by our habits. These are difficult to change, as Mark Twain said. But they are, at least, within our control. Our environment is not. There will be good times, when we are doing well at work and our families and friends are happy and supportive. There will also be bad times when work is uncertain and when illness or unhappiness affects our support systems. It is during these bad times that we need to be most buoyant, when we need a healthy body to help us to cope. Figure 73.4 also summarizes the medical concept of being under stress. Stress or pressure is part of every executive's life. On the whole he enjoys the challenge it provides and he is rewarded well because he copes well with stress. He becomes under stress when he fails to cope well,

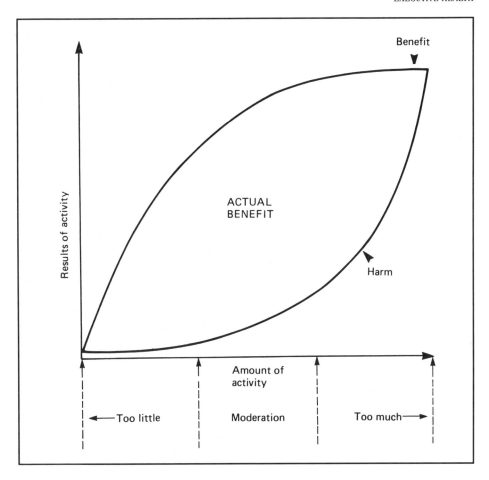

Figure 73.5   The 'rugby ball''

when he is sinking in his own sea. Many circumstances may contribute: excessive pressures at the time, poor support, poor body fitness, vulnerable personality are some examples. The downward trend can be reversed by reducing the pressures or increasing the support – provided that no irreversible physical or mental damage to the individual has occurred while he is down.

⁻What practical advice can be given to executives to help them to remain buoyant and so able to resist stress? The one word which best describes how to live well is 'moderation'. It was inscribed on the walls of the temple at Delphi to guide the Greeks. George Bernard Shaw wrote 'If you give up everything you like you can live to be a hundred, or at any rate it will seem like it!'

Figure 73.5 shows the body's response to stress in terms of performance and adds a second response – the harmful effects of stress on the body. These are minimal at low levels of stress, but increase greatly when stress levels become high. The gap between benefit and harm determines the net effect that stress has on the body: the gap is greatest at low stress levels.

Let us now apply this concept to the executive's life-style, looking first at the way he manages his body and then at the way he manages his work and family environment.

Smoking

Smoking has its benefits. Emotionally it stimulates but at the same time provides relaxation. Medically it reduces the weight. Unfortunately it became apparent to medical researchers in America and Britain that smokers became ill and died earlier than non-smokers. Their studies confirmed the high medical risk of cigarette smoking in terms of coronary heart disease and lung cancer – and subsequent research has confirmed this important association.

Doctors are convinced that the medical risks of cigarette smoking are so high that the accepted advantages of the habit cannot even start to tip the balance towards its support. The medical lobby against smoking grows stronger and at least on this occasion, doctors have practised what they preach as only 15 per cent of the profession in Britain now smoke. The dangers of smoking cigarettes are real, very unpleasant and proven.

These strictures only apply to cigarette smoking in excess. Unfortunately, excess is more than 2–3 cigarettes daily, and few smokers can stick at this level. The smoker, smoking 20 cigarettes per day who gives up at 35 should also be safe. Even better, the older smoker, providing no irreversible disease is present, will have removed the extra risk factor within three years of stopping smoking.

The dangers of smoking apply less to cigars and very little to pipes. The executive who badly needs to reduce tension should therefore stick to his pipe – empty if possible! The cigar smoked after dinner on occasions provides pleasure and quality of life – with no medical penalty. Filters sadly do not significantly reduce the risk of cigarette smoking; they reduce the risk of lung cancer but not the more important risk of heart disease.

There are many ways to stop smoking. Success needs careful planning so that motivation can be maintained during the period when smoking is stopped, and afterwards when temptation must be avoided. Acupuncture, hypnosis, aversion therapy can all help. Family doctors will be encouraging and can suggest therapeutic support such as nicotine chewing gum.

Alcohol

The cigarette smoker puts himself at risk. He can be considered a social nuisance and passive smoking does provide a small medical risk to others. But he is not an addict in the medical sense of the word. He does not need more and more of the drug to achieve the same results nor does he get the real addict's withdrawal symptoms. Nor does tobacco demean, degrade or destroy. Alcohol does all of these. Alcohol represents total destruction to the executive who becomes addicted to it, who becomes an alcoholic. Not only is he destroyed; so too are his family and his colleagues – and even those he has never seen, but may hurt with his inadequately controlled car. Despite this, public opinion is more aggressive towards tobacco smoking than towards alcohol. The reason probably lies in the social acceptability of alcohol; the fact that most of us drink moderately and enjoy it, doctors more than most. It is difficult to condemn others for what we condone ourselves.

Yet condemn them we must, and help them too. Alcoholism among executives is an international problem. The number of alcoholics in a population is always underestimated. At national level this may reflect a government's need for revenue (a *British Medical Journal* leader once started 'The government is far more addicted to alcohol than any individual alcoholic'). At company level, the alcoholic attempts to conceal his habit. If he can fool himself that he has no problem it is not surprising that he can fool other people.

Here are a few observations about this very important problem:

1   Although difficult to estimate, most informed sources agree that in Britain 6–7 per cent of executives (1 in 15) have an alcohol problem
2   For men, most doctors agree that a daily consumption of alcohol in excess of 6 or 7 units puts them at high risk from alcoholism (a unit is a single measure of spirits or a half pint of beer or a small glass of wine)
3   Half this daily consumption – 4 units – taken over 2–3 hours with an average meal will produce a blood level of approximately 80mg of alcohol in every 100ml of blood. This is the upper legal level for driving in Britain. Above this level, heavy fines and long periods of disqualification from driving are common. For many executives: 'there but for fortune . . .'
4   Women executives can drink only one half the amount of alcohol drunk by their male colleagues without risk of damaging their brains
5   Increased alcohol consumption is a common symptom of stress. It impairs performance by anaesthetizing the brain and by diverting its blood supply. Work suffers, stress increases; another vicious circle is started
6   The alcoholic can be recognized by his impaired performance, particularly when associated with irritability or absence from the office after lunch
7   If you suspect that colleagues or staff have an alcohol problem, face them with it at once and insist they seek medical help. Unless treated early, the alcoholic's hopes of recovery are small. Treated early, he can hope to resume a totally normal life.

Eating

Another way we reduce stress is to put food into our mouths. Unless this input is balanced by considerable physical activity or unless the individual is blessed with a high metabolic rate and so burns off excess fat, the result will be weight gain or obesity. Executives often entertain, so naturally they are at risk from weight gain.

Luckily, obesity is not too serious a health risk for young people. It does not increase the risk of cancer and in itself is not a risk factor for heart disease. But it can raise the blood pressure and the blood fats, both of which are risk factors for heart disease. The overweight executive will feel better slimmer and he should have his blood pressure and blood fats checked regularly. Current medical opinion recommends bran, dislikes animal fats and encourages moderation. It does not support drastic diets: just sensible care and good variety of food. Learning to leave food is perhaps the most important. Most British people are programmed to destroy all food put in front of them. However, Figure 73.5 showed that we get most pleasure at the moderate level. So try to leave any food you are not enjoying and encourage the cook to serve small helpings.

Exercise

Unfortunately a lot of exercise is needed to burn off excess food. Luckily exercise has many other advantages. Indeed, as was explained earlier, it is the sedentary life-style of the executive which helps to put him at risk from heart disease and sensible moderate exercise is the obvious answer.

The key word is moderate. With excess exercise comes an increasing risk of injury or illness and little medical benefit. Athletic fitness means exhausting training, means marathons. Medical fitness means keeping the body sensibly fit and this can easily be achieved by two or three 10 to 15 minutes sessions of jogging or Canadian Air Force exercises weekly. Here are some suggestions:

1 If you are unfit, start exercise gently. This is the high risk period. Kit yourself out well. Warm up for 5 minutes before exercise; it helps to avoid muscle and joint damage
2 Swimming, jogging, badminton and tennis provide appropriate, healthy exercise for executives
3 Squash and team sports such as rugby are less warmly recommended as they are vigorous and competitive and so can encourage the competitive executive to excess. Squash, however, is often a very appropriate exercise for executives – enjoyable and not too time-consuming. As a general rule executives under 40 are fit to play squash if they play regularly once weekly. Above 40 they need to play twice weekly to keep fit
4 Exercise need not be vigorous or with a ball. Climbing stairs and brisk walking during the working day or at airports carry great benefits
5 Ideally, exercise should be taken during or at the end of the working day – to burn off the unused fuel generated during the stressful day. But expediency is important. It is often easier to make time for exercise early in the morning and such exercise is far better than no exercise at all.

Sleep

The benefits which can be obtained from sleep also follow the slope of the benefit curve in Figure 73.5. Maximum benefit comes in the first 3–4 hours. After 7–8 hours there is little benefit. We all have an optimum period of sleep and usually know it. It varies from 6 to 8 hours. One hour in the afternoon can balance 2–3 hours lost in the night. Thus, a late night can be made more enjoyable by an hour's rest the afternoon before, and its bad effects reversed by an hour's sleep the next afternoon.

Under stress, the executive may buy time for extra work by missing sleep. He may get away with it for some time but chronic lack of sleep will affect performance and may cause sudden collapse.

Sex

Until the last few years it would have taken a brave doctor to quantify what is moderate in sex. The advent of AIDS and the increase in venereal disease, both usually the result of excessive indiscriminate sex, have changed this. Between couples frequency of sex is a question of mutual agreement. Certainly, there is no medical risk attached to sex. Quite the reverse – it provides happy healthy exercise and enhances relationships. The only recent medical input relates to faithfulness. Two studies, one in Japan and the other in France, revealed identical results; heart attacks during sex were very rare – but twice as common in 'away matches'. You can live a double life, but only for half as long!

A real problem for executives is the effect of their busy lives on their sexual drive. Partners usually interpret lack of performance as lack of interest and care. Another dangerous vicious circle may result.

Relaxation

For most executives life is hectic and every minute full. How to get everything done is their main concern. Relaxation is the natural antidote to all this hustle. Medical evidence supporting relaxation is mounting. It is now accepted that relaxation reduces blood pressure, pulse rate and blood fats – all risk factors for heart disease.

Relaxation can be achieved in two ways. The first is to carry out any activity which distracts the mind from work. A happy home life, religious activity, gardening, sport, hobbies; all of these are good forms of relaxation. The second form of relaxation is through a formal discipline such as yoga, transcendental meditation or autogenics. Sessions can be once daily for up to half-an-hour or for short periods during the day. Benson writes well about relaxation and has done much to demonstrate its value (see Further Reading).

Regular medical checks

The Americans probably have excessive medical checks – many cannot believe they are well until told so by their doctor. The British certainly have too few. When their relative value is compared it does seem remarkable that so many companies should service their cars and yet fail to 'service' their executives.

Regular medical checks take many forms and are usually recommended more often as the executive grows older. Ideally, a straightforward annual check is recommended. This should include weight and blood pressure recordings, together with a careful discussion of the executive's life-style. Every 2–4 years a more thorough medical with blood screening and testing and exercise cardiograms is valuable. Most GPs will carry out the simple annual check-up for NHS patients and the full checks can be arranged through the BUPA and PPP centres.

Air travel

Air travel for the executive soon loses its glamour. It is a frustrating and tiring business which can take up far too much of his time and energy. It is also a risk factor to his health – during flights he is even more sedentary than in his office, even more at risk to the temptations of excess alcohol and food. Some simple hints are:

1 Book in early and take a vigorous walk before the flight starts
2 Avoid alcohol completely while flying; spirits in particular actually cause dehydration by pushing fluid out from the body
3 Drink as much fluid as possible; ideally so that you need to walk to the toilet once an hour
4 When not drinking fluid, sleep; it is the best way to arrive fresh at your destination
5 Travel first-class when possible; it makes a tremendous difference to your comfort and health at the end of the trip.

THE WORK AND HOME ENVIRONMENTS

However well the executive looks after his body, his health ultimately will be determined by his happiness at work and at home. At work the fit between his personality and his job control the satisfaction that he achieves. His happiness at home will be influenced most by his choice of partner, and by their ability to discuss honestly their feelings about having a family. The more successful the executive is at work the more time he will want, or be asked, to spend there. The happier he is at home the more he will want to be there. In the end his happiness and that of his family will depend on his awareness of these conflicts and his ability to resolve them as well as he can.

Ten years ago I asked a large group of executives – 30–40-year-olds attending courses at Henley Management College – to look back over their managerial life and identify the source of their greatest stress so far. Sixty per cent identified this stress as coming from their family lives; 40 per cent from their work. This conclusion has been confirmed by a much more detailed and ambitious study in America by Holmes and Rahe. They set out to explore the concept that stress could cause illness. They chose to work with managers and they based their study on the idea that stability is safe and healthy. Stress, they argued, came from change.

A large number of American managers were asked to list the main changes that could affect their lives and then to rate their importance in comparison with the greatest change they could meet – death of a spouse. Figure 73.6 shows the resultant ratings. The scores from the changes were added together every 6 to 12 months to quantify the amount of stress in individuals. A typical result shows mental and physical illness occurring at times of high change scoring – providing scientific support for the version of 'Sod's Law' which states 'You get ill when you can't afford to'. In fact, illness came in the days or weeks after the change. The stress response boosts performance and at the same time discourages illness. It is during the flat time after the stressful period that we can become ill; or when stress goes on and on. The results seemed to confirm Holmes and Rahe's suggestion that change causes illness. There are two important applications of this concept:

Rank	Life event	Mean value
1	Death of spouse	100
2	Divorce	73
3	Marital separation	65
4	Jail term	63
5	Death of a close family member	63
6	Personal injury or illness	53
7	Marriage	50
8	Fired at work	47
9	Marital reconciliation	45
10	Retirement	45
11	Change in health of family member	44
12	Pregnancy	40
13	Sex difficulties	39
14	Gain of a new family member	39
15	Business readjustment	39
16	Change in financial state	38
17	Death of a close friend	37
18	Change to a different line of work	36
19	Change in number of arguments with spouse	35
20	High mortgage	31
21	Foreclosure of mortgage or loan	30
22	Change in responsibilities at work	29
23	Son or daughter leaving home	29
24	Trouble with in-laws	29
25	Outstanding personal achievement	28
26	Spouse begins or stops work	26
27	Children move to new school	26
28	Change in living conditions	25
29	Revision of personal habits	24
30	Trouble with boss	23
31	Change in work hours or conditions	20
32	Change in residence	20
33	Change in schools	20
34	Change in recreation	19
35	Change in church activities	19
36	Change in social activities	18
37	Mortgage or loan less than £10 000	17
38	Change in sleeping habits	16
39	Change in number of family get-togethers	15
40	Change in eating habits	15
41	Vacation	13
42	Christmas	12
43	Minor violations of the law	11

Figure 73.6   Life events points rating scale. (Adapted from: Holmes and Rahe)

The additive nature of stress

Life change units are relative, not absolute. A high life-change score does not mean that someone will become ill; just that they are more likely to. However, study of the table does show that several small changes in a short period can produce a much higher score than one big change. While surprising, this conclusion does seem to be borne out by what we see in general practice. Executives usually come through bereavement intact; but the same does not apply to their ability to cope with an event which actually scores a lot higher on the rating scale than bereavement – namely relocation. Relocation is a frequent event in many executives' lives. In one survey, IBM executives moved on an average every 27 months. Relocation scores 137 on the life-event rating. The executive must prove himself in a new job, his family must find a new house, his wife must start work again and the children must adapt to a new school. In my own practice, two tragedies have affected executives in recent years. I believe it to be no coincidence that both occurred four months after the executive had been moved to a new location and was having great difficulty adjusting to the change.

Management must recognize the pressures produced by relocation and moves must be thought through carefully. The executives concerned must be fully involved in the decision and have as much time as possible to plan it. Once they have moved, the manager and his family need all possible support for the next six months. The executive must involve his family fully in the decision to move and be prepared to take their views into account. In the last ten years more and more executives have declined moves for these reasons.

The important sources of stress

When the 43 life events are divided into their areas of origin it is immediately obvious that the majority come from this area of family life. There seems no doubt that in order to gain maximum fulfilment from his life, to be really happy, the executive must achieve the best possible balance between his work life and his home life. Family life provides him with his greatest risk factors; it also provides him with something worthwhile to work for and enormous pleasure. Not only this, it provides him with his most effective counsellor. The most important antidote to stress is to talk about what is happening. In this way the vicious circle by which lack of insight can lead to a totally irrational view of current problems is broken. When asked who provided them with their greatest help in times of stress, 80 per cent of the executives on our survey at Henley answered their wives.

How then can the executive check that he is achieving the right balance between his work and his family? At work, his performance will usually be checked once or twice yearly by his boss at an appraisal and counselling session. In addition, he will see his boss when things are out of control. From these meetings suggestions for future behaviour will be agreed. There is no reason why he should not use the same procedure to monitor his health and happiness. He has two resources:

1 *His doctor* A regular medical examination by an appropriate doctor should keep the executive aware of the effects of his life-style on his habits and his health. The same doctor would then be in the ideal position of knowing the

Complaints of:

Poor performance, lateness with work, indecision from partners and colleagues from work, family and social groups

Increased:

Eating, drinking, smoking, irritability, 'feeling tired', lack of concentration

Decreased:

Time for family, leisure, sense of humour, sleep, insight into problems, exercise, relaxation, preparation for holidays, sexual drive

At work, in general:

Inability to finish work in reasonable hours, too great a workload to tackle, frequently being late, rushing, exerting extra pressure on staff and long reports at the last minute. Altering appointments because of overbooking or over-commitment. Not taking holiday entitlement

At home and at work, in general:

Periods of poor health, change in sleep patterns, waking tired, more than one road traffic accident, minor accidents at home through carelessness, needing to take tranquilizers or sleeping tablets

Figure 73.7   Indicators for a crisis audit

executive well and also being available for consultation at times of medical crisis. It would be helpful, therefore, if companies made available such a service, either within the company or at a nearby medical centre
2   *His wife*   The same routine annual meeting could again apply. The agenda for discussion will be the happiness of all the family. Any changes agreed can be monitored at future meetings. The meeting must not be open to interruption or have a short time limit. Time is necessary for open, honest discussion.

As at work and with the doctor crisis meetings may also be appropriate. The reasons for such a crisis meeting serve as a reminder of the effects of stress on the executive (Figure 73.7).

FEMALE EXECUTIVES

I hope that this late specific mention of female executives will upset neither those who feel they should have had more space for their own particular problems earlier nor those who see themselves as no different from their male counterparts. The use of the male prefix throughout this chapter is partly for stylistic ease, and partly because most executives, particularly the more senior, are male. Considerable effort was needed to track down the small sample of women executives taking part in our Henley research project. Britain is still 20 or 30 years behind Scandinavian equality.

In general, women between 30 and 50 are protected against heart disease by their female hormones. However, recent findings show clearly, and the early results of our research confirm, that female executives, by achieving success in a previously male world, have lost this protection. Their risk of heart disease is the same as their male colleagues and as so many women managers smoke their risk of lung cancer is high. In addition women face the additional risk of breast cancer and female executives are well advised to schedule into their busy timetable an annual well-woman screen.

It is not surprising that the British female executive should have an increased health risk. She has needed to succeed in a chauvenistic world, for it has been suggested that female executives need to be 30 per cent more competent than their male counterparts to earn promotion. Her success at work can destroy her happiness at home. Many husbands cannot cope with a successful wife. Even if they do cope, they may well expect her to look after the home as well as work. Without a man at home life may be no easier; as Renèe Short said, 'What every working woman needs is a wife at home'. Perhaps female executives should be declared an endangered species and for them there is an even greater need for genuine concern for their health.

CONCLUSION

Achievement of good health and happiness must remain the important objective for every executive. Achieving success in both is partly a matter of luck, partly skill. Skills can be acquired; and even luck can be influenced but this requires careful planning. The executive who does control his life-style and discipline his habits has so much to gain. He really can help himself to better health and happiness.

USEFUL ORGANIZATIONS

The BUPA Medical Centre Ltd
Webb House
73 Pentonville Road
London W1

Tel. 071-837 8641

PPP Medical Centre
99 New Cavendish Street
London W1M 3FQ

Tel. 071-637 8941

FURTHER READING

Benson, H., *The Relaxation Response*, Morrow, New York, 1976
Carruthers, Malcolm, *F40 – Fitness on Forty Minutes a Week*, Futura, London, 1976

Cooper, Cary and Davidson, Marilyn, *High Pressure, Working Lives of Women Managers*, Fontana, London, 1982

Cranwell-Ward, Jane, *Managing Stress*, Gower, Aldershot, 1988

Fontana, David, *Managing Stress*, Routledge, London, 1989

Makin, P., Cooper, C. and Cox, C., *Managing People at Work*, BPS and Routledge, 1989

Melhuish, Andrew, *Work and Health*, Penguin, Harmondsworth, 1982

Reddy, Michael, *Counselling at Work*, BPS and Routledge, 1987

Royal Canadian Air Force, *Physical Fitness*, Penguin, Harmondsworth, 1971

Selye, Hans, *Stress Without Distress*, Lippincott, New York, 1974

Index